Rick Steves®

FRANCE

Rick Steves & Steve Smith

2020

≈ L'Indre

CONTENTS

Welcome to Rick Steves' Europe

Travel is intensified living—maximum thrills per minute and one of the last great sources of legal adventure. Travel is freedom. It's recess, and we need it.

I discovered a passion for European travel as a teen and have been sharing it ever since—through my tours, public television and radio shows, and travel guidebooks. Over the years, I've taught thousands of travelers how to best enjoy Europe's blockbuster sights—and experience "Back Door" discoveries that most tourists miss.

Written with my talented co-author, Steve Smith, this book offers you a balanced mix of France's lively cities and cozy towns, from the traditional heartland to jet-setting beach resorts. And it's selective—rather than listing dozens of beautiful châteaux in the Loire region, we cover only the top 10. Our self-guided museum tours, city walks, and driving tours give insight into France's vibrant history and today's living, breathing culture.

We advocate traveling simply and smartly. Take advantage of our money- and time-saving tips on sightseeing, transportation, and more. Try local, characteristic alternatives to pricey chain hotels and famous restaurants. In many ways, spending more money only builds a thicker wall between you and what you traveled so far to see.

We visit France to experience it—to become temporary locals. Thoughtful travel engages us with the world, as we learn to appreciate other cultures and new ways to measure quality of life.

Judging from the positive feedback we receive from readers, this book will help you enjoy a fun, affordable, and rewarding vacation—whether it's your first trip or your tenth.

Bon voyage! Happy travels!

Rick Steves

FRANCE

Bienvenue! You've chosen well. With its distinctive regions and renowned cuisine, France is Europe's most diverse, tasty, and exciting country to explore. It's a cultural bouillabaisse that surprises travelers with its varied, complex flavors.

A delightful blend of natural and man-made beauty, France offers chandeliered châteaux, forever coastlines, soaring cathedrals, Europe's highest mountain ranges, and museums showcasing cultural icons of the Western world.

In many ways, France is a yardstick of human achievement. Here, travelers can trace the path of European history, from magnificent prehistoric cave paintings to dazzling Roman ruins. In medieval times, France cultivated Romanesque and Gothic architecture—erecting towering cathedrals and inspiring copycat trends throughout Europe. With revolutionary zeal, French philosophers refined modern thought and politics. In the 16th and 17th centuries, the châteaux of the Loire and the grand palace of Versailles announced France's emergence as the first European superpower and first modern government. Later France gave birth to Impressionism and with that, the foundations of modern art. And the country remains at the forefront of technology, architecture, fashion, and cuisine.

France is a big country by European standards—and would be one of the biggest states if it ever joined the US (unlikely). It's a bit smaller than Texas, but has 66 million people (Texas has 26 million). This country features three

From chic attire (in Paris) to traditional garb (at a festival in Arles), the French wear it well.

mountain ranges, two very different coastlines, several cosmopolitan cities, and countless sleepy villages.

There are two Frances: Paris...and the rest of the country. France's government and cultural heart have always been centered in Paris, resulting in an overwhelming concentration of world-class museums, cutting-edge architecture, historic monuments, trendy energy, and famous cafés. Travelers can spend weeks in France and never leave Paris. Many do.

The other France venerates land, tradition, and a slower pace of life. Romantic hill towns and castles, meandering river valleys, and oceans of vineyards carpet this country's landscape. Wheat farms flourish in the north, dairy farms in the west, fruit orchards and lavender fields in the south...and vineyards and sunflowers just about everywhere. Even city dwellers venerate the soil *(le terroir)* that brings the flavor to their foods and wines.

France has more geographical diversity than any other nation in Europe. Paris and the land around it (called Ile de France) is the modern, bustling center. To the west are the dramatic D-Day beaches and thatch-roofed homes of Normandy; to the south lie the river valleys of the Loire and Dordogne, with elegant châteaux, medieval castles, and

Bon Appétit!

French cuisine is sightseeing for your taste buds. You're not paying just for the food—a good meal is a three-hour joyride for the senses, as rich as visiting an art gallery and as stimulating as a good massage.

Fine French restaurants may seem intimidating, but many servers speak English and are used to tourists. Here's an experience I shared with my co-author, Steve Smith, at a fine restaurant in Amboise, in the Loire Valley.

French restaurants open for dinner at about 19:00 and are most crowded at about 20:30—it's smart to reserve ahead for your splurge meal, which we did the day before. In France, you can order off the menu, which is called *la carte* and offers more selection, or you can order a multi-course, fixed-price meal, which, confusingly, is called a *menu* (a great value if you're hungry). Steve ordered a three-course *menu* and I ordered off *la carte*.

Aurore, our waitress, smiled as I ordered escargot (snails) for my first course. Getting a full dozen escargot rather than the typical six snails doubles the joy. Eating six, you're aware that the supply is limited. Eating twelve, for the first eight it seems like there's no end to your fun. Add a good white wine and you've got a full orchestral accompaniment.

A handwritten menu (a good sign), the perfect number of escargot, and a glass of wine to top it off

In France, slow service is good service (fast service rushes diners and digestion). After a pleasant pause, my main course arrived: tender beef with beans wrapped in bacon. Slicing through a pack of beans in their quiver of bacon, I let the fat do its dirty deed. A sip of wine, after a bite of beef, was ▶▶▶

▶▶▶ like an incoming tide washing the flavor ashore.

My crust of bread, a veteran from the escargot course, was called into action for a swipe of sauce. The French venerate fresh products and fine sauces. If the sauce is the medicine, the bread is the syringe. Thanks to the bread, I enjoyed one last encore of the meat and vegetables I'd just savored.

The next course was a selection of tasty cheeses. (It sounds like a lot of food but portions are smaller in France—what we cram onto one large plate they spread out over many courses.) Our cheese platter was a festival of mold on a rustic board. The vibrant-yet-mellow colors promised an array of tastes that made me want to sing with joy (out of consideration for Steve, I didn't).

Then came dessert. Mine was a café gourmand, an artfully presented assortment of five small desserts, including cinnamon-baked apple with butterscotch ice cream. That didn't keep me from reaching over for a snip of Steve's lemon tart with raspberry sauce.

Even after dessert, Aurore didn't rush us. Your server won't bring your bill until you ask for it. If you're in a rush, here's a good strategy: As you finish dessert, your server will ask if you'd like coffee. This gives you the perfect opening to ask for the bill.

Even if you're not a "foodie," I can't imagine a richer French sightseeing experience, one that brings together an unforgettable ensemble of local ingredients, culture, pride, and people. ∎

Your server brings you courses that can include your choice of cheeses or desserts.

hilltop villages. In the far southwest are the Spanish-tinged Languedoc-Roussillon and the overlooked Pyrenees. Closer to Italy, windswept Provence nurtures Roman ruins and rustic charm, while the Riviera celebrates sunny beaches and modern art. And to the east are Europe's highest snow-capped Alps, the vineyards of Burgundy, and the Germanic culture of Alsace.

The country is famous for its pâtés, foie gras, escargot, fine sauces, cheese (more than 350 different kinds), and delectable pastries. But the forte of French cuisine lies in its regional variety. You'll enjoy Swiss-like fondue in the Alps, Italian-style pasta on the Riviera, crêpes in Brittany, Spanish paella in Languedoc-Roussillon, seafood in Normandy, and sausage and sauerkraut in Alsace.

L'art de vivre—the art of living—is not just a cute expression; it's the foundation for good living in France. With five weeks of paid vacation, the French are obligated to slow down and enjoy life. It's no accident that the country is home to pastimes like café lounging, bike touring, barge cruising, and ballooning—all require a slower pace. You'll run headlong into that mindful approach to life at mealtime. The French insist on quality food and conversation. They don't rush lunch, and an evening's entertainment is often a meal with friends.

The socially minded French are proud of their cradle-to-grave social security system. On the other hand, French taxes are among the highest in Europe. The country sees more

Whether meeting a friend or cruising on a barge, the French cultivate the art of living.

France has Alps to inspire and D-Day beaches to ponder.

than its share of strikes, demonstrations, and slowdowns as workers try to preserve their hard-earned rights in a competitive global economy. Mainly Catholic, the French are not very devout, and are quick to separate church from state. France also has Europe's largest Muslim population. The influx of Muslim immigrants and their integration in French society is one of France's thorniest issues.

French people can come across as moody and complicated, though most will welcome you with a smile. Still, think where they've come from: In just a few generations, they've seen two debilitating world wars destroy their cities, villages, landscapes, and self-respect. But proud and resilient, they have risen from the ashes of the wars to generate the world's sixth-largest economy. Wine, agriculture, tourism, telecommunications, pharmaceuticals, cars, and Airbus planes are big moneymakers. Productivity is nothing new to a people who invented the metric system, pasteurization, high-speed trains, and the Concorde jet.

Highly cultured yet down to earth, France is fascinating. From the Swiss-like Alps to the *molto* Italian Riviera, and from the Spanish Pyrenees to *das* German Alsace, you can visit France and feel like you've sampled much of Europe— and never be more than a short stroll from a *bon vin rouge*.

France's Top Destinations

Mon Dieu! There's so much to see in France and so little time. This overview breaks the country's top destinations into must-see sights (to help first-time travelers plan their trip) and worth-it sights (for those with extra time or special interests), listed in book order. I've also suggested a minimum number of days to allow per destination.

ENGLAND

BELGIUM

English Channel

LUX.

G
E
R
M
A
N
Y

NORMANDY

REIMS & VERDUN

BRITTANY

NEAR PARIS

PARIS

ALSACE

THE LOIRE

BURGUNDY

SWITZ.

Atlantic Ocean

THE FRENCH ALPS

DORDOGNE

LYON

ITALY

PROVENCE

LANGUEDOC-ROUSSILLON

THE FRENCH RIVIERA

PLACES COVERED IN THIS BOOK

▲▲▲ Must See
▲▲ Try Hard to See
▲ Worthwhile

Mediterranean Sea

ANDORRA

SPAIN

100 Kilometers

100 Miles

MUST-SEE DESTINATIONS

The magical city of Paris, historic Normandy, the sun-dappled region of Provence, and the breathtaking Riviera coastline offer an excellent sampler of France.

▲▲▲Paris (allow 3 days)
The City of Light is not only the capital of France, but also the world capital of art, fashion, food, literature, and ideas, offering historic monuments, grand boulevards, corner cafés, chic boutiques, avant-garde architecture, and top-notch art galleries, including the Louvre (*Venus de Milo* and *Mona Lisa*) and the Orsay (Impressionists and more).

▲▲▲Normandy (2-3 days)
This region offers a pastoral mix of sweeping coastlines, half-timbered towns, and intriguing cities, including bustling Rouen (Gothic architecture and Joan of Arc sites), the cozy port town of Honfleur, and historic Bayeux (with its remarkable tapestry of the Battle of Hastings). Normandy's D-Day beaches and museums are profoundly moving, while the almost surreal island abbey of Mont St-Michel seems to float above it all.

▲▲▲Provence (2 days)
This beloved, hilly region is home to the cities of Arles (with Van Gogh sights and the evocative Roman Arena), Avignon (with the famous bridge and Palace of the Popes), and Orange (Roman theater), plus photogenic rock-top villages (such as Les Baux, Roussillon, and Vaison-la-Romaine). Attractions include the simply awe-inspiring Roman aqueduct of Pont du Gard and the inviting wine road of the Côtes du Rhône.

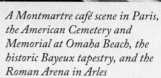

A Montmartre café scene in Paris, the American Cemetery and Memorial at Omaha Beach, the historic Bayeux tapestry, and the Roman Arena in Arles

▲▲▲The French Riviera (2 days)

Along the Riviera lies a string of coastal pearls, starring Nice (big city with a lively seafront promenade, Italianesque old town, and art museums), romantic Villefranche-sur-Mer, glitzy Monaco (casino and Prince's Palace), and easygoing Antibes (silky-sandy beaches and seafront hikes). Intriguing inland villages are Vence, St-Paul-de-Vence, and sky-high Eze-le-Village, with marvelous Mediterranean views.

Opposite: Monet's flowery gardens at Giverny
This page: A Riviera moment, canoeing on the Dordogne, and beautiful Amboise

WORTH-IT DESTINATIONS

You can weave any of these destinations—rated ▲ or ▲▲—
into your itinerary. Some places are easy to add based on
proximity (if you're going to Paris, Versailles is next door),
but even out-of-the-way destinations can merit the journey,
depending on your time and interests.

▲▲Near Paris (1 day)
Four very different sights make good day trips from Paris:
Europe's grandest palace at Versailles, the radiant cathedral of Chartres, Monet's flowery gardens at Giverny, and a
mouse-run amusement park (Disneyland Paris).

▲Brittany (1 day)
Windswept, rugged Brittany has an untouristed interior,
gorgeous coast, Celtic ties, and two notable towns—Dinan
(with Brittany's best medieval center) and the beach resort of
St-Malo—plus the sea-swept castle of Fort la Latte.

▲▲The Loire (2 days)
The river valleys of the Loire region host appealing towns
(such as Amboise and Chinon) and hundreds of castles
and palaces, including Chenonceau (arcing across its river),
the massive Château de Chambord, Villandry (wonderful
gardens), lavishly furnished Cheverny, and many more.

▲▲Dordogne (2 days)
Prehistoric caves, rock-sculpted villages, lazy canoe rides past
medieval castles, and bustling market towns such as pedestrian-friendly Sarlat-la-Canéda are among this region's charms.
Just east is the spectacular pilgrimage village of Rocamadour,
and to the west is St-Emilion, with vineyards and tastings.

▲Languedoc-Roussillon (1 day)

This sunny region with a Spanish flair boasts the medieval, walled town of Carcassonne (with towers, turrets, and cobblestones) and the lovely Mediterranean village of Collioure. Albi makes a good stop for its fortress-like cathedral and beautiful Toulouse-Lautrec museum.

▲▲The French Alps (2 days)

These majestic mountains feature the beautiful lakefront city of Annecy, Mont Blanc (Europe's highest peak), and the world-famous ski resort at its base, Chamonix, with lifts to stunning alpine views and trailheads, and hikes galore.

▲▲Burgundy (1-2 days)

An aged blend of vineyards and spirituality, Burgundy is home to the compact town of Beaune, renowned vineyards and wine roads, the well-preserved medieval abbey of Fontenay, the magnificent Romanesque church of Vézelay, and a medieval castle under construction at Guédelon.

▲Lyon (2 days)

This metropolitan city, wedged between Burgundy and Provence, features delicious yet affordable cuisine, a made-for-wandering old town, two Roman theaters, a terrific Gallo-Roman museum, the riveting French Resistance Center, and an impressive fine arts museum.

▲▲Alsace (1-2 days)

The Franco-Germanic region is dotted with adorable and colorful wine villages, half-timbered Colmar with a wonderful pedestrian-only center and world-class art, and the high-powered Euro-capital city of Strasbourg and its sensational cathedral.

▲Reims and Verdun (1 day)

Two very different sights, paired by proximity, are the champagne-soaked city of Reims with its historic cathedral and cellars serving the sparkling brew, and nearby Verdun, the site of horrific WWI battles, with unforgettable battle-field memorials and museums.

Carcassonne's castle walls, dining under medieval arches in Beaune, lovely lakeside Annecy, and cute wine villages along Alsace's Route du Vin

Planning Your Trip

To plan your trip, you'll need to design your itinerary—choosing where and when to go, how you'll travel, and how many days to spend at each destination. For more-detailed advice on sightseeing, accommodations, restaurants, and transportation, see the Practicalities chapter.

DESIGNING AN ITINERARY

As you read this book and learn your options...

Choose your top destinations.

The recommended whirlwind trip (on page 20) gives you an idea of how much you could see in 22 days, but it's best to adapt it to fit your interests and time frame.

Nearly every destination in this book can enjoyably fill a week or more of a focused trip, especially Paris, Normandy, the Loire, the Dordogne, Provence, and the French Riviera. Linking any two or three of these destinations would make a terrific trip.

France has something for everyone. Art lovers and museum-goers linger in Paris. Cyclists pedal between châteaux in the Loire, and canoeists paddle between castles in the Dordogne. Connoisseurs of wine and villages meander along the wine roads of Burgundy, Alsace, and the Côtes du Rhône.

Historians are at home in France. The Dordogne's prehistoric cave paintings literally rock. For ancient Roman ruins, roam through Provence. Medievalists marvel at the walled town of Carcassonne and the island abbey of Mont St-Michel. Revolutionaries and monarchists alike appreciate Paris and Versailles. WWII historians make a pilgrimage to Normandy's D-Day sites, while WWI students ponder Verdun.

Sun worshippers simmer on the Riviera while hikers love to go a-wandering in the Alps. If hill towns and sunny skies appeal, Provence and Languedoc deliver. Germanophiles think Alsace is *wunderbar,* foodies are fond of Lyon and Burgundy (but aren't disappointed elsewhere), and photographers want to go everywhere.

Decide when to go.

Late spring and fall are best, with generally good weather and fewer crowds, though summer brings festivals, livelier villages, reliable weather, and long hours at sights.

Weekends in May—with its many holidays—can be

A Van Gogh easel in Arles, a sound-and-light show at Chartres, and sunflowers in summer

Whirlwind Three-Week Tour of France by Car

While this trip is doable in 22 days, most will appreciate adding an extra day here and there to rest their engine.

Day	Plan
1	Fly into Paris (but save Paris sightseeing for your trip finale), pick up your car, and visit Giverny en route to **Honfleur (stay 1 night)**.
2	Morning in Honfleur, afternoon in Bayeux to see its tapestry and cathedral. Overnight in **Bayeux (2 nights)**.
3	Spend day touring D-Day sights: Arromanches, American Cemetery, and Pointe du Hoc (and Utah Beach Landing Museum, if you're moving fast).
4	Drive to Dinan and see its sights. In late afternoon, drive to Mont St-Michel and visit its abbey. Sleep on/near **Mont St-Michel or Dinan (1 night)**.
5	Head for château country in the Loire Valley. Tour Chambord, then settle in **Amboise (2 nights)** and take the self-guided town walk in this book.
6	Day trip to Chenonceau and Cheverny or Chaumont—or all three if you don't need more time for Amboise.
7	Leave early and head south to the Dordogne region, stopping en route at Oradour-sur-Glane. End in **Sarlat-la-Canéda (2 nights)** or a nearby riverside village.
8	If it's market day in Sarlat, start there (early), then take a relaxing canoe trip and tour a prehistoric cave. If it's not market day, start with a cave, then canoe and browse Sarlat late.
9	Head to Languedoc-Roussillon, lunch and sightsee in Albi, then overnight in **Carcassonne (1 night)**.
10	Morning in Carcassonne, then on to Arles, with a stop at the Pont du Gard. Stay in or near **Arles (2 nights)**.
11	All day for Arles and Les Baux (visit Les Baux early or late).
12	Make a beeline for the Riviera, staying in **Nice, Antibes, or Villefranche-sur-Mer (2 nights)**. Explore your home base in the afternoon.
13	Sightsee in Nice and Monaco.
14	Make the long drive north to the Alps and stay in **Chamonix (2 nights)**.
15	If the weather is even close to clear, take the mountain lifts up to Aiguille du Midi and beyond.

16	Allow another half-day for the Alps (in Chamonix or Annecy). Then head to Beaune in Burgundy for wine tasting. Stay in **Beaune (1 night)**.
17	Spend half of the day in and around Beaune, then move on to the Alsace city of **Colmar (2 nights)**.
18	Enjoy Colmar and the Route du Vin villages.
19	Return to Paris, visiting Verdun or Reims en route (consider dropping your car in Reims and training to Paris). Collapse in **Paris** hotel **(4 nights)**.
20	Sightsee Paris.
21	More time in Paris.
22	Finish your sightseeing in Paris, with possible side-trip to Versailles.

With Limited Time: Slice France into sections. If you only have 8-10 days, consider a loop linking Paris, Normandy, and the Loire. Or do a one-way trip, such as flying into Nice and out of Paris, seeing the Riviera, Provence, the Alps, and Burgundy along the way.

Whirlwind Three-Week Tour of France by Train (and Bus)

This itinerary is designed primarily for train travel, with some help from buses, minivan tours, and taxis. It takes 11 days of train travel to do this trip (also consider the cheaper Ouibus and Flixbus for some trips). If using only the train, buy an eight-day France rail pass, and make it stretch by buying point-to-point tickets for cheaper trips on day 5, day 13, and day 18. With only two weeks, end in Nice. *Bonne route and bon courage!*

Important: Book TGV (also called "InOui") train trips (marked here with a *) well in advance, particularly if traveling with a rail pass.

Day	Plan
1	Fly into **Paris (3 nights).**
2	Sightsee Paris.
3	More time in Paris.
4	Train* and bus (or Flixbus) to Mont St-Michel via Rennes (3 hours, arrive in Mont St-Michel about 13:00). Explore and stay on/near **Mont St-Michel (1 night).**
5	Train to Bayeux (2 hours, arrive by noon). Explore and stay in **Bayeux (2 nights).**
6	All day for D-Day beaches by minivan, taxi, bus, or a combination.
7	Train* to Amboise via Caen and St-Pierre des Corps (5 hours). See sights and sleep in **Amboise (2 nights).**
8	All day for touring Loire châteaux (by bus, bike, or minivan tour).
9	Early train* to Sarlat-la-Canéda (6 hours, arrive about 13:00). Explore and stay in **Sarlat (2 nights).**

busy anywhere, but June is generally quiet outside of Paris. In July and August, vacationing Europeans jam the Riviera, the Dordogne, and the Alps. And although many businesses close in August, you'll hardly notice.

Winter travel is fine for Paris, Nice, and Lyon, but small cities are buttoned up tight. The weather is gray, milder in the south (unless the wind is blowing), and colder and wetter in the north. Sights keep shorter hours and some tourist activities (such as English-language tours) disappear, though hotels and restaurants are much calmer. For specifics, see the climate chart in the appendix.

10	All day for caves and canoes (by train, bike, or minivan/taxi tour).
11	Train or bus to Carcassonne via Bordeaux (7 hours). Dinner and evening wall walk and sleep in **Carcassonne (1 night).**
12	In early morning, take another wall walk in Carcassonne. Train to Arles (3 hours; some with change in Narbonne). Afternoon and evening in Arles. Sleep in **Arles (2 nights).**
13	Train to Nîmes (30 minutes), then bus to Pont du Gard (50 minutes) to explore the ancient aqueduct. Bus to Avignon (50 minutes). Spend your afternoon/evening there and return to Arles by train (30 minutes).
14	Morning in Arles or Les Baux (by taxi or tour), afternoon train* to Nice via Marseille (4 hours). Sleep in **Nice (3 nights).**
15	All day for Nice.
16	All day for Villefranche-sur-Mer and Monaco.
17	Morning train* to Lyon (5 hours). Explore and stay in **Lyon (1 night).**
18	Morning in Lyon, then early afternoon train or Ouibus to Chamonix (4 hours). Explore and sleep in **Chamonix (2 nights).**
19	If the weather is even close to clear, take the mountain lifts up to Aiguille du Midi and beyond.
20	Linger in Chamonix, or take an early train* to Paris (7 hours) or Annecy (2 hours; Geneva Airport is one hour by bus from Annecy or 1.5 hours by shuttle from Chamonix). To extend your trip, spend a night in Burgundy (in Beaune) or two nights in Alsace (in Colmar); each is a 6.5-hour train ride from Chamonix. End in Paris.

Connect the dots.

Link your destinations into a logical route. Determine which cities you'll fly into and out of (Paris and Nice can make good bookends). Begin your search for transatlantic flights at Kayak.com.

Decide if you'll travel by car or public transportation or both. A car is useless in big cities, but a godsend for just about everywhere else. Normandy, the Dordogne, Languedoc and Provence have limited public transportation. Trains are faster and pricier than buses, though buses reach some places that trains don't. Well-run minivan tours are listed for every region in this book.

A trip to the City of Light is illuminating.

To determine approximate transportation times between destinations, study the driving chart in the Practicalities chapter or train schedules (www.sncf.com). If France is part of a bigger trip, consider budget flights; check Skyscanner.com for intra-European flights.

Write out a day-by-day itinerary.

Figure out how many destinations you can comfortably fit in your time frame. Don't overdo it—few travelers wish they'd hurried more. Allow enough days per stop (see estimates in "France's Top Destinations," earlier). Minimize one-night stands, especially consecutive ones. It can be worth a late-afternoon drive or train ride to get settled into a town for two nights. Allot sufficient time for transportation; whether traveling by car or train, it'll take you a half-day to get between most destinations.

Staying in a home base (such as Paris, Nice, or Amboise in the Loire) and taking day trips can be more time-efficient than changing locations and hotels.

Check the opening hours of your must-see sights; avoid visiting a town on the one day a week they're closed. Check if any holidays or festivals will fall during your trip—these attract crowds and can close sights (for the latest, visit France's tourist website, http://us.france.fr).

Give yourself some slack. Every trip—and every traveler—needs downtime for doing laundry, picnic shopping, people-watching, and so on. Pace yourself. Assume you will return.

Trip Costs Per Person

Run a reality check on your dream trip. You'll have major transportation costs in addition to daily expenses.

Flight: A round-trip flight from the US to Paris or Nice costs about $1,000-2,000, depending on where you fly from and when.

Public Transportation: For a three-week trip, allow $800 for buses and second-class trains ($900 for first class). Buying train tickets as you go can be fine for short rides, but expensive for long ones. To save money, buy a rail pass and make seat reservations (note that rail passes must be purchased outside of Europe), or lock in reserved tickets with advance-purchase discounts. In some cases, a short flight can be cheaper than taking the train. Make good use of Ouibus and Flixbus.

Car Rental: Allow roughly $250 per week, not including tolls, gas, parking, and insurance. If you need the car for three weeks or more, leasing can be cheaper.

AVERAGE DAILY EXPENSES PER PERSON

$195
Applies to most of France, allow 30 percent more for Paris.

Lodging
Based on two people splitting the cost of a $150 double room.
$75

Meals
$15 for breakfast, $20 for lunch and $40 for dinner
$75

City Transit
Buses or Métro
$10

Sights and Entertainment
This daily average works for most people.
$35

Budget Tips

Cut your daily expenses by taking advantage of the deals you'll find throughout France and mentioned in this book.

Some businesses—especially hotels and walking-tour companies—offer discounts to my readers (look for the RS% symbol in the hotel listings in this book).

Book your rooms directly with the hotel. Some hotels ▶▶▶

Rick Steves France

▶▶▶ offer a discount if you stay three nights or more (check online or ask). Or check Airbnb-type sites for deals.

It's easy to eat cheap in France. You can get tasty, inexpensive meals at bakeries (sandwiches, quiche, and mini-pizzas), cafés, *créperies*, department-store cafeterias, and takeout stands. Cultivate the art of picnicking in atmospheric settings.

City transit passes (for multiple rides or all-day usage) decrease your cost per ride in Paris: Buy a Navigo Easy travel card (which covers Paris as well as trips to outlying châteaux and the airports).

Avid sightseers buy combo-tickets or passes that cover multiple museums (like the worthwhile Paris Museum Pass). If a town doesn't offer deals, visit the sights that interest you most, and seek out free sights and experiences (people-watching counts).

When you splurge, choose an experience you'll always remember, such as a concert in Paris' Sainte-Chapelle or an alpine lift to panoramic views. Minimize souvenir shopping—how will you get it all home? Focus instead on collecting wonderful memories. ▪

Tasting wine, playing boules, *and taking public transportation*

BEFORE YOU GO

You'll have a smoother trip if you tackle a few things ahead of time. For more information on these topics, see the Practicalities chapter (and www.ricksteves.com, which has helpful tips and travel talks).

Make sure your travel documents are valid. If your passport is due to expire within six months of your ticketed date of return, you need to renew it. Allow up to six weeks to renew or get a passport (www.travel.state.gov). Beginning in 2021, you may also need to register with the European Travel Information and Authorization System (ETIAS).

Arrange your transportation. Book your international flights early. Figure out your main form of transportation within France: You can buy train tickets as you go, get a rail pass, rent a car, or book a cheap flight. Train travelers: You're required to make seat reservations for high-speed trains (your only option on some routes); book these as early as possible, particularly if using a rail pass, because trains can fill up and pass-holder reservations are limited.

Book rooms well in advance, especially if your trip falls during peak season or any major holidays or festivals.

Reserve or buy tickets ahead for major sights, saving you from long ticket-buying lines. Book an entry time online for the Eiffel Tower several months in advance. Some prehistoric caves in the Dordogne region take online reservations. For the greatest cave, Font-de-Gaume, there are no reservations; book a tour guide with tickets as far ahead as possible (at least six months).

Hire guides in advance. Popular guides can get booked up. If you want a specific guide, reserve by email as far ahead as possible—especially important for Paris, the D-Day beaches, Provence, and Burgundy's wine country.

Consider travel insurance. Compare the cost of the insurance to the cost of your potential loss. Check whether your existing insurance (health, homeowners, or renters) covers you and your possessions overseas.

Call your bank. Alert your bank that you'll be using your debit and credit cards in Europe. Ask about transaction fees, and get the PIN number for your credit card, particularly if driving (for gas stations and tollbooths). You don't need to bring euros for your trip; you can withdraw euros from cash machines in Europe.

Use your smartphone smartly. Sign up for an international service plan to reduce your costs, or rely on Wi-Fi in Europe instead. Download any apps you'll want on the road, such as maps, translation, transit schedules, and Rick Steves Audio Europe (see sidebar).

Rip up this book! Turn chapters into mini guidebooks: Break the book's spine and use a utility knife to slice apart chapters, keeping gummy edges intact. Reinforce the chapter spines with clear wide tape; use a heavy-duty stapler; or make or buy a cheap cover (see the Travel Store at www.ricksteves.com), swapping out chapters as you travel.

Pack light. You'll walk with your luggage far more than you think. Bring a single carry-on bag and a daypack. Use the packing checklist in the appendix as a guide.

∩ Stick This Guidebook in Your Ear!

My free Rick Steves Audio Europe app makes it easy for you to download my audio tours of many of Europe's top attractions and listen to them offline during your travels. For France, these include my Historic Paris and Rue Cler walks, and tours of the Louvre and Orsay museums, Versailles Palace, and Père Lachaise Cemetery. Sights covered by audio tours are marked in this book with this symbol: ∩. The app also offers insightful travel interviews from my public radio show with experts from France and around the globe. It's all free! You can download the app via Apple's App Store, Google Play, or Amazon's Appstore. For more info, see www.ricksteves.com/audioeurope.

Travel Smart

If you have a positive attitude, equip yourself with good information (this book), and expect to travel smart, you will.

Read—and reread—this book. To have an "A" trip, be an "A" student. Note opening hours of sights, closed days, crowd-beating tips, and whether reservations are required or advisable. Check the latest at www.ricksteves.com/update.

Be your own tour guide. As you travel, get up-to-date info on sights, reserve tickets and tours, reconfirm hotels and travel arrangements, and check transit connections. Visit local tourist information offices (TIs). Upon arrival in a new town, lay the groundwork for a smooth departure; confirm the train, bus, or road you'll take when you leave.

Outsmart thieves. Pickpockets abound in crowded places where tourists congregate. Treat commotions as

The Language Barrier and That French Attitude

You may have heard that the French are cold and refuse to speak English. This preconception is outdated. The French are as friendly as any other people (if a bit more formal). But be reasonable in your expectations: French waiters are paid to be efficient, not chatty.

The best advice? Slow down. Hurried, impatient travelers who don't recognize the pleasures of people-watching from a sun-dappled café often misinterpret French attitudes. With *beaucoup* paid vacation and 35-hour workweeks, your hosts can't fathom why anyone would rush through their time off. By making an effort to appreciate French culture, you're likely to have a richer experience.

The French take great pride in their customs and cling to a sense of their own cultural importance. They view formality as being polite, and prefer to avoid eye contact with strangers. When tourists stroll down the street with a big grin blurting "*Bonjour!*" to people they don't know, it's considered a little crazy rather than friendly.

Communication difficulties are exaggerated, but you'll get better treatment if you use the pleasantries. Learn these five phrases: *bonjour* (good day), *pardon* (pardon me), *s'il vous plaît* (please), *merci* (thank you), and *au revoir* (good-bye). Begin every encounter (for instance, when entering a shop) with "*Bonjour, madame* (or *monsieur*)," and end every encounter with "*Au revoir, madame* (or *monsieur*)."

When you attempt to speak French, you may be politely corrected—*c'est normal* (to be expected; they correct each other, too). The French are linguistic perfectionists; they take their language (and other languages) seriously. To ask a French person to speak English, say, "*Bonjour, madame* (or *monsieur*). *Parlez-vous anglais?*" They may smile and say "*non*," but as you struggle on, you may soon find out they speak more English than you speak French. This isn't a tourist-baiting tactic, but timidity on their part to speak another language less than fluently.

Practice the French survival phrases in this book (see the appendix), and have a translation app or a French/English dictionary handy. In transactions, a notepad and pen minimize misunderstandings; have vendors write down the price. For more tips, consider the *Rick Steves French Phrase Book & Dictionary* (available at www.ricksteves.com). ◼

smokescreens for theft. Keep your cash, credit cards, and passport secure in a money belt tucked under your clothes; carry only a day's spending money in your front pocket. Don't set valuable items down on counters or café tabletops, where they can be quickly stolen or easily forgotten.

Minimize potential loss. Keep expensive gear to a minimum. Bring photocopies of important documents (passport and cards) to aid in replacement if the originals are lost or stolen. Back up photos and files frequently.

Guard your time and energy. Taking a taxi can be a good value if it saves you a long wait for a cheap bus or an exhausting walk across town. To avoid long lines, follow the crowd-beating tips in this book, such as making advance reservations or sightseeing early or late.

Be flexible. Even if you have a well-planned itinerary, expect changes, strikes, closures, sore feet, bad weather, and so on. Your Plan B could turn out to be even better.

Going underground in Paris and on top of the world in the French Alps

Attempt the language. The French appreciate your effort. If you learn even just a few phrases, you'll get more smiles and make more friends. See the sidebar on page 30 for tips.

Connect with the culture. Interacting with locals carbonates your experience. Enjoy the friendliness of the French people. Ask questions; most locals are happy to point you in their idea of the right direction. Set up your own quest for the best croissant, sidewalk café, hill town, or the château you'd like to call home. When an opportunity pops up, make it a habit to say "yes."

France...here you come!

PARIS

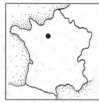

Paris—the City of Light—has been a beacon of culture for centuries. As a world capital of art, fashion, food, literature, and ideas, it stands as a symbol of all the fine things human civilization can offer. Come prepared to celebrate this, rather than judge our cultural differences, and you'll capture the romance and joie de vivre that this city exudes.

Paris offers sweeping boulevards, chatty crêpe stands, chic boutiques, and world-class art galleries. Sip decaf with deconstructionists at a sidewalk café, then step into an Impressionist painting in a tree-lined park. Pay homage to beloved Notre-Dame, recovering from a devastating fire. Cruise the Seine, zip to the top of the Eiffel Tower, and saunter down Avenue des Champs-Elysées. Master the Louvre and Orsay museums. Save some after-dark energy for one of the world's most romantic cities.

PLANNING YOUR TIME

If you have only one day, just do Day 1; for two days, add Day 2, and so on. When deciding where to plug in Versailles (see next chapter), remember that the main palace is closed on Mondays and especially crowded on Sundays, Tuesdays, and Saturdays (in that order).

Day 1: Follow this chapter's Historic Paris Walk. In the afternoon, tour the Louvre. Then enjoy the Place du Trocadéro scene and a twilight ride up the Eiffel Tower.

Day 2: Stroll the Champs-Elysées from the Arc de Triomphe to the Tuileries Garden. Tour the Orsay Museum. Take a nighttime tour by cruise boat, taxi/Uber, bus, or retro-chic Deux Chevaux car.

Day 3: Go early by train to Versailles. Tour the château's interior, then either sample the gardens or return to Paris for more sightseeing.

Day 4: Visit Montmartre and the Sacré-Cœur Basilica. Have lunch in Montmartre. Continue your Impressionist theme by touring the Orangerie. Enjoy dinner on Ile St. Louis, then a floodlit walk by Notre-Dame.

Day 5: Browse the morning market in the Rue Cler neighborhood, and spend the afternoon sightseeing at the Rodin Museum and the Army Museum and Napoleon's Tomb.

Day 6: Ride scenic bus #69 to the Marais and tour this neighborhood, including the Pompidou Center. In the afternoon, visit the Opéra Garnier, and end your day with rooftop views at the Galeries Lafayette or Printemps department stores.

Day 7: See more in Paris (such as Left Bank shopping, Père Lachaise Cemetery, Marmottan Museum), or day trip to Chartres or Giverny.

Orientation to Paris

Paris is magnificent, but it's also super-sized, crowded, and fast-paced. Take a deep breath, then use this orientation to the City of Light to help illuminate your trip.

PARIS: A VERBAL MAP

Central Paris (population 2.3 million) is circled by a ring road and split in half by the Seine River, which runs east-west. As you look downstream, the Right Bank (Rive Droite) is on your right, and the Left Bank (Rive Gauche) on your left. The bull's-eye on your map is Notre-Dame, on an island in the middle of the Seine and ground zero in Paris.

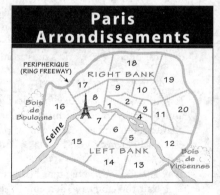

Twenty arrondissements (administrative districts) spiral out from the center, like an escargot shell. If your hotel's zip code is 75007, you know (from the last two digits) that it's in the 7th arrondissement. The city is riddled with Métro stops, and most Parisians locate addresses by the closest stop. So in Parisian jargon, the Eiffel Tower is on *la Rive Gauche* (the Left Bank) in the *7ème* (7th arrondissement), zip code 75007, Mo: Trocadéro (the nearest Métro stop).

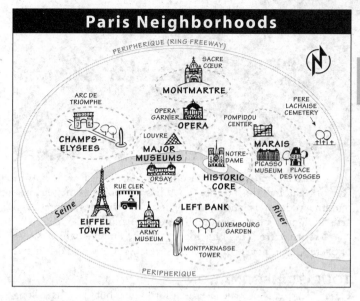

PARIS BY NEIGHBORHOOD

Paris is a big city, but its major sights cluster in convenient zones. Grouping your sightseeing, walks, dining, and shopping thoughtfully can save you lots of time and money.

Historic Core: This area centers on the Ile de la Cité ("Island of the City"), located in the middle of the Seine. On the Ile de la Cité, you'll find Paris' oldest sights, from Roman ruins to the medieval Notre-Dame and Sainte-Chapelle churches.

Major Museums Neighborhood: Located just west of the historic core, this is where you'll find the Louvre, Orsay, Orangerie, and Tuileries Garden.

Champs-Elysées: The greatest of the many grand, 19th-century boulevards on the Right Bank, the Champs-Elysées runs northwest from Place de la Concorde to the Arc de Triomphe.

Eiffel Tower Neighborhood: Dominated by the Eiffel Tower, this area also boasts the colorful Rue Cler, the Army Museum and Napoleon's Tomb, and the Rodin Museum.

Opéra Neighborhood: Surrounding the Opéra Garnier, this classy area on the Right Bank is home to a series of grand boulevards and monuments. Along with elegant sights such as the Opéra Garnier, the neighborhood also offers high-end shopping.

Left Bank: The Left Bank is home to...the Left Bank. Anchored by the large Luxembourg Garden, the Left Bank is the traditional neighborhood of Paris' intellectual, artistic, and café life.

Marais: Stretching eastward to Bastille along Rue de Rivoli/ Rue St. Antoine, this neighborhood has lots of recommended restaurants and hotels, shops, the delightful Place des Vosges, and artistic sights such as the Pompidou Center and Picasso Museum.

Montmartre: This hill, topped by the bulbous white domes of Sacré-Cœur, hovers on the northern fringes of your Paris map.

TOURIST INFORMATION

Paris' "TIs" can provide useful information but may have long lines. TIs sell Museum Passes and individual tickets to sights, but charge a small fee and may have longer lines than the museums (see "Sightseeing Strategies," later).

The main TI is located at the **Hôtel de Ville** (daily 10:00-18:30, 29 Rue de Rivoli—located on the north side of the Hôtel de Ville City Hall). You should find smaller TIs at **Gare du Nord** (daily 8:00-18:00), and at the **Puces St. Ouen** flea market (Sat-Mon 10:00-13:00 & 14:00-17:00, closed Tue-Fri, 120 Rue des Rosiers, tel. 01 58 61 22 90). In summer, TI kiosks may pop up in the squares in front of Notre-Dame and Hôtel de Ville. Both **airports** have handy TIs with long hours.

Event Listings: The weekly *L'Officiel des Spectacles* (available at any newsstand) is in French only but has easy-to-decipher listings of the most up-to-date museum hours, art exhibits, concerts, festivals, plays, movies, and nightclubs. The *Paris Voice*, with snappy English-language reviews of concerts, plays, and current events, is available online-only at www.parisvoice.com.

ARRIVAL IN PARIS

For a comprehensive rundown of the city's train stations, airports, and options for parking, see "Paris Connections" at the end of this chapter.

HELPFUL HINTS

Theft Alert: Paris is safe in terms of violent crime but is filled with thieves and scammers who target tourists. Don't be paranoid; just be smart. Wherever there are crowds (especially of tourists) there are thieves at work. They thrive near famous monuments and on Métro and train lines that serve airports and high-profile tourist sights. Pickpockets work busy lines (e.g., at ticket windows at train stations). Look out for groups of young girls who swarm around you (be very firm—even forceful—and walk away).

It's smart to wear a money belt, put your wallet in your front pocket, loop your day bag over your shoulders, and keep a tight hold on your purse or shopping bag. Watch out for your electronics; pickpockets snatch smartphones and tablets, too.

Muggings are rare, but they do occur. If you're out late, avoid dark riverfront embankments and any place with dim lighting and few pedestrians.

Paris has taken action to combat crime by stationing police at monuments, on streets, and on the Métro, and installing security cameras at key sights.

Tourist Scams: Be aware of the latest tricks, such as the "found ring" scam (a con artist pretends to find a "pure gold" ring on the ground and offers to sell it to you) or the "friendship bracelet" scam (a vendor asks you to help with a demo, makes a bracelet on your arm that seems like it can't easily be removed, and then asks you to pay for it). Don't be intimidated. They are removed with the pull of a string.

Distractions by a stranger can all be tricks that function as a smokescreen for theft. As you try to wriggle away from the pushy stranger, an accomplice picks your pocket. Be wary of a "salesman" monopolizing your attention, an "activist" asking you to sign a petition (and then bullying you into a contribution), someone posing as a deaf person to show you a small note to read, or a sidewalk hawker inviting you to play shell games (his thuggish accomplices are likely lurking nearby). Be skeptical of anything too good to be true, such as overly friendly people inviting you into impossibly friendly (or sexy) bars late at night.

Never agree to take a ride from strangers at train stations or airports. They may tell stories of problems with public transit—don't fall for it.

To all these scammers, simply say "no" firmly and step away purposefully. For reports from my readers on the latest scams, go to https://community.ricksteves.com/travel-forum/tourist-scams.

Pedestrian Safety: Parisian drivers are notorious for ignoring

PARIS

pedestrians. Paris' popular and cheap short-term electric-car rental program (Autolib') has put many of these small, silent machines on the streets—pay attention. Don't assume you have the right of way, even in a crosswalk. Bikes commonly go against traffic, so always look both ways, even on one-way streets.

Medical Help: There are a variety of English-speaking resources for medical help in Paris, including doctors who will visit your hotel. Try the American Hospital (63 Boulevard Victor Hugo, in Neuilly suburb, tel. 01 46 41 25 25, www.american-hospital.org) or SOS Médicins (SOS Doctors, tel. 3624, www.sosmedecins-france.fr).

Sightseeing Tips: For most sightseers, the best way to avoid long lines is to buy a Paris Museum Pass. You can also buy tickets in advance for certain sights. For more on these options, see "Sightseeing Strategies," later.

The Orsay, Rodin, Marmottan, and Picasso museums are closed on Mondays, as are the Catacombs, Petit Palais, Victor Hugo's House, Quai Branly, and the palace of Versailles (its gardens are open).

Many other sights are closed on Tuesdays, including the Louvre, Orangerie, Cluny, and Pompidou museums. The Champs-Elysées is traffic-free on the first Sunday of the month.

Wi-Fi: You'll find free hotspots at many cafés and in many public areas. In a café, order something, then ask the waiter for the Wi-Fi ("wee-fee") password (*"mot de passe"*; moh duh pahs).

Select Métro stations offer 20 minutes of free Wi-Fi, and more than 260 parks and other public areas offer two hours of free Wi-Fi (look for the Paris Wi-Fi logo to find a network).

The Orange network also has many hotspots and offers a two-hour pass for a small fee. If you come across one, click "Select Your Pass" to register.

Useful Apps: Gogo Paris reviews trendy places to eat, drink, relax, and sleep in Paris (www.gogocityguides.com/paris). The **RATP** app can help you plan Métro trips (see "Métro Resources" later in this chapter).

∩ For my free audio tours of some of Paris' best neighborhoods and sights (Historic Paris and Rue Cler, Louvre and Orsay museums, Versailles Palace, and Père Lachaise Cemetery), get the **Rick Steves Audio Europe** app (see page 28).

Public WCs: Many public toilets are free but you get what you pay for. If it's a pay toilet, the price will be clearly indicated, and the facility should be clean (thank Madame Pee-Pee who cleans). If there's an attendant, it's polite and sometimes required to leave a tip of €0.20-0.50. Booth-like toilets along the sidewalks provide both relief and a memory (don't leave small children inside unattended). The restrooms in museums are free and the best you'll find. Bold travelers can walk into any sidewalk café like they own the place and find the WC. Or do as the locals do—order a shot of espresso *(un café)* while standing at the café bar (then use the WC with a clear conscience). Keep toilet paper or tissues with you, as some WCs are poorly stocked.

Tobacco Stands *(Tabacs):* These little kiosks—usually just a counter inside a café—are handy and very local. Most sell public-transit tickets, postage stamps (though not all sell international postage), and...oh yeah, cigarettes. To find a kiosk, just look for a *Tabac* sign and the red cylinder-shaped symbol above certain cafés. A *tabac* can be a godsend for avoiding long Métro ticket lines, especially at the end of the month when ticket booths are crowded with locals buying next month's pass.

Winter Activities: The City of Light sparkles year-round. For what to do and see here in winter months, see www.ricksteves.com/pariswinter.

GETTING AROUND PARIS

Paris is easy to navigate. Your basic choices are Métro (in-city subway), suburban train (commonly called RER, rapid transit tied into the Métro system), public bus, tram, Uber, and taxi. Also consider the hop-on, hop-off bus and boat tours (described under "Tours in Paris," later). I've listed the handiest bus routes, Métro stops, and suburban train stations for each of my hotel neighborhoods in the Sleeping in Paris section.

You can buy tickets and passes at Métro stations and at many *tabacs*. Staffed ticket windows in stations are being replaced by ticket machines, so expect some stations to have only machines and an information desk. Some machines accept only credit cards and coins, though key stations always have machines that take small bills of €20 or less and chip-and-PIN cards (some American cards are accepted—try). These machines work logically with easy-to-follow instructions in English.

Information: The Métro, suburban train, and public bus systems share a helpful website: www.ratp.fr.

Public-Transit Tickets: Plans call for the old paper tickets used on the Métro, suburban trains (lines A-K), and buses to be replaced with plastic travel cards (called Navigo Easy, which can be shared and reloaded) and a smartphone app that can be used to download tickets and passes. The rollout may have happened by the time you visit. Until then, Métro, suburban trains, and buses all work on the same tickets. A **single ticket** costs €2. You can buy a *carnet* (kar-nay) of 10 tickets for about €15 (50 percent cheaper for ages 4-10). *Carnets* can be shared among travelers.

PARIS

Transit Basics

- The same tickets are good on the Métro, suburban trains (within the city), and city buses.
- Save money by buying a *carnet* of 10 discounted tickets or a Passe Navigo.
- Beware of pickpockets, and don't buy tickets from people roaming the stations.
- Find your train by its end-of-the-line stop.
- Insert your ticket into the turnstile, retrieve it, and keep it until the end of your journey.
- Safeguard your belongings; avoid standing near the train doors with luggage.
- At a stop, the door may open automatically. If it doesn't, open the door by either pushing a square button (green or black) or lifting a metal latch.
- Transfers *(correspondances)* between the Métro and suburban trains are free (but not between Métro/suburban trains and bus).
- Trash or tear used tickets after you complete your ride and leave the station (not before).

Passe Navigo: The weekly version of this pass covers all forms of transit from Monday to Sunday (expiring on Sunday, even if you buy it on, say, a Thursday). This chip-embedded card costs a one-time €5 fee (plus another €5 for the required photo; photo booths are in major Métro stations). The weekly unlimited pass (Navigo Semaine) costs about €23 and is good for all zones in the Paris region. You can buy your Passe Navigo at any Métro station in Paris.

Navigo or *Carnet?* The Navigo covers a far greater area than *carnet* tickets, including your trip from the airport (a €10.50 value alone), but cannot be shared. It's a great deal for visitors who use it for regional trips, or stay a full week (and start their trip early in the week). Two 10-pack *carnets*—enough for most travelers staying a week—cost €30, are shareable, and don't expire, but are only valid in the center of Paris.

Skip the **Paris Visite** travel card unless you plan to travel around the city extensively (1 day-€12, 2 days-€19.50, 3 days-€27, 5 days-€39).

By Métro

In Paris, you're never more than a 10-minute walk from a Métro

Key Words

French	English
station de Métro (stah-see-ohn duh may-troh)	Métro stop/station
direction (dee-rehk-see-ohn)	Direction
ligne (leen-yuh)	Line
A, B, C, D, E, F, G, H, I, J, K (ah, bay, say, day, euh, eff, zhay, ahsh, ee, jhee, kah)	A, B, C, D, E, F, G, H, I, J, K
Correspondence (koh-rehs-pohn-dahns)	connection/transfer
sortie (sor-tee)	exit
carnet (kar-nay)	discounted set of 10 tickets
Pardon, madame/monsieur. (par-dohn, mah-dahm/muhs-yuh)	Excuse me, ma'am/sir.
Je descends. (zhuh day-sahn)	I'm getting off.
Rendez-moi mon porte-monnaie! (rahn-day-mwah mohn porte-moh-nay)	Give me back my wallet!

station. Europe's best subway system allows you to hop from sight to sight quickly and cheaply (runs 5:30-1:00 in the morning, Fri-Sat until 2:00 in the morning). Learn to use it.

Using the Métro System: To get to your destination, determine the closest "Mo" stop and which line or lines will get you there. Lines are color-coded and numbered. You can tell their direction by the end-of-the-line stops. For example, the La Défense/Château de Vincennes line, also known as line 1 (yellow), runs between La Défense, on its west end, and Vincennes on its east end. Once in the Métro station, you'll see the color-coded line numbers and/or blue-and-white signs directing you to the train going in your direction (e.g., *direction: La Défense*). Insert your ticket in the turnstile, reclaim your ticket, pass through, and keep it until you exit the sys-

tem (some stations require you to pass your ticket through a turn-stile to exit). Fare inspectors regularly check for cheaters, accept absolutely no excuses, and have portable credit card machines to fine you on the spot: Keep that ticket or pay a minimum fine of €45.

Transfers are free and can be made wherever lines cross, provided you do so within 1.5 hours and don't exit the station. When you transfer, follow the appropriately colored line number and end-of-the-line stop to find your next train, or look for *correspondance* (connection) signs that lead to your next line.

When you reach your destination, blue-and-white *sortie* signs point you to the exit. Before leaving the station, check the helpful *plan du quartier* (map of the neighborhood) to get your bearings. At stops with several *sorties*, you can save time by choosing the best exit.

Métro Resources: Métro maps are free at Métro stations and included on freebie Paris maps at your hotel. For an interactive map of Paris' sights and Métro lines, with a trip-planning feature and information about each sight and station's history, see www.metro. paris. The free RATP mobile app can estimate Métro travel times, help you locate the best station exit, and tell you when the next bus will arrive (in English).

Beware of Pickpockets: Thieves dig public transit. You'll hear regular announcements in the Métro to beware of *les pickpockets*. Keep nothing of value in your pockets, and take care when buying tickets (watch your back). Be especially aware as you pass through the turnstile—if your pocket is picked, you end up stuck on the wrong side while the thief gets away. Stand away from Métro doors to avoid being a target for a theft-and-run just before the doors close. Any jostling or commotion—especially when boarding or leaving trains—is likely the sign of a thief or a team of thieves in action. Make any fare inspector show proof of identity (ask locals for help if you're not certain). Keep your bag close, hang on to your phone, and never show anyone your wallet.

By Suburban Train

The suburban train is an arm of the Métro, serving outlying destinations such as Versailles, Disneyland Paris, and the airports. Traditionally called RER (which you may see on signage), the line is undergoing a name change to simply "Train." These routes are indicated by thick lines on your subway map and identified by the letters A-K (see pronunciation guide in the "Transit Basics" sidebar). Throughout this chapter, you'll see it referred to as "RER/Train."

Within the city center, the suburban train works like the Métro and can be speedier if it serves your destination directly, because it makes fewer stops. Métro tickets are good on the suburban train; you can transfer between the Métro and suburban

Hop on the Bus, Gus

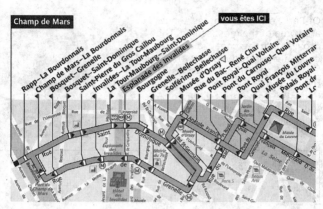

Just like the Métro, every bus stop has a name, and every bus is headed to one end-of-the-line stop or the other. This graphic shows the route map posted at the Invalides stop for bus #69.

First, find the stop on the chart—it says *"vous êtes ICI"* ("you are HERE") at Esplanade des Invalides. Next, find your destination stop—let's say Bosquet-Grenelle, located a few stops to the west. Now, find out exactly where to catch the bus going in that direction. On the route map, notice the triangle-shaped arrows pointing in the direction the bus is headed. You'll see that Esplanade des Invalides has two different bus stops—one for buses headed east, one for those going west. If you want to go west to Bosquet-Grenelle, head for that street corner to catch the bus. (One-way streets in Paris make it easy to get on the bus in the wrong direction.)

When the bus pulls up, double-check that the sign on the front of the bus has the end-of-the-line stop going in your direction—to "Champ de Mars," in this case.

train systems with the same ticket. But to travel outside the city (to Versailles or the airport, for example), you'll need a separate, more expensive ticket. The Passe Navigo card covers all suburban train trips, including to the airport and Versailles. Unlike the Métro, not every train stops at every station along the way; check the sign or screen over the platform to see if your destination is listed as a stop (*"toutes les gares"* means it makes all stops along the way), or confirm with a local before you board. For suburban trains, you may need to insert your ticket in a turnstile to exit the system.

By City Bus

Paris' excellent bus system is worth figuring out. Buses require less

Scenic Buses for Tourists

Of Paris' many bus routes, these are some of the most scenic. They provide a great, cheap, and convenient introduction to the city.

Bus #69 runs east-west between the Eiffel Tower and Père Lachaise Cemetery by way of Rue Cler, Quai d'Orsay, the Louvre, Ile St. Louis, and the Marais.

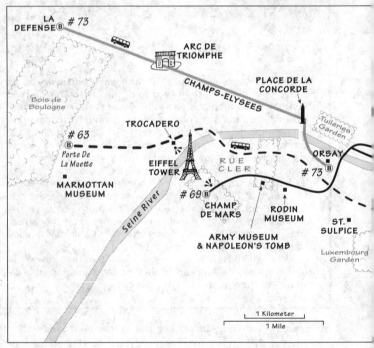

walking and fewer stairways than the Métro, and you can see Paris unfold as you travel.

Bus Stops: Stops are everywhere, and most come with a good city bus map, route maps for each bus that stops there, a frequency chart and schedule, live screens showing the time the next two buses will arrive, a *plan du quartier* map of the immediate neighborhood, and a *soirées* map explaining night service, if

Bus #63 is another good east-west route, connecting the Marmottan Museum, Trocadéro (Eiffel Tower), Pont de l'Alma, Orsay Museum, St. Sulpice Church, Luxembourg Garden, Latin Quarter/Panthéon, and Gare de Lyon.

Bus #73 is one of Paris' most scenic lines, starting at the Orsay Museum and running westbound around Place de la Concorde, then up the Champs-Elysées, around the Arc de Triomphe, and down Avenue Charles de Gaulle to La Défense and beyond.

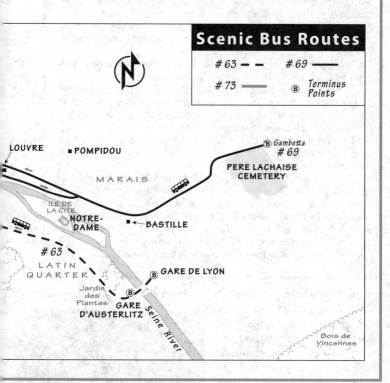

Scenic Bus Routes

# 63 – –	# 69 ——
# 73 ——	Ⓑ Terminus Points

available (there are even phone chargers at some locations). Bus-system maps are also available in any Métro station (and in the *Paris Pratique par Arrondissement* booklet sold at newsstands). For longer stays, consider buying the *Paris Urbain* book of transit info, including bus routes.

Using the Bus System: Buses use the same tickets and passes as the Métro and suburban trains. One Zone 1 ticket buys you a

PARIS

Scenic Bus Route #69

Why pay €35 for a tour company to give you an overview of Paris, when city bus #69 can do it for the cost of a Métro ticket? Get on the bus and settle in for a ride through some of the city's most interesting neighborhoods. Or use this line as a handy way to lace together many of Paris' most important sightseeing districts (you'll need a new ticket each time you board the bus).

Handy line #69 crosses the city east-west, running between the Eiffel Tower and Père Lachaise Cemetery, and passing these great monuments and neighborhoods: Eiffel Tower, Ecole Militaire, Rue Cler, Les Invalides (Army Museum and Napoleon's Tomb), Louvre museum, Ile de la Cité, Ile St. Louis, Hôtel de Ville, Pompidou Center, Marais, Bastille, and Père Lachaise.

If you're staying in the Marais or Rue Cler neighborhoods, line #69 is a useful route for just getting around town.

You can board daily until 22:30 (last departure from Eiffel Tower stop). It's best to avoid weekday rush hours (8:00-9:30 & 17:30-19:30) and hot days (no air-conditioning). Sundays are quietest, and it's easy to get a window seat. Evening bus rides are pretty from fall through spring (roughly Sept-April), when it gets dark early enough to see the floodlit monuments before the bus stops running.

In the Rue Cler area, eastbound line #69 leaves from the Eiffel Tower on Avenue Joseph Bouvard (the street that becomes Rue St. Dominique as it crosses the Champ de Mars, two blocks from the tower through the park). Board at one of the first few stops to secure a view seat. The first stop is at the southwestern end of the avenue; the second stop is at the eastern end (just before Avenue de la Bourdonnais).

bus ride anywhere in central Paris within the freeway ring road *(le périphérique)*. Use your Métro ticket or buy one on board for €0.10 more. These tickets are *sans correspondance*, which means you can't use them to transfer to another bus. (The ticket system has a few quirks—see "More Bus Tips," later.)

When a bus approaches, it's wise to wave to the driver to indicate that you want to be picked up. Board your bus through the front door. (Families with strollers can use any doors—the ones in the center of the bus are wider. To open the middle or back doors on long buses, push the green button located by those doors.) Validate your ticket in the

machine (stripe up) and reclaim it. With a Passe Navigo, scan it on
the purple touchpad. Keep track of which stop is coming up next by
following the onboard diagram or listening to recorded announcements. When you're ready to get off, push the red button to signal
you want a stop, then exit through the central or rear door. Even if
you're not certain you've figured out the system, do some joyriding.

More Bus Tips: Avoid rush hour (Mon-Fri 8:00-9:30 &
17:30-19:30), when buses are jammed and traffic doesn't move.
While the Métro shuts down at about 1:00 in the morning (even
later Fri-Sat), some buses continue much later (called *Noctilien*
lines, www.vianavigo.com). Not all city buses are air-conditioned,
so they can become rolling greenhouses on summer days. *Carnet*
ticket holders—but not those buying individual tickets onboard—
can transfer from one bus to another on the same ticket (within 1.5
hours, revalidate your ticket on the next bus). However, you can't
do a round-trip or hop on and off on the same line using the same
ticket. You can use the same ticket to transfer between buses and
trams, but you can't transfer between the bus and Métro/suburban
train systems (it'll take two tickets).

By Uber

Uber works in Paris like it does at home, and in general works
better than taxis in Paris (www.uber.com). Drivers are nicer and
more flexible than taxi drivers, it can be slightly cheaper than a taxi
outside of peak hours, and you can generally get a car wherever you
are within five minutes. Uber drivers can pick you up anywhere so
you don't have to track down a taxi stand, and you can text them if
you don't see the car. One downside is that Uber drivers can't use
the taxi/bus lanes during rush hour, so your trip may take longer at
busy times than it would in a cab.

By Taxi

Parisian taxis are reasonable, especially for couples and families.
The meters are tamper-proof. Fares and supplements (described
in English on the rear windows) are straightforward and tightly
regulated. Cabbies are legally required to accept four passengers,
though they don't always like it. If you have five in your group, you
can book a larger taxi in advance (your hotelier can call), or try your
luck at a taxi stand. A surcharge may be applied for a fifth rider.

Rates: The meter starts at €2.60 with a minimum charge of
about €7. A typical 20-minute ride (such as Bastille to the Eiffel
Tower) costs about €25 (versus about €1.45/person using a *carnet*
ticket on the Métro or bus, or about €15 via Uber). Taxis charge
higher rates at rush hour, at night, all day Sunday, and for extra
passengers. To tip, round up to the next euro (at least €0.50). The
A, B, or C lights on a taxi's rooftop sign correspond to hourly

rates, which vary with the time of day and day of the week (for example, the A rate of about €36/hour applies Mon-Sat 10:00-17:00). Tired travelers need not bother with the subtle differences in fares—if you need a cab, take it.

How to Catch *un Taxi*: You can try waving down a taxi, but it's often easier to ask someone for the nearest taxi stand (*"Où est une station de taxi?"*; oo ay ewn stah-see-ohn duh tahk-see). Taxi stands are indicated by a circled "T" on good city maps and on many maps in this book. To order a taxi in English, call the reservation line for the G7 cab company (tel. 01 41 27 66 99), or ask your hotelier or waiter to call for you. When you summon a taxi by phone, a set fee of €4 is applied for an immediate booking or €7 for reserving in advance (this fee will appear on the meter when they pick you up). You can also book a taxi using the cab company's app, which provides approximate wait times (surcharge similar to booking by phone). To download an app, search for either "Taxi G7" or "Taxis Bleus" (the two major companies, both available in English; note when entering your mobile number, you must include the international access code and your country code—use "+1" before the area code for a US/Canadian phone number).

If you need to catch an early morning train or flight, book a taxi the day before (especially for weekday departures; your hotelier can help). Some taxi companies require a €5 reservation fee by credit card for weekday morning rush-hour departures (7:00-10:00) and have a limited number of reservation spots.

By Bike

Paris is surprisingly easy by bicycle. The city is flat, and riders have access to more than 370 miles of bike lanes and many of the priority lanes for buses and taxis (be careful on these). You can rent from a bike-rental shop or use a city-operated bike-share program.

Though I wouldn't use bikes to get around routinely (traffic is a bit too intense), they're perfect for a joyride away from busy streets, especially on the riverside promenades. A four-mile stretch runs from near the Eiffel Tower to below the Bastille; the round-trip ride makes a wonderful hour-or-so long experience. (It could be much longer if you succumb to the temptations of the lounge chairs, hammocks, outdoor cafés, and simple delights of riverside Parisian life.) Bike-rental shops have good route suggestions.

TIs have a helpful "Paris à Vélo" map, which shows all the

dedicated bike paths. Many other versions are available for sale at newsstand kiosks, some bookstores, and department stores.

Bike About Tours is your best bet for bike rental, with good information and kid-friendly solutions such as baby seats, tandem attachments, and kid-sized bikes. Their office/coffee shop, called Le Peloton Café, offers bikes, tours, and artisan coffee (bike rent-al-€20/day during office hours, €25/24 hours, includes lock and helmet; Thu-Tue 9:30-17:30, closed Wed and Dec-Jan; shop/café near Hôtel de Ville at 17 Rue du Pont Louis Philippe, Mo: St-Paul, mobile 06 18 80 84 92, www.bikeabouttours.com).

Fat Tire Tours has a limited supply of bikes, so call ahead to check availability (€4/hour, €25/24 hours, includes lock and helmet, photo ID and credit-card imprint required for deposit; RS%—€2/day rental discount with this book, 2-discount maximum; office open daily 9:00-18:30, bike rental only after 11:00 as priority is given to those taking a tour, near the Eiffel Tower at 24 Rue Edgar Faure—see map on page 92, Mo: Dupleix or La Motte-Picquet Grenelle, tel. 01 82 88 80 96, www.fattiretours. com/paris).

The city's **Vélib'** program (from *vélo* + *libre* = "bike freedom") scatters 20,000 bikes at roughly 1,800 racks across town (non-electric bikes-free for the first 30 minutes, electric bikes-€1 for the first 30 minutes; the system is being overhauled—see www.velib-metropole.fr).

Tours in Paris

∩ To sightsee on your own, download my **free audio tours** that illuminate some of Paris' top sights and neighborhoods, including walks through Historic Paris and Rue Cler, and tours of the Louvre Museum, Orsay Museum, and Père Lachaise Cemetery (see sidebar on page 28 for details). Some tour companies offer a discount when you show this book (indicated in these listings with the abbreviation "RS%").

BY BUS OR PETIT TRAIN
Paris' cheapest "bus tour" is simply to hop on city bus #69 (see sidebar, earlier).

Hop-On, Hop-Off Bus Tours
Several companies offer double-decker bus services connecting Paris' main sights, giving you an easy once-over of the city with a basic recorded commentary. Buses normally run from about 9:30-19:00 in high season. You can hop off at any stop, tour a sight, then hop on a later bus. It's dang scenic—if you get a top-deck seat and the weather's decent. But because of traffic and stops, these buses

are sloooow. (Busy sightseers will do better using the Métro.) On the plus side, because the buses move so slowly, you have time to read my sight descriptions, making this a decent orientation tour—and there's free Wi-Fi. Buy tickets from the driver, or online and download directly to your smartphone.

L'OpenTour has the most options with reasonably frequent service on three routes covering central Paris (transfers between routes are OK). Their blue-and-green lines offer the best introduction and are most frequent (every 15 minutes in high season). You can catch the bus at just about any major sight (look for the Open Bus icon on public transit bus shelters and signs). L'OpenTour tickets are valid only for the days you purchase them, so get started early (1 day-€35, 2 days-€38, 3 days-€42, kids 4-11 pay €17 for 1, 2, or 3 days, days must be consecutive, allow 2 hours to complete a route with stops to visit a sight, tel. 01 42 66 56 56, www.paris. opentour.com). A combo-ticket covers the Batobus boats, described later (€47, kids 4-11-€21). L'OpenTour also runs night illumination tours that you can combine with a day pass for €48.

Big Bus Paris runs a fleet of buses around Paris on two routes with recorded narration—or use their better free app for sight descriptions (1 day-€34, 2 days-€38, kids 4-12-€17, €22 night tour, cheaper online, tel. 01 53 95 39 53, www.bigbustours.com).

City Sightseeing Tours' red buses run along two routes (11 stops each) and offer one advantage over the others: Your ticket is valid for 24 or 48 hours from the time you buy it—meaning that you could do an afternoon and a morning tour on consecutive days (1 day-€42, 2 days-€47, tickets valid for both routes, 3 buses/hour, 9 Avenue de l'Opèra, https://city-sightseeing.com).

Petit Train Tour

Another Paris offers tours on their blue *petit train* with see-through roofs (covered in the peak heat of summer) and huge view windows. Listening to simple yet informative audio commentary, passengers enjoy a leisurely ride through streets that large buses can't access. Tours cover neighborhoods such as the Marais, Latin Quarter, St. Germain-des-Prés, Louvre-Opéra, and "bohemian" Montparnasse-Montsouris-Porte de Vanves flea market. See their website for itinerary and departure details (€14-20, daily, 1.5 hours, disabled access, reservations required, mobile 06 31 99 29 38, www.another-paris.com, contact@another-paris.com).

BY BOAT
Seine Cruises

Several companies run one-hour boat cruises on the Seine. A typical cruise loops back and forth between the Eiffel Tower and the Pont d'Austerlitz, and drops you off where you started. For a fun experience, cruise at twilight or after dark. The first three companies are convenient to Rue Cler hotels, and run daily year-round (April-Oct 10:00-22:30, 2-3/hour; Nov-March shorter hours, runs hourly). Check their websites for discounts.

Bateaux-Mouches departs from Pont de l'Alma's right bank and has the biggest open-top, double-decker boats (higher up means better views). But this company caters to tour groups, making their boats jammed and noisy (€14, kids 4-12-€6, tel. 01 42 25 96 10, www.bateaux-mouches.fr).

Bateaux Parisiens has smaller covered boats with audioguides, fewer crowds, and only one deck. Skip this cruise if the boat lacks an outdoor deck. It leaves from right in front of the Eiffel Tower (€15, kids 3-12-€7, tel. 01 76 64 14 45, www.bateauxparisiens.com).

Vedettes de Paris boats also anchor below the Eiffel Tower and offer good outdoor seating on most of their boats. Their options include a one-way trip that drops off near Notre-Dame, or a round-trip with time to get out and explore the cathedral. They have a small bar on board so you can cruise with style (€15 standard one-hour cruise, €12 one-way, €16 round-trip with stop at Notre-Dame, tel. 01 44 18 19 50, www.vedettesdeparis.fr).

Vedettes du Pont Neuf offers essentially the same one-hour tour as the other companies with smaller boats; it starts and ends at Pont Neuf. The boats feature a live guide whose delivery (in English and French) may be as stiff as a recorded narration (€12, kids 4-12-€5, tip requested, nearly 2/hour, daily 10:30-22:30, tel. 01 46 33 98 38, www.vedettesdupontneuf.com).

Canauxrama runs a variety of relaxing cruises on the Seine or along the tranquil Canal St. Martin (boarding at Pont Neuf or Canal St. Martin, check online for routes, tel. 01 42 39 15 00, www.canauxrama.com).

Hop-On, Hop-Off Boat Tour

Batobus allows you to get on and off as often as you like at any of eight popular stops along the Seine. Boats make a continuous circuit and stop in this order: Eiffel Tower, Invalides, Orsay Museum, St. Germain-des-Prés, Notre-Dame, Jardin des Plantes, Hôtel de Ville, the Louvre, and Pont Alexandre III, near the Champs-Elysées (1

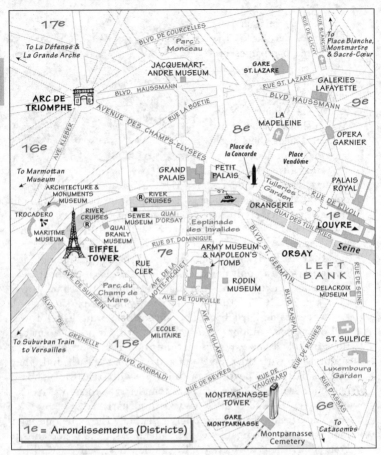

day-€17, 2 days-€19, April-Aug boats run every 20 minutes 10:00-21:30, Sept-March every 25 minutes 10:00-19:00, 45 minutes one-way, 1.5-hour round-trip, www.batobus.com). This is worthwhile as a scenic, floating alternative to the Métro, but if you just want a guided boat tour, the Seine cruises described earlier are a better choice. Combo-tickets covering L'OpenTour hop-on, hop-off buses (described earlier) are available, but skip the one-day ticket—you'll feel rushed trying to take full advantage of the bus and boat routes in a single day.

ON FOOT
Walking Tours

For food-oriented walking tours, see "Eating in Paris," later.

Paris Walks offers a variety of thoughtful and entertaining two-hour walks, led by British and American guides (€15-20, generally 2/day—morning and afternoon, private tours available,

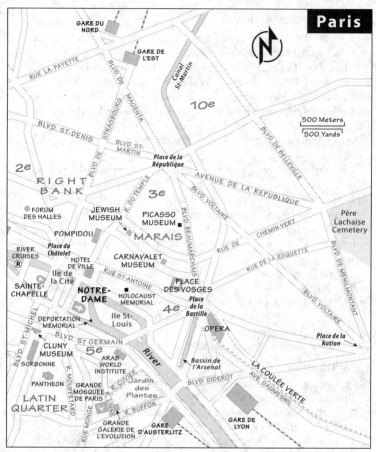

family-friendly and Louvre tours are a specialty, check current offerings online, tel. 01 48 09 21 40, www.paris-walks.com, paris@
paris-walks.com). Tours focus on the Marais, Montmartre, St.
Germain-des-Prés and the medieval Latin Quarter, Ile de la Cité/
Notre-Dame, the "Two Islands" (Ile de la Cité and Ile St. Louis),
the Revolution, and Hemingway's Paris. Specialty tours—such as
the Louvre, the Orsay, fashion, or chocolate—require reservations
and prepayment with credit card (deposits are nonrefundable).

Context Travel offers "intellectual by design" walking tours
geared for serious learners. Led by well-versed experts (historians,
architects, and academics), they range from traditional topics such
as French art history in the Louvre and the Gothic architecture
of Notre-Dame to more thematic explorations like immigration
and the changing face of Paris, jazz in the Latin Quarter, and the
history of the baguette. Book in advance—groups are limited to
six participants and can fill up fast (about €100/person, admission

PARIS

to sights extra, generally 3 hours, US tel. 800-691-6036, www.contexttravel.com, info@contexttravel.com). They also offer private tours and excursions outside Paris.

Fat Tire Tours offers high-on-fun and casual walking tours. Their two-hour Classic Paris Walking Tour covers most major sights (usually Mon, Wed, and Fri at 10:00 or 15:00). They also offer neighborhood walks, as well as a themed walk on the French Revolution. Their "Skip the Line" tours get you into major sights including Sainte-Chapelle, Catacombs, Eiffel Tower, and Versailles.

Reservations are required and can be made online, by phone, or in person at their office near the Eiffel Tower (€25/person for walking tours, €54-99/person for "Skip the Line" tours; RS%—€2 discount per person, 2-discount maximum; office generally open daily 9:00-18:00 or 19:00, shorter hours in winter, 24 Rue Edgar Faure, Mo: Dupleix, tel. 01 82 88 80 96, www.fattiretours.com/paris).

Paris Muse Tours offers guided scavenger-hunt-like tours to explore historic areas. Imagine yourself as a detective at the Louvre or a 19th-century art writer at the Orsay, or solve a real-life French Revolution murder mystery on the streets of Paris (€175-405 depending on group size, up to 8 people, 2.5 hours, mobile 06 73 77 33 52, www.parismuse.com, info@parismuse.com).

Local Guides
For many, Paris merits hiring a Parisian as a personal guide (€230-280 half-day, €400-500 full day).

Thierry Gauduchon is a terrific guide and a gifted teacher (mobile 06 19 07 30 77, tgauduchon@gmail.com).

Elisabeth Van Hest is another likable and very capable guide (tel. 01 43 41 47 31, mobile 06 77 80 19 89, elisa.guide@gmail.com). **Sylvie Moreau** also leads good tours (tel. 01 74 30 27 46, mobile 06 87 02 80 67, sylvie.ja.moreau@gmail.com).

Arnaud Servignat is a top guide who has taught me much about Paris (also does minivan tours of the countryside around Paris, mobile 06 68 80 29 05, www.french-guide.com, arnotour@icloud.com).

Joelle Valette-Coat is an effective teacher who takes her art seriously (tel. 01 46 06 74 95 or 06 86 28 32 20, jvalettecoat@hotmail.com).

Sylviane Ceneray is gentle and knowledgeable (mobile 06 84 48 02 44, www.paris-asyoulikeit.com).

Vincent Cabaret is a fine guide for Paris, day trips, and beyond, specializing in the Loire Valley and southwest (mobile 06 82 19 67 23, vincentcabaret@ymail.com).

ON WHEELS
Bike Tours

For contact information for these companies, see page 49.

Run by Christian (American) and Paul (New Zealander), **Bike About Tours** offers easygoing tours with a focus on the eastern half of the city (Marais, Latin Quarter, and Ile de la Cité). Their 3.5-hour tours run daily year-round at 10:00 (also at 14:30 May-Sept). Group tours have a 12-person maximum—reserve online to guarantee a spot, or show up and take your chances (€39, RS%—10 percent discount, show guidebook; helmets on request, private group tours available). They also offer day-trip bike tours of Versailles and the Champagne region.

Fat Tire Tours offers an extensive program of bike and walking tours (see earlier). Their young guides run three-hour bike tours of Paris day and night (adults-€34, students-€32; RS%—€4 discount per person, 2-discount maximum; reservations recommended but not required, especially in off-season). Kid-size bikes are available, as are tandem attachments (tours leave daily rain or shine at 10:30, April-Oct also at 15:00). Livelier night tours go past floodlit monuments and include a boat cruise on the Seine (€44, April-Oct daily at 18:30, less frequent in winter).

EXCURSIONS FROM PARIS

The following companies offer convenient transportation and a smidgen of guiding to destinations outside Paris.

Paris Webservices, a reliable outfit, offers private group day trips to Giverny and Versailles with well-trained, English-speaking chauffeur-guides in cushy minivans (figure €90-140/person for groups of 4 or more, RS%, tel. 01 45 56 91 67, or 09 52 06 02 59, www.pariswebservices.com, reservation@pariswebservices.com).

City Vision runs tours to several popular regional destinations, including the Loire Valley, Champagne region, D-Day beaches, and Mont St-Michel (2 Rue des Pyramides, Mo: Pyramides, www.pariscityvision.com). Their full-size bus tours are multilingual, mass-marketed, and mediocre at best, but can be worthwhile simply for the ease of transportation to the sights (about €50-170, destinations include Versailles, Giverny, Mont St-Michel, and more).

PARIS

Paris at a Glance

▲▲▲**Notre-Dame Cathedral** Paris' most beloved church will likely be closed for several years due to renovations following the 2019 fire. See page 60.

▲▲▲**Sainte-Chapelle** Gothic cathedral with peerless stained glass. **Hours:** Daily 9:00-19:00, Oct-March until 17:00. See page 69.

▲▲▲**Louvre** Europe's oldest and greatest museum, starring *Mona Lisa* and *Venus de Milo*. **Hours:** Wed-Mon 9:00-18:00, Wed, Fri, and first Sat of month until 21:45, closed Tue. See page 74.

▲▲▲**Orsay Museum** Nineteenth-century art, including Europe's greatest Impressionist collection. **Hours:** Tue-Sun 9:30-18:00, Thu until 21:45, closed Mon. See page 83.

▲▲▲**Eiffel Tower** Paris' soaring exclamation point. **Hours:** Daily mid-June-Aug 9:00-24:45, Sept-mid-June 9:30-23:45. See page 91.

▲▲▲**Champs-Elysées** Paris' grand boulevard. See page 104.

▲▲▲**Versailles** The ultimate royal palace (Château), with a Hall of Mirrors, vast gardens, and a grand canal, plus a queen's playground (Trianon Palaces and Domaine de Marie-Antoinette). **Hours:** Château April-Oct Tue-Sun 9:00-18:30, Nov-March until 17:30; Trianon/Domaine April-Oct Tue-Sun 12:00-18:30, Nov-March until 17:30; gardens generally April-Oct daily 8:00-20:30, Nov-March until 18:00; entire complex closed Mon year-round except the Gardens. See the next chapter.

▲▲**Riverside Promenades and Paris *Plages*** Traffic-free riverside areas for recreation and strolling; in summer, "beaches" add more fun. **Hours:** Promenades—always strollable; *Plages*—mid-July-mid-Aug 8:00-24:00. See page 74.

▲▲**Orangerie Museum** Monet's water lilies and modernist classics in a lovely setting. **Hours:** Wed-Mon 9:00-18:00, closed Tue. See page 90.

▲▲**Rue Cler** Ultimate Parisian market street. **Hours:** Stores open Tue-Sat plus Sun morning, dead on Mon. See page 95.

▲▲**Army Museum and Napoleon's Tomb** The emperor's imposing tomb, flanked by museums of France's wars. **Hours:** Daily 10:00-18:00, Nov-March until 17:00; tomb also open July-Aug until 19:00, tomb and Louis XIV-Napoleon I wing open April-Sept Tue until 21:00; Charles de Gaulle exhibit closed Mon year-round. See page 96.

▲▲**Rodin Museum** Works by the greatest sculptor since Michelangelo, with many statues in a peaceful garden. **Hours:** Tue-Sun 10:00-18:30, closed Mon. See page 97.

▲▲**Marmottan Museum** Art museum focusing on Monet. **Hours:** Tue-Sun 10:00-18:00, Thu until 21:00, closed Mon. See page 97.

▲▲**Cluny Museum** Medieval art with unicorn tapestries. **Hours:** Wed-Mon 9:15-17:45, closed Tue. See page 98.

▲▲**Arc de Triomphe** Triumphal arch marking start of Champs-Elysées. **Hours:** Exterior always viewable; interior daily 10:00-23:00, Oct-March until 22:30. See page 105.

▲▲**Opéra Garnier** Grand belle époque theater with a modern ceiling by Chagall. **Hours:** Generally daily 10:00-16:30, mid-July-Aug until 18:00. See page 109.

▲▲**Picasso Museum** World's largest collection of Picasso's works. **Hours:** Tue-Fri 10:30-18:00, Sat-Sun from 9:30, closed Mon. See page 112.

▲▲**Pompidou Center** Modern art in colorful building with city views. **Hours:** Permanent collection open Wed-Mon 11:00-21:00, closed Tue. See page 114.

▲▲**Père Lachaise Cemetery** Final home of Paris' illustrious dead. **Hours:** Mon-Fri 8:00-18:00, Sat from 8:30, Sun from 9:00, until 17:30 in winter. See page 115.

▲▲**Montmartre and Sacré-Cœur** Bohemian, hill-top neighborhood capped with a stunning white basilica and spectacular views. **Hours:** Daily 6:00-22:30; dome climb daily 8:30-20:00, Oct-April until 17:00. See page 116.

▲**Panthéon** Neoclassical monument and burial place of the famous. **Hours:** Daily 10:00-18:30, Oct-March until 18:00. See page 102.

▲**Ile St. Louis** Residential island behind Notre-Dame known for its restaurants. See page 67.

PARIS

Sightseeing Strategies

The best way to avoid long ticket-buying lines is with a Paris Museum Pass. If you forego the pass—or for sights not covered by the pass—I've outlined other options. All visitors must pass through (often slow) security checks at the most popular sights.

PARIS MUSEUM PASS
This pass admits you to many of Paris' most important sights, and allows you to skip most ticket-buying lines (but not security lines)—which can save hours of waiting, especially in summer. Another benefit is that you can pop into lesser sights that otherwise might not be worth the expense. Pertinent details about the pass are outlined here. For more info, visit www.parismuseumpass.com.

Buying the Pass
The pass pays for itself with four key admissions in two days (for example, the Louvre, Orsay, Sainte-Chapelle, and Versailles), and it lets you skip the ticket line at most sights (2 days-€48, 4 days-€62, 6 days-€74, no youth or senior discounts). Buy it in person upon arrival in Paris (it's not worth the cost or hassle to buy the pass online). The pass is sold at participating museums, monuments, TIs (small fee added)—including TIs at Paris airports—and some souvenir stores near major sights. Don't buy the pass at a major museum (such as the Louvre), where the supply can be spotty and lines long.

To determine whether the pass is a good value for your trip, tally up what you want to see from the list below.

Families: The pass isn't worth buying for children and teens, as most museums are free or discounted for those under age 18 (teenagers may need to show ID as proof of age). If parents have a Museum Pass, kids can usually skip the ticket lines as well. A few places may require everyone—even pass holders—to stand in line to collect your child's free ticket.

What the Paris Museum Pass Covers
Here's a list of key sights and their entry prices without the pass:

Louvre (€15)	Panthéon (€9)
Orsay Museum (€14)	Paris Sewer Museum (€4.40)
Orangerie Museum (€9)	Cluny Museum (€9)
Sainte-Chapelle (€10)	Pompidou Center (€14)
Arc de Triomphe (€12)	Picasso Museum (€14)
Rodin Museum (€12)	Conciergerie (€9)
Army Museum (€12)	Versailles (€30 total)

Notable sights *not* covered by the pass include the Eiffel Tower, Montparnasse Tower, Marmottan Museum, Opéra Garnier, Catacombs, Sacré-Cœur's dome, and the ladies of Pigalle.

Using the Pass

Plan carefully to make the most of your pass. Start using it only when you're ready to tackle the covered sights on consecutive days. The pass is activated at the time of first use and is time-based (not days-based). For example, a two-day pass gives you 48 hours of use from the time you first use it (e.g. if your first entry is at 13:00, you get 48 hours from 13:00). Make sure the sights you want to visit will be open when you want to go (many museums are closed Mon or Tue).

The pass provides the best value on days when sights close later, letting you extend your sightseeing day. Take advantage of late hours on selected evenings or times of year at the Arc de Triomphe, Pompidou Center, Sainte-Chapelle, Louvre, Orsay, and Napoleon's Tomb. On days that you don't have pass coverage, visit free sights and those not covered by the pass.

You can't skip security lines, though at a few sights (including the Louvre), pass holders may be able to skip to the front or enjoy "priority lines." Once past security, look for signs designating the entrance for reserved ticket holders. If it's not obvious, don't be shy—boldly walk to the front of the ticket line, hold up your pass, and ask the ticket taker: *"Entrez, pass?"* (ahn-tray pahs). You'll either be allowed to enter, or you'll be directed to a special entrance. For major sights, such as the Orsay Museum, I've identified pass-holder entrances on the maps in this book. Note that during peak times, the Louvre may not accept Museum Passes due to excessive crowds. You may need to make an advance reservation.

AVOIDING LINES WITHOUT A PASS

If you don't purchase a Paris Museum Pass, or if a sight is not covered by the pass, consider these options. Lines are shorter (and crowds are fewer) late in the day.

For many sights, you can buy **advance tickets** either at the sight's website (cheaper) or through a third party (for a fee). Some require you to choose a specific entry time, including the line-plagued Eiffel Tower, Louvre, and Catacombs, and the Marmottan Museum (special exhibits only). You can also buy advance tickets that allow you to skip the ticket-buying line for the Orsay, Sainte-Chapelle, and Monet's gardens at Giverny, as well as for activities and cultural events (Bateaux-Mouches cruises, Sainte-Chapelle concerts, and performances at the Opéra Garnier).

If you don't have a pass *and* can't buy tickets online, TIs, FNAC department stores, and travel-service companies such as Paris Webservices and Fat Tire Tours sell individual *"coupe-file"* **tickets** (pronounced "koop feel") for some sights. Compare your options: Some allow you to skip the ticket-buying line, others offer timed-entry and line-skipping, and still others provide a "host" to escort you into the sight (small fee at TIs, 10-20 percent surcharge elsewhere). FNAC stores are common, even on the Champs-Elysées (www.fnactickets.com, ask your hotelier for the nearest one); for Paris Webservices, see page 130.

Fat Tire Tours offers **"Skip the Line" tickets and tours** of major sights, including Sainte-Chapelle, Catacombs, Eiffel Tower, and Versailles (for contact info, see page 54).

Historic Paris Walk

Allow three to four hours for this three-mile self-guided walk, beginning at Ile de la Cité and ending at Pont Neuf (see the "Historic Paris Walk" map, later in this section).

🎧 You can download a free Paris Historic Walk audio tour.
• *Start near Notre-Dame Cathedral, the physical and historic bull's-eye of your Paris map. Access to the area around the cathedral is likely to change as reconstruction gets underway. Walk along the construction barriers to find the best view you can get of the cathedral's facade—near the entry to the Archeological Crypt is ideal, just off Rue de la Cité (see map). Start your tour here.*

Take in the scene around you: the church, the square in front, and the cityscape. You're looking at the symbolic heart of France.
• *Now turn your attention to the...*

❶ Notre-Dame Facade

Despite the 2019 fire, the main body of the church still stands strong. We'll get a better view of the damage later when we see the church from the side.

For now, find the circular window in the center of the fa-
cade, which frames a statue of a woman holding a baby. This church is dedicated to Mary, "Our Lady" (Notre Dame), the mother of Jesus. And there she is, cradling God, right in the heart of the facade, surrounded by the halo of the rose window.

Imagine the faith of the people who built this cathedral. They broke ground in 1163 with

Notre-Dame: The Fire, the Damage, and the Rebuild

At 18:50 on April 15, 2019, a fire ignited in the attic of Notre-Dame and quickly grew to an inferno. Paris came to a stand-still, transfixed with horror at the sight of its beloved church in flames. Within an hour, the 300-foot-long roof was reduced to cinders. Inside the church, parts of the stone ceiling broke apart and dropped to the floor far below, followed by massive, fiery, wooden roof beams. Soon after, the cathedral's soaring spire teetered, broke in two, and collapsed as the world gasped. That steeple—known as *la fleche* to Parisians ("the arrow")—was the needle around which this city spins. Incredibly, the fire was put out within nine hours, thanks to the heroic work of over 400 firefighters, mounting cranes while pumping water from the Seine.

The 13th-century lead roof and 19th-century spire were gone (400 tons of lead was lost in the fire). Inside the church, the nave was littered with fallen stones, the remains

of the steeple, and charred beams. Although most of the rib-arched stone ceiling support was intact, gaping holes opened to the sky. The falling debris caused some damage to the church's furnishings, but rescuers had managed to retrieve scores of priceless artifacts, including the Crown of Thorns, before the fire could reach them. The Grand Organ, one of Notre-Dame's most revered objects, with multiple keyboards and almost 8,000 pipes, was spared major damage.

No sooner had the smoke cleared than the French vowed to rebuild. Will they replicate Viollet-le-Duc's 19th-century spire, return to the 14th-century spire, or design something altogether new—perhaps a glassed-in greenhouse roof topped with a soaring futuristic spire? Whatever this great cathedral becomes, it's clear that Notre-Dame—like the people of Paris—is a survivor.

the hope that someday their great-great-great-great-great-great grandchildren might attend the dedication Mass, which finally took place two centuries later, in 1345. Look up the 200-foot-tall bell towers and imagine a tiny medieval community mustering the money and energy for construction. Master masons supervised, but the people did much of the grunt work themselves for free—hauling stones from distant quarries, digging a 30-foot-deep trench to lay the foundation, and treading on a wheel designed to lift the stones up, one by one.

PARIS

Notre-Dame Facade

BORED GARGOYLE

ENTHRALLED TOURISTS

Wow- What a great view!

← GARGOYLES

MARY IN ROSE WINDOW

Seine River

28 KINGS OF JUDAH

ST. DENIS (HOLDING HIS HEAD)

PORTAL OF MARY

LAST JUDGMENT

PORTAL OF ST. ANNE

To View of Flying Buttresses & Deportation Memorial

← To Right Bank

TOWER ENTRANCE

EXIT

ENTER

To Left Bank & Latin Quarter

DRINKING FOUNTAIN

POINT ZERO

WC

CHARLEMAGNE STATUE

HOTEL DIEU

Place du Parvis

To Sainte-Chapelle & 🇹

To Place St. Michel

• *Looking two-thirds of the way up Notre-Dame's left tower, you might spot Paris' most photographed gargoyle. Propped on his elbows on the balcony rail, he watches all the tourists below.*

St. Denis

If you could see through the barriers likely blocking the left doorway, you'd find a man with a misplaced head—that's **St. Denis,**

the city's first bishop and patron saint. He stands among statues of other early Christians who helped turn pagan Paris into Christian Paris. In the third century, Denis arrived from Italy to convert the Parisii. He settled here on the Ile de la Cité, back when there was a Roman temple on this spot and Christianity was suspect. Denis

proved so successful at winning converts that the Romans' pagan priests beheaded him as a warning to those forsaking the Roman gods. But those early Christians were hard to keep down. The man who would become St. Denis got up, tucked his head under his arm, headed north, paused at a fountain to wash it off, and continued until he found just the right place to meet his maker: Montmartre. The Parisians were convinced by this miracle, Christianity gained ground, and a church soon replaced the pagan temple.

• *Cross to the Left Bank over the Petit Pont bridge, then turn left along the river on Quai de Montebello. Stop on the next bridge (Pont au Double) for good views of the cathedral.*

Close your eyes and imagine the church in all its glory. Remove your metaphorical hat and "step inside" the church, to take a...

❷ Virtual Tour of Notre-Dame's Interior

Mentally "enter" the church—into a dark, earthly cavern lit with an unearthly light from the stained glass windows. Your eyes follow the slender columns up 10 stories to the praying-hands arches of the ceiling. Walk up the long central **nave** lined with columns and flanked by side aisles. The place is huge—it can hold up to 10,000 people.

The altar is at the center of this cross-shaped church. This was the holy spot for Romans, Christians... and even atheists. When the Revolutionaries stormed the church, they gutted it and turned it into a "Temple of Reason," complete with a woman dressed like Lady Liberty holding court at the altar.

If you were able to browse around the church, you'd see it's become a kind of Smithsonian for **artifacts** near and dear to the heart of the Parisian people. There's the venerated Crown of Thorns that supposedly Jesus wore (kept safely in the Treasury). A painting honors the scholar Thomas Aquinas (1225-1274), who studied at the University of Paris while writing his landmark theological works fusing faith and reason. And a statue of **Joan of Arc** (Jeanne d'Arc, 1412-1431), honors the French teenager who rallied her country's soldiers to try to drive English invaders from Paris.

The oldest feature inside the church is the blue-and-purple, **rose-shaped window** in the north transept—the only one of the three rose windows still with its original medieval glass. The newest feature is the huge white tarp covering the roof above to prevent rain from entering the church during reconstruction.

• *Now let's focus on the side of the church. Take the stairs down to the river (good for losing crowds and for Notre-Dame views). Climb back up at the next steps for the best viewpoint and to continue our tour.*

PARIS

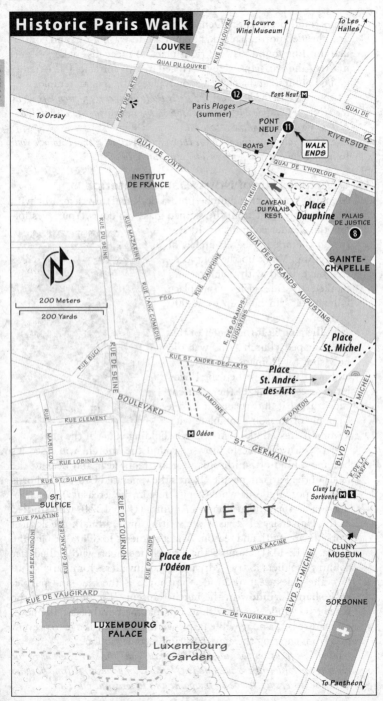

Historic Paris Walk

LOUVRE

QUAI DU LOUVRE

RUE DU LOUVRE

To Louvre Wine Museum

To Les Halles

To Orsay

PONT DES ARTS

⑫

Paris Plages (summer)

Pont Neuf Ⓜ

QUAI DE

QUAI DE CONTI

INSTITUT DE FRANCE

PONT NEUF

⑪

RIVERSIDE

BOATS

WALK ENDS

QUAI DE L'HORLOGE

CAVEAU DU PALAIS REST.

Place Dauphine

PALAIS DE JUSTICE

⑧

SAINTE-CHAPELLE

RUE DU SEINE

RUE MAZARINE

PONT NEUF

QUAI DES GRANDS AUGUSTINS

N

200 Meters

200 Yards

RUE DE L'ANC. COMEDIE

P.S.G.

RUE DAUPHINE

R. DES GRANDS AUGUSTINS

Place St. Michel

RUE BUCI

RUE ST. ANDRE-DES-ARTS

Place St. André-des-Arts

R. JARDINET

RUE DE SEINE

BOULEVARD

R. DANTON

MICHEL

RUE MABILLON

RUE CLEMENT

Ⓜ Odéon

ST. GERMAIN

BLVD. ST.

BLVD. ST.-MICHEL

RUE LOBINEAU

RUE ST. SULPICE

Cluny La Sorbonne Ⓜ Ⓣ

R. DE LA HARPE

ST. SULPICE

RUE PALATINE

LEFT

CLUNY MUSEUM

RUE SERVANDONI

RUE GARANCIERE

RUE DE TOURNON

RUE DE CONDE

Place de l'Odéon

RUE RACINE

SORBONNE

RUE DE VAUGIRARD

R. DE VAUGIRARD

LUXEMBOURG PALACE

Luxembourg Garden

To Panthéon

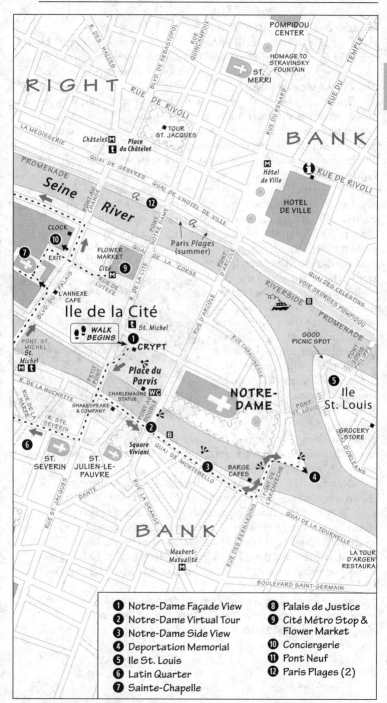

POMPIDOU CENTER

HOMAGE TO STRAVINSKY FOUNTAIN

ST. MERRI

R. DES HALLES

BLVD DE SEBASTOPOL

RUE QUINCAMPOIX

RUE DU TEMPLE

RUE DU RENARD

RIGHT

RUE DE RIVOLI

TOUR ST. JACQUES

BANK

LA MEGISSERIE

Châtelet M

Place du Châtelet t

M Hôtel de Ville

i RUE DE RIVOLI

QUAI DE GESVRES

QUAI DE L'HOTEL DE VILLE

HOTEL DE VILLE

PROMENADE

Seine

River

PONT AU CHANGE

PONT NOTRE-DAME

Paris Plages (summer)

PONT D'ARCOLE

QUAI DES CELESTINS

VOIE GEORGES POMPIDOU

CLOCK

EXIT

FLOWER MARKET

QUAI DE LA CORSE

RIVERSIDE

B

PROMENADE

Cité M

Ile de la Cité

BLVD DU PALAIS

L'ANNEXE CAFE

RUE DE LUTECE

R. DE LA CITÉ

WALK BEGINS

t St. Michel

CRYPT

GOOD PICNIC SPOT

PONT LOUIS PHILIPPE

PONT ST. MICHEL

St. Michel M t

R. DE LA HUCHETTE

PETIT PONT

Place du Parvis

CHARLEMAGNE STATUE WC

RUE D'ARCOLE

RUE CHANOINESSE

NOTRE-DAME

Ile St. Louis

GROCERY STORE

QUAI D'ORLEANS

SHAKESPEARE & COMPANY

R. STE. SEVERIN

Square Viviani

QUAI DE MONTEBELLO

B

BARGE CAFES

PONT AU DOUBLE

PONT ST. LOUIS

PONT DE L'ARCHEVECHE

RUE ST. JACQUES

ST. SEVERIN

ST. JULIEN-LE-PAUVRE

DANTE

RUE DE LA GRANGE

QUAI DE LA TOURNELLE

LA TOUR D'ARGENT RESTAURA

BANK

Maubert-Mutualité M

RUE DES BERNARDINS

BOULEVARD SAINT-GERMAIN

1 Notre-Dame Façade View
2 Notre-Dame Virtual Tour
3 Notre-Dame Side View
4 Deportation Memorial
5 Ile St. Louis
6 Latin Quarter
7 Sainte-Chapelle

8 Palais de Justice
9 Cité Métro Stop & Flower Market
10 Conciergerie
11 Pont Neuf
12 Paris Plages (2)

PARIS

❸ Notre-Dame Side View

From the side, you can really appreciate the devastation wrought by the 2019 fire. Before the fire, you'd have seen a green lead-covered roof topped with Violett-le-Duc's 300-foot steeple, and several statues adorning its base.

Those are gone completely, as is the lead roof and all windows—save for the three massive rose windows. But what's surprising is how much of the church survived. That's a testament to the medieval architects who designed this amazing structure. Their great technological innovation is what we've come to call the **Gothic style.**

In a glance, you can spot many of the elements of Gothic: pointed arches, the lacy stone tracery of the windows, pinnacles, statues on rooftops, and pointed steeples covered with the prickly "flames" (Flamboyant Gothic) of the Holy Spirit. Most distinctive of all are the flying buttresses. These 50-foot stone "beams" that stick out of the church were the key to the complex Gothic architecture. The pointed arches  built inside the church cause the weight of the roof to push outward rather than downward. The "flying" buttresses support the roof by pushing back inward.

Picture Quasimodo (the fictional hunchback) limping around along the railed balcony at the base of the roof among the "gargoyles." These grotesque beasts sticking out from pillars and buttresses represent souls caught between heaven and earth. They also function as rainspouts when there are no evil spirits to battle.

Nearby: The **Paris Archaeological Crypt,** which may be closed when you visit, is an intriguing 20-minute stop that lets you view Roman ruins from Emperor Augustus' reign (when this island became the birthplace of Paris), trace the street plan of the medieval village, and see diagrams of how early Paris grew (€8, covered by Museum Pass, Tue-Sun 10:00-18:00, closed Mon, good audioguide-€5, enter 100 yards in front of cathedral, tel. 01 55 42 50 10, www.crypte.paris.fr).

• *Continue along the river and cross the bridge (Pont de l'Archevêché) for views of the rear of the cathedral. Turn right to enter the park at the tip of the island. Look for the stairs at the Left Bank end of the park and head down to reach the...*

PARIS

❹ Deportation Memorial
(Mémorial de la Déportation)

This ▲ memorial to the 200,000 French victims of the Nazi concentration camps (1940-1945) draws you into their experience. France was quickly overrun by Nazi Germany, and Paris spent the war years under Nazi occupation. Jews and dissidents were rounded up and deported—many never returned.

Cost and Hours: Free, Tue-Sun 10:00-19:00, Oct-March until 17:00, closed Mon year-round, may randomly close at other times, free 40-minute audioguide may be available; at the east tip of Ile de la Cité, behind Notre-Dame and near Ile St. Louis (Mo: Cité); tel. 01 46 33 87 56.

Visiting the Memorial: As you descend the steps, the city around you disappears. Surrounded by walls, you have become a prisoner. Your only freedom is your view of the sky and the tiny glimpse of the river below. Enter the dark, single-file chamber up ahead. Inside, the circular plaque in the floor reads, "They went to the end of the earth and did not return."

The hallway stretching in front of you is lined with 200,000 lighted crystals, one for each French citizen who died. Flickering at the far end is the eternal flame of hope. The tomb of the unknown deportee lies at your feet. Above, the inscription reads, "Dedicated to the living memory of the 200,000 French deportees shrouded by the night and the fog, exterminated in the Nazi concentration camps." The side rooms are filled with triangles—reminiscent of the identification patches inmates were forced to wear—each bearing the name of a concentration camp. Above the exit as you leave is the message you'll find at many other Holocaust sites: "Forgive, but never forget."

• *To exit, climb the same stairs you descended. Before leaving the memorial park, look across the river (north) to the island called...*

❺ Ile St. Louis

If Ile de la Cité is a tugboat laden with the history of Paris, it's towing this classy little residential dinghy, laden only with high-rent apartments, boutiques, characteristic restaurants, and famous ice cream shops. Ile St. Louis wasn't developed until much later than Ile de la Cité (17th century). What was a swampy mess is now harmonious Parisian architecture and one of Paris' most exclusive neighborhoods.

PARIS

Look upstream (east) to the bridge (Pont Tournelle) that links Ile St. Louis with the Left Bank (which is now on your right). Where the bridge meets the Left Bank, you'll find one of Paris' most exclusive restaurants, La Tour d'Argent (with a flag flying from the rooftop). This restaurant was the inspiration for the movie *Ratatouille*. Because the top floor has floor-to-ceiling windows, your evening meal comes with glittering views—and a golden price (allow €200 minimum, though you get a photo of yourself dining elegantly with Notre-Dame floodlit in the background).

Ile St. Louis is a lovely place for an evening stroll (for details, see page 125). If you won't have time to come back later, consider taking a brief detour across the pedestrian bridge, Pont St. Louis, to explore this little island.

• *From the Deportation Memorial, cross the bridge to the Left Bank. Turn right and walk along the river until you reach the Pont au Double (the bridge leading to the facade of Notre-Dame). Carefully cross the street and continue on Quai de Montebello past a park until you see a cobbled lane on the left that leads to* **Shakespeare and Company,** *an atmospheric reincarnation of the original 1920s bookshop and a good spot to page through books (37 Rue de la Bûcherie). Before returning to the island, walk a block behind Shakespeare and Company, and take a spin through...*

❻ The Latin Quarter

This area (worth ▲) has a touristy fame relating to its intriguing, artsy, bohemian character. This was perhaps Europe's leading university district in the Middle Ages, when Latin was the language of higher education. The neighborhood's main boulevards (St. Michel and St. Germain) are lined with cafés—once the haunts of great poets and philosophers, now the hangouts of tired tourists. Exploring a few blocks up or downriver from here gives you a better chance of feeling the pulse of what survives of Paris' classic Left Bank. For colorful wandering and café-sitting, afternoons and evenings are best.

Although it may look more like the Greek Quarter today (cheap gyros abound), this area is the Latin Quarter, named for the language you'd have heard on these streets if you walked them in the Middle Ages. The University of Paris (founded 1215), one of the leading educational institutions of medieval Europe, was (and still is) nearby. Walking along Rue St. Séverin, you can still see the shadow of the medieval sewer system. The street slopes into a central channel of bricks. In the days before plumbing and toilets, when people still went to the river or neighborhood wells for their water, flushing meant throwing it out the window. At certain times of day, maids on the fourth floor would holler, *"Garde de l'eau!"*

("Watch out for the water!") and heave it into the streets, where it would eventually wash down into the Seine.

Consider a visit to the **Cluny Museum** for its medieval art and unicorn tapestries (see page 98). The **Sorbonne**—the University of Paris' humanities department—is also nearby; visitors can ogle at the famous dome, but aren't allowed to enter the building (two blocks south of the river on Boulevard St. Michel).

Don't miss **Place St. Michel.** This square is the traditional core of the Left Bank's artsy, liberal, hippie, bohemian district of poets, philosophers, winos, and *baba cool*s (neo-hippies). In less commercial times, Place St. Michel was a gathering point for the city's malcontents and misfits. In 1830, 1848, and again in 1871, the citizens took the streets from the government troops, set up barricades *Les Miz*-style, and fought against royalist oppression. During World War II, the locals rose up against their Nazi oppressors (read the plaques under the dragons at the foot of the St. Michel fountain). Even today, whenever there's a student demonstration, it starts here.

• *From Place St. Michel, look across the river and head toward the prickly steeple of the Sainte-Chapelle church. Cross the river on Pont St. Michel and continue north along the Boulevard du Palais. On your left, you'll see the doorway to Sainte-Chapelle (usually with a line of people).*

❼ Sainte-Chapelle

This triumph of Gothic church architecture, worth ▲▲▲, is a cathedral of glass like no other. It was speedily built between 1242 and 1248 for King Louis IX—the only French king who is now a saint—to house the supposed Crown of Thorns (moved to Notre Dame's treasury and now in safe keeping since the fire). Its architectural harmony is due to the fact that it was completed under the direction of one architect and in only six years—unheard of in Gothic times. Notre-Dame took more than 200 years.

Cost and Hours: €10, €15 combo-ticket with Conciergerie, free for those under age 18, covered by Museum Pass, advance tickets sold on church website and at FNAC stores; open daily 9:00-19:00, Oct-March until 17:00; audioguide-€3, 4 Boulevard du Palais, Mo: Cité, tel. 01 53 40 60 80, www.sainte-chapelle.fr. For info on upcoming church concerts, see page 123.

Avoiding Crowds: Security lines are shortest first thing in the morning (be in line by 9:00, or arrive at 10:00 after the early rush

PARIS

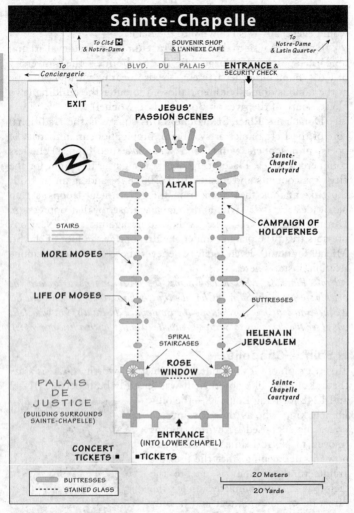

Sainte-Chapelle

To Cité Ⓜ & Notre-Dame

SOUVENIR SHOP & L'ANNEXE CAFÉ

To Notre-Dame & Latin Quarter

BLVD. DU PALAIS

ENTRANCE & SECURITY CHECK

To ← Conciergerie

EXIT

JESUS' PASSION SCENES

Sainte-Chapelle Courtyard

ALTAR

CAMPAIGN OF HOLOFERNES

STAIRS

MORE MOSES

LIFE OF MOSES

BUTTRESSES

SPIRAL STAIRCASES

HELENA IN JERUSALEM

ROSE WINDOW

Sainte-Chapelle Courtyard

PALAIS DE JUSTICE (BUILDING SURROUNDS SAINTE-CHAPELLE)

ENTRANCE (INTO LOWER CHAPEL)

CONCERT TICKETS ■

■TICKETS

BUTTRESSES
----- STAINED GLASS

20 Meters

20 Yards

subsides) and on weekends (when the courts are closed). They're longest on Tuesday and daily 13:00-14:00. To avoid this line, it may be worth rearranging the order of the walk: See Sainte-Chapelle first, then walk over to Notre-Dame (5 minutes away). Or see Sainte-Chapelle at the end of the day—being the last person in the chapel is an experience you'll never forget.

Visiting the Church: Though the inside is beautiful, the exterior is basically functional. The muscular buttresses hold up the stone roof, so the walls are essentially there to display stained glass. The lacy spire is Neo-Gothic—added in the 19th century. Inside, the layout clearly shows an *ancien régime* approach to worship. The low-ceilinged basement was for staff and other common folk—worshipping under a sky filled with painted fleurs-de-lis, a symbol of the king. Royal Christians worshipped upstairs. The paint job, a 19th-century restoration, helps you imagine how grand this small, painted, jeweled chapel was. (Imagine Notre-Dame painted like this...) Each capital is playfully carved with a different plant's leaves.

Climb the spiral staircase to the Chapelle Haute. Fill the place with choral music, crank up the sunshine, face the top of the altar, and really believe that the Crown of Thorns is there, and this becomes one awesome space.

Fiat lux. "Let there be light." From the first page of the Bible, it's clear: Light is divine. Light shines through stained glass like

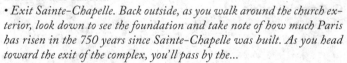

God's grace shining down to earth. Gothic architects used their new technology to turn dark stone buildings into lanterns of light. The glory of Gothic shines brighter here than in any other church.

The altar was raised up high to better display the Crown of Thorns, which cost King Louis more than three times as much as this church.

• *Exit Sainte-Chapelle. Back outside, as you walk around the church exterior, look down to see the foundation and take note of how much Paris has risen in the 750 years since Sainte-Chapelle was built. As you head toward the exit of the complex, you'll pass by the...*

❽ Palais de Justice

Sainte-Chapelle sits within a huge complex of buildings that has housed the local government since ancient Roman times. It was the

site of the original Gothic palace of the early kings of France. The only surviving medieval parts are Sainte-Chapelle and the Conciergerie prison.

Most of the site is now covered by the giant Palais de Justice, built in 1776, home of the French Supreme Court. The motto *Liberté, Egalité, Fraternité* over the doors is a reminder that this was also the headquarters of the Revolutionary government. Here they doled out justice, condemning many to imprisonment in the Conciergerie downstairs—or to the guillotine.

• *Now pass through the big iron gate to the noisy Boulevard du Palais. Cross the street to the wide, pedestrian-only Rue de Lutèce and walk about halfway down.*

PARIS

❾ Cité "Metropolitain" Métro Stop

Of the 141 original early-20th-century subway entrances, this is one of only a few survivors—now preserved as a national art treasure. (New York's Museum of Modern Art even exhibits one.) It marks Paris at its peak in 1900—on the cutting edge of Modernism, but with an eye for beauty. The curvy, plantlike ironwork is a textbook example of Art Nouveau, the style that rebelled against the erector-set squareness of the Industrial Age. Other similar Métro stations in Paris are Abbesses and Porte Dauphine.

The flower and plant market on Place Louis Lépine is a pleasant detour. On Sundays this square flutters with a busy bird market.

• *Pause here to admire the view. Sainte-Chapelle is a pearl in an ugly architectural oyster. Double back to the Palais de Justice, turn right onto Boulevard du Palais, and enter the Conciergerie (free with Museum Pass; pass holders can sidestep the ticket-buying line bottleneck).*

❿ Conciergerie

Though barren inside, this former prison echoes with history. The Conciergerie was the last stop for 2,780 victims of the guillotine,

including France's last *ancien régime* queen, Marie-Antoinette. Before then, kings had used the building to torture and execute failed assassins. (One of its towers along the river was called "The Babbler," named for the pain-induced sounds that leaked from it.) When the Revolution (1789) toppled the king, the progressive Revolutionaries proudly unveiled a modern and more humane way to execute people—the guillotine. The Conciergerie was the epicenter of the Reign of Terror—

the year-long period of the Revolution (1793-94) during which Revolutionary fervor spiraled out of control and thousands were killed. It was here at the Conciergerie that "enemies of the Revolution" were imprisoned, tried, sentenced, and marched off to Place de la Concorde for decapitation.

Cost and Hours: €9, €15 combo-ticket with Sainte-Chapelle, covered by Museum Pass, daily 9:30-18:00, videoguide-€6.50, 2

Boulevard du Palais, Mo: Cité, tel. 01 53 40 60 80, www.paris-conciergerie.fr.

Visiting the Conciergerie: Pick up a free map and breeze through the one-way, well-described circuit. You'll start in the spacious, low-ceilinged Hall of Men-at-Arms (Room 1), originally a guards' dining room warmed by four big fireplaces (look up the chimneys). During the Reign of Terror, this large hall served as a holding tank for the poorest prisoners. Then they were taken upstairs (in an area not open to visitors), where the Revolutionary tribunals grilled scared prisoners on their political correctness. Continue to the raised area at the far end of the room (Room 4, today's bookstore). This was the walkway of the executioner, who was known affectionately as "Monsieur de Paris."

Upstairs is a memorial room with the names of the 2,780 citizens condemned to death by the guillotine, including ex-King Louis XVI, Charlotte Corday (who murdered the Revolutionary writer Jean-Paul Marat in his bathtub), and—oh, the irony—Maximilien de Robespierre, the head rabble-rouser of the Revolution, who himself sent so many to the guillotine.

Just past the courtyard look up and notice the spikes still guarding from above. On October 16, 1793, Marie-Antoinette was awakened at 4:00 in the morning and led away. She walked the corridor, stepped onto the cart, and was slowly carried to Place de la Concorde, where she had her date with "Monsieur de Paris."

• *Back outside, turn left on Boulevard du Palais. On the corner is the city's oldest public clock. The mechanism of the present clock is from 1334, and even though the case is Baroque, it keeps on ticking.*

Turn left onto Quai de l'Horloge and walk along the river, past "The Babbler" tower. The bridge up ahead is the Pont Neuf, where we'll end this walk. At the first corner, veer left into a sleepy triangular square called Place Dauphine. It's amazing to find such coziness in the heart of Paris. From the equestrian statue of Henry IV, turn right onto Pont Neuf. Pause at the little nook halfway across.

⓫ Pont Neuf and the Seine

This "new bridge" is now Paris' oldest. Built during Henry IV's reign (about 1600), its arches span the widest part of the river. Unlike other bridges, this one never had houses or buildings growing on it. The turrets were originally for vendors and street entertainers. In the days of Henry IV, who promised his peasants "a chicken in every pot every Sunday," this would have been a lively scene. From the bridge, look downstream (west) to see the next bridge, the pedestrian-only Pont des Arts. Ahead on the Right Bank is the long Louvre museum. Beyond that, on the Left Bank, is the Orsay. And what's that tall black tower in the distance?

• *Our walk is finished. From here, you can tour the Seine by boat (the departure point for Seine River cruises offered by Vedettes du Pont Neuf is through the park at the end of the island—see page 51), continue to the Louvre, or head to the...*

PARIS

⑫ Riverside Promenades and Paris *Plages*

There's one traffic-free expanse on the Left Bank between the Eiffel Tower and the Orsay, and another on the Right Bank between the Louvre and the end of Ile St. Louis. Worth ▲▲, these areas are ideal for strolling, biking, having fun with the kids, dining—or, simply dangling one's feet over the water and being in the moment. In balmy weather, the embankment takes on a special energy. Each summer, the Paris city government trucks in potted palm trees, hammocks, and lounge chairs to create colorful urban beaches—the Paris *Plages*. For more on biking along the promenade, see page 48.

Cost and Hours: Free, promenades always open, *Plages* run mid-July–mid-Aug daily 8:00-24:00, on Right Bank of Seine, just north of Ile de la Cité, between Pont des Arts and Pont de Sully.

Sights in Paris

A 🎧 means the sight is covered by a free audio tour (via my Rick Steves Audio Europe app).

MAJOR MUSEUMS NEIGHBORHOOD

Paris' grandest park, the Tuileries Garden, was once the private property of kings and queens. Today it links the Louvre, Orangerie, and Orsay museums. And across from the Louvre are the tranquil, historic courtyards of the Palais Royal.

▲▲▲Louvre (Musée du Louvre)

This is Europe's oldest, biggest, greatest, and second-most-crowded museum (after the Vatican). Housed in a U-shaped, 16th-century palace (accentuated by a 20th-century glass pyramid), the Lou-

vre is Paris' top museum and one of its key landmarks. It's home to *Mona Lisa, Venus de Milo,* and hall after hall of Greek and Roman masterpieces, medieval jewels, Michelangelo statues, and paintings by the greatest artists from the Renaissance to the Romantics.

Touring the Louvre can be overwhelming, so be selective. Focus on the Denon wing, with Greek sculptures, Italian paintings (by Raphael and Leonardo), and, of course, French paintings (Neoclassical and Romantic), and the adjoining Sully wing, with Egyptian artifacts and more French paintings. For extra credit, tackle the Riche-

Major Museums Neighborhood

lieu wing, displaying works from ancient Mesopotamia, as well as French, Dutch, and Northern art.

Cost and Hours: €15, includes special exhibits, free on first Sat of month after 18:00, covered by Museum Pass—but during peak times, tickets may be limited and Museum Passes may not be accepted, timed-entry tickets available in advance at the website below; Wed-Mon 9:00-18:00; Wed, Fri, and first Sat of month until 21:45 (except on holidays); closed Tue, galleries start shutting 30 minutes before closing, last entry 45 minutes before closing.

Information: Tel. 01 40 20 53 17, recorded info tel. 01 40 20 51 51, www.louvre.fr.

When to Go: Crowds can be miserable on Sun, Mon (the worst day), Wed, and in the morning. Evening visits are quieter, and the glass pyramid glows after dark.

Buying a Museum Pass or Advance Ticket: With a Museum Pass or advance ticket, you can avoid long ticket-buying lines, and minimize the line for the security check. If you don't already have a Museum Pass, the **"Museum Pass Tabac"** (a.k.a. La Civette du Carrousel) sells them for no extra charge (cash only). It's just outside the Louvre entrance in the Carrousel du Louvre mall—to find it, follow *Museum Pass* signs inside the mall.

Timed-entry tickets are available **online** in advance (€2 fee; priority entry at the pyramid up to 30 minutes before your allotted time)—see the Louvre website for details. Skip-the-line tickets (extra fee) are sold at FNAC stores and by Paris tour companies; see page 60.

Buying Tickets at the Louvre: Inside the Louvre, tickets are sold in a side room under the pyramid—just line up for the next available self-service machine (machines only accept credit cards with a PIN) or ticket window.

Renovations: Expect changes to the room numbers in this tour as the museum undergoes renovations.

Getting There: Métro stop Palais Royal-Musée du Louvre is the closest. From the station, you can either exit above ground to go in the pyramid entrance, or stay underground to use the Carrousel du Louvre entrance. Eastbound bus #69 stops along the Seine River; the best stop is labeled Quai François Mitterrand. Westbound #69 stops in front of the pyramid (see the "Louvre Overview" map for stop locations). You'll find a taxi stand on Rue de Rivoli, next to the Palais Royal-Musée du Louvre Métro station.

Getting In: There are two entrances. Everyone must pass through security at the entrances.

Main Pyramid Entrance: There is no grander entry than through the main entrance at the pyramid in the central courtyard. The security line here can be very long, but if you have a ticket or a pass, you can use the VIP line.

Underground Mall Entrance: The less crowded underground entrance is accessed through the Carrousel du Louvre shopping mall. Enter the mall at 99 Rue de Rivoli (the door with the shiny metal awning) or directly from the Métro stop Palais Royal-Musée du Louvre (stepping off the train, exit to *Musée du Louvre-Le Carrousel du Louvre*). Once inside the mall, continue toward the inverted pyramid next to the Louvre's security entrance. There's no priority security line for Museum Pass holders here, but lines are generally shorter than the main pyramid entrance. (Don't follow signs to the *Passholders* entrance, which is at the pyramid, a long detour away.)

Once Inside: Once past security, everyone proceeds to the grand space beneath the glass pyramid with all the services. If you already have a ticket or Museum Pass, go directly to the galleries (our tour starts in the Denon wing). Otherwise, you can buy a ticket (see "Buying Tickets at the Louvre," above).

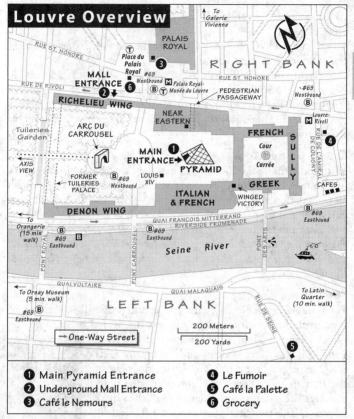

Louvre Overview

To Galerie Vivienne

PALAIS ROYAL

RUE ST. HONORE

Place du Palais Royal

❸ #69 Westbound

MALL ENTRANCE ❷

❻

RUE DE RIVOLI

RICHELIEU WING

RIGHT BANK

RUE ST. HONORE

Palais Royal–Musée du Louvre

PEDESTRIAN PASSAGEWAY

#69 Westbound

NEAR EASTERN

Tuileries Garden

ARC DU CARROUSEL

FRENCH

Cour Carrée

SULLY

Louvre–Rivoli

❹

RUE DE L'AMIRAL DE COLIGNY

AXIS VIEW

MAIN ENTRANCE → ❶ PYRAMID

FORMER TUILERIES PALACE

#69 Westbound

LOUIS XIV

GREEK

CAFES

ITALIAN & FRENCH

WINGED VICTORY

DENON WING

#69 Eastbound

To Orangerie (15 min walk)

#69 Eastbound

QUAI FRANCOIS MITTERRAND
RIVERSIDE PROMENADE

#69 Eastbound

PONT ROYAL

PONT CARROUSEL

Seine River

PONT DES ARTS

QUAI VOLTAIRE

QUAI MALAQUAIS

RUE DE SEINE

To Orsay Museum (5 min. walk)

#69 Eastbound

LEFT BANK

To Latin Quarter (10 min. walk)

→ One-Way Street

200 Meters

200 Yards

❺

❶ Main Pyramid Entrance
❷ Underground Mall Entrance
❸ Café le Nemours
❹ Le Fumoir
❺ Café la Palette
❻ Grocery

Expect Changes: The sprawling Louvre is constantly shuffling its deck. Rooms close, and pieces can be on loan or in restoration. If you can't find the artwork you're looking for, ask the nearest guard for its new location. Point to the photo in your book and ask, *"Où est, s'il vous plaît?"* (oo ay, see voo play).

Tours: Ninety-minute English-language **guided tours** leave twice daily from the *Accueil des Groupes* area, under the pyramid (normally at 11:00 and 14:00 plus 19:00 on Wed and Fri, possibly more often in summer; book in advance online, €12 plus admission, tour tel. 01 40 20 52 63). **Videoguides** (€5) provide commentary on about 700 masterpieces.

🎧 Download my free Louvre Museum **audio tour.**

Baggage Check: It's free to store your bag in slick self-service lockers under the pyramid. No bags bigger than a small day bag are allowed in the galleries. No bags bigger than airline carry-on size are allowed anywhere in the Louvre. Consider checking whatever you don't need—even if it's just a small bag—to make your visit more pleasant.

Services: WCs are located under the pyramid. Once you're in the galleries, WCs are scarce.

Eating near the Louvre: Try venerable Art Deco **$$** Café le Nemours or **$$$** Le Fumoir, which has a good-value two-course lunch *menu*. For a picnic in the adjacent Palais Royal gardens (enter from Place du Palais Royal), get supplies at the Franprix market on Rue St-Honoré.

◐ Self-Guided Tour

With more than 30,000 works of art, the Louvre is a full inventory of Western civilization. To cover it all in one visit is impossible. Let's focus on the Louvre's specialties—Greek sculpture, Italian painting, and French painting.

• *We'll start in the Sully wing, in Salle 16. To get there from the pyramid entrance, first enter the Denon wing, ascend several flights of escalators, and follow the crowds—then get out your map or ask for directions to the* Venus de Milo.

The Greeks

Venus de Milo (Aphrodite), late 2nd century BC: This goddess of love created a sensation when she was discovered in 1820 on the Greek island of Melos. The Greeks pictured their gods in human form (meaning humans are god-like), telling us they had an optimistic view of the human race. Venus' well-proportioned body captures the balance and orderliness of the Greek universe. The twisting pose gives a balanced S-curve to her body (especially noticeable from the back view) that Golden Age Greeks and succeeding generations found beautiful. Most "Greek" statues are actually later Roman copies. This is a rare Greek original.

• *Now head to Salle 6, behind* Venus de Milo.

Parthenon Friezes, mid-5th century BC: These stone fragments once decorated the exterior of the greatest Athenian temple of the Greek Golden Age. The temple glorified the city's divine protector, Athena, and the superiority of the Athenians, who were feeling especially cocky, having just crushed their archrivals, the Persians. A model of the Parthenon shows where the panels might have hung.

• *About 50 yards away, find a grand staircase. Climb it to the first floor and the...*

Winged Victory of Samothrace *(Victoire de Samothrace),* c. 190 BC: This woman with wings, poised on the prow of a ship, once stood on an island hilltop to commemorate a naval victory. Her clothes are windblown and sea-sprayed, clinging close enough to her body to win a wet T-shirt contest. Originally, her right arm was stretched high, celebrating the victory like a Super Bowl champion, waving a "we're number one" finger.

This is the *Venus de Milo* gone Hellenistic, from the time after the culture of Athens was spread around the Mediterranean by Alexander the Great (c. 325 BC). As *Victory* strides forward, the wind blows her wings and her back. Her feet are firmly on the ground, but her wings (and missing arms) stretch upward. She is a pillar of vertical strength, while the clothes curve and whip around her. These opposing forces create a feeling of great energy, making her the lightest two-ton piece of rock in captivity.

• *Facing* Winged Victory, *turn right (entering the Denon wing), and proceed to the large Salle 3.*

The Medieval World (1200-1500)

Cimabue, *The Madonna and Child in Majesty Surrounded by Angels (La Vierge et l'Enfant en Majesté Entourés de Six Anges),* c. 1280: During the Age of Faith (1200s), almost every church in Europe had a painting like this one. Mary was a cult figure—even bigger than the late-20th-century Madonna—adored and prayed to by the faithful for bringing Baby Jesus into the world. These holy figures are laid flat on a gold background like cardboard cutouts, existing in a golden never-never land, as though the faithful couldn't imagine them as flesh-and-blood humans inhabiting our dark and sinful earth.

Giotto, *St. Francis of Assisi Receiving the Stigmata (Saint François d'Assise Recevant les Stigmates),* c. 1295-1300: Francis of Assisi (c. 1181-1226), a wandering Italian monk of renowned goodness, kneels on a rocky Italian hillside, pondering the pain of Christ's torture and execution. Suddenly, he looks up, startled, to see Christ himself, with six wings, hovering above. Christ shoots lasers from his wounds to the hands, feet, and side of the empathetic monk, marking him with the stigmata. Francis' humble love of man and nature inspired artists like Giotto to portray real human beings with real emotions, living in a physical world of beauty.

• *Room 3 spills into the long Grand Gallery. Find the following paintings in the Gallery, as you make your way to the* Mona Lisa *(midway down the gallery, in the adjoining Salle 6—just follow the signs and the people).*

Italian Renaissance (1400-1600)

Leonardo da Vinci, *The Virgin and Child with St. Anne (La Vierge à l'Enfant Jésus avec Sainte-Anne),* c. 1510: Three generations—grandmother, mother, and child—are arranged in a pyramid, with Anne's face as the peak and the lamb as the lower right corner. It's as orderly as the geometrically perfect universe created by the Re-

PARIS

naissance god. There's a psychological kidney punch in this happy painting. Jesus, the picture of childish joy, is innocently playing with a lamb—the symbol of his inevitable sacrificial death. The Louvre has the greatest collection of Leonardos in the world—five of them. Look for the neighboring *Virgin of the Rocks* and *John the Baptist.* Leonardo was the consummate Renaissance Man; a musician, sculptor, engineer, scientist, and sometime painter, he combined knowledge from all these areas to create beauty.

Raphael, *La Belle Jardinière,* c. 1507: Raphael perfected the style Leonardo pioneered. This configuration of Madonna, Child, and John the Baptist is also a balanced pyramid with hazy grace and beauty. The interplay of gestures and gazes gives the masterpiece both intimacy and cohesiveness, while Raphael's blended brushstrokes varnish the work with an iridescent smoothness. With Raphael, the Greek ideal of beauty—reborn in the Renaissance—reached its peak.

Leonardo da Vinci, *Mona Lisa,* a.k.a. *La Joconde,* 1503-1506: Leonardo was already an old man when François I invited him to France. Determined to pack light, he took only a few paintings with him. One was a portrait of Lisa del Giocondo, the wife of a wealthy Florentine merchant.

Mona may disappoint you. She's smaller than you'd expect, darker, engulfed in a huge room, and hidden behind a glaring pane of glass. The famous smile attracts you first, but try as you might, you can never quite see the corners of her mouth. The overall mood is one of balance and serenity, but there's also an element of mystery. *Mona*'s smile and long-distance beauty are subtle and elusive, tempting but always just out of reach. *Mona* doesn't knock your socks off, but she winks at the patient viewer.

Paolo Veronese, *The Marriage at Cana (Les Noces de Cana),* 1562-1563: Venetian artists like Veronese painted the good life of rich, happy-go-lucky Venetian merchants. In a spacious setting of Renaissance architecture, colorful lords and ladies, decked out in their fanciest duds, feast on a great spread of food and drink. But believe it or not, this is a religious work showing the wedding celebration in which Jesus turned water into wine. With true Renaissance optimism, Venetians pictured Christ as a party animal, someone who loved the created world as much as they did.

• *Exit behind Mona into the Salle Denon (Room 76). Turn right for French Neoclassicism (Salle Daru, David and Ingres); then backtrack through the Salle Denon for French Romanticism (Room 77, Géricault and Delacroix).*

French Painting (1780-1850)

Jacques-Louis David, *The Coronation of Emperor Napoleon (Sacre de l'Empereur Napoléon),* 1806-1807: Napoleon holds aloft an imperial crown. This common-born son of immigrants is about to be crowned emperor of a "New Rome." He has just made his wife, Josephine, the empress, and she kneels at his feet. Seated behind Napoleon is the pope, who journeyed from Rome to place the imperial crown on his head. But Napoleon feels that no one is worthy of the task. At the last moment, he shrugs the pope aside.

The setting for the coronation was the ultra-Gothic Notre-Dame cathedral. But Napoleon wanted a location that would reflect the glories of Greece and the grandeur of Rome. So, interior decorators erected stage sets of Greek columns and Roman arches to give the cathedral the architectural political correctness you see in this painting. (The pietà statue on the right edge of the painting is still in Notre-Dame today.)

Jean-Auguste-Dominique Ingres, *La Grande Odalisque,* 1814: Take *Venus de Milo,* turn her around, lay her down, and stick a hash pipe next to her, and you have the *Grande Odalisque.* OK, maybe you'd have to add a vertebra or two. Using clean, polished, sculptural lines, Ingres (ang-gruh) exaggerates the S-curve of a standing Greek nude. As in the *Venus de Milo,* rough folds of cloth set off her smooth skin. Ingres gave the face, too, a touch of *Venus'* idealized features, taking nature and improving on it. Contrast the cool colors of this statue-like nude with Titian's golden girls. Ingres preserves *Venus'* backside for posterior—I mean, posterity.

Théodore Géricault, *The Raft of the Medusa (Le Radeau de la Méduse),* 1819: Clinging to a raft is a tangle of bodies and lunatics sprawled over each other. The scene writhes with agitated, ominous motion—the ripple of muscles, churning clouds, and choppy seas. The bodies rise up in a pyramid of hope, culminating in a flag wave. They signal frantically, trying to catch the attention of the tiny ship on the horizon, their last desperate hope...which did finally save them. Géricault uses rippling movement and powerful colors to catch us up in the excitement. This painting was based on the actual sinking of the ship *Medusa* off the coast of Africa in 1816. About 150 people packed onto the raft. After floating in the open seas for 12 days—suffering hardship and hunger, even resorting to cannibalism—only 15 survived.

Eugène Delacroix, *Liberty Leading the People (La Liberté Guidant le Peuple),* 1831: The year is 1830. Parisians take to the streets once again, *Les Miz*-style, to fight royalist oppressors. Leading them on through the smoke and over the dead and dying is the figure of Liberty, a strong woman waving the French flag. Does this symbol of victory look familiar? It's the *Winged Victory,* wingless and topless.

To stir our emotions, Delacroix uses only three major colors—the red, white, and blue of the French flag. France is the symbol of modern democracy, and this painting has long stirred its citizens' passion for liberty. This symbol of freedom is a fitting tribute to the Louvre, the first museum ever opened to  the common rabble of humanity. The motto of France is *Liberté, Egalité, Fraternité*—liberty, equality, and brotherhood for all.

• *Exit the room at the far end (past the Café Mollien) and go downstairs, where you'll bump into...*

More Italian Renaissance

Michelangelo, *Slaves (Esclaves),* 1513-1515: These two statues by the earth's greatest sculptor are a bridge between the ancient and modern worlds. Michelangelo, like his fellow Renaissance artists, learned from the Greeks. The perfect anatomy, twisting poses, and idealized faces appear as if they could have been created 2,000 years earlier.

The *Dying Slave* twists listlessly against his T-shirt-like bonds, revealing his smooth skin. This is probably the most sensual nude that Michelangelo, the master of the male body, ever created.

The *Rebellious Slave* fights against his bondage. His shoulders rotate one way, his head and leg turn the other. He even seems to be trying to release himself from the rock he's made of. Michelangelo said that his purpose was to carve away the marble to reveal the figures God put inside. This slave shows the agony of that process and the ecstasy of the result.

• *Tour over! But, of course, there's so much more. After a break (or on a second visit), consider a stroll through a few rooms of the Richelieu wing, which contain some of the Louvre's most ancient pieces.*

Nearby: Across from the Louvre are the lovely courtyards of the stately **Palais Royal.** Although the palace is closed to the public, the courtyards are open and free (directly north of the Louvre on Rue de Rivoli). Enter through a whimsical (locals say tacky) courtyard filled with stubby, striped columns and playful fountains (with fun, reflective metal balls). Next, you'll pass into another, perfectly Parisian garden. Bring a picnic and create your own quiet break, or have a drink at one of the outdoor cafés at the courtyard's northern end. This is Paris.

Exiting the courtyard at the side facing away from the Seine brings you to the Galeries Colbert and Vivienne, attractive examples of shopping arcades from the early 1800s.

▲▲▲Orsay Museum (Musée d'Orsay)

The Musée d'Orsay (mew-zay dor-say) houses French art of the 1800s and early 1900s (specifically, 1848-1914), picking up where the Louvre's art collection leaves off. For us, that means Impressionism, the art of sun-dappled fields, bright colors, and crowded Parisian cafés. The Orsay houses the best general collection anywhere of Manet, Monet, Renoir, Degas, Van Gogh, Cézanne, and Gauguin.

Cost and Hours: €14, €11 Tue-Wed and Fri-Sun after 16:30 and Thu after 18:00, free on first Sun of month and often right when the ticket booth stops selling tickets (Tue-Wed and Fri-Sun at 17:00, Thu at 21:00; they won't let you in much after that), covered by Museum Pass, combo-ticket with Orangerie Museum (€18) or Rodin Museum (€21). Museum open Tue-Sun 9:30-18:00, Thu until 21:45, closed Mon, last entry one hour before closing (45 minutes before on Thu), Impressionist galleries start shutting 45 minutes before closing, cafés and restaurant.

Information: Tel. 01 40 49 48 14, www.musee-orsay.fr.

Avoiding Lines: While everyone must wait to go through security, avoid the long ticket-buying lines with a Museum Pass, a combo-ticket, or by purchasing tickets in advance on the Orsay website; any of these entitle you to use a separate entrance. You can also buy tickets and Museum Passes (no mark-up; tickets valid 3 months) at newspaper kiosk just outside the Orsay entrance (along Rue de la Légion d'Honneur). If you're planning to get a combo-ticket with either the Orangerie or the Rodin Museum, consider starting at one of those museums instead, as they have shorter lines.

Getting There: The museum, at 1 Rue de la Légion d'Honneur, sits above the RER/Train-C Musée d'Orsay stop; the nearest Métro stop is Solférino, three blocks southeast of the Orsay. Bus #69 also stops at the Orsay. From the Louvre, it's a lovely 15-minute walk through the Tuileries Garden and across the pedestrian bridge to the Orsay.

Getting In: As you face the entrance, pass and ticket holders enter on the right (Entrance C). Ticket purchasers enter on the left (Entrance A). Security checks slow down all entrances.

Tours: Audioguides cost €5. English **guided tours** usually run Mon-Sat at 11:30 (€6/1.5 hours, none on Sun, tours may also run at 14:30 and Thu at 18:30.

🎧 Download my free Orsay Museum **audio tour.**

PARIS

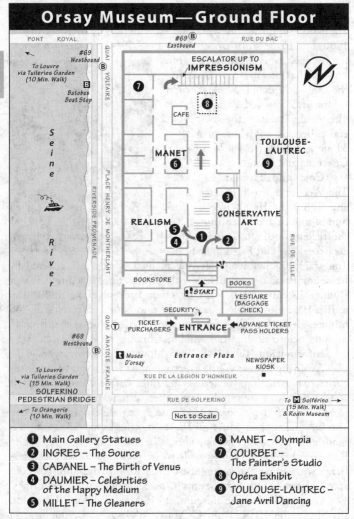

Orsay Museum—Ground Floor

1 Main Gallery Statues
2 INGRES – The Source
3 CABANEL – The Birth of Venus
4 DAUMIER – Celebrities of the Happy Medium
5 MILLET – The Gleaners
6 MANET – Olympia
7 COURBET – The Painter's Studio
8 Opéra Exhibit
9 TOULOUSE-LAUTREC – Jane Avril Dancing

➔ Self-Guided Tour

This former train station, the Gare d'Orsay, barely escaped the wrecking ball in the 1970s, when the French realized it'd be a great place to house the enormous collections of 19th-century art scattered throughout the city. The ground floor (level 0) houses early-19th-century art, mainly conservative art of the Academy and Salon, plus Realism. On the top floor (not visible from here) is the core of the collection—the Impressionist rooms. If you're pressed for time, go directly there.

Remember that the museum rotates its large collection often, so find the latest arrangement on your current Orsay map, and be ready to go with the flow.

Conservative Art

In the Orsay's first few rooms, you're surrounded by visions of idealized beauty—nude women in languid poses, Greek mythological figures, and anatomically perfect statues. This was the art adored by 19th-century French academics and the middle-class *(bourgeois)* public.

Jean-Auguste-Dominique **Ingres**' *The Source* (1856) is virtually a Greek statue on canvas. Like *Venus de Milo*, she's a balance of opposite motions. Alexandre **Cabanel** lays Ingres' *The Source* on her back. His *Birth of Venus* (1863) is a perfect fantasy, an orgasm of beauty.

Realism

The French Realists rejected idealized classicism and began painting what they saw in the world around them. For Honoré **Daumier,** that meant looking at the stuffy bourgeois establishment that controlled the Academy and the Salon. In the 36 bustlets of *Celebrities of the Happy Medium* (1835), Daumier, trained as a political cartoonist, exaggerates each subject's most distinct characteristic to capture with vicious precision the pomposity and self-righteousness of these self-appointed arbiters of taste (most were members of the French parliament).

Jean-François **Millet**'s *The Gleaners* (1867) shows us three gleaners, the poor women who pick up the meager leftovers after a field has already been harvest-

ed for the wealthy. Here he captures the innate dignity of these stocky, tanned women who bend their backs quietly in a large field for their small reward. This is "Realism" in two senses. It's painted "realistically," not prettified. And it's the "real" world—not the fantasy world of Greek myth, but the harsh life of the working poor.

For a Realist's take on the traditional Venus, find Edouard **Manet**'s *Olympia* (1863). Compare this uncompromising nude with Cabanel's idealized, pastel, Vaseline-on-the-lens beauty in *The Birth of Venus*. In *Olympia,* the sharp outlines and harsh, contrasting colors are new and shocking. Manet replaced soft-core porn with hard-core art.

Gustave **Courbet**'s *The Painter's Studio* (1855) takes us backstage, showing us the gritty reality behind the creation of pretty pictures. We see Courbet himself in his studio, working diligently on a Realistic landscape, oblivious to the confusion around him. Milling around are ordinary citizens, not Greek heroes.

At the far end of the gallery, you'll find the **Opéra Exhibit**—a glass floor over a model of Paris with the 19th-century, green-domed Opéra Garnier at the center. The Opéra, which opened in 1875, was the symbol of the belle époque, or "beautiful age," when Paris was a global center of prosperity, new technology, opera, ballet, painting, and joie de vivre.

Toulouse-Lautrec Detour

The Henri de **Toulouse-Lautrec** paintings near the Opéra Exhibit in Room 10 rightly belong with the Post-Impressionist works on level 2, but since you're already here, enjoy his paintings incarnating the artist's love of nightlife and show business. Every night, Toulouse-Lautrec put on his bowler hat and visited the Moulin Rouge to draw the crowds, the can-can dancers, and the backstage action. He worked quickly, creating sketches in paint that serve as snapshots of a golden era. In *Jane Avril Dancing* (1891), he depicts the slim, graceful, elegant, and melancholy dancer, who stood out above the rabble. Her legs keep dancing while her mind is far away.

Impressionism

The Impressionist collection is scattered randomly through Rooms 29-36 on the top floor.

Impressionist painters rejected camera-like detail for a quick style more suited to capturing the passing moment. Feeling stifled by the rigid rules and stuffy atmosphere of the Academy (the state-funded art school), the Impressionists took as their motto, "Out of the studio, into the open air." They grabbed their berets and scarves and went on excursions to the country, where they set up their easels (and newly invented tubes of premixed paint) on riverbanks and hillsides, or they sketched in cafés and dance halls. Gods, goddesses, nymphs, and fantasy scenes were out; common people and rural landscapes were in.

The quick style and everyday subjects were ridiculed and called childish by the "experts." Rejected by the Salon (where works were exhibited to the buying public), the Impressionists staged their own exhibition in 1874. They brashly took their name from an insult thrown at them by a critic who laughed at one of Monet's "impressions" of a sunrise. During the next decade, they exhibited their own work independently. The public, opposed at first, was slowly won over by the simplicity, the color, and the vibrancy of Impressionist art.

In Edouard **Manet**'s *Luncheon on the Grass* (*Le Déjeuner sur l'Herbe*, 1863), you can see that a new revolutionary movement was starting to bud—Impressionism. Notice the background: the messy brushwork of trees and leaves, the play of light on the pond, and the light that filters through the trees onto the woman who stoops in the haze. Also note the strong contrast of colors (white skin, black clothes, green grass).

Edgar **Degas** blends classical lines and Realist subjects with Impressionist color, spontaneity, and everyday scenes from urban Paris. He loved the unposed "snapshot" effect, catching his models off guard. Dance students, women at work, and café scenes are approached from odd angles that aren't always ideal but make the scenes seem more real. He gives us the backstage view of life. For instance, a dance rehearsal let Degas capture a behind-the-scenes look at bored, tired, restless dancers (*The Dance Class, La Classe de Danse*, c. 1873-1875). In the painting *In a Café* (*Dans un Café*, 1875-1876), a weary lady of the evening meets morning with a last, lonely, nail-in-the-coffin drink in the glaring light of a four-in-the-morning café.

Next up is Claude **Monet,** the father of Impressionism. In the 1860s, Monet (along with Renoir) began painting landscapes in the open air. He studied optics and pigments to know just the right colors he needed to reproduce the shimmering quality of reflected light. The key was to work quickly—at that "golden hour" (to use a modern photographer's term), when the light was just right. Then he'd create a fleeting "impression" of the scene. For example, you may see several canvases of the cathedral in Rouen. In 1893, Monet went to Rouen, rented a room across from the cathedral, set up his easel...and waited. He wanted to catch "a series of differing impressions" of the cathedral facade at various times of day and year. In all, he did 30 paintings of the cathedral, and each is unique.

Pierre-Auguste **Renoir** started out as a painter of landscapes, along with Monet, but later veered from the Impressionist's philosophy and painted images that were unabashedly "pretty." His best-known work is *Dance at the Moulin de la Galette* (*Bal du Moulin de la Galette*, 1876). On Sunday afternoons, working-class folk would dress up and head for the fields on Butte Montmartre (near Sacré-Cœur basilica) to dance,

drink, and eat little crêpes (galettes) till dark. Renoir liked to go there to paint the common Parisians living and loving in the afternoon sun. The sunlight filtering through the trees creates a kaleidoscope of colors, like the 19th-century equivalent of a mirror ball throwing darts of light onto the dancers. Like a photographer who uses a slow shutter speed to show motion, Renoir paints a waltzing blur.

Post-Impressionism

Post-Impressionism—the style that employs Impressionism's bright colors while branching out in new directions—is scattered all around the museum. You'll get a taste of the style with Paul Cézanne on the top floor, with much more on level 2.

Paul **Cézanne** (say-zahn) brought Impressionism into the 20th century. After the color of Monet and the warmth of Renoir, Cézanne's rather impersonal canvases can be difficult to appreciate (see *The Card Players, Les Joueurs de Cartes,* 1890-1895). Where the Impressionists built a figure out of a mosaic of individual brushstrokes, Cézanne used blocks of paint to create a more solid, geometrical shape. These chunks are like little "cubes." It's no coincidence that his experiments in reducing forms to their geometric basics inspired the...Cubists. Because of his style (not the content), he is often called the first modern painter.

Like Michelangelo, Beethoven, and a select handful of others, Vincent **van Gogh** put so much of himself into his work that art and life became one. In the Orsay's collection of paintings (level 2), you'll see both Van Gogh's painting style and his life unfold.

Encouraged by his art-dealer brother, Van Gogh moved to Paris. He met Monet, drank with Gauguin and Toulouse-Lautrec, and soaked up the Impressionist style. (For  example, see how he might build a bristling brown beard using thick strokes of red, yellow, and green side by side.) But the social life of Paris became too much for the solitary Van Gogh, and he moved to the south of France. At first, in the glow of the bright spring sunshine, he had a period of incredible creativity and happiness. But being alone in a strange country began to wear on him. A painting of his rented bedroom in Arles shows a cramped, bare-bones place (*Van Gogh's Room at Arles, La Chambre de Van Gogh à Arles,* 1889). He invited his friend Gauguin to join him, but after two months together arguing passionately about art, nerves got raw. Van Gogh threatened Gauguin with a razor, which drove his friend back to Paris. In crazed despair, Van Gogh cut off a piece of his own ear.

Vincent sought help at a mental hospital. The paintings he

finished in the peace of the hospital are more meditative—there are fewer bright landscapes and more closed-in scenes with deeper, almost surreal colors.

His final self-portrait shows a man engulfed in a confused background of brushstrokes that swirl and rave (*Self-Portrait, Portrait de l'Artiste,* 1889). But in the midst of this rippling sea of mystery floats a still, detached island of a face. Perhaps his troubled eyes know that in only a few months, he'll take a pistol and put a bullet through his chest.

Nearby are the paintings of Paul **Gauguin,** who got the travel bug early in childhood and grew up wanting to be a sailor. Instead, he became a stockbroker. At the age of 35, he got fed up with it all, quit his job, abandoned his wife (her stern portrait bust may be nearby) and family, and took refuge in his art.

Gauguin traveled to the South Seas in search of the exotic, finally settling on Tahiti. There he found his Garden of Eden.

Gauguin's best-known works capture an idyllic Tahitian landscape peopled by exotic women engaged in simple tasks and making music (*Arearea,* 1892). The native girls lounge placidly in unselfconscious innocence. The style is intentionally "primitive," collapsing the three-dimensional landscape into a two-dimensional pattern of bright colors. Gauguin intended that this simple style carry a deep undercurrent of symbolic meaning. He wanted to communicate to his "civilized" colleagues back home that he'd found the paradise he'd always envisioned.

French Sculpture

The open-air mezzanine of level 2 is lined with statues. Stroll the mezzanine, enjoying the work of great French sculptors, including Auguste **Rodin.** Born of working-class roots and largely self-taught, Rodin combined classical solidity with Impressionist surfaces to become one of the greatest sculptors since the Renaissance.

Rodin's *St. John the Baptist Preaching* (bronze, 1881) captures the mystical visionary who was the precursor to Christ, the man who would announce the coming of the Messiah. Rodin's inspiration came in the form of a shaggy peasant—looking for work as a model—whose bearing caught the artist's eye. Coarse and hairy, with both feet planted firmly, if oddly, on the ground, this sculpture's rough, "unfinished" look reflects light in the same way the rough Impressionist brushwork does—making the statue come alive, never quite at rest in the viewer's eye.

Rodin's sculptures capture the groundbreaking spirit of much of the art in the Orsay Museum. With a stable base of 19th-century stone, he launched art into the 20th century.

▲▲Orangerie Museum (Musée de l'Orangerie)

Located in the Tuileries Garden and drenched by natural light from skylights, the Orangerie (oh-rahn-zhuh-ree) is the closest you'll ever come to stepping right into an Impressionist painting. Start with the museum's claim to fame: Monet's *Water Lilies*. Then head downstairs to enjoy the manageable collection of select works by Utrillo, Cézanne, Renoir, Matisse, and Picasso.

Cost and Hours: €9, €6.50 after 17:00, free for those under age 18, €18 combo-ticket with Orsay Museum, €18.50 combo-ticket with Monet's Garden and House at Giverny, covered by Museum Pass; Wed-Mon 9:00-18:00, closed Tue; audioguide-€5, English guided tours (€6) usually Mon and Thu at 14:30 and Sat at 11:00, located in Tuileries Garden near Place de la Concorde (Mo: Concorde), 15-minute stroll from the Orsay, tel. 01 44 77 80 07, www.musee-orangerie.fr.

Visiting the Museum: Like Beethoven going deaf, a nearly blind Claude Monet (1840-1926) wrote his final symphonies on a monumental scale. Even as he struggled with cataracts, he planned a series of huge six-foot-tall canvases of water lilies to hang in special rooms at the Orangerie.

These eight mammoth, curved panels immerse you in Monet's garden. We're looking at the pond in his garden at Giverny—dotted with water lilies, surrounded by foliage, and dappled by the reflections of the sky, clouds, and trees on the surface. But the true subject of these works is the play of reflected light off the surface of the pond.

Working at his home in Giverny, Monet built a special studio with skylights and wheeled easels to accommodate the canvases. For 12 years (1914-1926), Monet worked on these paintings obsessively. Monet completed all the planned canvases, but he didn't live to see them installed here. In 1927, the year after his death, these rooms were completed and the canvases put in place. Some call this the first "art installation"—art displayed in a space specially designed for it in order to enhance the viewer's experience.

In the underground gallery are select works of other Impressionist heavyweights well worth your time. The museum is small enough to enjoy in a short visit, but complete enough to show the bridge from Impressionism to Modernism. And it's all beautiful.

EIFFEL TOWER AND NEARBY
▲▲▲Eiffel Tower (La Tour Eiffel)

Built on the 100th anniversary of the French Revolution (and in the spirit of the Industrial Revolution), the tower was the centerpiece of a World Expo designed simply to show off what people could build in 1889. For decades it was the tallest structure the world had ever known, and though it's since been eclipsed, it's still the most visited monument. Ride the elevators to the top of its 1,063 feet for expansive views that stretch 40 miles. Then descend to the two lower levels, where the views are arguably even better, since the monuments are more recognizable.

Cost and Hours: €25.50 to ride all the way to the top, €16.30 for just the two lower levels, €10.20 to climb the stairs to the first or second level, €19.40 to climb the stairs to the second level and take the elevator to the summit—must purchase summit elevator before entering tower, 50 percent cheaper for those under 25, 75 percent cheaper for those under 12, not covered by Museum Pass; open daily mid-June-Aug 9:00-24:45, Sept-mid-June 9:30-23:45, last ascent to top by elevator at 22:30 and to lower levels at 23:00 all year (stairs same except Sept-mid-June last ascent 18:30); cafés and great view restaurants, Mo: Bir-Hakeim or Trocadéro, RER/Train-C: Champ de Mars-Tour Eiffel (all about a 10-minute walk away).

Information: Tel. 08 92 70 12 39, www.toureiffel.paris.

Reservations Smart: It's wise to make a reservation well in advance of your visit. At www.toureiffel.paris, you can book a time slot for your ascent; this allows you to skip the long entry line.

Online ticket sales open up about 60 days before any given date (at 8:30 Paris time). Be sure of your date, as reservations are nonrefundable. To go all the way to the top, select "Lift entrance ticket with access to the summit" as your ticket type. You can either print your tickets (follow the specifications carefully) or download e-tickets to your phone. Note that email or text confirmations alone will not get you in; you must have a printed or electronic ticket showing the bar code.

If no slots are available, try buying a "Lift entrance ticket with access to 2nd floor"—the view from the second floor is arguably better anyway. Or, try the website again about a week before your visit—last-minute spots sometimes open up.

PARIS

Eiffel Tower & Nearby

Other Tips for Avoiding Lines: If you don't have a reservation, get in line to buy tickets 30 minutes before the tower opens. Going much later in the day is the next-best bet (after 19:00 May-Aug, after 17:00 off-season, after 16:00 in winter as it gets dark by 17:00). You can bypass some (but not all) lines with a reservation at either of the tower's view restaurants (Le Jules Verne or 58 Tour Eiffel). Or you can buy a "Skip the Line" tour (almost right up to the last minute) through Fat Tire Tours (see page 54).

When to Go: For the best of all worlds, arrive with enough light to see the views, then stay as it gets dark to see the lights. At the top of the hour, a five-minute display features thousands of sparkling lights (best viewed from Place du Trocadéro or the grassy park below).

Getting In: The perimeter of the tower is surrounded by glass walls for security purposes. So, while it's free to enter the area directly under the tower, you must first pass through an airport-like security check (allow 30 minutes or more at busy times; two entry points along Avenue Gustave-Eiffel). **If you have a reservation,** arrive at the tower at least 30 minutes before your entry time to pass security and look for either of the two entrances with green signs showing

Visiteurs avec Reservation (Visitors with Reservation), where attendants scan your ticket and put you on the first available elevator. **Without a reservation,** follow signs for *Individuels* or *Visiteurs sans Tickets* (avoid lines selling tickets only for *Groupes*). The stairs entrance (usually a shorter line) is at the south pillar (next to Le Jules Verne restaurant entrance).

Pickpockets: Beware. Street thieves plunder awestruck visitors gawking near the tower. And tourists in crowded elevators are like fish in a barrel for predatory pickpockets. *En garde.* A police station is at the Jules Verne pillar.

Security Check: Bags larger than 19" × 8" × 12" are not allowed, but there is no baggage check. All bags are subject to a security search. No knives, glass bottles, or cans are permitted.

Services: The Eiffel Tower information office is at the west pillar. Free WCs are at the base of the tower, behind the east pillar. Inside the tower itself, WCs are on all levels.

Background

The first visitor to the Paris World's Fair in 1889 walked beneath the "arch" formed by the newly built Eiffel Tower and entered the fairgrounds. This event celebrated both the centennial of the French Revolution and France's position as a global superpower. Bridge builder Gustave Eiffel (1832-1923) won the contest to build the fair's centerpiece by beating out rival proposals such as a giant guillotine.

The tower was nothing but a showpiece, with no functional purpose except to demonstrate to the world that France had the wealth, knowledge, and can-do spirit to erect a structure far taller than anything the world had ever seen. The original plan was to dismantle the tower as quickly as it was built after the celebration ended, but it was kept by popular demand.

The tower, including its antenna, stands 1,063 feet tall, or slightly higher than the 77-story Chrysler Building in New York. Its four support pillars straddle an area of 3.5 acres. Despite the tower's 7,300 tons of metal and 60 tons of paint, it is so well-engineered that it weighs no more per square inch at its base than a linebacker on tiptoes.

Visiting the Tower

There are three observation platforms, at roughly 200, 400, and 900 feet. If you want to see the entire tower, from top to bottom, then see it...from top to bottom.

There isn't a single elevator straight to the top *(le sommet)*. To get there, you'll first ride an elevator (or hike up the stairs) to the second level. (For the hardy, there are 360 stairs to the first level and another 360 to the second). Once on the second level, imme-

PARIS

diately line up for the next elevator, to the top. Enjoy the views from the "summit," then ride back down to the second level. When you're ready, head to the first level via the stairs (no line and can take as little as five minutes) or take the elevator down. Explore the shops and exhibits on the first level. To leave, you can line up for the elevator, but it's quickest and most memorable to take the stairs back down to earth.

Top Level: You'll find wind and grand, sweeping views on the tiny top level. The city lies before you (pick out sights with the help of the panoramic maps). On a good day, you can see for 40 miles. Do a 360-degree tour of Paris. Feeling proud you made it this high? You can celebrate your accomplishment with a glass of champagne from the bar.

Second Level: This level has the best views because you're closer to the sights, and the monuments are more recognizable. The second level has souvenir shops, WCs, and a small stand-up café. The world-class Le Jules Verne restaurant is on this level, but you won't see it; access is by a private elevator.

First Level: Here are more great views, all well described by the tower's panoramic displays. There's a private exhibition hall, a restaurant, and a public hall with a café, shop, and little theater. Pop-up restaurants and kiosks appear with every season—even a little playground for kids. In winter, part of the first level is often set up to host an ice-skating rink. The highlight is the breathtaking, vertigo-inducing, selfie-inspiring **glass floor.** Venture onto it and experience what it's like to stand atop an 18-story building and look straight down.

Back on the Ground: For a final look, stroll across the river to Place du Trocadéro or to the end of the Champ de Mars and look back for great views. However impressive it may be by day, the tower is an awesome thing to behold at twilight, when it becomes engorged with light, and virile Paris lies back and lets night be on top. When darkness fully envelops the city, the tower seems to climax with a spectacular light show at the top of each hour...for five glorious minutes.

Nearby, you can catch a boat for a Seine cruise (see page 50) or hop on bus #69 for a tour of the city (see page 46). The Trocadero viewpoint, which looks "right there," is a 20-minute walk away. The entertaining riverbank promenade starts on the south side of the river near here and stretches to the Orsay Museum. Also nearby are the Rue Cler area, Army Museum and Napoleon's Tomb, and Rodin Museum.

Near the Eiffel Tower
▲Paris Sewer Museum (Les Egouts de Paris)

Discover what happens after you flush. This quick, interesting, and slightly stinky visit (a perfumed hanky helps) takes you along a few hundred yards of water tunnels in the world's first underground sewer system. Pick up the helpful English self-guided tour, then drop down into Jean Valjean's world of tunnels, rats, and manhole covers. (Victor Hugo was friends with the sewer inspector when he wrote *Les Misérables*.) You'll pass well-organized displays explaining the history of water distribution and collection in Paris, from Roman times to the present (may be closed for renovation when you visit).

The evolution of this amazing network of sewers is fascinating. More than 1,500 miles of tunnels carry 317 million gallons of water daily through this underworld. It's the world's longest sewer system—so long, they say, that if it were laid out straight, it would stretch from Paris all the way to Istanbul.

Cost and Hours: €4.40, covered by Museum Pass, Sat-Wed 11:00-17:00, Oct-April until 16:00, closed Thu-Fri year-round, located where Pont de l'Alma greets the Left Bank—on the right side of the bridge as you face the river, Mo: Alma-Marceau, RER/Train-C: Pont de l'Alma, tel. 01 53 68 27 81.

▲▲Rue Cler

Paris is changing quickly, but a stroll down this market street introduces you to a thriving, traditional Parisian neighborhood and offers insights into the local culture. Although this is a wealthy district, Rue Cler retains the workaday charm still found in most neighborhoods throughout Paris. The shops lining the street are filled with the freshest produce, the stinkiest cheese, the tastiest chocolate, and the  finest wines (markets generally open Tue-Sat 8:30-13:00 & 15:00-19:30, Sun 8:30-12:00, dead on Mon). I'm still far from a gourmet eater, but my time spent tasting my way along Rue Cler has heightened my appreciation of good cuisine (as well as the French knack for good living).

🎧 For a self-guided walk, download my free Rue Cler audio tour.

▲▲Army Museum and Napoleon's Tomb (Musée de l'Armée)

Napoleon's tomb rests beneath the golden dome of Les Invalides church. In addition to the tomb, the complex of Les Invalides—a former veterans' hospital built by Louis XIV—has various military collections, together called the Army Museum, Europe's greatest military museum. Visiting the different sections, you can watch the art of war unfold from stone axes to Axis powers.

Cost and Hours: €12, €10 after 17:00 (16:00 Nov-March), free for military personnel in uniform, free for kids but they must wait in line for ticket, covered by Museum Pass, extra fee for special exhibits and evening concerts; open daily 10:00-18:00, Nov-March until 17:00; Napoleon's Tomb also open July-Aug until 19:00; Napoleon's Tomb and Louis XIV-Napoleon I wing open April-Sept Tue until 21:00; Charles de Gaulle exhibit closed Mon year-round, videoguide-€6, cafeteria, tel. 01 44 42 38 77, www.musee-armee.fr.

Getting There: The Hôtel des Invalides is at 129 Rue de Grenelle, a 10-minute walk from Rue Cler (Mo: La Tour Maubourg, Varenne, or Invalides). You can also take bus #69 (from the Marais and Rue Cler) or bus #63 from the St. Germain-des-Prés area.

Visiting the Museum: Pick up the free guide/map. At the center of the complex, Napoleon Bonaparte lies majestically dead inside several coffins under a grand dome—a goose-bumping pilgrimage for historians. The dome overhead glitters with 26 pounds of thinly pounded gold leaf.

Your visit continues through an impressive range of museums filled with medieval armor, cannons and muskets, Louis XIV-era uniforms and weapons, and Napoleon's horse—stuffed and mounted.

The best section is dedicated to the two World Wars. Walk through displays well described in English on the trench warfare of World War I, the victory parades, France's horrendous losses, and the humiliating Treaty of Versailles that led to World War II.

The WWII rooms use black-and-white photos, maps, videos, and a few artifacts to trace Hitler's rise, the Blitzkrieg that overran France, America's entry into the war, D-Day, the concentration camps, the atomic bomb, the war in the Pacific, and the eventual Allied victory. There's special insight into France's role (the French Resistance), and how it was Charles de Gaulle that actually won the war.

▲▲Rodin Museum (Musée Rodin)

This user-friendly museum with gardens is filled with passionate works by Auguste Rodin (1840-1917), the greatest sculptor since Michelangelo. You'll see *The Kiss, The Thinker, The Gates of Hell,* and many more, well displayed in the mansion where the sculptor lived and worked.

Cost and Hours: €12, free for those under age 18, free on first Sun of the month Oct-March, €21 combo-ticket with Orsay Museum, both museum and garden covered by Museum Pass; Tue-Sun 10:00-18:30, closed Mon; audioguide-€6, mandatory baggage check, self-service café in garden, 77 Rue de Varenne, Mo: Varenne, tel. 01 44 18 61 10, www.musee-rodin.fr.

Visiting the Museum: Auguste Rodin (1840-1917) was a modern Michelangelo, sculpting human figures on an epic scale, revealing through their bodies his deepest thoughts and feelings. Like many of Michelangelo's unfinished works, Rodin's statues rise from the raw stone around them, driven by the life force. With missing limbs and scarred skin, these are prefab classics, making ugliness noble. Rodin's people are always moving restlessly. Even the famous *Thinker* is moving; while he's plopped down solidly, his mind is a million miles away.

Exhibits trace Rodin's artistic development, explain how his bronze statues were cast, and show some of the studies he created to work up to his masterpiece, the unfinished *Gates of Hell.* Learn about Rodin's tumultuous relationship with his apprentice and lover, Camille Claudel. Mull over what makes his sculptures some of the most evocative since the Renaissance. And stroll the beautiful gardens, packed with many of his greatest works (including *The Thinker*) and ideal for artistic reflection.

▲▲Marmottan Museum (Musée Marmottan Monet)

In this private, intimate, and untouristy museum, you'll find the best collection anywhere of works by Impressionist headliner Claude Monet. Follow Monet's life through more than a hundred works, from simple sketches to the *Impression: Sunrise* painting that gave his artistic movement its start—and a name. The museum also displays some of the enjoyable large-scale canvases featuring the water lilies from his garden at Giverny.

Cost and Hours: €12, not covered by Museum Pass, €21.50 combo-ticket with Monet's garden and house at Giverny (lets you skip the line at Giverny); Tue-Sun 10:00-18:00, Thu until 21:00, closed Mon; audioguide-€3 (includes temporary exhibits), 2 Rue Louis-Boilly, Mo: La Muette, tel. 01 44 96 50 33, www.marmottan.fr.

Visting the Museum: Paul Marmottan (1856-1932) lived here amid his collection of exquisite 19th-century furniture and paintings. He donated his home and possessions to a private trust (which is why your Museum Pass isn't valid here). After Marmottan's death, the more daring art of Monet and others was added.

The 19th-century Marmottan mansion has three pleasant, manageable floors, all worth perusing. The ground floor has several rooms of Paul Marmottan's period furnishings and notable paintings by French artists. Temporary exhibits are usually displayed in a gallery on this floor. Upstairs is the permanent collection, featuring illuminated manuscripts and works by Monet's fellow Impressionists—Edgar Degas, Camille Pissarro, Paul Gauguin, Pierre-Auguste Renoir, Edouard Manet, and especially Berthe Morisot.

Monet's works—the core of the collection—are in the basement. In this one long room, you'll find some 50 paintings by Monet spanning his lifetime. They're generally (and very roughly) arranged in chronological order—from Monet's youthful discovery of Impressionism, to his mature "series" paintings, to his last great water lilies from Giverny.

LEFT BANK

Opposite Notre-Dame, on the left bank of the Seine, is the Latin Quarter. (For more about this neighborhood, see the "Historic Paris Walk," earlier).

▲▲Cluny Museum (Musée National du Moyen Age)

The Cluny is easy to visit and a treasure trove of Middle Ages (Moyen Age) art. Located on the side of a Roman bathhouse, it offers close-up looks at stained glass, Notre-Dame carvings, fine goldsmithing and jewelry, and rooms of tapestries. The highlights are several original stained-glass windows from Sainte-Chapelle and the exquisite series of six *Lady and the Unicorn* tapestries: A delicate, as-medieval-as-can-be noble lady introduces a delighted unicorn to the senses of taste, hearing, sight, smell, and touch. The museum is undergoing a multiyear renovation. Expect changes when you visit.

Cost and Hours: €9, includes audioguide, free on first Sun of month, covered by

Museum Pass; Wed-Mon 9:15-17:45, closed Tue; videoguide-€3; near corner of Boulevards St. Michel and St. Germain at 6 Place Paul Painlevé; Mo: Cluny-La Sorbonne, St. Michel, or Odéon; tel. 01 53 73 78 00, www.musee-moyenage.fr.

▲St. Sulpice Church

For pipe-organ enthusiasts, a visit here is one of Europe's great musical treats. The Grand Orgue at St. Sulpice Church has a rich history, with a succession of 12 world-class organists—including Charles-Marie Widor and Marcel Dupré—that goes back 300 years.

Patterned after St. Paul's Cathedral in London, the church has a Neoclassical arcaded facade and two round towers. Inside, in the first chapel on the right, are three murals of fighting angels by Delacroix: *Jacob Wrestling the Angel, Heliodorus Chased from the Temple,* and *The Archangel Michael* (on the ceiling). The fourth chapel on the right has a statue of Joan of Arc and wall plaques listing hundreds from St. Sulpice's congregation who died during World War I. The north transept wall features an Egyptian-style obelisk used as a gnomon on a sundial. The last chapel before the exit has a display on the Shroud of Turin.

Cost and Hours: Free, daily 7:30-19:30, Mo: St. Sulpice or Mabillon. See http://pss75.fr/saint-sulpice-paris for special concerts.

Sunday Organ Recitals: You can hear the organ played before and after Sunday Mass (10:45-11:00, 12:00-12:30, and 13:30-18:45; also during Sat Mass at 18:45; come appropriately dressed). The post-Mass offering is a high-powered 25-minute recital, usually performed by talented organist Daniel Roth.

▲Luxembourg Garden (Jardin du Luxembourg)

This lovely 60-acre garden is an Impressionist painting brought to life. Slip into a green chair pondside, enjoy the radiant flower beds, go jogging, play tennis or basketball, sail a toy sailboat, or take in a chess game or puppet show. Some of the park's prettiest (and quietest) sections lie around its perimeter (free, daily dawn until dusk, Mo: Odéon, RER/Train-B: Luxembourg).

PARIS

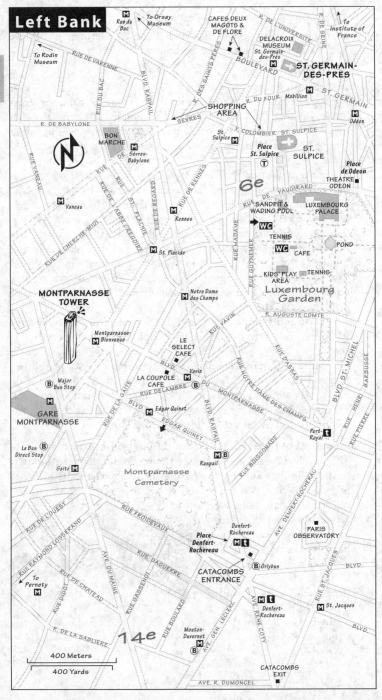

Left Bank

Rue du Bac M

To Orsay Museum

To Rodin Museum

RUE DE VARENNE

CAFES DEUX MAGOTS & DE FLORE

R. DE L'UNIVERSITE

R. DE SEINE

To Institute of France

DELACROIX MUSEUM

St. Germain-des-Prés

BOULEVARD ST. GERMAIN-DES-PRES

RUE DU BAC

BLVD. RASPAIL

RUE DES SAINTS PERES

SHOPPING AREA

R. DU FOUR Mabillion M ST. GERMAIN

SEVRES

R. DE BABYLONE

BON MARCHE

M Sèvres-Babylone

St. Sulpice M

COLOMBIER ST. SULPICE

Place St. Sulpice

ST. SULPICE

Odeon M

Place de Odeon

THEATRE ODEON

6e

RUE VANEAU

RUE DE BABYLONE

RUE DE SEVRES

RUE ST. PLACIDE

RUE DE REGARD

RUE DE RENNES

M Vaneau

RUE DE L'ABBE GREGOIRE

RUE DE CHERCHE-MIDI

Rennes M

RUE DE VAUGIRARD

SANDPIT & WADING POOL

RUE GUYNEMER

LUXEMBOURG PALACE

WC

TENNIS

WC CAFE

POND

M St. Placide

KIDS' PLAY AREA

TENNIS

Luxembourg Garden

RUE MADAME

MONTPARNASSE TOWER

Notre Dame des Champs M

R. AUGUSTE COMTE

Montparnasse-Bienvenue M

LE SELECT CAFE

BLVD. Vavin M

RUE VAVIN

RUE D'ASSAS

BLVD. ST. MICHEL

Major Bus Stop B

LA COUPOLE CAFE

RUE DELAMBRE

B DU MONTPARNASSE

RUE NOTRE DAME DES CHAMPS

RUE DE LA GAITE

BLVD. RASPAIL

M Edgar Quinet

EDGAR QUINET

Port-Royal

RUE HERRI

RUE PIERRE

BARBUSSE

GARE MONTPARNASSE M

Le Bus Direct Stop B

Gaité M

M B Raspail

RUE BOISSONADE

Montparnasse Cemetery

RUE DE L'OUEST

RUE FROIDEVAUX

AVE. DENFERT-ROCHEREAU

PARIS OBSERVATORY

RUE RAYMOND LOSSERAND

AVE. DU MAINE

RUE DAGUERRE

Place Denfert-Rochereau

Denfert-Rochereau M

B Orlybus

CATACOMBS ENTRANCE

BLVD.

To Pernety M

RUE DE CHATEAU

RUE DIDOT

RUE GASSENDI

Denfert-Rochereau M

RUE ST. JACQUES

M St. Jacques

BLVD.

R. DE LA SABLIERE

14e

RUE BOULARD

Mouton-Duvernet M

B

AVE. GEN. LECLERC

AVE. RENE COTY

400 Meters

400 Yards

CATACOMBS EXIT

AVE. R. DUMONCEL

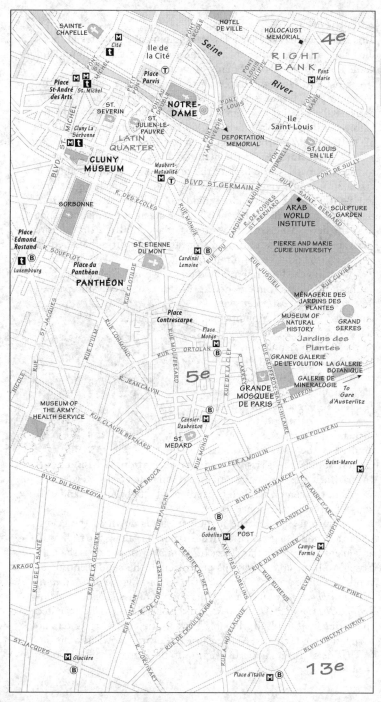

PARIS

▲Panthéon

This state-capitol-style Neoclassical monument celebrates France's illustrious history and people, balances a Foucault pendulum, and is the final resting place of many French VIPs.

Cost and Hours: €9, free for those under age 18, covered by Museum Pass, €3 for dome climb (not covered by Museum Pass); daily 10:00-18:30, Oct-March until 18:00, last entry 45 minutes before closing; audioguide-€3, Mo: Cardinal Lemoine, tel. 01 44 32 18 00, http://pantheon.monuments-nationaux.fr/.

Dome Climb: From the main floor, you can climb 206 steps to the colonnade at the base of the dome for views of the interior and a 360-degree view of the city. You're not so much high above Paris—it feels like you're in the middle of it. Buy your dome-climb ticket as you enter the sight, then join the queue at the meeting spot near the nave. An escort takes groups of about 50 at a time. Visits leave about every hour until 17:30 (or earlier—confirm the schedule as you go in) and take 40 minutes.

Visiting the Pantheon: Stand on the white-and-gray star bust at the head of the **nave** and take in the vast, evenly lit space—360 feet long, 280 feet wide, and 270 feet high. Monuments trace the celebrated struggles of the French people: St. Geneviève saving the fledgling city from Attila the Hun, and scenes of Joan of Arc (left transept). A Foucault pendulum swings gracefully at the end of a cable suspended from the towering dome. At the altar end of the  church stands the massive **Convention Nationale Monument.** "Marianne," the fictional woman who symbolized the Revolution, stands in the center, flanked by soldiers who fight for her and citizens who pledge allegiance to her.

A staircase behind the monument leads down to the **crypt,** where a panoply of greats is buried. Rousseau is along the right wall as you enter, while Voltaire faces him impishly from across the hall. Straight ahead up a few steps and through the small central rotunda are more greats (all to the left): Victor Hugo *(Les Misérables, The Hunchback of Notre-Dame),* Alexandre Dumas *(The Three Musketeers, The Count of Monte Cristo),* and Louis Braille (who invented the script for the blind). Double back to the central rotunda and turn left to find scientist Marie Curie (follow the glow), and various WWII dead (from Holocaust victims to the hero of the Resistance, Jean Moulin).

Montparnasse Tower

This sadly out-of-place 59-story superscraper has one virtue: If you can't make it up the Eiffel Tower, the sensational views from this tower are cheaper, far easier to access (a 40-second elevator ride), and make for a fair consolation prize. Come early in the day for clearest skies and shortest lines, and be treated to views from a comfortable interior and from up on the rooftop (consider their €6.50 breakfast with a view). Sunset is great but views are disappointing after dark. Some say it's the very best view in Paris, as  you can see the Eiffel Tower clearly...and you can't see the Montparnasse Tower at all.

Cost and Hours: €17, 30 percent discount with this book (2 people per book, not covered by Museum Pass); daily 9:30-23:30, Oct-March until 22:30; entrance on Rue de l'Arrivée, Mo: Montparnasse-Bienvenüe—from the Métro, stay inside the station and follow sparse *Tour* signs to exit #4; tel. 01 45 38 52 56, www.tourmontparnasse56.com.

▲Catacombs

Spiral down 60 feet below the street and walk a one-mile route through tunnels containing the anonymous bones of six million permanent Parisians. Lines to get in can be several hours long; it's essential to book online in advance. Once inside, allow an hour if you dawdle.

Cost and Hours: €13, not covered by Museum Pass, Tue-Sun 10:00-20:30, closed Mon; purchase a timed-entry ticket online in advance at the website below or consider Fat Tire Tours' "Skip the Line" ticket (see page 54); otherwise arrive by 9:30 or after 18:00 to minimize wait; ticket booth closes at 19:30, come no later than 19:00 or risk not getting in; well-done audioguide-€5, pick up English visitors guide for explanations of key stops, tel. 01 43 22 47 63, www.catacombes.paris.fr.

Getting There: It's at 1 Place Denfert-Rochereau. Take the Métro to Denfert-Rochereau and follow *Sortie 1,* then find the lion in the big traffic circle; if he looked left rather than right, he'd stare right at the green entrance to the Catacombs.

Visiting the Catacombs: In 1785, health-conscious Parisians looking to relieve congestion and improve the city's sanitary conditions emptied the church cemeteries and moved the bones here, to former limestone quarries, where incidentally, plaster of Paris was made. And in the mid-19th century, Baron Haussmann's many urban projects required the relocation of cemeteries, and these ancient, hand-dug quarries fit the bill. For decades, priests led ceremonial processions of black-veiled, bone-laden carts into the quarries, where the bones were stacked in piles five feet high and as much as 80 feet deep.

You'll descend 130 steps and land in a room with English posters describing 45 million years of ancient geology, then walk for 10 minutes through tunnels to reach the bones. Appreciate that some of these tunnels were originally built sans mortar. The sign, "Halt, this is the empire of the dead," announces your arrival at the bones. From here, shuffle along passageways of artfully arranged, skull-studded tibiae; admire 300-year-old sculptures cut into the walls of the catacombs; and see more cheery signs: "Happy is he who is forever faced with the hour of his death and prepares himself for the end every day." The highlight for me is the Crypt of the Passion (a.k.a. "the Barrel"), where bones are meticulously packed in a barrel shape hiding a support pillar.

Climb many steps to emerge far from where you entered and find a good WC and a ghoulish gift shop selling skulls and more. Note to wannabe Hamlets: An attendant checks your bag at the exit for stolen souvenirs.

CHAMPS-ELYSEES AND NEARBY
▲▲▲Champs-Elysées

This famous boulevard is Paris' backbone, with its greatest concentration of traffic (although it's delightfully traffic-free on the first Sunday of each month). From the Arc de Triomphe down Avenue des Champs-Elysées, all of France seems to converge on Place de la Concorde, the city's largest square. And though the Champs-Elysées has become as international as it is Parisian, a walk down the two-mile boulevard is still a must.

In 1667, Louis XIV opened the first section of the street, and it soon became *the* place to cruise in your carriage. (It still is today.)
By the 1920s, this boulevard was pure elegance—fancy residences, rich hotels, and cafés. Today it's home to big business, celebrity cafés, glitzy nightclubs, high-fashion shopping, and international people-watching. People gather here to celebrate Bastille Day (July 14), World Cup triumphs, and the finale of the Tour de France.

● **Self-Guided Walk:** Start at the Arc de Triomphe (Mo: Charles de Gaulle-Etoile; if you're planning to tour the Arc, do it before starting this walk, described next) and head downhill on the left-hand side. The arrival of McDonald's (at #140) was an unthinkable horror, but these days dining chez MacDo has become typically Parisian, and this branch is the most profitable McDonald's in the world.

The Lido (#116) is Paris' largest burlesque-type cabaret (and a multiplex cinema). Across the boulevard is the flagship store of leather-bag maker Louis Vuitton (#101). Fouquet's café (#99) is a popular spot for French celebrities, especially movie stars—note the names in the sidewalk in front. Enter if you dare for a €10 espresso. Ladurée café (#75) is also classy but has a welcoming and affordable takeout bakery.

Continuing on, you pass international-brand stores, such as Sephora, Disney, and the Gap. Car buffs should park themselves at the sleek café in the Renault store (#53, open noon-midnight). The car exhibits change regularly, but a Formula One racecar made from 300,000 Legos is usually on display.

You can end your walk at the round Rond Point intersection (Mo: Franklin D. Roosevelt) or continue to obelisk-studded Place de la Concorde, Paris' largest square.

On and Near the Champs-Elysées
▲▲Arc de Triomphe

Napoleon had the magnificent Arc de Triomphe commissioned to commemorate his victory at the 1805 battle of Austerlitz. The foot of the arch is a stage on which the last two centuries of Parisian history have played out—from the funeral of Napoleon to the goose-stepping arrival of the Nazis to the triumphant return of Charles de Gaulle after the Allied liberation. Examine the carvings on the pillars, featuring a mighty Napoleon and excitable Lady Liberty. Pay your respects at the Tomb of the Unknown Soldier. Then climb the 284 steps to the observation deck up top, with sweeping skyline panoramas and a mesmerizing view down onto the traffic that swirls around the arch.

Cost and Hours: Free to view exterior; steps to rooftop-€12, free for those under age 18, free on first Sun of month Nov-March, covered by Museum Pass; daily 10:00-23:00, Oct-March until 22:30, last entry 45 minutes before closing; Place Charles de Gaulle, use underpass to reach arch, Mo: Charles de Gaulle-Etoile, tel. 01 55 37 73 77, www.paris-arc-de-triomphe.fr.

Avoiding Lines: A Museum Pass lets you bypass the slooow un-

PARIS

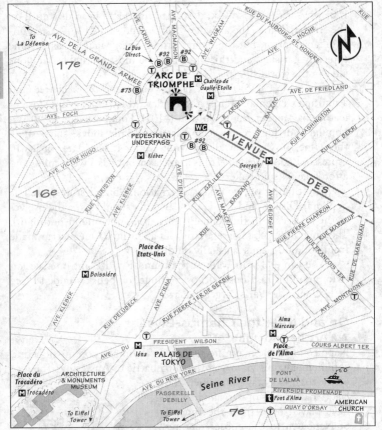

derground ticket line and the security line. You can tour much of the base of the Arc sans ticket, but you need one for the climb to the top (in a line you can't avoid). Lines disappear after 17:00.

▲Petit Palais (and Musée des Beaux-Arts)

This free museum displays a broad collection of paintings and sculpture from the 1600s to the 1900s on its ground floor, and an easy-to-appreciate collection of art from Greek antiquities to Art Nouveau in its basement. While the collection can be shuffled about during special exhibits, the part I describe is usually unaffected. Though it houses mostly second-tier art, there are a few diamonds in the rough (including works by Rembrandt, Courbet, Cézanne, Sisley, Pissarro, Degas, and Monet). The building is impressive, and was constructed along with the Grand Palais and Pont Alexandre III for the 1900 Paris Exhibition (World's Fair). The museum's classy café merits the detour alone—and if it's rain-

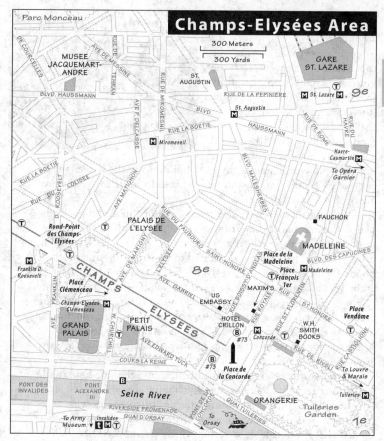

ing and your Museum Pass has expired, or you just need a clean WC, the Petit Palais is a worthwhile stop.

Cost and Hours: Free, Tue-Sun 10:00-18:00, Fri until 21:00 for special exhibits (fee), closed Mon; audioguide-€5; across from Grand Palais on Avenue Winston Churchill, a looooong block west of Place de la Concorde, Mo: Champs-Elysées Clemenceau; lovely café, tel. 01 53 43 40 00, www.petitpalais.paris.fr.

La Défense and La Grande Arche

Though Paris keeps its historic center classic and skyscraper-free, this district, nicknamed *"le petit Manhattan,"* offers an impressive excursion into a side of Paris few tourists see: that of a modern-day economic superpower. La Défense was first conceived more than 60 years ago as a US-style forest of skyscrapers that would accommodate the business needs of the modern world. Today La Défense is a thriving commercial and shopping center, home to 150,000 employees and 55,000 residents. It's also the single largest concentration of skyscrapers in all of Europe.

For a worthwhile visit, take the Métro to the La Défense Grande Arche stop, carefully follow *Sortie Grande Arche* signs (there are many), and climb to the base of La Grande Arche for distant city views. Then stroll about three-quarters of a mile gradually downhill among the glass buildings to the Esplanade de la Défense Métro station, and return home from there. Mall stores are open every day.

Visiting La Défense: The centerpiece of this ambitious complex is the mammoth **La Grande Arche de la Fraternité.** Inaugurated in 1989 on the 200th anniversary of the French Revolution, it was, like the Revolution, dedicated to human rights and brotherhood. The place is big—Notre-Dame Cathedral could fit under its arch. The "cloud"—a huge canvas canopy under the arch—is an attempt to cut down on the wind-tunnel effect this gigantic building creates. You can take a pricey elevator to the **panoramic rooftop** for a view over the skyscrapers and Parisian suburbs, but I wouldn't as you're too far from the city center for worthwhile views (€15, daily 10:00-19:00).

Drop down the arch's steps and glide onto the vast **Esplanade** (a.k.a. "le Parvis"), surveying the skyscraping scene.

In France, getting a building permit often comes with a requirement to dedicate two percent of the construction cost to art. Hence the Esplanade is a virtual open-air modern art gallery, sporting pieces by Joan Miró (blue, red, and yellow), Alexander Calder (red), Anthony Caro (long, brown, folded-steel sculpture that resembles the meltdown of a bridge support), and Yaacov Agam (the fountain with colorful stripes and rhythmically dancing spouts), among others. Just behind Yaacov's fountain, find *La Défense de Paris,* the statue that gave the area its name; it recalls the 1870 Franco-Prussian war—a rare bit of old Paris out here in the 'burbs.

As you descend the Esplanade, notice how the small gardens with benches and areas for *boules* are designed to integrate tradition into this celebration of modern commerce. Note also how the buildings tend to decrease in height and increase in age as you approach Paris' center. Your walk ends at the amusing fountain of Bassin Takis, where you'll find the Esplanade de la Défense Métro station that zips you out of all this modernity and directly back into town. Before descending into the Métro, take one last look back to La Grande Arche to appreciate how far you've come.

Opéra Neighborhood

200 Meters
200 Yards

To Musée
Jacquemart-André &
Parc Monceau

BD. HAUSSMANN   PRINTEMPS

RUE DE PROVENCE

R. DE MOGADOR

RUE DE LA CHAUSSÉE

RUE LA FAYETTE

RUE DES MATHURINS   Havre
Caumartin   GALERIES
LAFAYETTE   R. GLUCK   Chaussée d'Antin
La Fayette

RUE AUBER

RUE PASQUIER

R. DE SURENE

BD. MALESHERBES

BD. D'ANJOU

R. CHAUVEAU
LAGARDE

RUE TRONCHET

RUE VIGNON

RUE GODOT DE MAUROY

OPERA
GARNIER

FRAGONARD
PERFUME
MUSEUM   RUE SCRIBE   CAFE DE
LA PAIX   Place de
l'Opéra   CAPUCINES

Place
de la
Madeleine   LA
MADELEINE   Madeleine   RUE DE SÈZE   BD. DES   Opéra   RUE DU 4 SEPT

RUE DES CAPUCINES   Quatre
Septembre

R. DES   RUE DANOU   RUE ST. AUGUSTIN

RUE BOISSY D'ANGLAS

R. DE SURENE

HOTEL
RITZ   Place
Vendôme   RUE DE LA PAIX   RUE LE GRAND   AVE. DE L'ANTIN   PASSAGE
STE. ANNE   PASSAGE CHOISEUL

R. ST. FLORENTIN   R. DUPHOT   CAMBON   RUE DES   PETITS CHAMPS

HOTEL
CRILLON   Concorde   RUE ST.   RUE
MARCHÉ

Place
de la
Concorde   RUE DE RIVOLI   R. CASTIGLIONE   HONORÉ   RUE DE LA BOURDIE   RUE ST ROCH   Pyramides

RUE 29
JUILLET   RUE DES
PYRAMIDES   RUE ST. ANNE

- - -   Place de la Madeleine
Shopping Walk

OPERA NEIGHBORHOOD

The glittering Garnier opera house anchors this neighborhood of broad boulevards and grand architecture. This area is also nirvana for high-end shoppers, with the opulent Galeries Lafayette and Printemps stores, and the sumptuous shops that line Place Vendôme and Place de la Madeleine (see "Shopping in Paris," later, for a self-guided shopping walk of this area).

▲▲Opéra Garnier
(Opéra National de Paris—Palais Garnier)

A gleaming grand theater of the belle époque, the Palais Garnier was built for Napoleon III and finished in 1875. From Avenue de l'Opéra, once lined with Paris' most fashionable haunts, the facade suggests "all power to the wealthy." To see the interior, you have several choices: Take a guided tour (your best look), tour the public areas on your own (using the audioguide), or attend a per-

Baron Georges-Eugène Haussmann

The elegantly uniform streets that make Paris so Parisian are the work of Baron Haussmann (1809-1891), who oversaw the modernization of the city in the mid-19th century. He cleared out the cramped, higgledy-piggledy, unhygienic medieval cityscape and replaced it with broad, straight boulevards lined with stately buildings and linked by modern train stations.

The quintessential view of Haussmann's work is from the pedestrian island immediately in front of the Opéra Garnier. You're surrounded by Paris circa 1870, when it was the capital of the world. Gaze down the surrounding boulevards to find the column of Place Vendôme in one direction, and the Louvre in another. Haussmann's uniform, cohesive buildings are all five stories tall, with angled, black slate roofs and formal facades. The balconies on the second and fifth floors match those of their neighbors, creating strong lines of perspective as the buildings stretch down the boulevard.

But there was more than aesthetics to the plan. In pre-Haussmann Paris, angry rioters would take to the narrow streets, setting up barricades to hold back government forces (as made famous in Victor Hugo's *Les Misérables*). With Haussmann's new design, government troops could circulate easily and fire cannons down the long, straight boulevards. A whiff of "grapeshot"—chains, nails, and other buckshot-type shrapnel—could clear out any revolutionaries in a hurry.

formance. Its golden decor (mostly gold paint, not gilding) features statues, columns, and chandeliers, all set off by colorful ceiling paintings. Note that the auditorium is sometimes off-limits due to performances and rehearsals.

Cost and Hours: €12, not covered by Museum Pass, generally daily 10:00-16:30, mid-July-Aug until 18:00, closes for rehearsals and performances—most reliably open 10:00-13:00; 8 Rue Scribe, Mo: Opéra, RER/Train-A: Auber, www.operadeparis.fr/en/visits/palais-garnier.

Tours: The €5 audioguide gives a good self-guided tour. Guided tours in English run July-Aug at 11:00 and 14:30 daily; Sept-June Wed, Sat, and Sun only; check website below for off-season tours and to confirm times year-round, arrive 30 minutes early for security screening (€17, includes entry, 1.5 hours, tel. 01 42 46 72 40 or 01 71 25 24 23, www.cultival.fr/en, contact@cultival.fr).

Nearby: The illustrious Café de la Paix faces the Opera's front and has been a meeting spot for the local glitterati for generations. If you can afford the coffee, this spot offers a delightful break.

High-End Shopping

The upscale Opéra neighborhood hosts some of Paris' best shopping. Even window shoppers can appreciate this as a ▲ "sight." Just behind the Opéra, the **Galeries Lafayette** department store is a magnificent cathedral to consumerism, under a stunning stained-glass dome. The area between **Place de la Madeleine,** dominated by the Madeleine Church (looking like a Roman temple), and the octagonal **Place Vendôme,** is filled with pricey shops and boutiques, giving travelers a whiff of the exclusive side of Paris (for more on shopping in this area, see page 119).

MARAIS NEIGHBORHOOD AND NEARBY

Naturally, when in Paris you want to see the big sights—but to experience the city, you also need to visit a vital neighborhood. The Marais fits the bill, with trendy boutiques and art galleries, edgy cafés, narrow streets, leafy squares, Jewish bakeries, aristocratic mansions, and fun nightlife—and it's filled with real Parisians. It's the perfect setting to appreciate the flair of this great city.

The Marais extends along the Right Bank of the Seine, from the Bastille to the Pompidou Center. The main east-west axis is formed by Rue St. Antoine, Rue des Rosiers (the heart of Paris' Jewish community), and Rue Ste. Croix de la Bretonnerie. The centerpiece of the neighborhood is the stately Place des Vosges. Don't waste time looking for the Bastille, the prison of Revolution fame. It's Paris' most famous nonsight. The building is long gone, and just the square remains, good only for its nightlife and as a jumping-off point for the Marais Walk or a stroll through La Coulée Verte.

For a map of this area, see page 136.

Place des Vosges and West
▲▲Place des Vosges

Henry IV built this centerpiece of the Marais in 1605 and called it "Place Royale." As he'd hoped, it turned the Marais into Paris' most exclusive neighborhood. Walk to the center, where Louis XIII, on horseback, gestures, "Look at this wonderful square my dad built." Study the architecture: nine pavilions (houses) per side. The two highest—at the front and back—were for the king and queen (but were never used). Warm red brickwork—some real, some fake—is topped with sloped slate roofs, chimneys, and another quaint relic of a bygone era: TV antennas.

The insightful writer **Victor Hugo** lived at #6 from 1832 to 1848. (It's at the southeast corner of the square, marked by the French flag.) This was when he wrote much of his most important work, including *Les Misérables.* Inside this free museum (if it's not closed for renovations) you'll wander through eight plush rooms, enjoy a fine view of the square, and find good WCs (free, Tue-Sun 10:00-18:00, closed Mon; tel. 01 42 72 10 16, http://maisonsvictorhugo.paris.fr).

Sample the flashy art galleries ringing the square (the best ones are behind Louis). Ponder a daring new piece for that blank wall at home and take a peek into the courtyard of the Hôtel le Pavillon de la Reine (#28) for a glimpse into refined living—my hotel doesn't look like this. Or consider a pleasant break at one of the recommended eateries on the square.

▲Carnavalet Museum (Musée Carnavalet)

The tumultuous history of Paris—starring the Revolutionary years—is well portrayed in this converted Marais mansion (at 23 Rue de Sévigné, if it's open after a lengthy renovation). The museum contains models of medieval Paris, maps of the city over the centuries, paintings of Parisian scenes, French Revolution paraphernalia—including a small guillotine—and fully furnished rooms re-creating life in Paris in different eras.

▲▲Picasso Museum (Musée Picasso)

Whatever you think about Picasso the man, as an artist he was unmatched in the 20th century for his daring and productivity. The

Picasso Museum has the world's largest collection of his work— some 400 paintings, sculptures, sketches, and ceramics—spread across five levels of this mansion in the Marais. A visit here walks you through the full range of this complex man's life and art.

Cost and Hours: €14, covered by Museum Pass, free on first Sun of month and for those under age 18 with ID; open Tue-Fri 10:30-18:00, Sat-Sun from 9:30, closed Mon, last entry 45 minutes before closing; audioguide-€5, 5 Rue de Thorigny, Mo: St. Sébastien-Froissart, St-Paul, or Chemin Vert, tel. 01 42 71 25 21, www.musee-picasso.fr.

Visiting the Museum: The museum's fine audioguide is updated with each change to the exhibit. Floors 1 and 2 are the core of the museum with selections from its permanent collection. Floor 3 always features paintings from Picasso's personal collection— works of his that he never sold, and paintings by contemporaries (such as Miró, Matisse, Cézanne, and Braque) who inspired him.

Early Years and Early Cubism: In 1900, Picasso set out to make his mark in Paris, the undisputed world capital of culture. The brash Spaniard quickly became a poor, homesick foreigner, absorbing the styles of many painters while searching for his own artist's voice. When his best friend committed suicide, Picasso plunged into a **Blue Period,** painting emaciated beggars, hard-eyed pimps, and himself, bundled up against the cold, with eyes all cried out (*Autoportrait,* 1901).

In 1904, Picasso got a steady girlfriend, and suddenly saw the world through rose-colored glasses (the **Rose Period,** though the museum has very few works from this time). With his next-door neighbor, Georges Braque, Picasso invented Cubism, a fragment-ed, "cube"-shaped style. He'd fracture a figure (such as the mu-sician in *Man with a Mandolin,* 1911) into a barely recognizable jumble of facets. Picasso sketched reality from every angle, then pasted it all together, a composite of different views.

Cubist Experiments: Modern art was being born. The first stage had been so-called Analytic Cubism: breaking the world down into small facets, to "analyze" the subject from every angle. Now it was time to "synthesize" it back together with the real world (Synthetic Cubism). Picasso created "constructions" that were es-sentially still-life paintings (a 2-D illusion) augmented with glued-on, real-life materials—wood, paper, rope, or chair caning (the real 3-D world). In a few short years, Picasso had turned painting in the direction it would go for the next 50 years.

During the gray and sad years of World War II, Picasso stayed in Paris. His beloved mother had died, and he endured an endless, bitter divorce while juggling his two longtime, feuding mistress-es—as well as the occasional fling.

Later Years: At war's end, Picasso left Paris and all that emo-tional baggage behind, finding fun in the sun in the south of France. Sixty-five-year-old Pablo Picasso was reborn, enjoying worldwide fame. Picasso's Riviera works set the tone for the rest of his life—sunny, lighthearted, childlike, experimenting in new media, and using motifs of the sea, Greek mythology (fauns, centaurs), and animals (birds, goats, and pregnant baboons). Picasso was fertile to the end, still painting with bright thick colors at age 91.

▲Jewish Art and History Museum (Musée d'Art et Histoire du Judaïsme)

This is a fine museum of historical artifacts and rare ritual objects spanning the Jewish people's long cultural heritage. It empha-sizes the cultural unity maintained by this continually dispersed population. You'll learn about Jewish traditions, and see exquisite costumes and objects central to daily life and religious practices. Novices may find the displays beautiful and thought-provoking but not especially meaningful. Those with a background in Judaism or who take the time with the thoughtful audioguide and posted information will be rewarded.

Cost and Hours: €10, includes audioguide, covered by Museum Pass; Tue-Fri 11:00-18:00, Sat-Sun from 10:00, open later during special exhibits—Wed until 21:00 and Sat-Sun until 19:00, closed Mon year-round, last entry 45 minutes before closing; 71 Rue du Temple, Mo: Rambuteau or Hôtel de Ville a few blocks farther away, RER/Train-B: Châtelet-Les Halles; tel. 01 53 01 86 60, www.mahj.org.

Holocaust Memorial (Mémorial de la Shoah)

This sight, commemorating the lives of the more than 76,000 Jews deported from France in World War II, has several facets: a WWII deportation memorial, a museum on the Holocaust, and a Jewish resource center. Displaying original deportation records, the museum takes you through the history of Jews in Europe and France, from medieval pogroms to the Nazi era. But its focal point is underground, where victims' ashes are buried.

Cost and Hours: Free, Sun-Fri 10:00-18:00, Thu until 22:00, closed Sat and some Jewish holidays, audioguides-€5, 17 Rue Geoffroy l'Asnier, tel. 01 42 77 44 72, www.memorialdelashoah.org.

▲▲Pompidou Center (Centre Pompidou)

One of Europe's greatest collections of far-out modern art is housed in the Musée National d'Art Moderne, on the fourth and fifth floors of this colorful exoskeletal building. Created ahead of its time, the modern and contemporary art in this collection is still waiting for the world to catch up. The Pompidou Center and the square that fronts it are lively, with lots of people, street theater, and activity inside and out—a perpetual street fair. Kids of any age enjoy the fun, colorful fountain (an homage to composer Igor Stravinsky) next to the Pompidou Center.

Cost and Hours: €14, free on first Sun of month, Museum Pass covers permanent collection and escalators to sixth-floor panoramic views (plus occasional special exhibits); permanent collection open Wed-Mon 11:00-21:00, closed Tue, ticket counters close at 20:00; rest of the building open until 22:00 (Thu until 23:00); arrive after 17:00 to avoid crowds (mainly for special exhibits); free "Centre Pompidou" app, café on mezzanine, pricey view restaurant on level 6, Mo: Rambuteau or Hôtel de Ville, tel. 01 44 78 12 33, www.centrepompidou.fr.

Visiting the Museum: The Pompidou's "permanent" collection...isn't. But while the paintings (and other pieces) change, the museum generally keeps the artists and various styles in a set order.

You'll find this general scheme: ground floor—all services; basement—always photography exhibits and always free; floors 1 and 6—temporary exhibits (galleries 1-4); floors 4 and 5—the museum (what you're likely here for). The museum starts on floor 5 with a one-way route, with the collection displayed in chronological order filling rooms in numerical order. It's that easy.

Use the museum's floor plans (posted on the wall) to find specific artists. See the classics—Picasso, Matisse, etc.—but be sure to leave time to browse the thought-provoking and fun art of more recent artists.

As you tour the Pompidou, remember that most of the artists, including foreigners, spent their formative years in Paris. In the 1910s, funky Montmartre was the mecca of Modernism—the era of Picasso, Braque, and Matisse. In the 1920s, the center shifted to the grand cafés of Montparnasse, where painters mingled with American expats such as Ernest Hemingway and Gertrude Stein. During World War II, it was Jean-Paul Sartre's Existentialist scene around St. Germain-des-Prés. After World War II, the global art focus moved to New York, but by the late 20th century, Paris had reemerged as a cultural touchstone for the world of modern art.

View Art: The sixth floor has stunning views of the Paris cityscape. Your Pompidou ticket or Museum Pass gets you there, or you can buy the €5 View of Paris ticket (good for the sixth floor only; doesn't include museum entry).

East of Place des Vosges

▲▲Père Lachaise Cemetery (Cimetière du Père Lachaise)

Littered with the tombstones of many of the city's most illustrious dead, this is your best one-stop look at Paris' fascinating, romantic past residents. More like a small city, the cemetery is big and confusing, but it holds the graves of Frédéric Chopin, Molière, Edith Piaf, Oscar Wilde, Gertrude Stein, Jim Morrison, Héloïse and Abélard, and many more.

Cost and Hours: Free, Mon-Fri 8:00-18:00, Sat from 8:30, Sun from 9:00, until 17:30 in winter; two blocks from Mo: Gambetta (do not go to Mo: Père Lachaise) and two blocks from bus #69's last stop; tel. 01 55 25 82 10, searchable map available at unofficial website: www.pere-lachaise.com.

Visiting the Cemetery: Enclosed by a massive wall and lined with 5,000 trees, the peaceful, car-free lanes and dirt paths of Père Lachaise cemetery encourage parklike meandering. Named for Father *(Père)* La Chaise, whose job was listening to Louis XIV's sins, the cemetery is relatively new, having opened in 1804 to accommodate Paris' expansion. Today, this 100-acre city of the dead (pop. 70,000) still accepts new residents, but real estate prices are sky high (a 21-square-foot plot costs more than €11,000).

This cemetery, with thousands of graves and tombs crammed every which way, has only a few pedestrian pathways to help you navigate. The map available from a nearby florist can also help guide you. I recommend taking a one-way tour through the cemetery, starting from the convenient Métro/bus stops at Place Gambetta, connecting a handful of graves from some of this necropolis'

best-known residents, and taking a last bow at either the Père Lachaise or Philippe Auguste Métro stops, or a nearby bus #69 stop.

🎧 Download my free Père Lachaise Cemetery audio tour.

MONTMARTRE

Paris' highest hill, topped by Sacré-Cœur Basilica and rated ▲▲, is best known as the home of cabaret nightlife and bohemian artists. Struggling painters, poets, dreamers, and drunkards came here for cheap rent, untaxed booze, rustic landscapes, and views of the underwear of high-kicking cancan girls at the Moulin Rouge. These days, the hill is equal parts charm and kitsch—still vaguely village-like but mobbed with tourists and pickpockets on sunny weekends. Come for a bit of history, a getaway from Paris' noisy boulevards, and the view (to beat the crowds, it's best on a weekday or early on weekend mornings). For restaurants, see page 161.

▲Sacré-Cœur

You'll spot Sacré-Cœur, the Byzantine-looking white basilica atop Montmartre, from most viewpoints in Paris. Though only 130 years old, it's impressive and iconic, with a climbable dome, and marks Paris' highest natural point (430 feet). The church was finished only a century ago by Parisians humiliated by German invaders. Roman Catholics built it as a kind of penance for how the surrounding neighborhood sowed rebelliousness and division. Many French people were disgusted that in 1871 their government actually shot its own citizens, the Communards, who held out here on Montmartre after the French leadership surrendered to the Prussians.

Cost and Hours: Church-free, daily 6:00-22:30; dome-€6, not covered by Museum Pass, daily 8:30-20:00, Oct-April until 17:00; modest dress required, tel. 01 53 41 89 00, www.sacre-coeur-montmartre.com.

Getting There: You can take the Métro to the Anvers stop (to avoid the stairs up to Sacré-Cœur, use one more Métro ticket and ride up on the funicular). Alternatively, from Place Pigalle, you can take bus #40, which drops you right by Sacré-Cœur

PARIS

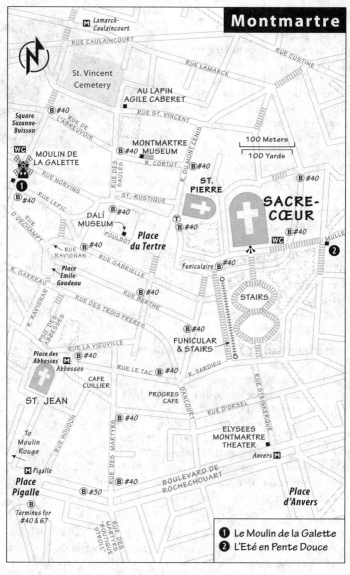

Montmartre

- Lamarck-Caulaincourt
- RUE CAULAINCOURT
- RUE LAMARCK
- RUE CUSTINE
- St. Vincent Cemetery
- AU LAPIN AGILE CABERET
- RUE ST. VINCENT
- Square Suzanne-Buisson
- RUE DE L'ABREUVOIR
- B #40
- MOULIN DE LA GALETTE
- WC
- ❶
- B #40
- RUE NORVINS
- RUE LEPIC
- MONTMARTRE MUSEUM
- B #40
- R. CORTOT
- RUE DES SAULES
- ST.-RUSTIQUE
- R. DI MONT-CENIS
- ST. PIERRE
- B #40
- B #40
- SACRE-CŒUR
- B #40
- WC
- ❷
- MULLE
- 100 Meters
- 100 Yards
- DALÍ MUSEUM
- B #40
- RUE D'ORCHAMPT
- POULBOT
- Place du Tertre
- T
- B #40
- RUE RAVIGNAN
- B #40
- RUE GABRIELLE
- Funiculaire B #40
- R. GARREAU
- Place Emile-Goudeau
- R. RAVIGNAN
- B #40
- RUE BERTHE
- STAIRS
- PSG. DES ABBESSES
- RUE DES TROIS FRERES
- B #40
- FUNICULAR & STAIRS
- Place des Abbesses
- B #40
- Abbesses
- RUE LA VIEUVILLE
- RUE LE TAC B #40
- R. TARDIEU
- ST. JEAN
- CAFE CUILLIER
- RUE HOUDON
- PROGRES CAFE
- DANCOURT
- RUE D'ORSEL
- RUE STEINKERQUE
- B #40
- ELYSEES MONTMARTRE THEATER
- To Moulin Rouge
- Pigalle
- RUE DES MARTYRS
- B #40
- Anvers
- Place Pigalle
- B #30
- BOULEVARD DE ROCHECHOUART
- Place d'Anvers
- B
- Terminus for #40 & 67
- RUE DES MARTYRS "BOUTIQUE STROLL"

❶ Le Moulin de la Galette
❷ L'Eté en Pente Douce

(Funiculaire stop, costs one Métro ticket, 4/hour). A taxi from near the Seine saves time and avoids sweat (about €20, €25 at night).

Visiting the Church: The Sacré-Cœur (Sacred Heart) Basilica's exterior, with its onion domes and bleached-bone pallor, looks ancient, but it was finished only a century ago by Parisians humiliated by German invaders. The five-domed, Roman-Byzantine-looking basilica took 44 years to build (1875-1919). It stands on a foundation of 83 pillars sunk 130 feet deep, necessary because the ground beneath was honeycombed with gypsum mines. The exterior is laced with gypsum, which whitens with age.

Take a clockwise spin around the crowded interior to see impressive mosaics, a statue of St. Thérèse, a scale model of the church, and three stained-glass windows dedicated to Joan of Arc. Pause near the Stations of the Cross mosaic to give St. Peter's bronze foot a rub. For an unobstructed panoramic view of Paris, climb 260 feet (300 steps) up the tight and claustrophobic spiral stairs to the top of the dome.

Nearby: To lose the crowd and feel Montmartre's pulse, explore a few blocks behind Place du Tertre. Go down Rue du Mont Cenis and turn left on Rue Cortot (past the Montmartre Museum). At Rue des Saules take a few steps downhill to see the vineyards that still supply cheap wine, then backtrack up Rue des Saules to the hilltop.

▲Montmartre Museum (Musée de Montmartre)

This 17th-century home re-creates the traditional cancan-and-cabaret Montmartre scene, with paintings, posters, photos, music, videos, and memorabilia. It offers the best look at the history of Montmartre and the amazing period from 1870 to 1910 when so much artistic action was percolating in this neighborhood, plus a chance to see the studio of Maurice Utrillo.

Cost and Hours: €12, includes good 45-minute audioguide, not covered by Museum Pass, daily 10:00-19:00, Oct-March until 18:00, last entry 45 minutes before closing, 12 Rue Cortot, tel. 01 49 25 89 39, www.museedemontmartre.fr.

Pigalle

Paris' red light district, the infamous "Pig Alley" to WWII servicemen, is at the foot of Butte Montmartre. *Ooh la la.* It's more racy than dangerous. Walk from Place Pigalle to Place Blanche, teasing desperate barkers and fast-talking temptresses. In bars, a €150 bottle of (what would otherwise be) cheap champagne comes with a friend. Stick to the bigger streets, hang on to your wallet, and exercise good judgment. Cancan can cost a fortune, as can con artists in topless bars. After dark, countless tour buses line the streets, reminding us that tour guides make big bucks by bringing their groups to touristy nightclubs like the famous Moulin Rouge (Mo: Pigalle or Abbesses).

Shopping in Paris

Shopping in chic Paris is altogether tempting—even reluctant shoppers can find good reasons to indulge. Wandering among elegant boutiques provides a break from the heavy halls of the Louvre, and, if you approach it right, a little cultural enlightenment. Even if you don't intend to buy anything, budget some time for window shopping, or, as the French call it, *faire du lèche-vitrines* ("window licking").

Before you enter a Parisian store, remember the following points:

- In small stores, always say, *"Bonjour, Madame* or *Mademoiselle* or *Monsieur"* when entering. And remember to say *"Au revoir, Madame* or *Mademoiselle* or *Monsieur"* when leaving.
- The customer is not always right. In fact, figure the clerk is doing you a favor by waiting on you.
- Except in department stores, it's not normal for the customer to handle clothing. Ask first before you pick up an item: *"Je peux?"* (zhuh puh), meaning, "Can I?"
- By law the price of items in a window display must be visible, often written on a slip of paper set on the floor or framed on the wall—a good indication of the shop's general price range.
- For clothing size comparisons between the US and France, see the appendix.
- Forget returns (and don't count on exchanges).
- Observe French shoppers. Then imitate.
- Saturday afternoons are *très* busy.
- Stores are generally closed on Sunday. Exceptions include the Galeries Lafayette store near the Opéra Garnier, the Carrousel du Louvre (underground shopping mall at the Louvre with a Printemps department store), and some shops near Sèvres-Babylone, along the Champs-Elysées, and in the Marais.
- Some small stores don't open until 14:00 on Mondays.
- Don't feel obliged to buy. If a shopkeeper offers assistance, just say, *"Je regarde, merci."*
- For information on VAT refunds and customs regulations, see the Practicalities chapter.

Department Stores (Les Grands Magasins)

Parisian department stores begin with their showy perfume and purse sections, almost always central on the ground floor, and worth a visit to see how much space is devoted to these luxuries. Helpful information desks are usually located at the main entrances near the perfume section (with floor plans in English). Stores generally have affordable restaurants (some with view terraces) and a good selection of fairly priced souvenirs and toys. Opening hours are customarily Monday through Saturday from 10:00 to 19:00 or 20:00. The major stores are open on Sundays and later on Thursdays, and all are jammed on Saturdays. You'll find both Galeries Lafayette and Printemps stores in several neighborhoods. The most convenient and most elegant sit side by side behind the Opéra Garnier, complementing that monument's similar, classy ambience (Mo: Chaussée d'Antin-La Fayette, Havre-Caumartin, or Opéra, see map on page 109).

Boutique Strolls

Give yourself a vacation from sightseeing by sifting through window displays, pausing at corner cafés, and feeling the rhythm of neighborhood life. (Or have you been playing hooky and doing this already?) Though smaller shops are more intimate, sales clerks are still formal—so mind your manners.

Most shops are closed on Sunday, which is the perfect day to head for the **Marais,** where many shops remain open on Sunday (and close on Saturday) and most of the neighborhood is off-limits to cars. For eclectic, avant-garde boutiques, peruse the artsy shops between Place des Vosges and the Pompidou Center.

Place de la Madeleine to Place de l'Opéra

The ritzy streets connecting several high-priced squares—Place de la Madeleine, Place de la Concorde, Place Vendôme, and Place de l'Opéra—form a miracle mile of gourmet food shops, glittering jewelry stores, posh hotels, exclusive clothing boutiques, and people who spend more on clothes in one day than I do in a year. This walk highlights the value Parisians place on outrageously priced products.

Start at Eglise de la Madeleine (Mo: Madeleine). In the northeast corner at #24 is the black-and-white awning of **Fauchon.** Founded on this location in 1886, this bastion of over-the-top edibles became famous around the world, catering to the refined tastes of the rich and famous. **Hédiard** (#21, northwest corner of the square) is older than Fauchon, and it's weathered the tourist mobs a bit better, though it may be closed for renovation during your visit. Hédiard's small red containers—of mustards, jams, coffee, candies, and tea—make great souvenirs.

Step inside tiny **La Maison des Truffe** (#19) to get a whiff of the product—truffles, those prized, dank, and dirty cousins of mushrooms. Check out the tiny jars in the display case. Ponder how something so ugly, smelly, and deformed can cost so much. The venerable **Mariage Frères** (#17) shop demonstrates how good tea can smell and how beautifully it can be displayed. At **Caviar Kaspia** (#16), you can add caviar, eel, and vodka to your truffle collection.

Continue along, past **Marquise de Sévígné chocolates** (#11) and Fauchon's new razzle-dazzle hotel, then cross to the island in the middle of **Boulevard Malesherbes.** When the street officially opened in 1863, it ushered in the Golden Age of this neighborhood. Continue across Boulevard Malesherbes. Straight ahead is **Patrick Roger Chocolates** (#3), famous for its chocolates, and even more so for M. Roger's huge, whimsical, 150-pound chocolate sculptures of animals and fanciful creatures.

Turning right down **Rue Royale,** there's Dior, Chanel, and Gucci. At Rue St. Honoré, turn left and cross Rue Royale, pausing in the middle for a great view both ways. Check out **Ladurée** (#16) for an out-of-this-world pastry break in the busy 19th-century tea salon, or to just pick up some world-famous macarons. Continue east down **Rue St. Honoré.** The street is a three-block parade of chic boutiques—L'Oréal cosmetics, Jimmy Choo shoes, Valentino, and so on. Looking for a €1,000 handbag? This is your spot.

Find the shortcut on the left at #362 or turn left on Rue de Castiglione to reach **Place Vendôme.** This octagonal square is *très* elegant—enclosed by symmetrical Mansart buildings around a 150-foot column. On the left side is the original Hôtel Ritz, opened in 1898. The square is also known for its upper-crust jewelry and designer stores—Van Cleef & Arpels, Dior, Chanel, Cartier, and others (if you have to ask how much...).

Leave Place Vendôme by continuing straight, up **Rue de la Paix**—strolling by still more jewelry, high-priced watches, and crystal—and enter **Place de l'Opéra:** You're in the middle of Right Bank glamour. Here you'll find the Opéra Garnier (described on page 109). If you're shopping till you're dropping, the Galeries Lafayette and Printemps department stores are located a few blocks up Rue Halévy.

Sèvres-Babylone to St. Sulpice

This Left Bank shopping area lets you sample smart clothing boutiques and clever window displays—and be tempted by tasty treats—while enjoying one of Paris' more attractive and boutique-filled neighborhoods.

Start at the Sèvres-Babylone Métro stop (take the Métro or bus #87). You'll find the **Bon Marché,** Paris' oldest department store. Continue along Rue de Sèvres, working your way to Place St. Sulpice and making detours left and right as the spirit moves you.

You'll pass some of Paris' smartest boutiques and coolest cafés, such as **Hermès** (at #17), and **Au Sauvignon Café** (at #10). Make a short detour up Rue du Cherche-Midi and find Paris' most celebrated bread—beautiful round loaves with designer crust—at the low-key **Poilâne** at #8. At the end of your walk, spill into Place St. Sulpice, with its big, twin-tower church. **Café de la Mairie** is a great spot to sip a *café crème,* admire the lovely square, and consider your next move. If you'd like more shopping options, you're in the heart of boutique shopping. As for me, stick a *fourchette* in me—I'm done.

Entertainment in Paris

Paris is brilliant after dark. Save energy from your day's sightseeing and experience the City of Light lit. Whether it's a concert at Sainte-Chapelle, a boat ride on the Seine, a walk in Montmartre, a hike up the Arc de Triomphe, or a late-night café, you'll see Paris at its best.

Jazz and Blues Clubs

With a lively mix of American, French, and international musicians, Paris has been an internationally acclaimed jazz capital since World War II. You'll pay €12-25 to enter a jazz club (may include one drink; if not, expect to pay €5-10 per drink; beer is cheapest). See *L'Officiel des Spectacles* under "Concerts" for listings, or, even better, the *Paris Voice* website. You can also check each club's website (all have English versions), or drop by the clubs to check out the calendars posted on their front doors. Music starts after 21:00 in most clubs. Some offer dinner concerts from about 20:30 on. Here are several good bets:

Caveau de la Huchette: This fun, characteristic old jazz/dance club fills an ancient Latin Quarter cellar with live jazz and frenzied dancing every night (admission about €15, €10 for those under 25, drinks from €7, daily from 21:30, no reservations needed, buy tickets at the door, 5 Rue de la Huchette, Mo: St. Michel, tel. 01 43 26 65 05, www.caveaudelahuchette.fr).

Other Venues: For a spot teeming with late-night activity and jazz, go to the two-block-long Rue des Lombards, at Boulevard Sébastopol, midway between the river and the Pompidou Center (Mo: Châtelet). **Au Duc des Lombards** is one of the most popular and respected jazz clubs in Paris, with concerts nightly in a great, plush, 110-seat theater-like setting (€30-55, €60-90 with dinner, buy online and arrive early for best seats, reasonable drink prices, shows usually at 19:30 and 21:30, 42 Rue des Lombards, tel. 01 42 33 22 88, www.ducdeslombards.fr). **Le Sunside** is just a block away. The club offers two little stages (ground floor and downstairs): "Le Sunset" stage tends toward contemporary world jazz; "le Sunside" stage features more traditional and acoustic jazz (concerts €20-30, a few are free; 60 Rue des Lombards, tel. 01 40 26 46 60, www.sunset-sunside.com).

Classical Concerts

For classical music on any night, consult *L'Officiel des Spectacles* magazine (check "Classique" under "Concerts" for listings), and look for posters at tourist-oriented churches. From March through November, these churches regularly host concerts: St. Sulpice, St. Germain-des-Prés, La Madeleine, St. Eustache, St. Julien-le-Pauvre, and Sainte-Chapelle.

Sainte-Chapelle: Enjoy the pleasure of hearing Mozart, Bach, or Vivaldi, surrounded by 800 years of stained glass (unheated—bring a sweater). The acousti-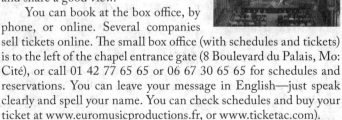cal quality is surprisingly good. There are usually two concerts per evening, at about 19:00 and 20:30; specify which one you want when you buy or reserve your ticket. Tickets start around €35— the more you pay, the closer you sit, though there isn't a bad seat in the chapel. Seats are unassigned within each section, so arrive at least 30 minutes early to get through the security line and snare a good view.

You can book at the box office, by phone, or online. Several companies sell tickets online. The small box office (with schedules and tickets) is to the left of the chapel entrance gate (8 Boulevard du Palais, Mo: Cité), or call 01 42 77 65 65 or 06 67 30 65 65 for schedules and reservations. You can leave your message in English—just speak clearly and spell your name. You can check schedules and buy your ticket at www.euromusicproductions.fr, or www.ticketac.com).

Other Venues: Look also for daytime concerts in parks, such as the Luxembourg Garden. Even the Galeries Lafayette department store offers concerts. Many of these concerts are free *(entrée* *libre),* such as the Sunday atelier concert sponsored by the American Church (generally Sept-June at 17:00 but not every week and not in Dec, 65 Quai d'Orsay, Mo: Invalides, RER/Train-C: Pont de l'Alma, tel. 01 40 62 05 00, www.acparis.org). The Army Museum offers inexpensive afternoon and evening classical music concerts all year round (for programs—in French only—see www.musee-armee.fr). There are also concerts at the Louvre's auditorium (www.louvre.fr/en/auditorium-louvre/music).

Opera

Paris is home to two well-respected opera venues. The **Opéra Bastille** is the massive modern opera house that dominates Place de la Bastille. Come here for state-of-the-art special effects and modern interpretations of classic ballets and operas. In the spirit of this everyman's opera, unsold seats are available at a big discount to seniors and students 15 minutes before the show. Standing-room-only tickets for €15 are also sold for some performances (Mo: Bastille).

The **Opéra Garnier,** Paris' first opera house, hosts opera and ballet performances. Come here for grand belle époque decor (Mo: Opéra; generally no performances mid-July-mid-Sept). To get tickets for either opera house, it's easiest to reserve online at www.operadeparis.fr, or call 01 71 25 24 23 outside France or toll tel. 08 92 89 90 90 inside France (office closed Sun). You can also buy tickets in person at their ticket offices (open Mon-Sat: Opéra Bastille 14:30-18:30, Opéra Garnier 11:30-18:30; both also open an hour before show; closed Sun).

Evening Sightseeing

Various museums (including the Louvre, Orsay, Pompidou, and Marmottan) are open late on different evenings—called *visites nocturnes*—offering the opportunity for more relaxed, less crowded visits. An elaborate sound-and-light show (Les Grandes Eaux Nocturnes) takes place in the gardens at Versailles on some Saturday evenings in summer (see the next chapter).

Seine River Cruises

Several companies offer cruises after dark as well as dinner cruises on huge glass-domed boats (or open-air decks in summer) with departures along the Seine, including from the Eiffel Tower. **Bateaux Parisiens** is considered the best of the lot for dinner (www.bateauxparisiens.com).

Night Walks

Go for an evening walk to best appreciate the City of Light. Break for ice cream, pause at a café, and enjoy the sidewalk entertainers as you join the post-dinner Parisian parade. (Avoid poorly lit areas and stick to main thoroughfares.)

Trocadéro and Eiffel Tower: Worth ▲▲▲, this is one of Paris' most spectacular views at night. Take the Métro to the Trocadéro stop and join the party on Place du Trocadéro for a magnificent view of the glowing Eiffel Tower. It's a festival of hawkers, gawkers, drummers, and entertainers.

Champs-Elysées and the Arc de Triomphe: The ▲▲ Avenue des Champs-Elysées is best after dark. Start at the Arc de Triomphe (open late), then stroll down Paris' glittering grand promenade.

Ile St. Louis and Notre-Dame: This ▲▲ stroll features floodlit views of Notre-Dame and a taste of the Latin Quarter. Find your way to the east end of Rue St. Louis-en-l'Ile, stopping for dinner—or at least a Berthillon ice cream (at #31) or Amorino Gelati (at #47). At the west end of Ile St. Louis, cross Pont St. Louis to Ile de la Cité, with a knockout view of Notre-Dame. Wander to the Left Bank on Quai de l'Archevêché, and drop down to the river for the best floodlit views.

▲Deux Chevaux Car Tours

If rumbling around Paris and sticking your head out of the rolled-back top of a funky old 2CV car *à la* Inspector Clouseau sounds like your kind of fun, consider this. The informal student-drivers are not professional guides (you're paying for their driving services), though they speak some English. Appreciate the simplicity of the car. It's France's version of the VW "bug" and hasn't been made since 1985. Ask your  guide to honk the horn, to run the silly little wipers, and to open and close the air vent—*c'est magnifique!*

They'll pick you up and drop you at your hotel or wherever you choose. **4 Roues Sous 1 Parapluie** ("4 wheels under 1 umbrella") offers several tours with candy-colored cars and drivers dressed in striped shirts and berets (for 2 people it's about €50/person for an hour and €70/person for 90 minutes; 10 percent tip appropriate if you enjoyed your ride, longer tours available, maximum 3 people/car, tel. 01 58 59 27 82, mobile 06 67 32 26 68, www.4roues-sous-1parapluie.com, info@4roues-sous-1parapluie.com).

▲Nighttime Bus Tours

GoBe's Paris by Night tour connects all the great illuminated sights of Paris with a 100-minute bus ride in 12 languages. You'll stampede on with a United Nations of tourists, get a set of headphones, dial up your language, and listen to a recorded spiel. Uninspired as it is, the ride provides an entertaining overview of the city at its floodlit and scenic best. Bring your city map to stay oriented as you go. You're always on the bus, but the driver slows for photos at viewpoints (€32, kids-€21, 1.75 hours, departs from 2 Rue des Pyramides April-Oct at 22:00, Nov-March at 20:00, reserve one day in advance, arrive 30 minutes early to wait in line for best seats, Mo: Pyramides, tel. 01 44 55 61 00, www.gobe.com). GoBe also offers a Paris by Night tour in a small-group minibus, which follows a similar route. For all GoBe tours, buy tickets through your hotel (no booking fee, brochures in lobby) or directly at the GoBe office at 2 Rue des Pyramides.

▲▲▲Floodlit Paris Driving Tour by Taxi or Uber

Seeing the City of Light floodlit is one of Europe's great travel experiences and a great finale to any day in Paris. I recommend a circular, one-hour route—from Notre-Dame to the Eiffel Tower along the Left Bank, then back along the Right Bank. Start at Notre-Dame (there's a taxi stand there—just in front, on left), at any convenient point along the route, or from your hotel. Review with the driver exactly where you hope to stop *("arrêt")* before you start.

Traffic can be sparse, and lights shine between 22:00 and 24:00 every night. Sunday is the best night, as there's less traffic. Complete your tour by midnight when lights are shut off at major monuments. Your other timing consideration: The Eiffel Tower twinkles for only the first five minutes of each hour after dark. If you start at Notre-Dame at half past the hour, you should be right on time for the sparkles.

This suggested loop costs around €50 (more on Sun) via taxi and around €40 by Uber. If your cabbie was easy to work with, add a 10 percent tip; if not, tip just 5 percent. You don't need to tip with Uber (though you can). Drivers can take up to four people in a cab or regular sedan, though this is tight for decent sightseeing (with three, everyone gets a window).

Sleeping in Paris

I've focused my recommendations on three safe, handy, and colorful neighborhoods: the village-like Rue Cler (near the Eiffel Tower); the artsy and trendy Marais (near Place de la Bastille); and the historic island of Ile St. Louis (next door to Notre-Dame).

If you're looking on your own for accommodations (beyond this book's listings), consider the classy Luxembourg Garden neighborhood (on the Left Bank) and the less polished, less central, but less pricey Montmartre neighborhood. For lower rates or greater selection, look farther from the river (prices drop proportionately with distance from the Seine), but be prepared to spend more time on the Métro or the bus getting to sights. For some travelers, short-term, Airbnb-type rentals can be a good alternative; search for places in my recommended hotel neighborhoods. I also list a few bed-and-breakfast agencies and give suggestions for sleeping near Paris' airports.

I rank accommodations from $ budget to $$$$ splurge. The French use stars to rate hotels based on their amenities (indicated by asterisks in this book). To get the best deal, contact hotels directly (via their website, phone, or email). When you go direct, the owner avoids a roughly 20 percent commission and may be able to offer you a discount. Book any accommodations well in advance, especially if you'll be traveling during peak season or if your trip coincides with a major holiday or festival (see the appendix). For more information and tips on hotel rates and deals, making reservations, finding a short-term rental, and chain hotels, see the "Sleeping" section in the Practicalities chapter.

RUE CLER NEIGHBORHOOD

(7th arr., Mo: Ecole Militaire, La Tour Maubourg, Invalides)
Rue Cler is so French that when I step out of my hotel in the morning, I feel like I must have been a poodle in a previous life. How such coziness lodged itself between the high-powered government district, the Eiffel Tower, and Les Invalides, I'll never know. This is a neighborhood of wide, tree-lined boulevards, stately apartment buildings, and lots of Americans. Hotels here are a fair value, considering the elegance of the neighborhood. And for sightseeing, you're within walking distance of the Eiffel Tower, Army Museum, Seine River, Champs-Elysées, and Orsay and Rodin museums.

Become a local at a Rue Cler café for breakfast, or join the afternoon crowd for *une bière pression* (a draft beer). On Rue Cler you can eat and browse your way through a street full of cafés, pastry shops, delis, cheese shops, and colorful outdoor produce stalls. Afternoon *boules* (outdoor bowling) on the Esplanade des Invalides or in the Champ de Mars park is a relaxing spectator sport. The manicured gardens behind the golden dome of the Army Museum are free, peaceful, and filled with flowers (at southwest corner of grounds, closes at about 19:00), and the riverside promenade along the Seine is a fine place to walk, run, bike, or just sit and watch the river of people stroll by.

Services: ComAvenue has computers (€5/hour), Wi-Fi, and consultants who can help if you have problems with your laptop (Mon-Fri 10:00-19:00, closed Sat-Sun, 24 Rue du Champ de Mars, tel. 01 45 55 00 07). You can buy your Paris Museum Pass at **Tabac La Cave à Cigares** on Avenue de la Motte-Picquet, across

PARIS

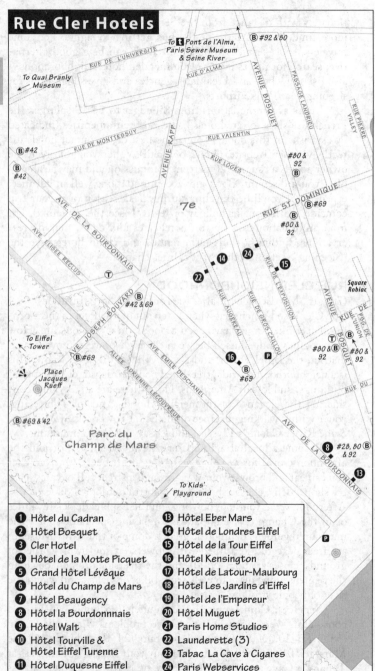

Rue Cler Hotels

To Pont de l'Alma, Paris Sewer Museum & Seine River

To Quai Branly Museum

#92 & 80

RUE DE L'UNIVERSITE

RUE D'ALMA

AVENUE BOSQUET

PASSAGE LANDRIEU

RUE PIERRE VILLEY

#42

#42

RUE DE MONTTESSUY

RUE VALENTIN

RUE LOGES

AVENUE RAPP

#80 & 92

RUE ST. DOMINIQUE

#69

7e

AVE. DE LA BOURDONNAIS

#80 & 92

AVE. ELISEE RECLUS

RUE DE L'EXPOSITION

Square Robiac

AVENUE BOSQUET

RUE DE GRENELLE

#42 & 69

AVE. JOSEPH BOUVARD

RUE AUGEREAU

RUE DE GROS CAILLOU

RUE DE L'UNION

To Eiffel Tower

#69

ALLEE ADRIENNE LECOUVREUR

AVE. EMILE DESCHANEL

#69

#80 & 92

#80 & 92

Place Jacques Rueff

RUE DU

#69 & 42

Parc du Champ de Mars

AVE. DE LA BOURDONNAIS

#28, 80 & 92

To Kids' Playground

1 Hôtel du Cadran
2 Hôtel Bosquet
3 Cler Hotel
4 Hôtel de la Motte Picquet
5 Grand Hôtel Lévêque
6 Hôtel du Champ de Mars
7 Hôtel Beaugency
8 Hôtel la Bourdonnnais
9 Hôtel Walt
10 Hôtel Tourville & Hôtel Eiffel Turenne
11 Hôtel Duquesne Eiffel
12 Hôtel de France Invalides

13 Hôtel Eber Mars
14 Hôtel de Londres Eiffel
15 Hôtel de la Tour Eiffel
16 Hôtel Kensington
17 Hôtel de Latour-Maubourg
18 Hôtel Les Jardins d'Eiffel
19 Hôtel de l'Empereur
20 Hôtel Muguet
21 Paris Home Studios
22 Launderette (3)
23 Tabac La Cave à Cigares
24 Paris Webservices

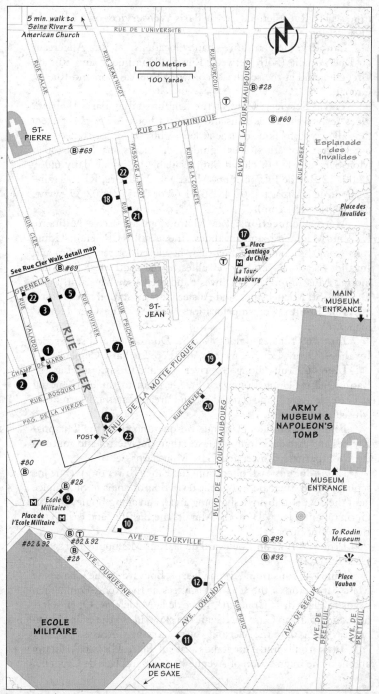

PARIS

5 min. walk to
Seine River &
American Church

RUE DE L'UNIVERSITE

100 Meters
100 Yards

RUE MALAR

RUE JEAN NICOT

RUE SURCOUF

BLVD. DE LA-TOUR-MAUBOURG

Ⓣ

Ⓑ #28

ST-
PIERRE

Ⓑ #69

RUE ST. DOMINIQUE

Ⓑ #69

RUE FABERT

Esplanade
des
Invalides

RUE CLER

PASSAGE J. NICOT

RUE DE LA COMETE

Ⓐ 22

Ⓐ 18

RUE AMELIE

Ⓐ 21

Place des
Invalides

Ⓐ 17
Place
Santiago
du Chile

Ⓣ

See Rue Cler Walk detail map

GRENELLE

Ⓑ #69

Ⓜ La Tour-
Maubourg

RUE DUVIVIER

RUE PSICHARI

ST-
JEAN

RUE CLER

RUE VALADON

Ⓐ 22

Ⓐ 5

Ⓐ 3

Ⓐ 1

CHAMP DE MARS

Ⓐ 2

Ⓐ 6

Ⓐ 7

MAIN
MUSEUM
ENTRANCE
↓

RUE BOSQUET

PSG. DE LA VIERGE

AVENUE DE LA MOTTE-PICQUET

Ⓐ 19

RUE CHEVERT

Ⓐ 20

ARMY
MUSEUM &
NAPOLEON'S
TOMB

Ⓐ 4

POST

Ⓐ 23

7e

BLVD. DE LA-TOUR-MAUBOURG

MUSEUM
ENTRANCE
↓

#80
Ⓑ

Ⓑ #28

Ⓜ Ecole
Militaire

Ⓐ 9

Place de
l'Ecole Militaire

Ⓜ

Ⓑ
#82 & 92

Ⓑ Ⓣ
#82 & 92

Ⓐ 10

AVE. DE TOURVILLE

Ⓑ #92

To Rodin
Museum

#28

AVE. DUQUESNE

Ⓑ #92

Place
Vauban

AVE. LOWENDAL

AVE. DE SEGUR

RUE BIXIO

AVE. DE
BRETEUIL

AVE. DE
BRETEUIL

ECOLE
MILITAIRE

Ⓐ 12

Ⓐ 11

MARCHE
DE SAXE

from where Rue Cler ends, or at **Paris Webservices** on 12 Rue de l'Exposition.

Laundry: Here are three handy locations: on Rue Augereau, on Rue Amélie (both between Rue St. Dominique and Rue de Grenelle), and at the southeast corner of Rue Valadon and Rue de Grenelle.

Travel Services: Contact the helpful staff at **Paris Webservices** to buy the Paris Museum Pass, to book *"coupe-file"* tickets that allow you to skip the line at key sights, or for assistance with hotels, transportation, local guides, or excursions (office open Mon-Sat 9:00-17:00, closed Sun; available by phone daily 6:00-22:00, 12 Rue de l'Exposition, Mo: Ecole Militaire, RER/Train-C: Pont de l'Alma, tel. 01 45 56 91 67 or 09 52 06 02 59, www.pariswebservices.com).

Métro Connections: Key Métro stops are Ecole Militaire, La Tour Maubourg, and Invalides. The useful RER/Train-C line runs from the Pont de l'Alma (may be closed for renovation) and Invalides stations, serving Versailles to the southwest; the Marmottan Museum to the northwest; and the Orsay Museum, Latin Quarter (St. Michel stop), and Austerlitz train station to the east.

Bus Routes: For stop locations, see the "Rue Cler Hotels" map.

Line #69 runs east along Rue St. Dominique and serves Les Invalides, Orsay, Louvre, Marais, and Père Lachaise Cemetery.

Line #63 runs along the river (Quai d'Orsay), serving the Latin Quarter along Boulevard St. Germain to the east (ending at Gare de Lyon), and Trocadéro and areas near the Marmottan Museum to the west.

Line #92 runs along Avenue Bosquet, north to the Champs-Elysées and Arc de Triomphe (faster than the Métro) and south to the Montparnasse Tower and Gare Montparnasse.

Line #86 runs eastbound from the Eiffel Tower on Avenue Joseph Bouvard, then along Avenue de la Bourdonnais to St. Sulpice (and the Sèvres-Babylone shopping area), and along Boulevards St. Germain and Henry IV to the Marais, the Bastille, and east to the Bois de Vincennes.

Line #28 runs on Boulevard de la Tour Maubourg and serves Gare St. Lazare.

Line #42 runs from Avenue Joseph Bouvard in the Champ de Mars park, crosses the Champs-Elysées at the Rond-Point, then heads to Place de la Concorde, Place de la Madeleine, Opéra Garnier, and finally to Gare St. Lazare—a slow ride to the train station but less tiring than the Métro if you're carrying suitcases.

Taxi: You'll find taxi stands just off Place L'Ecole Militaire and near the intersection of Avenue Bosquet and Rue de Grenelle.

In the Heart of Rue Cler

Many of my readers stay in the Rue Cler neighborhood. If you want to disappear into Paris, choose a hotel elsewhere. The following hotels are within Camembert-smelling distance of Rue Cler.

$$$$ Hôtel du Cadran,*** a well-placed *boule* toss from Rue Cler, is comfortable and *très* stylish with a wine bar in its lobby and designer rooms. The hotel has rooms in two locations a block apart. The main hotel has 40 tight rooms and their 12-room annex (called **Hôtel Cadran Coleur**) has larger rooms, though you'll sleep well in either (RS% includes big breakfast—use code "RICK"; 10 Rue du Champ de Mars, tel. 01 40 62 67 00, www.cadranhotel.com, resa@cadranhotel.com).

$$$ Hôtel Bosquet*** is an exceptionally good hotel in an ideal location, with comfortable public spaces and well-configured rooms that are large by local standards and feature effective darkness blinds. The staff is politely formal (RS%—use code "RSDEAL"; good but pricey breakfast buffet with eggs and sausage, 19 Rue du Champ de Mars, tel. 01 47 05 25 45, www.hotel-paris-bosquet. com, hotel@relaisbosquet.com).

$$$ Cler Hotel*** is a smart boutique hotel with appealing decor, a small outdoor patio, and a killer location right on Rue Cler. Rooms are well-designed, and the young owners are eager to please (RS%, 24 bis Rue Cler, tel. 01 45 00 18 06, www.clerhotel.com, contact@clerhotel.com).

$$$ Hôtel de la Motte Picquet,*** at the corner of Rue Cler and Avenue de la Motte-Picquet, is an intimate and modest little place with 16 compact yet comfortable-enough rooms. The terrific staff makes staying here a pleasure (RS%—use code "STEVE-SMITH"; family rooms, good—and free—breakfast served in a minuscule breakfast room, easy bike rental, 30 Avenue de la Motte-Picquet, tel. 01 47 05 09 57, www.hotelmottepicquetparis. com, book@hotelmottepicquetparis.com).

$$$ Grand Hôtel Lévêque*** is overpriced and undermaintained but has a terrific location on Rue Cler (29 Rue Cler, tel. 01 47 05 49 15, www.hotel-leveque.com, info@hotelleveque.com)

$$ Hôtel du Champ de Mars*** is a top choice, brilliantly located barely 10 steps off Rue Cler. This plush little hotel has a small-town feel from top to bottom. The adorable rooms are snug but lovingly kept by hands-on owners Françoise and Stéphane, and single rooms can work as tiny doubles. It's popular, so book well ahead (continental breakfast only, 30 yards off Rue Cler at 7 Rue du Champ de Mars, tel. 01 45 51 52 30, www.hotelduchampdemars. com, hotelduchampdemars@gmail.com).

$$ Hôtel Beaugency*** has 30 smallish rooms, most with double beds, and a lobby that you can stretch out in. It's a fair value on a quieter street a short block off Rue Cler (free breakfast for Rick

Steves readers, 21 Rue Duvivier, tel. 01 47 05 01 63, www.hotel-beaugency.com, infos@hotel-beaugency.com).

Near Ecole Militaire Métro Stop

These listings are a five-minute walk from Rue Cler, near the Ecole Militaire Métro stop or RER/Train-C: Pont de l'Alma (may be closed for renovation).

$$$$ Inwood Hotels has three sister hotels in this neighborhood; all are ****, well-located, and offer top comfort and professional service—for a price (be clear about cancellation policies before booking). Public spaces and rooms are polished. The first two offer Rick Steves readers free breakfast; use www.inwood-hotels.com for booking at all three. **Hôtel la Bourdonnais,** near the Champ de Mars park, is the largest of the three and closest to the Eiffel Tower (113 Avenue de la Bourdonnais, tel. 01 47 05 45 42, labourdonnais@inwood-hotels.com). **Hôtel Walt** has a sharp interior courtyard terrace (37 Avenue de la Motte-Picquet, tel. 01 45 51 55 83, lewalt@inwood-hotels.com). **Hôtel Tourville** is the most intimate (6 Avenue de Tourville, tel. 01 47 05 62 62, letourville@inwood-hotels.com).

$$$ Hôtel Duquesne Eiffel,*** a few blocks farther from the action, is handsome and hospitable. It features a welcoming lobby, a street-front terrace, comfortable rooms (some with terrific Eiffel Tower views), and connecting rooms that work well for families (RS%, big, hot breakfast—free for Rick Steves readers, 23 Avenue Duquesne, tel. 01 44 42 09 09, www.hde.fr, contact@hde.fr).

$$$ Hôtel Eiffel Turenne*** is a good choice with sharp, well-maintained rooms, a pleasing lounge, and a service-oriented staff (20 Avenue de Tourville, tel. 01 47 05 99 92, www.hoteleiffelturenne.com, reservation@hoteleiffelturenne.com, friendly Emma).

$$ Hôtel de France Invalides** is a fair midrange option run by a brother-sister team (Alain and Marie-Hélène). It has contemporary decor and 60 rooms, some with knockout views of Invalides' golden dome (but with some traffic noise and no air-con). Rooms on the courtyard are quieter, smaller, and cheaper (RS%, connecting rooms possible, first breakfast free for Rick Steves readers—maximum of two per party, 102 Boulevard de la Tour Maubourg, tel. 01 47 05 40 49, www.hoteldefrance.com, contact@hoteldefrance.com).

$$ Hôtel Eber Mars,*** a few steps from Champ de Mars park, has warm public spaces, an I-try-harder owner (Monsieur Eber), a very narrow elevator, and comfortable, mostly bigger-than-average rooms (free continental breakfast for Rick Steves readers who book direct, 117 Avenue de la Bourdonnais, tel. 01 47 05 42 30, www.hotelebermars.com, reservation@hotelebermars.com).

Closer to Rue St. Dominique (and the Seine)

$$$ Hôtel de Londres Eiffel*** is my closest listing to the Eiffel Tower and the Champ de Mars park. Here you get immaculate, warmly decorated but tight rooms (several are connecting for families), comfy public spaces, and a terrific staff that can't do enough to help. It's less convenient to the Métro (10-minute walk), but very handy to buses #69, #80, and #92, and to RER/Train-C: Pont de l'Alma (some Eiffel Tower view rooms, 1 Rue Augereau, tel. 01 45 51 63 02, www.hotel-paris-londres-eiffel.com, info@londres-eiffel.com, helpful Cédric and Arnaud).

$ Hôtel de la Tour Eiffel** is a solid value on a quiet street near several of my favorite restaurants. The rooms are well-designed and comfortable with air-conditioning (but no breakfast). The six sets of connecting rooms are ideal for families (RS%, 17 Rue de l'Exposition, tel. 01 47 05 14 75, www.hotel-toureiffel.com, hte7@wanadoo.fr).

$ Hôtel Kensington** is a fair budget value close to the Eiffel Tower. It's an unpretentious place offering basic comfort (some partial Eiffel Tower views, no air-con but ceiling fans, 79 Avenue de la Bourdonnais, tel. 01 47 05 74 00, www.hotel-eiffel-kensington.com, hotelkensignton@gmail.com).

Near La Tour Maubourg Métro Stop

These listings are within three blocks of the intersection of Avenue de la Motte-Picquet and Boulevard de la Tour Maubourg.

$$$$ Hôtel de Latour-Maubourg*** owns a peaceful manor-home setting with 17 plush, mostly large and wonderfully traditional rooms, a small patio, and free spa for clients (across from the Métro station at 150 Rue de Grenelle, tel. 01 47 05 16 16, www.latourmaubourg.com, info@latourmaubourg.com).

$$$ Hôtel Les Jardins d'Eiffel*** is a big place on a quiet street, with impersonal service, a peaceful patio, and a lobby you can stretch out in. The 81 well-configured rooms—some with partial Eiffel Tower views, some with balconies—offer a bit more space and quiet than other hotels (RS%, parking garage, 8 Rue Amélie, tel. 01 47 05 46 21, www.hoteljardinseiffel.com, reservations@hoteljardinseiffel.com).

$$$ Hôtel de l'Empereur*** is stylish and delivers smashing views of Invalides from many of its fine rooms. All rooms have queen- or king-size beds, are well-designed with hints of the emperor, and are large by Paris standards (some view rooms, family rooms, strict 7-day cancellation policy, 2 Rue Chevert, tel. 01 45 55 88 02, www.hotelempereurparis.com, contact@hotelempereur.com).

$$$ **Hôtel Muguet***** is quiet, well-located, well-run, and reasonable, with tastefully appointed rooms and a helpful staff (some view rooms, strict 7-day cancellation policy, 11 Rue Chevert, tel. 01 47 05 05 93, www.hotelparismuguet.com, contact@ hotelparismuguet.com).

MARAIS

Those interested in a more central, diverse, and lively urban locale should make the Marais their Parisian home. This is jumbled, medieval Paris at its finest, where classy stone mansions sit alongside trendy bars, antique shops, and fashion-conscious boutiques. The streets are an intriguing parade of artists, students, tourists, immigrants, and baguette-munching babies in strollers. The Marais is also known as a hub of the Parisian gay and lesbian scene.

In the Marais you have these major sights close at hand: Victor Hugo's House, Jewish Art and History Museum, Pompidou Center, and Picasso Museum. You're also a manageable walk from Paris' two islands (Ile St. Louis and Ile de la Cité), home to Notre-Dame and Sainte-Chapelle. The Opéra Bastille, La Coulée Verte Promenade-Park, Place des Vosges (Paris' oldest square), the Jewish Quarter (Rue des Rosiers), the Latin Quarter, and nightlife-packed Rue de Lappe are also walkable. Strolling home (day or night) from Notre-Dame along Ile St. Louis is marvelous.

Most of my recommended hotels are located a few blocks north of the Marais' main east-west drag, Rue St. Antoine/Rue de Rivoli. For those who prefer a quieter home with fewer tourists, I list several hotels in the northern limits of the Marais, near Rue de Bretagne, the appealing commercial spine of this area.

Services: A busy **SNCF Boutique** is just off Rue St. Antoine at 2 Rue de Turenne (Mon-Fri 8:00-20:30, Sat 10:00-20:30, closed Sun).

Laundry: Launderettes are scattered throughout the Marais; ask your hotelier for the nearest. Here are two that you can count on: on Impasse Guémenée (north of Rue St. Antoine), and on Rue du Petit Musc (south of Rue St. Antoine).

Métro Connections: Key Métro stops in the Marais are, from east to west: Bastille, St-Paul, and Hôtel de Ville (Sully-Morland, Pont Marie, and Rambuteau stops are also handy). Métro connections are excellent, with direct service to the Louvre, Champs-Elysées, Arc de Triomphe, and La Défense (all on line 1); the Rue Cler area, Place de la Madeleine (see "Boutique Strolls," page 120), and Opéra Garnier/Galeries Lafayette (line 8 from Bastille stop);

and four major train stations: Gare de Lyon, Gare du Nord, Gare de l'Est, and Gare d'Austerlitz (all accessible from Bastille stop).

Bus Routes: For stop locations, see the "Marais Hotels" map.

Line #69 on Rue St. Antoine takes you eastbound to Père Lachaise Cemetery and westbound to the Louvre, Orsay, and Rodin museums, plus the Army Museum and Rue Cler, ending at the Eiffel Tower.

Line #87 runs down Boulevard Henri IV, crossing Ile St. Louis and serving the Latin Quarter along Boulevard St. Germain, before heading to St. Sulpice Church/Luxembourg Garden, ending at the Musée d'Orsay. The same line, running in the opposite direction, brings you to Gare de Lyon.

Line #96 runs on Rues Turenne and Rivoli, serves Ile de la Cité and St. Sulpice Church (near Luxembourg Garden), and ends at Gare Montparnasse.

Taxi: You'll find taxi stands on the north side of Rue St. Antoine (where Rue Castex crosses it), on Place de la Bastille (where Boulevard Richard Lenoir meets the square), on the south side of Rue St. Antoine (in front of St. Paul Church), and behind the Hôtel de Ville on Rue du Lobau (where it meets Rue de Rivoli).

Near Place des Vosges

(3rd and 4th arr., Mo: Bastille, St-Paul, or Hôtel de Ville)

$$$$ Hôtel le Pavillon de la Reine,***** 15 steps off the beautiful Place des Vosges, merits its stars with top service and comfort and exquisite attention to detail, from its melt-in-your-couch lobby to its luxurious rooms (free access to spa and fitness room, parking, 28 Place des Vosges, tel. 01 40 29 19 19, www.pavillon-de-la-reine.com, contact@pavillon-de-la-reine.com).

$$$ Hôtel Bastille Spéria*** is situated a short block off Place de la Bastille, offering business-type service and OK comfort in a happening location. The 42 rooms have uninspiring decor but are well configured and relatively spacious (1 Rue de la Bastille, Mo: Bastille, tel. 01 42 72 04 01, www.hotelsperia.com, info@hotelsperia.com).

$$$ Hôtel St. Louis Marais*** is an intimate and sharp little hotel that sits on a quiet street a few blocks from the river. The handsome rooms have character...and spacious bathrooms (skip their 3 annex rooms, 1 Rue Charles V, Mo: Sully-Morland, tel. 01 48 87 87 04, www.saintlouismarais.com, marais@saintlouis-hotels.com).

$$ Hôtel Jeanne d'Arc*** is a lovely hotel that's ideally located for connoisseurs of the Marais who don't need air-conditioning. Here, artful decor meets stone walls and oak floors, rooms are thoughtfully appointed, and corner rooms are wonderfully bright

PARIS

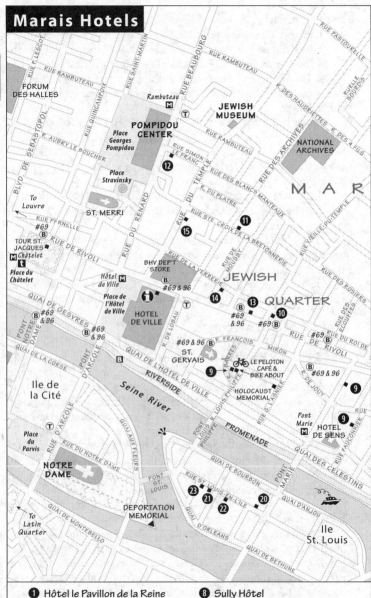

Marais Hotels

1 Hôtel le Pavillon de la Reine
2 Hôtel Bastille Spéria
3 Hôtel St. Louis Marais
4 Hôtel Jeanne d'Arc
5 Hôtel Castex
6 Hôtel de Neuve
7 Hôtel Pratic

8 Sully Hôtel
9 MIJE Hostels (3)
10 Hôtel Caron de Beaumarchais
11 Hôtel de la Bretonnerie
12 Hôtel Beaubourg
13 Hôtel de Nice
14 Hôtel du Loiret

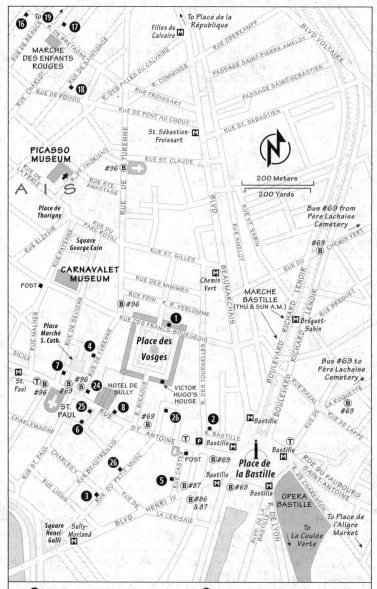

15 D'Win Hôtel

16 Hôtel Jacques de Molay

17 Hôtel du Vieux Saule

18 Hôtel Saintonge

19 To Hôtel Picard

20 Hôtel du Jeu de Paume

21 Hôtel de Lutèce

22 Hôtel des Deux-Iles

23 Hôtel Saint-Louis

24 SNCF Boutique

25 Monoprix (Grocery)

26 Launderette (2)

in the City of Light. Rooms on the street can have some noise until the bars close (family rooms, some view rooms, 3 Rue de Jarente, Mo: St-Paul, tel. 01 48 87 62 11, www.hoteljeannedarc.com, information@hoteljeannedarc.com).

$$$ Hôtel Castex*** is a well-located place—on a quiet street near Place de la Bastille—with narrow and tile-floored rooms. Their system of connecting rooms allows families total privacy between two rooms, each with its own bathroom (free buffet breakfast for Rick Steves readers, just off Place de la Bastille and Rue St. Antoine at 5 Rue Castex, Mo: Bastille, tel. 01 42 72 31 52, www.castexhotel.com, info@castexhotel.com).

$$ Hôtel de Neuve*** is a small, central, and dignified place with classical music in the lobby and high tea in the afternoon. Rooms are plush, quiet, and a good value in this pricey area (free breakfast for Rick Steves readers—use code "RICKSTEVES" when booking, behind the Monoprix at 14 Rue de Neuve, Mo: St-Paul, tel. 01 44 59 28 50, www.hoteldeneuveparis.com, bonjour@hoteldeneuveparis.com).

$$ Hôtel Pratic,** just off the quiet and charming Place du Marché Ste. Catherine, works for budget travelers who don't mind squeezing sideways to make it past the bed into the bathroom. The half-timbered interior gives the lobby a trace of character, but also makes for dark hallways. Rooms are clean with modern amenities (some view rooms, no elevator, 6 floors, no air-con, 9 Rue d'Ormesson, tel. 01 48 87 80 47, www.pratichotelparis.com, pratic.hotel@wanadoo.fr).

$ Sully Hôtel,* right on Rue St. Antoine, is a basic, cheap place run by affable Monsieur Zeroual. The rooms are frumpy, dimly lit, and can smell of smoke, the entry is dark and narrow (need I say more?), but the price fits. Two can spring for a triple for more room (family rooms, no elevator, no air-con, 48 Rue St. Antoine, Mo: St-Paul, tel. 01 42 78 49 32, www.sullyhotelparis.com, sullyhotel@orange.fr).

¢ MIJE Youth Hostels: The Maison Internationale de la Jeunesse et des Etudiants (MIJE) runs three classy, old residences, ideal for budget travelers who are at least 18 years old or traveling with someone who is. Each is well maintained, with simple, clean, single-sex (unless your group takes a whole room) one- to four-bed rooms. The hostels are **MIJE Fourcy** (biggest and loudest, dirt-cheap dinners available with a membership card, 6 Rue de Fourcy, just south of Rue de Rivoli), **MIJE Fauconnier** (no elevator, 11 Rue du Fauconnier), and **MIJE Maubisson** (smallest and quietest, no outdoor terrace, 12 Rue des Barres). None have double beds or air-conditioning. All have private showers in every room—but bring your own towel or buy one there (includes breakfast, required membership-€3 extra/person, Wi-Fi in common areas only, rooms locked 12:00-15:00). They share the same contact information (tel. 01 42 74 23 45, www.mije.com, info@mije.com) and Métro stop (St-Paul).

Near the Pompidou Center
(4th arr., Mo: St-Paul, Hôtel de Ville, or Rambuteau)
These hotels are farther west, closer to the Pompidou Center than to Place de la Bastille.

$$$ Hôtel Caron de Beaumarchais* transports you to the 18th century, with a small lobby that's cluttered with bits from an elegant old Marais house. If you want traditional French decor, stay here. Located on a busy street, it's well cared for and filled with character (12 Rue Vieille du Temple, tel. 01 42 72 34 12, www.carondebeaumarchais.com, hotel@carondebeaumarchais.com).

$$ Hôtel de la Bretonnerie* makes a fine Marais home. Located three blocks from the Hôtel de Ville, it has a warm, welcoming lobby and helpful staff. Its 30 good-value rooms are on the larger side with an antique, open-beam warmth (family rooms, free breakfast for Rick Steves readers who book direct, no air-con, between Rue Vieille du Temple and Rue des Archives at 22 Rue Ste. Croix de la Bretonnerie, tel. 01 48 87 77 63, www.hotelparismaraisbretonnerie.com, hotel@bretonnerie.com).

$$ Hôtel Beaubourg* is a top value on a small street in the shadow of the Pompidou Center. The place is surprisingly quiet, and the 28 plush and traditional rooms are well appointed (bigger doubles are worth the extra cost, 11 Rue Simon Le Franc, Mo: Rambuteau, tel. 01 42 74 34 24, www.hotelbeaubourg.com, reservation@hotelbeaubourg.com).

$$ Hôtel de Nice,* on the Marais' busy main drag, features a turquoise-and-fuchsia "Marie-Antoinette-does-tie-dye" decor. This character-filled place is littered with paintings and layered with carpets, and its 23 Old World rooms have thoughtful touches. Rooms on the street come with some noise though the air-conditioning helps; bathrooms are tight (reception on second floor, 42 bis Rue de Rivoli, tel. 01 42 78 55 29, www.hoteldenice.com, contact@hoteldenice.com).

$$ Hôtel du Loiret* is a budget place renting decent rooms with tight bathrooms (no air-con, expect some noise, 8 Rue des Mauvais Garçons, tel. 01 48 87 77 00, www.hotel-du-loiret.fr, hotelduloiret@hotmail.com).

$$ D'Win Hôtel is a solid two-star value in the thick of the Marais, with a helpful staff and 40 relatively spacious and quiet rooms (family rooms, no elevator, 20 Rue du Temple, tel. 01 44 54 05 05, www.dwinhotel.com, contact@dwinhotel.com).

Near Rue de Bretagne

(3rd arr., Mo: Filles du Calvaire, République, or Temple)

Called the Haut (upper) Marais, this appealing neighborhood attracts those wanting a quieter, more local vibe with easy access to the heart of the Marais. Appealing Rue de Bretagne is the backbone of this area, with broad sidewalks and plenty of cafés and shops, plus the lively Marché des Enfants Rouges market area. The beautiful park where Rue de Bretagne meets Rue des Archives is a draw for kids and adults. Allow 15 minutes to walk from these hotels to the Marais' main drag, Rue St. Antoine. The hotels are all within a short walk of Rue de Bretagne and a bit cheaper than in the heart of the Marais.

$$$ Hôtel Jacques de Molay*** delivers *très* modern comfort, a fitness room, bar, and nice public spaces (94 Rue des Archives, Mo: République, tel. 01 42 72 68 22, www.hotelmolay.fr, contact@hotelmolay.fr).

$$ Hôtel du Vieux Saule,*** well located across from the Marché des Enfants Rouges, offers 26 simple rooms at fair rates (small, free sauna for guests, 6 Rue de Picardie, Mo: République, Filles du Calvaire, or Temple, tel. 01 42 72 01 14, www.hotelvieuxsaule.com, reserv@hotelvieuxsaule.com).

$$ Hôtel Saintonge*** is a handsome and well-maintained place with good prices. Its very comfortable rooms feature wooden beams and stone floors (16 Rue de Saintonge, Mo: Filles du Calvaire, tel. 01 42 77 91 13, www.saintlouissaintonge.com, saintonge@saintlouis-hotels.com).

¢ Hôtel Picard** owns a great location and a cheery lobby and breakfast room, though its rooms are worn and tired. Still, the price is right for budget travelers (no air-con, elevator, 26 Rue de Picardie, Mo: République or Filles du Calvaire, tel. 01 48 87 53 82, hotel.picard@orange.fr, gentle Pascal runs the place).

ILE ST. LOUIS

(4th arr., Mo: Pont Marie)

The peaceful, residential character of this river-wrapped island, with its brilliant location and homemade ice cream, has drawn Americans for decades. There are no budget deals here—all of the hotels are three-star or more—though prices are respectable considering the level of comfort and wonderful location. The island's village ambience and proximity to the Marais, Notre-Dame, and the Latin Quarter make this area well worth considering. The following hotels are on the island's main drag, Rue St. Louis-en-l'Ile, where I list several restaurants (see page 157). For hotel locations, see the "Marais Hotels" map, earlier. There are no Métro stops on Ile St. Louis; expect a five-minute walk to the closest station—

Pont Marie—or a bit farther to Cité. Bus #69 works well for Ile St-Louis residents.

$$$$ Hôtel du Jeu de Paume** occupies a 17th-century tennis center. Its magnificent lobby and cozy public spaces make it a fine splurge. Greet Lemon (luh-moe), *le chien*, then take a spin in the glass elevator for a half-timbered treehouse experience. The 30 rooms are carefully designed and tasteful, though not particularly spacious (you're paying for the location and public areas). Most rooms face a small garden courtyard; all are pin-drop peaceful (apartments for 4-6 people, 54 Rue St. Louis-en-l'Ile, tel. 01 43 26 14 18, www.jeudepaumehotel.com, info@jeudepaumehotel.com).

The next two places share the same hands-on owner and comfort. **$$$ Hôtel de Lutèce**** comes with a welcoming wood-paneled lobby and a real fireplace (though fires are no longer allowed in Paris). Rooms are traditional and warm, and those on lower floors have high ceilings. Most have wood-beam ceilings and good space for storage. Twin rooms are larger and the same price as doubles; most beds are doubles, and there are a few good triples. Rooms with bathtubs are on the street side, while those with showers are on the quieter courtyard (65 Rue St. Louis-en-l'Ile, tel. 01 43 26 23 52, www.hoteldelutece.com, info@hoteldelutece.com).

$$$ Hôtel des Deux-Iles** has a few true singles, a larger breakfast room, is a bit cheaper than the Lutèce, but is otherwise hard to distinguish—you can't go wrong in either place (59 Rue St. Louis-en-l'Ile, tel. 01 43 26 13 35, www.hoteldesdeuxiles.com, isle@hoteldesdeuxiles.com).

$$$ Hôtel Saint-Louis** blends character with modern comforts. The sharp rooms come with cool stone floors and exposed beams. Rates are reasonable...for the location (some rooms with balcony, iPads available for guest use, 75 Rue St. Louis-en-l'Ile, tel. 01 46 34 04 80, www.saintlouisenlisle.com, isle@saintlouis-hotels.com).

AT OR NEAR PARIS' AIRPORTS

At Charles de Gaulle Airport: These places are located a few minutes from the terminals, outside the T-3 RER/Train-B stop, and have restaurants. For locations, see the map on page 162.

$$$ Novotel** is a step up from cookie-cutter airport hotels (tel. 01 49 19 27 27, www.novotel.com, h1014@accor.com).

$$ Hôtel Ibis CDG Airport** is huge and offers standard airport accommodations (tel. 01 49 19 19 19, www.ibishotel.com, h1404@ accor.com).

Near Orly Airport: These chain hotels are your best options near Orly. Both have free shuttles *(navettes)* to the terminals. **$$$ Hôtel Mercure Paris Orly***** provides high comfort for a high price (tel. 08 25 80 69 69, www.accorhotel.com, h1246@accor. com). **$$ Hôtel Ibis Orly Aéroport**** is reasonable and basic (tel. 01 56 70 50 60, www.ibishotel.com, h1413@accor.com).

APARTMENT RENTALS

Consider this option if you're traveling as a family, in a group, or staying at least a few nights. Intrepid travelers around the world are accustomed to using Airbnb and VRBO when it comes to renting a vacation apartment; search for places in my recommended hotel neighborhoods. In Paris, you have many additional options among rental agencies, and I've found the following to be the most reliable. Their websites are good and essential to understanding your choices: **Paris Perfect,** www.parisperfect.com; **Adrian Leeds Group,** www.adrianleeds.com; **France Homestyle,** www.francehomestyle. com; **Home Rental Service,** www.homerental.fr; **Haven in Paris,** www.haveninparis.com; **Paris Home,** www.parishome2000.com; **Cobblestone Paris Rentals,** www.cobblestoneparis.com; **Paris for Rent,** www.parisforrent.com); and **Cross-Pollinate,** www.cross-pollinate.com.

BED-AND-BREAKFASTS

Several agencies can help you go local by staying in a private home in Paris. While prices and quality can range greatly, most rooms have a private bath and run from €85 to €150. Most owners won't take bookings for fewer than two nights. To limit stair-climbing, ask whether the building has an elevator. These agencies have a good selection: **Alcôve & Agapes,** www.bed-and-breakfast-in-paris.com; and **Meeting the French,** http://en.meetingthefrench. com.

Eating in Paris

The Parisian eating scene is kept at a rolling boil. Entire books (and lives) are dedicated to the subject. Paris is France's wine-and-cuisine melting pot. There is no "Parisian cuisine" to speak of (only French onion soup is truly Parisian), but it draws from the best of France. Paris could hold a gourmet Olympics and import nothing.

My restaurant recommendations are mostly centered on the same great neighborhoods as my hotel listings; you can come home exhausted after a busy day of sightseeing and find a good selection of eateries right around the corner. And evening is a fine time to explore any of these delightful neighborhoods, even if you're sleeping elsewhere. Serious eaters looking for even more suggestions should consult the always appetizing www.parisbymouth.com, an eating-and-drinking guide to Paris.

To save piles of euros, go to a bakery for takeout, or stop at a café for lunch. Cafés and brasseries are happy to serve a *plat du jour* (plate of the day, about €16-24) or a chef-like salad (about €12-16) day or night. To save even more, consider picnics (tasty takeout dishes available at charcuteries). Try eating your big meal at lunch, when many fine restaurants offer their dinnertime fixed-price *menus* at a reduced price.

Linger longer over dinner—restaurants expect you to enjoy a full meal. Most restaurants I've listed have set-price *menus* between €26 and €40. In most cases, the few extra euros you pay are well spent and open up a variety of better choices. Remember that a service charge is included in the prices (so little or no tipping is expected).

I rank restaurants from **$** budget to **$$$$** splurge. For more advice on eating in Paris, including restaurant pricing; dining in French restaurants, cafés, and brasseries; getting takeout and assembling a picnic; and a rundown of French cuisine—see the "Eating" section of the Practicalities chapter.

RUE CLER NEIGHBORHOOD
On Rue Cler
(Mo: Ecole Militaire)

$ Café du Marché boasts the best seats on Rue Cler. The owner's philosophy: Brasserie on speed—crank out good enough food at fair prices to appreciative locals and savvy tourists. It's high-energy, with young waiters who barely have time to smile...*très* Parisian. This place works well if you don't mind average quality and want to eat an inexpensive one-course meal among a commotion of people. The chalkboard lists your choices: good, hearty salads or more filling *plats du jour.* Arrive before 19:00 to avoid waiting (serves continuously, daily 11:00-23:00, no reservations, at the corner of Rue Cler and Rue du Champ de Mars, 38 Rue Cler, tel. 01 47 05 51 27).

$$ Tribeca Restaurant, next door to Café du Marché, fills a broad terrace along Rue Cler and offers a wide selection at good prices. Choose from kid-pleasing burgers and Italian dishes or try the roasted Camembert *à la crème* (pizzas, pastas, and salads; daily, tel. 01 45 55 12 01).

$ L'Eclair, a few doors down, is a bar-meets-bistro place with

PARIS

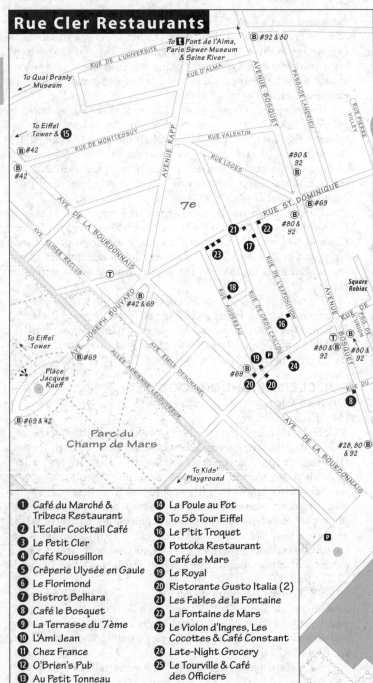

Rue Cler Restaurants

To 🇹 Pont de l'Alma, Paris Sewer Museum & Seine River

Ⓑ #92 & 80

To Quai Branly Museum

RUE DE L'UNIVERSITE

RUE D'ALMA

To Eiffel Tower & ⑮

Ⓑ #42

RUE DE MONTTESSUY

Ⓑ #42

RUE VALENTIN

RUE RAPP

AVENUE BOSQUET

PASSAGE LANDRIEU

RUE PIERRE VILLEY

RUE LOGES

#80 & 92

Ⓑ

7e

RUE ST. DOMINIQUE

Ⓑ #69

AVE. DE LA BOURDONNAIS

#80 & 92

㉑   ㉒

AVE. ELISEE RECLUS

㉓   ⑰

RUE DE L'EXPOSITION

Square Robiac

Ⓣ

⑱

RUE AUGEREAU

RUE DE GROS CAILLOU

AVENUE

RUE DE L'UNION

RUE DES DE

AVE. JOSEPH BOUVARD

Ⓑ #42 & 69

AVE. EMILE DESCHANEL

⑯

Ⓣ

BOSQUET

#80 & 92

#80 & 92

To Eiffel Tower

Ⓑ #69

ALLEE ADRIENNE LECOUVREUR

⑲   P

#69   Ⓑ

㉔

Place Jacques Rueff

⑳   ⑳

RUE DU

⑧

Ⓑ #69 & 42

Parc du Champ de Mars

AVE. DE LA BOURDONNAIS

#28, 80 Ⓑ & 92

To Kids' Playground

- ❶ Café du Marché & Tribeca Restaurant
- ❷ L'Eclair Cocktail Café
- ❸ Le Petit Cler
- ❹ Café Roussillon
- ❺ Crêperie Ulysée en Gaule
- ❻ Le Florimond
- ❼ Bistrot Belhara
- ❽ Café le Bosquet
- ❾ La Terrasse du 7ème
- ❿ L'Ami Jean
- ⓫ Chez France
- ⓬ O'Brien's Pub
- ⓭ Au Petit Tonneau
- ⓮ La Poule au Pot
- ⓯ To 58 Tour Eiffel
- ⓰ Le P'tit Troquet
- ⓱ Pottoka Restaurant
- ⓲ Café de Mars
- ⓳ Le Royal
- ⓴ Ristorante Gusto Italia (2)
- ㉑ Les Fables de la Fontaine
- ㉒ La Fontaine de Mars
- ㉓ Le Violon d'Ingres, Les Cocottes & Café Constant
- ㉔ Late-Night Grocery
- ㉕ Le Tourville & Café des Officiers

PARIS

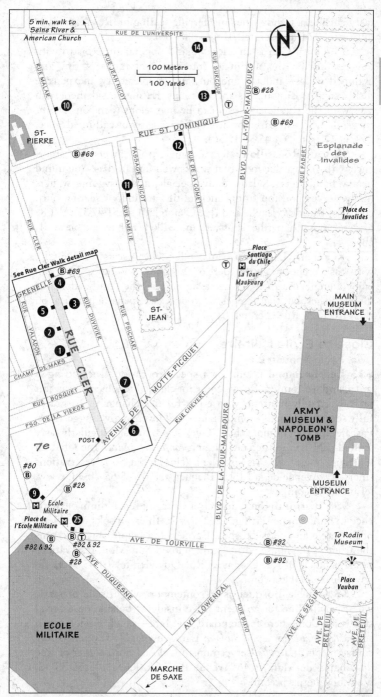

5 min. walk to
Seine River &
American Church

RUE DE L'UNIVERSITE

14

RUE SURCOUF

100 Meters
100 Yards

RUE MALAR

13

T

B #28

10

B #69

ST-
PIERRE

RUE JEAN NICOT

RUE ST. DOMINIQUE

BLVD. DE LA-TOUR-MAUBOURG

RUE FABERT

Esplanade
des
Invalides

B #69

12

RUE DE LA COMETE

PASSAGE J. NICOT

11

RUE AMELIE

RUE CLER

Place des
Invalides

Place
Santiago
du Chile

T

See Rue Cler Walk detail map

B #69

GRENELLE

4

RUE DUVIVIER

RUE PSICHARI

M La Tour-
Maubourg

5

3

RUE VALADON

2

1

ST-
JEAN

CHAMP DE MARS

RUE CLER

AVENUE DE LA MOTTE-PICQUET

7

RUE BOSQUET

RUE CHEVERT

MAIN
MUSEUM
ENTRANCE

PSG. DE LA VIERGE

POST

6

ARMY
MUSEUM &
NAPOLEON'S
TOMB

7e

BLVD. DE LA-TOUR-MAUBOURG

MUSEUM
ENTRANCE

#80
B

B #28

9

M Ecole
Militaire

Place de
l'Ecole Militaire

M

25

B

T

B #82 & 92

AVE. DE TOURVILLE

B #92

To Rodin
Museum

B
#82 & 92

B
#28

AVE. DUQUESNE

AVE. LOWENDAL

RUE BIXIO

RUE DE SEGUR

AVE. DE BRETEUIL

AVE. DE BRETEUIL

Place
Vauban

B #92

ECOLE
MILITAIRE

MARCHE
DE SAXE

tasty cuisine, a trendy vibe, and terrific seating on Rue Cler (daily until late, 32 Rue Cler, tel. 01 44 18 09 04).

$ Le Petit Cler is an adorable and popular little bistro with long leather booths, a vintage interior, tight ranks of tiny and cramped tables—indoors and out, and simple, tasty, inexpensive dishes such as €10 omelets and €9 soups. Eating outside here with a view of the Rue Cler action can be marvelous (delicious *pots de crème,* daily, opens early for dinner, arrive early or call in advance, 29 Rue Cler, tel. 01 45 50 17 50).

$$ Café Roussillon offers a younger, pub-meets-café ambience with good-value food that works well for families. You'll find hearty hamburgers, salads, daily specials, and easygoing waiters (daily, serves nonstop from lunch until late, indoor seating only, corner of Rue de Grenelle and Rue Cler, tel. 01 45 51 47 53). While less charming than other spots, it's more likely to have a table available.

$ Crêperie Ulysée en Gaule offers cheap seats on Rue Cler with basic crêpes to go. Readers of this book who buy a drink can enjoy a crêpe at a table for takeaway prices. The family adores its Greek dishes, but their crêpes are your least expensive hot meal on this street (28 Rue Cler, tel. 01 47 05 61 82).

Close to Ecole Militaire
(Mo: Ecole Militaire)

$$$ Le Florimond is fun for a special occasion. The setting is warm and welcoming. Locals come for classic French cuisine at fair prices. Friendly Laurent, whose playful ties change daily, gracefully serves one small room of tables and loves to give suggestions. Pascale, his chef of more than 20 years, produces particularly tasty stuffed cabbage, lobster ravioli, and *confit de canard.* The Château Chênaie house wine is excellent (closed Sat-Sun, reservations smart, 19 Avenue de la Motte-Picquet, tel. 01 45 55 40 38, www.leflorimond.com).

$$$ Bistrot Belhara delivers a vintage French dining experience in an intimate setting. Chef-owner Thierry cooks up a blend of inventive and classic dishes. Earnest and helpful Frédéric runs the front of the house with a smile (closed Sun-Mon, reservations smart, a block off Rue Cler at 23 Rue Duvivier, tel. 01 45 51 41 77, www.bistrotbelhara.com).

$$ Café le Bosquet is a contemporary Parisian brasserie where you'll dine for a decent price inside or outside on a broad sidewalk. Come here for standard café fare—salad, French onion soup, *steak-frites,* or a *plat du jour.* Lanky owner "Jeff" offers three-course meals and *plats* (serves nonstop, closed Sun, corner of Rue du Champ de Mars at 46 Avenue Bosquet, tel. 01 45 51 38 13, www.bosquetparis.com).

$$$ La Terrasse du 7ème is a sprawling, happening café with grand outdoor seating and a living room-like interior with comfy love seats. Located on a corner, it overlooks a busy intersection with a constant parade of people and traffic. Chairs face the street, as a meal here is like dinner theater—and the show is slice-of-life Paris (good *salades*, French onion soup, and foie gras, nonstop service daily until at least 24:00, 2 Place de L'Ecole Militaire, tel. 01 45 55 00 02).

Between Rue de Grenelle and the River, East of Avenue Bosquet
(Mo: La Tour-Maubourg)

$$$$ L'Ami Jean offers authentic Basque specialties in a snug-but-convivial atmosphere with red peppers and Basque stuff dangling from the ceiling. While pricey, portions are hearty and delicious. Parisians detour long distances to savor the gregarious chef's special cuisine and fun atmosphere. For dinner arrive before 19:30 or reserve ahead (€80 six-course dinner *menu*, more accessible lunch *menu* for €35, closed Sun-Mon, 27 Rue Malar, tel. 01 47 05 86 89, www.lamijean.fr).

$$ Chez France is a simple place lined with red-velvet booths where the focus is on food, not charming ambience—the dining room gets very warm when filled. You must order from the two- or three-course *menu*. Sit back and trust Régis and Arnaud to manage your meal (good choices of classic French cuisine, fine wine options, closed Sun, 9 Rue Amelie, tel. 01 45 51 50 08).

$$ O'Brien's Pub is a relaxed Parisian rendition of an Irish pub/sports bar, where locals toss darts and order fine red wine with gourmet hamburgers (daily, 77 Rue St. Dominique, tel. 01 45 51 75 87). Along with their pubby barroom they have appealing streetside seating.

$$$ Au Petit Tonneau is a small, authentic French bistro with original, time-warp decor, red-checked tablecloths, and carefully prepared food from a limited menu. Away from the Rue Cler tourist crush, this place is real, the cuisine is delicious, and the experience is what you came to France for (good à la carte choices or three-course *menu* that changes with the season, well-priced wines, closed Mon, 20 Rue Surcouf, tel. 01 47 05 09 01, charming owner Arlette at your service).

The Paris Food Scene

Food Tours

Note that several of the listings under Cooking Classes below also offer food tours.

Paris by Mouth offers well-respected yet casual small-group tours, with a maximum of seven foodies per group. Tours are organized by location, street market, or flavor, and led by local food writers (€110/3 hours, includes tastings, www.parisbymouth.com, tasteparisbymouth@gmail.com).

At **Edible Paris,** friendly Canadian Rosa Jackson designs personalized itineraries based on your interests. She and her colleagues also lead three-hour "food-guru" tours of Paris (unguided itineraries-€125-200, guided tours-€300 for 1-2 people, larger groups welcome, mobile 06 81 67 41 22, www.edible-paris.com, rosa@rosajackson.com).

Cooking Classes

At **Les Secrets Gourmands de Noémie,** charming and knowledgeable Noémie shares her culinary secrets with hands-on fun in the kitchen. Courses tackle savory and sweet dishes with the possibility of an add-on market tour (€65-130, 92 Rue Nollet, Mo: La Fourche, mobile 06 64 17 93 32, www.lessecretsgourmandsdenoemie.com).

Cook'n with Class gets rave reviews for its range of convivial cooking classes from breads to *macarons* to croissants to wine and cheese. There's a maximum of six students. Tasting courses are offered as well (€85-200, 6 Rue Baudelique, Mo: Jules Joffrin or Simplon, mobile 06 31 73 62 77, www.cooknwithclass.com/paris).

La Cuisine Paris has a great variety of classes in English, rea-

---

$$ La Poule au Pot is the neighborhood's Old World café, worth a stop to sip a coffee or have a simple meal amid decor that can't have changed in, like, forever (closed Sat-Sun, 121 Rue de l'Université, tel. 01 47 05 16 36).

Between Rue de Grenelle and the River, West of Avenue Bosquet

(Mo: Ecole Militaire unless otherwise noted)

$$$$ 58 Tour Eiffel, on the tower's first level, provides a feast for both your belly and your eyes, with incredible city views. Dinner here is pricey and requires a reservation (two seatings: 18:30 with €86-125 *menus*, and 21:00 with €95-175 *menus*—priciest *menus* buy you more courses and better views; reserve long in advance, especially if you want a view, no jeans or tennis shoes at dinner). During the day they serve a €40 *picque-nique-chic* lunch, which is packaged in a little basket (€15 for kids, daily 11:30-16:30, reservations are a

sonable prices, and a beautiful space in central Paris (€70-100, €160 for 4-hour class with market tour, also offers gourmet visit to Versailles, 80 Quai de l'Hôtel de Ville, tel. 01 40 51 78 18, www. lacuisineparis.com).

REED is the creation of Catherine Reed, who also runs a restaurant with the same name a few blocks from Rue Cler. Classes are limited to eight students and focus on practical skills—from basic techniques to classic French gastronomy (€145, Sun and Wed at 10:30, 11 Rue Amelie, tel. 01 45 55 88 40, www.reedrestaurant. com).

If you're looking for an upscale demonstration course, you'll find it at **Le Cordon Bleu** (tel. 01 53 68 22 50, www.lcbparis.com) or **Ritz Escoffier Ecole de Gastronomie** (tel. 01 43 16 30 50, www. ritzparis.com).

Wine Tasting

Several of the above-mentioned cooking outfits also offer wine-tasting options, but **Ô Château** is decisively wine-centric, though it also has a respectable restaurant. Their team of sommeliers teach wine-tasting classes in fluent English while you sit in the 18th-century residence of Madame de Pompadour. Classes range from an introductory, "Tour de France" tasting with six wines and Champagne (€59), to wine-tasting lunches with five wines plus cheeses and charcuterie (€75), or three-course dinners with wine pairings (€99). Each tasting lasts about two hours and is usually limited to 12 people. Register online using code "RS2020" for a 10-percent discount, or check the website for last-minute deals (68 Rue Jean-Jacques Rousseau, Mo: Louvre-Rivoli or Etienne Marcel, tel. 01 44 73 97 80, www.o-chateau.com).

good idea, Mo: Bir-Hakeim or Trocadéro, RER/Train-C: Champ de Mars-Tour Eiffel, tel. 01 72 76 18 46, toll tel. 08 25 56 66 62, www.restaurants-toureiffel.com). With a reservation, you ride up for free in the restaurant elevator.

$$ Le P'tit Troquet is a petite eatery taking you back to the Paris of the 1920s. Anna serves while hubbie José cooks a tasty range of traditional choices. The homey charm of the tight little dining room makes this place a delight (€36 three-course dinner *menu* available for €25 at lunch, dinner service from 18:30, closed Sun, reservations smart, 28 Rue de l'Exposition, tel. 01 47 05 80 39, www.leptittroquet.fr).

$$$ Pottoka attracts locals willing to book ahead and crowd into this shoebox for a chance to sample tasty Basque cuisine. Service is friendly, wines are reasonable, and the focus is on food rather than decor (daily, reservations smart, 4 Rue de l'Exposition, tel. 01 45 51 88 38, www.pottoka.fr).

PARIS

$$ Café de Mars is a relaxed place featuring creative cuisine that draws from many countries—and there's always a good vegetarian option. With its simple setting and reasonable prices, it feels more designed for neighbors than tourists. It's also comfortable for single diners thanks to a convivial counter (closed Sun-Mon, 11 Rue Augereau, tel. 01 45 50 10 90, www.cafedemars.com).

$ Le Royal is a tiny neighborhood fixture offering the cheapest meals in the area. This humble time-warp place, with prices and decor from another era, comes from an age when cafés sold firewood and served food as an afterthought. Parisians dine here because "it's like eating at home." Gentle Guillaume is a fine host (closed Sat-Sun, 212 Rue de Grenelle, tel. 01 47 53 92 90).

Affordable Italian: You'll find several good places in the area. **$$ Ristorante Gusto Italia** is fun, tight, and characteristic (two locations—199 and 21 Rue de Grenelle, tel. 01 45 55 00 43).

The Rue St-Dominique Lineup
(Mo: Ecole Militaire or RER/Train-C: Pont de l'Alma)
A terrific string of restaurants gathers a few short blocks from the Eiffel Tower. Find the western end of Rue St. Dominique between Rue Augereau and Rue de l'Exposition for the next five restaurants. Each is distinct, offering a different experience and price range. None is really cheap, but they're all a good value, delivering top-quality cuisine.

$$$$ Les Fables de la Fontaine is a fine place to relax over a gourmet dinner with appealing seating inside or out on a picturesque square. It has a Michelin star yet maintains fair prices and friendly staff. While the chef's specialty is fish, he also serves a few meat dishes (€75 tasting *menu,* less for à la carte, book ahead on weekends, daily, 131 Rue St. Dominique, tel. 01 44 18 37 55, www.lesfablesdelafontaine.net).

$$$ La Fontaine de Mars, a longtime favorite and neighborhood institution, is charmingly situated on a tiny, jumbled square with tables jammed together for the serious business of eating. Reserve in advance for a table on the ground floor or square, and pass on the upstairs room (superb foie gras and desserts, daily, 129 Rue St. Dominique, tel. 01 47 05 46 44, www.fontainedemars.com).

$$$$ Le Violon d'Ingres makes for a good excuse to dress up and dine finely in Paris. Glass doors open onto a chic eating scene—hushed and elegant. Service is formal yet helpful; the cuisine is what made this restaurant's reputation (order à la carte or consider their €130 seven-course tasting *menu,* cheaper lunch *menu,* daily, reservations essential, 135 Rue St. Dominique, tel. 01 45 55 15 05, www.maisonconstant.com).

$$$ Les Cocottes attracts a crowd of trendy Parisians and tourists with its fun energy and creative dishes served in *cocottes*—small cast-iron pots (tasty soups, daily, nonstop service from noon until late, go early as they don't take reservations, 135 Rue St. Dominique, tel. 01 45 50 10 28).

$$ Café Constant is a cool, two-level place that feels more like a small bistro-wine bar than a café. Delicious dishes are served in a snug setting. Arrive as early as you want to get a table downstairs—the upstairs seating lacks character (daily, opens at 7:00 for breakfast, meals served nonstop 12:00-23:00, no reservations, corner of Rue Augereau and Rue St. Dominique, next to recommended Hôtel de Londres Eiffel at 139 Rue Saint-Dominique, tel. 01 47 53 73 34).

MARAIS

The trendy Marais is filled with diners enjoying fine food in colorful and atmospheric eateries. The scene is competitive and changes all the time. I've listed an assortment of places—all handy to recommended hotels—that offer good food at decent prices, plus a memorable experience.

On Romantic Place des Vosges

(Mo: St-Paul or Bastille)
This square offers Old World Marais elegance, a handful of eateries, and an ideal picnic site until dusk, when the park closes. Strolling around the arcade after dark is more important than dining here—fanciful art galleries alternate with restaurants and cafés. Choose a restaurant that best fits your mood and budget; most have arcade seating and provide big space heaters to make outdoor dining during colder months an option. Also consider just a drink on the square at Café Hugo.

$$$ La Place Royale offers an exceptional location on the square with comfortable seating inside or out, and is good for a relaxed lunch or dinner. Come here for the setting and snag an outdoor table under the arches. The hearty cuisine is priced well and served nonstop all day, and the lengthy wine list is reasonable. The €42 dinner *menu* comes with three courses, a half-bottle of wine per person, and coffee; or just order a salad—or split one before a main course—and call it good (lunch specials, daily, reserve ahead to dine outside under the arcade, 2 bis Place des Vosges, tel. 01 42 78 58 16).

$$ Café Hugo, named for the square's most famous resident, serves salads and basic café fare with a Parisian energy. The food's just OK, but the setting's terrific, with good seating under the arches (daily, 22 Place des Vosges, tel. 01 42 72 64 04).

PARIS

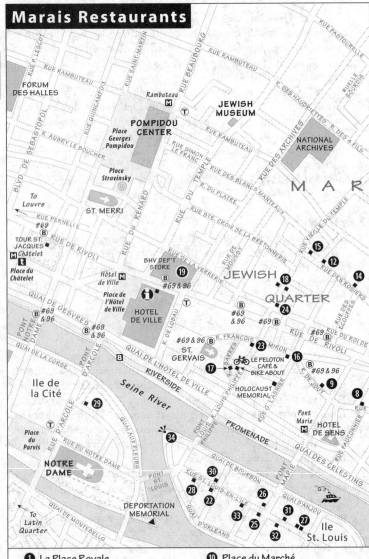

Marais Restaurants

1 La Place Royale
2 Café Hugo
3 Chez Janou
4 Le Petit Marché
5 Brasserie Bofinger
6 Le Temps des Cerises
7 Crêpolog & La Cerise sur la Pizza
8 Chez Mademoiselle
9 Le Metropolitan

10 Place du Marché
Ste. Catherine Eateries
11 Les Bougresses
12 Chez Marianne
13 Le Loir dans la Théière
14 Falafel Row
15 La Droguerie Crêperie
16 Au Bourguignon du Marais
17 L'Ebouillanté

PARIS

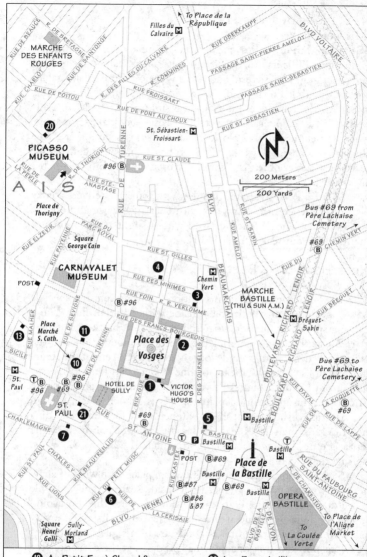

18 Au Petit Fer à Cheval &
   La Belle Hortense
19 BHV Cafeteria
20 Breizh Café
21 Monoprix (Grocery)
22 Late-Night Grocery
23 La Perla Bar
24 Le Pick-Clops
25 Nos Ancêtres les Gaulois
26 Les Fous de l'Île
27 L'Orangerie & Auberge de la
   Reine Blanche
28 Café Med
29 Au Bougnat
30 Bakery
31 Bakery & 38 Saint Louis Deli
32 Berthillon Ice Cream
33 Amorino Gelati
34 Good Picnic Spot

Near Place des Vosges
(Mo: Chemin Vert)

$$$ Chez Janou, a Provençal bistro, tumbles out of its corner building and fills its broad sidewalk with happy eaters. It's relaxed and charming, with helpful and patient service. The curbside tables are inviting, but I'd sit inside (with very tight seating) to immerse myself in the happy commotion. The style is French Mediterranean, with an emphasis on vegetables (daily—book ahead or arrive when it opens at 19:00, 2 blocks beyond Place des Vosges at 2 Rue Roger Verlomme, tel. 01 42 72 28 41, www.chezjanou.com). They serve 81 varieties of *pastis* (licorice-flavored liqueur, browse the list above the bar).

$$$ Le Petit Marché, popular with tourists, delivers a cozy bistro experience inside and out with friendly service and a tasty cuisine that blends French classics with a slight Asian influence (daily, 9 Rue du Béarn, tel. 01 42 72 06 67).

Near Place de la Bastille
(Mo: Bastille or St. Paul)

$$$ Brasserie Bofinger, an institution for over a century, specializes in seafood and traditional cuisine with Alsatian flair. You'll eat in a sprawling interior, surrounded by brisk, black-and-white-attired waiters. Come here for the one-of-a-kind ambience in the elaborately decorated ground-floor rooms, reminiscent of the Roaring Twenties. Reserve ahead to dine under the grand 1919 *coupole* (avoid eating upstairs). If you've always wanted one of those pricey picturesque seafood platters, this is a good place, though the Alsatian dishes are far cheaper (open daily for lunch and dinner, fun kids' menu, 5 Rue de la Bastille, don't be confused by the lesser "Petite" Bofinger across the street, tel. 01 42 72 87 82, www. bofingerparis.com).

$$$ Le Temps des Cerises is a warm place with wads of character, a young and lively vibe, tight inside seating, and a couple of outdoor tables. (There are a few more upstairs that I'd avoid.) Come for a glass of wine at the small zinc bar, and stay for a very tasty dinner. Owner Ben takes good care of his guests and serves generous portions (reasonable wine list, daily, at the corner of Rue du Petit Musc and Rue de la Cerisaie, 31 Rue de la Cerisaie, tel. 01 42 72 08 63).

$ Crêpes and Pizza: Two budget finds sit side-by-side where Rue St-Paul meets Rue Neuve St-Pierre. Both are open daily and have good but limited seating inside and out. **Crêpolog** dishes out a tasty range of appetizer, main course, and dessert crêpes using fresh batter (tel. 01 43 48 28 34, Mo: St. Paul). **La Cerise sur la Pizza** ("Cherry on the Pizza") fires up great-looking pizza (eat there or to go, tel. 01 42 78 15 59, Mo: St. Paul).

In the Heart of the Marais
(Mo: St-Paul)

$$$ Chez Mademoiselle's country-elegant, candlelit decor recalls charming owner Alexia's previous career as a French *comédienne*. Enjoy a French-paced (a.k.a. slow) dinner in a relaxing atmosphere (tables have generous spacing) inside or at a sidewalk table. Ingredients are fresh and prepared simply. Let Alexia share her enthusiasm for her seasonal dishes before you choose. The tender *château filet* is served all year, but most dishes follow the seasons (good wine list, daily from 19:30, 16 Rue Charlemagne, tel. 01 42 72 14 16).

$$ Le Metropolitan is a tiny, easygoing bistro serving top-quality cuisine to those in the know. The young chef's dishes are creative and delicious. Come early (opens at 19:00) or book ahead (closed Sun, 8 Rue de Jouy, tel. 09 81 20 37 38, www.metroresto.fr).

$$ On Place du Marché Ste. Catherine: This small, romantic square, just off Rue St. Antoine, is cloaked in extremely Parisian, leafy-square ambience. It feels like the Latin Quarter but classier. On a balmy evening, this is a neighborhood favorite, with a handful of restaurants offering mediocre cuisine (you're here for the setting). It's also family-friendly: Most places serve French hamburgers, and kids can dance around the square while parents breathe. Survey the square. You'll find three French bistros with similar features and menus: **Le Marché, Chez Joséphine,** and **Le Bistrot de la Place** (all open daily, cheaper for lunch, tight seating on simple chairs indoors and out). At Chez Joséphine the cuisine takes a back seat to its lively drink scene—I'd choose between the other two.

$$ Les Bougresses, just off the charming square, offers less romance but more taste. Stepping inside, you feel like you've joined a food lovers' party with owners Mika and Constantin overseeing the conviviality (inside seating only, daily from 18:30, 6 Rue de Jarente, tel. 01 48 87 71 21).

In the Jewish Quarter, Rue des Rosiers
(Mo: St-Paul or Hôtel de Ville)

$$ Chez Marianne is a neighborhood fixture that serves tasty Jewish cuisine in a fun atmosphere with Parisian *élan*. Choose from several indoor zones with a cluttered wine shop/deli feeling, or sit outside. You'll select from two dozen *zakouskis* (hot and cold hors d'oeuvres) to assemble your *plat*. Vegetarians will find great options (takeaway falafel sandwiches, long hours daily, corner of Rue des Rosiers and Rue des Hospitalières-St-Gervais, tel. 01 42 72 18 86).

$$ Le Loir dans la Théière ("The Dormouse in the Teapot"—think Alice in Wonderland) is a cozy, mellow teahouse offering a welcoming ambience for tired travelers (laptops and smartphones are not welcome). It's ideal for lunch but slammed on weekends.

They offer a daily assortment of creatively filled quiches and bake an impressive array of homemade desserts that are proudly displayed in the dining room (daily 9:00-19:00 but only dessert-type items offered after 15:00, 3 Rue des Rosiers, tel. 01 42 72 90 61).

$ Falafel Row is a series of inexpensive joints serving filling falafel sandwiches (and other Jewish dishes to go or to eat in) that line Rue des Rosiers between Rue des Ecouffes and Rue Vieille du Temple. Take a stroll along this short stretch to compare, then decide. Their takeout services draw a constant crowd (long hours most days, most are closed Fri evening and all day Sat).

$ La Droguerie, a hole-in-the-wall crêpe stand on Rue des Rosiers near Rue Vieille du Temple, is a good budget option if falafels don't work for you but cheap does. Grab a stool, or get a crêpe to go and smile with the friendly owner/crêpe master (daily 12:00-22:00, 56 Rue des Rosiers).

Close to Hôtel de Ville
(Mo: Hôtel de Ville)

$$$ Au Bourguignon du Marais is a dressy wine bar/bistro for Burgundy lovers, where excellent wines (Burgundian only, available by the glass) blend with a good selection of well-designed dishes and efficient service. The *œufs en meurette* are mouthwatering and the *bœuf bourguignon* could feed two (daily, pleasing indoor and outdoor seating on a perfect Marais corner, 52 Rue François Miron, tel. 01 48 87 15 40).

$ L'Ebouillanté is a breezy café, romantically situated near the river on a broad, cobbled pedestrian lane behind a church. With great outdoor seating on flimsy chairs and an artsy interior, it's good for an inexpensive and relaxing tea, snack, or lunch—or for dinner on a warm evening. Their €15 *bricks*—paper-thin, Tunisian-inspired pancakes stuffed with what you would typically find in an omelet—come with a small salad (daily 12:00-21:30, closes earlier in winter, a block off the river at 6 Rue des Barres, tel. 01 42 74 70 57).

$$ Au Petit Fer à Cheval delivers classic seating ideal for admiring the Marais' active night scene. The horseshoe-shaped zinc bar carbonates rich conversation—and the rear room is Old-World adorable, but the few outdoor tables are street-theater perfect. The food is fairly priced, standard café fare (daily, 30 Rue Vieille du Temple, tel. 01 42 72 47 47).

$ BHV Department Store's fifth-floor cafeteria provides nice views, good prices, and many main courses to choose from, with a salad bar, pizza by the slice, and pasta. It's family-easy (daily, 11:00-19:00, hot food served until 16:00, open later Wed, at intersection of Rue du Temple and Rue de la Verrerie, one block from Hôtel de Ville).

Close to Rue de Bretagne

(Mo: Filles du Calvaire or Rambuteau)

$$ Breizh Café is worth the hike for some of the best Breton crêpes in Paris ("Breizh" means Brittany). This simple joint serves organic crêpes—both sweet and savory—and small rolls made for dipping in rich sauces and salted butter. They talk about cider like a somme-lier would talk about wine. Try a sparkling cider, a Breton cola, or my favorite—*lait ribot,* a buttermilk-like drink (closed Mon, serves nonstop 11:30-late, reservations highly recommended, 109 Rue du Vieille du Temple, tel. 01 42 72 13 77, www.breizhcafe.com).

ILE ST. LOUIS

(Mo: Pont Marie)

These recommended spots—ranging from rowdy to petite, rustic to elegant—line the island's main drag, Rue St. Louis-en-l'Ile (see map on page 152).

$$ Nos Ancêtres les Gaulois ("Our Ancestors the Gauls"), famous for its rowdy, medieval-cellar atmosphere, is made for hun-gry warriors and wenches who like to swill hearty wine. For dinner they serve up rustic, all-you-can-eat fare with straw baskets of raw veggies and bundles of *saucisson* (cut whatever you like with your dagger), plates of pâté, a meat course, cheese, a dessert, and all the wine you can stomach for €40. The food is perfectly edible; burp-ing is encouraged. If you want to overeat, drink too much wine, be surrounded by tourists (mostly French), and holler at your friends while receiving smart-aleck buccaneer service, you're home. If you stay later, the atmosphere progresses from sloppy to frat party (daily, 39 Rue St. Louis-en-l'Ile, tel. 01 46 33 66 07).

$$ Les Fous de l'Ile is a tasty, lighthearted mash-up of a col-lector's haunt, art gallery, and bistro. It's a fun place to eat bistro fare with gourmet touches for a good price (2- or 3-course *menus* or *plat du jour* only, daily, serves nonstop, 33 Rue des Deux Ponts, tel. 01 43 25 76 67).

$$$ L'Orangerie is an inviting, rustic-yet-elegant place with soft lighting, comfortable spacious seating, and a hushed ambience. The cuisine blends traditional with modern touches (closed Mon, 28 Rue St. Louis-en-l'Ile, tel. 01 46 33 93 98).

$$ Auberge de la Reine Blanche—woodsy, cozy, and tight— welcomes diners willing to rub elbows with their neighbors. Ear-nest owner Michel serves basic French cuisine at reasonable prices. Along with like-mother-made-it comfort food, he serves good din-ner salads (closed Wed, 30 Rue St. Louis-en-l'Ile, tel. 01 46 33 07 87).

$ Café Med, near the pedestrian bridge to Notre-Dame, is a tiny, cheery *crêperie* with good-value salads, crêpes, pasta, and several meat dishes (daily, 77 Rue St. Louis-en-l'Ile, tel. 01 43 29 73 17). Two less atmospheric *crêperies* are just across the street.

$$ Au Bougnat, a short walk away on Ile de la Cité, is a place that delivers good cuisine at very fair prices with oodles of ambience. It's a short hop from Notre-Dame and where local cops and workers get sandwiches, coffee, and reasonably priced *menus* (daily, 26 Rue Chanoinesse, tel. 01 43 54 50 74).

Ice-Cream Dessert: Half the people strolling Ile St. Louis are licking an ice-cream cone because this is the home of the famous *les glaces Berthillon* (now sold throughout Paris, though still made here on Ile St. Louis). The original **Berthillon** shop, at 31 Rue St. Louis-en-l'Ile, is marked by the line of salivating customers (closed Mon-Tue). For a less famous but satisfying treat, the Italian gelato a block away at **Amorino Gelati** is giving Berthillon competition (no line, bigger portions, easier to see what you want, and they offer small tastes—Berthillon doesn't need to, 47 Rue St. Louis-en-l'Ile, tel. 01 44 07 48 08). Having a little of each is not a bad thing.

ON THE LEFT BANK
Near the Odéon Theater

(Mo: Odéon)

$$$ Brasserie Bouillon Racine takes you back to 1906 with an Art Nouveau carnival of carved wood, stained glass, and old-time lights reflected in beveled mirrors. It's like having dinner with Gustav Klimt and a bunch of tourists. The over-the-top decor and energetic waiters give it an inviting conviviality. Check upstairs before choosing a table. There's Belgian beer on tap and a fascinating history on the menu (daily, serves nonstop, 3 Rue Racine, tel. 01 44 32 15 60, www.bouillon-racine.com).

$$$ La Méditerranée is all about seafood from the south served in a pastel and dressy setting...with similar clientele. The scene and the cuisine are sophisticated yet accessible, and the view of the Odéon is *formidable* (daily, reservations smart, facing the Odéon at 2 Place de l'Odéon, tel. 01 43 26 02 30, www.la-mediterranee.com).

$$ Café de l'Odéon, on a square with the venerable theater, is a place to savor a light meal with a stylish young crowd (but only in good weather, as it's all outdoors). The menu offers a limited selection of cheese and meat platters at fair prices—you'll feel like a winner eating light but well in such a Parisian setting (good salads, reasonable *plats,* May-Oct daily 12:00-23:00, no reservations, Place de l'Odéon, tel. 07 72 36 69 13).

$$$$ Le Comptoir Restaurant is a trendy, less tourist-friendly splurge where trusting foodies who book well in advance enjoy gourmet dishes with a modern flair. In a lively and jammed, streetfront setting, you'll choose from either a delicious, five-course

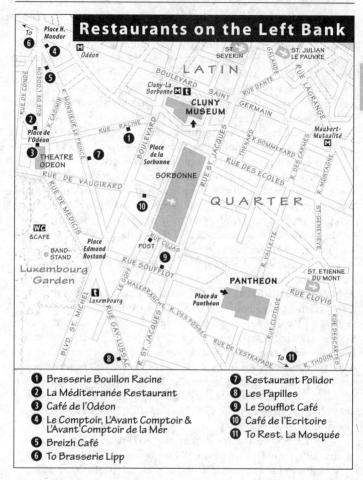

Restaurants on the Left Bank

1. Brasserie Bouillon Racine
2. La Méditerranée Restaurant
3. Café de l'Odéon
4. Le Comptoir, L'Avant Comptoir & L'Avant Comptoir de la Mer
5. Breizh Café
6. To Brasserie Lipp
7. Restaurant Polidor
8. Les Papilles
9. Le Soufflot Café
10. Café de l'Ecritoire
11. To Rest. La Mosquée

€60 fixed *menu*, or do your best to order à la carte (daily, reservations smart but only accepted Mon-Fri for those ordering the five-course *menu*, 9 Carrefour de l'Odéon, tel. 01 44 27 07 97).

$$ L'Avant Comptoir and **L'Avant Comptoir de la Mer** are two stand-up-only hors d'oeuvres bars sitting next door to the mothership restaurant (described earlier). They serve an array of both French-Basque tapas and seafood tapas on sleek zinc counters. With illustrated menu cards hanging from the ceilings, these popular (and pretty intense) places are designed to make the cuisine from the pricey Le Comptoir more accessible. At the walk-up counters outside, you can get top quality sandwiches, crêpes, or seafood to go (for less and with less commotion). But step inside for the foodie bar and it's another world (daily 12:00-23:00, 3 Carrefour de l'Odéon, tel. 01 44 27 07 97).

$$ Breizh Café serves gourmet crêpes a short hop from Boulevard St. Germain. The staff is welcoming, the outside terrace is generous, and the interior has a stone-wall-and-oak-floor warmth (daily, 1 Rue de l'Odéon, tel. 01 42 49 34 73).

$$$ Brasserie Lipp is the place to experience an unspoiled yet famous brasserie. The cool two-level interior is awash with worn leather booths and faded decor that looks like it dates to when the place opened in 1880. Come for the ambience and good-enough cuisine (daily, 151 Boulevard St. Germain, tel. 01 45 48 53 91).

$$ Restaurant Polidor is the Parisian equivalent of a beloved neighborhood diner. A fixture here since 1845, it's much loved for its unpretentious quality cooking, fun old-Paris atmosphere, and fair value. Noisy, happy diners sit tightly at shared tables, savoring classic bourgeois *plats* from every corner of France. The drawers you see at the back? They hold napkins for regulars (daily 12:00-14:30 & 19:00-23:00, cash only, no reservations, good wines by the glass, 41 Rue Monsieur-le-Prince, tel. 01 43 26 95 34).

Between the Panthéon and the Cluny Museum
(Mo: Cluny-La Sorbonne or RER/Train-B: Luxembourg)

$$$ Les Papilles is worth the walk. You'll dine surrounded by bottles of wine in a warm, woody bistro and eat what's offered… and you won't complain. It's one *menu*, no choices, and no regrets. Choose your wine from the shelf or ask for advice from the burly, rugby-playing owner, then relax and let the food arrive. Reserve ahead and make sure that you're OK with what he's cooking (closed Sun-Mon, 30 Rue Gay Lussac, tel. 01 43 25 20 79, www.lespapillesparis.fr).

$$ Le Soufflot, named after the architect of the Panthéon, delivers dynamite views of the inspiring dome. Dine on café cuisine or just enjoy a drink (16 Rue Soufflot, tel. 01 43 26 57 56).

$$ Café de l'Ecritoire sits among other cafés on an appealing little square surrounding a gurgling fountain and facing Paris' legendary Sorbonne University—just a block from the Cluny Museum. It's a typical brasserie with salads, *plats du jour,* and good seating inside and out (daily, 3 Place de la Sorbonne, tel. 01 43 54 60 02).

$$ Restaurant La Mosquée transports diners to Morocco with its dazzling Arabic ambience and cuisine at fair prices. It's tucked into the back of the Grande Mosquée de Paris and serves tasty baked goods, teas, and even tastier meals—including several varieties of couscous and tagine (daily 9:00-late, 39 Rue Geoffroy-Saint-Hilaire, tel. 01 43 31 38 20).

IN MONTMARTRE, NEAR SACRE-CŒUR

For locations, see the map on page 117.

(Mo: Abbesses or Anvers)

$$$ Le Moulin de la Galette is a fine place to dine *chez* Renoir under the famous windmill. Along with the stylish decor, there's well-respected cuisine (daily, 83 Rue Lepic, tel. 01 46 06 84 77).

$ L'Eté en Pente Douce is a good budget choice, hiding under some trees just downhill from the crowds on a classic neighborhood corner. It features cheery indoor and outdoor seating, cheap *plats du jour* and salads, vegetarian options, and good wines (daily, many steps below Sacré-Cœur to the left as you leave, 23 Rue Muller, tel. 01 42 64 02 67).

AT GARE DE LYON

$$$$ Le Train Bleu is a grandiose restaurant with a low-slung, leather-couch café-bar area built right into the train station for the Paris Exhibition of 1900 (which also saw the construction of the Pont Alexandre III). It's simply a grand-scale-everything experience, with over-the-top belle époque decor that speaks of another age, when going to dinner was an event—a chance to see and be seen. Forty-one massive paintings of scenes along the old rail lines tempt diners to consider a getaway. Reserve ahead for dinner, or drop in for a drink before your train leaves (up the stairs opposite track L, tel. 01 43 43 09 06, www.le-train-bleu.com).

Paris Connections

Budget plenty of time to reach your departure point. Paris is a big, crowded city, and getting across town or from terminal to terminal on time is a goal you'll share with millions of others. Factor in traffic delays and walking time through huge stations and vast terminals. Always keep your luggage safely near you. Thieves prey on jet-lagged and confused tourists using public transportation.

BY PLANE
Charles de Gaulle Airport

Paris' main airport (airport code: CDG, www.charlesdegaulleairport.co.uk) has three terminals: T-1, T-2, and T-3 (see map). Most flights from the US use T-1 or T-2. You can travel between terminals on the free CDGVAL shuttle train (departs every 5 minutes, 24/7) or by shuttle bus (on the arrivals level). Allow 30 minutes to travel between terminals and an hour for total

PARIS

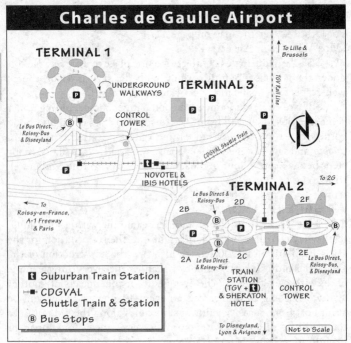

Charles de Gaulle Airport

TERMINAL 1

UNDERGROUND WALKWAYS

TERMINAL 3

CONTROL TOWER

To Lille & Brussels

TGV Rail Line

Le Bus Direct, Roissy-Bus & Disneyland

CDGVAL Shuttle Train

To 2G

NOVOTEL & IBIS HOTELS

TERMINAL 2

To Roissy-en-France, A-1 Freeway & Paris

Le Bus Direct & Roissy-Bus

2B   2D   2F

2A   Le Bus Direct   2C
     & Roissy-Bus

2E   Le Bus Direct, Roissy-Bus, & Disneyland

TRAIN STATION (TGV + 🚆) & SHERATON HOTEL

CONTROL TOWER

🚆 Suburban Train Station
⊶■ CDGVAL Shuttle Train & Station
Ⓑ Bus Stops

To Disneyland, Lyon & Avignon

Not to Scale

travel time between your gates at T-1 and T-2. All three terminals have access to ground transportation.

When leaving Paris, make sure you know which terminal you are departing from (if it's T-2, you'll also need to know which hall you're leaving from—they're labeled *A* through *F*). Plan to arrive at the airport three hours early for an overseas flight, and two hours for flights within Europe (particularly on budget airlines, which can have especially long check-in lines). For airport and flight info, visit www.parisaeroport.fr.

Services: All terminals have Paris Tourisme information desks, where you can get city maps, buy a Paris Museum Pass, and get tickets for the RoissyBus or suburban RER/Train-B to Paris—a terrific time- and hassle-saver (to buy a Passe Navigo card, you must go to the airport train station). You'll also find ATMs *(distributeurs),* free (but slow) Wi-Fi, shops, cafés, and bars. If you're returning home and want a VAT refund, look for tax-refund centers in the check-in area.

Terminal 1 (T-1)

This circular terminal has three key floors—arrivals *(arrivées)* on the top floor, and two floors for departures *(départs)* below. The terminal's round shape can be confusing—if you feel like you're going around in circles, you probably are.

PARIS

Arrival Level *(niveau arrivée):* After passing through immigration and customs, you'll exit between doors *(porte)* 34 and 36. Nearby are a snack stand and an ATM. Walk counterclockwise around the terminal to find the Paris Tourisme desk (door 6). Walk clockwise to find ground transportation: Le Bus Direct, Roissy-Bus, and the Disneyland shuttle bus (door 34), car rental counters (doors 24-30), and taxis (door 24).

Departure Levels *(niveaux départ):* Scan the departure screen to find out which hall you should go to for check-in. Halls 1-4 are on floor 2, and 5-6 are downstairs on floor 1. Also on floor 1 are the CDGVAL shuttle train, cafés, a post office (La Poste), pharmacy, boutiques, and a handy grocery. Boarding gates and duty-free shopping are located on floor 3, which is only accessible with a boarding pass.

Terminal 2 (T-2)

This long, horseshoe-shaped terminal is divided into six halls, labeled *A* through *F*. If arriving here, be ready for long walks and short train rides to baggage claim and exits. It's a busy place, so take a deep breath and follow signage carefully. A Paris Tourisme counter is located near gate 6/8 in each hall. Shuttle buses *(navettes)* circulate between T-2 halls A, C, and F, and to terminals T-1 and T-3 on the arrivals level. To locate bus stops for Le Bus Direct, RoissyBus, and the Disneyland shuttle—marked on the "Charles de Gaulle Airport" map—follow *bus* signs and bus icons.

T-2 has a **train station,** with suburban trains into Paris (described later), as well as longer-distance trains to the rest of France (including high-speed TGV trains, also called "InOui" trains). It's located between T-2C/D and T-2E/F, below the Sheraton Hotel (prepare for a long walk to reach your train). Shuttle buses to **airport hotels** leave from above the train station at T-2.

Car-rental offices, post offices, pharmacies, and ATMs are all well signed. T-2E/F has duty-free shopping arcades, and other T-2 halls have smaller duty-free shops. You can stash your bags at Baggage du Monde, above the train station in T-2 (daily 6:00-21:30, tel. 01 48 16 02 15, www.bagagesdumonde.com).

Getting Between Charles de Gaulle Airport and Paris

Buses, suburban trains, airport vans, and taxis link the airport's terminals with central Paris. If you're traveling with two or more companions, carrying lots of baggage, or are just plain tired, taxis (or Uber) are worth the extra cost, but keep in mind that they can be slow on weekdays during rush-hour traffic. Total travel time to your hotel should be around 1.5 hours by bus and Métro, one hour by train and Métro, and 50 minutes by taxi. At the airport, using buses and taxis requires shorter walks than the suburban train.

Transfers to Métro lines often involve stairs and long corridors. For more information, check the "Getting There" tab at www.charlesdegaulleairport.co.uk.

By RoissyBus: This bus drops you off at the Opéra Métro stop in central Paris (€12, runs 6:00-23:00, 3-4/hour, 50 minutes; buy ticket at airport Paris Tourisme desk, ticket machine, or on bus; tel. 3246, www.ratp.fr). The RoissyBus arrives on Rue Scribe; to get to the Métro entrance or nearest taxi stand, turn left as you exit the bus and walk counterclockwise around the lavish Opéra building to its front. A taxi to any of my listed hotels costs about €15 from here.

By Le Bus Direct (formerly Air France Bus): Several bus routes drop travelers at convenient points in and near the city, though it's a bit slower (€17 one-way, €30 round-trip, runs 5:45-22:30, 2/hour, Wi-Fi and power outlets, toll tel. 08 92 35 08 20, www.lebusdirect.com). You can book tickets online (must print out and bring with you), buy at ticket machines or ticket windows at stops (credit card only, availability varies by stop), or pay the driver (cash only, see www.lebusdirect.com for round-trip and group discount details). **Bus #2** goes to Porte Maillot (with connections to Beauvais Airport), the Arc de Triomphe (Etoile stop, 1 Avenue Carnot, 50 minutes, the Trocadéro (10 Place du Trocadéro, near Avenue d'Eylau), and ends near the Eiffel Tower at 19 Avenue de Suffren (1.25 hours, see map on page 92 for Trocadéro and Eiffel Tower stops). **Bus #4** runs to Gare de Lyon (45 minutes) and the Montparnasse Tower/train station (1.25 hours; see the map on page 100). **Bus #3** goes to Orly Airport (€21, 1.25 hours). All Le Bus Direct stops in Paris are identified with an airplane icon above the shelter.

You can return to the airport on Le Bus Direct coaches at any of the above locations (though you might need to cross the street to head in the right direction).

By Suburban Train: Paris' commuter RER/Train-B is the fastest public transit option for getting between the airport and the city center (€10.50, runs 5:00-24:00, 4/hour, about 35 minutes; you may still see maps and signage referring to these trains only by their old name, "RER").

RER/Train-B runs directly to well-located RER/Train-B/Métro stations (including Gare du Nord, Châtelet-Les Halles, St. Michel, and Luxembourg); from there, you can hop the Métro to get exactly where you need to go. RER/Train-B is handy and cheap, but it can require walking with your luggage through big, crowded stations—especially at Châtelet-Les Halles, where a transfer to the Métro can take 10-15 minutes and may include stairs.

To reach RER/Train-B from the airport terminal, follow *Paris by Train* signs. (If you land at T-1 or T-3, you'll need to take the CDGVAL shuttle to reach the train station.) The train station at T-2 is busy with long ticket-window lines (the other airport train station, between T-1 and T-2, is quieter). To save time, buy tickets/travel cards at a Paris Tourisme info desk or from the green ticket machines at the station (labeled *Paris/Ile de France*, takes cash and some American credit cards). For step-by-step instructions on taking RER/Train-B into Paris, see www.parisbytrain.com (see the options under "Airport"). Beware of thieves on the train; wear your money belt and keep your bags close.

To return to the airport on RER/Train-B from central Paris, allow plenty of time to get to your departure gate (plan for a 15-minute Métro or bus ride to the closest RER/Train-B station, a 15-minute wait for your train, a 35-minute train ride, plus walking time through the stations and airport). Your Métro or bus ticket is not valid on RER/Train-B to the airport (but a Passe Navigo is). When you catch your train, make sure the sign over the platform shows *Aéroport Roissy-Charles de Gaulle* as a stop served. (The line splits, so not every RER/Train-B serves the airport.) If you're not clear, ask another rider, *"Air-o-por sharl duh gaul?"*

By Airport Van: Shuttle vans carry passengers to and from their hotels, with stops along the way to drop off and pick up other riders. Shuttles require you to book a precise pickup time in advance—even though you can't know if your flight will arrive on time. For that reason, they work best for trips *from* your hotel to the airport. Though not as fast as taxis, shuttle vans are a good value for single travelers and big families (about €30 for one person, per-person price decreases the more you have in your party; have hotelier book at least a day in advance). Several companies offer shuttle service; I usually just go with the one my hotel uses. For groups of three or four, take a taxi or Uber instead.

By Taxi or Uber: Taxis charge a flat rate into Paris (€55 to the Left Bank, €50 to the Right Bank. Taxis can carry three people with bags comfortably, and are legally required to accept a fourth passenger (though they may not like it; beyond that, there's an extra passenger supplement). Larger parties can wait for a larger vehicle. Don't take an unauthorized taxi from cabbies greeting you on arrival. Official taxi stands are well signed. For taxi trips from Paris to the airport, have your hotel arrange it. Specify that you want a real taxi *(un taxi normal),* not a limo service that costs €20 more (and gives your hotel a kickback). For weekday-morning departures (7:00-10:00), reserve at least a day ahead (€7 reservation fee payable by credit card).

Uber offers Paris airport pickup and drop-off for the same rates as taxis, but since they can't use the bus-only lanes (normal taxis can), expect some added time.

Paris Webservices Private Car: This professional car service works well from the airport because your driver meets you inside

PARIS

the terminal and waits if you're late (two people-€90 one-way, €5-10/extra person up to 7, tel. 01 45 56 91 67 or 09 52 06 02 59, www.pariswebservices.com). They also offer guided tours.

By Rental Car: Car-rental desks are well signed from the arrival halls. Be prepared for a maze of ramps as you drive away from the lot—get directions from the rental clerks when you do the paperwork. For information on parking in Paris, see the end of this chapter.

When returning your car, allow ample time to reach the drop-off lots (at T-1 and T-2), especially if flying out of T-2. Check your rental company's exact drop-off location—there are several, and imperfect signage can make return lots confusing to find.

Orly Airport

This easy-to-navigate airport (airport code: ORY, www.airport orly.com) feels small, but it has all the services you'd expect at a major airport: ATMs and currency exchange, car-rental desks, cafés, shops, post offices, and more. Orly is good for rental-car pickup and drop-off, as it's closer to Paris and easier to navigate than Charles de Gaulle Airport.

Orly has four terminals (1-4). At all terminals, arrivals are on the ground level (level 0) and departures are on level 1. You can connect the terminals with the free Orlyval shuttle train (well signed).

Services: There are Paris Tourisme desks in the arrivals area (a good spot to buy the Paris Museum Pass and tickets for public transit into Paris) and offer free Wi-Fi.

Getting Between Orly Airport and Paris

Shuttle buses *(navettes)*, suburban trains, airport vans, and taxis connect Paris with Orly. Bus stops and taxis are centrally located at arrivals levels and are well signed.

By Bus or Tram: Bus bays are found in the Sud terminal outside exits L and G, and in the Ouest terminal outside exit D.

Le Bus Direct route #1 runs to Gare Montparnasse, Eiffel Tower, Trocadéro, and Arc de Triomphe/Etoile stops (all stops have connections to Métro lines). For Rue Cler hotels, take Le Bus Direct to the Eiffel Tower stop (20 Avenue de Suffren—see map on page 92), then walk 15 minutes across the Champ de Mars park to your hotel. Buses depart from the arrivals level—look for signs to *navettes* (€12 one-way, €20 round-trip, 4/hour, 40 minutes to the Eiffel Tower, buy ticket from driver or book online. See www. lebusdirect.com for details on round-trip and group discounts.

For the cheapest (but slow) access to central Paris (best for the Marais area), take **tram line 7** from outside Terminal 4 (direction: Villejuif-Louis Aragon) to the Villejuif station to catch Métro line 7 (you'll need one Métro ticket for the tram and one for the Métro—buy a *carnet* of 10 tickets at the Paris Tourisme desk in the terminal, 4/hour, 45 minutes to Villejuif Métro station, then 15-minute Métro ride to the Marais).

By Suburban Train: The next two options take you to **RER/ Train-B,** with access to the Luxembourg Garden area, Notre-Dame Cathedral, handy Métro line 1 at the Châtelet stop, Gare du Nord, and Charles de Gaulle Airport.

The **Orlybus** goes directly to the Denfert-Rochereau Métro and RER/Train-B stations (€8, 3/hour, 30 minutes). The pricier but more frequent—and more comfortable—**Orlyval shuttle train** takes you to the Antony RER/Train-B station (about €12, 6/hour, 40 minutes, buy ticket to Paris—not just to Antony—before boarding, smart to purchase your 10-ticket *carnet* for the Métro here, too). The Orlyval train is well signed and leaves from the departure level. Once at the RER/Train-B station, take the train in direction: Mitry-Claye or Aéroport Charles de Gaulle to reach central Paris.

For access to Left Bank neighborhoods (including Rue Cler) via **RER/Train-C,** take the bus marked *Go C Paris* five minutes to the Pont de Rungis station (€2 shuttle only, €6.25 combo-ticket includes RER/Train-C), then catch RER/Train-C to St. Michel, Musée d'Orsay, Invalides, or Pont de l'Alma (direction: Versailles Château Rive Gauche or Pontoise, 4/hour, 35 minutes).

By Airport Van: From Orly, figure about €23 for one person or €30 for two (less per person for larger groups and kids).

By Taxi: Taxis wait outside baggage claim areas. Allow 30 minutes for a taxi ride into central Paris (fixed fare: €30 for Left Bank, €35 for Right Bank).

By Uber: Head toward exit B, following signs for *Pre-Ordered Vehicles*. Meet your Uber driver in the lot labeled *Parking Pro* (same fixed rate as taxis for central Paris).

Beauvais Airport

Budget airlines such as Ryanair use this small airport with two terminals (T-1 and T-2), offering dirt-cheap airfares but leaving you 50 miles north of Paris. Still, this airport has direct buses to Paris and is handy for travelers heading to Normandy or Belgium (car rental available). The airport is basic, waiting areas can be crowded, and services sparse (airport code: BVA, toll tel. 08 92 68 20 66, www.aeroportparisbeauvais.com).

Getting Between Beauvais Airport and Paris

Buses depart from a stop between the two terminals (€17 one-way, 2/hour, 1.5 hours to Paris, buy ticket online to save time, http://tickets.aeroportbeauvais.com). Buses arrive at Porte Maillot on the west edge of Paris (where you can connect to Métro line 1 and RER/Train-C); the closest taxi stand is next door at the Hôtel Hyatt Regency Paris Etoile. To head back to Beauvais Airport from Porte Maillot, catch the bus in the parking lot at 22 Boulevard Pershing next to the Hyatt Regency.

Trains connect Beauvais' city center and Paris' Gare du Nord (20/day, 1.5 hours). To reach the Beauvais train station, take the Hôtel/Aéroport Navette shuttle or local bus #12 (each hourly, 25 minutes).

Taxis run from Beauvais Airport to the Beauvais train station or city center (€20), or to central Paris (allow €150 and 1.5 hours).

Connecting Paris' Airports
Charles de Gaulle and Orly

Le Bus Direct #3 directly and conveniently links Charles de Gaulle and Orly airports (€21, stops at Charles de Gaulle T-1 and T-2 and Orly Ouest exit B-C or Sud exit L, roughly 2/hour 5:45-23:00, 1 hour, www.lebusdirect.com).

Suburban **RER/Train-B** connects Charles de Gaulle and Orly but requires a transfer to the Orlyval train. It isn't as easy as the Le Bus Direct mentioned above, but it's faster when there's traffic (€19, 5/hour, 1.5 hours). This line splits at both ends: Heading from Charles de Gaulle to Orly, take trains that serve the Antony stop (direction: St-Rémy-les-Chevreuse), then transfer to the Orlyval shuttle train; heading from Orly to Charles de Gaulle, take trains that end at the airport—Aéroport Charles de Gaulle-Roissy, not Mitry-Claye.

Taxis take about one hour and are easiest, but pricey (about €85, book online for best rates, http://city-airport-taxis.com); shuttle services are a cheaper option.

Charles de Gaulle (or Orly) and Beauvais

You can connect Charles de Gaulle or Orly to Beauvais via Gare du Nord, then a train to the town of Beauvais. From there, you can take a shuttle, local bus, or taxi to Beauvais Airport. From Charles de Gaulle, take **RER/Train-B** to Gare du Nord; from Orly, take the **Orlybus or Orlyval shuttle** train (described earlier, under "Orly Airport") to the suburban train station to pick up RER/Train-B to Gare du Nord.

Taxis between Charles de Gaulle and Beauvais take one hour and cost about €120; from Orly, it's about a 1.5-hour taxi ride and about €150 (http://city-airport-taxis.com).

BY TRAIN

Paris is Europe's rail hub, with six major stations and one minor station, and trains heading in different directions:

- Gare du Nord (northbound trains)
- Gare Montparnasse (west- and southwest-bound trains)
- Gare de Lyon (southeast-bound trains)
- Gare de l'Est (eastbound trains)
- Gare St. Lazare (northwest-bound trains)
- Gare d'Austerlitz (southwest-bound trains)
- Gare de Bercy (smaller station with non-TGV trains mostly serving cities in Burgundy)

The main train stations all have free Wi-Fi, banks or currency exchanges, ATMs, train information desks, cafés, newsstands, and clever pickpockets (pay attention in ticket lines—keep your bag firmly gripped in front of you). Not all have baggage checks.

Any train station has schedule information, can make reservations, and can sell tickets for any destination, although it may be handier to buy tickets from a neighborhood SNCF office.

Each station offers two types of rail service: long distance to other cities, called Grandes Lignes (major lines, TGV—also called "InOui"—or TER trains); and commuter service to nearby areas, called Banlieue, Transilien, or suburban trains lines A-K. You also may see ticket windows identified as *Ile de France*. These are for Transilien trains serving destinations outside Paris in the Ile de France region (usually no more than an hour from Paris). When arriving by Métro, follow signs for *Grandes Lignes-SNCF* to find the main tracks. Métro and suburban train lines A-K, as well as buses and taxis, are well marked at every station.

Budget plenty of time before your departure to factor in ticket lines and making your way through large, crowded stations. Paris train stations can be intimidating, but if you slow down, take a deep breath, and ask for help, you'll find them manageable and efficient. Bring a pad of paper and a pen for clear communication at ticket/info windows. It helps to write down the ticket you want. For instance: "28/05/20 Paris-NordLyon dep. 18:30." All stations have a central information booth *(accueil);* bigger stations have roving helpers, usually wearing red or blue vests. They're capable of answering rail questions more quickly than the staff at the information desks or ticket windows. I make a habit of confirming my track number and departure time with these helpers (all rail staff speak English). To make your trip go more smoothly, be sure to review the train tips on page 1141.

Gare du Nord

The granddaddy of Paris' train stations serves cities in northern France and international destinations north of Paris, including Co-

PARIS

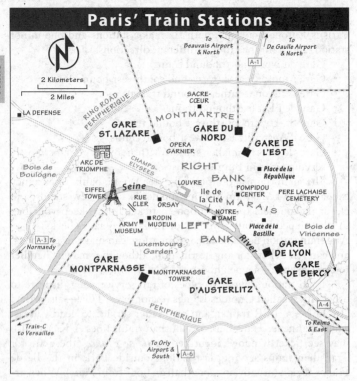

Paris' Train Stations

2 Kilometers

2 Miles

To Beauvais Airport & North

To De Gaulle Airport & North

A-1

LA DEFENSE

RING ROAD PERIPHERIQUE

SACRE-CŒUR

MONTMARTRE

GARE ST. LAZARE

OPERA GARNIER

GARE DU NORD

GARE DE L'EST

Bois de Boulogne

ARC DE TRIOMPHE

CHAMPS-ELYSEES

RIGHT BANK

Place de la République

EIFFEL TOWER

Seine

LOUVRE

Ile de la Cité

POMPIDOU CENTER

PERE LACHAISE CEMETERY

RUE CLER

ORSAY

MARAIS

NOTRE-DAME

ARMY MUSEUM

RODIN MUSEUM

LEFT BANK

Place de la Bastille

Bois de Vincennes

A-3 To Normandy

Luxembourg Garden

River

GARE DE LYON

GARE MONTPARNASSE

MONTPARNASSE TOWER

GARE D'AUSTERLITZ

GARE DE BERCY

A-4

PERIPHERIQUE

To Reims & East

Train-C to Versailles

To Orly Airport & South

A-6

penhagen, Amsterdam, and the Eurostar to London. The station is undergoing a €600-million renovation that won't be finished until 2024—expect changes and construction disruptions.

Look for circulating information-helpers. A helpful TI kiosk (labeled *Paris Tourist Office*) opposite track 8 sells Paris Museum Passes and fast-pass *"coupe-file"* tickets (credit cards only).

Key Destinations Served by Gare du Nord Grandes Lignes: Brussels by Thalys (at least hourly, 1.5 hours), **Bruges** (at least hourly, 2.5-3 hours, change in Brussels), **Amsterdam** by Thalys (9/day direct, 3.5 hours), **Berlin** (4/day, 8.5 hours, change in Cologne or Dortmund), **Koblenz** (4/day, 5 hours, change in Cologne, more from Gare de l'Est that don't cross Belgium), and **London** by Eurostar (1-2/hour, 2.5 hours).

By Banlieue/Suburban Lines: Charles de Gaulle Airport (4/hour, 35 minutes, track 41-44), and **Pontoise** (2/hour, 50 minutes).

Gare Montparnasse

This big, modern station covers three floors, serves lower Normandy and Brittany, and has TGV service to the Loire Valley and southwestern France, as well as suburban service to Chartres. Trains to Chartres usually depart from tracks 18-24.

Most services are provided on the top level (second floor up, Hall 1), where all trains arrive and depart. Baggage check *(consignes)* is by track 24, and the main rail information office *(accueil)* is opposite track 16. As you face the tracks, to the far left and outside are Le Bus Direct buses to Orly and Charles de Gaulle airports (on Rue du Commandant René Mouchotte).

City buses are out front, between the train station and the Montparnasse Tower (down the escalator through the glassy facade). Bus #96 is good for connecting to Marais and Luxembourg area hotels, while #92 is ideal for Rue Cler hotels (both easier than the Métro).

Key Destinations Served by Gare Montparnasse: Chartres (14/day, 1 hour), **Amboise** (8/day in 1.5 hours with change in St-Pierre-des-Corps, requires TGV reservation; non-TGV trains leave from Gare d'Austerlitz), **Pontorson/Mont St-Michel** (5/day, 5.5 hours, via Rennes or Caen), **Dinan** (6/day, 4 hours, change in Rennes and Dol), **Bordeaux** (20/day, 2.5 hours), **Sarlat** (4/day, 5 hours, change in Bordeaux), **Toulouse** (6/day, 4.5 hours, more with change in Bordeaux), **Albi** (4/day, 6.5-9 hours, change in Montauban or Toulouse), **Tours** (8/day, 1 hour), and **Hendaye** (8/day, 5 hours, connect here to **San Sebastian** by local train).

Gare de Lyon

This huge, bewildering station offers TGV and regular service to southeastern France, Italy, Switzerland, and other international destinations. Grandes Lignes and Banlieue lines share the same tracks. Platforms are divided into two areas: Hall 1 (tracks A-N) and Hall 2 (tracks 5-23). Hall 3 is underground with more ticket offices, food services, and quieter waiting areas—but no trains.

Le Bus Direct coaches—to Gare Montparnasse (easy transfer to Orly Airport) and direct to Charles de Gaulle Airport—stop outside the station's main entrance. They are signed *Navette-Aéroport*. To find them, exit Hall 1 with your back to track A. Walk down the ramp toward the Café Européen. Turn right at the street (Boulevard Diderot), walk a block, and find the shelter with the airplane icon. For more on Le Bus Direct, see page 164.

Hall 2 has the best services—including a train information office, pharmacy, and a handy Monop grocery store. You'll find baggage check *(consignes)* in Hall 2 down the ramp, opposite track 17, and in Hall 1, downstairs by track M. Car rental is out the exit past track M (Hall 1).

Don't leave the station without at least taking a peek at the recommended Le Train Bleu Restaurant in Hall 1, up the stairs opposite tracks G-L (no elevator, see listing on page 161).

Key Destinations Served by Gare de Lyon: Disneyland (RER/Train-A to Marne-la-Vallée-Chessy, at least 3/hour, 45 minutes), **Beaune** (roughly hourly at rush hour but few midday, 2.5 hours, most require change in Dijon; direct trains from Paris' Bercy station take an hour longer), **Dijon** (TGV trains only, roughly hourly, 1.5 hours; see Gare de Bercy for local trains), **Chamonix** (7/day, 5.5-7 hours, some change in Switzerland), **Annecy** (hourly, 4 hours, many with change in Lyon), **Lyon** (hourly, 2 hours), **Avignon** (hourly direct, 2.5 hours to Avignon TGV station; 5/day in 3.5 hours to Avignon Centre-Ville Station, more connections with change—3-4 hours), **Arles** (hourly, 4 hours, transfer in Avignon or Nîmes), **Nice** (hourly, 6 hours, may require change), **Carcassonne** (8/day, 5.5 hours, 1 change usually in Bordeaux), **Zürich** (4/day direct, 4 hours), **Venice** (4/day, 9.5-11.5 hours with 1-3 changes; 1 direct overnight—see "Specialty Trains from Paris," later), **Rome** (2/day, 11-12 hours, 1-3 changes), **Bern** (1/day direct, 6/day with change in Basel, 4-5 hours), **Interlaken** (5/day with change in Basel, 5-5.5 hours, 8/day more from Gare de l'Est), and **Barcelona** (2-4/day direct, 6.5 hours).

Gare de l'Est

This two-floor station (with underground Métro) serves northeastern France and international destinations east of Paris. All trains depart at street level from tracks 1-30. Most services are opposite tracks 12-20 (baggage lockers, car rental, WC, small grocery store, shops, and Métro access).

Key Destinations Served by Gare de l'Est: Colmar (12/day with TGV, 2.5 hours, 3 direct, others change in Strasbourg), **Strasbourg** (hourly with TGV, under 2 hours), **Reims** Centre station (8/day by direct TGV, 45 minutes), **Verdun** (5/day direct to Meuse TGV station and shuttle bus, 1.5 hours; 3.5 hours by regional train with transfer), **Interlaken** (12/day, 6 hours, 1-2 changes, faster trains from Gare de Lyon), **Zürich** (12/day, 5-7 hours, 1-2 changes, faster direct trains from Gare de Lyon), **Frankfurt** (4 direct/day, 4 hours; 3 more/day with change in Karlsruhe, 4.5 hours), **Munich** (1/day direct, 6/day with 1 change, 6 hours), and **Berlin** (6/day, 8.5 hours, 1 change; trains run via Germany, not Belgium).

Gare St. Lazare

This compact station serves upper Normandy, including Rouen and Giverny. All trains arrive and depart one floor above street level. Grandes Lignes to all destinations listed next depart from tracks 18-27; Banlieue trains depart from 1-16. Baggage check is available near the station at Annexx Lockers (6 Rue de Constantinople, www.lockers.fr). There's also a three-floor shopping mall (Monop grocery store, pharmacy, clothing stores, and more).

SNCF Boutiques

You can save time and stress by buying train tickets or making train reservations at an SNCF Boutique. These small branch offices of the French national rail compa- ny are conveniently located throughout Paris, with offices near some of my rec- ommended hotels and museums and at Charles de Gaulle and Orly airports. Arrive when they open to avoid lines (generally open Mon-Sat 8:30-19:00 or 20:00, closed Sun).

Marais
- 2 Rue de Turenne, Mo: St. Paul

Farther North on the Right Bank
- 2 Rue Chauveau Lagarde, Mo: Madeleine
- 82 Avenue de la Grande Armée, Mo: Porte Maillot (near Hôtel Concorde-Lafayette and Beauvais Airport bus stop)

Latin Quarter/Luxembourg Garden
- 54 Boulevard St. Michel, Mo: Cluny-Sorbonne
- 79 Rue de Rennes, Mo: St. Sulpice

Farther South on the Left Bank
- 3 Avenue du Général Leclerc, Mo: Denfert-Rochereau (near Catacombs)
- 30 Avenue d'Italie, in Centre Commerciale Galaxie, Mo: Place d'Italie

You can also buy tickets in train stations of the towns I sug- gest for day trips from Paris, such as Versailles, Fontainebleau, Melun (for Vaux-le-Vicomte), Chartres, Chantilly, Vernon (for Giverny), and Pontoise (for Auvers-sur-Oise).

Key Destinations Served by Gare St. Lazare: Giverny (train to Vernon, 8/day Mon-Sat, 6/day Sun, 45 minutes), **Pontoise** (1-2/hour, 45 minutes), **Rouen** (nearly hourly, 1.5 hours), **Le Havre** (hourly, 2.5 hours, some change in Rouen), **Honfleur** (13/day, 2-3.5 hours, via Lisieux, Deauville, or Le Havre, then bus), **Bayeux** (9/day, 2.5 hours, some change in Caen), **Caen** (14/day, 2 hours), and **Pontorson/Mont St-Michel** (2/day, 4-5.5 hours, via Caen; more trains from Gare Montparnasse).

Gare d'Austerlitz

This small station currently provides non-TGV service to the Loire Valley, southwestern France, and Spain. All tracks are at street level. Baggage check and WCs (with pay showers that include towel and soap) are opposite track 4. To get to the Métro and RER/Train-C, you must walk outside and along either side of the station. Car rental is across the river at Gare de Lyon (a level 10-minute walk—follow signs opposite track 1).

Key Destinations Served by Gare d'Austerlitz: Orly Airport (via RER/Train-C, 4/hour, 35 minutes), **Versailles** (via RER/Train-C, 4/hour, 35 minutes), **Amboise** (3/day direct in 2 hours, more with transfer; faster TGV connection from Gare Montparnasse), **Sarlat** (1/day, 6.5 hours, requires change to bus in Souillac, 3 more/day via Gare Montparnasse), and **Cahors** (5/day, 5 hours; slower trains from Gare Montparnasse).

Gare de Bercy

This smaller station mostly handles southbound non-TGV trains such as to **Dijon** (6/day, 3 hours), but some TGV trains do stop here in peak season (Mo: Bercy, one stop east of Gare de Lyon on line 14, exit the Bercy Métro station and it's across the street). Facilities are limited—just a WC and a sandwich-fare takeout café.

Specialty Trains from Paris
Low-Cost TGV Trains to Elsewhere in France

A TGV train called OuiGo (pronounced "we go") offers rock-bottom fares and no-frills service to select French cities also served by regular TGV trains. Departures from TGV stations at Gare de Lyon, Gare Montparnasse, Gare de l'Est, Charles de Gaulle Aiport, and near Disneyland at Marne-la-Vallée. From central Paris, most routes to western France depart from Montparnasse Vaugirard station in Hall 2, most east-bound service departs from Gare de l'Est, and most south-bound service leaves from Gare de Lyon. You must print your ticket within four days of departure (or download it to your phone), arrive 30 minutes before departure, and activate your ticket. Rail passes are not accepted, and you can only bring one carry-on-size bag plus one handbag for free (children's tickets allow you to bring a stroller). Larger or extra luggage is €5/bag if you pay when you buy your ticket. If you just show up without paying in advance, it's €20/bag on the train—yikes. There's no food service on the train (BYO), but children under age 12 pay only €5 for a seat. The website explains it all in easy-to-understand English (https://en.oui.sncf/en/ouigo).

To Brussels and Amsterdam by Thalys Train

The pricey high-speed Thalys train has the monopoly on the rail route between Paris and Brussels. Without a rail pass, for the Paris-Amsterdam train, you'll pay about €80-205 first class, €35-135 second class (compared to €38-50 by bus); for the Paris-Brussels train it's €65-140 first class, €30-100 second class (€20-30 by bus). Even with a rail pass, you need to pay for train reservations (first class-€25-30, includes a light meal; second class-€20-25). Book early for the best rates (discounted seats are limited, www.thalys.com).

Thalys also operates a slower, cheaper Paris-to-Brussels train called IZY (2-3/day, 2.5 hours, tickets from €10 for standing room to €29 full fare, rail passes not accepted, luggage limits, online only at www.izy.com). Thalys and IZY trains both use Gare du Nord. For another cheap option, try Flixbus or OuiBus (see "Paris Bus Connections," later).

To London by Eurostar Train

The fastest and most convenient way to get from the Eiffel Tower to Big Ben is by rail. Eurostar zips you (and up to 800 others in 18 sleek cars) from downtown Paris to downtown London at 190 mph in 2.5 hours (1-2/hour). The tunnel crossing is a 20-minute, silent, 100 mph nonevent. Your ears won't even pop.

Eurostar Tickets and Fares: A one-way ticket between London and Paris can vary widely in price; for instance, $45-200 (Standard class), $160-310 (Standard Premier), and $400 (Business Premier). Fares depend on how far ahead you reserve and whether you're eligible for any discounts—available for children (under 12), youths (under 26), and adults booking months ahead or round-trip tickets. You can book tickets 4-9 months in advance. Tickets can be exchanged before the scheduled departure for a fee (about $45 plus the cost of any price increase), but only Business Premier class allows any refund.

Buy tickets online using the print-at-home eticket option (see www.ricksteves.com/eurostar or www.eurostar.com). You can also order by phone through Rail Europe (US tel. 800-387-6782) for home delivery before you go, or through Eurostar (French toll tel. 08 92 35 35 39, priced in euros) to pick up at the station. In continental Europe you can buy your Eurostar tickets at any major train station in any country, at neighborhood SNCF offices (see the "SNCF Boutiques" sidebar, earlier), or at any travel agency that handles train tickets (booking fee).

If you have a Eurail Global Pass, seat reservations are available at Eurostar departure stations, through US agents, or by phone with Eurostar (generally harder to get at other train stations and travel agencies; $35 in Standard, $45 in Standard Premier, can sell out).

Taking the Eurostar: Eurostar trains depart from and arrive at Paris' Gare du Nord. Check in at least 45 minutes in advance (remember that times listed on tickets are local times—departure from Paris is French time, arrival in London is British time). Pass through airport-like security, show your passport to customs officials, and locate your departure gate (shown on a TV monitor). There's a reasonable restaurant before the first check-in point, but only a couple of tiny sandwich-and-coffee counters in the cramped waiting area.

To Italy by Thello Train

The direct night train that runs between Paris and Venice (with stops in Dijon, Milan, and a few other northern Italian cities) is operated under the private brand Thello (pronounced "Tell-o"; rail passes not accepted). For the best prices, buy your ticket up to six months in advance (www.ricksteves.com/rail or www.thello.com)—or consider flying.

BY BUS, CAR, OR CRUISE SHIP
Paris Bus Connections

Buses generally provide the cheapest—if less comfortable and more time-consuming—transportation to major European cities. The bus is also the cheapest way to cross the English Channel; book at least two days in advance for the best fares.

Eurolines is the old standby; two relative newcomers (Ouibus and Flixbus, see below) are cutting prices drastically, adding more destinations, and ramping up onboard comfort with Wi-Fi and snacks. These companies provide service usually between train stations and airports within France and to many international destinations. If the schedule works for you, it's a handy and cheap way to connect Paris airports with other French destinations (Blois, Rouen, and Caen, for example) and skip central Paris train stations.

OuiBus has routes mostly within France but serves some European cities as well (central Paris stop is at Gare de Bercy, Mo: Bercy, easy online booking, www.ouibus.com). German-run **Flix-Bus** connects key cities within France and throughout Europe, often from secondary airports and train stations (central Paris stop is near Gare de Bercy at 208 Quai de Bercy, handy eticket system and easy-to-use app, tel. 01 76 36 04 12, www.flixbus.com). **Eurolines'** buses depart from several locations in Paris (toll tel.

08 92 89 12 00; from the US, dial 011 33 1 41 86 24 21, www.eurolines.com).

Parking in Paris

Street parking is generally free at night (20:00-9:00) and all day Sunday. To pay for streetside parking, use a credit card. Meters limit street parking to a maximum of two hours.

Underground garages are plentiful in Paris. You'll find them under Ecole Militaire, St. Sulpice Church, Les Invalides, the Bastille, and the Panthéon; all charge about €25-50/day (€50-70/3 days, €10/day more after that, for locations see www.parisfranceparking.com). Some hotels offer parking for less—ask your hotelier.

For a longer stay, park at an airport (about €20/day) and take public transport or a taxi into the city. Orly is closer and easier for drivers to navigate than Charles de Gaulle.

Le Havre Cruise Port

Ships visiting "Paris" actually call at the industrial city of Le Havre, France's second-biggest port (after Marseille), and the primary French port on the Atlantic.

Paris and Le Havre are connected by train (about 3 hours each way). To get from the port to the Le Havre train/bus station, you can ride a cruise-line shuttle bus or take a taxi. From there, trains leave about every 1-2 hours for the three-hour journey to Paris' St. Lazare station (fewer on weekends).

For port information, see www.lehavretourisme.com (choose "To Discover," then "The cruise destination"). For more about Le Havre, see my *Rick Steves Scandinavian & Northern European Cruise Ports* guidebook.

NEAR PARIS

Versailles • Chartres • Giverny • Disneyland Paris

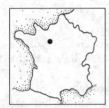

Efficient trains bring dozens of day trips within the grasp of temporary Parisians. Europe's best palace at Versailles, the awesome cathedral of Chartres, the flowery gardens at Giverny that inspired Monet, and a mouse-run amusement park await the traveler looking for a refreshing change from urban Paris.

Versailles

Every king's dream, Versailles (vehr-"sigh") was the residence of French monarchs and the cultural heartbeat of Europe for about 100 years—until the Revolution of 1789 changed all that. The Sun King (Louis XIV) created Versailles, spending freely from the public treasury to turn his dad's hunting lodge into a palace fit for the gods (among whom he counted himself). Louis XV and Louis XVI spent much of the 18th century gilding Louis XIV's lily. In 1837, about 50 years after the royal family was evicted by citizen-protesters, King Louis-Philippe (then a constitutional monarch rather than a divine one) opened the palace as a museum. Today you can visit parts of the huge palace and wander through acres of manicured

NEAR PARIS

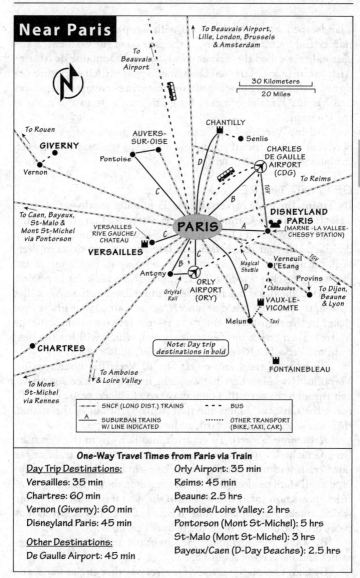

Near Paris

To Beauvais Airport,
Lille, London, Brussels
& Amsterdam

To Beauvais Airport

30 Kilometers
20 Miles

To Rouen

GIVERNY

Vernon

Pontoise

AUVERS-SUR-OISE

CHANTILLY

Senlis

CHARLES DE GAULLE AIRPORT (CDG)

To Reims

To Caen, Bayeux, St-Malo & Mont St-Michel via Pontorson

VERSAILLES RIVE GAUCHE/ CHÂTEAU

VERSAILLES

PARIS

DISNEYLAND PARIS
(MARNE -LA VALLEE- CHESSY STATION)

Antony

OrlyVal Rail

ORLY AIRPORT (ORY)

Magical Shuttle

Verneuil l'Etang

Provins

Châteaubus

VAUX-LE-VICOMTE

To Dijon, Beaune & Lyon

Melun   Taxi

CHARTRES

Note: Day trip
destinations in bold

FONTAINEBLEAU

To Mont St-Michel via Rennes

To Amboise & Loire Valley

| | SNCF (LONG DIST.) TRAINS | | BUS |
| A | SUBURBAN TRAINS W/ LINE INDICATED | | OTHER TRANSPORT (BIKE, TAXI, CAR) |

One-Way Travel Times from Paris via Train

Day Trip Destinations:	Orly Airport: 35 min
Versailles: 35 min	Reims: 45 min
Chartres: 60 min	Beaune: 2.5 hrs
Vernon (Giverny): 60 min	Amboise/Loire Valley: 2 hrs
Disneyland Paris: 45 min	Pontorson (Mont St-Michel): 5 hrs
	St-Malo (Mont St-Michel): 3 hrs
Other Destinations:	Bayeux/Caen (D-Day Beaches): 2.5 hrs
De Gaulle Airport: 45 min	

gardens sprinkled with fountains and studded with statues. Europe's next-best palaces are just Versailles wannabes.

Worth ▲▲▲, Versailles offers three blockbuster sights. The main attraction is the palace itself, called the **Château.** Here you walk through dozens of lavish, chandeliered rooms once inhabited by Louis XIV and his successors, starring the magnificent Hall of Mirrors. Next come the expansive **Gardens** behind the palace, a landscaped wonderland crossed with footpaths and dotted with statues and fountains. Finally, at the far end of the Gardens, is the pastoral area called the **Trianon Palaces and Domaine de Marie-Antoinette** (a.k.a. Trianon/Domaine), a vast walled enclosure designed for frolicking blue bloods and featuring several small palaces and Marie's Hamlet—perfect for getting away from the mobs at the Château.

Visiting Versailles can seem daunting because of its size and hordes of visitors. But if you follow my tips, a trip here during even the busiest times is manageable.

GETTING THERE

By Train: The town of Versailles is 35 minutes southwest of Paris. Take **RER/Train-C** from any of these stations: Gare d'Austerlitz, St. Michel, Musée d'Orsay, Invalides, Pont de l'Alma, or Champ de Mars. Use your Passe Navigo or buy a round-trip ticket to "Versailles Rive Gauche/Château" from an easy-to-figure-out ticket machine or ticket window (€7.10 round-trip, credit card or coins, 4/hour). If the ticket machine doesn't immediately offer a Versailles option, try pressing "Ile de France." Swipe your pass or insert your ticket in the turnstile to enter the system (as you would with the Métro). Then check the departure board, which will list the next train to "Versailles Rive Gauche/Château" and its track.

Board your train and relax. On all Versailles-bound trains, Versailles Rive Gauche/Château is the final stop. Once you arrive, exit through the turnstiles (you may need to insert your ticket). To reach the Château, follow the flow: Turn right out of the station, then left at the first boulevard, and walk 10 minutes.

Returning to Paris: To get back into Paris from the Versailles Rive Gauche/Château train station, just hop on the train at the same train station—all trains from here zip back to the city, stopping at all stations along line C. The monitor above the ticket turnstiles shows how many minutes until the next train leaves and from which track. Remember, your RER/Train-C ticket covers any connecting Métro ride once you're back downtown.

By Taxi: The 30-minute ride (without traffic) between Versailles and Paris costs about €65.

By Car: Get on the *périphérique* freeway that circles Paris, and take the toll-free A-13 autoroute toward Rouen. Exit at Versailles, follow signs to *Versailles Château,* and avoid the hectic Garden lots by parking in the big pay lot at the foot of the Château on Place d'Armes (€5/hour).

PLANNING YOUR TIME

Versailles merits a full sightseeing day. In general, allow 1.5 hours each for the Château, the Gardens (includes time for lunch), and the Trianon/Domaine. Add another two hours for round-trip transit, and you're looking at nearly an eight-hour day. If you have more time to spend at Versailles, consider one of the lesser sights near the palace: the Equestrian Performance Academy (www. acadequestre.fr) or the King's Vegetable Garden (www.potager-du-roi.fr).

Versailles is all about crowd management; a well-planned visit can make or break your experience. Take this advice to heart. Here's what I'd do on a first visit:

- Get a pass in advance (see "Passes," later).
- In high season, avoid holidays, Sundays, Tuesdays, and Saturdays—in that order—when crowds smother the palace interior. Thursdays and Fridays are best.
- Leave Paris by 8:00, get in line before the palace opens at 9:00, and follow my self-guided tour of the Château interior. Have lunch. Spend the afternoon touring the Gardens and the Trianon Palaces/Domaine de Marie-Antoinette. To shorten your visit, skip the Trianon/Domaine, which takes 1.5 hours to see, plus a 30-minute walk each way.
- An alternate plan is to see the Trianon/Domaine first. Arrive in Versailles around 11:00 and catch the "TRI" shuttle bus from the train station to the Trianon/Domaine (see the "Getting Around the Gardens" sidebar, later) to get there when it opens at noon. Then work your way back through the Gardens to the Château, arriving after the crowds have died down (usually by 14:00, later on Sun).

ORIENTATION TO VERSAILLES

Cost: Buy either a Paris Museum Pass or a Versailles Le Passeport Pass, both of which give you access to the most important parts of the complex (see "Passes," next). If you don't get a pass, buy individual tickets for each of the three different sections. (Booking a tour also saves you time; see later.)

    Château: €18, includes audioguide, free for kids 17 and under. Free on the first Sunday Nov-March.

    Trianon Palaces and Domaine de Marie-Antoinette: €12, no audioguide, free for kids 17 and under. Covers all the buildings within this walled enclosure. Free on the first Sunday Nov-March.

    Gardens: The gardens are free Mon, Wed, Thu and

NEAR PARIS

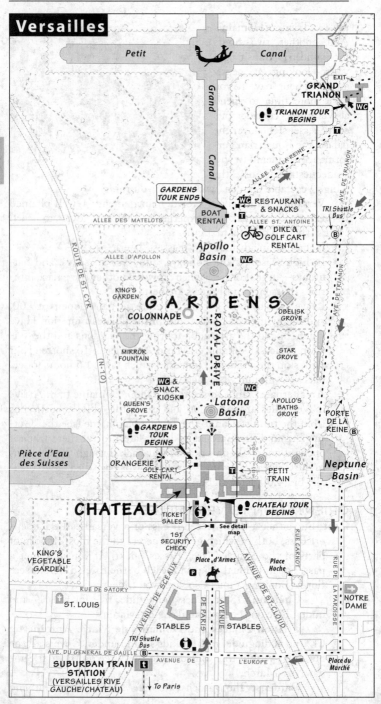

Versailles

- Petit Canal
- Grand Canal
- GRAND TRIANON
- EXIT
- WC
- TRIANON TOUR BEGINS
- T
- AVE. DE TRIANON
- ALLÉE DE LA REINE
- GARDENS TOUR ENDS
- WC — RESTAURANT & SNACKS
- BOAT RENTAL
- T
- ALLÉE ST. ANTOINE
- BIKE & GOLF CART RENTAL
- TRI Shuttle Bus
- B
- ALLÉE DES MATELOTS
- ALLÉE D'APOLLON
- Apollo Basin
- WC
- KING'S GARDEN
- GARDENS
- COLONNADE
- ROYAL DRIVE
- OBELISK GROVE
- AVE. DE TRIANON
- ROUTE DE ST. CYR (N-10)
- MIRROR FOUNTAIN
- STAR GROVE
- WC & SNACK KIOSK
- WC
- Pièce d'Eau des Suisses
- QUEEN'S GROVE
- Latona Basin
- APOLLO'S BATHS GROVE
- PORTE DE LA REINE
- B
- GARDENS TOUR BEGINS
- ORANGERIE
- GOLF-CART RENTAL
- T
- PETIT TRAIN
- Neptune Basin
- CHATEAU
- TICKET SALES
- i
- CHATEAU TOUR BEGINS
- See detail map
- 1ST SECURITY CHECK
- KING'S VEGETABLE GARDEN
- Place d'Armes
- P
- RUE CARNOT
- Place Hoche
- RUE DE LA PAROISSE
- NOTRE DAME
- RUE DE SATORY
- ST. LOUIS
- AVENUE DE SCEAUX
- AVENUE DE PARIS
- DE PARIS
- AVENUE
- AVENUE DE ST-CLOUD
- STABLES
- STABLES
- TRI Shuttle Bus
- B
- i
- AVE. DU GENERAL DE GAULLE
- AVENUE DE
- L'EUROPE
- Place du Marché
- SUBURBAN TRAIN STATION (VERSAILLES RIVE GAUCHE/CHATEAU)
- t
- To Paris

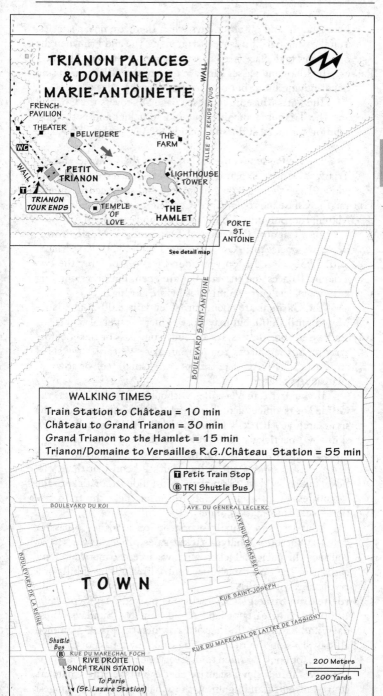

NEAR PARIS

TRIANON PALACES
& DOMAINE DE
MARIE-ANTOINETTE

FRENCH PAVILION

THEATER

BELVEDERE

THE FARM

WC

WALL

ALLEE DU RENDEZVOUS

WALL

PETIT TRIANON

LIGHTHOUSE TOWER

TRIANON TOUR ENDS

TEMPLE OF LOVE

THE HAMLET

PORTE ST. ANTOINE

See detail map

BOULEVARD SAINT-ANTOINE

WALKING TIMES

Train Station to Château = 10 min
Château to Grand Trianon = 30 min
Grand Trianon to the Hamlet = 15 min
Trianon/Domaine to Versailles R.G./Château Station = 55 min

T Petit Train Stop
B TRI Shuttle Bus

BOULEVARD DU ROI

AVE. DU GENERAL LECLERC

AVENUE DE BASSEUX

BOULEVARD DE LA REINE

RUE SAINT-JOSEPH

TOWN

RUE DU MARECHAL DE LATTRE DE TASSIGNY

Shuttle Bus
B RUE DU MARECHAL FOCH
RIVE DROITE
SNCF TRAIN STATION

To Paris
(St. Lazare Station)

200 Meters
200 Yards

Nov-March, and on other days when there are no Spectacles. You'll pay on Sat-Sun as well as on many Tue and Fri, when the Spectacles take place (see "Spectacles in the Gardens," later).

Passes: The following passes can save money and allow you to skip ticket-buying lines (but not the long security checks).

The Paris Museum Pass (see page 58) covers the Château and the Trianon/Domaine area (a €30 value) and is the best solution for most. It doesn't include the Gardens on Spectacle days.

The **Le Passeport** pass (€20) covers the Château and the Trianon/Domaine area. On Spectacle days, it's €27. You can add an English language tour for €10 and skip security lines.

Hours: The **Château** is open April-Oct Tue-Sun 9:00-18:30, Nov-March Tue-Sun until 17:30, closed Mon year-round.

The **Trianon Palaces and Domaine de Marie-Antoinette** are open April-Oct Tue-Sun 12:00-18:30, Nov-March until 17:30, closed Mon year-round (off-season only the two Trianon Palaces and the Hamlet are open, not other outlying buildings), last entry 45 minutes before closing.

The **Gardens** are open April-Oct daily 8:00-20:30, Nov-March until 18:00, but may close earlier for special events.

Buying Passes and Tickets: Ideally, buy your pass or ticket before arriving at the palace. You can purchase Versailles tickets at any Paris TI, FNAC department store (small fee), or at www.chateauversailles.fr.

If you arrive in Versailles without a pass or a ticket, the **GuidaTours** office (across from the train station, under the stone arch at #10) sells Château tickets (€18) as well as VIP skip-the-line tickets (€30; you'll leave from their office, go directly in with the group, then disperse; departures with demand, still some security line wait). I'd consider their VIP tickets on busy days. Skip their €40 guided tour ticket. The **Versailles TI** also sells tickets (for a fee; near the train station—see "Information," later).

Your last and (usually) worst option is to buy a pass or ticket at the busy **Château ticket-sales office** (to the left as you face the palace). Ticket windows accept American credit cards. For the ticket machines (in back) you'll need bills or a credit card with a PIN.

Crowd-Beating Strategies: Versailles is packed May-Sept 9:30-14:00, so come early or late. Avoid holidays, Sundays, Tuesdays, and Saturdays (in that order), when the place is jammed all day. To skip the ticket-buying line, buy a pass or ticket in advance, or book a guided tour. Everyone must go through the same two (often slow) security checkpoints: at the Château's courtyard entry and again at the Château entrance (longest lines 10:00-12:00). Consider seeing the Château late in the afternoon, when crowds die down.

Pickpockets: Assume pickpockets are working the tourist crowds.

Information: Check the excellent website for updates and special events—www.chateauversailles.fr. The palace's general contact number is tel. 01 30 83 78 00. You'll pass the city TI on your walk from the train station to the palace—it's just past the Pullman Hôtel and sells palace tickets (10 percent fee, open Tue-Sun 8:30-19:00, Mon 9:30-18:00, shorter hours in winter, free Wi-Fi, tel. 01 39 24 88 88). The information office at the Château is to the left as you face the palace (WCs, toll tel. 08 10 81 16 14).

Tours: The 1.5-hour English **guided tour** gives you access to a few extra rooms (the itinerary varies) and lets you skip the regular security line (€10, plus €18 palace entry if you don't have it; generally at least 5 tours in English between 9:00 and 15:00 April-Oct; off-season likely only at 9:30 and 14:00). Book in advance on the palace's website, or reserve immediately upon arrival at the guided-tours office (to the right of the Château, good WCs). Tours often sell out by 12:00 (and sometimes by 10:00), though more are usually available than indicated online.

A free and worthwhile **audioguide** to the Château is included in your admission. Other podcasts and digital tours are available in the "multimedia" section at www.chateauversailles.fr.

🎧 Download my free Versailles **audio tour.** (Note that my tour and the included palace audioguide complement each other—"A" students enjoy listening to both.)

Baggage Check: Free and located just after Château entry security. You must retrieve your items one hour before closing (maximum size is same as airlines allow for carry-on bags). Large bags and baby strollers are not allowed in the Château and the two Trianons.

Services: WCs are plentiful and well-signed in the Château, but fewer and farther between in the Gardens.

Eating: At the Château, the **$ Grand Café d'Orléans** offers good-value self-service meals (sandwiches and small salads, great for picnicking in the Gardens). In the Gardens, you'll find several cafés and snack stands with fair prices. One is located near the Latona Fountain (less crowded) and others are in an atmospheric cluster at the Grand Canal (more crowds and more choices, including two restaurants).

Across from the train station, there's a McDonald's, a Starbucks (both with WCs), and the Ibis hotel's buffet breakfast (perfect for early birds). In Versailles town center, the best choices are on the lively Place du Marché Notre-Dame, with a

Kings and Queens and Guillotines

• *You could read this on the train ride to Versailles. Relax...the palace is the last stop.*

Come the Revolution, when they line us up and make us stick out our hands, will you have enough calluses to keep them from shooting you? A grim thought, but Versailles raises these kinds of questions. It's the architectural embodiment of the *ancien régime,* a time when society was divided into rulers and the ruled, when you were born to be rich or to be poor. To some it's the pinnacle of civilization; to others, the sign of a civilization in decay. Either way, it remains one of Europe's most impressive sights.

Versailles was the residence of the king and the seat of France's government for a hundred years. Louis XIV (r. 1643-1715) moved out of the Louvre in Paris, the previous royal residence, and built an elaborate palace in the forests and swamps of Versailles, 10 miles west. The reasons for the move were partly personal—Louis XIV loved the outdoors and disliked the sniping environs of stuffy Paris—and partly political.

Louis XIV was creating the first modern, centralized state. At Versailles, he consolidated his government's scattered ministries so that he could personally control policy. More importantly, he invited France's nobles to Versailles in order to control them. Living a life of almost enforced idleness, the "domesticated" aristocracy couldn't interfere with the way Louis ran things. With 18 million people united under one king (England had only 5.5 million), a booming economy, and a powerful military, France was Europe's number-one power.

Around 1700, Versailles was the cultural heartbeat of Europe, and French culture was at its zenith. Throughout Europe, when you said "the king," you were referring to the French king—Louis XIV. Every king wanted a palace like Versailles. Everyone learned French. French taste in clothes, hairstyles, table manners, theater, music, art, and kissing spread across the Continent. That cultural dominance continued, to some extent, right up to the 20th century.

Louis XIV

At the center of all this was Europe's greatest king. He was a true Renaissance Man, a century after the Renaissance: athletic, good-looking, a musician, dancer, horseman, statesman, patron of the

supermarket nearby, or along traffic-free Rue de Satory, on the opposite (south) side as you leave the Château.

Spectacles in the Gardens: The Gardens and fountains at Versailles come alive at selected times, offering a glimpse into Louis XIV's remarkable world. The Sun King had his engineers literally reroute a river to fuel his fountains and feed his plants. Even by today's standards, the fountains are impres-

arts, and lover. For all his grandeur, he was one of history's most polite and approachable kings, a good listener who could put even commoners at ease in his presence.

Louis XIV called himself the Sun King because he gave life and warmth to all he touched. He was also thought of as Apollo, the Greek god of the sun. Versailles became the personal temple of this god on earth, decorated with statues and symbols of Apollo, the sun, and Louis XIV himself. The classical themes throughout underlined the divine right of France's kings and queens to rule without limit.

Louis XIV was a hands-on king who personally ran affairs of state. All decisions were made by him. Nobles, who in other countries were the center of power, became virtual slaves dependent on Louis XIV's generosity. For 70 years he was the perfect embodiment of the absolute monarch. He summed it up best himself with his famous expression—*"L'état, c'est moi!"* (lay-tah say-mwah): "The state, that's me!"

Another Louis or Two to Remember

Three kings lived in Versailles during its century of glory. Louis XIV built it and established French dominance. Louis XV, his great-grandson (Louis XIV reigned for 72 years), carried on the tradition and policies, but without the Sun King's flair. During Louis XV's reign (1715-1774), France's power abroad was weakening, and there were rumblings of rebellion from within.

France's monarchy was crumbling, and the time was ripe for a strong leader to reestablish the old feudal order. They didn't get one. Instead, they got Louis XVI (r. 1774-1792), a shy, meek bookworm, the kind of guy who lost sleep over revolutionary graffiti... because it was misspelled. Louis XVI married a sweet girl from the Austrian royal family, Marie-Antoinette, and together they retreated into the idyllic gardens of Versailles while revolutionary fires smoldered.

sive. Check the Versailles website for current hours and to find out what else might be happening during your visit.

On nonwinter weekends, the Gardens' fountains are in full squirt. The whole production, called **Les Grandes Eaux Musicales,** involves 55 fountains gushing for an hour in the morning, then again for about two hours in the afternoon, all accompanied by loud classical music (€9.50; early April-late Oct Sat-Sun 11:00-12:00 & 15:30-17:00, Tue mid-May-June 11:00-12:00 & 14:30-16:30, plus some Fri—check www.chateauversailles.fr). Pay at the entrance to the Gardens, unless you've bought Le Passeport—in which case you've already paid (automatically tacked on to Passeport price on Spectacle days).

Even on high-season Tue and Fri when the fountains don't run, you still get all-day music with the **Les Jardins Musicaux** program (€9.50, April-mid-May and July-Oct 10:00-18:30).

On certain summer weekend nights you get the big shebang: **Les Grandes Eaux Nocturnes,** which presents whimsical lighted displays leading between gushing fountains and a fireworks show over the largest fountain pool (€26-42, mid-June-mid-Sept Sat 20:30-22:40, fireworks at 22:50). On these nights, the Royal Serenade option lets you go into the palace with costumed characters (€42 combo-ticket).

Starring: Luxurious palaces, endless gardens, Louis XIV, Marie-Antoinette, and the *ancien régime*.

❍ SELF-GUIDED TOUR

On this self-guided tour, you'll see the Château (the State Apartments of the king as well as the Hall of Mirrors), the landscaped Gardens in the "backyard," and the Trianon Palaces and Domaine de Marie-Antoinette, located at the far end of the Gardens. If your time is limited or you don't enjoy walking, I give you permission to skip the Trianon/Domaine, which is a hefty 30-minute hike (each way) from the Château.

This commentary covers the basics. For background, first read the "Kings and Queens and Guillotines" sidebar. For a detailed room-by-room rundown, consider the guidebook called *The Châteaux, the Gardens, and Trianon* (sold at Versailles).

The Château

• *Stand in the huge courtyard and face the palace. The golden Royal Gate in the center of the courtyard—nearly 260 feet long and decorated with 100,000 gold leaves—is a replica of the original. If you don't already have a pass or ticket, the ticket-sales office is to the left; guided-tour sales are to the right. The entrance to the Château is marked Entrance A (where the line usually is). Before entering (or while standing in line*

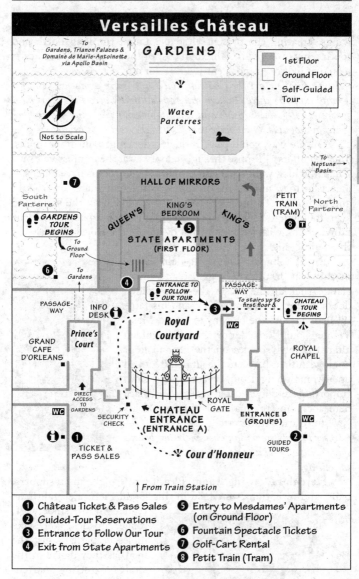

Versailles Château

GARDENS

- 1st Floor
- Ground Floor
- - - - Self-Guided Tour

To Gardens, Trianon Palaces & Domaine de Marie-Antoinette via Apollo Basin

Water Parterres

Not to Scale

To Neptune Basin

South Parterre

GARDENS TOUR BEGINS

To Ground Floor

To Gardens

HALL OF MIRRORS

KING'S BEDROOM

QUEEN'S

KING'S

STATE APARTMENTS (FIRST FLOOR)

PETIT TRAIN (TRAM)

North Parterre

ENTRANCE TO FOLLOW OUR TOUR

PASSAGE-WAY

To stairs up to first floor &

CHATEAU TOUR BEGINS

PASSAGE-WAY

INFO DESK

Royal Courtyard

WC

Prince's Court

GRAND CAFE D'ORLEANS

DIRECT ACCESS TO GARDENS

SECURITY CHECK

ROYAL CHAPEL

CHATEAU ENTRANCE (ENTRANCE A)

ROYAL GATE

ENTRANCE B (GROUPS)

WC

WC

TICKET & PASS SALES

GUIDED TOURS

Cour d'Honneur

↑ From Train Station

1. Château Ticket & Pass Sales
2. Guided-Tour Reservations
3. Entrance to Follow Our Tour
4. Exit from State Apartments
5. Entry to Mesdames' Apartments (on Ground Floor)
6. Fountain Spectacle Tickets
7. Golf-Cart Rental
8. Petit Train (Tram)

at the entrance), take in the Château and the open-air courtyard on the other side of the golden Royal Gate.

The section of the palace with the clock is the original château, once a small hunting lodge where little Louis XIV spent his happiest boyhood years. Naturally, the Sun King's private bedroom (the three arched windows beneath the clock) faced the rising sun. The palace and grounds are laid out on an east-west axis.

Once king, Louis XIV expanded the lodge by attaching wings, creating the present U-shape. Later, the long north and south wings were built. The total cost of the project has been estimated at half of France's entire GNP for one year.

• *As you finally enter the Château, you'll find an information desk (get a map) and bag check. Follow the crowds directly across the courtyard, where you'll go back inside and line up for your free (and worth-the-wait) audioguide. Now make your way to the start of our tour.*

On the way, you'll pass through a dozen ground-floor rooms. The first offers a glimpse through a doorway at the impressive Royal Chapel, which we'll see again upstairs. Later rooms have videos of palace history, models of Versailles at different stages of growth, and paintings of Louis XIV, XV, and XVI. Climb the stairs and keep following the flow. You'll eventually reach a palatial golden-brown room, with a doorway that overlooks the Royal Chapel. Let the tour begin.

Royal Chapel: Dut-dutta-dah! Every morning at 10:00, the organist and musicians struck up the music, these big golden doors opened, and Louis XIV and his family stepped onto the balcony to attend Mass. While Louis looked down on the golden altar, the lowly nobles on the ground floor knelt with their backs to the altar and looked up—worshipping Louis worshipping God. Important religious ceremonies took place here, including the marriage of young Louis XVI to Marie-Antoinette.

• *Enter the next room, an even more sumptuous space with a fireplace and a colorful painting on the ceiling.*

Hercules Drawing Room: Pleasure ruled. The main suppers, balls, and receptions were held in this room. Picture elegant par-

tygoers in fine silks, wigs, rouge, lipstick, and fake moles (and that's just the men) as they dance to the strains of a string quartet.

On the wall opposite the fireplace is an appropriate painting showing Christ in the middle of a Venetian party. The work—by Paolo Veronese, a gift from the Republic of Venice—was one of Louis XIV's favorites, so the king had the room decorated around it.

• *From here on it's a one-way tour—getting lost is not allowed.*

The King's Wing: The names of the rooms generally come from the paintings on the ceilings. For instance, the **Venus Room** was the royal make-out space, where couples would cavort beneath the goddess of love, floating on the ceiling. In the **Diana Room,** Louis and his men played pool on a table that stood in the center of the room, while ladies sat surrounding them on Persian-carpet cushions, and music wafted in from next door. Louis was a good pool player, a sore loser, and a king—thus, he rarely lost.

Also known as the Guard Room (as it was the room for Louis' Swiss bodyguards), the **Red Room** is decorated with a military flair. The **Mercury Room** may have served as Louis' official (not actual) bedroom, where the Sun King would ritually rise each morning to warm his subjects. The **Apollo Room** was the grand throne room. Louis held court from a 10-foot-tall, silver-and-gold canopied throne on a raised platform placed in the center of the room (the platform is there, though not the throne). Even when the king was away, passing courtiers had to bow to the empty throne.

The final room of the King's Wing is the **War Room,** depicting Louis' victories—in marble, gilding, stucco, and paint.

• *Next you'll visit the magnificent...*

Hall of Mirrors: No one had ever seen anything like this hall when it was opened. Mirrors were still a great luxury at the time,

and the number and size of these monsters was astounding. The hall is nearly 250 feet long. There are 17 arched mirrors, matched by 17 windows letting in that breathtaking view of the Gardens. Imagine this place lit by the flames of thousands of candles, filled with ambassadors, nobles, and guests dressed in silks and powdered wigs. At the far end of the room sits the king, on the canopied throne moved in temporarily from the Apollo Room. Servants glide by with silver trays of hors d'oeuvres, and an orchestra fuels the festivities. The mirrors reflect an age when beautiful people loved to look at themselves.

In another age altogether, Germany and the Allies signed the Treaty of Versailles, ending World War I (and, some say, starting World War II) right here, in the Hall of Mirrors.

• *Partway down the Hall of Mirrors, turn left through the heart of the palace, to the...*

King's Bedroom and Council Rooms: Louis XIV's bedroom is elaborately decorated, and the decor changed with the season. Look out the window and notice how this small room is at the

Getting Around the Gardens

On Foot: It's a 45-minute walk without stops from the palace, down to the Grand Canal, past the two Trianon palaces, to the Hamlet at the far end of Domaine de Marie-Antoinette.

By Bike: A bike-rental station is by the Grand Canal. A bike won't save you that much time, and you can't take it inside the grounds of the Trianon/Domaine, but it's fun pedaling around the greatest royal park in Europe (about €8/hour or €18/half-day, kid-size bikes and tandems available, daily 10:00-18:30).

By *Petit Train*: The slow-moving hop-on, hop-off tram leaves from behind the Château (see map on page 189) and makes a one-way loop, stopping at the Grand Trianon and Petit Trianon (entry points to Domaine de Marie-Antoinette), then the Grand Canal before returning to the Château (€8 round-trip, €4.50 one-way, free for kids 10 and under, 4/hour, Tue-Sun 11:30-19:00, Mon 11:00-17:00, shorter hours in winter).

By Golf Cart: These make for a fun drive through the Gardens, but you can't drive it in the Trianon/Domaine, and there are steep late fees. To go out to the Hamlet, sightsee quickly, and get back within your allotted hour, rent at the Grand Canal and put the pedal to the metal (€32/hour, €8.50/15 minutes after that, 4-person limit per cart, rental stations by the canal and behind the Château—near the *petit train* stop). Return your cart to the place you started.

By Shuttle Bus: Phébus runs an hourly "TRI" shuttle bus between the train station (Versailles Rive Gauche/Château, leaves from curb directly in front of station) and the Trianon/Domaine (doesn't stop at the Château). It's ideal if you're visiting the Trianon/Domaine first, before the Château, or if you want to return to the station straight from the Trianon/Domaine (€2—pay driver, or one Métro ticket, May-late Aug only, check current schedule for "Ligne TRI" at www.phebus.tm.fr). Buses depart from the train station Tue-Sun at :40 after the hour 8:40-19:40, and from a stop near the Trianon at :08 after the hour 9:08-20:08 (see the "Domaine de Marie-Antoinette map," later). Schedules are available at the Phébus office across from the train station (closed at lunch and on weekends).

exact center of the immense horseshoe-shaped building, overlooking the main courtyard and—naturally—facing the rising sun in the east. It symbolized the exact center of power in France.

• *This ends our tour of the Château. The* **Queen's Wing** *of the Château will most likely have reopened when you visit after an extensive renovation. (If it's open, you'll pass through an additional half-dozen sparkling rooms where France's queens had their apartments.) Otherwise, you'll make your way toward the exit through several unremarkable rooms (described in the audioguide).*

The Gardens

Louis XIV was a divine-right ruler. One way he proved it was by controlling nature like a god. These lavish grounds—elaborately

planned, pruned, and decorated—showed everyone that Louis was in total command. Louis loved his gardens and, until his last days, presided over their care. He personally led VIPs through them and threw his biggest parties here. With their Greco-Roman themes and incomparable beauty, the Gardens further illustrated his immense power.

The Gardens are vast. For some, a stroll through the landscaped shrubs around the Château and quick view down the Royal Drive is plenty. But it's worth the 10-minute walk down the Royal Drive to the Apollo Basin and back (even if you don't continue further to the Trianon/Domaine). To trace the route of this tour, see the "Versailles" map earlier in this chapter.

As you walk, consider that a thousand orange trees were once stored beneath your feet in greenhouses. On sunny days, they were wheeled out in their silver planters and scattered around the grounds. The warmth from the Sun King was so great that he could even grow orange trees in chilly France.

With the palace behind you, it seems as if the grounds stretch out forever. Versailles was laid out along an eight-mile axis that included the grounds, the palace, and the town of Versailles itself, one of the first instances of urban planning since Roman times and a model for future capitals, such as Washington, DC, and Brasilia. A promenade leads from the palace to the Grand Canal, where France's royalty floated up and down in imported Venetian gondolas.

Trianon Palaces and Domaine de Marie-Antoinette

Versailles began as an escape from the pressures of kingship. But in a short time, the Château became as busy as Paris ever was. Louis XIV needed an escape from his escape, so he built a smaller palace out in the boonies. Later, his successors retreated still farther from the Château and French political life, ignoring the

real world that was crumbling all around them. They expanded the Trianon area, building a fantasy world of palaces, ponds, pavilions, and pleasure gardens—the enclosure called Marie-Antoinette's Domaine.

Grand Trianon: Delicate, pink, and set amid gardens, the Grand Trianon was the perfect summer getaway. This was the king's private residence away from the main palace. Louis XIV usually spent a couple of nights a week here (more in the summer) to escape the sniping politics, strict etiquette, and 24/7 scrutiny of official court life.

Louis XIV built the palace (1670-1688) near the tiny peasant village of Trianon (hence the name) and faced it with blue-and-white ceramic tiles. When those began disintegrating almost immediately, the palace was renovated with pink marble. It's a one-story structure of two wings connected by a colonnade, with gardens in back.

• *To enter the Grand Trianon, you must first pass through its security checkpoint. Pick up the free palace brochure and follow the simple one-way route through the rooms.*

The rooms are a complex overlay of furnishings from many different kings, dauphins, and nobles who lived here over the centuries. Louis XIV alone had three different bedrooms. Concentrate on the illustrious time of Louis XIV (1688-1715) and Napoleon Bonaparte (1810-1814). Use your map to find the Mirror Room, Louis XIV's Bedchamber, the Emperor's Family Drawing Room, and the Malachite Room (Napoleon's living room).

Domaine de Marie-Antoinette: Near the Grand Trianon are the **French Pavilion** (small cream-colored building where Marie-Antoinette spent summer evenings with family and a few friends), **Marie-Antoinette's Theater,** and the octagonal **Belvedere** palace.

You'll find the **Hamlet** 10 minutes past the Belvedere palace. Marie-Antoinette longed for the simple life of a peasant—not the hard labor of real peasants, who sweated and starved around her, but the fairy-tale world of simple country pleasures. She built this complex of 12 thatched-roof buildings fronting a lake as her own private "Normand" village. The main building is the Queen's House—actually two buildings connected by a wooden skywalk.

Domaine de Marie-Antoinette

Petit Canal

HORSESHOE FOUNTAIN

200 Meters
200 Yards

EXIT

GRAND TRIANON

WC

WALK BEGINS

ALLÉE DE LA REINE

From Château

To Grand Canal, Apollo Basin & Château

WC

WALK ENDS

WALL

AVE. DE TRIANON

AVE. DE PETIT TRIANON

FRENCH PAVILION

THEATER

BELVEDERE

ROCK — GROTTO

PETIT TRIANON

To Château

TEMPLE OF LOVE

ALLÉE ST. ANTOINE

FARM

WALL

ALLÉE DU RENDEZVOUS

LIGHTHOUSE TOWER

MILL

PIGEON COOP

THE HAMLET

QUEEN'S HOUSE

PORTE ST. ANTOINE

T Petit Train Stop
B TRI Shuttle Bus

B TRI Shuttle Bus

To Château

It's the only one without a thatched roof. Like any typical peasant farmhouse, it had a billiard room, library, elegant dining hall, and two living rooms.

After touring the Hamlet, head back toward the Petit Trianon. Along the way (in about five minutes), you'll see the white dome of the **Temple of Love.** The gray, cubical **Petit Trianon** from the 1760s is a masterpiece of Neoclassical architecture, built by the same architect (Ange-Jacques Gabriel) who created the Opera House in the main palace. It has four distinct facades,

each a perfect and harmonious combination of Greek-style columns, windows, and railings.

Louis XV built the Petit Trianon as a place to rendezvous with his mistress Madame de Pompadour. He later gave it to his next mistress, Countess du Barry. After the crown passed to Louis XVI, it became the principal residence of Marie-Antoinette, who was uncomfortable with the court intrigue in the big Château. As you tour the Petit Trianon, you'll see portraits and historical traces of this intriguing cast of characters.

Marie-Antoinette made the Petit Trianon her home base. On the lawn outside, she installed a carousel. Despite her bad reputation with the public, Marie-Antoinette was a sweet girl from Vienna who never quite fit in with the fast, sophisticated crowd at Versailles. At the Petit Trianon, she could get away and re-create the charming home life that she remembered from her childhood. Here she played, while in the cafés of faraway Paris, revolutionaries plotted the end of the *ancien régime*.

TOWN OF VERSAILLES

The town of Versailles gives an opportunity to enjoy a classic, small French town that doesn't feel touristy, and can be a good overnight stop, especially for drivers. Park in the palace's main lot while looking for a hotel, or leave your car there overnight (see page 180).

The pleasant town center—around Place du Marché Notre-Dame—hosts a thriving open market defined by four L-shaped halls. The two halls closest to the palace (Carré à la Marée and Carré aux Herbes, Tue-Sat 7:30-13:00 & 15:30-19:00, Sun 7:30-13:00, closed Mon) are worth a wander. The square itself hosts regular markets (food market Sun, Tue, and Fri mornings until 13:00; clothing market all day Wed-Thu and Sat). Nearby streets have a variety of reasonably priced restaurants, cafés, and shops.

SLEEPING IN VERSAILLES

$ **Hôtel de France***** is in a 17th-century townhouse just outside the gates of the palace. It offers Old World class, mostly air-conditioned, traditional rooms with thick tapestries and rugs, a pleasant courtyard, a bar, and a restaurant (23 rooms, just off parking lot across from Château at 5 Rue Colbert, tel. 01 30 83 92 23, www.hoteldefranceversailles.com, reception@hdfversailles.com).

$ **Hôtel le Cheval Rouge,***** built in 1676 as Louis XIV's stables, now boards tourists. Tucked into a corner of Place du Marché, this modest hotel has a big courtyard with pay parking and sufficiently comfortable rooms connected by long halls (40 rooms, no air-con, 18 Rue André Chénier, tel. 01 39 50 03 03, www.chevalrougeversailles.fr, chevalrouge@sfr.fr).

$ **Hôtel Ibis Versailles***** offers a good weekend value and modern comfort, with 85 air-conditioned rooms (good buffet breakfast open to public and served daily until 10:00; pay parking, across from train station at 4 Avenue du Général de Gaulle, tel. 01 39 53 03 30, www.ibishotel.com, h1409@accor.com).

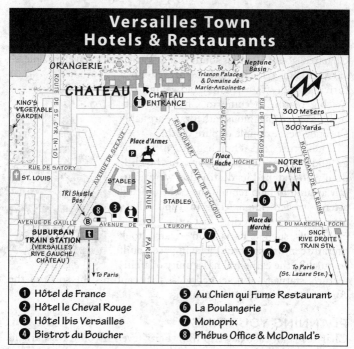

Versailles Town Hotels & Restaurants

❶ Hôtel de France
❷ Hôtel le Cheval Rouge
❸ Hôtel Ibis Versailles
❹ Bistrot du Boucher
❺ Au Chien qui Fume Restaurant
❻ La Boulangerie
❼ Monoprix
❽ Phébus Office & McDonald's

EATING IN VERSAILLES

The Place du Marché Notre-Dame market square—a 15-minute walk from the Château (veer left as you leave the Château)—is lined with colorful and inexpensive eateries with good seating inside and out. Troll the various options or try one of these:

$$$ Bistrot du Boucher reeks with fun character inside and has good seating outside. They like their meat dishes best here, though you'll find a full menu of choices (bargain lunch *menu*, daily, 12 Rue André Chénier, tel. 01 39 02 12 15, Nolan).

$$ Au Chien qui Fume is a decent choice, with cozy seating inside and out, a playful staff, and reliable, traditional cuisine (lunch deals, closed Sun, 72 Rue de la Paroisse, tel. 01 39 53 14 56).

$ La Boulangerie has mouthwatering sandwiches, salads, quiches, and more (Tue-Sat until 20:00, Sun until 13:30, closed Mon, 60 Rue de la Paroisse).

Breakfast: The **Hôtel Ibis Versailles,** across from the train station, offers a good buffet breakfast daily until 10:00 (€10.50). It's great for early birds who want to fuel up before sightseeing.

Supermarket: A big **Monoprix** is centrally located between the Versailles Rive Gauche/Château train station and Place du Marché Notre-Dame (entrances from Avenue de l'Europe and at 5 Rue Georges Clemenceau, Mon-Sat 8:30-21:00, closed Sun).

Chartres

Chartres, about 50 miles southwest of Paris, gives travelers a pleasant break in a lively, midsize town with a
thriving, pedestrian-friendly old center. But
the big reason to come to Chartres (shar-
truh) is to see its famous cathedral—arguably
Europe's best example of pure Gothic.

Chartres' old church burned to the
ground on June 10, 1194. Some of the children who watched its destruction were actually around to help rebuild the cathedral and
attend its dedication Mass in 1260. That's
astonishing, considering that other Gothic
cathedrals, such as Paris' Notre-Dame, took
literally centuries to build. Having been built
so quickly, the cathedral has a unity of archi-
tecture, statuary, and stained glass that captures the spirit of the
Age of Faith like no other church.

PLANNING YOUR TIME

Chartres is an easy day trip from Paris (even if you leave Paris in
the afternoon and return later in the evening). But with its statues
glowing in the setting sun—and with hotels and restaurants much
less expensive than those in the capital—Chartres also makes a
worthwhile overnight stop. If you'll be here at night, don't miss
the dazzling light show—Chartres en Lumières—when dozens of
Chartres' most historic buildings are colorfully illuminated, adding to the town's after-hours appeal (mid-April-mid-Oct; details at
TI). Chartres' historic center is quiet Sunday and Monday, when
most shops are closed.

Chartres is a one-hour ride from Paris' Gare Montparnasse
(14/day, about €16 one-way; see the "Paris Connections" section
of the previous chapter for Gare Montparnasse details). Jot down
return times to Paris before you exit the Chartres train station (last
train generally departs Chartres around 21:30).

Upon arrival in Chartres, head for the cathedral. Allow an
hour to savor the church on your own as you follow my self-guided
tour. But don't miss the mesmerizing cathedral tour at noon led
by Malcolm Miller; also consider the informative tour at 14:45 by
Anne-Marie Woods (details on both tours later). Take another
hour or two to wander the appealing old city. On Saturday and
Wednesday mornings, a small outdoor market sets up a few short
blocks from the cathedral on Place Billard.

Orientation to Chartres

Tourist Information: The TI is in the historic Maison du Saumon building (Mon-Sat 10:00-18:00, Sun until 17:00, closes earlier Nov-March, 8 Rue de la Poissonnerie, tel. 02 37 18 26 26, www. chartres-tourisme.com). It offers specifics on cathedral tours and also rents audioguides for the old town (€5.50, €8.50/double set, about 2 hours). Skip the Chartres Pass sold here.

The TI has a small map that shows the floodlit Chartres en Lumières sites, and information on the Petit Train you can take to see them all (check the website or ask at the TI for details).

Arrival in Chartres: Exiting Chartres' **train** station, you'll see the spires of the cathedral dominating the town. It's a 10-minute walk up Avenue Jehan de Beauce to the cathedral. The free minibus, called the Filibus, runs to near the cathedral (line: Relais des Portes, 3/hour, Mon-Sat 8:30-19:00), or you can take a taxi for about €7. The last train to Paris usually leaves around 21:30 (verify for your day of travel).

If arriving **by car,** you'll have fine views of the cathedral and city as you approach from the A-11 autoroute. Pay underground parking is on Place des Epars and Place Châtelet, both a short walk from the cathedral. Free parking is available in the lower medieval town (Parking Trois Détours), a 15-minute uphill walk to the cathedral following my Chartres Walk.

Helpful Hints: To get online, try the free Chartres **Wi-Fi** on Place des Epars or Place Châtelet. A **launderette** is a few blocks from the cathedral (by the TI) at 16a Place de la Poissonnerie (daily 7:00-21:00). If you need to call a **taxi,** try tel. 02 37 36 00 00.

Sights in Chartres

▲▲▲CHARTRES CATHEDRAL

The church is (at least) the fourth one on this spot dedicated to Mary, the mother of Jesus, who has been venerated here for some 1,700 years. There's even speculation that the pagan Romans dedicated a temple here to a mother-goddess. In earliest times, Mary was honored next to a natural spring of healing waters (not visible today).

In 876, the church acquired the torn veil (or birthing gown) supposedly worn by Mary when she gave birth to Jesus. The 2,000-year-old veil (now on display) became the focus of worship at the church. By the 11th century, the cult of saints was strong. And Mary, considered the "Queen of All Saints," was hugely popular. God was enigmatic and scary, but Mary was maternal and accessible, providing a handy go-between for Christians and their Cre-

NEAR PARIS

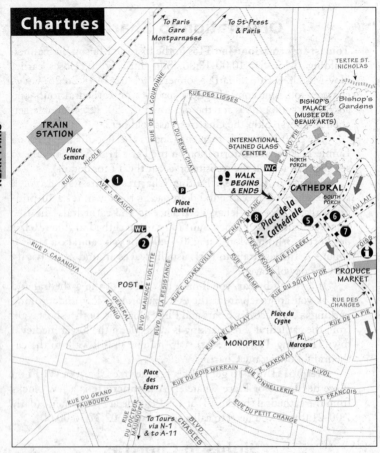

ator. Chartres, a small town of 10,000 with a prized relic, found itself in the big time on the pilgrim circuit.

When the fire of 1194 incinerated the old church, the veil was feared lost. Lo and behold, several days later, townspeople found it miraculously unharmed in the crypt (beneath today's choir). Whether the veil's survival was a miracle or a marketing ploy, the people of Chartres were so stoked, they worked like madmen to erect this grand cathedral in which to display it. Thinkers and scholars gathered here, making the small town with its big-city church a leading center of learning in the Middle Ages (until the focus shifted to Paris' university).

By the way, the church is officially called the Cathédrale Notre-Dame de Chartres. Many travelers think that "Notre-Dame" is in Paris. That's true. But more than a hundred churches dedicated to Mary—"Notre-Dames"—are scattered around France, and Chartres Cathedral is one of them.

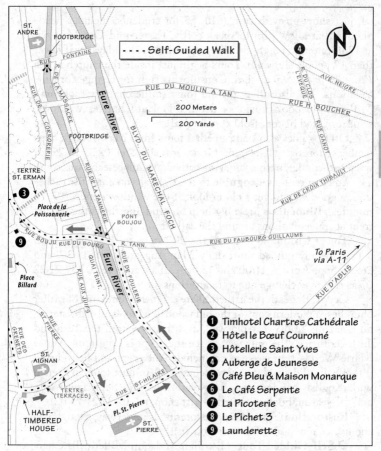

Self-Guided Walk

200 Meters
200 Yards

ST. ANDRE
FOOTBRIDGE
RUE FONTAINE
R. DE LA MASSACRE
RUE DE LA CORROIRERIE
Eure River
RUE DU MOULIN A TAN
RUE H. BOUCHER
R. DES CLOS L'EVEQUE
AVE. NEIGRE
RUE GANOT
BLVD. DU MARECHAL FOCH
FOOTBRIDGE
RUE DE LA TANNERIE
TERTRE ST. ERMAN
Place de la Poissonnerie
PONT BOUJOU
RUE DE CROIX THIBAULT
RUE BOUJU
RUE DU BOURG
R. TANN
RUE DU FAUBOURG GUILLAUME
To Paris via A-11
RUE D'ABLIS
Place Billard
QUAI TEINT
RUE AUX JUIFS
RUE DE FOULERIE
Eure River
RUE DES GRENETS
RUE ST. PIERRE
ST. AIGNAN
TERTRE (TERRACES)
RUE ST-HILAIRE
Pl. St. Pierre
HALF-TIMBERED HOUSE
ST. PIERRE

❶ Timhotel Chartres Cathédrale
❷ Hôtel le Bœuf Couronné
❸ Hôtellerie Saint Yves
❹ Auberge de Jeunesse
❺ Café Bleu & Maison Monarque
❻ Le Café Serpente
❼ La Picoterie
❽ Le Pichet 3
❾ Launderette

Cathedral: Free to enter, open daily 8:30-19:30. Mass usually Mon-Sat at 11:45 (in the crypt), daily at 18:00, plus Sun also at 9:00 (Gregorian) and 11:00. Confirm times by phone or online—tel. 02 37 21 59 08, www. cathedrale-chartres.org (click "Infos Pratiques," then "Horaires des Messes").

Cathedral Tours: A fascinating English scholar who moved here almost 60 years ago at age 24, **Malcolm Miller** has dedicated his life to studying this cathedral and sharing its wonder through his guided lecture tours. He's slowing down a bit, but his 1.25-hour tours are still riveting even if you've taken my self-guided tour. No reservation is need-

ed; just show up with cash (€10, €5 for students, includes head-phones that allow him to speak softly, Easter-mid-Oct Mon-Sat at 12:00; no tours on Sun in Aug, on religious holidays, or if fewer than 12 people show up). Tours begin just inside the church at the *Visites de la Cathédrale* sign. Consult this sign for changes or can-cellations. He also offers private tours (millerchartres@aol.com). Miller's guidebook provides a detailed look at Chartres' windows, sculpture, and history (sold at cathedral).

Other guides also lead cathedral tours from May through Sep-tember (Mon-Sat at 14:45, meet inside gift shop, tel. 02 37 21 75 02, www.cathedrale-chartres.org, visitecathedrale@diocesechartres.com).

You can rent a **videoguide** to the right as you enter the cathe-dral, a good way to get a closer look at the window details (€7, 70 minutes). **Binoculars** are a big help for studying the cathedral art (rent at souvenir shops around the cathedral).

Tower Climb: €6 to climb the 200 steps to the rooftop with a French-only guided tour; daily May-Aug at 11:00, 14:30, and 16:00, Sept-April at 11:00 and 15:00; call ahead at tel. 02 37 21 22 07 as this may change due to renovations.

Crypt: Beneath the cathedral are extensive remnants of earlier churches, a modern copy of the old wooden Mary-and-baby statue, an amazing 2,000-year-old well, and frescoes from the 12th and 13th centuries. The only way to see the crypt is on a tour. Anne-Marie Woods' tour (see earlier) includes the crypt and helps bring it to life, but I'd avoid the more frequent 30-minute tours in French with English handout (€4, 5/day late June-mid-Sept, fewer Sun and off-season, book at cathedral gift shop, tel. 02 37 21 75 02).

Restoration: A multiyear restoration is underway, though you should see few signs of it when you visit.

◑ Self-Guided Tour: Historian Malcolm Miller calls Char-tres a picture book of the entire Christian story, told through its statues, stained glass, and architecture. In this "Book of Chartres," the text is the sculpture and windows, and its binding is the ar-chitecture. The complete narrative can be read—from Creation to Christ's birth (north side of church), from Christ and his followers up to the present (south entrance), and then to the end of time, when Christ returns as judge (west entrance). The remarkable co-hesiveness of the text and the unity of the architecture are due to the fact that nearly the entire church was rebuilt in just 30 years (a blink of an eye for cathedral building).

• *Start outside, taking in the...*

❶ Main Entrance (West Facade): Chartres' soaring (if mis-matched) steeples announce to pilgrims that they've arrived. Com-pare the **towers.** The right (south) tower, with a Romanesque stone

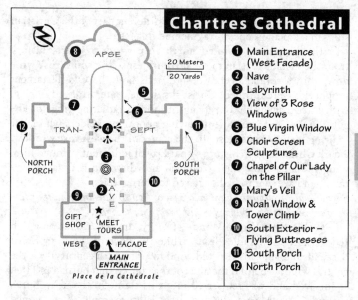

Chartres Cathedral

❶ Main Entrance (West Facade)
❷ Nave
❸ Labyrinth
❹ View of 3 Rose Windows
❺ Blue Virgin Window
❻ Choir Screen Sculptures
❼ Chapel of Our Lady on the Pillar
❽ Mary's Veil
❾ Noah Window & Tower Climb
❿ South Exterior – Flying Buttresses
⓫ South Porch
⓬ North Porch

NEAR PARIS

steeple, survived the fire. The left (north) tower lost its wooden steeple in the fire. In the 1500s, it was topped with the flamboyant Gothic steeple we see today.

• *Enter the church (from a side entrance if the main one is closed) and wait for your pupils to enlarge.*

❷ **Nave:** The place is huge—the nave is 427 feet long, 20 feet wide, and 120 feet high. Try to picture the church in the Middle Ages—painted in greens, browns, and golds (like colorful St. Aignan Church in the old town). It was packed with pilgrims, and was a rough cross between a hostel, a soup kitchen, and a flea market. Taking it all in from the nave, notice that, as was typical in medieval churches, the windows on the darker north side feature Old Testament themes—awaiting the light of Christ's arrival. And the windows on the brighter south side are New Testament.

• *On the floor, midway up the nave, find the...*

❸ **Labyrinth:** The broad, round labyrinth inlaid in black marble on the floor is a spiritual journey. Labyrinths like this were common in medieval churches. Pilgrims enter from the west rim, by foot or on their knees, and wind around, meditating, on a metaphorical journey to Jerusalem. About 900 feet later, they hope to meet God in the middle.

• *Walk up the nave to where the transept crosses. As you face the altar and gleaming choir, north is to the left.*

❹ **The Rose Windows:** The three big, round "rose" (flower-shaped) windows over the entrances receive sunlight at different times of day. All three are predominantly blue and red, but each has different "petals," and each tells a different part of the Christian story in a kaleidoscope of fragmented images.

The brilliantly restored **north rose window** charts history from the distant past up to the birth of Jesus. The **south rose window,** with a similar overall design, tells how the Old Testament prophecies were fulfilled. Christ sits in the center (dressed in blue, with a red background), setting in motion radiating rings of angels, beasts, and instrument-playing apocalyptic elders who labor to bring history to its close. In the center of the **west rose window,** a dark Christ rings in history's final Day of Judgment. Around him, winged angels blow their trumpets and the dead rise, face judgment, and are sent to hell or raised to eternal bliss.

• *Now walk around the altar to the right (south) side and find the window with a big, blue Mary (second one from the right).*

❺ **The Blue Virgin Window:** Mary, dressed in blue on a rich red background, cradles Jesus, while the dove of the Holy Spirit descends on her. This very old window (mid-12th century) was the central window behind the altar of the church that burned in 1194. It survived and was reinserted into this frame in the new church around 1230. Mary's glowing dress is an example of the famed "Chartres blue," a sumptuous color made by mixing cobalt oxide into the glass (before cheaper materials were introduced).

• *Now turn around and look behind you.*

❻ **The Choir Screen: Life of Mary:** The choir (enclosed area around the altar where church officials sat) is the heart *(coeur)* of the church. A stone screen rings it with **41 statue groups** illustrating Mary's life. The **plain windows** surrounding the choir date from the 1770s, when the dark mystery of medieval stained glass was replaced by the open light of the French Enlightenment.

• *Do an about-face and find the chapel with Mary on a pillar.*

❼ **Chapel of Our Lady on the Pillar:** A 16th-century statue of Mary and baby—draped in cloth, crowned and sceptered—sits on a 13th-century column in a wonderful carved-wood alcove. This is today's pilgrimage center, built to keep visitors from clogging up the altar area.

• *Double back a bit around the ambulatory, heading toward the back of the church. In the next chapel you encounter (Chapel of the Sacred Heart of Mary), you'll find a gold frame holding a fragment of Mary's venerated veil. These days it's kept—for its safety and preservation—out of the light and behind bulletproof glass.*

❽ **Mary's Veil:** This veil (or tunic) was supposedly worn by Mary when she gave birth to Jesus. In the frenzy surrounding the fire of 1194, the veil mysteriously disappeared, only to reappear three days later (recalling the Resurrection). This was interpreted by church officials and the townsfolk as a sign from Mary that she wanted a new church, and thus the building began.

• *Return to the west end and find the last window on the right (near the tower entrance).*

❾ The Noah Window and Tower Climb: Read Chartres' windows in the medieval style: from bottom to top. In the bottom diamond, God tells Noah he'll destroy the earth. Next, Noah hefts an axe to build an ark, while his son hauls wood (diamond #2). Two by two, he loads horses (cloverleaf, above left), purple elephants (cloverleaf, right), and other animals. The psychedelic ark sets sail (diamond #3). Waves cover the earth and drown the wicked (two cloverleafs). The ark survives (diamond #4), and Noah releases a dove. Finally, up near the top (diamond #7), a rainbow (symbolizing God's promise never to bring another flood) arches overhead, God drapes himself over it, and Noah and his family give thanks.

• *To climb the north tower, you'll need to join a tour (see page 202). Then exit the church through the main entrance or the door in the south transept to view its south side.*

❿ South Exterior: Flying Buttresses: Six flying buttresses (the arches that stick out from the upper walls) push against six pillars lining the nave inside, helping to hold up the heavy stone ceiling and sloped, lead-over-wood roof. The result is a tall cathedral held up by slender pillars buttressed from the outside, allowing the walls to be opened up for stained glass.

⓫ South Porch: The three doorways of the south entrance show the world from Christ's time to the present, as Christianity triumphs over persecution. On the center door, **Jesus** holds a book and raises his arm in blessing. He's a simple, itinerant, bareheaded, barefoot rabbi, but underneath his feet, he tramples symbols of evil: the dragon and lion. Christ is surrounded by his **apostles,** who spread the good news to a hostile world.

The final triumph comes above the door in the **Last Judgment.** Christ sits in judgment, raising his hands, while Mary and John beg him to take it easy on poor humankind. Beneath Christ the souls are judged—the righteous on our left, and the wicked on our right, who are thrown into the fiery jaws of hell.

• *Reach the north side by circling around the back end of the church.*

⓬ North Porch: In the "Book of Chartres," the north porch is chapter one, from the Creation up to the coming of Christ. Imagine all this painted and covered with gold leaf in preparation for the dedication ceremonies in 1260, when the Chartres generation could finally stand back and watch as their great-grandchildren, carrying candles, entered the cathedral.

OTHER SIGHTS IN CHARTRES

Chartres Town

Chartres' old town bustles with activity (except Sun and Mon) and merits exploration. You can rent an audioguide from the TI, or

better, just wander (follow the route shown on the map on page 200).

In medieval times, Chartres was actually two towns—the pilgrims' town around the cathedral, and the industrial town along the river, which was powered by watermills. An easy 45-minute loop takes you around the cathedral, through the old pilgrims' town, down along the once-industrial riverbank, and back to the cathedral. Along the way you'll discover a picnic-perfect park behind the cathedral, see the colorful pedestrian zone, and wander quiet alleys and peaceful lanes.

International Stained Glass Center
(Centre International du Vitrail)

This low-key center on the north side of the cathedral is worth a visit to learn about the techniques behind the mystery of this

fragile but enduring art. Panels describe the displays, many of which are original windows. Ask at the entrance about the 25-minute video in English describing the process of blown glass and the 10-minute French-only video explaining how it is turned into stained glass (easy to follow for non-French speakers).

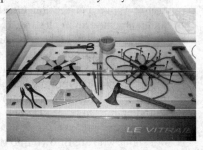

The center also offers five-day classes; call ahead or email for topics and dates.

Cost and Hours: €7, Mon-Fri 9:30-12:30 & 13:30-17:45, Sat from 10:00 & 14:30, Sun 14:30-17:45, 5 Rue du Cardinal Pie, 50 yards from cathedral, tel. 02 37 21 65 72, www.centre-vitrail.org.

Sleeping in Chartres

$$ Timhotel Chartres Cathédrale,*** a block up from the train station, is comfortable and well run. Don't let the facade fool you—inside is a comfy place with a huge fireplace in the lobby and 48 well-kept rooms. Several rooms connect—good for families—and many have partial cathedral views (good buffet breakfast—extra, but one breakfast per couple free for Rick Steves readers; mini-bars, elevator, air-con, handy and safe pay parking, 6 Avenue Jehan de Beauce, tel. 02 37 21 78 00, www.timhotel.com, chartres@timhotel.fr).

$ Hôtel le Bœuf Couronné*** is more like a vintage two-star hotel, with 17 colorful, good-value rooms and a handy location half-way between the station and cathedral (elevator, no air-con, good restaurant with views of the cathedral, reserve ahead for pay parking, 15 Place Châtelet, tel. 02 37 18 06 06, www.leboeufcouronne.com, resa@leboeufcouronne.fr).

$ Hôtellerie Saint Yves, which hangs on the hillside just behind the cathedral, delivers well-priced simplicity with 50 spic-and-span rooms in a renovated monastery with meditative garden areas. Single rooms have no view; ask for a double room with views of the lower town (small bathrooms, good breakfast—extra, 3 Rue des Acacias, tel. 02 37 88 37 40, www.maison-st-yves.com, reception@saintyves.net).

Hostel: A 20-minute walk from the historic center, **¢ Auberge de Jeunesse** is located in a modern building with good views of the cathedral from its terrace (includes breakfast, dirt cheap meals, 23 Avenue Neigre, tel. 02 37 34 27 64, www.auberge-de-jeunesse-chartres.fr, auberge-jeunesse-chartres@wanadoo.fr).

Eating in Chartres

Dining out in Chartres is a good deal—particularly if you've come from Paris. Troll the places basking in cathedral views, and if it's warm, find a terrace table (several possibilities). Then finish your evening cathedral-side, sipping a hot or cold drink at Le Serpente.

$$ Café Bleu offers a great view terrace and an appealing interior. It serves classic French fare at acceptable prices (closed Tue, 1 Cloître Notre-Dame, tel. 02 37 36 59 60).

$$ Le Café Serpente saddles up next door to the cathedral, with terrific view tables and an adorable collector's interior. The cuisine is good, basic bistro fare and fairly priced. Simple dishes and to-go food are available from the room at the back (daily, 2 Cloître Notre-Dame, tel. 02 37 21 68 81).

$ La Picoterie efficiently serves up inexpensive fare such as omelets, crêpes, and salads in its cozy dining room (daily, 36 Rue des Changes, tel. 02 37 36 14 54).

$$ Le Pichet 3 is run by endearing Marie-Sylvie and Xavier. This local-products shop and snug bistro make a fun stop. Sit on the quiet terrace or peruse the artsy inside. Laura—the daughter—serves a tasty *assiette végétarienne* and a good selection of *plats*. Try the local specialty, *la poule au pot*, and the rabbit with plums (Thu-

Mon, closed Mon evening and all day Tue-Wed, 19 Rue du Cheval Blanc, tel. 02 37 21 08 35).

$ Maison Monarque offers decadent pastries and light lunches with a cathedral view (closed Mon-Tue, 49 Rue des Changes, tel. 02 34 40 04 00).

Giverny

Claude Monet's gardens at Giverny are like his paintings—brightly colored patches that are messy but balanced. Flowers were his brushstrokes, a bit untamed and slapdash, but part of a carefully composed design. Monet spent his last (and most creative) years cultivating his garden and his art at Giverny (zhee-vayr-nee), the spiritual home of Impressionism. Visiting the Marmottan and/or the Orangerie museums in Paris before your visit here heightens your appreciation of these gardens.

In 1883, middle-aged Claude Monet, his wife Alice, and their eight children from two families settled into this farmhouse, 50 miles northwest of Paris. Monet, already a famous artist and happiest at home, would spend 40 years in Giverny, traveling less with each passing year. He built a pastoral paradise complete with a Japanese garden and a pond full of floating lilies.

GETTING THERE

Minivan and big bus tours take groups to Giverny. The trip is also doable in a half-day by car or public transportation by train with a connection by bus, taxi, bike, or hike.

By Tour: Minivan tours will pick you up at your hotel and whisk you painlessly there and back. Paris Webservices tours are best, with informative drivers and ample time to savor the experience (figure around €100/person or €65 for transport only—see page 55). Big bus tour companies do a Giverny day trip from Paris for around €50 (5 hours, includes entry, get details at your hotel or www.pariscityvision.com).

By Car: From Paris' *périphérique* ring road, follow A-13 toward Rouen, exit at *Sortie 14* to Vernon, and follow *Centre Ville* signs, then signs to *Giverny*. You can park at Monet's house or in nearby lots. Romantics can take the scenic route from the same exit by following tiny D-201 over the river and through the woods.

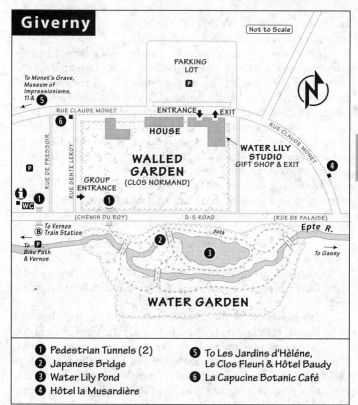

Giverny

Not to Scale

PARKING LOT

To Monet's Grave,
Museum of
Impressionisms,
TI & ❺

RUE CLAUDE MONET

ENTRANCE   EXIT

HOUSE

❻

RUE DE PRESSOIR

RUE GENTE LEROY

WALLED
GARDEN
(CLOS NORMAND)

WATER LILY
STUDIO
GIFT SHOP & EXIT

RUE CLAUDE MONET

❹

GROUP
ENTRANCE

❶

WC

❶

(CHEMIN DU ROY)   D-5 ROAD   (RUE DE FALAISE)

Epte R.

To Vernon
Train Station

❷

Path

❸

To Gasny

To
Bike Path
& Vernon

WATER GARDEN

NEAR PARIS

❶ Pedestrian Tunnels (2)
❷ Japanese Bridge
❸ Water Lily Pond
❹ Hôtel la Musardière

❺ To Les Jardins d'Hèléne,
   Le Clos Fleuri & Hôtel Baudy
❻ La Capucine Botanic Café

By Train: This option is less expensive than a tour and puts you in charge of your own time, but because trains are not frequent, be prepared for a six-hour excursion. Take the Rouen-bound train from Paris Gare St. Lazare Station to Vernon, about four miles from Giverny (normally leaves from tracks 20-25, 45 minutes, about €30 round-trip). The train that leaves Paris at around 8:15 is ideal for this trip, with departures about every two hours after that (8/day Mon-Sat, 6/day Sun). Before boarding, use an information desk in Gare St. Lazare to get return times from Vernon to Paris.

Getting from Vernon's Train Station to Giverny: From the Vernon station to Monet's garden, you have four options: bus, taxi, bike, or hike. The Vernon-Giverny **bus** works well with most trains from Paris for the 15-minute run to Giverny (generally every 2 hours 9:15-15:15, €10 round-trip, pay driver). A bus-and-train timetable is available at the bus stops, on the bus, and online (www.giverny.org/transpor)—note return times. To reach the bus stop, across from the L'Arrivée de Giverny café, walk through the station and keep straight. Don't dally in the station—the bus may leave soon after your train arrives.

Returning to the station, the bus leaves Giverny from the same stop where it drops you off (near the pedestrian underpass—see map; TI and good WCs on the north side of the underpass). Buses generally run hourly in the morning and afternoon (every two hours midday, at :10 after the hour, last departure about 19:10, confirm times by checking schedule upon arrival). Get to the stop at least 15 minutes early to ensure a space. If you miss the return bus and can't wait for the next one, ask any approachable service personnel to call a taxi.

Taxis wait in front of the station in Vernon (allow €15 one-way for up to 3 people). Try Damien Taxi at mobile 06 03 30 85 47 or tel. 02 77 02 94 97 (for other taxis call 06 77 49 32 90 or 06 50 12 21 22).

Another option is to rent a **bike** at L'Arrivée de Giverny café (opposite the station, closed Mon, tel. 02 32 21 16 01) and take a 30-minute ride along a well-signed, paved bike path *(piste cyclable)* that runs from near Vernon along an abandoned railroad right-of-way.

Hikers can go on **foot** to Giverny (4 level miles, about 1.5 hours one way) following the bike path and take a bus or taxi back.

Extension to Rouen: Consider combining your morning Giverny visit with an afternoon excursion to nearby Rouen—together they make an efficient and memorable day trip from Paris. Note that Rouen's museums are closed on Tuesdays. From Vernon (the halfway point between Rouen and Paris), it's about 40 minutes by train to Rouen; the return trip from Rouen back to Paris takes 70-90 minutes. Plan to arrive at Monet's garden when it opens (at 9:30) so you can be back to the Vernon train station by 13:00. You'll land in Rouen by 14:00 and have just enough time to see Rouen's cathedral and surrounding medieval quarter. If you leave Rouen around 18:00, you'll pull into Paris about 19:15, having spent a wonderful day sampling rural and urban Normandy.

Orientation to Giverny

Giverny is a tiny village about four miles from the town of Vernon. All of Giverny's sights and shops string along Rue Claude Monet, which runs in front of Monet's house. The **TI** is located by the WCs in the parking lot near the road to Vernon (see map, daily April-Sept, closed off-season, 80 Rue Claude Monet, tel. 02 32 64 45 01).

NEAR PARIS

Sights in Giverny

▲Monet's Garden and House

There are two gardens, split by a busy road, plus the house, which displays Monet's prized collection of Japanese prints. The gardens are always flowering with something; they're at their most colorful April through July.

Cost and Hours: €9.50, not covered by Paris Museum Pass, €17 combo-tickets available with nearby Museum of Impressionisms, €18.50 with Paris' Orangerie, or €21.50 with Marmottan Museum; daily April-Oct 9:30-18:00, closed Nov-late March; tel. 02 32 51 90 31, http://fondation-monet.com.

Crowd-Beating Tips: Though lines may be long and tour groups may trample the flowers, true fans still find magic in the gardens. Minimize crowds by arriving a little before 9:30, when it opens, or come after 16:00 and stay until it closes. The busiest months are May and June. Sunday mornings are busiest in any season when cruise groups arrive in force.

Advance ticket and combo-ticket holders skip the ticket-buying line and use the nifty group entrance, a huge advantage in high season. You can buy advance tickets online or at any FNAC store in Paris, or at the TI in Vernon. Alternately, buy combo tickets with either the Orangerie or Marmottan Museum in Paris, or the Museum of Impressionisms here (described later).

Guided Tours: Enthusiasts can take a 1.5-hour guided tour of the gardens for €80 (1-4 people, http://giverny.org/guide/ariane/).

Visiting the House and Gardens: There are two parts to the gardens, the **Walled Garden** (next to the house) and the **Water Garden** (across the road). Most visitors use the main entry and start in the Walled Garden (Clos Normand). Those able to use the group entrance should start with the Water Garden and end with the Walled Garden and house.

In the **Walled Garden,** smell the pretty scene. Monet cleared this land of pine trees and laid out symmetrical beds, split down the middle by a "grand alley" covered with iron trellises of climbing roses. He did his own landscaping, installing flowerbeds of lilies, irises, and clematis. In his carefree manner, Monet throws together hollyhocks, daisies, and poppies. The color scheme of each flowerbed contributes to the look of the whole garden.

In the southwest corner of the Walled Garden (near the group entrance), you'll find a pedestrian tunnel that leads under the road to the **Water Garden,** with Monet's famous pond and lilies. Follow the meandering path to the Japanese bridge, under weeping willows, over the pond filled with water lilies, and past countless scenes that leave artists aching for an easel. Find a bench and linger for a while. Monet landscaped like he painted—he built an Impressionist pattern of blocks of color. After he planted the gardens, he painted them, from every angle, at every time of day, in all kinds of weather.

End your visit with a wander through Monet's charming, I-could-retire-here **home,** with pretty furnishings, Japanese prints, old photos, and rooms filled with copies of his and other artists' paintings. The gift shop at the exit is the actual sky-lighted studio where Monet painted his masterpiece Water-Lily series (displayed at the Orangerie Museum in Paris). Many visitors spend more time in this tempting gift shop than in the gardens themselves.

Village of Giverny

The village is a sight in itself, with flowery lanes home to a few souvenir shops, art galleries, and cafés. Cars are not allowed to enter the center of the village.

Museum of Impressionisms (Musée des Impressionnismes)

This bright, modern museum, dedicated to the history of Impressionism and its legacy, houses temporary exhibits of Impressionist art. Check its website for current shows or just drop in. Meander through its colorful, picnic-friendly gardens for more color.

Cost and Hours: €7.50, €17 combo-ticket with Monet's Garden and House, daily April-Oct 10:00-18:00, closed Nov-March and for 10 days in mid-July to change exhibitions; to reach it, turn left after leaving Monet's place and walk 200 yards; tel. 02 32 51 94 00, www.mdig.fr.

Claude Monet's Grave

Monet's grave is a 15-minute walk from his door. Turn left out of his house and walk down Rue Claude Monet, pass the Museum of Impressionisms and the Hôtel Baudy, and find it in the backyard of the white church Monet attended (Eglise Sainte-Radegonde). Look for flowers, with a cross above. The inscription says: *Here lies our beloved Claude Monet, born 14 November 1840, died 5 December 1926; missed by all.*

Vernon Town

If you have extra time at Vernon's train station, take a five-minute walk into town and sample the peaceful village. From the station, pass Café de l'Arrivée on your left, follow the street as it curves left, and keep straight. You'll find a smattering of half-timbered Norman homes near Hôtel de Ville, several good cafés and shops, and the town's towering Gothic church.

Sleeping and Eating in Giverny

Sleeping: $ Hôtel la Musardière** is nestled in the village of Giverny two blocks from Monet's home (exit right when you leave Monet's) with 10 sweet rooms that Claude himself would have felt at home in (family rooms available). There's also a reasonable and homey **$ crêperie-restaurant** with outdoor tables (daily with non-stop service, 123 Rue Claude Monet, tel. 02 32 21 03 18, www.lamusardiere.fr, hotelmusardieregiverny@wanadoo.fr).

$$ Les Jardins d'Héléne chambres d'hôte is a warm, comfy place with good public spaces, floral rooms, and a large garden. Owner Isabelle makes a good host (includes breakfast, cash only, 15-minute walk from Monet's home at 12 Rue Claude Monet, tel. 02 32 21 30 68 or 06 47 98 14 87, www.giverny-lesjardinsdhelene.com, lesjardinsdhelene@outlook.com).

$ Le Clos Fleuri is a family-friendly B&B with three spacious and very comfortable rooms, each with a king-size bed and a private terrace facing the grassy garden. The rooms also share handy cooking facilities. It's a 15-minute walk from Monet's place and is run by charming, English-speaking Danielle (with Australian heritage), who serves up a good included breakfast (cash only, 5 Rue de la Dîme, tel. 02 32 21 36 51, www.giverny-leclosfleuri.fr, leclosfleuri27@yahoo.fr).

Eating: You'll find various snack places just outside the entrance to Monet's home. Your best lunch option is a block to the left at **$ La Capucine** self-serve restaurant. Eat tasty, cheap soups, salads, and quiches at a table in the warm interior or the welcoming garden (daily 10:00-18:00).

Rose-colored **$$ Hôtel Baudy,** once a hangout for American Impressionists, offers an appropriately pretty setting for lunch or dinner. The decor looks as though it has not changed since painters hung their brushes here (outdoor tables in front, good-value *menus,* popular with tour groups at lunch, daily, 5-minute walk past Museum of Impressionisms at 81 Rue Claude Monet, tel. 02 32 21 10 03). Don't miss a stroll through the artsy gardens behind the restaurant.

Disneyland Paris

Europe's Disneyland is a remake of California's, with most of the same rides and smiles. The main difference is that Mickey Mouse speaks French, and you can buy wine with your lunch. My kids went ducky for it.

The Disneyland Paris Resort is a sprawling complex housing two theme parks (Disneyland Paris and Walt Disney Studios), a few entertainment venues, and several hotels. With upwards of 15 million visitors a year, it is Europe's single leading tourist destination.

Disneyland Paris: This park has cornered the fun market, with classic rides and Disney characters. You'll find familiar favorites wrapped in French packaging, like Sleeping Beauty Castle *(Le Château de la Belle au Bois Dormant)* and Pirates of the Caribbean *(Pirates des Caraïbes).*

Walt Disney Studios: This zone has a Hollywood focus geared for an older crowd, with animation, special effects, and movie magic "rides." The cinema-themed rides include the Studio Tram Tour: Behind the Magic (a slow-motion ride that goes mostly outdoors through a "movie backlot"); and Moteurs... Action! Stunt Show Spectacular (an actual movie sequence is filmed with stunt drivers, audience bit players, and brash MTV-style hosts). The top thrill rides include the Rock 'n' Roller Coaster (which starts out by accelerating from a standstill to nearly 60 miles per hour in less than three seconds), and the Twilight Zone Tower of Terror (which drops passengers from a precarious 200-foot-high perch). Gentler attractions include a re-creation of the parachute jump in *Toy Story* and a *Finding Nemo*-themed ride (Crush's Coaster) that whisks you through the ocean current.

GETTING THERE

Disneyland is easy to get to, and may be worth a day—if Paris is handier than Florida or California.

By Bus or Train from Downtown Paris: The slick 45-minute RER/Train-A trip is the best way to get to Disneyland from Paris. Take the train to Marne-la-Vallée-Chessy (check the signs over the platform to be sure Marne-la-Vallée-Chessy is served, because the line splits near the end). Catch it from one of these stations: Charles de Gaulle-Etoile, Auber, Châtelet-Les Halles, or Gare de Lyon (at least 3/hour, drops you 45 minutes later right in the park, about €10 each way). The last train back to Paris leaves shortly after midnight. When returning, remember to use the same RER/Train-A ticket for your Métro connection in Paris.

The all-day Mobilis ticket is a smart purchase for some Disney day-trippers, as it covers your Paris Métro rides for the day and the round-trip train to Disneyland (about €18 for zones 1-5 ticket). Buy it at any Métro station, fill in your name and date of travel on the ticket, and validate it the day you use it.

Disneyland Express runs buses to Disneyland from several stops in central Paris (including Opéra, Madeleine, Châtelet, and Gare du Nord). A single ticket combines transportation and entrance to Disneyland (about €100 for ages 3-11, free for ages 2 and under, €115 for adults; several morning departures to choose from and one return time of 20:00, book tickets online, www.disneylandparis-express.com).

By Bus or Train from the Airport: Both of Paris' major airports (Charles de Gaulle and Orly) have direct shuttle buses to Disneyland Paris (€23; about hourly and takes 45 minutes, www.magicalshuttle.co.uk). Fast TGV trains (also called "InOui") run from Charles de Gaulle to near Disneyland in 10 minutes (2/hour; shuttle bus takes you from train station to Disneyland).

By Car: Disneyland is about 40 minutes (20 miles) east of Paris on the A-4 autoroute (direction Nancy/Metz, exit #14). Parking is about €30/day at the park.

ORIENTATION TO DISNEYLAND

Cost: A variety of single and multiday tickets and packages (including transportation, lodging, and/or meals) are sold for Disneyland Paris and/or Walt Disney Studios. Regular prices are discounted about 25 percent Nov-March, and promotions are offered occasionally (check www.disneylandparis.com).

Hours: Disneyland—daily 10:00-22:00, mid-May-Aug until 23:00, until 20:00 in winter, open later on weekends, hours fluctuate with the seasons—check website for precise times. Walt Disney Studios—daily 10:00-19:00.

Skipping Lines: The free Fastpass system is a worthwhile time-saver for the most popular rides (see website for details). At the ride, check the Fastpass sign to see when you can return and skip the line. Insert your park admission ticket into the Fastpass machine, which spits out a ticket printed with your return time. You'll also save time by buying park tickets in advance (at airport TIs, some Métro stations, or along the Champs-Elysées at the Disney Store).

Avoiding Crowds: Saturday, Sunday, Wednesday, public holidays, and any day in July and August are the most crowded. After dinner, crowds are gone.

Information: Disney brochures are in every Paris hotel. For more info and to make reservations, call 01 60 30 60 53, or try www.disneylandparis.com.

Eating with Mickey: Food is fun and not outrageously priced. (Still, many smuggle in a picnic.) The Disneyland Hotel restaurant Inventions offers a buffet dinner with Disney characters (roughly €70/adult, €40/child).

SLEEPING AT DISNEYLAND

Most are better off sleeping in the real world (i.e., Paris), though with direct buses and freeways to both airports, Disneyland makes a convenient first- or last-night stop. Seven different Disney-owned hotels offer accommodations at or near the park in all price ranges. Prices are impossible to pin down, as they vary by season and by the package deal you choose (deals that include park entry are usually a better value, with more in the **$$$$** range). To reserve any Disneyland hotel, call 01 60 30 60 53, or check www.disneylandparis.com. The prices you'll be quoted include entry to the park. **Hotel Cheyenne**** and **Hotel Santa Fe**** offer fair midrange values, with frequent shuttle service to the park (or a 20-minute walk). A cheaper option is **Davy Crockett's Ranch Hotel,** but you'll need a car to stay there. The most expensive is the **Disneyland Hotel,****** right at the park entry, about three times the price of the Santa Fe. The **Vienna House Dream Castle Hotel****** is another higher-end choice, with nearly 400 rooms done up to look like a lavish 17th-century palace (40 Avenue de la Fosse des Pressoirs, tel. 01 64 17 90 00, www.dreamcastle-hotel.com, info@dreamcastle-hotel.com).

NORMANDY

Rouen • Honfleur • Bayeux • D-Day Beaches • Mont St-Michel

Sweeping coastlines, half-timbered towns, and thatched roofs decorate the rolling green hills of Normandy (Normandie). Parisians call Normandy "the 21st arrondissement." It's their escape—the nearest beach. Brits consider this area close enough for a weekend escape (you'll notice that the BBC comes through loud and clear on your car radio). Americans find it a rare place where their country played a pivotal role in European history.

Despite the peacefulness you sense today, the region's past is filled with war. Normandy was founded by Viking Norsemen who invaded from the north, settled here in the ninth century, and gave the region its name. A couple hundred years later, William the Conqueror invaded England from Normandy. His 1066 victory is commemorated in a remarkable tapestry at Bayeux. A few hundred years after that, France's greatest cheerleader, Joan of Arc (Jeanne d'Arc), was convicted of heresy in Rouen and burned at the stake by the English, against whom she rallied France during the Hundred Years' War. And in 1944, Normandy was the site of a WWII battle that changed the course of history.

The rugged, rainy coast of Normandy harbors pristine beaches, wartime bunkers, and enchanting fishing villages like Honfleur. And, on the border Normandy shares with Brittany, the almost surreal island-abbey of Mont St-Michel rises serene and majestic, oblivious to the tides of tourists.

PLANNING YOUR TIME

For many, Normandy makes the perfect jet-lag antidote: A good first stop for your trip is Rouen, which is a few hours by car or train from Paris' Charles de Gaulle or Beauvais airports. Plan on four

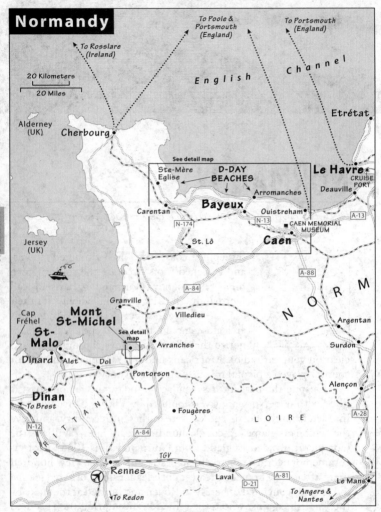

NORMANDY

nights for a first visit to Normandy: Honfleur and Mont St-Michel each merit an overnight and the D-Day beaches merit two. At a minimum, you'll want a full day for the D-Day beaches and a half-day each in Honfleur, Bayeux, and Mont St-Michel.

If you're driving between Paris and Honfleur, Giverny (see previous chapter) and Rouen make good detours. The WWII memorial museum in Caen works well as a stop between Honfleur and Bayeux (and the D-Day beaches). Mont St-Michel must be seen early or late to avoid the masses of midday tourists. Dinan, just 45 minutes by car from Mont St-Michel, offers a fine introduction to Brittany (see next chapter). Drivers can enjoy Mont St-Michel as a day trip from Dinan.

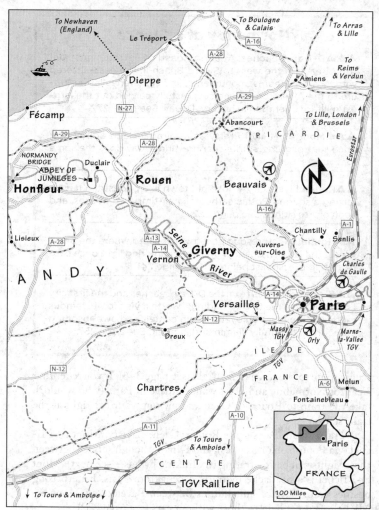

Winter travelers should note that many sights on the D-Day beaches and in Bayeux are closed in January. For practical information about travel, current events, concerts, and more in Normandy, see www.normandie-tourisme.fr.

GETTING AROUND NORMANDY
On Your Own

This region is best explored by **car.** If you're driving into Honfleur from the north, take the impressive Normandy Bridge (Pont de Normandie, €6 toll); if you're coming the from Rouen area, follow the Route of the Ancient Abbeys (described later). If you're driving from Mont St-Michel into Brittany, follow my recommended

NORMANDY

Normandy at a Glance

▲▲▲**D-Day Beaches** Atlantic coastline—stretching from Utah Beach in the west to Sword Beach in the east—littered with WWII museums, monuments, and cemeteries left in tribute to the Allied forces who successfully carried out the largest military operation in history: D-Day. See page 272.

▲▲▲**Mont St-Michel** Pretty-as-a-mirage island abbey that once sent pilgrims' spirits soaring—and today does the same for tourists. See page 310.

▲▲**Rouen** Lively city whose old town is a pedestrian haven, mixing a soaring Gothic cathedral, half-timbered houses, and Joan of Arc sights. See page 222.

▲▲**Honfleur** Picturesque port town, located where the Seine greets the English Channel, whose shimmering light once captivated Impressionist painters. See page 241.

▲▲**Bayeux** Six miles from the D-Day beaches and the first city liberated after the D-Day landings, worth a visit for its famous medieval tapestry, enjoyable town center, and awe-inspiring cathedral, beautifully illuminated at night. See page 257.

scenic route to the town of St-Malo (see page 346). If you're renting a car for Normandy and don't want to drive in Paris (who would?), take the train to Rouen or Caen and pick up your car right at the train station.

Trains from Paris serve Rouen, Caen, Bayeux, Mont St-Michel (via Pontorson or Rennes), and Dinan, though service between these sights can be frustrating (try linking by bus—see next). Mont St-Michel is a headache by train, except from Paris. Enterprising businesses in Bayeux run shuttles between Bayeux and Mont St-Michel—a great help to those without cars (see page 272).

Buses link Giverny, Honfleur, Arromanches, and Mont St-Michel to train stations in nearby towns (less frequent on Sundays). To plan ahead, visit the websites for **Bus Verts** (for Le Havre, Honfleur, Bayeux, Arromanches, and Caen, www.busverts.fr), **Keolis** (for Mont St-Michel, https://keolis-armor.com), and **Tibus** or **Illenoo** (for Dinan and St-Malo, www.tibus.fr or www.illenoo-services.fr). Bus companies commonly offer good-value and multi-ride discounts—for example, Bus Verts offers a 20 percent discount on a shareable four-ride ticket.

With a Tour or Shuttle

Another good option is to use an **excursion tour** to link destinations. **Westcapades** provides trips to Mont St-Michel from Dinan and St-Malo (for details, see page 331).

Private shuttles make it easy to link Paris and Normandy without driving or connecting by train. **Albion Transport** (run by American Adrienne O'Donoghue) organizes private transfers between Paris airports or hotels and key Normandy destinations such as Honfleur, Bayeux, and Caen (€450 for up to 3 people, €600 for 4-8 people, extra fee for stops en route at Giverny or Honfleur, tel. 02 31 78 88 88, mobile 06 80 28 65 61, www.albion-voyages.com).

D-Day Beaches

For specifics on getting around the D-Day Beaches, see that section of this chapter.

NORMANDY'S CUISINE SCENE

Normandy is known as the land of the four C's: Calvados, Camembert, cider, and *crème*. The region specializes in cream sauces, organ meats (sweetbreads, tripe, and kidneys—the gizzard salads are great), and seafood *(fruits de mer)*. You'll see *crêperies* offering inexpensive and good-value meals everywhere. A galette is a savory buckwheat crêpe enjoyed as a main course; a crêpe is sweet and eaten for dessert.

Dairy products are big, too. Local cheeses are Camembert (mild to very strong; see sidebar), Brillat-Savarin (buttery), Livarot (spicy and pungent), Pavé d'Auge (spicy and tangy), and Pont l'Evêque (earthy).

What, no local wine? *Eh oui,* that's right. Here's how to cope. Fresh, white Muscadet wines are made nearby (in western Loire); they're cheap and a good match with much of Normandy's cuisine. But Normandy is proud of its many apple-based beverages. You can't miss the powerful Calvados apple brandy or the Bénédictine brandy (made by local monks). The local dessert, *trou Normand,* is apple sorbet swimming in Calvados. The region also produces three kinds of alcoholic apple ciders: *Cidre* can be *doux* (sweet), *brut* (dry), or *bouché* (sparkling—and the strongest). You'll also find bottles of Pommeau, a tasty blend of apple juice and Calvados (sold in many shops), as well as *poiré,* a tasty pear cider. And don't leave Normandy without sampling a *kir Normand,* a mix of crème de cassis and cider. Drivers in Normandy should be on the lookout for *Route du Cidre* signs (with a bright red apple); this tourist trail leads you to small producers of handcrafted cider and brandy.

NORMANDY

Camembert Cheese

This cheap, soft, white, Brie-like cheese is sold all over France (and America) in distinctive, round wooden containers. The Camembert region has long been known for its cheese, but local legend has it that today's cheese got its start in the French Revolution, when a priest on the run was taken in by Marie Harel, a Camembert farm woman. The priest repaid the favor by giving her the secret formula for his hometown cheese—Brie.

From cow to customer, Camembert takes about three weeks to make. High-fat milk from Norman cows is curdled with rennet, ladled into round, five-inch molds, sprinkled with *Penicillium camemberti* bacteria, and left to dry. In the first three days, the cheese goes from the cow's body temperature to room temperature to refrigerator cool (50 degrees). Two weeks later, the ripened and aged cheese is wrapped in wooden bands and labeled for market. Like wines, Camembert cheese is controlled by government regulations and must bear the "A.O.C." (Appellation d'Origine Contrôlée) stamp of approval.

Rouen

This 2,000-year-old city mixes Gothic architecture, half-timbered houses, and contemporary bustle like no other place in France. Busy Rouen (roo-ahn) is France's fifth-largest port and Europe's biggest food exporter (mostly wheat and grain). Its cobbled and traffic-free old town is a delight to wander.

Rouen was a regional capital during Roman times, and France's second-largest city in medieval times (with 40,000 residents—only Paris had more). In the ninth century, the Normans made Rouen their capital. William the Conqueror called it home before moving to England. After that, Rouen walked a political tightrope between England and France for centuries and was an English base during the Hundred Years' War. Joan of Arc was burned here (in 1431).

Rouen's historic wealth was built on its wool industry and trade—for centuries, it was the last bridge across the Seine River before the Atlantic. In April 1944, as America and Britain weakened German control of Normandy prior to the D-Day landings,

Allied bombers destroyed 50 percent of Rouen. Although the industrial suburbs were devastated, most of the historic core survived, keeping Rouen a pedestrian haven.

PLANNING YOUR TIME

If you want a dose of a smaller—yet lively—French city, Rouen is an easy day trip from Paris, with convenient train connections to Gare St. Lazare (nearly hourly, 1.5 hours). For a memorable day trip from Paris, combine Rouen with Giverny.

If you're planning to rent a car as you leave Paris, save headaches by taking the train to Rouen and picking up a rental car there (spend a quiet night in Rouen and pick up your car the next morning). Or take an early train to Rouen, pick up keys to a rental car, stash your bags in it, leave it in the secure rental lot at the train station, and visit Rouen on foot before heading out to explore Normandy. This plan also works in reverse—drop your car in Rouen and visit the city before taking a train to Paris.

Those relying on public transportation can visit Rouen on the way from Paris to other Normandy destinations, thanks to the good bus and train service.

Orientation to Rouen

Although Paris embraces the Seine, Rouen ignores it. The area we're most interested in is bounded by the river to the south, the Museum of Fine Arts (Esplanade Marcel Duchamp) to the north, Rue de la République to the east, and Place du Vieux Marché to the west. It's a 20-minute walk from the train station to the Notre-Dame Cathedral. Everything else of interest is within a 10-minute walk of the cathedral.

TOURIST INFORMATION

The TI faces the cathedral and rents €5 audioguides covering the cathedral, Rouen's historic center, and the history of Joan of Arc in Rouen (though this book's self-guided walk is plenty for most). If driving, get information about the Route of the Ancient Abbeys (TI open Mon-Sat 9:00-19:00, Sun 9:30-12:30 & 14:00-18:00; Oct-April Mon-Sat 9:30-12:30 & 14:00-18:00, closed Sun; 25 Place de la Cathédrale, tel. 02 32 08 32 40, www.rouentourisme. com).

ARRIVAL IN ROUEN

By Train: Rue Jeanne d'Arc cuts straight from Rouen's train station through the town center to the Seine River. Day-trippers can **walk** from the station down Rue Jeanne d'Arc toward Rue du Gros Horloge—a busy pedestrian mall in the medieval center and near

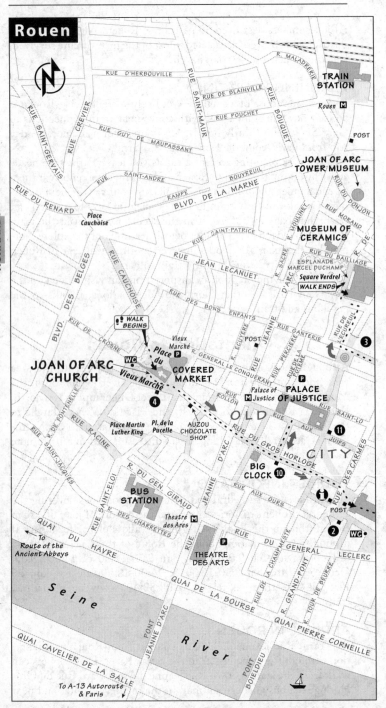

NORMANDY

Rouen

N

RUE D'HERBOUVILLE

RUE SAINT-MAUR

RUE DE BLAINVILLE

RUE FOUCHET

RUE BOUQUET

TRAIN STATION

Rouen Ⓜ

POST

RUE CREVIER

RUE SAINT-GERVAIS

RUE GUY DE MAUPASSANT

RUE SAINT-ANDRÉ

RAMPE

BOUVREUIL

RUE DU RENARD

BLVD. DE LA MARNE

JOAN OF ARC TOWER MUSEUM

RUE DU DONJON

RUE MORAND

Place Cauchoise

RUE SAINT-PATRICE

MUSEUM OF CERAMICS

R. SACRE

RUE CAUCHOISE

RUE JEAN LECANUET

RUE DU BAILLIAGE

ESPLANADE MARCEL DUCHAMP

Square Verdrel

WALK ENDS

BLVD. DES BELGES

RUE DE CROSNE

RUE DES BONS ENFANTS

R. ÉCUYÈRE

RUE GANTERIE

RUE DE L'ÉCUREUIL

❸

WALK BEGINS

Vieux Marché

Place du Vieux Marché

WC

COVERED MARKET

R. GÉNÉRAL LE CONQUÉRANT

POST

RUE JEANNE

RUE PERCIÈRE

RUE DE LA POTERNE

JOAN OF ARC CHURCH

Vieux Marché

❹

RUE ROLLON

Palace of Ⓜ **Justice**

PALACE OF JUSTICE

OLD

RUE SAINT-LO

R. DE FONTENELLE

RUE RACINE

Place Martin Luther King

Pl. de la Pucelle

AUZOU CHOCOLATE SHOP

RUE DU GROS HORLOGE

RUE AUX

CITY

❶❶

RUE SAINT-JACQUES

RUE SAINTELOI

R. DU GEN. GIRAUD

RUE JEANNE D'ARC

BIG CLOCK ❿

RUE AUX OURS

RUE DES CARMES

BUS STATION

R. DES CHARRETTES

Théatre des Arts Ⓜ

ℹ️

POST

❷

WC

RUE DU GÉNÉRAL LECLERC

QUAI DU HAVRE

THEATRE DES ARTS

P

RUE

RUE DE LA CHARPENTERIE

RUE GRAND-PONT

RUE TOUR DE BEURRE

To Route of the Ancient Abbeys

S e i n e

QUAI DE LA BOURSE

QUAI PIERRE CORNEILLE

QUAI CAVELIER DE LA SALLE

PONT JEANNE D'ARC

R i v e r

PONT BOIELDIEU

To A-13 Autoroute & Paris

NORMANDY

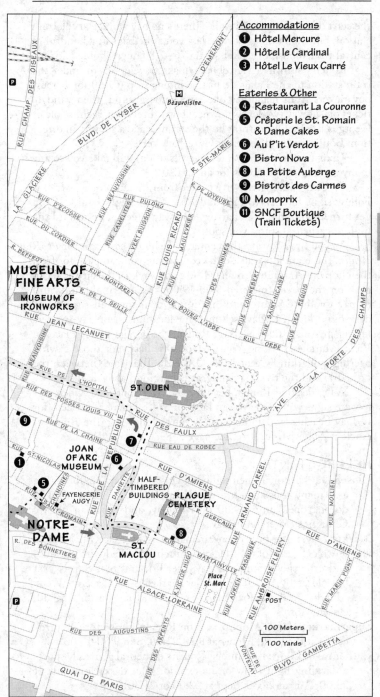

Accommodations
1 Hôtel Mercure
2 Hôtel le Cardinal
3 Hôtel Le Vieux Carré

Eateries & Other
4 Restaurant La Couronne
5 Crêperie le St. Romain & Dame Cakes
6 Au P'it Verdot
7 Bistro Nova
8 La Petite Auberge
9 Bistrot des Carmes
10 Monoprix
11 SNCF Boutique (Train Tickets)

the start of my self-guided walk. There's no bag storage at the train station, but the Holibag service lets you store bags at a handful of central Rouen businesses (tel. 02 35 76 47 80, www.holibag.io).

Rouen's **subway** (Métrobus) whisks travelers from under the train station to the Palais de Justice in one stop (€1.60 for 1 hour; buy tickets from machines one level underground, then validate ticket on subway two levels down; subway direction: Technopôle or Georges Braque). Returning to the station, take a subway in direction: Boulingrin and get off at Gare-Rue Verte.

Taxis (to the right as you exit the station) will take you to any of my recommended hotels for about €10.

By Car: Finding the city center from the autoroute is tricky. Follow signs for *Centre-Ville* and *Rive Droite* (right bank). If you get turned around on the narrow, one-way streets, aim toward the highest cathedral spires you spot.

As you head toward the center, you should see signs for *P&R Relais*. These are lots outside the core where you can park for free, then hop on a tram into town (€1.60 each way). In the city, you can park on the street (metered 9:00-19:00, free overnight and Sun) or pay for more secure parking in one of many well-signed underground lots (€15/day; see map for locations). For day-trippers taking my self-guided walk of Rouen, the garage under Place du Vieux Marché (Parking Vieux Marché) is best. For those staying overnight, Parking Cathédrale–Office du Tourisme (between the cathedral and the river) is handy, as is Parking Palais de Justice.

When leaving Rouen, head for the riverfront road, where autoroute signs will guide you to Paris or to Le Havre and Caen (for D-Day beaches and Honfleur). If you're following The Route of Ancient Abbeys from here, see page 238.

HELPFUL HINTS

Closed Days: Many Rouen sights are closed midday (12:00-14:00), and many museums are closed on Tuesdays. The cathedral doesn't open until 14:00 on Monday, and the Joan of Arc Church is closed on Friday.

Market Days: The best open-air market is on Place St. Marc, a few blocks east of St. Maclou Church. It's filled with antiques and other good stuff (all day Tue, Fri, and Sat; Sun is best but closes by 13:30). A smaller market is on Place du Vieux Marché, near the Joan of Arc Church (Tue-Sun until 13:30, closed Mon).

Supermarket: A big **Monoprix** is on Rue du Gros Horloge (groceries at the back, Mon-Sat 8:30-21:00, Sun 9:00-13:00).

Cathedral of Light: In summer, Rouen's cathedral generally sports a dazzling light show on its exterior after dark (June-July at 23:00, Aug at 22:30, Sept at 22:00 or 21:30).

Wi-Fi: You'll find Wi-Fi at several cafés within a few blocks of the train station on Rue Jeanne d'Arc.

Taxi: Call **Les Taxi Blancs** at 02 35 61 20 50.

Car Rental: Agencies with offices in the train station include **Europcar** (tel. 02 35 88 21 20), **Avis** (tel. 02 35 88 60 94), and **Hertz** (tel. 02 35 70 70 71). All are closed Sunday and for lunch (Mon-Sat 12:30-14:00).

SNCF Boutique: For train tickets, visit the SNCF office at the corner of Rue aux Juifs and Rue Eugène Boudin (Mon-Sat 10:00-13:00 & 14:00-18:15, closed Sun).

Rouen Walk

On this 1.5-hour self-guided walk, you'll see the essential Rouen sights (all but the Joan of Arc Museum and Bell Tower Panorama are free) and experience the city's pedestrian-friendly streets. This walk is designed for day-trippers coming by train, but works just as well for drivers (ideally, park at the underground garage at Place du Vieux Marché, where the walk begins).

We'll stroll the length of Rue du Gros Horloge to Notre-Dame Cathedral, visit the plague cemetery (Aître St. Maclou), pass the church of St. Ouen, and end at the Museum of Fine Arts, a short walk back to the train station or parking lot. The map on page 224 highlights our route.

• *If arriving by train, walk down Rue Jeanne d'Arc and turn right on Rue du Guillaume le Conquérant (notice the Gothic Palace of Justice building across Rue Jeanne d'Arc—we'll get to that later). This takes you to the back door of our starting point...*

▲Place du Vieux Marché

Surrounded by half-timbered buildings, this old market square houses a cute, covered produce-and-fish market, a park commemorating Joan of Arc's burning, and a modern church named after her. Find the tall, aluminum-and-concrete cross in the small garden behind the market stalls, near the entrance to the church. That towering cross marks the spot where Rouen publicly punished and executed people. The pillories stood here, and during the Revolution, the town's guillotine made 800 people "a foot shorter at the top." In 1431, Joan of Arc—only 19 years old—was burned right here. Find her flaming statue (built into the wall of the church, facing the cross). As the flames engulfed her, an English soldier said, "Oh my God, we've killed a saint." Nearly 500 years later, Joan was canonized, and the soldier was proven right.

• *Now step inside...*

NORMANDY

▲Joan of Arc Church (Eglise Jeanne d'Arc)

This modern church is a tribute to the young woman who was canonized in 1920 and later became the patron saint of France. The church, completed in 1979, feels Scandinavian inside and out—another reminder of Normandy's Nordic roots. Sumptuous 16th-century windows, salvaged from a church lost during World War II, were worked into the soft architectural lines. The pointed, stake-like support columns to the right seem fitting for a church dedicated to a woman burned at the stake. This is an uplifting place to be, with a ship's-hull vaulting and sweeping wood ceiling sailing over curved pews and a wall of glass below. Make time to savor this unusual sanctuary.

Cost and Hours: Free, Mon-Thu & Sat 10:00-12:00 & 14:00-18:00, Fri & Sun 14:00-18:00, closed during Mass, 50-cent English pamphlet describes the stained-glass scenes. A clean public WC is 30 yards straight ahead from the church doors.

• *Turn left out of the church.*

Ruined Church and Julia Child

As you leave the church, you're stepping over the ruins of a 15th-century church (destroyed during the French Revolution). The charming half-timbered building just beyond—overflowing with flags and geraniums—is the recommended Restaurant La Couronne, reputedly the oldest restaurant in France. It was here, in 1948, that American chef and author Julia Child ate her first French meal, experiencing a culinary epiphany that changed her life (and the eating habits of a generation of Americans). Inside the restaurant's front doors find historic photos of happy diners, including Julia (three doors in on the right).

• *Leave the square with the church on your left and join the busy pedestrian street, Rue du Gros Horloge. An important thoroughfare in Roman times, it's been the city's main shopping street since the Middle Ages. A block up on your right (at #163) is Rouen's most famous chocolate shop.*

Auzou and Houses That Lean Out

The friendly *chocolatiers* at Auzou would love to tempt you with their chocolate-covered almond "tears *(larmes)* of Joan of Arc." Although you must resist touching the chocolate fountain, you are welcome to taste a tear (delicious). The first one is free; a small bag costs about €9.50.

Before moving on, notice the architecture. The higher floors of the Auzou house lean out, evidence that the building dates from before 1520, when such street-crowding construction was prohibited. (People feared that houses leaning over the street like this would block breezes and make the city more susceptible to disease.) Look around the corner and down the lane behind the Auzou

NORMANDY

Joan of Arc (1412-1431)

The teenager who rallied French soldiers to drive out English invaders was the illiterate daughter of a humble farmer. One summer day, in her dad's garden, 13-year-old Joan heard a heavenly voice accompanied by bright light. It was the first of several saints (including Michael, Margaret, and Catherine) to talk to her during her short life.

In 1429, the young girl was instructed by the voices to save France from the English. Dressed in men's clothing, she traveled to see the king and predicted that the French armies would be defeated near Orléans—as they were. King Charles VII equipped her with an ancient sword and a banner that read "Jesus, Maria," and sent her to rally the troops.

Soon "the Maid" (la Pucelle) was bivouacking amid rough soldiers, riding with them into battle, and suffering an arrow wound to the chest—all while liberating the town of Orléans. On July 17, 1429, she held her banner high in the cathedral of Reims as Charles was officially proclaimed king of a resurgent France.

Joan and company next tried to retake Paris (1429), but the English held out. She suffered a crossbow wound through the thigh, and her reputation of invincibility was tarnished. During a battle at Compiègne (1430), she was captured and turned over to the English for £10,000. The English took her to Rouen, where she was chained by the neck inside an iron cage while the local French authorities (allied with the English) plotted against her. The Inquisition—insisting that Joan's voices were "false and diabolical"—tried and sentenced her to death for being a witch and a heretic.

On May 30, 1431, Joan of Arc was tied to a stake on Rouen's old market square (Place du Vieux Marché). She yelled, "Rouen! Rouen! Must I die here?" Then they lit the fire; she fixed her eyes on a crucifix and died chanting, "Jesus, Jesus, Jesus."

After Joan died, her place in history was slowly rehabilitated. French authorities proclaimed her trial illegal (1455), and she quickly became the most important symbol of French nationhood. Over the centuries, prominent writers and artists were inspired by her, politicians co-opted her fame for their own purposes, and common people rallied around her idealized image. Finally, the Catholic Church beatified (1909) and canonized her (1920) as St. Joan of Arc.

building to see a fine line of half-timbered Gothic facades. Study the house next to Auzou, at #161. You can tell it was built after 1520 (because its facade is flat) and that it's Renaissance (because of the characteristic carved wooden corner-posts). We'll see more houses like this later on our walk.

• *Your route continues past a medieval McDonald's to busy Rue Jeanne*

The Hundred Years' War (1336-1453)

It would take a hundred years to explain all the causes, battles, and political maneuverings of this century-plus of warfare between France and England. Here's the Hundred Years' War in 100 seconds:

In 1300, before the era of the modern nation-state, the borders between France and England were fuzzy. French-speaking kings had ruled England, English kings owned the south of France, and English merchants dominated trade in the north. Dukes and lords in both countries were aligned more along family lines than by national identity. When the French king died without a male heir (1328), both France and England claimed the crown, and the battle was on.

England invaded the more populous France (1345) and—thanks to skilled archers using armor-penetrating longbows—won big battles at Crécy (1346) and Poitiers (1356). Despite a truce, roving bands of English mercenaries stayed behind and supported themselves by looting French villages. The French responded with guerrilla tactics.

In 1415, with Henry V's big victory at Agincourt, the English took still more territory. But rallied by the heavenly visions of young Joan of Arc, the French slowly drove the invaders out. Paris was liberated in 1436, and when Bordeaux fell to French forces (1453), the fighting ended without a treaty.

d'Arc. Pause here and look both ways. With the 19th-century Industrial Age, France expanded its transportation infrastructure. A train line connecting Paris to Rouen arrived in the early 1840s, and major roads like this were plowed through to get traffic efficiently to the station. The facades here date from the 1860s and are in the Haussmann style so dominant in Paris in that era.

Cross the street and continue straight to the...

▲Great Clock (Gros Horloge)

This impressive, circa-1528 Renaissance clock, the Gros Horloge (groh or-lohzh), decorates the former City Hall. Originally, the clock had only an hour hand but no minute hand. In the 16th century, an hour hand offered sufficient precision; minute hands became necessary only in a later, faster-paced age (forget second hands). The silver orb above the clock makes one revolution in 29 days. (The cycle of the moon let people know the tides—of practical value here as Rouen was a seaport.) The town medallion (sculpted into the stone below the clock) features a sacrificial lamb, which has both religious meaning (Jesus is the Lamb of God) and commercial significance (wool was the source of Rouen's wealth). The clock's artistic highlight fills the underside of the arch (walk underneath and stretch your back), with the "Good Shepherd" and loads of sheep.

Bell Tower Panorama: To see the inner workings of the clock and an extraordinary panorama over Rouen and its cathedral, climb the clock tower's 100 steps. You'll tour several rooms with the help of a friendly, 40-minute audioguide and learn about life in Rouen when the tower was built. The big one- and two-ton bells ring on the hour—a deafening experience if you're in the tower. Don't miss the 360-degree view outside from the very top (€7, includes audioguide, Tue-Sun 10:00-13:00 & 14:00-19:00, shorter hours off-season, closed Mon year-round).

• *Walk under the Gros Horloge and continue straight a half-block, then take a one-block detour left (up Rue Thouret) to see the...*

Palace of Justice (Palais de Justice)

Rouen is the capital of Normandy, and this impressive building is its parliament. The section on the left is the oldest, in Flamboyant Gothic style dating from 1550. Normandy was an independent little country from 911 to 1204, and since then, while a part of France, it's had an independent spirit and has enjoyed a bit of autonomy.

The parliament building fronts the historic Rue aux Juifs (Street of the Jews)—a reminder that this was the Jewish quarter from the 10th century until the early 14th century, when the Jews were expelled from France. Their homes were destroyed and the city took their land. Later, the empty real estate was used for the parliament.

• *Double back and continue up Rue du Gros Horloge. In a block, high on the left, you'll see a stone plaque dedicated to hometown hero Cavelier de la Salle, who explored the mouth of the Mississippi River, claimed the state of Louisiana for France, and was assassinated in Texas in 1687. Soon you'll reach...*

▲▲Notre-Dame Cathedral (Cathédrale Notre-Dame)

This cathedral is a landmark of art history. You're seeing essentially what Claude Monet saw as he painted 30 different studies of this frilly Gothic facade at various times of day. Using the physical building only as a rack upon which to hang light, mist, dusk, and shadows, Monet was capturing "impressions." One of these paintings is in Rouen's Museum of Fine

Arts; others are at the Orsay Museum in Paris. Find the plaque showing one of the paintings (in the corner of the square, about 30 paces to your right if exiting the TI).

Cost and Hours: Free, Tue-Sun 9:00-19:00, Mon from 14:00; Nov-March until 18:00 and closed 12:00-14:00; Mass: Tue-Sat at 10:00, July-Aug also at 18:00, Sun and holidays at 8:30, 10:30, and 12:00.

❷ Self-Guided Tour

There's been a church on this site for more than a thousand years. Charlemagne honored it with a visit in the eighth century before the Vikings sacked it a hundred years later. The building you see today was constructed between the 12th and 14th centuries, though lightning strikes, wars (the cathedral was devastated in WWII bombing), and other destructive forces meant constant rebuilding.

• *We'll start outside, facing the...*

Central Facade: Look up at the elaborate, soaring **facade,** with bright statues on either side of the central portal—later, we'll meet some of their friends face-to-face inside the cathedral. The facade is another fine Rouen example of Flamboyant Gothic, and the dark spire, soaring nearly 500 feet high, is awe-inspiring. Why such a big cathedral here? Until the 1700s, Rouen was the second-largest city in France—rich from its wool trade and its booming port. On summer evenings, there's usually a colorful light show on the cathedral's facade (see "Helpful Hints," earlier).

Above the **main door** is a marvelous depiction of the Tree of Jesse. Jesse, King David's father, is shown reclined, resting his head on his hand, looking nonplussed. The tree grows from Jesse's back; the figures sprouting from its branches represent the lineage of Jesus. Many statues on the facade are headless. In 1562, during the French Wars of Religion, Protestant iconoclasts held the city for six months—more than enough time to deface the church.

• *Head inside.*

Cathedral Interior: Look down the center of the **nave.** This is a classic Gothic nave—four stories of pointed-arch arcades, the top filled with windows to help illuminate the interior. Today, the interior is lighter than intended because clear glass has replaced the original colored glass (destroyed over the centuries by angry Protestants, horrible storms, changing tastes, and WWII bombs).

Circle counterclockwise around the church, starting down the right aisle. The side chapels and windows, each dedicated to a different saint, display the changing styles through the centuries.

At the high altar, look across and up at the north transept **rose window,** which dates from around 1300. It survived a hurricane in 1683. During World War II the glass was taken out, but the original stone tracery did not survive. On the right (in the south transept) is a **chapel dedicated to Joan of Arc.** Its focal point is a touching statue of the saint being burned. The chapel's modern 1956 windows replaced those destroyed in the war.

Passing through an iron gate after the high altar, you come to several **stone statues.** Each is "bolted" to the wall—as they originally were in their niches high above the street centuries ago. These figures were lifted from the facade during a cleaning and provide a rare chance to stand toe-to-toe with a medieval statue.

Several **stone tombs** on your left date from when Rouen was the Norman capital. The first tomb is for Rollo, the first duke of Normandy who died about 932 (he's also the great-great-great-great grandfather of William the Conqueror, seventh duke of Normandy, c. 1028). Rollo was chief of the first gang of Vikings (the original "Normans") who decided to settle here. Called the Father of Normandy, Rollo died at the age of 80, but he is portrayed on his tomb as if he were 33 (as was the fashion, because Jesus died at that age). Thanks to later pillage and plunder, only Rollo's femur is inside the tomb.

And speaking of body parts, the next tomb once contained the heart of English King **Richard the Lionheart,** famous for his military exploits in the Third Crusade (he died in 1199). Over the years, people forgot about the heart, and it was only rediscovered in 1838. It was eventually analyzed by forensic scientists, who concluded that the king had died from a festering arrow wound (not poison, as popularly thought). Look across the altar to the radiant stained-glass window (we'll get there soon but the view is best from here).

Smile at the cute angels on your right and circle behind the altar. The beautiful **windows** with bold blues and reds are generally from the 13th century. Opposite Richard the Lionheart's tomb is a fine window dedicated to St. Julian, patron of hoteliers and travelers (with pane-by-pane descriptions in English on an easel below).

Continue a few paces, then look up to the **ceiling** over the nave (directly above Rollo's femur). You can see the lighter-colored patchwork where, in 1999, a fierce winter storm caused a spire to crash through the roof.

• *Exit while you can, through the side door of the north transept. (If the door is closed, leave through the main entrance, turn right, then loop back alongside the church.)*

North Transept Facade: Outside, look back at the **facade** over the door of the north transept. The fine-but-dirty tympanum (the area over the door) shows a graphic Last Judgment. Jesus stands between the saved (on the left) and the damned (on the right). Notice the devil grasping a miser, who clutches a bag of coins. On the far right, look for the hellish hot tub, where even a bishop (pointy hat) is eternally in hot water. And is it my imagination, or are those saved souls on the far left high-fiving each other?

Most of the facade has been cleaned—blasted with jets of water—but the limestone carving like this is still black. It's too delicate to survive the hosing. A more expensive laser cleaning has begun, and the result is astonishing.

• *From this courtyard, a gate deposits you on a traffic-free street facing the elegant Art Nouveau facade of the recommended Dame Cakes tea shop. This was originally the workshop of the church's lead 19th-century craftsman, Ferdinand Marrou. To showcase his work, he fashioned the wrought iron on this door as well as the fine touches inside.*

Turn right and walk along the appealing Rue St. Romain for one last church sight.

Spire View: In a short distance, look up through an opening above the entrance to the Joan of Arc Museum and gaze back at the cathedral's prickly **spire.** Made of cast iron in the late 1800s—about the same time Gustave Eiffel was building his tower in Paris—the spire is, at 490 feet, the tallest in France. You can also see the smaller (green) spires, one of which was blown over in that violent 1999 storm and crashed—all 30 tons of it—through the roof to the cathedral floor. Replaced in 2013, you can bet it's now securely bolted down.

• *To learn more about Rouen's most famous figure, consider touring the...*

▲Joan of Arc Museum (Historial Jeanne d'Arc)

Rouen's Archbishop's Palace, where in 1431 Joan of Arc was tried and sentenced to death, now hosts a multimedia experience that tells her story. Equipped with headphones, you'll walk for 75 minutes through a series of rooms, each with a brief video presentation that tries very hard to teach and entertain. Your tour ends in the Officialité—the room where the trial took place. You're then set free to explore exhibits examining the role Joan of Arc has played in French culture over the centuries. The complete experience is entertaining and informative, but slow-moving—both kids and adults may find it a little boring.

Cost and Hours: €10.50, required tours depart on the quarter-hour Tue-Sun from 10:00, last tour generally at 17:15, closed 12:00-13:00 and Mon year-round, 7 Rue St. Romain, tel. 02 35 52 48 00, www.historial-jeannedarc.fr.

• *From the museum, continue down atmospheric Rue St. Romain. At #26, find the shop marked...*

Fayencerie Augy

Monsieur Augy and his family welcome shoppers to browse his studio/gallery/shop and see Rouen's earthenware "china" being made in the traditional faience style (Mon-Sat 10:00-19:00, closed Sun, shipping available, 26 Rue St. Romain, www.fayencerie-augy.com). First, the clay is molded and fired. Then it's dipped in white enamel, dried, lovingly hand painted, and fired a second time. Rouen was the first city in France to make this colorfully glazed faience earthenware. In the 1700s, the town had 18 factories churning out the popular product. For more faience, visit the local Museum of Ceramics (see "Sights in Rouen").

• *Peer down Rue des Chanoines (next to Augy) for a skinny example of the higgledy-piggledy streets common in medieval Rouen. Back on Rue St. Romain, walk along the massive Archbishop's Palace, which (after crossing Rue de la République) leads to the fancy...*

St. Maclou Church (Eglise St. Maclou)

This church's unique, bowed facade is textbook Flamboyant Gothic. Notice the flame-like tracery decorating its gable. Because this was built at the very end of the Gothic age—and construction took many years—the carved wooden doors are from the next age: the Renaissance (c. 1550). Study the graphic Last Judgment above the doors, and imagine the mindset of the frightened parishioners who worshipped here. If it's open, the bright and airy interior is worth a quick peek (closed Tue-Fri).

• *Leaving the church, turn right, and then take another right (giving the little boys on the corner wall a wide berth). Wander past a fine wall of half-timbered buildings fronting Rue Martainville, to the back end of St. Maclou Church.*

Half-Timbered Buildings

Because the local stone—a chalky limestone from the cliffs of the Seine River—was of poor quality (your thumbnail is stronger), and because local oak was plentiful, half-timbered buildings became a Rouen specialty from the 14th through 19th century. There are still 2,000 half-timbered buildings in town; about 100 date from before 1520. Cantilevered floors were standard until the early 1500s. These top-heavy designs made sense: City land was limited, property taxes were based on ground-floor square footage, and the cantilevering minimized unsupported spans on upper floors. The oak beams provided the structural skeleton of the building, which was then filled in with a mix of clay, straw, or whatever was available.

Until the Industrial Age, this was the textile district where cloth was processed, dyed, and sold. When that industry moved across the river in the 19th century, the neighborhood was mothballed and forgotten. After World War II it was recognized as historic and preserved. Eventually rents went up, and gentrification crept in.

• *A block after the church, on the left at 186 Rue Martainville, a short lane leads to the...*

NORMANDY

▲Plague Cemetery (Aître St. Maclou)

During the great plagues of the Middle Ages, as many as two-thirds of the people in this parish died. For the decimated community, dealing with the corpses was an overwhelming task. This half-timbered courtyard (c. 1520, free to enter, daily 9:00-18:00) was a mass grave, an ossuary where the bodies were "processed." (Expect lots of construction around the courtyard as the place is getting a major facelift). Bodies were dumped into the grave (an open pit where the well is now) and drenched in liquid lime to help speed decomposition. Later, the bones were stacked in alcoves above the once-open arcades that line this courtyard. Notice the colonnades with their ghoulish carvings of gravediggers' tools, skulls, crossbones, and characters doing the "dance of death." In this *danse macabre*, Death, the great equalizer, grabs people of all social classes. As you leave, spy the dried black cat (in tiny glass case to the left of the door). Perhaps to overcome evil, it was buried during the building's construction.

Nearby: Farther down Rue Martainville, at Place St. Marc, a colorful market is lively Sunday until about 13:30 and all day Tuesday, Friday, and Saturday.

• *Our walk is over. To return to the train station or reach the Museum of Fine Arts directly, turn right from the boneyard, then right again at the little boys (onto Rue Damiette), and hike up a pleasing antique row to the vertical St. Ouen Church (a seventh-century abbey turned 15th-century church; lush park behind). Turn left when you see St. Ouen Church and continue down traffic-free Rue de l'Hôpital (which becomes Rue Gante-rie). Turn right on Rue de l'Ecureuil to find the museum directly ahead. To continue to the train station, turn left onto Rue Jean-Lecanuet, then right onto Rue Jeanne d'Arc.*

Sights in Rouen

These museums, within blocks of one another, are all free and never crowded.

▲Museum of Fine Arts (Musée des Beaux-Arts)

Paintings from many periods are beautifully displayed in this overlooked two-floor museum, including works by Caravaggio, Peter Paul Rubens, Paolo Veronese, Jan Steen, Velázquez, Théodore Géricault, Jean-Auguste-Dominique Ingres, Eugène Delacroix, and several Impressionists. With its free admission and calm interior, this museum is worth a short visit for the Impressionists and a surgical hit of a few other key artists. The museum café is good for a peaceful break.

Cost and Hours: Free, €11 for frequent and impressive special exhibitions—check website; open Wed-Mon 10:00-18:00, closed

Tue; bag check available, a few blocks below train station at Esplanade Marcel Duchamp, tel. 02 35 71 28 40, www.musees-rouen-normandie.fr.

Visiting the Museum: Pick up the essential museum map at the info desk as you enter, then climb the grand staircase that divides the museum into two wings.

Turning right when you reach the second floor, you'll pass through a few rooms, then start seeing some names you recognize: Ingres and Jacques-Louis David (Room 2.21) and then a good collection of works by Géricault (Room 2.22). Turn left into Room 2.33, with one of Monet's famous paintings of the Rouen cathedral facade. Now loop through this wing to enjoy scenes inspired by Normandy's landscape and works by Impressionist greats (Monet, Sisley, Pissarro, Renoir, Degas, and Corot). Make a point to appreciate beautiful paintings by Impressionists whose names you may not recognize. Room 2.25 showcases a scene of Rouen's busy port in 1855.

Paintings on the other side of the grand staircase are devoted to French painters from the 17th and 18th centuries (Boucher, Fragonard, and Poussin) and Italian works, including several by Veronese. A gripping Caravaggio canvas (Room 2.4), depicting the flagellation of Christ, demands attention with its dramatic lighting and realistic faces.

Stairs at the rear, near the Caravaggio, lead down to an intriguing collection of paintings by 16th-century Dutch and Belgian artists and temporary exhibits. On the other side of the first floor, pass through the bookstore to find a collection of modern paintings: several by hometown boy Raymond Duchamp-Villon (brother of the famous Dadaist Marcel Duchamp), a few colorful Modiglianis, and a grand-scale Delacroix.

Museum of Ironworks (Musée le Secq des Tournelles, a.k.a. Musée de la Ferronnerie)

This deconsecrated church houses a vast collection of iron objects, many of them more than 1,500 years old. Locks, chests, keys, tools, thimbles, coffee grinders, corkscrews, and flatware from centuries ago—virtually anything made of iron is on display. You can duck into the entry area for a glimpse of a medieval iron scene without passing through the turnstile.

Cost and Hours: Free, no English explanations, Wed-Mon 14:00-18:00, closed Tue, behind Museum of Fine Arts at 2 Rue Jacques Villon, tel. 02 35 88 42 92, www.museelesecqdestournelles.fr.

Museum of Ceramics (Musée de la Céramique)

This fine old mansion is filled with examples of Rouen's famous faience earthenware, dating from the 16th to 18th century. There are also examples of Sèvres and Delft wares—but not a word of English.

Cost and Hours: Free, Wed-Mon 14:00-18:00, closed Tue, 1 Rue Faucon, tel. 02 35 07 31 74, www.museedelaceramique.fr.

Joan of Arc Tower (La Tour Jeanne d'Arc)

This misnamed and massive tower (1204) was once part of Rouen's brooding castle. Joan was a prisoner in the castle before her execution, but the actual tower where she was kept is no longer standing. Cross the deep moat and find three small floors (and 122 spiral steps) covering tidbits of Rouen's and Joan's history. The top floor gives a good peek at an impressive wood substructure—but no views.

Cost and Hours: Free, Tue-Sun 14:00-16:00, closed Mon, one block uphill from the Museum of Fine Arts on Rue du Bouvreuil, tel. 02 35 98 16 21, www.donjonderouen.com.

NEAR ROUEN
The Route of the Ancient Abbeys
(La Route des Anciennes Abbayes)

This driving route—punctuated with medieval abbeys, apples, cherry trees, and Seine River views—provides a pleasing detour for those with cars connecting Rouen and Honfleur or the D-Day beaches. The only "essential" stop on this drive is the Abbey of Jumièges, about 45 minutes from Rouen.

From Rouen to Duclair: Leaving Rouen, follow the Seine along its right bank and track signs carefully for D-982 to Duclair. Fifteen minutes west of Rouen, drivers can stop to admire the gleaming Romanesque church at the **Abbey of St. Georges de Boscherville** (skip the abbey grounds). This perfectly intact and beautiful church makes for interesting comparisons with the ruined church at Jumièges. The recommended Chambres d'Hôtes Les Hostises de Boscherville next door is good for a snack or lunch—and a peaceful night's sleep.

From Duclair to Jumièges: Leaving Duclair, follow D-65 to Jumièges and the **Abbey of Jumièges,** a spiritual place for lovers of evocative ruins (worth ▲; €6.50, helpful English handout, daily 9:30-18:30, mid-Sept-mid-April 9:30–13:00 & 14:30-17:30; ask to borrow the detailed English booklet or pay €7 for the well-done *Itineraries* book, or download the free Jumièges app to see virtual reconstructions of the original abbey; tel. 02 35 37 24 02, www.abbayedejumieges.fr).

Founded in AD 654 as a Benedictine abbey, it was leveled by Vikings in the 9th century, then rebuilt by William the Conqueror in the 11th century. This magnificent complex thrived for centuries as Normandy's largest abbey. It was part of the great monastic movement that reestablished civilization in Normandy from the chaos that followed the fall of Rome (for more about the power of the Benedictines, read about Cluny Abbey on page 922).

The abbey was destroyed again during the French Revolution, when it was used as a quarry, and it has changed little since then. Today there is no roof, and many walls are entirely gone. But what remains of the abbey's Church of Notre-Dame is awe-inspiring. Study its stark Romanesque facade standing 160 feet high. Stroll down the nave's center; notice the three levels of arches and the soaring rear wall capped by a lantern tower to light the choir. Find a seat in the ruined apse and imagine the church before its destruction. You'll discover brilliant views of the ruins and better appreciate its importance by wandering into the park.

Decent lunch options lie across the street from the abbey, and there's a TI for the village of Jumièges in front of the parking lot.

From Jumièges Onward: From near Jumièges you can cross the Seine on the tiny, free, and frequent car ferry to the D-913, then connect with the A-13 (better), or continue following the right bank of the Seine and cross it at the Pont de Tancarville bridge (€5). For a grand view, cross even farther west on the magnificent Normandy Bridge, near Honfleur (Pont de Normandie, €6). By any route, allow 75 minutes from Jumièges to Honfleur, or two hours to Bayeux.

Sleeping in Rouen

These hotels are perfectly central, within two blocks of Notre-Dame Cathedral.

$$$ Hôtel Mercure*** is a modern business hotel with a professional staff, a lobby/bar you can stretch out in, and 125 well-equipped and thoughtfully appointed rooms. Suites come with good views of the cathedral, but are pricey and not much bigger than a double, "privilege" rooms have balconies and at least partial views of the cathedral, and standard rooms are cheapest but fine (air-con, elevator, pay parking garage, spendy breakfast, 7 Rue Croix de Fer, tel. 02 35 52 69 52, www.mercure.com, h1301@accor.com).

$$ Hôtel le Cardinal** is a good value with 15 sharp, well-designed rooms, most with point-blank views of the cathedral and all with queen-size beds and modern bathrooms (larger but pricier fourth-floor rooms with balconies and great cathedral views, reception often unstaffed as owners do the cleaning, elevator, 1 Place de la Cathédrale, tel. 02 35 70 24 42, www.cardinal-hotel.fr, info@cardinal-hotel.fr).

$ Hôtel Le Vieux Carré** is an adorable 13-room place a block from the Museum of Fine Arts. You're greeted by a leafy,

NORMANDY

half-timbered courtyard where lunch and afternoon tea are served, a cozy lobby, and welcoming owners. Rooms are a little tight (mostly double beds) but clean and traditional with floral wallpaper (no elevator but just three floors, 34 Rue Ganterie, tel. 02 35 71 67 70, www.hotel-vieux-carre.com, vieuxcarre.rouen@gmail.com).

Near Rouen: To sleep peacefully within a 20-minute drive of town, consider sleepy St-Martin-de-Boscherville, where you can stay at **$ Chambres d'Hôtes Les Hostises de Boscherville.** Christel has four tasteful and spacious rooms, a big garden, and point-blank views to the abbey church—and is the only game in town when it comes to dinner (includes breakfast, book ahead for her cheap-and-tasty €18 "light" dinner of salad, killer quiche, cheese, dessert, and wine, 1 Route de Quevillon, 76840 St-Martin-de-Boscherville, tel. 02 35 34 19 81, www.chambrehôtenormandie. com, hostises.boscherville@gmail.com).

Eating in Rouen

To find the best eating action, prowl the streets between the St. Maclou and St. Ouen churches (Rues Martainville and Damiette) for *crêperies,* wine bars, international cuisine, and traditional restaurants. This is Rouen's liveliest area at night (except Sunday and Monday, when many places are closed).

$$$$ Restaurant La Couronne is a venerable and cozy place to dine very well. Reserve ahead to experience the same cuisine that Julia Child tasted when she ate her first French meal here in 1948 (31 Place du Vieux Marché, tel. 02 35 71 40 90, www.lacouronne. com.fr).

$ Crêperie le St. Romain, between the cathedral and St. Maclou Church, is an excellent budget option. Here you'll find filling crêpes with small salads in a warm setting (tables in the rear are best, lunch Tue-Sat, dinner Thu-Sat, closed Sun-Mon, 52 Rue St. Romain, tel. 02 35 88 90 36).

$ Au P'it Verdot is a lively wine bar-café where locals gather for a glass of wine and meat-and-cheese plates in the thick of restaurant row (appetizers only, Tue-Sat 18:00-24:00, closed Sun-Mon, 13 Rue Père Adam, tel. 02 35 36 34 43).

$ Bistro Nova is a nifty and quirky place to eat well in a warm, friendly setting at good prices. The menu changes daily, but one meat, one fish, and one veggie *plat* are always available (excellent wine list, lunch and dinner, closed Sun-Mon, 2 Place du Lieutenant Aubert, tel. 02 35 70 20 25).

$$ La Petite Auberge, a block off Rue Damiette, is the most traditional place I list. It has an Old World interior, a nice terrace, and good prices—and it's open Sundays (good escargot and *en-*

trecôte with Camembert, reservations smart, closed Mon, 164 Rue Martainville, tel. 02 35 70 80 18).

Lunch Places: For lunch only, try one of these two options.

$$ Dame Cakes is ideal if you need a Jane Austen fix at lunch or teatime. The decor is from a more precious era, and the baked goods are out of this world. Locals adore the tables in the back garden, while tourists eat up the cathedral view from the first-floor room (Mon-Sat 10:30-19:00, closed Sun, 70 Rue St. Romain, tel. 02 35 07 49 31).

$ Bistrot des Carmes is ideal in good weather with tables gathered in a leafy square hidden a few blocks from the cathedral. You'll enjoy its friendly vibe (closed Sun, 37 Place des Carmes, tel. 02 35 71 66 89).

Rouen Connections

Rouen is well served by trains from Paris and Caen, making Bayeux and the D-Day beaches a snap to reach.

From Rouen by Train to: Paris' Gare St. Lazare (nearly hourly, 1.5 hours), **Bayeux** (14/day, 2.5 hours, change in Caen), **Caen** (14/day, 1.5 hours), **Pontorson/Mont St-Michel** (3/day, 5 hours, change in Caen; more with change in Paris, 7 hours).

By Train and Bus to: Honfleur (5/day Mon-Sat, 2/day Sun, 1-hour train to Le Havre, then find Bay D at bus station just outside train station for 30-minute bus trip over Normandy Bridge to Honfleur).

Route Tips for Drivers: Those continuing to Honfleur or the D-Day beaches should consider the Route of the Ancient Abbeys, outlined earlier, under "Sights in Rouen."

Honfleur

Gazing at its cozy harbor lined with skinny, soaring houses, it's easy to overlook the historic importance of Honfleur (ohn-flur). For more than a thousand years, sailors have enjoyed this port's ideal location, where the Seine River greets the English Channel. William the Conqueror received supplies shipped from Honfleur. Samuel de Champlain sailed from here in 1603 to North America, where he founded Quebec City.

NORMANDY

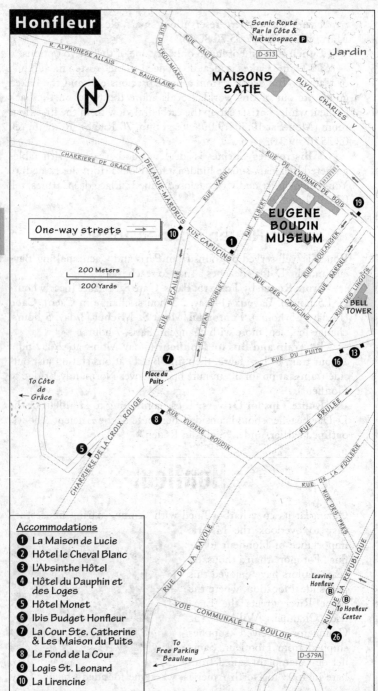

Honfleur

Scenic Route
Par la Côte &
Naturospace

Jardin

MAISONS
SATIE

R. ALPHONESE ALLAIS
R. BAUDELAIRE
R. DU TROU MIARD
RUE HAUTE
D-513

CHARRIERE DE GRÁCE
R. L DELARUE-MARDRUS
BLVD. CHARLES V
RUE DE L'HOMME DE BOIS

RUE VARIN
RUE CAPUCINS

EUGENE
BOUDIN
MUSEUM

One-way streets →

RUE BUCAILLE
RUE JEAN DOUBLET
RUE DES CAPUCINS

RUE BOULANGERE
RUE BARBEL
RUE DES LINGOTS

BELL
TOWER

200 Meters
200 Yards

RUE DU PUITS

RUE BRULEE

To Côte
de
Grâce

Place du
Puits

RUE EUGENE BOUDIN

CHARRIERE DE LA CROIX ROUGE

RUE DE LA FOULERIE

RUE DES PRES

RUE DE LA BAVOLE

Leaving
Honfleur

To Honfleur
Center

VOIE COMMUNALE LE BOULOIR

RUE DE LA REPUBLIQUE

To
Free Parking
Beaulieu

D-579A

Accommodations
1 La Maison de Lucie
2 Hôtel le Cheval Blanc
3 L'Absinthe Hôtel
4 Hôtel du Dauphin et
   des Loges
5 Hôtel Monet
6 Ibis Budget Honfleur
7 La Cour Ste. Catherine
   & Les Maison du Puits
8 Le Fond de la Cour
9 Logis St. Leonard
10 La Lirencine

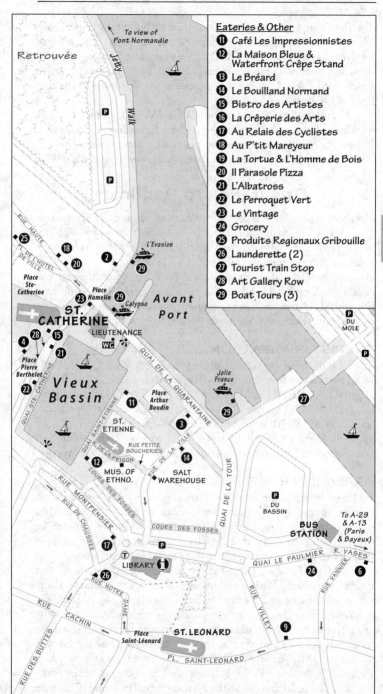

Eateries & Other

11 Café Les Impressionnistes
12 La Maison Bleue & Waterfront Crêpe Stand
13 Le Bréard
14 Le Bouilland Normand
15 Bistro des Artistes
16 La Crêperie des Arts
17 Au Relais des Cyclistes
18 Au P'tit Mareyeur
19 La Tortue & L'Homme de Bois
20 Il Parasole Pizza
21 L'Albatross
22 Le Perroquet Vert
23 Le Vintage
24 Grocery
25 Produits Regionaux Gribouille
26 Launderette (2)
27 Tourist Train Stop
28 Art Gallery Row
29 Boat Tours (3)

NORMANDY

Retrouvée

To view of
Pont Normandie

Jetty Walk

RUE HAUTE

PL. DE L'HOTEL
DE VILLE

Place
Ste-Catherine

L'Evasion

Place
Hamelin

ST. CATHERINE

Calypso

Avant Port

LIEUTENANCE

WC

Place
Pierre
Berthelot

Vieux Bassin

Place
Arthur
Boudin

Jolie
France

ST. ETIENNE

RUE SAINTE-ETIENNE

R. DE LA PRISON

RUE PETITE
BOUCHERIES

MUS. OF
ETHNO.

RUE DE LA VILLE

SALT
WAREHOUSE

QUAI DE LA QUARANTAINE

QUAI DE LA TOUR

P
DU
MOLE

P

P
DU
BASSIN

BUS
STATION

To A-29
& A-13
(Paris
& Bayeux)

COURS DES FOSSES

RUE MONTPENSIER

RUE DE CHAUSSÉE

QUAI LE PAULMIER

R. VASES

RUE VANNIER

LIBRARY

RUE NOTRE DAME

RUE VILLEY

RUE CACHIN

RUE DES BUTTES

Place
Saint-Léonard

ST. LEONARD

PL. SAINT-LEONARD

QUAI STE. CATHERINE

The charming town was also a favorite of 19th-century Impressionists who were captivated by Honfleur's unusual light—the result of its river-meets-sea setting. The 19th-century artist Eugène Boudin lived and painted in Honfleur, attracting Monet and other creative types from Paris. In some ways, modern art was born in the fine light of idyllic little Honfleur.

Honfleur escaped the bombs of World War II, and today offers a romantic port enclosed on three sides by sprawling outdoor cafés. Long eclipsed by the gargantuan port of Le Havre just across the Seine, Honfleur happily uses its past as a bar stool...and sits on it.

Orientation to Honfleur

Honfleur is popular—expect crowds on weekends and during summer. All of Honfleur's appealing lanes and activities are within a short stroll of its old port, the Vieux Bassin. The Seine River flows just east of the center, the hills of the Côte de Grâce form its western limit, and Rue de la République slices north-south through the center to the port. Honfleur has two can't-miss sights—the harbor and St. Catherine Church—and a handful of other intriguing monuments. But really, the town itself is its best sight.

TOURIST INFORMATION

The TI is in the glassy public library (Mediathèque) on Quai le Paulmier, two blocks from the Vieux Bassin (Mon-Sat 9:30-19:00, Sun 10:00-17:00; Sept-June Mon-Sat until 18:30 and closed daily for lunch 12:30-14:00; closed Sun afternoon Nov-Easter; free WCs, tel. 02 31 89 23 30, www.ot-honfleur.fr). Here you can rent a €5 audioguide for a self-guided town walk, pick up regional bus and train schedules, and get limited information on the D-Day beaches.

ARRIVAL IN HONFLEUR

By Bus: Get off at the small bus station (gare routière), and confirm your departure at the information counter. To reach the TI and old town, turn right as you exit the station and walk five minutes up Quai le Paulmier. Note that the bus stop on Rue de la République is closer to some accommodations (see the "Honfleur" map).

By Car: Follow Centre-Ville signs, then find your hotel and unload your bags (double-parking is OK for a few minutes). Parking is a headache in Honfleur, especially on summer and holiday weekends. Some hotels offer pay parking (worth considering); otherwise, your hotelier knows where you can park for free. If you don't mind paying for convenience, Parking du Bassin across from the TI is central (€3/hour, €24/24 hours). To save piles of euros, find Parking du Môle or Parking Bassin de l'Est (€5/day). Free parking is available farther out at the Naturospace Museum (15-minute walk up Boulevard Charles V, near the beach), on the road near the recommended Hôtel Monet, and at Parking Beaulieu (take Rue St-Nichol to Rue Guillaume de Beaulieu). Street parking, metered during the day, is free from 20:00 to 8:00. See the "Honfleur" map for parking locations.

HELPFUL HINTS

Museum Pass: The €13 museum pass, sold at participating museums, covers the Eugène Boudin Museum, Maisons Satie, and the Museum of Ethnography and Norman Popular Arts (www.musees-honfleur.fr).

Market Day: The area around St. Catherine Church becomes a colorful open-air market every Saturday (9:00-13:00). A smaller organic-food-only market takes place here on Wednesday mornings, and a flea market takes center stage here the first Sunday of every month and also on Wednesday evenings in summer.

Grocery Store: There's one near the TI (long hours daily July-Aug, closed Mon off-season, 16 Quai le Paulmier).

Regional Products: Visit **Produits Regionaux Gribouille** for any Norman delicacy you can dream up. Ask about cider and Calvados tastings (generally closed Wed, 16 Rue de l'Homme de Bois, tel. 02 31 89 29 54).

Wi-Fi: Free Wi-Fi is available on the port and at several cafés, including the recommended **L'Albatross** and **Le Perroquet Vert.**

Laundry: Lavomatique is a block behind the TI, toward the port (self-service only, daily 7:30-21:30, 4 Rue Notre-Dame). **La Lavandière** has handy drop-off service (Mon-Sat 8:30-12:30 & 14:00-18:00, closed Sun, two blocks from the harbor at 41 Rue de la République).

Taxi: Call 06 08 60 17 98.

Tourist Train: Honfleur's handy *petit train* toots you up the Côte de Grâce—the hill overlooking town—and back in about 45 minutes (€7, June-Sept daily 10:30-17:30, off-season weekends only, departures on the hour except at lunchtime, leaves from across gray swivel bridge that leads to Parking du Môle).

Sights in Honfleur

▲▲Vieux Bassin (Old Port)

If you're an early riser, you can watch the morning light at it shines brilliantly on Honfleur's harbor. Take a prebreakfast walk to savor the quiet scene that Monet would have loved.

No matter when you go, start by standing near the water facing Honfleur's square harbor, with the merry-go-round across the

NORMANDY

lock to your left, and survey
the town. The word "Honfleur"
is Scandinavian, meaning the
shelter *(fleur)* of Hon (a Viking
warlord). This town has been
sheltering residents for about
a thousand years. During the
Hundred Years' War (14th century), the entire harbor was fortified by a big wall with twin

gatehouses (the one surviving gatehouse, La Lieutenance, is on
your right). A narrow channel allowing boats to pass was protected
by a heavy chain.

After the walls were demolished around 1700, those skinny
houses on the right side were built for the town's fishermen. How
about a room on the top floor, with no elevator? Imagine moving
a piano or a refrigerator into one of these units today. The spire
halfway up the left side of the port belongs to Honfleur's oldest
church. The port, once crammed with fishing boats, now harbors
sleek sailboats.

Walk toward the Lieutenance gatehouse. In front of the barrel-vaulted arch (once the entry to the town), you can see a bronze
bust of Samuel de Champlain—the explorer who, 400 years ago,
sailed with an Honfleur crew—famous for their maritime skills—
to make his discoveries in the New World. Champlain is acknowl-
edged as the founder of the Canadian city of Quebec—which remains French-speaking to this day.

Turn around to see various tour and fishing boats and the
masts of the high-flying Normandy Bridge (described later) in the
distance. Fisherfolk catch flatfish, scallops, and tiny shrimp daily
to bring to the Marché au Poisson, located 100 yards to your right
(look for white metal structures with blue lettering). Wednesday
through Saturday, you may see fishermen's wives selling *crevettes*
(shrimp) and more. You can buy them *cuites* (cooked) or *vivantes*
(alive and wiggly). They are happy to let you sample one (rip off the
cute little head and tail, and pop what's left into your mouth—*dél-
icieuse!*), or buy a cupful to go for a few euros.

You'll probably see artists sitting at easels around the harbor,
as Boudin and Monet did. Many consider Honfleur the birthplace
of 19th-century Impressionism. This was a time when people began
to revere the out-of-doors, and pretty towns like Honfleur and the
nearby coast made perfect subjects (and still do), thanks to the unusual luminosity of the region. And with the advent of new railway
lines in the late 1800s, artists could travel to the best light like
never before. Monet came here to visit the artist Boudin, a hometown boy, and the battle cry of the Impressionists—"Out of the

studio and into the light!"—was born. Artists set up their easels along the harbor to catch the light playing on the line of buildings, slate shingles, timbers, geraniums, clouds, and reflections in the water—much as they still do today.

Old Honfleur

A chance to study the Lego-style timber-frame houses of Honfleur awaits just off the harbor. On the southern quay, next to the Church of St. Etienne (today's skippable Museum of the Sea), head up Rue de la Prison (past the worthwhile Museum of Ethnography, described later) and bend around to Rue des Petites Boucheries for some prime examples. The oldest beams of these buildings were numbered so they could be disassembled and moved. The street is named for butcher shops that once lined the lane—the ancient wood shed just before the passage is a surviving example. Walking through the slate-sided passage, you'll pop out onto Rue de la Ville with more historic Norman architecture. Across the way is one of three huge 17th-century salt warehouses (today used for exhibitions). It's worth entering to see the huge stone hall with its remarkable wooden ceiling and imagine the importance of salt as a preservative before refrigeration existed.

Strategically positioned Honfleur guarded Paris from a naval attack up the Seine. That's why the king fortified it with a wall in the 1300s. In the 1600s, when England was no longer a threat, the walls were torn down, leaving the town with some wide boulevards (like the one in front of the TI) and plenty of stones (like those that made the salt warehouse).

▲▲St. Catherine Church (Eglise Ste. Catherine)

St. Catherine's replaced an earlier stone church, destroyed in the Hundred Years' War. In those chaotic times, the town's money was spent to fortify its walls, leaving only enough funds to erect a wooden church. The unusual wood-shingled exterior suggests that this church has a different story to tell than most. In the last months of World War II, a bomb fell through the church's roof—but didn't

explode—leaving this unique church intact for you to visit today.

Cost and Hours: Free, daily 9:00-18:30, Sept-June until 17:15, Place Ste-Catherine.

Visiting the Church: Walk inside. You'd swear that if it were turned over, the building would float—the legacy of a community of sailors and fishermen, with loads of talented boat-builders (and no church architect). When workers put up the first (left) nave in 1466, it soon became apparent that more space was needed—so a second was built in 1497 (on the right). Because it felt too much like a market hall, they added side aisles.

The oak columns were prepared as if the wood was meant for a ship—soaked in seawater for seven years and then dried for seven years. Notice some pillars are full-length and others are supported by stone bases. Trees come in different sizes, yet each pillar had to be the same length.

The pipe organ (from 1772, rebuilt in 1953) behind you is popular for concerts, and half of the modern pews are designed to flip so that you can face the music. Take a close look at the balustrade (below the organ) with carved wooden panels featuring 17 musical instruments used in the 16th century.

Find a seat, and enjoy the worshipful ambience of this beautiful space. But don't sit in the box in the center; this was reserved for the local noble lord and his family. If you want to gossip, head to the "cackling zone"—an open-air porch (outside, about halfway up on the right) where historically (and perhaps hysterically) people gathered after Mass.

Bell Tower: The church's bell tower was built away from the church to avoid placing too much stress on the wooden church's roof, and to help minimize fire hazards. Notice the funky shingled chestnut beams that run from its squat base to support the skinny tower, and find the small, faded wooden sculpture of a tiny St. Catherine over the door. Until recently the bell ringer lived in the bell tower. (The tower interior may be open to visit on summer weekends.)

HONFLEUR'S MUSEUMS AND GALLERIES

Eugène Boudin established Honfleur's artistic tradition in the 1800s. The town remains a popular haunt for artists, many of whom display their works in Honfleur's many art galleries (the best ones are along the streets between St. Catherine Church and the port). As you stroll around the town taking in its old sights, take time to enjoy today's art, too.

▲Eugène Boudin Museum

This pleasing little museum opened in 1869 and has several interesting floors with many paintings of Honfleur and the surrounding countryside, giving you a feel for Honfleur in the 1800s.

Cost and Hours: €8, covered by museum pass; May-Sept Wed-Mon 10:00-12:00 & 14:00-18:00, no lunchtime closure July-Aug, shorter hours Oct-April, closed Tue year-round; good but

Eugène Boudin (1824-1898)

Born in Honfleur, Boudin was the son of a harbor pilot. As an

amateur teenage artist, he found work in an art-supply store that catered to famous artists from Paris (such as landscapists Corot and Millet) who came to paint the seaside. Boudin himself studied in Paris and his work was exhibited there, but he kept his hometown roots.

At age 30 Boudin met the teenage Claude Monet. Monet had grown up in nearby Le Havre and, like Boudin, sketched the world around him—beaches, boats, and small-town life. Boudin encouraged him to don a scarf, set up his easel outdoors, and paint the scene exactly as he saw it. Today, we say: "Well, duh!" But "open-air" painting was unorthodox for artists trained to thoroughly study their subjects in the perfect lighting of a controlled studio setting. Boudin didn't teach Monet as much as give him the courage to follow his artistic instincts.

In the 1860s and 1870s, Boudin spent summers at his farm (St. Siméon) on the outskirts of Honfleur, hosting Monet, Edouard Manet, and other hangers-on. They taught Boudin the Impressionist techniques of using bright colors and building a subject with many individual brushstrokes. Boudin adapted those "strokes" to build subjects with "patches" of color. In 1874, Boudin joined the renegade Impressionists at their "revolutionary" exhibition in Paris.

skippable audioguide-€2, elevator, Rue de l'Homme de Bois, tel. 02 31 89 54 00, www.musees-honfleur.fr.

Visiting the Museum: Pick up a museum map at the ticket counter, tip your beret to Eugène Boudin, and climb the stairs (or take the elevator). The first floor has good WCs, kids' activity rooms, and some traditional *Normand* furnishings.

Second Floor: Making a right off the stairs leads you into a large room usually featuring special exhibits. A left off the stairs leads through a room of temporary exhibits to the *Peintures du 19eme Siècle* room, a small gallery of 19th-century paintings. Focus your time here. Boudin's artwork is shown alongside that of his colleagues and contemporaries (usually Claude Monet and Gustave Courbet), letting you see how those masters took Boudin's approach to the next level. Boudin loved his outdoor world and filled his paintings with port scenes, the sea, and big skies. Find the glass display case in the rear titled *Précurseur de l'Impressionisme*, with little pastel drawings, and follow Boudin's art chronologically, as it evolves. Nearby cases feature some of Boudin's first beach scenes and portraits.

When Boudin and other Honfleur artists showed their work in Paris, they created enough of a stir that Normandy came into vogue. Many Parisian artists (including Monet and other early Impressionists) traveled to Honfleur to dial in to the action. Boudin himself made a big impression on the father of Impressionism by introducing Monet to the practice of painting outside. This collection of Boudin's paintings—which the artist gave to his hometown—shows how his technique developed, from realistic portrayals of subjects (outlines colored in, like a coloring book) to masses of colors catching light (Impressionism). Boudin's beach scenes at the end of the room, showing aristocrats taking a healthy saltwater dip, helped fuel that style. His skies were good enough to earn him the nickname "King of Skies."

Third Floor: Follow the steps that lead up from the Boudin room to the small, enjoyable Hambourg/Rachet collection, which is largely from the mid-20th century. Finally, return to the main stairway and climb to another wing on the third floor to find a worthwhile collection of 20th-century works by artists who lived and learned in Honfleur, including the Fauvist painter Raoul Dufy and Yves Brayer. There's an exceptional view of the Normandy Bridge through the big windows.

▲Maisons Satie

If Honfleur is over-the-top cute, this museum, housed in composer Erik Satie's birthplace, is a burst of witty charm—just like the musical genius it honors. If you like Satie's music, this is a delight—a 1920s "Yellow Submarine." If not, it can be a ho-hum experience. Allow an hour for your visit.

Cost and Hours: €6.30, includes audioguide, covered by museum pass; May-Sept Wed-Mon 10:00-19:00, off-season 11:00-18:00, closed Jan-mid-Feb and Tue year-round; last entry one hour before closing, 5-minute walk from harbor at 67 Boulevard Charles V, tel. 02 31 89 11 11, www.musees-honfleur.fr.

Visiting the Museum: As you wander from room to room with your included audioguide, infrared signals transmit bits of Satie's dreamy music, along with a first-person story. As if you're living as an artist in 1920s Paris, you'll drift through a weird and whimsical series of old-school installations—winged pears, strangers in windows, and small girls with green eyes. The finale—performed by you—is the *Laboratory of Emotions* pedal-go-round, a self-propelled carousel where your feet create the music (pedal softly). For a relaxing finale, enjoy the 12-minute movie (plays by request, French only) featuring modern dance springing from *Pa-*

rade, Satie's collaboration with Pablo Picasso and Jean Cocteau. You'll even hear the boos and whistles that greeted these ballets' debuts.

▲Museum of Ethnography and Norman Popular Arts (Musée d'Ethnographie et d'Art Populaire Normand)

Honfleur's engaging little Museum of Ethnography and Norman Popular Arts (pick up English translation at the desk) is located in the old prison and courthouse a short block off the harbor in the heart of Old Honfleur. It re-creates typical rooms from Honfleur's past and crams them with objects of daily life—costumes, furniture, looms, and an antique printing press. You'll see the old yard and climb through two stories of furnished rooms. The museum paints a picture of daily life in Honfleur during the time when its ships were king and the city had global significance. (Skip the adjacent Museum of the Sea.)

Cost and Hours: €4.20, Tue-Sun 10:00-12:00 & 14:00-18:30, shorter hours off-season, closed mid-Nov-mid-Feb and Mon year-round, Rue de la Prison, www.musees-honfleur.fr.

HONFLEUR WALKS AND DRIVES
▲Côte de Grâce Walk (or Drive)

For good exercise and a bird's-eye view of Honfleur and the Normandy Bridge, go for an uphill 30-minute walk (or quick drive) up to the Côte de Grâce—best in the early morning, late afternoon, or at sunset. From St. Catherine Church, **walk** up Rue du Puits and then follow the blue-on-white *Rampe du Mont Joli* signs to reach the splendid view over Honfleur and the Normandy Bridge at the top. This viewpoint alone justifies the climb.

Drivers should head up Rue Brulée and make a right on Rue Eugène Boudin, then take a hard left at Rue de Puits and follow *Côte de Grâce* signs.

At the top, walkers and drivers can continue past the viewpoint for about 300 yards along a country lane to the **Chapel of Notre-Dame de Grâce,** built in the early 1600s by the mariners and people of Honfleur (open daily 8:30-17:30). Model boats hang from the ceiling, pictures of boats balance high on the walls, and several stained-glass windows are decorated with images of sailors at sea praying to the Virgin Mary. Find the 23 church bells hanging on a wood rack 20 steps to the right as you leave the church and imagine the racket they make (the bells ring four times an hour). Below the chapel, a lookout offers a sweeping view of superindustrial Le Havre and the Seine estuary where the river hits the Manche (English Channel).

Jetty/Park Walk

Take a level stroll along the water past the Hôtel le Cheval Blanc to find the mouth of the Seine River and big ships at sea. Strolling on a cobbled walkway, you'll pass a defunct lighthouse across the water, kid-friendly parks carpeted with flowers and grass, and the lock connecting Honfleur to the Seine and the sea. Grand and breezy vistas of the sea and smashing views of the Normandy Bridge reward the diligent walker (allow 20 minutes to reach the best views).

NEAR HONFLEUR

Boat Excursions

Boat trips in and around Honfleur depart from various docks between Hôtel le Cheval Blanc and the opposite end of the outer port (Easter-Oct usually about 11:00-17:00). The tour boat *Calypso* takes good 45-minute spins around Honfleur's harbor (€8, Jetée de la Lieutenance, mobile 06 71 64 50 46). Other cruises run to the Normandy Bridge, which, unfortunately, means two boring trips through the locks (€11/1.5 hours, choose between *Jolie France*, near Parking du Môle, Jetée du Transit, mobile 06 71 64 50 46, www. promenade-en-bateau-honfleur.fr; or *L'Evasion* near Hôtel le Cheval Blanc, Quai des Passagers, mobile 06 31 89 21 10).

Normandy Bridge (Pont de Normandie)

The 1.25-mile-long Normandy Bridge is the longest cable-stayed bridge in the Western world (€6 toll each way, not worth a detour). This is a key piece of European expressway that links the Atlantic ports from Belgium to Spain. View the bridge from Honfleur (better from an excursion boat or the Jetty Walk described earlier, and best at night, when bridge is floodlit). Also consider visiting the bridge's free Exhibition Hall (just before tollbooth on Le Havre side, daily 8:00-19:00). The Seine finishes its winding journey here, dropping only 1,500 feet from its source, 450 miles away. The river flows so slowly that, in certain places, a stiff breeze can send it flowing upstream.

▲Etrétat

France's answer to the White Cliffs of Dover, these chalky cliffs soar high above a calm, crescent beach and make an exceptional excursion from Honfleur. Walking trails lead hikers from the small seaside resort of Etrétat along a vertiginous route with sensational views (and crowds of hikers in summer and on weekends). You'll recognize these cliffs—and the arches and stone spire that decorate them—from countless Impressionist paintings, including several at the Eugène Boudin Museum in Honfleur. The small, Coney Island-like town holds plenty of cafés and a TI (Place Maurice Guillard, tel. 02 35 27 05 21, www.etretat.net).

Getting There: Etrétat is north of Le Havre. To get here by car (50 minutes), cross the Normandy Bridge and follow A-29, then exit at *sortie Etrétat.* Buses serve Etrétat from Le Havre's *gare routière,* adjacent to the train station (5/day, 1 hour, www.keolis-seine-maritime.com).

Sleeping in Etrétat: $$$$ Dormy House has a brilliant setting and makes a nice splurge for a room and/or restaurant with a view (Route du Havre at the edge of Etrétat, tel. 02 35 27 07 88, www.dormy-house.com, info@etretat-hotel.com).

Nightlife in Honfleur

Nightlife in Honfleur centers on the old port. Several bar/cafés line the high-building side of the port, including these down-and-dirty watering holes: pub-like **L'Albatross** (a fun and smoky clubhouse) and **Le Perroquet Vert** (also cool but more existential—"those lights are so..."). **Le Vintage,** just off the port, has a lively bar scene and live piano and jazz on weekend nights (closed Tue, 8 Quai des Passagers, tel. 02 31 89 05 28).

Sleeping in Honfleur

Though Honfleur is popular in summer, it's busiest on weekends and holidays (blame Paris). English is widely spoken (blame vacationing Brits). A few moderate accommodations remain, but most hotels are pretty pricey.

HOTELS

$$$ La Maison de Lucie*** is a fine *Normand* splurge and greets its guests with a garden courtyard, sumptuous lounges, and rooms filled with thoughtful touches and fine furnishings (suites available, 44 Rue des Capucines, tel. 02 31 14 40 40, www.lamaisondelucie.com, info@lamaisondelucie.com).

$$$ Hôtel le Cheval Blanc*** is an impersonal waterfront splurge with port views from all of its 35 plush and pricey rooms (many with queen beds), plus a rare-in-this-town elevator and a spa, but no air-conditioning—noise can be a problem with windows open (family rooms, pay parking, 2 Quai des Passagers, tel. 02 31 81 65 00, www.hotel-honfleur.com, info@hotel-honfleur.com).

$$ L'Absinthe Hôtel*** offers 11 tasteful rooms with king-size beds in two locations. The traditional rooms in the main (reception) section come with wood-beamed decor and share a cozy public lounge with a fireplace. Six rooms are located above their next-door restaurant and have views of the modern port and three-star, state-of-the-art comfort. There are minimal hotel services as their focus is their restaurant (includes breakfast, air-con in both buildings, private pay parking, 1 Rue de la Ville, tel. 02 31 89 23 23, www.absinthe.fr, reservation@absinthe.fr).

$$ Hôtel du Dauphin et des Loges*** combines two hotels in adjacent locations and delivers very central and fairly priced rooms.

The main building (Hôtel du Dauphin with reception) has narrow stairs (normal in Honfleur), an Escher-esque floor plan, and Wi-Fi in the lobby only. The Hôtel des Loges is more comfortable with larger rooms, Wi-Fi in all rooms, and slightly higher rates (RS%, a stone's throw from St. Catherine Church at 10 Place Pierre

Berthelot, tel. 02 31 89 15 53, www.hoteldudauphin.com, info@ hotelhonfleur.com).

$$ Hôtel Monet,** on the road to the Côte de Grâce and a 15-minute walk down to the port, is a fair value, particularly for drivers. This tranquil spot offers 16 small but comfortable rooms, all with private patios that surround a gravel parking area (family rooms, free and easy parking, Charrière du Puits, tel. 02 31 89 00 90, www.hotel-monet-honfleur.com, contact@hotel-monet-honfleur.com). Reception is closed 13:00-17:00.

$ Ibis Budget Honfleur is modern, efficient, trim, and cheap, with prefab bathrooms and an antiseptically clean ambience (family rooms, reception closed 21:00-6:00 but automatic check-in with credit card available 24 hours, elevator, across from bus station and main parking lot on Rue des Vases, tel. 08 92 68 07 81, www. ibisbudget.com, h2716-re@accor.com).

CHAMBRES D'HOTES

The TI has a long list of Honfleur's many *chambres d'hôtes* (rooms in private homes), but most are too far from the town center. Those listed here are good values.

$$ La Cour Ste. Catherine is an enchanting bed-and-breakfast with six big, tasteful rooms—each with a separate sitting area—surrounding a perfectly *Normand* courtyard with fine plantings and small sitting areas placed just so. There's a cozy lounge area ideal for cool evenings and a gourmet, home-cooked dinner (€32, must book ahead). They also have free loaner bikes and serve light snacks, wine, and other drinks all day (includes good breakfast, cash only, pay parking, 200 yards up Rue du Puits from St. Catherine Church at #74, tel. 02 31 89 42 40, www.coursaintecatherine. com, coursaintecatherine@orange.fr).

$$ Le Fond de la Cour, kitty-corner to La Cour Ste. Catherine and run by British expats Amanda and Craig, offers a good mix of crisp, modern, and comfortable accommodations around a peaceful courtyard. They have cottages that can sleep four, and four comfortable doubles (doubles include English-style breakfast, free street parking nearby, limited private pay parking, 29 Rue Eugène Boudin, mobile 06 72 20 72 98, www.lefonddelacour.com, amanda.ferguson@orange.fr).

$$ Les Maisons du Puits is an assembly of several small "apartments" for 2-4 people, all centrally situated and reasonably priced (14 Rue du Puits, mobile 06 03 98 64 91, www.lesmaisonsdupuits.com, lesmaisonsdupuits@gmail.com).

$$ Logis St. Leonard is a sweet three-room place on Honfleur's quiet side (longer walk but few tourists) where guests are given the run of the house—well, almost. Overseen by earnest Anne-Marie, it's decorated with oodles of personal touches and has a fine garden (cash only, includes breakfast, mobile 06 63 72 72 38, annemariecarneiro14@gmail.com).

$ La Lirencine is central and a good value, with three quite comfortable rooms with kitchenettes and a shared terrace. Charming Annick Proffit is your host (cash only, 3 Rue Lucie Delarue Mardrus, mobile 06 70 70 98 65, www.lalirencine.fr, chambrecharmehonfleur14@gmail.com).

Eating in Honfleur

Eat seafood, crêpes, or cream sauces here. Choose between an irresistible waterfront table at one of many lookalike places lining the harbor, or finer dining elsewhere in town. It's best to call ahead to reserve (particularly on weekends).

DINING ALONG THE HARBOR

Survey the eateries lining the harbor (all open Wed when other places are closed). The food isn't great, but you'll find plenty of salads, crêpes, and seafood—and a great setting. Heaters and canopies make dining outdoors a good option even in chilly weather. On a languid evening, it's hard to pass up. Even if you dine elsewhere, come to the harbor for a before- or after-dinner drink. **Café Les Impressionnistes** and **La Maison Bleue,** on the Quai St. Etienne side of the harbor, own the best views of Honfleur.

BETTER FOOD, NO VIEWS

While I wouldn't blame you for enjoying a forgettable meal in an unforgettable setting on the harborfront, consider these finer alternatives a couple of blocks away.

$$$$ Le Bréard is a fine place to dial it up a little and eat very well for a fair price. The decor is low key but elegant, the cuisine is inventive, delicious, and not particularly *Normand,* and the service is excellent (closed Mon, 7 Rue du Puits, tel. 02 31 89 53 40).

$$ Le Bouilland Normand hides a block off the port on a pleasing square and offers true *Normand* cuisine at reasonable pric-es. Annette, Claire, and chef-hubby Bruno provide quality dishes and enjoy serving travelers (closed Wed and Sun, dine inside or out, 7 Rue de la Ville, tel. 02 31 89 02 41).

$$ Bistro des Artistes is a two-woman operation with a pleasant 10-table dining room (call ahead for a window table). Hardworking Anne-Marie cooks up huge portions; one course is plenty...and maybe a dessert (great salads, closed Wed, 30 Place Berthelot, tel. 02 31 89 95 90).

$ La Crêperie des Arts serves up crêpes in a comfortable set-ting with a huge fireplace, and is a good, centrally located budget option (closed Tue-Wed, 13 Rue du Puits, tel. 02 31 89 14 02).

$ Au Relais des Cyclistes, on a busy street near the TI, is an eclectic, lively, pub-like place for a simple, inexpensive meal with fun indoor and outdoor seating (closed Thu, 10 Place de la Porte de Rouen, tel. 02 31 89 09 76).

$$ Au P'tit Mareyeur is whisper-formal, intimate, all about seafood, and a good value. The ground floor and upstairs rooms offer equal comfort and ambience (€38 Bouillabaisse Honfleuraise, closed Tue-Wed and Jan, 4 Rue Haute, tel. 02 31 98 84 23, Julie speaks some English).

At **$$ La Tortue,** the owner/chef prepares tasty cuisine, in-cluding good vegetarian dishes, and serves it in a cozy setting (open daily in summer, closed Tue-Wed rest of year, tel. 02 31 81 24 60, 36 Rue de l'Homme de Bois).

$$ L'Homme de Bois combines handsome ambience with authentic *Normand* cuisine that is loved by locals, so book a day ahead. Fish is their forte (daily, a few outside tables, skip the up-stairs room, 30 Rue de l'Homme de Bois, tel. 02 31 89 75 27).

Breakfast: If it's even close to sunny, skip your hotel breakfast and eat on the port, where several cafés offer *petit déjeuner* (€4-7 for continental fare, €7-14 for more elaborate choices—the Bagel Burger at **L'Albatross** is filling). Morning sun and views are best from the high side of the harbor.

Dessert: Honfleur is ice-cream crazy, with gelato and tradi-tional ice-cream shops on every corner. If you need a Ben & Jerry's ice-cream fix or a scrumptious dessert crêpe, find the **waterfront stand** at the southeast corner of the Vieux Bassin.

Nighttime Food to Go: Order a pizza to go until late from **$ Il Parasole** (2 Rue Haute, tel. 02 31 98 94 29), and enjoy a picnic dinner with port views a few steps away at the Lieutenance gatehouse.

Honfleur Connections

There's no direct train service to Honfleur, so you must connect by bus or car. Buses #39 (express) and #20 (local) link Honfleur with train service in Caen and Deauville. Some trips also run to Le Havre on these lines. Bus #50 runs between Le Havre, Honfleur, and Lisieux. Although train and bus service usually is coordinated, confirm your connection with the helpful staff at Honfleur's bus station (English info desk open Mon-Fri 9:30-12:00 & 13:15-18:00, in summer also Sat-Sun, tel. 02 31 89 28 41, www.busverts. fr). If the station is closed, you can get schedules at the TI. Rail-pass holders will save money by connecting through Deauville, as bus fares increase with distance.

From Honfleur by Bus and/or Train to: Caen (bus #39 2/day, 1 hour; slower bus #20 12/day Mon-Sat, 7/day Sun, 2 hours); **Bayeux** (bus #39 or #20 to Caen, then 20-minute train to Bayeux); **Rouen** (bus-and-train combo 6/day Mon-Sat, 3/day Sun, includes 30-minute bus ride over Normandy Bridge to Le Havre, then easy transfer to 1-hour train to Rouen); **Paris'** Gare St. Lazare (13/day, 2-3.5 hours, by bus to Caen, Lisieux, Deauville, or Le Havre, then train to Paris; buses from Honfleur meet most Paris trains).

Route Tips for Drivers: If driving to Rouen, see the Route of the Ancient Abbeys (described earlier, under "Sights in Rouen."). If connecting to the D-Day beaches, consider taking the scenic route *"par la côte"* to Trouville, which goes past sea views, thatched hamlets, and stupendous mansions. From Honfleur, drive to the port, pass Hôtel du Cheval Blanc, and stick to this road (D-513) to Trouville, then follow signs for A-13 to Caen.

Bayeux

Only six miles from the D-Day beaches, Bayeux was the first city liberated after the landing on June 6, 1944. Incredibly, the town was spared the bombs of World War II. The Allied Command needed an intact town from which to administer the push to Berlin. And after a local chaplain made sure London knew that his city was neither strategically important nor a German headquarters, a scheduled bombing raid was canceled—making Bayeux the closest city to the D-Day landing site not destroyed. Even without its famous medieval tapestry and proximity to the D-Day beaches, Bayeux would be worth a visit for its enjoyable town center and awe-inspiring cathedral, beautifully illuminated at night. Its location and manageable size (pop. 14,000) make Bayeux an ideal home base for visiting the area's sights, particularly if you lack a car.

Orientation to Bayeux

Bayeux grew up along the Aure River. Its main street (Rue St. Jean) was a Roman road. The river powered the town's waterwheels and flushed its waste as its industry grew. The TI is located in the old fish market over the river, and the nearby waterwheel was part of the tanning and dyeing industry in the 15th century. Across from the Bayeux Tapestry museum, another waterwheel once powered a flour mill (now a recommended crêpe restaurant); its lock created a mill pond which did double-duty as the bishop's fish pond.

TOURIST INFORMATION

The information-packed TI is on a small bridge two blocks north of the cathedral. Ask for bus schedules to the beaches and inquire about special events, concerts, and short tours of local sights. They have an excellent—and free—D-Day booklet *(Normandy, Land of Liberty)*, but WWII buffs may prefer the D-Day maps (€5-8) showing troop deployments and more (June-Aug daily 9:00-19:00, April-May and Sept-Oct Mon-Sat 9:30-12:30 & 14:00-18:00, Sun 10:00-13:00 & 14:00-18:00; shorter hours off-season; on Pont St. Jean leading to Rue St. Jean, tel. 02 31 51 28 28, www.bessin-normandie.com).

ARRIVAL IN BAYEUX

By Train and Bus: Trains and buses share the same station (no bag check). It's a 15-minute **walk** from the station to the Bayeux Tapestry museum, and 15 minutes from the tapestry to Place St. Patrice. To reach the tapestry, the cathedral, and recommended hotels, cross the major street in front of the station and follow Rue de Cremel toward *l'Hôpital*, then turn left on Rue Nesmond. Find signs to the *Tapisserie* (tapestry) or continue on to the cathedral. **Taxis** usually wait at the station—allow €9 to any recommended hotel or sight in Bayeux, and €21 to Arromanches (€32 after 19:00 and on Sundays, taxi tel. 02 31 92 92 40 or mobile 06 70 40 07 96).

By Car: A handy ring road circles Bayeux with well-signed parking and hotels. Look for the cathedral spires and follow signs for *Centre-Ville*, and then signs for the *Tapisserie* or your hotel. Pay parking lots are in the town center (including at the Hôtel de Ville near the TI; and at Place St. Patrice, 3-hour limit, free 12:00-14:00 and overnight 19:00-9:00). You can park for free along the ring road below the station and at a few lots in the city (the TI has a map of free parking, or ask your hotelier).

By Private Shuttle from Paris: Albion Transport offers top-notch transfers to Bayeux direct from Paris airports, train stations, or hotels. Their Bayeux office is next to the train station (tel. 02 31 78 88 88, mobile 06 80 28 65 61, www.albion-voyages.com). For more information, see "Getting Around Normandy" at the beginning of this chapter.

HELPFUL HINTS

Sightseeing Tips: Bayeux's three main museums—the Bayeux Tapestry, Battle of Normandy Memorial Museum, and MAHB—offer combo-tickets that save you money if you see more than one sight. A combo-ticket covering two sights is €12; for all three it's €15 (buy at the first sight you visit). Note that many sights close in January.

Market Days: The Saturday open-air market on Place St. Patrice is Bayeux's best, though the Wednesday market on pedestrian Rue St. Jean is pleasant. Both end by 13:00. Don't leave your car on Place St. Patrice on a Friday night, as it will be towed early Saturday.

Grocery Store: Carrefour City, at Rue St. Jean 14, is next to the recommended Hôtel Churchill (long hours Mon-Sat, Sun until 14:00).

Laundry: A launderette is a block behind the TI, on Rue Maréchal Foch. Another launderette is near Place St. Patrice, at 69 Rue des Bouchers (both open daily 7:00-21:00).

Bike Rental: These two places rent both electric and standard bikes. **Vélos Location** is across from the TI and delivers to outlying hotels (daily 8:00-20:30, closes earlier off-season, inside grocery store at Impasse de Islet, tel. 02 31 92 89 16, www.velosbayeux.com). **Maison du Vélo** is near the train station at 4 Rue de la Résistance (tel. 02 31 21 52 50, www.lamaisonduvelobayeux.fr).

Taxi: Call 02 31 92 92 40 or mobile 06 70 40 07 96.

Car Rental: Bayeux offers two choices. **Hertz** allows you to drop off in a different city and is open daily, but it's not very central—you'll need to take a cab (Mon-Fri 8:00-20:00, Sat-Sun 8:00-12:00 & 14:00-17:00, at the Total gas station on Route de Cherbourg, tel. 02 31 92 03 26). **Renault Rent** is just below the train station on the ring road at the Renault dealership, but you must return your car here (Mon-Sat 7:30-19:30, closed Sun, 16 Boulevard Sadi Carnot, tel. 02 31 51 18 51). Allow about €50-70/day with a 200-kilometer limit, which is sufficient to see the key sights from Arromanches to Utah Beach—you'll drive about 180 kilometers. Handier rental options are in Caen (see "Caen Memorial Museum" on page 306).

Calvados Tasting: For a fun and easy cider or Calvados sampling, drop by the recommended **Logis les Remparts** B&B (Tue-Sat 10:00-19:00, closed Sun-Mon, 4 Rue Bourbesneur, tel. 02 31 92 50 40).

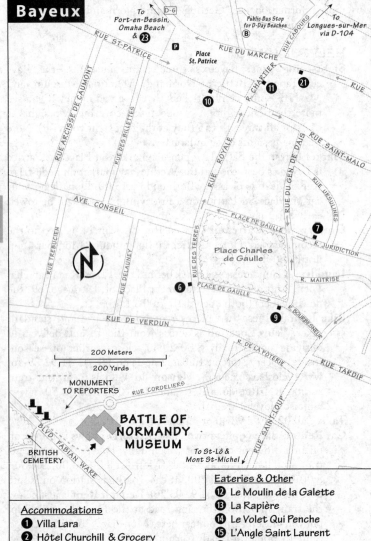

Bayeux

NORMANDY

Eateries & Other

12 Le Moulin de la Galette
13 La Rapière
14 Le Volet Qui Penche
15 L'Angle Saint Laurent
16 Le Pommier
17 Au P'tit Bistrot
18 La Fringale
19 To Le 49
20 Bike Rental (2)
21 Launderette (2)
22 Renault Car Rental
23 To Hertz Car Rental
24 Bayeux Shuttle
25 Albion Transport

Accommodations

1 Villa Lara
2 Hôtel Churchill & Grocery
3 Hôtel le Lion d'Or
4 Hôtel Reine Mathilde & Le Garde Manger
5 Hôtel au Georges VII & Café
6 Le Petit Matin
7 Manoir Sainte Victoire
8 Le Clos de La Croix
9 Logis les Remparts & Calvados
10 Hôtel d'Argouges
11 Hôtel Mogador

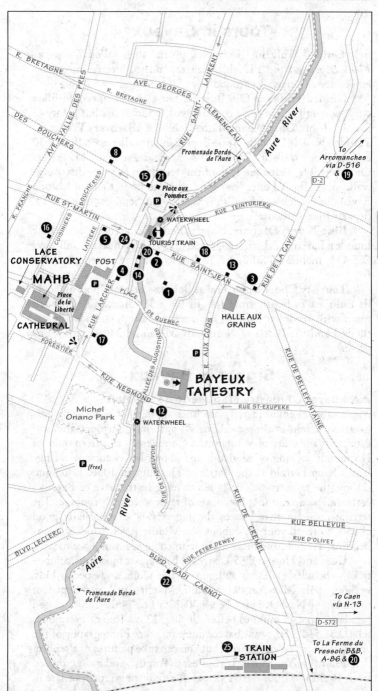

NORMANDY

Tours in Bayeux

Self-Guided Walking Tour: Pick up the map called *Découvrez Vieux Bayeux* at the TI, which corresponds to bronze info plates embedded in sidewalks around town.

Guided Walks of Old Bayeux: For a chatty, anecdote-filled stroll through the historic center—with no interiors but plenty of factoids—join Christèle or Marie-Noëlle of **Discovery Walks** for a guided walk (€15, daily April-Sept, 2-hour walk generally at 9:30 and 1.5-hour walk at 17:00, rain or shine, leave from TI, private tours possible year-round, confirm schedule at www.discovery-walks.org). The **TI** offers morning and afternoon tours of historic Bayeux in French and English (€5, July-mid-Sept, get times at TI, departs from cathedral).

Bike Tours of Bayeux: Hugo at Petite Reine runs electric bike tours of Bayeux (2 hours-€45) and the D-Day beaches (all day-€75-115, mobile 06 80 87 87 37, https://us.petitereinenormandie.fr).

Touristy Choo-Choo Train: Bayeux's hop-on, hop-off tourist train leaves hourly from the TI for a 35-minute ride through town with recorded English commentary. Stops include the cathedral and the Battle of Normandy Memorial Museum (€7, pay driver).

Sights in Bayeux

▲▲▲Bayeux Tapestry (Tapisserie de Bayeux)

Made of wool embroidered onto linen cloth, this historically precious document is a mesmerizing 70-yard-long cartoon. The tapestry tells the story of William the Conqueror's rise from duke of Normandy to king of England, and shows his victory over England's King Harold at the Battle of Hastings in 1066. Long and skinny, the tapestry was designed to hang in the nave of Bayeux's cathedral as a reminder for locals of their ancestor's courage. The terrific museum that houses the tapestry is an unusually good chance to teach your kids about the Middle Ages. Models, mannequins, a movie, and more make it an engaging, fun place to visit.

Cost and Hours: €9.50, covered by Bayeux museums combo-ticket, includes excellent audioguide for adults and special kids' version; daily May-Aug 9:00-19:00, March-April and Sept-Oct until 18:30; Nov-Dec and Feb 9:30-12:30 & 14:00-18:00, closed Jan; last entry 45 minutes before closing, 13 bis Rue de Nesmond, tel. 02 31 51 25 50, www.bayeuxmuseum.com. Photography of the actual tapestry is not allowed, but you can take pictures of a replica.

Planning Your Visit: It's busiest in August, and most crowded from 10:00 to 17:00. Arrive before 10:00, during lunch, or late in the day (lunchtime is most reliably quiet). As the audioguide cannot be paused, you're limited to 25 minutes with the tapestry. It's a strict one-way route. Allow at least a full hour for your complete museum visit.

Film: When buying your ticket, get the schedule for the English version of the 16-minute battle film (runs every 40 minutes). Because you can watch the film only after viewing the tapestry, and the last show time is about an hour before closing, arriving late means no film.

Visiting the Museum: Your visit starts with the actual **tapestry,** accompanied by an included audioguide that gives a

NORMANDY

top-notch, fast-moving, 25-minute scene-by-scene narration complete with period music (no pausing or rewinding—if you lose your place, find subtitles in Latin). Remember, the tapestry is Norman propaganda: The English (the bad guys, referred to as *les goddamns*, after a phrase the French kept hearing them say) are shown with mustaches and long hair; the French (*les* good guys) are clean-cut and clean-shaven—with even the backs of their heads shaved for a better helmet fit.

Appreciate the fun details—such as the bare legs in scene 4 or Harold's pouting expressions in various frames—and look for references to places you may have visited (like Dinan). Pay strict attention to scene 23, where Harold takes his oath to William; the importance of keeping one's word is the point of the tapestry. Get close and (almost) feel the tapestry's texture. The most famous scene is Harold's death: This marks the end of the intense battle—and victory for William.

Next, you'll climb upstairs into a room filled with engaging **exhibits,** including a full-size replica of a Viking ship much like the one William used to cross the Channel (Normans inherited their weaponry and seafaring skills from the Norsemen). You'll also see mannequins (find William looking unmoved with his new crown), a replica of the Domesday Book (an inventory of noble's lands as ordered by William), and models of castles (who knew that the Tower of London was a Norman project?). Good explanations outline the events surrounding the invasion and the subsequent creation of the tapestry, and a touchscreen lets you see the back side of the embroidery.

Your visit finishes with a **film** that ties it all together one last

The Battle of Hastings

Because of this pivotal battle, the most memorable date of the Middle Ages is 1066. England's king, Edward the Confessor, was about to die without an heir. The big question: Who would succeed him—Harold, an English nobleman and the king's brother-in-law, or William, duke of Normandy and the king's cousin? Edward chose William, and sent Harold to Normandy to give William the news. On the journey, Harold was captured. To win his release, he promised he would be loyal to William and not contest the decision. To test his loyalty, William sent Harold to battle for him in Brittany. Harold was successful, and William knighted him. To further test his loyalty, William had Harold swear on the relics of the Bayeux cathedral that when Edward died, he would allow William to ascend the throne. Harold returned to England, Edward died...and Harold grabbed the throne.

William, known as William the Bastard, invaded England to claim the throne. Harold met him in southern England at the town of Hastings, where their forces fought a fierce 14-hour battle. Harold was killed, and his Saxon forces were routed. William—now "the Conqueror"—marched to London, claimed his throne, and became king of England (though he spoke no English).

The advent of a Norman king of England muddied the political waters and set in motion 400 years of conflict between England and France—not to be resolved until the end of the Hundred Years' War (1453). The Norman conquest of England brought that country into the European mainstream (but still no euros). The Normans established a strong central English government. Historians speculate that had William not succeeded, England would have remained on the fringe of Europe (like Scandinavia), and French culture (and language) would have prevailed in the New World—which would have meant no communication issues for us in France. Hmmm.

time (in the cinema upstairs, skippable if you're pressed for time). Just before the theater you reach a full-sized replica of the tapestry (which you are welcome to photograph).

▲Bayeux Cathedral

This massive building, as big as Paris' Notre-Dame, dominates the small town of Bayeux. Make a point to enjoy the cathedral rising over the town late in the afternoon, when the facade is bathed in light, or after dark, when the entire church is illuminated.

Cost and Hours: Free, daily July-Aug 8:30-19:00, Sept-June until 18:00, 4 Rue du Général de Dais.

Visiting the Cathedral: To start your visit, find the small **square** opposite the front entry (info board about the cathedral facade in rear corner). Notice the two towers—originally Romanesque, they were capped later with tall Gothic spires. The cathedral's west facade is structurally Romanesque, but with a decorative Gothic "curtain" added.

Now step inside the cathedral. The magnificent view of the **nave** from the top of the steps shows a mix of Romanesque (ground floor) and soaring Gothic (upper floors). Historians believe the Bayeux tapestry originally hung here. Imagine it draped halfway up the big Romanesque arches. Try to visualize this scene with the original, richly colored stained glass in all those upper windows. Rare 13th-century stained-glass bits are in the high central window above the altar; the other glass (below) is from the 19th and 20th centuries.

Walk down the nave and notice the areas between the big, round **arches.** That busy zigzag patterning characterizes Norman art in France as well as in England. These 11th-century Romanesque arches are decorated with a manic mix of repeated geometric shapes: half-circles, hash marks, full circles, and diagonal lines. Notice also the creepy faces eyeing you, especially the ring of devil heads lining the third arch on the right.

More 13th-century Norman Gothic is in the **choir** (the fancy area behind the central altar). Here, simple Romanesque carvings lie around Gothic arches whose characteristically tall, thin lines add a graceful verticality to the interior.

For maximum 1066 atmosphere, step into the beautifully lit **crypt** (beneath the central altar), which originally was used as a safe spot for the cathedral's relics. The small crypt displays two freestanding columns and bulky capitals with fine Romanesque carvings. During a reinforcement of the nave, these two columns were replaced. Workers removed the Gothic veneer and discovered their true inner Romanesque beauty. Orange angel-musicians on other columns add color to this somber room.

Nearby: Leaving the church's front entry, turn right and walk to the top of the steps. Look high on the church's spire to spy a little rectangular stone house. This was the **watchman's home,** from which he'd keep an eye out for incoming English troops during the Hundred Years' War...and for Germans five centuries later (it didn't work—the Germans took the town in 1940). Bayeux was liberated on D-Day plus one: June 7. According to an interesting (but likely false) legend, about the only casualty that day was the lookout, who supposedly was shot while watching from the window of this stone house.

The big tree ahead is a **Liberty Tree.** These were planted in cities throughout France in 1793 (when the king was beheaded) to celebrate the end of the Old Regime and the people's hard-won freedom. When the tree was planted, the cathedral kicked off a decade in which it was not considered a church but a revolutionary "temple of reason."

Place Charles de Gaulle

A block in front of the cathedral (up Rue Maîtrise) is a big, grassy-yet-historic square—once the site of a 10th-century castle. The statue in the center is Poppa, the mistress or wife of the Viking conqueror Rollo who, in 911, became first duke of Normandy. The people of Normandy came from this union (not to mention many English royals—Rollo's descendants include William the Conqueror). On June 14, 1944, this square hosted the first public appearance of Charles de Gaulle in newly freed France. The self-appointed leader of the Free French Forces, now with Churchill's endorsement, proceeded to rally the French to rise up and help push out the Germans. This event helped initiate de Gaulle's legitimacy as head of the Free French. Bayeux later served as the first administrative capital of post-Nazi-occupied France.

River Walk (Promenade Bords de l'Aure)

Join the locals and promenade along the meandering walking path that follows the little Aure River for about 2.5 miles through Bayeux. Find the waterwheel behind the TI to its right and keep walking (path marked on city maps).

Lace Conservatory (Conservatoire de Dentelles)

This conservatory offers a chance to watch workers design and weave intricate lace *(dentelle),* just as artisans did in the 1600s, when lace was an important Bayeux industry, competing to break the Venetian monopoly on this required bit of formal wear. Enter to the clicking sound of the small wooden bobbins used by the lacemakers, and appreciate the concentration their work requires. You can also see examples of lace from the past and pick up some nifty souvenirs. The community helps fund this teaching workshop to keep the tradition alive. The conservatory building is nicknamed the "Adam and Eve House" for its carved 15th-century facade (find Adam, Eve, and the snake).

Cost and Hours: Free, Mon-Sat 9:30-12:30 & 14:30-18:00 except Mon and Thu until 17:00, closed Sun, across from cathedral entrance, 6 Rue du Bienvenu, tel. 02 31 92 73 80, http://dentelledebayeux.free.fr.

▲MAHB (Musée d'Art et d'Histoire Baron Gérard)

For a break from D-Day and tapestries, MAHB offers a modest review of European art and history in a beautiful display space within what was once the Bayeux bishop's palace. The 14 rooms on two floors are laid out in chronological order (prehistory, ancient Rome, medieval, and early modern) and descriptions are translated into English. Bayeux was born during the Roman Empire and you'll see ample evidence of that. In the stern Court of Justice—a court-room from French revolutionary times (1793)—a bust of Lady Liberty (Marianne) presides over the tribunal like a secular goddess, backed by some Napoleonic stained glass (1806). You'll see a fine little collection of 18th- and 19th-century paintings donated by Baron Henri-Alexandre Gérard more than a century ago. Notable are an early work—*Le Philosophe (The Philosopher)*—by Neoclassical master Jacques-Louis David and, by Antoine-Jean Gros, *Sappho*—a moonlit version of the Greek poetess' suicide that influenced Géricault and Delacroix. Lace lovers will enjoy several rooms of exquisite lace with drawers full of bobbins and artful creations. Your visit is capped with an exhibit dedicated to the ceramics of Bayeux.

Cost and Hours: €7.50, covered by Bayeux museums combo-ticket, daily May-Sept 9:30-18:30, shorter hours off-season, near the cathedral at 37 Rue du Bienvenu, tel. 02 31 92 14 21, www.bayeuxmuseum.com.

Battle of Normandy Memorial Museum (Musée Mémorial de la Bataille de Normandie)

This museum provides a manageable overview of WWII's Battle of Normandy. With its many maps and timelines of the epic battle to liberate northern France, it's aimed at military history buffs. You'll get a good briefing on the Atlantic Wall (the German fortifications stretching along the coast—useful before visiting Longues-sur-Mer), learn why Normandy was selected as the landing site, understand General Charles de Gaulle's contributions to the invasion, and realize the key role played by aviation. You'll also appreciate the challenges faced by doctors, war correspondents, and civil engineers (who had to clean up after the battles—the gargantuan bulldozer on display looks useful).

Cost and Hours: €7.50, covered by Bayeux museums combo-ticket, daily May-Sept 9:30-18:30, Oct-Dec and Feb-April 10:00-12:30 & 14:00-18:00, closed Jan, last entry one hour before closing, on Bayeux's ring road, 20 minutes on foot from center on Boulevard Fabian Ware, free parking, tel. 02 31 51 25 50, www.bayeuxmuseum.com.

Film: A 25-minute film with original footage gives a good summary of the Normandy invasion from start to finish, and highlights the slog that continued even after the beaches were liberated (normally shown in English May-Sept at 10:30, 12:00, 14:00, 15:30, and 17:00; Oct-April at 10:30, 14:45, and 16:15).

Nearby: A right out of the museum leads along a footpath to the **Monument to Reporters,** a grassy walkway lined with white roses and stone monuments listing, by year, the names of reporters who have died in the line of duty from 1944 to today. Some years have been kinder to journalists than others. Notice how many names from recent years are Arabic.

The path continues to the **British Military Cemetery,** decorated with 4,144 simple gravestones marking the final resting places of these fallen soldiers. The cemetery memorial's Latin inscription reads, *"We Who Were Conquered by William Have Liberated His Fatherland."* Interestingly, this cemetery has soldiers' graves from all countries involved in the Battle of Normandy (even Germany) except the United States, which requires its soldiers to be buried on US property—such as the American Cemetery at Omaha Beach.

Sleeping in Bayeux

Drivers should also see "Sleeping in Arromanches," on page 284.

NEAR THE TAPESTRY

$$$$ Villa Lara***** owns the town's most luxurious accommodations smack in the center of Bayeux. Most of the 28 American-size, spacious rooms have brilliant views of the cathedral (best after dark), and a few have small terraces. Hands-on owner Rima and her attentive staff take top-notch care of their guests (pricey but excellent breakfast, elevator, exercise room, comfortable lounges, free and secure parking, between the tapestry museum and TI at 6 Place de Québec, tel. 02 31 92 00 55, www.hotel-villalara.com, info@hotel-villalara.com).

$$$ Hôtel Churchill,*** on a traffic-free street across from the TI, could not be more central. The hotel has 46 plush-and-pricey rooms—some with traditional furnishings, and others quite modern. All have big beds and surround convivial public spaces peppered with historic photos of Bayeux's liberation (family rooms, no elevator, 14 Rue St. Jean, tel. 02 31 21 31 80, www.hotel-churchill.fr, info@hotel-churchill.fr).

$$ Hôtel le Lion d'Or,*** General Eisenhower's favorite hotel in Bayeux, draws a loyal American and British clientele who love the historic aspect of staying here. It has an atmospheric Old World bar, 31 stylish rooms, and a responsive staff (no elevator, no air-con, limited pay parking, restaurant with fair prices, 71 Rue St. Jean, tel. 02 31 92 06 90, www.liondor-bayeux.fr, info@liondor-bayeux.fr).

$ Hôtel Reine Mathilde** is a solid, centrally located value with 16 sharp rooms above an easygoing brasserie, and 10 pricier and larger rooms with three-star comfort in two annexes nearby (family rooms, some rooms with air-con, no elevator, reception one block from TI at 23 Rue Larcher, tel. 02 31 92 08 13, www.hotel-bayeux-reinemathilde.fr, info@hotel-bayeux-reinemathilde.fr).

¢ Hôtel au Georges VII offers 10 no-star, no-frills rooms (some with only a sink or a shower) with just enough comfort. The rooms are up a tight staircase above a central café, and the bartender doubles as the receptionist. Reception closes at 19:00 (19 Rue St. Martin, tel. 02 31 92 28 53, www.georges-7.com, augeorges7@ orange.fr).

CHAMBRES D'HOTES IN THE TOWN CENTER

$$ Le Petit Matin, run by friendly Pascal, is a central, kid-friendly, and handsome bed-and-breakfast with good public spaces, five stylish rooms with big bathrooms, and a magnifique back garden with play toys and tables (breakfast included, on Place Charles de Gaulle at 9 Rue des Terres, tel. 02 31 10 09 27, www.lepetitmatin. fr, lepetitmatin@hotmail.fr).

$$ Manoir Sainte Victoire is a classy, 17th-century building with three top-quality rooms over a small garden at very fair prices (run by the friendly Bunels). Each has a small kitchenette and views of the cathedral (32 Rue de la Jurisdiction, tel. 02 31 22 74 69, mobile 06 85 02 67 97, www.manoirsaintevictoire.com, contact@ manoirsaintevictoire.com).

$$ At Le Clos de La Croix, friendly Gilles and Mickaël offer five big and comfortable rooms tastefully decorated with antique and modern touches. The 18th-century mansion has many public spaces and a splendid back garden. Some rooms have cathedral or garden views (includes breakfast, 2-night minimum, cash or Paypal only, free and handy parking, 16 Rue des Bouchers, mobile 06 16 99 61 50, www.closdelacroix.fr, contact@closdelacroix.fr).

$ Logis les Remparts, run by bubbly Christèle, is a delightful, three-room bed-and-breakfast situated above an atmospheric Calvados cider-tasting shop. The big and beautifully decorated rooms are a great value—one is a huge, two-room suite (breakfast extra, stays under €200 are cash only, a few blocks above the cathedral on parklike Place Charles de Gaulle at 4 Rue Bourbesneur, tel. 02 31 92 50 40, www.lecornu.fr, lecornu.bayeux@gmail.com).

NEAR PLACE ST. PATRICE

These hotels just off the big Place St. Patrice are a 10-minute walk up Rue St. Martin from the TI (a 15-minute walk to the tapestry).

$$ Hôtel d'Argouges* (dar-goozh) is named for its builder, Lord d'Argouges. This tranquil retreat has a mini château feel with classy public spaces, lovely private gardens, and 28 standard-comfort rooms. The hotel is impeccably run by Frederic and his staff (big family rooms, good breakfast, no air-con, no elevator, secure free parking, just off Place St. Patrice at 21 Rue St. Patrice, tel. 02 31 92 88 86, www.hotel-dargouges.com, info@hotel-dargouges. com).

$ Hôtel Mogador** is a modest, good-value, 14-room place with a tiny courtyard. Ask for a renovated room, and choose be-

NORMANDY

tween wood-beamed quarters on the busy square, or quieter rooms *sans* beams off the street (20 Rue Alain Chartier at Place St. Patrice, tel. 02 31 92 24 58, www.hotelmo.fr, lemogador@gmail.com).

IN THE COUNTRYSIDE NEAR BAYEUX

$ La Ferme du Pressoir is a lovely, traditional B&B on a big working farm immersed in the Norman landscape about 20 minutes south of Bayeux (see the "D-Day Beaches" map, later). If you've ever wanted to stay on a real French farm yet rest in cozy comfort, this is the place. The five rooms are filled with wood furnishings and decorated with bright garden themes. Guests share a kitchenette, and larger groups can stay in a cottage with its own kitchen. The experience is vintage Normandy—and so are the kind owners, Jacques and Odile (good family rooms, includes good breakfast, Le Haut St-Louet, just off A-84, exit at Villers Bocage, detailed directions on website, tel. 02 41 40 71 07, www.bandbnormandie.com, lafermedupressoir@bandbnormandie.com).

Eating in Bayeux

You'll find many restaurants along Rue St. Jean, a traffic-free street lined with cafés, *crêperies*, and inexpensive dining options. As there's more demand for good restaurants than supply in Bayeux, you're smart to book a day ahead for the **$$$** listings below. Drivers can also consider the short drive to Arromanches for seaside dining options (see "Eating in Arromanches," later).

$ Le Moulin de la Galette is like eating in an Impressionist painting. Enjoy a big selection of tasty crêpes, salads, and *plats* at good prices in a dreamy setting right on the small river. There's fine seating inside, but the place is very popular so book ahead or come when it opens at 18:30 (effective heaters, closed Wed, 38 Rue de Nesmond, tel. 02 31 22 47 75).

$$$ La Rapière is a wood-beamed eatery—calm and romantic—filled with locals enjoying a refined meal and a rare-these-days cheese platter for a finale. Reservations are wise (Mon-Sat 18:30-21:15, closed Sun, 53 Rue St. Jean, tel. 02 31 21 05 45, www.larapiere.net, charming Linda).

$ Le Volet Qui Penche is a fun-loving, wine-shop-meets-bistro run by playful, English-speaking Pierre-Henri and Stéphane. They serve salads, escargot, charcuterie-and-cheese platters, and a small selection of meaty à la carte dishes as well as a vast selection of wines and cider by the glass (food service 18:00-21:00 most days—making early dinners easy, closed Sun, near the TI at 3 Passage de l'Islet, tel. 02 31 21 98 54).

$$$ L'Angle Saint Laurent is a tasteful and elegant place run by a husband-and-wife team (Caroline speaks English and manages the floor while Sébastien cooks). Come here for a special meal of *Normand* specialties done in a contemporary gourmet style. The selection is limited and changes with the season (good wine list, closed Mon, 2 Rue des Bouchers, reserve in advance, tel. 02 31 92 03 01, www.langlesaintlaurent.com).

$ Le Garde Manger, a popular, family-friendly eatery, offers basic grub all day (omelets, big salads, bigger burgers) with a marvelous outside terrace and partial cathedral views (daily 12:00-22:00, a block from Rue St. Jean at 23 Rue Larcher).

$$ Le Pommier, with street appeal inside and out, is a good place to sample regional products with clever twists in a relaxed yet refined atmosphere. Owner Thierry mixes old and new in his cuisine and decor, and focuses on organic food (good vegetarian *menu*, open daily, 38 Rue des Cuisiniers, tel. 02 31 21 52 10, www. restaurantlepommier.com).

$$$ Au P'tit Bistrot is a small eatery with a snappy interior and a good reputation for its carefully prepared food. Warmly run by Magalie (whose husband is *le chef*), it's a mix of modern and traditional (closed Sun-Mon, 31 Rue Larcher, tel. 02 31 92 30 08).

$ La Fringale is Bayeux's low-key diner with a big selection of basic café fare. It's also nicely located on the main pedestrian street and has tables available when others don't (closed Sun, 43 Rue St. Jean, tel. 02 31 22 72 52).

$$ Le 49, in an elegant old farmhouse, is barely outside Bayeux but merits the short drive for its delicious and beautifully presented cuisine at fair prices. The service is friendly, the setting is calm, and there's a pleasant outside terrace or indoor seating in a mod setting. You should have no trouble landing a table (closed Sun-Mon, 49 Route de Courseulles, Saint-Vigor-le-Grand, mobile 06 08 16 70 06).

Bayeux Connections

From Bayeux by Train to: Paris' Gare St. Lazare (9/day, 2.5 hours, some change in Caen), **Amboise** (4/day, 5 hours, change in Caen and Tours' St-Pierre-des-Corps), **Rouen** (14/day, 2.5 hours, change in Caen), **Caen** (20/day, 20 minutes), **Honfleur** (2/day, 20-minute train to Caen, then 1-hour express bus #39; or train to Caen and slower bus #20, 12/day Mon-Sat, 7/day Sun, 2 hours); bus info tel. 02 31 89 28 41, www.busverts.fr), **Pontorson/Mont St-Michel** (3/day, 2 hours to Pontorson, then bus to Mont St-Michel; also consider faster shuttle vans described on the next page).

By Bus to the D-Day Beaches: Bus Verts du Calvados offers minimal service to D-Day beaches with stops in Bayeux at Place St. Patrice and at the train station (schedules at TI, www.busverts. fr). Lines #74/#75 run east to Arromanches and Juno Beach (5/

NORMANDY

day in summer; 3/day Mon-Sat and none on Sun in off-season; 30 minutes to Arromanches, 50 minutes to Juno Beach). Line #70 runs west to the American Cemetery and Vierville-sur-Mer (6/day in summer; 3/day Mon-Sat in off-season, none on Sun; 35 minutes to American Cemetery, 45 minutes to Vierville-sur-Mer). Going round-trip by bus often leaves you stuck with either too much or too little time at either sight; consider a taxi one way and a bus the other (see taxi info under Bayeux's "Helpful Hints," earlier).

By Shuttle Van to Mont St-Michel: Two services run shuttle-van day trips to Mont St-Michel for €65 round-trip (about 1.5 hours each way, plus at least 3 hours at Mont St-Michel): **Hôtel Churchill** (small discount for hotel guests, www.hotel-churchill.fr) and **Bayeux Shuttle** (includes skip-the-line abbey ticket, www.bayeuxshuttle.com). Either trip is a terrific deal, as you'll get a free tour of Normandy along the way from your knowledgeable driver. Both run morning and afternoon trips when demand justifies.

Route Tips for Drivers: Drivers connecting Bayeux with Mont St-Michel should use the speedy, free A-84 autoroute (from near the train station, follow signs to *Villars-Bocage*, then take A-84 toward Rennes).

D-Day Beaches

The 54 miles of Atlantic coast north of Bayeux—stretching from Utah Beach in the west to Sword Beach in the east—are littered with WWII museums, monuments, cemeteries, and battle remains left in tribute to the courage of the British, Canadian, and American armies that successfully carried out the largest military operation in history: D-Day. (It's called *Jour J* in French.) It was on these serene beaches, at the crack of dawn on June 6, 1944, that the Allies (roughly one-third Americans and two-thirds British and Canadians) finally gained a foothold in France. From this moment, Nazi Europe was destined to crumble.

> *"The first 24 hours of the invasion will be decisive... The fate of Germany depends on the outcome... For the Allies, as well as Germany, it will be the longest day."*
> —Field Marshal Erwin Rommel, April 22, 1944
> (from *The Longest Day*, by Cornelius Ryan)

June 6, 2019 marked the 75th anniversary of the landings. It was a particularly poignant commemoration, given how very few D-Day veterans are still alive. Locals talk of the last visits of veterans with heartfelt sorrow; they have adored seeing the old soldiers in their villages and fear losing the firsthand accounts of the battles. All along this rambling coast, locals will never forget what the troops and their families sacrificed all those years ago. A warm regard for Americans has survived political disputes, from de Gaulle to Trump. This remains particularly friendly soil for Americans—a place where US soldiers are still honored and the image of the US as a force for good remains largely untarnished.

PLANNING YOUR TIME

I've listed the prime D-Day sites from east to west, starting with Arromanches (the British sector) and then the American sectors (with a stop-by-stop tour of Omaha Beach and its related sights, followed by Utah Beach). Finally, I backtrack east to cover the Canadian sector. In the British and Canadian sectors, urban sprawl makes it harder to envision the events of June 1944, but the American sector looks today very much as it did 70 years ago. To best appreciate the beaches, avoid visiting at high tide if you can. For more information on touring the D-Day beaches, www.normandie-tourisme.fr is a useful resource.

D-Day Sites in One Day

If you have only one day, I'd spend it visiting the exciting sites and impressive museums along the beaches and miss the Caen Memorial Museum. (To squeeze in the Caen Memorial Museum, visit it on your way to or from the area.) Note that the American Cemetery closes at 18:00 mid-April-mid-Sept and at 17:00 the rest of the year—and you'll want at least an hour there.

If you're traveling by car, begin on the cliffs above Arromanches. From there, visit the Port Winston artificial harbor and the D-Day Landing Museum, then continue west to Longues-sur-Mer and tour the German gun battery there. Spend your afternoon visiting the American Cemetery and its thought-provoking visitors center, walking on Omaha Beach at Vierville-sur-Mer, and exploring the Pointe du Hoc Ranger Monument. Consider a quick stop at the German Military Cemetery on your way home. With an extra half-day, see the impressive Utah Beach sights.

Canadians will want to start at the Juno Beach Centre and Canadian Cemetery (in Courseulles-sur-Mer, 10 minutes east of Arromanches).

Day-Tripping to the Beaches from Paris: If you're staying in Paris and considering a day trip to the D-Day beaches by train and rental car, think twice: Going by train to Caen, picking up a car, driving to your first stop, then returning to Paris will take at least seven hours. Note that Sunday train service to Bayeux is limited. A better alternative is to book a service to meet you at the Bayeux or Caen train station and drive you around the D-Day sites (see

NORMANDY

NORMANDY

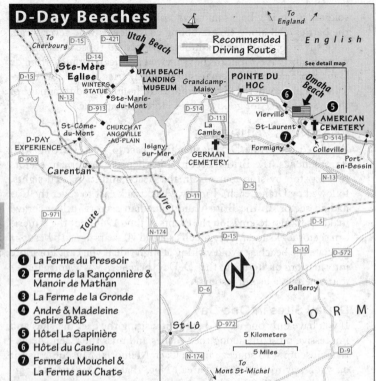

D-Day Beaches

To England

Recommended Driving Route

English

To Cherbourg — D-15 — D-421 — Utah Beach

D-14

Ste-Mère Eglise

WINTERS STATUE

D-15 — N-13

Ste-Marie-du-Mont
D-913

St-Côme-du-Mont

D-DAY EXPERIENCE

CHURCH AT ANGOVILLE-AU-PLAIN

D-903

Carentan

Taute

UTAH BEACH LANDING MUSEUM

Grandcamp-Maisy

D-514

D-113

La Cambe

Isigny-sur-Mer

GERMAN CEMETERY

POINTE DU HOC

D-514

Vierville

St-Laurent

Formigny

Omaha Beach

❻

AMERICAN CEMETERY ❺

❼

D-514

Colleville

Port-en-Bessin

See detail map

Vire

D-5

N-13

D-11

D-971

N-174

D-15

D-10

D-572

D-6

Balleroy

St-Lô

D-972

N-174

N O R M

5 Kilometers

5 Miles

D-9

To Mont St-Michel

❶ La Ferme du Pressoir
❷ Ferme de la Rançonnière & Manoir de Mathan
❸ La Ferme de la Gronde
❹ André & Madeleine Sebire B&B
❺ Hôtel La Sapinière
❻ Hôtel du Casino
❼ Ferme du Mouchel & La Ferme aux Chats

"By Taxi Minivan" and "By Minivan Tour," later), or take a private shuttle for a cushy connection from Paris (see page 221). The Caen Memorial Museum also runs a good D-Day tour program for day-trippers.

GETTING AROUND THE D-DAY BEACHES
On Your Own

Though the minivan excursions listed later teach important history lessons, **renting a car** is a far less expensive way to visit the beaches, particularly for three or more people (for rental suggestions, see Bayeux's "Helpful Hints" on page 259, or rental options in Caen on page 307).

Very limited **bus service** links Bayeux, the coastal town of Arromanches, and the most impressive sites of D-Day (see Bus Verts du Calvados info on page 271)—but it's not practical for anything more than one sight. Going by **bike** is dicey as roads are narrow (no bike lanes), with plenty of blind curves and relentless traffic.

By Taxi Minivan (Unguided)

Taxi minivans shuttle up to seven people between the key sites at

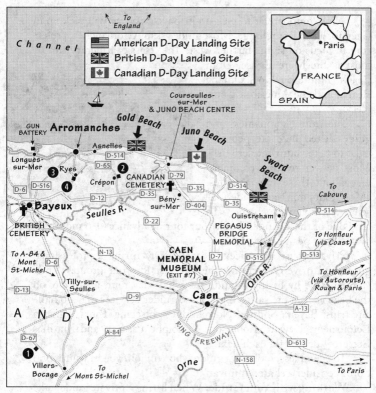

reasonable rates (which vary depending on how far you go). Allow €280 for a six-hour taxi day to visit the top Utah and Omaha Beach sites. No guiding is included; you are paying strictly for transport. Figure about €22 each way between Bayeux and Arromanches, €37 between Bayeux and the American Cemetery, and €110 for a 2.5-hour visit to Omaha Beach sites from Bayeux or Arromanches (50 percent surcharge after 19:00 and on Sun, taxi tel. 02 31 92 92 40 or mobile 06 70 40 07 96, www.taxisbayeux.com, taxisbayeux@orange.fr).

Abbeilles Taxis offer D-Day excursions from Caen (about €230/5-hour visit, tel. 02 31 52 17 89, www.taxis-abbeilles-caen.com).

By Minivan Tour (Guided)

An army of small companies and private guides offers all-day guided excursions to the D-Day beaches. I've worked hard to find guides who respect the importance of your time and these sights. Anyone can get you around the beaches, but you should expect your guide to deliver clear history lessons and be at your side constantly. My recommendations meet and exceed these standards.

Most tours prefer to pick up in Bayeux; a few will pick up in Caen for a small surcharge. Most guides skip Arromanches, preferring to focus on sights farther west: The "classic" itinerary run by most is Ste-Mère Eglise, Utah Beach, Pointe du Hoc, Omaha Beach, and the American Cemetery.

The tour companies and guides listed here are people I trust to take your time seriously. Most deliver riveting commentary about these moving sites. (Most tours don't go inside museums, which is a shame.) To land one of these guides, book your tour in advance (3-6 months is best during peak periods).

Private tours are pricey because you're hiring a professional guide and driver/vehicle for the day just for your group. While you can save by hiring a guide for a half-day tour, a full day on the beaches is more satisfying. (These guides/services may do half-day trips: Bayeux Shuttle, Normandy Sightseeing Tours, Vanessa Letourneur, Edward Robinson, Rodolphe Passera, and Mathias Leclere—details for each next.)

To spend less, look for a guide who will join you in your rental car or consider a shared minivan tour.

Working with Your Guide: When hiring a private guide, take charge of your tour if you have specific interests (some guides can get lost in battle minutiae that you don't have time for). The best route for a one-day tour with a private guide is to start in Arromanches and end at Point du Hoc or the American Cemetery. If you're doing the "classic tour," request extra time at the American Cemetery to see the excellent visitors center, and ask your guide to make time for the Utah Beach Landing Museum or one of the paratrooper museums in Ste-Mère Eglise (entry is cheap and seeing at least one museum is worthwhile).

While some companies discourage children, others (including Dale Booth, Normandy Sightseeing Tours, Mathias Leclere, Sylvain Kast, and Edward Robinson) welcome them.

Tours in a Shared Minivan

These tour companies offer shared tours designed for individual sign-ups. Figure about €110/person for a day and €65/person for a half-day. (These companies also run private tours.)

Bayeux Shuttle's vans come with tablets that show effective video clips as you travel, and their guides are well trained. You can visit their office in Bayeux and usually book at the last minute. All departures are assured (€60 half-day tour, €100 all-day tour, office open daily about 7:45-18:00, across from the Bayeux TI at Impasse de Islet, tel. 09 70 44 49 89, www.bayeuxshuttle.com).

Normandy Sightseeing Tours delivers a French perspective with capable guides and will pick you up anywhere you like—for a price (€70 half-day tour, €100 all-day tour, tel. 02 31 51 70 52, www.normandy-sightseeing-tours.com).

Overlord Tours is also a good choice (www.overlordtour. com).

The Caen Memorial Museum runs a busy program of half- and full-day tours covering the American and Canadian sectors in combination with a visit to the museum (handy for those with limited time—see museum listing on page 306).

Tours with a Private Guide

Costs are about the same for all guides listed here. Private groups should expect to pay €500-650 for up to eight people for an all-day tour and €250-330 for a half-day.

Expat Guides: These (mostly British) guides, like a band of brothers, are passionate about teaching and offer excellent private tours. All have their own vehicles. While some are happy to ride in your car, let them do the driving. They work together and can help you find a guide if the first one you call is booked.

- **Dale Booth Normandy Tours,** led by Dale Booth (tel. 02 14 16 66 14, www.dboothnormandytours.com, dboothholidays@sfr. fr). Dale's wife Debbie provides inexpensive chauffeur service to D-Day sights with an audio tour (www.visitsinnormandy. com).
- **Normandy Battle Tours,** led by Stuart Robertson (tel. 02 33 41 28 34, www.normandybattletours.com, stuart@ normandybattletours.com).
- **Battle of Normandy Tours,** guided by Edward Robinson (www.battleofnormandytours.com, edrobinson@ battleofnormandytours.com).

French Guides: These guides speak fluent English and are excellent teachers. Most have family connections to the area.

- **Rodolphe Passera,** owner of American Heroes Tours (mobile 06 30 55 63 39, www.normandyamericanheroes.com, rudy@ normandyamericanheroes.com).
- **Sylvain Kast** (mobile 06 17 44 04 46, www.d-day-experience-tours.com, sylvainkast@yahoo.fr).

NORMANDY

NORMANDY

Countdown to D-Day

1939

On September 1, Adolf Hitler invades the Free City of Danzig (today's Gdańsk, Poland), sparking World War II.

1940

Germany's Blitzkrieg ("lightning war") quickly overwhelms France, Nazis goose-step down Avenue des Champs-Elysées, and the country is divided into Occupied France (the north) and Vichy France (the south, administered by right-wing French). Just like that, nearly the entire Continent is fascist.

1941

The Allies (Britain, Soviet Union, and others) peck away at the fringes of "Fortress Europe." The Soviets repel Hitler's invasion at Moscow, while the Brits (with American aid) battle German U-boats for control of the seas. On December 7, Japan bombs the US naval base at Pearl Harbor, Hawaii. The US enters the war against Japan and its ally, Germany.

1942

Three crucial battles—at Stalingrad, El-Alamein, and Guadalcanal—weaken the German forces and their ally Japan. The victorious tank battle at El-Alamein in the deserts of North Africa soon gives the Allies a jumping-off point (Tunis) for the first assault on the Continent.

1943

More than 150,000 Americans and Brits, under the command of George Patton and Bernard "Monty" Montgomery, land in Sicily and begin working their way north through Italy. Meanwhile, Germany has to fend off tenacious Soviets on their eastern front.

1944

On June 6, 1944, the Allies launch "Operation Overlord," better known as D-Day. The Allies amass three million soldiers and six million tons of *matériel* in England in preparation for the biggest

---

- **Vanessa Letourneur** can guide anywhere in Normandy (mobile 06 98 95 89 45, www.normandypanorama.com).
- **Mathias Leclere** (www.ddayguidedtours.com).
- **Magali Desquesne** (mobile 06 88 75 86 17, www.dday4you. com, mag.ddayguide@gmail.com).

HELPFUL HINTS

Good Booklet: A free visitor's guide *(D-Day Normandy, Land of Liberty)* gives succinct reviews of D-Day museums and sights with current opening times. It's available at TIs, but you usually need to ask for it (downloadable at www.normandie-tourisme.fr).

amphibious invasion in history—across the English Channel to France, then eastward toward Berlin. The Germans, hunkered down in northern France, know an invasion is imminent, but the Allies keep the details top secret. On the night of June 5, more than 180,000 soldiers board ships and planes in England, not knowing where they are headed until they're under way. Each one carries a note from General Dwight D. Eisenhower: "The tide has turned. The free men of the world are marching together to victory."

At 6:30 on June 6, 1944, Americans spill out of troop transports into the cold waters off a beach in Normandy, code-named Omaha. The weather is bad, seas are rough, and the prep bombing has failed. The soldiers, many seeing their first action, are dazed, confused, and weighed down by heavy packs. Nazi machine guns pin them against the sea. Slowly, they crawl up the beach on their stomachs. More than a thousand die. They hold on until the next wave of transports arrives.

Americans also see action at Utah Beach, while the British and Canadian troops storm Sword, Juno, and Gold. All day long, Allied confusion does battle with German indecision—the Nazis never really counterattack, thinking D-Day is just a ruse, not the main invasion. By day's end, the Allies have taken all five beaches along the Normandy coast and soon begin building two completely artificial harbors, code-named "Mulberry," providing ports for the reconquest of western Europe. The stage is set for the eventual end to the war.

1945

Having liberated Paris (August 26, 1944), the Allies' march on Berlin bogs down, hit by poor supply lines, bad weather, and the surprising German counterpunch at the Battle of the Bulge. Finally, in the spring, the Americans and Brits cross the Rhine, Soviet soldiers close in on Berlin, Hitler shoots himself, and—after nearly six long years of war—Europe is free.

Guided Tours at Individual Sites: Tours in English are generally available in high season for free or a very low fee at Arromanches, Longues-sur-Mer, the American Cemetery, Point du Hoc, the Utah Beach Landing Museum, and the Juno Beach Centre. Some are quick 20-minute orientation tours; others last two hours.

Get times at area TIs, check each site's website, or see www.bayeux-bessin-tourisme.com.

TV and Films About D-Day: D-Day guides recommend some preparatory viewing before your visit. The top two movies are *The Longest Day* (for the big D-Day story) and *Saving Private*

Ryan (for a realistic sense of what it was like to land here and battle your way into France). *Band of Brothers,* a powerful 11-hour HBO miniseries telling the story from D-Day preparations, through the landing, and on to the end of the war, is simply the best.

Food Strategies: The D-Day landing sites are rural, and you won't find a grocery on every corner. Plan ahead if you want to picnic, or find groceries in Arromanches or Port-en-Bessin.

Tides: Tides will affect your experience of the beaches throughout the region, changing what you can see and your access to the sand. Avoid visiting the beaches at high tide if possible. Most TIs have tide tables to help you plan (when searching tide charts, the nearest reference point is Port-en-Bessin).

Arromanches

This small town—part of Gold Beach (in the British landing zone)—was ground zero for the D-Day invasion. The Allies decided it would be easier to build their own port than to try to take one from the Nazis—and one here would surprise the enemy. And so, almost overnight, Arromanches sprouted the immense harbor Port Winston, which gave the Allies a foothold in Normandy from which to begin their victorious push toward Berlin and the end of World War II.

Today a touristy-but-fun little town that offers a pleasant cocktail of war memories, cotton candy, and trinket shops, Arromanches makes a good home base for drivers touring the D-Day beaches. Here you'll find an evocative beach, rusty hardware with English descriptions scattered around town, a good waterfront museum, a bluff with great views, and a theater with a thrilling little film. The town's pleasant seaside promenade is a great place from which to view the port.

Wander the wide beach, sit on the seawall after dark, listen to the surf, and contemplate the events that took place here almost 75 years ago.

Orientation to Arromanches

Tourist Information: The service-oriented TI in the town center has good D-Day information, bus schedules, and a listing of area hotels and *chambres d'hôtes* (daily mid-June-Aug 9:30-19:00, off-season 10:00-13:00 & 14:00-17:00, 2 Avenue Maréchal Joffre, tel. 02 31 22 36 45, www.bayeux-bessin-tourisme.com). The TI offers short orientation walking tours to the beach and landing museum—call ahead for the schedule.

Arrival in Arromanches: The bus stop is at the top of town

Arromanches

English   Channel

More of "Port Winston" artificial harbor in distance

Note: Map shows beach at low tide.

Beach

To Longues-sur-Mer via Coastal Path (on foot only)

BEACHFRONT PROMENADE

RUSTED REMAINS OF ARTIFICIAL HARBOR

D-DAY LANDING MUSEUM

PONTOON SECTION

Beach

RUE JOFFRE

WC

SHERMAN TANK

Pl. du 6 Juin 1944

RUE DU COL. JOB

RUE COL. MICHEL

R. PETIT FONT.

TOWER

D-514

CAMPGROUND

BLVD. LONGUET

R. JOURDAN

RUE LAURENT

PONTOON SECTION

To Courseulles-sur-Mer, Gold, Juno & Sword Beaches

To Bayeux, Longues-sur-Mer & Omaha Beach

POST

CHURCH

360 THEATER

D-514

D-514

One-way streets

D-22

To Caen

200 Meters

200 Yards

❶ Hotel Les Villas d'Arromanches
❷ Hôtel de la Marine
❸ Hôtel d'Arromanches & Restaurant "Le Pappagall"
❹ L'Hôtel Idéal de Mountbatten
❺ The Mary Celeste Pub
❻ Supermarket
❼ Arromanches Militaria Shop & Bakery

NORMANDY

across from the post office. You can pay to park at the big parking lot by the D-Day Landing Museum (€.50/15 minutes, free 19:00-9:00). For free parking and less traffic, look for the lot between the small grocery store and L'Hôtel Ideal de Mountbatten as you enter town.

Services and Shopping: An **ATM** is across from the museum parking lot. A small **market** is a long block above the beach, across from L'Hôtel Ideal de Mountbatten (closed Sun afternoon and Mon). **Arromanches Militaria** sells all sorts of D-Day relics and WWII paraphernalia (daily 10:00-19:00, in a tight space at 11 Boulevard Gilbert Longuet). To get an Arromanches-based **taxi,** call mobile 06 66 62 00 99.

Sights in Arromanches

Arromanches' key sight, the Port Winston artificial harbor, is best seen from two vantage points—above town on the bluff (with the Arromanches 360° theater), and from the seawall in town (near the D-Day Landing Museum).

▲▲▲Port Winston Artificial Harbor

Arromanches is all about its artificial harbor—the remains of which can be seen to this day. Winston Churchill's brainchild, the prefab harbor was made by the British and affectionately nicknamed Port Winston by the troops. To appreciate the massive undertaking of creating this harbor in a matter of days, start on the bluff overlooking the site of the impressive harbor. See the presentation at the cliff-top Arromanches 360° theater then head down to the D-Day Landing Museum and a nearby viewing area.

Getting to the Bluff: Drive two minutes toward Courseulles-sur-Mer and pay to park in the big, can't-miss-it lot overlooking the sea. Your other options are to hike 10 steep minutes from Arromanches' center up the hill behind the town's D-Day Landing Museum, or take the free minibus from the museum (runs every 10 mins daily June-Sept, Sat-Sun only Oct-mid-Nov and April-May, none in winter). I'd minibus up and walk down.

Viewing the Harbor from the Bluff: Survey the coast from the observation platform. To the left is the American sector, with Omaha Beach and then Utah Beach (notice the sheer cliffs typical of Normandy's coastline). Below and to the right lie the British and Canadian sectors (level landscape, no cliffs).

Along the beaches below, the Allies arrived in the largest amphibious attack ever, launching the liberation of Western Europe. On D-Day +1—June 7, 1944—17 old ships sailed 100 miles across the English Channel under their own steam to Arromanches. Their crews sank them so that each bow faced the next ship's stern, forming a sea barrier. Then 500 tugboats towed 115 football-field-size cement blocks (called "Phoenixes") across the channel. These were also sunk (with the ships and Phoenixes making a semicircle). This created a four-mile-long breakwater about a mile offshore. Finally, engineers set up seven floating steel pierheads with extendable legs, then linked these to shore with four floating roads made of concrete pontoons. (You'll see sections of pontoon roads at various locations along the beaches). Soldiers placed 115 antiaircraft guns on the Phoenixes and pontoons, protecting a port the size of Dover, England. Within just six days of operation, 54,000 vehicles, 326,000 troops, and 110,000 tons of goods had crossed the English Channel. An Allied toehold in Normandy was secure. Eleven months later, Hitler was dead and the war was over.

▲▲Arromanches 360° Theater

The domed building at the cliff-top houses the powerful film *Normandy's 100 Days*. The screens surrounding you show archival footage and photographs of the endeavor to liberate Normandy (works in any language). In addition to honoring the many Allied and German soldiers who died, it reminds us that 20,000 French civilians were killed in aerial bombardments. The experience is intense—as loud and slickly produced as anything at the D-Day beaches.

Cost and Hours: €6.50, €22.50 combo-ticket with Caen Memorial Museum; 2 shows/hour (on the hour and half-hour), daily May-Aug 9:30-18:00, April-May and Sept from 10:00, Oct-mid-Nov 10:00-17:30, these are first and last show times, closed most of Jan, Chemin du Calvaire, tel. 02 31 06 06 45, www. arromanches360.com.

• *To return to the town center from the bluff, follow signs to Musée du Débarquement—the D-Day Landing Museum. The walk down is easy and delivers fine views and a Sherman tank (follow the small road in front of the Arromanches 360° theater).*

▲D-Day Landing Museum (Musée du Débarquement)

This museum, facing the harbor, makes a worthwhile hour-long visit and is the best way to appreciate how the artificial harbor was built. While gazing through windows at the site of this amazing undertaking, you can study helpful models, videos, and photographs illustrating the construction and use of the prefabricated harbor. Screens over the first big model show a virtual reconstruction of Port Winston. Those blimp-like objects tethered to the port prevented German planes from getting too close (though the German air force was largely irrelevant by this time). Ponder the overwhelming task of building this harbor in just 12 days, while battles raged. The essential 15-minute film (up the stairs behind the cashier) uses British newsreel footage to illustrate the construction of the port. Another video (7 minutes, far end of ground floor) recalls the night of the first landings.

Cost and Hours: €8.30, daily May-Aug 9:00-19:00, Sept until 18:00, Oct-Dec and Feb-April 10:00-12:30 & 13:30-17:00, closed Jan, Place du 6 Juin, tel. 02 31 22 34 31, www.arromanches-museum.com.

Viewing the Harbor from near the Museum: Find the round bulkhead on the seawall, near the entrance to the D-Day Landing Museum. Stand facing the sea. Designed to be temporary (it was used for 6 months), the harbor was supposed to wash out to sea over time—which is exactly what happened with its twin harbor at Omaha Beach (which lasted only 12 days, thanks to a terrible storm). If the tide is out, you'll see rusted floats mired on the sand close in—these supported the pontoon roads. Imagine the traffic

NORMANDY

pouring in past the many antiaircraft guns poised to defend against the invasion.

On the hill beyond the museum, there's a partially viewable Sherman tank, one of 50,000 deployed during the landings. Stroll to the east side of the museum and find a section of a pontoon road with a bulldozer, an antiaircraft gun, and a searchlight. Walk down to the beach and wander among the concrete and rusted litter of the battle—and be thankful that all you hear are birds and surf.

Sleeping in Arromanches

Arromanches, with its pinwheels and seagulls, has a salty beach-town ambience that makes it a good overnight stop. For evening fun, have a drink at The Mary Celeste pub, a block from the beach on Rue Colonel René Michel.

Drivers should also consider my sleeping recommendations near Omaha Beach (see "Sleeping near Omaha Beach," later).

$$ Hotel Les Villas d'Arromanches*** has a privileged location, perched above the sea in its own park at the town's entry, a short walk to the center. While faded on the outside, the hotel has an attractive, manor-house feel within, featuring bright and tastefully designed rooms and a handsome wine-bar lounge. Plans are afoot to attach a new building with more rooms, a spa, and a fitness room (free and easy parking, 1 Rue du Lieutenant-Colonel de Job, tel. 02 31 21 38 97, www.lesvillasdarromanches.com, contact@lesvillasdarromanches.com).

$$ Hôtel de la Marine*** has a knockout location with point-blank views to the artificial harbor from most of its 33 comfortable rooms, and charming Sylvie at the reception (family rooms, elevator, good view restaurant, Quai du Canada, tel. 02 31 22 34 19, www.hotel-de-la-marine.fr, hotel.de.la.marine@wanadoo.fr).

$ Hôtel d'Arromanches,** on the main pedestrian drag near the TI, is a good value, with nine small, straightforward rooms (some with water views), all up a tight stairway that feels like a tree house. Here you'll find the cheery, recommended Restaurant "Le Pappagall" run by English-speaking Luis (2 Rue Colonel René Michel, tel. 02 31 22 36 26, www.hoteldarromanches.fr, reservation@hoteldarromanches.fr).

$ L'Hôtel Ideal de Mountbatten,*** located a long block up from the water, is a 12-room, two-story, motel-esque place with generously sized, stylish, clean, and good-value lodgings—and welcoming owners Sylvie and Laurent (family rooms, reception closed 14:00-16:00, easy parking—free when you book direct, short block below the main post office at 20 Boulevard Gilbert Longuet, tel. 02 31 22 59 70, www.hotelarromancheslideal.fr, contact@hotelarromanchelideal.fr).

IN THE COUNTRYSIDE NEAR ARROMANCHES

$$ Ferme de la Rançonnière is a 35-room, country-classy oasis buried in farmland a 15-minute drive from Bayeux or Arromanches. It's flawlessly maintained, from its wood-beamed, stone-walled rooms to its traditional restaurant (good *menu* options) and fireplace-cozy lounge/bar (family rooms, bike rental, service-oriented staff, 4.5 miles southeast of Arromanches in Crépon, tel. 02 31 22 21 73, www.ranconniere.fr, ranconniere@wanadoo.fr).

The same family has two other properties nearby: The **$$ Manoir de Mathan** has 21 similarly traditional but bigger rooms a few blocks away in the same village (comparable prices to main building, Route de Bayeux, Crépon). An eight-minute drive away, in the village of Asnelles, are seven slick, glassy, modern seaside **$$ apartments** right along the beachfront promenade (2 Impasse de l'Horizon, www.gites-en-normandie.eu). For any of these, check in at the main hotel. Book directly so they can help you choose the property and room that works best for you.

$ La Ferme de la Gronde lies midpoint between Bayeux and Arromanches with five large traditional rooms in a big stone farmhouse overlooking wheat fields and lots of grass, with outdoor tables (includes breakfast, 2 big comfortable apartments ideal for families, well-signed from D-516 on Route de l'Eglise in Magny-en-Bessin, tel. 02 31 21 33 11, www.chambres-gite-normandie.fr, info@chambres-gite-normandie.fr).

At **¢ André and Madeleine Sebire**'s B&B, you'll experience a real Norman farm. The hardworking owners offer four modest, homey, and dirt-cheap rooms in the middle of nowhere (includes breakfast, 2 miles from Arromanches in the tiny Ryes at Ferme du Clos Neuf, tel. 02 31 22 32 34, emmanuelle.sebire@wanadoo.fr, little English spoken). Follow signs into Ryes, then go down Rue de la Forge (kitty-corner from the restaurant). Turn right just after the small bridge, onto Rue Tringale, and go a half-mile to a sign on the right to *Le Clos Neuf*. Park near the tractors.

Eating in Arromanches

You'll find cafés, *créperies,* and shops selling sandwiches to go (ideal for beachfront picnics). The **bakery** next to the recommended Arromanches Militaria store makes good sandwiches, quiches, and tasty pastries. Many restaurants line Rue Maréchal Joffe, the bustling pedestrian zone a block inland. The following restaurants at recommended hotels are also reliable:

$$ Restaurant "Le Pappagall" serves basic café fare in a cheery setting (daily in high season, closed Wed and possibly other days off-season, Hôtel d'Arromanches).

$$ Hôtel de la Marine allows you to dine or drink in style—

NORMANDY

NORMANDY

and with good quality cuisine—right on the water (ideal outdoor seating for a drink in nice weather, daily).

Arromanches Connections

From Arromanches by Bus to: Bayeux (bus #74/#75, 5/day in summer; 3/day Mon-Sat and none on Sun in off-season), **Juno Beach** (bus #74/#75, 20 minutes, www.busverts.fr). The bus stop is near the main post office, four long blocks above the sea (the stop for Bayeux is on the sea side of the street; the stop for Juno Beach is on the post office side).

American D-Day Sites

The American sector, stretching west of Arromanches, is divided between Omaha and Utah beaches. Omaha Beach starts just a few miles west of Arromanches and has the most important sights for visitors. Utah Beach sights are farther away (on the road to Cherbourg), but were also critical to the ultimate success of the Normandy invasion. The American Airborne sector covers a broad area behind Utah Beach and centers on Ste-Mère Eglise.

Omaha Beach

Omaha Beach is the landing zone most familiar to Americans. This well-defended stretch was where US troops suffered their greatest losses. Going west from Arromanches, I've listed four powerful stops (and a few lesser ones): the massive German gun battery at Longues-sur-Mer (which secured the west end of the beach), the American Cemetery, Omaha Beach itself (at Vierville-sur-Mer, the best stop on the beach), and Pointe du Hoc.

• *The D-514 coastal road links to all the sights in this section—just keep heading west. I've provided specific driving directions where they'll help. Allow about an hour driving time plus whatever time you spend at each stop.*

▲Longues-sur-Mer Gun Battery

Four German casemates (three with guns intact)—built to guard against seaborne attacks—hunker down at the end of a country road. The guns, 300 yards inland, were arranged in a semicircle to maximize the firing range east and west, and are the only original coastal ar-

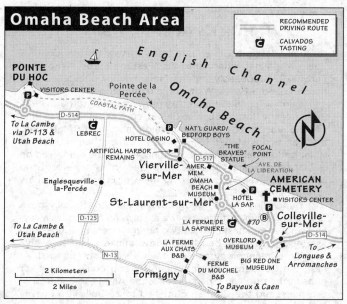

tillery guns remaining in place in the D-Day region. (Much was scrapped after the war, long before people thought of tourism.) This battery, staffed by 194 German soldiers, was more defended than the better-known Pointe du Hoc. The Longues-sur-Mer Battery was a critical link in Hitler's Atlantic Wall defense, which consisted of more than 15,000 defensive structures stretching from Norway to the Pyrenees. These guns could hit targets up to 12 miles away with relatively sharp accuracy if linked to good target information. The Allies had to take them out.

Cost and Hours: Free and always open (and a good spot for a picnic); on-site TI open April-Oct daily 10:00-13:00 & 14:00-18:00. The TI's €5.70 booklet is helpful, and guided tours are offered several times a day (€5, one-hour tour, details at TI, tel. 02 31 21 46 87).

Getting There: You'll find the guns 10 minutes west of Arromanches off D-514 on Rue de la Mer (D-104). Follow *Port-en-Bessin* signs from Arromanches; once in Longues-sur-Mer, turn right at the town's only traffic light and follow *Batterie* signs to the free and easy parking lot (with WC).

Visiting the Battery: Walk in a clockwise circle, seeing the inland gun bunkers first and then the command bunker closer to the bluff before circling back to the parking lot. Enter the third bunker you pass. It took seven soldiers to manage each gun, which could be loaded and fired six times per minute (the shells weighed

Hitler's Atlantic Wall

Germany defended its empire from Norway to the border of Spain with what Hitler called his "Festung Europa" (Fortress Europe), a supposedly impenetrable military shield, of which the so-called "Atlantic Wall" was a cornerstone.

German-controlled territory grew from 1941 through 1942. But, after the Battle of Britain defeat, costly campaigns in Russia, the start of the Africa campaign, and the US entry into the war, things stalled for Germany. Rather than expanding, Hitler concentrated on consolidating. In 1942 he embarked on perhaps the greatest engineering project in history—fortifying (where necessary) almost 2,000 miles of European coastline in his Atlantic Wall.

Depending on the geography, Hitler strategically positioned huge gun batteries (to fire at ships up to 10 miles away) and smaller gun nests (about two per mile were needed—such as along the D-Day beaches). These bunkers had to evolve quickly as technology and Germany's situation changed. At first, the Germans had air superiority and could leave their guns in the open air. Then, in 1943, the Allies took control of the skies, and the German guns had to be built into heavily fortified bunkers.

A half-million people—mostly forced labor—worked furiously on the Atlantic Wall as D-Day approached, and German commanders wondered exactly where the Allies would strike.

40 pounds). Climbing above the bunker you can see the hooks that secured the camouflage netting that protected the bunker from Allied bombers.

Head down the path (toward the sea) between the second and third bunkers until you reach a lone observation bunker (look for the low-lying concrete roof just before the cliffs). This was designed to direct the firing; field telephones connected the observation bunker to the gun batteries by underground wires. Peer out to sea from inside the bunker to appreciate the strategic view over the Channel. From here you can walk along the glorious *Sentier du Littoral* (coastal path) above the cliffs and see bits of Arromanches' artificial harbor in the distance, then walk the road back to your car. (You can drive five minutes down to the water on the road that leads from the parking area.)

• *Continue west on D-514, passing two small sights of note—Port-en-Bessin and the Big Red One Museum—before arriving at the American Cemetery.*

Near Longues-sur-Mer
Port-en-Bessin

This sleepy-sweet fishing port west of Longues-sur-Mer has a historic harbor, lots of harborfront cafés, a small grocery store, and easy, free parking. Drive to the end of the village, cross the short bridge to the right, and park. While the old harbor was too small to be of use during the invasion, this was the terminus of PLUTO (Pipe Line Under the Ocean), an 80-mile-long underwater fuel line from England. This (and an American version that terminated at Ste-Honorine, one town over) kept the war machine going after the Normandy toehold was established.

Big Red One Museum

In humble Colleville-sur-Mer, this museum is a roadside warehouse filled with D-Day artifacts. This labor of love—one of many small D-Day museums in the area—is the life's work of Pierre, who for 30 years (since he was a boy) has been scavenging and gathering D-Day gear—and he is still finding good stuff. "Big Red One" refers to the nickname of the 1st Infantry Division, the US Army troops in the first wave (with the 29th Infantry Division) to assault Omaha Beach. Pierre is happy to show visitors around—his passion for his collection adds an extra dimension to your D-Day experience. Near the museum, the main street of little Colleville-sur-Mer is lined with WWII photos.

Cost and Hours: €5, June-Aug daily 10:00-19:00, spring and fall Wed-Mon 10:00-12:00 & 14:00-18:00, closed in winter, Le Bray, Colleville-sur-Mer, tel. 02 31 21 53 81.

▲▲▲WWII Normandy American Cemetery and Memorial

The American Cemetery is a pilgrimage site for Americans visiting Normandy. Crowning a bluff just above Omaha Beach, 9,386 brilliant white, marble tombstones honor and remember the Americans who gave their lives on the beaches below to free Europe. France has given the US permanent free use of this 172-acre site, which is immaculately maintained by the American Battle Monuments Commission.

A fine modern visitors center prepares you for your visit. Plan to spend at least 1.5 hours at this stirring site. If you come late in

the day, a moving flag ceremony takes place at 17:00 at the main flagpole.

Cost and Hours: Free, daily 9:00-18:00, mid-Sept-mid-April until 17:00, tel. 02 31 51 62 00, tel. 02 31 51 62 00, www.abmc. gov. Guided 45-minute tours are offered a few times a day in high season (call ahead to confirm times). The best WC is in the basement of the visitors center.

Getting There: The cemetery is just outside Colleville-sur-Mer, a 30-minute drive northwest of Bayeux. Follow signs on D-514 toward Colleville-sur-Mer; at the big roundabout in town (at the Overlord Museum, described later), follow signs leading to the cemetery (plenty of free parking).

Visiting the Cemetery

From the parking lot, stroll in a counterclockwise circle through the lovingly tended, parklike grounds, making four stops: at the visitors center, the bluff overlooking Omaha Beach, memorials to the fallen and the missing, and finally the cemetery itself.

Visitors Center: The low-slung, modern building is mostly underground. On the arrival level (after security check) are computer terminals providing access to a database containing the Roll of Honor—the names and story of each US serviceman and woman whose remains lie in Europe. Out the window, a rectangular pond points to the infinite sea.

The exhibit downstairs does more than recount the battle. It humanizes the men who fought and died, and are now buried, here. First find a large theater playing the video *Letters,* a touching 16-minute film with excerpts of letters home from the servicemen who now lie at rest here (shown on the half-hour, you can enter late). Next is a smaller, open theater with a moving eight-minute video, *On Their Shoulders.* From here, worthwhile exhibits and more videos (one includes an interview with Dwight Eisenhower) tell the stories of the brave individuals who gave their lives to liberate people they could not know, and shows the few possessions they left behind (about 25,000 Americans died in the battle for Normandy).

A lineup of informational plaques on the left wall provides a worthwhile and succinct overview of key events from September 1939 to June 5, 1944. Starting with June 6, 1944, the plaques present the progress of the landings in three-hour increments. Omaha Beach was secured within eight hours of the landings; within 24 hours it was safe to jump off your landing vehicle and slog onto the shore.

You'll exit the visitors center through the Sacrifice Gallery, with photos and bios of several individuals buried here, as well as those of some survivors. A voice reads the names of each of the cemetery's permanent residents on a continuous loop.

Bluff Overlooking Omaha Beach: Walk through a parkway along the bluff designed to feel like America (with Kentucky bluegrass) to a viewpoint overlooking the piece of Normandy beach called "that embattled shore, the portal of freedom." An orientation table looks over the beach and sea. Gazing at the quiet and peaceful beach, it's hard to imagine the horrific carnage of June 6, 1944. You can't access the beach directly from here (the path is closed for security)—but those with a car can drive there easily; see the Omaha Beach listing, later. A walk on the beach is a powerful experience.

• *With your back to the sea, climb the steps to reach the memorial (on the left).*

Memorial and Garden of the Missing: Overlooking the cemetery, you'll find a striking memorial with a soaring statue representing the spirit of American youth. Around the statue, giant reliefs of the Battle of Normandy and the Battle of Europe are etched on the walls. Behind is the semicircular Garden of the Missing, with the names of 1,557 soldiers who perished but whose remains were never found. A small bronze rosette next to a name indicates one whose body was eventually recovered.

Cemetery: Finally, wander through the peaceful and poignant sea of headstones that surrounds an interfaith chapel in the distance. Names, home states, and dates of death are inscribed on each tombstone, with dog-tag numbers etched into the lower backs. During the campaign, the dead were buried in temporary cemeteries throughout Normandy. After the war, the families of the soldiers  could decide whether their loved ones should remain with their comrades or be brought home for burial. (About two-thirds were returned to America.)

Among the notable people buried here are General Theodore Roosevelt Jr., his brother Quentin (who died in World War I but was moved here at the request of the family), and the Niland brothers (whose story inspired *Saving Private Ryan*). There are 33 pairs of brothers lying side by side, 1 father and son, 149 African Americans, 149 Jewish Americans, and 4 women. From the three generals buried here to the youngest casualty (a teen of just 17), each grave is of equal worth.

• *To visit Omaha Beach itself, return up the long driveway to the round-*

NORMANDY

about (at the Overlord Museum) and follow signs to St-Laurent-sur-Mer (D-514). But first consider popping into the Overlord Museum.

Near the American Cemetery
Overlord Museum
While there are several museums more worth your sightseeing energy, you'll drive right by this purpose-built warehouse filled with Normandy's most impressive collection of WWII-era vehicles. Offering a good balance of American, British, and German exhibits, the museum's highlights include Germany's 88mm antiaircraft and antitank gun (formidable and feared by the Allies), a strafed German Panther tank (the best tank of the Third Reich), a Sherman tank, and a battlefield crane (recalling the on-the-go construction that took place in the field). You'll also see a horse—a reminder that much of the German war machine was actually powered by horses—and a Jeep, one of 640,000 made for the war.

Cost and Hours: €8, daily June-Aug 9:30-19:00, off-season 10:00-18:30, Oct-March until 17:30, closed Jan, tel. 02 31 22 00 55, www.overlordmuseum.com).

• *As you continue west on D-514, just before St-Laurent-sur-Mer, be on the lookout for the well-signed...*

La Ferme de la Sapinière Calvados Tasting
La Ferme de la Sapinière is a stony apple farm welcoming guests with lots of free tastes along with a few photos of this family's (seven generations on this same farmstead) war experience. Drop-ins are welcome for tastings or you can join a one-hour tour in English that explains the growing, pressing, and fermenting of apples in Normandy (followed by tasting).

Cost and Hours: Open daily for tasting 9:30-19:30 except closed Sun Oct-March; tour/tasting-€3.50, April-mid-Nov Mon-Sat at 14:30, no tours on Sun, wise to call first; tel. 02 31 22 40 51, www.producteur-cidre.com. The farm is just off D-514 (Route de Port-en-Bessin) between the American Cemetery and St-Laurent-sur-Mer.

• *From the farm, return to westbound D-514. At the next roundabout, follow signs to Vierville s/Mer par la Côte to get to Omaha Beach.*

Omaha Beach Sights from St-Laurent to Vierville
Omaha Beach has five ravines (or "draws"), which provided avenues from the beach past the bluff to the interior. These were the goal of the troops that day. You'll drive down one (Avenue de la Libération)—passing the small Omaha Beach Memorial Museum—to reach the beach and two commemorative statues. Then drive west along the beach to the National Guard Memorial before leaving the beach up a second ravine.

On Omaha Beach

Walking on Omaha Beach is a powerful ▲▲▲ experience for history buffs. (While the beach is about 300 yards wide at low tide, it disappears at high tide.) Let the modern world melt away here and try to put yourself in those soldiers' combat boots:

You're wasted from lack of sleep and nervous anticipation. Now you get seasick, too, as you're about to land in a small, flat-bottomed boat, cheek-to-jowl with 29 other soldiers. Your water-soaked pack feels like a boulder, and your gun feels even heavier. The boat's front ramp drops open, and you run for your life through water and sand for 500 yards onto this open beach, dodging bullets from above (the landings had to occur at low tide so that mines and obstacles would be visible). Your only protection is the defensive obstacles left by the Germans.

Omaha Beach witnessed by far the most intense battles of any along the D-Day beaches. The hills above were heavily fortified with machine gun and mortar nests. (The aerial, naval, and supporting rocket fire that the Allies poured onto the German defenses failed to put them out of commission.) A single German machine gun could fire 1,200 rounds a minute. That's right—1,200. It's amazing that anyone survived. It's estimated that on the first day of the campaign, the Allies suffered 10,500 casualties (killed, wounded, and missing), 6,000 of whom were Americans. The highest casualty rates occurred at Omaha Beach. More than 4,000 troops were killed and wounded here that day, many of whom drowned after being hit.

If the tide's out, you may notice remains of rusted metal objects just below the surface. Omaha Beach was littered with obstacles to disrupt the landings. Thousands of metal poles and "Czech hedgehogs" (made from Czech steel), miles of barbed wire, and more than six million mines were scattered along this shore. At least 150,000 tons of metal were taken from the beaches after World War II, and they still didn't get it all. They never will.

Omaha Beach Memorial Museum
(Musée Memorial d'Omaha Beach)

Skip the museum (for most visitors, it's not worth the entry), but WWII junkies should make a quick stop in the parking lot. On display is a rusted metal obstacle called a "Czech hedgehog"—thousands of these were placed on the beaches by the Germans to stop and immobilize landing craft and foil the Allies' advance. Find the American 155mm "Long Tom" gun nearby, and keep it in mind for your stop at Pointe du Hoc (this artillery piece is similar in size to the German guns that US Army Rangers targeted at that site). The Sherman tank here is one of the best examples of the type that landed on the D-Day beaches.

• *You'll hit the beach at a roundabout. Park your car for a look at the two memorials, and to take a stroll on the beach. (If parking is tight or you want a quieter beach experience, turn right along the water and find a spot farther down along the road.)*

▲▲Omaha Beach Focal Point

Omaha was the most difficult of the D-Day beaches to assault. Nicknamed "Bloody Omaha," nearly half of all D-Day casualties were suffered here.

Two American assault units landed on Omaha Beach—the 1st Infantry Division (the "Big Red One," a veteran formation) and the 29th Infantry Division (a National Guard citizen army unit with little combat experience). For those troops, everything went wrong.

The four-mile-long beach is surrounded on three sides by cliffs, which were heavily armed by Germans. The Allies' preinvasion bombing was ineffective, and about 500 Germans manning 11 gun nests pummeled the beach all day. Thanks to the concave shape of the beach, German artillery was positioned to hit every landing ship. It was an amphitheater of death. If the tide is out, you'll see little skinny lakes between the sandbars. These were blood red on D-Day.

Those who landed first and survived were pinned down, played dead, and came in with the tide over a period of four hours. Troops huddled against the beachhead for six to eight hours awaiting support—or death. But reinforcements kept coming, and thanks to navy ships that moved in dangerously close to shallow water, then turned broadside so they could fire at the Germans, the attack ended successfully. By the end of the day, 34,000 Americans had landed on the beach, and the Germans had been pushed back. In the next 34 days, these troops built 34 airfields. The final assault leading to Berlin was under way.

Memorial Statues

You're at the center of Omaha Beach. While only Americans landed on this beach, the flags recognize eight nations that took part in the invasion. A striking modern metal statue (*The Braves*, 2004) rises from the waves in honor of the liberating forces and symbolizes the rise of freedom on the wings of hope. Next to that is a much older memorial from 1949. Built by thankful French, it was funded by selling scrap metal after the war and honors

the two assaulting divisions, the 29th and 1st. You can read the motto of the 1st Division: "No mission too difficult. No sacrifice too great. Duty first."

• *Drive west from here along the beachfront, nicknamed "Golden Beach" before the war for its lovely sand.*

Beachfront Drive

While movie images may give the impression that the D-Day beaches were wild, they were actually lined with humble beach hotels and vacation cottages much like those you see today. After about 300 yards, you'll pass a small memorial down on your left. This marks the site of the first temporary American cemetery (which was moved after about three days, as it provided a sad welcome to newly landed troops).

• *Drive until you see a wharf stretching out from the Hôtel du Casino, at the base of the next ravine, where you'll find a couple of battlements and monuments. Park in the lot across from the hotel and walk toward the boxy gray monument by the flagpoles. Find the bronze statues of soldiers.*

Bedford Boys and Artificial Harbor

These two bronze soldiers commemorate the so-called "Bedford Boys" and the little Virginia town of Bedford that contributed 35 men to the landing forces—19 were killed.

Look out to the ocean. It was here that the Americans assembled their own floating bridge and artificial harbor (à la Arromanches; for a description, find the panel near the blue telescope). The harbor was under furious construction for 12 days before being destroyed by an unusually vicious June storm (the artificial port at Arromanches and a makeshift port at Utah Beach survived and were used until November 1944).

• *Walk down the steps of the boxy gray monument next to the statues.*

National Guard Memorial

The 29th Infantry Division, a National Guard unit, was one of the American assault units that landed on Omaha Beach on D-Day. While well-trained and disciplined, these troops were less experienced than the battle-tested 1st Division, their landing partners. A memorial to their sacrifices is built atop an 88mm German artillery casement.

Peer down through the cage into the gun station. Rather than being aimed out to sea, this gun was aimed at the beach. It could shoot all the way across the beach in two seconds at the rate of two well-aimed shots per minute. Notice the desperate bullet holes all around the gun. Its twin was several miles away at the opposite end of Omaha Beach. In 1944 the Germans built this gun station and hid it inside the facade of a fake beach hotel. A second gun casement with two 50mm guns, a few steps to the west, added to the Omaha Beach carnage.

The nearby pier offers good views—handy if the tide is in. This is also a good place to walk along the beach.

• *From here, drive uphill on D-517 to return to coastal road D-514 at Vierville-Sur-Mer (as you head up, immediately look above and to your left to find two small concrete window frames high in the cliff that served as German machine gun nests).*

When you hit D-514, turn right (west) and head toward Pointe du Hoc. Along the way, just past the turnoff for the hamlet of Englesqueville la Percée (D-125), you'll have an opportunity to quench your thirst.

Lebrec Calvados Tasting

A 10th-century fortified farm on the left offers Calvados tastings. To try some, cross the drawbridge and park on the right. Ring the rope bell and meet charming owners Soizic and Bernard Lebrec. They're happy to offer a free three-part tasting: cider, Pommeau (a mix of apple juice and Calvados), and a six-year-old Calvados. Consider their enticing selection of drinkable souvenirs. Bernard likes to share his family's D-Day scrapbook (his farm was requisitioned as a military base in 1944). Ask to see the farm's own D-Day monument. Erected in September 1944—before the war was even over—it's likely one of the earliest in France (farm tel. 09 60 38 60 17).

• *Rejoin D-514, and at next roundabout, follow signs to Pointe du Hoc.*

▲▲▲Pointe du Hoc Ranger Monument

The intense bombing of the beaches by Allied forces is best understood at this bluff. This point of land was the Germans' most heavily fortified position along the Utah and Omaha beaches. The cliffs are so severe here that the Germans turned their defenses around to face what they assumed would be an attack from inland. Yet US Army Rangers famously scaled the impossibly steep cliffs to disable the gun battery. Pointe du Hoc's bomb-cratered, lunar-like landscape and remaining bunkers make it one of the most evocative of the D-Day sites.

Cost and Hours: Free, always open; visitors center open daily 9:00-18:00, mid-Sept-mid-April until 17:00, tel. 02 31 51 62 00, www.abmc.gov/cemeteries-memorials. It's off route D-514, 20 minutes west of the American Cemetery, in Cricqueville-en-Bessin.

Crowd Control: The sight is most crowded in the afternoons. Try to avoid 14:00-16:00 on peak days.

Visiting Pointe du Hoc

Two paths lead to the site, one from each end of the long parking lot (take one path out and the other back).

The visitors center is at the eastern end of the lot. If you have time, stop here for the WCs and to see the eight-minute film explaining the daring Ranger mission from a personal perspective, through interviews with survivors. But if the security line is long, skip it, or save it for later.

Follow either gravel path to the site (both with info panels focusing on individual Rangers). The path to the western end of the site leads past a big French 155mm gun barrel from World War I. While state-of-the-art in 1917, in World War II this gun was still formidable. Six of these were what Pointe du Hoc was all about. The other path near the visitors center leads to an opening (on the left) that's as wide as a manhole cover and about six feet deep. This was a machine gun nest that had three soldiers crammed inside—a commander, a gunner, and a loader.

Lunar Landscape: The craters are the result of 10 kilotons of bombs—nearly the explosive power of the atomic bomb at Hiroshima—but dropped over seven weeks. This was a jumbo German gun battery, with more than a mile of tunnels connecting its battlements. Its six 155mm guns could fire as far as 13 miles—good enough to hit anything on  either beach. For the American D-Day landings to succeed, this nest had to be taken out. So the Allies pulverized it with bombs, starting in April 1944 and continuing until June 6—making this the most intensely bombarded of the D-Day targets. Even so, the heavily reinforced bunkers survived.

Walk around. The battle-scarred German bunkers and the cratered landscape remain much as the Rangers left them. You can identify the gun placements by the short, circular, concrete walls, sometimes with the rusted remains of a gun support sticking out of the center. The guns sat in wide-open placements. You can crawl in and out of the bunkers at your own risk, or stick to the viewing platforms with helpful information panels. Work your way to the bunker with the tall stone memorial at the cliff edge.

Dagger Memorial: The memorial represents the Ranger dagger used to help scale the cliffs. Here, it's thrust into the command center of the battery. Exploring the heavily fortified interior of this observation bunker (officers' quarters, enlisted quarters, and command room) with its charred ceiling and battered hardware, you can imagine the fury of the attack that finally took this station. The slit is only for observing. This bunker was the "eyes" of the guns—from here spotters directed the firing via hard-wired telephone, sending coordinates to the gunners at the six 155mm guns. The bronze plaque in the larger room honors the Rangers who did not return from this mission.

Walk down the steps to the front of the bunker for the greatest impact. Peer over the cliff and think about the 225 handpicked Rangers who attempted a castle-style assault on the gun battery (they landed on the beach down to the right). They used rocket-propelled grappling hooks connected to 150-foot ropes, and climbed ladders borrowed from London fire departments.

Timing was critical; the Rangers had just 30 minutes to get off the beach before the rising tide would overcome them. Fortunately, the soldiers successfully surprised the Germans and climbed to the top in two hours—the Germans had prepared no defense for an attack up the cliffs. The most dangerous part of the Ranger's mission occurred after reaching the top, when they faced an intense German counterattack. The Rangers used the bomb craters as foxholes until reinforcements arrived.

Then it was the Americans' turn to be surprised. After taking control of the clifftop, the Rangers found that the guns had been moved—the Germans had put telegraph poles in their place as decoys. The Rangers eventually found the operational guns hidden a half-mile inland and destroyed them.

Three American presidents (Eisenhower in 1963, Reagan in 1984, and Clinton in 1994) have stood at this bunker to honor the heroics of those Rangers.

Viewing Platform: Navigate the craters inland about 100 yards to another bunker capped with a viewing platform. Climb up top to appreciate the intensity of the blasts that made the craters and disabled phone lines—cutting communication between the command bunker and the guns to render them blind.

• *Our tour of the American Omaha Beach sights is finished. But to consider the other side of the conflict, it's worth visiting the German Military Cemetery at La Cambe. To get there from Pointe du Hoc, follow D-514 west, then turn off in Grandcamp following signs to La Cambe and Bayeux (D-199). After crossing over the autoroute, turn left at the first country road and follow it around to the cemetery.*

▲German Military Cemetery at La Cambe (Cimetière Militaire Allemand)

To ponder German losses, visit this somber, thought-provoking final resting place of 21,000 German soldiers. Compared to the American Cemetery at St-Laurent, this site is more about humility than hero appreciation. The cemetery was not inaugurated until 1961—it took that long to identify bodies and find next of kin.

Cost and Hours: Free, daily April-Oct 8:00-19:00, off-season generally 9:00-17:00, tel. 02 31 22 70 76. Good WCs are in the back of the visitors center.

Getting There: La Cambe is 15 minutes south of Pointe du Hoc and 20 minutes west of Bayeux (from the autoroute, follow signs reading *Cimetière Militaire Allemand*).

Visiting the Cemetery: The largest of six German cemeteries in Normandy, it's appropriately bleak, with two graves per simple marker and dark basalt crosses in groups of five scattered about. The tall circular mound in the middle—with a cross, topped by a grieving mother and father—covers the remains of about 300 mostly unknown soldiers. You can climb to the top for a different perspective over the cemetery.

Wandering among the tombstones, notice the ages of the soldiers who gave their lives for a cause some were too young to understand. "Strm" indicates storm trooper—the most ideologically motivated troops that bolstered the German army. About a fifth of the dead are unidentified, listed as "Ein Deutscher Soldat." You'll also notice many who died after the war ended—a reminder that over 5,000 German POWs perished in France clearing the minefields their comrades had planted.

A field hospital was sited in this area during the war, and originally American troops were buried here. After the war, those remains were moved to the current American Cemetery or returned to the US. A small visitors center—with a focus on building peace—has information about German war cemeteries, a small display showing the German soldiers' last letters home, and a case of their artifacts. Visiting here, you can imagine the complexity of dealing with this for today's Germans.

Sleeping near Omaha Beach

With a car, you can sleep in the countryside, find better deals on accommodations, and wake up a stone's throw from many landing sites. Besides these recommended spots, you'll pass scads of good-value *chambres d'hôtes* as you prowl the D-Day beaches. The last two places are a few minutes toward Bayeux on D-517 in the village of Formigny.

$$ Hôtel la Sapinière** is a find just a few steps from the beach at Vierville-sur-Mer. A grassy, beach-bungalow kind of place, it has 15 sharp rooms, all with private patios, and a lighthearted, good-value restaurant/bar (family rooms, outside St-Laurent-sur-Mer 10 minutes west of the American Cemetery—take D-517 down to the beach, turn right and keep going to 100 Rue de la 2ème Division D'Infanterie US, tel. 02 31 92 71 72, www. la-sapiniere.fr, sci-thierry@wanadoo.fr).

$$ Hôtel du Casino*** is a good place to experience Omaha

Beach. This average-looking hotel has surprisingly comfortable rooms and sits alone overlooking the beach in Vierville-sur-Mer, between the American Cemetery and Pointe du Hoc. All rooms have views, but the best face the sea: Ask formal owner Madame Clémençon for a *côté mer* (elevator, view restaurant with *menus* from €30, café/bar on the beach below, Rue de la Percée, tel. 02 31 22 41 02, www.logishotels.com, hotel-du-casino@orange.fr). Don't confuse this with Hôtel du Casino in St-Valery-en-Caux.

$ La Ferme aux Chats sits on D-517 across from the church in the center of Formigny and has a cozy lounge with a library of D-Day information, and four clean, comfortable, modern rooms (includes breakfast, tel. 02 31 51 00 88, www.lafermeauxchats.fr, info@fermeauxchats.fr).

At **¢ Ferme du Mouchel,** animated Odile rents three colorful and good rooms with impeccable gardens in a lovely farm setting in the village of Formigny (cash only, includes breakfast, 3-day minimum in summer, tel. 02 31 22 53 79, mobile 06 15 37 50 20, www.ferme-du-mouchel.com, odile.lenourichel@orange.fr). Follow the sign from the main road (D-517), then turn left down the tree-lined lane when you see the *Le Mouchel* sign.

Utah Beach

Utah Beach, added late in the planning for D-Day, proved critical. This was where two US paratrooper units (the 82nd and the 101st Airborne Divisions) dropped behind enemy lines the night before the invasion, as dramatized in *Band of Brothers* and *The Longest Day*. Many landed off-target. It was essential for the invading forces to succeed here, then push up the peninsula (which had been intentionally flooded by the Nazis) to the port city of Cherbourg.

Utah Beach itself was taken in 45 minutes at the cost of 194 American lives. More paratroopers died (over 1,000) preparing the way for the actual beach landing. Fortunately for the Americans who stormed this beach, it was defended not by Germans but mostly by conscripted Czechs, Poles, and Russians who had little motivation for this fight.

While the brutality on this beach paled in comparison with the carnage on Omaha Beach, most of the paratroopers missed their targets—causing confusion and worse—and the units that landed here faced a three-week battle before finally taking Cherbourg. Ultimately over 800,000 Americans (and 220,000 vehicles) landed on Utah Beach over a five-month period.

• *These stops are listed in the order you'll find them coming from Bayeux or Omaha Beach. For the first two, take the Utah Beach exit (D-913) from N-13 and turn right (see the "D-Day Beaches" map on page 274).*

Allow 40 minutes to reach Angoville-au-Plain if you come direct from Bayeux, and another 45 minutes to drive between the Utah Beach sites, plus time at each stop.

Church at Angoville-au-Plain

At this simple Romanesque church, two young American medics—Kenneth Moore and Robert Wright—treated the wounded while battles raged only steps away. On June 6, American paratroopers landed around Angoville-au-Plain, a few miles inland of Utah Beach, and met fierce resistance from German forces. The two medics (who also parachuted in) set up shop in the small church, and treated both American and German soldiers for 72 hours straight, saving many lives. German patrols entered the church on a few occasions. The medics insisted that the soldiers park their guns outside or leave the church—incredibly, they did. In an amazing coincidence, this 12th-century church is dedicated to two martyrs who were doctors.

An informational display outside the church recounts the events here; an English handout is available inside. Pass through the small cemetery and enter the church. Inside, several wooden pews toward the rear still have visible bloodstains. Find the new window that honors the American medics and another that honors the paratroopers.

After surviving the war, both Wright and Moore returned to the US and led full lives. Robert Wright's wish was to be buried here; you'll find his grave in the cemetery to the left of the church.

Cost and Hours: €3 requested donation for brochure, daily 9:00-18:00, 2 minutes off D-913 toward Utah Beach.

• *As you continue toward the beach, you'll see a* **statue** *on the left a few minutes after passing through Ste-Marie-du-Mont. This honors paratrooper Richard Winters, a hero of the 101st Airborne Division's "Easy Company," who landed near here. Winters was the leader of the company portrayed in Band of Brothers.*

▲▲▲Utah Beach Landing Museum (Musée du Débarquement)

This is the best museum located on the D-Day beaches, and worth the 45-minute drive from Bayeux. For the Allied landings to succeed, many coordinated tasks had to be accomplished: Para-troopers had to be dropped inland, the resistance had to disable bridges and cut communications, bombers had to soften German defenses by delivering their payloads on target and on time, the infan-

try had to land safely on the beaches, and supplies had to follow the infantry closely. This thorough yet manageable museum pieces those many parts together in a series of fascinating exhibits and displays.

Cost and Hours: €8, daily June-Sept 9:30-19:00, Oct-Nov and Jan-May 10:00-18:00, closed Dec, last entry one hour before closing, tel. 02 33 71 53 35, off D-913 at Plage de la Madeleine, www.utah-beach.com. Park in the "obligitaire" lot, then walk five minutes to reach the museum.

Film and Tours: Check for the next English video time as you pay. Guided tours of the museum and the beachfront are offered twice a day (€4, call ahead for times or ask when you arrive, tips are appropriate).

Visiting the Museum

Built around the remains of a concrete German bunker, the museum nestles in the sand dunes on Utah Beach with floors above and below beach level. Your visit follows a one-way route past rooms of artifacts. It starts with background about the American landings on Utah Beach (over 20,000 troops landed on the first day alone) and the German defense strategy (Rommel was in charge of maintaining the western end of Hitler's Atlantic Wall). See the outstanding 12-minute film, *Victory in the Sand*, which sets the stage.

Highlights of the museum are the displays of innovative invasion equipment with videos demonstrating how it all worked (most were built for civilian purposes and adapted to military use): the remote-controlled Goliath mine, the LVT-2 Water Buffalo and Duck amphibious vehicles, and the wooden Higgins landing craft. Next, see a fully restored B-26 bomber with its zebra stripes and 11 menacing machine guns—find the one at the rear, without which the landings would not have been possible (the yellow bomb icons painted onto the cockpit indicate the number of missions a plane had flown).

Upstairs is a large, glassed-in room overlooking the beach. From here, you'll peer over re-created German trenches and get a sense for what it must have been like to defend against such a massive and coordinated onslaught.

Outside the museum, find the beach access where Americans first broke through Hitler's "Atlantic Wall." Pile into the Higgins boat replica (this one is made of steel—those used in the landings were made from plywood). You can hike up to the small bluff, which is lined with monuments to the branches of military service that participated in the fight. A gun sits atop a buried battlement under the flags, part of a vast underground network of German defenses. And all around is the hardware of battle frozen in time.

• *To reach the next several sights, follow the coastal route D-421 and signs to Ste-Mère Eglise.*

▲Ste-Mère Eglise

This celebrated village lies 15 minutes west of Utah Beach and was the first village to be liberated by the Americans. The area around Ste-Mère Eglise was the center of action for American paratroopers, whose objective was to land behind enemy lines before dawn on D-Day and wreak havoc in support of the Americans landing at Utah Beach that day.

For *The Longest Day* movie buffs, Ste-Mère Eglise is a necessary pilgrimage. It was in and near this village that many paratroopers, facing terrible weather and heavy antiaircraft fire, landed off-target—and many landed in the town. American paratrooper Private John Steele dangled from the town's church steeple for two hours (a parachute has been reinstalled on the steeple near where Steele became snagged). Though many paratroopers were killed in the first hours of the invasion, the Americans eventually overcame their poor start and managed to take the town. (Steele survived his ordeal by playing dead). These troops who dropped (or glided) in behind enemy lines in the dark played a critical role in the success of the Utah Beach landings by securing roads and bridges.

Today, the village greets travelers with flag-draped streets (and plenty of pay parking). The 700-year-old **medieval church** on the town square now holds two contemporary stained-glass windows. One, in the back, celebrates the heroism of the Allies (made in 1984 for the 40th anniversary of the invasion). The window in the left transept features St. Michael, patron saint of paratroopers (made in 1969 for the 25th anniversary).

The **TI** on the square across from the church has loads of information (July-Aug Mon-Sat 8:30-18:00, Sun 10:00-16:00; Sept and April-June closes Mon-Sat 12:00-14:00 and on Sun; shorter hours off-season; 6 Rue Eisenhower, tel. 02 33 21 00 33, www.ot-baieducotentin.fr).

Museums in and near Ste-Mère Eglise
▲Airborne Museum

This four-building collection is dedicated to the daring aerial landings that were essential to the success of D-Day. During the invasion, in the Utah Beach sector alone, 23,000 men were dropped from planes or landed in gliders, along with countless vehicles and tons of supplies.

Cost and Hours: €10, daily May-Aug 9:00-19:00, April and Sept 9:30-18:30, shorter hours off-season and closed Jan, 14 Rue Eisenhower, tel. 02 33 41 41 35, www.airborne-museum.org.

Visiting the Museum: Your visit to the museum unfolds across four buildings (allow a full hour to visit). In the first building, you'll see a **Waco glider,** one of 104 such gliders flown into Normandy at first light on D-Day to land supplies in fields to support the paratroopers. These gliders could normally be used only once. Feel the canvas fuselage and check out the bare-bones interior.

The second, larger building holds a **Douglas C-47** plane that dropped paratroops and supplies. Here you'll find mannequins of soldiers (including Gen. Dwight Eisenhower) with their uniforms, displays of their personal possessions and weapons, and a movie that venerates President Ronald Reagan's 1984 trip to Normandy.

A third structure, labeled **Operation Neptune,** puts you into the paratrooper's experience starting with a night flight and jump, then tracks your progress on the ground past enemy fire using elaborate models and sound effects. Don't miss the touching video just before the exit showing the valor of Gen. Theodore Roosevelt Jr. on D-Day.

The fourth building houses temporary exhibits and a cushy **theater** showing a good 20-minute film focusing on the airborne invasion.

• *From Ste-Mère Eglise, head 10 minutes on N-13 (back toward Bayeux) to St-Côme-du-Mont.*

▲D-Day Experience/Dead Man's Corner

This unique museum is dedicated to the paratroopers of the 101st Airborne Division (a.k.a. the "Screaming Eagles"), the first to land in Normandy. The museum has three parts: the "Dead Man's Corner" exhibit that focuses on the battles that raged around this vital location, the D-Day Experience section, and an IMAX film about the battle of Carentan. It's a labor of museum love, with lots of artifacts and uniforms.

The highlight is the D-Day Experience with two creative exhibits designed to help you feel what it might have been like to be in the 101st. You'll enter a briefing room for a 10-minute review of your mission by a hologram commander. Then you'll climb into an authentic Douglas C-47 (built in 1943, it actually flew on D-Day), buckle in, survive a simulated flight through flak across the English Channel, and then crash-land before you can parachute out.

Cost and Hours: €12, daily April-Sept 9:30-19:00, Oct-March 10:00-18:00, 2 Vierge de l'Amont (D-913), St-Côme-du-Mont, tel. 02 33 23 61 95, www.dday-experience.com.

Canadian D-Day Sites

The Canadians' assignment for the Normandy invasions was to work with British forces to take the city of Caen. They hoped to make quick work of Caen, then move on. That didn't happen. The

Germans poured most of their reserves, including tanks, into the city and fought ferociously for a month. The Allies didn't occupy Caen until August 1944.

Juno Beach Centre

Located on the beachfront in the Canadian sector, this facility—inaugurated in 2003—is dedicated to teaching travelers about the vital role Canadian forces played in the invasion, and about Canada in general. Canada declared war on Germany two years before the United States, a fact little recognized by most Americans today (after the US and Britain, Canada contributed the largest number of troops to D-Day—14,000). The Centre includes many thoughtful exhibits that bring to life Canada's unique ties with Britain, the US, and France, and explains how the war front affected the home front in Canada.

Cost and Hours: €7, €11 with guided tour of Juno Beach—highly recommended, daily April-Sept 9:30-19:00, Oct and March 10:00-18:00, Nov-Dec and Feb 10:00-17:00, closed Jan, tel. 02 31 37 32 17, www.junobeach.org.

Tours: The best way to appreciate this sector of the D-Day beaches is to take a tour with one of the Centre's capable Canadian guides, who will take you down into two bunkers and a tunnel of the German defense network (€5.50 for tour alone, €11 with admission, 45 minutes; April-Oct generally at 10:30 and 14:30, July-Aug also at 11:30, 13:30, 14:30, and 16:30; verify times prior to your visit). If you can't make a tour, ask for the brochure that gives a self-guided tour of the beaches.

Getting There: It's in Courseulles-sur-Mer, about 15 minutes east of Arromanches off D-514. Approaching from Arromanches, as you enter the village of Grave-sur-Mer, watch for the easy-to-miss *Juno Beach-Mémorial* sign marking the turnoff on the left; you'll drive the length of a sandy spit (passing a marina) to the end of the road at Voie des Français Libres, where you'll find the parking lot.

Visiting the Juno Beach Centre: Your visit begins with a short film designed to give you a sense of what soldiers were thinking as their boats neared the shore. Then you'll view informative exhibits about the various Canadian forces and their contributions to the invasion. You'll learn about the campaigns that Canadian soldiers were most involved with (such as the disastrous raid on Dieppe) and understand the immense challenges they faced during and after the landings. A scrolling list honors the 45,000 Canadians who died in World War II and a large hall highlights the vital roles women played in the war. Your visit ends with a powerful, 12-minute film that captures Canada's D-Day experience.

Take advantage of the center's eager-to-help, red-shirted "student-guides" (young Canadians working a seven-month stint here). Ask about the bulky "kiosks" in front of the center and get their take on other D-Day sites.

Nearby: Between the main road and the Juno Beach Centre, you'll spot a huge stainless-steel double cross (by a row of French flags). This is La Croix de Lorraine, marking the site where General de Gaulle returned to France (after four years of exile) on June 14, 1944. A small memorial just beyond is dedicated to the 16,000 Polish soldiers who fought in the Battle of Normandy.

Canadian Cemetery

This small, touching cemetery hides a few miles above the Juno Beach Centre. To me, it captures the understated nature of Canadians perfectly. Surrounded by pastoral farmland with distant views to the beaches, you'll find 2,000 graves marked with maple leaves and the soldiers' names and ages. Most fell in the first weeks of the D-Day assault. Like the American Cemetery, this is Canadian territory on French land.

Getting There: From Courseulles-sur-Mer, follow signs to Caen on D-79. After a few kilometers, follow D-35 toward Reviers (and Bayeux). The cemetery is on Route de Reviers.

Caen Memorial Museum

Caen, the modern capital of lower Normandy, has the most thorough (and by far the priciest) WWII museum in France. Located at the site of an important German headquarters during World War II, its official name is Caen-Normandy Memorial: Center for History and Peace (Mémorial de Caen-Normandie: Cité de l'Histoire pour la Paix). With thorough coverage of the lead-up to World War II and of the war in both Europe and the Pacific, accounts of the Holocaust and Nazi-occupied France, the Cold War aftermath, and more, it effectively puts the Battle of Normandy into a broader context and is worth ▲▲.

It's like a history course that prepares you for the D-Day sites, but it's a lot to take in with a single visit (which is why tickets are valid 24 hours). If you have the time and attention span, it's as good as it gets. If forced to choose, I prefer the focus of many of the smaller D-Day museums at the beaches.

Town of Caen: The old center of Caen is appealing and, with its château and abbeys, makes a tempting visit. But, I'd focus on Bayeux and the D-Day beaches. Bayeux or Arromanches—which are much smaller—make the best base for most D-Day sites, though train travelers with limited time might find urban Caen more practical.

The **TI** is on Place St. Pierre, 10 long blocks from the train station—take the tram to the St. Pierre stop (Mon-Sat 9:30-18:30, until 19:00 July-Aug, Sun 10:00-13:00 & 14:00-17:00 except closed Sun Oct-March, drivers follow *Parking Château* signs, tel. 02 31 27 14 14, www.caenlamer-tourisme.fr).

If Caen is your first stop on a longer trip, consider **renting a car** after arriving at the train station. Avis, Europcar, Enterprise, and Sixt are directly across the street and Hertz is just down the block at 24 Rue de la Gare.

A looming château, built by William the Conqueror in 1060, marks the city's center. To the west, modern Rue St. Pierre is a popular shopping area and pedestrian zone. The more historic Vagueux quarter to the east has many restaurants and cafés.

GETTING THERE

By Car: From Bayeux, it's a straight shot on the N-13 to Caen (30 minutes). From Paris or Honfleur, follow the A-13 autoroute to Caen. When approaching Caen, take the *Périphérique Nord* (ringroad expressway) to *sortie* (exit) #7—the museum is a half-mile from here. Look for white *Le Mémorial* signs. When leaving the museum, follow *Toutes Directions* signs back to the ring road.

By Train or Bus: By train, Caen is two hours from Paris (12/day) and 20 minutes from Bayeux (20/day). The modern train station sits next to the *gare routière,* where buses from Honfleur arrive (2/day express or 7-12/day local). There's no baggage storage at the station, though it is available (and free) at the museum. Car rental offices are nearby (see "Town of Caen," above).

Taxis usually wait in front of the train station and will get you to the museum in 15 minutes (about €18 one-way—more expensive on Sun). A **tram-and-bus** combination takes about 30 minutes (Mon-Sat only): Take the tram right in front of the train station (line A, direction: Campus 2, or line B, direction: St. Clair; buy €1.40 ticket from machine and validate on tram and again on bus, good for entire trip). Get off at the third tram stop (Bernières), then transfer to frequent bus #2 (cross the street). For transit maps, see www.twisto.fr.

To return to the station, take bus #2 across from the museum (museum has schedule, buy ticket from driver and validate); transfer to the tram at the Quatrans stop in downtown Caen. Either line A or line B will take you to the station (Gare SNCF stop).

ORIENTATION TO CAEN MEMORIAL MUSEUM

Cost and Hours: €20, ticket valid 24 hours, free for all veterans and kids under 10 (ask about good family rates), €22.50 combo-ticket with Arromanches 360° theater (see page 283). Open March-Sept daily 9:00-19:00; Oct-Dec and Feb Tue-Sun 9:30-18:00, closed Mon; closed most of Jan (Esplanade Général Eisenhower).

Information: Tel. 02 31 06 06 44—as in June 6, 1944, www.memorial-caen.fr.

Planning Your Time: Allow at least two hours for your visit. The museum is divided into two major wings: one devoted to the years before and during World War II, and the other to the Cold War years and later. Focus on the WWII wing.

Visitor Information: English descriptions are posted at every exhibit (but if you read every word, you'd be here for days). The €4.50 audioguide is well done and adds insight to the exhibits—a kid's version is also available.

Services: The museum provides free baggage storage and free supervised childcare for children under age 10. The large gift shop has plenty of books in English.

Eating: An all-day sandwich shop/café with reasonable prices sits above the entry area, and there's a restaurant with garden-side terrace (lunch only). Picnicking in the gardens is an option.

Minivan Tours: The museum offers good-value minivan tours covering the key sites along the D-Day beaches and is a top option for day-trippers from Paris. The all-day "D-Day Tour" package (€135) includes pickup/drop off at the Caen train station, a tour of the museum followed by lunch, and a five-hour tour of the American sector (there's a similar tour option to Juno Beach). There's also a €95 half-day minivan tour that includes free entry to the museum (no tour) but does not include lunch. It's appropriate to tip if you were satisfied with your tour.

NORMANDY

VISITING THE MUSEUM

Find *Début de la Visite* signs and begin your museum tour here with a downward-spiral stroll, tracing (almost psychoanalyzing) the path Europe and America followed from the end of World War I to the rise of fascism to World War II. Rooms are decorated to immerse you in the pre-WWII experience.

The **"World Before 1945"** exhibits deliver a thorough description of how World War II was fought—from General Charles de Gaulle's London radio broadcasts to Hitler's early missiles to wartime fashion to the D-Day landings. Videos, maps, and countless displays relate the stories of the Battle of Britain, Vichy France, German death camps, the Battle of Stalingrad, the French Resistance, the war in the Pacific, and finally, liberation. Several powerful displays summarize the terrible human costs of World War II, from the destruction of Guernica in Spain to the death toll (21 million Russians died during the war; Germany lost 7 million; the US lost 300,000). A smaller, separate exhibit (on your way back up to the main hall) covers D-Day and the Battle of Normandy, though the battle is better covered at other D-Day museums described in this chapter.

Next, don't miss the 25-minute film, *Saving Europe*, an immersive and, at times, graphic black-and-white film covering the agonizing 100 days of the Battle of Normandy (runs every half-hour 10:00-18:00, English subtitles).

At this point, you've completed your WWII history course. Next comes the **"World After 1945"** wing, which sets the scene for the Cold War with photos of European cities destroyed during World War II and insights into the psychological battle waged by the Soviet Union and the US for the hearts and minds of their people until the fall of communism (you'll even see a real Soviet MiG 21 fighter jet). The wing culminates with an important display recounting the division of Berlin and its unification after the fall of the Wall.

Two more stops are outside the rear of the building. I'd skip the first, a re-creation of the former **command bunker** of German General Wilhelm Richter, with exhibits on the Nazi Atlantic Wall defense in Normandy. Instead, finish your tour with a walk through the **US Armed Forces Memorial Garden** (Vallée du Mémorial). On a visit here, I was bothered at first by the seemingly unaware laughing of lighthearted children, unable to appreciate the gravity of their surroundings. Then I read this inscription on the pavement: "From the heart of our land flows the blood of our youth, given to you in the name of freedom." And their laughter made me happy.

Mont St-Michel

For more than a thousand years, the distant silhouette of this island abbey has sent pilgrims' spirits soaring. Today, it does the same for tourists. Mont St-Michel, one of the top pilgrimage sites of Christendom through the ages, floats like a mirage on the horizon. For centuries devout Christians endeavored to make a great pilgrimage once in their

lifetimes. If they couldn't afford Rome, Jerusalem, or Santiago de Compostela, they came here, earning the same religious merits. Today, several million visitors—and a steady trickle of pilgrims—flood the single street of the tiny island each year. If this place seems built for tourism, in a sense it was. It's accommodated, fed, watered, and sold trinkets to generations of travelers visiting its towering abbey.

The easiest way to get to Mont St-Michel is by car, but train, bus, and minivan options are also available. A fast TGV train serves nearby Rennes, and Flixbus runs direct and cheap bus service to the island from Paris' Gare de Bercy. Also, minivan shuttle services can zip you here from Bayeux. See "Mont St-Michel Connections" and "Bayeux Connections" for more details.

Orientation to Mont St-Michel

Mont St-Michel is surrounded by a vast mudflat and connected to the mainland by a bridge. Think of the island as having three parts: the Benedictine abbey soaring above, the spindly road leading to the abbey, and the medieval fortifications below. The lone main street (Grand Rue), with the island's hotels, restaurants, and trinkets, is mobbed in-season from 11:00 to at least 16:00. Though several tacky history-in-wax museums tempt visitors with hustlers out front, these are commercial gimmicks with no real artifacts. The only worthwhile sights are the abbey at the summit and a ramble on the ramparts, which offers mudflat views and an escape from the tourist zone.

The "village" on the mainland side of the causeway (called La Caserne) was built to accommodate tour buses. It consists of a lineup of modern hotels, a handful of shops, vast parking lots, and efficient shuttle buses zipping to and from the island every few minutes.

The tourist tide comes in each morning and recedes late each

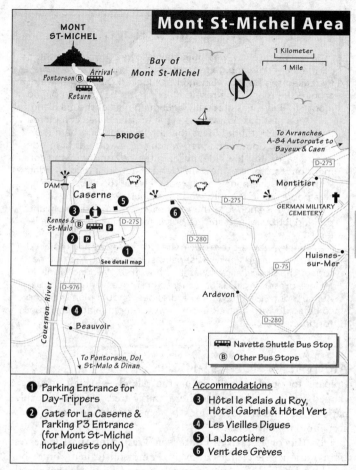

Mont St-Michel Area

MONT
ST-MICHEL

Pontorson ⓑ Arrival

Return

Bay of
Mont St-Michel

1 Kilometer

1 Mile

← BRIDGE

To Avranches,
A-84 Autoroute to
Bayeux & Caen

D-275

DAM

La
Caserne

❸

ⓘ ❺

Rennes &
St-Malo ⓑ P

❷ P

D-275

❻

Montitier

D-275

GERMAN MILITARY
CEMETERY

D-280

❶

See detail map

D-976

Couesnon River

❹

Beauvoir

To Pontorson, Dol,
St-Malo & Dinan

D-280

Ardevon

D-75

Huisnes-
sur-Mer

🚐 Navette Shuttle Bus Stop
ⓑ Other Bus Stops

NORMANDY

❶ Parking Entrance for
Day-Trippers

❷ Gate for La Caserne &
Parking P3 Entrance
(for Mont St-Michel
hotel guests only)

Accommodations

❸ Hôtel le Relais du Roy,
Hôtel Gabriel & Hôtel Vert

❹ Les Vieilles Digues

❺ La Jacotière

❻ Vent des Grèves

afternoon. To avoid crowds, arrive late in the afternoon, sleep on
the island or nearby on the mainland, and depart early.

TOURIST INFORMATION

On the mainland, near the parking lot's shuttle stop, look for the
helpful **Visitors Center** with convenient WCs (daily April-Sept
9:00-19:00, off-season 10:00-18:00, www.accueilmontsaintmichel.
fr). The official **TI** is on the island (just inside the town gate, daily
July-Aug 9:15-19:00, March-June and Sept-Oct 9:15-12:30 &
14:00-18:00, shorter hours off-season; tel. 02 33 60 14 30, www.
ot-montsaintmichel.com). A post office and ATM are 50 yards beyond the island TI. While either office can inform you about English tour times for the abbey, bus schedules, and tide tables *(horaires
des marées)*, the Visitors Center at the parking lot is far less crowded.

An Island Again

In 1878, a causeway was built that allowed Mont St-Michel's pilgrims to come and go regardless of the tide. The causeway increased the flow of visitors, but blocked the flow of water around the island. The result: Much of the bay silted up, and Mont St-Michel was gradually becoming part of the mainland.

An ambitious project to keep it an island was completed in 2015. The first phase was the construction of a dam (bar-rage) on the Couesnon River, which traps water at high tide and releases it at low tide, flushing the bay and forcing sedi-ment out to the sea. The dam is an attraction in its own right, with informative panels and great views of the abbey from its sleek and picnic-friendly wood benches. Parking lots at the foot of the island were then removed and a huge mainland parking lot built, with shuttle buses ferrying visitors to the is-land.

Finally, workers tore down the old causeway and replaced it with the super-sleek, artistically swooping bridge you see today. The bridge allows water to flow freely around Mont St-Michel, preserving its island character. Those wanting to expe-rience Mont St-Michel at its natural best should plan their trip to coincide with high tide (see www.ot-montsaintmichel.com for tide tables).

ARRIVAL IN MONT ST-MICHEL

Prepare for lots of walking as the island—a small mountain capped by an abbey—is entirely traffic-free. For good expla-nations of your arrival options by car or train/bus, visit www. accueilmontsaintmichel.fr.

By Bus or Taxi from Pontorson Train Station: The nearest train station is five miles away in Pontorson (called Pontorson/ Mont St-Michel). Few trains stop here, and Sunday service is al-most nonexistent. Trains are met by buses that take passengers to the foot of the island (€3, 10 buses/day July-Aug, 8/day Sept-June, fewer on Sun, 20 minutes). Or take a taxi to the shuttle stop in the Mont St-Michel parking lot (about €20, €26 after 19:00 and on weekends/holidays; tel. 02 33 60 26 89, mobile 06 32 10 54 06).

By Bus or Van from Regional Train Stations: Buses con-necting with fast trains from Rennes and Dol-de-Bretagne stations drop you near the shuttle stop in the parking lot. From Bayeux, it's faster by shuttle van.

By Flixbus: Flixbuses from Paris' Gare de Bercy stop in the huge parking lot near the shuttle stop (at the P7 parking area).

By Car: Day-trippers are directed to a sea of parking (remem-ber your parking-area number). Expect parking jams in high sea-son between 10:00 and noon. To avoid extra walking, take your

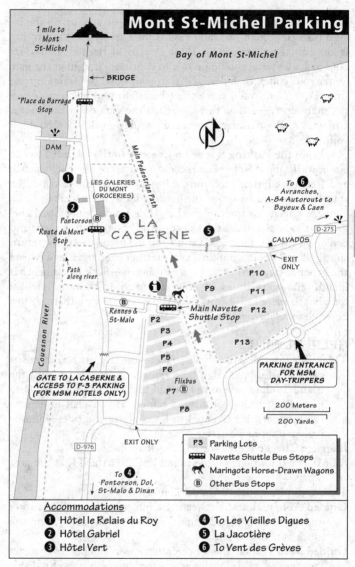

Mont St-Michel Parking

1 mile to Mont St-Michel

Bay of Mont St-Michel

BRIDGE

"Place du Barrage" Stop

DAM

LES GALERIES DU MONT (GROCERIES)

Main Pedestrian Path

To **6**, Avranches, A-84 Autoroute to Bayeux & Caen

D-275

1

2

Pontorson **B**

3

LA CASERNE

5

CALVADOS

"Route du Mont" Stop

Path along river

EXIT ONLY

Couesnon River

i

P10

P9

P11

Rennes & St-Malo **B**

P2

Main Navette Shuttle Stop

P12

P3

P4

P5

P13

P6

PARKING ENTRANCE FOR MSM DAY-TRIPPERS

Flixbus

GATE TO LA CASERNE & ACCESS TO P-3 PARKING (FOR MSM HOTELS ONLY)

P7 **B**

P8

200 Meters

200 Yards

D-976

EXIT ONLY

To **4**, Pontorson, Dol, St-Malo & Dinan

P3	Parking Lots
🚌	Navette Shuttle Bus Stops
🐎	Maringote Horse-Drawn Wagons
B	Other Bus Stops

Accommodations

1 Hôtel le Relais du Roy

2 Hôtel Gabriel

3 Hôtel Vert

4 To Les Vieilles Digues

5 La Jacotière

6 To Vent des Grèves

NORMANDY

parking ticket with you and pay at the machines near the visitors center (€12/24 hours—no re-entry, machines take cash and US credit cards, parking tel. 02 14 13 20 15). If you arrive after 19:00 and leave before 11:00 the next day, the fee is €4.50.

If you're staying at a hotel on the island or in La Caserne, you'll receive a parking-gate code from your hotel (ending with "V"). As you approach the parking areas from Bayeux, don't enter the parking lot at the main entry. Instead, follow wheelchair and bus icon signs until you come to a gate. Those staying on the island turn right here and follow signs for *Parking P3* (the parking is close to the shuttle bus). Those staying at the foot of the island in La Caserne should be able to continue straight at the gate (enter your code), then drive right to your hotel (€9 fee). Coming from Ponterson, you'll reach the wheelchair and bus icons *before* the main entry—follow these to reach the gate described above. Changes to the parking system are possible—ask when booking your hotel.

From the Parking Lot or La Caserne to the Island: You can either **walk** (about 50 level and scenic minutes) or pile onto the free and frequent **shuttle bus** (runs 7:30-24:00, 12-minute trip). The shuttle makes four stops: at the parking lot Visitors Center, in La Caserne village (in front of the Les Galeries du Mont St-Michel grocery), near the dam at the start of the bridge, and at the island end of the bridge, about 200 yards from the island itself. The return shuttle stop is about a hundred yards farther from the island (where the benches start). Most stops are unsigned—sleek wood benches identify the stops. Buses are often crammed. If it's warm, prepare for a hot (if mercifully short) ride. You can also ride either way in a horse-drawn *maringote* wagon (€6.50).

HELPFUL HINTS

Tides: The tides here rise above 50 feet—the largest and most dangerous in Europe. High tides *(grandes marées)* lap against the island TI door, where you should find tide tables posted (also posted at parking lot visitors center). If you plan to explore the mudflats, it's essential to be aware of the tides—and be prepared for muddy feet.

Baggage Check: There is no bag check available.

ATM: You'll find one on the island just after the TI, at the post office.

Taxi: Call 02 33 60 26 89 or 02 33 60 26 89.

Guided Abbey Tours: Between the information in this chapter and the tours (and audio tours) available at the abbey, a private guide is not necessary.

Guided Mud Walks: The TI can refer you to companies that run inexpensive guided walks across the bay (with some English).

Crowd-Beating Tips: If you're staying overnight, arrive after 16:00 and leave by 11:00 to avoid the worst crowds. During the day you can skip the human traffic jam on the island's main street by following this book's suggested walking routes (under "Sights in Mont St-Michel"); the shortcut works best if you want to avoid both crowds and stairs. If you're here from mid-July through August, consider touring the abbey after dinner (it's open until midnight).

NORMANDY

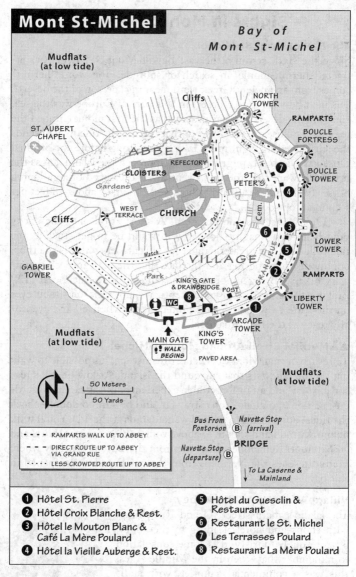

Mont St-Michel

Bay of Mont St-Michel

Mudflats (at low tide)

Cliffs

NORTH TOWER

RAMPARTS

BOUCLE FORTRESS

ST. AUBERT CHAPEL

ABBEY

REFECTORY

CLOISTERS

Gardens

BOUCLE TOWER

ST. PETER'S

7

WEST TERRACE

CHURCH

Cliffs

Cem.

4

6 **3**

LOWER TOWER

Watch

VILLAGE

5

GABRIEL TOWER

Park

2

RAMPARTS

KING'S GATE & DRAWBRIDGE

POST

GRAND RUE

Mudflats (at low tide)

8

WC

1

LIBERTY TOWER

MAIN GATE

KING'S TOWER

ARCADE TOWER

WALK BEGINS

PAVED AREA

Mudflats (at low tide)

N

50 Meters

50 Yards

Bus From Pontorson

Navette Stop (arrival)

B

Navette Stop (departure) B

BRIDGE

To La Caserne & Mainland

- - - - RAMPARTS WALK UP TO ABBEY

- - - DIRECT ROUTE UP TO ABBEY VIA GRAND RUE

· · · · · LESS CROWDED ROUTE UP TO ABBEY

1 Hôtel St. Pierre

2 Hôtel Croix Blanche & Rest.

3 Hôtel le Mouton Blanc & Café La Mère Poulard

4 Hôtel la Vieille Auberge & Rest.

5 Hôtel du Guesclin & Restaurant

6 Restaurant le St. Michel

7 Les Terrasses Poulard

8 Restaurant La Mère Poulard

Best Light and Views: Mont St-Michel faces southwest, making morning light along the sleek bridge eye-popping. Early risers win with the best light and the fewest tourists.

After dark, the island is magically floodlit. Views from the ramparts are sublime. But for the best view, exit the island and walk out on the bridge a few hundred yards. This is the reason you came.

Sights in Mont St-Michel

The Bay of Mont St-Michel

Since the sixth century, the vast Bay of Mont St-Michel has attracted hermit-monks in search of solitude. The word "hermit" comes from an ancient Greek word meaning "person of the desert." The next best thing to a desert in this part of Europe was the sea. Imagine the desert this bay provided as the first monk climbed the rock to get close to God. Add to that the mythic tide, which sends the surf speeding eight miles in and out. Long before the original causeway was built, pilgrims would approach the island across the mudflat, aware that the tide swept in "at the speed of a galloping horse" (well, maybe a trotting horse—12 mph, or about 18 feet per second at top speed).

Quicksand was another peril. A short stroll onto the sticky sand helps you imagine how easy it would be to get stuck as the tide rolled in. The greater danger for adventurers today is the thoroughly disorienting fog and the fact that the sea can encircle unwary hikers. (Bring a mobile phone, and if you're stuck, dial 112.) Braving these devilish risks for centuries, pilgrims kept their eyes on the spire crowned by their protector, St. Michael, and eventually reached their spiritual goal.

▲▲Mudflat Stroll Around Mont St-Michel

To resurrect that Mont St-Michel dreamscape, it's possible to walk out on the mudflats that surround the island. At low tide, it's reasonably dry and an unforgettable experience. But it can be hazardous, so don't go alone, don't stray far, and be sure to double-check the tides—or consider a guided walk (details at the TI). You'll walk on mucky mud and sink in to above your ankles, so wear shorts and go barefoot. Remember the scene from the Bayeux tapestry where Harold rescues the Normans from the quicksand? It happened in this bay.

Village Walk Up to the Abbey

The island's main street (Grand Rue), lined with shops and hotels leading to the abbey, is grotesquely touristy. It is some consolation to remember that, even in the Middle Ages, this was a commercial gauntlet, with stalls selling souvenir medallions, candles, and fast food. With only seven full-time residents (not counting a handful of monks and nuns at the abbey), the village lives solely for tourists.

To avoid the crowds, veer left as you approach the island's main entry and walk under the stone arch of the freestanding building.

Follow the cobbled ramp up to the abbey. This is also the easiest route up, thanks to the long ramps, which help you avoid most stairs. To trace the route, see the "Mont St-Michel" map, earlier.

If you opt to trek up through the village on Grand Rue, don't miss the following stops:

Restaurant La Mère Poulard: Before the drawbridge, on your left, peek through the door of Restaurant La Mère Poulard. The original Madame Poulard (the maid of an abbey architect who married the village baker) made quick and tasty omelets here. These were popular with pilgrims who, back before there was a causeway or bridge, needed a quick meal before they set out to beat the tide. The omelets are still a hit with tourists—even at rip-off prices. Pop in for a minute just to enjoy the show as old-time-costumed cooks beat eggs. (When it comes to the temptation of an omelet on this island, I'd make like a good pilgrim and fast.)

King's Gate: During the Middle Ages, Mont St-Michel was both a fortress and a place of worship. The abbot was a feudal land-lord with economic, political, and religious power. Mont St-Michel was the abbot's castle as well as a pilgrimage destination. Entering the town, you'll pass two fortified gates before reaching the actual village gate, the King's Gate, with its Hollywood-style drawbridge and portcullis. The old door has a tiny door within it, complete with a guard's barred window (open it). The other gates you passed were added for extra defensive credit. Imagine breaching the first gate and being surrounded by defensive troops. The highest tides bring saltwater inside the lowest gate.

Main Street Tourist Gauntlet: Stepping through the King's Gate, you enter the old town commercial center. Look back at the City Hall (flying the French flag, directly over the King's Gate). Climb a few steps and notice the fine half-timbered 15th-century house above on the right. (To skirt the main street crowds, stairs lead from here to the ramparts and on to the abbey—see "Ramparts" under the Abbey listing, later.) Once upon a time this entire lane was lined with fine half-timbered buildings with a commotion of signs hanging above the cobbles. After many fires, the wooden buildings were replaced by stone. As you climb, you'll see a few stone arches and half-timbered facades that pilgrims also passed by, five centuries ago.

St. Peter's Church (Eglise St-Pierre): At the top of the commercial stretch (on the left) is St. Peter's Church. A statue of Joan of Arc (from 1909, when she became a saint) greets you at the door. She's here because of her association with St. Michael, whose voice inspired her to rally the French against the English. St. Peter's feels alive (giving a sense of what today's barren abbey church might once have felt like). The church is dedicated to St. Peter, patron saint of fishermen, who would have been particularly beloved by the island's parishioners. Tour the small church counterclockwise. Just left of the entry is the town's only surviving 15th-century stained-glass window. In the far-left rear of the church (past its granite foundation) find the 1772 painting of pilgrims crossing the mudflat under the protection of St. Michael, who seems to be surfing on a devil's face over a big black cloud. To the right of the main altar lies the headless tomb of a 15th-century noblewoman (notice the empty pillow). During the Revolution heads were lopped off statues like this one, as France's 99 percent rose up against their 1 percent in 1789. From the center of the altar area, the fine carvings you see on the lectern and tall chairs are the work of prisoners held here during the Revolution. The church is busy with Masses (daily at 11:00 and special services for pilgrims).

Pilgrims' Stairs to the Abbey: A few steps farther up you'll pass a hostel for pilgrims on the right (Stella Maris, dark-red doors). Reaching the abbey, notice the fortified gate and ramparts necessary to guard the church entry back in the 14th century. Today the abbey, run by just a handful of monks and nuns, welcomes the public.

▲▲▲Abbey of Mont St-Michel

Mont St-Michel has been an important pilgrimage center since AD 708, when the bishop of Avranches heard the voice of Archangel Michael saying, "Build here and build high." Michael reassured the bishop, "If you build it...they will come." Today's abbey is built on the remains of a Romanesque church, which stands on the remains of a Carolingian church. St. Michael, whose gilded statue decorates the top of the spire, was the patron saint of many French kings, making this a favored site for French royalty through the ages. St. Michael was particularly popular in Counter-Reformation times, as the Church employed his warlike image in the fight against Protestant heresy.

This abbey has 1,200 years of history, though much of its story was lost when its archives were taken to St-Lô for safety during World War II—only to be destroyed during the D-Day fighting. As you climb the stairs, imagine the centuries of pilgrims and monks who have worn down the edges of these same stone steps. Don't expect well-furnished rooms; those monks lived simple lives with few comforts.

Cost and Hours: €10; May-Aug daily 9:00-19:00, until 24:00 Mon-Sat early July-Aug; Sept-April daily 9:30-18:00; closed Dec 25, Jan 1, and May 1; may close during music festival in late Sept; last entry one hour before closing; allow 20 minutes on foot uphill from the island TI, www.mont-saint-michel.monuments-nationaux.fr. Mass is held Mon-Sat at 12:00 and Sun at 11:15 (www.abbaye-montsaintmichel.com).

When to Go: To avoid crowds, arrive before 10:00 or after 16:00 (the place gets really busy by 11:00). In summer, consider a **nighttime visit.** You'll enjoy the same access with mood-lighting effects (bordering on cheesy) and no crowds (€15, €13 at TI, early July-Aug Mon-Sat 19:00-24:00, last entry one hour before closing, daytime tickets aren't valid for re-entry, but you can visit before 19:00 and stay on). The last shuttle bus leaves the island for the mainland parking lot at midnight.

Tours: The excellent audioguide gives greater detail (€3, €5/2 people). You can also take a 1.25-hour English guided tour (free but tip requested, 2-4 tours/day, first and last tours usually around 11:00 and 15:00, confirm times at TI, meet at top terrace in front of church). These tours can be good, but come with big crowds. You can start a tour, then decide if it works for you—but I'd skip it, instead following my directions, next.

➋ **Self-Guided Tour:** Your visit is a one-way route, so there's no way to get lost—just follow the crowds. You'll climb to the ticket office, then climb some more. Along that final stony staircase, monks and nuns (who live in separate quarters on the left) would draw water from a cistern from big faucets on the right. At the top (just past the WC) is a small view terrace, with a much better one just around the corner.

You've climbed the mount. Stop and look back to the church. Now go through the room marked *Accueil*, with interesting models of the abbey through the ages.

• *Emerging on the other side, find your way to the big terrace, walk to the round lookout at the far end, and face the church.*

West Terrace: In 1776, a fire destroyed the west end of the church, leaving this unplanned grand view terrace. The original extent of the church is outlined with short walls. In the paving stones, notice the stonecutter numbers, which are generally not exposed like this—a reminder that stonecutters were paid by the piece. The buildings of Mont St-Michel are made of granite stones quarried from the Isles of Chausey (visible on a clear day, 20 miles away). Tidal power was ingeniously harnessed to load, unload, and even transport the stones, as barges hitched a ride with each incoming tide.

As you survey the Bay of Mont St-Michel, notice the polder land—farmland reclaimed by Normans in the 19th century with the help of Dutch engineers. The lines of trees mark strips of land regained in the process. Today, the salt-loving plants covering this land are grazed by sheep whose salty meat is considered a local treat. You're standing 240 feet above sea level.

The bay stretches from Normandy (on the right as you look to the sea) to Brittany (on the left). The Couesnon River below marks the historic border between the two lands. Brittany and Normandy have long vied for Mont St-Michel. In fact, the river used to pass Mont St-Michel on the other side, making the abbey part of Brittany. Today, it's just barely—but definitively—on Norman soil. The new dam across this river was built in 2010. Central to the dam is a system of locking gates that retain water upriver during high tide and release it six hours later, in effect flushing the bay and returning sediment to a mudflat at low tide (see the "An Island Again" sidebar, earlier).

• *Now enter the...*

Abbey Church: Sit on a pew near the altar, under the little statue of the Archangel Michael (with the spear to defeat dragons and evil, and the scales to evalu-

ate your soul). Monks built the church on the tip of this rock to be as close to heaven as possible. The downside: There wasn't enough level ground to support a sizable abbey and church. The solution: Four immense crypts were built under the church to create a platform to support each of its wings. While most of the church is Romanesque (see the 11th-century round arches behind you), the light-filled apse behind the altar was built later, when Gothic arches were the rage. In 1421, the crypt that supported the apse collapsed, taking that end of the church with it. None of the original windows survive (victims of fires, storms, lightning, and the Revolution).

In the chapel to the right of the altar stands a grim-looking 12th-century statue of St. Aubert, the man with the vision to build the abbey. Directly in front of the altar, look for the glass-covered manhole (you'll see it again later from another angle). Take a spin around the apse and find the suspended pirate-looking ship.

• *Follow Suite de la Visite signs to enter the...*

Cloisters: A standard abbey feature, this peaceful zone connected various rooms. Here monks could meditate, read the Bible, and tend their gardens (growing food and herbs for medicine). The great view window is enjoyable today (what's the tide doing?), but was not part of the original design. The more secluded a monk could be, the closer he was to God. (A cloister, by definition, is an enclosed place.) Notice how the columns are staggered. This efficient design allowed the cloisters to be supported with less building material (a top priority, given the difficulty of transporting stone this high up). Carvings above the columns feature various plants and heighten the cloister's Garden-of-Eden ambience. The statues of various saints, carved among some columns, were defaced—literally—by French revolutionaries.

• *Continue on to the...*

Refectory: At its peak, the abbey was home to about 50 monks. This was the dining hall where they consumed both food and the word of God in near silence as one monk read in a monotone from the Bible during meals (pulpit on the right near the far end). The monks gathered as a family here in one undivided space under one big arch (an impressive engineering feat in its day). The abbot ate at the head table; guests sat at the table below the cross. The clever columns are thin but very deep, allowing maximum light and solid support. From 966 until 2001, this was a Benedictine abbey. In 2001, the last three Benedictine monks checked out, and a new order of monks from Paris took over.

• *Stairs lead down one flight to a...*

Stone Relief of St. Michael: This romanticized scene (carved in 1860) depicts the legend of Mont St-Michel: The archangel Michael wanted to commemorate a hard-fought victory over the devil with the construction of a monumental abbey on a nearby island. He sent his message to the bishop of Avranches—St. Aubert—who saw Michael twice in his dreams. But the bishop didn't trust his dreams until the third time, when Michael drove his thumb into the bishop's head, leaving a mark that he could not ignore. Notice the urgent gesture of Michael's hand and arm as the saint points to the uninhabited mount. The bishop finally got the message, and the first chapel was consecrated in 709.

• *Continue down the stairs another flight to the...*

Guests' Hall: St. Benedict wrote that guests should be welcomed according to their status. That meant that when kings (or other VIPs) visited, they were wined and dined without a hint of monastic austerity. This room once exploded in color, with gold stars on a blue sky across the ceiling. (This room's decoration was said to be the model for Sainte-Chapelle in Paris.) The floor was composed of glazed red-and-green tiles. The entire space was bathed in glorious sunlight, made divine as it passed through a filter of stained glass. The big double fireplace, kept out of sight by hanging tapestries, served as a kitchen—walk under it, imagine an entire wild boar on a spit, and see the light.

• *Hike up the stairs through a chapel to the...*

Hall of the Grand Pillars: Perched on a pointy rock, the huge abbey church had four sturdy crypts like this to prop it up. You're standing under the Gothic portion of the abbey church—this was the crypt that collapsed in 1421. Notice the immensity of the columns (15 feet around) in the new crypt, rebuilt with a determination not to let it fall again. Now look up at the round hole in the ceiling and recognize it as the glass "manhole cover" from the church altar above.

• *To see what kind of crypt collapsed, continue on to the...*

Crypt of St. Martin: This simple 11th-century vault, one of the oldest on the mount, is textbook Romanesque. It has minimal openings, since the walls needed to be solid and fat to support the buildings above. As you leave, notice the thickness of the walls.

• *Walking on, study the barnacle-like unplanned stone construction, added haphazardly over the centuries, yet all integrated. Next, you'll find the...*

Ossuary (identifiable by its big treadwheel): The monks celebrated death as well as life. This part of the abbey housed the hospital, morgue, and ossuary. Because the abbey graveyard was small, it was routinely emptied, and the bones were stacked here.

During the Revolution, monasticism was abolished. Church property was taken by the secular government, and from 1793 to 1863, Mont St-Michel was used as an Alcatraz-type prison. Its first inmates were 300 priests who refused to renounce their vows. (Victor Hugo complained that using such a place as a prison was like keeping a toad in a reliquary.) The big treadwheel from 1820—the kind that did heavy lifting for big building projects throughout the Middle Ages—is from the decades when the abbey was a prison. Teams of six prisoners marched two abreast in the wheel, hamster-style, powering two-ton loads of stone and supplies up Mont St-Michel. Spin the rollers of the sled next to the wheel.

From here, you'll pass through a chapel (with a rare fragment of a 13th-century fresco above), walk up the Romanesque-arched North-South Stairs, pass through the Promenade of the Monks (appreciate the fine medieval stonework, built directly into the granite rock of the island), go under more Gothic vaults, and finally descend into the vast...

Scriptorium Hall (a.k.a. Knights Hall): This important room is where monks decorated illuminated manuscripts and transcribed texts. It faces north so its big windows would let in lots of flat, indirect light, the preference of artists throughout time. You'll then spiral down to the gift shop, exiting out the back door (follow signs to the *Jardins*).

• *You'll emerge into the rear garden. From here, look back from where you just came and up at a miracle (merveille) of medieval engineering.*

The "Merveille": This was an immense building project—a marvel back in 1220. Three levels of buildings were created: the lower floor for storage, the middle floor for work and study, and the top floor for meditation (in the cloister, open to the heavens). It was a medieval skyscraper. The vision was even grander—the place where you're standing was to be built up in similar fashion to support an expansion of the church. But the money ran out, and the project was abandoned. As you leave the garden, notice the tall narrow windows of the refectory on the top floor.

• *Exiting the abbey, you'll pop out midway on the steps you climbed to get here. You could descend here straight into tourist hell. But for a little rampart romance, go down only until you find the short stairway on the left. Climb up the dozen steps and circle right, following a well-fortified outer rampart with a few awe-inspiring viewpoints before heading back down to the King's Gate and the bridge. (From near the high point, try to spot the former schoolhouse—operational until 1972—with its school bell, small playground, and tree.)*

Ramparts: Mont St-Michel is ringed by a fine example of 15th-century fortifications. They were built to defend against a new weapon: the cannon. They were low, rather than tall—to make a smaller target—and connected by protected passageways, which enabled soldiers to zip quickly to whichever zone was under attack. The five-sided Boucle Tower (1481) was crafted with no blind angles, so defenders could protect it and the nearby walls in all directions. And though the English conquered all of Normandy in the early 15th century, they never took this well-fortified island. Because of its stubborn success against the English in the Hundred Years' War, Mont St-Michel became a symbol of French national identity.

NEAR MONT ST-MICHEL
German Military Cemetery (Cimetière Militaire Allemand)

Located three miles from Mont St-Michel, near tiny Huisnes-sur-Mer, this somber cemetery-mortuary houses the remains of 12,000 German WWII soldiers brought to this location from all over France. The stone blocks on the steps up indicate the regions in France from where they came. From the upstairs lookout, take in the sensational views over Mont St-Michel. The cemetery is well-signed east of Mont St-Michel (off D-275 at 3 Rue du Mont de Huisnes).

Sleeping in Mont St-Michel

Sleep on or near the island so that you can visit Mont St-Michel early and late. What matters is being here before or after the crush of tourists, and seeing the island floodlit after dark. Sleeping on the island—inside the walls—is a memorable experience for medieval romantics who don't mind small and overpriced rooms of average quality, and baggage hassles. To reach a room on the island, you'll need to carry your bags 15 minutes from the *navette* (shuttle) stop. Take only what you need for one night in a smaller bag, but don't leave any luggage visible in your car.

Hotels and *chambres d'hôtes* near the island are a better value (if less romantic). Those listed next are within walking distance of the free and frequent shuttle to the island.

ON THE ISLAND

Because most visitors day-trip here, finding a room is generally no problem. Though some pad their profits by requesting that guests buy dinner from their restaurant, requiring it is illegal. Higher-priced rooms generally have bay views.

The following hotels, all on Grand Rue, are listed in order of altitude from lowest to highest.

$$$ Hôtel St. Pierre*** and **Hôtel Croix Blanche***** sit side by side and share the same owners and reception desk (at St. Pierre). Each provides comfortable rooms at inflated prices, some with good views (family rooms, lower rates at Hôtel Croix Blanche, tel. 02 33 60 14 03, www.auberge-saint-pierre.fr, contact@auberge-saint-pierre.fr).

$$$ Hôtel le Mouton Blanc*** delivers a higher price value, with 15 rooms split between two buildings. Rooms in the main building have wood beams and all are freshly renovated with contemporary decor (tel. 02 33 60 14 08, www.lemoutonblanc.fr, contact@lemoutonblanc.fr).

$$ Hôtel la Vieille Auberge** is a small place with good rooms at fair prices (pricier but worthwhile view room with deck; check in at their restaurant, but book through Hôtel St. Pierre, listed above).

$$ Hôtel du Guesclin** has the cheapest and best-value rooms I list on the island and is the only family-run hotel left there. Rooms have simple decor and provide basic comfort (tel. 02 33 60 14 10, www.hotelduguesclin.com, hotel.duguesclin@wanadoo.fr).

ON THE MAINLAND

Modern hotels with easy parking and quick shuttle-bus access gather in La Caserne near the bridge to the island.

$$ Hôtel le Relais du Roy*** houses small but well-config-ured and plush rooms above comfy public spaces. Most rooms are on the riverside, with countryside views, and many have small bal-conies allowing "lean-out" views to the abbey (bar, restaurant, 8 Route du Mont Saint-Michel, tel. 02 33 60 14 25, www.le-relais-du-roy.com, reservation@le-relais-du-roy.com).

$$ Hôtel Gabriel*** has 45 modern rooms, with flashy col-ors and OK rates (includes breakfast, Route du Mont Saint-Mi-chel, tel. 02 33 60 14 13, www.hotelgabriel-montsaintmichel.com, hotelgabriel@le-mont-saint-michel.com).

$ Hôtel Vert** provides 54 motel-esque, comfortable rooms at good rates (family rooms, Route du Mont Saint-Michel, tel. 02 33 60 09 33, www.hotelvert-montsaintmichel.com, stmichel@

le-mont-saint-michel.com). They also have a small launderette for guests.

CHAMBRES D'HOTES

Simply great values, these places are a short-to-medium walk from the shuttle buses (allowing you to skip the parking mess and cost).

$ Les Vieilles Digues, where charming, English-speaking Danielle will pamper you, is toward Pontorson on the main road (on the left if you're coming from Mont St-Michel). It has a lovely garden and six spotless and homey rooms, all with showers (but no Mont St-Michel views). Ground-floor rooms have private patios on the garden (includes good breakfast, easy parking, 68 Route du Mont St-Michel, tel. 02 33 58 55 30, www.lesvieillesdigues.com, les.vieillesdigues@yahoo.fr). A pedestrian path offers a level walk along the Couesnon River to the shuttle buses a half-mile away.

$ La Jacotière is closest to Mont St-Michel and within easy walking distance of the regional bus stop and the island shuttle buses (allowing you to avoid all parking fees). Welcoming Véronique offers six comfortable rooms and views of the island from the cool backyard garden (studio with great view from private patio, family rooms, includes breakfast, tel. 02 33 60 22 94, www.lajacotiere.fr, la.jacotiere@wanadoo.fr). Drivers coming from Bayeux should keep right well before the main parking lot entry: As the road bends to the left away from the bay, stay straight and look for a Calvados products store standing alone on the right. Follow the small service lane in front of the store signed *sauf véhicule autorisé*—La Jacotière is the next building. Those coming from Pontorson should pass the main parking lot entrance then turn left near the Calvados products store.

¢ Vent des Grèves is about a mile down D-275 from Mont St-Michel (green sign; if arriving from the north, it's just after Auberge de la Baie) and in walking distance to the shuttle buses (along a busy road). Gentle Estelle (who speaks English) and Stéphane (who tries) offer comfortable rooms in two buildings for a steal. The main building has five bright, big, and modern rooms with good views of Mont St-Michel and a common deck with tables to let you soak it all in. The newer section has four sharper rooms in an apartment-like setting with a full living room (includes breakfast, 27 Rue de la Côte, tel. 02 33 48 28 89, www.ventdesgreves.com, ventdesgreves@orange.fr).

NORMANDY

Eating in Mont St-Michel

Puffy omelets (*omelette montoise*, or *omelette tradition*) are Mont St-Michel's specialty. Also look for mussels, seafood platters, and locally raised lamb *pré-salé* (a saltwater-grass diet gives the meat a unique taste, but beware of impostor lamb from New Zealand—ask where your dinner was raised). Muscadet wine (dry, white, and cheap) from the western Loire valley is made nearby and goes well with most regional dishes.

The cuisine served at most restaurants is low quality, similar, and geared to tourists (with *menus* from €18 to €29, cheap crêpes, and full à la carte choices). Pick a restaurant for its view. Window-shop the places that face the bay from the ramparts walk (several access points—one is across from the post office at the bottom of the village) and arrive early to land a view table. Unless noted, the following restaurants are open daily for lunch and dinner.

$$ Hôtel du Guesclin is the top place for a traditional meal, with white tablecloths and beautiful views of the bay from its inside-only tables (closed Thu, book a window table in advance; see details under "Sleeping in Mont St-Michel—On the Island," earlier).

$$ Restaurant le St. Michel is lighthearted, reasonable, family-friendly, and run by helpful Patricia (decent omelets, mussels, salads, and pasta; open daily for lunch, open for dinner July-Aug, closed Thu-Fri off-season, test its toilet in the rock, across from Hôtel le Mouton Blanc, tel. 02 33 60 14 37).

$$ Café La Mère Poulard is a stylish three-story café-*crêperie*-restaurant one door up from Hôtel le Mouton Blanc. (Don't confuse it with the Restaurant La Mère Poulard by the drawbridge.) It's worth considering for its upstairs terrace, which offers the best outside table views up to the abbey (when their umbrellas don't block it). **La Vieille Auberge** has a broad terrace with the next-best views to the abbey. **La Croix Blanche** owns a small deck with abbey views and window-front tables with bay views, and **Les Terrasses Poulard** has indoor views to the bay.

Groceries: In La Caserne, **Les Galeries du Mont St-Michel** is stocked with souvenirs and enough groceries to make a credible picnic (daily 9:00-20:00).

Picnics: This is the romantic's choice. The small lanes above the main street hide scenic picnic spots, such as the small park at the base of the ancient treadwheel ramp to the upper abbey. You'll catch late sun by following the ramp that leads you through the *gendarmerie* and down behind the island (on the left as you face the main entry to the island). Sandwiches, pizza by the slice, salads, and drinks are all available to go at shops (open until 19:00) along the main drag. You'll find a better selection at the modest grocery on the mainland.

Mont St-Michel Connections

BY TRAIN, BUS, OR TAXI

Bus and train service to and from Mont St-Michel can be a challenge. You may find that you're forced to arrive and depart early or late—leaving you with too much or too little time on the island. Understand all of your options.

From Mont St-Michel to Paris: Most travelers take the regional bus from Mont St-Michel's parking lot to Rennes or Dol de Bretagne and connect directly to a high-speed train (4/day via Rennes, about 3 hours total from Mont St-Michel to Paris' Gare Montparnasse via fastest train from Rennes; €15 for bus to Rennes; not covered by rail pass, buy ticket from driver, all explained in English at https://keolis-armor.com). You can also take a short bus ride to Pontorson (see next) to catch the infrequent local train to Paris. Flixbus runs direct service from Mont St-Michel to Paris' Gare de Bercy.

From Mont St-Michel via Pontorson: The nearest train station to Mont St-Michel is five miles away, in Pontorson (called Pontorson/Mont St-Michel). It's connected to Mont St-Michel by bus or by taxi (see details earlier, under "Arrival in Mont St-Michel"). Trains go from Pontorson to Paris (3/day, 5.5 hours, transfer in Caen, St-Malo, or Rennes) and Bayeux (2/day, 2 hours; faster by shuttle van—see page 271).

From Mont St-Michel by Bus to: Rennes (4/day direct, 2 hours) and **St-Malo** (1/day, one hour, round-trip ticket required). Bus tel. 02 99 19 70 70, https://keolis-armor.com.

Taxis are more expensive, but are helpful when trains and buses don't cooperate. Figure €100 from Mont St-Michel to St-Malo, and €110 to Dinan (50 percent more on Sun and at night).

BY CAR

From Mont St-Michel to St-Malo, Brittany: The direct (and free) freeway route takes 40 minutes. For a scenic drive into Brittany, take the following route: Head to Pontorson, follow *D-19* signs to St-Malo, then look for *St. Malo par la Côte* and join D-797, which leads along *La Route de la Baie* to D-155 and

NORMANDY

on to the oyster capital of Cancale. In Cancale, keep tracking *St. Malo par la Côte* and *Route de la Baie* signs. You'll be routed through the town's port (good lunch stop), then emerge on D-201. Take time to savor Pointe du Grouin, then continue west on D-201 as it hugs the coast to St-Malo (see page 357).

From Mont St-Michel to Bayeux: Take the free and zippy A-84 toward Caen.

BRITTANY

Dinan • St-Malo • Fougères

The bulky peninsula of Brittany ("Bretagne" in French; "Breizh" in Breton) is windswept and rugged, with a well-discovered coast, a forgotten interior, strong Celtic ties, and a craving for crêpes. This region of independent-minded locals is linguistically, physically, and culturally different from Normandy—and, for that matter, the rest of France. Tradition is everything here, where farmers and fishermen still play a big part in the region's economy.

The Couesnon River skirts the western edge of Mont St-Michel and has long marked the border between Normandy and Brittany. The constant moving of the riverbed made Mont St-Michel at times Norman and at other times Breton. To end the bickering, the border was moved a few miles to the west—making Mont St-Michel a Normandy resident for good.

In 1491, the French King Charles VIII forced Brittany's 14-year-old Duchess Anne to marry him (at Château de Langeais in the Loire Valley). Their union made feisty, independent Brittany a small, unhappy cog in a big country (the Kingdom of France). Brittany lost its freedom but, with Anne as queen, gained certain rights, such as free roads. Even today, more than 500 years later, Brittany's freeways have no tolls, which is unique in France.

Locals take great pride in their distinct Breton culture. In Brittany, music stores sell more Celtic albums than anything else. It's hard to imagine that this music was forbidden as recently as the 1980s. During that repressive time, many of today's Breton pop stars were underground artists. And not long ago, a child would lose French citizenship if christened with a Celtic name.

But *les Bretons* are now free to wave their black-and-white-striped flag, sing their songs, and *parler* their language (there's a

BRITTANY

Breton TV station and radio station). Look for *Breizh* (abbreviated BZH) bumper stickers and flags touting the region's Breton name. Like their Irish counterparts, Bretons are chatty, their music is alive with stories of struggles against an oppressor, and their identities are intrinsically tied to the sea.

PLANNING YOUR TIME

With one full day, spend the morning in Dinan and the afternoon either along the Rance River (walking or biking are best, but driving works) or along Brittany's wild coast, where you can tour Fort la Latte and enjoy the massive views near Cap Fréhel. Try to find a few hours for St-Malo—ideally when connecting Mont St-Michel with Brittany. The coastal route between Mont St-Michel and St-Malo—via the town of Cancale (famous for oysters and a good place for lunch), with a stop at Pointe du Grouin (fabulous ocean views)—gives travelers with limited time a worthwhile glimpse at this photogenic province.

GETTING AROUND BRITTANY

By Car: This is the ideal way to scour the ragged coast and watery towns. Expressways here are free, with a 110 km/hr speed limit. Traffic is generally negligible, except in summer, on sunny weekends along the coast, and around St-Malo and the big city of Rennes.

By Train and Bus: Trains provide barely enough service to Dinan and St-Malo (on Sun, service to Dinan all but disappears). Key transfer points by train include Rennes and the small town of Dol-de-Bretagne. Some trips are more convenient by bus (including Rennes to Dinan and Dinan to St-Malo).

By Minivan Tour: Westcapades runs daylong minivan tours covering Dinan, St-Malo, and Mont St-Michel. Designed for day-trippers from Paris, the tours leave from St-Malo or Rennes (pick-ups also possible from Dinan; €98/day includes abbey entry, tel. 02 23 23 01 96, www.westcapades.com, contact@westcapades.com).

A different tour option starts at the Rennes TGV station, includes Mont St-Michel and key D-Day beaches, and ends at the train station in either Bayeux or Caen. Another runs to the Loire Valley.

BRITTANY'S CUISINE SCENE

Though the endless coastline suggests otherwise, there is more than seafood in this rugged Celtic land. Crêpes are to Bretons what pasta is to Italians: a basic, reasonably priced, daily necessity. Galettes are savory buckwheat crêpes, commonly filled with ham, cheese, eggs, mushrooms, spinach, seafood, or a combination. Purists insist that a galette should not have more than three or four fillings—overfilling it masks the flavor (which is the point in certain places).

Oysters *(huîtres),* the second food of Brittany, are available all year. Mussels, clams, and scallops are often served as main courses, and you can also find galettes with scallops and *moules marinières* (mussels steamed in white wine, parsley, and shallots). Farmers compete with fishermen for the hearts of locals by growing fresh vegetables, such as peas, beans, and cauliflower.

For dessert, look for *far breton,* a traditional flan-like cake often served with prunes. Dessert crêpes, made with white flour, come with a variety of toppings. Or try *kouign amann,* a puffy, cara-melized Breton cake (in Breton, *kouign* means "cake" and *amann* means "butter"). At bakeries, seek out *gâteau breton,* a traditional Breton shortbread cake made with butter, of course.

Cider is the locally produced drink. Order *une bolée de cidre brut, demi-sec* or *doux* (a traditional bowl of hard apple cider, from dry to sweet) with your crêpes. Breton beer is strong and delicious; try anything local (Sant Erwann is one of my favorites).

Dinan

If you have time for only one stop in Brittany, do Dinan. Hefty ramparts corral its half-timbered and cobbled quaintness into Brittany's best medieval town center. While simply charming today, Dinan was once a formidable city—a residence of the duke of Brittany, a strategic port, and a trading center with powerful guilds and good connections with England and Holland. But in the 13th century, ships outgrew its river port, and

the harbor action migrated to nearby St-Malo. This impeccably preserved ancient city escaped the bombs of World War II, and today its stout, mile-long ramparts are like an elevated parkway. Given a chance to replace their venerable walls with a wide, modern boulevard, the people of Dinan chose instead to keep their slice of history—and the traffic congestion that comes with it.

While Dinan has a touristy icing—plenty of *crêperies*, shops selling Brittany kitsch, and colorful flags—it's a workaday Breton town filled with about 10,000 people who appreciate their beautiful, peaceful surroundings. It's also conveniently located, about a 45-minute drive from Mont St-Michel. For a memorable day, spend your morning exploring Dinan and your afternoon walking, biking, or boating the Rance River.

Orientation to Dinan

Dinan's old city, wrapped in medieval ramparts, gathers on a hill well above the Rance River. The vast Place du Guesclin (gek-lan) welcomes you with acres of parking, Château de Dinan, and the TI. A few blocks from there, Place des Merciers marks the center for shoppers. From the old cobbled core, a steep lane leads down to a small river port—once the reason for the town and now a springboard for vacation paddles and pedals.

BRITTANY

TOURIST INFORMATION

At the TI, pick up a map and bus schedules and ask about boat trips on the Rance River (Mon-Sat 9:30-19:00, Sun 10:00-12:30 & 14:30-18:00; Sept-June Mon-Sat 9:30-12:30 & 14:00-18:00, closed Sun; just off Place du Guesclin near Château de Dinan at 9 Rue du Château, tel. 02 96 87 69 76, www.dinan-capfrehel.com).

ARRIVAL IN DINAN

By Train: To get to the town center from Dinan's Old World train station, hop a taxi (see "Helpful Hints," later) or walk 20 steady minutes (see the town map). If walking, veer left out of the train station—passing Hôtel de la Gare (baggage storage available—see "Helpful Hints," later)—and walk up Rue Carnot. Turn right on Rue Thiers following *Centre Historique/Office de Tourisme* signs, then go left across big Place Duclos-Pinot, passing just left of Café de la Mairie. To reach the TI and Place du Guesclin, go to the right of the café (on Rue du Marchix).

By Bus: Dinan's intercity bus stops are at the train station and in front of the post office on Place Duclos-Pinot, minutes from Place du Guesclin. To reach the historic core, cross the square, passing to the left of Café de la Mairie (for more on buses, see "Dinan Connections," later).

By Car: Follow *Centre Historique/Office de Tourisme* signs and park on Place du Guesclin (pay nearby; free overnight from 19:00-9:00 except on Thu market days). If you enter Dinan near the train station, drive the route described earlier (see "By Train"), and keep to the right of Café de la Mairie to reach Place du Guesclin. Check with your hotelier before leaving your car overnight on Place du Guesclin; it will be towed before 6:00 on market or festival days. You can park for free all day behind the Château de Dinan, but space is limited—arrive early or late (coming from Place du Guesclin, take the first right under the medieval arch after passing the château and keep right).

HELPFUL HINTS

Market Days: Every Thursday, a big open-air market is held on Place du Guesclin (8:00-13:00). On Wednesdays in July and August, there's a flea market on Place St. Sauveur.

Baggage Storage: The recommended Hôtel de la Gare (across from the train station) will store your bags, as will the launderette listed next.

Laundry: A self-serve launderette is a few blocks from Place Duclos-Pinot at 19 Rue de Brest (Tue-Fri 8:30-12:00 & 13:45-19:00, Sat 8:30-18:00, closed Sun-Mon, tel. 02 22 13 19 72).

Supermarkets: Groceries are upstairs in the **Monoprix** (Mon-Sat 9:00-19:30, closed Sun, 7 Rue du Marchix). Or try **Carrefour**

BRITTANY

BRITTANY

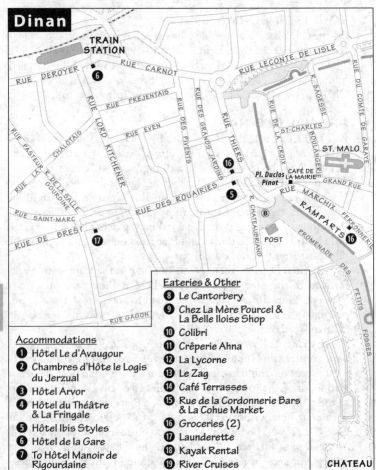

Dinan

TRAIN STATION

RUE DEROYER
RUE CARNOT
RUE LECONTE DE LISLE
RUE DU COMTE DE GARAYE
❻
RUE PREJENTAIS
RUE LORD KITCHENER
CHALOTAIS
RUE PASTEUR
R. DE LA SALLE
RUE EVEN
RUE DES FIVENTS
RUE DES GRANDS JARDINS
RUE THIERS
RUE DE LA CROIX
ST-CHARLES
K. SAGESSE
BOULANGERIE
ST. MALO
❶❻
Pl. Duclos Pinot
CAFÉ DE LA MAIRIE
GRAND RUE
RUE MARCHIX FERRONNERIE
RUE LA FOURRIE
GOURDINE
❺
R. CHATEAUBRIAND
B
RAMPARTS
❶❻
RUE SAINT-MARC
RUE DE BREST
❶❼
POST
PROMENADE DES PETITS FOSSES
RUE GAGON

Eateries & Other

❽ Le Cantorbery
❾ Chez La Mère Pourcel & La Belle Iloise Shop
❿ Colibri
⓫ Crêperie Ahna
⓬ La Lycorne
⓭ Le Zag
⓮ Café Terrasses
⓯ Rue de la Cordonnerie Bars & La Cohue Market
⓰ Groceries (2)
⓱ Launderette
⓲ Kayak Rental
⓳ River Cruises

Accommodations

❶ Hôtel Le d'Avaugour
❷ Chambres d'Hôte le Logis du Jerzual
❸ Hôtel Arvor
❹ Hôtel du Théâtre & La Fringale
❺ Hôtel Ibis Styles
❻ Hôtel de la Gare
❼ To Hôtel Manoir de Rigourdaine

CHATEAU

City on Place Duclos-Pinot (Mon-Sat 7:00-21:00, Sun 8:00-13:00).

Bike Rental: The recommended Hôtel Le d'Avaugour has a few bikes for rent. For more bike rentals, inquire at the TI.

Kayak Rental: Club Canoë Kayak rents kayaks and canoes; you can go upstream almost to Léhon, and downstream to Taden (€10/1 hour, €30/day, cash only, July-Aug daily 10:00-18:00, Sept-June by reservation only, tel. 02 96 39 01 50, www.dinanrancekayak.fr).

Taxi: Call 06 08 00 80 90 (www.taxi-dinan.com). Figure about €50 to St-Malo, €90 to Rennes, and €120 to Mont St-Michel.

Tourist Train: The *petit train* runs a circuit connecting the port and upper old town (€8, Easter-Sept Mon-Sat 11:00-17:00, Sun 14:00-17:00, runs hourly, leaves on the hour in the old

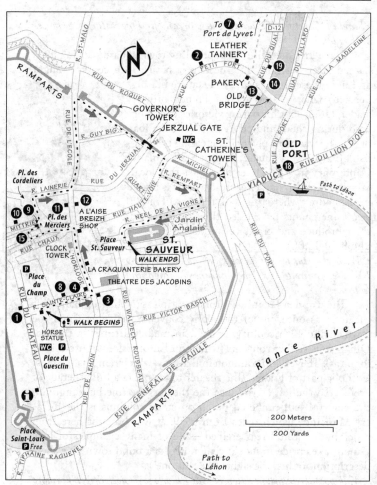

town from in front of Théâtre des Jacobins, a block off Place du Guesclin, and returns from the port on the half hour, stopovers at the port allowed).

Picnic Park: The small but flowery Jardin Anglais hides behind the Church of St. Sauveur.

Dinan Walk

Frankly, I wouldn't go through a turnstile in Dinan. The attraction is the town itself. Enjoy the old town center, ramble around the ramparts, and explore the old riverfront harbor. Here are some ideas, laced together as a relaxed one-hour walk (not including exploring the port). As you wander, notice the pride locals take in their Breton culture.

• *Start in the center of Place du Guesclin, and find the statue of the horseback rider.*

Place du Guesclin: This sprawling town square/parking lot is named after Bertrand du Guesclin, a native 14th-century knight and hero (described as small in stature but big-hearted) who became a great French military leader, famous for his daring victories over England during the Hundred Years' War (like Joan of Arc, he was a key player in defeating the English). On this very square, he beat Sir Thomas of Canterbury in a nail-biter of a joust that locals talk about to this day. (Bertrand's heart is buried in the church where this walk finishes.) For 700 years, merchants have filled this square to sell their produce and crafts (in modern times, it's Thu 8:00-13:00).

• *With the statue of Guesclin behind you, follow Rue Ste. Claire to the right, into the old town and to the...*

Théâtre des Jacobins: Fronting a pleasant little square, this theater was once one of the many convents that dominated the town in the 13th century. In fact, in medieval times, a third of Dinan consisted of convents (which, in Europe, are not exclusively for nuns). They're still common in Brittany, which remains the most Catholic part of France. The theater today offers a full schedule of events. To the left as you face the theater, the fine building with the colorful half-timbered porch on stone columns is the **Keratry Mansion,** which dates from 1559. It was brought here from a nearby town and reassembled—one of many examples of how Dinan takes pride in its old center. (Posts around town give short descriptions of historic sights like this one.)

• *Walk past the mansion down Rue de l'Horloge ("Clock Street") toward the clock tower. Under the next porch on your left, you'll see...*

Anybody's Tombstone: The tombstone without a head is a town mascot. It's a prefab tombstone, mass-produced during the Hundred Years' War, when there was more death than money in France. A portrait bust would be attached to this generic body and they'd chip the deceased's coat of arms onto the blank banner for a proper, yet economical, burial.

• *On your right, 20 yards farther down, is...*

La Craquanterie: This shop specializes in Breton cookies and treats. Look for *caramels au beurre salé* (salted butter caramels), *kouign amann* (extremely rich butter cake), *gâteau breton* (traditional cake), *craquants* (crisp cookies with salted butter), and the Breton answer to Nutella—*Craquamel*. There's a good chance your hotel will serve these local treats at breakfast.

BRITTANY

• *Continue a few steps to the...*

Clock Tower: Five hundred years ago, Dinan built this 150-foot tall tower so people would know when to start and stop working. Back when most towns only had church bell towers, this proud and modern civic tower was a symbol of the power of the town's merchants. The tower's 156 steps (the last 12 are on a ladder) lead past the clock's original mechanism—from 1498, one of the oldest in Europe—to a 360-degree sweeping city view. Warning: Plug your ears at the quarter-hour (€4, daily June-Sept 10:00-18:30, April-May 14:00-18:00, closed Oct-March).

• *At the next corner find the store...*

A l'Aise Breizh: This store, with its distinctive name (meaning "take it easy in Brittany"), has been riding the wave of Brittany's cultural renewal since 1996. You may have seen their slogan on bumper stickers throughout the region. Inside, you'll find fun clothing and whimsical souvenirs designed in Brittany.

• *You're in the middle of Dinan's...*

Old Town Center: The arcaded, half-timbered buildings around you are Dinan's oldest. They date from the time when property taxes were based on the square footage of the ground floor. To provide shelter from both the rain and taxes, buildings started with small ground floors, then expanded outward as they got taller. Notice the stone bases supporting the wood columns. Because trees didn't come in standard lengths, builders adjusted the size of the pedestals. Medieval shopkeepers sold goods in front of their homes under the shelter of these traditional porches.

• *Ducking for cover at **Le Pole Nord** (a local favorite for ice cream), turn left under the covered arcade, enjoying the architecture along the way. At the end, angle left and cross to the small well on Place des Merciers.*

Place des Merciers: From this spot spin 360 degrees counter-clockwise. Looking back at Le Pole Nord, admire the woody structures. This arcade originally continued left 100 yards past the four modern black lampposts to the next arcade. In the 19th century Dinan had about 1,000 buildings with fine wooden porches, but a 1907 fire destroyed much of the center, and only 17 survive today.

A block to the left is La Belle Iloise, a shop filled with canned fish from Brittany (described later). Behind you, enjoy the swaying, half-timbered facade of Chez La Mère Pourcel. On its lower left side, find the colorful carved statue of St. Michael. Below him, a well-beaten cornerstone protects the building from carriages careening down Rue de la Cordonnerie. Across the lane is a shop with regional products and a window full of traditional Breton ceramic cups with "ears" as handles and folk paintings inside. The mugs are based on the traditional Breton bowls that every local was raised with—hand-painted with designs of costumed Bretons and each kid's first name.

• *Walk a few paces up narrow Rue de la Cordonnerie and stop.*

Rue de la Cordonnerie: Many Breton streets are named for the key commerce that took place there in medieval times. This street, literally "Cobblers' Lane," is now nicknamed "Street of Thirst" for its many pubs. Rue de la Cordonnerie is a good example of a medieval lane, with overhanging buildings whose roofs nearly touch. After a disastrous 18th-century fire, a law required that the traditional thatch be replaced by safer slate. Enjoy the details of the buildings on this characteristic lane.

• *Take your first right (passing a public WC) into a little park where a gate leads to a modern market.*

La Cohue: There's been a market here since the 13th century, but the ambience of La Cohue today is very 21st century. It has a produce stand, wine store, cheese shop, bakery, and more (Tue-Sun 8:00-14:00, Fri-Sat until 19:00, closed Mon).

• *Explore the market. Then double back to Place des Merciers along Rue du Petit Pain, where you reach the shop selling tinned fish.*

La Belle Iloise: For three generations, a fishing family has respected the traditions of canning their fresh catch. Their factory, which is based in southern Brittany and has outlets all over France, produces tasty sardine, mackerel, and tuna spreads.

• *Make your way left past the black lampposts to the end of the square. (The building with the arched stone facade at the end—Les Cordeliers—once a Franciscan monastery, is now a middle school.) Turn right and walk a block down Rue de la Lainerie ("Street of Wool Shops") to the top of a hill. Stop at the top of Rue du Jerzual.*

Rue du Jerzual: Peer down this street that connects the town and its river port. Notice the waist-high stone and wooden shelves that front many of the buildings.

Here, medieval merchants could display their products and tempt passersby. These days, the street is lined with welcoming art galleries and inviting craft shops. (From here it's a 10-minute walk down to the port—described later, under "Sights in Dinan.")

• *Head left down Rue de l'Ecole (past Café Les Affranchis) 200 yards to the medieval gate. Ten yards before the stone gate, walk right through the wrought-iron gate onto the ramparts (called Chemin de Ronde, daily 8:00-21:00, until 17:00 off-season). Turn right and walk out onto Governor's Tower.*

Governor's Tower and the Ramparts: Although the old port town was repeatedly destroyed, these ramparts were never taken by force. If an attacker got by the *contrescarpe* (second outer wall, now covered in vegetation) and through the (dry) moat, he'd be pummeled by ghastly stuff dropped through the holes lining the ramparts. Cannon slots on the 15th-century Governor's Tower enabled defenders to shoot in all directions. Today, the ramparts protect the town's residential charm and are lined by private gardens.

• *Continue along the ramparts. At the next tower (Jerzual), look left down to Rue du Jerzual, which leads to the port (a worthwhile if steep detour). Now continue down the steps onto Rue Michel and turn right. Take the first left, onto Rue du Rempart, which dead-ends at a rampart park. On the left is a round tower called...*

St. Catherine's Tower: This part of Dinan's medieval defense system allows strategic views of the river valley and over the old port. Below you can see the medieval bridge and the path that leads along the river to the right to Léhon (described later, under "Sights in Dinan"). To the left, the Rance River flows toward the sea; behind you are the English gardens.

• *Leave the ramparts, walk through the gardens to the front of the church, and go inside.*

Church of St. Sauveur: When it was built a thousand years ago, this church sat lonely here, as all other activity was focused around the port far below. Step in to see its striking, modern stained-glass windows and beautifully lit nave. Pick up the simple English explanation. The old wood balcony above the entry heaves under the weight of its organ. A capital in the center of the back wall is decorated with camels. According to legend, a local crusader promised to build this church if he survived his crusade. Apparently he was fortunate.

The gangly church is terribly asymmetrical—built in many stages over the centuries. Notice an older section of wall on the right of the nave: The simple, round Romanesque arches bear traces of the original red bull's-blood paint, surviving from the 12th century. The fourth chapel on the left has its original 15th-century stained glass (with four Breton saints lined up below the four evangelists). The rest of the church's windows are post-World War II (c. 1950). And in the vase atop the upright tomb in the left transept, no longer beats the heart of the Dinan hero, Bertrand du Guesclin.

• *Your tour is over. Good lunch cafés are on the square (see "Eating in Dinan," later), and you are a block below the main Rue de l'Horloge.*

BRITTANY

Sights in Dinan

Dinan's Old Port

This port was the birthplace of Dinan a thousand years ago. For centuries, this is where people lived and worked, and today it's a great place for a riverside drink or meal. The once-thriving port is connected to the sea—15 miles away—by the Rance River (and a bike path that parallels it). The town grew prosperous by taxing river traffic. The tiny medieval bridge dates to the 15th century. Because the port area was so exposed, the towns-folk retreated to the bluff behind

its current fortifications. The viaduct high above was built in 1850 to alleviate congestion and to send traffic around the town. Before then, the main road crossed the little medieval bridge, heading up Rue du Jerzual to Dinan.

Getting There: Walkers following my self-guided walk (described earlier) can reach Dinan's modest little port by continuing steeply down Rue du Jerzual (which becomes Rue du Petit Fort). Just before reaching the port, notice the unusual wood-topped building on the left-hand side. This was the town's **leather tannery**—those wooden shutters could open to dry the freshly tanned hides while the nearby river flushed away the waste (happily, swimming was not in vogue then). The last business on the right before the port is a killer bakery, **La Maison de Tatie Jeanne,** with delicious local specialties, including *far breton* and *kouign amann* (you'll also find good picnic fixings and drinks to go, closed Wed). You deserve a baked break.

Drivers can park at the pay lot under the viaduct for easy port access.

▲Rance River Valley

The best thing about Dinan's port is the access it provides to lush riverside paths that amble along the gentle Rance River Valley. You can walk, bike, drive, or boat in either interesting direction (perfect for families).

On Foot: For a breath of fresh Brittany air and an easy walk, visit the flower-festooned village of **Léhon.** Trails follow either side of the river to reach it, though the more scenic one starts across Dinan's medieval bridge (turn right, and walk 35 minutes to Léhon).

Arriving in pristine little Léhon—a town of character, as the sign reminds you—visitors are greeted by a beautiful ninth-century abbey that rules the roost (find the cloisters). Explore the village's

BRITTANY

flowery cobbled lanes, but skip the town-topping castle ruin. Enjoy a meal at the adorable **$ La Marmite de l'Abbaye** restaurant, with seating inside or out. Your hostess, sweet Breton Madame Borgnic, serves wood-fire grilled meats for lunch and dinner (arrive for the 12:00 or 13:30 service, closed Mon-Tue, tel. 02 96 87 39 39).

The trail continues on well past Léhon, but you'll need a bike to make a dent in it. The villages of Evran and Treverien are both reachable by bike (allow 45 minutes from Dinan to Evran, and an additional 25 minutes to Treverien).

By Bike: The Rance River Valley could not be more bike-friendly, as there's nary a foot of elevation gain (for bike rentals, ask the Dinan TI). Here's what I'd do with three hours and a bike: Pedal to Léhon (following the "On Foot" route, earlier—but be aware that rain can make the trail too muddy), then double back to Dinan and follow the bike path along the river downstream to the Port de Lyvet.

To reach the Port de Lyvet, ride through Dinan's port, staying on the old-city side of the river. You'll join a parade of ocean-bound boats as the river opens up, becoming more like an inlet of the sea. It's a breezy, level 30-minute ride past rock faces, cornfields, and slate-roofed farms to the tiny **Port de Lyvet** (cross bridge to reach village). **$ Le Lyvet Gourmand** café/restaurant is well positioned in the village on the right after the bridge (crêpes, salads, omelets, and such, closed Wed, tel. 02 96 41 45 48). Serious cyclists should continue on to St-Suliac via La Vicomté (described later, under "By Car").

By Boat: Boats depart from Dinan's port, at the bottom of Rue du Jerzual, 50 feet to the left of the medieval bridge on the Dinan side (schedules depend on tides, get details at TI). The snail-paced, one-hour cruise on the *Jaman V* runs upriver to Léhon (the trip is far better on foot or bike), taking you through a lock and past pretty scenery (€14, April-Oct 4-5/day except none on Mon, see schedule on-

line—click on *Horaires*, tel. 02 96 39 28 41, www.vedettejamaniv. com). A longer cruise with **Compagnie Corsaire** goes to St-Malo (€35 round-trip—return is by bus, €31 one-way, April-Sept, frequency varies with tide—almost daily July-Aug, slow and scenic 2.5 hours one-way, tel. 08 25 13 81 00, www.compagniecorsaire. com, or ask at TI). Enjoy St-Malo (described later in this chapter), then take the bus back; return by bus takes 30-40 minutes.

By Car: Meandering the Rance River Valley by car requires a good map (orange Michelin #309 worked for me). Drivers connecting Dinan and St-Malo can include this short Rance joyride detour: From Dinan, go down to the port, then follow D-12 with the river to your right toward Taden, then toward Plouër-sur-Rance (Dinan's port-front road is occasionally blocked, in which case you'll join this route beyond the port). Stay straight through La Hisse, then drop down and turn right, following signs to *La Vicomté-sur-Rance*. Cross the Rance on the bridge and find the cute **Port de Lyvet** (lunch café described earlier), then continue to La Vicomté and find D-29 north toward St-Malo.

A little before Pleudihen-sur-Rance, take a 10-minute detour toward **La Cale de Mordreuc** to see "L9," a seal who settled here in 2000 after being rescued and fed for six months in a nearby aquarium. She refused to return to her seal colony near Mont St-Michel and has been the town's top attraction ever since. If she's not around, savor the views from the café on the harbor.

Back on the main road, track your way to **St-Suliac,** a pretty little port town—classified in *les plus beaux villages de France*—with a handful of restaurants, a small grocery store, and a *boulangerie.* Stroll the ancient alleys, find a bench on the grassy waterfront, and contemplate lunch. **$ Au Galichon** serves good crêpes with salad in a traditionally Breton setting (closed Mon, 5 Rue de la Grande Cohue, tel. 02 99 58 49 49). **$$ La Ferme du Boucanier** is a good higher-end choice with live music on weekends and a well-respected chef (closed Tue-Wed, 10 Rue du Pavé, tel. 02 23 15 06 35). From here, continue on to St-Malo or return to Dinan.

Sleeping in Dinan

Weekends and summers are tight; book ahead if you can. Dinan likes its nightlife, so be wary of rooms over loud bars, particularly on lively weekends.

IN THE OLD CENTER

$$ Hôtel Le d'Avaugour**** is Dinan's most central four-star hotel, with an efficient staff, stay-awhile lounge areas, full bar, and backyard garden oasis. It faces busy Place du Guesclin, near the town's medieval wall. The wood-furnished rooms have queen- or king-sized beds and modern hotel amenities but no air-con (rooms over garden are best). Likable owner Nicolas strongly encourages two-night stays (bikes for rent, 1 Place du Champ, tel. 02 96 39 07 49, www.avaugourhotel.com, contact@avaugourhotel.com).

$ Chambres d'Hôte le Logis du Jerzual is just about as cozy as it gets, with five warmly decorated rooms and thoughtful touches throughout. Gentle Sylvie Ronserray and her son Guillaume welcome guests to their terraced yard in this haven of calm close to the action: It's just up from the port but a long, steep walk below the main town (includes breakfast, deals for stays of two nights or longer, no elevator, 25 Rue du Petit Fort, tel. 02 96 85 46 54, www.logis-du-jerzual.com, sylvie.logis@bbox.fr). Get parking advice when you book.

$ Hôtel Arvor* is a good value with a fine stone facade, ideally located in the old city a block off Place du Guesclin. It's well-run, with 24 slightly tired but comfortable rooms, a cozy lounge, and nine "apartments," all with small kitchens and room to stretch (good breakfast, pay parking, 5 Rue Pavie, tel. 02 96 39 21 22, www.hotelarvordinan.com, contact@hotelarvordinan.com).

¢ Hôtel du Théâtre is ideal for budget travelers, with four central, surprisingly sharp, clean rooms above a luminous café/bar, across from Hôtel Arvor (no elevator, 2 Rue Ste. Claire, tel. 02 96 39 06 91, theatredinan@free.fr, owner Mickael speaks some English).

CLOSER TO THE TRAIN STATION

$$ Hôtel Ibis Styles,* with its shiny, predictable comfort, stands tall between Place du Guesclin and the train station. It works especially well for bus and train travelers, as it's central, reasonably priced, and next to the bus stop. They may have rooms when others don't (air-con, elevator, 1 Place Duclos-Pinot, tel. 02 96 39 46 15, https://ibis.accorhotels.com, h5977@accor.com).

¢ Hôtel de la Gare* faces the station and offers the full Breton Monty, with *charmant* Laurence and Claude (who both love Americans), a local-as-it-gets café hangout, and surprisingly quiet, clean, and comfy rooms for a steal. The hotel has no email of its own (though there is guest Wi-Fi, thanks to the owners' son) and you won't find it on Booking.com, so call to book (family rooms, Place de la Gare, tel. 02 96 39 04 57).

NEAR DINAN

$ Hôtel Manoir de Rigourdaine* is *the* place to stay if you have a car and two nights to savor Brittany. Overlooking a splendid scene of green meadows and turquoise water, this well-renovated farmhouse comes with wood beams, characteristic public spaces, verdant grounds with short and scenic hikes nearby, and three-star rooms at great rates. Owner Patrick takes good care of

BRITTANY

his guests (15-minute drive north of Dinan, tel. 02 96 86 89 96, www.hotel-rigourdaine.fr, hotel.rigourdaine@wanadoo.fr). From Dinan, drop down to the port and follow D-12 toward Taden, then follow signs to *Plouër-sur-Rance*, then *Langrolay*, and look for signs to the hotel. If coming from the St-Malo area, take D-137 toward Rennes, then N-176 toward Dinan. Take the Rance Plouër exit, and follow signs to *Langrolay* until you see hotel signs. If coming from Rennes, take D-137 toward St-Malo, then N-176 toward Saint-Brieuc, take the Plouër-sur-Rance exit, and look for signs to *Langrolay* and then the hotel.

Eating in Dinan

Dinan has good restaurants for every budget. Since galettes (savory crêpes) are the specialty, *crêperies* are a nice, inexpensive choice—and available on every corner. Be daring and try the crêpes with scallops and cream, or go for the egg-and-cheese crêpes. For a good dinner, book Le Cantorbery a day ahead if you can, or think about walking, riding, or driving to nearby Léhon for a charming village experience (see "Rance River Valley," earlier).

$$ Le Cantorbery is the place to go in Dinan for a classic meal served with grace by owner Madame Touchais. It's a warm place (literally), where the fish is mouthwatering, and meats are grilled in the cozy dining-room fireplace *à la tradition*. For dessert, don't miss the *Palet Breton*, a dense cake topped with ice cream, caramel, and salted butter (closed Wed except July-Aug, just off Place du Guesclin at 6 Rue Ste. Claire, indoor dining only, tel. 02 96 39 02 52).

$$$ Chez La Mère Pourcel has warm Breton ambience, an elegant interior, and great, artfully prepared cuisine (closed Wed, 3 Place des Merciers, tel. 02 96 39 03 80).

$$ Colibri is the talk of Dinan, so it's smart to book ahead. The cuisine is inventive Breton, but you'll find international touches as well from the talented chef. The interior is contemporary but warm—and the prices are very reasonable (closed Sun-Mon, 14 Rue de la Mittrie, tel. 02 96 83 97 89).

$ Crêperie Ahna rocks Dinan. Locals jam the place: The price is right, the dishes are tasty, and owner Greg sets the tone for a fun experience. The Ahna crêpe with duck breast is delicious, and his vanilla rum is excellent. The cuisine goes well beyond crêpes; the do-it-yourself *pierrades*—where you cook your meat or fish on a hot stone at your table—are a treat (mostly inside seating, closed Sun-Mon, reservations recommended, 7 Rue de la Poissonnerie, tel. 02 96 39 09 13).

$$ La Lycorne is Dinan's place to go for a healthy serving of mussels prepared 20 different ways and great desserts. The cook-at-your-table *pierrades* are a good deal. The ambience is medieval, especially if you order *Potence Flambée*—meat or fish served on mini gallows. It's situated on a traffic-free street (closed Mon except July-Aug, 6 Rue de la Poissonnerie, tel. 02 96 39 08 13, www. restaurant-lycorne-dinan.com).

$ La Fringale is a shoebox place next to Café du Théâtre, serving dirt-cheap-yet-tasty *paninis,* salads, and omelets to go (daily 8:00-20:00, 1 Rue de l'Horloge, mobile 06 71 30 07 56).

At the Old Port: Have a before-dinner drink—or a meal if the waterfront setting matters more than the cuisine—at one of the many places on the river. **$$ Le Zag,** with a privileged river-front setting, is famous in Dinan for its pizza, but it also cooks up delicious seafood. It has a bohemian, laid-back feel with easygoing wait staff and a fun bar scene (next door). It's good in any weather (closed Mon, 7 Rue du Port, tel. 02 96 80 55 84). **$$ Café Terrasses** is decent, with nice outdoor seating and moderately priced *menus* (daily March-Oct, tel. 02 96 39 09 60).

Nightlife: So many lively pub-like bars line the narrow, pedestrian-friendly **Rue de la Cordonnerie** that the street is nicknamed "Rue de la Soif" ("Street of Thirst"). When the weather is good, you can sit outside at a picnic table and strike up a conversation with a friendly, tattooed Breton.

Dinan Connections

Trains from Dinan generally require a change in Dol-de-Bretagne; for some long-distance connections it may be better to take the bus to Rennes, then catch a train from there. For regional destinations the bus is generally better (bus service provided by Tibus for St-Malo and Dinard, www.tibus.fr; by Illenoo for Rennes, www. illenoo-services.fr).

From Dinan by Train to: Dol-de-Bretagne (7/day, 25 minutes), **Paris'** Gare Montparnasse (10/day, 3.5 hours, change in Dol-de-Bretagne, or in Dol and Rennes), **Pontorson/Mont St-Michel** (2/day, 1.5-2.5 hours, change in Dol, then bus or taxi from Pontorson, see "Mont St-Michel Connections" on page 327, **St-Malo** (6/day, 1-2 hours, transfer in Dol, bus is better—see next), **Amboise** (3/day, 4.5-6 hours, via Dol, Le Mans, and Tours or via Paris).

By Bus to: Rennes (with good train connections to many destinations, on Rennes to Dinard line #7, 7/day, 1 hour), **St-Malo** (line #10, 5/day, none on Sun except in summer, 45 minutes; faster, cheaper, and better than train, as bus stops are more central), **Mont St-Michel** (3/day, 3.5 hours, transfer in Rennes via line #7), **Dinard** (7/day, fewer on Sun, 45 minutes, line #7). All buses depart from Place Duclos-Pinot (near the main post office), and most make a stop at the train station, too.

St-Malo

Come here to experience a true Breton beach resort. The old city
(called Intra Muros) is your
target, with pretty beaches,
powerful ramparts encircling the
town, and island fortifications
littering the bay. The inner city
can feel almost claustrophobic,
thanks to the concentration of
tall stone buildings hemmed in
by towering ramparts, though its
pedestrian streets feel more open
and lively. The town feels best up
top on the walls, which are *the* sight here.

St-Malo is packed in July and August, when the 8,000 people
who call the old city home become a minority within their own
walls as they host hordes of French holiday-makers. And St-Malo
became a literary destination for travelers thanks to the bestselling
novel *All the Light We Cannot See* by Anthony Doerr, winner of the
2015 Pulitzer Prize for fiction. This story, about a young German
who joins the Nazi Army and a blind French girl who flees Paris
for St-Malo with her father, brings wartime St-Malo to life and
describes the impact of the conflict on average folks on both sides.

Established as a Gallic city in the 1st century BC, St-Malo
became an important fortress town under Roman rule in the fourth
century thanks to its seafront location protecting access to the
Rance River. The town emerged after the fall of the Roman Empire
as a monastic center, then faded in importance. But St-Malo rose
again from the ashes of irrelevance in the 17th and 18th centuries,
becoming an important base for merchant ships and government-
sanctioned pirates defending France against threats from England
and Holland.

Today's city feels simultaneously old and new. St-Malo has
no important interiors: The cathedral, rebuilt after 1944, has little
touristic interest, and the castle houses the city government. The
city itself is the attraction—a stony wonder with some of Europe's
finest ramparts in an unforgettable setting, mixing family-friendly
beaches and craggy coastline. Simply walking the walls makes a
visit here unforgettable.

St-Malo is a 45-minute drive—or a manageable bus or train
ride—from Dinan. (There's no baggage storage in town.) If you
have a whole day here, stroll St-Malo's ramparts, cruise to Dinard,
and walk to Alet.

St-Malo's Seafaring Past

St-Malo has been a sailor's town since its origin as an ancient monastic settlement about 1,500 years ago. After the fall of the Roman Empire, Norse and Viking invasions drove people from unfortified settlements to monasteries, which provided security and stability, allowing communities like this one to grow and evolve. By the 1100s, St-Malo was a powerful, fortified island, guarding access to the Rance River Valley from one direction and the English Channel from the other. The town later joined the Hanseatic League (Europe's association of great trading cities), giving it economic heft. Its intrepid sailors further enriched the city in the 16th century (and later) by fishing for cod off the distant coast of Newfoundland.

Then St-Malo became notorious as the home of the corsairs—French mercenaries working for the king of France, and famous for daring raids on rival countries' ships. Unlike other pirates, these swashbuckling sailors were semilegal, as they were considered the king's combatants. Until the late 1700s, St-Malo's corsairs enriched themselves—and the king—by wreaking economic havoc on England, Spain, and Holland. You'll see the statue of the last and best-known corsair of St-Malo, Robert Surcouf, as you stroll the rampart walls. The stony fortress city of St-Malo was a haven for these very wealthy, king-endorsed pirates of France.

Orientation to St-Malo

St-Malo's seafront walled city (your focus) is ringed by water on all sides. Nice beaches border the walls to the north and west providing access to historic forts and good strolling at low tide. Most access points to St-Malo lie to the east (including roads from Mont St. Michel, Dinan, and the train and bus stations). Ferries arrive south of the walled city.

TOURIST INFORMATION

St-Malo's glassy TI is just outside the walls across from the main city gate (Porte St. Vincent) on Esplanade St. Vincent (Mon-Sat 9:00-19:30, Sun 10:00-18:00; closed at lunchtime April-June and Sept; shorter hours and closed Sun off-season; tel. 08 25 13 52 00, www.saint-malo-tourisme.com). The TI's free map is useless—buy the better "pocket map" (with good English information), and get bus, train, and ferry schedules. You can pay €12 to rent an audioguide to tour the city (€50 deposit) or be happy with my walking tour.

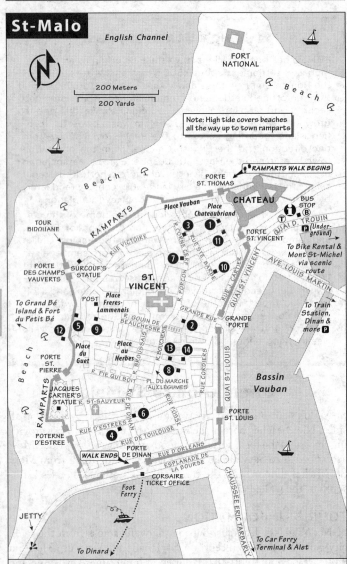

St-Malo

English Channel

N

200 Meters
200 Yards

Note: High tide covers beaches all the way up to town ramparts

FORT NATIONAL

Beach

Beach

RAMPARTS WALK BEGINS

PORTE ST. THOMAS

CHATEAU

BUS STOP

Place Vauban

Place Chateaubriand

TOUR BIDOUANE

RAMPARTS

RUE VICTOIRE

PORTE ST. VINCENT

QUAI DU TROUIN

P (Underground)

To Bike Rental & Mont St-Michel via scenic route

AVE. LOUIS MARTIN

PORTE DES CHAMPS VAUVERTS

SURCOUF'S STATUE

ST. VINCENT

R. PORCON

R. CORNE CERF

RUE STE. BARBE

RUE CARTIER

QUAI ST. VINCENT

To Grand Bé Island & Fort du Petit Bé

POST

Place Freres-Lammenais

R. GOUIN DE BEAUCHESNE

GRANDE RUE

GRANDE PORTE

To Train Station, Dinan & more P

Beach

Place du Guet

Place au Herbes

R. BOUCHERIE

R. BROUSSAIS

Bassin Vauban

PORTE ST. PIERRE

RAMPARTS

JACQUES CARTIER'S STATUE

R. PIE QUI BOIT

R. ST-SAUVEUR

RUE DE DINAN

RUE FOSSE

RUE CORDIERS

QUAI ST. LOUIS

PL. DU MARCHE AUX LEGUMES

PORTE ST. LOUIS

POTERNE D'ESTREE

RUE D'ESTREES

RUE DE TOULOUSE

WALK ENDS

PORTE DE DINAN

RUE D'ORLEANS

ESPLANADE DE LA BOURSE

Foot Ferry

CORSAIRE TICKET OFFICE

JETTY

CHAUSSEE ERIC TABARLY

To Dinard

To Car Ferry Terminal & Alet

Accommodations

1 Hôtel France et Chateaubriand & Restaurants
2 Hôtel du Louvre
3 Hôtel le Nautilus
4 Hôtel Quic en Groigne

Eateries & Other

5 Le Corps de Garde Crêperie
6 La Brigantine
7 Le Bistro de Jean
8 Breizh Café
9 Brasserie Amoricaine
10 La Java Café
11 Hôtel de l'Univers Bar
12 Bar de l'Embraque
13 La Maison du Beurre Bordier
14 Launderette

BRITTANY

ARRIVAL IN ST-MALO

By Train: From the modern TGV station, it's a five-minute bus ride on the #1, #2, or #3 lines to Porte St. Vincent (€1.30). If you'd rather walk, go for 15 minutes straight out of the station, then track the pointed spire in the distance for another five minutes.

By Bus: The main bus stops are near Porte St. Vincent and the TI, and at the train station (confirm which stop your bus uses—some stop at both). Buses from Dinan typically stop at the train station, but those to Mont St-Michel leave near the TI and Porte St. Vincent. Flixbus serves St-Malo, stopping at the train station.

By Car: Come early to avoid traffic and to find a convenient parking space. Follow *Intra-Muros/Office de Tourisme* signs to the old center, and park as close as possible to Porte St. Vincent (near the merry-go-round). A big underground parking lot is opposite Porte St. Vincent (descend near the TI), and smaller surface lots and street parking are scattered around the walls, mostly to the east. In peak season, you can park in the spacious pay parking lot just outside of town (Parking Paul Féval), and take the free Express Féval shuttle to Porte St. Vincent (runs daily, 2/hour until 22:00).

HELPFUL HINTS

Services: Pay WCs are located in some gates *(portes)* leading to the old city.

Laundry: Inside the walls, there's a launderette on the corner of Rue de la Herse and Halle des Grands Degrés (daily 7:00-21:00).

Car Rental: **Avis** (tel. 02 23 18 07 18) and **Europcar** (tel. 02 99 56 75 17) are both inside the train station.

Bike Rental: You'll find shops willing to rent you a bike, but St-Malo is not bike-friendly. It's better to bike from Dinan, ride here, then explore St-Malo on foot (2-hour ride from Dinan north past Port de Lyvet—see page 341 and get directions at TI).

Minivan Tour: **Westcapades** guarantees minivan departures at least three times a week from St-Malo. Tours can include Dinan, Mont St-Michel, or the D-Day beaches (see page 331).

Sights in St-Malo

▲St-Malo's Ramparts

To reach the ramparts, climb the stairs inside Porte St. Thomas (behind the Hôtel France et Chateaubriand). Then tour the walls counterclockwise. You'll take a rewarding half-mile-long romp around medieval fortifications with segments dating from the 1100s. (Note that the ramparts described here are the scenic ones: The stretch not described is not worth your time or energy.) Read the information panels as you go. Along the way, stairs provide access to the beach and the town. Walk down to the beaches if the tides allow (along with Mont St-Michel, St-Malo has Europe's greatest tidal changes). The walls are at their best and most peaceful early in the day.

Here are your rampart highlights:

View from Porte St. Thomas: Imagine the strategic importance of this city. The fortified islands were built during the wars of Louis XIV (late 1600s) by his military architect, Vauban, to defend the country against British and Dutch naval attacks. You can tour the closer forts (€6 each) when tides allow. Both offer visits with a French-only tour (skippable, though the views back to St-Malo from near the forts alone merit the effort). **Fort National** is nearest. Farther along is the **Fort du Petit Bé.** Built in the 1600s, it sits behind Ile du Grand Bé, where the famous poet Chateaubriand is buried. A garrison of 177 French soldiers manned this fort until 1885. During WWII, Germans used these forts as part of their Atlantic Wall defense. They occupied the forts and the city of St-Malo through much of World War II with almost no damage. But as the Allies pushed into France after D-Day, Hitler ordered St-Malo's Nazi commander to fight to the end. This led to the near-total destruction of the city in one horrible week in August 1944.

Continue along the ramparts. The tree trunks below, planted like little forests on the sand, form part of St-Malo's breakwater and must be replaced every 20 years. These help break the powerful waves that pound the seawalls when storms scream in off the English Channel. High tides cover those trunks.

Continue along to the next tower—the defensive-minded **Tour Bidouane.** Climb the steps and find a helpful orientation table and more views. Locate Fort la Latte, about 11 miles in the distance (described on page 356). Fort la Latte was part of Vauban's elaborate defense network (with Forts National and Bé).

View from Porte des Champs Vauverts: Cross the short bridge to the flagpoles, occasionally flying blue-and-white Québec flags in honor of St-Malo's sister city, Québec City. The great Breton navigator Jacques Cartier, who visited the future site of Québec City during early Canadian explorations, lived in and sailed from St-Malo. Cartier's statue is further along the wall; the statue here is of the famed pirate, Robert Surcouf, who won fortune and fame in the late 1700s by operating slave ships and raiding dozens of (mostly British) ships and seizing their cargo for the French.

Mean Bulldogs: Next, pass St-Malo's best positioned *crêperie* (consider a coffee or breakfast break), then find the *Chiens du Guet* restaurant sign (with two dogs). At one time, 24 bulldogs were kept in the small, enclosed area behind the restaurant, then let loose late at night to patrol the defenses and no-man's-land along these ramparts.

Porte St. Pierre: Next is a big, square park on the ramparts still defended by cannon. The statue, commemorating Jacques Cartier, was inaugurated in 1984 by Canadian Prime Minister Pierre Trudeau on the 450th anniversary of Cartier's first voyage to Canada. Below on the pretty beach is the recommended **Bar de l'Embraque**—a nifty outdoor-only bar/café ideal at sunset (see "Eating in St-Malo," later).

As you continue along the ramparts, notice that much of the fine stonework of both the city and the ramparts feels rebuilt. Remember, St-Malo was decimated by American bombs during World War II as part of the campaign to liberate France, and 80 percent of St-Malo was leveled. Even though they look old, most of the town's buildings date from 1945 or later. The quality of St-Malo's rebuild is a testament to the feisty pride and spirit of its people.

Rounding the corner, look for a long, concrete jetty pointing across the bay to the belle époque resort town of Dinard (described later). Consider a walk out to the end of the jetty, where the views back to St-Malo justify the detour. Across the bay, you'll also spot the green, circular park at the tip of Alet (also described later). Big ferries sail to England from the harbor in front of you.

Porte de Dinan: With the most interesting section of the ramparts behind you, this is a good place to descend and check out the harbor action and the *pétanque* (a.k.a. *boules*) courts below the walls on the left (you may see locals playing *boule bretonne*—more like lawn bowling and with bigger balls). The Corsaire ticket kiosk marks the departure point for a fun little foot ferry to Dinard (10 minutes each way with great views, described next). They also offer cruises to Cap Fréhel and Fort La Latte.

Strolling the Old Town

After walking the ramparts, see the old town with a stroll through the town center from Porte de Dinan to Porte St. Vincent, eating, browsing, and shopping as you go. The liveliest shopping streets are Rue de Dinan, the delightful Place du Marché aux Légumes (with its medieval timber market hall), Rue de la Vieille Boucherie, and Rue Porcon de la Barbinais. Drop by **La Maison du Beurre Bordier** to appreciate the art of handmade butter and cheese. With the help of a small exhibit, the welcoming staff explains how their artisanal butter and cheese are crafted. The **$$$** bistro next door allows you to sample dishes that show off their work (shop open Tue-Sat 9:00-13:00 & 15:30-19:30, Sun 9:00-13:00, closed Mon, bistro open Tue-Sat for lunch and Thu-Sat for dinner, 9 Rue de l'Orme, tel. 02 23 18 25 81).

BRITTANY

NEAR ST-MALO
Dinard

This upscale-traditional resort comes with a kid-friendly beach and an old-time, Coney Island-style, beach-promenade feel. In the late 1800s, this was France's number-one beach resort (before the Mediterranean became popular). This explains the many elaborate seaside villas you'll walk past.

A scenic little foot ferry *(Bus de Mer)* shuttles passengers between St-Malo and Dinard in 10 minutes (€8 round-trip, worthwhile for the views alone, runs roughly 9:30-18:00, later in summer, none Nov-March). Boats depart from near Porte de Dinan on the south side of the old city—buy tickets from the kiosk labeled *Compagnie Corsaire*. Buses also run from Dinan (see "Dinan Connections," earlier).

There's plenty in Dinard to keep you busy for a half- or full day. To reach the town's popular promenade, face the ferry-ticket office, turn right, and follow the path that leads to a small cove with a couple of restaurants. Continue following the seaside on the circular *Promenade du Moulinet,* where rich Brits settled during the belle époque and great views of St-Malo await. To get to the family-friendly beach (Plage de l'Ecluse), face the ferry-ticket office and turn left to reach this quieter beach via the yacht club. Along the way you'll see photogenic trees framing views of St-Malo. Dinard's market day is Saturday on Place Crolard (until 12:30).

Alet

The park and village of Alet is just a few minutes' drive past St-Malo's port (a pleasant 20-minute walk south from the ramparts), but it feels a world apart. A splendid 30-minute walking path leads around Alet's forested point with stunning views of crashing waves, the city of Dinard, the open sea, and St-Malo. The entire park is picnic-perfect. WWII bunkers cap the small hill, and a few rusted defenses are scattered throughout the park. Inside one of the bunkers is the small **Mémorial 39/45** museum, which explains the strategic value of St-Malo, its WWII battles, and German defenses (€6, must join a one-hour guided tour in French only—printed English text provided, tel. 02 99 82 41 74, www.ville-saint-malo.fr). Several pleasing cafés face the bay near the Tour Solidor (a 14th-century fortification at the mouth of the Rance River).

Getting There: By **car** from St-Malo's TI or train station, follow *Toutes Directions* signs south until you spot signposts for *Alet* and *Alet/Mémorial.* These lead to and through the park, where you can drive right to the top of the hill and park for free. Those preferring a somewhat longer stroll should follow signs to *Alet,* then *Tour Solidor* (parking a few blocks before the tower on or near Place

St. Pierre). To reach the start of the walking path from here, walk to the sea, turn right, and climb the stairs at the end of the small bay before making a hard left.

On **foot** from St-Malo, buy the TI map and walk from Porte St. Louis along Quai St. Louis. Cross the drawbridge and continue along the dike (Digue des Sablons), hugging the bay through the Port de Plaisance. Follow *Mémorial* signs up and into the park.

Sleeping in St-Malo

Overnighting here gives you more time to enjoy the sunset and sea views from the town walls. To reach these hotels, it's best to park outside the walls and walk in through Porte St. Vincent.

$$$ Hôtel France et Chateaubriand*** is a venerable Old World establishment near Porte St. Vincent, with 80 tired rooms at inflated rates (secure pay parking, 12 Place Chateaubriand, tel. 02 99 56 66 52, www.hotel-chateaubriand-st-malo.com).

$$ Hôtel du Louvre*** is a modern hotel inside the city walls with comfortable rooms at fair rates (elevator, pay parking, 2 Rue des Marins, tel. 02 99 40 86 62, www.hotel-louvre-saint-malo.com, contact@hoteldulouvre-saintmalo.com).

$ Hôtel le Nautilus** is a solid, colorful value, run by the affable team of Loïck and Jean-Michel. It's conveniently located inside the walls near Porte St. Vincent (elevator, pay parking, 9 Rue de la Corne de Cerf, tel. 02 99 40 42 27, www.hotel-lenautilus-saint-malo.com, info@lenautilus.com).

$ Hôtel Quic en Groigne is a well-run and popular place with sharp rooms and great prices (8 Rue d'Estrées, tel. 02 99 20 22 20, www.quic-en-groigne.com).

Eating in St-Malo

St-Malo is all about seafood and crêpes. There's no shortage of restaurants, many serving the local specialty of mussels *(moules)* and oysters *(huîtres)*. Look also for bakeries selling *ker-y-pom*, traditional apple-filled shortbread biscuits that are the best-tasting specialty in town, especially when warmed.

$$$ Le Chateaubriand offers two choices. The **ground-floor restaurant** delivers a grand, Old World aura and a full range of choices at decent prices (daily, indoor and outdoor dining). At **Le 5,** their "gourmet" restaurant five floors up, you pay more for the sea views but the *menu* is a good value (closed Mon-Tue, Place Chateaubriand, tel. 02 99 56 66 52).

$ Le Corps de Garde Crêperie is on the walls and has St-Malo's cheapest, killer-view tables; there's a pleasant ambience indoors or out. They serve breakfast for morning wall-walkers from

BRITTANY

9:15-10:30 and good-enough crêpes at fair prices from 11:30-22:00 (daily, 3 Montée Notre Dame, tel. 02 99 40 91 46).

$ La Brigantine offers delicious crêpes but no view (closed Tue-Wed except July-Aug, 13 Rue de Dinan, tel. 02 99 56 82 82).

$$ Le Bistro de Jean serves traditional French bistro fare in an intimate setting (closed Sun, 6 Rue de la Corne de Cerf, tel. 02 99 40 98 68).

$$ Breizh Café has a smart, wood-accented interior and the best gourmet crêpes in St-Malo (closed Mon-Tue, reservations recommended, 6 Rue de l'Orme, tel. 02 99 56 96 08).

$$ Brasserie Amoricaine is an Old World kind of spot with white tablecloths under wood beams, serving good-value fare and affordable wine. Their flaming lobster is a memorable experience (closed Sun-Mon, 6 Rue du Boyer, tel. 02 99 40 89 13).

Nightlife: The oldest café in St Malo (open since 1820) also has the longest name (too long to repeat here) and 2,874 dolls along its walls. Locals call it **La Java** and gather here for beer, wine, and *les bons temps*. Even if you aren't staying overnight in St-Malo, it's worth taking a peek at the quirky decor any time of day (near Porte St. Vincent at 3 Rue Ste. Barbe, tel. 02 99 56 41 90, www.lajavacafe. com). The bar at **Hôtel de l'Univers** reeks of swashbuckling, local character, and everything nautical (daily, Place Chateaubriand, tel. 02 99 40 89 52).

Beach Life: For St-Malo's best view beach bar and good prices, find a seat at **Bar de l'Embraque** and soak up the view (lunch only or drinks before dinner, ideal at sunset, open daily, on the Plage de Bon Secours, 4 Rue de la Harpe, tel. 02 23 15 99 13).

St-Malo Connections

From St-Malo by Train to: Dinan (6/day, 1-2 hours, transfer in Dol-de-Bretagne, bus is better—see below), **Pontorson** (with bus connections to **Mont St-Michel;** 2/day, 2 hours, transfer in Dol), **Rennes** (10/day, 1 hour).

By Bus to: Dinan (5/day, none on Sun except in summer, 45 minutes; faster and better than train, as bus stops are more central).

By Train/Bus to Mont St-Michel: (2/day, 1-2.5 hours, train to Pontorson, bus to Mont St-Michel).

By Direct Bus to Mont St-Michel: (1/day at 9:15, return trip departs from Mont St-Michel at 15:45, less off-season, €23, round-trip ticket required, https://keolis-armor.com).

Scenic Drives near St-Malo

▲▲Scenic Drive on the Western Emerald Coast

For drivers, the western Emerald Coast *(Côte d'Emeraude)* between Cap Fréhel and St-Malo offers the best look at Brittany's raw beauty. You'll drive past sleepy villages, sweeping views of sandy beaches with wind-sculpted rocks and immense cliffs overlooking crashing waves (see "Brittany" map, earlier). The highlight is Fort la Latte, a medieval castle built on a rocky spur over the ocean.

Allow a half-day for the entire trip. Your drive covers the area between St-Malo and the town of Pléhérel-Plage (about 34 miles, or 55 kilometers). If you don't have much time and just want to see the fort, it's about an hour's scenic drive from St-Malo or Dinan. During summer or on a weekend, do this drive early to avoid crowds. If it's Saturday and off-season, consider starting at the market in Dinard (described earlier). Here's a brief explanation of the route.

Driving from St-Malo to Pléhérel-Plage: Take D-168 west, which becomes D-786 near Ploubalay. The road is busy until Ploubalay but opens up nicely west of there. Continue toward Matignon, detouring to St-Jacut-de-la-Mer and Pointe du Chevet (described next) before continuing on to Fort la Latte, Cap Fréhel, and finally, Pléhérel-Plage.

Driving from Dinan to Pléhérel-Plage: Drive north on the D-2 to Ploubalay, then follow the route described from St-Malo.

Pointe du Chevet

After Ploubalay, the first worthwhile detour is up the narrow peninsula to Pointe du Chevet. From D-786, follow D-62, passing just outside the sweet little town of St-Jacut-de-la-Mer. Follow imperfect signage a few miles to Pointe du Chevet (just keep heading north). You'll come to a parking area near the end of the peninsula—turn left and continue down a tiny lane, parking where the road ends. Beautiful views (and few people) surround you. If the tide is out, you can hike to an island or study the impressive rows of wooden piers sunk into the bay. These are used to grow mussels, which cling to the wooden poles; farmers eventually harvest them using a machine that pushes a ring around the poles.

From here, return to D-786 heading toward Matignon and

BRITTANY

follow signs to *Fort La Latte* and *Cap Fréhel*. Start with Fort la Latte.

▲▲Fort la Latte

This mighty fortress is a 25-minute drive west of Pointe du Chevet. From the parking lot, it's a 10-minute walk to memorable views of a medieval castle hugging a massive rock above the ocean. The skippable English flier gives general background about the castle's history. The castle itself is well-presented in English with unusually good information panels at all key stops.

Cost and Hours: €6.50, daily 10:30-18:00, July-Aug until 19:00, shorter hours off-season, closed Jan, tel. 02 96 41 57 11, www.castlelalatte.com.

Visiting the Fort: The first fort on this site was made from wood and built as a lookout for invading Normans. What you see today dates from the 14th and 15th centuries, when wars between England and France caught Brittany in the middle for well over a hundred years. While the castle was never successfully attacked from the sea, in 1597 its garrison of 25 men was overwhelmed by a force of 2,000 soldiers coming overland. Later, Louis XIV's military architect Vauban oversaw work shoring up the castle's outer defenses. It was used well into the 18th century.

Touring the site, take time to read the information panels and appreciate the carefully tended plantings. You'll cross two impressive drawbridges (the second separates the castle from the mainland), peer into a dungeon (*l'oubliette* in French—"the forgotten") that still holds a prisoner, check the water level of the cistern, then wander ramparts towering high above the ocean. The guardroom houses a small gift shop (there's a good book about the castle in English). The small chapel was added in the 18th century, replacing the original chapel, and is dedicated to St. Michael, protector of warriors. The largest structure inside the fort is the governor's lodge (closed to the public because the owners—from the same family that restored the place in the 1930s—live here).

The highlight of a visit to Fort la Latte is the climb to the top of the castle keep, with a magnificent 360-degree view. You can only reach the very top lookout by ladder, but the views from the more accessible level below are still sensational. As you gaze out from this invincible castle, clinging for its life to a rock, think of Fort la Latte as a symbol of Brittany's determination to remain independent from France. It's no surprise that Hollywood used this castle in the 1958 film *The Vikings* with Kirk Douglas.

Behind the keep, the low-slung *four à rougir les boulets* served as a kiln to heat cannonballs. The defenders aimed hot shots at ships to set them afire. That's cool. One hundred cannon balls could be heated at a time. Don't miss the three-story, round, archer's tower with crossbows in place. From the castle's end, a cannon sits on a wheeled base, allowing it to swivel as it points out to the infinite sea.

If you want to stretch your legs, back at the entrance a trail behind the ticket kiosk runs to Cap Fréhel. Just a 10-minute walk up this path rewards you with sensational views back to the fort; it takes 75 minutes to walk all the way to Cap Fréhel. There's also a short trail from the ticket kiosk down to a rocky beach, giving you a sea-level perspective of the fortress.

Cap Fréhel and Pléhérel-Plage

Too-popular Cap Fréhel is a five-minute drive west of Fort La Latte at the tip of a long peninsula. It features walking paths over soaring cliffs with views in all directions. You'll park near Cap Fréhel's stone lighthouse and pay a small fee to enter the site (café nearby). The place can be crazy on weekends and summer afternoons. While views from the trails are sufficiently expansive, it is possible to climb the lighthouse each afternoon from April to September (small fee, Mon-Fri 15:00-17:00, Sat-Sun 14:30-17:30).

While Cap Fréhel offers immediate access to good trails, consider skipping the entry (and crowds) and continuing west on D-34, stopping at pullouts with access to bluff trails (with one that parallels the road). Parking at Plage de la Fosse is an ideal stop with trails down to a gorgeous beach below.

Finish your beach excursion by continuing west 10 minutes to the small town of Pléhérel-Plage, where beachfront parking is available at a beach called Plage de l'Anse du Croc. You can walk forever on this beautiful beach if the tide is out far enough.

From Pléhérel-Plage, return east to Dinan or St-Malo by following signs to the town of Fréhel, then Matignon, then eventually Dinan and St-Malo.

▲▲Scenic Drive Between St-Malo and Mont St-Michel

If you have less time, consider this lovely ride—worth ▲▲▲ if it's clear (see route on the "Brittany" map, earlier). This quick taste-of-Brittany driving tour samples a bit of the rugged peninsula's coast, with lots of views but no dramatic forts. Allow two hours for the drive between Mont St-Michel and St-Malo, including stops (a more direct route takes 45 minutes). On a weekend or in summer, the drive will take longer—start early. These directions are from St-Malo to Mont St-Michel, but the drive works just as well in reverse order.

St-Malo to Cancale: From St-Malo, take the scenic road hugging the coast east on D-201 to Pointe du Grouin. To find the road, leave St-Malo following *Paramé/Cancale* signs. D-201 skirts in and out of camera-worthy views as you follow signs for *Rothéneuf.* As you drive toward Cancale, you will be surrounded by fields of cauliflowers, potatoes, and onions, reminding you that tourism and agriculture form the economic base of Brittany.

Fans of quirky sights can make a quick stop at *Les Rochers Sculptés* in Rothéneuf. At the end of the 19th century, a Catholic abbot decided to devote his life to sculpture after he became deaf and mute. With a hammer and chisel, he worked for 15 years creating his story out of the rock of a sea cliff (small fee, daily in summer 9:00-19:00, shorter hours off-season, short introduction provided in English, tel. 02 99 56 23 95). You could make this stop longer by having lunch right here at **$$$$ Le Bénétin,** a mod restaurant serving fresh food with panoramic views (daily April-Sept, tel. 02 99 56 97 64).

Back on the road to Cancale, signs lead to short worthwhile detours to the coast; these are my favorites:

Ile Besnard and Dunes des Chevrêts: A five-minute detour off D-201 leads to this pretty, sandy beach arcing alongside a crescent bay. There are sea-piercing rocks to scramble on, a nature trail above the beach, and a view restaurant (**$$ La Perle Noire,** tel. 02 99 89 01 60). It's a 10-minute drive from Rothéneuf: Follow signs to *Ile Besnard* and *Dunes des Chevrêts* to the very end (past the campground), and park at the far end of the lot.

Pointe du Grouin: This striking rock outcrop yields views from easy trails in all directions. Park near Hôtel Pointe du Grouin (outdoor café with views), and continue on foot. Pass the *sémaphore du Grouin* (signal station), where paths lead everywhere. Breathe in the sea air. Can you spot Mont St-Michel in the distance? The big rock below is Ile des Landes, an island earmarked for a fort during the French Revolution. The fort was never built, and the island remains home to thousands of birds. What fool would build on an island in this bay?

Cancale: Return to your car and leave Pointe du Grouin, following signs to *Cancale,* Brittany's appealing oyster capital. Follow *le port* signs leading to a quiet harbor and turn left. Slurp oysters at the outdoor stands. There are several types. *Belon* are flat and round—they're finer and pricier than the more common *creuse*. *Pied de cheval* are older and even more expensive as they are wild, unlike most oysters growing in the seabeds in front of you. Size is rated from #5 (smallest) to #0 (biggest). The port is lined with more than 30 restaurants showing off the label *Site remarquable du goût* (extraordinary place to taste).

Consider a meal at **$$ Le Narval,** named after the fishing boat of Chef Gégé's grandfather. It serves fine seafood and meat dishes (reservations smart, tel. 02 99 89 63 12).

Cancale to Mont St-Michel: Cancale is a 45-minute drive from Mont St-Michel. Head out of Cancale toward Mont St-Michel on D-76 to D-155, then D-797, and drive along the *Route de la Baie,* which skirts the bay and passes big-time oyster farming, windmill towers (most lacking their sails), flocks of sheep, and, at low tide, grounded boats waiting for the sea to return. On a clear day, look for Mont St-Michel in the distance. On a foggy day, look harder.

Fougères

The very Breton city of Fougères, worth ▲, is a handy stop for drivers traveling between the Loire châteaux and Mont St-Michel.

Fougères has one of Europe's largest medieval castles, a lovely old city center, and a panoramic park viewpoint. Drivers follow *Centre-Ville* signs, then *Château,* and park at the free lot just past the château.

For a memorable loop through new and old Fougères, start at the parking lot near the château. Walk into Fougères with the water-filled moat on your left, then follow the *Château* sign. Stop for a peek in the handsome **Church of St. Sulpice** (English handout inside)—the woodwork is exceptional, especially the choir stalls and altar. Then walk through **Porte Sainte Anne,** the only remaining gate to the walled city. The château is on your left, but there's no reason to visit it unless you need more exercise or want to pick up a town map at the ticket office (€8.50, includes audioguide, June-Sept daily 10:00-19:00, shorter hours and closed Mon off-season, closed Jan, tel. 02 99 99 79 59, www.chateau-fougeres.com).

Next, walk up Rue de la Pinterie (fine views) to the top of the street, then turn right on Rue Nationale at the TI. You are now in the Haute Ville (modern Fougères). Keep walking toward St. Léonard Church, passing the old belfry on a square on your right. At the church, enter the **Jardin Public** and enjoy its floral panorama. From here all paths lead down to the old town. At the bottom of the garden, find various types of *fougères* (ferns). To finish the loop, exit the Jardin Public following signs to the château and cross the little Nançon River. You'll land in the Basse Ville, the old medieval town with lovely half-timbered houses on Place du Marchix. The château is ahead, and you'll find a gaggle of cafés and *crêperies* nearby with good choices and prices.

THE LOIRE

Amboise • Chinon • Beaucoup de Châteaux

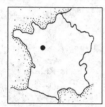

As it glides gently east to west, officially separating northern from southern France, the Loire River has come to define this popular tourist region. The importance of this river and the valley's prime location, in the center of the country just south of Paris, have made the Loire a strategic hot potato for more than a thousand years. The Loire was the high-water mark for the Moors as they pushed into Europe from Morocco. Today, this region is still the dividing line for the country—for example, weather forecasters say, "north of the Loire...and south of the Loire..."

Because of its history, the Loire Valley is home to more than a thousand castles and palaces of all shapes and sizes. When a "valley address" became a must-have among 16th-century hunting-crazy royalty, rich Renaissance palaces replaced outdated medieval castles. Hundreds of these castles and palaces are open to visitors, and it's castles that you're here to see. Old-time aristocratic château-owners, struggling with the cost of upkeep, enjoy financial assistance from the government if they open their mansions to the public.

Today's Loire Valley is carpeted with fertile fields, crisscrossed by rivers, and laced with rolling hills. It's one of France's most important agricultural regions. The region is also under some development pressure, thanks to TGV bullet trains (also called "InOui" trains) that link it to Paris in well under two hours, and cheap flights to England that have made it a prime second-home spot for many Brits, including Sir Mick Jagger.

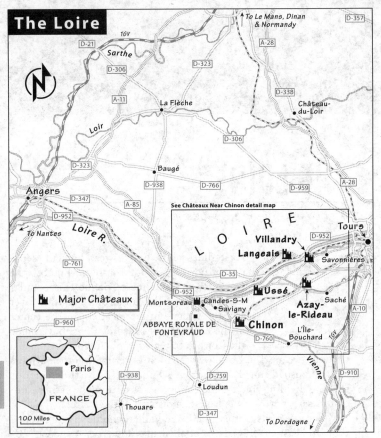

The Loire

To Le Mans, Dinan & Normandy

D-357

TGV

D-21

Sarthe

D-306

D-323

A-28

D-338

A-11

La Flèche

Château-du-Loir

Loir

D-306

D-323

Baugé

D-938

D-766

D-959

A-28

Angers

D-347

A-85

L O I R E

Tours

D-952

Villandry

Savonnières

D-952

Langeais

To Nantes

Loire R.

D-761

D-35

Ussé

Saché

Major Châteaux

Montsoreau

Candes-S-M

Savigny

Azay-le-Rideau

A-10

D-960

ABBAYE ROYALE DE FONTEVRAUD

Chinon

L'Île-Bouchard

D-760

See Châteaux Near Chinon detail map

Vienne

TGV

Paris

FRANCE

D-938

D-759

D-347

Loudun

Thouars

D-910

100 Miles

To Dordogne

LOIRE

CHOOSING A HOME BASE

This is a big, unwieldy region, so I've divided it into two halves: east and west of the sprawling city of Tours. Each area is centered around a good, manageable town—**Amboise** (east) or **Chinon** (west)—to use as a home base for exploring nearby châteaux. Which home base should you choose? That will depend on which châteaux you'd like to visit; for ideas, scan the "Loire Valley Châteaux at a Glance" sidebar, later. For first-time visitors, Amboise is, hands-down, the better choice.

Châteaux-holics and gardeners can stay longer and sleep in both towns. Avoid driving across traffic-laden Tours; the A-85 autoroute (toll) is the quickest way to link Amboise with châteaux near Chinon (about an hour). Thanks to this uncrowded freeway, sleepy Azay-le-Rideau is another good base for destinations west of Tours; it also works as a base for sights on both sides.

East of Tours: Amboise and, to a lesser extent, **Blois** or

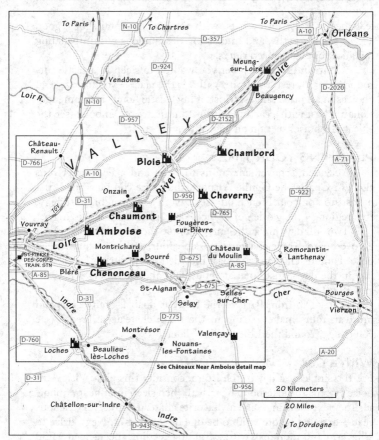

To Paris ↑ N-10 / To Chartres | To Paris → A-10 | Orléans
D-357
D-924
Meung-sur-Loire
Vendôme
Loir R.
N-10
D-957
D-2152
Beaugency
D-2020
Château-Renault
D-766
A-10
Blois
Chambord
A-71
Onzain
River
D-956
Cheverny
D-922
Chaumont
Fougères-sur-Bièvre
D-765
Vouvray
Amboise
Loire
Montrichard
Château du Moulin
Romorantin-Lanthenay
ST-PIERRE-DES-CORPS TRAIN. STN
Bourré
D-675
A-85
A-85
Bléré
Chenonceau
Selles-sur-Cher
Cher
To Bourges
St-Aignan
D-675
Indre
D-31
Seigy
Vierzon
D-775
Montrésor
Valençay
D-760
Loches
Beaulieu-lès-Loches
Nouans-les-Fontaines
A-20
See Châteaux Near Amboise detail map
D-31
D-956
20 Kilometers
Châtellon-sur-Indre
Indre
20 Miles
D-943
↓ To Dordogne

Chenonceaux, make the best home bases for this area. Amboise and Blois have handy car or bus/minivan access to these important châteaux: elegant Chenonceau, urban Blois, epic Chambord, canine-crazy Cheverny, royal Amboise, and garden-showy Chaumont-sur-Loire. Amboise has minivan service to area sights, and drivers appreciate its small scale and easy parking; Blois has better train connections from Paris and better low-cost transportation to nearby sights in high season but lacks the small-town warmth of Amboise. The peaceful town of Chenonceaux works for drivers and hardy bicyclists. Most visitors choose Amboise for its just-right size and more varied tourist appeal.

West of Tours: Chinon, Azay-le-Rideau, and their nearby châteaux don't feel as touristy; these towns appeal to gardeners and road-less-traveled types. The key châteaux in this area are historic Chinon, fairy-tale Azay-le-Rideau, fortress-like Langeais, and garden-lush Villandry. Lesser sights include the châteaux at Rivau and Ussé, plus the historic Abbaye Royale de Fontevraud. Azay-le-Rideau is best for cyclists, with convenient rental shops, good access to bike paths, and interesting destinations within pedaling distance for experienced riders.

Château Hotels: If ever you wanted to sleep in a castle surrounded by a forest, the Loire Valley is the place—you have several choices in all price ranges. Most of my "castle hotel" recommendations are best with a car and within 15 minutes of Amboise (see the "Near Amboise" section on page 387).

PLANNING YOUR TIME

With frequent, convenient trains to Paris and a few direct runs right to Charles de Gaulle Airport, the Loire can be a good first or last stop on your French odyssey. Avoid a château blitz strategy; this region—"the garden of France"—is a pleasant place to linger.

Two full days are sufficient to sample the best châteaux. Don't go overboard. Three châteaux, possibly four, are the recommended dose. Famous châteaux are least crowded early, during lunch, and late in the day. Most open at about 9:00 and close between 18:00 and 19:00.

A day trip from Paris to the Loire is doable. Shuttle bus and minivan tours make getting to the main châteaux a breeze (see "Getting Around the Loire Valley," later).

With a Car

For the single best day in the Loire, consider this plan: Visit Amboise's sights the afternoon of arrival, then sleep in or near Amboise. The next morning, visit my favorite château—graceful Chenonceau—arriving before 9:00 to be one of the first in. Next, drive to Cheverny (40 minutes), with a fun dog-feeding spectacle at 11:30 and good lunch options. End your day at monumental Chambord, a 15-minute drive from Cheverny. Energetic travelers could visit Chaumont on their way back to Amboise. To see the dog feeding at Cheverny, you need to stay on task and leave Chenonceau by 10:30—or visit these sights in reverse order, starting with Chambord (arrive close to 9:00 opening), then Cheverny, and ending at Chenonceau (this means more crowds at Chenonceau).

With a second full day, you could move to (or day-trip to) Chinon, visiting Villandry (and its gardens) or Azay-le-Rideau en route, then devote your afternoon to the château and old town in Chinon.

Try to see one château on your drive in (for example, if arriving from the north, visit Chambord, Chaumont, or Blois; if coming from the west or the south, see Azay-le-Rideau or Villandry). If you're coming from Burgundy, don't miss the one-of-a-kind Château de Guédelon (see page 912 in the Burgundy chapter). If you're driving to the Dordogne from the Loire, the A-20 autoroute via

Limoges (near Oradour-sur-Glane) is fastest and toll-free until Brive-la-Gaillarde.

The best map of the area is Michelin #518, covering all the sights described in this chapter. The Tours TI's free map of Touraine—the area surrounding Tours—is also good.

Without a Car

Sleep in Amboise and take a minivan excursion (see the next section). This is easily the best plan for most visitors and allows easy access to all châteaux described in this chapter.

Budget travelers with one day can catch the public bus or train from Amboise to the town of Chenonceaux, tour Chenonceau, then return to Amboise in the afternoon to enjoy its château and Leonardo's last stand at Clos-Lucé. With a second day, take the short (and cheap) train ride to Blois; from here, visit massive Chambord and classy Cheverny (using the château shuttle bus or renting a bike to see Chambord). Try to budget time to also visit Blois itself before returning to Amboise. With more time, those connecting Paris with Amboise or Chinon can lay over in Blois en route (lockers available near the station and at Blois château).

Minivan excursions from Tours are the best option for most nondrivers staying in Chinon. Budget travelers based in Chinon or Azay-le-Rideau can bike to Langeais, Ussé, and Villandry (better from Azay), and/or take the train to Azay-le-Rideau and Langeais (but keep in mind that bike and train trips are long and not a good option for most).

GETTING AROUND THE LOIRE VALLEY

Traveling by car is the easiest way to get around, and day rentals are reasonable. Trains, a few buses, minivan tours, taxis, and bikes allow those without a car to reach the well-known châteaux. But even the less-famous châteaux are accessible: Take a taxi, arrange a custom minivan excursion (affordable for small groups), or ride a bike (great option for those with time and stamina).

By Car

You can rent a car most easily at the St-Pierre-des-Corps TGV station just outside Tours; rentals are also available in Amboise (see page 373). Parking is free at all châteaux except Chambord.

By Train

With easy access from Amboise and Chinon, the big city of Tours is the transport hub for travelers bent on using trains or buses to explore the Loire (but has little else to offer visitors—I wouldn't sleep there). Tours has two important train stations and a major bus station (with service to several châteaux). The main train station is

Loire Valley Châteaux at a Glance

Which châteaux should you visit? Here's a quick summary. Local TIs sell bundled tickets that save you money and time (see page 372).

Châteaux East of Tours

▲▲▲**Chenonceau** Elegant château arching over the Cher River, with lovely gardens. **Hours:** Daily 9:00-19:30, July-Aug until 20:00, closes earlier off-season. See page 395.

▲▲▲**Chambord** Epic grandeur (440 rooms) and fun rooftop views in an evocative setting surrounded by a forest. **Hours:** Daily 9:00-18:00, Oct-March until 17:00. See page 411.

▲▲**Blois** Urban château with a beautiful courtyard and fun sound-and-light show. **Hours:** Daily 9:00-18:30, July-Aug until 19:00, Oct until 18:00, shorter hours off-season. See page 401.

▲▲**Cheverny** Intimate-feeling château with lavish furnishings and daily feeding of hunting dogs. **Hours:** Daily 9:15-18:30, Nov-March 10:00-17:00. See page 415.

▲▲**Chaumont-sur-Loire** Imposing setting over the Loire River, notable for its historic connections to America and impressive Festival of Gardens. **Hours:** Daily 10:00-20:00, shorter hours Oct-mid-April. See page 417.

Chenonceau   *Chambord*

Tours SNCF, and the smaller, suburban TGV station (located between Tours and Amboise) is St-Pierre-des-Corps. Check schedules carefully, as service is sparse on some lines. The châteaux of Amboise, Blois, Chenonceau, Chaumont (via the town of Onzain plus a long walk), Langeais, Chinon, and Azay-le-Rideau all have train and/or bus service from Tours' main SNCF station; Amboise, Blois, Chenonceau, and Chinon are also served from the St-Pierre-des-Corps station. Look under each sight for specifics, and seriously consider a minivan excursion (described next).

▲**Amboise** Supposed burial place of Leonardo da Vinci, with terrific views over Amboise. **Hours:** Daily 9:00-18:00, July-Aug until 20:00, shorter hours Nov-March. See page 371.

▲**Clos-Lucé (in Amboise)** Leonardo da Vinci's final home and gardens, with models of his creations. **Hours:** Daily 9:00-19:00, July-Aug until 20:00; shorter hours Nov-Jan. See page 379.

Châteaux West of Tours
▲▲**Azay-le-Rideau** Set on a romantic reflecting pond, with a fairy-tale facade and beautifully furnished rooms. **Hours:** Daily 9:30-18:00, July-Aug until 23:00, Oct-March 10:00-17:15. See page 432.

▲▲**Villandry** Average palace boasting the best gardens in the Loire—and possibly all of France. **Hours:** Daily 9:00-19:00, March and Oct until 18:00, Nov-Feb until 17:00. See page 438.

▲**Langeais** Fortress-like setting above an appealing little village with evocative 15th- and 16th-century rooms. **Hours:** Daily July-Aug 9:00-19:00, April-June and Sept-mid-Nov 9:30-18:30, mid-Nov-March 10:00-17:00. See page 436.

LOIRE

Chaumont-sur-Loire   *Azay-le-Rideau*

By Shuttle Bus/Van or Minivan Tour
Shuttle services and minivan tours offer affordable transportation to many of the valley's châteaux. Shuttles connect Amboise, Tours, or Blois with key châteaux in peak season (€6-20), and minivan tours combine several châteaux into a painless day tour (about €40/person for scheduled half-day itineraries from Amboise or Tours, €60 for all day; allow €150/person for all-day guided tours that include wine tastings, châteaux visits, and lunch; figure €240 for custom groups of up to 7 for 4 hours, €400 for 8 hours). Most of these services depart from TIs (who can book them for you) and can save

you time (in line) and money (on admissions) when you purchase your château ticket at a discounted group rate from the driver.

By Shuttle Bus: Between April and October, an excursion bus does a loop route connecting Blois, Chambord, Cheverny, and (skippable) Beauregard, allowing visits to the châteaux with your pick of return times (€6). Unfortunately the service doesn't run daily, so you'll need to confirm the schedule in advance. It departs from the train station in Blois, an easy train ride from Amboise or Tours and a good place to bed down (for shuttle details, see "Blois Connections" on page 410). **Public buses** also connect Tours, Amboise, and Chenonceaux (see "Amboise Connections" on page 392).

By Minivan Tour: Tour operators **Acco-Dispo, Touraine Evasion, Loire Valley Tours,** and **A La Française Tours** offer half- and full-day itineraries from Amboise and/or Tours that hit all the main châteaux (see "Amboise Connections" on page 392). **Eco Shuttle** runs similar excursions from Blois (see page 410).

Minivan excursions also leave from the Tours TI office (outside the Tours SNCF train station) to many châteaux; some include wine tasting (book at www.tours-tourisme.fr, tel. 02 47 70 37 37, easy connections from Amboise, Blois, or Chinon; see "By Train," earlier).

By Taxi

Taxi excursions can be affordable—particularly when split among several people and especially from the Blois train station to nearby châteaux, or from Amboise to Chenonceau. For details, see "Blois Connections" on page 410, and "Amboise Connections" on page 392.

By Bike

Cycling options are endless in the Loire, where the elevation gain is generally manageable. (However, if you have only a day or two, rent a car or stick to the châteaux easily reached by buses and minivans.) Amboise, Chenonceaux, Blois, Azay-le-Rideau, and Chinon all make good biking bases and have rental options (ask at TIs). A network of nearly 200 miles of bike paths and well-signed country lanes connect many châteaux near Amboise. Pick up the free bike-path map at any TI, buy the more detailed map available at TIs, or study the route options at www.cycling-loire.com. Your bike rental company will be able to advise you as well.

About five miles from Chinon, a 30-mile bike path runs along the Loire River, passing by Ussé and Langeais. It meets the Cher River at Villandry and continues along the Cher to Tours and beyond. To follow this route, get the *La Loire à Vélo* brochure at any area TI.

Détours de Loire can help you plan your bike route. They can

Hot-Air Balloon Rides

In France's most popular regions, you'll find hot-air balloon companies eager to take you for a ride (Burgundy, the Loire,  Dordogne, and Provence are best suited for ballooning). It's not cheap, but it's unforgettable—a once-in-a-lifetime chance to sail serenely over châteaux, canals, vineyards, Romanesque churches, and villages. Balloons don't go above 3,000 feet and usually fly much lower than that, so you get a bird's-eye view of France's sublime landscapes.

Most companies offer similar deals and work this way: Trips range from 45 to 90 minutes of air time, to which you should add two hours for preparation, champagne toast, and transport back to your starting point. Deluxe trips add a gourmet picnic, making it a four-hour event. Allow about €200 for a short tour, and about €300 for longer flights. Departures are, of course, weather-dependent, and are usually scheduled first thing in the morning or in early evening. If you've booked ahead and the weather turns bad, you can reschedule your flight, but you can't get your money back. Most balloon companies charge about €25 more for a bad-weather refund guarantee; unless your itinerary is very loose, it's a good idea.

Flight season is April through October. It's smart to bring a jacket for the breeze, though temperatures in the air won't differ too much from those on the ground. Heat from the propane flames that power the balloon may make your hair stand up—I wear a cap. Airsickness is usually not a problem, as the ride is typically slow and even. Baskets have no seating, so count on standing the entire trip. Group (and basket) size can vary from 4 to 16 passengers. Area TIs have brochures. **France Montgolfières** gets good reviews and offers flights in the areas that I recommend (tel. 03 80 97 38 61, US tel. 917/310-0783, www.france-balloons.com). Others are Aérocom Montgolfière (tel. 02 54 33 55 00, www.aerocom.fr) and Touraine Montgolfière (tel. 02 47 30 10 80, www.touraine-montgolfiere.fr).

also deliver rental bikes to most places in the Loire for reasonable rates. They have a full range of bikes—kid-size, tandems, and electric—and will shuttle luggage to your next stop if you reserve ahead. They have shops in Amboise, Blois, and Tours, allowing one-way rentals between these and their partner shops (www.detoursdeloire.com).

TOURS IN THE LOIRE VALLEY

Local Guides: An expert in all things Loire, **Fabrice Maret** lives in Blois but can meet you in Amboise to give an excellent walking tour of the city and its sights, or guide you around the area's châteaux using your rental car (€260/day plus transportation from Blois, tel. 02 54 70 19 59, www.chateauxloire.com, info@chateauxloire.com).

To experience the Loire Valley off the beaten path, consider **Loire Valley à la Carte,** where passionate and longtime resident Catherine Canteau Cohen can organize or guide your day from soup to nuts (tel. 07 81 61 19 58, www.loirevalleyalacarte.com, contact@loirevalleyalacarte.com).

THE LOIRE VALLEY'S CUISINE SCENE

Here in "the garden of France," locally produced food is delicious. Look for seasonal vegetables, such as white and green asparagus, and *champignons de Paris*—mushrooms grown in local caves, not in the capital. Around Chinon, pears and apples are preserved *tapées* (dried and beaten flat for easier storage), rehydrated in alcohol, and served in tasty recipes. Loire Valley rivers yield fresh trout *(truite),* shad *(alose),* and smelt *(éperlan),* which are often served fried *(friture).* Various dishes highlight *rillons,* big chunks of cooked pork, while *rillettes,* a stringy pile of *rillons,* make for a cheap, mouthwatering sandwich spread (add a baby pickle, called a *cornichon).*

Locally raised pork is a staple, but don't be surprised to see steak, snails, *confit de canard* (a Dordogne duck specialty), and seafood on menus—the Loire borrows much from neighboring regions. The area's wonderful goat cheeses include Crottin de Chavignol *(crottin* means horse dung, which is what this cheese, when aged, resembles), Saint-Maure de Touraine (soft and creamy), and Selles-sur-Cher (mild). For dessert, try a delicious *tarte tatin* (upside-down caramel-apple tart). Regional pastries include *sablés* (shortbread cookies) from Sablé-sur-Sarthe.

WINES OF THE LOIRE

Loire wines are overlooked, and that's a shame—there is gold in them thar grapes. The Loire is France's third-largest producer of wine and grows the greatest variety of any region. Four main grapes are grown in the Loire: two reds (gamay and cabernet franc) and two whites (sauvignon blanc and chenin blanc).

The Loire is divided into four subareas, and the name of a wine (its *appellation*) generally refers to where its grapes were grown. The Touraine subarea covers the wines of Chinon and Amboise. Using 100 percent cabernet franc grapes, growers in Chinon and Bourgueil are the main (and best) producers of reds. Thanks to soil variation and climate differences year in and out, wines made from a single grape have an intriguing range in taste. The best white wines are the Sancerres (my opinion), made on the less-touristed eastern edge of the Loire. Less expensive, but still tasty, are Touraine Sauvignons and the sweeter Vouvray, whose *chenin blanc* grapes are grown not far from Amboise. Vouvray is also famous for its light and refreshing sparkling wines (called *vins pétillants*)—locals will tell you the only proper way to begin any meal in this region is with a glass of it, and I can't disagree (try the *rosé pétillant* for a fresh sensation). A dry rosé is popular in the Loire in the summer and can be made from a variety of grapes.

You'll pass scattered vineyards as you travel between châteaux, though there's no scenic wine road to speak of (the closest thing is around Bourgueil). It's best to call ahead before visiting a winery.

East of Tours

The area east of Tours includes the good home-base towns of Amboise and Blois (each with their own châteaux), and several of the area's top châteaux: popular Chenonceau (in the town of Chenonceaux—another fine home base), massive Chambord, lavish Cheverny, and the strategically-located-up-a-cliff Chaumont.

Amboise

Straddling the widest stretch of the Loire River, Amboise is an inviting town with a pleasing old quarter below its hilltop château. A

castle has overlooked the Loire from Amboise since Roman times. Leonardo da Vinci retired here...just one more of his many brilliant ideas.

As the royal residence of François I (r. 1515-1547), Amboise wielded far more importance than you'd imagine from a lazy walk through its center. In fact, its residents are pretty conservative, giving the town an attitude—as if no one told them they're no longer the second capital of France. Locals keep their wealth to themselves; consequently, many grand mansions hide behind nondescript facades.

With or without a car, Amboise is an ideal small-town home base for exploring the best of château country.

Orientation to Amboise

Amboise (pop. 14,000) covers ground on both sides of the Loire, with the "Golden Island" (Ile d'Or) in the middle. The train station is on the north side of the Loire, but nearly everything else is on the south (château) side. Pedestrian-friendly Rue Nationale parallels the river a few blocks inland and leads from the base of Château d'Amboise through the town center and past the clock tower—once part of the town wall—to the Romanesque Church of St-Denis.

TOURIST INFORMATION

The information-packed TI is on Quai du Général de Gaulle (April-June and Sept-Oct Mon-Sat 9:30-18:00, Sun 10:00-13:00 & 14:00-17:00; July-Aug Mon-Sat 9:00-19:00, Sun 10:00-18:00; Nov-March shorter hours Mon-Sat, closed Sun; tel. 02 47 57 09 28, www.amboise-valdeloire.com). Pick up the city map, and consider purchasing tickets to key area châteaux (saving money and time in ticket lines—see "Helpful Hints," later). Ask about sound-and-light shows (generally summers only).

The TI stores bags for a small fee and can recommend local guides. They can also help you organize tours to the châteaux with a shuttle bus or minivan service. All minivan tours from Amboise leave from the TI.

ARRIVAL IN AMBOISE

By Train: Amboise's train station is birds-chirping peaceful. You can't store bags here, but you can leave them at the TI or at some châteaux (see "Baggage Storage," later). Allow 20 minutes to walk to the TI from the station: Turn left out of the station (you may have to cross under the tracks first), make a quick right, and walk down Rue Jules Ferry five minutes to the end, then turn right and cross the long bridge leading over the Loire River to the town center. It's a €10 taxi ride from the station to central Amboise, but taxis seldom wait at the station (see "Helpful Hints" for taxi phone numbers).

By Car: Drivers set their sights on the flag-festooned château that caps the hill. Most parking is free; hotels can help you locate a spot (the big parking area downriver from the TI has lots of free parking, handy for day-trippers).

HELPFUL HINTS

Save Time and Money: The TI sells tickets in bundles of two or more to sights and châteaux around Amboise and Chinon, which saves on entry fees—and, more importantly, time spent in line. You may also get discounted tickets if you take a mini-van tour (see "Getting Around the Loire Valley," earlier).

Market Days: Popular open-air markets are held on Friday (smaller but more local) and Sunday (the big one) in the parking lot behind the TI on the river (both 8:30-13:00).

Regional Products: Galland, at 29 Rue Nationale, sells fine food and wine products from the Loire (daily 9:30-19:00).

Bookstore: Lu & Approuvé has a big selection of maps and the Michelin Green Guide *Châteaux of the Loire* in English; they also sell English translations of bike-route books (Mon-Sat 8:00-19:00, Sun 9:30-12:30, a block from the TI at 5 Quai du Général de Gaulle).

Baggage Storage: Besides the **Amboise TI,** which stores bags for €2 each, most châteaux offer free storage if you've paid admission.

Laundry: The nearest launderette is at **Supermarket LeClerc,** on the outskirts of town on Avenue Léonard de Vinci.

Supermarket: Near the TI, **Carrefour City** is open long hours and on Sundays (at 5 Quai du Général de Gaulle), though the specialty shops on pedestrian-only Rue Nationale are infinitely more pleasing.

Bike Rental: You can rent a bike (electric or standard, leave your passport or a photocopy) at **Locacycle** (daily, full-day rentals can be returned the next morning, 2 Rue Jean-Jacques Rousseau, tel. 02 47 57 00 28).

Taxi: There's no taxi station, so you must call for one (tel. 02 47 57 13 53, 06 12 92 70 46, 02 47 57 30 39, or 06 88 02 44 10).

Car Rental: It's easiest to rent cars at the St-Pierre-des-Corps train station (TGV service from Paris), a 15-minute drive from Amboise. Figure €10 for a taxi from Amboise to either place. Both of these places are closed Sun.

On the outskirts of Amboise, **Désiré Automobile** at the Renault dealership rents cars (roughly €60/day for a small car with 100 kilometers free, closed Sun, about a mile downriver from the TI at 105 Avenue de Tours, tel. 02 47 57 17 92, www. renaultamboise.com, renault-amboise@orange.fr).

A bit pricier, **Europcar** is outside Amboise on Route de Chenonceaux at the Total gas station (tel. 02 47 57 07 64, reservation tel. 02 47 85 85 85, www.europcar.com).

Tourist Train: The *petit train,* with hourly departures from the TI, makes a 40-minute circuit around the city and is useful as a way to reach Clos-Lucé (€7, in peak season runs Mon-Sat 11:00-17:00, Sun from 14:00).

LOIRE

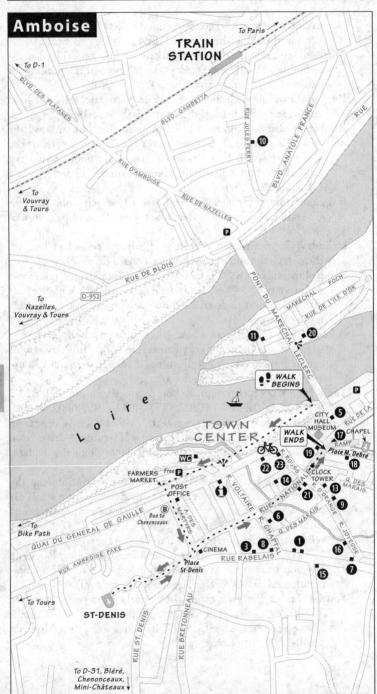

Amboise

TRAIN STATION

To Paris

To D-1

BLVD DES PLATANES

BLVD. GAMBETTA

RUE D'AMBOISE

RUE JULES FERRY

RUE DE NAZELLES

BLVD. ANATOLE FRANCE

RUE

10

To Vouvray & Tours

P

RUE DE BLOIS

D-952

To Nazelles, Vouvray & Tours

PONT DU MARECHAL LECLERC

MARECHAL FOCH

RUE DE L'ILE D'OR

11

20

WALK BEGINS

TOWN CENTER

WALK ENDS

CITY HALL MUSEUM

5

RUE DE LA

CHAPEL

17

RAMP

Place M. Debré

18

19

WC

22 **23**

R. ROUSS

14

R. NATIONAL

CLOCK TOWER

21

R. D'ORANGE

13

Q. DES MARAIS

9

FARMERS MARKET

Free P

POST OFFICE

i

R. VOLTAIRE

RUE—

R. CHAPTAL

6

Q. DES MARAIS

R. JOYEUS

(B) Bus to Chenonceaux

A. DES MARTYRS

QUAI DU GENERAL DE GAULLE

To Bike Path

3

8

1

16

RUE AMBOISE PARE

CINEMA

RUE RABELAIS

15

7

Place St-Denis

To Tours

ST-DENIS

RUE ST-DENIS

RUE BRETONNEAU

To D-31, Bléré, Chenonceaux, Mini-Châteaux

Loire

LOIRE

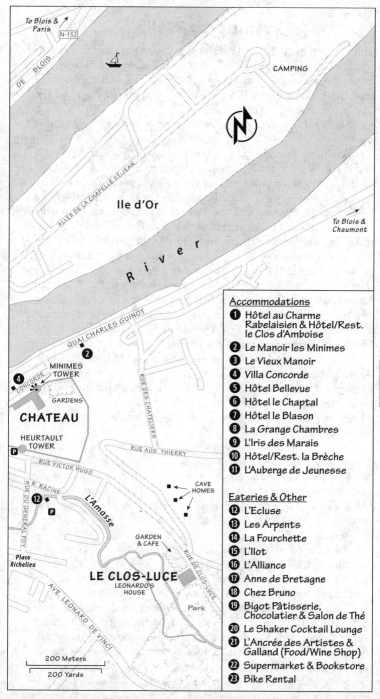

Accommodations

1 Hôtel au Charme Rabelaisien & Hôtel/Rest. le Clos d'Amboise

2 Le Manoir les Minimes

3 Le Vieux Manoir

4 Villa Concorde

5 Hôtel Bellevue

6 Hôtel le Chaptal

7 Hôtel le Blason

8 La Grange Chambres

9 L'Iris des Marais

10 Hôtel/Rest. la Brèche

11 L'Auberge de Jeunesse

Eateries & Other

12 L'Ecluse

13 Les Arpents

14 La Fourchette

15 L'Ilot

16 L'Alliance

17 Anne de Bretagne

18 Chez Bruno

19 Bigot Pâtisserie, Chocolatier & Salon de Thé

20 Le Shaker Cocktail Lounge

21 L'Ancrée des Artistes & Galland (Food/Wine Shop)

22 Supermarket & Bookstore

23 Bike Rental

Amboise Walk

This short, self-guided walk starts at the banks of the Loire River, winds past the old church of St-Denis, and meanders through the heart of town to a fine little city museum. You'll end near the entrance to Château Royal d'Amboise and Leonardo's house. Use the "Amboise" map to orient yourself.

• *Climb to the top of the embankment overlooking the river from near the bridge.*

Amboise Riverbank: Survey the town, its island, bridge, and castle (see "Sights in Amboise," later, to learn more about the castle). If you have a passion for anything French—philosophy, history, food, wine—you'll feel it here, along the Loire. This river, the longest in the country and the natural boundary between northern and southern France, is the last "untamed" river in the country (there are no dams or mechanisms to control periodic flooding). The region's châteaux line up along the Loire and its tributaries, because before trains and trucks, stones for big buildings were best shipped by boat. You may see a few of the traditional flat-bottomed Loire boats moored here. The bridge spanning the river isn't just any bridge. It marks a strategic river crossing and a longtime political border. That's why the first Amboise castle was built here. In the 15th century, this was one of the biggest forts in France.

The half-mile-long "Golden Island" (Ile d'Or) is the only island in the Loire substantial enough to withstand flooding and to have permanent buildings (including a soccer stadium, hostel, and 13th-century church). It was important historically as the place where northern and southern France came together. Truces were made here.

• *Walk downstream on the footpath above busy Quai du Général de Gaulle. After about a quarter-mile, you'll see a parking lot below and to your right, where farmers markets take place on Friday and Sunday mornings. When you spot the post office across the street, cross Quai du Général de Gaulle. Walk up Avenue des Martyrs de la Résistance and turn right at Place St-Denis to find the old church standing proudly on a bluff to the right.*

Church of St-Denis (Eglise St-Denis): Ever since ancient Romans erected a Temple of Mars here, this has been a place of worship. According to legend, God sent a bolt of lightning that knocked down the statue of Mars, and Christians took over the spot. The current Romanesque church dates from the 12th century. A cute little statue of St. Denis (above the entry's arch) greets you as you step in. The delightful carvings capping the many columns inside date from Romanesque times. The lovely (but poorly lit) pastel-painted *Deposition* to the right of the choir is restored to its 16th-century brilliance. The medieval stained glass in the windows, likely destroyed in the French Revolution, was replaced with 19th-century glass. A plaque in the rear of the church lists Amboise residents who died in World War I.

From the steps of the church, look out to the hill-capping Amboise château. For a thousand years, it's been God on this hill and the king on that one. It's interesting to ponder how, throughout French history, the king's power generally trumped the Church's, and how the Church and the king worked to keep people down—setting the stage for the French Revolution.

• *Retrace your steps down from the church and across Place St-Denis, go past Amboise's cinema, continue walking straight, and follow Rue Nationale through the heart of town toward the castle.*

Rue Nationale: In France, districts around any castle or church officially classified as historic are preserved. The broad, pedestrianized Rue Nationale, with its narrow intersecting lanes, survives from the 15th century. At that time, when the town spread at the foot of the king's castle, this was the "Champs-Elysées" of Amboise. Supporting the king and his huge entourage was a serious industry. The French king spilled money wherever he stayed.

As you walk along this spine of the town, spot rare surviving bits of rustic medieval oak in the half-timbered buildings. The homes of wealthy merchants rose from the chaos of this street. Side lanes can be more candid—they often show what's hidden behind modern facades.

Stop when you reach the impressive **clock tower** (Tour de l'Horloge), built into part of the 15th-century town wall. This was once a fortified gate, opening onto the road to the city of Tours. Imagine the hefty wood-and-iron portcullis (fortified door) that dropped from above.

• *At the intersection with Rue François I (where you'll be tempted by the Bigot chocolate shop), turn left a couple of steps to the...*

City Hall Museum: This free museum is worth a quick peek for its romantic interior, town paintings, and historic etchings (a flier gives some English explanations, inconsistent hours, usually open July-Aug daily 10:00-12:30 & 14:00-19:00, otherwise closed). In the room dedicated to Leonardo da Vinci are his busts and photos of the gripping deathbed painting of him with caring King François I at his side (the original is on loan to the château). In the Salle des Rois (Kings' Room), find portraits of Charles VIII (who coldcocked himself at Amboise's castle; more on this later) and other nobles; I like to admire their distinct noses.

Upstairs, in the still-functioning city assembly hall (last room), notice how the photo of the current president faces the lady of the Republic. (According to locals, her features change with the taste of the generation, and the bust of France's Lady Liberty is often modeled on famous supermodels of the day.)

LOIRE

• *Retrace your steps along Rue François I to* **Place Michel Debré,** *at the base of the Château Royal d'Amboise and the end of this walk. Here, at one of the most touristy spots in the Loire, tourism's importance to the local economy is palpable. Notice the fat, round 15th-century fortified tower, whose interior ramp was built for galloping horses to spiral up to castle level (but without a horse, you'll have to walk up the long ramp). Beyond the château is Leonardo's last residence at Clos-Lucé.*

Sights in Amboise

CHATEAUX

▲Château Royal d'Amboise

This historic heap, built mostly in the late 15th century, became the favored royal residence in the Loire under Charles VIII. Charles is famous for accidentally killing himself by walking into a door lintel on his way to a tennis match (seriously). Later, more careful occupants include Louis XII (who moved the royal court to Blois) and François I (who physically brought the Renaissance here in 1516, in the person of Leonardo da Vinci).

Cost and Hours: €13, daily 9:00-18:00, July-Aug until 20:00, shorter hours Nov-March, skip the unnecessary audioguide, Place Michel Debré, tel. 02 47 57 00 98, www.chateau-amboise.com.

Visiting the Château: After climbing the long ramp to the ticket booth and picking up the free and well-done English brochure, your first stop is the petite **chapel** where Leonardo da Vinci is supposedly buried. This flamboyant little Gothic chapel is where the king began and ended each day in prayer. It comes with two fireplaces "to comfort the king" and two plaques "evoking the final resting place" of Leonardo (one in French, the other in Italian). Where he's actually buried, no one seems to know. Look up at the ceiling to appreciate the lacy design.

Enter the **castle rooms** across from Leonardo's chapel. The three-floor route takes you chronologically from Gothic-style rooms to those from the early Renaissance and on to the 19th century. The first room, **Salle des Gardes,** shows the château's original, much larger size; drawings in the next room give you a better feel for its original look. Some wings added in the 15th and 16th centuries have disappeared. (The little chapel you just saw was once part of the bigger complex.)

You'll pass the sumptuous **council chambers** (Salle du Conseil) where the king would meet with his key staff (find his throne). King **Henry II's bedroom** is livable. The second son of François I, Henry is remembered as the husband of the ambitious and unscrupulous Catherine de' Medici—and for his tragic death in a jousting tournament.

The rose-colored top-floor rooms are well-furnished from the post-Revolutionary 1800s and demonstrate the continued interest among French nobility in this château. Find the classy portrait of King Louis-Philippe, the last Louis to rule France.

The **Minimes Tower** delivers grand views from its terrace. From here, the strategic value of this site is clear: The visibility is great, and the river below provided a natural defense.

The bulky tower climbs 130 feet in five spirals—designed for a mounted soldier in a hurry. Walk a short distance down the spi-

ral ramp and exit into the **gardens.** Each summer, bleachers are set up for sound-and-light spectacles—a faint echo of the extravaganzas Leonardo orchestrated for the court. Modern art decorating the garden reminds visitors of the inquisitive and scientific Renaissance spirit that Leonardo brought to town. The flags are those of France and Brittany—a reminder that, in a sense, modern France was created at the nearby château of Langeais when Charles VIII (who was born here) married Anne of Brittany, adding her domain to the French kingdom.

Spiral down the **Heurtault Tower** (through the gift shop). As with the castle's other tower, this was designed to accommodate a soldier on horseback. As you gallop down to the exit, notice the cute little characters and scenes left by 15th-century stone carvers. While they needed to behave when decorating churches and palaces, here they could be a bit racier and more spirited.

Leaving the Château: The turnstile puts you on the road to Château du Clos-Lucé (described next; turn left and hike straight for 10 minutes). Along the way, you'll pass **troglodyte houses**—both new and old—carved into the hillside stone (a type called *tuffeau,* a sedimentary rock). Originally, poor people resided here—the dwellings didn't require expensive slate roofing, came with natural insulation, and could be dug essentially for free, as builders valued the stone quarried in the process. Today wealthy stone lovers are renovating them into stylish digs worthy of *Better Homes and Caves.* You can see chimneys high above. Unfortunately, none are open to the public.

▲Château du Clos-Lucé and Leonardo da Vinci Park

In 1516, Leonardo da Vinci packed his bags (and several of his favorite paintings, including the *Mona Lisa*) and left an imploding Rome for better wine and working conditions in the Loire Valley. He accepted the position of engineer, architect, and painter to

France's Renaissance king, François I. This "House of Light" is the plush palace where Leonardo spent his last three years. (He died on May 2, 1519.) François, only 22 years old, installed the 65-year-old Leonardo here just so he could enjoy his intellectual company.

The house is a kind of fort-château of its own, with a forti-fied rampart walk and a 16th-century chapel. Two floors of finely decorated rooms are open to the public, but most of the furnishings are neither original nor compelling (though you can stare face-to-face at a copy of Leonardo's *Mona Lisa* and see a recreation of the artist's studio and study). Come here to learn about the genius of Leonardo and to see well-explained models of his inventions, displayed inside the house and out in the huge park.

Leonardo attracted disciples who stayed active here, using this house as a kind of workshop and laboratory. The place survived the Revolution because the quick-talking noble who owned it was sympathetic to the cause; he convinced the Revolutionaries that, philosophically, Leonardo would have been on their side.

Cost and Hours: The €16 admission (includes house and gardens) is worth it for Leonardo fans with two hours to fully appreciate this sight. Skip the special exhibit (*Da Vinci et la France*, in the garden) and its €5 supplement. Open daily 9:00-19:00, July-Aug until 20:00, shorter hours Nov-Jan, last entry one hour before closing, tel. 02 47 57 00 73, www.vinci-closluce.com.

Getting There: It's a 10-minute walk uphill at a steady pace from Château Royal d'Amboise, past troglodyte homes (see end of previous listing). You can also take the *petit train* (listed under "Helpful Hints," earlier). If you park in the nearby lot, leave nothing of value visible in your car.

Tours: Follow the helpful free English handout. A free app in English includes background information and audio tours of the château and grounds.

Eating: Several garden cafés, including one just behind the house and others in the park, are reasonably priced and appropriately meditative. For a view over Amboise, choose the terrace *crê-perie*.

Visiting the Château and Gardens: Your visit begins with a tour of Leonardo's elegant yet livable Renaissance **home.** This little residence was built in 1450—just within the protective walls of the town—as a guesthouse for the king's château nearby. Today it re-creates (with Renaissance music) the everyday atmosphere Leonardo enjoyed while he lived here, pursuing his passions to the very end. Find the touching sketch in Leonardo's bedroom of François I comforting his genius pal on his deathbed.

The basement level is filled with **sketches** recording the storm patterns of Leonardo's brain and **models** of his remarkable inventions (inspired by nature and built according to his notes). Helpful descriptions—written and visual—reveal his vision for these way-before-their-time inventions. Leonardo was fascinated by water. All he lacked was steam power. It's hard to imagine that this Roman candle of creativity died nearly 500 years ago. Imagine Leonardo's résumé letter to kings of Europe: "I can help your armies by designing tanks, flying machines, wind-up cars, gear systems, extension ladders, and water pumps." The French considered him a futurist who never really implemented his visions.

Exit into the rose garden, then find another less-compelling room with 40 small models of his inventions. Don't waste time on the French-only video above the souvenir shop.

Your visit finishes with a stroll through the whimsical and expansive **park grounds,** with life-size models of Leonardo's inventions (including some that kids can operate), "sound stations" (in English), and translucent replicas of some of his paintings. The models and explanations make clear that much of what Leonardo observed and created was based on his intense study of nature.

OTHER SIGHTS AND ACTIVITIES
▲Château Royal d'Amboise Sound-and-Light Show: *The Prophecy of Amboise*

This summer-only show is considered one of the best shows of its kind in the area. Although it's entirely in French, you can rent an English audioguide. Over 100 volunteer locals from toddlers to pensioners re-create a hermit-monk's prophecy of the improbable rise of François I to become king and master of France. Dramatic lighting effects combine with lavish costumes, battle scenes, and fireworks to make this a most entertaining event. Dress warmly.

Cost and Hours: €20 with audioguide, family deals, about 20 performances a year, 1.5-hour show runs several days per week, July 22:30-24:00, Aug 22:00-23:30, tel. 02 47 57 14 47, www.renaissance-amboise.com. Buy tickets online or from the ticket window on the ramp to the château (opens at 20:30). Seats are usually available up until the start time.

Mini-Châteaux

This five-acre park on the edge of Amboise (on the route to Chenonceaux) shows the major Loire châteaux in 1:25-scale models, forested with 2,000 bonsai trees. For children, it's a fun introduction to the real châteaux they'll be visiting (and there's a cool toy

The Loire and Its Many Châteaux: A Historical Primer

It's hard to overstate the importance of the Loire River to France. Its place in history goes back to the very foundation of the country. As if to proclaim its storied past, the Loire is the last major wild river in France, with no dams and no regulation of its flow.

Traditional flat-bottomed boats moored along embankments are a reminder of the age before trains and trucks, when river traffic safely and efficiently transported heavy loads of stone and timber. With prevailing winds sweeping east from the Atlantic, barge tenders raised their sails and headed upriver; on the way back, boats flowed downstream with the current.

With this transportation infrastructure providing (relatively) quick access to Paris and the region's thick forests—offering plenty of timber, firewood, and hunting terrain—it's no wonder that castles were built here in the Middle Ages. The first stone fortresses went up a thousand years ago, and many of the pleasure palaces you see today rose over the ruins of those original defensive keeps.

The Hundred Years' War—roughly 1336 to 1453—was a desperate time for France. Because of a dynastic dispute, the English had a legitimate claim to the French throne, and by 1415 they controlled much of the country, including Paris. France was at a low ebb, and its king and court retreated to the Loire Valley to rule what remained of their realm. Chinon was the refuge of the dispirited king, Charles VII. He was famously visited there in 1429 by the charismatic Joan of Arc, who inspired the king to get off his duff and send the English packing.

The French kings continued to live in the Loire region for the next two centuries, having grown comfortable with their château culture. The climate was mild, hunting was good, the rivers made nice reflections, wealthy friends lived in similar luxury nearby, and the location was close enough to Paris—but still far enough away. Charles VII ruled from Chinon, Charles VIII preferred Amboise, Louis XII reigned from Blois, and François I held court in Chambord and Blois.

This was a kind of cultural Golden Age. With peace and stability, there was no need for fortifications. The most famous luxury hunting lodges, masquerading as fortresses, were built during this period—including Chenonceau, Chambord, Chaumont, Amboise, and Azay-le-Rideau. Kings (François I), writers (Rabelais), poets (Ronsard), and artists (Leonardo da Vinci) made the Loire a cultural hub. Many years later, these same châteaux attracted other notables, including Voltaire, Molière, and perhaps Benjamin Franklin.

Because French kings ruled effectively only by being constantly on the move among their subjects, many royal châteaux were used infrequently. The entire court (usually over 2,000 individuals)—and its trappings—had to be portable. A castle kept empty and cold 11 months of the year would suddenly become the busy center of attention when the king came to town. As you visit the castles, imagine the royal roadies setting up a kingly room—hanging tapestries, unfolding chairs, wrestling big trunks with handles—in the hours just before the arrival of the royal entourage. The French

word for furniture, *mobilier,* literally means "mobile."

When touring the châteaux, you'll notice the impact of Italian culture. From the Renaissance onward, Italian ways were fancy ways. French nobles and court ministers who traveled to Italy returned inspired by the art and architecture they saw. Kings imported Italian artists and architects. It's no wonder that the ultimate French Renaissance king, François I, invited the famous Italian artist, Leonardo da Vinci, to join his court in Amboise. Tastes in food, gardens, artists, and women were all influenced by Italian culture.

Women had a big impact on Loire château life. Big personalities like kings tickled more than one tiara. Louis XV famously decorated the palace of Chenonceau with a painting of the Three Graces—featuring his three favorite mistresses.

Châteaux were generally owned by kings, their ministers, or their mistresses. A high-maintenance and powerful mistress could get her own place even when a king's romantic interest shifted. In many cases, the king or minister would be away at work or at war for years at a time—leaving home-improvement decisions to the lady of the château, who had unlimited money. That helps explain the emphasis on comfort and the feminine touch you'll enjoy while touring many of the Loire châteaux.

In 1525, François I moved to his newly built super-palace at Fontainebleau, and political power left the Loire. From then on, châteaux were mostly used as vacation rentals and hunting retreats. They became refuges for kings again during the French Wars of Religion (1562-1598)—a sticky set of squabbles over dynastic control that pitted Protestants (Huguenots) against Catholics. Its conclusion marked the end of an active royal presence on the Loire. With the French Revolution in 1789, symbols of the Old Regime, like the fabulous palaces along the Loire, were ransacked. Fast talking saved some châteaux, especially those whose owners had personal relationships with Revolutionary leaders.

Only in the 1840s did the châteaux of the Loire become appreciated for their historic value. The Loire was the first place where treasures of French heritage were officially recognized and protected by the national government. In the 19th century, Romantic Age writers—such as Victor Hugo and Alexander Dumas—visited and celebrated the châteaux. Aristocrats on the Grand Tour stopped here. The Loire Valley and its historic châteaux found a place in our collective hearts and are treasured to this day.

store). Essential English information is posted throughout the sight. You'll find other kid-oriented attractions at Mini-Châteaux; consider feeding the fish in the moat (a great way to get rid of that old baguette), or take a self-driving boat for a spin.

Cost and Hours: Adults–€14, kids under 13–€10.50, daily 10:00-18:30, July-Aug from 9:30, Sept-Oct 10:30-18:00, closed Nov-mid-April, last entry one hour before closing, tel. 02 47 23 44 57, www.parcminichateaux.com.

Wine Tasting in Amboise

Caveau des Vignerons (Vins d'Amboise) is a small "cellar" offering tastings of cheeses, pâtés, and mediocre regional wines from seven different vintners (daily mid-March-mid-Nov 10:30-19:00, under Château d'Amboise, across from L'Epicerie restaurant, tel. 02 47 57 23 69).

Biking from Amboise

La Voie Royale is a suggested 26-mile loop connecting Amboise and Chenonceaux in a roughly four-hour round-trip ride along quiet, mostly car-free paths (get details at TI). The more direct— if less scenic—ride to Chenonceaux is about eight miles each way (allow 1.5 hours one way) and is signed for bikes. Leading past Leonardo's Clos-Lucé, the first two miles are uphill, and the entire ride is on a road with some traffic. Serious cyclists can continue to Chaumont in 1.5 hours, connecting Amboise, Chenonceaux, and Chaumont in an all-day, 37-mile pedal (see "Bike Route" on the "Near Amboise" map, later in this section). The most appealing pedal from Amboise leaves from the lower riverfront parking lot near the TI and follows the Loire downstream along a dedicated bike path, though you won't see any great castles. The village of Lussault-sur-Loire makes an easy destination (2.5 miles one-way), or keep on pedaling to Montlouis, two miles past Lussault.

Canoe Trips from Amboise or Chenonceaux

Paddling under the Château de Chenonceau is a memorable experience. **Canoe Company** offers rentals on the Cher river (€12-25/person depending on how far you go, mobile 06 70 13 30 61 or 06 37 01 89 92, www.canoe-company.fr).

NEAR AMBOISE
Wine Tasting in Vouvray

In the nearby town of Vouvray, 10 miles toward Tours from Amboise, you'll find wall-to-wall opportunities for wine tasting (but less impressive vineyards than in other parts of France). From Amboise you can take the speedy D-952 there, or joyride on the more appealing D-1 (see the "Near Amboise" map, later in this section).

For tips on wine tasting, see the "French Wine-Tasting 101" sidebar on page 1124. Here are two top choices for testing the local sauce:

The big **Cave des Producteurs** is a smart place to start. It has an English-speaking staff, English-language tours of the winery, and a good selection from the 33 producers they represent, including wines from other Loire areas (free wine tasting, €3 cellar tour, daily 9:00-12:30 & 14:00-19:00, no midday closure July-Aug, English tour usually at 11:30 and 15:30—call or check online to confirm times, 38 La Vallée Coquette in Vouvray, tel. 02 47 52 75 03, www.cavedevouvray.com). It's just west of Vouvray in Rochecorbon. Go past the smaller Cave des Producteurs outlet you'll see along D-952 in Vouvray, turn when you see the blue signs to *Moncontour,* then follow the small brown signs to *Cave des Producteurs.*

For a more intimate experience, drop by **Marc Brédif,** where you'll find a top-quality selection of Vouvray wines, excellent dessert wines, and red wines from Chinon and Bourgueil. You can also tour their impressive 1.2 miles of 10th-century cellars dug into the hillside (free wine tasting, small fee for cellar tour, Mon-Sat 10:30-12:00 & 14:30-18:00, Sun 10:00-13:00, tel. 02 47 52 50 07, www.deladoucette.fr—select "Domaine Brédif" under "Domaines"). Coming from Amboise, you'll pass it on D-952 after Vouvray; it's on the right, after the blue *Moncontour* signs.

Sleeping in Amboise

Amboise is busy in the summer, but there are lots of reasonable hotels and *chambres d'hôtes* in and around the city.

IN THE TOWN CENTER

$$$$ Hôtel au Charme Rabelaisien** is a luxurious, well-managed 10-room place. Big doors open onto a lovely courtyard with manicured gardens and a heated pool. The beautifully decorated rooms have every comfort conceivable, and welcoming Olivier is ready to help (air-con, elevator, private parking, 25 Rue Rabelais, tel. 02 47 57 53 84, www.hotel-acr.com, info@hotel-acr.com).

$$$ Le Manoir les Minimes** is a good place to experience the refined air of château life in a 17th-century mansion, with antique furniture and precious art objects in the public spaces. Its 15 large, modern rooms work for those seeking luxury digs in Amboise. (Tall folks take note: Top-floor attic rooms have low ceilings.) Several rooms have views of Amboise's château (family rooms, air-con, closed much of winter, three blocks upriver from bridge at 34 Quai Charles Guinot, tel. 02 47 30 40 40, www.manoirlesminimes.com, reservation@manoirlesminimes.com).

$$ Hôtel le Clos d'Amboise** is a smart, urban refuge opening onto beautiful gardens and a small, heated swimming pool.

Those with time to linger will be tempted by stay-awhile lounges, a lovely garden terrace, and well-designed traditional rooms with warm colors and carpets (RS%, family rooms, air-con, elevator, sauna, easy and free parking, 27 Rue Rabelais, tel. 02 47 30 10 20, www.leclosdamboise.com, infos@leclosamboise.com). They also offer meals at their **$$ restaurant**—best experienced on a warm night in the garden (see "Eating in Amboise," later).

$$ Le Vieux Manoir*** is an entirely different splurge. American expats Gloria and Bob Belknap restored this secluded but central one-time convent with an attention to detail that Martha Stewart would envy. The gardens are delightful—as is the atrium-like breakfast room—and its six bedrooms are lovingly decorated. Knowledgeable Gloria is a one-person tourist office. Bob and Gloria are slowing down, so pack your patience or skip this place (cottages, includes good  breakfast, air-con, no TVs, free parking, 13 Rue Rabelais, tel. 02 47 30 41 27, www.le-vieux-manoir.com, le_vieux_manoir@yahoo. com).

$$ Villa Concorde hunkers below the castle with four luxurious apartments. Helpful owner Karine will check you in, and then you're on your own (no reception, etc.). These well-furnished apartments come with washers/dryers, kitchens, and air-con (studios, some bigger units can sleep up to 6, 3-night minimum May-Sept, free transfer from train station possible—book ahead, 26 Rue de la Concorde, tel. 02 47 50 64 42, www.villaconcorde.com, info@ villaconcorde.com).

$$ Hôtel Bellevue*** is a decent midrange place with 30 comfortable-enough rooms. It's centrally located on the main road, overlooking the river where the bridge hits the town (there's no air-con so avoid it in summer). Its stylish bar/bistro has a good selection of local wines by the glass (family rooms, elevator, 12 Quai Charles Guinot, tel. 02 47 57 02 26, www.hotel-bellevue-amboise. com, contact@hotel-bellevue-amboise.com).

$ Hôtel le Chaptal** is a solid, central budget bet with smallish but tastefully designed rooms and air-con (family rooms, 11 Rue Chaptal, tel. 02 47 57 14 46, http://hotel-chaptal.com, infos@ hotel-chaptal-amboise.com).

$ Hôtel le Blason** is housed in a 15th-century, half-timbered building on a busy street. Run by helpful Damien, it has tight but comfortable and clean rooms with double-paned windows and ceiling fans. Top-floor rooms have air-conditioning, sloped ceilings, and low beams (quieter rooms in back and on top floor, family rooms, secure pay parking, 11 Place Richelieu, tel. 02 47 23 22 41, www.leblason.fr, hotel@leblason.fr).

CHAMBRES D'HOTES

The heart of Amboise offers several solid bed-and-breakfast options.

$ **La Grange Chambres** welcomes with an intimate, flowery courtyard and four comfortable rooms, each tastefully restored with modern conveniences. There's also a common room with a fridge and tables for do-it-yourself dinners (includes breakfast, reserve with credit card but pay in cash only, where Rues Chaptal and Rabelais meet at 18 Rue Chaptal, tel. 02 47 57 57 22, www. la-grange-amboise.com, lagrange-amboise@orange.fr). Adorable Yveline Savin also rents a small two-room cottage and speaks fluent *franglais.*

$ **L'Iris des Marais** is a budget B&B with three artsy and homey rooms and a wild garden where you can enjoy a peaceful picnic (family rooms, includes continental breakfast, 14 Quai des Marais, tel. 02 47 30 46 51, www.irisdesmarais.com, vianney. frain@wanadoo.fr).

NEAR THE TRAIN STATION

$ **Hôtel la Brèche,**** a sleepy place near the station, has 14 good-value rooms and a top-notch restaurant. Many of the comfortable rooms overlook the peaceful graveled garden and all but two have air-con. While rooms on the street side are larger, those facing the garden are quieter (excellent breakfast, easy and free parking, 15-minute walk from town center and 2-minute walk from station, 26 Rue Jules Ferry, tel. 02 47 57 00 79, www.labreche-amboise. com, info@labreche-amboise.com).

Hostel: ¢ **L'Auberge de Jeunesse** (Centre Charles Péguy) is ideally located on the western tip of the "Golden Island," a 10-minute walk from the train station. It's open to people of all ages and popular with student groups. There are a handful of double rooms—some with partial views to the château—so book ahead (reception open daily 15:00-20:00, no curfew, on Ile d'Or, email is useless—call no more than two weeks ahead to book, tel. 02 47 30 60 90).

NEAR AMBOISE

The area around Amboise is peppered with accommodations of every shape, size, and price range. This region offers drivers the best chance to experience château life at affordable rates—and my recommendations justify the detour. For locations, see the "Near

Amboise" map, later. Also consider the recommended accommodations in Chenonceaux.

$$$$ Château de Pray** allows you to sleep in a 700-year-old fortified castle with hints of its medieval origins. A few minutes from Amboise, the château's 19 rooms aren't big or luxurious, but they come with character and history—and with tubs in most bathrooms (about half have air-con). The lounge is small, but the backyard terrace compensates in agreeable weather. A newer annex offers four more-modern rooms (sleeping up to

three each) with lofts, terraces, and castle views. A big pool and the restaurant's vegetable garden lie below the château (3-minute drive upriver from Amboise toward Chaumont on D-751 before the village of Chargé, Rue du Cèdre, tel. 02 47 57 23 67, www.chateaudepray.fr, contact@chateaudepray.fr). The **$$$$ dining room,** cut into the hillside rock in the old *orangerie,* is an OK place to splurge, but I prefer dining outside on a beautiful terrace when the weather agrees (four-course *menus* from €59, reservations required, closed Mon-Tue).

$$$ Château de Perreux* rents big rooms in a majestic 18th-century castle overlooking a huge park just 10 minutes by car from Amboise. Here, upscale bed-and-breakfast service meets château-hotel ambience with 11 plush and tastefully designed rooms and a pool. Top-floor rooms lie under impressive wooden beams. A casual €26 dinner is available for guests who book ahead (family rooms, air-con, elevator, Wi-Fi on main floor only, on D-1 between Nazelles and Pocé-sur-Cisse; coming from Amboise, turn left at the *Château de Perreux* sign, 36 Rue de Pocé, tel. 02 47 57 27 47, www.chateaudeperreux.fr, info@chateaudeperreux.fr).

$$$ Château des Arpentis,* a medieval château-hotel centrally located just minutes from Amboise, makes a classy splurge. Flanked by woods and acres of grass, and fronted by a stream and a moat, you'll come as close as you can to château life during the Loire's Golden Age. Its 13 rooms are big with handsome decor—and the pool is even bigger. The place has laissez-faire management, the reception is

not staffed regularly, and there's no restaurant, but terrace-table picnics are encouraged (family rooms, air-con, elevator, tel. 02 47 23

00 00, www.chateaudesarpentis.com, contact@chateaudesarpentis. com). It's on D-31 just southeast of Amboise; from the roundabout above the Supermarket Leclerc, follow *Autrèche* signs, then look for small sign on the right next to a tall flagpole.

At **$$$ Château de Nazelles Chambres,***** gentle owners Véronique and Olivier Fructus offer six rooms in a 16th-century hillside manor house that comes with a cliff-sculpted pool, manicured gardens, a guest kitchen (picnics are encouraged), views over Amboise, and a classy living room with billiards. The bedrooms in the main building are traditional, while the rooms cut into the hillside come with private terraces and rock-walled bathrooms. They also rent a very comfortable two-room cottage with living area, kitchen, and private garden (RS%, family rooms, includes breakfast, 16 Rue Tue-La-Soif, Nazelles-Négron, tel. 02 47 30 53 79, www.chateau-nazelles.com, info@chateau-nazelles.com). From D-952, take D-5 into Nazelles, then turn left on D-1 and quickly veer right onto the little lane between the Town Hall and the post office (La Poste)—don't rely on GPS.

$$ Le Moulin du Fief Gentil is a lovely 16th-century mill house with five large and immaculate rooms set on four acres with a backyard pond (fishing possible in summer, dinner picnics anytime, fridge and microwave at your disposal), and the possibility of home-cooked dinners by English-speaking owner Florence (includes breakfast, four-course dinner *menu* with wine—must reserve in advance, cash only, Wi-Fi in mechanical mill room, 3 Rue de Culoison, tel. 02 47 30 32 51, mobile 06 64 82 37 18, www. fiefgentil.com, contact@fiefgentil.com). It's located on the edge of Bléré, a 15-minute drive from Amboise and 7 minutes from Chenonceaux—from Bléré, follow signs toward *Luzillé;* it's on the right.

$$ L'Auberge de Launay,*** five miles upriver from Amboise, gets positive reviews for its easy driving access to many châteaux, fair prices, and good restaurant (ask for a room on the garden, 4 miles from Amboise, across the river toward Blois, 9 Rue de la Rivière in Limeray, tel. 02 47 30 16 82, www.aubergedelaunay.com, info@aubergedelaunay.com). The star of this place is the country-classy **$$ restaurant** (closed Sun except for hotel guests in season).

$ La Chevalerie owners Ljubisa and Martine Aleksic rent four simple bargain *chambres* that are family-friendly, with a swing set, tiny pond, shared kitchens, and connecting rooms. The owners speak French and German—but not English (includes basic breakfast, cash only, in La Croix-en-Touraine, tel. 02 47 57 83 64, lyoubisa.aleksic@orange.fr). From Amboise, take D-31 toward Bléré, look for the *Chambres d'Hôtes* sign on your left at about three miles, and then turn left onto C-105; keep left and continue to the end of the road.

LOIRE

Eating in Amboise

The epicenter of the city's dining action is along Rue Victor Hugo, between Place Michel Debré and the château. While most of these restaurants are forgettable, the lively street atmosphere makes for fun dining, particularly on warm nights.

A handful of talented chefs run more intimate, less-central places offering limited-but-top-quality selection and excellent value. Some offer just two selections for both *entrée* (starters) and *plat* (main course). For these places, because selection and seating are limited, it's smart to check to see what's cooking, then book a day ahead.

LIMITED-SELECTION RESTAURANTS

$$ L'Ecluse ("The Lockhouse") is a top choice. Here, you can dine outside under a weeping willow to the sound of Amboise's small stream, or stick to the sharply-decorated interior. Choose between a delicious two- or three-course *menu* (no à la carte, closed Sun-Mon, a block below the château's entrance on Rue Racine, tel. 02 47 79 94 91).

$$ Les Arpents is the talk of Amboise with a new chef making a splash with inventive and delicious cuisine at reasonable prices. Book ahead, particularly to land a table in the courtyard (reservations smart, closed Sun-Mon, 5 Rue d'Orange, tel. 02 36 20 92 44, https://restaurant-lesarpents.fr).

$ La Fourchette is Amboise's tiny family diner, with simple decor and a handful of tables inside and out. Hardworking owners make everything fresh in their open kitchen. Book ahead—the morning of the same day is fine (closed Wed, on a quiet corner near Rue Nationale at 9 Rue Malebranche, mobile 06 11 78 16 98).

$ L'Ilot is an intimate yet convivial half-timbered place where tables gather around a central stone island. *Le* chef presides over all from his island, adding a very personal touch. *La* cuisine is generally tasty but can be inconsistent (air-con, closed Fri, 52 Rue Rabelais, tel. 02 47 57 66 58).

$$$ L'Alliance is a low-key place offering the kind of fresh French cuisine normally found in more formal restaurants, and it's open when most other places are closed. Here, you'll get quality ingredients prepared with an original twist, not fine decor (children's menu, good but pricey cheese tray, closed Tue-Wed for lunch, 14 Rue Joyeuse, tel. 02 47 30 52 13).

DINING ON RUE VICTOR HUGO, BELOW THE CHATEAU

These places all offer good outdoor seating.

$ Anne de Bretagne serves very basic café fare at cheap prices with the best view seats over Place Michel Debré (Montée Abdel-Kader, tel. 02 47 57 05 46).

$$ Chez Bruno is your best bet on restaurant row. It's a lively and popular wine-bar-meets-café with uneven floors, lowbrow decor, and simple yet surprisingly tasty food. People come here for classic French dishes at affordable prices (closed Sun-Mon, 38 Place Michel Debré, reservations smart, tel. 02 47 57 73 49).

$$ Bigot Pâtisserie's Salon de Thé sells luscious quiches and omelets along with delightful homemade ice cream and a terrace view. Say *bonjour* to the friendly staff, and try their specialty pastry, *puits d'amour*—"Well of Love" (Mon-Fri 9:00-19:30, Sat-Sun 8:30-20:00, where Place Michel Debré meets Rue Nationale one block off the river, tel. 02 47 57 04 46).

ELSEWHERE IN AMBOISE

Cross the bridge for the best castle views, and consider a relaxing aperitif or after-dinner drink at **$$ Le Shaker Cocktail Lounge.** It's also an ideal choice for a light meal on a warm evening. The place is young, fun, lively, and great for kids. The menu and food quality are limited, but the French burgers and ceasar salad are good (daily from 18:30 until later than you'll stay awake, 3 Quai François Tissard).

$$ Hôtel le Clos d'Amboise—one of my recommended hotels—offers outside tables overlooking its lovely gardens and good, if not exceptional, cuisine. Prices are fair, and it makes a good choice on Sunday or Monday when most other places are closed—or if you just want an intimate and peaceful evening (daily, for details, see "Sleeping in Amboise," earlier).

$ L'Ancrée des Artistes is a reliable, centrally located *crêperie*. This young-at-heart place has music to dine by and easygoing servers (three-course crêpe *menus*, good meat dishes grilled on stones—called *pierres*, and casserole-like *cocottes*, daily July-Aug, off-season closed Sun evening and Mon, 35 Rue Nationale, tel. 02 47 23 18 11).

$$$ Hôtel la Brèche is a deservedly trendy place with excellent service and delicious cuisine at reasonable prices. Dine in a warm, traditional dining room or in the large garden. Stretch your legs and cross the river to the restaurant (closed Sun-Mon; for details, see "Sleeping in Amboise," earlier).

NEAR AMBOISE

For an elegant castle dining experience, consider making the quick drive to **Château de Pray.** Call ahead to get a spot on the terrace, or skip it altogether (for details, see "Sleeping in Amboise," earlier).

LOIRE

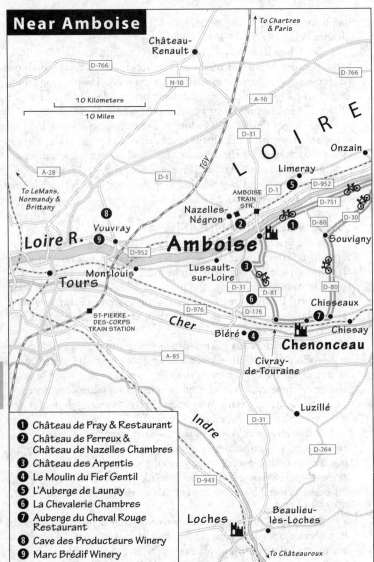

Near Amboise

To Chartres & Paris

LOIRE

10 Kilometers
10 Miles

Château-Renault

D-766

N-10

D-766

A-10

D-31

TGV

D-5

Onzain

Limeray

A-28

To LeMans, Normandy & Brittany

AMBOISE TRAIN STN.

Nazelles-Négron

D-1

❺

D-952

D-751

D-80

D-30

❷

❶

Souvigny

Vouvray

❽

❾

Loire R.

D-952

Amboise

❸

Lussault-sur-Loire

❻

D-80

Chisseaux

❼

Montlouis

Tours

D-31

D-81

D-176

ST-PIERRE-DES-CORPS TRAIN STATION

D-976

Cher

Bléré

❹

Chissay

Chenonceau

A-85

Civray-de-Touraine

Luzillé

D-31

Indre

D-764

D-943

❶ Château de Pray & Restaurant
❷ Château de Perreux & Château de Nazelles Chambres
❸ Château des Arpentis
❹ Le Moulin du Fief Gentil
❺ L'Auberge de Launay
❻ La Chevalerie Chambres
❼ Auberge du Cheval Rouge Restaurant
❽ Cave des Producteurs Winery
❾ Marc Brédif Winery

Loches

Beaulieu-lès-Loches

To Châteauroux

Amboise Connections

By Bus

Buses leave for **Chenonceaux** once or twice daily (Mon-Sat only—none on Sun, 25 minutes, departs Amboise about 9:45, returns from Chenonceaux at about 12:20, allowing you about 1.5 hours at the château during its most crowded time; in summer, there's also

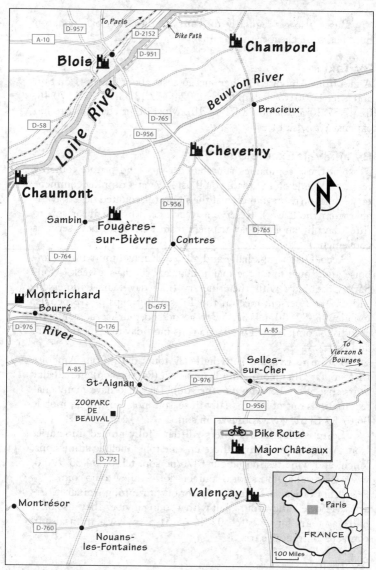

an afternoon departure at about 15:00 with a return from Chenonceaux at about 17:50; confirm times with the TI). The Amboise stop (direction: Chenonceaux)—called Théâtre—is between Place St-Denis and the river on the west side of Avenue des Martyrs de la Résistance, across from the Théâtre de Beaumarchais; in Chenonceaux, the bus stops across the street from the TI (a 5-minute walk to the château entrance). For more flexibility, consider taking a train back instead (see page 401, www.thetrainline.com).

Buses also go regularly to **Tours** (8/day Mon-Sat, none on Sun, buses are cheaper than trains).

By Taxi

A taxi from Amboise to Chenonceau costs about €29 (€41 on Sun and after 19:00, €7 pickup fee, call 02 47 57 13 53, 06 12 92 70 46, 02 47 57 30 39, or 06 88 02 44 10). Most other châteaux are too expensive to visit by cab.

By Minivan Excursion

Most of these companies run shared tours (and private tours by request). While on the road, you'll usually get a running commentary—but you're on your own at the sights (discounted tickets available from the driver). Reserve a week ahead by email, or two to three days by phone. (Day-trippers from Paris find these services convenient.)

Acco-Dispo runs half- and all-day English tours from Amboise and Tours to all the major châteaux six days a week (Mon-Sat). Costs vary with the itinerary (half-day tours-€40/person, full-day-€62/person; meet at the TI, small groups of 2-8 people, mobile 06 82 00 64 51, www.accodispo-tours.com, contact@accodispo.com). Acco-Dispo also runs multiday tours of the Loire and Brittany.

Touraine Evasion runs half-day tours daily from Amboise that stop at Chambord and Chenonceau (€40/person) and all-day tours that add Cheverny (€62/person). They also have many château options out of Tours (daily in season, none in winter, mobile 06 07 39 13 31, www.tourevasion.com).

Loire Valley Tours offers all-day, fully-guided itineraries from Amboise and Tours. These upscale tours include admissions, lunch, and wine tasting (about €170/person, tel. 02 54 33 99 80, www.loire-valley-tours.com, contact@loire-valley-tours.com).

A la Française Tours is a newer outfit running similar itineraries as Loire Valley Tours, but with a younger vibe. They also offer half-day tours for €82 (tel. 02 46 65 51 57, www.alafrancaise.fr, contact@alafrancaise.fr).

By Train

Amboise provides decent train connections both within the Loire and beyond.

Within the Loire: From Amboise, you can reach **Chenonceaux** (trains are more frequent, but slower and pricier than the bus; 6/day, 1 hour, transfer at St-Pierre-des-Corps—check connections to avoid long waits), **Blois** (14/day, 20 minutes, bus or taxi excursions from there to Chambord and Cheverny—see "Blois Connections" on page 410), **Chaumont** (14/day, 35 minutes, take 10-minute train to Onzain on the Amboise-Blois route, 25-minute walk—you can see château from station), **Tours** (12/day, 25 minutes, allows connections to châteaux west of Tours), **Chinon** (7/day, 2 hours, transfer in Tours), and **Azay-le-Rideau** (6/day, 1.5 hours, transfer in Tours).

To Destinations Beyond the Loire: Frequent trains link Amboise to the regional train hub of St-Pierre-des-Corps in suburban Tours (20/day, 15 minutes). There you'll find reasonable connections to distant points (including the TGV to Paris' Gare Montparnasse). Transferring in Paris can be the fastest way to reach many French destinations, even in the south.

From Amboise you can catch the train to: **Paris Gare Montparnasse** (8/day, 1.5 hours with change to TGV at St-Pierre-des-Corps, requires TGV reservation), **Paris Gare d'Austerlitz** (3/day direct, 2 hours, no reservation required, more with transfer), **Sarlat-la-Canéda** (3/day, 6 hours, change at St-Pierre-des-Corps, then TGV to Bordeaux, then train through Bordeaux vineyards to Sarlat), **Limoges** (10/day, 4 hours, near Oradour-sur-Glane, requires bus from Limoges—see page 504), **Pontorson/Mont St-Michel** (5/day, 5.5 hours with several transfers), **Bayeux** (4/day, 5 hours, best requires transfers at St-Pierre-des-Corps and Caen, more with transfer in Paris leaving from Gare St. Lazare), **Beaune** (6/day, 6 hours, transfers at Nevers and/or St-Pierre-des-Corps; more with multiple connections and reservations), **Bourges** (roughly hourly—though fewer midday, 2-3 hours, change at St-Pierre-des-Corps).

LOIRE

Chenonceau

Château de Chenonceau is the toast of the Loire and worth ▲▲▲. This 16th-century Renaissance palace arches gracefully over the Cher River and is impeccably maintained, with fresh flower arrangements in the summer and roaring log fires in the winter. The château itself, understandably the most popular in the region, is wonderfully organized for visitors. But it's also one of the most-visited châteaux in France—so carefully follow my crowd-beating tips.

While Chenonceau is the name of the château, and Chenonceaux is the name of the town, they're pronounced the same: shuh-nohn-soh. The town itself—a one-road village with well-priced hotels and some fine eating options—makes a good home base for drivers (see recommendations later, under "Town of Chenonceaux").

Tourist Information: The ignored TI is on the main road from Amboise as you enter the village (July-Aug daily 9:30-19:00, closed at lunchtime on Sun; Sept-June Mon-Sat 9:30-13:00 &

14:00-18:00—until 17:00 in winter, closed Sun; tel. 02 47 23 94 45).

GETTING THERE

From Amboise, you can get here by **train** (6/day, 1 hour, transfer at St-Pierre-des-Corps) or faster, by **bus,** which drops off at the TI (1-2/day, Mon-Sat only, none on Sun, 25 minutes—see page 392 for details on this bus). There are also frequent train connections from Tours (10/day, 30 minutes). The unstaffed train station sits between the village and the château.

There may be **shuttles** running from Amboise; ask at the TI. Minivan **excursions** from Amboise and Tours are also available (see "By Minivan Excursion to Nearby Châteaux" under "Amboise Connections" on page 394).

You can also take a **taxi** from Amboise (€29 one-way, €41 on Sun and after 19:00, €7 pickup fee; for contact info, see "Taxi" under "Helpful Hints" for Amboise on page 373).

If **driving,** plan on a 15-minute walk from the parking lot to the château. Don't leave any valuables visible in your car.

ORIENTATION TO CHATEAU DE CHENONCEAU

Cost and Hours: €14.50, €11.50 for kids under 18, daily 9:00-19:00, July-Aug until 20:00, closes earlier off-season. The château's gardens may stay open later on selected evenings in summer (with music to enjoy as you stroll).

Information: Tel. 02 47 23 90 07, www.chenonceau.com.

Crowd-Beating Tips: Spaces are tight inside the château, so smart travelers plan around Chenonceau's crowds. This place gets slammed in high season—come early (by 9:00) or late (after 17:00). Avoid slow ticket lines by purchasing your ticket in advance (at area TIs) or from the ticket machines at the main entry (US credit cards work but instructions in English are hit-or-miss—withdraw your card at the prompt *"retirez"*).

Tours: The interior is fascinating—but only if you take advantage of the excellent 20-page **booklet** (included with entry), or rent the wonderful **videoguide** (€4). Pay for the guide when buying your ticket (before entering the château grounds), then pick it up just inside the château's door.

Services: WCs are available by the ticket office and behind the old stables.

Eating: A reasonable **$$** cafeteria is next door to the hospital room. Fancy **$$$** meals are served in the *orangerie* behind the stables (Restaurant l'Orangerie). There's a cheap *crêperie/* sandwich shop at the entrance gate. While picnics are not allowed on the grounds, there are picnic tables in a park near the parking lot.

Boat Trips: In summer, the château has rental **rowboats**—an idyllic way to savor graceful château views (€7/30 minutes, July-Aug daily 10:00-19:00, 4 people/boat, not available when the river is low).

BACKGROUND

Find a riverside view of the château to get oriented. Although earlier châteaux were built for defensive purposes, Chenonceau was

the first great pleasure palace. Nicknamed the "château of the ladies," it housed many famous women over the centuries. The original owner, Thomas Bohier, was away on the king's business so much that his wife, Katherine Briçonnet, made most of the design decisions during construction of the main château (1513-1521).

In 1547, King Henry II gave the château to his mistress, Diane de Poitiers, who added an arched bridge across the river to access the hunting grounds. She enjoyed her lovely retreat until Henry II died (pierced in a jousting tournament in Paris); his vengeful wife, Catherine de' Medici, unceremoniously kicked Diane out (and into the château of Chaumont, described later). Catherine added the three-story structure on Diane's bridge. She died before completing her vision of a matching château on the far side of the river, but not before turning Chenonceau into *the* place to see and be seen by the local aristocracy. (Whenever you see a split coat of arms, it belongs to a woman—half her husband's and half her father's.)

VISITING THE CHATEAU

Strut like an aristocrat down the tree-canopied path to the château. (There's a fun plant maze partway up on the left.) You'll cross three moats and two bridges, and pass an old round tower, which predates the main building. Notice the tower's fine limestone veneer, added so the top would better fit the new château.

The main château's original **oak door** greets you with the coats of arms of the first owners. The knocker is high enough to be used by visitors on horseback. The smaller door within the large one could be for two purposes: to slip in after curfew, or to enter during winter without letting out all the heat.

Once inside, you'll tour the château in a clockwise direction. Take time to appreciate the beautiful brick floor tiles and lavishly decorated ceilings. As you continue, follow your pamphlet or videoguide, and pay attention to these details:

LOIRE

In the **guard room,** the best-surviving tiles from the original 16th-century floor are near the walls—imagine the entire room covered with these faience tiles. And though the tapestries kept the room cozy, they also functioned to tell news or recent history (to the king's liking, of course). The French-style joist beams feature Catherine de' Medici's monogram. You'll see many more tapestries and monograms in this château.

The superbly detailed **chapel,** with its original 1521 wood gallery above the entry, survived the vandalism of the Revolution because the fast-thinking lady of the palace filled it with firewood. Angry masses were supplied with mallets and instructions to smash everything royal or religious. While this room was both, all they saw was stacked wood. The hatch door provided a quick path to the kitchen and an escape boat downstairs. The windows, blown out during World War II, are replacements from the 1950s. Look for graffiti in English left behind by the guards who protected Mary, Queen of Scots (who stayed here after her marriage to King François II).

The centerpiece of the **bedroom of Diane de Poitiers** is, ironically, a severe portrait of her rival, Catherine de' Medici, at 40 years old. Notice the various monograms in the room. You've already seen Catherine's Chanel-like double-C insignia. Henri II flaunts his singular H. And combining the two seems to form mirrored Ds...perhaps showing Henri's preference for his mistress Diane.

The 16th-century tapestries are among the finest in France. Each one took an average of 60 worker-years to make. Study the complex compositions of the *Triumph of Charity* (over the bed) and the violent *Triumph of Force.*

At 200 feet long, the three-story **Grand Gallery** spans the river. The upper stories house double-decker ballrooms and a small museum. Notice how differently the slate and limestone of the checkered floor wear after 500 years. Imagine grand banquets here. Catherine, a contemporary of Queen Elizabeth I of England, wanted to rule with style. She threw wild parties and employed her ladies to circulate and soak up all the political gossip possible from the well-lubricated Kennedys and Rockefellers of her realm. Parties included grand fireworks displays and mock naval battles on the river. The niches once held statues—Louis XIV took a liking to them, and they now decorate the palace at Versailles.

In summer and during holidays, you can take a quick walk outside for more good palace **views:** Cross the bridge, pick up a re-entry ticket, then stroll the other bank of the Cher (across the river from the château). During World War I, the Grand Gallery served as a military hospital, where more than 2,200 soldiers were cared for—picture hundreds of beds lining the gallery. And in World War II, the river you crossed marked the border between the collaborationist Vichy government and Nazi-controlled France. Back then, Chenonceau witnessed many prisoner swaps, and at night, château staff would help resistance fighters and Jews cross in secret. Because the gallery was considered a river crossing, the Germans had their artillery aimed at Chenonceau, ready to destroy the "bridge" to block any Allied advance.

Double back through the gallery to find the sensational state-of-the-art (in the 16th century) **kitchen** below. It was built near water (to fight the inevitable kitchen fires) and in the basement; because heat rises, it helped heat the palace. Cross the small bridge (watch your head) to find the stove and landing bay for goods to be ferried in and out.

From here, find the **Muse/Three Graces Room** (with a painting featuring King Louis XV's three favorite mistresses), then visit the King Louis XIV Room.

Back on the main floor, the staircase leading **upstairs** wowed royal guests. It was the first nonspiral staircase they'd seen...quite a treat in the 16th century. When open, the balcony provides lovely views of the gardens, which originally supplied vegetables and herbs. (Diane built the one to the right; Catherine, the prettier one to your left.) The estate is still full of wild boar and deer—the primary dishes of past centuries. You'll see more lavish bedrooms on this floor. Small side rooms show fascinating old architectural sketches of the château. The walls, 20 feet thick, were honeycombed with the flues of 224 fireplaces and passages for servants to do their pleasure-providing work unseen. There was no need for plumbing: Servants fetched, carried, and dumped everything.

Above the Grand Gallery is the **Medici Gallery,** now a mini-museum for the château. Displays in French and English cover the lives of six women who made their mark on Chenonceau (one of them had a young Jean-Jacques Rousseau, who would later become an influential philosopher, as her personal secretary). There's also a timeline of the top 10 events in the history of the château and a cabinet of curiosities.

Go to the **top floor** to peek inside the somber bedchamber and mourning room of Louise de Lorraine, widow of Henri III. Stabbed by a renegade Dominican monk, the king dictated this message for his wife on his deathbed: "My dear, I hope that I shall bear myself well. Pray to God for me and do not move from there." Louise took him literally and spent the last 11 years of her life in meditation and prayer at Chenonceau. Perpetually dressed in the then-traditional mourning color, she became known as the White Queen. Take a close look at the silver teardrops that adorn the black walls before paying homage at the 16th-century portrait of Henri III.

To end your visit, escape the hordes by touring the **two gardens**

LOIRE

with their postcard-perfect views of the château. The upstream garden hasn't changed since Diane de Poitiers first commissioned it in 1547. Designed in the austere Italian style, the water fountain was revolutionary in its time for its forceful jet. The downstream garden of Catherine de' Medici is more relaxed, with tree roses and lavender gracing its lines in high season.

Military Hospital Room and Traditional Farm: These sights are best seen after you've toured the château and gardens. The military hospital room (with effective English explanations) is located in the château stables and gives an idea of what the Grand Gallery was like when it housed wounded soldiers during World War I. You can taste the owner's wines in the atmospheric **Cave des Dômes** below. Just past the stables you can stroll around a traditional farm. Imagine the production needed to sustain the château while making your way through the vegetable and flower gardens toward the exit.

TOWN OF CHENONCEAUX

This one-road, sleepy village makes a good home base for drivers and a workable base for train travelers who don't mind connections.

Sleeping: Hotels are a good value in Chenonceaux, and there's one for every budget. You'll find them *tous ensemble* on Rue du Dr. Bretonneau, all with free and secure parking.

$$$ Auberge du Bon Laboureur** turns heads with its ivied facade, lush terraces, and stylish indoor lounges and bars. The staff is a tad stiff, but past the formal pleasantries are lovely four-star rooms with every comfort at three-star prices (family rooms and suites, heated pool, air-con, fine gardens, finer restaurant, 6 Rue du Dr. Bretonneau, tel. 02 47 23 90 02, www.bonlaboureur.com, contact@bonlaboureur.com).

$$ Hôtel la Roseraie* has a flowery terrace, bar, and 22 handsome rooms—request one that overlooks the gardens. Sabine, Jerome, and dog Layla run a good show with fair prices for three-star comfort (air-con, pool, closed mid-Nov-March, 7 Rue du Dr. Bretonneau, tel. 02 47 23 90 09, www.hotel-chenonceau.com, laroseraie-chenonceaux@orange.fr). The traditional dining room and sweet terrace are ideal for a nice dinner—available for guests and nonguests alike who reserve ahead (daily May-Sept 19:00-21:00, closed Tue off-season and mid-Nov-mid-March).

$ Relais Chenonceaux greets guests with a nice patio and a mix of rooms. The best rooms are in the annex; those in the main building are plain and above a restaurant (family rooms, tel. 02 47 23 98 11, 10 Rue du Dr. Bretonneau, www.chenonceaux.com, info@chenonceaux.com).

$ Hostel du Roy** offers 30 spartan but well-priced rooms, some around a garden courtyard, and a mediocre but cheap restaurant. Hardworking Nathalie runs the place with papa's help (family rooms, 9 Rue du Dr. Bretonneau, tel. 02 47 23 90 17, www. hostelduroy.com, hostelduroy@wanadoo.fr).

Eating: You'll find eating options for all budgets. All of these are listed earlier, under "Sleeping": Reserve ahead to dine in formal style at the country-elegant and Michelin-starred **$$$$ Auberge du Bon Laboureur** restaurant (€55 and €90 *menus*). **$$$ Hôtel la Roseraie** serves good fixed-price meals in a lovely dining room or on a garden terrace (*menus* for €30 or €43). **$$ Relais Chenonceaux** dishes up savory crêpes, salads, and *plats* in a pleasant interior or on its terrace. The price is right for the basic cuisine at **$ Hostel du Roy,** with an all-you-can-eat salad bar for €10 and a cheap *plat du jour.*

La Maison des Pages has some bakery items, sandwiches, cold drinks to go, and just enough groceries for a modest picnic (closed Wed, on the main drag between Hostel du Roy and Hôtel la Roseraie).

For a French treat and no tourists in sight, book ahead and drive about a mile to Chisseaux and dine at the *très* traditional **$$ Auberge du Cheval Rouge.** You'll enjoy some of the region's fine cuisine at affordable prices, either inside a pretty dining room or on a verdant patio (closed Tue-Wed, 30 Rue Nationale, Chisseaux, tel. 02 47 23 86 67, www.auberge-duchevalrouge.com).

Connections: From Chenonceaux it's easy to get by train to **Tours** (10/day, 30 minutes), with connections to **Chinon, Azay-le-Rideau,** and **Langeais.** To reach **Amboise,** you can either take the train (6/day, 1 hour, transfer at St-Pierre-des-Corps) or bus (1-2/day, Mon-Sat only, none on Sun, 25 minutes, departs Chenonceaux at about 12:20, in summer also at about 17:50, catch bus across the street from the TI, tel. 02 47 05 30 49, www.remi-centrevaldeloire.fr).

Blois

Bustling Blois (pronounced "blwah") feels like the Big Apple after all of those rural villages and castles. Blois owns a rich history, dolled-up pedestrian areas, and a darn impressive château smack in its center. With convenient access to Paris, Blois makes a handy base for train travelers; Chambord and Cheverny are within reach by excursion bus (cheap, high season only) or taxi (which also serve

Chaumont). Frequent train service to Paris and Amboise enables easy stopovers in Blois.

From this once powerful city, the medieval counts of Blois governed their vast lands and vied with the king of France for dominance. The center of France moved from Amboise to Blois in 1498, when Louis XII inherited the throne (after Charles VIII had his unfortunate head-banging incident in Amboise). The château you see today is living proof of this town's 15 minutes of fame. But there's more to humble Blois than just its château. Visit the flying-buttressed St. Nicholas Church, find the medieval warren of lanes and lovely rose garden below St. Louis Cathedral, and relax in a café on Place Louis XII.

Orientation to Blois

Unlike most other Loire châteaux, Blois' Château Royal sits smack in the city center, with no forest, pond, moat, or river to call its

own. It's an easy walk from the train station, near ample underground parking, and just above the TI. Below the château, Place Louis XII marks the hub of traffic-free Blois, with cafés and shops lining its perimeter. Rue du Commerce, leading up from the river, is Blois' primary shopping street. Atmospheric cafés and restaurants hide in the medieval tangle of lanes below St. Louis Cathedral and around St. Nicholas Church. Blois was heavily bombed in World War II, leaving much of the old town in ruins, but the château survived. Today, the city largely ignores its river and celebrates Saturdays with a lively market (until about 13:00) centered on Place Louis XII. Sundays are awfully quiet in Blois.

ARRIVAL IN BLOIS

Train travelers can walk 10 minutes straight out of the station downhill on Avenue du Dr. Jean Laigret to the TI and château (follow *Château* signs), or take a two-minute taxi from in front of the station.

Drivers follow *Centre-Ville* and *Château* signs (metered parking along Avenue du Dr. Jean Laigret or inside at Parking du Château—first 30 minutes free, then about €2/2 hours).

TOURIST INFORMATION

The TI may have moved by the time you visit. Its new location is below the château entrance, just off Place du Château (see the

"Blois" map). They sell discounted tickets when purchased for several châteaux (daily April-Sept 9:00-19:00, Oct-March 10:00-17:00, tel. 02 54 90 41 41, www.bloischambord.com). To explore the center of Blois, use the TI's walking-tour map (red and purple routes are best), or just follow my suggested walking route under "Other Sights and Activities," later. The TI has schedules for the Navette Châteaux bus, Navette Azalys shuttle, and Eco Shuttle minivan exursions to Chambord and Cheverny (see "Blois Connections," later). They also have information on bike rentals and bike paths.

HELPFUL HINTS

Baggage Storage: You have several good choices for bag storage in Blois. **Détours de Loire** can store large suitcases for a small fee (free if you rent a bike—see next listing). The **TI** and the recommended **Hôtel Anne de Bretagne** will also store bags for a small fee. You can store smaller bags in the château's free **lockers** with paid admission—so you can drop off your luggage, tour the château and town, and even take an excursion to Chambord and Cheverny, provided you reclaim your bag before the château closes.

Bike Rental: Détours de Loire bike rental is a block below the train station at 39 Avenue du Dr. Jean Laigret (tel. 02 54 56 07 73, https://detoursdeloire.com). You can rent a bike for a 26-mile one-way ride to Amboise, stopping at garden-rich Chaumont-sur-Loire on the way, then return to Blois by train with your bike. See "Biking from Blois," later, for route ideas.

Launderette: A self-service launderette is at 6 Rue St-Lubin (daily 7:00-21:00).

Local Guide: Fabrice Maret lives in Blois and is a skilled teacher (see page 370 for details).

Sights in Blois

▲▲CHATEAU ROYAL DE BLOIS

Size up the château from the big square before entering. A castle has inhabited this site since the 900s. Even though parts of the building date from the Middle Ages, notice the complete absence of defensive towers, drawbridges, and other fortifications. Gardens once extended behind the château and up the hill to a forest (where the train station is today). A walk around the building's perimeter (to the right as you face it) reveals more of its beautiful Renaissance facade.

Kings Louis XII and François I built most of the château you see today, each calling it home during their reigns. That's Louis looking good on his horse in the niche. The section on the far right

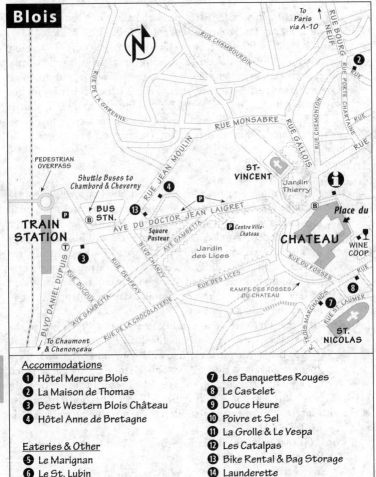

Blois

To Paris via A-10

RUE CHAMBOURDIN

RUE BOURG NEUF

RUE PORTE CHARTAINE

RUE DE LA GARENNE

RUE MONSABRE

RUE GALLOIS

RUE CHEMONTON

PEDESTRIAN OVERPASS

Shuttle Buses to Chambord & Cheverny

RUE JEAN MOULIN

ST-VINCENT

Jardin Thierry

Place du

TRAIN STATION

BUS STN.

AVE DU DOCTOR JEAN LAIGRET

Square Pasteur

Centre Ville-Château

CHATEAU

WINE COOP

BLVD DANIEL DUPUIS

RUE DUCOUX

RUE DESERAY

BLVD CHANZY

AVE GAMBETTA

Jardin des Lices

RUE DU FOSSE

RUE DES LICES

RAMPE DES FOSSES DU CHATEAU

RUE TROIS MARCHANDS

RUE ST. LAUMER

AVE GAMBETTA

RUE DE LA CHOCOLATERIE

ST. NICOLAS

To Chaumont & Chenonceau

Accommodations
1. Hôtel Mercure Blois
2. La Maison de Thomas
3. Best Western Blois Château
4. Hôtel Anne de Bretagne

Eateries & Other
5. Le Marignan
6. Le St. Lubin
7. Les Banquettes Rouges
8. Le Castelet
9. Douce Heure
10. Poivre et Sel
11. La Grolle & Le Vespa
12. Les Catalpas
13. Bike Rental & Bag Storage
14. Launderette

LOIRE

looks like a church but was actually the château's most important meeting room (more on this later).

Cost and Hours: €12, €6.50 for kids under 18, €20 combo-ticket with House of Magic or sound-and-light show, €27 covers all three, daily 9:00-18:30, July-Aug until 19:00, Oct until 18:00, Nov-March 9:00-12:30 & 14:30-17:30.

Information: Tel. 02 54 90 33 33, www.chateaudeblois.fr.

Sound-and-Light Show: This 45-minute 3-D "show" takes place in the center courtyard and features projections with a historical narrative of the château (€10.50, covered by château combo-tickets, free headset provides English translation, daily April-mid Sept at about 22:00).

Tours: At the ticket office, pick up the helpful brochure, then

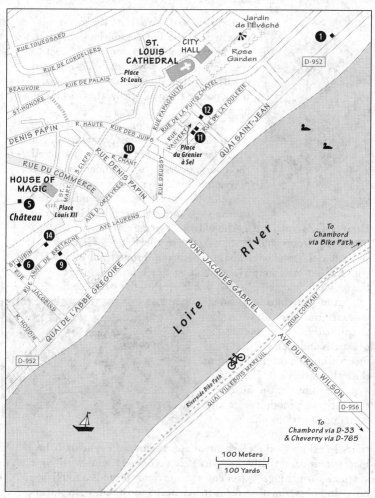

read the well-presented displays in each room. The snazzy "Histo-pad" with images and sound is free, but the less-techy audioguide is €3 (go figure).

Visiting the Château: Begin in the **courtyard,** where four wings—ranging from Gothic to Neoclassical—underscore this château's importance over many centuries. Stand with your back to the entry to get oriented. The medieval parts of the château are the brick-patterned sections (to your left and behind you), both built by Louis XII. While work was underway on Chambord, François I (who apparently was addicted to home renovation) added the elaborate Renaissance wing (to your right; early 16th century), centered on a protruding spiral staircase and slathered with his emblematic salamanders. Gaston d'Orléans inherited the place in the 1600s

and wanted to do away with the messy mismatched styles. He demolished a church that stood across from you (the chapel to your left is all that remains) and replaced it with the clean-lined, Neoclassical structure you see today. Luckily, that's as far as he got.

Visit the interior counterclockwise, and focus on the Renaissance wing. Begin in the far-right corner (where you entered the courtyard) and walk under the stone porcupine (Louis' symbol of royal power—it could throw off protective quills) and up the steps into the dazzling **Hall of the Estates-General.** This is the oldest surviving part of the château (predating Louis and François), where the Estates-General met twice to deliberate who would inherit the throne from Henry III, who had no male heir. (Keep reading to see how Henry resolved the problem, and skip the silly virtual-reality show if offered.)

Continue into the small **lapidary museum** (down a few steps), with an engaging display of statues and architectural fragments from the original château (love the gargoyles). There's also a good exhibit on the history of the castle with models of its construction at various phases.

About halfway down, stone stairs spiral up to the plush **royal apartments of François I.** Immerse yourself in richly tiled, ornately decorated rooms with some original furnishings (excellent explanations posted). You'll see busts and portraits of some of the château's most famous residents (including portraits from François' lineage several rooms down). You'll also enter the stunning **Queen's Room,** where Catherine de' Medici died, and near the end, learn about the dastardly 1588 murder of the duke of Guise, which took place in these apartments. In the late 1500s, the devastating Wars of Religion pitted Protestant against Catholic and took a huge toll on this politically and religiously divided city—including the powerful Guise brothers. King Henry III (Catherine de' Medici's son) had the devoutly Catholic duke assassinated to keep him off the throne.

The Neoclassical wing is of less interest; end your visit with a walk through the small **fine-arts museum.** Located just over the château's entry, this 16th-century who's-who portrait gallery lets you put faces to the characters that made this château's history.

OTHER SIGHTS AND ACTIVITIES
House of Magic (Maison de la Magie)

The home of Jean-Eugène Robert-Houdin, the illusionist whose name was adopted by Harry Houdini, offers an interesting but overpriced history of illusion and magic. Kids enjoy the gift shop. Several daily 30-minute shows have no words, so they work in any language (the good English brochure helps you navigate the place). A fun dragon snorts his stuff on the outside of the building on the half-hour.

Cost and Hours: €10, €7 for kids under 18, covered by château combo-tickets described earlier; daily 10:00-12:30 & 14:00-18:30, magic "séance" schedule posted at entry—usually at 11:15, 14:45 or 15:15, and 17:15; at the opposite end of the square from the château, tel. 02 54 90 33 33, www.maisondelamagie.fr.

A Walk Through Blois' Historic Center

There's little to do along the river except to cross Pont Jacques Gabriel for views back to the city. But Blois' old town is worth a ramble. Although much of the historic center was destroyed by WWII bombs, it has been rebuilt with traffic-free streets and pleasing squares.

For a taste of medieval Blois, drop down the steps below the Maison de la Magie and turn right into Place Louis XII, ground zero in the old city; from here, walk down Rue St-Lubin (after a few blocks it turns into Rue des Trois Marchands). Follow along as the street curves to the left and continue until you see the church of **St. Nicholas.** The towering church, with its flying buttresses, dates from the late 1100s, and is worth a peek inside for its beautifully lit apse and its blend of Gothic and Romanesque styles. Find Rue Anne de Bretagne skirting left and behind the church and track it back to Place Louis XII. From here, pedestrian-friendly streets like Rue St-Martin lead north to Rue du Commerce, the town's main shopping drag, and to peaceful medieval lanes below Blois' other hill, crowned by **St. Louis Cathedral.** Finish your walk with a steep climb up from cute Place du Grenier à Sel to the rose garden that sits just below the cathedral and Hôtel de Ville. The esplanade above the rose garden offers rooftop views over the city.

Biking from Blois

Blois is well-positioned as a starting point for biking forays into the countryside. Cycling from Blois to Chambord is a level, 1.5-hour, one-way ride along a well-marked, 13-mile route, much of it an elaborate bike-only lane that follows the river's left (eastern) bank. You can loop back to Blois without repeating the same route and connect to a good network of other bike paths (the TI's free *Les Châteaux à Vélo* map shows area bike routes). Hardy riders can bike one-way to Amboise via Chaumont by renting at the Détours de Loire bike shop (see "Helpful Hints" for Blois, earlier).

Sleeping in Blois

Blois has a scarcity of worthwhile hotels.

$$$ Hôtel Mercure Blois**** is modern, and made for businesspeople, but it's reliable, with big, superior two-level rooms and a riverfront location a 15-minute walk below the château (air-con, elevator, pay parking, 28 Quai Saint-Jean, tel. 02 54 56 66 66, www.mercure.com).

$$ La Maison de Thomas is a mod B&B that doubles as a wine-tasting boutique specializing in Loire vintages. It's an old building, but all five rooms have been updated with Euro-chic decor (includes breakfast, cash only, uphill from the château near the pedestrian main drag at 12 Rue Beauvoir, ask for directions to street parking, tel. 09 81 84 44 59, www.lamaisondethomas.fr, resa@lamaisondethomas.fr, Guillaume).

$$ Best Western Blois Château* has stylish decor, small-but-sharp rooms, all the comforts you'd expect from this chain, and is ideally located for train travelers (air-con, elevator, across from the train station at 8 Avenue du Dr. Jean Laigret, tel. 02 54 56 85 10, www.bestwestern.fr, contact@hotelblois-gare.fr).

$ Hôtel Anne de Bretagne,** run by helpful Sandra, offers a solid two-star value with 29 well-appointed rooms (with good fans but no air-con), a central location near the château and train station, and a welcoming terrace. Ask for a room on the quiet side of the building facing the terrace. They also rent bikes—best to book in advance (family rooms, no elevator, 150 yards uphill from Parking du Château, 5-minute walk below the train station at 31 Avenue du Dr. Jean Laigret, tel. 02 54 78 05 38, www.hotelannedebretagne.com, contact@hotelannedebretagne.com).

Eating in Blois

If you're stopping in Blois around lunchtime, plan on eating at one of the places in the lower part of town. **Le Marignan,** on the square in front of the château, works for a drink to watch the stately mansion opposite the château becoming the "dragon house," as monsters crane their long necks out its many windows on the half-hour.

Diners can start their evening with a drink at the popular watering hole **Le St. Lubin,** a café-bar (closed Sun, 16 Rue St-Lubin).

BETWEEN THE CHATEAU AND THE RIVER

The traffic-free streets between the château and the river are home to many cafés with standard, easy meals.

$$ Les Banquettes Rouges, a block above St. Nicholas Church's left transept, is your best bet for foodie pleasures. It features fine regional dishes with creative twists—try the duck or pan-fried veal liver. You'll dine in a red booth—as the name suggests (closed Sun-Mon, reservations smart, 16 Rue des Trois Marchands, tel. 02 54 78 74 92, www.lesbanquettesrouges.com).

$ Le Castelet, also near St. Nicholas, is simple and cheap with decent vegetarian choices (closed Sun and Wed, 40 Rue St-Lubin, tel. 02 54 74 66 09).

$$ Douce Heure is a cheery *salon gourmand* on Place Louis XII's southwest corner. The extensive menu of homemade beverages includes iced teas, traditional hot chocolate, and fruit cocktails—the strawberry, raspberry, and rose are excellent (good salads, quiches, and wraps; great desserts, Mon-Sat 12:00-19:00, closed Sun, 4 Rue Anne de Bretagne).

ELSEWHERE IN BLOIS

$$ Poivre et Sel, just a few blocks from the Pont Jacques, offers new takes on traditional French cuisine in a faux-rustic setting. Dine on the ground floor or in the open loft. Weekend reservations are recommended (Mon-Tue and Thu-Sat 12:00-14:00 & 19:00-22:00, closed Sun and Wed, 9 Rue du Chant des Oiseaux, tel. 02 54 78 07 78).

Between the Cathedral and the River: To dine cheaply on an atmospheric square with few tourists in sight, find Place du Grenier à Sel (a block from the river, below St. Louis Cathedral) and consider these places: **$$ La Grolle** specializes in *savoyard* cuisine with fondues, raclettes, *tartiflette,* and other melted-cheese dishes, with lighter options available in summer (closed Sun-Mon, 5 Rue Vauvert, tel. 02 36 23 64 65). Next door, **$$ Le Vespa** does a basic Franco-Italian mix, including pizzas (pleasant interior seating, closed Sun-Mon except in summer, 11 Rue Vauvert, tel. 02 54 78 44 97).

LOIRE

Save room for dessert and try the crêpes and good salads at **$ Les Catalpas** (daily 12:00-14:00 & 19:00-23:00, 1 Rue du Grenier à Sel, tel. 02 54 56 86 86).

Blois Connections

By Shuttle

Two companies offer handy service from the Blois train station to key châteaux. Look for the buses across the parking lot from the station. You can also board these shuttles below and behind the Blois château (3 minutes later than the train station departure).

Transports du Loir-et-Cher (TLC) runs bus trips to **Chambord, Cheverny,** and (skippable) Villesavin and Beauregard (several departures per week April-Oct, no service Nov-March). The bus is marked *Navette-Châteaux*. Morning departures from Blois station are usually at 9:30 and 11:15 and head to Chambord; from Chambord, departures link Cheverny and Beauregard with a few return-trip options to Blois. The schedule is inconsistent—verify times at a TI or online at www.bloischambord.com—click "visiter sans voiture" (€3 bus fare, discounts offered on châteaux entries including the Château Royal in Blois; buy tickets from TI or bus driver).

Navette Azalys runs to **Chaumont** (3 daily morning trips, 2 afternoon returns, €4.50 round-trip, check schedule with TI or at www.bloischambord.com).

By Minivan Excursion

Eco Shuttle offers several daily excursions to surrounding châteaux leaving from the Blois train station and from Place du Château by the TI. Look for excursions to Chambord (€25/person) or Chambord and Cheverny (€39). Book ahead at the TI or online (tel. 06 49 26 34 35, www.ecoshuttle41.com).

By Taxi

Blois taxis wait in front of the station and offer excursion fares to **Chambord, Chaumont,** or **Cheverny** (rates posted in taxi shelter, about €36 one-way from Blois to any of these three châteaux, €110 round-trip to Chambord and Cheverny, €160 for Chambord and Chenonceau, more expensive on Sun, 8-person minivans available, tel. 02 54 78 07 65). These rates are per cab, making the per-person price downright reasonable for groups of three or four.

By Train

From Blois to: Amboise (14/day, 20 minutes), **Tours** (roughly hourly, 40 minutes), **Chinon** (6/day, 2 hours, transfer in Tours and possibly in St-Pierre-des-Corps), **Azay-le-Rideau** (7/day, 1.5 hours, transfer in Tours and possibly in St-Pierre-des-Corps), **Paris** (4/day direct to Gare d'Austerlitz, 1.5 hours, more with transfer in St-Pierre-des-Corps or Orléans).

Chambord

With its huge scale and prickly silhouette, Château de Chambord, worth ▲▲▲, is the granddaddy of the Loire châteaux. It's surrounded by Europe's largest enclosed forest park, a game preserve

defined by a 20-mile-long wall and teeming with wild deer and boar. Chambord (shahm-bor) began as a simple hunting lodge for bored Blois counts and became a monument to the royal sport and duty of hunting. (Hunting was considered important to keep the animal population under control and the vital forests healthy.)

The château's massive architecture is the star attraction—particularly the mind-boggling double-helix staircase. Six times the size of your average Loire castle, the château has 440 rooms and a fireplace for every day of the year. The château is laid out as a keep in the shape of a Greek cross, with four towers and two wings surrounded by stables. Its four floors are each separated by 46 stairs, creating sky-high ceilings. The ground floor has reception rooms, the first floor up has the royal apartments, the second floor up houses temporary exhibits and a hunting museum, and the rooftop offers a viewing terrace to plot your next hunting adventure. Special exhibits describing Chambord at key moments in its history help animate the place. Because hunters could see best after autumn leaves fell, Chambord was a winter palace (which helps explain the 365 fireplaces). Only 80 of Chambord's rooms are open to the public—but that's plenty.

If you hate crowds, you'll like Chambord. Because it's so huge, it's relatively easy to escape the hordes. It helps that there's no one-way, mandatory tour route—you're free to roam like a duke surveying his domain.

GETTING THERE

Without a car from Blois, you have several options (see "Blois Connections," earlier). Shuttle buses drop you 200 yards in front of the château, a 10-minute walk to the "village." It's a level 1.5-hour bike ride from Blois to Chambord (see "Biking from Blois," earlier). Minivan excursions also run from Amboise (see "Amboise Connections" on page 394).

With a car, allow 20 minutes to drive from Blois, 45 minutes from Amboise, 55 minutes from Chenonceaux, and 15 minutes from Cheverny. You'll pay €6 to park (pay at machines near the

LOIRE

lots when you arrive to avoid end-of-day lines, credit cards only, US cards work—except for American Express). If you have trouble with the machine, pay at the ticket office as you approach the château.

ORIENTATION TO CHATEAU DE CHAMBORD

Cost and Hours: €14.50, daily 9:00-18:00, Oct-March until 17:00. One ticket office is in Chambord's "village" near the main parking area; another is inside the château.

Information: Château tel. 02 54 50 40 00, www.chambord.org.

Tours: This château requires helpful information to make it come alive. The free handout is useful, and most rooms have some explanations. For a lot more context, rent the €6.50 "Histopad" tablet guide inside the château. Or take a guided tour in English (€5, July-Sept daily at 11:15).

Services: The primary ticket office and TI are located together in a flashy building near the closest parking area to the château. Nearby you'll also find a "village" of shops and services, including souvenir shops, a wine-tasting room, and several choices for a quick meal. There's a WC behind the primary ticket office and another at the château itself. The bookshop inside the château has a good selection of children's books.

Cruising the Grounds: A network of leafy lanes crisscrosses the vast expanse contained within the 20-mile-long wall. Explore the park on a bike (€7/hour), a 4-person pedalcart (€20/hour), or a golf cart (€28/45 minutes, great value for 2-4 people). Your roaming area is more restricted in the golf cart, but you'll cover lots more ground than on foot. You can also rent electric boats (€20/30 minutes—which is plenty), and cruise the château-front canal. Bikes, boats, and carts are all rented on the canal between the "village" and the château.

Gardens: The original Renaissance gardens behind the château can be accessed with a château entry ticket. The best views of the gardens are from the château's rooftop terrace.

Horse and Bird of Prey Show: The 45-minute show is not worth most people's time or money (€16, less for kids or with château combo-ticket, mid-July-Aug daily in morning and afternoon except no Mon show, fewer off-season, reserve ahead, reservations@chambord.org).

Views: The best view of the château depends on the light. Walk out of the back of the château into the gardens for fine views, or walk straight out the main entrance a few hundred yards for exquisite looks back to the château. On the "village" side, cross the small river in front of the château and turn right for more views.

BACKGROUND

Starting in 1518, a young François I created this "weekend retreat," employing 1,800 workmen for 15 years. (You'll see his signature salamander symbol everywhere.) François I was an absolute monarch—with an emphasis on absolute. In 32 years of rule (1515-1547), he never once called the Estates-General to session (a rudimentary parliament in *ancien régime* France). This imposing hunting palace was another way to show off his power. Countless guests, like Charles V—the Holy Roman Emperor and most powerful man of the age—were invited to this pleasure palace of French kings...and were totally wowed.

The grand architectural plan of the château—modeled after an Italian church—feels designed as a place to worship royalty. Each floor of the main structure is essentially the same: Four equal arms of a Greek cross branch off a monumental staircase, which leads up to a cupola. From a practical point of view, the design pushed the usable areas to the four corners. This castle, built while the pope was erecting a new St. Peter's Basilica, is like a secular rival to the Vatican.

Construction started the year Leonardo died, 1519. The architect is unknown, but an eerie Leonardo-esque spirit resides here. The symmetry, balance, and classical proportions combine to reflect a harmonious Renaissance vision that could have been inspired by Leonardo's notebooks.

Typical of royal châteaux, this palace of François I was rarely used. Because any effective king had to be on the road to exercise his power, royal palaces sat empty most of the time. In the 1600s, Louis XIV renovated Chambord, but he visited it only six times (for about two weeks each visit). And while the place was ransacked during the Revolution, the greatest harm to Chambord came later, from neglect.

VISITING THE CHATEAU

I've covered the highlights, floor by floor.

Ground Floor: This stark level shows off the general plan—four wings, small doors to help heated rooms stay warm, and a massive staircase. In a room just inside the front door, on the left, you can watch a worthwhile, 18-minute video—look for a screen on the side wall for viewing with English subtitles.

The attention-grabbing **double-helix staircase** dominates the open vestibules and invites visitors to climb up. Its two spirals are interwoven, so people can climb up and down and never meet. Find the helpful explanation of the staircase posted on the wall. From the staircase, enjoy fine views of the vestibule action, or just marvel at the playful Renaissance capitals carved into its light tuff stone.

First Floor Up: Here you'll find the most interesting rooms.

Starting opposite a big ceramic stove (added in the 18th century), tour this floor basically clockwise. You'll enter the lavish apartments in the **king's wing** and pass through the grand bedrooms of Louis XIV, his wife Maria Theresa, and, at the far end after the queen's boudoir, François I (follow *Logis de François 1er* signs). These theatrical bedrooms place the royal beds on raised platforms—getting them ready for some nighttime drama. The furniture in François' bedroom was designed so it could be easily disassembled and moved with him.

A highlight of the first floor is the seven-room **Museum of the Count of Chambord** (Musée du Comte de Chambord). The last of the French Bourbons, Henri d'Artois (a.k.a. the count of Chambord) was next in line to be king when France decided it didn't need one. He was raring to rule—you'll see his coronation outfits and even souvenirs from the coronation that never happened. Watch the short video about the man who believed he should have become King Henry V but who lived in exile from the age of 10. Although he opened the palace to the public and saved it from neglect, he actually visited this château only once, in 1871.

The **chapel,** tucked off in a side wing, is interesting only for how unimpressive and remotely located it is. It's dwarfed by the mass of this imposing château—clearly designed to trumpet the glories not of God, but of the king of France.

Second Floor: Beneath beautiful coffered ceilings (notice the "F" for François) is a series of ballrooms that once hosted post-hunt parties. From here, you'll climb up to the rooftop, but first lean to the center of the staircase and look down its spiral.

Rooftop: A pincushion of spires and chimneys decorates the rooftop viewing terrace. From a distance, the roof—with its frilly forest of stone towers—gives the massive château a deceptive lightness. From here, ladies could scan the estate grounds, enjoying the spectacle of their ego-pumping men out hunting. On hunt day, a line of beaters would fan out and work inward from the distant walls, flushing wild game to the center, where the king and his buddies waited. The showy lantern tower of the tallest spire glowed with a nighttime torch when the king was in.

Gaze up at the grandiose tip-top of the tallest tower, capped with the king's fleur-de-lis symbol. It's a royal lily—not a cross—that caps this monument to the power of the French king.

In the Courtyard: In the far corner, next to the summer café, a door leads to the Rolls-Royce of **carriage rooms** and the fascinating **lapidary rooms.** Here you'll come face-to-face with original stonework from the roof, including the graceful lantern cupola, with the original palace-capping fleur-de-lis. Imagine having to hoist that load. The volcanic tuff stone used to build the spires was soft and easy to work, but not very durable—particularly when so exposed to the elements. Several displays explain the ongoing renovations to François' stately pleasure dome. On the opposite side of the courtyard, find the château **kitchen,** with good English explanations.

Cheverny

This stately hunting palace, a ▲▲ sight, is one of the more lavishly furnished Loire châteaux. Because the immaculately preserved Château de Cheverny (shuh-vehr-nee) was built and decorated in a relatively short 30 years, from 1604 to 1634, it has a unique architectural harmony and unity of style. From the start, this château has been in the Hurault family, and Hurault pride shows in its flawless preservation and

intimate feel (it was opened to the public in 1922). The charming viscount and his family still live on the third floor (not open to the public, but you'll see some family photos). Cheverny was spared by the French Revolution; the count's relatives were popular then, as today, even among the village farmers.

GETTING THERE
You can reach Cheverny by shuttle or minivan excursion from Blois (see "Blois Connections" on page 410), or by minivan excursion from Amboise or Tours (see "Amboise Connections" on page 394). Drivers can park for free at the château.

ORIENTATION TO CHATEAU DE CHEVERNY
Cost and Hours: €12, €16 combo-ticket includes Tintin "adventure" rooms, family deals available; daily 9:15-18:30, Nov-March 10:00-17:00; tel. 02 54 79 96 29, www.chateau-cheverny.fr.

Eating and Sleeping: The château sits alongside a pleasant village, with a small grocery store and cafés offering good lunch options (the town also has a few hotels).

VISITING THE CHATEAU
As you walk across the manicured grounds toward the gleaming château, the sound of hungry hounds may follow you. Lined up across the facade are sculpted medallions with portraits of Roman emperors, including Julius Caesar (above the others in the center).

LOIRE

As you enter the château, pick up the excellent self-guided tour brochure, which describes the interior beautifully.

Your visit starts in the lavish **dining room,** decorated with leather walls and a sumptuous ceiling. Next, as you climb the stairs to the private apartments, look out the window and spot the *orangerie* across the gardens. It was

here that the *Mona Lisa* was hidden (along with other treasures from the Louvre) during World War II.

On the first floor, turn right from the stairs and tour the I-could-live-here **family apartments** with silky bedrooms, kids' rooms, and an intimate dining room. On the other side of this floor is the impressive **Arms Room** with weapons, a sedan chair, and a snare drum from the count of Chambord (who would have been king; see page 411). The **King's Bedchamber** is literally fit for a king. Study the fun ceiling art, especially the "boys will be boys" cupids.

On the top floor, peek inside the **chapel** before backtracking down to the ground floor. Browse the left wing and find a family tree going back to 1490, a grandfather clock with a second hand that's been ticking for 250 years, and a letter of thanks from George Washington to this family for their help in booting out the English.

Leaving the château, consider a short stroll through the gardens to the *orangerie,* which today houses a kids' play area and a garden café.

OTHER SIGHTS AT THE CHATEAU
Dog Kennel
Barking dogs remind visitors that the viscount still loves to hunt (he goes twice a week year-round). The kennel (200 yards in front of the château, look for *Chenil* signs) is especially interesting when the 70 hounds are fed (daily at 11:30). The dogs—half English foxhound and half French Poitou—are bred to have big feet and bigger stamina. They're given food once a day (two pounds each in winter, half that in summer), and the feeding *(la soupe des chiens)* is a fun spectacle that shows off their strict training. Before chow time, the hungry hounds fill the little kennel rooftop and watch the trainer (who knows every dog's name) bring in troughs stacked with delectable raw meat. He opens the gate, and the dogs gather enthusiastically around the food without touching it—yelping hysterically.

Only when the trainer says to eat can they dig in. You can see the dogs at any time, but the feeding show is fun to plan for.

More Château Sights

Near the kennel, **Tintin** comic lovers can enter a series of fun rooms designed to take them into a Tintin "adventure" (called *Les Secrets de Moulinsart*—it's in French, ask for English translations); hunters can inspect an antler-filled **trophy room;** and gardeners can prowl the château's fine **kitchen and flower gardens** (free, behind the dog kennel).

Wine Tastings at the Château Gate

Opposite the entry to the château sits a slick wine-tasting room, **La Maison des Vins.** It's run by an association of 32 local vintners. Their mission: to boost the Cheverny reputation for wine (which is fruity, light, dry, and aromatic compared to the heavier, oaky wines made farther downstream). For most, the best approach is to enjoy four free tastes from featured bottles of the day, offered with helpful guidance (€6-11 bottles). Wine aficionados can pay to sample among the 96 bottles by using modern automated dispensers (3 wines-€4, 7 wines-€6.50). Even if just enjoying the free tasting, wander among the spouts. Each gives the specs of that wine in English (daily 11:00-13:15 & 14:15-19:00, open during lunch July-Aug, closed in winter, tel. 02 54 79 25 16, www. maisondesvinsdecheverny.fr).

Chaumont-sur-Loire

A castle has been located on this spot since the 11th century; the current version is a ▲▲ sight (▲▲▲ for garden or horse lovers).

The first priority at Chaumont (show-mon) was defense; the second, it seems, was gardening. Gardeners will appreciate the elaborate Festival of Gardens that unfolds next to the château every year, and modern-art lovers will enjoy how works have been incorporated into the gardens, château, and stables. If it's cold, you'll also appreciate that the château is heated in winter (rare in this region).

GETTING THERE

The train between Blois and Amboise can drop you (and your bike) in Onzain, a 25-minute roadside walk across the river to the château (14 trains/day, 10 minutes from Amboise). Other options include biking (Chaumont is about 11 level miles from Amboise or Blois), taxi (about €36 from Blois train station), or the shuttle from Blois (see "Blois Connections" on page 410).

To avoid the hike up, drivers should skip the river-level entrance (closed in winter) and park up top behind the château (open all year). From the river, drive up behind the château (direction: Montrichard); at the first roundabout follow signs to *Château* and *Festival des Jardins*.

ORIENTATION TO DOMAINE DE CHAUMONT-SUR-LOIRE

Cost and Hours: €18 combo-ticket covers château, stables, and Festival of Gardens; €14 off-season combo-ticket covers château and stables (gardens closed); open daily 10:00-20:00, Oct-mid-Nov until 18:00, mid-Nov-mid-April until 17:00, stables open 11:00-17:00, last entry 45 minutes before closing.

Information: Tel. 02 54 20 99 22, www.domaine-chaumont.fr.

Tours: A good English handout and posted explanations in each room make the €4 videoguide less essential.

Festival of Gardens: This annual exhibit, with 25 elaborate gardens arranged around a different theme each year, draws rave reviews from international gardeners. It's as impressive as the Chelsea Flower Show in England, but without the crowds—if you love contemporary garden design, you'll love this. When the festival is on, you'll find several little cafés and reasonable lunch options scattered about the hamlet. Chaumont also hosts a winter garden festival inside several greenhouses.

BACKGROUND

The Chaumont château you see today was built mostly in the 15th and 16th centuries. Catherine de' Medici forced Diane de Poitiers to swap Chenonceau for Chaumont; you'll see tidbits about both women inside.

There's a special connection to America here. Jacques-Donatien Le Ray, a rich financier who owned Chaumont in the 18th century, was a champion of the American Revolution. He used his wealth to finance loans in the early days of the new republic (and even let Benjamin Franklin use one of his homes in Paris rent-free for nine years). Unfortunately, the US never repaid the loans in full and eventually Le Ray went bankrupt.

Ironically, the American connection saved Chaumont during the French Revolution. Le Ray's son emigrated to New York and became an American citizen, but returned to France when his father deeded the castle to him. During the Revolution, he was able to turn back the crowds set on destroying Chaumont by declaring that he was now an American—and that all Americans were believers in *liberté, égalité,* and *fraternité.*

Today's château offers a good look at a top defense design from the 1500s: on a cliff with a dry moat, big and small drawbridges with classic ramparts, loopholes for archers, and handy holes through which to dump hot oil on attackers.

VISITING THE CHATEAU

Your walk through the palace—restored mostly in the 19th century—is described by the flier you'll pick up when you enter (or in more detail with the audioguide). As the château has more rooms than period furniture, your tour is peppered with modern-art exhibits that fill otherwise empty spaces. The first "period" rooms you'll visit (in the east wing) show the château as it appeared in the 15th and 16th centuries. Your visit ends in the west wing, which features furnishings from the 19th-century owners.

The castle's medieval **entry** is littered on the outside with various coats of arms. As you enter, take a close look at the two drawbridges (a new mechanism allows the main bridge to be opened with the touch of a button). Once inside, the heavy defensive feel is replaced with palatial luxury. Peek into the courtyard—during the more stable mid-1700s, the fourth wing, which had enclosed the courtyard, was taken down to give the terrace its river-valley view. The château kitchens are down the steps from the entry, though there's little of interest to see unless you enjoy wild art installations.

Entering the ground floor château rooms, signs direct you along a one-way loop path *(suite de la visite)* through the château's three wings. Catherine de' Medici, who missed her native Florence, brought a touch of Italy to all her châteaux, and her astrologer (Ruggieri) was so important that he had his own (plush) room—next to hers. **Catherine's bedroom** has a 16th-century throne—look for unicorns holding a shield. The Renaissance-style bed is a reproduction from the 19th century. Peer into the chapel below before leaving her room.

The exquisitely tiled **Salle de Conseil** has a grand fireplace and elaborate tapestries designed to keep this conference room warm. The treasury box in the **guard room** is a fine example of 1600s-era locksmithing. The lord's wealth could be locked up here as safely as possible in those days, with a false keyhole, no handles, and even an extra-secure box inside for diamonds.

The **King's room** offers a fascinating collection of medallions. Look for the case of ceramic portrait busts dating from 1772, when Le Ray invited the Italian sculptor Jean-Baptiste Nini to work for him. In addition to Marie Antoinette, Voltaire, and Catherine the Great, you'll find several medallions depicting Benjamin Franklin. A big spiral staircase leads up through many unfurnished rooms and galleries of contemporary art. Instead, head downstairs to find rooms decorated in 19th-century style. The **dining room**'s fanciful limestone fireplace is exquisitely carved. Find the food (frog legs, snails, goats for cheese), the maid with the bellows, and even the sculptor with a hammer and chisel at the top (maid and sculptor on the left). Your visit ends with a stroll through the 19th-century library, the billiards room, and the living room. The porcupines over the fireplace and elsewhere are thanks to the Duke of Orléans, who adopted the porcupine as his emblem in 1394.

In the **courtyard,** study the entertaining spouts and decor on the walls, and remember that this space was originally enclosed on all sides. Chaumont has one of the best château views of the Loire River—rivaling Amboise for its panoramic tranquility.

Veer right, leaving the château to find the **stables** *(écuries)* which were entirely rebuilt in the 1880s. The medallion above the gate reads *pour l'avenir* (for the future), which shows off an impressive commitment to horse technology. Inside, circle clockwise—you can almost hear the clip-clop of horses walking. Notice the deluxe horse stalls, padded with bins and bowls for hay, oats, and water, complete with a strategically placed drainage gutter. The horse kitchen *(cuisine des chevaux)* produced mash twice weekly for the horses, which were named for Greek gods and great châteaux. You'll also see an impressive display of riding harnesses, saddles, and several carriages parked and ready to go.

The **estate** is set in a 19th-century landscape, with woodlands and a fine lawn. More English than French, it has rolling open terrain, follies such as a water tower, and a designer *potager* (vegetable garden) with an imaginative mix of edible and decorative plants. Its trees were imported from throughout the Mediterranean world to be enjoyed—and to fend off any erosion on this strategic bluff.

West of Tours

You'll find several worthwhile sights in the area west of Tours, including Azay-le-Rideau, Langeais, Villandry, Rivau, Ussé, and the Abbaye Royale de Fontevraud. The town of Chinon makes a good home base for seeing these sights, as each is no more than a 30-minute drive away. Trains provide access to many châteaux (via Tours) but are time-consuming, so you're better off with your own car or a minivan excursion (see "Chinon Connections," later).

Chinon

This pleasing, sleepy town straddles the Vienne River and hides its ancient streets under a historic royal fortress. Henry II (Henry Plantagenet of England), Eleanor of Aquitaine, Richard the Lionheart, and Joan of Arc all called this town home for a while. Today's Chinon (shee-nohn) is best known for its popular red wines and enjoys a fraction of the visitors that Amboise does.

Orientation to Chinon

Chinon stretches out along the Vienne River, and everything of interest to travelers lies between it and the hilltop fortress. Charming Place du Général de Gaulle—ideal for café-lingering—is in the center of town. Rue Rabelais is Chinon's traffic-free shopping street, with restaurants, bars, and cafés—and is as lively as it gets in peaceful Chinon.

TOURIST INFORMATION

The **main TI** is by the river in the town center, a 15-minute walk from the train station. You'll find discounted Châteaux tickets, wine-tasting and bike-rental information, and an English-language brochure with a self-guided town walk (TI open daily 9:30-13:00 & 14:00-18:00, shorter hours and closed Sun off-season, 1 Rue Rabelais, tel. 02 47 93 17 85, www.azay-chinon-valdeloire.com). A **TI annex** is located near the fortress entrance on Rue Porte du Château (daily June-Sept 10:00–13:00 & 14:00–18:00).

HELPFUL HINTS

Market Days: A bustling market takes place all day Thursday (food in the morning only) on Place Jeanne d'Arc (east end of town). There's also a sweet little market on Saturday and Sunday mornings, around Place du Général de Gaulle.

Laundry: Salon Lavoir is near the bridge at 7 Quai Charles VII (daily 7:00-21:00).

Bike and Canoe Rental: Clan Canoë Kayak & Vélo is on the river, next to the campground (bikes-€16/day; canoes-€11/2 hours or €20/half-day, includes shuttle; €15-26 to combine bike and canoe in a half/full day; cash only, closed off-season, Quai Danton, mobile 06 23 82 96 33). For more on biking and canoeing, see "Other Chinon Activities," later.

Taxi: Call 02 47 93 37 88 or 06 50 97 87 30.

Car Rental: It's best to rent at the St-Pierre-des-Corps train station. Otherwise, ask at the TI.

Parking: You'll find metered but cheap parking in town. Or park

for free at the fortress (castle) and take the elevator down to
the town.

Traditional Riverboat Cruise: One-hour rides on flat-bottom
boats are available in high season—get the schedule at the TI
(€11, next to bike/canoe rental described earlier).

Best Views: You'll find terrific rooftop views from the fortress and
along Rue du Coteau St-Martin (between St. Mexme Church
and the fortress—see map), and rewarding river views to Chinon by crossing the bridge in the center of town and turning
right (small riverfront café May-Sept).

Chinon Walk

Chinon offers a peaceful world of quiet cobbled lanes, historic
buildings, and few tourists. Follow this self-guided walk (or the
TI's brochure) and read plaques at key buildings to gain a good
understanding of this city's historic importance.

• *Begin this short walk from the highest point of the bridge that crosses the
Vienne River, and enjoy the great view.*

Chinon Riverbank: Chinon is sandwiched between the Vienne River (which flows into the Loire River only a few miles from
here) and an abrupt cliff. People have lived along the banks of this
river since prehistoric times. The Gallo-Romans built the first defenses in Chinon 1,600 years ago, and there's been a castle up on
that hill for more than a thousand years—which pretty much predates every other castle you'll visit in the Loire area. The castle
walls are extensive: That skinny, rounded clock tower on the right
actually sits in the middle of the castle and served as a key entrance
to the the fortress during the Middle Ages. Starting in 1044, the
fortress-castle became an important outpost for the king of France,
and by 1150 Henry II Plantagenet (king of England) made this
the center of his continental empire. A few hundred years later,
Charles VII took refuge behind those walls during the Hundred
Years' War, during which Chinon was France's capital city.

Down on the water, you'll see reproductions of the traditional
wooden boats once used to shuttle merchandise up and down the
river; some boats ventured as far west as the Atlantic.

• *Walk toward the city, then make a right along the riverbank and find
the big statue that honors a famous Renaissance writer and satirist.*

Rabelais Statue: The great French writer François Rabelais
was born here in 1494. You'll see many references to him in his
proud hometown. His best-known work, *Gargantua and Pantagru-
el,* describes the amusing adventures of father-and-son giants and
was set in Chinon. Rabelais' vivid humor and savage wit are, for
many, quintessentially French—there's even a French word for it:
rabelaisien. In his bawdy tales, Rabelais critiqued society in ways

that deflected outright censorship—though the Sorbonne called his work obscene. Also a monk and a doctor, Rabelais is considered the first great French novelist, and his farces were a voice against the power of the Church and the king.

• *Turn your back on Rabelais and follow the cobbled sidewalk leading to the center of Chinon's main square.*

Place du Général de Gaulle: The town wall once sat on the wide swath of land running from this square down to the river, effectively walling the city off from the water. This explains why, even now, Chinon seems to turn its back on its river. In medieval times, the market was here, just outside the wall. The Town Hall building, originally an arcaded market, was renovated only in the 19th century. Today it flies three flags: Europe, France, and Chinon (with its three castles). From here, you can see the handy elevator that connects the town with its castle.

• *Turn left down...*

Rue Voltaire: If the old wall still stood, you'd be entering town through the east gate. Walk along a fine strip of 16th-, 17th-, and 18th-century houses to find a trio of fun wine-tasting possibilities. A half-block to the right is the funky little **Musée Animé du Vin,** at the next corner is the laid-back **Cave Voltaire wine shop,** and a right turn on the next small lane leads to **Caves Painctes** and the quarry where the stone for the castle originated (all covered later, under "Sights in Chinon").

• *Continue a few blocks farther down Rue Voltaire into the historic city center.*

Old Town: In the immediate post-WWII years, there was little money or energy to care for beautiful old towns. But in the 1960s, new laws and sensitivities kicked in, and old quarters like this were fixed up and preserved. Study the local architecture. **La Maison Rouge** (at #38) is a fine example of the town's medieval structures: a stone foundation and timber frame, filled in with whatever was handy. With dense populations crowding within the protective town walls, buildings swelled wider at the top to avoid blocking congested streets. **La Maison Bleue** next door features slate siding and looks like it belongs in Normandy. The plaque tells us that Joan of Arc dismounted her horse at this spot in 1429.

Pop into the ancient **bookshop** on the corner. I asked the owner where he got his old prints. He responded, "Did you ever enjoy a friend's mushrooms and ask him where he found them? Did he tell you?"

The **town museum** (Musée Le Carroi) is across the street. Its plaque recalls that this building housed an Estates-General meeting, convened by Charles VII, in 1428. Just around the corner, find a good tower view (and a public WC).

• *From here the street changes names to Rue Haute St-Maurice. You can*

LOIRE

continue in the same direction and find the Caves Plouzeau wine cellars at #94 (described later). If you'd rather visit the castle, turn around, walk back, and climb up Rue Jeanne d'Arc or take the elevator to the fortress.

Sights in Chinon

Forteresse Royale de Chinon

Chinon's castle (or fortress) is more ruined and older than the more famous and visited châteaux of the Loire. It comes without a hint of pleasure palace. While there's not much left, its rich history and terrific views make the castle a popular destination for historians and French tourists.

Cost and Hours: €10.50, daily 9:30-18:00, May-Aug until 19:00, Nov-Feb until 17:00, tel. 02 47 93 13 45, www.forteressechinon.fr.

Castle Tours: Your admission includes an informative self-guided tour booklet that leads you through various automated information stations. Free English-language tours can help bring the ruins to life. It's worth planning your visit around them (45 minutes, generally twice daily March-Oct, check locally for times).

Getting There: It's a bracing walk up from town, or walk behind the main square, Place du Général de Gaulle, to find the free "panoramic" elevator (and still climb 5 minutes). A free parking lot is 100 yards above the castle entry.

Background: England's King Henry II and Eleanor of Aquitaine, who ruled a vast realm from Scotland to the Spanish border, reigned from here around 1150. They had eight children (among them two future kings, including Richard the Lionheart). And it was in this castle that Joan of Arc pleaded with Charles VII to muster the courage to rally the French and take the throne back from the nasty English. Charles  had taken refuge in this well-fortified castle during the Hundred Years' War, making Chinon France's capital city during that low ebb in Gallic history.

Visiting the Castle: The castle has three structures separated by moats. Enter via the oldest part, the 12th-century Fort Saint-Georges. Crossing a dry moat, you'll land in the big courtyard of the Château du Milieu; at the far end is Fort Coudray. The fortress comes with commanding views of the town, river, and château-studded countryside.

Follow the arrows through eight stark and stony rooms, enjoying the clever teaching videos. There's a small museum devoted to the legendary Joan of Arc and her myth, developed through the centuries to inspire the French to pride and greatness. Chinon—both the city and the castle—developed as its political importance grew. It was the seat of French royalty in the 14th century. Most of the stones were quarried directly below the castle and hauled up through a well. The resulting caverns keep stores of local wine cool to this day.

WINE SIGHTS AND TASTINGS

Chinon reds are among the most respected in the Loire. Most of these places are in town and reachable on foot; the last two are outside of town and require a car.

La Cave Voltaire

At the most convenient of Chinon's wine-tasting options, English-speaking sommelier Patrice would love to help you learn about his area's wines. He serves wonderful cheese, *rillettes*, and sausage appetizers and has wines from all regions of France—but the best, of course, are from Chinon. It's a good place to come before dinner or for a light meal. The ambience inside is wine-shop cozy, but the tables outside are hard to resist (daily 10:30-23:30, Nov-March closed Mon, near Place du Général de Gaulle at 13 Rue Voltaire, tel. 02 47 93 37 68).

Caves Plouzeau

This place offers an opportunity to walk through long, atmospheric *caves*—complete with mood lighting—that extend under the château to a (literally) cool tasting room and reasonably priced wines (free tasting, €7-15/bottle, Tue-Sat 11:00-13:00 & 15:00-19:00, closed Sun-Mon, Oct-March shorter hours and closed Sun-Wed, at the western end of town on 94 Rue Haute St-Maurice, tel. 02 47 93 16 34, www.plouzeau.com).

Caves Painctes

At this *cave*, summer travelers can sample Chinon wines and walk through the cool quarry from which stones for the castle and town's houses were cut. This rock (tuff) is soft and easily quarried, and when exposed to oxygen, it hardens. The *caves*, 300 feet directly below the castle, were dug as the castle was built. Its stones were hauled directly up to the building site with a treadmill-powered hoist. Converted to wine cellars in the 15th century, the former quarry is a pilgrimage site of sorts for admirers of Rabelais, who featured it prominently in his writings. The English tour takes about an hour and includes a 20-minute video and a tasting of three local wines. Designed to promote Chinon wines, it's run by a local winemakers' association (€3; July-Aug Tue-Sun at 11:00, 15:00,

LOIRE

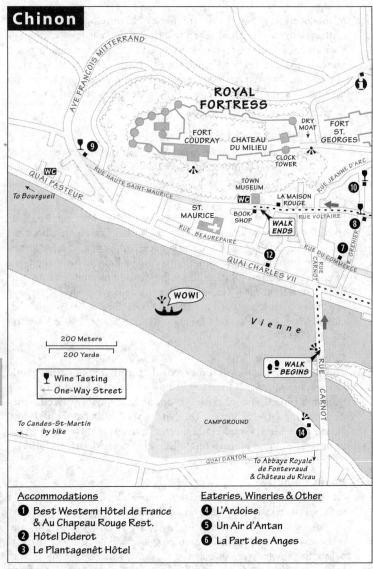

Chinon

ROYAL FORTRESS

FORT COUDRAY

CHATEAU DU MILIEU

DRY MOAT

FORT ST. GEORGES

CLOCK TOWER

AVE FRANÇOIS MITTERRAND

RUE HAUTE SAINT-MAURICE

QUAI PASTEUR

WC

To Bourgueil

TOWN MUSEUM

WC

ST. MAURICE

BOOK SHOP

LA MAISON ROUGE

RUE JEANNE D'ARC

RUE VOLTAIRE

WALK ENDS

RUE BEAUREPAIRE

RUE DU COMMERCE

QUAI CHARLES VII

RUE CARNOT

Vienne

WOW!

WALK BEGINS

RUE CARNOT

200 Meters
200 Yards

♀ Wine Tasting
← One-Way Street

To Candes-St-Martin
by bike

CAMPGROUND

QUAI DANTON

To Abbaye Royale
de Fontevraud
& Château du Rivau

LOIRE

Accommodations
1 Best Western Hôtel de France
  & Au Chapeau Rouge Rest.
2 Hôtel Diderot
3 Le Plantagenêt Hôtel

Eateries, Wineries & Other
4 L'Ardoise
5 Un Air d'Antan
6 La Part des Anges

16:30, and 18:00; closed Sept-June and Mon year-round; off Rue
Voltaire on Impasse des Caves Painctes, tel. 02 47 93 30 44).

Château du Petit Thouars

Château du Petit Thouars offers a fun wine-tasting experience just
10 minutes west of Chinon (near Abbaye Royale de Fontevraud),
featuring a castle and vineyards that produce fine white, rosé, and
red wines. You can drop by for a free tasting, or better yet, book

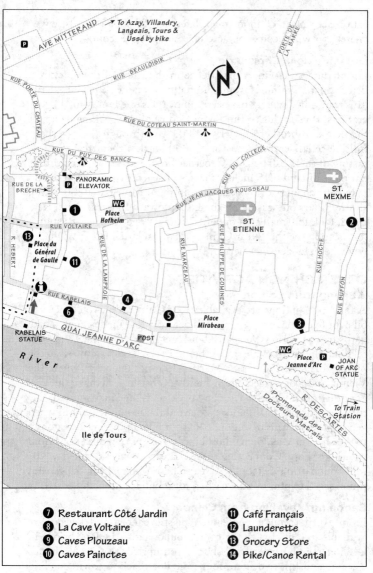

7 Restaurant Côté Jardin
8 La Cave Voltaire
9 Caves Plouzeau
10 Caves Painctes
11 Café Français
12 Launderette
13 Grocery Store
14 Bike/Canoe Rental

ahead for a tour and be greeted by the friendly, young, and English-fluent castle owners (French Sébastien and Canadian D'Arcy) who are as excited about this place as you are. Both understand the art of wine-making and love sharing their knowledge (€5 for basic vineyards tour and tasting, €15 for more elaborate tasting and cellar tour, €40 for memorable and family-friendly picnic and tasting package, closed Sun; well-signed in St-Germain sur Vienne and La Chausée area—follow the dirt road to the castle; for location see "Near Chinon" map, later; tel. 02 47 95 96 40, www.chateaudptwines.com, contact@chateaudptwines.com).

Domaine de la Chevalerie

For an authentic winery experience in the thick of the vineyards, drive about 25 minutes from Chinon to Domaine de la Chevalerie. This traditional winery has been run by the same family for 14 generations. If you're lucky, fun-loving and English-speaking daughter Stéphanie or brother Olivier will take you through the cavernous hillside cellars crammed with 180,000 bottles, then treat you to a tasting of their 100 percent Cabernet Franc reds from seven different plots of land (€15 includes tastes of several wines, drop in and take your chances or book an appointment Mon-Sat 10:00-18:30, shorter hours off-season; off the D-35, toward Langeais from Restigné, look for small sign on left, 7 Rue du Peu Muleau, Restigné; for location see the "Near Chinon" map, later, tel. 02 47 97 46 32, www.domainedelachevalerie.fr).

OTHER CHINON ACTIVITIES
▲Biking from Chinon

A few good options are available from Chinon, but you'll need to bike for five miles on regular roads before riding on designated bike paths to destinations you care about (get maps from the TI or your bike shop). A reasonable ride—thanks to the level terrain—is to the pretty village of Candes-St-Martin (10 miles one way), where the Vienne and Loire rivers meet. Hardy cyclists can manage the longer ride from Chinon to Ussé and back, and some may want to venture even farther to Villandry. To avoid the monumental hill when leaving town in this direction, take your bike in the free elevator up to the château level, then follow bike icon signs (get directions from your bike shop). Connecting these château towns is a full-day, 40-mile round-trip ride (see the "Near Chinon" map, later, for general route; see "Helpful Hints," earlier, for rental location and costs).

Canoeing/Kayaking from Chinon

From April through September, plastic canoes and kayaks are available to rent next to the campground across the lone bridge in Chinon. The outfitters will shuttle you upriver to tiny Anché for a scenic and fun two-hour, four-mile float back to town—ending with great Chinon fortress views. They also offer a 10-mile, half-day float that starts in Chinon and ends downriver in the sweet little village of Candes-St-Martin. Or do your own biathlon by canoeing one way and biking back (see "Helpful Hints," earlier, for rental location and costs).

Nighttime in Chinon

Café Français, run by Jean François (a.k.a. "Jeff"), is a character-istic local hangout and *the* place for late-night fun in this sleepy town (open Tue-Sat from 18:00 and Sun from 19:00 until you shut it down, closed Mon year-round and Sun off-season, live music less likely off-season, behind Town Hall at 37 Rue des Halles, tel. 02 47 93 32 78).

CHATEAUX NEAR CHINON

The best châteaux within day-trip distance of Chinon are Azay-le-Rideau (on an island in a river), Langeais (imposing 15th-century fortress), and Villandry (amazing gardens)—all covered in their own sections later in this chapter. But the following châteaux are closer and worth consideration.

Château du Rivau

Gleaming white and medieval, this château sits wedged between wheat and sunflower fields, and makes for a memorable 15-minute drive from Chinon. Its owners have spared little expense in their decades-long renovation of the 15th-century castle and its exten-sive gardens. The 14 different flower and vegetable gardens and orchards are kid-friendly (with elf and fairy guides) and lovingly tended with art installations, topiaries, hammocks, birds, a maze, and more (the medieval castle interior is skippable). The stables near the entry show projections about "Heroic Horses" from his-tory (with English subtitles) and an overview of the gardens across the seasons. A good little café serves reasonable meals in a lovely setting.

LOIRE

Cost and Hours: €11, daily 10:00-18:00, May-Sept until 19:00, closed Nov-March, skip the unnecessary audioguide, in Lémeré on D-749—from Chinon follow *Richelieu* signs, then signs to the château; tel. 02 47 95 77 47, www.chateaudurivau.com.

Ussé

This château, famous as an inspiration for Charles Perrault's classic version of the Sleeping Beauty story, is worth a quick photo stop for its fairy-tale turrets and gardens, but don't bother touring the interior of this pricey pearl. The best view, with reflections and a golden-slipper picnic spot, is just across the bridge.

Cost and Hours: €15, daily 10:00-19:00, mid-Feb-March and Sept-mid-Nov until 18:00, closed in winter, along D-7 20 minutes north of Chinon on the Indre River, tel. 02 47 95 54 05, www.chateaudusse.fr.

Sleeping in Chinon

Hotels are a good value in Chinon. If you stay overnight here, walk out to the river and cross the bridge for a floodlit view of the château walls.

$ Best Western Hôtel de France*** offers good comfort in 28 rooms on Chinon's best square; many have partial views of the fortress (family rooms and suites, several rooms have balconies over the square, some have thin walls, nice courtyard terrace, air-con, easy pay parking near the hotel, 49 Place du Général de Gaulle, tel. 02 47 93 33 91, www.bestwestern-hoteldefrance-chinon.com, hoteldefrance@bw-chinon.fr).

$ Hôtel Diderot,** a handsome 18th-century manor house on the eastern edge of town, is the closest hotel I list to the train sta-

tion. The hotel, run by Floridian Jamie and her French husband Jean-Pierre, surrounds a carefully planted courtyard (where you'll park). Rooms in the main building vary in size and decor, but all are well maintained, with personal touches. Ground-floor rooms come with private patios. The four good family rooms have connecting rooms, each with a private bathroom (limited pay parking, 4 Rue de Buffon, drivers should look for signs from Place Jeanne d'Arc, tel. 02 47 93 18 87, www.hoteldiderot.com, hoteldiderot@hoteldiderot.com).

$ Le Plantagenêt*** has 33 comfortable rooms and may have space when others don't. There's a peaceful garden courtyard—picnics encouraged if you buy drinks from hotel—and an onsite washer/dryer. Superior rooms in *Maison Bourgeoise* have a more historic feel (air-con, 12 Place Jeanne d'Arc, tel. 02 47 93 36 92, www.hotel-plantagenet.com, resa@hotel-plantagenet.com).

OUTSIDE CHINON, NEAR LIGRÉ

$$ Le Clos de Ligré lets you sleep in peace, surrounded by vineyards and farmland. A 10-minute drive from Chinon, it has room to roam, a large pool, and a *salon* library room with a baby grand piano. English-speaking Martine offers cavernous and creatively decorated rooms (good family rooms, includes big breakfast, €35 dinner serves up the works in a traditional setting, cash only, 37500 Ligré, tel. 02 47 93 95 59, mobile 06 61 12 45 55, www.le-clos-de-ligre.com, descamps.ligre@gmail.com). From Chinon, drive toward Richelieu on D-749, turn right on D-115 at the *Ligré par le vignoble* sign, and continue for about five kilometers. Turn left, following signs to *Ligré*; at the Dozon winery turn left and look for signs to *Le Clos de Ligré* (see the "Near Chinon" map, later).

Eating in Chinon

For a low-stress meal with ambience, choose one of the cafés on the photogenic Place du Général de Gaulle. Unless otherwise noted, these restaurants are closed Sunday and Monday.

$$ Au Chapeau Rouge offers a traditional and elegant *gastronomique* experience in a lovely dining room or at outdoor tables facing the square. Regional products are used in creative specialties: Try *poires tapées* (dried local pears) or the decadent *déclinaison autour de la fraise*—a strawberry dessert medley (reservations recommended, 49 Place du Général de Gaulle, tel. 02 47 98 08 08, www.auchapeaurouge.fr).

$$ L'Ardoise means "the chalkboard," which is how the menu is presented, reflecting the bistro feel of the place. Dine here to sample carefully prepared, stylishly presented regional cuisine in a lively dining room (reservations smart, 42 Rue Rabelais, tel. 02 47 58 48 78, www.lardoisechinon.com).

$ Un Air d'Antan is a tiny, easygoing diner with tasty cuisine at amazing prices, a fun interior, and small patio (54 Bis Rue Rabelais, tel. 02 47 95 37 52).

$$ La Part des Anges is an intimate two-person love affair with food in a charming setting. Virginie creates contemporary cuisine based on timeless French technique while husband Hervé serves with aplomb and manages the baby (good lunch options, limited outdoor seating, closed Mon-Tue, 5 Rue Rabelais, tel. 02 47 93 99 93).

$ Restaurant Côté Jardin is an unprententious place that's all about welcoming service and traditional French cuisine at low prices. The owner is a retired butcher, so expect ample meat dishes. Along with regional specialties, you'll find French classics such as coq au vin and *coquilles St. Jacques* (scallops). Linger in the secluded garden courtyard and order one of the best deals in town—the €15 *menu* that includes a starter, the *plat du jour*, and dessert (30 Rue du Commerce, tel. 02 47 93 10 97).

Groceries: Carrefour City is across from the Hôtel de Ville, on Place du Général de Gaulle (Mon-Sat 7:00-21:00, Sun 9:00-13:00).

NEAR CHINON

For a memorable countryside meal, drive 25 minutes to **$$ Etape Gourmande** at Domaine de la Giraudière, in Villandry (see listing on page 440). A trip here combines well with visits to Villandry and Azay-le-Rideau.

LOIRE

Chinon Connections

By Minivan to Loire Châteaux: Acco-Dispo, Loire Valley Tours, Touraine Evasion, and A La Française Tours offer fixed-itinerary minivan excursions from Tours (see "Amboise Connections" on page 394). Take the train to Tours from Chinon (see next), or get several travelers together to book your own van from Chinon.

By Train/Bus to Tours: Trains and SNCF buses link Chinon daily with **Tours** (8/day, 1 hour, connections to other châteaux and minibus excursions from Tours) and to the regional rail hub of St-Pierre-des-Corps in suburban Tours (TGV trains to distant destinations, and the fastest way to Paris). Traveling by train to the nearby châteaux (except for Azay-le-Rideau) requires careful schedule coordination with a transfer in Tours and healthy walks from the stations to the châteaux. Fewer trains run on weekends.

To Loire Châteaux: **Azay-le-Rideau** (7/day, 20 minutes direct, plus long walk to château, or take SNCF bus to town center, www.oui.sncf/bus), **Langeais** (8/day, 2 hours, transfer in Tours), **Amboise** (7/day, 2 hours, transfer in Tours), **Chenonceau** (4/day, 2 hours, transfer in Tours), **Blois** (6/day, 2 hours, transfer in Tours and possibly in St-Pierre-des-Corps).

To Destinations Beyond the Loire: **Paris Gare Montparnasse** (8/day, 3-4 hours, transfer in Tours and sometimes also St-Pierre-des-Corps), **Sarlat-la-Canéda** (1/day, 7 hours, change at St-Pierre-des-Corps, then TGV to Libourne or Bordeaux-St. Jean, then train through Bordeaux vineyards to Sarlat), **Pontorson/Mont St-Michel** (1/day, 8 hours with change at Tours main station, Le Mans, and Rennes, then bus from Rennes), **Bayeux** (2/day, 6-8 hours with change in Tours and Caen, more via Tours, St-Pierre-des-Corps, and Paris leaving from Gare St. Lazare).

Azay-le-Rideau

This charming 16th-century château, worth ▲▲, sparkles on an island in the Indre River, its image romantically reflected in the slow-moving waters. The build-ing is a prime example of an early-Renaissance château. With no defensive purpose, it was built simply for luxurious living in a luxurious setting. The ornamental facade is perfectly harmonious, and the interior—with its grand staircases and elegant loggias—is Italian-inspired. The

château stays open late in summer, with mood lighting and music to accompany your visit.

Azay-le-Rideau (ah-zay luh ree-doh) is also the name of the endearing little town, with a small but pleasing pedestrian zone and a fine boutique hotel. It's one of the best bases for bike riders, with its designated bike paths and small roads to nearby châteaux.

Tourist Information: Azay-le-Rideau's TI is just below Place de la République, a block to the right of the post office (July-Aug daily 9:30-19:00; April-June and Sept daily 9:30-13:00 & 14:00-18:00; shorter hours Oct-March; 4 Rue du Château, tel. 02 47 45 44 40, www.azay-chinon-valdeloire.com). The TI sells reduced-price tickets to all area châteaux and offers info for bike rentals.

GETTING THERE

Azay-le-Rideau is served by both SNCF trains and buses from Tours (7/day, 30 minutes) and Chinon (7/day, 20 minutes). Buses stop in the city center and save you the long half-mile walk from the train station (see "Chinon Connections," earlier). From Amboise, it's a doable but long train ride (7/day, 1.5 hours, transfer in Tours). From Azay's station, it's about a 25-minute walk to the town center (taxi tel. 02 47 45 96 42 or 06 17 76 42 92). Walk down from the station, turn left, and follow *Centre-Ville* signs. Drivers can head for the château and park there.

ORIENTATION TO CHATEAU D'AZAY-LE-RIDEAU

Cost and Hours: €11, daily 9:30-18:00—July-Aug until 23:00, Oct-March 10:00-17:15, last entry one hour before closing, storage lockers. The château stays open late in summer with fun mood lighting and music to accompany your visit.

Information: Tel. 02 47 45 42 04, www.azay-le-rideau.fr.

Tours: The free and helpful château plan, combined with excellent explanations posted in all rooms, makes the €3 audioguide unnecessary except for serious students.

BACKGROUND

The château was built between 1518 and 1527 by a filthy-rich banker—Gilles Berthelot, treasurer to the king of France. The structure has a delightfully feminine touch: Because Gilles was often away for work, his wife, Philippa, supervised the construction. The castle was so lavish that the king, François I, took note, giving it the ultimate compliment: He seized it, causing its owner to flee. Because this château survived the Revolution virtually unscathed, its interior capably demonstrates three centuries of royal styles. The French government purchased it in 1905.

LOIRE

Near Chinon

Accommodations
1 To Le Clos de Ligré
2 Hôtel la Croix Blanche & Le Plantagenet Rest.

Eateries
3 Etape Gourmande at Domaine de la Giraudière
4 Le Saut aux Loups Mushroom Caves & Restaurant

Wine Tasting
5 Château du Petit Thouars
6 Domaine de la Chevalerie

LOIRE

VISITING THE CHATEAU

The château plan guides you in and around the château, starting inside on the first floor up. Rooms are elaborately furnished and decorated but not dissimilar to others you may see in this region. You'll climb to the castle attic *(comble)*, wander under a strikingly beautiful roof support cut from 500-year-old oak trees, and learn about the resident bats hanging around the room (now that's original). Then work your way down through more sumptuous Renaissance rooms loaded with elaborate tapestries, colossal fireplaces, and intricately carved wood chests. Pause to admire the king's portrait gallery in the "Apartement du XVII Siècle" (three Louis, three Henrys, and François I).

For many, the highlight of a visit is the romantic garden, designed in the 19th century to enhance the already beautiful château. Take a spin on the path around the castle to enjoy romantic views and find the rare-in-France sequoia and cedar trees.

TOWN OF AZAY-LE-RIDEAU

The town's appealing center may convince you to set up here. It works well as a base for visiting sights west of Tours by car or bike

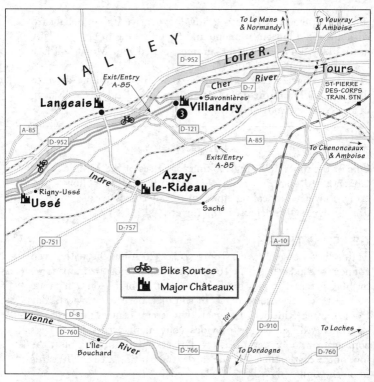

(but not by train, as the station is a half-mile walk from the town center). It's also close to the A-85 autoroute, offering drivers reasonable access to châteaux near Amboise.

Sleeping: Ideally located on a traffic-free street between Place de la République (easy parking) and the château, **$$ Hôtel de Biencourt***** is a good choice. This sharp yet affordable hotel has thoughtfully appointed rooms, a pleasing garden terrace, and a calming lounge area (some rooms with air-con, no elevator, shared fridge, picnics OK on terrace, closed mid-Nov-late March, 7 Rue de Balzac, tel. 02 47 45 20 75, www.hotelbiencourt.com, contact@hotelbiencourt.fr, helpful owners Xavier and Bruno).

Eating: The village has shops with all you need to create a fine picnic. As for restaurants, you'll find fresh and creative cuisine and reasonable prices at **$$ Côté Cour.** Friendly Sandrine offers a few select choices—local products and mostly organic foods—served in a warm interior or on a great outdoor terrace (closed Tue for dinner and all day Wed, facing the château gate at 19 Rue Balzac, tel. 02 47 45 30 36).

$$ La Ripaille has a large selection of dishes (à la carte only) and a generous courtyard terrace (at the foot of the château's access lane, 5 Rue de Pineau, tel. 02 47 52 81 89).

$ L'Epicerie de Julie is a tiny, inexpensive Italian deli-bistro with a limited but cheap menu and friendly Julie in charge (daily until 19:00, longer hours in summer, closed Sun-Mon, 17 Place Gambetta, tel. 02 47 42 06 45).

If you have a car, seriously consider the 15-minute drive to dine at **$$$ Domaine de la Giraudière** in Villandry (see "Eating in and Near Villandry," later).

Langeais

One of the most imposing-looking fortresses of the Middle Ages, Château de Langeais—rated ▲—was built mostly for show. Towering above its appealing little village, it comes with a moat, a drawbridge, lavish defenses, and turrets.

GETTING THERE

Trains link Langeais with Tours (7/day, 20 minutes), with seven connections a day between Tours and Chinon (most by train, some by SNCF bus, 2 hours total, just as fast by bike—on a separate path—for experienced riders). In summer, buses run twice a day from Azay-le-Rideau to Langeais (www.remi-centrevaldeloire.fr).

The A-85 autoroute provides convenient access for drivers coming from points east or west. Drivers should turn right at the foot of the castle, then hug the castle; the parking area is 200 yards in on the right.

ORIENTATION TO CHATEAU DE LANGEAIS

Cost and Hours: €10, daily July-Aug 9:00-19:00, April-June and Sept-mid-Nov 9:30-18:30, mid-Nov-March 10:00-17:00, last entry one hour before closing, tel. 02 47 96 72 60, www. chateau-de-langeais.com.

Eating: The château is within easy walking distance of several cafés and restaurants.

BACKGROUND

Langeais occupies a key site on the Loire River, 15 miles downstream on the road to Tours (which for a time was the French capital), and about halfway from Paris along the trading route to Brittany and the Atlantic. This location made Langeais a player in historic events, though the only remaining part of the original castle is the thousand-year-old tower standing across from the castle's garden. (That

castle, an English stronghold, was destroyed by the French king in the Hundred Years' War.)

The "new" castle, built in the 15th century, dates from the age of cannons, which would have made quick work of its tough-looking facade. In fact, the imposing walls were mostly for show. This is a transitional piece of architecture: part medieval and part Renaissance. The mullioned windows overlooking the courtyard indicate this was a fancy residence more than a defensive fortress. While Langeais makes a show of its defenses, castles built just 50 years later (such as Azay-le-Rideau) give not a hint of fortification.

VISITING THE CHATEAU

The interior is late Middle Ages chic. It's the life's work of a 19th-century owner who was a lover of medieval art. He decorated and furnished the rooms with 15th- and 16th-century artifacts or good facsimiles. Most of what you see is modern-made in 16th-century style.

Langeais tries hard to give visitors a feel for royal life in the 15th century—and it succeeds. The palace is decked out as palaces were—designed to impress, and ready to pack and move. The rooms are well-furnished and well-explained with handy information sheets. The video in the first room sets the stage for your visit. Here's a sampling of what you'll see.

The **banquet room** table would have groaned with food and luxury items—but just one long, communal napkin and no forks. Belgian tapestries on the walls still glimmer with 500-year-old silk thread. In an upstairs **bedroom,** it looks like the master has just left—gloves and other accessories are lying on the bedcovers, and shoes sit below the bed. There were bedrooms for show, and bedrooms for sleeping.

As you wander, notice how the rooms—with hanging tapestries, foldable chairs, and big chests with handles—could have been set up in a matter of hours. Big-time landowners circulated through their domains, moving every month or so. Also notice how each piece of furniture had multiple uses—such as a throne that doubled as a writing desk.

In the so-called **Wedding Hall,** wax figures re-create the historic marriage that gave Langeais its 15 minutes of château fame in 1491. It was here that King Charles VIII secretly wed 14-year-old Anne (duchess of Brittany), a union that brought independent Brittany into France's fold. The gowns are accurate and impressive, and it's interesting to see how short everyone was in the Middle Ages. An eight-minute sound-and-light show explains the event—usually in English at :15 past each hour.

The top-floor museum has a rare series of 16th-century **tapestries** featuring nine heroes—biblical, Roman, and medieval. This

LOIRE

is one of just three such sets in existence, with seven of the original nine scenes surviving.

Finish your visit by enjoying commanding **town views** from the ramparts.

Villandry

Château de Villandry (vee-lahn-dree) is famous for its extensive gardens, considered to be the best in the Loire Valley, and possibly all of France. Its château is an aver-age Loire palace, but the grounds— arranged in elaborate geometric patterns and immaculately main-tained—make it a ▲▲ sight (worth ▲▲▲ for gardeners). Still, if you're visiting anyway, it's worth the extra euros to tour the château as well.

GETTING THERE
In summer, buses run twice a day from the train station in Tours to Villandry, though the best option for most is to take a minivan excursion from Amboise or Tours (see "Amboise Connections" on page 394). Tours is easily accessible by train from Amboise (25 minutes) and Chinon (1 hour). Villandry is a popular bike destination (2 hours from Chinon, 1 hour from Azay-le-Rideau).

Drivers will find free parking located across from the entry (hide valuables in your trunk).

ORIENTATION TO CHATEAU DE VILLANDRY
Cost and Hours: €11, €7 for gardens only, daily 9:00-19:00, March and Oct until 18:00, Nov-Feb until 17:00.

Information: Tel. 02 47 50 02 09, www.chateauvillandry.fr.

Tours: The excellent handout leads you through the château's 19th-century rooms. Skip the unnecessary audioguide.

Services: Storage lockers are available.

Gardens: You can stay as late as you like in the gardens, though you must enter before the ticket office closes and exit through the back gate after 19:00.

BACKGROUND
Finished in 1536, Villandry was the last great Renaissance châ-teau built on the Loire. It's yet another pet project of a fabulously wealthy finance minister of François I—Jean le Breton. While serving as ambassador to Italy, Jean picked up a love of Italian Re-

naissance gardens. When he took over this property, he razed the 12th-century castle (keeping only the old tower), put up his own château, and installed a huge Italian-style garden. The château was purchased in 1906 by the present owner's great-grandfather, and the garden—a careful reconstruction of what the original might have been—is the result of three generations of passionate dedication.

VISITING THE CHATEAU AND GARDENS

The **château**'s 19th-century rooms feel so lived-in that you'll wonder if the family just stepped out to get their poodle bathed. Don't miss the 15-minute *Four Seasons of Villandry* slideshow just inside the château. With period music and no narration, it delivers a glimpse at the gardens throughout the year in a relaxing little theater (ask at the ticket window or you may miss it). The literal high point of your château visit is the spiral climb to the top of the keep—the only surviving part of the medieval castle—where you'll find a 360-degree view of the gardens, village, and surrounding countryside. The extra cost for visiting the château seems worth it when you take in the panorama.

The lovingly tended **gardens** are well-described by your handout. Follow its recommended route through the four garden types. The 10-acre Renaissance garden, inspired by the 1530s Italian-style original, is full of symbolism. Even the herb and vegetable sections are put together with artistic flair. The earliest Loire gardens were practical, grown by medieval abbey monks who needed vegetables to feed their community and medicinal herbs to cure their ailments. And those monks liked geometrical patterns. Later Italian influence brought decorative ponds, tunnels, and fountains. Harmonizing the flowers and vegetables was an innovation of 16th-century Loire châteaux. This example is the closest we have to that garden style. Who knew that lentils, chives, and cabbages could look this good?

The 85,000 plants—half of which come from the family greenhouse—are replanted twice a year by 10 full-time gardeners. They use modern organic methods: ladybugs instead of pesticides and a whole lot of hoeing. The place is as manicured as a putting green—just try to find a weed. Stroll under the grapevine trellis, through a good-looking salad zone, and among Anjou pears (from the nearby region of Angers). If all the topiary and straight angles seem too rigid, look for the sun garden in the back of the estate, which has "wilder" perennial borders favored by the Brits. Charts posted throughout identify everything in English.

Bring bread for the piranha-like carp who prowl the fanciful moat. Like the carp swimming around other Loire châteaux, they're so voracious, they'll gather at your feet to frantically eat

LOIRE

your spit. Don't miss the fine views from the Belvedere lookout (near the garden exit).

EATING IN AND NEAR VILLANDRY

The pleasant little village of Villandry has several cafés and restaurants, a small grocery store, and a bakery.

$$ Etape Gourmande at Domaine de la Giraudière offers a wonderfully rustic farmhouse dining experience. Gentle owner Alexandra takes time with every client and the country-gourmet cuisine is simply delicious. Choose just a starter and dessert, a starter and main course, or all three if you're starved. The dining room is hunting-lodge cozy, and there's lovely outdoor seating under the shade of generous trees (daily 12:00-14:30 & 19:30-21:00, closed mid-Nov-mid-March, reservations smart, a half-mile from Villandry's château toward Druye; for location see the "Near Chinon" map, earlier; tel. 02 47 50 08 60, www.letapegourmande.com). This place works well for lunch, as it's well-signed between Villandry and Azay-le-Rideau on D-121.

Abbaye Royale de Fontevraud

The Royal Abbey of Fontevraud (fohn-tuh-vroh) is a 15-minute journey west from Chinon. This once vast 12th-century abbey provides keen insight into medieval monastic life. The "abbey" was actually a 12th-century monastic city, the largest such compound in Europe—with four monastic complexes, all within a fortified wall.

ORIENTATION

Cost and Hours: €12; daily April-Oct 9:30-19:00, Nov-March until 18:00, closed Jan and on major holidays.

Information: Tel. 02 41 51 73 52, www.fontevraud.fr.

Tours: English information panels are posted throughout the abbey, making the well-done, €4.50 audioguide a little less essential. Kids love the iPad "treasure hunt" (€4.50). You can also buy the simple but useful English booklet.

Parking: Parking here is confusing. Follow *Parking Abbaye* signs, then signs toward *Hôtel de la Croix Blanche,* and park as close to the abbey as you can (you may end up parking by private apartments—that's OK).

BACKGROUND

The order of Fontevraud, founded in 1101, was an experiment of rare audacity. This was a double monastery, where both men and women lived under the authority of an abbess while observing the rules of St. Benedict (but influenced by the cult of the Virgin Mary). Men and women lived separately and chastely within the abbey walls. The order thrived, and in the 16th century, this was the administrative head of more than 150 monasteries. Four communities lived within these walls until the Revolution. In 1804, Napoleon made the abbey a prison, which actually helped preserve the building. It functioned as a prison for 150 years, until 1963, with five wooden floors filled with cells. Designed to house 800 inmates, the prison was notoriously harsh. Life expectancy here was eight months.

VISITING THE ABBEY

Follow *sens de la visite* signs to tour the abbey (basically clockwise).

Your visit begins in the bright, 12th-century, Romanesque **abbey church.** Sit inside on the steps, savor the ethereal setting, and feel the weight of this Romanesque structure. Appreciate the finely carved capitals and have fun with the clever touch-screen monitors. At the end of the nave are four painted sarcophagi belonging to Eleanor of Aquitaine; her second husband, Henry II, the first of England's Plantagenet kings; their son Richard the Lionheart; and his sister-in-law. These are the tops of the sarcophagi only. Even though we know these Plantagenets were buried here (because they gave lots

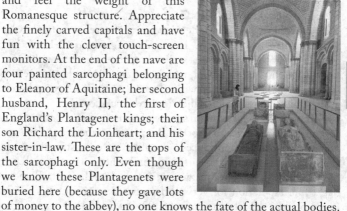

of money to the abbey), no one knows the fate of the actual bodies.

You'll leave the church through the right transept into the big **cloister.** This was the center of the abbey, where the nuns read, exercised, checked Facebook, and washed their hands. While visiting the abbey, remember that monastic life was extremely simple: nothing but prayers, readings, and work. Daily rations were a loaf of bread and a half-liter of wine per person, plus soup and smoked fish. English information panels in this section change regularly, covering different themes about life at the abbey.

Next is the **chapter house,** where the nuns' meetings took place. Renaissance paintings feature portraits of the women who ran this abbey, wearing black habits. The **community room/ treasury** comes next. The only heated room in the abbey, it's where the nuns embroidered linen and where today you'll see gripping fragments from a 12th-century Last Judgment and other important abbey treasures—as well as excellent information on the history of the abbey.

Climb steps up to see the cavernous **Grand Dortoir** (dormitory), where hundreds of monks could sleep. An adjacent room offers rotating exhibits usually well described in English. Back down the steps, the **refectory,** built to feed 400 silent monks at a time, was later the prison work yard, where inmates built wooden chairs (exposition rooms above provide insight into this period).

Your abbey visit continues with the unusual, honeycombed, 12th-century **kitchen** (accessed from outside), with five bays covered by 18 chimneys to evacuate smoke. It likely served as a smokehouse for fish farmed in the abbey ponds. Abbeys like this were industrious places, but focused on self-sufficiency rather than trade.

Finish your visit with a refreshment at the **garden café** or in the fancy hotel below and contemplate a wander through the abbey's **medicinal gardens.**

SLEEPING AND EATING

$$$ Hôtel la Croix Blanche*** welcomes travelers with flowery terraces and cushy comfort. This ambitious restaurant-hotel, just outside the abbey, combines a stylish hunting-lodge feel with comfortable public spaces, a pool, and 24 rooms (Place Plantagenêts—see the "Near Chinon" map, earlier; tel. 02 41 51 71 11, www.hotel-croixblanche.com, bonjour@hotel-croixblanche.com).

The abbey faces the main square of a charming little town with several handy eateries, a grocery shop, and a wine bar. The *boulangerie* opposite the entrance to the abbey serves tasty quiche and sandwiches at good prices, but you'll find other options as well.

$$ Le Plantagenet restaurant at the Hôtel la Croix Blanche has a fine reputation for very well-prepared cuisine at fair prices (daily, 5 Place des Plantagenets, tel. 02 41 51 71 11).

NEAR FONTEVRAUD: MUSHROOM CAVES

For an unusual fungus find close to the abbey of Fontevraud, visit the mushroom caves called **Le Saut aux Loups.** France is one of the world's top mushroom producers, so mushrooms matter. Climb to a cliff ledge and enter 16 chilly rooms bored into limestone to discover everything about the care and nurturing of mushrooms. You'll see them raised in planters, plastic bags, logs, and straw bales, and you'll learn about their incubation, pasteurization, and fermentation. Abandoned limestone quarries like this are fertile homes for mushroom cultivation, and have made the Loire Valley the mushroom capital of France since the 1800s. You'll ogle at the weird shapes and never take your 'shrooms for granted again. The growers harvest a ton of mushrooms a month in these caves; shiitakes are their most important crop. Pick up the English booklet and follow the fungus. Many visitors come only for the on-site mushroom restaurant, whose wood-fired *galipettes* (stuffed mushrooms with crème fraîche and herbs) are the kitchen's forte (€12 for three *galipettes*).

Cost and Hours: €7, daily 10:00-18:00, July-Aug until 19:00, closed mid-Nov-Feb, dress warmly, just north of Fontevraud at Montsoreau's west end along the river, for location see the "Near Chinon" map, earlier, tel. 02 41 51 70 30, www.troglosautauxloups.com.

LOIRE

DORDOGNE

Sarlat-la-Canéda • Dordogne River Valley • Cro-Magnon
Caves • Oradour-sur-Glane • St-Emilion • Rocamadour •
Lot River Valley

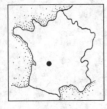

The Dordogne River Valley is a delicious brew,
blending natural and man-made beauty. Walnut orchards, tobacco plants, sunflowers, and
cornfields carpet the valley, while stone fortresses patrol the cliffs above. During much of
the on-again, off-again Hundred Years' War
this strategic river—so peaceful today—separated warring England and France. Today's
Dordogne River carries more travelers than goods, as the region's
economy relies heavily on tourism.

The joys of the Dordogne include rock-sculpted villages, formidable castles, fertile farms surrounding I-should-retire-here cottages, magnificent vistas, lazy canoe rides, and a local cuisine worth
loosening your belt for. You'll also find an amazing cache of prehistoric artifacts. Limestone caves decorated with prehistoric artwork
litter the Dordogne region.

PLANNING YOUR TIME

Although tourists inundate the region in the summer, the Dordogne's charm is protected by its relative inaccessibility. Given the
time it takes to get here by car or train, allow a minimum of two
nights (ideally three) and most of two days. Whirlwind travelers
could consider flying here: Inexpensive flights connect Paris with
the region's main city, Brive-la-Gaillarde (where you can rent a car,
one hour to Sarlat) and bullet trains link Paris with Bordeaux in
two hours (easy car rental, two-hour drive to Sarlat).

Your sightseeing obligations are prehistoric cave art; the Dordogne River Valley, with its villages and castles; the town of Sarlat-
la-Canéda (often shortened to "Sarlat," pronounced sar-lah); and,
with more time, the less-traveled Lot River Valley.

Dordogne at a Glance

▲▲▲**Dordogne River Valley** A lovely mix of natural and man-made attractions, with medieval villages, lush farmland, and cliff-top fortresses—enjoyable by car or canoe. See page 466.

▲▲▲**Cro-Magnon Caves** Prehistoric caves famous throughout the world. For a rundown of options, see "Prehistoric Sights at a Glance" on page 482.

▲▲▲**Oradour-sur-Glane** Ruined village machine-gunned and burned by Nazi SS troops in 1944 and now preserved as a war memorial. See page 503.

▲▲**Sarlat-la-Canéda** Regional market town with a seductive tangle of cobblestone streets peppered with beautiful buildings and traffic-free lanes. See page 453.

▲▲**Lot River Valley** Overlooked but beautiful valley, home to dramatically situated villages like St-Cirq-Lapopie. See page 518.

▲**Eastern Dordogne** Remote and less visited area, highlighted by spectacular hill towns and the pilgrimage village of Rocamadour. See page 508.

▲**St-Emilion** Prosperous little town devoted to Bordeaux wine on the western edge of the region. See page 505.

If you're connecting the Dordogne with the Loire region by car, the fastest path is usually via the free A-20 autoroute (exit at Souillac or Brive for Sarlat-la-Canéda and nearby villages). Break up your trip from the north by stopping in the martyr village of Oradour-sur-Glane. If you're connecting the Dordogne and Carcassonne, explore the Lot River Valley on your way south (see "Route of the Bastides" on page 536). If heading west, taste the Bordeaux wine region's prettiest town, St-Emilion.

Those serious about visiting the Dordogne's best caves need to plan carefully and book ahead when possible (explained on page 490).

The following three-day itinerary is designed for drivers, but it's doable—if you're determined—by taxi rides, a canoe trip (the best way to see the Dordogne regardless of whether you've got a car), and a minivan tour.

Day 1—Sarlat-la-Canéda and the Dordogne Valley: Enjoy a morning in Sarlat (best on a market day—Sat or Wed), then spend the afternoon on a canoe trip, with time at the day's end to explore

Beynac and/or Castelnaud. If it's not market day in Sarlat, do the canoe trip, Beynac, and Castelnaud first, and enjoy the late afternoon and evening in Sarlat. (Because the town's essential sights are outdoors, my self-guided Sarlat walk works great after dinner.) The sensational views from Castelnaud's castle and Domme are best in the morning; visit Beynac's castle or viewpoint late in the day for the best light. With a little lead time, some canoe-rental companies can pick up nondrivers in Sarlat. Taxis are reasonable between Sarlat and the river villages.

Day 2—Prehistoric Caves: Your day will depend on whether you've booked the cave(s) in advance (about half the caves can be booked ahead—see details in each cave listing, later).

Lacking reservations, start your day in Les Eyzies-de-Tayac at the Prehistory Welcome Center and the National Museum of Prehistory for your cave-art introduction. From there, head to the fascinating Grotte de Rouffignac (no prebooking but you can usually get in). If you're here in July or August, reverse this plan starting with Rouffignac (to beat crowds).

Serious cave dwellers can add Lascaux II or IV replica caves which offer excellent introductions to cave art (though you need to book their tours ahead).

Without a car, this day's full list of activities is only possible by taxi or excursion tour (I list several excellent tour companies). By train, you can link Sarlat-la-Canéda and Les Eyzies-de-Tayac, though you have to transfer, and some connections aren't great.

Day 3—Other Sights: Head east and upriver to explore Rocamadour, Gouffre de Padirac, and storybook villages such as Carennac, Autoire, and Loubressac. Though Rocamadour is accessible by train and a short taxi ride, the rest of these places are feasible only with your own wheels, by taxi, or on an excursion tour.

CHOOSING A HOME BASE

Sarlat-la-Canéda is the only viable solution for train travelers. Drivers should also consider sleeping in a riverside village. For a château hotel experience that won't break the bank, sleep near the Lascaux caves at Château de la Fleunie (30 minutes north of Sarlat; see page 500). For the best view hotel I've found in the area, try Hôtel de l'Esplanade in Domme (see page 472).

GETTING AROUND THE DORDOGNE

This region is a joy with a car but tough without one. Think about renting a car for a day, renting a canoe or electric bike, or taking a minivan excursion. If you're up for a splurge, take a hot-air balloon ride.

On Your Own

By Train: Connecting the Dordogne's sights by train is hopeless. The lone helpful train runs from Sarlat-la-Canéda to Les Eyzies-de-Tayac, with the Prehistory Welcome Center and museum and the Grotte de Font-de-Gaume (2-3/day, 1-2.5 hours, transfer in Le Buisson, some long waits, 15-minute walk from station to museum, 40-minute walk from station to Font-de-Gaume cave).

By Car: Roads are small, slow, and scenic. There's no autoroute near Sarlat-la-Canéda; count on more travel time than usual. Little Sarlat is routinely snarled with traffic on market days—particularly Saturdays. You can rent a car in Sarlat (see Sarlat's "Helpful Hints," later), though bigger cities, such as Libourne, Périgueux, and Brive-la-Gaillarde, offer greater selection and drop-off flexibility. In summer (mid-June–mid-Sept), you'll pay to park in most villages' riverfront lots between 10:00 and 19:00. Leave nothing in your car at night—thieves enjoy the Dordogne, too.

By Taxi: To taxi from Sarlat-la-Canéda to Beynac or La Roque-Gageac, allow €28 one-way (€39 at night and on Sun); from Sarlat to Les Eyzies-de-Tayac, allow €47 one-way (€68 at night and on Sun). Christoph or Corinne can often pick you up within a few minutes if you call. Book your rides (even short transfers) in advance, as there are very few taxis around. **Christoph Kusters** speaks fluent English and also does tours—next page (mobile 06 08 70 61 67, www.taxialacarte.com, taxialacarte@gmail.com). Corinne Brouqui, who runs Beynac-based **Taxi Corinne,** is helpful, speaks a little English, and is eager to provide good service (can provide regional as well as local transport, tel. 05 53 29 42 07, mobile 06 72 76 03 32).

By Bike: Cyclists find the Dordogne beautiful but hilly, with lots of traffic on key roads with no bike lanes. You can pick up a basic bike for the day in Sarlat-la-Canéda; serious riders will be impressed with **Liberty Bike**'s services and **Aquitaine Bike**'s fleet and tours (described later, under Sarlat's "Helpful Hints"). The most pleasing ride is along the abandoned rail line that starts just outside Sarlat and runs to Souillac.

By Boat: Nondrivers should rent a canoe, my favorite way to explore a small but gorgeous slice of this region. A canoe offers easy access to the river's sights and villages at your own pace, and some canoe companies will pick you up in Sarlat-la-Canéda for no extra charge (based on their schedule). Because a canoe costs only

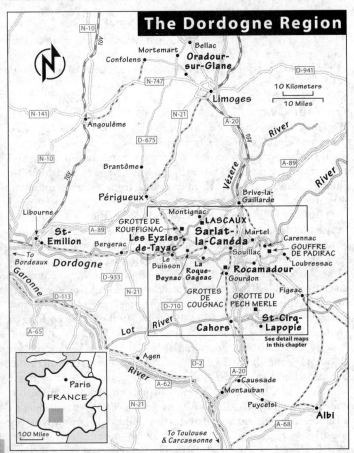

The Dordogne Region

DORDOGNE

about €20/person (for the trip I recommend), and you can spend all day on and off the river touring sights I cover, this is a swimmingly good deal. For the same scenery with less work (and no ability to visit villages and castles en route), you can take a boat cruise from Beynac or La Roque-Gageac (€10).

WITH A TOUR

Custom Taxi/Minivan Excursions

You have several good options. Book the first two companies listed well ahead as they are popular.

Private Tours: Gentle **Christoph** and lively **Sarissa Kusters** speak flawless English and provide top service in their Wi-Fi-equipped Mercedes van (7 people) or Tesla SUV (6 people), whether you need a taxi from the train station in Sarlat-la-Canéda to the town center, a pickup in Paris or Oradour-sur-Glane, or a day-long tour. They can organize your trip, book cave visits, and give good running commentary. Ask about their transfer and tour options to St-Emilion/Bordeaux, Oradour-sur-Glane, and even Carcassonne (€44/hour, less after 6 hours, €110 night tour of illuminated castles and villages, mobile 06 08 70 61 67, www.taxialacarte.com, taxialacarte@gmail.com).

Exploreo Tours is run by passionate world traveler (and fluent English speaker) David Lascoux. He offers a variety of half- and full-day minivan trips in the Dordogne region with expert commentary. Individuals should ask about shared tours (for 4—€120/day, €55/half-day, tel. 09 67 72 58 96, www.exploreo24.com, exploreo24@gmail.com).

Béatrice Mollaret and **Bruno Eluere**—a fun, very French guide team headquartered in Sarlat-la-Canéda—create tours tailor-made for travelers wanting to dig into Dordogne culture and get off the beaten track (9 Cours des Fontaines, mobile 06 79 63 28 47, contact@dordogne-fellow-traveller.com).

Caves and Castles is run by a British couple (Steve and Judie Burman) who offer tours to the area's main sights for a day or more. They offer translation services for French-only cave visits, and Steve has plenty of tricks to keep families happy and kids entertained (British mobile 44-789-972-0482, www.cavesandcastles.com).

Allo Philippe Taxi offers transportation only and is run by French-speaking Philippe. For excursions, he charges €45/hour for up to four people (€68/hour on Sun, tel. 05 53 59 39 65, mobile 06 08 57 30 10, www.allophilippetaxi.com, allophilippetaxi@wanadoo.fr).

Shared Tours: Ophorus Excursions offers a full range of informative half- and full-day trips—for individuals or private groups—to caves, castles, and villages, including Sarlat (options also include the Lot River Valley, Rocamadour, or St-Emilion) in a comfortable minivan with competent, English-fluent guides and up to eight fellow travelers (€75/half-day, €150/day, tel. 05 56 15 26 09, www.ophorus.com, info@ophorus.com).

Hot-Air Balloon Rides

If ever you were going to spring for a hot-air balloon ride in France, the Dordogne is the place to do it. Balloons take you high above its gorgeous river and hilly terrain capped with golden stone castles and villages. **Montgolfières du Périgord** is conveniently based in La Roque-Gageac and offers a variety of flights with well-trained pilots (one-hour flight about €220/person, departures in good weather generally just after sunrise and just before sunset, tel. 05 53 28 18 58, www.montgolfiere-du-perigord.com, perigordballoons@wanadoo.fr).

DORDOGNE

THE DORDOGNE'S CUISINE SCENE

Gourmets flock to this area for its geese, ducks, and wild mushrooms. The geese produce (involuntarily) the region's famous foie gras. (They're force-fed, denied exercise during the last weeks of their lives, and slaughtered for their livers, meat, and fluffy down—see sidebar on page 480.) Foie gras tastes like butter and costs like gold. The main duck specialty is *confit de canard* (duck meat preserved in its own fat—sounds terrible, but tastes great).

You'll also see *magret de canard* (sautéed duck breast), smoked duck, and anything fried in duck fat on menus.

Pommes de terre sarladaises are mouthwatering, thinly sliced potatoes fried in duck fat and commonly served with *confit de canard*. Wild truffles are dirty black mushrooms that grow underground, generally on the roots of oak trees. Farmers traditionally locate them with sniffing pigs and then charge a fortune for their catch (roughly $300 per pound). Local *cèpe* mushrooms are commonly pan-fried with parsley and garlic—look for omelets cooked this way.

Native cheeses are Cabécou (a silver-dollar-size, pungent, nutty-flavored goat cheese) and Echourgnac (made by local Trappist monks). You'll find walnuts *(noix)* in salads, cakes, liqueurs, salad dressings, and more.

Wines to sample are Bergerac (red, white, and rosé), Pecharmant (red, must be at least four years old), Cahors (a full-bodied red), and Monbazillac (sweet dessert wine). The *vin de noix* (sweet walnut liqueur) is delightful before dinner.

DORDOGNE MARKETS

Markets are a big deal in rural France, and nowhere more so than in the Dordogne. I've listed good markets for every day of the week, so there's no excuse for drivers not to experience one. Here's what to look for:

Strawberries *(fraises):* For the French, the Dordogne is the region famous for the very tastiest strawberries. Available from April to November, they're gorgeous, and they smell even better than they look. Buy *une barquette* (small basket), and suddenly your two-star hotel room is a three-star. Look also for *fraises des bois*, the tiny, sweet, and less visually appealing strawberries found in nearby forests.

Fresh Veggies: Outdoor markets allow you to meet the farmers, and give you a chance to buy directly from them. (See what's fresh, and look for it on your menu this evening.) Subtly check out the hands of the person helping customers—if they're not gnarled and rough from working the fields, move on.

Cheeses *(fromages):* The region is famous for its Cabécou goat cheese (described earlier), though often you'll also find Auvergne cheeses (St. Nectaire and Cantal are the most common) from just east of the Dordogne (usually in big rounds) and Tomme and Brebis (sheep cheeses) from the Pyrenees to the south.

Truffles *(truffes):* Only the bigger markets will have these ugly, jet-black mushrooms on display. Truffle season is during off-season (Nov-Feb), when you'll find them at every market. During summer, the fresh truffles you might see are *truffes d'été,* a less desirable and cheaper, but still tasty, species. If you see truffles displayed at other times, they've been sterilized (a preservative measure that can reduce flavor). On Sarlat-la-Canéda market days, you may find a man in the center of Place de la Liberté with a photo of his grandfather and his truffle-hunting dog. From November to mid-March there's a truffle market on Saturday mornings on Rue Fénelon (details at TI).

Anything with Walnuts *(aux noix): Pain aux noix* is a thick-as-a-brick bread loaf chock-full of walnuts. *Moutarde de noix* is walnut mustard. *Confiture de noix* is a walnut spread for hors d'oeuvres. *Gâteaux de noix* are tasty cakes studded with walnuts. *Liqueur de noix* is a marvelous creamy liqueur, great over ice or blended with a local white wine.

Goose or Duck Livers and Pâté (foie gras): This spread—which you are not supposed to spread but rather to eat in small chunks on warm toast—is made from geese (better) and ducks (still good) or from a mix of the two. You'll see two basic forms: *entier* and *bloc.* Both are 100 percent foie gras; *entier* is a piece cut right from the product, whereas *bloc* has been blended. Foie gras is best accompanied by a sweet white wine (such as the locally produced Monbazillac or Sauternes from Bordeaux). You can bring the un-opened tins back into the US, *pas de problème.*

Confit de Canard: At butcher stands, look for chunks of duck smothered in white fat, just waiting for someone to take them home and cook them up. If you have kitchen access, try it: Scrape off some of the fat, then sauté the chunks until they're crispy on the outside and heated through. Save some of that fat for roasting potatoes.

Dried Sausages *(saucissons secs):* Long tables piled high with dried sausages covered in herbs or stuffed with local goodies are a common sight in French markets. You'll always be offered a mouthwatering sample. Some of the variations you'll see include *porc, canard* (duck), *fumé* (smoked), *à l'ail* (garlic), *cendré* (rolled in ashes), *aux myrtilles* (with blueberries), *sanglier* (wild boar), and even *âne* (donkey)— and, but of course, *aux noix* (with walnuts).

Olive Oil *(huile d'olive):* You'll find stylish bottles of various olive oils, as well as vegetable oils flavored with truffles, walnuts, chestnuts *(châtaignes),* and hazelnuts *(noisettes)*—good for cooking, ideal on salads, and great as gifts. Pure walnut oil, pressed at local mills from nuts grown in the region, is a local specialty, best on salads. Don't cook with pure walnut oil, as it will burn quickly.

Olives and Nuts *(olives et noix):* These interlopers from Provence find their way to every market in France.

Brandies and Liqueurs: Armagnac and Cognac are made a few hours away, as are southwestern fruit-flavored liquors like *pomme verte;* they're usually available from a seller or two.

Dordogne Market Days

The best markets are in Sarlat-la-Canéda (Sat and Wed, in that order), followed by the markets in Cahors on Saturday, St-Cyprien on Sunday, and Le Bugue on Tuesday. Markets usually shut down by 13:00.

Sunday: St-Cyprien (lively market, 10 minutes west of Beynac, difficult parking) and St-Geniès (a tiny, intimate market with few tourists; halfway between Sarlat and Montignac)

Monday: Les Eyzies-de-Tayac (April-Oct) and a tiny one in Beynac (mid-June-mid-Sept)

Tuesday: Cénac (you can canoe from here) and Le Bugue (great market 20 minutes west of Beynac)

Wednesday: Sarlat (big market) and Montignac (near Lascaux)

Thursday: Domme (good market)

Friday: Souillac (transfer point to Cahors, Carcassonne) and La Roque-Gageac (May-Sept)

Saturday: Sarlat and Cahors (both are excellent), the little *bastide* village of Belvès (small market), and Montignac

Sarlat-la-Canéda

Sarlat–la-Canéda is a pedestrian-filled banquet of a town, serenely set amid forested hills with no blockbuster sights. Still, Sarlat delivers a seductive tangle of traffic-free, golden cobblestone lanes peppered with beautiful buildings, lined with foie gras shops (geese hate Sarlat), and stuffed with tourists. The town is warmly lit at night and ideal for after-dinner strolls. It's just the right  size—large enough to have a theater with four screens, but small enough that everything is an easy meander from the town center. And though undeniably popular with tourists, it's the handiest home base for those without a car.

Orientation to Sarlat-la-Canéda

Rue de la République slices like an arrow through the circular old town. The action lies east of Rue de la République. Sarlat's smaller half has few shops and many quiet lanes.

TOURIST INFORMATION

The TI is 50 yards to the right of the Cathedral of St. Sacerdos as you face it (July-Aug Mon-Sat 9:00-19:30, Sun 10:00-13:00 & 14:00-18:00; April-June and Sept until 18:30; Oct Mon-Sat 9:00-12:00 & 14:00-17:00, Sun 10:00-13:00; shorter hours and closed Sun Nov-March; on Rue Tourny, tel. 05 53 31 45 45, www. sarlat-tourisme.com). Ask for information on caves and renting a car, bike, or canoe. The TI also sells tickets for the panoramic elevator ride (€5, cash only, or buy at the elevator with a chip credit card).

DORDOGNE

ARRIVAL IN SARLAT-LA-CANEDA

By Train: The sleepy train station keeps a lonely vigil (without a shop, café, or hotel in sight). It's a mostly downhill, 20-minute walk to the town center (taxis are about €10, book ahead, mobile 06 08 70 61 67 or tel. 05 53 59 02 43). To walk into town, turn left out of the station and follow Avenue de la Gare as it curves downhill, then turn right at the bottom, on Avenue Thiers, to reach the town center. Some trains (such as those from Limoges and Cahors) arrive at nearby Souillac, which is poorly connected to Sarlat's train station by bus (2-3/day, schedule at www.transperigord.fr).

By Car: The hilly terrain around Sarlat-la-Canéda creates traffic funnels unusual for a town of this size. Hotels know the best strategies for parking. The closest parking to the center is metered and easy on nonmarket and off-season days (about €2/hour, free 19:00-9:00). On market days, avoid the center by parking along Avenue du Général de Gaulle (at the north end of town), or in one of the signed lots on the ring road. You'll also find free parking at Place des Cordeliers, a 5-minute walk north of Place de la Petite Rigaudie.

HELPFUL HINTS

Market Days: Sarlat has been an important market town since the Middle Ages. Outdoor markets still thrive on Wednesday morning and all day Saturday. Saturday's market swallows the entire town and is best in the morning (produce and food vendors leave around noon). Come before 9:00, have breakfast or coffee on the square (the recommended **Brasserie le Glacier** serves breakfast), and watch them set up. On Thursday evenings (starting at 18:00), a small organic market enlivens the town's lower side (best in summer; just south of the old center at Place du 14 Juillet) and a lively bric-a-brac market runs till midnight on Rue de la République. From November to March, a truffle market takes place on Saturday mornings on Rue Fénelon. For tips on what to look for at the market, see "Dordogne Markets," earlier.

Supermarkets: There's a **Petit Casino** grocery at 32 Rue de la République. The **Carrefour** grocery at 23 Avenue Gambetta is bigger. Both are open daily.

Wi-Fi: The recommended **Brasserie le Glacier** has free Wi-Fi for customers, as do other central cafés.

Laundry: **Le Lavandou** launderette sits across from the recommended Hôtel la Couleuvrine (self-serve daily 24 hours, 10 Place de la Bouquerie, mobile 06 81 30 57 81).

Biking: Sarlat-la-Canéda is surrounded by beautiful country lanes that would be ideal for biking were it not for all those hills and cars (consider renting an electric bike). Villages along the Dor-

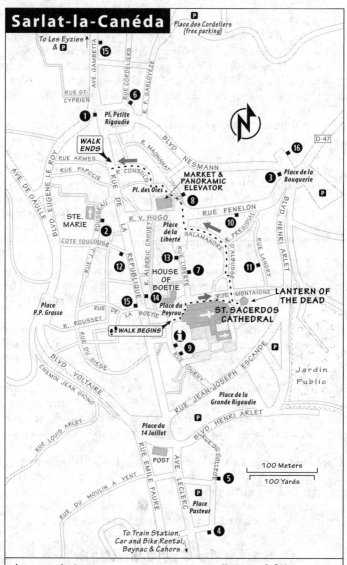

Sarlat-la-Canéda

Place des Cordeliers (free parking)

To Les Eyzies & P

WALK ENDS

Pl. Petite Rigaudie

RUE ST-CYPRIEN

AVE. GAMBETTA

RUE CORDELIERS

R. F. SARLOVÈZE

BLVD. NESSMANN

R. MAGNANAT

RUE ARMES

RUE PAPUCIE

RUE DES CONSULS

RUE DE LA

AVE. DE GAULLE

BLVD. EUGÈNE LE ROY

RUE J.J. ROUSSEAU

CÔTE TOULOUSE

STE. MARIE

Pl. des Oies

MARKET & PANORAMIC ELEVATOR

RUE FENELON

R. V. HUGO

Place de la Liberté

SALAMANDRE

R. ALBÉRIC CAHUET

R. PRÉSIDIAL

RUE LIBERTÉ

RUE D'ALBUSSE

RUE LANDRY

BLVD. HENRI ARLET

Place de la Bouquerie

D-47

HOUSE OF BOETIE

RUE DE LA RÉPUBLIQUE

Place P.P. Grasse

RUE DE LA BOETIE

R. ROUSSET

Place du Peyrou

WALK BEGINS

RUE MONTAIGNE

LANTERN OF THE DEAD

ST. SACERDOS CATHEDRAL

Jardin Public

BLVD. VOLTAIRE

CHEMIN JEAN GIONO

RUE DU SIÈGE

RUE JEAN-JOSEPH ESCANDE

RUE TOURNY

Place de la Grande Rigaudie

RUE LOUIS ARLET

Place du 14 Juillet

BLVD. HENRI ARLET

POST

AVE. LECLERC

RUE ÉMILE FAURE

RUE DU COLLÈGE

RUE DU MOULIN A VENT

Place Pasteur

To Train Station, Car and Bike Rental, Beynac & Cahors

100 Meters

100 Yards

DORDOGNE

<u>Accommodations</u>
1 Hôtel Plaza Madeleine
2 La Villa des Consuls
3 Hôtel la Couleuvrine
4 Hôtel Montaigne
5 Côté Jardin
6 Les Cordeliers
7 Les Chambres du Glacier & Brasserie
8 La Maison du Notaire Royal

<u>Eateries & Other</u>
9 Chez le Gaulois
10 L'Adresse
11 Le Présidial
12 Pizzeria Romane
13 Le Régent
14 Maison Massoulier
15 Grocery (2)
16 Launderette

dogne River make good biking destinations, though expect traffic (bike-rental places can advise quieter routes) and some serious ups and downs between Sarlat and the river. There's a lovely 16-mile bike-only lane from Sarlat to Souillac following an old rail right-of-way—see "Dordogne Scenic Loop," later (Liberty Cycle rental, described next, is located at the trail's start).

Liberty Cycle rents bikes and offers short bike tours from Sarlat (1 Route de Souillac, Madrazès, daily, delivery to hotel possible, mobile 07 81 24 78 79, www.liberty-cycle.com, guillaume@liberty-cycle.com). At the southern edge of Castelnaud, **Bike Bus** also offers rentals and tours (daily, tel. 05 53 31 10 61, www.bike-bus.com). From Castelnaud, you have access to a bike path that starts along the Dordogne and follows a smaller river for six miles. **Aquitaine Bike,** run by a British-American couple, can deliver top quality hybrid and road bikes to your hotel in and near Sarlat and provides route advice, customized self-guided tours, and roadside assistance (4-day minimum, tours available, tel. 05 53 30 35 17, mobile 06 32 35 56 50, www.aquitainebike.com, aquitainebike@gmail.com). The TI has info on bike rental outside Sarlat.

Taxi: Call friendly **Christoph Kusters** (mobile 06 08 70 61 67, www.taxialacarte.com, taxialacarte@gmail.com, also offers regional day trips—see "With A Tour," earlier) or **Taxi Sarlat** (tel. 05 53 59 02 43).

Car Rental: Try **Europcar** (Le Pontet, at south end of Avenue Leclerc on roundabout, Place du Maréchal de Lattre de Tassigny, 15-minute walk from center—for location, see the "Greater Sarlat-la-Canéda" map later in this section, tel. 05 53 30 30 40).

Cooking Classes: Le Chèvrefeuille offers family-friendly market tours and cooking classes that focus on Périgord cuisine ($150/day includes market tour, €75 for cooking class only). Courses are run by friendly British expats and are situated in the countryside about a half-hour drive from Sarlat (see page 493).

Sarlat-la-Canéda Walk

This short self-guided walk, rated ▲▲, starts facing the Cathedral of St. Sacerdos (a few steps from the TI). The walk works well in the day—when sights are open—but in some ways it's better after dinner, when the gaslit lanes and candlelit restaurants twinkle. (You can always circle back the next day to sights that interest you.) See the "Sarlat-la-Canéda" map to help navigate.

• Start in front of the Cathedral of St. Sacerdos, on the...

Place du Peyrou: An eighth-century Benedictine abbey once stood where the Cathedral of St. Sacerdos is today. It provided the stability for Sarlat to develop into an important trading city during the Middle Ages. The old Bishop's Palace, built right into the cathedral (on the right, with its top-floor Florentine-style loggia), recalls Sarlat's Italian connection. The Italian bishop was the boyfriend of Catherine de' Medici (queen of France)—a relationship that landed him this fine residence. After a short stint here, he split to Paris with loads of local money. And though his departure scandalized the town, it left Sarlat with a heritage of Italian architecture. (Notice the fine Italianate house of Etienne de la Boëtie on the opposite side of the square and the similar loggia to its right.)

Another reason for Sarlat's Italo-flavored urban design was its loyalty to the king during wartime. Sarlat's glory century was from about 1450 to 1550, after the Hundred Years' War (see sidebar on page 230). Loyal to the French cause—through a century of war—Sarlat was rewarded by the French king, who gave the town lots of money to rebuild itself in stone. Sarlat's new nobility needed fancy houses, complete with ego-boosting features. Many of Sarlat's most impressive buildings date from this prosperous era, when the Renaissance style was in vogue and everyone wanted an architect with an Italian résumé.

• *Take a closer look (opposite the cathedral) at...*

The House of Étienne de la Boëtie: This house was a typical 16th-century merchant's home—family upstairs and open ground floor (its stone arch now filled in) with big, fat sills to display retail goods. Pan up, scanning the crude-but-still-Renaissance carved reliefs. It was a time when anything Italian was trendy (when yokels "stuck a feather in their cap and called it macaroni"). La Boëtie (lah bow-ess-ee), a 16th-century bleeding-heart liberal who spoke and wrote against the rule of tyrannical kings, remains a local favorite.

Notice how the house just to the left arches over the small street. This was a common practice to maximize buildable space in the Middle Ages. Sarlat enjoyed a population boom in the mid-15th century after the Hundred Years' War ended.

• *If you're doing this walk during the day, head into the cathedral now. After hours, skip ahead to the Lantern of the Dead (see next page).*

Cathedral of St. Sacerdos: Though the cathedral's facade has a few well-worn 12th-century carvings, most of it dates from the 18th and 19th centuries. Step inside. The faithful believed that Mary delivered them from the great plague of 1348, so you'll find a full complement of Virgin Marys here and throughout the town. The Gothic interiors in this part of France are simple, with clean lines and nothing extravagant. The first chapel on the left is the baptistery. Locals would come here to give thanks after they made the pilgrimage to Lourdes for healing and returned satisfied. The

DORDOGNE

second column on the right side of the nave shows a long list of hometown boys who gave their lives for France in World War I.

• *Exit the cathedral's front door and turn right, walk uphill on the first lane (Rue de Montaigne), then go right again through a short walkway that leads behind the church. Here you'll find a bullet-shaped building ready for some kind of medieval takeoff, known as the...*

Lantern of the Dead (Lanterne des Morts): Dating from 1147, this is the oldest monument in town. In four horrible days, a quarter of Sarlat's population (1,000 out of 4,000) died in a plague. People prayed to St. Bernard of Clairvaux for help. He blessed their bread—and instituted hygiene standards while he was at it, stopping the disease. This lantern was built in gratitude—but I'm not clear on what they did with it other than have small meetings inside.

• *Facing the church, go back the way you came, toward an adorable house with its own tiny tower. Cross one street and keep straight, turn left a block later on Impasse de la Vieille Poste, make a quick right on Rue d'Albusse, and then take a left onto...*

Rue de la Salamandre: The salamander—unfazed by fire or water—was Sarlat's mascot. Befitting its favorite animal, Sarlat was also unfazed by fire (from war) and water (from floods). Walk a few steps down this "Street of the Salamander" and find the Gothic-framed doorway just below on your right. Step back and notice the tower that housed the staircase. Spiral staircase towers like this (Sarlat has about 20) date from about 1600 (after the wars of religion between the Catholics and Protestants), when the new nobility needed to show off.

• *Continue downhill, passing under the salamander-capped arch, and pause near (or better, sit down at) the café on the...*

Place de la Liberté: This has been Sarlat's main market square since the Middle Ages, though it was expanded in the 18th century. Sarlat's patriotic Town Hall stands behind you (with a café perfectly situated for people-watching). You can't miss the dark **stone roofs** topping the buildings across the square. They're typical of this region: Called *lauzes* in French, the flat limestone rocks were originally gathered by farmers clearing their fields, then made into cheap, durable roofing material (today few people can afford them). The unusually steep pitch of the *lauzes* roofs—which last up to 300 years—helps distribute the weight of the roof (about 160 pounds per square foot) over a greater area. Although most *lauzes* roofs have been replaced by roofs made from more affordable materials, a great number remain. The small windows in the roof are critical: They provide air circulation, allowing the lichen that coat the porous stone to grow—sealing gaps between the stones and effectively waterproofing the roof. Without that layer, the stone would crumble after repeated freeze-and-thaw cycles.

• *Walk right, to the "upper" end of the square. The bulky Church of Ste. Marie, right across from you, today serves as Sarlat's...*

Covered Market and Panoramic Elevator: Once a parish church dedicated to St. Marie, with a massive *lauzes* roof and a soaring bell tower, this building was converted into a gunpowder factory and then a post office before becoming today's **indoor market** (daily 8:30-13:00). Marvel at its tall, strangely modern, seven-ton doors, and imagine the effort it took to deliver and install them in the center of this tight-laned town.

On the opposite side of this building (walk through if it's open, or around if it's closed), you'll find the entrance to a modern, glass-sided **panoramic elevator,** which whisks tourists up through the center of the ancient church's bell tower for bird's-eye views over Sarlat's rooftops. Your elevator operator doubles as a guide, who gives a quick history of Sarlat at the top. If they gather enough English-speakers, the spiel

is in English; otherwise, it'll be in French and you'll use the good English handout (feel free to ask questions). Because the elevator is open-air, it doesn't run in the rain (€5, buy timed-entry ticket at machines, chip credit card required, rarely a wait, cash-only tickets available at TI; 5/hour, visit lasts 12 minutes, generally open daily in summer 10:00-14:00 & 17:00-21:00, in spring and fall 10:00-13:00 & 14:00-18:00, shorter hours off-season).

• *When you've returned to earth, double back into Place de la Liberté and climb up the small ramp opposite the market's big doors to meet the "Boy of Sarlat"—a statue marking the best view over Place de la Liberté. Notice the cathedral's tower to the left, with a salamander swinging happily from its spire. Just below you on the stairs are several shops.*

Foie Gras and Beyond: Tourist-pleasing stores line the streets of Sarlat and are filled with the finest local products. The shop near the "boy" sells it all, from truffles to foie gras to walnut wine to truffle liqueur. To better understand what you're looking at, read the foie gras sidebar on page 480.

• *Turn left behind the boy and trickle like medieval rainwater down the ramp into an inviting square. Here you'll find a little gaggle of geese.*

Place des Oies: Feathers fly when geese are traded on this "Square of the Geese" on market days (Nov-March). Birds have been serious business here since the Middle Ages. Even today, a typical Sarlat menu reads, "duck, duck, goose." Trophy homes surround this cute little square on all sides.

DORDOGNE

Check out the wealthy merchant's home to the right as you enter the square—the **Manoir de Gisson**—with a tower built big enough to match his ego. The owner was the town counsel, a position that arose as cities like Sarlat outgrew the Middle Ages. Town counsels replaced priests in resolving civil conflicts and performing other civic duties. Touring the interior of the manor reveals how the wealthy lived in Sarlat (study the big poster next to the entry). You'll climb up one of those spiral staircase towers, ogle at several rooms carefully decorated with authentic 16th- to 18th-century furniture, and peek inside the impressive *lauzes* roof. It's fun to gaze out the windows and imagine living here, surrounded by 360 degrees of gorgeous cityscape (€8, daily April-Sept 10:00-18:30, until 19:00 July-Aug, closes earlier off-season, borrow English booklet, tel. 05 53 28 70 55, www.manoirdegisson.com).

• *Walk to the right along Rue des Consuls. Just before Le Mirandol restaurant, turn right toward a...*

Fourteenth-Century Vault and Fountain: For generations, this was the town's only source of water, protected by the Virgin Mary (find her at the end of the fountain). Opposite the restaurant and fountain, find the wooden doorway (open late June-Aug only) that houses a massive Renaissance stairway. These showy stairways, which replaced more space-efficient spiral ones, required a big house and a bigger income. Impressive.

• *Follow the curve along Rue des Consuls, and enter the straight-as-an-arrow...*

Rue de la République: This "modern" thoroughfare, known as *La Traverse* to locals, dates from the mid-1800s, when blasting big roads through medieval cities was standard operating procedure (it's traffic-free in afternoons in high season). It wasn't until 1963 that Sarlat's other streets would become off-limits to cars, thanks to France's forward-thinking minister of culture, André Malraux. The law that bears his name has served to preserve and restore important monuments and neighborhoods throughout France. Eager to protect the country's architectural heritage, private investors, cities, and regions worked together to create traffic-free zones, rebuild crumbling buildings, and make sure that no cables or ugly wiring marred the ambience of towns like this. Without the Malraux Law, Sarlat might well have more "efficient" roads like Rue de la République slicing through its old town center.

• *Our walk is over, but make sure you take time for a poetic ramble through the town's quiet side—or, better yet, stroll any of Sarlat's lanes after dark. This is the only town in France illuminated by gas lamps, which cause the warm limestone to glow, turning the romance of Sarlat up even higher. Now may also be a good time to find a café and raise a toast to Monsieur Malraux.*

Sleeping in Sarlat-la-Canéda

Sarlat-la-Canéda is the train traveler's best Dordogne home base. Book early here for July and August. Parking can be a headache (ask your hotelier for help). Drivers will find rooms and parking easier just outside of town or in the nearby villages and destinations described later, under "The Best of the Dordogne River Valley" (most are a 15-minute drive away).

HOTELS IN THE TOWN CENTER

$$$ Hôtel Plaza Madeleine**** is a central and upscale value with formal service, a handsome pub/wine-bar, stylish public spaces, and 39 very sharp rooms with every comfort. You'll find a pool out back, a sauna, and a whirlpool bath—all free for guests (connecting rooms for families, big breakfast buffet, air-con, elevator, pay garage parking, at north end of ring road at 1 Place de la Petite Rigaudie, tel. 05 53 59 10 41, www.plaza-madeleine.com, contact@plaza-madeleine.com).

$ La Villa des Consuls,** a cross between a B&B and a hotel, occupies a 17th-century home buried on Sarlat's quiet side with 11 lovely, spacious rooms, each with a small kitchen and many with a living room. The rooms surround a small courtyard and come with wood floors, private decks, and high ceilings (family rooms, higher prices for 1-night stays, air-con, adorable owners help with hauling bags from the street, reception closed 12:00-15:30 and after 19:00, 3 Rue Jean-Jacques Rousseau, tel. 05 53 31 90 05, www.villaconsuls.fr, villadesconsuls@aol.com).

$ Hôtel la Couleuvrine** offers 27 simple rooms with character at fair rates in a historic building with a handy location—across from the launderette and with easy parking (for Sarlat). Some rooms have tight bathrooms, and a few have private terraces (family rooms, elevator, on ring road at 1 Place de la Bouquerie, tel. 05 53 59 27 80, www.la-couleuvrine.com, contact@la-couleuvrine.com). Half-pension is encouraged during busy periods and in the summer—figure €38 per person beyond the room price for breakfast and a good dinner in the classy restaurant.

$ Hôtel Montaigne,** a good value located a block south of the pedestrian zone, is run by the hardworking Martinat family. The 28 rooms are simple, comfortable, and air-conditioned. Of the hotels I list, this is the one nearest to the train station (family rooms, elevator, easy parking nearby, Place Pasteur, tel. 05 53 31 93 88, www.hotelmontaigne.fr, contact@hotelmontaigne.fr).

HOTELS NORTH OF TOWN

The following hotels are a 10-minute walk north of the old town on Avenue de Selves. All have easy parking. For locations, see the "Greater Sarlat-la-Canéda" map.

$$$ Au Grand Hôtel de Sarlat**** feels *très* American, with a big lobby, professional staff, and 38 pricey-for-Sarlat rooms in a modern shell with a year-round swimming pool and pleasant grounds (RS%, includes big breakfast, air-con, elevator, pay parking, 93 Avenue de Selves, tel. 05 53 31 50 00, http://au-grand-hotel-de-sarlat.com, augrandhotelsarlat@gmail.com).

$ Hôtel de Compostelle*** features a cheery, spacious lobby and 23 sharp, generously sized, and air-conditioned rooms, many with decks. There are several good family rooms at good rates—and the kids will enjoy the pool (elevator is one floor up, pay parking, 66 Avenue de Selves, tel. 05 53 59 08 53, www.hotel-compostelle-sarlat.com, info@hotel-compostelle-sarlat.com).

$ Hôtel le Madrigal,** one block past Hôtel de Compostelle (same owners—check in may be at Hôtel de Compostelle), is a charming nine-room hotel with good two-star rooms and rates, all with queen-size beds, air-conditioning, and smallish bathrooms (family rooms, fitness room, pay parking, 50 Avenue de Selves, tel. 05 53 59 21 98, www.hotel-madrigal-sarlat.com, info@hotel-madrigal-sarlat.com).

CHAMBRES D'HOTES

These *chambres d'hôtes* are central and compare well with the hotels listed earlier.

$ Côté Jardin is a fine spread with good rates run by gregarious Michelle. She rents three top-comfort rooms, each with its own terrace, surrounding a large garden. Her breakfast room is beyond cozy (air-con, 13 Rue du Collège, mobile 06 03 11 52 96, www.sarlatcotejardin.com, msimonet24@gmail.com).

$ Les Cordeliers, owned by gentle Brits Chris and Amanda Johnson, offers high-end comfort at two-star prices. Most of the seven cushy rooms are huge; all are air-conditioned and well-furnished; and a small kitchen is at your disposal with serve-yourself snacks and drinks. The building has sky-blue shutters and overlooks a picturesque square at the north end of the old center (big breakfast with fresh fruit and eggs extra, closed Nov-Feb, 51 Rue des Cordeliers, mobile 06 76 78 04 01, www.hotelsarlat.com, info@hotelsarlat.com).

$ Les Chambres du Glacier, where kind Monsieur Da Costa and son Bruno offer four cavernous, simple, but surprisingly comfortable rooms above an outdoor café, is in the thick of Sarlat's pedestrian zone (perfect for market days). Rooms come with sky-high ceilings, big and soundproof windows over Sarlat's world, polished

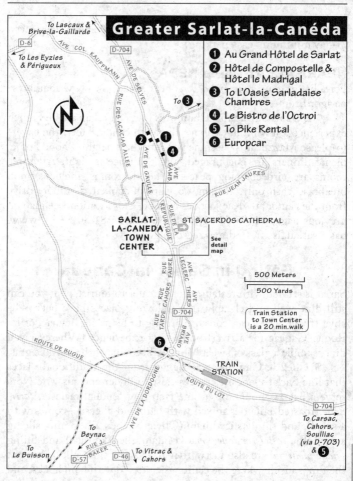

Greater Sarlat-la-Canéda

1. Au Grand Hôtel de Sarlat
2. Hôtel de Compostelle & Hôtel le Madrigal
3. To L'Oasis Sarladaise Chambres
4. Le Bistro de l'Octroi
5. To Bike Rental
6. Europcar

To Lascaux & Brive-la-Gaillarde

To Les Eyzies & Périgueux

D-6

D-704

AVE. COL. KAUFFMANN

AVE. DE SEIVES

RUE DES ACACIAS ALLEE

To ❸

❷ ❶

❹

AVE DE GAULLE

AVE. GAMBETTA

RUE JEAN JAURES

SARLAT-LA-CANEDA TOWN CENTER

RUE DE LA REPUBLIQUE

ST. SACERDOS CATHEDRAL

See detail map

RUE FAURE

RUE LECLERC

AVE. THIERS

500 Meters

500 Yards

RUE TARDE

RUE CAHORS

D-704

AVE. BRIAND

Train Station to Town Center is a 20 min. walk

ROUTE DE BUGUE

❻

TRAIN STATION

ROUTE DU LOT

AVE. DE LA DORDOGNE

To Beynac

RUE J. BAKER

D-704

To Carsac, Cahors, Soulliac (via D-703) & ❺

To Le Buisson

D-57

D-46

To Vitrac & Cahors

DORDOGNE

wood floors, cheap furnishings, and bathrooms you can get lost in (family rooms, no air-con, includes continental breakfast, Place de la Liberté, tel. 05 53 29 99 99, www.leglacier-sarlat.fr, contact. leglacier@gmail.com).

¢ **La Maison du Notaire Royal,** run by English-speaking Pierre-Henri Toulemon and French-speaking Diane, has four large and homey rooms with a private entry in a 17th-century home located a few steps above the main square. Guests have access to a fridge, microwave, and sweet garden tables (includes breakfast, cash only, no deposit required, cheap parking, call a day ahead to confirm arrival time, look for big steps from northeast corner of Place de la Liberté, 4 Rue Magnanat, tel. 05 53 31 26 60, mobile 06 08 67 76 90, www.sarlat-chambres-hotes.com, contact@toulemon. com). They also rent a cottage a few blocks from the town center with living room, kitchen, and three bedrooms that can sleep seven (3-day minimum, easy parking).

NEAR SARLAT-LA-CANEDA

For a list of good *chambres d'hôtes* near Sarlat, try www.chambres-perigord.com.

¢ **L'Oasis Sarladaise Chambres** gives travelers a true French experience a few minutes above the town center. Here, the eager-to-please Mazzocatos welcome you into their neighborhood home, picnic dinners are encouraged, and the price is right. All three rooms are bird-chirping peaceful (family rooms, includes good breakfast, cash only, air-con, no English spoken, 5-minute drive from the center at 9 Rue Jacques Monod—for location, see map on previous page; tel. 05 53 31 07 43, mobile 06 81 30 57 81, www.oasis-sarladaise.fr, fred.mazzo@orange.fr).

Eating in Sarlat-la-Canéda

Sarlat is stuffed with restaurants that cater to tourists, but you can still dine well and cheaply. The following places have been reliable. If you have a car, consider driving to Domme, Beynac, or La Roque-Gageac for a riverfront dining experience. Wherever you dine, sample a glass of sweet Monbazillac wine with your foie gras.

$ Chez le Gaulois is a change from the traditional places that line Sarlat's lanes. Pyrenees-raised Olivier and his wife Nora serve a hearty mountain cuisine featuring fondue, raclette, *tartiflette* (roasted potatoes mixed with ham and cheese—comes with a salad), and thinly sliced ham (Olivier spends all evening slicing away). The *cassolette de légumes* (a ratatouille-like dish) and filling *salade plein sud* are also tasty. They have a few sidewalk tables, but the fun is inside where the ceiling is cluttered with ham hocks, and the soundtrack is jazz (closed Sun-Mon except in July-Aug, near the TI at 1 Rue Tourny, tel. 05 53 59 50 64).

$$$ L'Adresse is Sarlat's small, foodie bistro serving delicious cuisine with creative twists. You'll experience an open kitchen and young staff; inside seating is tight but fun, and there's a nice terrace in front. Book ahead, particularly if you want a table on the terrace (well-priced *menus* with good choices, closed Sun-Mon, 10 Rue Fénelon, tel. 05 53 30 56 19).

$$$ Le Présidial is a lovely, formal place for a refined meal of regional cuisine in a historic mansion. The setting is exceptional—you're greeted with beautiful gardens (where you can dine in good weather), and the interior comes with high ceilings, stone walls, and rich wood floors (closed Sun, reservations recommended, 6 Rue Landry, tel. 05 53 28 92 47, www.lepresidial.fr).

$ Pizzeria Romane is a cheap, spacious, and family-friendly

DORDOGNE

eatery where you can watch your tasty pizza bake in the oven and enjoy it in the smoke-free patio, or get it to go (lots of salads, daily July-Aug, otherwise closed Sun, on the quiet side of Sarlat at 3 Côte de Toulouse, tel. 05 53 59 23 88).

On Place de la Liberté: The next two places are your best bet for a decent meal on Sarlat's made-for-people-watching main square. Skip them if you can't eat outside.

$$ Le Régent serves everything from pizza and burgers to traditional dishes. Of its two terraces, the upstairs terrace is quieter but removed from the action. The €28 *menu* gives a good taste of Sarlat's specialties, and they serve until late (daily, tel. 05 53 31 06 36).

$ Brasserie le Glacier offers main-square views from its outdoor tables and good-enough café fare served nonstop from 11:00-22:00. Come here for friendly service (Filomena has the big smile), big salads, pizza, or *un plat* (daily, tel. 05 53 29 99 99, also rents rooms—see Les Chambres du Glacier under "Sleeping in Sarlat-la-Canéda," earlier).

North of the Center: Overlooking a busy road a few blocks north of the old town, **$$ Le Bistro de l'Octroi** must provide top cuisine and competitive prices to draw locals—and it does. Quality bistro fare (mostly meat dishes) is served on a generous terrace and within the pleasant interior. The three-course *menus* offer many options at good prices—order two starters if you prefer (daily, 111 Avenue des Selves—for location see the "Greater Sarlat-la-Canéda" map, tel. 05 53 30 83 40, www.lebistrodeloctroi.fr).

Pastries: At **$ Maison Massoulier,** a classy pastry shop with sidewalk tables along Rue de la République, you can enjoy decadent desserts with a hot drink while people-watching (daily, 33 Rue de la République, tel. 05 53 59 00 85).

Sarlat-la-Canéda Connections

Sarlat's TI has train schedules. Souillac and Périgueux are the train hubs for points within the greater region. For all the following destinations, you could go west on the Libourne/Bordeaux line (transferring in either city, depending on your connection), or east by infrequent bus to Souillac (bus leaves from Sarlat train station). I've listed the fastest path in each case. For any travel to the southeast, it's easier to take a train from Souillac.

From Sarlat-la-Canéda by Train to: Les Eyzies-de-Tayac (2-3/day, 1-2.5 hours, transfer in Le Buisson), **Paris** (4/day, 5 hours, change in Bordeaux), **Amboise** (3/day, 6 hours, via Bordeaux, then TGV to Tours' St-Pierre-des-Corps, then local train to Amboise), **Bourges** (6/day, 7 hours, 2 changes), **Limoges/Oradour-sur-Glane** (4/day, 4 hours, change in Le Buisson and Périgueux—then

DORDOGNE

15-minute walk to catch bus to Oradour-sur-Glane), **Cahors** (5/day, 3 hours, 2 changes), **Albi** (6/day, 6 hours with 2-3 changes, some require bus from Sarlat to Souillac), **Carcassonne** (5/day, 7 hours, 1-2 changes usually in Bordeaux and/or Toulouse), **St-Emilion** (5/day, 2 hours, change in Bordeaux).

   To Beynac, La Roque-Gageac, Castelnaud, and Domme: These are accessible only by taxi or bike (best rented in Sarlat). See Sarlat's "Helpful Hints" for specifics.

The Best of the Dordogne River Valley

The most striking stretch of the Dordogne lies between Carsac and Beynac. Traveling by canoe is the best way to savor the highlights of the Dordogne River Valley, though several scenic sights lie off the river and require a car or bike. Following my "Dordogne Scenic Loop" (next page), you'll easily link Sarlat-la-Canéda with La Roque-Gageac, Beynac and its château, and Castelnaud before returning to Sarlat.

PLANNING YOUR TIME

Drivers should allow a minimum of a half-day to sample the river valley. Drive slowly to savor the scenery and to stay out of trouble (there are some narrow, cliff-hanging roads). The area is picnic-perfect, but buy your supplies before leaving Sarlat; pickings are slim in the villages (though view cafés are abundant). Vitrac (near Sarlat) is the best place to park for a canoe ride down the river. La Roque-Gageac, Beynac, and Domme have good restaurants. There are a few good places to witness the *gavage* (feeding of the geese and ducks to make foie gras) between the river and Sarlat—their dinnertime is generally about 18:00.

   In riverfront villages, you'll pay a small fee to park during the day. Parked cars are catnip to thieves: Take everything out or stow belongings out of sight.

   In this section I've given distances in kilometers; drivers can match these with your rental car's odometer.

   Key villages along these routes are described in detail later in this chapter, under "Dordogne Towns and Sights."

Dordogne Scenic Loop

Following these directions, beginning and ending in Sarlat-la-Canéda, you can see this area by car or bike, a ▲▲▲ experience covering 27 hilly miles. Cyclists can cut seven miles off this distance and still see most of the highlights by following D-704 from Sarlat toward Cahors, then taking the Montfort turnoff (well-signed after the big Leclerc grocery store at the roundabout) and tracking signs to Montfort—see the "Dordogne Canoe Trips & Scenic Loop Drive" map. Once in Montfort, follow the river downstream to La Roque-Gageac. Along the way, you'll pass cornfields busy growing feed for ducks and geese—locals are appalled that humans would eat the stuff.

From Sarlat to Beynac and Back: Leave Sarlat on D-704 following signs toward *Cahors*. You'll soon pass the Rougié foie gras outlet store, then the lime-stone **quarry** that gives the houses in this area their lemony color.

In about five minutes, be on the lookout for the little signposted turnoff on the right to the *Eglise de Carsac* (Church of Carsac). Set peacefully among cornfields, with its WWI monument, bonsai-like plane trees, and simple, bulky Romanesque exterior, the **Eglise de Carsac** church is part of a vivid rural French scene. Take a break here and enter the church (usually open). The stone capitals behind the altar are exquisitely medieval, and the chapel to the left of the altar reminds us how colorful medieval churches were.

Continue on, following signs to *Montfort*. About a kilometer west of Carsac, pull over to enjoy the scenic viewpoint (overlooking a bend in the river known as Cingle de Montfort). Across the Dordogne River, fields of walnut trees stretch to distant castles, and the nearby hills are covered in oak trees. This area is nicknamed "black Périgord" for its thick blanket of oaks, which stay leafy throughout the winter. The fairy-tale castle you see is **Montfort,** once the medieval home of Simon de Montfort, who led the Cathar Crusades in the early 13th century. Today it's considered mysterious by locals. (It's rumored that the castle is now the home of a brother of the emir of Kuwait.) A plaque on the rock near where you parked honors those who fought Nazi occupiers in this area in 1943.

Pass under Montfort's castle (which you can't tour; its cute little village has a few cafés and restaurants lassoed in a small pedestrian zone). If you're combining a canoe trip with this drive, cross the river following signs to *Domme,* and find my recommended canoe rental on the right side (see "Dordogne Canoe Trip," next).

The touristy *bastide* (fortified village) of **Domme** is well worth a side-trip from Vitrac or La Roque-Gageac for its sensational views (best early in the day). The driving route continues to the more important riverfront villages of **La Roque-Gageac,** then on to **Castelnaud,** and finally to **Beynac** (all described later in this chapter). From Beynac, it's a quick run back to Sarlat.

Dordogne Canoe Trip

For a refreshing break from the car or train, explore the riverside castles and villages of the Dordogne by canoe, a trip worth ▲▲▲. My recommended route is a nine-mile paddle from Vitrac to Beynac. This is the most interesting, scenic, and handy trip if you're based in or near Sarlat. Vitrac, on the river close to Sarlat, is a good starting point. And, with its mighty castle and good cafés and restaurants, Beynac delivers the perfect finale to your journey. Allow 2 hours for this paddle at a relaxed pace in spring and fall, and up to 2.5 hours in summer when the river is usually at its lowest flow.

Planning Your Trip: The trip is fun even in light rain—but steady, heavy rains can make the current too fast to handle. Prolonged droughts can have the opposite effect. Check river levels before you rent.

Beach your boat wherever it works to take a break—it's light enough that you can drag it up high and dry to go explore. (The canoes aren't worth stealing, as they're cheap and clearly color-coded for their parent company.) It's OK if you're a complete novice—the only whitewater you'll encounter will be the rare wake of passing tour boats...and your travel partner frothing at the views.

Renting a Canoe or Kayak: You can rent plastic boats—hard, light, and indestructible—from many area outfits. Whether a two-person canoe or a one-person kayak, they're stable enough for beginners (canoes are easier to manage in the river and more comfortable). Some rental places will pick you up at an agreed-upon spot, even in Sarlat, if they aren't too busy and you can give a precise pickup time and location (and be flexible on the return time). Also, consider hiring a taxi/driver to connect your canoe float with a visit to a prehistoric cave (see "Helpful Hints," earlier).

All companies let you put in anytime between 9:30 and 16:00 (start no later than 15:00 to allow time to linger when the mood strikes; they'll pick you up at about 18:00). They all charge about the same and most accept cash only (two-person canoe–€15-20/person, one-person kayak–€16-26). You'll get a life vest and, for about €2 extra, a watertight bucket in which to store your belongings. (The bucket is bigger than you'd need for just a camera, watch, wallet, and phone; if that's all you have bring a resealable plastic baggie or something similar for dry storage.) You must have shoes that stay on your feet; travelers wearing flip-flops will be invited to purchase more appropriate footwear (sold at most boat launches for around €10).

Périgord-Aventure et Loisirs has a pullout arrangement in Beynac (to get to their Vitrac put-in base, from the main roundabout in the town of Vitrac, cross the Dordogne, and turn right). They may be able to pick you up in Sarlat for free (RS%—10 percent discount with this book, arrange in advance, return times to Sarlat based on driver availability, tip the driver a few euros for this helpful service; tel. 05 53 28 23 82, mobile 06 83 27 30 06, www.perigordaventureloisirs.com, info@perigordaventureloisirs.com). Allow time to explore Beynac after your river paddle and before the return shuttle trip. Périgord-Aventure also arranges a longer, 14-mile trip from Carsac to Beynac, adding the gorgeous Montfort loop *(Cingle de Montfort)*. Ask about their canoe, hike, and bike options, such as the canoe trip to Beynac, followed with a walk along a riverside trail to Castelnaud, and ending with a mountain-bike ride on uneven terrain back to your starting point in Vitrac (€30, no discounts, reserve in advance, start or end the loop wherever you like).

The Nine-Mile Paddle from Vitrac to Beynac: Here's a rundown of the two-hour Vitrac-Beynac adventure: Leave **Vitrac**, paddling at an easy pace through lush, forested land. The fortified hill town of Domme will be dead ahead. Pass through Heron Gulch, and after about an hour you'll come to **La Roque-Gageac** (one of two easy and worthwhile stops before Beynac).

Paddle past La Roque-Gageac's wooden docks (with the tour boats) to the stone ramp leading up to the town. Do a 180-degree turn and beach thyself, dragging the boat high and dry. From there you're in La Roque-Gageac's tiny town center, with a TI and plenty of cafés, snacks, and ice-cream options. Enjoy the town before heading back to your canoe and into the water.

When leaving La Roque-Gageac, float backward for a bit to enjoy the village view. About 15 minutes farther downstream, you'll approach views of the feudal village and castle of **Castelnaud**. Look for the castle's huge model of medieval catapults silhouetted menacingly against the sky (it's a steep but worthwhile climb to

DORDOGNE

Dordogne Canoe Trips & Scenic Loop Drive

To Sarlat

LE PETIT VERSAILLES

BEYNAC

To St-Cyprien, Les Eyzies & Truffe en Périgord

Bike Route to Sarlat

D-703

6

FINISH

D-57

FAYRAC

5

D-703

LE LYS DE CASTELNAUD B&B

DIVE ROCK

LA ROQUE-GAGEAC

3

MONTGOLFIÈRES DU PÉRIGORD

D-53

CASTELNAUD

4

Dordogne

White Cliffs

Heron Gulch

River

D-703

EASY CANOE PULLOUTS

2

Cénac

D-57

D-50

D-46

LA TOUR DE CAUSE B&B

St-Cybranet

To Salviac

1 Start Point (Périgord-Aventure et Loisirs at Vitrac)
2 Pont de Cénac
3 La Roque-Gageac
4 Castelnaud
5 Snack Stand & Views
6 Beynac & End Point

tour this castle). You'll find two grassy pullouts flanking the bridge below the castle. The bridge arches make terrific frames for castle views. Nearby, there's a small market and charcuterie with all you need for a picnic. The local café serves good-enough fare with views (near where you pull out).

Another 15 minutes downstream brings views of **Château de Fayrac** on your left. The lords of Castelnaud built this to spy on Beynac during the Hundred Years' War (1336-1453). It's another 15 minutes to your last stop: **Beynac.** The awesome Beynac castle—looming high above the town—gets more impressive as you approach. Slow down and enjoy the ride (sometimes there's a snack stand with the same views at the bridge on the right). Keep to the right as you approach the Périgord-Aventure depot. You'll see the ramp just before the parking lot and wooden dock (where the tour boats generally tie up). Do another 180-degree turn, and beach yourself hard. The office is right there. Return your boat, and explore Beynac.

Other Canoe Options: All along the river you'll see canoe companies, each with stacks of plastic canoes. Depending on their location and relations with places to pull out, each one works best on a particular stretch of the river. All have essentially the same

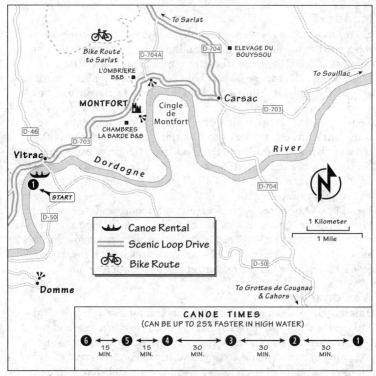

policies. Below Domme in Cénac, **Dordogne Randonnées** has canoes and kayaks for the scenic two-hour stretch to a pullout just past Beynac (to reach their office coming from Sarlat or Beynac, take the first left after crossing the bridge to Cénac, tel. 05 53 28 22 01). In La Roque-Gageac, **Canoe-Dordogne** rents canoes for the worthwhile two-hour float to Château des Milandes, allowing canoers to stop in Beynac along the way (tel. 05 53 29 58 50). For a lazier, no-paddle alternative, a boat cruise on the river to Castelnaud and back—either from Beynac or La Roque-Gageac—is great for landlubbers (€10, 1 hour, described in the next section).

Dordogne Towns and Sights

The towns and sights described coincide with the Dordogne River Valley scenic loop and canoe trip outlined earlier. These villages are a joy to wander early and late in the day. In high season, expect mobs of tourists and traffic in the afternoons. Those with a car can enjoy tranquil rural accommodations at great prices in these cozy villages. Read about the villages next, then make your choice—you can't go wrong.

Montfort

There's more to this castle-topped village than meets the eye—leave most tourists behind and find a handful of cafés, restaurants, and *chambres d'hôtes*, including these recommended listings (for locations, see the "Dordogne Canoe Trips & Scenic Loop Drive" map).

Sleeping near Montfort: $$ Chambres la Barde has five good rooms in a warm, recently built stone home with friendly French owners, a swimming pool, cozy lounge, big grass yard, communal kitchen, and views to Montfort castle from most rooms' terraces (family rooms, includes breakfast, cash only, well-signed behind Montfort castle at 135 Route de la Plage de Caudon, tel. 05 53 28 24 34, mobile 06 09 63 19 71, www.labardemontfort.com, frederique.drouin5@gmail.com).

$$ L'Ombrière, with four elegant rooms and welcoming German hosts Niels and Lena, is a calm B&B overlooking a walnut grove with many picnic spaces (includes breakfast, attic rooms have air-con, on east edge of Montfort village—watch for signs, tel. 07 89 68 18 89, www.lombriere.com, contact@lombriere.com).

▲▲Domme

This busy little town merits a stop for its stunning view and is ideal early in the day. Otherwise, come late, when crowds recede and the light is divine. If you come for lunch or dinner, arrive early enough to savor the cliff-capping setting, and if you come on market day (Thu) expect to hoof it up from a parking lot well below (cars not allowed in old town until the market is over). On other days, follow signs up to *La Bastide de Domme,* and drive right through the narrow gate of the fortified town walls. Park at the pay lot near the view *(Panorama).* You'll find picnic-perfect benches, cafés, and a view you won't soon forget. While the main street is lined with touristy shops that make the town feel greedy, you can lose yourself in some of the unusually picturesque back lanes, where roses climb over rustic doorways.

Sleeping and Eating in Domme: The town has many forgettable restaurants, but a few places stand out.

$$$ Cabanoix et Châtaigne is a small bistro serving delicious Dordogne fare blended with international flavors. Enjoy the sunset from Domme's viewpoint, then come here to dine in a quaint courtyard with colorful shutters. Book a table ahead—local foodies are all over this place (€33-40 *menus,* July-Aug open daily for lunch and dinner, Sept-June usually closed Tue; from the viewpoint, walk past the church several blocks down Grand Rue and turn left to 3 Rue Geoffroy de Vivans; tel. 05 53 31 07 11, www. restaurantcabanoix.com).

$$ Hôtel de l'Esplanade* delivers the valley's most sensational views from many of its 15 comfortable and traditional bed-

rooms and restaurant tables. If you come for the **$$$** restaurant (closed Mon lunch), book ahead for view seating. Both the hotel and the restaurant are traditional, formal, and a bit stiff (air-con, tel. 05 53 28 31 41, www.esplanade-perigord.com, esplanade.domme@wanadoo.fr).

$$ Belvédère Café owns a privileged position at the viewpoint and serves standard café fare at good prices with million-dollar views from its outside tables. Try to eat here at sunset (daily for lunch and dinner, closed Oct-March, at *Le Panorama*, tel. 05 53 31 12 01).

▲▲▲La Roque-Gageac

Whether you're joyriding, paddling the Dordogne, or taking a hot-air balloon ride, La Roque-Gageac (lah rohk-gah-zhahk) is an essential stop—and a strong contender on all the "cutest towns in France" lists. Called by most simply "La Roque" ("The Rock"), it looks sculpted out of the rock between the river and the cliffs. It also is a fine base for touring the region.

At the upstream end of town, you'll find parking and an ATM, the **TI** (closed off-season, tel. 05 53 29 17 01), a WC, swings and slides for kids, canoe rental, and *pétanque (boules)* courts. A small market brightens La Roque-Gageac on Friday mornings in summer. Though busy with day-trippers, the town is tranquil at night.

Visiting La Roque-Gageac: Stand along the river just downstream from the boat ticket office and survey La Roque-Gageac: It's a one-street town stretching along the river. The highest stonework (on the far right) was home to the town's earliest inhabitants in the 10th century. High above (about center), 12th-century cave dwellers built a settlement during the era of Norman (Viking) river raids. Long after the Vikings were tamed, French soldiers used this lofty perch as a barracks while fighting against

England in the Hundred Years' War. Sturdy modern supports now reinforce the cave.

Now locate the exotic foliage around the church on the right. Tropical gardens (bamboo, bananas, lemons, cactus, and so on) are a village forte, because limestone absorbs heat. Notice the two

DORDOGNE

church chapels extending over the cliff—when level land is scarce, necessity is the mother of invention.

The wooden boats on the river are modeled after boats called *gabarres*, originally built here to take prized oak barrels filled with local wine down to Bordeaux. Unable to return against the river current, the boats were routinely taken apart for their lumber. Today, tourists, rather than barrels, fill the boats on river cruises (described later). These actual boats (dolled up) were used by Johnny Depp in the movie *Chocolat*, to the delight of viewers and Juliette Binoche alike.

Looking downstream, notice the fanciful castle built in the 19th century by a British aristocrat (whose family still nurtures Joan of Arc dreams in its turrets). The old building just beyond that (downstream end of town) actually is historic—it's the quarantine house, where lepers and out-of-town visitors who dropped by in times of plague would be kept (after their boats were burned).

Walk along the main drag to get a closer look at the village. La Roque-Gageac frequently endures winter floods that would leave you (standing where you are now) underwater. When there's a big rain in central France, La Roque-Gageac floods two days later. The first floors of all the riverfront buildings are vacated off-season. The new riverfront wall, finished in 2014, was pushed out into the river, adding 13 feet of width to the street. Notice the openings at sidewalk level allowing water to flow through in heavy rains. A house about five buildings downriver from Hôtel la Belle Etoile has high-water marks engraved on its wall (*inondation* means "flood").

Climb into the town by strolling up the cobbled lane to the right of Hôtel la Belle Etoile. Where the stepped path ends, veer right to find the exotic plants and viewpoint (in front of the simple church). From here you can make out Château de Castelnaud downriver, and the village of Domme capping its hill to the left. A left turn at the end of the stepped path takes you to more views and a nice loop that connects back to the river.

Boat Tours: Tour boats cruise from La Roque-Gageac to Castelnaud and back (one-hour cruise-€10, includes audioguide, 2/hour, April-Nov daily, tel. 05 53 29 40 44).

Hot-Air Balloon Rides: Montgolfières du Périgord, located in La Roque-Gageac, offers a range of flights (see listing on page 449).

Sleeping and Eating: Along with Beynac, this is one of the region's most beautiful villages. Park in the lot at the eastern end of town if you're staying in La Roque-Gageac, and take everything of value out of your car.

$$ Manoir de la Malartrie is a wonderful splurge. It has five country-classy rooms and two family apartments with oak-meets-leather public areas, all surrounding a big, heated pool and impeccable terraced gardens (begging for a picnic). Your gentle hostess Ouaffa manages her place with elegance (3-night minimum in summer, air-con, free parking, barely downstream from the village—10-minute walk to town on trail above road, tel. 05 53 29 03 51, mobile 06 18 61 61 18, www.chambresdhotes-lamalartrie.com, lamalartrie@orange.fr).

$ Hôtel la Belle Etoile,* a well-managed hotel-restaurant in the center of La Roque-Gageac, is a terrific value. Hostess Danielle and chef Régis (ray-geez) offer good, basic rooms overlooking the river, a nice terrace, and a fine restaurant (air-con, free parking, closed Nov-March, tel. 05 53 29 51 44, www.belleetoile.fr, hotel.belle-etoile@wanadoo.fr). Régis is the third generation of his family to be chef here and he takes his job seriously. Come to the **$$ restaurant** for a memorable dinner of classic French cuisine with modern accents in a romantic setting. The *œufs cocottes* are really good (closed for lunch Wed and all day Mon; book a few days ahead).

$ L'Auberge des Platanes,** across from La Roque-Gageac's TI and parking lot, rents 21 rooms above a sprawling café—guests take a backseat to café clients. Half the rooms are basic and traditional; the other half are modern and pricier (a few rooms have air-con, tel. 05 53 29 51 58, www.aubergedesplatanes.com, contact@aubergedesplatanes.com).

▲▲Château de Castelnaud

This castle may look a tad less mighty than Château de Beynac (down the river), but it packs a powerful medieval punch. The concise

handout escorts you room by room through the castle-museum. The exhibits—which focus on warfare (armor, crossbows, and catapults) are well organized and slicker than Beynac's, but the castle is also more touristy and lacks personality.

Cost and Hours: €11; daily July-Aug 9:00-20:00, April-June and Sept 10:00-19:00, Oct and Feb-March until 18:00, shorter hours Nov-Jan, last entry one hour before closing; tel. 05 53 31 30 00, www.castelnaud.com.

Activities: From mid-July to August, the castle offers daily demonstrations of medieval warfare and guided visits in English (call ahead for times), and a sound-and-light show—in French only—takes place in the courtyard of the castle after dark.

Getting There: From the river, it's a steep 30-minute hike through the village to the castle. Drivers must park in the pay lot

DORDOGNE

(5-minute walk uphill from the castle). You can stop at Castelnaud on your canoe trip or hike an hour from Beynac along a riverside path (though it's tricky to follow in parts—it hugs the river as it passes through campgrounds and farms—determined walkers do fine).

Visiting the Castle: After passing the ticket booth, read your essential handout and follow the *suite de la visite* signs. Start by climbing through the tower. Every room has a story to tell, and many have displays of costumed mannequins, suits of armor, weaponry (including the biggest and most artistic crossbows I've ever seen), and artifacts from the Hundred Years' War. Other rooms show informative videos (with English subtitles)—don't miss the catapult video where you'll learn that the big ones could fire only two shots per hour and required up to 250 men to manage. Kids eat it up, in part thanks to the children's guide with fun puzzles. The upper courtyard has a 150-foot-deep well (drop a pebble). On your way back down, you'll see a sparsely furnished medieval kitchen and an iron forge with an interesting video. The rampart views are as unbeatable as the four siege machines are formidable. A few cafés and fun medieval shops await at the foot of the castle.

Sleeping near Castelnaud: This village is ideally situated between La Roque-Gageac and Beynac. **$ La Tour de Cause** is where Belgian owners Igor and Nico have found their heaven, amid their renovated farmhouse with five top-quality rooms. Some have immense walk-in showers, and the upstairs rooms have beautiful wood-beam high ceilings. There's also a big pool, fine gardens, and, best of all, a *pétanque* court. Your hosts are talented chefs and happy to prepare a refreshing €35 three-course dinner with wine—if you book ahead (3-night minimum July-Aug, includes breakfast, no air-con, cash only, tel. 05 53 30 30 51, mobile 06 37 32 44 17, www.latourdecause.com, info@latourdecause.com). From the Dordogne River, cross the bridge to Castelnaud, follow signs toward *Daglan,* then make a hard right turn in the hamlet of Pont de Cause and park near their gate.

▲▲▲Beynac

Four miles downstream from La Roque-Gageac, Beynac (bay-nak) is the other must-see Dordogne village. It's also home to one of the most imposing castles in France.

This well-preserved medieval village winds like a sepia-tone film set from the castle above to the river below (easy parking at the top avoids the

steep climb). The stone village—with cobbled lanes that retain their Occitan (old French) names—is just plain pretty, best late in the afternoon and downright dreamy after dark. For the best light, tour the castle late, or at least walk out to the sensational viewpoint, then have a dinner here.

Drivers can **park** at pay lots located on the river (busy), way up at the castle (quieter, follow signs to *Château de Beynac*), or halfway between. The same parking ticket works at all three lots (park below, explore the lower village, then drive to the top for the castle). The **TI** is near the river, across from Hôtel du Château (closed in winter, tel. 05 53 29 43 08). Pick up the *Plan du Village* in English for a simple self-guided walking tour, and get information on hiking and canoes. A few steps down from the TI is the post office (ATM outside). If you need a lift, call Beynac-based Bernard at **Taxi Corinne** (see page 447). From mid-June to mid-September, a cute little market sets up on Monday mornings in the riverfront parking lot.

Château de Beynac: Beynac's brooding, cliff-clinging château, worth ▲▲, soars 500 feet above the Dordogne River (€8, daily 10:00-19:00, off-season until 18:30, last entry 45 minutes before closing, tel. 05 53 29 50 40, www.chateau-beynac. com). Spring for the essential and well-done €3 audioguide that can be shared by many (no headphones needed). This castle is the ultimate for that top-of-the-world, king-

of-the-castle feeling. During the Hundred Years' War (see sidebar on page 230), the castle of Beynac housed the French, while the English set up camp across the river at Castelnaud. This authentic, sparsely furnished castle is best for its valley views, but it still manages to evoke a memorable medieval feel. (These castles never had much furniture in any case.) When buying your ticket, notice the list showing the barons of Beynac *(Beynac et Ses Barons)*—Richard the Lionheart *(Coeur de Lion)* spent 10 years here.

You're free to wander on your own. As you tour the castle, swords, spears, and crossbows keep you honest, and two stone WCs keep kids entertained. The furnishings show how soldiers parked their swords and hung their crossbows before sitting down to dinner and drink (soldiers drank over two quarts of wine per day). Circling up through the castle, find your way to the highest crenellated terraces for sensational views. This is the closest look

DORDOGNE

you'll have to a *lauzes* roof. Just down the river, mighty Casteln-aud—which seems so imposing from up close—looks like a child's playset.

Walks and Viewpoints: A busy road separates Beynac from its river. Traffic-free lanes climb steeply uphill from the river to the château—the farther you get from the road, the more medieval the village feels. A pedestrian sidewalk runs along the river connecting to a riverfront trail, which begins across from Hôtel Bonnet at the eastern end of town and follows the river toward Castelnaud, of-fering great views back toward Beynac. For able route-finders, this is a level one-hour hike to the village of Castelnaud. Make time to walk at least a few hundred yards along this trail to enjoy the view to Beynac.

One of the Dordogne's most commanding views lies a short walk from the castle at the **top of the village** (easy parking, not essential if you toured the castle). Step just outside the village's upper end and take the enclosed lane to the right of the little cem-etery. Stroll uphill to an odd glass structure. Castelnaud's castle hangs on the hill in the distance straight ahead. Château de Fayrac (owned by a Texan) is just right of the rail bridge and was originally constructed by the lords of Castelnaud to keep a close eye on the castle of Beynac. The Château de Marqueyssac, on a hill to the left, was built by the barons of Beynac to keep a close eye on the boys at Castelnaud—touché. More than a thousand such castles were erected in the Dordogne alone during the Hundred Years' War.

Boat Tours: Boats leave from Beynac's riverside parking lot for relaxing, 50-minute river cruises to Château de Fayrac and back (€10, nearly hourly, departures Easter-Oct daily 10:00-12:30 & 14:00-18:00, more frequent July-Aug, tel. 05 53 28 51 15).

Sleeping in or near Beynac: $$$ Domaine de Monre-cour*** is a classy place a few minutes west of Beynac. It features a mix of elegant rooms in the château and cheaper rooms in a family friendly annex. Public spaces are fit for a lord, with sweeping views from terraces and two pools (one pool for the annex peasants, the other for château nobles comes with castle views). There's a *gas-tronomique* restaurant—**$$$ La Table de Monrecour**—as well (in the village of St-Vincent de Cosse, tel. 05 53 28 33 59, www.monrecour.com, contact@monrecour.com).

$ Hôtel Pontet** is a good budget option in Beynac, with 10 modern and clean rooms (air-con, no elevator, Wi-Fi best in lobby, 100 yards from the river on the main street; when reception is closed—11:00-14:00 and after 19:00—check in at the Hostel-lerie Maleville restaurant on the river, tel. 05 53 29 50 06, www.hostellerie-maleville.com, hostellerie.maleville@orange.fr).

$ Le Petit Versailles does its name justice, with five immacu-late rooms that Louis would have appreciated. The place has a quiet terrace and garden, and—best of all—the welcoming Fleurys, Jean-Claude and Françoise (three rooms have fine views, all have big beds, includes large English breakfast, cash only, no smoking anywhere, laundry facilities, Route du Château, mobile 06 71 88 59 72, www.lepetitversailles.fr, info@lepetitversailles.fr). With the river on your right, take the small road—wedged between the hill and Hôtel Bonnet—for a half-mile, turn right when you see the *Résidence de Versailles* sign and continue 100 yards, then take a right down a steep driveway.

$ Hôtel du Château,** centrally situated at Beynac's main intersection, is a work in progress that comes with a pool, bar, restaurant, and terrace-café. Welcoming owner Stéphanie is renovating the rooms with taste and air-conditioning (ask for a renovated room or sleep elsewhere, tel. 05 53 29 19 20, www.hotel-chateau-dordogne.com, contact@hotel-beynac-dordogne.com).

Eating in Beynac: Beynac has a few worthwhile places to eat and a bakery with handy picnic-ready lunch items (across from the TI). Have a drink up high at the café opposite the castle entry (see next), or down below at the **P'tit Malo** café, which hides right on the river (walk down the steps across from Hôtel du Château); stay for dinner if the spirit moves you.

$ Café des Remparts, Beynac's scenic eatery, faces the castle at the top of the town and serves copious salads, omelets, and *plats*. I can't imagine leaving Beynac without relaxing at their view-perfect café for at least a drink or an ice cream (*glace à la noix*—walnut ice cream—cannot get more local). Sophie promises a free house aperitif with this book in 2020 and usually keeps the place open until at least 19:30—plenty late for most Americans to have dinner. Call ahead to be sure they're open (daily, closed in winter, across from castle, tel. 05 53 29 57 76).

The recommended **$ Hôtel du Château's restaurant** serves reliable cuisine at fair prices in an air-conditioned room or outside on the terrace across from the river.

$$ La Petite Tonnelle, cut into the rock, has a romantic interior and a fine terrace out front. Locals love it for its tasty cuisine served at fair prices, though the service can be erratic. It's a block up from Hôtel du Château (good *menu* options, closed Sun-Mon, on the road to the castle, tel. 05 53 29 95 18, www.restaurant-petite-tonnelle.fr).

BEYOND THE SCENIC LOOP
Foie Gras Farms
During the evenings, many farms in this area let you witness the force-feeding of geese for the "ultimate pleasure" of foie gras. Look for *Gavage* signs, but beware: It can be hard for the squeamish to watch (read the sidebar for a description before you visit).

DORDOGNE

Foie Gras and Force-Feeding the Geese and Ducks

Force-feeding geese and ducks has the result of quickly fattening their livers, the principal ingredient of the Dordogne specialty foie gras. Among animal-rights activists, the practice is as controversial as bullfighting (and their case is well-documented). But talking to local farmers, it's fascinating to hear the other side of the story. While awful conditions certainly exist in some places, here in the Dordogne, farmers pride themselves on treating their animals in what they consider a humane manner. Here's their take:

French enthusiasts of *le gavage* (as the force-feeding process is called) say the animals are calm, in no pain, and are designed to take in food in this manner because of their massive gullets and expandable livers (used to store lots of fat for their long migrations). Geese and ducks do not have a gag reflex, and the linings of their throats are tough (they swallow rocks to store in their gizzards for grinding the food they eat). They can eat lots of food easily, without choking. Dordogne ducks and geese live lives at least as comfy as the chickens, cows, and pigs that many people have no problem eating, and they are slaughtered as humanely as any nonhuman can expect in this food-chain existence.

The quality of foie gras depends on a stress-free environment; the birds do best with the same human feeder and a steady flow of good corn. These mostly free-range geese and ducks live six months (most of our factory-farmed chickens in the US live less than two months, and are plumped with hormones). Their "golden weeks" are the last three or four, when they go into the pen to have their livers fattened. With two or three feedings a

Elevage du Bouyssou

This big, homey goose farm, a short drive from Sarlat, is run by a couple passionate about their work. Denis Mazet (the latest in a long line of goose farmers here) spends five hours a day feeding his gaggle of geese. His wife, Nathalie—clearly in love with country life—speaks wonderful English and enthusiastically shows guests around their idyllic farm. Each evening, she leads a one-hour, kid-friendly tour. You'll meet the goslings, do a little unforced feeding, and hear how every part of the goose (except heads and feet) is used—even feathers (for pillows). Nathalie explains why locals see

day, their liver grows from about a quarter-pound to nearly two pounds. A goose with a fattened liver looks like he's waddling around with a full diaper under his feathers. (Signs and placards in the towns of the region show geese with this unique and, for foie-gras lovers, mouthwatering shape.) The same process is applied to ducks to get the marginally less exquisite and less expensive duck-liver foie gras.

The varieties of product you'll be tempted to buy (or order in restaurants) can be confusing. Here's a primer: first, *foie gras* means "fattened liver"; *foie gras d'oie* is from a goose, and *foie gras de canard* is from a duck (you'll also see a blend of the two). *Pâté de foie gras* is a "paste" of foie gras combined with other meats, fats, and seasonings (think of liverwurst). Most American consumers get the chance to eat foie gras only in the form of pâtés—and be careful, because *pâté* in French refers to a pork spread.

The *foie gras d'oie entier* (a solid chunk of pure goose liver) is the most expensive and prized version of canned foie gras, costing about €22 for 130 grams (about a tuna-can-size tin). The *bloc de foie gras d'oie* is made of chunks of pure goose liver that have been pressed together; it's more easily spreadable (figure €15 for 130 grams). The *medaillons de foie gras d'oie* must be at least 50 percent foie gras (the rest will be a pâté filler, about €10 for 130 grams). Stay away from *mousse,* a mixture of several things, with or without wings or liver. When choosing, read the label carefully: *éleveur en Dordogne/Périgord* means that the animal was actually raised locally; *produit en Dordogne/ Périgord/France* means it was processed here, but may have originated elsewhere. It's also trendy to label products *artisan conserveur*—"conserved artisanally"—but again, this promises only that the product was canned locally. Note: Airport security may require you to carry these in your checked baggage, not your carry-on. For foie gras farm visits, see "Beyond the Scenic Loop," earlier.

After a week in the Dordogne, I leave feeling a strong need for foie gras detox.

DORDOGNE

force-feeding as humane (comparable to raising any other animal for human consumption) before you step into the dark barn where about a hundred geese await another dinner. The tour finishes in the little shop. They raise and slaughter a thousand geese annually, producing about 1,500 pounds of foie gras—most of which is sold directly to visitors at good prices.

Cost and Hours: Free; tours July-Aug daily at 18:30, Sept-June Mon-Sat at 18:30; shop open 9:00-19:30, tel. 05 53 31 12 31, mobile 06 38 95 48 80, www.elevagedubouyssou.com, elevagedubouyssou@gmail.com.

Getting There: Leave Sarlat on the Cahors-bound road (D-704), go about seven kilometers, turn left at the cement plant (where you see the *Camping Aqua-Viva* sign), and follow *Bouyssou* signs until you reach the farm (the last section winds up several curves; keep going—you'll hear the geese).

Truffle Hunting (Truffe en Périgord)

Learn everything there is to know about this dirty delicacy on a two-hour tour with truffle expert Edouard and his adorable dogs (also experts in this field). In sometimes rough but understandable English, you'll hear about the different truffle varieties and techniques for hunting the "black diamond." You'll then head out in the field to accompany the hunt.

Cost and Hours: €10 daily by appointment only, no tours in Aug, avoid morning tour groups in July, tel. 05 53 29 20 44, mobile 06 79 02 48 02, French-only website at www.truffe-perigord.com, pechalifour@gmail.com.

Getting There: From St. Cyprien (3 kilometers away), follow signs toward *Campagne/Le Bugue,* and then *Péchalifour* and *Truffes du Périgord.*

Cro-Magnon Caves

The area around the town of Les Eyzies-de-Tayac—about a 30-minute drive from Sarlat or the Dordogne Valley—has a rich history of prehistoric cave art. The paintings you'll see in this area's caves are famous throughout the world for their remarkably modern-looking technique, beauty, and mystery.

For a rundown of your cave options, see "Prehistoric Sights at a Glance." And to fully appreciate the art you'll see, take time to read the following information, written by Gene Openshaw, on the purpose of the art and the Cro-Magnon style of painting.

CAVE ART 101

From 18,000 to 10,000 BC, long before Stonehenge, before the pyramids, before metalworking and farming, back when mammoths and saber-toothed cats still roamed the earth, prehistoric people

painted deep inside limestone caverns in southern France and northern Spain. These are not crude doodles with a charcoal-tipped stick. They're sophisticated, costly, and time-consuming engineering projects planned and executed by dedicated artists supported by a unified and stable culture—the Magdalenians.

The Magdalenians (c. 18,000-10,000 BC): These hunter-gatherers of the Upper Paleolithic period (40,000-10,000 BC) were driven south by the Second Ice Age. (Historians named them after the Madeleine archaeological site near Les Eyzies-de-Tayac.) The Magdalenians flourished in southern France and northern Spain for eight millennia—long enough to chronicle the evolution and extinction of several animal species. (Think: Egypt lasted a mere 3,000 years; Rome lasted 1,000; America fewer than 250 so far.)

Physically, the people were Cro-Magnons. Unlike hulking, beetle-browed Neanderthals, Cro-Magnons were fully developed *Homo sapiens* who could blend in to our modern population. We know these people by the possessions found in their settlements: stone axes, flint arrowheads, bone needles for making clothes, musical instruments, grease lamps (without their juniper wicks), and cave paintings and sculptures. Many objects are beautifully decorated.

The Magdalenians did not live in the deep limestone caverns they painted (which are cold and difficult to access). But many did live in the shallow cliffside caves that you'll see throughout your Dordogne travels, which were continuously inhabited from prehistoric times until the Middle Ages.

The Paintings: Though there are dozens of caves painted over a span of more than 8,000 years, they're all surprisingly similar. These Stone Age hunters painted the animals they hunted—bison or bulls (especially at Lascaux and Grotte de Font-de-Gaume), horses, deer, reindeer, ibex (mountain goats), wolves, bears, and cats, plus animals that are now extinct—mammoths (the engravings at Grotte de Rouffignac), woolly rhinoceroses (at Grotte de Font-de-Gaume), and wild oxen.

Besides animals, you'll see geometric and abstract designs, such as circles, squiggles, and hash marks. There's scarcely a *Homo sapiens* in sight (except the famous "fallen hunter" at Lascaux), but there are human handprints traced on the wall by blowing paint through a hollow bone tube around the hand. The hunter-gatherers

Cro-Magnon Caves near Sarlat-la-Canéda

To Perigueux &
St-Emilion
via A-89

D-45

D-32

2 Kilometers

2 Miles

**GROTTE DE
ROUFFIGNAC**

St-Léon

D-706

**LA ROQUE
ST-CHRISTOPHE**

MAISON FORTE
DE REIGNAC

D-710

River

D-65

D-47

**ABRI DU
CAP BLANC**

Les Eyzies-
de-Tayac

D-48

**GROTTE
DE FONT-
DE-GAUME**

CHATEAU DE
COMMARQUE

Le Bugue

Vézère

(PREHISTORY
WELCOME CENTER
& MUSEUM)

D-47

D-703

LA TRUFFE
EN PERIGORD

D-35

D-48

LE CHEVREFEUILLE
CHAMBRES

D O R D O G N E

D-703

St-Cyprien

River

Le Buisson

D-51

D-703

D-29

DORDOGNE

D-25

Dordogne

D-25

D-703

D-53

Siorac-en-
Périgord

CHATEAU
DES MILANDES

To Bergerac
& St-Emilion

D-710

D-53

Belvès

D-53

Paris

FRANCE

100 Miles

■   Prehistoric Sites

🦆   Foie Gras Farm

▓▓▓   Scenic Loop

To D-6089 & A-89: Périgueux

To A-20: Limoges, Oradour-sur-Glane & Mortemart

D-45

CHATEAU DE LA FLEUNIE

Montignac

INTERNATIONAL CENTER FOR CAVE ART & LASCAUX IV

D-706

LASCAUX II

D-65

D-64

D-62

D-60

D-704

St-Geniès

D-48

D-60

Salignac-Eyvigues

D-62

To Souillac & A-20

D-47

D-704

See Greater Sarlat detail map

Sarlat-la-Canéda

To Souillac

V A L L E Y

BIKE PATH

D-703

D-57

D-704

ELEVAGE DU BOUYSSOU

D-704A

Dordogne River

BEYNAC

D-46

MONTFORT

Carsac

D-703

La Roque-Gageac

Vitrac

CASTELNAUD

D-703

D-50

D-57

Cénac

Domme

D-50

See Dordogne Canoe Trips detail map

L O T

D-46

D-704

GROTTES DE COUGNAC

To Cahors, "Eastern Dordogne", Grotte du Pech Merle & Lot River Valley

Gourdon

DORDOGNE

painted the animals they hunted, but none of the plants they gathered.

Style: The animals stand in profile, with unnaturally big bodies and small limbs and heads. Black, red, and yellow dominate (with some white, brown, and violet). The thick black outlines are often wavy, suggesting the animal in motion. Except for a few friezes showing a conga line of animals running across the cave wall, there is no apparent order or composition. Some paintings are simply superimposed atop others. The artists clearly had mastered the animals' anatomy, but they chose to simplify the outlines and distort the heads and limbs for effect, always painting in the distinct Magdalenian style.

Many of the cave paintings are on a Sistine Chapel-size scale. The "canvas" was huge: Lascaux's main caverns are more than a football field long; Grotte de Font-de-Gaume is 430 feet long; and Grotte de Rouffignac meanders six miles deep. The figures are monumental (one bull at Lascaux is 17 feet long). All are painted high up on walls and ceilings, like the woolly rhinoceros of Grotte de Font-de-Gaume.

Techniques: Besides painting the animals, these early artists also engraved them on the wall by laboriously scratching outlines into the rock with a flint blade, many following the rock's natural contour. A typical animal might be made using several techniques—an engraved outline that follows the natural contour, reinforced with thick outline paint, then colored in.

The paints were mixed from natural pigments dissolved in cave water and oil (animal or vegetable). At Lascaux, archaeologists have found more than 150 different minerals on hand to mix paints. Even basic black might be a mix of manganese dioxide, ground quartz, and a calcium phosphate that had to be made by heating bone to 700 degrees Fahrenheit, then grinding it.

No paintbrushes have been found, so artists probably used a sponge-like material made from animal skin and fat. They may have used moss or hair, or maybe even finger-painted with globs of pure pigment. Once they'd drawn the outlines, they filled everything in with spray paint—either spit out from the mouth or blown through tubes made of hollow bone.

Imagine the engineering problems of painting one of these caves, and you can appreciate how sophisticated these "primitive" people were. First, you'd have to haul all your materials into a cold, pitch-black, hard-to-access place. Assistants erected scaffolding to reach ceilings and high walls, ground up minerals with a mortar and pestle, mixed paints, tended the torches and oil lamps, prepared the "paintbrushes," laid out major outlines with a connect-the-dots series of points...then stepped aside for Magdalenian Michelangelos to ascend the scaffolding and create.

DORDOGNE

Dating: Determining exactly how old this art is—and whether it's authentic—is tricky. (Because much of the actual paint is mineral-based with no organic material, carbon-dating techniques are often ineffective.) As different caves feature different animals, prehistorians can deduce which caves are relatively older and younger, since climate change caused various animal species to come and go within certain regions. In several cases, experts confirmed the authenticity of a painting because the portrayals of the animals showed anatomical details not previously known—until they were discovered by modern technology. (For instance, in Grotte de Rouffignac, the mammoths are shown with a strange skin flap over their anus, which was only discovered during the 20th century on a preserved mammoth found in Siberian permafrost.) They can also estimate dates by checking the amount of calcium glaze formed over the paint, which can sometimes only be seen by infrared photography.

Why? No one knows the purpose of the cave paintings. Interestingly, the sites the artists chose were deliberately awe-inspiring, out of the way, and special. They knew their work here would last for untold generations, as had the paintings that came before theirs. Here are some theories of what this first human art might mean.

It's no mystery that hunters would paint animals, the source of their existence. The first scholar to study the caves, Abbé Henri Breuil, thought the painted animals were magic symbols made by hunters to increase the supply of game. Or perhaps hunters thought that if you could "master" an animal by painting it, you could later master it in battle. Some scholars think the paintings teach the art of hunting, but there's very little apparent hunting technique shown. Did they worship animals? The paintings definitely depict an animal-centered (rather than a human-centered) universe.

The paintings may have a religious purpose, and some of the caverns are large and special enough that rituals and ceremonies could have been held there. But the paintings show no sacrifices, rituals, or ceremonies. Scholars writing on primitive art in other parts of the world speculate that art was made by shamans in a religious or drug-induced trance, but France's paintings are very methodical.

The order of paintings on the walls seems random. Could it be that the caves are a painted collage of the history of the Magdalen-

Prehistoric Sights at a Glance

You can reserve ahead only for Lascaux II and IV, Grotte du Pech Merle, and Abri du Cap Blanc. For the other caves, it's first-come, first-served.

▲▲▲**Grotte de Font-de-Gaume** Last prehistoric multicolored paintings open to public, with strict limits on the number of daily visitors. **Hours:** Mid-May-mid-Sept Sun-Fri 9:30-17:30, mid-Sept-mid-May Sun-Fri 9:30-12:30 & 14:00-17:30, closed Sat year-round. **Reservations:** Not available, but some area guides and transport services may be able to secure advance tickets. Without a guide, be in line by 7:30 in summer, 8:30 in spring and fall, and 9:00 in winter. Required 45-minute tour (likely in French). See page 494.

▲▲**International Center for Cave Art at Lascaux** Exact replicas of the world's most famous cave paintings, and an interactive center on cave art. **Hours:** Lascaux IV—daily July-Aug 9:00-21:00; late March-June and Sept-Nov until 19:00, shorter hours in winter and closed Jan. Lascaux II—shorter hours and closed mid-Nov-late March. **Reservations:** Book in advance online, especially in high season. Required 40-minute tour for Lascaux IV, 75-minute tour for Lascaux II; allow up to 3 hours. See page 498.

▲▲**Grotte de Rouffignac** Etchings and paintings of prehistoric creatures, such as mammoths, in a large cave accessed by a little train. **Hours:** Daily July-Aug 9:00-11:30 & 14:00-18:00, April-June and Sept-Oct 10:00-11:30 & 14:00-17:00, closed Nov-March. **Reservations:** Not available or necessary, arrive by 8:30 in mid-July-Aug, otherwise 30 minutes early. Visit lasts one hour. See page 500.

▲▲**Grottes de Cougnac** Oldest paintings (30,000 years) open to public, showing rust-and-black ibex, mammoths, giant deer, and a few humans, on a tour more focused on cave geology than art. **Hours:** Mid-July-Aug daily 10:00-17:45; April-mid-July and Sept daily 10:00-11:30 & 14:30-17:00; Oct Mon-Sat 14:00-16:00, closed Sun; closed Nov-March. **Reservations:** Not available. Arrive 10 minutes before it opens in summer. Required 70-minute tour (with minimal English explanation). See page 502.

ians, with each successive generation adding its distinct animal or symbol to the collage, putting it in just the right spot that established their place in history?

The fact that styles and subject matter changed so little over the millennia might imply that the artists purposely chose timeless images to relate their generation with those before and after. Perhaps they simply lived in a stable culture that did not value innova-

▲▲**Grotte du Pech Merle** Vivid cave art of mammoths, bison, and horses, plus Cro-Magnon footprint and good museum, about an hour south of the Dordogne in the Lot River Valley. **Hours:** Daily July-Aug 9:15-17:00, April-June and Sept-early Nov 9:30-12:00 & 13:30-17:00, limited off-season hours and closed in Jan. **Reservations:** Book a week ahead in summer to join a rare English tour, or reserve a French tour and use English translations (fewer visitors allowed on weekends). Without reservations, arrive by 9:30. Allow two hours for a complete visit. See page 520.

▲**National Museum of Prehistory at Les Eyzies** More than 18,000 well-displayed artifacts offer good background information for patient students. **Hours:** July-Aug daily 9:30-18:30; closed Tue Sept-June, closed at lunchtime Oct-May. **Reservations:** Not necessary, but reserve if you want a tour. Allow one hour to visit. See page 492.

▲**Abri du Cap Blanc** 14,000-year-old carvings that use natural contours of cave to add dimension, but no cave paintings. **Hours:** Mid-May-mid-Sept Sun-Fri 10:00-18:00, mid-Sept-mid-May Sun-Fri 10:00-12:30 & 14:00-18:00, closed Sat year-round, last entry at about 16:15. **Reservations:** Book a tour time by phone, or just show up at the Font-de-Gaume ticket office. Required 45-minute tour (often with some English, usually 6/day); call for times. See page 496.

▲**La Roque St-Christophe** Terraced cliff dwellings where prehistoric people lived. **Hours:** Daily July-Aug 10:00-20:00, April-June and Sept until 18:30, shorter hours off-season. **Reservations:** Not available or necessary. Allow 45 minutes to visit. See page 497.

Prehistory Welcome Center at Les Eyzies Free, helpful intro to region's important prehistoric sites. **Hours:** Mon-Fri 9:30-18:30, Sun from 10:30, off-season closes one hour earlier; closed all day Sat except July-Aug. **Reservations:** Not necessary. Allow 30 minutes to visit. See page 492.

DORDOGNE

tion. Or were these people too primitive to invent new techniques and topics?

Maybe the paintings are simply the result of the universal human drive to create, and these caverns were Europe's first art galleries, bringing the first tourists.

Very likely there is no single meaning that applies to all the paintings in all the caves. Prehistoric art may be as varied in meaning as current art.

Picture yourself as a Magdalenian viewing these paintings: You'd be guided by someone into a cold, echoing, and otherworldly chamber. In the darkness, someone would light torches and lamps, and suddenly the animals would flicker to life, appearing to run around the cave, like a prehistoric movie. In front of you, a bull would appear, behind you a mammoth (which you'd never seen in the flesh), and overhead a symbol that might have tied the whole experience together. You'd be amazed that an artist could capture the real world and reproduce it on a wall. Whatever the purpose—religious, aesthetic, or just plain fun—there's no doubt the effect was (and is) thrilling.

Today, you can visit the caves and share a common experience with a caveman. Feel a bond with these long-gone people...or stand in awe at how different they were from us. Ultimately, the paintings are as mysterious as the human species.

PLANNING YOUR TIME

While the cave art here is amazing, it can be a headache to strategize. Delicate caves come with strict restrictions, and many of them are in out-of-the-way locations—making it time-consuming to fit a cave visit into your vacation (allow three hours for a typical visit, including transit time from Sarlat). Try to visit a cave on your way in or out of the area—Lascaux is north of Sarlat, Cougnac and Pech Merle are to the south. The most famous cave with original art, Font-de-Gau-

me, is so restricted that getting in is nigh impossible. Some caves (like Lascaux IV) require long visits. But several caves are easier to plan for and visit, and well worth a traveler's time, provided you come prepared. Use the "Prehistoric Sights at a Glance" sidebar to determine which cave(s) best fit into your itinerary.

You'll learn that some caves are privately owned or owned by a community. This does not mean that they have the right to do as they please. Irrespective of ownership, the caves are strictly monitored and maintained by the French government, which also determines the number of daily visitors that a cave can handle.

If seeing the very best matters, plan way ahead and book a local guide or transport service to the best cave: Grotte de Font-de-Gaume. If you don't score an entry here, the best alternative is Rouffignac (no reservations available, but you can generally show up and get in without too long a wait—call ahead to see how busy they are). Abri du Cap Blanc is bookable in advance, but it only has carvings, not paintings. Grotte du Pech Merle is easy to book ahead and has good English descriptions but requires a considerable detour, unless you're heading to or from the south.

Procrastinators who arrive in the Dordogne without cave reservations can show up and take their chances; see tips in each listing.

HELPFUL HINTS

Drivers Fare Best: All the prehistoric caves listed here (except Grotte du Pech Merle) are within 45 min of Sarlat-la-Canéda. But public transit is scarce: Without a car you'll be like a caveman without a spear (see page 448 for guided tours that connect some of these sights).

Reserve Ahead or Get Up Early: Be clear on which caves take reservations (see the "Prehistoric Sights at a Glance" sidebar), and try to reserve your choice; other caves are first-come, first-served. That means it's essential to arrive early to secure a ticket, and then find something to do nearby if you have time to kill. How early you need to arrive varies by cave; I've suggested times for caves where you can't make a reservation. July and August are busiest, and rainy weather anytime sends sightseers scurrying for the caves. The caves are quieter from October to April (and Rouffignac closes entirely Nov-March); in high season, Saturdays are best (unless it's a holiday)—but note that Grotte de Font-de-Gaume and Abri du Cap Blanc are closed that day, as is the Prehistory Welcome Center.

Cave Tips: Read "Cave Art 101" (earlier) to gain a better understanding of what you'll see. Dress warmly, even if it's hot outside. Tours can last up to an hour, and the caves are all a steady, chilly 55 degrees Fahrenheit, with 98 or 99 percent humidity. On a tour, lag behind the group to have the paintings to yourself for a few moments. Photos, daypacks, big purses, and strollers are not allowed. (You can take your camera—without using it—and check the rest at the site.)

Local Guide: Angelika Siméon is a passionate guide/lecturer eager to teach you about the caves and well worth spending a day with. She handles cave reservations and makes your cave visit easy and educational (book ahead; €195/half-day, €285/day, prices are for two people, tel. 05 53 35 19 30, mobile 06 24 45 96 28, angelika.simeon@wanadoo.fr).

Les Eyzies-de-Tayac

This single-street town is the touristy hub of a cluster of Cro-Magnon caves, castles, and rivers. It merits a stop for its Prehistory Welcome Center, National Museum of Prehistory, and (if you can

DORDOGNE

get in) the Grotte de Font-de-Gaume cave, a 15-minute walk or two-minute drive outside of town. Les Eyzies-de-Tayac is world-famous because it's where the original Cro-Magnon man was discovered in 1870. That breakthrough set of bones was found just behind the hotel of Monsieur Magnon—Hôtel le Cro-Magnon, which is in business to this day on the western end of the main street. The name "Cro-Magnon" translates as "Mr. Magnon's Hole."

Orientation: Les Eyzies-de-Tayac's TI is below the museum on the main drag (July-Aug daily 9:30-18:30, closed off-season 12:30-14:00 and Sun afternoons, ask about bike rentals, tel. 05 53 06 97 05, www.lascaux-dordogne.com). The train station is a level 500 yards from the town center (turn right from the station to get into town).

Sights in Les Eyzies-de-Tayac

Prehistory Welcome Center
(Pôle International de la Préhistoire)

You could start your prehistoric explorations at the Pôle International de la Préhistoire (PIP) as you enter town from the east (Sarlat). This glass-and-concrete facility is a helpful resource for planning a visit to the region's important prehistoric sites. The low-slung building houses timelines, a good eight-minute film (English subtitles), and exhibits that work together to give visitors a primer on the origins of humanity. The English-speaking staff is happy to provide maps of the region and give suggestions on places to visit. Park here (for free), then walk out the center's back door 200 yards on a pedestrian-only lane to the National Museum of Prehistory.

Cost and Hours: Free; Mon-Fri 9:30-18:30, Sun from 10:30, off-season closes one hour earlier, closed Sat except July-Aug; free parking across the street, located east of downtown Les Eyzies-de-Tayac at 30 Rue du Moulin—watch for tall silver *PIP* sign, tel. 05 53 06 06 97, www.pole-prehistoire.com.

▲National Museum of Prehistory
(Musée National de Préhistoire)

This well-presented, modern museum houses more than 18,000 bones, stones, and crude little doodads that were uncovered locally. It takes you through prehistory—starting 400,000 years ago—and is good preparation for your cave visits. Appropriately located on a cliff inhabited by humans for 35,000 years (above Les Eyzies-de-Tayac's TI), the museum's sleek design is intended to help it blend into the surrounding rock. Inside, the many worthwhile exhibits include videos demonstrating scratched designs, painting techniques, and how spearheads were made. You'll also see full-size models of Cro-Magnon people and animals that stare at racks of arrowheads. The museum's handheld English explanations require patience to correlate to the exhibits.

Cost and Hours: €6, €8 with temporary exhibits, daily 9:30-18:30, closed Tue Sept-June, closed at lunchtime Oct-May, last entry 45 minutes before closing, tel. 05 53 06 45 65, www.musee-prehistoire-eyzies.fr.

Information: For context, read the "Cave Art 101" sidebar before you go.

Tours: To get the most out of your visit, consider a private or semiprivate English-language guided tour; for details, call 05 53 06 45 65 or email reservation.prehistoire@culture.gouv.fr.

Visiting the Museum: Pick up the museum layout with your ticket. Notice the timeline shown on the stone wall starting a mere 7 million years ago. Then enter, walking in the footsteps of your ancestors, and greet the 10-year-old Turkana Boy, whose bone fragments were found in Kenya in 1984 by Richard Leakey and date from 1.5 million years ago.

Spiral up the stairs to the first floor, which sets the stage by describing human evolution and the fundamental importance of tools. You'll also see a life-size re-creation of *Megaloceros*—a gigantic deer (with even bigger antlers)—and a skeleton of an oversized steppe bison, both of which appear in some of the area's cave paintings.

The more engaging second floor highlights prehistoric artifacts found in France. Some of the most interesting objects you'll see are displayed in this order: a handheld arrow launcher, a 5,000-year-old flat-bottomed boat (pirogue) made from oak, prehistoric fire pits, amazing cavewoman jewelry (including a necklace labeled *La Parure de St-Germain-la-Rivière*, made of 70 stag teeth—pretty impressive, given that stags only have two teeth each), engravings on stone (find the unflattering yet impressively realistic female figure), a handheld lamp used to light cave interiors (*lampe façonnée*, found at Lascaux), and beautiful replicas of horses (much like the sculptures at the cave of Abri du Cap Blanc).

Your visit ends on the cliff edge, with a Fred Flintstone-style photo op on a stone ledge (through the short tunnel) that some of our ancient ancestors once called home.

Sleeping and Eating near
Les Eyzies-de-Tayac

$$ Le Chèvrefeuille, halfway between Les Eyzies-de-Tayac and the river at St-Cyprien, is a family-friendly place offering homey comfort in a farm setting. Ian and Sara Fisk moved to France from

DORDOGNE

England to raise their children. Five rustic guest rooms and two small apartments in various configurations handle singles to family groups (includes breakfast, cash only, free loaner bikes, pay laundry facilities, cooking classes for families and adults, market tours possible, big swimming pool, large grass and play areas, *pétanque* court, closed mid-Oct-April except for apartments, tel. 05 53 59 47 97, www.lechevrefeuille.com, info@lechevrefeuille.com). From near Les Eyzies, head south on D-48 about six kilometers, turn right into the small hamlet of Pechboutier, and look for their sign.

Caves and Other Sights near Les Eyzies-de-Tayac

I've arranged these geographically, and included sights that can be handy if you have time to kill while awaiting your cave appointment: the ruined-but-rebuilding Château de Commarque, the stately-for-a-cave Maison Forte de Reignac, and the evocative troglodyte terraces of La Roque St-Christophe. Most of the caves and other sights listed here are within a 20-minute drive of Les Eyzies. Two caves are easier to visit from other bases: the Grottes de Cougnac is south of the river, and Grotte du Pech Merle—listed on page 520—is an hour and a half south, near the Lot River Valley.

JUST EAST OF LES EYZIES-DE-TAYAC

The Grotte de Font-de-Gaume and Abri du Cap Blanc are barely outside of Les Eyzies, and managed by the same outfit; tickets for either one can be purchased in person at the Font-de-Gaume ticket office.

▲▲▲Grotte de Font-de-Gaume

Even if you're not a connoisseur of Cro-Magnon art, you'll dig this cave—the last one in France with prehistoric multicolored (poly-chrome) paintings still open to the public. (Lascaux—45 minutes down the road—has replica caves; the other cave paintings open to the public are mono-chrome.) This cave, made millions of years ago—not by a river, but by the geological activity that created the Pyrenees Mountains—is entirely natural. It contains 15,000-year-old  paintings of 230 animals, 82 of which are bison.

On a carefully guided and controlled 100-yard walk, you'll see

DORDOGNE

about 20 red-and-black bison—often in elegant motion—painted with a moving sensitivity. When two animals face each other, one is black, and the other is red. Your guide, with a laser pointer and great reverence, will trace the faded outline of the bison and explain how, 15 millennia in the past, cave dwellers used local minerals and the rock's natural contours to give the paintings dimension. Some locals knew about the cave long ago, when there was little interest in prehistory, but the paintings were officially discovered in 1901 by the village schoolteacher.

Warning: Access to Font-de-Gaume is extremely restricted, and individual reservations are not accepted. The 78 tickets available each day meets only a fraction of the demand. Area guides snap up 26 of these ahead of time; the 52 remaining spots are given out on a first-come basis (see details below).

If you must see Font-de-Gaume, book through a guide service long ahead or line up for tickets early on the morning of the day you want to visit. It would be pretty clear that you're not going to get a ticket if you show up and all 52 spots are already taken. Drivers who can't get a ticket here should try the other interesting caves I recommend. Rouffignac is the best backup (you're already partway there).

Cost and Hours: €10, 17 and under free, includes required 45-minute tour; open mid-May–mid-Sept Sun-Fri 9:30-17:30, mid-Sept–mid-May Sun-Fri 9:30-12:30 & 14:00-17:30, closed Sat year-round; no photography or large bags, tel. 05 53 06 86 00, www.eyzies.monuments-nationaux.fr. Those planning to also visit Abri du Cap Blanc (described next) can reserve and buy tickets here.

Getting Tickets: The 52 tickets for individuals are doled out in person each morning starting at 9:30. In summer, plan to be in line by 7:30, in spring and fall no later than 8:30, and in the dead of winter you should be OK if you arrive by 9:00. Be aware that there are minimal facilities for the ticket queue (no shelters, no WCs, no food services, etc.) There are 52 numbered seats outside the entrance, so you'll know where you are in line. (Each person can buy only one ticket, so you can't send one member of your party ahead for the whole group.) You must check in at least 20 minutes before your tour time.

Local guide Angelika Siméon (see page 491) and some of the recommended minivan services on page 448 may be able to get tickets, but you must reserve at least six months ahead and hire that service for a tour.

Tours: English tours are available but limited; expect to visit with a French guide. Depending on the guide, the actual tour can be either illuminating and enthusiastic, or uninspiring. Don't fret if you're not on an English tour—most important is experiencing the art itself. You can buy an informative book afterward.

Getting There: The cave is at the corner of D-47 and D-48, about a two-minute drive (or a 15-minute walk) east of Les Eyzies-de-Tayac (toward Sarlat). There's easy on-site parking. After checking in at the ticket house, walk 400 yards on an uphill path to the cave entrance (where there's a free, safe bag check and a WC).

▲Abri du Cap Blanc

In this prehistoric cave (a 10-minute drive from Grotte de Font-de-Gaume), early artists used the rock's natural contours to add dimension to their sculpture. Your guide spends the tour in a single stone room explaining the 14,000-year-old carvings. The small museum helps prepare you for your visit, and the useful English handout describes what the French-speaking guide is talking about (some guides add English commentary). Look for places where the artists smoothed or roughened the surfaces to add depth. Keep in mind that you'll be seeing carvings, not cave paintings. Impressive as these carvings are, their subtle majesty is lost on some.

Cost and Hours: €8, ages 18 and under free; includes required 45-minute tour, 6 tours/day (35 people each), call for tour times and to reserve. The cave is open mid-May to mid-Sept Sun-Fri 10:00-18:00, mid-Sept-mid-May Sun-Fri 10:00-12:30 & 14:00-18:00, closed Sat year-round, last entry at about 16:15, no photos, tel. 05 53 59 60 30.

Getting Tickets: Buy tickets at the sight or book by phone. You can also buy a ticket in person at the Font-de-Gaume ticket office (see previous listing).

Getting There: Abri du Cap Blanc is well-signed and is located about seven kilometers after Grotte de Font-de-Gaume on the road to Sarlat. From the parking lot, walk 200 yards down to the entry. Views of the Château de Commarque (described next) are terrific as you arrive.

▲Château de Commarque

This mystical medieval castle ruin is ripe for hikers wanting to get away from it all. Owner Hubert de Commarque acquired his family's ancestral castle in 1968 and has been digging it out of the forest ever since. (The Commarque clan has the world's only family crest that features the Ark of the Covenant—people call Hubert "Indiana Jones.") While not as striking as other castles in the region, this Back Door alternative offers fewer crowds and a chance to explore a ruined castle that's coming back to life before your eyes. Note that it requires a long hike to visit (good walking shoes are essential).

Cost and Hours: €8, daily 11:00-19:00, July-Aug until 20:00, April and Oct until 18:00, closed Nov-March, last entry one hour before closing, WCs at parking lot, www.commarque.com.

Getting There: The château is well-signed off D-47 between Sarlat and Les Eyzies—see the "Cro-Magnon Caves near Sarlat-la-Canéda" map. Hearty hikers can walk from Abri du Cap Blanc to the castle in 25 minutes (ask for trail conditions at the site). Signs also direct drivers from here.

Visiting the Castle: From the remote and secluded parking lot, it's a 20-minute walk down through a forest of chestnut trees to a clearing, where the mostly ruined castle appears...like a mirage. Helpful information panels allow you to scour the complex and learn. Near the entrance, peek into the chapel for photos of the overgrown hillside just 50 years ago. Then hike up to the 12th-century keep, which is a work in progress; areas that are completed feature modest exhibits, and the top of the tallest tower provides panoramic views.

Walking out into the field and looking back, you can see that Château de Commarque sits on layers of history: in the river-gouged lower level are troglodyte dwellings; just above are fortified early medieval settlements, where 9th-century residents holed up from Viking attacks; and at the top, there's a 12th-century castle that is being resurrected in the 21st century. There's even some 15,000-year-old cave art. It's not open to the public but you can watch a video about the art in the château.

NORTHEAST OF LES EYZIES-DE-TAYAC

I've listed the following stops—an elegant manor burrowed into the side of a cliff, a medieval cave dwelling, and one of the region's most famous stops for cave art—in the order you reach them traveling northeast from Les Eyzies along the Vézère River on D-706.

Maison Forte de Reignac

For over 700 years, a powerful lord ruled from this unusual home carved from a rock face high above the Vézère River. After a short but steep hike to the entry, you'll climb through several floors of well-furnished rooms, some with lit fireplaces. Kids love this tree-house-like place. Your tour concludes in a room that houses torture devices and highlights man's creative abilities to inflict unthinkable pain...and a slow death. (This section may be too gruesome for young kids.) The loaner English handout provides good context.

Cost and Hours: €9, daily 10:00-19:00, July-Aug until 20:00, Oct-Nov and March until 18:00, closed Dec-Feb; just north of the village of Tursac, tel. 05 53 50 69 54, www.maison-forte-reignac.com. From Les Eyzies-de-Tayac, it's a twisty 10-minute drive up D-706 (direction: La Roque St-Christophe).

▲La Roque St-Christophe

Five fascinating terraces carved by the Vézère River have provided shelter to people here for 55,000 years. Although the terraces were

DORDOGNE

inhabited in prehistoric times, there's no prehistoric art on display—the exhibit (except for one small cave) is entirely medieval.

Cost and Hours: €10, daily July-Aug 10:00-20:00, April-June and Sept until 18:30, shorter hours off-season, last entry 45 minutes before closing, lots of steps; eight kilometers north of Les Eyzies-de-Tayac—soon after passing Maison Forte de Reignac—follow signs to *Montignac*; tel. 05 53 50 70 45, www.roque-st-christophe.com.

Background: The official recorded history goes back to AD 976, when people settled here to steer clear of the Viking raiders who'd routinely sail up the river. (Back then, in this part of Europe, the standard closing of a prayer wasn't "amen," but "and deliver us from the Norseman, amen.") A clever relay of river watchtowers kept an eye out for raiders. When they came, cave dwellers gathered their kids, hauled up their animals (see the big, re-created winch), and pulled up the ladders. Although there's absolutely nothing old here except for the gouged-out rock (with holes for beams, carved out of the soft limestone), it's easy to imagine the entire village—complete with butcher, baker, and candlestick maker—in this family-friendly exhibit. This place is a dream for kids of any age who hold fond tree-house memories.

Visiting the Terraces: There's a free parking lot across the stream, with picnic tables, a WC, and, adjacent to the babbling brook, a pondside café (selling salads, sandwiches, and drinks—the nearby pretty village of St-Léon provides more lunch choices). Climb through the one-way circuit, which is slippery when damp. Panels show the medieval buildings that once filled this space; don't miss the English translations on the back side. Allow at least 45 minutes for your visit.

▲▲International Center for Cave Art
(Lascaux Centre International de l'Art Pariétal)

The region's—and the world's—most famous cave paintings are at Lascaux, 14 miles north of Sarlat-la-Canéda and Les Eyzies-de-Tayac. The Lascaux caves were discovered accidentally in 1940 by four kids and their dog. From 1948 to 1963, more than a million people climbed through the prehistoric wonderland of incredibly vivid and colorful paintings—but the visitors tracked in fungus on their shoes and changed the temperature and humidity with their heavy breathing. In just 15 years, the precious art deterio-

rated more than during the previous 15,000 years, and the caves were closed to the public.

Today you can only see replicas here. Seeing the real thing at one of the other caves is thrilling, but coming to Lascaux and taking one of the scheduled tours is a great introduction to the region's cave art. Forget that these are copies and enjoy being swept away by the prehistoric majesty of it all.

To plan your visit, know the lingo: **Lascaux I** is the original cave. In 1983, a replica of the cave called **Lascaux II** was built next to the original—accurate to within one centimeter, reproducing the best 40-yard-long stretch, and showing 90 percent of the paintings found in Lascaux. **Lascaux III** is an exhibit designed to travel abroad. And **Lascaux IV** is the newest razzle-dazzle replica—opened in 2017, reproducing 100 percent of the original cave, and designed with the latest technology. Visitors can tour Lascaux II or IV—or both—depending on their interest (descriptions on the next page). The Lascaux caves are a constant 56 degrees year-round, so dress warmly.

At the end of your visit, the pleasant town of Montignac is close and worth a wander if you have time to kill.

Cost and Hours: Lascaux IV—€20 includes tour, audioguide, 3-D film, and many exhibits, open daily July-Aug 9:00-21:00, late March-June and Sept-Nov until 19:00, shorter hours in winter and closed Jan, last ticket sold two hours before closing; Lascaux II—€14, by guided tour only, open July-Aug 9:00-19:00, late March-June and Sept-early Nov 10:00-12:30 & 14:00-18:00, closed mid-Nov-late March.

Getting Tickets: Reservations for the few daily English tours are essential for either cave (most reliable English tours are usually around 10:00 or 11:00). Book in advance on the Lascaux website at www.lascaux.fr/en. Tickets also sold at the sight.

Information: Located on Avenue de Lascaux in Montignac; tel. 05 53 50 99 10, www.lascaux.fr/en.

Eating: Lascaux IV has a good cafeteria with fair prices and outdoor seating. The pleasant town of Montignac is less than a mile away with cafés and food shops.

Visiting the Caves: These replica caves each took years to create. The prehistoric reindeer, horses, and bulls of the original Lascaux cave were painstakingly reproduced by talented artists, using

DORDOGNE

the same dyes, tools, and techniques their predecessors used 15,000 years ago.

Lascaux IV gives a thorough overview of the original cave but has a circus-like feel in high season: Groups of 35 are processed every six minutes, and you wade through huge parking lots to get there. It's housed in the International Center for Cave Art, a sight in itself built into the hillside next to the original cave. Your visit to this state-of-the-art center starts with a well-done, 40-minute guided tour of the replica caves. Then you are set free with a tablet to view interactive exhibits that explain the role Lascaux played in prehistory, scientific research analyzing cave art, and the link from cave art to modern art. The thought-provoking, what-do-these-paintings-mean, 3-D film is a fine way to finish your visit. Plan to spend a minimum of 1.5 hours here.

Lascaux II sits a half-mile above Lascaux IV in the woods and offers a more intimate, quiet, and intensive look at the caves on a 75-minute tour with a group of 20 people.

Sleeping and Eating near Lascaux: $$-$$$ Château de la Fleunie*** allows you to bed down in a medieval castle at digestible prices. Built between the 12th and 16th centuries, this castle shares its land with pastures and mountain goats, a big pool (unheated), worn tennis courts, and play toys. Rooms are located in three buildings: the main château, an attached wing, and the modern pavilion. The château's rooms are Old World-worn with musty and dated bathrooms (many big rooms for families), while the pavilion offers contemporary rooms with private view decks (family rooms, half-pension possible—about €40 more/person). Stay-awhile terraces overlook the scene and its riddled-with-character **$$ restaurant** (€30-70 *menus,* cheaper "grill" restaurant open in high season, 10-minute drive north of Montignac on D-45 road toward Aubas, near Condat-sur-Vézère, tel. 05 53 51 32 74, www.lafleunie.com, lafleunie@free.fr).

NORTHWEST OF LES EYZIES
▲▲Grotte de Rouffignac

At Rouffignac you'll ride a clunky little train down a giant subterranean riverbed, exploring about half a mile of this six-mile-long gallery with black-on-white paintings and engravings. The cave itself was long known to locals, but the 15,000-year-old drawings were officially "discovered" only in 1956. With a little planning, you'll have no trouble getting a ticket to this fascinating cave. Dress warmly as you'll be sitting during your visit.

Cost and Hours: €8, daily July-Aug 9:00-11:30 & 14:00-18:00, April-June and Sept-Oct 10:00-11:30 & 14:00-17:00, closed Nov-March; essential videoguide-€1.50; one-hour guided tours run 2-3/hour, no reservations; tel. 05 53 05 41 71, www. grottederouffignac.fr.

Getting Tickets: It's really crowded only mid-July–Aug—during these months the ticket office opens at 9:00 and closes when tickets are sold out for the day—usually by noon. Arrive by 8:30 in summer and 30 minutes early at other times of year (you may get an entry time for a bit later in the day). Weekends tend to be quietest, particularly Saturday.

Getting There: Grotte de Rouffignac is well-signed from the route between Les Eyzies-de-Tayac and Périgueux (don't take the first turnoff, for *Rouffignac;* wait for the *Grotte de Rouffignac* sign); allow 25 minutes from Les Eyzies-de-Tayac.

Visiting the Cave: Your tour will be in French (with highlights described in English), but the videoguide explains it all. Before the tour begins, read your videoguide's background sections and the displays in the cave entry area. Once on the tour it's easy to follow along. Here's the gist of what they're saying on the stops of your train ride:

The cave was created by the underground river. It's entirely natural, but it was much shallower before the train-track bed was excavated. As you travel, imagine the motivation and determination of the artists who crawled more than a half-mile into this dark and mysterious cave. They left behind their art...and the wonder of people who crawled in centuries later to see it all.

You'll ride about five minutes before the first stop. Along the way, you'll see crater-like burrows made by hibernating bears long before the first humans drew here. There are hundreds of them—not because there were so many bears, but because year after year, a few of them would return, preferring to make their own private place to sleep (rather than using some other bear's den). After a long winter nap, bears would have one thing on their mind: Cut those toenails. The walls are scarred with the scratching of bears in need of clippers.

Stop 1: The guide points out bear scratches on the right. On the left, images of woolly mammoths etched into the walls can be seen only when lit from the side (as your guide will demonstrate). As the rock is very soft here, these were simply gouged out by the artists' fingers.

Stop 2: Look for images of finely detailed rhinoceroses outlined in black. Notice how the thicker coloring under their tummies suggests the animals' girth. The rock is harder here, so nothing is engraved. Soon after, your guide will point out graffiti littering the ceiling—made by "modern" visitors who were not aware of the prehistoric drawings around them (with dates going back to the 18th century).

Stop 3: On the left, you'll see woolly mammoths and horses

DORDOGNE

engraved with tools in the harder rock. On the right is the biggest composition of the cave: a herd of 10 peaceful mammoths. A mysterious calcite problem threatens to cover the art with ugly white splotches.

Off the Train: When you get off the train, notice how high the original floor was (today's floor was dug out in the 20th century to allow for visitors). Imagine both the prehistoric makers and viewers of this art crawling all the way back here with pretty lousy flashlight substitutes. The artists lay on their backs while creating these 60 images (unlike at Lascaux, where they built scaffolds).

The ceiling is covered with a remarkable gathering of animals. You'll see a fine 16-foot-long horse, a group of mountain goats, and a grandpa mammoth. Art even decorates the walls far down the big, scary hole. When the group chuckles, it's because the guide is explaining how the mammoth with the fine detail (showing a flap of skin over its anus) helped authenticate the drawings: These couldn't be fakes, because no one knew about this anatomical detail until the preserved remains of an actual mammoth were found in Siberian permafrost in modern times. (The discovery explained the painted skin flap, which had long puzzled French prehistorians.)

SOUTH OF THE RIVER

Of the caves listed in this section, this is the farthest from Les Eyzies-de-Tayac and Sarlat (about 30 minutes from each). It's roughly on the way between the Dordogne Valley and the A-20 autoroute.

▲▲Grottes de Cougnac

Located 23 kilometers south of Sarlat-la-Canéda and three well-signed kilometers north of Gourdon on D-704, this cave holds fascinating rock formations and the oldest (20,000-25,000-year-old) paintings and drawings open to the public. Family-run and less developed than other sites, it provides a more intimate look at cave art, as guides take more time to explain the caves (your guide should give some explanations in English—ask). The art you see is single-color outlines or silhouettes (in red, yellow, or black). It's just one small part of the full tour, which focuses heavily on the cave's geology and unique formations—you'll see spaghetti-style stalactites, curtain stalactites, and much more.

Cost and Hours: €8.50, includes required 70-minute tour; these hours correspond to first/last tour times: mid-July-Aug daily 10:00-17:45; April-mid-July and Sept daily 10:00-11:30 & 14:30-17:00; Oct Mon-Sat 14:00-16:00, closed Sun; closed Nov-March; free WCs, consider the decent €5 English-language booklet. Tel. 05 65 41 47 54, www.grottesdecougnac.com.

Getting Tickets: Because access is first-come, first-served (and groups are limited to 25), plan your visit carefully. There are no online reservations. You can call right at 9:30 or 14:30 (when the ticket office opens) to check on availability, or show up 20 minutes before the ticket office opens to assure entry. During busy times (in summer and in bad weather), they're most crowded 11:00-12:00 and 15:00-17:00. At quieter times, you can usually stop by before 11:00 and get in. Outside of July and August, be careful not to arrive too close to the last tour before lunch (11:30)—if that tour is full, you'll have to wait for the 14:30 departure. Note: If you have time to kill, you're only minutes from the town of Gourdon (with shops, restaurants, and a historic center).

Visiting the Cave: The 70-minute tour, likely in French, begins in a cave below the entrance, where the guide explains the geological formations (you'll learn that it takes 70 years for water to make it from the earth's surface into the cave). From this first cave, you'll return to the fresh air and walk eight minutes to a second cave. Inside, you'll twist and twist through forests of stalagmites and stalactites before reaching the grand finale: the drawings you came to see. They are worth the wait. Vivid depictions (about 10) of ibex, mammoths, and giant deer *(Megaloceros)*, as well as a few nifty representations of humans, are outlined in rust or black. The rendering of the giant deer's antlers is exquisite, and many drawings use the cave's form to add depth and movement. The art is subtle—small sketches here and there, rather than the grand canvases of some of the more famous caves—but powerful.

Oradour-sur-Glane

Lost in lush countryside, two hours north of Sarlat-la-Canéda, Oradour-sur-Glane is a powerful experience—worth ▲▲▲. French children know this town well, as most come here on school trips. **Village des Martyrs,** as it is known, was machine-gunned and burned on June 10, 1944, by Nazi troops. With cool

attention to detail, the Nazis methodically rounded up the entire population of 642 townspeople, of whom about 200 were children. The women and children were herded into the town church, where they were tear-gassed and machine-gunned as they tried to escape the burning chapel. Oradour's men were tortured and executed.

The town was then set on fire, its victims left under a blanket of ashes.

The reason for the mass killings remains unclear. Some say the Nazis wanted revenge for the kidnapping of one of their officers, but others believe the Nazis were simply terrorizing the populace in the wake of D-Day. Today, the ghost town, left untouched for more than 70 years (by order of President Charles de Gaulle), greets every pilgrim who enters with only one English word: Remember.

ORIENTATION TO ORADOUR-SUR-GLANE

Cost and Hours: Entering the village is free, but the museum costs €8 (audioguide-€2). Both are open daily mid-May-mid-Sept 9:00-19:00, off-season until 17:00 or 18:00, last visit one hour before closing, tel. 05 55 43 04 30, www.oradour.org. Allow two hours for your visit.

Getting There: For **drivers** coming from the south, Oradour-sur-Glane is well-signed off the (mostly free) A-20. Those driving from the north should take A-10 to Poitiers, then follow signs toward *Limoges* and turn south at Bellac. **Bus** #12 links Oradour-sur-Glane with the train station in Limoges (2-3/day, 40 minutes, schedule on Oradour website, consider taking the bus one way to Oradour and taxi the other; Limoges TI tel. 05 55 34 46 87). Those without a car should consider hiring a **taxi;** Christoph Kusters can pick you up in Limoges and take you to Oradour and other sights on the way to your Dordogne hotel (reverse this plan if leaving the Dordogne; see listing under "Getting Around the Dordogne" on page 447).

VISITING ORADOUR-SUR-GLANE

Follow *Village Martyrs* signs to the parking lot and enter at the rust-colored **underground museum** (Centre de la Mémoire). The pricey-for-what-it-offers museum gives a standard timeline of the rise of Hitler and WWII events, shows haunting footage of everyday life in Oradour before the attack, and offers a day-by-day account of the town's destruction. While thorough explanations are posted, and the 13-minute subtitled movie adds drama, the museum is skippable for some. At the bookshop, consider picking up a €3 English map to better navigate the site (which has almost no posted information).

From the museum's back door, you pop out at the edge of the ruined village itself. It's shocking just how big and how ruined it is—a harrowing embodiment of the brutality and pointlessness of war.

Join other hushed visitors to walk the length of Oradour's **main street,** past gutted, charred buildings and along lonely streetcar tracks. *Lieu de Supplice* signs show where the townsmen were tormented and murdered. The plaques on the buildings provide the names and occupations of the people who lived there (*laine* means wool, *sabotier* is a maker of wooden shoes, *couturier* is a tailor, *quincaillerie* is a hardware store, *cordonnier* is shoe repair, *menuisier* is a carpenter, and *tissus* are fabrics). You'll pass several cafés and butcher shops and a hôtel-restaurant. This village was not so different from many you have seen on your trip.

At the end of main street, visit the modest **church,** with its bullet-pocked altar. Then double back through the upper part of the village, bearing right at the long, straight street to the **cemetery.** The names of all who died in the massacre on that June day are etched into the rear wall of the cemetery, around an austere pillar. In front of the pillar, glass cases display ashes of some of the victims. Leaving the cemetery, jog right and cut through the hedges to find the entrance to the easy-to-miss, bunker-like **underground memorial,** where you'll see displays of people's possessions found after the attack: eyeglasses, children's toys, sewing machines, cutlery, pocket watches, and so on.

Nearby: The adorable village of **Mortemart** lies 15 minutes north with a good café (closed Mon) wedged between its ancient market hall and low-slung château (a block off the main road, to the right; wander behind for a sweet scene).

St-Emilion

Two hours due west of Sarlat-la-Canéda and just 40 minutes from Bordeaux, pretty St-Emilion is carved like an amphitheater into the bowl of a limestone hill. Its tidy streets connect a few inviting squares with heavy cobbles and scads of well-stocked wine shops. There's little to do in this well-heeled town other than enjoy the setting and sample the local sauce. Sunday is market day.

They've been making wine in St-Emilion for more than 1,800 years—making it the oldest wine producer in the Bordeaux region (though it accounts for barely 5 percent of Bordeaux's famous red wine). Blending cabernet franc and merlot grapes, St-Emilion wines are also the most robust in Bordeaux. About 60 percent of the grapes you see are merlot.

DORDOGNE

The helpful **TI** is located at the top of the town on Place des Créneaux, across from the town's highest bell tower (open daily year-round, Place Pioceau, tel. 05 57 55 28 28, www.saint-emilion-tourisme.com). The TI rents bikes and has helpful English-language handouts outlining self-guided cycling routes as well as themed, well-marked walking routes through the vineyards. Ask also about their English-language guided tours (see "Tours and Views," below).

Getting There: It's a 20-minute walk from St-Emilion's train station into town. Electric tuk-tuks run between the station and the village (April-Oct, small fee). Taxis don't wait at the station, but you can call one from there (5 trains/day from Sarlat-la-Canéda, 2 hours; 6/day Mon-Fri from Bordeaux, 4/day Sat-Sun). You can also get off in Libourne (5 miles away), with better train service, easy car rental, and taxis, but just one daily bus to St-Emilion.

Drivers will find pay parking in lots at the upper end of the town or along the wall.

Wine Tasting and Wine Shops: Next to the TI, **Maison du Vin** is a fair starting point for an introduction to wine (free, daily, tel. 05 57 55 50 55, www.maisonduvinsaintemilion.com). They also offer wine-tasting classes (usually daily mid-July-Aug, Sat only April-June and Sept-Oct, register in advance).

Keepers of small shops greet visitors in flawless English, with a free tasting table, maps of the vineyards, and several open bottles. Americans may represent only about 15 percent of the visitors, but we buy 40 percent of their wine. **Cercle des Oenophiles** is an easygoing place where you can taste wines and tour nearby cellars storing more than 400,000 bottles (free, daily except closed 12:30-14:00, 12 Rue Guadet, tel. 05 57 74 45 55).

Château Visits and Excursions: The TI can send you to tastings at selected châteaux (no charge, but a tasting fee may apply). It also offers a variety of tours (some on an open-deck bus, smaller groups in electric tuk-tuks) through the vineyards—in English and French; some include a tasting at one château (€14-25, 1 hour, usually May-mid-Sept only; verify times on TI website.

Tours and Views: The TI offers guided tours in St-Emilion (€9 each). The interesting 45-minute underground tour makes three stops at sights that otherwise aren't open to visitors: the catacombs (sorry, no bones), monolithic church, and Trinity Chapel (English tour daily, usually at 14:00, more in French, thorough English handout given on French tours). The city walking tour takes 1.5 hours and covers aboveground sights and St-Emilion's back streets.

You can climb the bell tower in front of the TI for a good view (€2, ask at TI for key), but the view is best from the Tour du Roy several blocks below (also €2).

Quickie Vineyard Loop: This 10-kilometer loop can be done in 20 minutes by car, and in 2 relaxed hours by bike. Leave the upper end of St-Emilion on D-243E-1 and head to St-Christophe des Bardes. Pass through the village (direction: St-Genès), then follow signs to the right to *St. Laurent des Combes*. Joyride your way down through hillsides of vines, then find signs looping back to St-Emilion's lower end via D-245, turning right on D-122.

If you need a driver, local guide **Robert Faustin** offers good service, speaks enough English, and arranges visits to wineries—he knows them all (tel. 05 57 25 17 59, mobile 06 77 75 36 64, robert. faustin@wanadoo.fr).

Sleeping in St-Emilion: There are no cheap hotels in St-Emilion. *Chambres d'hôtes* hidden among the surrounding vineyards offer a better value—ask the TI for a list. Hotel prices skyrocket during the VinExpo festival at the end of June and during harvest time (late Sept).

$$$ Au Logis des Remparts*** offers good comfort, a pool, and a tranquil garden with vineyards (tel. 05 57 24 70 43, www. logisdesremparts.com, contact@logisdesremparts.com).

At **$$ Logis des Cordeliers Chambres,** gentle Valérie, who speaks just enough English, rents four comfortable rooms in a restored 18th-century mansion. Three rooms offer the best view in town of the Tour du Roy (includes breakfast, 7 Rue Porte Brunet, mobile 07 82 78 01 55, www.logis-des-cordeliers.com, contact@ logis-des-cordeliers.com).

$ L'Auberge de la Commanderie** has 17 modern rooms at midrange prices (air-con, elevator, free parking, closed Jan-Feb, tel. 05 57 24 70 19, www.aubergedelacommanderie.com, contact@ aubergedelacommanderie.com).

Eating in St-Emilion: Skip most of the cafés lining the street by the TI and instead head to the melt-in-your-chair square, Place du Marché.

$ Amelia-Canta Café is *the* happening spot on this popular square, with reasonable *plats du jour,* salads, and veggie options (daily March-Nov, 2 Place de l'Eglise Monolithe, tel. 05 57 74 48 03).

$$ L'Envers du Décor wine bar-bistro is about fun, wine, and food—in that order. Meat dishes are their forte (daily, a few doors from the TI at 11 Rue du Clocher, tel. 05 57 74 48 31).

$$ Logis de la Cadène has street appeal with a pleasing patio terrace, a warm interior, and very pricey fine cuisine (closed Sun-Mon, just above Amelia-Canta Café at 3 Place du Marché du Bois, tel. 05 57 24 71 40, www.logisdelacadene.fr).

At **$$ Les Cordeliers,** enjoy a few bites or a bubbly aperitif in the 14th-century cloister (daily May-Sept 11:00-19:00, until 20:00

on weekends and mid-July-mid-Aug, Oct-April 14:00-18:00, 2 bis Rue de la Porte Brunet, tel. 05 57 24 42 13).

The Overlooked Eastern Dordogne

This remote, less-visited section of the Dordogne (Quercy *région*) is detour-worthy for those with more time. Its undisputed highlight is the pilgrimage town of Rocamadour, but there's much more to see. For a good introduction to this area, follow this self-guided driving tour connecting Sarlat and Rocamadour.

Eastern Dordogne Driving Tour

The direct route from Sarlat to Rocamadour takes about 75 minutes. To follow a more scenic route from the Sarlat area to Rocamadour, drive upriver from Souillac, connecting these worthwhile stops: Martel, Carennac, Château de Castelnau-Bretenoux, Loubressac, and Autoire. Allow 45 minutes from Sarlat to Souillac, then 15 minutes to Martel, and 20 minutes to Carennac (Château de Castelnau-Bretenoux and Loubressac are within 10 minutes of Carennac; Autoire is about 10 minutes beyond Loubressac). From Carennac or Autoire, it's 25 minutes south to Rocamadour. On Mondays, these towns are very quiet, and most shops are closed.

• *Start by taking D-803 east from Souillac's center to...*

  Martel: This well-preserved medieval town of 1,500 souls and seven towers offers a good chance to stretch your legs and stock up on picnic items (market days are Wed and Sat on the atmospheric Place des Consuls). Lacking a riverfront or a hilltop setting, Martel is largely overlooked by tourists. Park in the ample lot along the main road, then walk behind the post office to find the market square, with the TI in a smaller, adjoining square. Buy a copy of the TI's well-done walking-tour pamphlet (TI closed 12:30-14:00 and Sun), and enjoy the handsome pedestrian area lined with historic buildings. The walking tour starts at Martel's terrific main square (Place des Consuls)—with a medieval covered market and reasonable lunch cafés—and connects the town's seven towers and the fortress-like church of St. Maur. The town is said to be named for Charles Martel, Charlemagne's grandfather and role model, who stopped the Moors' advance into northern France in 732.

• *From Martel, continue east on D-803 toward Vayrac and Bétaille, then cross the Dordogne on D-20 and turn right to find...*

  Carennac: This jumble of peaked roofs and half-timbered

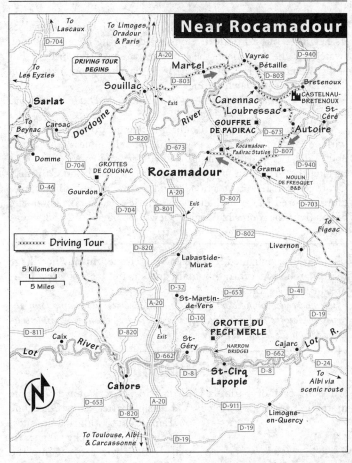

Near Rocamadour

To Lascaux
D-704
To Limoges, Oradour & Paris
A-20
DRIVING TOUR BEGINS
Vayrac
Bétaille
D-940
Martel
D-803
To Les Eyzies
Souillac
Bretenoux
CASTELNAU-BRETENOUX
St-Céré
Exit
Carennac
Loubressac
Autoire
D-807
GOUFFRE DE PADIRAC
D-673
Sarlat
To Beynac
Carsac
Dordogne
River
D-820
D-673
Rocamadour-Padirac Station
Domme
GROTTES DE COUGNAC
D-704
Rocamadour
Gramat
MOULIN DE FRESQUET B&B
D-940
D-46
Gourdon
A-20
D-807
D-703
D-801
Exit
To Figeac
Driving Tour
D-802
Livernon
5 Kilometers
5 Miles
D-820
Labastide-Murat
D-32
D-653
D-41
A-20
St-Martin-de-Vers
D-811
Caix
River
D-820
D-820
D-10
GROTTE DU PECH MERLE
D-19
Exit
St-Géry
NARROW BRIDGE!
Cajarc
Lot R.
Lot
D-662
D-662
D-24
D-8
St-Cirq Lapopie
D-8
To Albi via scenic route
Cahors
D-653
A-20
D-911
Limogne-en-Quercy
D-820
To Toulouse, Albi & Carcassonne
D-19
D-19

DORDOGNE

walls, lassoed between the river and D-20, begs to be photographed. Park along D-20 and wander the village to the river on foot. Find the fortified Prieuré St.-Pierre, explore its evocative church, and examine its exquisitely carved tympanum. It was built as an outpost of the Cluny Abbey in the 10th century and then fortified in the 1500s during the French Wars of Religion (a series of civil wars between Catholic and Protestant factions). You can pay a small fee to enter the tranquil, two-story cloister; in the chapter house, you'll see a life-size statue group surrounding the body of Christ. Cross the small bridge behind the restaurant for more village views.

• *From here, head east on D-30, tracking the Dordogne River. On the left you'll pass the splendidly situated and once-powerful military castle called...*

Château de Castelnau-Bretenoux: This château has views in all directions and a few well-furnished rooms. The reddish-golden stone and massive 12th-century walls make an impression, as does its height—almost 800 feet. Consider detouring for a closer look (watch for the turnoff on the left, over the one-lane bridge), but skip the interior. The village of Bretenoux has good markets on Tuesday and Saturday mornings.

• *From D-30, turn right on D-14 and then left on D-118. You'll come to...*

Loubressac: Mystical Loubressac hangs atop a beefy ridge, with outlandish views and a gaggle of adorable homes at its eastern end. Take a loop stroll through the village, and consider a *café* or meal at the *très* traditional and reasonable **$ Hôtel Lou Cantou****. Or, if you're really on vacation, spend the night, have dinner (restaurant closed Mon), and let owner Marie-Claude take good care of you (half the rooms have valley views, tel. 05 65 38 20 58, www. lou-cantou.fr, lou_cantou@orange.fr).

• *From here it's a short hop on D-118 to lovely little...*

Autoire: Snuggled in a welcoming cirque, this idyllic village rotates around its central fountain and square. It's just a few minutes beyond Loubressac.

• *From here you can follow signs to Gramat, then on to Rocamadour. The caves of Gouffre de Padirac (described later) are also nearby, and well-signed from this area.*

Rocamadour

An hour east of Sarlat-la-Canéda, this historic town with its dramatic rock-face setting is a ▲▲ sight after dark. Once one

of Europe's top pilgrimage sites, today it feels more tacky than spiritual. Still, if you can get into the medieval mindset, its dramatic setting—combined with the memory of the countless thousands of faithful who trekked from all over Europe to worship here—overwhelms the kitschy tourism and makes it a worthwhile two-hour stop.

Those who visit only during the day might wonder why they bothered, as there's little to do here except climb the pilgrims' steps (with scads of people who aren't pilgrims) to a few churches, and then stare at the view. Travelers who arrive late and spend the night enjoy fewer crowds—and a floodlit spectacle. To scenically connect Rocamadour and Sarlat, follow the driving tour outlined in the previous section.

Orientation to Rocamadour

Rocamadour has three basic levels, connected by steps and trails or elevators. The bottom level (La Cité Médiévale, or simply La Cité) is a single, long pedestrian street lined with shops and restaurants. The sanctuary level (Cité Religieuse)—the main attraction—is up 223 holy steps from La Cité. Its centerpiece is a church with seven chapels gathered around a small square. A switchback trail, the Way of the Cross (Chemin de la Croix), leads from the sanctuary to the top level. The top level consists of a cliff-capping château (public access to ramparts only) and—a 15-minute walk away—a small town, called L'Hospitalet. You can drive between the upper town (where you'll approach from the north) and the lower town (where you'll approach from the south), which both have free parking lots.

TOURIST INFORMATION

There are two TIs in Rocamadour: the glassy TI that most drivers come to first, in the village of **L'Hospitalet** above Rocamadour (daily July-Aug 9:30-19:00, April-June and Sept-Oct 10:00-12:30 & 14:00-18:00, closed Nov-March); and another on the level pedestrian street in **La Cité Médiévale** (same hours in summer, off-season 10:00-12:00 & 14:00-17:00, tel. 05 65 33 22 00, www.vallee-dordogne.com).

ARRIVAL IN ROCAMADOUR

By Train: Five daily trains (transfer in Brive-la-Gaillarde) leave you 2.5 miles from the village at an unstaffed station. It's about a €10-15 taxi ride to Rocamadour (see "Helpful Hints—Taxi").

By Car: Most of the parking lots around Rocamadour are free, but not those near the TI in L'Hospitalet. It's best to park in the **upper lot:** From L'Hospitalet, follow *P Château* signs all the way to the western end of town until you see the *ascenseur incliné* (elevator). From here, it's easy to walk or take the elevator down to the sanctuary.

You could park in the **lower lot,** but it takes more effort to get up to the sanctuary: Follow signs to *La Cité* and park at *Parking de la Vallée*. Hike 15 minutes up into La Cité Médiévale, or take the little tourist train—called *le petit train* (4/hour, €4 round-trip); then either climb the stairs or take the elevator up to the sanctuary.

HELPFUL HINTS

Elevators: This vertical town has two handy elevators. From top to bottom, the *ascenseur incliné* (€2.60 one-way, €4.20 round-trip) connects the sanctuary with the château and parking lot at the top. The *ascenseur cité/sanctuaire* (€2.10 one-way, €3.10 round-trip) links the lower town with the sanctuary. If you buy

DORDOGNE

a round-trip, keep the receipt for your return ride. If no one is staffing the ticket window, press the button to call the elevator, then pay as you exit. The elevators are within 50 yards of one another at the sanctuary level and both stop running at night (after 19:00 in peak season, earlier off-season).

Views After Dark: If you're staying overnight, don't miss the views of a floodlit Rocamadour from the opposite side of the valley (doable by car, on foot, or by tourist train; see next). It's best as a half-hour (round-trip) stroll. From the town's southeast end (Porte du Figuier), follow the quiet road down, cross the bridge, and head up the far side of the gorge opposite the town. Leave before it gets dark, as the floodlighting is best just after twilight. Wear light-colored or reflective clothing, or take a flashlight—it's a dark road with no shoulder. Within the town, climb the steps to just below the sanctuary, and consider a drink with a view at the Hôtel Sainte Marie.

Tourist Train: Most useful for connecting the valley parking lot to the lower town (explained earlier), the *petit train* is an option for enjoying the view after dark—with 50 other travelers, a bad sound system blaring worthless multilingual commentary, a flashing yellow light, and a view-cramping rooftop (€6, 30-minute round-trip, 2 trips/evening April-Sept, departures starting at twilight—the first one is by far the best, check at the TI or call 05 65 33 65 99). Or you can walk the same route in 30 minutes (see earlier), and take much better photos.

Money: There's an ATM in the upper town (next to the TI) and one in the lower town (near the elevator).

Taxi: Call 06 86 18 71 55.

Sights in Rocamadour

IN THE UPPER TOWN (L'HOSPITALET)

If you're coming from Sarlat or from the north, your first view of Rocamadour is the same as the one seen by medieval pilgrims—at the top of the gorge from the hamlet of **L'Hospitalet,** named for the hospitality it gave pilgrims. Stop here for the TI and sweeping views. Facing the view, a right turn leads to the *Château* parking lot described earlier (for most, this is the best place to park for the sanctuary); a left leads down to the La Cité Médiévale and valley parking.

Taking in the view, imagine the impact of this sight in the 13th century, as awestruck pilgrims first gazed on the sanctuary cut from the limestone cliffs. It was through L'Hospitalet's fortified gate that medieval pilgrims gained access to the "Holy Way," the path leading from L'Hospitalet to Rocamadour.

Of the sights below, the cave is right in the town itself, and the château is a two-minute drive (or 15-minute walk from the TI).

Grotte Préhistorique des Merveilles

This cave, located next to the upper TI, has the usual geological formations and a handful of small, blurred cave paintings. It's of no interest if you have seen or will see other prehistoric caves—its sole advantages are that it requires little effort to visit (with only about 10 steps down), and the guide can answer questions in English on the 45-minute French tour.

Cost and Hours: €7.50, daily July-Aug 9:30-19:00, April-June and Sept 10:30-12:00 & 14:00-18:00, Oct until 17:00, closed Nov-March, decent handout available, tel. 05 65 33 67 92, www.grotte-des-merveilles.com.

Château

Dating from the 14th century, the original château fortified a bluff that was an easy base for bandits to attack the wealthy church below. Today's structure is a 19th-century private house that was transformed into a reception spot for pilgrims. It's *privé* unless you are a pilgrim (in which case you can sleep here). All it offers tourists is a short rampart walk for a grand view (not worth the entry fee; turnstile requires exact change).

The zigzag **Way of the Cross** (Chemin de la Croix—a path marked with 14 Stations of the Cross, with a chapel for each station) gives religious purpose to the 15-minute hike between the château and the sanctuary below.

BETWEEN THE UPPER AND LOWER TOWNS (LA CITE RELIGIEUSE)

▲Sanctuary of Our Lady of Rocamadour

These sights form the heart of your vertical sightseeing. Be sure to read the "Rocamadour's Religious History" sidebar before beginning your visit.

Cost and Hours: Free, open daily generally 8:00-19:00.

Getting There: To reach the sights from the château's parking lot in the upper town, descend the paved Way of the Cross path or take the elevator and walk downhill about 150 yards. If you're coming from the lower town, ride the elevator up or climb the Grand Escalier steps (like a good pilgrim), passing a plaque listing key medieval pilgrims, such as St. Bernard, St. Dominique, and St. Louis (the only French king to become a saint; he brought the Crown of Thorns to Paris and had Sainte-Chapelle constructed to house it). Either way, your destination will be signed *Sanctuaires*.

Rocamadour's Religious History

Rocamadour was once one of Europe's top pilgrimage sights. Today tourists replace the pilgrims, enjoying a dramatically situated one-street town under a pretty forgettable church—all because of a crude little thousand-year-old black statue of the Virgin Mary.

Of France's roughly 200 "Black Virgins," this was perhaps the most venerated. Black Virgins date to the end of the pagan era—when black typically symbolized fertility and mother-hood. For newly converted (and still reluctant) pagans, it was easier to embrace the Virgin if she was black.

A thousand years ago, many Europeans expected the world to end, and pilgrimages became immensely popular. About that time, the first pilgrims came here—to a little cave in a cliff—to pray to a crude statue of a Black Virgin. Then, in 1166, a remarkably intact body was found beneath the thresh-old of the troglodyte chapel. People assumed this could only be a hermit (certainly a saintly hermit) who had lived in this cave. He was given the name Amadour (servant of Mary), and the place was named Rocamadour (the rock of the servant of Mary).

Suddenly, this humble site was on the map. Like Mont St-Michel, a single-street town sprouted at its base to handle the needs of its growing pilgrim hordes. During Europe's great age of pilgrimages (12th and 13th centuries), the greatest of pilgrims (St. Louis, St. Dominique, Richard the Lionheart, and so on) all trekked to this spot to pray. Rocamadour became a powerful symbol of faith and hope.

During the 14th century, up to 8,000 people lived in Ro-camadour, earning their living off the pilgrims—who arrived in numbers of up to 20,000 a day. But with the Wars of Religion and the Age of Enlightenment, pilgrimages declined...and so did Rocamadour.

During the Romantic Age of the 19th century, pilgrim-ages were again in vogue, and Rocamadour rebounded. Local bishops rebuilt the château above the sanctuary, making it a pilgrims' reception center, and connecting it to the church with the Way of the Cross. But there hasn't been a bona fide miracle here for eight centuries...and that's not good for the pilgrimage business.

Since the mid-20th century, Rocamadour has become more a tourist attraction, and today, its 650 inhabitants earn a living off its million visitors a year. Many of those visitors are French: In 2016, the viewers of a French television channel voted it the "favorite village of the French." So it's no surprise that the vast majority of those who climb the holy steps to the sanctuary are tourists—more interested in burning calories than incense.

⊙ Self-Guided Tour: Find the concrete bench on the small square facing the cliff. Though the buildings originated much earlier, most of what you see was rebuilt in the 19th century. Crammed onto a ledge on a cliff, the church couldn't follow the standard floor plan, so its seven chapels surround the square (called the *parvis*) rather than the church. The bishop's palace and the Chapel of St. Blaise de la Divine Miséricorde are behind you. The bishop's palace has a gift shop selling various pilgrimage mementos, including modern versions of the medallions that pilgrims prized centuries ago as proof of their visit (€13 for a tiny one). The two most historic chapels are straight ahead on either side of the steps.

• *Walk up the flight of steps to the cliff, where a tomb is cut into the rock.*

This is where the miraculously preserved body of **St. Amadour** was found in 1166. Places of pilgrimage do better with multiple miracles, so, along with its Black Virgin and the miracle of St. Amadour's body, Rocamadour has the **Sword of Roland.** The rusty sword of Charlemagne's nephew sticks in the cliffside, 30 feet above Amadour's tomb and a bit to the right. According to medieval sources, Roland was about to die in battle, but the great warrior didn't want his sword to fall into enemy hands. He hurled it from the far south of France, and it landed here—stuck miraculously into the Rocamadour cliffs just above the Black Virgin. (The sword is clearly from the 18th century, but never mind.)

St. Michael's Chapel is built around the original cave to your left (open only to pilgrims, with little to see inside). A few steps farther along, the tiny **Chapel of St-Louis** is sculpted into the rock with a view terrace just beyond. Since 2011, this chapel has been dedicated to "Notre-Dame du Rugby," honoring a sport that's revered in southwestern France by displaying jerseys on the wall.

Backtrack to the **Chapel of Our Lady** (Chapelle Notre-Dame), the focal point for pilgrims. Step inside. Sitting above the altar is the much-venerated Black Virgin, a 12th-century statue (covered with a thin plating of blackened silver) that depicts Mary presenting Jesus to the world. The oldest thing in the sanctuary—from the ninth century—is a simple rusted bell hanging from the ceiling. The suspended sailboat models are a reminder that sailors relied on Mary for safe passage, and the marble plaque on the left wall lists "incontestable" years of miracles, mostly from sailors who were in danger of being shipwrecked.

The adjacent **Church of St. Sauveur** is the sanctuary's main place of worship. You can't miss the dazzling organ, installed in 2013. The impressive wooden balcony was designed for the monks. Imagine attending a Mass here in centuries past, when pilgrims filled the church and monks lined those balconies. While Rocamadour's church seems more like a tourist attraction, it remains a sacred place of worship. A sign reminds tourists "to admire, to contemplate, to pray. You're welcome to respectfully visit." A bulletin board on the wall usually displays fliers for pilgrimages to Lourdes or Santiago de Compostela. Rocamadour has been both a key destination and staging point for pilgrims for centuries.

• *From here, you can walk down the Grand Escalier to the lower town. Or walk under the Church of St. Sauveur to find the Way of the Cross (Chemin de la Croix) and elevators up (Château par ascenseur) or down (La Cité par ascenseur). The passage under the church is lined with votive plaques, many of them saying "Merci à Notre-Dame" (thank you to the Virgin Mary) or "Reconnaissance" (in appreciation).*

IN THE LOWER TOWN (LA CITE MEDIEVALE)

Rocamadour's town is basically one long street traversing the cliff below the sanctuary. For eight centuries it has housed, fed, and sold souvenirs to countless visitors. There's precious little here other than tacky trinket shops, but I enjoy popping into the **Galerie le Vieux Pressoir** (named for its 13th-century walnut millstone). It fills a medieval vaulted room with the fine art of a talented couple: Richard Begyn and Veronique Guinard (about 50 yards up from the elevator).

Of Rocamadour's 11 original **gates,** seven survive (designed to control the pilgrim crowds). In the 14th century, as many as 20,000 people a day from all over Europe would converge on this spot. From the western end of town, 223 steps lead up to the church at the sanctuary level. Traditionally, pilgrims kneel on each and pray an "Ave Maria" to Our Lady.

NEAR ROCAMADOUR
▲Gouffre de Padirac

A 20-minute drive northeast of Rocamadour is the huge sinkhole of Padirac, with its underground river and miles of stalagmites and stalactites (but no cave art). Though it's an impressive cave, if you've seen caves already, it may feel tame in comparison (and there's little English). But the mechanics of the visit are easy, and there's not much to communicate anyway. Here's the drill: After paying, get your included tablet guide, hike the stairs (with big views of the sinkhole—a round shaft about 100 yards wide and deep), or ride the elevator to the river level. Line up and wait for your boat. Pack into the boat with about a dozen others for the slow row past a fantasy world of hanging cave formations that your tablet describes expertly. Get out and hike a big circle with your group and guide, enjoying lots of caverns, underground lakes, and mighty stalagmites and stalactites. Get back on the boat and retrace your course. Two elevators zip you back to the sunlight. The visit takes 1.5 hours (crowds make it take longer in summer). Dress warmly. For a knickknack Padirac, don't miss the shop.

Cost and Hours: €14.50, includes essential tablet guide, reserve online at least 24 hours ahead in high season, open daily mid-July-Aug 8:00-21:30, April-mid-July and Sept-early Nov 9:30-18:00, closed mid-Nov-March, tel. 05 65 33 64 56, www.gouffre-de-padirac.com.

Sleeping in Rocamadour

Hotels are a good deal here. Those in the upper town (L'Hospitalet) have views down to Rocamadour and easier parking, but the spirit of St. Amadour is more present below, in the lower town (La Cité, which I prefer). Every hotel—including the ones I recommend—has a restaurant where they'd like you to dine. None of the hotels I list has air-conditioning.

In the Upper Town (L'Hospitalet): **$ Hôtel Belvédère**** has 17 well-maintained, modern, and appealing rooms with access to a nearby pool. Seven rooms have views over Rocamadour, and four have valley views (rooms #14-18 have best views, free parking, tel. 05 65 33 63 25, www.hotel-le-belvedere.fr, lebelvedere-rocamadour@orange.fr).

In the Lower Town (La Cité): **$$ Maison d'hôte Les Pirondeaux** rents three high-end rooms at the foot of the sanctuary, some with kitchenettes, some good for families (check in at the Sainte Marie café next door, tel. 05 65 33 63 07 or mobile 06 87 82 28 27, www.chambrehotesrocamadour.fr, contact@chambreshotesrocamadour.fr).

$ Hôtel-Restaurant le Terminus des Pèlerins,** at the western end of the pedestrian street in La Cité Médiévale, has 12 immaculate, homey rooms with wood furnishings; the best have balconies and face the valley. Reserved, motherly owner Geneviève was born in this hotel (family rooms, tel. 05 65 33 62 14, www.terminus-des-pelerins.fr, contact@terminus-des-pelerins.com).

Eating in Rocamadour

Both of these are in the upper town, L'Hospitalet.

$$ Hôtel Belvédère has the best interior view from its modern dining room. Come early to get a windowside table, ideally for a meal just before sunset (daily, tel. 05 65 33 63 25; also recommended under "Sleeping in Rocamadour," earlier).

The **$ Bar l'Esplanade** hunkers cliffside below Hôtel Belvédère and owns unobstructed views from the tables in its garden café. It's open for lunch, dinner, drinks, and snacks (daily, tel. 05 65 33 18 45).

Grocery Store: There's a small one on Place de l'Europe in the upper town (daily 8:00-20:00).

Lot River Valley

An hour and a half south of the Dordogne, the overlooked Lot
River meanders through a strikingly
beautiful valley under stubborn cliffs and
past tempting villages. If you have a car,
the prehistoric cave paintings at Grotte
du Pech Merle, the breathtaking town of
St-Cirq-Lapopie, and the fortified bridge
at Cahors are *the* sights in this valley. The
bridge can be also visited by train as it's
not far from Cahor's train station. These
sights can be combined to make a terrific
day for drivers willing to invest the time
(doable as a long day trip from the Sarlat area). They also work well as a day trip
from Rocamadour, but are best to visit

when connecting the Dordogne with Albi, Puycelsi, or Carcassonne. (If you're going to or coming from the south, you can scenically connect this area with Albi via Villefranche-de-Rouergue and
Cordes-sur-Ciel.)

St-Cirq-Lapopie

This spectacularly situated village, clinging to a ledge sailing
above the Lot River, knows only two directions—straight up and

way down. In St-Cirq-
Lapopie, there's little to
do but wander the ram-
bling footpaths, inspect
the flowers and stones,
and thrill over the vistas.
You'll find picnic perches,
a gaggle of galleries and
restaurants, and views
from the bottom and top
of the village that justify

the pain. Leave no stone unturned in your quest to find the vil-
lage's best view (the overlook from the rocky monolith behind the
TI makes a good start). In this town, every building seems historic.
You'll lose most tourists by wandering downhill from the church.

The **TI** is across from the recommended Auberge du Som-
bral (daily 10:00-13:00 & 14:00-18:00, July-Aug 10:00-19:00,
Oct-April until 17:00 and closed Sun, tel. 05 65 31 31 31). Pick
up the visitor's guide in English, with brief descriptions of 22 historic buildings, and ask for information on area hikes. The Chemin

d'Hallage trail makes a fine hike: It was cut into the rock to allow boats to be pulled along the river.

St-Cirq-Lapopie is slammed on weekends and in high season (mid-June-mid-Sept), but is peaceful early and after hours all year. Come early and spend a few hours, or arrive later and spend the night—your first views of St-Cirq-Lapopie are eye-popping enough to convince you to stay (find a good pullout and savor the view). The lanes are steep—those with imperfect knees but still wanting a lovely village retreat should sleep an hour south in the level, quiet hilltop village of Puycelsi (see page 537).

Getting There: St-Cirq-Lapopie is well-signed 40 minutes east of Cahors, 75 minutes south of Rocamadour, and just 15 minutes from the cave paintings of Grotte du Pech Merle. Allow 1.5 hours from Sarlat.

Arriving by car from the west, you'll pass the town across the Lot River, then cross a narrow bridge and climb. There are five pay parking lots from well below to above the village. The *Village* lot (parking #4) is closest—but in high season you may be directed to lower lots, leaving you a good climb to the center.

Sleeping and Eating in St-Cirq-Lapopie: The village has all of 18 rooms, none of which are open off-season (mid-Nov-March).

$ Auberge du Sombral,** run by English-speaking Marion, is a good value in the town center across from the TI. She'll welcome you with a cozy lobby area and eight comfortable, traditional rooms in various sizes, most with double beds and sharp bathrooms (no air-con, no elevator, tel. 05 65 31 26 08, www.lesombral.com, aubergesombral@gmail.com). The good **$** restaurant serves reliable lunches (every day but Wed) in its lovely dining room or on the front terrace.

As restaurants go, **$ Lou Bolat Brasserie** works for a quick meal. It serves low-risk light fare (salads, crêpes, pizza, and *plats*) in a low-stress setting, with good views from the pleasant side terrace (daily for lunch and dinner May-Sept, otherwise lunch only, at the upper end of town, just off the main road by the post office, tel. 05 65 30 29 04).

$$ L'Oustal delivers delicious cuisine with modern touches at affordable prices inside its small dining room or on its intimate terrace (beneath the towering church, tel. 05 65 31 20 17).

$$ Le Gourmet Quercynois has the most ambience inside and out and serves reliable regional cuisine (daily, a block below the main road on Rue de la Peyrolerie, tel. 04 65 31 21 20).

Picnicking: This town was made for picnics; consider picking up dinner fixings in the hamlet of La Tour de Faure. There's a small **Proxi** grocery store on the other side of the river just west of the bridge to St-Cirq-Lapopie, and a bakery a short way east of the bridge.

DORDOGNE

▲▲Grotte du Pech Merle

This cave, about 30 minutes east of Cahors, has prehistoric paintings of mammoths, bison, and horses—rivaling the better-known cave art at Grotte de Font-de-Gaume. With 700 visitors allowed per day and a remote setting, it's a snap to get a reservation compared to other caves, but that also makes it a bit less special. Still, it has fascinating cave art and interesting stalactite and stalagmite formations. And the mud-preserved Cro-Magnon footprint is one of a kind.

Cost and Hours: €13.50, daily July-Aug 9:15-17:00, April-June and Sept-early Nov 9:30-12:00 & 13:30-17:00, limited off-season hours and closed in Jan, fewer visitors on weekends, tel. 05 65 31 27 05, www.pechmerle.com. Before you visit, read "Cave Art 101" on page 482.

Getting Tickets: It's smart to reserve in advance by phone or online and try to snag an English tour (only a few per week), as private groups can fill the cave's quota. Book a week ahead in summer; if you visit without a reservation July-Aug, try to arrive by 9:30.

Visiting the Cave: Allow a total of two hours for your visit, starting at the good museum that gives a succinct overview of human evolution. Next, see a 20-minute film (with English subtitles) that prepares you for the cave art you'll see here, and finish with a one-hour tour of the caves. If you can't join an English tour, ask for the English translations or spring for the €4.50 booklet. But don't worry about the language barrier; you'll be well prepared for the cave if you tour the museum and watch the film first.

The cave is unusual as it's owned and operated by residents of the nearby village of Cabrerets, where you'll find bakeries, groceries, and cafés. A café on the Peche Merle site offers light meals.

▲Cahors and the Pont Valentré

Cahors is home to one of Europe's best medieval monuments, the **Pont Valentré.** This massive fortified bridge was built in 1308 to keep the English out of Cahors. It worked. Learn the story of the devil on the center tower, then cross the bridge and have a view drink at the riverside café. Consider walking up the trail across the road away from the city: A short, steep hike leads to terrific views (the rock is dangerous if the trail is wet). This trail was once part of the pilgrimage route to Santiago de Compostela in northwest Spain. Imagine that cars were allowed to cross this bridge until recently.

To find the bridge as you're approaching Cahors by car, follow signs to *Centre-Ville, Gare SNCF,* then *Toutes Directions,* and finally *Pont Valentré.* Turn left at the river and find parking lots a few blocks down and a fine riverside promenade to the bridge.

On the city side of the bridge, several wine boutiques offer a good selection of Cahors wines at fair prices.

If you need an urban fix, walk for 10 minutes on the street that continues straight from the bridge (Rue de Président Wilson) and find the old city *(Vielle Ville)* after crossing Boulevard Gambetta. Cahors' thriving, pedestrian-friendly center is filled with good lunch options, cafés, cool gardens, and riverside parkways. To find this area by car, follow *Centre-Ville* and *St. Urcisse Eglise* signs, and park where you can.

If you feel like bedding down in this untouristed city with a view of the bridge, sleep at the modern **$$ Hotel Divona** (113 Avenue André Breton, tel. 05 65 21 18 39, www.divona-hotel-cahors.com, contact@hoteldivona.fr).

DORDOGNE

LANGUEDOC-ROUSSILLON

Albi • Carcassonne • Collioure

From the 10th to the 13th century, this mighty and independent region controlled most of southern France. The ultimate in mean-spirited crusades against the Cathars (or Albigensians) began here in 1208, igniting Languedoc-Roussillon's meltdown and eventual incorporation into the state of France.

The name *languedoc* comes from the *langue* (language) that its people spoke: *Langue d'oc* ("language of Oc" or Occitan—*Oc* for the way they said "yes") was the dialect of southern France; *langue d'oïl* was the dialect of northern France (where *oïl* later became *oui*, or "yes"). Languedoc-Roussillon's language faded with its power.

The Moors, Charlemagne, and the Spanish have all called this area home, with the Roussillon part corresponding closely with its Catalan corner, near the border with Spain. The Spanish influence is still *muy* present, particularly in the south, where restaurants serve paella and the siesta is still respected.

While sharing many of the same attributes as Provence (climate, wind, grapes, and sea), this sunny, southwesternmost region of France is allocated little time by most travelers. Lacking Provence's cachet, sophistication, and tourism, Languedoc-Roussillon (long-dohk roo-see-yohn) feels more real. Pay homage to Henri de Toulouse-Lautrec in Albi; spend a night in Europe's greatest fortress city, Carcassonne; scamper up to a remote Cathar castle; and sift through sand in Collioure. That wind you feel—*la tramontane*—is this region's version of Provence's mistral wind.

Languedoc-Roussillon

To Clermont-Ferrand

To Cahors & Sarlat-la-Canéda [A-20]
[D-820] Gorges de L'Aveyron
To Figeac
Rodez
La Malène
[A-75]
St-Antonin
Caussade [D-922]
[N-88]
[D-964] [D-115]
Penne
Cordes-sur-Ciel
Millau
Bruniquel [D-600]
Puycelsi
Castelnau
River
Tarn
Gaillac
Albi [D-999]
To Bordeaux
[A-68]
MIDI-PYRENEES
[D-612] [D-607]
[A-75]
[A-61]
Toulouse [N-126]
See Near Carcassonne Area detail map
[D-908]
To Lourdes & Cirque de Gavarnie
Castres [D-622]
Bardou Mons
[D-33]
Mazamet [D-907]
To Arles & Nice
[D-118] [D-612] St-Pons
[D-820] Castelnaudary
Caunes-Minervois **Minerve** Béziers
LASTOURS Azillanet
Canal du Midi
[A-61] [D-620] Olonzac [D-5]
Canal du Midi [A-9]
[D-119] **Carcassonne** Narbonne
[D-118] LANGUEDOC-ROUSSILLON
[N-20]
Limoux
Mediterranean Sea
Foix [D-613]
Couiza
20 Kilometers [D-117] [D-14] **PEYREPERTUSE**
20 Miles Cubières **QUERIBUS**
Quillan St-Paul Maury [D-117]
[D-2]
Ax [N-20]
Perpignan
P [N-116] [A-9]
ANDORRA F R A N C E [D-914]
y **Collioure**
r Céret [D-618]
e Banyuls
n [D-618] Cerbère
e Portbou
Paris [N-260]
FRANCE Cadaqués
[C-38] Figueres (DALI MUSEUM)
100 Miles Ripoll S P A I N To Barcelona [E-15]

PLANNING YOUR TIME

Languedoc-Roussillon is a logical stop between the Dordogne and Provence—or on the way to Barcelona, which is not far over the border.

If you are driving between the Dordogne and Carcassonne, Albi or Puycelsi make a good day or overnight stop (figure about two autoroute hours from Albi to either place; Puycelsi is 40 minutes closer to the Dordogne). By train, Carcassonne and Albi take about the same travel time from the Dordogne's Sarlat-la-Canéda (7 hours).

Plan your arrival in popular Carcassonne carefully: Get there late in the afternoon, spend the night, and leave no later than 11:00 the next morning to miss most day-trippers.

Collioure lies a few hours from Carcassonne and is your Mediterranean beach-town vacation from your vacation, where you'll want two nights and a full day. The most exciting Cathar castles—Peyrepertuse and Quéribus—work well as stops between Carcassonne and Collioure on a scenic drive.

GETTING AROUND LANGUEDOC-ROUSSILLON

Albi, Carcassonne, and Collioure are all accessible by train, but a car is essential for seeing the remote sights. Pick up your rental car in Albi or Carcassonne, and buy Michelin maps #344 and #338. Roads can be pencil-thin, and traffic slow. To find the Cathar castle ruins or the village of Minerve, you'll need wheels of your own and a good map—or a minivan tour (see page 541).

If you're connecting Languedoc with eastern regions like Provence, D-5 between Béziers and Olonzac will take you between long lines of plane trees and along sections of the Canal du Midi.

For a side trip from Albi, choose from a scenic one-hour detour route connecting Albi and points north, or with a bit more time, follow the "Route of the Bastides" (for either, see page 536). If you really want to joyride, take a half-day drive through the glorious Lot River Valley via Villefranche-de-Rouergue, Cajarc, and St-Cirq-Lapopie (see the Dordogne chapter).

LANGUEDOC-ROUSSILLON'S CUISINE SCENE

Hearty peasant cooking and full-bodied red wines are Languedoc-Roussillon's tasty trademarks. While the cuisine shares common roots with Provence (olives, olive oil, tomatoes, anchovies, onions, herbs, and garlic), you'll find a distinctly heartier cuisine in Languedoc-Roussillon. Be adventurous. Cassoulet, an old Roman concoction of goose, duck, pork, mutton, sausage, and white beans, is the main-course specialty. You'll also see *cargolade*, a satisfying stew of snail, lamb, and sausage. Local cheeses are Roquefort and Pelardon (a nutty-tasting goat cheese). Corbières, Minervois, and  Côtes du Roussillon are the area's good-value red wines. The local brandy, Armagnac, tastes just like Cognac and costs less.

Albi

Albi, an enjoyable river city of sienna-tone bricks, half-timbered buildings, and a marvelous traffic-free center, is worth a stop for two world-class sights: its towering, red-brick cathedral and the Toulouse-Lautrec Mu-seum. Lost in the Dordo-gne-to-Carcassonne shuf-fle and overshadowed by its big brother Toulouse, unpretentious yet digni-fied Albi rewards the stray tourist well. For most, Albi works best as a day stop, though some will be smitten by its charm and lured into spending a night.

Orientation to Albi

Albi's cathedral is home base. For our purposes, this is the city cen-ter—all sights, pedestrian streets, and hotels fan out from here and are less than a 10-minute walk away. The Tarn River hides below and behind the cathedral. The best city view is from the 22 Août 1944 bridge. Albi is dead quiet on Sundays and Monday mornings.

TOURIST INFORMATION

The main TI is across the square from the **cathedral,** at 42 Rue Mariès (daily 9:30-18:00, shorter hours Nov-Feb; tel. 05 63 36 36 00, www.albi-tourisme.fr). The TI sells a worthwhile combo-ticket that includes the Toulouse-Lautrec museum and the cathedral choir for €13 (saves €2). Ask about concerts in the cathedral, and pick up a map of the city center with walking tours and the map of *La Route des Bastides Albigeoises* (hill towns near Albi).

ARRIVAL IN ALBI

By Train: There are two stations in Albi; you want Albi-Ville. It's a level 15-minute walk to the town center: Exit the station, take the second left onto Avenue Maréchal Joffre, and then take another left on Avenue du Général de Gaulle. Go straight across Place La-pérouse and find the traffic-free street to the left that leads into the city center. This turns into Rue Ste. Cécile, the main shopping street that takes you to my recommended hotels and the cathedral.

    By Car: Follow *Centre-Ville* and *Cathédrale* signs (if you lose

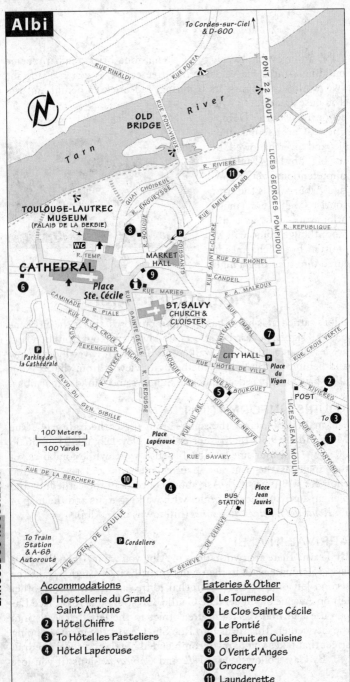

Albi

To Cordes-sur-Ciel & D-600

RUE RINALDI

RUE PORTA

PONT 22 AOUT

OLD BRIDGE

Tarn River

RUE PONT-VIEUX

LICES GEORGES POMPIDOU

R. RIVIERE

QUAI CHOISEUL

R. ENGUEYSSE

RUE EMILE GRAND

R. REPUBLIQUE

TOULOUSE-LAUTREC MUSEUM (PALAIS DE LA BERBIE)

WC

R. TEMP.

R. SOUGUE

POISSANTS

RUE SAINTE-CLAIRE

RUE DE RHONEL

MARKET HALL

CATHEDRAL

Place Ste. Cécile

RUE MARIES

RUE CANDEIL

R. A. MALROUX

ST. SALVY CHURCH & CLOISTER

CAMINADE

R. PIALE

RUE DE LA CROIX BLANCHE

RUE SAINTE CECILE

PENITENTS TIMBAL

RUE TIMBAL

RUE CROIX VERTE

Parking de la Cathédrale

RUE BERENGUIER

R. LAUTREC

R. VERDUSSE

R. ROQUELAURE

CITY HALL

RUE L'HOTEL DE VILLE

Place du Vigan

R. RIVIERES

POST

To

BLVD. DU GEN. SIBILLE

RUE DU SEL

RUE PORTE NEUVE

RUE DE BOURGUET

LICES JEAN MOULIN

RUE SAINT-ANTOINE

100 Meters
100 Yards

Place Lapérouse

RUE SAVARY

RUE DE LA BERCHERE

AVE. GEN. DE GAULLE

Place Jean Jaurès

BUS STATION

R. GENEVE R. DE GENEVE

To Train Station & A-68 Autoroute

Cordeliers

Accommodations
1 Hostellerie du Grand Saint Antoine
2 Hôtel Chiffre
3 To Hôtel les Pasteliers
4 Hôtel Lapérouse

Eateries & Other
5 Le Tournesol
6 Le Clos Sainte Cécile
7 Le Pontié
8 Le Bruit en Cuisine
9 O Vent d'Anges
10 Grocery
11 Launderette

LANGUEDOC-ROUSSILLON

your way, follow the tall church tower). Some sections of the sur-
face-level Parking de la Cathédrale are free (on Boulevard Sibille);
reasonably priced pay garages are under the market hall *(Marché
Couvert)* and Place du Vigan. If you find a spot on the street, note
that parking meters are free between 12:00-14:00 and 19:00-
8:00—as well as all day Sunday; otherwise pay by the hour.

HELPFUL HINTS

Market Days: The beautiful Art Nouveau market hall, a block
    past the cathedral square, hosts a market daily except Monday
    (7:00-14:00). On Saturday mornings, a lively farmers market
    gathers around the market hall and the TI.

Supermarkets: Carrefour City is across from the recommended
    Hôtel Lapérouse (long hours, 14 Place Lapérouse). There's also
    a grocery at the market hall in the city center.

Baggage Storage: The **Toulouse-Lautrec Museum** has lockers in
    all sizes accessible only during the museum's open hours.

Laundry: Do your washing at **Lavomatique,** above the river at 10
    Rue Emile Grand (daily 7:00-21:00).

Taxi: Call **Albi Taxi Radio** (mobile 06 12 99 42 46).

Tourist Train: The *petit train* leaves from Place Ste. Cécile in front
    of the cathedral and makes a 45-minute scenic loop around
    Albi (€7, daily in high season).

Sights in Albi

Everything of sightseeing interest is within a few blocks of the towering cathedral. (I've included walking directions to connect some
of the key sights.) Get oriented in the main square (see map).

Place Ste. Cécile

Grab the lone bench or a café table on the far side of Place Ste.
Cécile. With the church directly in front of you, the bishop's palace (with the Toulouse-Lautrec Museum inside) is a bit to the
right. The TI is hard on your right, and the market hall is a block
behind it.

    Why the big church? At its peak, Albi was the administrative
center for 465 churches. Back when tithes were essentially legally
required taxes, everyone gave their 10 percent, or *"dime,"* to the
church. The local bishop was filthy rich, and with all those *dimes,*
he had money to build a dandy church. In medieval times, there
was no interest in making a space so people could step back and
get a perspective on such a beautiful building. A clutter of houses
snuggled right up to the church's stout walls, and only in the 19th
century were things cleared away. (Just in the past few years the
cars were also cleared out.)

Why so many bricks? Because there were no stone quarries nearby. Albi is part of a swath of red-brick towns from here to Toulouse (nicknamed "the pink city" for the way its bricks dominate that townscape). Notice on this square the buffed brick addresses next to the sluggish stucco ones. As late as the 1960s, the town's brickwork was considered low-class and was covered by stucco. Today, the stucco is being peeled away, and Albi has that brick pride back.

▲▲Ste. Cécile Cathedral (Cathédrale Ste. Cécile)

When the heretical Cathars were defeated in the 13th century, this massive cathedral was the final nail in their coffin. Big and bold, it made it clear who was in charge. The imposing exterior and the stunning interior drive home the message of the Catholic (read: "universal") Church in a way that would have stuck with any medieval worshipper. This place oozes power—get on board, or get run over.

Cost and Hours: It's free to enter the **church** (daily 9:00-18:30 except Nov-April closed 13:15-14:00). Once inside, you'll pay €5 to visit the **choir** (includes excellent audioguide describing art throughout the church, open daily from 9:30 except Sun when it closes from 10:15 until Mass is over—usually 14:00, last entry one hour before the church closes). The treasury (a single room of reliquaries and church art) isn't worth the entry fee or the climb.

Organ Concerts: From mid-July to mid-August, concerts are held at the cathedral at 16:00 on Wed and Sun, and sometimes at St. Salvy Church on Wed (ask TI for schedule).

⊙ Self-Guided Tour: Visit the cathedral using the following commentary, which you can supplement with an excellent audioguide (it's especially good if you want to know more about the church's Last Judgment mural; pick it up as you enter the choir).

• Begin facing the...

Exterior: The cathedral looks less like a church and more like a fortress, as it was a central feature of the town's defensive walls. Notice how high the windows are (out of stone-tossing range). The simple Gothic style was typical of this region—designed to be sensitive to the antimaterialistic tastes of the local Cathars.

The top (from the gargoyles and newer, brighter bricks upward) is a fanciful, 19th-century, Romantic-era renovation. The church was originally as plain and austere as the bishop's palace

The Cathars

The Cathars were a heretical group of Christians who grew in numbers from the 11th through the 13th century under tolerant rule in Languedoc-Roussillon. They saw life as a battle between good (the spiritual) and bad (the material), and they considered material things evil and of the devil. Although others called them "Cathars" (from the Greek word for "pure") or "Albigensians" (for their main city, Albi), they called themselves simply "friends of God." Cathars focused on the teachings of St. John, and recognized only baptism as a sacrament. They refused to eat meat or eggs—or anything else that resulted from sexual reproduction (fish was OK).

Travelers encounter traces of the Cathars in their Languedoc sightseeing because of the Albigensian Crusades (1209-1240s). The king of France wanted to consolidate his grip on southern France. The pope needed to make a strong point that the only acceptable Christianity was Roman style (Cathars did not tithe to the church, making them a financial as well as a spiritual threat). The king and the pope discovered a mutual interest in waging a genocidal war against the Cathars, who never amounted to more than 10 percent of the local population and had coexisted happily with their non-Cathar neighbors. After a terrible generation of torture and mass burnings, the Cathars were wiped out. The last Cathar was burned in 1321.

Today, tourists find haunting castle ruins (once Cathar strongholds) high in the Pyrenees, and eat meaty, if misnamed, *salades Cathar.*

(the similar, bold brick building to the right). Imagine the church with a rooftop more like that of the bishop's palace.

• *Walk to the bottom of the cathedral's steps and gaze up at the extravagant Flamboyant Gothic...*

Entry Porch: The entry was built about two centuries after the original plain church (1494), when concerns about Cathar sensitivities were long passé. Originally colorfully painted, it provided one fancy entry.

• *Head into the cathedral's...*

Interior: The inside of the church—also far from plain—looks essentially as it did in 1500. The highlights are the vast Last Judgment mural (west wall, under the organ) and the ornate choir (east end).

• *Walk toward the front of the altar and find a good spot to view the...*

Last Judgment Mural: The oldest art in the church (1474), this is also the biggest Last Judgment painting from the Middle Ages. The dead come out of the ground, then line up (above) with a printed accounting of their good and bad deeds displayed in ledgers on their chests. Judgment, here we come. Those on the left (God's right) look confident and comfortable. Those on the right—the hedonists—look edgy. The assembly above the risen dead (on the left) shows the heavenly hierarchy: The pope and bishops sit closest to the center; then more bishops and priests—before kings—followed by monks; and then, finally, commoners like you and me.

Get closer. Inspect both sides of the arch to find seven frames illustrating a wonderland of gruesome punishments that sinners could suffer through while attempting to earn a second chance at salvation. Those who fail to do so end up in the black clouds of hell (upper right).

But where's Jesus—the key figure in any Judgment Day painting? The missing arch in the middle (cut out in late Renaissance times to open the way to a new chapel) once featured Christ overseeing the action. Go back to the last pew and find the black-and-white image on a small stand. The picture provides a good guess at how this painting would have looked—though no one knows for sure.

The **altar** in front of the Last Judgment is the newest art in the church. But this is not the front of the church at all—the altar is to the west. Turn 180 degrees and head east, for Jerusalem (where most medieval churches point).

• *Stop in front of the choir—a fancy, more intimate room within the finely carved stone "screen." Pick up the audioguide that's included with the choir admission.*

Choir of the Canons: In the Middle Ages, nearly all cathedrals had ornate Gothic choir screens like this one. These highly decorated walls divided the church into a private place for clergy and a general zone for the common rabble. The screen enclosed the altar and added mystery to the Mass. In the 16th century, with the success of the Protestant movement and the Catholic Church's Counter-Reformation, choir screens were removed. (In the 20th century, the Church took things one step further, and priests actually turned and faced their parishioners.) Later, French Revolution atheists destroyed most of the choir screens that remained—Albi's is a rare survivor.

Follow the plan (in English) as you stroll around the choir. You'll see colorful Old Testament figures along the Dark Ages exterior columns and New Testament figures in the enlightened interior. Stepping inside the choir, marvel at the fine limestone carving. Scan each of the 72 unique little angels just above the wood-paneled choir stalls. Check out the brilliant ceiling, which hasn't been touched or restored in 500 years. A bishop, impressed by the fresco technique of the Italian Renaissance, invited seven Bolognese artists to do the work. Good call.

• *Exit the cathedral through the side door, next to where you paid for the choir. You'll pass a WC on your way to the...*

▲▲Toulouse-Lautrec Museum (Musée Toulouse-Lautrec)

The Palais de la Berbie (once the fortified home of Albi's archbishop) has the world's largest collection of Henri de Toulouse-Lautrec's paintings, posters, and sketches.

Cost and Hours: €10, mid-June-Sept daily 9:00-18:00; otherwise daily 10:00-12:00 & 14:00-18:00 except closed Tue Oct-March; audioguide-€4 (for most, the printed English explanations in most rooms are sufficient), lockers available, on Place Ste. Cécile.

Information: Tel. 05 63 49 48 70, www.musee-toulouse-lautrec.com.

Background: Henri de Toulouse-Lautrec, born in Albi in 1864, was crippled from youth. After he broke his right leg at age 13 and then his left leg the next year (probably due to a genetic disorder), the lower half of his body stopped growing. His father, once very engaged in parenting, lost interest in his son. Henri moved to the fringes of society, where he gained an affinity for people who didn't quite fit in. He later made his mark painting the dregs of the Parisian underclass with an intimacy only made possible by his life experience.

Visiting the Museum: From the turnstile, walk down a few steps and enter the main floor collection.

The first room is filled with intriguing **portraits** of Toulouse-Lautrec painted by artists on whom he made an impact. There's also a rare self-portrait on display.

In the next sections we see his earliest classical paintings (of horses and pets) and his **boyhood doodles.** Find the dictionary he scribbled all over as a schoolkid. In the 1880s, Henri was stuck in Albi, far from any artistic action. During these years, he found inspiration in nature, in the pages of magazines, and by observing people. This was his Impressionistic stage.

Next, go down a few more steps to see some of his first portraits of family and friends, most done in an Impressionist style.

Step into the next room for his most famous stuff: paintings of the prostitutes and brothels of **Paris.** In 1882, Henri moved to the big city to pursue his passion. In these early Paris works, we see his trademark shocking colors, and down and dirty street-life scenes emerge. Compare his art-school work and his street work: Henri augmented his classical training with vivid life experience. His subjects were from bars, brothels, and cabarets...Toto, we're not in Albi anymore. In these exploratory years, he dabbled in any style he encountered. The naked body emerged as one of his fascinations.

Henri started making money in the 1890s by selling illustrations to magazines and newspapers. Back then, his daily happy hour included brothel visits—1892-1894 was his prostitution period. He respected the ladies, feeling both fascination and empathy toward them. The **prostitutes** accepted him the way he was and let him into their world...which he sketched brilliantly. He shows the prostitutes as real humans—they are neither glorified nor vulgarized in his works.

At the far end of this room, notice the big *Au Salon de la Rue des Moulins* (1894). There are two versions: the quick sketch, then the finished studio version. With

this piece, Toulouse-Lautrec arrived—no more sampling. The artist has established his unique style, oblivious to society's norms: colors (strong), subject matter (society's underbelly), and moralism (none). Henri's trademark use of cardboard was simply his quick, snapshot way of working: He'd capture these slice-of-life impressions on the fly on cheap, disposable material, intending to convert them to finer canvas paintings later, in his studio. But the cardboard quickies survive as Toulouse-Lautrec masterpieces.

Spiral up two flights through a room showing off a rare, 13th-century terra-cotta tile floor original to the building. Enter the next room on the left to find Lautrec's famous **advertising posters,** which were his bread and butter. He was an innovative advertiser, creating simple, bold, and powerful lithographic images. Look for displays of his original lithograph blocks (simply prepare the stone with a backward image, apply ink—which sticks chemically to the black points—and print posters). Four-color posters meant creating four different blocks. Many of the displayed works show different stages of the printing process—first with black ink, then the red layer, then the finished poster. The **Moulin Rouge** poster established his business reputation in Paris—strong symbols, bold and simple: just what, where, and when. Across the room, cabaret singer and club owner Aristide Bruant (*dans son cabaret*—"in his cabaret") is portrayed as bold and dashing.

The next room has more advertising posters, several featuring the dancer Jane Avril. Henri was fascinated by cancan dancers (whose legs moved with an agility he'd never experience), and he captured them expertly. Next, continue through several more rooms with more posters (check out those lips on Yvette Guilbert), portraits of Parisian notables and misfits, and finally the darker works he painted before his death.

One thing you will not see (because it's away on loan) is Toulouse-Lautrec's **cane,** which offers more insight into this tortured artistic genius. To protect him from his self-destructive lifestyle, loved ones had him locked up in a psychiatric hospital. But, with the help of this clever hollow cane, he still got his booze. Friends would drop by with hallucinogenic absinthe, his drink of choice—also popular among many other artists of the time. With these special deliveries, he'd restock his cane, which even came equipped with a fancy little glass.

In 1901, at age 37, alcoholic, paranoid, depressed, and syphilitic, Toulouse-Lautrec returned to his mother—the only woman who ever really loved him—and died in her arms. The art world didn't mourn. Obituaries, speaking for the art establishment, said good riddance to Toulouse-Lautrec and his ugly art. Although no one in the art world wanted Henri's pieces, his mother and his best friend—a boyhood pal and art dealer named Maurice Joyant—recognized his genius and saved his work. They first offered it to the Louvre, which refused. Finally, in 1922, the mayor of Albi accepted the collection and hung Toulouse-Lautrec's work here in what had previously been a sleepy museum of archaeology.

Your visit continues with a few rooms showing off the one-time grandeur of the Palais de la Berbie and two captivating paintings by 17th-century master Georges de La Tour.

If you still have stamina, you can climb up to the next floor, with a good exhibit of modern art. You'll see works by Toulouse-Lautrec's classmates and contemporaries, including paintings by Matisse, Degas, Brayer, and Vuillard.

• *Leaving the museum, curl around to the right, following the hulking building to find a gorgeous garden overlooking a fine...*

▲Albi Town View

Albi is here because of its river access to Bordeaux (which connected the town to global markets). In medieval times, the fastest, most economical way to transport goods was down rivers like this. The lower, older bridge (Pont Vieux) was first built in 1020. Prior to its construction, the weir (look just beyond this first bridge) provided a series of stepping stones that enabled people to cross the river. The garden of the bishop's palace dates from the 17th century (when the palace at Versailles inspired the French to create fancy gardens). The palace itself grew from the 13th century until 1789, when the French Revolution ended the power of the bishops, and the state confiscated the building. Since 1905, it's been a museum.

• *The last two sights are in the town center, roughly behind the cathedral.*

St. Salvy Church and Cloister (Eglise St. Salvi et Cloître)

Although this church (the oldest in town) is nothing special, the cloister creates a delightful space embracing an ancient well (now planted) and modern garden. Look for the easy-to-miss entrance on the main shopping street, Rue Ste. Cécile, a block off the main square. Delicate arches surround an enclosed courtyard, providing a peaceful interlude from the shoppers that fill the pedestrian streets. Notice the church wall from the courtyard. It was the only stone building in Albi in the 11th century; the taller parts, added later, are made of brick.

This is one of many little hidden courtyards throughout town. In the rough-and-tumble Middle Ages, most buildings faced inward. If doors are open, you're welcome to pop in to courtyards.

• *Leave the cloister, go up the steps, and find a sweet square with quiet cafés.*

Market Hall (Marché Couvert)

Albi's elegant Art Nouveau market is good for picnic-gathering and people-watching. There are fun lunch counters on its main floor and a grocery store on the lower level (Tue-Sun 7:00-14:00, closed Mon, 2 blocks from cathedral). On Saturdays, a lively farmers market sets up outside the market hall.

Sleeping in Albi

Hotels listed below do not have elevators unless noted.

$$ Hostellerie du Grand Saint Antoine** is Albi's oldest hotel (established in 1784) and the most traditional place I list. Guests enter an inviting, spacious lobby that opens onto an enclosed garden. Some of the 44 rooms are Old World cozy, while others have a modern flair (great breakfast, elevator, private pay parking, a block above big Place du Vigan at 17 Rue Saint-Antoine, tel. 05 63 54 04 04, www.hotel-saint-antoine-albi.com, courriel@hotel-saint-antoine-albi.com).

$$ Hôtel Chiffre* is a modern and impersonal place, with 38 simple yet comfortable rooms (elevator, pay parking garage, near Place du Vigan at 50 Rue Séré de Rivières, tel. 05 63 48 58 48, contact@hotelchiffre.com).

$ Hôtel les Pasteliers is a cool, homey place with appealing lounges, a service-oriented owner, and simple-yet-comfortable rooms with air-conditioning at terrific prices (pay secured parking, 3 Rue Honoré de Balzac, tel. 05 63 54 26 51, www.hotellespasteliers.com, contact@hotellespasteliers.com).

$ Hôtel Lapérouse is one block from the old city and a 10-minute walk to the train station. This family-run hotel offers 24 modest rooms and enthusiastic owners, Quentin and Christèle. Spring for one of the two rooms with a balcony over the big pool and quiet garden where picnics and aperitifs are encouraged (no air-con, reception closed 12:00-15:00 and after 20:00, 21 Place La-

pérouse, tel. 05 63 54 69 22, www.hotel-laperouse.com, contact@
hotel-laperouse.com).

Eating in Albi

Albi is filled with reasonable restaurants that serve a meaty local
cuisine, including plenty of duck dishes. If you're adventurous,
search out these local specialties: tripe (cow intestines), andouillette (sausages made from pig intestines), *foie de veau* (calf liver),
and *tête de veau* (calf's head). Besides the restaurants listed below,
there are many tempting cafés on the squares behind St. Salvy's
cloister and in front of the market hall.

$ **Le Tournesol** is a good (primarily lunch) option for vegetar-
ians, since that's all they do. The food is delicious (vegan options
available), the setting is bright with many windows and a good terrace, and the service is friendly. Try the wonderful homemade tarts
(open daily for lunch, dinner on Fri-Sat in high season, closed Sun
in off-season, 11 Rue de l'Ort en Salvy, tel. 05 63 38 38 14).

$ **Le Clos Sainte Cécile,** a short block behind the cathedral,
is an old-school place (literally and figuratively) transformed into a
delightful family-run restaurant with a charming courtyard laced
with cheery lights and covered with umbrellas. Friendly waiters
serve regional dishes including good salads, *confit de canard,* and
foie gras (closed Tue-Wed, 3 Rue du Castelviel, tel. 05 63 38 19 74).

$ **Le Pontié** is Albi's go-to brasserie with a big selection (pizza,
salads, *plats,* and such) and a large terrace. Interior seating is pleasant, and prices are fair (daily, Place du Vigan, tel. 05 63 54 16 34).

$$ **Le Bruit en Cuisine** offers refined food that blends the
modern with the traditional. Interior tables are OK, but you'll have
a spectacular view of the cathedral (and catch a memorable sunset)
from the broad, lamp-lit terrace (lunch *menu* based on market of
the day, evening *menu* with good choices, reservations recommend-
ed, closed Sun-Mon, 22 Rue de la Souque, tel. 05 63 36 70 31).

$ **O Vent d'Anges,** on the market hall square, is Albi's hap-
pening wine bar-café, with tables sprawling over several terraces.
It's good for an evening aperitif or small plates that can make a
meal. Big tasty salads and a delicious house burger are served dur-
ing lunch only (Wed-Sat 17:30 until late plus Thu-Sat lunch in
summer, 9 Place St-Julien, tel. 05 81 02 62 33).

Albi Connections

You'll connect to just about any destination through Toulouse.

From Albi by Train to: Toulouse (11/day, 70 minutes), **Car-
cassonne** (12/day, 2.5 hours, change in Toulouse), **Sarlat-la-Cané-
da** (6/day, 5-8 hours with 2-3 changes), **Paris** (6/day, 7-8.5 hours,

change in Toulouse; also a night train with change in Toulouse—may not run every day).

Near Albi

ROUTE OF THE BASTIDES

The hilly terrain north of Albi was tailor-made for medieval villages to organize around for defensive purposes. Here, along the Route of the Bastides (La Route des Bastides Albigeoises), scores of fortified villages *(bastides)* spill over hilltops, above rivers, and between wheat fields, creating a ▲ detour for drivers. These planned communities were the medieval product of community efforts organized by local religious or military leaders. Most *bastides* were built during the Hundred Years' War (see sidebar on page 230) to establish a foothold for French or English rule in this hotly contested region, and to provide stability to benefit trade. Unlike other French hill towns, *bastides* were not safe havens provided by a castle. Instead, they were a premeditated effort by a community to collectively construct houses as a planned defensive unit, *sans* castle.

Connect these *bastides* as a day trip from Albi, or as you drive between Albi and the Dordogne. I've described the top *bastides* in the order you'll reach them on these driving routes.

Day Trip from Albi: For a good 80-mile loop route northwest from Albi, cross the 22 Août 1944 bridge and follow signs to *Cordes-sur-Ciel* (the loop without stops takes about 2.5 hours). The view of Cordes as you approach is memorable. From Cordes, follow signs to *Saint-Antonin-Noble-Val,* an appealing, flat "hill town" on the river, with few tourists. Then turn south and west past vertical little Penne, Bruniquel (signed from Saint-Antonin-Noble-Val), Larroque, Puycelsi (my favorite), and, finally, Castelnau-de-Montmiral (with a lovely main square), before returning to Albi. Each of these places is worth exploring if you have the time.

On the Way to the Dordogne: For a one-way scenic route north to the Dordogne that includes many of the same *bastides,* leave Albi, head toward Toulouse, and make time on the free A-68. Exit at Gaillac, go to its center, and track D-964 to Castelnau-de-Montmiral, Puycelsi, and on to Bruniquel. From here you can head directly to Caussade on D-115 and D-964, then hop on the A-20 northbound (toward *Cahors/Paris*); from here, exits for Cahors, St-Cirque-Lapopie, Rocamadour, and Sarlat-la-Canéda are all well marked.

Cordes-sur-Ciel

It's hard to resist this brilliantly situated hill town about 20 miles north of Albi, but I would (in high season, at least). Enjoy the fantastic view on the road from Albi, and consider a detour up into town only if the coast looks clear (read: off-season). Cordes, once an important Cathar base, has slipped over the boutique-filled edge to the point where it's hard for me to find the medieval town. But it's a dramatic setting filled with steep streets, beautiful half-timbered buildings, and great views (www.cordessurciel.fr).

Bruniquel

This overlooked, *très* photogenic, but less-tended village will test your thighs as you climb the lanes upward to the Châteaux de Bruniquel (small fee, daily 10:00-18:00, July-Aug until 19:00, closed Nov-Feb). Don't miss the dramatic view up to the village from the river below as you drive along D-964 (about an hour northwest of Albi).

▲Puycelsi

Forty minutes north of Albi, this town crowns a high bluff overlooking thick forests and sweeping pastures. Drive to the top (passing a signed, lower lot) to find

parking and an unspoiled, level village with a couple of cafés, a bistro with a view, small grocery, bakery, a few *chambres d'hôtes*, and one sharp little hotel.

From the parking lot, pass the Puycelsi Roc Café and make your way through town. Appreciate the fine collection of buildings with lovingly tended flowerbeds. At the opposite side of the village, a rampart walk yields fine views, reminding us of the village's history as a *bastide*. The parklike ramparts near the parking area come with picnic benches, grand vistas (ideal at sunset), and a WC. It's a good place to listen to the birds and feel the wind.

As you wander, consider the recent history of an ancient town like this. In 1900, 2,000 people lived here with neither running water nor electricity. Then things changed. Millions of French men lost their lives in World War I; Puycelsi didn't escape this fate, as the monument (by the parking lot) attests. World War II added to the exodus and by 1968 the village was down to three families. But then running water replaced the venerable cisterns, and things started looking up. Today, there is just enough commercial activity to keep locals happy. The town has a stable population of 110, all marveling at how lucky they are to live here.

Sleeping in Puycelsi: An overnight here is my idea of vacation. Church bells keep a vigil, ringing on the hour throughout the night.

$$ L'Ancienne Auberge is *the* place to sleep, with eight surprisingly smart and comfortable rooms, some with sublime views. Owner/chef Dorothy moved here from New Jersey many moons ago and is eager to share her passion for this region (air-con in some rooms, Place de l'Eglise, tel. 05 63 33 65 90, www.ancienne-auberge.com, contact@ancienne-auberge.com). Ask about their self-catering apartments that can accommodate up to five people, and consider dinner at their view bistro Jardin de Lys (described below).

$ Delphine de Laveleye Chambres is another great choice just behind L'Ancienne Auberge. Warm Delphine and her dogs fill a cave-like, 17th-century house with a variety of rooms, ranging from a small romantic room for two to a three-bedroom suite with a kitchen, all hovering above a small garden and pool (family rooms, cash only, tel. 05 63 33 13 65, mobile 06 72 92 69 59, delphine@chezdelphine.com).

Eating in Puycelsi: The **$$ Jardin de Lys** bistro-café clings to the hillside, offering breathtaking views and all-day service. Come for a drink at least, or, better, for dinner based on original recipes and cooked with fresh products (daily for lunch, Mon-Sat for dinner, tel. 05 63 60 23 55). **$$ Puycelsi Roc Café,** at the parking lot, has standard café fare, a warm interior, and pleasant outdoor tables (daily for lunch and dinner in high season, tel. 05 63 33 13 67).

Castelnau-de-Montmiral

This overlooked village (30 minutes northwest of Albi) has quiet lanes leading to a perfectly preserved *bastide* square surrounded by fine arcades and filled with brick half-timbered facades. Ditch your car below and wander up to the square, where a TI, restaurant, café, and small *pâtisserie* await. Have a drink or lunch on the square.

Carcassonne

Medieval Carcassonne is a 13th-century world of towers, turrets, and cobblestones. Europe's ultimate walled fortress city, it's also stuffed with tourists. At 10:00, salespeople stand at the doors of their main-street shops, a gauntlet of tacky temptations poised and ready for their daily ration of customers—consider yourself

warned. But early, late, or off-season, a quieter Carcassonne is an evocative playground for any medievalist. Forget midday—spend the night. In fact, this is one city that can be well seen with a late afternoon arrival. There's only one "sight" to enter, and the majesty of the place can best be enjoyed after-hours.

Locals like to believe that Carcassonne got its name this way: 1,200 years ago, Charlemagne and his troops besieged this fortress-town (then called La Cité) for several years. A cunning townsperson named Madame Carcas saved the town. Just as food was running out, she fed the last few bits of grain to the last pig and tossed him over the wall. Splat. Charlemagne's bored and frustrated forces, amazed that the town still had enough food to throw fat party pigs over the wall, decided they would never succeed in starving the people out. They ended the siege, and the city was saved. Madame Carcas *sonne*-d (sounded) the long-awaited victory bells, and La Cité had a new name: Carcas-sonne.

It's a good story...but historians suspect that Carcassonne is a Frenchified version of the town's original name (Carcas). As a teenage backpacker on my first visit to Carcassonne, I wrote this in my journal: "Before me lies Carcassonne, the perfect medieval city. Like a fish that everyone thought was extinct, somehow Europe's greatest Romanesque fortress city has survived the centuries. I was supposed to be gone yesterday, but here I sit imprisoned by choice—curled in a cranny on top of the wall. The wind blows away the sounds of today, and my imagination 'medievals' me. The moat is one foot over and 100 feet down. Small plants and moss upholster my throne."

More than 40 years later, on my most recent visit, Carcassonne "medievaled" me just the same. Let this place make you a kid on a rampart, too.

Orientation to Carcassonne

Contemporary Carcassonne is neatly divided into two cities: the magnificent La Cité (the fortified old city, with 200 full-time residents taking care of lots more tourists) and the lively Ville Basse (modern lower city). Two bridges, the busy Pont Neuf and the traffic-free Pont Vieux, both with great views, connect the two parts. The train station is separated from Ville Basse by the Canal du Midi.

LANGUEDOC-ROUSSILLON

TOURIST INFORMATION

The main TI, in **Ville Basse,** is useful only if you're walking to La Cité (28 Rue de Verdun). A far more convenient branch is in **La Cité,** a block to your right (on Impasse Agnès de Montpellier) after entering the main gate (Narbonne Gate—or Porte Narbonnaise). Both TIs have similar hours (July-Aug daily 9:00-19:00; April-June and Oct Mon-Sat 9:00-18:00, Sun 10:00-13:00; Nov-March daily 9:30-12:30 & 13:30-17:30; tel. 04 68 10 24 30, www. tourisme-carcassonne.fr). If you arrive by train, the most convenient TI is the small kiosk across the canal from the **train station** (generally daily 9:30-13:00, plus July-Sept 14:00-18:30, closed Oct-May...but you never know).

At any TI, pick up a map of La Cité and the excellent (and free) *Walks* booklet that includes biking ideas. Ask about walking tours of La Cité or rent their €3 audioguide for a self-guided tour (or follow my tour later in this section).

ARRIVAL IN CARCASSONNE

By Train: The train station is located in Ville Basse, a 30-minute walk from La Cité. The nearest pay baggage storage is a few blocks away (at the recommended Hôtel Astoria). You have three basic options for reaching La Cité: taxi, bus, or on foot.

Taxis charge €12 for the short trip to La Cité but cannot enter the city walls. Taxis usually wait in front of the train station.

Two cheaper options run to La Cité from the Chénier stop (on Boulevard Omer Sarraut, at the far edge of the park a block from the station): **public bus #4** (€1, hourly Mon-Sat, none Sun) and the rubber-tired **train-bus** (€2 one-way, €3 round-trip, hourly 11:00-19:00, daily June-Aug, Mon-Sat only Sept-mid-Oct, no service mid-Oct-June). Schedules for both are posted in the bus shelter.

An **airport bus** departs from in front of the station to Carcassonne's airport, scheduled to coincide with departing flights (€6); most departures also stop at La Cité en route. A taxi to the airport costs around €20.

The 30-minute **walk** through Ville Basse to La Cité ends with a good uphill climb. Walk straight out of the station, cross the canal, then follow the route shown on the "Carcassonne Overview" map in this chapter (starting up Rue Clemenceau). La Cité is sign-posted.

By Car: Follow signs to *Centre-Ville,* then *La Cité.* You'll come to a drawbridge at the Narbonne Gate, the walled city's main entrance, where day-trippers will find several huge public pay lots (€10/6 hours). Free parking can be found on both sides of the river, but it's more plentiful on the Ville Basse side (along the river just north of the Pont Neuf or along Quai Bellevue; see map on the next page). Leave nothing on display; theft is common in public lots. Allow 15 minutes on foot over uneven surfaces to hotels in the old town.

HELPFUL HINTS

Market Days: Pleasing Place Carnot in Ville Basse hosts a thriving nontouristy open market (Tue, Thu, and Sat mornings until 13:00; Sat is the biggest and worth the detour).

Supermarkets: There's a small one in the train station. You'll also find a **Monoprix** department store (with a grocery section) where Rues Clemenceau and de la République cross, a few blocks from the train station.

Summer Festivals: Carcassonne becomes colorfully medieval during many special events each July and August. Highlights are the *spectacle équestre* (jousting matches) and July 14 (Bastille Day) fireworks. The TI has details on these and other events.

Laundry: Try **Laverie Express** (daily 8:00-22:00, 5 Square Gambetta at Hôtel Ibis; from Là Cité, cross Pont Vieux and turn right).

Bike Rental: Bike riding is very popular thanks to the scenic towpath that follows the canal (start at the train station). Ask at the TI for bike rental locations.

Taxi: Call 04 68 71 50 50.

Car Rental: The airport has all the rental companies, but is 30 minutes from Carcassonne.

Guided Excursions from Carcassonne: Vin en Vacances offers daylong vineyard tours that mix wine tasting with local food, sightseeing, and cultural experiences. It's run by charming Wendy Gedney and her terrific team, all of whom have excellent knowledge of the region and its wines. Tours include stops at two wineries, lunch, and visits to key sights such as the Cathar castles (€125-€145/person, see website for other tour options, mobile 06 42 33 34 09, www.vinenvacances.com, enquiries@vinenvacances.com).

Minivan Service: Friendly **Didier** provides comfortable transportation for up to eight passengers to the village of Minerve, all area châteaux and sights, airports, and hotels. He's not a guide and speaks just enough English (for 4 passengers plan on about €220/half-day, €400/day, €30/person for the Châteaux of Lastours; bike transport also possible; mobile 06 03 18 39 95, www.catharexcursions.com, bod.aude11@orange.fr).

Tourist Train or Horse Carriage: You have two options for taking a 20-minute loop around La Cité in high season (both cost €8 and begin at the Narbonne Gate): The tourist train has headphone English commentary and loops outside the wall,

LANGUEDOC-ROUSSILLON

TRAIN STATION

To Albi via D-118 & Caunes-Minervois

13

14

Canal du Midi

PONT MARENGO

R. DE MONTPELLIER

10

RUE H. BERNARD

RUE M.

D'ILENA

To Cité

T
B

BLVD. OMER SARRAUT

ALLEE

RUE CROZALS

RUE DE LA LIBERTE

RUE GEORGES

RUE

VILLE BASSE

(NEW CITY)

BLVD. DE VARSOVIE

RUE DU QUATRE SEPTEMBRE

CLEMENCEAU

BLVD. JEAN JAURES

RUE DU PALAIS

RUE DE LA REPUBLIQUE

RUE JEAN BRINGER

RUE MAZAGRAN

11

RUE DU DOCTEUR ALBERT TOMEY

RUE BARBES

RUE DES ETUDES

RUE JULES SAUZEDE

RUE VICTOR HUGO

RUE COSTE

BLVD. DE VARSOVIE

RUE DE VERDUN

Place Carnot

RUE REBOULH

Square Gambetta

BLVD. LITTRE

RUE ANTOINE

RUE COURTEJAIRE

RUE DE VERDUN

R. DU PONT

BLVD. MARCOU

RUE AIME RAMOND

BRASSERS

RUE ARAGO

RUE VOLTAIRE

C. PELLETAN

R. 3 COURONNES

To Cathar Castles via D-118

BOULEVARD BARBES

Place du Général de Gaulle

BLVD. C. ROUMENS

RUE DE LA DIGUE

RUE DE METZ

RUE LARAIGNON

CAPITAINE CAZAUX

RUE BASSE

R. JOSEPH FOUX

P
(Free)

RUE 24 FEVRIER

RUE DES RAMES

QUAI BELLEVUE

RUE GEN. LAPERRINE

Cimetière Saint-Michel

RUE SAINT-MICHEL

RUE TESSEYRE

RUE OURLIAC

RUE ANDRIEU

QUAI DU PAICHEROU

Aude River

CHEMIN DE LA JASSO

Parque Elle

N

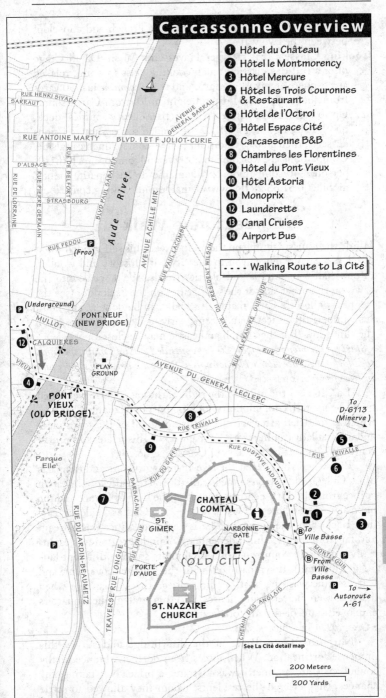

Carcassonne Overview

1. Hôtel du Château
2. Hôtel le Montmorency
3. Hôtel Mercure
4. Hôtel les Trois Couronnes & Restaurant
5. Hôtel de l'Octroi
6. Hôtel Espace Cité
7. Carcassonne B&B
8. Chambres les Florentines
9. Hôtel du Pont Vieux
10. Hôtel Astoria
11. Monoprix
12. Launderette
13. Canal Cruises
14. Airport Bus

- - - - Walking Route to La Cité

LANGUEDOC-ROUSSILLON

while the horse-and-carriage ride is in French and clip-clops between the two walls.

Cooking Classes: Brit Heather Hayes and Aussie David Crago offer a full-day classic French cooking class in a fun, relaxed atmosphere at a working farm and wine *domaine* just 50 yards from the Canal du Midi and eight miles from Carcassonne. Up to eight cooks can learn to prepare savory soufflés, duck, quail, fish or guinea fowl, classic French sauces, and delicious desserts, then enjoy a traditional three-course lunch canalside. Companions are welcome to observe and join for lunch (€110/person, €40/companion, 29 Domaine de Millepetit, Trèbes, mobile 06 51 63 29 04, www.canaldumidicooking.com).

Carcassonne Walk

While the tourists shuffle up the main street, this self-guided walk, rated ▲▲▲, introduces you to the city with history and wonder, rather than tour groups and plastic swords. We'll sneak into the town on the other side of the wall...through the back door (see the "Carcassonne's La Cité" map). This walk can be done at any hour. It's wonderfully peaceful and scenic early or late in the day, when the sun is low (but the church and castle may be closed).

• *Start on the modern asphalt 20 steps outside La Cité's main entrance, the Narbonne Gate (Porte Narbonnaise). Pause a moment to simply take in Europe's best-preserved fortress city.*

La Cité: On the pillar to the right of the gate, you're welcomed by a 12-foot-tall, contemporary-looking bust of Madame Carcas—which is modeled after a 16th-century original of the town's legendary first lady (for her story, see page 539). This relates to a ninth-century siege, during the days of Charlemagne.

But, when you gaze at the awe-inspiring turrets and ramparts of La Cité (as old Carcassonne is called), you're really looking at an edifice from the 13th-century crusade of the king of France and the pope against the heretical Cathars (see "The Cathars" sidebar, earlier). Back then, the notion of a Paris-centered France was a dream and far from reality. This independently minded region was essentially a different country whose inhabitants spoke a different language (Occitan). It sympathized with the Cathar movement, and Carcassonne was one of its leading cities. This was an age when defenses were better than offenses, and this strategic headquarters employed state-of-the-art fortifications.

• *Cross the bridge toward the...*

Narbonne Gate: Pause at the drawbridge and survey this immense fortification. When forces from northern France finally conquered Carcassonne, it was a strategic prize. Not taking any chances, they evicted the residents, whom they allowed to settle

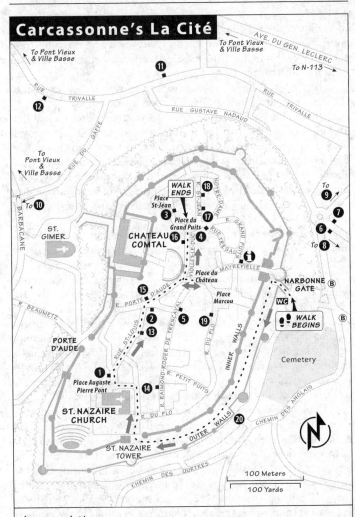

Carcassonne's La Cité

Accommodations
1. Hôtel de la Cité
2. Best Western Hôtel le Donjon
3. Maison des Remparts & Place St. Jean Eateries
4. Chambres le Grand Puits
5. Hostel Carcassonne
6. Hôtel du Château
7. Hôtel le Montmorency
8. To Hôtel Mercure
9. To Hôtel de l'Octroi & Hôtel Espace Cité
10. To Carcassonne B&B
11. Chambres les Florentines
12. Hôtel du Pont Vieux

Eateries & Other
13. Comte Roger
14. Auberge des Lices
15. Le Jardin de la Tour
16. L'Escargot
17. Le Jardin de L'Escargot
18. Le Chaudron
19. Gérard Sion Galerie (Photos)
20. Parking Entrance for Hôtels le Donjon & la Cité

LANGUEDOC-ROUSSILLON

in the lower town (Ville Basse)—as long as they stayed across the river. (Though it's called "new," this lower town actually dates from the 13th century.) La Cité remained a French military garrison until the 18th century.

This drawbridge was made crooked to slow attackers' rush to the main gate and has a similar effect on tourists today.

This is La Cité's biggest gate and worth a closer look. High above, between the two big turrets, a statue of Mary blesses all who enter. She may be blessing you, but not if you're an enemy: The drawbridge is outfitted with "murder holes" to attack people from above, a heavy portcullis (a big iron grate) that dropped down, and huge doors bolstered by beefy sliding beams. Notice the arrow slits. (In fact, you're already dead.) Behind you is a barbican, an extra defensive tower.

• *Don't enter the city yet. After crossing the drawbridge, lose the crowds and walk left between the walls. At the first short set of stairs, climb to the outer-wall walkway and linger while facing the inner walls.*

Wall Walk: The Romans built Carcassonne's first wall, upon which the bigger medieval wall was constructed. Identify the ancient Roman bits by looking about one-third of the way up and finding the smaller rocks mixed with narrow stripes of red bricks (and no arrow slits). The outer wall that you're on was not built until the 13th century (after the French defeated the city), more than a thousand years after the Roman walls went up. The massive walls you see today, with 52 towers, defended an important site near the intersection of north-south and east-west trade routes.

Look over the wall and down at the moat below (now mostly used for parking). Like most medieval moats, it was never filled with water (or even alligators). A ditch like this—which was originally even deeper—effectively stopped attacking forces from rolling up against the wall in their mobile towers and spilling into the city. Another enemy tactic was to "undermine" (tunnel underneath) the wall, causing a section to cave in. Notice the small, square holes at foot level along the ramparts. Wooden extensions of the rampart walkways outside the walls (which we'll see later, at the castle) once plugged into these holes so that townsfolk could drop nasty, sticky things on anyone trying to tunnel underneath. When you see a new section of a wall like this, it's often an indication that the spot was once successfully undermined.

In peacetime the area between the two walls *(les lices)* was used for medieval tournaments, jousting practice, and markets. But during times of war, it was always kept clear so defenders could see and target anyone approaching.

During La Cité's Golden Age, the 1100s, independent rulers with open minds allowed Jews and Cathars to live and prosper within the walls, while troubadours wrote poems of ideal love. This liberal attitude made for a rich intellectual life but also led to La Cité's downfall. The Crusades aimed to rid France of the dangerous Cathar movement (and their liberal sympathizers), which led to Carcassonne's defeat and eventual incorporation into the kingdom of France.

The walls of this majestic fortress were partially reconstructed in 1855 as part of a program to restore France's important monuments (led by the Neo-Gothic architect Eugène Viollet-le-Duc). The tidy crenellations and the pointy tower roofs are generally from the 19th century.

As you continue your wall walk to higher points, the lack of guardrails is striking. This would never fly in the US, but in France, if you fall, it's your own fault (so be careful). Note the lights embedded in the outer walls. This fortress, like most important French monuments, is beautifully illuminated every night (for directions to a good nighttime view, see "Night Wall Walk" under "Sights in Carcassonne," later).

• *You could keep working your way around the walls (though you may be detoured inside for a stretch if special events block your path). If you do the entire wall walk, you'll see five authentic Roman towers just before returning to the Narbonne Gate. Walking the entire circle between the inner and outer gate is a terrific 30-minute stroll (and fantastic after dark).*

But for this tour, we'll stop at the first possible entrance into La Cité, the...

Inner Wall Tower (St. Nazaire Tower): The tower has the same four gates it had in Roman times. Before entering, notice the squat tower on the outer wall—this was another barbican (placed opposite each inner gate for extra protection). Barbicans were generally semicircular—open on the inside to expose anyone who breached the outer defenses. Notice the holes in the barbican for supporting a wooden catwalk.

As you breach the wall and enter the old town, study the ornate defenses. Look to the right. Damn. More arrow slits—you're dead again. Look up to see a slot for the portcullis and the frame for a heavy wooden door. Imagine the heavy beams that would have bolstered the door against battering rams. The beam hole on the left goes back eight feet so the beam could slide. The entry is at an angle (to provide better cover). At the inner set of doors, you can see centuries-old, rusty parts of the hinge.

Once safely inside the wall, pretend you're a defender. Hook right and station yourself in the first arrow slit, where the design gives you both range and protection. Notice how, from here, you can guard the entrance through the outer wall (immediately opposite).

• *Opposite the tower stands the...*

LANGUEDOC-ROUSSILLON

St. Nazaire Church (Basilique St. Nazaire): This was a cathedral until the 18th century, when the bishop moved to the lower town. Today, due to the depopulation of the basically dead-except-for-tourism Cité, it's not even a functioning parish church. Step inside. Notice the Romanesque arches of the nave and the delicately vaulted Gothic arches over the altar and transepts. After its successful conquest of this region in the 13th-century Albigensian Crusades, France set out to destroy all the Romanesque churches and replace them with Gothic ones—symbolically asserting its northern rule with this more northern architectural style. With the start of the costly Hundred Years' War in 1337, the expensive demolition was abandoned. Today, the Romanesque remainder survives, and the destroyed section has been rebuilt Gothic, leaving us with one of the best examples of Gothic architecture in southern France. When the lights are off, the interior—lit only by candles and 14th-century stained glass (some of finest in southern France)—is evocatively medieval. A plaque near the door says that St. Dominique (founder of the Dominican order) preached at this church in 1213.

• *The ivy-covered luxury hotel in front of the church entrance is...*

Hôtel de la Cité: This hotel sits where the bishop's palace did 700 years ago. Today, it's a worthwhile detour to see how the privileged few travel. You're welcome to wander in. Find the cozy bar/library (reasonable beer and wine by the glass). Stepping into the rear garden, turn right for super wall views.

While little of historic interest survives in La Cité, along with this bishop's palace, it was once filled with abbeys, monasteries, the headquarters of the local Inquisition, fortified noble mansions, and one huge castle within this castle—our next stop.

• *Leaving the hotel, turn left and take the right fork at the medieval flat-iron building. Notice the surviving timbers and medieval wattle-and-daub construction (spaces between the oak posts were filled in with twigs and sticks, then finished with a layer of clay, mud, or dung). You can see the beams were roughed up so the daub finish would attach more firmly.*

Follow Rue St. Louis for several blocks. Merge right onto Rue de la Porte d'Aude, then look for a small view terrace on your left, a block up.

Château Comtal: Originally built in 1125, Carcassonne's third layer of defense was enlarged in later reconstructions. From this impressive viewpoint you can see the wooden rampart extensions (rebuilt in modern times) that once circled the entire city wall. (Notice the empty peg holes to the left of the bridge.) During sieges, these would be covered with wet animal skins as a fire retardant. Château Comtal is a worthwhile visit for those with time and interest (see "Sights in Carcassonne," later). Or just take a stroll through the tranquil garden moat (free), where you'll see people enjoying a very scenic picnic.

• *Fifty yards away, opposite the entrance to the castle, is...*

Place du Château: This busy little square sports a modest statue honoring the man who saved the city from deterioration and neglect in the 19th century. The bronze model (considered fairly accurate) circling the base of the statue shows Carcassonne's walls as they looked before their fanciful 1855 Neo-Gothic reconstruction by Viollet-le-Duc (who also restored Paris' Notre-Dame Cathedral).

• *It's downhill from here to the Narbonne Gate (where this walk started). But first, one last stop. Backtrack a few steps to face the château entry, then turn right and walk one block to...*

Place du Grand Puits: This huge well is the oldest of Carcassonne's 22 wells. In an age of starve-'em-out sieges, it took more than stout walls to keep a town safe—you also needed a steady supply of water and food.

• *Our walk is finished. You can return to the Château Comtal entrance gate to tour the castle. Or, if you turn left at the fountain, you'll pop out in the charming, restaurant-lined Place St-Jean; a hard left here takes you down into the château's moat garden and a small gate (on the right side of the castle), which leads to the most impressive part of the city wall (around the Porte d'Aude).*

Sights in Carcassonne

▲▲▲Night Wall Walk

Save some post-dinner energy for a don't-miss walk around the same walls you visited today (great dinner picnic sites as well). The effect at night is mesmerizing: The embedded lights become torches and unfamiliar voices become the enemy. You can enter and exit the old city from two locations: Porte d'Aude, on the west side, or from the main Narbonne Gate, on the east side. From either point you can walk 15 minutes down to the Pont Vieux (old bridge) and find an unforgettable view of the  floodlit walled town. Ideally, take one route down and the other back up (see the La Cité map).

▲▲Château Comtal and Rampart Walk

Your best look at Carcassonne's medieval architecture is a walk through this castle-within-the-castle, followed by a walk atop the city ramparts (possible only with a castle ticket). Grab the basic flier in English (and rent the €3 audioguide for the full story—

as narrated by Eugène Viollet-le-Duc, the man who restored the old city in the 19th century), cross the drawbridge over the garden moat, and once inside the courtyard, enter the château on your left and climb to the top of the stairs.

Start your visit in a small theater, where a short video sets the stage. Next is a big model of La Cité (made in 1910 to show the city as it looked in 1300). Enjoy the black-and-white images of old Carcassonne on the walkway above. From here, a self-guided tour with posted English explanations (and your audioguide) leads you around the inner ramparts of Carcassonne's castle. You'll see the underpinnings of the towers and of the catwalks that hung from the walls, and learn all about medieval defense systems. The views are terrific. Your visit ends with a museum showing bits of St. Nazaire Church and fragments from important homes.

From the castle you can climb out onto the actual city ramparts and circle about two-thirds of the old town. The north rampart is open all the way to the main Narbonne Gate, but there's no exit and you'll need to backtrack. The west rampart lets you circle all the way to the St. Nazaire Tower, from where you can exit (drop off your audioguide before entering the west rampart). I'd explore both sections.

Cost and Hours: €9, daily 10:00-18:30, Oct-March 9:30-17:00, last entry 45 minutes before closing, tel. 04 68 11 70 70, www.remparts-carcassonne.fr.

Porte d'Aude, Pont Vieux, and Riverside Walks
The stretch of fortification behind Château Comtal is particularly interesting. The impressive gate called Porte d'Aude is central to this section and allows access from the walls down a path to Pont Vieux, a 14th-century bridge that spans the Aude River with 12 massive arches. It was built to connect La Cité with the Ville Basse, which was first populated with outcasts from La Cité. Agreements and treaties between the two towns (which did not always get along) were signed here. Today the pedestrian-only bridge provides brilliant views day or night and access to walking paths along the river. Those paths run along each side of the river, offering occasional views to the fortress and a verdant escape for runners and walkers.

Canal du Midi
Completed in 1681, this sleepy 155-mile canal connects France's Mediterranean and Atlantic coasts and, at about its midpoint, runs directly in front of the train station in Carcassonne. Before railways, Canal du Midi was clogged with commercial traffic; today, it entertains only pleasure craft. Two companies offer **canal cruises** that leave from in front of the station. Bateau Cocagne runs 1.5-2.5-hour trips (about €9-11, April-Oct 2-4/day, www.bateau-

cocagne-canal-carcassonne.fr). Carcassonne Navigation boats run similar trips and also has longer lunch and dinner cruises (www.carcassonne-navigationcroisiere.com). Travelers with limited time are best off biking along the canal: The path is level, pedaling is a breeze and you can cover far more territory than by boat—for bike rental locations, ask at the TI.)

Gérard Sion Galerie

Duck into this impressive photo gallery in the old town before selecting which Cathar castles you want to visit (brilliant shots of many monuments in Languedoc-Roussillon, generally daily 10:00-12:30 & 14:00-19:00, just up from Place Marcou at 27 Rue du Plô).

Nightlife in Carcassonne

There are several low-key ways to enjoy La Cité after dark. For relief from all the medieval kitsch, savor a pricey drink in four-star, library-meets-bar ambience at the **Hôtel de la Cité** bar. To taste the liveliest square, with loads of tourists and strolling musicians, sip a drink or nibble a dessert on **Place Marcou.** Near the château, the recommended **L'Escargot** morphs into a convivial bar after dinner is finished.

For a peaceful drink and floodlit views from outside the wall, pause at the recommended **Hôtel du Château**'s broad terrace, below the Narbonne Gate (2 Rue Camille Saint-Saëns). To be a medieval poet, share a bottle of wine in your own private niche somewhere remote on the ramparts.

Le Bar à Vins is the only real nightclub in the old town. It's a down and dirty bar with a huge open-air terrace offering lively music, plenty of drinks, and a fun garden scene in the moonshadow of the wall...without any tourists (daily 12:00 until late in high season, 6 Rue du Plô, tel. 04 68 47 38 38). They serve gut-bomb bar food without a full-service kitchen.

Sleeping in Carcassonne

Sleep within or near the old walls, in La Cité. I've also listed a hotel near the train station. In the summer, when La Cité is jammed with tourists, consider sleeping in quieter Caunes-Minervois. July and August are most expensive, when the town is packed. At other times of the year, prices drop and there are generally plenty of rooms. Hotels have air-conditioning and elevators, unless noted.

IN LA CITÉ

Pricey hotels, good B&Bs, and an excellent youth hostel offer a full range of rooms inside the walls. The Hôtel de la Cité and Best

LANGUEDOC-ROUSSILLON

Western Hôtel le Donjon offer private pay parking near the castle moat (pass the small cemetery, heading slightly uphill, and find the attendant; includes bag transfers); they also validate parking in the main lot below the Narbonne Gate (no bag transfers; you must show your reservation or have the attendant call your hotel).

$$$$ Hôtel de la Cité***** offers 59 rooms with deluxe everything in a beautiful building next to St. Nazaire Church. Peaceful gardens, a swimming pool and spa, royal public spaces, the elegant Barbacane restaurant, and reliable luxury are yours—for a price (family rooms, pay parking, Place Auguste-Pierre Pont, tel. 04 68 71 98 71, www.hoteldelacite.com, h8613@accor.com).

$$ Best Western Hôtel le Donjon** has 61 well-appointed rooms, a lobby with wads of character, and a great location inside the walls. Rooms are split between three buildings in La Cité (the main building, a lookalike annex across the street, and the cheaper **Maison des Remparts** a few blocks away). The main building is most appealing, and the rooms with terraces on the garden are delightful (pay parking, 2 Rue Comte Roger, tel. 04 68 11 23 00, www.hotel-donjon.fr, info@bestwestern-donjon.com).

$ Chambres le Grand Puits, across from Maison des Remparts, is a splendid value. It has one cute double room and two cavernous apartment-like rooms that could sleep five, with kitchenette, private terrace, and sweet personal touches. Inquire in the small boutique, and say *bonjour* to happy-go-lucky Nicole (includes self-serve breakfast, cash only, no elevator, no air-con, 8 Place du Grand Puits, tel. 04 68 25 16 67, http://legrandpuits.free.fr, nicole.trucco@club-internet.fr).

¢ Hostel Carcassonne is big, clean, and well-run, with an outdoor garden courtyard, self-service kitchen, TV room, bar, washer/dryer, and a welcoming ambience. If you ever wanted to bunk down in a hostel, consider doing it here—all ages are welcome. Reserve ahead for summer (€11/person membership, includes breakfast, rental towels, Rue du Vicomte Trencavel, tel. 04 68 25 23 16, www.hifrance.org or www.hihostels.com, carcassonne@hifrance.org).

JUST OUTSIDE LA CITE

Sleeping just outside La Cité offers the best of both worlds: quick access to the ramparts, less claustrophobic surroundings, and easy parking.

$$$ Hôtel du Château** and **$$ Hôtel le Montmorency*** are adjacent hotels that lie barely below La Cité's main gate and are run by the same family. Check-in, parking, and breakfast for both hotels are at Hôtel du Château. Guests enjoy an easy walk to La Cité, a snazzy pool, hot tub, view terraces to the walls of Carcassonne, a lazy hound, and a sweet cat. Hôtel du Château gives four-star comfort with 17 sumptuous rooms (RS%—use code "RICK-

STEVES," pay parking, 2 Rue Camille Saint-Saëns, tel. 04 68 11 38 38, www.hotelduchateau.net, contact@hotelduchateau.net). Hôtel Montmorency, a short walk behind Hôtel du Château, has a split personality. Half the rooms are neon-colored mod, and half are purely Provençal and a bit smaller. Several have views to the ramparts, and many come with private decks or terraces (RS%—use code "RICKSTEVES," no elevator but only one floor up, pay parking, 2 Rue Camille Saint-Saëns, tel. 04 68 11 96 70, www. hotelmontmorency.com, contact@hotelmontmorency.com).

$$ Hôtel Mercure** hides a block behind the Hôtel le Montmorency, a five-minute walk to La Cité. It rents 80 snug but comfy air-conditioned rooms and has a refreshing garden, good-sized pool, big elevators, a restaurant, and a warm bar-lounge. A few rooms have views of La Cité (many family rooms, free parking, 18 Rue Camille Saint-Saëns, tel. 04 68 11 92 82, www.mercure. com, h1622@accor.com).

CLOSE TO LA CITE

These places are on either side of the Pont Vieux, about 15 minutes below La Cité and 15 to 20 minutes from the train station on foot.

$$ Hôtel les Trois Couronnes,** a modern hotel in a con-crete shell just across Pont Vieux, offers 44 rooms with terrific views up to La Cité—and 26 nonview rooms that you don't want (indoor pool with views, pay parking garage, 2 Rue des Trois Couronnes, tel. 04 68 25 36 10, www.hotel-destroiscouronnes.com, contact@ hotel-destroiscouronnes.com). Their reasonably priced restaurant also has a good view.

$$ Hôtel de l'Octroi* delivers colorful, contemporary com-fort, efficient service, and a young vibe from its full-service bar to its small, stylish pool and 21 rooms (RS%—use code "RICK-STEVES," family rooms, no elevator, pay parking, 143 Rue Tri-valle, tel. 04 68 25 29 08, www.hoteloctroi.com).

$ Hôtel Espace Cité, three blocks downhill from the main gate to La Cité, is a fair value, with 48 small-but-clean, cookie-cutter rooms (no elevator, limited free parking—otherwise pay parking in garage, 132 Rue Trivalle, tel. 04 68 25 24 24, www. hotelespacecite.fr, espace-cite@hotelespacecite.fr)

$ Carcassonne Bed and Breakfast is a meticulously main-tained, five-room *chambres d'hôte* that sits a 15-minute walk below La Cité and 20 minutes from the train station. Rooms are beauti-fully furnished, some have views of Carcassonne, and there's a nice courtyard to relax in (12 Rue Fernand Merlane, tel. 04 68 25 80 34, www.carcassonnebandb.com, info@carcassonnebandb.com).

$ Chambres les Florentines is a good-value B&B run by charming Madame Mistler. The five rooms are spacious, tradi-tional, and homey; one room has a big deck and grand views of La

Cité (cash only, family rooms, includes breakfast, no air-con, no elevator, pay parking, 71 Rue Trivalle, tel. 04 68 71 51 07, www. lesflorentines.net, lesflorentines11@gmail.com).

$ Hôtel du Pont Vieux, with welcoming Catherine and Jean-Michel, offers 19 sharp rooms, a peaceful garden, and a small rooftop terrace with million-dollar views. Four rooms come with views to La Cité; others look over the garden (secure parking garage—reserve ahead, no elevator, 32 Rue Trivalle, tel. 04 68 25 24 99, www.hotelpontvieux.com, info@hoteldupontvieux.com).

NEAR THE TRAIN STATION

$ Hôtel Astoria has some of the cheapest hotel beds that I list in town, divided between a main hotel and an annex across the street. Book ahead—it's popular. The updated annex rooms have air-conditioning; rooms in the main building are simple—the cheapest have a shared bath (no elevator, pay parking—reserve ahead, bike rentals, baggage storage for small fee; from the train station, walk across the canal, turn left, and go two blocks to 18 Rue Tourtel; tel. 04 68 25 31 38, www.astoriacarcassonne.com, info@astoriacarcassonne.com).

IN CAUNES-MINERVOIS

To experience unspoiled, tranquil Languedoc-Roussillon, sleep surrounded by vineyards in the characteristic village of Caunes-Minervois. Comfortably nestled in the foothills of the Montagne Noire, Caunes-Minervois is a 25-minute drive from Carcassonne. Take route D-118 or follow signs toward *Mazamet* to a big round-about and find D-620. The town offers an eighth-century abbey, two cafés, several restaurants, a pizzeria, a handful of wineries, and no other tourists. The friendly staff at the town's TI (in the abbey) is eager to help you explore the region. Caunes-Minervois makes an ideal base for exploring the area's wine roads.

$ Hôtel d'Alibert, in a 15th-century home with character, sits in the heart of the village. It has a mix of nicely renovated and Old World traditional rooms. It's managed with a relaxed je ne sais quoi by Frédéric "call me Fredo" Dalibert and his son, who can help plan your wine-tasting excursion (includes breakfast, Place de la Mairie, tel. 04 68 78 00 54, www.hotel-dalibert.com, frederic.dalibert@wanadoo.fr). Tasty meals are offered most days in his cozy restaurant with great courtyard tables.

$ L'Ancienne Boulangerie is a cozy B&B option a few doors down from Hôtel d'Alibert with a comfortable lounge and nifty shared terrace. Home-cooked dinners are possible if you book a day ahead (cash only, includes breakfast, tel. 04 68 76 27 17, www. ancienneboulangerie.com, ancienne.boulangerie@orange.fr).

Eating in Carcassonne

For a social outing in La Cité, take your pick from a food circus of basic eateries on a leafy courtyard—often with strolling musicians in the summer—on lively Place Marcou. If rubbing elbows with too many tourists gives you hives, go local and dine below in Ville Basse (the new city). Cassoulet (described on page 524) is the traditional must. It's a rustic peasant's dish—beloved for sure, but locals will remind you "there's no gourmet cassoulet" (tip: a dash of vinegar helps the digestion); big salads provide a lighter alternative. For a local before-dinner drink, try a glass of Muscat de Saint-Jean-de-Minervois.

IN LA CITE

$$$ Comte Roger has a quiet elegance that seems out of place in this touristy town. If you want one fine meal in the old town, book a table here to enjoy Chef Pierre's fresh Mediterranean cuisine. Ask for a table on the vine-covered patio, or eat in their stylish dining room. Their €50 *menu* is the best gourmet value in town. Pierre's cassoulet comes closer than anyone to breaking the "no gourmet cassoulet" rule (closed Sun-Mon, 14 Rue St. Louis, tel. 04 68 11 93 40, www.comteroger.com).

$$ Auberge des Lices, serving traditional plates with a rustic-plush ambience, is hidden down a quiet lane and has a courtyard with cathedral views (vegetarian options, daily July-Aug, closed Tue-Wed Sept-June, 3 Rue Raymond Roger Trencavel, tel. 04 68 72 34 07).

$$ Le Jardin de la Tour, run with panache by Elodie for many years, offers good cassoulet, duck, seafood, and a list of first-course plates designed for sharing family-style. Inside you'll feel like you're dining in an antique shop; outside, enjoy the peaceful atmosphere in the parklike garden (closed Sun-Mon, lunch served July-Aug only, 11 Rue de la Porte d'Aude, tel. 04 68 25 71 24).

$$ L'Escargot, casual and welcoming, feels like a wine bar with tapas. The tight seating, sizzle of an open kitchen, minimal tables, wine-bottle walls, and popular following combine to create a convivial bustle. Thomas and his black-shirted staff serve several gourmet salads and give their Spanish and French plates an extra twist: anise in the escargot, apple in the foie gras...and definitely no cassoulet. Reserve ahead during busy times (lunch from 12:15 and two dinner seatings: 19:00 and 21:00, three seating zones: peaceful streetside, quiet basement, busy ground-floor kitchen area, closed Wed and in winter, 7 Rue Viollet-Le-Duc, tel. 04 68 47 12 55, https://restaurant-lescargot.com).

When L'Escargot is full, they send people two blocks away

to their branch **Le Jardin de L'Escargot,** with the same formula (decor, menu, and prices) at 4 Rue St. Jean.

$$ Le Chaudron takes its cassoulet seriously. It's carefully traditional, served with a salad, and may be the best in town. You'll dine in a peaceful outdoor setting under the shade of trees, in the simple interior room, or the more refined and spacious upstairs space (daily July-Aug, closed Mon-Tue off-season, 6 Rue St Jean, tel. 04 68 71 09 08).

Castle Views On Place St. Jean: On this great little square in La Cité, several eateries compete for your business. All have outside terrace tables with views to the floodlit Château Comtal. **$$ Restaurant Adélaïde** is a lively bistro with good prices; they serve a three-course *menu* with cassoulet as well as big salads (daily except closed Mon Sept-May, tel. 04 68 47 66 61). Kid-friendly **$ Le Créneau,** with more commotion and energy, serves creative tapas, pizzas, and Spanish plates. They have a cafeteria vibe inside and a sunny, castle-view roof terrace. Owner-chef Paul is enthusiastic about his oysters and escargot (daily, tel. 04 68 71 81 53).

Picnics: Basic supplies can be gathered at shops along the main drag (generally open until at least 19:30, better to buy outside La Cité). For your beggar's banquet, picnic on the city walls or in the little park above Place Marcou.

IN VILLE BASSE

$$ Restaurant les Trois Couronnes, just across the Pont Vieux in the recommended Hôtel les Trois Couronnes, gives you a panorama of Carcassonne from the top floor of a concrete hotel (open daily for dinner only, closed Jan, call ahead, 2 Rue des Trois Couronnes, tel. 04 68 25 36 10).

Carcassonne Connections

From Carcassonne by Train to: Albi (10/day, 3 hours, change in Toulouse), **Collioure** (8/day, 2 hours, most require change in Narbonne), **Sarlat-la-Canéda** (5/day, 7 hours, 1-2 changes usually in Bordeaux and/or Toulouse), **Arles** (4/day direct, 2.5 hours, more with transfer in Narbonne), **Nice** (3/day, 6.5 hours with change in Marseille), **Paris** (Gare de Lyon: 8/day, 5.5 hours, 1 change usually in Bordeaux), **Toulouse** (nearly hourly, 1 hour), **Barcelona** (1/day direct, 2.5 hours, 5/day with change in Narbonne, 3 hours).

Cathar Sights near Carcassonne

The land around Carcassonne is carpeted with vineyards and littered with romantically ruined castles, ancient abbeys, and photogenic villages. To the south, the castle remains of Peyrepertuse and

Quéribus make terrific stops between Carcassonne and Collioure (allow 2 hours from Carcassonne on narrow, winding roads; from the castles it's another 1.5 hours to Collioure). You can also link them on a fine loop trip from Carcassonne.

Northeast of Carcassonne, two Cathar sights and the gorge-sculpted village of Minerve (45 minutes from Carcassonne), work well for Provence-bound travelers or as a day trip from Carcassonne.

Getting There: Public transportation is hopeless; taxis for up to six people cost about €300 for a daylong excursion (taxi tel. 04 68 71 50 50). See page 541 for excursion bus and minivan tours to these places.

SOUTH OF CARCASSONNE
▲▲Chateaux of Hautes Corbières

About two hours south of Carcassonne, in the scenic foothills of the Pyrenees, lies a series of surreal, mountain-capping castle ruins. Like a Maginot Line of the 13th century, these cloud-piercing castles were strategically located between France and the Spanish kingdom of Roussillon. As you can see by flipping through the picture books in Carcassonne's tourist shops, these crumbled ruins are an impressive contrast to the restored walls of La Cité. You'll want a hat (there's no shade) and sturdy walking shoes—prepare for a vigorous climb.

Getting There: Connect two of these castles (but visit just one) along this incredibly scenic, 2.5-hour drive. You can either make a loop from Carcassonne or continue on to the seaside village of Collioure.

From Carcassonne drive to Limoux, then Couiza. At Couiza follow little D-14 to Bugarach (passing through Languedoc's only spa town, Rennes-le-Château). Near Bugarach, views open to rocky ridgelines hovering above dense forests. You'll soon see signs leading the way to Peyrepertuse. At Cubières, canyon lovers can detour to the **Gorges de Galamus,** driving partway into the teeth of white-rock slabs that seem to squeeze closer the farther in you go (those looping back to Carcassonne can do the whole canyon on their way back). **Peyrepertuse** is a short hop from Cubières; you'll pass snack stands and view cafés on the twisty drive up. After visiting this Cathar castle, your next destination—**Quéribus**—is a well-signed, 15-minute drive away.

From Quéribus it's a 1.5-hour drive to Collioure (follow signs in direction: Maury, then direction: Perpignan). If returning to Carcassonne, follow signs for Maury, then St-Paul-de-Fenouillet, then drive through the Gorges de Galamus and track D-14 to Bugarach, Couiza, Limoux, and Carcassonne.

Sleeping near Peyrepertuse and Quéribus: To really get

LANGUEDOC-ROUSSILLON

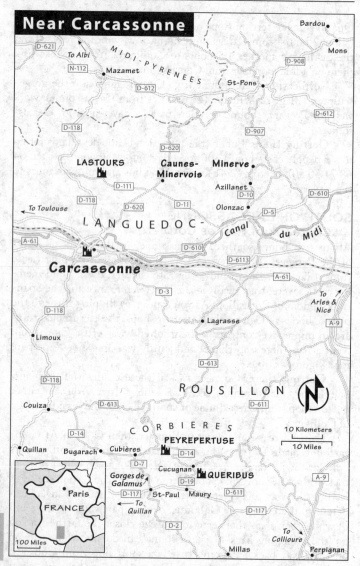

Near Carcassonne

Bardou

Mons

D-621

To Albi

MIDI-PYRENEES

N-112 Mazamet

D-908

St-Pons

D-612

D-612

D-907

D-118

D-620

LASTOURS

Caunes-Minervois

Minerve

Azillanet

D-10

D-610

To Toulouse

D-111

D-118

D-620

D-11

Olonzac

D-5

LANGUEDOC-

Canal   du   Midi

A-61

D-610

Carcassonne

D-6113

A-61

D-3

To Arles & Nice

D-118

Lagrasse

A-9

Limoux

D-613

ROUSILLON

D-611

Couiza

D-613

N

10 Kilometers

10 Miles

D-14

CORBIERES

PEYREPERTUSE

Quillan Bugarach Cubières

D-14

D-7

Cucugnan

QUERIBUS

A-9

Gorges de Galamus

D-19

D-117 St-Paul Maury D-611

To Quillan

D-2

D-117

To Collioure

Millas

Perpignan

Paris

FRANCE

100 Miles

To Quillan

away (and I mean really), sleep in the little village of Cucugnan, located between the castles. **$ L'Ecurie de Cucugnan** is a friendly bed-and-breakfast with five comfortable rooms at great rates, a view pool, and a shady garden. Joël, winemaker and owner, doesn't speak English, but his wife—a teacher—does (includes breakfast, full house rental available, 18 Rue Achille Mir, tel. 04 68 33 37 42, www.ecuriedecucugnan.com, ecurie.cucugnan@orange.fr).

$$ Ferrairolles Eco Guesthouse, about 16 miles from the

castle ruins, is an elegant four-room guesthouse run by dynamic Dutchwoman Rolinka Bloeming (who doubles as a Rick Steves' Europe tour guide). Located on the scenic route from Carcassonne to Collioure in remote Villeneuve-les-Corbières, it's 30 minutes from the Mediterranean and surrounded by Cathar castles, canyons, hiking trails, and vineyards (includes breakfast, nice pool, ask about vegetarian dinners with wine, mobile 06 47 53 16 34, www. rolinkablooming.com, rolinka.blooming@gmail.com).

▲▲Peyrepertuse

The most spectacular Cathar castle is Peyrepertuse (pay-ruh-pair-twos), where the ruins rise from a splinter of cliff: Try to spot it on your drive up from the village. From the parking lot, you'll first hike downhill, curling around the back of the rock wall, then hike steeply up 15 minutes through a scrubby forest to the fortress. The views are sensational in all directions (including to Quéribus, sticking up from an adjacent ridge). But what's most amazing is that they could build this place at all. This was a lookout in the Middle Ages, staffed with 25 very lonely men. Today, it's a scamperer's paradise with weed-infested structures in varying states of ruin. Let your imagination soar, but watch your step as you try to reconstruct this eagle's nest—the footing is tricky. Don't miss the St. Louis stairway to the upper castle ruins—another stiff, 10-minute climb straight up.

Cost and Hours: €7, daily 9:00-19:00, July-Aug until 20:00, shorter hours off-season & closed Jan, theatrical audioguide-€4 (narrated from the perspective of a French captain posted here), free handout gives plenty of background, tel. 04 30 37 00 77, www. chateau-peyrepertuse.com).

▲Quéribus

While Peyrepertuse rides along a high ridge, this bulky castle caps a mountaintop and delivers more amazing views (find the snow-covered peaks of the Pyrenees). It owns a similar history to Peyrepertuse but has an easier (but still uphill) footpath to access the site and gentler climbing within the ruins. It's famous as the last Cathar castle to fall, and was abandoned after 1659, when the border between France and Spain was moved farther south into the high Pyrenees.

Cost and Hours: €7.50, daily May-Sept 9:30-19:00, July-Aug until 20:00, shorter hours off-season, theatrical audioguide-€4, good handout, tel. 04 68 45 03 69, www.cucugnan.fr.

NORTH OF CARCASSONNE

The next two Cathar sights provide an easy excursion north from Carcassonne, offering a taste of this area's appealing countryside.

LANGUEDOC-ROUSSILLON

They tie in well with a visit to the village of Caunes-Minervois (where I recommend sleeping—see page 554).

Châteaux of Lastours

Ten scenic miles north of Carcassonne, four ruined castles cap a rugged hilltop and give visitors a handy (if less dramatic) look at  the region's Cathar castles. These castles, which once surrounded a fortified village, date from the 11th century. The village welcomed Cathars (becoming a bishop's seat at one point) but paid dearly for this tolerance with destruction by French troops in 1227. But three of the four castles still have their towers intact.

From the village of Lastours you can hike to the castles, then drive to an impressive viewpoint. Hikers park at the lot as they enter the village, walk 500 yards upriver to the modern ticket and information office, then walk 20 minutes uphill to the castles (ask for the good brochure with your ticket and allow at least an hour for a reasonable tour; good shoes and water are smart). Don't leave sans making the short drive into the village and up to the **belvedere** for a smashing panorama over the castles.

Cost and Hours: Castles and belvedere viewpoint-€7, viewpoint only-€3; daily July-Aug 9:00-20:00, April-June and Sept 10:00-18:00, Oct daily and Nov-March weekends only 10:00-17:00; closed Jan-Feb; tel. 04 68 77 56 02.

Getting There: From Carcassonne, follow signs to *Mazamet*, then *Conques-sur-Orbiel*, then *Lastours*.

Eating: An idyllic and inexpensive lunch awaits near the lower entry at **$$ Le Moulin de Lastours,** where a small bakery has a few tables serenely overlooking the river (good quiche and sandwiches, closed Tue off-season, tel. 04 68 25 23 14).

▲Minerve

A onetime Cathar hideout with Celtic origins, the photogenic village of Minerve is sculpted out of a swirling canyon that provided a natural defense. Strong as it was, it couldn't keep out the pope's armies, and the village was razed during the vicious Albigensian Crusades of the early 1200s.

Getting There: Located between Carcassonne and Béziers, Minerve is seven miles north of Olonzac and 45 minutes by car from Carcassonne. It makes for a good stop between Provence and Carcassonne. As you approach Minerve, don't miss the view from the bus parking lot near the bridge to the village.

Visiting Minerve: As you arrive, follow the *P* signs to the pay parking lot above the village (good WCs). Take in the views from the cliff at the parking lot, then walk 200 yards past canyon views to enter the village and find

the **TI** (Rue des Martyrs, tel. 04 68 91 81 43, www.minervois-caroux.com). Pick up the brochure with a simple self-guided tour of the village describing Minerve's history. Hikers should ask about trails into and above the canyon.

Minerve has cool cafés, one hotel, a nifty little bookshop, a few wine shops, and a smattering of art galleries. You'll also find two small museums: a prehistory museum and the compact **Hurepel de Minerve,** with models from the Cathar era and excellent English descriptions that effectively describe this terrible time (€3.50, free for children under 14, interesting for kids, daily 10:00-13:00 & 14:00-18:00, closed Nov-March, Rue des Martyrs, tel. 04 68 91 12 26).

After your village stroll, explore the canyon below by walking down to the riverbed: follow *Access Remparts* signs from below Café de la Place. Metal steps head down to the river, and a short-but-rough trail across the riverbed leads up to a catapult and terrific views back to Minerve. From the viewpoint, backtrack down and over to the village side of the river; from there pick up signs to *Poterne* to return to the town up a cobbled lane.

Sleeping and Eating in Minerve: Stay here and melt into southern France (almost literally, if it's summer).

$ Relais Chantovent's unpretentious and spotless rooms are designed for those who come to get away from it all, with no phones or TV...and ample quiet. All rooms have queen-size beds (tel. 04 68 91 14 18, www.relaischantovent-minerve.fr, contact@relaischantovent-minerve.fr). Its sharp **$$ restaurant** has a marvelous view from its deck and deserves your business; it's popular, so reserve ahead (open for lunch Thu-Tue 12:15-14:00, and for dinner Thu-Sat and Mon 19:30-21:00, closed Wed).

$ Café de la Place has a good patio and some tables with views (light snacks).

LANGUEDOC-ROUSSILLON

Collioure

Surrounded by less-appealing
resorts, lovely Collioure is
blessed with a privileged
climate and a romantic setting.
By Mediterranean standards,
this seaside village should be
slammed with tourists—it has
everything. But, outside of peak
times, it is remarkably quiet.

Collioure is a pastel treat with six petite and pebbly beaches, leafy
squares under a once-mighty castle, and a lighthouse to mark where
the Pyrenees meet the sea.

Just 15 miles from the Spanish border, Collioure (Cotlliure in
Catalan) shares a common history and independent attitude with
its Catalan siblings across the border. Undeniably French yet with
a proud strain of Catalan, it flies the yellow and red flag of Catalunya, displays street names in French and Catalan, and sports a few
business names with *el* and *els*, rather than *le* and *les*. Less than a
century ago, most villagers spoke Catalan; today that language is
enjoying a resurgence as Collioure rediscovers its roots.

Come here to unwind and regroup. Even with its crowds of
vacationers in peak season (July and August are busy), Collioure is
what many look for when they head to the Riviera—a sunny, relaxing splash in the Mediterranean.

PLANNING YOUR TIME

Check your ambition at the station. Enjoy a slow coffee on *la Med,*
lose yourself in the old town's streets, compare the *gelati* shops on
Rue Vauban, sample the fine local wines, and relax on a pebble-
sand beach (water shoes are helpful). The hills above Collioure
deliver fantastic views whether from your car or the tourist train
(described later).

Orientation to Collioure

Most of Collioure's shopping, sights, and hotels are in the old
town, near the Château Royal. You'll find memorable views of the
old town from across the bay near the recommended Hôtel Boramar and brilliant views from the hills above. You can walk from
one end of Collioure to the other in 20 minutes.

TOURIST INFORMATION

The TI hides behind the main beachfront cafés at 5 Place du 18 Juin (July-Sept Mon-Sat 9:15-18:45, Sun 10:15-17:45; same hours April-June and Oct except closes Mon-Sat at 17:45; shorter hours and closed Sun Nov-March; tel. 04 68 82 15 47, www.collioure. com).

ARRIVAL IN COLLIOURE

By Train: Walk out of the station (no baggage storage), turn right, and follow Rue Aristide Maillol downhill for about 10 minutes until you see Hôtel Restaurant La Frégate. Before leaving the station, check the schedule for Spanish side-trips or for your next destination (station staffed generally 9:15-13:00 & 14:30-18:00).

By Car: Collioure is 16 miles south of Perpignan. From the autoroute, take the *Perpignan-Sud Sortie* exit and follow signs to *Argelès-sur-Mer* (also called *Argelès*). Pass Argelès, staying on D-914, and follow signs to *Collioure par la Corniche.* To reach the center, follow *Collioure Centre-Ville* signs, and turn left onto Rue de la République.

Parking is a challenge and almost impossible in summer—arrive early or late (all lots are numbered; see "Collioure" map for locations). There's a central pay lot (Parking Glacis, P-4) accessed from the bottom of Rue de la République, behind the post office (about €15/24 hours). You may find a space at Parking Haut Douy (P-3, as you drop downhill toward the city center (5-minute walk to the center, 3-hour limit, €6). The best deal is Parking de la Stade (P-5), a 15-minute walk from the center past Fort Miradou (on Route du Pla de las Fourques, about €1/hour). In high season, it's easiest to park at the remote Parking Cap Dourats on the Route de Madeloc (€12/24 hours) and take the free shuttle bus into town (3/hour, daily 10:00-20:00, July-Aug until 24:00). Leave nothing of value in your car.

HELPFUL HINTS

Market Days: Markets are held on Wednesday and Sunday mornings on Place Général Leclerc, across from Hôtel Frégate.

Laundry: Ask at the TI for the nearest launderette.

Taxi: Call 04 68 82 09 30 or mobile 07 62 12 68 68.

Tourist Train: Collioure's *petit train* leaves from the main square (next to bridge, bottom of Rue République, where you'll find a ticket booth with departures posted). It winds on tiny lanes through vineyards, climbs 300 yards above sea level to a five-minute photo stop at Fort St. Elme, and then drops down through more lovingly terraced vineyards, cork trees, and cactus to the neighboring village of Port Vendres before returning to your starting point. There's good recorded narration in English. You can hop out at Fort St. Elme and hike down or wait for the next train (if there's an empty place). You can also disembark at Port Vendres (€8 round-trip, 45 minutes, departures at least on the hour 10:00-18:00; €12 one-way with fort entry—return to town on foot, www.petit-train-touristique.com).

Sights in Collioure

There's no important sight here except what lies on the beach and the views over Collioure. Indulge in a long seaside lunch, inspect the colorful art galleries, catch up on your diary, and maybe take a hike. Collioure's bay caters to more than just sun-loving tourists. Don't be surprised to see French Marines playing commando in their rafts. Sightseeing here is most romantic in the evening, when yellow lamps reflect warm pastels and deep blues.

▲View from the Beach

Walk out to the jetty's end, past the church and the little chapel, and find a spot along the rail. Collioure has been popular since well before your visit. For more than 2,500 years, people have battled to control its enviable position on the Mediterranean at the foot of the Pyrenees. The mountains rising behind Collioure provide a natural defense, and its port gives it a commercial edge, making Collioure an irresistible target. A string of forts defended Collioure's land-locked side. Panning from left to right, you'll see the low-slung remains of a 17th-century fort, the still-standing Fort St. Elme (built by powerful Spanish king and Holy Roman Emperor Charles V) at the top of a hill, and then the 2,100-foot-high observation tower of Madeloc, capping the mountain peak. Topping the village to the far right is the 18th-century *citadelle*, Fort Mirador, now home to a French Marine base and commando training center. Scattered ruins crown several other hilltops.

Back to the left, that old windmill (1344) was originally used for grain; today it grinds out olive oil. The stony soil and dry weather conditions in the hills above Collioure are ideal for growing grapes. Those beautiful terraced vineyards, averaging 250 days of sunshine a year, grow primarily grenache, syrah, and mourvèdre grapes, which make terrific reds and rosés.

Collioure's medieval town hunkers down between its church and royal château. The town was batted back and forth between the French and Spanish for centuries. Locals just wanted to be left alone—as Catalans (most still do today—notice the yellow-and-red Catalan flag flying above the château). The town was Spanish for nearly 400 years before becoming definitively French in 1659 (thanks to Louis XIV). After years of obscurity, Collioure was re-discovered by artists drawn to its pastel houses and lovely setting. Henri Matisse, André Derain, Pablo Picasso, Georges Braque, Raoul Dufy, and Marc Chagall were all inspired to paint here at one time or another. You may recognize Collioure in paintings in many museums across Europe.

Château Royal (Royal Castle)

The 800-year-old castle, built over Roman ruins, served as home over the years to Majorcan kings, Crusaders, Dominican monks, and Louis XIV (who had the final say on the appearance we see now). Today it's a sprawling vacant shell, giving tourists a place to prowl, offering rampart walks, harbor views, and a home to local history and art exhibits.

Cost and Hours: €4, daily 10:00-18:00, July-Aug until 19:00, Oct-May 9:00-17:00, tel. 04 68 82 06 43.

Notre-Dame des Anges
(Our Lady of the Angels Church)

This waterfront church is worth a look (daily 8:30-16:30). Supporting a guiding light (for ships as well as souls), the church's foundations are built into the sea, and its one-of-a-kind lighthouse/bell tower helped sailors return home safely. The highlight is its over-the-top golden altar, unusual in France but typical of Catalan churches across the border. Drop €1 in the box to the left of the altar: lights, cameras, reaction—*oh là!*

Path of Fauvism (Chemin du Fauvisme)

Art lovers will enjoy meandering along the harborfront (Boulevard Boramar) and seeing seven copies of paintings by Derain and Matisse—inspired by the artists' stays in Collioure in 1905—mounted as panels along sidewalk walls. Two additional panels are along Avenue du Mirador in the quieter part of town. The Maison du Fauvisme office, behind the TI at 10 Rue de la Prud'homie, sells "Path of Fauvism" fliers (ask about walking tours).

If you enjoyed seeing these copies, you can view a good collection of original paintings by Derain and Matisse in the museum in Céret (see "Near Collioure," later) and in the recommended Hôtel les Templiers.

Stroll Around the Bay

A highlight of any Collioure visit is to walk the length of the harbor and the various scooped-out beaches of the bay. Playing on the town's heritage of inspiring artists, there are empty picture frames for your photo fun. Between the church and the castle, look for memorial winches (by the Copacabana restaurant, for example) that recall the days when anchovy boats were hauled onto the beach—back when anchovies didn't ornament tourist salads but helped hungry locals get through the winter. An easy promenade runs around the base of the château to the Port d'Avall beach. Opposite the carrousel is Anchois Roque (a traditional anchovy shop). Just beyond that is the Cellier Dominicain, offering a good wine tasting (see below). Follow the promenade to the end of the line (La Balette), where you'll find the laid-back Balco del Mar bar with exceptional views of Collioure. From here, you can return the way you came, or climb up the stairs to the road, then make your way up to a stone windmill before coming back to town (see "Walks and Hikes," next page).

Beaches (Plages)

You'll usually find the best sand-to-stone ratio at Plage de Port d'Avall or Plage St. Vincent (chaise lounge rental-about €10/day, paddleboat/kayak rentals-€20/hour, summer only). The tiny Plage de la Balette is quietest but rocky, with brilliant views of Collioure and a stone skipper's nirvana. All three spots come with beach showers.

Wine Tasting

Collioure and the surrounding area produce well-respected wines, and many shops offer informal tastings of the sweet Banyuls and Collioure reds and rosés. **Cellier Dominicain** is ideal for tasting, with a fine selection at good prices and a helpful staff who offer cellar tours at 16:00 (free tasting, €5 for tours, daily 9:00-12:00 & 14:00-18:00, closed Sun in off-season, near the Hôtel Triton on Place Orphila, tel. 04 68 82 05 63). For a good selection of wines from many wineries and fair prices, try **Vins d'Auteurs** (next to Hôtel Frégate at 6 Place Maréchal Leclerc, daily, tel. 04 68 55 45 22).

Inviting Evening Spots in Collioure

Collioure has no shortage of cafés and bars where you can enjoy views of the village, sip a drink beachside, or mix it up with locals in the old town. **Balco del Mar** is the place to savor a seaside drink with memorable views of Collioure's old town (daily 11:00 to late, near Plage de la Balette, behind and below La Voile restaurant). The cafés along the harborfront on the old city side offer a sandy scene (see "Eating in Collioure"). The recommended **Paco,** tucked in the old town, is a lively Spanish-feeling pub crammed with locals (open late). **Café Sola** is a local and lively standby (2 Rue de la République, next to the recommended Hôtel Casa Pairal).

WALKS AND HIKES

The views described here offer different perspectives of this splendid area.

▲Views Below the Stone Windmill

Stone steps lead five minutes up behind Collioure's modern art museum to fine views that are positively peachy at sunset. Find the museum's gateway behind Hôtel Triton, and walk through its stony backyard. Red *le moulin* signs recommend a clockwise loop up to the windmill and back: Bear left (hugging the museum's back) and climb up the steps to a small, square structure with fine views. From here, you can huff up another five minutes to the windmill itself (interesting to see, though the views are less obstructed from below). The windmill is also the starting point for the next hike.

▲Hike to Fort St. Elme

This vertical hike is best done early or late (there's no shade) and is worth the sweat, even if you don't make it to the top (trail starts from windmill described above, allow 30 minutes from there each way). You can't miss the square castle lurking high above Collioure. The privately owned castle has a rich history (built in 1552 by Holy Roman Emperor Charles V) and exhibits of medieval armor and weaponry—pick up the English booklet that explains them (€7, daily 10:30-19:00, shorter hours off-season, closed mid-Nov-mid-Feb, mobile 06 64 61 82 42, www.fortsaintelme.com). The most practical way to get here is to take the tourist train (which sells a combo-ticket for the ride and fort at a discount) and hop off here. Then you can either walk down or wait for a later train (see "Helpful Hints," earlier). Cheaters can drive here via Port Vendres.

▲▲Drive/Hike Through Vineyards to Madeloc Tower (Tour de Madeloc)

Check your vertigo at the hotel, fasten your seatbelt, and take this drive-and-hike combination high above Collioure. The narrow road, hairpin turns, and absence of guardrails only add to the experience, as Collioure shrinks to Lego size and the clouds become

LANGUEDOC-ROUSSILLON

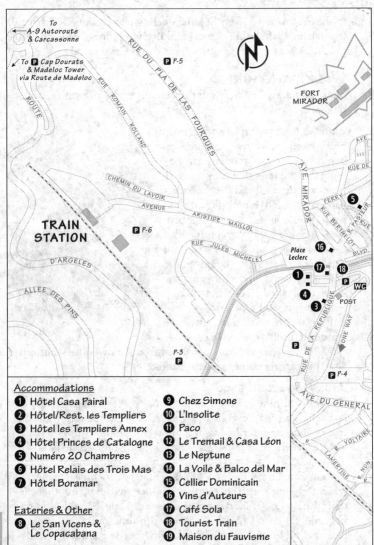

Accommodations
1 Hôtel Casa Pairal
2 Hôtel/Rest. les Templiers
3 Hôtel les Templiers Annex
4 Hôtel Princes de Catalogne
5 Numéro 20 Chambres
6 Hôtel Relais des Trois Mas
7 Hôtel Boramar

Eateries & Other
8 Le San Vicens &
   Le Copacabana
9 Chez Simone
10 L'Insolite
11 Paco
12 Le Tremail & Casa Léon
13 Le Neptune
14 La Voile & Balco del Mar
15 Cellier Dominicain
16 Vins d'Auteurs
17 Café Sola
18 Tourist Train
19 Maison du Fauvisme

your neighbors. Drive as far as you like on this route—the views become exceptional quickly and turnouts allow for panorama appreciation and easy turnarounds. The road is popular with bicycle riders. If you plan to go up to Madeloc Tower, be aware that there's no shade—do this hike early or late in the day.

Leave Collioure, heading toward Perpignan, and look for signs reading *Tour de Madeloc* at the roundabout. Climb through steep and rocky terraced vineyards, following *Tour* signs and negotiating countless hairpin turns. About eight kilometers past the

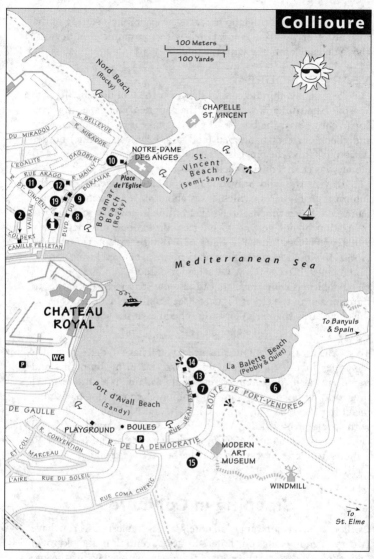

Collioure

100 Meters
100 Yards

Nord Beach
(Rocky)

CHAPELLE
ST. VINCENT

R. BELLEVUE
R. MIRADOR
DU MIRADOU
L'EGALITE
DAGOBERT
RUE ARAGO
ST. VINCENT
VAUBAN
COLBERT
CAMILLE PELLETAN
BLVD DU BORAMAR
R. MAILLY

NOTRE-DAME
DES ANGES

St.
Vincent
Beach
(Semi-Sandy)

10
11
12
19
9
8
2

Place
de l'Eglise

Boramar
Beach
(Rocky)

Mediterranean Sea

CHATEAU
ROYAL

To Banyuls
& Spain

La Balette Beach
(Pebbly & Quiet)

14
13
7
6

WC
P

Port d'Avall Beach
(Sandy)

ROUTE DE PORT-VENDRES
RUE JEAN BART

DE GAULLE
R. CONVENTION
ET COLL
MARCEAU
L'AIRE RUE DU SOLEIL
RUE COMA CHERIC
R. DE LA DEMOCRATIE

PLAYGROUND
BOULES
P

MODERN
ART
MUSEUM

15

WINDMILL

To
St. Elme

roundabout, turn right at the intersection toward *Balcon de Madeloc* (where you see a sign to *Port Vendres*). In three more kilometers (about 20 minutes after you leave Collioure), you'll come to a fork in the road with a paved path (marked by a "no entry" symbol that applies to cars) and a road leading downhill. Park at the fork, and walk up the paved path. The views are everywhere and magnificent—the Pyrenees on one side, and the beach towns of Port Vendres and Collioure on the other. Just 15 minutes of walking will get you to Pyrenees views; allow 30 minutes at a slow-yet-steady pace along the splintered ridgetop to reach the eagle's-nest setting of the ancient tower (La Tour), now fitted with communication devices. Here you can commune with the gods.

NEAR COLLIOURE

The 15-mile, 40-minute coastal drive via the Col de Banyuls into Spain is beautiful and well worth the countless curves, even if you don't venture past the border. If you do make it to the border, park and check out the abandoned (and strangely lost-in-time) border station. It's from the pre-EU era, when passports were stamped and money was changed with each new country.

To visit the wild **Salvador Dalí Theater-Museum,** take the autoroute to Figueres, which takes about an hour each way (museum-€14; buy a timed-entry ticket online in advance to avoid the frustration of not getting in on busy days; open July-Sept daily 9:00-20:00; Oct-June Tue-Sun 9:30-18:00—except from 10:30 Nov-Feb, closed Mon; last entry 45 minutes before closing, Spanish tel. 34-972-677-500, www.salvador-dali.org).

Ambitious train travelers can also day-trip to Spain, either to Barcelona or to the closer Figueres (see "Collioure Connections" at the end of this chapter). Get train schedules at the station.

Céret

To see the art that Collioure inspired, you'll have to drive 25 winding miles inland to this pleasing town, featuring fountains and mountains at its doorstep. Céret's claim to fame is its **modern art museum,** with works by some of Collioure's more famous visitors, including Picasso, Joan Miró, Chagall, and Matisse (€5.50, more with special exhibits, daily 10:00-19:00, Oct-June until 17:00 and closed Mon, tel. 04 68 87 27 76, www.musee-ceret.com). Allow 40 minutes to Céret by car, or ride the bus from Perpignan—ask at Collioure's TI.

Sleeping in Collioure

Collioure has a fair range of hotels at favorable rates. You have two good choices for your hotel's location: central, in the old town (closer to train station); or across the bay, with views of the old town (10-minute walk from the central zone, with easier parking). Unless noted, hotels have air-conditioning and elevators.

IN THE OLD TOWN

To orient you to the hotel locations, I've used the landmark Hôtel Frégate, at the edge of the old town, a 10-minute walk down from the train station.

$$ **Hôtel Casa Pairal,***** opposite Hôtel Frégate and hiding

down a short alley (behind Café Sola), is a Mediterranean-elegant oasis. Enter to the sounds of a fountain gurgling in the flowery courtyard. Reclining lounges await in the garden and by the pool. The rooms are quiet and tastefully designed; "privilege" rooms, on the first floor, have high ceilings and higher prices; some have small balconies over a courtyard (no elevator, pay parking—reserve ahead, good breakfast, Impasse des Palmiers, tel. 04 68 82 05 81, www.hotel-casa-pairal.com, contact@hotel-casa-pairal.com).

$ **Hôtel les Templiers,**** with three buildings in the heart of the old town, has wall-to-wall paintings in its main building, a perennially popular café-bar, low-key management, and good-value rooms. The paintings are payments in kind and thank-yous from artists who have stayed here: In the bar is a black-and-white photo of the hotel's owner with Picasso. In the main (and best) building—where you'll check in—choose between a view to the castle or facing the quieter back lane; many rooms here have traditional Catalan furniture. The annex, a five-minute walk away on Rue de la République, is a notch lower in quality and price. Across the street from the main hotel is a third building with a few cheaper, last-resort rooms (main hotel is a block toward beach from Hôtel Frégate along drainage canal at 12 Quai de l'Amirauté, tel. 04 68 98 31 10, www.hotel-templiers.com, contact@hotel-templiers.com).

$ **Hôtel Princes de Catalogne***** offers 30 comfortable, spacious, well-maintained rooms. For maximum quiet, get a room on the mountain side, or *côté montagne* (some view rooms, family rooms, limited free parking, next to Hôtel Casa Pairal, Ruedes Palmiers, tel. 04 68 98 30 00, www.hotel-princescatalogne.com, contact@hotel-princescatalogne.com).

$ **Numéro 20 Chambres,** with eager-to-help hosts Véronique and Noël, is a good budget value. Their four rooms are simple, clean, spacious, and suitable for families, with small fridges, coffeemakers, and microwaves (family rooms, cash only, no air-con, no elevator, on pedestrian street two blocks past Hôtel Frégate at 20 Rue Pasteur, tel. 04 68 82 15 31, mobile 06 17 50 16 89, www.collioure-chambre-peroneille.fr, numero20ruepasteur@gmail.com).

ACROSS THE BAY

$$$ **Hôtel Relais des Trois Mas****** clings to the hill above the La Balette beach and delivers 23 modern and comfortable rooms, many with killer views (lower rooms can be a bit musty). They have the best view pool and whirlpool in Collioure (no elevator but just two floors, several large suites, free valet parking, Michelin-star $$$$ **restaurant** with good-value dinner *menus* from €55 and lunch *menus* from €35, Route de Port Vendres, tel. 04 68 82 05 07, www.relaisdestroismas.com, contact@relaisdes3mas.com).

$ **Hôtel Boramar,**** across the bay from Collioure's center,

is understated and modest (like its owner Thierry), but well maintained (also like Thierry) and a terrific value. Ten of the 14 rooms
face the water, many with balconies, and a fine breakfast terrace
faces the beach (family rooms, no air-con, no elevator, Wi-Fi in
lobby, Rue Jean Bart, tel. 04 68 82 07 06, www.hotel-boramar.fr,
hotelboramar.collioure@orange.fr).

Eating in Collioure

Test the local wine and eat anything Catalan, including the fish
and anchovies (hand-filleted, as no machine has ever been able to
accomplish this precise task). All of my recommended restaurants
have indoor and outdoor tables, and most are in the old town. Several delicious *gelati* shops and a Grand Marnier crêpe stand next to
the Copacabana restaurant fuel after-dinner strollers with the perfect last course. Many restaurants close in bad weather and through
the winter.

Eating Cheaply: Small places sell a variety of meals to go (*à
emporter;* ah em-pohr-tay) for budget-minded romantics wanting
to dine on the bay. There's a shady harborside park under Château
Royal with handy benches and fine views.

HARBORFRONT STRIP

A string of waterside eateries (behind the TI) delivers café fare
with a view, mostly mediocre values, and a fun beachside scene. All
are open daily. **$$$ Le San Vicens** has the most serious kitchen
and menu (2 Boulevard du Boramar, tel. 04 68 87 09 86). **$$ Le
Copacabana** next door has great seating but a limited menu from the
beachside tables—drop by here for a drink or dessert (6 Boulevard
du Boramar, tel. 04 68 82 06 74). Just off the beach, **$$$ Chez
Simone,** a lighthearted and popular place, serves enticing tapas,
tartines, and *plats* with sea views. Tapas sampler plates are a fun
way to enjoy some variety (daily, 7 Rue Mailly, tel. 04 34 29 93 47).
$$ L'Insolite is a modest place offering salads, burgers, seafood,
and a nicer view from a quieter perch near the church, with outdoor
tables only (4 Place de l'Eglise, tel. 04 68 82 22 94).

IN THE OLD TOWN

$$ Paco, close and dark, is a lively little pub, drenched in south-
of-the-border character. The offerings of French/Catalan cuisine,
served to a mostly local crowd, are limited to salads, tapas, and a
few other dishes (daily, some outdoor seating, on a tiny lane two
blocks off the harbor at 18 Rue Rière, tel. 04 68 82 90 91).

$$ Le Tremail is a reasonable choice for contemporary seafood and Catalan specialties served outside or in. With its colorful
tile decor, it feels Spanish. It's a small and cozy place one block

LANGUEDOC-ROUSSILLON

from the bay, where Rue Arago and Rue Mailly meet (daily year-round, 1 Rue Arago, tel. 04 68 82 16 10).

$$ Casa Léon offers some of the town's freshest Mediterranean cuisine, served in a tight-but-fun interior or at outside tables. The massive *parriade de poissons* seafood plate (€34) is their specialty, though the anchovy dishes and dorado are also delicious (daily, closed Mon off-season, next door to Le Tremail at 2 Rue Rière, tel. 04 68 82 10 74).

$$$ Hôtel-Restaurant les Templiers, with painting-lined walls, a tiled floor, and cushioned benches, is popular with locals and dishes up Catalan-inspired plates of reliable value (daily, 12 Quai de l'Amirauté, tel. 04 68 98 31 10).

HARBORFRONT SOUTH OF THE CASTLE

Some of your best values are just south of the castle, facing the Port d'Avall beach. When you take your harborside stroll, drop into each to consider an evening meal, and, if you like the Neptune, reserve the table of your dreams.

$$$ Le Neptune is an elegant restaurant where you'll want to wear your nicest; it's borderline stuffy but clearly offers the best dressy value in town. Foodies will love the adventurous and well-presented dishes, and those on a budget will dine elegantly with their €40 *menu*. There are harbor views for all, with outdoor seating below and a covered dining room on top that feels al fresco (daily, closed Tue-Wed in off-season, 9 Route de Port-Vendres, tel. 04 68 82 02 27).

$$ La Voile ("The Sail"), next to Le Neptune, perches under three decorative sails with open seating, a long counter facing the sea, and a yacht-club vibe. It's casual with hearty fish dishes and good dinner salads. They take no reservations and close with bad weather (9 Route de Port-Vendres, mobile 06 34 89 01 95). Their harborside bar below, **Balco del Mar,** is inviting any time of day.

Collioure Connections

From Collioure by Train to: Carcassonne (8/day, 2 hours, most require change in Narbonne), **Paris** (8/day, 6-7 hours, 2-4 changes), **Barcelona,** Spain (8/day, 2.5-4 hours, most change in Perpignan or Portbou), **Figueres,** Spain (6/day, 1-2 hours, most change in Perpignan or Portbou), **Avignon/Arles** (8/day, 3.5-4.5 hours, several transfer points possible).

PROVENCE

Arles • Avignon • Pont du Gard • Les Baux • St-Rémy-de-Provence • Orange • Côtes du Rhône Villages • Hill Towns of the Luberon

The magnificent region of Provence is shaped like a giant wedge of quiche. From its sunburned crust, fanning out along the Mediterranean coast from the Camargue to Marseille, it stretches north along the Rhône Valley to Orange. The Romans were here in force and left many ruins—some of the best anywhere (the region's name comes from its status as the first Roman province). Seven popes, artists such as Vincent van Gogh and Paul Cézanne, and author Peter Mayle all enjoyed their years in Provence. This destination features a splendid recipe of arid climate, oceans of vineyards, dramatic scenery, lively cities, and adorable hill-capping villages.

Explore the ghost town that is ancient Les Baux, and see France's greatest Roman ruins—the Pont du Gard aqueduct and the theater in Orange. Admire the skill of ball-tossing *boules* players in small squares in every Provençal village and city. Spend a few Van Gogh-inspired starry, starry nights in Arles or St-Rémy-de-Provence. Youthful but classy Avignon bustles in the shadow of its brooding Palace of the Popes. It's a short hop from Arles or Avignon into the splendid scenery and villages of the Côtes du Rhône and Luberon regions.

PLANNING YOUR TIME

Make Arles or Avignon your sightseeing base—particularly without a car. Italophiles prefer smaller Arles, while poodles pick urban Avignon. **Arles** has a blue-collar quality; the entire city feels like Van Gogh's bedroom. **Avignon**—double the size of Arles—feels sophisticated, with more nightlife and shopping, and makes a good base for nondrivers thanks to its convenient public-transit

options. For drivers who prefer a smaller-town base, St-Rémy-de-Provence is well situated. To measure the pulse of rural Provence, spend at least one night in a village (such as Vaison-la-Romaine or Roussillon) or in the countryside. These villages can be terminally quiet from mid-October to Easter.

When budgeting your time, plan a full day for sightseeing in Arles and Les Baux (for example, spend most of the day in Arles—best on Wed or Sat, when it's market day—and visit Les Baux in the late afternoon or early evening); a half-day for Avignon; and a day or two for the villages and sights in the countryside.

Pont du Gard is a short hop west of Avignon and on the way to/from Languedoc-Roussillon for drivers. Les Baux works well by car from Avignon and better from Arles, and in high season by bus from Arles. The town of Orange ties in tidily with a trip to

Provence at a Glance

▲▲▲**Arles** Workaday town of evocative Roman ruins, Van Gogh memories, Provençal "bullgames," and easy pedestrian zones. See page 584.

▲▲▲**Pont du Gard** West of Avignon, a huge stone structure—part bridge and part aqueduct—heralding the greatness of ancient Rome. See page 640.

▲▲▲**Les Baux** Rock-top village sitting in the shadow of its ruined medieval citadel. See page 645.

▲▲**Avignon** History-rich city, famous for its medieval bridge and Gothic Palace of the Popes. See page 615.

▲▲**Orange** Leafy café-lined streets and the best-preserved Roman theater in existence. See page 656.

▲▲**Côtes du Rhône Wine Road Drive** Soak up picturesque villages and vineyards, unfurling along a scenic wine-tasting route. See page 673.

▲▲**Hill Towns of the Luberon** Enticing terrain of age-old vineyards, limestone mountains, and sturdy little villages. See page 680.

▲**St-Rémy-de-Provence** Fun village that's home to a bustling market, with Van Gogh's psychiatric ward and the ancient Roman city of Glanum nearby. See page 651.

▲**Vaison-la-Romaine** Lively little town atop a 2,000-year-old Roman site. See page 663.

the Côtes du Rhône villages. The Côtes du Rhône is ideal for wine connoisseurs and an easy stop for those heading to or from the north, as is Vaison-la-Romaine. Isle-sur-la-Sorgue (the most accessible small town by train) is conveniently located between Avignon and the Luberon.

GETTING AROUND PROVENCE

By Bus or Train: Public transit is good between cities and decent to some towns, but marginal at best to the smaller villages. Frequent trains link Avignon, Arles, and Nîmes (no more than an hour between each). Avignon has good train connections with Orange and adequate service to Isle-sur-la-Sorgue.

Buses connect many smaller towns, though service can be sporadic. From Arles you can catch a bus to Stes-Maries-de-la-Mer (in

Public Transportation in Provence

To Lyon & Paris

P R O V E N C E

Montélimar
Rhône
Nyons
Buis-les-
Baronnies
Vaison-la-Romaine
Orange
CÔTES
DU RHÔNE
To Grenoble
Châteauneuf-du-Pape
Uzès
PONT
DU GARD
Avignon
Isle-sur-
la-Sorgue
Roussillon
Avignon TGV
Cavaillon
Apt
Nîmes
Tarascon
LUBERON
Lourmarin
Rhône
St-
Rémy
To
Montpellier,
Carcassonne
& Barcelona
(Spain)
Les
Baux
Arles
Rhône
Aigues-
Mortes
C A M A R G U E
Aix-
en-Provence
To Nice
Aix
TGV
Petit
Rhône
Toulon
Stes-
Maries-
de-la-Mer
Marseille
Cassis
Stn.
Les
Calanques
La Ciotat
Cassis
Not to Scale

Mediterranean
Sea

Rail
TGV High Speed Rail
Bus
Boat
Airports
(Not All Shown)

Note: In some cases regular
train lines and TGV lines share
the same track

the Camargue) or St-Rémy. From Avignon, you can bus to Pont du Gard, St-Rémy, Isle-sur-la-Sorgue (also by train), and to some Côtes du Rhône villages.

While a tour of the Côtes du Rhône or Luberon is best on your own by car, a variety of minivan tours and basic bus excursions are available. (TIs in Arles and Avignon also have information on bus excursions to regional sights that are hard to reach sans car; see "Tours in Provence.")

By Car: The region is made for a car, though travel time between some sights will surprise you—thanks, in part, to narrow roads and endless roundabouts (for example, figure an hour from

PROVENCE

Les Baux to Pont du Gard, and almost two hours from Arles to Vaison-la-Romaine). Michelin map #527 (1:275,000 scale) covers this area perfectly. Michelin maps #332 (Luberon and Côtes du Rhône) and #340 (Arles area) are also worth considering. Be wary of thieves: Park only in well-monitored spaces and leave nothing valuable in your car. Drivers are smart to offload bags at hotels before sightseeing.

By Bike: Wind, heat, and hilly terrain make this region a challenge to bike. If you're determined, I list bike rental options in most cities (including electric bikes). **Telecycles** will deliver your bike to hotels within about 12 miles of St-Rémy (tel. 04 90 92 83 15 or mobile 06 11 64 04 69, www.telecycles-location.com). Check also with **Sun-e-Bike** for handy electric bike rentals throughout Provence (www.location-velo-provence.com).

TOURS IN PROVENCE
Tours with a Wine Focus
Wine Safari
Dutchman Mike Rijken runs a one-man show, taking travelers through the region he adopted 25 years ago. His English is fluent, and though his focus is on wine and wine villages, Mike knows the region thoroughly and is a good teacher of its history (per person: €80/half-day, €140/day, 2-6-person groups; pickups possible in Arles, Avignon, Lyon, Marseille, or Aix-en-Provence; tel. 04 90 35 59 21, mobile 06 19 29 50 81, www.winesafari.net, mikeswinesafari@orange.fr).

Le Vin à la Bouche
Charming Céline Viany—a sommelier and easy-to-be-with tour guide—is an expert on her region and its chief product (from €200/half-day or €250/day for 2 people, price depends on pickup location and number of clients, tel. 04 90 46 90 80, mobile 06 76 59 56 30, www.levinalabouche.com, contact@degustation-levinalabouche.com).

Avignon Wine Tour
For a playful perspective on wines of the Côtes du Rhône region, contact François Marcou (€110/person for all-day wine tours that include 4 tastings, €80/person for half-day tours, €350 for private groups, less in winter, mobile 06 28 05 33 84, www.avignon-wine-tour.com, contact@avignon-wine-tour.com).

Wine Uncovered
Passionate Englishman Olivier Hickman takes small groups on focused tours of selected wineries in Châteauneuf-du-Pape and in the villages near Vaison-la-Romaine. Olivier knows his subject matter inside and out. His in-depth tastings include a half-day tour of

two or three wineries (€40-75/person for half-day to full-day tours, prices subject to minimum tour fees, mobile 06 75 10 10 01, www. wine-uncovered.com, olivier.hickman@orange.fr).

Tours du Rhône

Low-key American Doug Graves, who owns a small wine *domaine* in the Côtes du Rhône, runs custom tours of Châteauneuf-du-Pape, the villages of the Côtes du Rhône, and the Luberon Valley (per person: €135/day, up to 4 people, includes lunch; mobile 06 37 16 04 56, www.toursdurhone.com, doug@masdelalionne.com).

Winery Plus Tours

This company offers small group tours centered on wine and food with a good dose of history and local culture. Experienced guide and wine connoisseur Joe McLean leads walking and photography tours, as well as wine tours focusing on the wines of Uzès, Châteauneuf-du-Pape, and the Côtes du Rhône (per person: about €70-95/half-day, €140-170/day, prices include pickup from Uzès hotels; custom tours possible from Arles and Avignon, no tours on Sun, mobile 06 73 08 23 97, www.wineryplustours.com, contact@wineryplustours.com).

Provence & Wine

Sommelier Romain Gouvernet is a young and sincere wine guide concentrating on Châteauneuf-du-Pape and the Luberon. Ask about his evening wine tours (per person: €90/half-day, €140/day; mobile 06 86 49 56 76, www.provenceandwine.com, provenceandwine@gmail.com).

Cultural and Historical Tours
Imagine Tours

This organization offers personalized cultural excursions that highlight the "true heart of Provence and Occitania." Itineraries are adapted to your interests, and your guide can meet you at your hotel or the departure point of your choice (€190/half-day, €315/day, prices for up to 4 people starting from near Avignon or Arles, mobile 06 89 22 19 87, www.imagine-tours.net, imagine.tours@gmail.com). They can also help plan your itinerary, book hotel rooms, or address other travel issues.

Local Guides

Catherine D'Antuono is a smart, capable, licensed guide for Aix-en-Provence and the region. She guides tours as far west as Pont du Gard and as far east as St-Tropez (€480/day for 2 people, €15 extra for each additional person, 8-person maximum, mobile 06 17 94 69 61, www.provence-travel.com, tour.designer@provence-travel.com).

The Rules of *Boules*

The game of *boules*—also called *pétanque*—is the horseshoes of France. Invented here in the early 1900s, it's a social yet serious sport, and endlessly entertaining to watch—even more so if you understand the rules.

The game is played with heavy metal balls and a small wooden target ball called a *cochonnet* (piglet). Whoever gets his *boule* closest to the *cochonnet* is awarded points. Teams commonly have specialist players: a *pointeur* and a *tireur*. The *pointeur*'s goal is to lob his balls as close to the target as he can. The *tireur*'s job is to blast away opponents' *boules.*

In teams of two, each player gets three *boules.* The starting team traces a small circle in the dirt (in which players must stand when launching their *boules*), and tosses the *cochonnet* about 30 feet to establish the target. The *boule* must be thrown underhand, and can be rolled, launched sky-high, or rocketed at its target. The first *pointeur* shoots, then the opposing *pointeur* shoots until his *boule* gets closer. Once the second team lands a *boule* nearest the *cochonnet,* the first team goes again. If the other team's *boule* is very near the *cochonnet,* the *tireur* will likely attempt to knock it away.

Once all *boules* have been launched, the tally is taken. The team with a *boule* closest to the *cochonnet* wins the round, and they receive a point for each *boule* closer to the target than their opponents' nearest *boule.* The first team to get to 13 points wins. A regulation *boules* field is 10 feet by 43 feet, but the game is played everywhere—just scratch a throwing circle in the sand, toss the *cochonnet,* and you're off.

Discover Provence was founded by England-born Sarah Pernet, who has lived in Aix-en-Provence since 2001. She and her small team offer a variety of well-organized, easygoing, small-group tours to the Luberon, Cassis, Arles, and St-Rémy (from €130/person for half-day, mobile 06 16 86 40 24, www.discover-provence.net, sarah@discover-provence.net).

Basic Transportation-Only Tours
Visit Provence
This company runs day tours from Avignon, Arles, Marseille, Nice, and Aix-en-Provence. Tours provide introductory commentary, but no guiding at sights. They use eight-seat, air-conditioned minivans (per person: about €65-80/half-day, €100-125/day). Ask about their cheaper big-bus excursions, or consider hiring a van and

driver for your private use (allow about €300/half-day, €500/day, tel. 04 90 14 70 00, www.provence-reservation.com).

THE ROMANS IN PROVENCE

Provence is littered with Roman ruins. Many scholars claim the best-preserved ancient Roman buildings are not in Italy, but in France. These ancient stones will be an important part of your sightseeing agenda in this region, so it's worth learning about how they came to be.

Classical Rome endured from about 500 BC through AD 500—spending about 500 years growing, 200 years peaking, and 300 years declining. Julius Caesar conquered Gaul—which included Provence—during the Gallic Wars (58-51 BC), then crossed the Rubicon River in 49 BC to incite civil war within the Roman Republic. He erected a temple to Jupiter on the future site of Paris' Notre-Dame Cathedral.

The concept of one-man rule lived on with his grandnephew, Octavian (whom he had also adopted as his son). Octavian killed Brutus, eliminated his rivals (Mark Antony and Cleopatra), and united Rome's warring factions. He took the title "Augustus" and became the first in a line of emperors who would control Rome for the next 500 years—ruling like a king, with the backing of the army and the rubber-stamp approval of the Senate. Rome morphed from a Republic into an Empire: a collection of many diverse territories ruled by a single man.

Augustus' reign marked the start of 200 years of peace, prosperity, and expansion known as the *Pax Romana*. At its peak (c. AD 117), the Roman Empire had 54 million people and stretched from Scotland in the north to Egypt in the south, as far west as Spain and as far east as modern-day Iraq. To the northeast, Rome was bounded by the Rhine and Danube Rivers. On Roman maps, the Mediterranean was labeled *Mare Nostrum* ("Our Sea"). At its peak, "Rome" didn't just refer to the city, but to the entire civilized Western world.

The Romans were successful not only because they were good soldiers, but also because they were smart administrators and businessmen. People in conquered territories knew they had joined the winning team and that political stability would replace barbarian invasions. Trade thrived. Conquered peoples were welcomed into the fold of prosperity, linked by roads, education, common laws and gods, and the Latin language.

Provence, with its strategic location, benefited greatly from Rome's global economy and grew to become an important part of its worldwide empire. After Julius Caesar conquered Gaul, Emperor Augustus set out to Romanize it, building and renovating cities in the image of Rome. Most cities had a theater (some had several), baths, and aqueducts; the most important cities had sports arenas. The Romans also erected an elaborate infrastructure of roads, post offices, schools (teaching in Latin), police stations, and water-supply systems.

A typical Roman city (such as Nîmes, Arles, Orange, or Vaison-la-Romaine) was a garrison town, laid out on a grid plan with two main roads: one running north-south (the *cardus*), the other east-west (the *decumanus*). Approaching the city on your chariot, you'd pass by the cemetery, which was located outside of town for hygienic reasons. You'd enter the main gate and wheel past warehouses and apartment houses to the town square (forum). Facing the square were the most important temples, dedicated to the patron gods of the city. Nearby, you'd find bathhouses; like today's fitness clubs, these served the almost sacred dedication to personal vigor. Also close by were businesses that catered to the citizens' needs: the marketplace, bakeries, banks, and brothels.

Aqueducts brought fresh water for drinking, filling the baths, and delighting the citizens with bubbling fountains. Men flocked

to the stadiums in Arles and Nîmes to bet on gladiator games; eager couples attended elaborate plays at theaters in Orange, Arles, and Vaison-la-Romaine. Marketplaces brimmed with exotic fruits, vegetables, and animals from the far reaches of the empire.

Some cities in Provence were more urban 2,000 years ago than they are today. For instance, experts believe that Roman Arles had a population of between 70,000 and 100,000—almost double today's size. Think about that when you visit.

When it came to construction, the Romans eventually discovered a magic building ingredient: concrete. A mixture of volcanic ash, lime, water, and small rocks, concrete—easier to work than stone and longer-lasting than wood—served as flooring, roofing, filler, glue, and support. Builders would start with a foundation of brick, then fill it in with poured concrete. They would then cover important structures, such as basilicas, in sheets of expensive marble (held on with nails), or decorate floors and walls with mosa-

PROVENCE

Le Mistral

Provence lives with its vicious mistral winds, which blow 30-60 miles per hour, about 100 days out of the year. Locals say it blows in multiples of threes: three, six, or nine days in a row. The mistral clears people off the streets and turns lively cities into ghost towns. You'll likely spend a few hours or days taking refuge. The winds are strongest between noon and 15:00.

When the mistral blows, it's everywhere, and you can't escape. Author Peter Mayle said it could blow the ears off a donkey (I'd include the tail). According to the natives, it ruins crops, shutters, and roofs (look for stones holding tiles in place on many homes). They'll also tell you that this pernicious wind has driven many people crazy (including young Vincent van Gogh). A weak version of the wind is called a *mistralet*.

The mistral starts above the Alps and Massif Central mountains and gathers steam as it heads south, gaining momentum as it screams over the Rhône Valley (which acts like a funnel between the Alps and the Cévennes mountains) before exhausting itself when it hits the Mediterranean. And though this wind rattles shutters everywhere in the Riviera and Provence, it's strongest over the Rhône Valley...so Avignon, Arles, and the Côtes du Rhône villages bear its brunt. While wiping the dust from your eyes, remember the good news: The mistral brings clear skies.

ics—proving just how talented the Romans were at turning the functional into art.

PROVENCE'S CUISINE SCENE

The almost extravagant use (by French standards) of garlic, olive oil, herbs, and tomatoes makes Provence's cuisine France's liveliest. To sample it, order anything *à la provençale*. Among the area's spicy specialties are ratatouille (a mixture of vegetables in a thick, herb-flavored tomato sauce), aioli (a rich, garlicky mayonnaise spread over vegetables, potatoes, fish, or whatever), tapenade (a paste of pureed olives, capers, anchovies, herbs, and some-

times tuna), *soupe au pistou* (thin yet flavorful vegetable soup with a sauce—called *pistou*—of basil, garlic, and cheese), and *soupe à l'ail* (garlic soup, called *aigo bouido* in the local dialect). Look for *riz de Camargue* (the reddish, chewy, nutty-tasting rice that has taken over the Camargue area) and *taureau* (bull's meat). The native goat cheeses are *banon de banon* or *banon à la feuille* (dipped in brandy and wrapped in chestnut leaves) and spicy *picodon*. Don't miss the region's prized Cavaillon melons (cantaloupes) or its delicious cherries and apricots, which are often turned into jams and candied fruits.

Wines of Provence: Provence also produces some of France's great wines at relatively reasonable prices (€5-10/bottle on average). Look for wines from Gigondas, Rasteau, Cairanne, Beaumes-de-Venise, Vacqueyras, and Châteauneuf-du-Pape. For the cheapest but still tasty wines, look for labels showing Côtes du Rhône Villages or Côtes de Provence. If you like rosé, you win. Rosés from Tavel are considered among the best in Provence. For reds, splurge for Châteauneuf-du-Pape or Gigondas, and for a fine apéritif wine or a dessert wine, try the Muscat from Beaumes-de-Venise.

PROVENCE MARKET DAYS

Provençal market days offer France's most colorful and tantalizing outdoor shopping. The best markets are on Monday in Cavaillon, Tuesday in Vaison-la-Romaine, Wednesday in St-Rémy, Thursday in Nyons or Orange, Friday in Lourmarin and Bonnieux, Saturday in Arles, Uzès, and Apt, and, best of all, Sunday in Isle-sur-la-Sorgue. Crowds and parking problems abound at these popular events—arrive by 9:00, or, even better, sleep in the town the night before.

Arles

Arles (pronounced "arl") is an amiable slice of Provence, with evocative Roman ruins, an eclectic assortment of museums, made-for-ice-cream pedestrian zones, and squares that play hide-and-seek with visitors.

Back in Roman times, the city earned the imperial nod by helping Julius Caesar defeat his archrival Pompey at Marseille, and grew into an important port. Site of the first bridge over the Rhône River, Arles was a key stop on the Roman road from Italy to Spain, the Via Domitia. After reigning as the seat of an important archbishop and as a trading center for centuries, the city became a sleepy afterthought of little importance in the 1700s. Vincent van Gogh settled here in the late 1800s, but left only a chunk of his ear. American bombers destroyed much of Arles in World War II as the townsfolk hid out in its underground Roman galleries.

Today Arles, while touristic, feels like a backwater. A city in search of an economy, workaday Arles feels unpolished and even a little dirty compared to nearby Avignon and Nîmes. But to me, that's part of its charm. Locals display a genuine joie de vivre that's hard to sense in Arles' larger, more cosmopolitan neighbors.

PLANNING YOUR TIME

For a helpful overview to your Arles sightseeing, start at the Ancient History Museum. Drivers should try to do this museum on their way into Arles—then head to the city-center sights, linked by my Arles City Walk. For cost-efficient sightseeing, get one of the city's sightseeing passes, which cover the ancient monuments and the Ancient History Museum.

Orientation to Arles

Arles faces the Mediterranean, turning its back on Paris. And although the town is built along the Rhône, it largely ignores the river. Landmarks hide in Arles' medieval tangle of narrow, winding streets. Hotels have good, free city maps, and helpful street-corner signs point you toward sights and hotels.

TOURIST INFORMATION

The TI is on the ring road Boulevard des Lices, at Esplanade Charles de Gaulle (daily 9:00-18:45; Oct-March Mon-Sat 9:00-16:45, Sun 10:00-13:00; tel. 04 90 18 41 20, www.arlestourisme.com). Ask about walking tours and "bullgames" in Arles and nearby towns (Provence's more humane version of bullfights—see "Experiences in Arles," later). The TI sells worthwhile city sightseeing passes (see "Helpful Hints," later).

ARRIVAL IN ARLES

By Train or Bus: The train station is on the river, a 10-minute walk from the town center. There are two good options for baggage storage (see "Helpful Hints," later). The main bus station is on big Boulevard Georges Clemenceau, but some buses stop at the train station.

To reach the town center or Ancient History Museum from the train station without walking, wait for the free **Navia shuttle** at the glass shelter facing away from the station (cross the street and veer left, 2/hour Mon-Sat 7:00-19:00, none Sun). The bus makes a counterclockwise loop around Arles, stopping near most of my

PROVENCE

recommended hotels (see "Arles" map for stops). **Taxis** usually wait in front of the station (if there's not a taxi waiting, call 04 90 96 52 76 or the posted telephone numbers, or ask the info desk staff to call for you). Though the rides are short, allow €12 to any of my recommended hotels.

By Car: I'd avoid driving in old Arles. Enter on foot after stowing your car (at least temporarily) at Arles' only parking garage, **Parking des Lices,** near the TI on Boulevard des Lices (about €2/hour, €18/24 hours). All of my recommended hotels are within a 10-minute walk of this garage. Most hotels have parking deals for a nearby lot (ask before you arrive).

Lots and curbside parking spots in Arles center are metered 9:00-19:00 every day May-Sept (some limited to 2.5 hours). You'll find metered lots along the city wall at Place Lamartine (except Tue night, when it is restricted). To find these, first follow signs to *Centre-Ville,* then *Gare SNCF* (train station) until you come to the roundabout with a Monoprix department store to the right. The hotels I list are no more than a 15-minute walk from here.

HELPFUL HINTS

Sightseeing Tips: Arles has a smart ticket-and-hours plan for its sightseeing. Ancient monuments, such as the Roman Arena and Classical Theater, share the **same hours** (daily 9:00-19:00, April and Oct until 18:00, Nov-March 10:00-17:00).

A €9 entry fee gets you access to all of Arles' monuments (but not its museums). The good-value **Pass Liberté** (€12) covers any four monuments and one museum of your choice (I recommend the Ancient History Museum). The **Pass Avantage** (€16) covers all monuments and museums and is worthwhile if you plan to visit two or more museums. Both passes offer a discount at the Fondation Van Gogh. Buy your pass at the TI or any included sight.

Van Gogh Trail: The TI has placed various "Van Gogh easels" around town marking points where Vincent set up his easel and painted. Many (but not all) are incorporated into my "Arles City Walk."

Market Days: The big markets are on Wednesdays and Saturdays.

Crowds: An international photo event jams hotels the second weekend of July. The let-'er-rip, twice-yearly Féria draws crowds over Easter and in mid-September.

Baggage Storage and Bike Rental: Taco & Co stores luggage and rents bikes; it's located by the bus stop across from the train station (€5/bag, bike rental €7/half-day, €10/day, Mon-Sat 9:00-18:00, closed Sun, tel. 04 82 75 73 45, www.tacoandco. fr). The recommended **Hôtel Régence** will store your bags (€3/bag, daily 7:30-22:00, closed in winter, 5 Rue Marius

PROVENCE

Jouveau). They also rent bikes (€7/half-day, €15/day, one-way rentals within Provence possible, same hours as baggage storage). From Arles you can ride to Les Baux (25 miles round-trip)—but it's a darn steep climb. Those in great shape can consider biking into the Camargue (level 30-40-mile round-trip, forget it on windy days).

Laundry: A launderette is at 41 Rue du 4 Septembre. Another is near the bus station at 34 Boulevard Georges Clemenceau. Both are open long hours daily.

Car Rental: Europcar and **Hertz** are downtown (Europcar is at 61 Avenue de Stalingrad, tel. 04 90 93 23 24; Hertz is closer to Place Voltaire at 10 Boulevard Emile Combes, tel. 04 90 96 75 23).

Local Guides: Charming **Agnes Barrier** knows Arles and nearby sights intimately. Her tours cover Van Gogh and Roman history (€145/3 hours, mobile 06 11 23 03 73, agnes.barrier@ hotmail.fr). **Alice Vallat** offers scheduled visits of Arles' key sights that leave from the TI, usually at 16:00 several days a week (€25/person for 1.5-hour group tour, €145 for 3-hour private tour, mobile 06 74 01 22 54, www.guidearles.com, alice.vallat13@gmail.com). Ask about her city tours that add wine tasting.

Public Pools: Arles has three pools (indoor and outdoor). Ask at the TI or your hotel for hours and locations.

GETTING AROUND ARLES

In this flat city, everything's within **walking** distance. Only the Ancient History Museum is far enough out to consider a shuttle or taxi ride. The riverside promenade provides a scenic and direct stroll to the Ancient History Museum (as well as to the train station).

The free **Navia shuttle** circles the town, stopping at the train station and along Rue du 4 Septembre, then along the river. It's useful for access to my recommended hotels and the Ancient History Museum (see "Arles" map for stop locations, 2/hour, Mon-Sat 7:00-19:00, none Sun).

Arles City Walk

The joy of Arles is how its compact core mixes ancient sights, Van Gogh memories, and a raw and real contemporary scene that is easily covered on foot. All dimensions of the city come together in this self-guided walk.

Length of This Walk: If you enter the sights described (which I recommend, even if briefly), this walk will take most of a day. If

Arles

<u>Arles City Walk</u>
1. The Yellow House (Easel)
2. Starry Night over the Rhône (Easel)
3. Rue Voltaire
4. Old Town
5. Arena (Easel)
6. Roman Arena
7. Alpilles Mountains View
8. L'Entrée du Jardin Public (Easel)
9. Classical Theater
10. Republic Square
11. Cryptoporticos
12. St. Trophime Church
13. St. Trophime Cloisters
14. Rue de la République
15. Espace Van Gogh (Easel)
16. Fondation Van Gogh
17. Rue du Docteur Fanton
18. Place du Forum & Café Terrace at Night (Easel)

<u>Other</u>
19. Bag Storage/Bike Rental (2)
20. Launderette (2)
21. To Europcar Car Rental
22. Hertz Car Rental

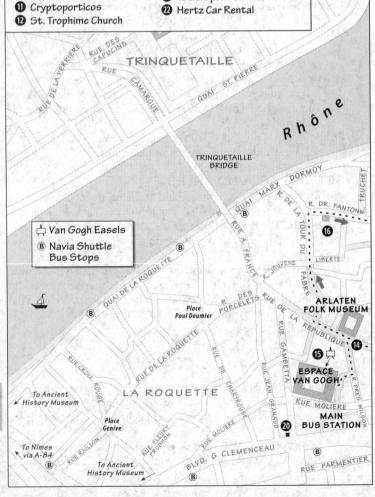

PROVENCE

P

SNCF Bus to
TGV Station B

19

Navia Shuttle
#20 & 57 B

RUE GORODICHE

AVE. PAULIN TALABOT

TRAIN
STATION

AVE. DE STALINGRAD

To
Les Baux,
Fontvielle,
Avignon &
21

BRASSERIE

MONOPRIX
PARKING

N

100 Meters

100 Yards

River

2

1 WALK BEGINS

Place
Lamartine

MONOPRIX
DEP'T
STORE

BLVD. EMILE COMBES

PETANQUE

CAVALERIE GATE P

JULES FERRY

R. TERRIN

RUE CAVALERIE

RUE JOUVEAU

R.L. BLUM

QUAI MARX DORMOY

RUE METRAS

19

B

3

R. PUITS

RUE BALZAC

RUE VOLTAIRE

Place
Voltaire

B

4

RUE
EUZEBY

RUE CONDORCET

R. LA FONTAINE

BATHS OF
CONSTANTINE

REATTU
MUSEUM

RUE GRAND PRIEURE

RUE GRILLE

L'AMPHITHEATRE

R. A. TARDIEU
DU FOUR

RUE BOILEAU

RUE PORTAGNEL

22

RUE DU QUATRE SEPTEMBRE

R. REATTU

RUE BARBES

R. RASPAIL

R.A.

20

5

PARVIS DES ARENOISES

RUE REFUGE

R. RENAN

ST. SUVAGE

RUE SUISSES

R. VERNON

R. DE L'HOTEL DE VILLE

R. DOISNEAU

R. FAURE

E. BRIAND

6

ROMAN

ARENA

ROND-POINT DES ARENES

7

B

NOTRE
DAME

RUE MADELEINE

BLVD. EMILE COMBES

17

WALK
ENDS

18

Place
du Forum

R. NICOLA

RUE DES ARENES

R. DIDEROT

B

RUE BALZE

RUE DE LA CALADE

HOTEL LE
CALENDAL

WC 11

ST. TROPHIME

9

CLASSICAL
THEATER

R. L'AGNEAU

12

13

Place de la
République

CLOISTERS

R. JEAN JAURES

RUE DU CLOITRE

10

R. EMILE PARRERE

ANCIENT
CITY WALLS

8

Jardin
d'Ete

MONTEE VAUBAN

TOUR
DES
MOURGUES

RUE ROTONDE

TAXIS
T

PLAYGROUND

B

BLVD. DES LICES

Esplanade
Charles
de Gaulle

i

POST

P

B

PARKING
DES LICES
(DU CENTRE)

RUE E. FASSIN

AVE. ALYSCAMPS

AVE. VICTOR
HUGO

To
LUMA
Foundation

PROVENCE

the walk seems long, you could split it up and do the latter half in the evening.

Tours: To trace the route of this walk, see the "Arles" map, earlier.

Sightseeing Tips: Most sights on this walk are covered by the city's sightseeing passes—sold at the TI and included sights (see "Helpful Hints," earlier). I've also listed the full prices for sights, if you're not using a sightseeing pass. To better understand the ancient sites along this route, visit the Ancient History Museum before taking this walk (see "Sights in Arles," later).

BACKGROUND

The life and artistic times of Dutch artist **Vincent van Gogh** form a big part of Arles' draw, and the city does a fine job of highlighting its Van Gogh connection with its Van Gogh Trail: Throughout town, about a dozen steel-and-concrete panels, or "easels," provide then-and-now comparisons, depicting the artist's paintings alongside the current view of that painting's subject.

In the dead of winter in 1888, 35-year-old Van Gogh left big-city Paris for Provence, hoping to jump-start his floundering career and social life. He was as inspired as he was lonely. Coming from the gray skies and flat lands of the north, Vincent was bowled over by everything Provençal—the sun, bright colors, rugged landscape, and raw people. For the next two years he painted furiously, cranking out a masterpiece every few days.

Of the 200-plus paintings that Van Gogh made in the south, none permanently resides in the city that so moved him. (But there is always at least one here on loan, displayed at the Fondation Van Gogh gallery, which we'll visit on this stroll). But walking the same streets he knew and seeing the places he painted, you can understand how Arles inspired him.

⊘ SELF-GUIDED WALK

• *Start at the north gate of the city, just outside the medieval wall on Place Lamartine (100 yards in front of the medieval gate, with the big Monoprix store across the street to the right, beyond the roundabout). A four-foot-tall easel shows Van Gogh's painting.*

❶ *The Yellow House* Easel

Vincent arrived in Arles on February 20, 1888, to a foot of snow. He rented a small house here on the north side of Place Lamartine. The house was destroyed in 1944 by an errant bridge-seeking bomb, but the four-story building behind it still stands (find it in the painting). The house (which stood where the street runs today) had four rooms, including a small studio and the cramped trapezoid-shaped bedroom made famous in his paintings. It was painted yellow inside and out, and Vincent named it…"The Yellow House." In the distance, the painting shows the same bridges you see today.

In those days, a short walk from Place Lamartine led to open fields. Donning his straw hat, Vincent set up his easel outdoors and painted quickly, capturing what he saw and felt—the blossoming fruit trees, gnarled olive trees, peasants sowing and reaping, jagged peaks, and windblown fields, all lit by a brilliant sun that drove him to use ever-brighter paints.

• *Walk to the river.*

As you walk, you'll pass: on the right, an eight-foot-tall stone monument in honor of two WWII American pilots killed in action during the liberation of Arles (erected in 2002 as a post-9/11 sign of solidarity with Americans); a post celebrating Arles' nine sister cities (left); and a big concrete high school and tour bus parking lot (right).

At the river, find the easel in the wall where ramps lead down. The Roman bridge stood here (look for a few stones directly across), and just upstream are the remains of a modern bridge bombed by the Allies in World War II.

• *Now, turn your attention to the…*

❷ *Starry Night over the Rhône* Easel

One night, Vincent set up his easel along the river and painted the stars boiling above the city skyline. Vincent looked to the night sky for the divine and was the first to paint outside after dark, adapting his straw hat to hold candles (which must have blown the minds of locals back then). As his paintings progressed, the stars became larger and more animated (like Vincent himself). The lone couple in the painting pops up again and again in his work. (Note: This painting is not the *Starry Night* you're probably thinking of—that one was painted later, in St-Rémy.)

• *With your back to the river, angle right through the scruffy park of plane trees (a kind of sycamore). Continue into town through the park and between the stumpy 14th-century stone towers where the city gates once stood. Walk a block up Rue de la Cavalerie to the decorative (if dry) fountain with the colorful old mosaic.*

❸ Rue Voltaire

Van Gogh first walked into town down this street in 1888. When he saw this fountain, it was just a year old. Its mosaic celebrates the high culture of Provence (she's the winged woman who obviously loves music and reading). But this neighborhood was Arles' 19th-century red light district, and the far-from-home Dutchman spent many lonely nights in its bars and brothels. Though it's no longer the rough area it was in Van Gogh's day, this street still has a certain edgy local color with humble shops, bars, and bakeries.

• Stay left and keep walking to Place Voltaire, a center of this working-class neighborhood (the local Communist Party headquarters is across the square on the left). Stop at the top end of the square under the plane tree in front of Brasserie le Pitchounet.

❹ Old Town

Take a slow 360-degree spin tour to just enjoy the rough elegance of the architecture. Pretend you're a one-eared painter looking for a place to set up your easel. You've left the bombed-out part of town and entered the old town, with buildings predating World War II. The stony white arches of the ancient Roman Arena ahead mark your destination. As you hike up Rue Voltaire, notice the shutters, which contribute to Arles' character. The old town is strictly protected: These traditional shutters come in a variety of styles but cannot be changed.

• Keep straight up Rue Voltaire, climb to the Roman Arena, and find the Arena *easel at the top of the stairs, to the right.*

❺ *Arena* Easel

All summer long, fueled by sun and alcohol, Vincent painted the town. He loved the bullfights in the arena and sketched the colorful surge of the crowds, spending more time studying the people than watching the bullfights (notice how the bull is barely visible). Vincent had little interest in Arles' antiquity—it was people and nature that fascinated him.

• At this point you can take a break from your town walk and visit the Roman Arena or read about it as you circle clockwise to the left.

❻ Roman Arena (Amphithéâtre)

This well-preserved arena is worth ▲▲ and is still in use today. Nearly 2,000 years ago, gladiators fought wild animals to the delight of 20,000 screaming fans. Now local daredevils still fight wild animals here—"bullgame" posters around the arena advertise upcoming spectacles (see "Experiences in Arles," later). Don't miss the tower climb for fantastic views over Arles, the arena, and the Rhône River.

Cost and Hours: €9 combo-ticket with Classical Theater; daily 9:00-19:00, April and Oct until 18:00, Nov-March 10:00-17:00, Rond-point des Arènes, tel. 04 90 49 36 86, www.arenes-arles.com.

Visiting the Arena: After passing the ticket kiosk, find the helpful English display under the second arch, where you can read about the arena's history and renovation. Then climb up and take a seat in the theater.

Thirty-four rows of stone bleachers extended all the way to the top of those vacant **arches** that circle the arena. All arches were numbered to help distracted fans find their seats. The many passageways you'll see (called *vomitoires*) allowed for rapid dispersal after the games—fights would break out among frenzied fans if they couldn't leave quickly.

The arena takes its name from the central **floor** where the action took place—"arena" derives from the Latin word for sand, which was spread across the floor to absorb the blood. Wild animals were caged in passages and storage areas underneath the floor and hoisted up on an elevator to make surprise appearances. (While Rome could afford exotic beasts, places like Arles made do with snarling local fauna...bulls, bears, and lots of boars.) The standard fight was as real as professional wrestling is today—mostly just crowd-pleasing.

The arena is a fine example of Roman engineering...and propaganda. In the spirit of "give them bread and circuses," games were free—sponsored by city bigwigs. The idea was to create a populace that was thoroughly Roman—enjoying the same activities, entertainment, and thoughts (something like how US television contributes to the psyche of the American masses).

After Rome fell and stability was replaced by Dark Ages chaos, this huge structure was put to good use: Throughout medieval times and until the early 1800s, the stadium became a fortified town with towers added, arches bricked up, and 200 humble homes crammed within its circular defenses. Parts of three of the medieval **towers** survive.

Inside the arena, circumnavigate along its upper level and savor the receding views of arches and fine stonework. To climb one of the medieval towers and enjoy magnificent **views** over Arles and the arena, find the *"To the Tower"* sign near the ticket booth and exit.

• *Exit at street level and turn right, and after a quarter of the way around, turn left (where the metal fence ends and you hit the little street). Go up the cute stepped lane (Rue Renan). Take three steps and turn around to study the arena. (You can lean on the bollard, put there by yours truly for your sightseeing convenience.)*

The big stones are Roman; the little medieval stones—more like rubble—filling the two upper-level archways are a reminder of the arena's time as a fortified town in the Middle Ages. You can even see roof lines and beam holes where the Roman structure provided a solid foundation to lean on.

• *Hike up the pretty, stepped lane through the parking lot, keeping to the left of the stark and stony church to the highest point in Arles. Take in the countryside view.*

❼ Alpilles Mountains View

This view pretty much matches what Vincent van Gogh, an avid walker, would have seen. Imagine him hauling his easel into those fields under intense sun, leaning against a ferocious wind, struggling to keep his hat on. Vincent carried his easel as far as the medieval Abbey of Montmajour, that bulky structure on the hill in the distance. The St. Paul Hospital, where he was eventually treated in St-Rémy, is on the other side of the Alpilles mountains (which look more like hills to me), several miles beyond Montmajour.

• *Cross in front of the church to return to the arena, and continue circling it clockwise. At the high point (where the arena was rebuilt after WWII bombing), turn left and walk out Rue de Porte de Laure. (You'll pass the ancient Classical Theater on your right, which we'll visit later.) If you're ready for a break, the recommended* **Hôtel Le Calendal** *has a handy self-service bar with drinks, great little sandwiches, and a welcoming garden out back. After a couple of charming blocks, go right, down the curved staircase into the park. At the bottom of the stairs continue toward the busy street. Take the second right (through the gate and into the park) and find the...*

❽ *L'Entrée du Jardin Public* Easel

Vincent spent many a sunny day painting in the leafy Jardin d'Eté. In another letter to his sister, Vincent wrote, "I don't know whether you can understand that one may make a poem by arranging colors...In a similar manner, the bizarre lines, purposely selected and multiplied, meandering all through the picture may not present a literal image of the garden, but they may present it to our minds as if in a dream."

• *Hike through the park and uphill toward the three-story surviving tower of the ancient Classical Theater. At the ancient tower, follow the white metal fence to the left, enjoying peeks at "le jardin" of stone—a collection of ancient carved bits of a once-grand Roman theater. Go up four steps and around to the right to the corner of the fence for a fine view of the...*

❾ Classical Theater (Théâtre Antique)

This first-century BC Roman theater once seated 10,000...just like the theater in nearby Orange. But unlike Orange, here in Arles there was no hillside to provide structural support. Instead, this elegant, three-level structure had 27 buttress arches radiating out behind the seats.

Cost and Hours: €9 combo-ticket with Roman Arena, same hours as Arena.

Visiting the Theater: Start with the 10-minute video, which provides background information that makes it easier to imagine the scattered stones back in place (crouch in front to make out the small English subtitles).

Then walk into the theater and pull up a stone seat in a center aisle. (For more context, read the description of Orange's Roman theater on page 657 while you rest.) Imagine that for 500 years, ancient Romans gathered here for entertainment. The original structure was much higher, with 33 rows of seats covering three levels to accommodate demand. During the Middle Ages, the old theater became a convenient town quarry—much of St. Trophime Church was built from theater rubble. Precious little of the original theater survives—though it still is used for events, with seating for 2,000 spectators.

Two lonely Corinthian columns are all that remain of a three-story stage wall that once featured more than 100 columns and statues painted in vibrant colors (a model in the Ancient History Museum shows the complete theater). Principal actors entered through the central arch, over which a grandiose statue of Caesar Augustus stood (it's now on display at the Ancient History Museum).

• *From the theater, walk downhill on Rue de la Calade. As you stroll, enjoy the fine facades of 17th- and 18th-century mansions. Take the first left into a big square.*

❿ Republic Square (Place de la République)

This square used to be called "Place Royale"...until the French Revolution. The obelisk was the former centerpiece of Arles' Roman

PROVENCE

Circus (outside of town). The lions at its base are the symbol of the city, whose slogan is (roughly) "the gentle lion." Observe the age-old scene: tourists, peasants, shoppers, pilgrims, children, and street musicians. The City Hall (Hôtel de Ville) has a stately facade, built in the same generation as Versailles. Where there's a City Hall, there's always a free WC (if you win the Revolution, you can pee for free at the mayor's home). Notice the flags: The yellow-and-red of Provence is the same as the yellow-and-red of Catalunya, its linguistic cousin in Spain.

• *Today's City Hall sits upon an ancient city center. Inside, admire the engineering of the ceiling and find the entrance to an ancient cryptoportico (foundation).*

⓫ Cryptoporticos (Cryptoportiques)

This dark, drippy underworld of Roman arches was constructed to support the upper half of Forum Square (necessary for a big, level square in a town built on a slope). Two thousand years ago, most of this gallery of arches was at or above street level; modern Arles has buried about 20 feet of its history over the millennia. Through the tiny windows high up you would have seen the sandals of Romans on their way to the forum. Other than dark arches and broken bits of forum littering the dirt floor, there's not much down here beyond ancient memories (€4.50, same hours as Arena).

• *The highlight of Place de la République is...*

⓬ St. Trophime Church

Named after a third-century bishop of Arles, this church, worth ▲▲, sports the finest Romanesque main entrance I've seen anywhere. The Romanesque and Gothic interior—with tapestries, relics, and a rare painting from the French Revolution when this was a "Temple of Reason"—is worth a visit.

Cost and Hours: Free, daily 9:00-12:00 & 14:00-18:30, Oct-March until 17:00.

Exterior: Like a Roman triumphal arch, the church **facade** trumpets the promise of Judgment Day. The tympanum (the semi-circular area above the door) is filled with Christian symbolism. Christ sits in majesty, surrounded by symbols of the four evangelists: Matthew (the winged man), Mark (the winged lion), Luke (the ox), and John (the eagle). The 12 apostles are lined up below Jesus. It's Judgment Day...some are saved and others aren't. Notice the condemned

(on the right)—a chain gang doing a sad bunny-hop over the fires of hell. For them, the tune trumpeted by the three angels above Christ is not a happy one. Below the chain gang, St. Stephen is being stoned to death, with his soul leaving through his mouth and instantly being welcomed by angels. Study the exquisite detail. In an illiterate world, long before the vivid images of our Technicolor time, this was colorfully painted, like a neon billboard over the town square. It's full of meaning, and a medieval pilgrim understood it all.

Interior: Just inside the door on the right, a yellow chart locates the interior highlights and helps explain the carvings you just saw on the tympanum. The tall 12th-century Romanesque nave is decorated by a set of tapestries (typical in the Middle Ages) showing scenes from the life of Mary (17th century, from the French town of Aubusson).

This church is a stop on the ancient pilgrimage route to Santiago de Compostela in northwest Spain. For 800 years pilgrims on their way to Santiago have paused here...and they still do today. Notice the modern-day pilgrimages advertised on the far right near the church's entry.

• *To reach the adjacent peaceful cloister, leave the church, turn left, then left again through a courtyard.*

⓭ St. Trophime Cloisters

Worth seeing if you have an Arles sightseeing pass (otherwise €5.50, same hours as Arena), the cloisters' many small columns were scavenged from the ancient Roman theater and used to create an oasis of peace in Arles' center. Enjoy the delicate, sculpted capitals, the rounded Romanesque arches (12th century), and the pointed Gothic ones (14th century). The pretty vaulted hall exhibits 17th-century tapestries showing scenes from the First Crusade to the Holy Land. There's an instructive video and a chance to walk outside along an angled rooftop designed to catch rainwater: Notice the slanted gutter that channeled the water into a cistern and the heavy roof slabs covering the tapestry hall below.

• *From Place de la République, exit on the far corner (opposite the church and kitty-corner from where you entered) to stroll a delightful pedestrian street.*

⓮ Rue de la République

Rue da la République is Arles' primary shopping street. Walk downhill, enjoying the scene and popping into shops that catch your interest.

Near the start is **Maison Soulier Bakery.** Inside you'll be tempted by *fougasse* (bread studded with herbs, olives, and bacon bits), *sablés Provençal* (cookies made with honey and almonds), *tarte* *lavande* (a sweet almond lavender tart), and big crispy meringues (the egg-white-and-sugar answer to cotton candy—a cheap favorite of local kids). They also have sandwiches and salads if you feel like a picnic on the square. A few doors down is **Restaurant L'Atelier** (around the corner, with two prized Michelin stars), **L'Occitane en Provence** (local perfumes), **Puyricard Chocolate** (with enticing €1 treats and *calisson*, a sweet almond delight), as well as local design and antique shops. The fragile spiral columns on the left (just before the tourist-pleasing Lavender Boutique on the corner) show what 400 years of weather can do to decorative stonework. The big Arlaten Folk Museum is up on the right.

• *Take the first left onto Rue Président Wilson. (Wilson was so honored by the French for his noble efforts to create the League of Nations—a proto-UN—after World War I.) Just after the butcher shop (Chez Mère Grand, with local pork-and-bull sausages hanging above a counter filled with precooked dishes to take home and heat up), turn right to find the* **Hôtel Dieu,** *a hospital made famous by one of its patients: Vincent van Gogh.*

⓰ Espace Van Gogh Easel

In December 1888, shortly after his famous ear-cutting incident (see *Café Terrace at Night* easel, described later), Vincent was admitted into the local hospital—today's Espace Van Gogh cultural center. The Espace—with its exhibit space, classrooms, and library—is free (there's a handy WC inside). It surrounds a flowery courtyard (open to the public) that the artist loved and painted when he was being treated for blood loss, hallucinations, and severe depression that left him bedridden for a month. The citizens of Arles circulated a petition demanding that the mad Dutch-

man be kept under medical supervision. Félix Rey, Vincent's kind doctor, worked out a compromise: The artist could leave during the day so that he could continue painting, but he had to sleep at the hospital at night. Look through the postcards sold in the courtyard to enjoy a tour of Arles through the eyes of Vincent. Find a painting of Vincent's ward—that's right here—showing nuns attending to patients in a gray hall *(Ward of Arles Hospital).*

• *Return to Rue de la République. Take a left and continue two blocks downhill. Take the second right up Rue Tour de Fabre and follow signs to* Fondation Van Gogh. *After a few steps, you'll pass* **La Main Qui Pense** *(The Hand That Thinks) pottery shop and workshop, where Cécile Cayrol is busy creating and teaching. A couple of blocks farther down, turn right onto Rue du Docteur Fanton. On your immediate right is the...*

⓰ Fondation Van Gogh

This art foundation, worth ▲, delivers a refreshing stop for modern-art lovers and Van Gogh fans, with two temporary exhibits per year in which contemporary artists pay homage to Vincent with thought-provoking interpretations of his works. You'll also see at least one original work by Van Gogh (painted during his time in the region). The gift shop has a variety of souvenirs, prints, and postcards.

Cost and Hours: €9, discount with sightseeing passes; daily 11:00-19:00, July-Aug from 10:00, Oct-March until 17:45, closed Mon off-season—check website for current hours and what's on; audioguide-€3, 35 Rue du Docteur Fanton, tel. 04 90 49 94 04, www.fondation-vincentvangogh-arles.org.

• *Continue on Rue du Docteur Fanton.*

⓱ Rue du Docteur Fanton

A string of recommended restaurants is on the left. On the right is the **Crèche Municipale.** Open workdays, this is a free government-funded daycare where parents can drop off their infants up to two years old. The notion: No worker should face financial hardship in order to receive quality childcare. At the next corner is the recommended **Soleileïs,** Arles' top ice cream shop.

After the ice cream shop, turn right and step into **Bar El Paseo** at 4 Rue des Thermes. This little restaurant is run by the Leal family, famous for its "dynasty" of bullfighters and proud of its bullfighting lore. They've lovingly wallpapered the place with photos and bullfighting memorabilia. The main museum-like room is full of bull—including the mounted heads of three big ones who died in the local arena and a big black-and-white photo of Arles' arena packed to capacity. You're welcome to look around...and even more welcome to buy a glass of Spanish Rioja wine or sangria.

• *A few steps farther is...*

⓲ Forum Square (Place du Forum) and *Café Terrace at Night* Easel

Named for the Roman forum that once stood here, **Forum Square,** worth ▲, was the political and religious center of Roman Arles. Still lively, this café-crammed square is a local watering hole and popular for a *pastis* (anise-based aperitif). The bistros on the square can put together a passable salad or

plat du jour—and when you sprinkle on the ambience, that's €14 well spent.

At the corner of Grand Hôtel Nord-Pinus, a plaque shows how the Romans built a foundation of galleries to make the main square level in order to compensate for Arles' slope down to the river. The two columns are all that survive from the upper story of the entry to the forum.

The statue on the square is of **Frédéric Mistral** (1830-1914). This popular poet, who wrote in the local dialect rather than in French, was a champion of Provençal culture. After receiving the Nobel Prize in Literature in 1904, Mistral used his prize money to preserve and display the folk identity of Provence. He founded a regional folk museum (the Arlaten Folk Museum) at a time when France was rapidly centralizing and regions like Provence were losing their unique identities. (The local mistral wind—literally "master"—has nothing to do with his name.)

• *Facing the brightly painted yellow café, find your final Van Gogh easel*—**Café Terrace at Night.**

In October 1888, lonely Vincent—who dreamed of making Arles a magnet for fellow artists—persuaded his friend Paul Gauguin to come. He decorated Gauguin's room with several humble canvases of sunflowers (now some of the world's priciest paintings), knowing that Gauguin had admired a similar painting he'd done in Paris. Their plan was for Gauguin to be the "dean" of a new art school in Arles, and Vincent its instructor-in-chief. At first, the two got along well. They spent days side by side, rendering the same subjects in their two distinct styles. At night they hit the bars and brothels. Van Gogh's well-known *Café Terrace at Night* captures the glow of an absinthe buzz at Café la Nuit on Place du Forum.

After two months together, the two artists clashed over art and personality differences (Vincent was a slob around the house, whereas Gauguin was meticulous). The night of December 23, they were drinking absinthe at the café when Vincent suddenly went ballistic. He threw his glass at Gauguin. Gauguin left. Walking through Place Victor Hugo, Gauguin heard footsteps behind him and turned to see Vincent coming at him, brandishing a razor. Gauguin quickly fled town. The local paper reported what happened next: "At 11:30 p.m., Vincent van Gogh, painter from Holland, appeared at the brothel at no. 1, asked for Rachel, and gave her his cut-off earlobe, saying, 'Treasure this precious object.' Then he vanished." He woke up the next morning at home with his head wrapped in a bloody towel and his earlobe missing. Was Vincent emulating a successful matador, whose prize is cutting off the bull's ear?

The **bright-yellow café**—called Café la Nuit—was the subject of one of Vincent van Gogh's most famous works in Arles. Although his painting showed the café in a brilliant yellow from the glow of gas lamps, the facade was bare limestone, just like the other cafés on this square. The café is now a tourist trap that its current owners painted to match Van Gogh's version...and to cash in on the Vincent-crazed hordes who pay too much to eat or drink here.

In spring 1889, the bipolar genius (a modern diagnosis) checked himself into the St. Paul Monastery and Hospital in St-Rémy-de-Provence (described later, under "Sights in St-Rémy"). He spent a year there, thriving in the care of nurturing doctors and nuns. Painting was part of his therapy, so they gave him a studio to work in, and he produced more than 100 paintings. Alcohol-free and institutionalized, he did some of his wildest work. With thick, swirling brushstrokes and surreal colors, he made his placid surroundings throb with restless energy.

Eventually, Vincent's torment became unbearable. In the spring of 1890, he left Provence to be cared for by a sympathetic doctor in Auvers-sur-Oise, just north of Paris. On July 27, he wandered into a field and shot himself. He died two days later.

• *With this walk, you have seen the best of Arles. The colorful Roquette District, the Arlaten Folk Museum, and the Réattu Museum are each a short walk away (all described next). But I'd rather enjoy a drink on the Place du Forum and savor the joy of experiencing the essence of Provence.*

Sights in Arles

IN THE CENTER

Many of Arles' city-center sights (such as the Roman Arena and St. Trophime church) are covered on my self-guided walk. Here are a few more worthwhile things to see on your visit.

▲▲Arlaten Folk Museum (Museon Arlaten)

This is the leading museum in Provence for traditional culture and folklore. After a long closure for renovation, it may reopen by the time you visit. When it does, it is expected to resume its place as one of the top attractions in Arles.

Cost and Hours: Reopening in 2020—check ahead for price and open days. Tel. 04 13 31 51 99, www.museonarlaten.fr.

La Roquette District

To escape the tourist beat in Arles, take a detour into the town's little-visited western fringe. Find Rue des Porcelets near the Trinquetaille Bridge and stroll several blocks into pleasing Place Paul Doumer, where you'll find a lively assortment of cafés, bakeries, and bistros catering to locals (see "Eating in Arles," later, for my suggestions). Continue along Rue de la Roquette and turn right on charming Rue Croix Rouge to reach the river. Those walking to or from the Ancient History Museum can use this appealing stroll as a shortcut.

▲Réattu Museum (Musée Réattu)

Housed in the former Grand Priory of the Knights of Malta, this modern-art collection, while always changing, is a stimulating and well-lit mix of new and old. Picasso loved Arles and came here regularly for the bullfights. At the end of his life in 1973, he gave the city a series of his paintings, some of which are always on display here. The permanent collection usually includes a series of works by homegrown Neoclassical artist Jacques Réattu.

Cost and Hours: €8; Tue-Sun 10:00-18:00, Nov-Feb until 17:00, closed Mon year-round; 10 Rue du Grand Prieuré, tel. 04 90 49 37 58, www.museereattu.arles.fr.

Baths of Constantine (Thermes de Constantin)

These partly intact Roman baths were built in the early fourth century when Emperor Constantine declared Arles an imperial residence. Roman cities such as Arles had several public baths like this, fed by aqueducts and used as much for exercising, networking, and chatting with friends as for bathing (like today's athletic clubs). These baths were located near the Rhône River for easy water disposal. You can get a pretty good look at the baths through the fence. If you enter you'll walk elevated metal corridors at the original floor level. Imagine the elaborate engineering: the hypocaust system for heating the floor and big tubs with various temperatures—hot, tepid, and cold—next to a sauna and steam room heated by slave-stoked, wood-burning ovens.

Cost and Hours: €4, daily 9:00-19:00, April and Oct until 18:00, Nov-March 10:00-17:00.

ON THE OUTSKIRTS

▲▲Ancient History Museum (Musée Départemental Arles Antique)

This museum, just west of central Arles along the river, provides valuable background on Arles' Roman history: Visit it first, before delving into the rest of the city's sights (drivers should stop on the way into town).

Located on the site of the Roman chariot racecourse (the arc of which defines today's parking lot), this air-conditioned, all-on-one-floor museum is full of models and original sculptures that re-create the Roman city, making workaday life and culture easier to imagine.

PROVENCE

While the museum's posted descriptions of most of its treasures are only in French, the audioguide does a fine job describing the exhibits in English. For a deeper understanding of Provence's ancient roots, read "The Romans in Provence," earlier.

Cost and Hours: €8, free first Sun of the month, Wed-Mon 10:00-18:00, closed Tue, audioguide-€2, Presqu'île du Cirque Romain, tel. 04 13 31 51 03.

Getting There: Drivers will see signs for the museum at the city's western end. To reach the museum from the city center *sans* car, take the €1 **Navia shuttle** (see "Getting Around Arles," earlier). The museum is about a 20-minute **walk** from the city center: Turn left at the river and take the riverside path under two bridges to the big, modern blue building (or better, stroll through Arles' enjoyable La Roquette neighborhood, described earlier). As you approach the museum, you'll pass the verdant Hortus Garden—designed to recall the Roman circus and chariot racecourse that were located here. A **taxi** ride costs about €12 (museum can call a taxi for your return).

Visiting the Museum: The permanent collection is housed in a large hall flooded with natural light. Highlights include models of the ancient city and its major landmarks, a 2,000-year-old Roman boat, statues, mosaics, and sarcophagi. Here's what you'll see:

A wall **map** of the region during the Roman era greets visitors and shows the geographic importance of Arles: Three important Roman trade routes—vias Domitia, Grippa, and Aurelia—all converged on or near Arles.

After a small exhibit on pre-Roman Arles you'll come to fascinating **models of the Roman city** and the impressive Roman structures in (and near) Arles. These breathe life into the buildings, showing how they looked 2,000 years ago.

Start with the **model of Roman Arles** and ponder the city's splendor when Arles' population was almost double that of today. Find the forum—it's still the center of town, although only two columns survive (the smaller section of the forum is where today's Place du Forum is built). The next model shows the grandeur of the forum in greater detail.

At the museum's center stands the original **statue of Julius Caesar,** which once graced Arles' ancient theater's magnificent stage wall. To the left of Julius, find a **model of Arles' theater** and its wall, as well as models of the ancient town's other major buildings. Find the arena with its movable cover to shelter spectators from sun or rain, the floating wooden bridge over the widest, slowest part of the river—giving Arles a strategic advantage—and the hydraulic mill of Barbegal with its 16 waterwheels cascading water down a hillside.

Step down into the hall to Julius's right and find the large model of the **chariot racecourse.** Part of the original racecourse was just outside the windows, and although long gone, it likely resembled Rome's Circus Maximus. The rest of this hall is dedicated to the museum's newest and most exciting exhibit: a **Gallo-Roman vessel** and much of its cargo (English translations on panels). This almost-100-foot-long Roman barge was hauled out of the Rhône in 2010, along with some 280 amphorae and 3,000 ceramic artifacts. It was typical of flat-bottomed barges used to shuttle goods between Arles and ports along the Mediterranean (vessels were manually towed upriver). This one hauled limestone slabs and big rocks—no wonder it sank. A worthwhile 20-minute video about the barge's recovery (with English subtitles) plays continuously in a tiny theater at the end of the hall.

Elsewhere in the museum, you'll see displays of pottery, jewelry, metal, and glass artifacts. You'll also see well-crafted mosaic floors that illustrate how Roman Arles was a city of art and culture. The many **statues** are all original, except for the greatest—the *Venus of Arles,* which Louis XIV took a liking to and had moved to Versailles.

Frank Gehry Tower and LUMA Arles

The buzz in Arles is the 180-foot-tall Gehry-designed aluminum tower rising in a rundown neighborhood southeast of the center. The once thriving railyard quarter, which never recovered after WWII bombings, will enjoy this futuristic facelift. The tower is part of the new LUMA Arles and will provide a space for independent artists and special expositions. The project promises to revitalize this zone with galleries and apartments (opens in 2020, 45 Chemin des Minimes, tel. 04 90 47 76 17, www.luma-arles.org).

NEAR ARLES
The Camargue

Knocking on Arles' doorstep, the Camargue region, occupying the vast delta of the Rhône River, is one of Europe's most important wetlands. This marshy area exists where the Rhône splits into two branches (big and little), just before it flows into the Mediterranean. Over the millennia, a steady flow of sediment has been deposited

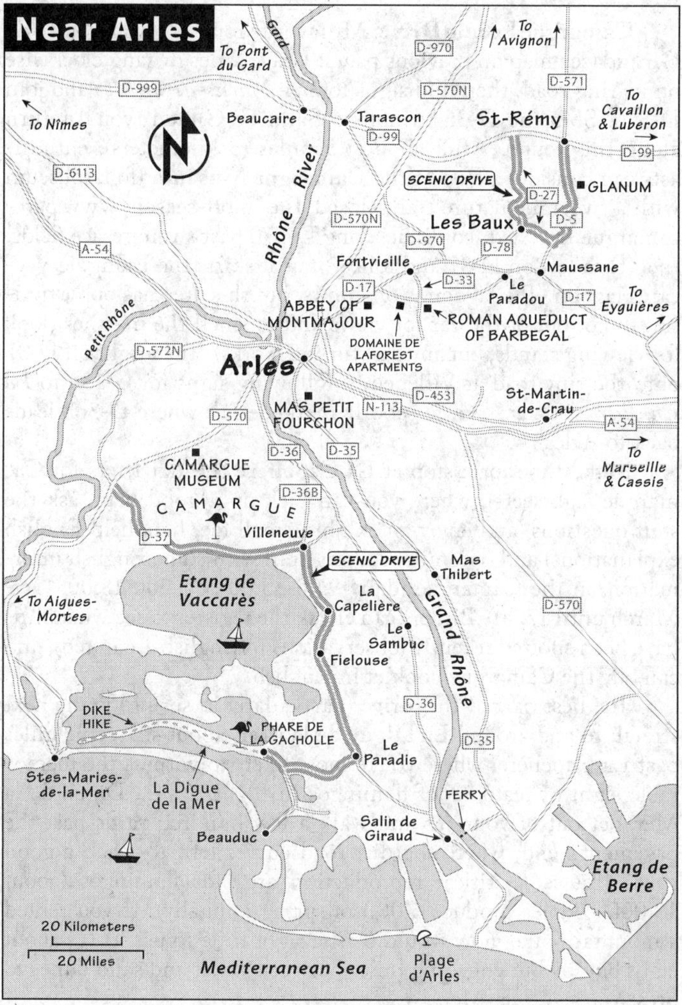

Near Arles

at the mouth of the rivers—thoroughly land-locking villages that once faced the sea.

Today the Camargue Regional Nature Park is a protected "wild" area, where pink flamingos, wild bulls, nasty boars, nastier mosquitoes (in every season but winter—come prepared), and the famous white horses wander freely through lagoons and tall grass. The dark bulls are harder to spot than the white horses and flamingos, so go slow and make use of the viewing platforms.

The best time to visit is in spring, when the flamingos are out in full force; the worst time to visit is in summer, when birds are fewest and the mosquitoes are most abundant.

PROVENCE

Camargue Scenic Drive: My favorite route is toward **Salin de Giraud** (see map on previous page): Leave Arles driving clockwise on its ring road, then find signs to *Stes-Maries-de-la-Mer* and join D-570. Skip the D-36 turnoff to Salin de Giraud (you'll return along this route). After about 3.5 miles (6 kilometers), enthusiasts can consider a stop at the **Camargue Museum** (folk museum with a two-mile nature trail, closed Tue in off-season, www.parc-camargue.fr). Next, continue along D-570 past swampy rice fields, then turn left on D-37 and follow it as it skirts the Etang de Vaccarès lagoon. The lagoon is off-limits, but this area has opportunities to get out of the car for views and to smell the marshes (look for viewing stands, but any dirt turnoff works). Turn right off D-37 onto the tiny road at Villeneuve, following signs for C-134 to *La Capelière* and *La Fiélouse* (poorly marked—it's where D-36b leads back to Arles).

Make time for a stop at **La Capelière** (headquarters for Camargue sightseers), where you can pick up a good map, ask the staff questions, and enjoy an exhibit (small fee, handheld English explanations) and one-mile walking trail with some English information on the Camargue (daily 9:00-13:00 & 14:00-18:00, Oct-March until 17:00). Birders can check the register to see what birds have been spotted recently (observations in English are in red), and can buy the Camargue booklet in English.

The best part of this drive (particularly in spring) is the next stretch to and around **La Digue de la Mer,** about six scenic miles past La Capelière, where you're most likely to witness the memorable sight of platoons of flamingos in flight. At La Digue de la Mer, get out of your car and walk a few hundred yards past the pavement's end, where the dirt road curves left, to reach a good spot. This is a critical reproduction area for flamingos (about 13,000 couples produce 5,000 offspring annually). If you rented a mountain bike, now would be the right time to use it: It's about eight bumpy but engaging miles between water and sand dunes to Stes-Maries-de-la-Mer.

From here, most will want to retrace their route back to Villeneuve, then continue straight onto D-36b, which leads back to Arles.

Experiences in Arles

▲▲Markets

On Wednesday and Saturday mornings, Arles' ring road erupts into an open-air festival of fish, flowers, produce...and everything Provençal. The main event is on Saturday, with vendors jamming the ring road from Boulevard Emile Combes to the east, along Boulevard des Lices near the TI (the heart of the market), and continuing down Boulevard Georges Clemenceau to the west. Wednesday's market runs only along Boulevard Emile Combes, between Place Lamartine and Avenue Victor Hugo; the segment nearest Place Lamartine is all about food, and the upper half features clothing, tablecloths, purses, and so on. On the first Wednesday of the month, a flea market doubles the size of the usual Wednesday market along Boulevard des Lices near the TI. Both markets are open until about 12:30.

▲▲Bullgames *(Courses Camarguaises)*

Provençal "bullgames" are held in Arles and in neighboring towns. Those in Arles occupy the same seats that fans have used for nearly 2,000 years, and deliver the city's most memorable experience—the *courses camarguaises* in the ancient arena. The nonviolent bullgames are more sporting than bloody bullfights (though traditional Spanish-style bullfights still take place on occasion). The bulls of Arles (who, locals insist, "die of old age") are promoted in posters even more boldly than their human foes. In the

bullgame, a ribbon *(cocarde)* is laced between the bull's horns. The *razeteur,* dressed in white and carrying a special hook, has 15 minutes to snare the ribbon. Local businessmen encourage a *razeteur* by shouting out how much money they'll pay for the *cocarde.* If the bull pulls a good stunt, the band plays the famous "Toreador" song from *Carmen.* The following day, newspapers report on the games, including how many *Carmen*s the bull earned.

Three classes of bullgames—determined by the experience of the *razeteurs*—are advertised in posters: The *Course de Protection* is for rookies. The *Trophée de l'Avenir* comes with more experience. And the *Trophée des As* features top professionals. During Easter *(Féria de Pâques)* and the fall rice-harvest festival *(Féria du Riz),* the arena hosts traditional Spanish bullfights (look for *corrida*) with outfits, swords, spikes, and the whole gory shebang. (Nearby villages stage *courses camarguaises* in small wooden bullrings nearly every weekend; TIs have the latest schedule.)

Bullgame tickets usually run €11-20; bullfights are pricier (€36-100). Schedules for bullgames vary (usually July-Aug on Wed and Fri)—ask at the TI or check www.arenes-arles.com.

Boules

The local "*boul*ing alleys" are by the Alyscamps necropolis (a block outside the ring road and sometimes by the river on Place Lamartine). Watch the old boys congregate for a game of *pétanque* after

PROVENCE

their afternoon naps (see "The Rules of *Boules*" sidebar, earlier in this chapter, for more on this popular local pastime).

Sleeping in Arles

Hotels are a great value here—most are air-conditioned, though few have elevators. The Calendal, Musée, and Régence hotels offer exceptional value.

$$ Hôtel le Calendal*** is a service-with-a-smile place ideally located between the Roman Arena and Classical Theater. The hotel opens to the street with airy lounges and a lovely palm-shaded courtyard, providing an enjoyable refuge. You'll find snacks and drinks in the café/sandwich bar (daily 8:00-20:00). The soothing rooms show a modern flair with creations from local artists (and explanations of their art). Rooms come in all shapes and sizes (some with balcony, family rooms, air-con, free spa for adults, ask about parking deals, just above arena at 5 Rue Porte de Laure, tel. 04 90 96 11 89, www.lecalendal.com, contact@lecalendal.com). They also run the nearby budget Hostel Arles City Center, described later.

$ Hôtel du Musée** is a quiet, affordable manor-home hideaway tucked deep in Arles (if driving, call the hotel from the street—they'll open the barrier so you can drive in to drop off your bags). This delightful place comes with 29 tasteful rooms, a flowery courtyard, and comfortable lounges. Lighthearted Claude and English-speaking Laurence are good hosts (family rooms, no elevator, pay parking garage, follow *Réattu Museum* signs to 11 Rue du Grand Prieuré, tel. 04 90 93 88 88, www.hoteldumusee.com, contact@hoteldumusee.com).

$ Hôtel de la Muette** is an intimate, good-value hotel located in a quiet corner of Arles, run by hardworking owners Brigitte and Alain. Its sharp rooms and bathrooms come with tiled floors and stone walls (RS%, family rooms, no elevator, pay private garage, 15 Rue des Suisses, tel. 04 90 96 15 39, www.hotel-muette.com, hotel.muette@wanadoo.fr).

$ Hôtel Régence** is a top budget deal with a riverfront location, comfortable, Provençal rooms, and easy parking. Of all the hotels I list, this one is the closest to the train station—a 10-minute walk (family rooms, choose river-view or quieter courtyard rooms, no elevator; from Place Lamartine, turn right after passing between towers to reach 5 Rue Marius Jouveau; tel. 04 90 96 39 85, www.hotel-regence.com, contact@hotel-regence.com). Gentle Valérie and Eric speak English.

$ Hôtel Acacias*** sits just off Place Lamartine and inside the old city walls. It's a modern hotel with small, clean, and comfortable rooms (family rooms, air-con, pay parking garage, 2 Rue

PROVENCE

de la Cavalerie, tel. 04 90 96 37 88, https://hotel-arles.brithotel.fr, arles@brithotel.fr).

¢ **Hostel Arles City Center** offers good four-bed dorm rooms, a shared kitchen, and homey living area. It's a great value for backpackers and those on a shoestring. Check in next door at the recommended Hôtel le Calendal (air-con, just above the Roman Arena at 26 Place Pomme, mobile 06 99 71 11 89, www.arles-pelerins.fr).

NEAR ARLES

Many drivers, particularly those with families, prefer staying outside Arles in the peaceful countryside, with easy access to the area's sights. For locations, see the "Near Arles" map.

$$ Mas Petit Fourchon is a grand farmhouse with spacious rooms on a sprawling property a few minutes from Arles. There's acres of room to roam and a big, heated pool (includes breakfast, some rooms with air-con, 1070 Chemin de Nadal in the Fourchon suburb; take exit 6 from N-113 toward *l'hôpital*, turn right just after the hospital and follow signs; tel. 04 90 96 16 35, www.petitfourchon.com, info@petitfourchon.com).

$ Domaine de Laforest, a few minutes' drive below Fontvieille, near the aqueduct of Barbegal, is a 320-acre spread engulfed by vineyards, rice fields, and swaying trees. The sweet owners (Sylvie and mama Mariette) rent eight well-equipped and comfortable two-bedroom apartments with great weekly rates (may be rentable for fewer days, air-con, washing machines, pool, big lawn, swings, 1000 Route de l'Aqueduc Romain, mobile 06 23 73 44 59, www.domaine-laforest.com, contact@domaine-laforest.com).

Eating in Arles

You can dine well in Arles on a modest budget (most of my listings have *menus* for under €25). Sunday is a quiet night for restaurants, though eateries on Place du Forum are open. For a portable snack, try Maison Soulier Bakery (see my "Arles City Walk," earlier), and for groceries, use the big Monoprix supermarket/department store on Place Lamartine (Mon-Sat 8:30-19:30, closed Sun).

FOR LUNCH OR A LIGHT DINNER

$ Café Factory République is a youthful, creative, and fun-loving place run by jovial Gilles. He's fun to talk with and serves sandwiches, hearty salads, and a wide variety of drinks. While not really a dinner place, he takes orders until 18:00 (Mon-Sat 8:00-19:00, closed Sun, 35 Rue de la République, tel. 04 90 54 52 23, skinniest WC in France).

$ Le Comptoir du Calendal, in the recommended Hôtel le Calendal, serves light, seasonal fare either curbside overlooking the

PROVENCE

Arles Hotels & Restaurants

Accommodations

1. Hôtel/Comptoir Le Calendal & Hostel Arles City Center
2. Hôtel du Musée
3. Hôtel de la Muette
4. Hôtel Régence
5. Hôtel Acacias
6. To Mas Petit Fourchon
7. To Domaine de Laforest

Eateries

8. Café Factory République
9. L'Atelier & A Côté
10. Le Criquet
11. Place du Forum Eateries
12. Cuisine de Comptoir
13. Rue du Dr. Fanton Eateries
14. Soleileïs Ice Cream
15. Pizza 22
16. Oscar
17. Le Gibolin
18. Maison Soulier Bakery

RUE DES CAPUCINS

RUE ROBESPIERRE

RUE DE LA VERRIERE

RUE

RUE CAMARGUE

TRINQUETAILLE

QUAI ST. PIERRE

Rhône

TRINQUETAILLE BRIDGE

QUAI MARX DORMOY

R. DE LA FANTON

R. TRUCHET

R. DR. FANTON

FONDATION VAN GOGH

RUE A. FRANCE

RUE DE LA TOUR DU FABRE

R. JOUVENE

LIBERTE

B Navia Shuttle Bus Stops

QUAI DE LA ROQUETTE

RUE DE LA RÉPUBLIQUE

ARLATEN FOLK MUSEUM

R. DES PORCELETS

RUE DE LA ROQUETTE

Place Paul Doumier

15 16 17

RUE DE LA RÉPUBLIQUE

RUE GAMBETTA

ESPACE VAN GOGH

RUE CROIX ROUGE

RUE DE CHARTROUSE

RUE JEAN GRANAUD

RUE MOLIERE

R. PRES. WILSON

To Ancient History Museum

LA ROQUETTE

MAIN BUS STATION

Place Genive

RUE FLEURY PRUDHON

To Nîmes via A-84

RUE RAILLON

To Ancient History Museum

BLVD. G. CLEMENCEAU

B

RUE PARMENTIER

PROVENCE

N

100 Meters
100 Yards

River

SNCF Bus to TGV Station

Navia Shuttle #20 & 57

TRAIN STATION

To Les Baux, Fontvielle, Avignon & **7**

RUE GORODICHE

RUE PAULIN TALABOT

AVE. DE STALINGRAD

BRASSERIE

Place Lamartine

MONOPRIX PARKING

MONOPRIX DEP'T STORE

BLVD. EMILE COMBES

PETANQUE

CAVALERIE GATE

RUE CAVALERIE

JULES FERRY

R. TERRIN

RUE JOUVEAU

4 **5**

R. PUITS

RUE BALZAC

R. L. BLUM

RUE METRAS

QUAI MARX DORMOY

R. GRILLE

Place Voltaire

RUE VOLTAIRE

RUE CONDORCET

R. EUZEBY

R. LA FONTAINE

RUE BOILEAU

RUE PORTAGNEL

BATHS OF CONSTANTINE

REATTU MUSEUM

RUE GRAND PRIEURE

2

RUE REATTU

RUE DU QUATRE SEPTEMBRE

L'AMPHITHEATRE

R. A. BARBES

R. A. TARDIEU

DU FOUR

RUE REFUGE

R. RENAN

SAUVAGE

RUE SUISSES

R. VERNON

R. DOISNEAU

R. GASPAIL

R. RASPAIL

RUE A. BRIAND

3

ROND-POINT DES ARENES

PARVIS DES ARENES

ROMAN ARENA

NOTRE DAME

14

RUE DES ARENES

RUE BABE CHIOT

R. NICOLAS

R. DIDEROT

ROND-POINT DES ARENES

11

Place du Forum

FAVORIN

RUE DE L'HOTEL DE VILLE

RUE BALZE

RUE DE LA CALADE

RUE MADELEINE

BLVD. EMILE COMBES

WC

ST. TROPHIME

Place de la République

8

CLOISTERS

CLASSICAL THEATER

PORTE DE LAURE

1

R. L'AGNEAU

10

R. EMILE BARRERE

RUE DU CLOITRE

9 **18**

RUE ROTONDE

RUE JEAN JAURES

Jardin d'Ete

ANCIENT CITY WALLS

MONTEE VAUBAN

PLAYGROUND

TOUR DES MOURGUES

TAXIS

BLVD. DES LICES

AVE. ALYSCAMPS

AVE. VICTOR HUGO

Esplanade Charles de Gaulle

POST

PARKING DES LICES (DU CENTRE)

RUE E. FASSIN

To **6** & LUMA Foundation

PROVENCE

arena, in its lovely courtyard, or inside the café—order at the counter (delicious and cheap little sandwiches and salads, daily 8:00-20:00, guest computer available, 5 Rue Porte de Laure, tel. 04 90 96 11 89).

FINER DINING

One of France's most recognized chefs, Jean-Luc Rabanel, runs two very different places 50 yards from Place de la République. They sit side by side at 7 Rue des Carmes. **$$$$ L'Atelier** is a top-end place with two Michelin stars (contemporary tasting *menus* only—around €125, closed Mon-Tue, tel. 04 90 91 07 69). And next door is **$$$ A Côté,** a place with all the quality, none of the pretense, and meals at a fraction of the price. It offers a smart wine bar/bistro ambience and fine cuisine. This is a wonderful opportunity to sample the famous chef's talents with the €32 three-course *menu* (limited selection of wines by the glass, closed Mon-Tue, tel. 04 90 47 61 13, www.rabanel.com).

$$ Le Criquet, possibly the best value in Arles, is a sweet little place two blocks above the arena, serving well-presented and delicious Provençal classics with joy at good prices. Sisters Lili and Charlotte serve while mama and papa run the kitchen. Their mouthwatering €25 *bourride* is the house specialty: a creamy fish soup thickened with aioli and lots of garlic and stuffed with mussels, clams, calamari, and more—but every dish is tasty here. They have a lovely dining room and a petite terrace (closed Mon-Tue, 21 Rue Porte de Laure, tel. 04 90 96 80 51).

OTHER EATERIES
Place du Forum

The most charming square in town is also the most touristy. While you feel sure Van Gogh sipped his *pastis* here, these days he'd avoid it. Still, if you want to enjoy forgettable food with unforgettable atmosphere under a starry, starry night, Place du Forum is a winner.

For dinner: Circle the square to compare the ambience and crowds. You don't need a reservation here, so keep your options open. Your best bets for a good **$$** meal are probably **Le Tambourin** at the top of the square (good dinner salads and more) and **Mon Bar Brasserie** at the bottom (most local crowd, decent-value plates). **La Taverne du Forum** always seems the liveliest with the least lively food. **Le Comptoir d'Italie** serves your basic Italian grub, pizzas, and salads. **Apostrophe Café** has a younger vibe, more modern food, and smoothies. **Le Café La Nuit** may have the best street appeal, but it's a tourist trap designed to hook those with Vincent fantasies.

Before-Dinner Drink or Dessert: You can eat at a better restaurant elsewhere and enjoy the ambience of Place du Forum for an aperitif or dessert. Any bar can serve you a *pastis*—one of the most local rituals you can enjoy in Arles. This anise-based aperitif is served straight with ice, along with a carafe of water—dilute to taste. And the ice cream shop on the square has a handful of tables, giving you a front-row seat to the Provençal ambience.

Just off Place du Forum

$ Cuisine de Comptoir offers light and cheap dinners of *tartine*—a cross between pizza and bruschetta, served with soup or salad for €11—and offers a fun array of pizza-style *tartine* toppings. This Provençal answer to a pizzeria—run by Vincent—has indoor seating only (closed Sun, off lower end of square at 10 Rue de la Liberté, tel. 04 90 96 86 28).

On Rue du Docteur Fanton

$$$ Le Galoubet is a popular local spot, blending a warm interior, traditional French cuisine, and gregarious service, thanks to owner Frank. It's the most expensive and least flexible place on the street, serving *menus* only. If it's cold, a roaring fire keeps you toasty (closed Sun-Mon, great fries and desserts, at #18, tel. 04 90 93 18 11).

$$ Les Filles du 16 is a warm, affordable place to enjoy a good Provençal two- or three-course dinner. The choices, while tasty, are limited, so check the selection before sitting down (closed Sat-Sun, at #16, tel. 04 90 93 77 36).

$$ Le Plaza la Paillotte buzzes with happy diners enjoying delicious, well-presented Provençal cuisine. Attentive owners Stéphane and Graziela (he cooks, she serves) welcome diners with a comfortable terrace and a smart interior (open daily, at #28, tel. 04 90 96 33 15).

Ice Cream: At **Soleileïs**, Marijtje scoops up fine ice cream made with organic milk, fresh fruit, all-natural ingredients, and creative flavors that fit the season. There's also a shelf of English books for exchange (daily 14:00-18:30, closed in winter, at #9).

In the La Roquette District

For a less-touristy-feeling dining experience, wander into the La Roquette neighborhood (described earlier, under "Sights in Arles").

$ Pizza 22 fires up the best pizza in Arles with inviting tables on Place Paul Doumer (closed Tue, 22 Place Paul Doumer, tel. 04 86 63 65 60).

$ Oscar is an intriguing place with a young chef, an open kitchen, and a dining room that feels like a retro-chic art gallery/diner hybrid. The silverware sits in a jar on your table next to the napkin dispenser, while revolving photo exhibits decorate the walls. They offer eight or so seasonal plates designed to be eaten family style (about €12 each, three will fill two people). They also serve good wines by the glass (closed Wed, may be closed by the time of your visit, 20 Rue des Porcelets, tel. 04 90 99 53 12).

$$ Le Gibolin, while less convivial, is an intimate place with a warm interior where you'll eat surrounded by wine bottles and locals. There is no à la carte, just two- or three-course *menus* (closed Sun-Mon, 13 Rue des Porcelets, tel. 04 88 65 43 14).

Arles Connections

BY TRAIN
Note that Intercité trains in and out of Arles require a reservation. These include connections with Nice to the east and Bordeaux to the west (including intermediary stops). Ask at the station.

Compare train and bus schedules: For some nearby destinations the bus may be the better choice, and it's usually cheaper.

From Arles by Train to: Paris (hourly, 4 hours, transfer in Avignon or Nîmes; or take the SNCF bus to Avignon TGV Station and train from there), **Avignon Centre-Ville** (hourly, 20 minutes), **Nîmes** (hourly, 30 minutes), **Orange** (4/day direct, 30 minutes, more with transfer in Avignon), **Aix-en-Provence Centre-Ville** (hourly, 2 hours, transfer in Marseille, train may separate midway—be sure your section is going to Aix-en-Provence), **Marseille** (hourly, 1 hour), **Cassis** (7/day, 2 hours), **Carcassonne** (4/day direct, 2.5 hours, more with transfer in Narbonne, direct trains may require reservations), **Beaune** (hourly, 5 hours, transfer in Lyon), **Nice** (hourly, 4 hours, most require transfer in Marseille), **Barcelona** (3/day, 4.5 hours, transfer in Nîmes), **Italy** (3/day, transfer in Marseille and Nice; from Arles, it's 5 hours to Ventimiglia on the border, 8 hours to Milan, 9 hours to Cinque Terre, 11 hours to Florence, and 13 hours to Venice or Rome).

BY BUS
Arles' main bus station is located on Boulevard Georges Clemenceau, a few blocks from the TI. Most buses to regional destinations depart from here, and most bus trips cost under €2. Get schedules at the TI or from the bus company (closed Sun, tel. 08 10 00 08 18, www.lepilote.com).

From Arles Train Station to Avignon TGV Station: The direct SNCF bus is your best option (€8, 8/day, 1 hour, included with rail pass). Though less convenient, you can also take the train from Arles to Avignon's Centre-Ville Station, then catch the shuttle train to the TGV station (see page 616).

From Arles by Bus to St-Rémy: Cartreize bus #57 connects Arles to St-Rémy-de-Provence (6/day, daily July-Aug, Sat-Sun only in early May-June and Sept, none in off-season; departs from the train station, not the bus station; 50 minutes to St-Rémy, then runs to Avignon). Bus #54 also goes to St-Rémy (5/day Mon-Fri, 3/day Sat, none on Sun, 1 hour).

By Bus to Other Destinations: Nîmes (8/day Mon-Fri, 2/day Sat-Sun, 1 hour), **Aix-en-Provence** (faster than trains, 6/day Mon-Fri, 4/day Sat-Sun, 1.5 hours), **Fontvieille** (6/day Mon-Sat, 2/day Sun, 20 minutes), **Camargue/Stes-Maries-de-la-Mer** (bus #20, 6/day Mon-Sat, 3/day Sun, departs from both the bus and train station, 1 hour).

Avignon

Famous for its nursery rhyme, medieval bridge, and brooding Palace of the Popes, contemporary Avignon (ah-veen-yohn) bustles and prospers behind its mighty walls. For nearly 100 years (1309-1403) Avignon was the capital of Christen- dom, home to seven popes. (And, for a difficult period after that—during the Great Schism when there were two competing popes—Avignon was "the other Rome.") During this time, it grew from a quiet village into a thriving city. Today, with its large student population and fashion- able shops, Avignon is an intriguing

blend of medieval history, youthful energy, and urban sophistica- tion. Street performers entertain the international throngs who fill Avignon's ubiquitous cafés and trendy boutiques. And each July the city goes pedal to the metal during its huge theater festival (with about 2,000 performances, big crowds, higher prices, and hotels booked up long in advance).

Orientation to Avignon

Cours Jean Jaurès, which turns into Rue de la République, runs straight from the Centre-Ville train station to Place de l'Horloge and the Palace of the Popes, splitting Avignon in two. The larger eastern half is where the action is. Climb to the Jardin du Rochers des Doms for the town's best view, tour the pope's immense palace, lose yourself in Avignon's back streets (following my self-guided

"Discovering Avignon's Back Streets Walk"), and go organic in its vibrant market hall.

TOURIST INFORMATION

The TI is located on the main street linking the Centre-Ville train station to the old town (Mon-Sat 9:00-18:00 except Sat until 17:00 Nov-March, Sun 10:00-17:00 except until 12:00 Nov-March, daily until 19:00 in July, 41 Cours Jean Jaurès, tel. 04 32 74 32 74, www.avignon-tourisme.com).

At the TI, pick up a map with several good (but tricky to follow) walking tours and ask about guided tours in English. They offer a worthwhile two-hour walking tour that covers Avignon at the time of the popes (€21, Aug-Sept Wed 10:30, also on Sun in Aug, reserve at TI, on their website, or call).

Also ask about the Baladine and City Zen minibuses that loop through the old city (see "Helpful Hints," next page) and get bike maps for good rides in the area, including the Ile de la Barthelasse.

ARRIVAL IN AVIGNON
By Train

Avignon has two train stations: Centre-Ville and TGV (linked to downtown by shuttle trains). Some TGV trains stop at Centre-Ville—verify your station in advance.

The **Centre-Ville station** *(Gare Avignon Centre-Ville)* gets all non-TGV trains (and a few TGV trains). To reach the town center, cross the busy street in front of the station and walk through the city walls onto Cours Jean Jaurès. Baggage storage is close by (see "Helpful Hints," later).

The **TGV station** *(Gare TGV),* on the outskirts of town, has easy car rental, but no baggage storage (see "Helpful Hints," later, for options). Car rental, buses, and taxis are outside the north exit *(sortie nord).* To reach the city center, take the **shuttle train** from platform A or B to the Centre-Ville station (€1.60, included with rail pass, 2/hour, 5 minutes, buy ticket from machine on platform or at *billeterie* in main hall). A **taxi** ride be-

tween the TGV station and downtown Avignon costs about €18.

If you're connecting from the TGV station to other points, you'll find **buses** to Arles' Centre-Ville station at the second bus shelter (€7.50, 9/day, hourly, included with rail pass, schedule posted on shelter and available at TGV station info booths).

If you're **driving,** Arles is well-signed from the TGV station.

If driving to St-Rémy-de-Provence, Les Baux, or the Luberon, leave the station following signs to *Avignon Sud,* then *La Rocade.* You'll soon see exits to Arles (follow those for St-Rémy and Les Baux) and Cavaillon (for Luberon villages).

By Bus
The efficient bus station *(gare routière)* is 100 yards to the right as you exit the Centre-Ville train station, beyond and below Hôtel Ibis (helpful info desk open Mon-Sat 7:00-19:30, closed Sun, tel. 04 90 82 07 35).

By Car
Avignon is essentially traffic-free in the old center. There are several safe underground parking lots clearly signposted. For those day-tripping in and wanting the most central garage, follow signs to *Centre,* then to the *Centre Historique* and then *P Palais des Papes* (from where, after parking, you'll climb the stairs and arrive at the pope's doorstep, €12 half-day, €20/24 hours).

You can also park for free at the edge of town at lots with complimentary shuttle buses to the center (no shuttles on Sunday; see "Avignon" map).

Follow *P Gratuit* signs for **Parking de l'Ile Piot,** across Pont Daladier on Ile de la Barthelasse, with shuttles to Place Crillon; or to **Parking des Italiens,** along the river east of the Palace of the Popes, with shuttles to Place Pie (allow 30 minutes to walk from either parking lot to the center). Street parking is €1-3/hour for a maximum of four hours Mon-Sat 9:00-19:00 (free 19:00-9:00 and all day Sunday).

No matter where you park, leave nothing of value in your car.

HELPFUL HINTS
Book Ahead for July: During the July theater festival, rooms are almost impossible to come by—reserve early, or stay in Arles or St-Rémy.

Local Help: David at **Imagine Tours,** a nonprofit group whose goal is to promote this region, can help with hotel emergencies and special-event tickets (mobile 06 89 22 19 87, www.imagine-tours.net, imagine.tours@gmail.com). If you don't get an answer, leave a message.

English Bookstore: Try **Camili Books & Tea,** a secondhand bookshop with a refreshing courtyard and hot drinks (Tue-Sat 12:00-19:00, closed Sun-Mon, free Wi-Fi, 155 Rue Carreterie, in Avignon's northeast corner—see "Avignon" map).

Baggage Storage: La Consigne will either be in the Centre-Ville train station or a few blocks away under the modern arcade at 1 Avenue Maréchal de Lattre de Tassigny (€6-10/day; June-Aug

Avignon

Ile de la Barthelasse

VIEW WALK

SHUTTLE BOAT

ST. BENEZET BRIDGE

PORTE DU ROCHER

BLVD. DE LA

❶

PORTE DU RHONE

❷

PETIT PALAIS MUSEUM

Jardin du Rocher des Doms

River

Rhône

N-580

de l'Ile Piot

PONT E. DALADIER

R. REMPART DU RHONE

R. GRANDE FUSTERIE

Palace Square

❼

N.D. DES DOMS

PALACE OF THE POPES

R. BANASTERIE

R. ST. ETIENNE

RUE BALANCE

DISCOVERING BACK STREETS WALK BEGINS

PORTE DE L'OULLE

Place Crillon

#5 Ⓑ

RUE VERNET

PEYROLERIE

ST. PIERRE

Place Carnot

WELCOME TO AVIGNON WALK BEGINS

Place de l'Horloge

R. FAVART

R. MARCHANDS

SYNA-GOGUE

R. VIEUX SEXTIER

ALLEE DE L'OULLE

BLVD. DE L'OULLE

RUE REMPART DE L'OULLE

RUE VICTOR HUGO

RUE D'ANNANELLE

RUE JOSEPH VERNET

R. PETITE FUST.

R. ST. AGRICOL

RUE RACINE

RUE LA BOUQUERIE

RUE GALANTE

RUE BANCASSE

RUE ROUGE

PATRICK MALLARD PASTRIES

CALVET MUSEUM

❺

RUE VERNET

Place St. Didier

R. ROI

OLD CITY WALLS

R. REMPART ST-DOMINIQUE

RUE VELOUTERIE

RUE JOSEPH VERNET

RUE SAINT-CHARLES

RUE DE LA REPUBLIQUE

MUSEE LAPIDAIRE

ANGLADON MUSEUM

R. H. FABRE

ⓘ

BLVD. RASPAIL

COLLECTION LAMBERT

COURS JEAN JAURES

❺

RUE SAINT-MICHEL

RUE PERDIGUIER

❹

Place des Corps-Saints

PORTE ST. ROCH

RUE REMPART SAINT-ROCH

POST

Ⓑ

Place de la Republique

PORTE ST. MICHEL

RUE

To Nimes via A-9

BLVD. SAINT- ROCH

PORTE ST. CHARLES

PORTE DE LA REPUBLIQUE

P   P

AVE. DE   7EME GENIE

BUS STATION

❻

AVE. EISENHOWER

CENTRE-VILLE TRAIN STATION

AVE. MONCLAR

AVE. SAINT-RUF

200 Meters

200 Yards

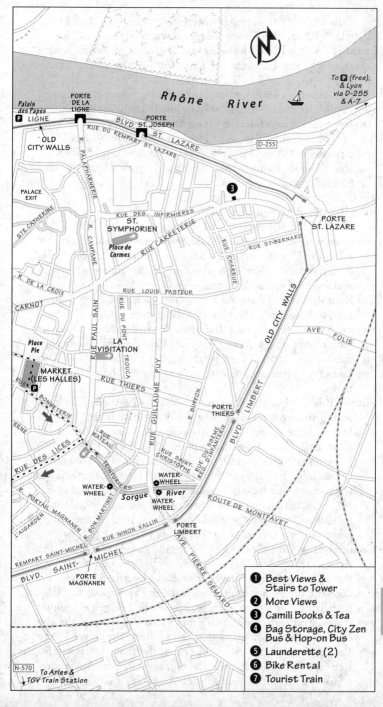

Best Views & Stairs to Tower

More Views

Camili Books & Tea

Bag Storage, City Zen Bus & Hop-on Bus

Launderette (2)

Bike Rental

Tourist Train

PROVENCE

daily 8:00-21:00; Sept-May Mon-Sat 9:00-18:00, closed Sun, tel. 09 82 45 20 24, www.consigne-avignon.fr).

Laundry: At **La Blanchisseuse,** you can drop off your laundry and pick it up the same day (daily 7:00-21:00, several blocks west of the TI at 24 Rue Lanterne, tel. 04 90 85 58 80). The launderette at 66 Place des Corps-Saints, where Rue Agricol Perdiguier ends, is handy to most hotels (daily 7:00-20:00).

Grocery Store: Carrefour City is central and has long hours daily (2 blocks from TI, toward Place de l'Horloge on Rue de la République). A second Carrefour City is near Les Halles at 19 Rue Florence (same hours). See the "Avignon Hotels & Restaurants" map for locations.

Taxi: Dial 04 90 82 20 20 to get a cab.

Bike Rental: Rent pedal and electric bikes and scooters near the train station at **Provence Bike** (April-Oct 9:00-18:30, 7 Avenue St. Ruf, tel. 04 90 27 92 61, www.provence-bike.com), or ask at the TI about other options. You'll enjoy riding on the Ile de la Barthelasse (the TI has bike maps), but biking is better in and around Isle-sur-la-Sorgue and Vaison-la-Romaine.

Car Rental: The TGV station has counters for all the big companies; only Avis is at the Centre-Ville station.

Shuttle Vans: Wave down a **Baladine** electric minivan along its loop route through Avignon, or use **City Zen** minibuses with fixed stops (€0.50, 4/hour for either). City Zen minibuses also link remote parking lots with the city center. The TI has route maps.

Shuttle Boat: A free shuttle boat, the *Navette Fluviale,* plies back and forth across the river (as it did in the days when the town had no functioning bridge) from near St. Bénezet Bridge (3/hour, daily April-June and Sept 10:00-12:15 & 14:00-18:00, July-Aug 11:00-20:45; Oct-March weekends and Wed afternoons only). It drops you on the peaceful Ile de la Barthelasse, with its recommended riverside restaurant, grassy walks, and bike rides with memorable city views. If you stay on the island for dinner, check the schedule for the last return boat—or be prepared for a taxi ride or a 30-minute walk back to town.

Commanding City Views: For great views of Avignon and the river, walk or drive across Daladier Bridge, or ferry across the Rhône on the *Navette Fluviale* (described above). I'd take the boat across the river, walk the view path to Daladier Bridge, and then cross back over the bridge (45-minute walk). You can enjoy other impressive vistas from the top of the Jardin du Rochers des Doms, from the tower in the Palace of the Popes, from the end of the famous, broken St. Bénezet Bridge, and from the entrance to Fort St. André, across the river in Villeneuve-lès-Avignon.

Tours in Avignon

Local Guides

Isabelle Magny is a good local guide for the city and region (€160/half-day, €330/day, no car, mobile 06 11 82 17 92, isabellemagny@sfr.fr). **Nina Seffusatti** is also good (same prices as Isabelle, mobile 06 14 80 30 37, nina.seffusatti@wanadoo.fr).

Food Tour

The **Avignon Gourmet Walking Tour** is a wonderful experience if you like to eat. Charming and passionate Aurélie meets small groups daily (except Sun and Mon) at the TI at 9:00 for a well-designed three-hour, eight-stop walk. Her tour is filled with information and tastes of top-quality local foods and drinks, and finishes in the market hall (€59/person, 2-8 people per group, mobile 06 35 32 08 96, www.avignongourmetours.com). Book in advance on her website.

Tourist Train

The little train leaves regularly (generally on the half hour) from in front of the Palace of the Popes and offers a decent overview of the city, including the Jardin du Rochers des Doms and St. Bénezet Bridge (€9, 2/hour, 45 minutes, recorded English commentary, mid-March-Oct daily 10:00-18:00, until 20:00 July-Aug).

Hop-On, Hop-Off Bus

Visite Avignon's open-top double-decker bus does a one-hour loop through the old city, up to the Jardin du Rocher des Doms, crosses the river onto Ile de la Barthelasse, then travels into Villeneuve-les-Avignon, with 18 stops including the Tower of Philip the Fair (€16, hourly departures, main stop between TI and train station on Cours Jean Jaurès, www.visiteavignon.com).

Minivan Excursions from Avignon

Several minivan tour companies based in Avignon offer transportation to destinations described in this book, including Pont du Gard, the Luberon, and the Camargue (see "Tours in Provence" on page 578).

Walks in Avignon

For an excellent city overview, combine these two self-guided walks. "Welcome to Avignon" covers the major sights, while "Discovering Avignon's Back Streets" leads you along the lanes less taken, delving beyond the surface of this historic city. To trace both routes, see the "Avignon" map, earlier in this section.

PROVENCE

WELCOME TO AVIGNON WALK

Start this ▲▲ tour where the Romans did, on Place de l'Horloge, in front of City Hall (Hôtel de Ville).

Place de l'Horloge

In ancient Roman times this was the forum, and in medieval times it was the market square. The square is named for the clock tower (now hiding behind the more recently built City Hall) that, in its day, was a humanist statement. In medieval France, the only bells in town rang from the church tower to indicate not the hours but the calls to prayer. With the dawn of the modern age, secular clock towers like this rang out the hours as people organized their lives independent of the Church.

Taking humanism a step further, the City Hall, built after the French Revolution, obstructed the view of the old clock tower while celebrating a new era. The slogan "liberty, equality, and brotherhood" is a reminder that the people supersede the king and the Church. And today, judging from the square's jammed cafés and restaurants, it is indeed the people who rule.

The square's present popularity arrived with the trains in 1854. Facing City Hall, look left down the main drag, Rue de la République. When the trains came to Avignon, proud city fathers wanted a direct, impressive way to link the new station to the heart of the city—so they destroyed existing homes to create Rue de la République and widened Place de l'Horloge.

• Walk slightly uphill past the neo-Renaissance facade of the theater and the carousel (public WCs behind). Look back to see the late Gothic bell tower. Then veer right at the Palace of the Popes and continue into...

Palace Square (Place du Palais)

Pull up a concrete stump just past the café. These bollards effectively keep cars from double-parking in areas designed for people. Many of the metal ones slide up and down by remote control to let privileged cars come and go.

Now take in the scene. This grand square is lined with the Palace of the Popes, the Petit Palais, and the cathedral. In the 1300s the entire headquarters of the Roman Catholic Church was moved to Avignon. The Church purchased the city of Avignon and gave it a complete makeover. Along with clearing out vast spaces like this square and building a three-acre palace, the Church erected more than three miles of protective wall (with 39 towers), "appropriate" housing for cardinals (read: mansions), and residences for its entire bureaucracy. The city was Europe's largest construction zone. Avignon's population grew from 6,000 to 25,000 in short order. (Today, only 13,000 people live within the walls.) The limits of pre-papal Avignon are outlined on your city map: Rues Joseph Vernet,

Henri Fabre, des Lices, and Philonarde all follow the route of the city's earlier defensive wall (about half the diameter of today's wall).

The imposing facade behind you, across the square from the Palace of the Popes' main entry, was "the papal mint," which served as the finance department for the Holy See. The Petit Palais (Little Palace) seals the uphill end of the square and was built for a cardinal; today it houses medieval paintings.

Avignon's 12th-century Romanesque cathedral, just to the left of the Palace of the Popes, has been the seat of the local bishop for more than a thousand years.

• *You can visit the massive **Palace of the Popes** (described later), but it works better to visit that palace at the end of this walk, then continue directly to my "Discovering Avignon's Back Streets Walk."*

Now is a good time to take in the...

Petit Palais Museum (Musée du Petit Palais)

This former cardinal's palace now displays the Church's collection of (mostly) art. You'll find some English information but not a lot of detail. Still, a visit here before going to the Palace of the Popes helps furnish and populate that otherwise barren building. You'll see bits of statues and tombs—an inventory of the destruction of exquisite Church art that was wrought by the French Revolution (which tackled established French society with Taliban-esque fervor). Then you'll see many rooms filled with religious Italian paintings, organized in chronological order from early Gothic to late Renaissance. Room 10 holds two paintings by Botticelli.

Cost and Hours: Free, Wed-Mon 10:00-13:00 & 14:00-18:00, closed Tue, ask about summer sound-and-light shows in main courtyard, at north end of Palace Square, tel. 04 90 86 44 58, www.petit-palais.org.

• *From Palace Square, head up to the cathedral (enjoy the viewpoint overlooking the square from its front porch), and fill your water bottle just past the gate. Now climb the ramp to the top of a rocky hill, passing "the popes' vineyard," to where Avignon was first settled. Atop the hill is an inviting café and pond in a park—the Jardin du Rocher des Doms. At the far side (the top end with the green suicide-prevention fence) is a viewpoint high above the river from where you can see Avignon's beloved broken bridge.*

▲Jardin du Rocher des Doms

Enjoy the view from this bluff. On a clear day, the tallest peak you see (far to the right), with its white limestone cap, is Mont Ventoux ("Windy Mountain"). Below and just to the right, you'll spot free passenger ferries shuttling across the river, and—tucked amidst the trees on the far side of the river—the recommended restaurant, Le Bercail, a local favorite. The island in the river is the Ile de la Bar-

thelasse, a lush nature preserve where Avignon can breathe. In the distance to the left is the TGV rail bridge.

Medieval Avignon was administered by the Vatican and independent of the rest of France. The Rhône River marked the border of Vatican territory in medieval times. Fort St. André—across the river on the hill—was in the kingdom of France. The fort was built in 1360, shortly after the pope moved to Avignon, to counter the papal incursion into this part of Europe. Avignon's famous bridge was a key border crossing, with towers on either end—one was French, and the other was the pope's. The French one, across the river, is the Tower of Philip the Fair (described later, under "More Sights in Avignon").

Cost and Hours: Free, park gates open daily 7:30-20:00, June-Aug until 21:00, Oct-March until 18:00.

• *Take the walkway down to the left (passing the popes' vineyard again) and find the stairs leading down to the tower. You'll catch glimpses of the...*

Ramparts

The only bit of the rampart you can walk on is accessed from St. Bénezet Bridge (accessible only with your ticket to the bridge). Just after the papacy took control of Avignon, the walls were extended to take in the convents and monasteries that had been outside the city. What you see today was partially restored in the 19th century.

• *When you come out of the tower on street level, turn left to walk inside the city wall to the entry to the old bridge.*

▲St. Bénezet Bridge (Pont St. Bénezet)

This bridge, whose construction and location were inspired by a shepherd's religious vision, is the "Pont d'Avignon" of nursery-rhyme fame. The ditty (which you've probably been humming all day) dates back to the 15th century: *Sur le Pont d'Avignon, on y danse, on y danse, sur le Pont d'Avignon, on y danse tous en rond* ("On the bridge of Avignon, we will dance, we will dance, on the bridge of Avignon, we will dance all in a circle").

PROVENCE

And the bridge was a big deal even outside its kiddie-tune fame. Built between 1171 and 1185, it was strategic—one of only three bridges crossing the mighty Rhône in the Middle Ages, important to pilgrims, merchants, and armies. It was damaged several times by floods but always rebuilt. In the winter of 1668 most of it was knocked out for the last time by a disastrous icy flood. The townsfolk decided not to rebuild this time, and for more than a century, Avignon had no bridge across the Rhône. While only four arches survive today, the original bridge was huge: Imagine a 22-arch, half-mile-long bridge extending from Vatican territory across the island to the lonely Tower of Philip the Fair, which marked the beginning of France (see displays of the bridge's original length).

Cost and Hours: €5, includes audioguide, €14.50 combo-ticket includes Palace of the Popes, daily 9:00-19:00, July-Aug until 20:00, Nov-Feb 9:30-17:45, last entry one hour before closing, tel. 04 90 27 51 16.

• *To get to the Palace of the Popes from here, walk away from the river and follow the signs to* Palais des Papes.

▲▲Palace of the Popes (Palais des Papes)

In 1309 a French pope was elected (Pope Clément V). His Holiness decided that dangerous Italy was no place for a pope, so he moved the whole operation to Avignon for a secure rule under a supportive French king. The Catholic Church literally bought Avignon (then a two-bit town) and built the Palace of the Popes, where the popes resided until 1403. Eventually, Italians demanded a Roman pope, so from 1378 on, there were twin popes—one in Rome and one in Avignon—causing a schism in  the Catholic Church that wasn't fully resolved until 1417.

Cost and Hours: €12, includes multimedia Histopad; €14.50 combo-ticket includes St. Bénezet Bridge, daily 9:00-19:00, July-Aug until 20:00, Nov-Feb 9:30-17:45, last entry one hour before closing; tel. 04 90 27 50 00, www.palais-des-papes.com.

Visiting the Palace: Visitors follow a tangled one-way route through mostly massive rooms equipped with an iPad they call "The Histopad"—an earnest effort to bring these old papal spaces to life. There's a lot of history here, but artifacts are sparse and wall frescos are faint: Without guiding help, it's mostly meaningless. Old-fashioned English-language boards in each room provide a little info, but your visit becomes greatly enriched if you master the included Histopad—the staff is happy to help you with it. Nine posts during the tour activate a time-tunnel effect, taking you back to the 14th century as you furnish the rooms by pointing your iPad. While in this mode, you can click on various points in the room for more info.

The palace was built stark and strong, before the popes knew how long they'd be staying (and before the affluence and fanciness of the Renaissance and Baroque ages). This was the most fortified palace of the time (remember, the pope left Rome to be more secure). With 10-foot-thick walls, it was a symbol of power.

This largest surviving Gothic palace in Europe was built to accommodate 500 people as the administrative center of the Holy See and home of the pope. Seven popes ruled from here, making this the center of Christianity for nearly 100 years. The last pope checked out in 1403, but the Church owned Avignon until the French Revolution in 1791. During this interim period, the palace still housed Church authorities. Avignon residents, many of whom had come from Rome, spoke Italian for a century after the pope left, making the town a cultural oddity within France.

The palace is pretty empty today—nothing portable survived both the pope's return to Rome and the French Revolution. Just before the gift shop exit, you can climb the tower (Tour de la Gâche) for grand views. The artillery room is now a gift shop channeling all visitors on a full tour of knickknacks for sale.

• You'll exit at the rear of the palace, where my next walk, "Discovering Avignon's Back Streets," begins. Or, to return to Palace Square, make two rights after exiting the palace.

DISCOVERING AVIGNON'S BACK STREETS WALK

Use the map earlier in this section to navigate this easy, level, 30-minute walk, worth ▲▲. We'll begin in the small square (Place de la Mirande) behind the Palace of the Popes. If you've toured the palace, this is where you exit. Otherwise, from the front of the palace, follow the narrow, cobbled Rue de la Peyrolerie—carved out of the rock—around the palace on the right side as you face it.

• Our walk begins at the...

Hôtel La Mirande: Avignon's finest hotel welcomes visitors. Find the atrium lounge, check out the queenly garden, and consider a coffee break amid the understated luxury (€12 afternoon tea served daily 15:00-18:00, see listing under "Eating in Avignon," later).

• Turn left out of the hotel and left again on Rue de la Peyrolerie ("Coppersmiths Street"), then take your first right on Rue des Ciseaux d'Or ("Street of the Golden Scissors"). On the small square ahead you'll find the...

Church of St. Pierre: The original walnut doors were carved in 1551, when tales of New World discoveries raced across Europe. (Notice the Indian headdress, top center of left-side door.) The fine Annunciation (eye level on right-side door) shows Gabriel giving Mary the exciting news in impressive Renaissance 3-D. The niches on the facade are empty except for one mismatched Mary and Child filling the center niche. (The original was ransacked by the Revolution.) Now take 10 steps back from the door and look way up. The tiny statue breaking the skyline of the church is a tiny, naked baby—that's Bacchus, the pagan god of wine, with oodles of grapes. What's he doing sitting atop a Christian church? No one knows. The church's interior—with its art amped up as a Counter-Reformation answer to the Protestant threat—holds a beautiful Baroque altar.

• *Facing the church door, turn left and pass the recommended* L'Epicerie *restaurant, then follow the alley, which was covered and turned into a tunnel during the town's population boom. It leads into...*

Place des Châtaignes: The cloister of St. Pierre is named for the chestnut *(châtaigne)* trees that once stood here (now replaced by plane trees). The practical atheists of the French Revolution destroyed the cloister, leaving only faint traces of the arches along the church side of the square.

• *Continue around the church and cross the busy street. At the start of little Rue des Fourbisseurs at the right corner, find the big...*

15th-Century Building: With its original beamed eaves showing, this is a rare vestige from the Middle Ages. Notice how this building widens the higher it gets. A medieval loophole based taxes on ground-floor square footage—everything above was tax-free. Walking down Rue des Fourbisseurs ("Street of the Animal Furriers"), notice how the top floors almost touch. Fire was a constant danger in the Middle Ages, as flames leapt easily from one home to the next. In fact, the lookout guard's primary responsibility was watching for fires, not the enemy. Because of fires, this is the only 15th-century home surviving in town. After this period, buildings were made of fire-resistant stone, like those across the street.

• *Walk down Rue des Fourbisseurs past lots of shops and turn left onto the traffic-free Rue du Vieux Sextier ("Street of the Old Sexy People"); another left under the first arch leads in 10 yards to one of France's oldest synagogues.*

Synagogue: Jews first arrived in Avignon with the Diaspora (exile after the Romans destroyed their great temple) in the first century. Avignon's Jews were nicknamed "the Pope's Jews" because of the protection that the Church offered to Jews expelled from France. Although the original synagogue dates from the 1220s, in the mid-19th century it was completely rebuilt in a Neoclassical Greek-temple style by a non-Jewish architect. This is the only synagogue under a rotunda. It's an intimate, classy place—where a community of 500 local Jews worships—dressed with white colonnades and walnut furnishings (free, Mon-Fri 9:00-11:00, ring doorbell at #6, closed Sat-Sun and holidays, 2 Place Jerusalem).

• *Retrace your steps to Rue du Vieux Sextier and turn left. A few steps down the street (on the right) is Patrick Mallard—an inviting pastry shop. It's one of two shops authorized to sell Avignon's one-of-a-kind, thistle-shaped candy called* papalines d'Avignon *(dark chocolate wrapped in pink-hued chocolate and filled with a liquor made from local plants).*

Continue down Rue du Vieux Sextier to the big square (across the busy street) and find the big, boxy market building with the vertical (hydroponic) garden growing out its front wall.

Market (Les Halles): In 1970, the town's open-air market was replaced by this modern one (more efficient, with a parking garage overhead, hoping to compete with supermarkets in the suburbs). The market's jungle-like hydroponic green wall reflects the changes of seasons and helps mitigate its otherwise stark exterior (Tue-Sun until 13:00, closed Mon). Step inside for a sensual experience of organic breads, olives, and festival-of-mold cheeses. Cheap cafés, bars, and good cheese shops are mostly on the right—the stinky fish stalls are on the left. This is a terrific place for lunch (doors close weekdays at 13:30,  Sat-Sun at 14:00)—especially if you'd fancy a big plate of mixed seafood with a glass of white wine (see "Eating in Avignon," later, for several good lunch options).

• *Walk through the market and exit out the back door, then turn left on Rue de la Bonneterie ("Street of Hosiery"), which has recently transitioned from a busy street for cars to a more peaceful—and therefore more prosperous—pedestrian zone lined with triple-A shops (alternative, arty, and artisan). Track the street for five minutes to the plane trees, where it becomes...*

Rue des Teinturiers: This "Street of the Dyers" is a bohemian-friendly, tree- and stream-lined lane, home to earthy cafés and galleries. This was the cloth industry's dyeing and textile center in the 1800s. The stream is a branch of the Sorgue River. Those stylish Provençal fabrics and patterns you see for sale everywhere were first made here, based on printed fabrics originally imported from India.

About three small bridges down, you'll pass the Grey Penitents chapel on the right. The upper facade shows the GPs, who dressed up in robes and pointy hoods to do their anonymous good deeds back in the 13th century. (While the American KKK dresses in hoods to hide their hateful racism, these hoods symbolized how all are equal in God's eyes.) As you stroll on, you'll see the work of amateur sculptors, who have carved whimsical car barriers out of limestone. Fun restaurants on this atmospheric street are recommended later, under "Eating in Avignon."

• *Farther down Rue des Teinturiers, you'll come to the...*

Waterwheel: Standing here, imagine the Sorgue River—which hits the mighty Rhône in Avignon—being broken into several canals in order to turn 23 such wheels. Starting in about 1800, waterwheels powered the town's industries. The little cogwheel above the big one could be shoved into place, kicking another machine into gear behind the wall.

• *If you're ready for a meal or drinks in the Rue des Teinturiers quarter, see "Eating in Avignon," later. To return to the center of town, double back on Rue des Teinturiers and turn left on Rue des Lices, which traces the first medieval wall. (A "lice" is the no-man's-land along a protective wall.) After a long block you'll pass a striking four-story building that was a home for the poor in the 1600s, an army barracks in the 1800s, a fine-arts school in the 1900s, and is a deluxe condominium today (much of this neighborhood is going high-class residential). Eventually you'll return to Rue de la République, Avignon's main drag.*

More Sights in Avignon

Most of Avignon's top sights are covered earlier by my self-guided walks. With more time, consider these options.

Anglandon Museum (Musée Anglandon)

Visiting this museum is like being invited into the elegant home of a rich and passionate art collector. It houses a small but enjoyable collection of art from Post-Impressionists to Cubists (including Paul Cézanne, Vincent van Gogh, Edgar Degas, and Pablo Picasso), with re-created art studios and furnishings from many periods. It's a quiet place with a few superb paintings and good temporary exhibits.

Cost and Hours: €8, Tue-Sun 13:00-18:00, closed Mon, 5 Rue Laboureur, tel. 04 90 82 29 03, www.anglandon.com.

Calvet Museum (Musée Calvet)

This fine-arts museum, ignored by most, impressively displays a collection highlighting French Baroque works and Northern masters such as Hieronymus Bosch and Pieter Bruegel. You'll find a

PROVENCE

few gems upstairs: a painting each by Manet, Sisley, Géricault, and David. On the ground floor is a room dedicated to more modern artists, with works by Soutine, Bonnard, and Vlamnick. The Calvet Museum's antiquities collection, Le Musée Lapidaire, is hosted in a church a few blocks away at 27 Rue de la République.

Cost and Hours: Free, includes audioguide and Le Musée Lapidaire, Wed-Mon 10:00-13:00 & 14:00-18:00, closed Tue, in the western half of town at 65 Rue Joseph Vernet, tel. 04 90 86 33 84, www.musee-calvet.org.

Collection Lambert

This modern art museum, situated in a grand 18th-century mansion, features works from the 1960s to the present. It came from the famous art dealer Yvon Lambert, who was determined to make well-known contemporary art accessible outside Paris. The recommended Le Violette restaurant in the courtyard is worth the visit alone.

Cost and Hours: €10, Tue-Sun 11:00-18:00, closed Mon except July-Aug when it's open until 19:00, 5 Rue Violette, tel. 04 90 16 56 20, www.collectionlambert.fr.

NEAR AVIGNON
▲Tower of Philip the Fair (Tour Philippe-le-Bel)

Built to protect access to St. Bénezet Bridge in 1307, this hulking tower, located in nearby Villeneuve-lès-Avignon, offers a terrific view over Avignon and the Rhône basin.

Cost and Hours: €2.50; Tue-Sun 10:00-12:30 & 14:00-18:00, Feb-April and Nov 14:00-17:00 only, closed Dec-Jan and Mon year-round.

Getting There: To reach the tower from Avignon, drive five minutes (cross Daladier Bridge, follow signs to *Villeneuve-lès-Avignon*), or take bus #5 (2/hour, bus stops just outside Place du Crillon, see the "Avignon" map).

Sleeping in Avignon

Hotel values are better in Arles. Avignon is crazy during its July festival—you must book long ahead and pay inflated prices. Drivers should ask about parking discounts through hotels.

NEAR CENTRE-VILLE STATION

These listings are a 5- to 10-minute walk from the Centre-Ville train station.

$$ Hôtel Bristol** is a big, professionally run place on the main drag, offering predictable "American" comforts at fair rates. Enjoy spacious public spaces, large rooms, big elevators, and a generous buffet breakfast (family rooms, pay parking—reserve ahead, 44 Cours Jean Jaurès, tel. 04 90 16 48 48, www.bristol-avignon. com, contact@bristol-avignon.com).

$ Hôtel Ibis Centre Gare*** offers tight-but-tasteful comfort and quiet near the central train and bus stations (42 Boulevard St. Roch, tel. 04 90 85 38 38, www.ibishotel.com, h0944@accor.com).

$ Hôtel Colbert** is on a quiet lane, with a dozen spacious rooms gathered on four floors around a skinny spiral staircase (no elevator). Patrice decorates each room as if it were his own, with a colorful (occasionally erotic) flair. There are warm public spaces and a sweet little patio (some tight bathrooms, rooms off the patio can be musty, closed Nov-March, 7 Rue Agricol Perdiguier, tel. 04 90 86 20 20, www.lecolbert-hotel.com, contact@avignon-hotel-colbert.com).

$ At Hôtel Boquier,** helpful owner Frédéric offers 13 quiet, good-value, and homey rooms under wood beams in a central location (family rooms, steep and narrow stairways to some rooms, no elevator, pay parking nearby, near the TI at 6 Rue du Portail Boquier, tel. 04 90 82 34 43, www.hotel-boquier.com, contact@ hotel-boquier.com).

¢ Hôtel les Corps Saints,** run by young Agnes and Fabrice, rents 16 bright rooms with tight baths at fair rates (no elevator, 17 Rue Agricol Perdiguier, tel. 04 90 86 14 46, www.hotel-les-corps-saints.fr, corpssaints.avignon@gmail.com).

IN THE CENTER, NEAR PLACE DE L'HORLOGE

$$$$ Hôtel d'Europe,***** one of Avignon's most prestigious addresses, lets peasants sleep affordably—but only if they land one of the six reasonable *"classique"* rooms. With formal staff, spacious lounges, and a shady courtyard, the hotel is located on the handsome Place Crillon, near the river (pay garage parking, near Daladier Bridge at 12 Place Crillon, tel. 04 90 14 76 76, www.heurope. com, reservations@heurope.com). Readers seeking top comfort should compare this hotel with Hôtel la Mirande, next.

$$$$ Hôtel la Mirande***** pampers its guests with traditional luxury in a quiet, central location behind the Palace of the Popes. The welcoming staff delivers service with a smile, public spaces are comfy and welcoming, and the rooms are exquisitely decorated. The hotel also houses a well-respected restaurant (4 Place de l'Amirande, tel. 04 90 14 20 20, www.la-mirande.fr).

$$$ Hôtel de l'Horloge**** is as central as it gets—on Place de l'Horloge. It offers 66 comfortable rooms, some with terraces and views of the city and the Palace of the Popes (1 Rue Félicien David, tel. 04 90 16 42 00, www.hotel-avignon-horloge.com, hotel. horloge@hotels-ocre-azur.com).

$$$ Hôtel Mercure Palais des Papes,**** about a block from

Avignon Hotels & Restaurants

To ℙ (free), Villeneuve & 16

15

ℙ de l'Ile Piot

N-580

Île de la Barthelasse

VIEW WALK

ST. BENEZET BRIDGE

PORTE DU ROCHER

SHUTTLE BOAT

BLVD. DE LA

PORTE DU RHONE

10

PETIT PALAIS MUSEUM

Palace Square

Jardin du Rocher des Doms

N.D. DES DOMS

PALACE OF THE POPES

Rhône River

PONT E. DALADIER

RUE DU RHONE

RUE GRANDE FUSTERIE

ST. ETIENNE

RUE BALANCE

PORTE DE L'OULLE

#5 ℬ

Place Crillon

6

VERNET

24   14

19

RUE

9

PEYROLERIE

7

R. BANASTERIE

17

R. RHONE

8

Place de l'Horloge

20

ST. PIERRE

Place Carnot

30

13

RUE

SYNA-GOGUE

RUE JOSEPH

RUE PETITE FUST

R. ST. AGRICOL

R. FAVART

R. MARCHANDS

R. BANCASSE

RUE GALANTE

RUE ROUGE

R. VIEUX SEXTIER

23

ALLEE DE L'OULLE

BLVD. DE L'OULLE

RUE DE L'OULLE

RUE REMPART DE L'OULLE

ℙ

ℙ

RUE VICTOR HUGO

RUE D'ANNANELLE

CALVET MUSEUM

R. VERNET

RUE DE LA REPUBLIQUE

RUE LA BOUQUERIE

Place St. Didier

R. ROI

OLD CITY WALLS

RUE REMPART ST-DOMINIQUE

RUE VELOUTERIE

RUE JOSEPH VERNET

34

Musée Lapidaire

ANGLADON MUSEUM

21

R. H. FABRE

RUE SAINT-MICHEL

PORTE ST. ROCH

BLVD. RASPAIL

22   4

COLLECTION LAMBERT

RUE SAINT CHARLES

COURS JEAN JAURES

RUE PERDIGUIER

1   5   3

Place des Corps-Saints

31

PORTE ST. MICHEL

RUE

To Nimes via A-9

RUE REMPART SAINT-ROCH

POST

Place de la République

AVE. DE 7EME GENIE

PORTE ST. CHARLES

BLVD. SAINT-ROCH

PORTE DE LA REPUBLIQUE

ℙ   ℙ

2

BUS STATION

🚲

CENTRE-VILLE TRAIN STATION

AVE. EISENHOWER

AVE. MONCLAR

AVE. SAINT-RUF

PROVENCE

200 Meters

200 Yards

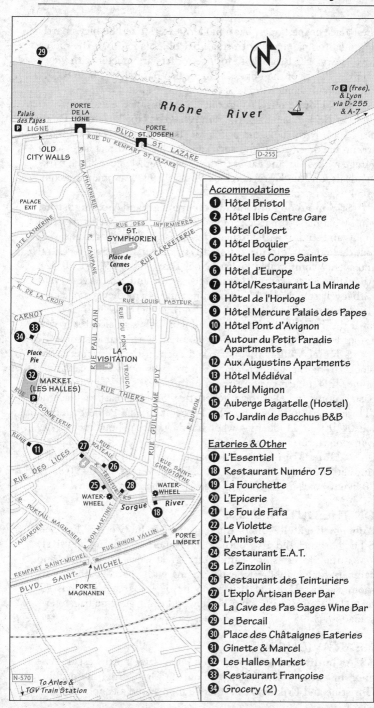

<u>Accommodations</u>
1 Hôtel Bristol
2 Hôtel Ibis Centre Gare
3 Hôtel Colbert
4 Hôtel Boquier
5 Hôtel les Corps Saints
6 Hôtel d'Europe
7 Hôtel/Restaurant La Mirande
8 Hôtel de l'Horloge
9 Hôtel Mercure Palais des Papes
10 Hôtel Pont d'Avignon
11 Autour du Petit Paradis Apartments
12 Aux Augustins Apartments
13 Hôtel Médiéval
14 Hôtel Mignon
15 Auberge Bagatelle (Hostel)
16 To Jardin de Bacchus B&B

<u>Eateries & Other</u>
17 L'Essentiel
18 Restaurant Numéro 75
19 La Fourchette
20 L'Epicerie
21 Le Fou de Fafa
22 Le Violette
23 L'Amista
24 Restaurant E.A.T.
25 Le Zinzolin
26 Restaurant des Teinturiers
27 L'Explo Artisan Beer Bar
28 La Cave des Pas Sages Wine Bar
29 Le Bercail
30 Place des Châtaignes Eateries
31 Ginette & Marcel
32 Les Halles Market
33 Restaurant Françoise
34 Grocery (2)

PROVENCE

the Palace of the Popes, has a modern exterior and 86 big, smartly designed rooms, many with small balconies (about half the rooms have views over Place de l'Horloge, others are quieter with views over the Palace of the Popes, 1 Rue Jean Vilar, tel. 04 90 80 93 00, www.mercure.com, h1952@accor.com).

$$$ **Hôtel Pont d'Avignon,****** just inside the walls near St. Bénezet Bridge, is part of the same chain as Hôtel Mercure Palais des Papes, with the same prices for its 87 rooms. There's an airy atrium breakfast room and small garden terrace (direct access to a garage makes parking easier than at the other Mercure hotel, parking deals, on Rue Ferruce, tel. 04 90 80 93 93, www.mercure.com, h0549@accor.com).

$$ **Autour du Petit Paradis Apartments** and **Aux Augustins,** run by Sabine and Patrick, offer 22 contemporary, well-furnished rooms and studios with kitchenettes spread over two locations. Autour du Petit Paradis, in a restored 17th-century mansion, is central and plenty comfortable (5 Rue Noël Biret, tel. 04 90 81 00 42); Augustins is less central with larger rooms and a nicer courtyard with lovely stonework dating from its time as a medieval monastery (16 Rue Carreterie, tel. 04 84 51 01 44). Either place will pick you up at the TGV station for a fee, and neither has an elevator (www.autourdupetitparadis.com, contact@autourdupetitparadis.com).

$ **Hôtel Médiéval,**** burrowed deep in the old center a few blocks from the Church of St. Pierre, was built as a cardinal's home. This stone mansion's grand staircase leads to 35 comfortable, pastel rooms (no elevator, kitchenettes, 5 blocks east of Place de l'Horloge, behind Church of St. Pierre at 15 Rue Petite Saunerie, tel. 04 90 86 11 06, www.hotelmedieval.com, hotel.medieval@wanadoo.fr, run by Régis).

¢ **Hôtel Mignon*** is a sleepable, homey one-star place with tiny bathrooms (no elevator, 12 Rue Joseph Vernet, tel. 04 90 82 17 30, www.hotel-mignon.com, reservation@hotel-mignon.fr).

ON THE OUTSKIRTS

Auberge Bagatelle offers dirt-cheap beds in two buildings—a $ budget hotel and a ¢ youth hostel—and has a young and lively vibe, café, grocery store, launderette, great views of Avignon, and campers for neighbors (cheaper rooms with shared bath, family rooms, across Daladier Bridge on Ile de la Barthelasse, bus #5, tel. 04 90 86 30 39, www.hostelworld.com, auberge.bagatelle@wanadoo.fr).

NEAR AVIGNON

$$ At **Jardin de Bacchus,** a 15-minute drive northwest of Avignon by car and convenient to Pont du Gard, English-speaking Christine and Erik offer two double rooms (and a couple of apart-

ments) in their village home overlooking the famous rosé vineyards of Tavel (includes breakfast, good €30 dinner if booked in advance, swimming pool, great patio, possible bike rentals, mobile 06 74 41 77 94, www.jardindebacchus.fr, jardindebacchus@gmail.com). By car, it's just off the A-9 autoroute (exit 22).

Eating in Avignon

Avignon offers a good range of restaurants and settings, from lively squares to atmospheric streets. Skip the crowd-pleasing places on Place de l'Horloge and enjoy better value and atmosphere elsewhere. Avignon is brimming with delightful squares and back streets lined with little restaurants eager to feed you. At the finer places, reservations are generally smart (especially on weekends); your hotel can call for you.

FINE DINING WORTH THE SPLURGE

$$$$ La Mirande, inside the recommended five-star hotel just behind the Pope's Palace, transports you into a historic and aristocratic world. What was once a cardinal's palace today is a romantic oasis where you'll dine in 18th-century splendor with elegant service and presentation. Dress as nicely as you can (dine inside or in the queenly garden, closed Tue-Wed, €50 *plats,* enticing five-course €65 *menu* must be ordered by everyone in your party, 4 Place de l'Amirande, tel. 04 90 14 20 20, www.la-mirande.fr).

$$$ L'Essentiel is modern, spacious, and bright, with traditional French dishes. It has classy presentation and ambience, and seating indoors or outdoors on a romantic back terrace (€36-48 *menus,* closed Sun-Mon, reservations recommended, 2 Rue Petite Fusterie, tel. 04 90 85 87 12, www.restaurantlessentiel.com).

$$$ Restaurant Numéro 75 fills the well-worn Pernod mansion (of *pastis* liquor fame) with a romantic, chandeliered, Old World dining hall that extends to a leafy, gravelly courtyard. They serve delightful lunch salads, fish is a forte, and the French cuisine is beautifully presented (Mon-Sat 12:00-14:00 & 19:30-22:00, closed Sun, 75 Rue Guillaume Puy, tel. 04 90 27 16 00, www.numero75.com).

$$$ La Fourchette is an inviting, dressy place graced with warm colors and spacious indoor-only seating. The cuisine mixes traditional French with Provençal. Book ahead for this popular place (closed Sun-Mon, 17 Rue Racine, tel. 04 90 85 20 93, www. la-fourchette.net).

DINING WELL IN THE OLD CENTER ON A MODERATE BUDGET

$$$ **L'Epicerie** sits alone under green awnings on the romantic Place St-Pierre square and is ideal for dinner outside (or in the small but cozy interior). It has an accessible menu with Mediterranean dishes and big, splittable *assiettes* (sample plates), each with a theme (daily, 10 Place St-Pierre, tel. 04 90 82 74 22, Magda speaks English).

$$$ **Le Fou de Fafa** is a warm, spacious, 12-table place where delightful Antonia serves while her husband cooks (inside dining only, book ahead or arrive early, Tue-Sat from 18:30, closed Sun-Mon, 17 Rue des Trois Faucons, tel. 04 32 76 35 13).

$$ **Le Violette,** in the peaceful courtyard of the Collection Lambert modern art museum, serves fresh modern cuisine and is gorgeous when lit by the museum rooms at night (July-Aug daily, Sept-June closed Sun and Mon, 5 Rue Violette, tel. 04 90 85 36 42).

$$ **L'Amista** ("the spot to meet friends") is a cozy, youthful, and welcoming place on a quiet lane with indoor and outdoor seating. Run by Delphine, it offers a fun Provençal/Spanish-inspired menu that always includes vegetarian options. Tapas-style plates are great for sharing (daily 12:00-15:00 & 18:30-22:00, closed Sun-Mon off-season, 23 Rue Bonneterie, tel. 09 86 19 36 86).

$$ **Restaurant E.A.T.,** whose name stands for "Estaminet, Arômes et Tentations" (a small restaurant with aroma and temptations), is just off Place du Crillon. It's locally popular, serving eclectic and fun options with international twists (closed Wed, reservations recommended, 8 Rue Mazan, tel. 04 90 83 46 74, www. restaurant-eat.com).

BOHEMIAN CHIC, CANALSIDE ON RUE DES TEINTURIERS

Rue des Teinturiers' fun concentration of midrange, popular-with-the-locals eateries justifies the long walk on a balmy evening. (In bad weather, it's dead.) It's a trendy, youthful area, spiffed up but with little hint of tourism. You'll find wine bars, vegetarian options, and live music at rickety metal tables under shady trees along the canal. I'd walk the street's entire length to find the best ambience before making a choice. Note that the finer Restaurant Numéro 75, listed earlier, is just around the corner.

$$ **Le Zinzolin** is a big bohemian diner serving European cuisine with a few vegetarian options, including lots of salads in the

summer. The atmosphere is good inside and out (daily, 22 Rue des Teinturiers, tel. 04 90 82 41 55).

$$$ Restaurant des Teinturiers, run by chef Guillaume, combines a casual setting with upscale nouvelle French cuisine and presentation. Guests leave comments on the chalkboard about their "semi-gastronomic meals" (closed Wed and Sun, reservations smart, near the waterwheel at 5 Rue des Teinturiers, tel. 04 90 33 43 83, www.restaurantdesteinturiers.com).

Drinks in the Rue des Teinturiers Quarter: For a break from sightseeing or a relaxing night spot for a drink, this pedestrian-only street has two particularly good watering holes: a craft beer place at the start and a laid-back hippie wine bar at the lazy waterwheel. **L'Explo Artisan Beer Bar** is like a beer-lovers club on a canal. It's mod, minimal, and cheap, with a convivial terrace. They serve 10 craft beers (no bottles) all on tap, and sausage and cheese plates to help soak it up (closed Sun-Mon, 2 Rue des Teinturiers, tel. 04 90 31 06 35). **La Cave des Pas Sages,** a down-and-dirty wine bar, is just right to linger with the locals over a cheap glass of regional wine or beer. Choose from the blackboard by the bar that lists all the open bottles, then join the gang outside by the canal (Mon-Sat 12:00-24:00, closed Sun, 41 Rue des Teinturiers, tel. 04 32 74 25 86).

LOCAL FAVORITE ACROSS THE RHÔNE

$$$ Le Bercail offers a fun opportunity to cross the river, get out of town, and take in the country air with a terrific riverfront view of Avignon, all while enjoying big portions of Provençal cooking. Make a reservation before trekking out there (daily May-Oct, often closed off-season, tel. 04 90 82 20 22, www.restaurant-lebercail.fr). Take the free shuttle boat (located near St. Bénezet Bridge) to the Ile de la Barthelasse, turn right, and walk five minutes. As the boat usually stops running at about 18:00 (20:45 in July-Aug), you can either taxi back or walk 25 minutes along the pleasant riverside path and over Daladier Bridge.

GOOD BUDGET PLACES IN THE CENTER
Place des Châtaignes

This "square of the chestnut trees" (technically Place du Cloître Saint-Pierre) offers cheap meals and a fun commotion of tables.

$ La Pause Gourmande, a tiny bakery/deli with the best tables on the square, is great for salads, sandwiches, and daily *plats* (great *fougasse;* Mon-Sat 6:00-20:00, closed Sun, tel. 04 90 86 10 84).

$ Crêperie La Flourdiliz is a cheery, traditional Breton place with an open kitchen, a classy-for-a-*crêperie* interior, and great seating on the square (closed Sun-Tue, tel. 04 90 22 28 14).

PROVENCE

$ La Cantine is a convenient place popular for its self-serve, pay-by-weight, cafeteria line (Tue-Sat 11:00-16:00, closed Sun-Mon, a few steps away at 6 Rue Armand de Pontmartin, tel. 09 72 88 67 44).

Place des Corps-Saints

This welcoming square offers the best feeling of a neighborhood dining, drinking, and simply living outdoors together. It's great for outdoor dining in Avignon, with several eateries in all price ranges sharing the same great setting under big plane trees. Survey the scene: tables crammed into every nook and cranny, standard café fare, Italian options, a pizza joint, a wine bar, and finer dining choices. **$ Ginette & Marcel: Bistrot à Tartines** serves salads, big slices of toast with a variety of toppings, and has tasty desserts (daily 11:00-late, tel. 04 90 85 58 70).

Les Halles and Place Pie

Avignon's youth make their home on Place Pie, a big square filled with cafés. At the south end of the square is Les Halles, Avignon's farmers market hall (described in my "Discovering Avignon's Back Streets Walk," earlier). Les Halles is an ideal lunch spot, with a handful of wonderfully characteristic and cheap places serving locals the freshest of food surrounded by all that market fun (closed Mon and after 13:00). If picnicking, there are plenty of benches under the trees outside on the square.

Les Halles Orientation: Use the main aisle to orient yourself (enter under vertical garden). The first place on the left is **Comptoir du Sud** (fun sampling of edibles from the South); down the aisle on the right is a traditional café where you can BYOC (C for croissant); the mid-center aisle on the right is the "250 cheeses shop"; at the end of the center aisle on the right, behind bakery with dangling hats, is **Cuisine Centr'Halles** (described below); the WC is in the far-left corner, and **fish bars** are in the two back corners. Either shop will assemble the plate of your fishy dreams at a painless price (€18 for an assortment for two). While the prices at both these places are about the same, the place in the far-left corner feels like a little restaurant (open daily) and the one in the far-right corner more like a picnic at the marina (Fri-Sun only, Natalies).

$$$ Cuisine Centr'Halles is where Jonathan Chiri (an American chef who landed here 14 years ago) serves €20 tasting plates (land or sea) offering the best of the market in an elegant setting. He also runs two-hour market tours (€40, includes tapenade cooking and tasting with wine, Wed-Sat 9:00, mobile 06 46 89 85 33, www.jonathanchiri.com).

$ Restaurant Françoise is a fine deli-café a block off Place Pie, where fresh-baked tarts—savory and sweet—and a variety of salads and soups make a healthful meal, and vegetarian options are plentiful. Order at the counter and eat inside or out (Mon-Sat 8:00-21:00, closed Sun, 6 Rue Général Leclerc, tel. 04 32 76 24 77).

Avignon Connections

BY TRAIN

There are two train stations in Avignon: the suburban TGV station and the Centre-Ville station in the city center (€1.60 shuttle trains connect the stations, buy ticket from machine on platforms or at a counter, included with rail pass, 2/hour, 5 minutes). TGV trains usually serve the TGV station only, though a few depart from Centre-Ville station (check your ticket). The TGV station has a broad choice of car rental agencies; only Avis is at Centre-Ville station. Some cities are served by slower local trains from Centre-Ville station as well as by faster TGV trains from the TGV station; I've listed the most convenient stations for each trip.

From Avignon's Centre-Ville Station to: Arles (roughly hourly, 20 minutes, less frequent in the afternoon), **Orange** (hourly, 20 minutes), **Nîmes** (hourly, 30 minutes), **Isle-sur-la-Sorgue** (hourly on weekdays, 5/day on weekends, 30 minutes), **Lyon** (hourly, 2 hours; faster from TGV station), **Carcassonne** (8/day, 7 with transfer in Narbonne or Nîmes, 3 hours), **Barcelona** (2/day, 6 hours with changes).

From Avignon's TGV Station to: Nice (hourly, most by TGV, 4 hours, many require transfer in Marseille), **Marseille** (hourly, 35 minutes), **Cassis** (7/day, transfer in Marseille, 1.5 hours), **Aix-en-Provence TGV** (hourly, 30 minutes), **Lyon** (hourly, 70 minutes, slower from Centre-Ville station), **Paris' Gare de Lyon** (hourly direct, 2.5 hours), **Paris' Charles de Gaulle airport** (7/day, 3 hours), **Barcelona** (1/day direct, 4 hours).

BY BUS

The bus station *(gare routière)* is just past and below Hôtel Ibis, to the right as you exit the train station. Nearly all buses leave from this station (a few leave from the ring road outside the station—ask, buy tickets on bus or at bus station). Service is reduced or nonexistent on Sundays and holidays. Check your departure time beforehand, and make sure to verify your destination with the driver. Buses are cheap in this region, figure €1.50-5 for most trips. When connecting big cities (like Avignon and Aix-en-Provence), check FlixBus and Ouibus schedules as well as the local lines listed below (see the "Transportation" section of the Practicalities chapter for more on these bus companies).

PROVENCE

From Avignon to Pont du Gard: Take bus #A15 to this famous Roman aqueduct (5/day Mon-Fri, 3/day Sat-Sun, 1 hour).

By Bus to Other Regional Destinations: Arles train station (8/day, 1 hour, leaves from TGV station), **Nîmes** (10/day, 1 hour), **Aix-en-Provence** (6/day Mon-Sat, 3/day Sun, 75 minutes, faster and easier than train), **Uzès** (5/day, 80 minutes, stops at Pont du Gard); **St-Rémy-de-Provence** (Cartreize #57 bus, 12/day Mon-Fri, 6/day Sat-Sun, 45 minutes); **Orange** (Mon-Sat hourly, 5/day Sun, 45 minutes—take the train instead); **Isle-sur-la-Sorgue** (bus #6, 12/day Mon-Sat, 2/day Sun, 45 minutes). For the **Côtes du Rhône** area, the bus runs to **Vaison-la-Romaine, Sablet,** and **Séguret** (10/day Mon-Sat, 2/day Sun), **Nyons** (3-6/day; all buses pass through Orange—faster to take train to Orange, and transfer to bus there). Buses to the **Luberon** area are too infrequent to be workable.

Pont du Gard

Throughout the ancient world, aqueducts were like flags of stone that heralded the greatness of Rome. A visit to this impressively preserved sight still works to proclaim the wonders of that age.

In the first century AD, the Romans built a 30-mile aqueduct that ran to Nîmes, one of ancient Europe's largest cities. While most of it ran on or below the ground, at Pont du Gard the aqueduct spans a canyon on a massive bridge over the Gardon River—one of the most remarkable surviving Roman ruins anywhere. The aqueduct supported a small canal that dropped one inch for every 350 feet, supplying the city of Nîmes with nine million gallons of water per day (about 100 gallons per second).

Allow about a full four hours for visiting Pont du Gard (including transportation time from Avignon).

GETTING THERE

The famous aqueduct is between Remoulins and Vers-Pont du Gard on D-981, 17 miles from Nîmes and 13 miles from Avignon.

By Car: Pont du Gard is a 30-minute drive due west of Avignon (follow N-100 from Avignon, tracking signs to *Nîmes* and *Remoulins,* then *Pont du Gard* and *Rive Gauche*), and 45 minutes northwest of Arles (via Tarascon on D-6113). If going to Arles from Pont du Gard, follow signs to *Nîmes* (not *Avignon*), then D-6113, or faster A-54 (autoroute) to Arles.

By Bus: Buses run to Pont du Gard (on the Rive Gauche side) from Avignon (#A15, 5/day Mon-Fri, 3/day Sat-Sun, 1 hour), Nîmes, and Uzès.

PROVENCE

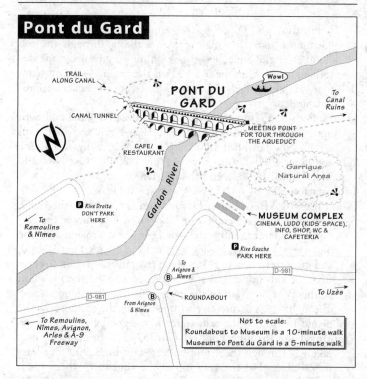

Buses stop at the traffic roundabout 400 yards from the museum (stop name: Rond Point Pont du Gard; see "Pont du Gard" map). If leaving by bus, make sure you're waiting on the correct side of the traffic circle (stops have schedules posted), and wave your hand to signal the bus to stop for you—otherwise, it may drive on by. Buy your ticket when you get on and verify your destination with the driver.

By Taxi: From Avignon, it's about €60 for a taxi to Pont du Gard (tel. 04 90 82 20 20). Consider splurging on a taxi to the aqueduct in the morning, then take the early afternoon bus back.

ORIENTATION TO PONT DU GARD

There are two riversides at Pont du Gard: the Left Bank (Rive Gauche) and the Right Bank (Rive Droite). Park on the Rive Gauche (parking validated with ticket purchase), where you'll find the museums, ticket booth, TI, cafeteria, WCs, and shops—all built into a modern plaza. A restaurant and ice-cream kiosk are on the Rive Droite side. You'll see the aqueduct in two parts: first the informative museum complex, then the actual river gorge spanned by the ancient bridge.

Cost: €8.50 Discovery Pass includes access to the aqueduct, mu-

PROVENCE

seum, film, and outdoor *garrigue* nature area; €6 extra for a 45-minute tour that may include walking through the top channel of the aqueduct—book online in advance, tour described below. Skip the €15.50 Pass Patrimoine—the museum tour is too long. Kids 6-17 pay €7 for any of the ticket options; kids under 6 are free.

Hours: Pont du Gard open daily May 9:00-21:00, June and Sept until 22:00; July-Aug until 23:00; Feb-April and Oct until 20:00, Nov-Jan until 18:00. Museum open daily April-June and Sept 9:00-19:00, July-Aug until 20:00, Oct-Nov and March until 18:00, Dec-Feb until 17:00.

Information: Tel. 04 66 37 50 99, www.pontdugard.fr.

Pont du Gard After Hours: During summer months, the site is open late so that people can hike, enjoy a picnic or the riverside restaurant, and watch the light show projected on the monument. The parking lot is staffed and guarded until 24:00, and after the museum closes you'll pay only €5/person to enter (free for kids under 17). If you don't care to see the museum, seeing Pont du Gard in the evening is dramatic (and cheap). The light show is projected from the north, so those in the picnic area and at the restaurant enjoy a good view.

Walking Tour Through Pont Du Gard: The 45-minute tour may take you through the 4-foot-wide, 6-foot-high, 900-foot-long water channel at the very top of the aqueduct, where you'll walk the route of the water high above the river below. Guides range in quality from mediocre to excellent, provide commentary in French and English, and lead groups of up to 30 people. The massive calcium buildup lining the channel from more than 400 years of flowing water is impressive to see. Manhole cover-like openings allow light in, though a flashlight is helpful to discern details.

Canoe Rental: Floating under Pont du Gard by canoe is an unforgettable experience. **Collias Canoes** will pick you up at Pont du Gard (or elsewhere, if prearranged) and shuttle you to the town of Collias. You'll float down the river to the nearby town of Remoulins, where they'll pick you up and take you back to Pont du Gard (€23, kids under 12-€12, usually 2 hours—though you can take as long as you like, reserve the day before in July-Aug, tel. 04 66 22 87 20, www.canoe-collias.com).

Plan Ahead for Swimming and Hiking: Pont du Gard is perhaps best enjoyed on your back and in the water—bring along a swimsuit and flip-flops for the rocks. (Local guides warn that the bridge can create whirlpools and be dangerous to swim under.) The best Pont du Gard viewpoints are up steep hills with uneven footing—bring good shoes, too.

PROVENCE

SIGHTS AT PONT DU GARD
▲Museum

In this state-of-the-art museum (well presented in English), you'll enter to the sound of water and understand the critical role fresh water played in the Roman "art of living." You'll see copies of lead pipes, faucets, and siphons; walk through a mock rock quarry; and learn how they moved those huge rocks into place and how those massive arches were made. A wooden model shows how Roman engineers determined the proper slope. While actual artifacts from the aqueduct are few, the exhibit shows the immensity of the undertaking as well as the payoff. Imagine the jubilation when this extravagant supply of water finally tumbled into Nîmes. A relaxing highlight is the scenic video of a helicopter ride along the entire 30-mile course of the aqueduct, from its start at Uzès all the way to the Castellum in Nîmes.

Other Activities

Skip the 15-minute film showing aqueduct images with no captions or information (in the museum building). The nearby kids' museum, called *Ludo,* offers a scratch-and-sniff teaching experience (in English) of various aspects of Roman life and the importance of water. The extensive outdoor *garrigue* natural area, closer to the aqueduct, features historic crops and landscapes of the Mediterranean.

▲▲▲Viewing the Aqueduct

A broad walkway from the museum complex leads in 10 minutes to the aqueduct. Until a few years ago, this was an actual road—

adjacent to the aqueduct—that had spanned the river since 1743. Before crossing the bridge, walk to a terrific riverside viewpoint by continuing under the aqueduct on a stony path, then find two staircases about 50 yards apart leading down to an unobstructed view of the world's second-highest standing Roman structure. (Rome's Colosseum is only six feet taller.)

This was the biggest bridge in the whole 30-mile-long aqueduct. The arches are twice the width of standard aqueducts, and the main arch is the largest the Romans ever built—80 feet across (the width of the river). The bridge is about 160 feet high and was originally about 1,200 feet long.

Though the distance from the source (in Uzès, on the museum side of the site) to Nîmes was only 12 miles as the eagle flew, engi-

PROVENCE

neers chose the most economical route, winding and zigzagging 30 miles. The water made the trip in 24 hours with a drop of only 40 feet. Ninety percent of the aqueduct is on or under the ground, but a few river canyons like this required bridges. A stone lid hides a four-foot-wide, six-foot-tall chamber lined with waterproof mortar that carried the stream for more than 400 years. For 150 years, this system provided Nîmes with good drinking water. Expert as the Romans were, they miscalculated the backup caused by a downstream corner, and had to add the thin extra layer you can see just under the lid to make the channel deeper.

The stones that jut out—giving the aqueduct a rough, unfinished appearance—supported the original scaffolding. The protuberances were left, rather than cut off, in anticipation of future repair needs. The lips under the arches supported wooden templates that allowed the stones in the round arches to rest on something until the all-important keystone was dropped into place. Each stone weighs from two to six tons. The structure stands with no mortar (except at the very top, where the water flowed)—taking full advantage of the innovative Roman arch, made strong by gravity.

Cross to the right bank for a closer look and the best views. Soon find steps leading up a short, steep trail (marked *View Point/Bellevedere*). Follow the short-but-rugged trail with the river to your right to several superb lookouts above the aqueduct.

Back on the museum side, steps lead up to the top of the Rive Gauche side of the aqueduct, where tours meet to enter the water channel. From here you can follow the canal path along a trail (marked with red-and-white horizontal lines) to find remains of the Roman canal (spur trails off this path lead to more panoramic views). Hikers can continue along the path, following the red-and-white markings that lead through a forest, after which you'll come across more remains of the canal (much of which are covered by vegetation). There's not much left to see because of medieval cannibalization—frugal builders couldn't resist the precut stones as they constructed area churches. The path continues for about 15 miles, but there's little reason to go farther.

Les Baux

The hilltop town of Les Baux crowns the rugged Alpilles (ahl-pee) mountains, evoking a tumultuous medieval history. Here, you can imagine the struggles of a strong community that lived a rough-and-tumble life—thankful more for their top-notch fortifications than for their dramatic views. It's mobbed with tourists most of the day, but Les Baux rewards those who arrive by 9:00  or after 17:30. (Although the hilltop citadel's entry closes at the end of the day, once you're inside, you're welcome to live out your medieval fantasies all night long, even with a picnic.) Sunsets are dramatic, the castle is brilliantly illuminated after dark, and nights in Les Baux are ghost town-peaceful.

GETTING THERE

By Car: Les Baux is a 20-minute drive from Arles. Follow signs for *Avignon,* then *Les Baux.* Drivers can combine Les Baux with St-Rémy (15 minutes away).

On arrival in Les Baux, drivers pay to park near the village or several blocks below. Parking is all metered and squirreled all around the site (first hour is free, €3-4/hour after that, half the meters accept coins). You can park a 15-minute walk away for free at the quarry-cave called Carrières de Lumières, but arrive early to land a spot (described later, under "Near Les Baux").

By Taxi: You can taxi from St-Rémy, then take another taxi to return to St-Rémy or to your home base. Figure €35 for a taxi one-way to Les Baux from Arles, €60 from Avignon, and €20 from St-Rémy (mobile 06 13 07 55 00).

By Minivan Tour: The best option for many is a minivan tour, which can be both efficient and economical (easiest from Avignon; see page 578).

Orientation to Les Baux

Les Baux is actually two visits in one: castle ruins perched on an almost lunar landscape, and a medieval town below. Savor the castle, then tour—or blitz—the lower town's polished-stone gauntlet of boutiques. While the town, which lives entirely off tourism, is packed with shops, cafés, and tourist knickknacks, the castle above stays manageable because crowds are dispersed over a big area. The town's main drag leads directly to the castle—just keep going uphill (a 10-minute walk).

Tourist Information: The TI is immediately on the left as you enter the village (daily 9:00-18:00, shorter hours and closed Sun in off-season). The TI can call a cab for you if you need one.

Sights in and near Les Baux

▲▲▲CASTLE RUINS (CHATEAU DES BAUX)

The sun-bleached ruins of the stone fortress of Les Baux are carved into, out of, and on top of a rock 650 feet above the valley floor.

Many of the ancient walls of this striking castle still stand as a testament to the proud past of this once-feisty village.

Cost: €9, €11 if there's "entertainment" (described below), €16 Pass Provence combo-ticket with Carrières de Lumières and Yves Brayer Museum (€18 if there is entertainment at Les Baux), entry fees include excellent audioguide.

Hours: Daily 9:00-19:00 (July-Aug until 20:00), March and Oct 9:30-18:30, Nov-Feb 10:00-17:00, www.chateau-baux-provence.com. If you're inside the castle when the entry closes, you can stay as long as you like.

Entertainment: Every weekend from April through early September and daily in summer, the castle presents medieval pageantry, tournaments, demonstrations of catapults and crossbows, and jousting matches. Pick up a schedule as you enter (or check online).

Picnicking: While no food or drink is sold inside the castle grounds, you're welcome to bring your own and use one of several picnic tables (the best view table is at the edge near the siege weaponry). Sunset dinner picnics are memorable.

Background: Imagine the importance of this citadel in the Middle Ages, when the Lords of Baux were notorious warriors

Les Baux

1 Le Mas d'Aigret Hôtel
2 Hostellerie de la Reine Jeanne

To Views, Carrières de Lumières
& St-Rémy
via most scenic route

D-27

100 Meters

100 Yards

To St-Rémy,
Maussane &
Le Paradou

P

D-27A

RUE PORTE MAGE

PORTE
MAGE

WC

DONJON

MUSEUM OF
SANTONS

Place
St-Louis
Jou

Uphill !

CASTLE
RUINS

P

GRAND RUE

LOWER

MANVILLE
MANSION
CITY HALL

EYGUIERES
GATE

TOWN

NEUVE

RENAISSANCE
WINDOW

CITADEL

YVES BRAYER
MUSEUM

FOURS

CHATEAU

R. L'ORME

CHAPEL OF
PENITENTS

ST.
VINCENT

WC

TICKETS &
ENTRY TO
CASTLE RUINS

Cemetery

TRENCAT

ST. BLAISE
CHAPEL

Cliffs

D-27

Cliffs

To Arles &
Fontvielle

CHARLOUN-RIEU
MONUMENT

PROVENCE

(who could trace their lineage back to one of the "three kings" of Christmas-carol fame, Balthazar). In the 11th century, Les Baux was a powerhouse in southern France, controlling about 80 towns. The Lords of Baux fought the counts of Barcelona for control of Provence...and eventually lost. But while in power, these guys were mean. One ruler enjoyed forcing unransomed prisoners to jump off his castle walls.

In 1426, Les Baux was incorporated into Provence and France. Not accustomed to playing second fiddle, Les Baux struggled with the French king, who responded by destroying the fortress in 1483. Later, Les Baux regained some importance and emerged as a center of Protestantism. Arguing with Rome was a high-stakes game in the 17th century, and Les Baux's association with the Huguenots brought destruction again in 1632 when Cardinal Richelieu (under King Louis XIII) demolished the castle. Louis rubbed salt in the wound by billing Les Baux's residents for his demolition expenses. The once-powerful town of 4,000 was forever crushed.

Visiting the Castle: Buy your ticket and inspect the models of Les Baux before its 17th-century destruction. Pick up your in-cluded audioguide when you enter. As you wander, key in the number for any of the 30 narrated stops that interest you.

The sight is exceptionally well presented. As you walk on the windblown spur (*baux* in French), you'll pass kid-thrilling medieval siege weaponry (go ahead, try the batter-ing ram). Good displays in English and big paintings in key locations help reconstruct the place. Imagine 4,000 people living up here. Notice the water-catchment system (a slanted field that caught rainwater and drained it into cisterns—necessary during a siege) and find the reservoir cut into the rock below the castle's highest point. Look for post holes throughout the stone walls that reveal where beams once supported floors.

For the most sensational views, climb to the blustery top of the citadel—hold tight if the mistral wind is blowing.

▲LOWER TOWN

After your castle visit, you can shop and eat your way back through the lower town. Or, escape some of the crowds by visiting these minor but worthwhile sights as you descend. I've linked the sights with walking directions.

• *Follow the main drag about 100 yards through the town and look for the flags marking...*

Manville Mansion City Hall

The 15th-century City Hall offers art exhibits under its cool vaults. It often flies the red-and-white flag of Monaco amid several others, a reminder that the Grimaldi family (longtime rulers of the tiny principality of Monaco) owned Les Baux until the French Revolution (1789). In fact, in 1982, Princess Grace Kelly and her royal husband, Prince Rainier Grimaldi, came to Les Baux to receive the key to the city.

Exit left and walk uphill 20 steps to the empty 1571 **Renaissance window frame.** This beautiful stone frame stands as a reminder of this town's Protestant history. This was probably a place of Huguenot worship—the words carved into the lintel, *Post tenebras lux,* were a popular Calvinist slogan: "After the shadow comes the light."

• *Continue walking uphill, and turn right on the first street to find the...*

Yves Brayer Museum (Musée Yves Brayer)

This enjoyable museum lets you peruse three small floors of luminous paintings (Van Gogh-like Expressionism) by Yves Brayer (1907-1990), who spent his final years here in Les Baux. Like Van Gogh, Brayer was inspired by all that surrounded him, and by his travels through Morocco, Spain, and the rest of the Mediterranean world. Ask about the English information sheet at the entry.

Cost and Hours: €8, covered by Pass Provence combo-ticket, daily 10:00-12:30 & 14:00-18:30, shorter hours and closed Tue and all of Jan-Feb in off-season, tel. 04 90 54 36 99, www.yvesbrayer. com.

• *Next door is...*

St. Vincent Church

This 12th-century Romanesque church was built short and wide to fit the terrain. The center chapel on the right (partially carved out of the rock) houses the town's traditional Provençal processional chariot. Each Christmas Eve, a ram pulls this cart—holding a lamb, symbolizing Jesus, and surrounded by candles—through town to the church.

• *As you leave the church, WCs are to the left (dug into the stone wall) and up the stairs. Directly in front of the church is a vast view, making clear the strategic value of this rocky bluff's natural fortifications. A few steps away is the...*

Chapel of Penitents

The elaborate Nativity scene painted by Yves Brayer covers the entire interior and illustrates the local legend that says Jesus was born in Les Baux.

• *As you leave the church, turn left and find the old town "laundry"—*

with a pig-snout faucet and 14th-century stone washing surface designed for short women.

Continue past the Yves Brayer Museum again, keep left, and curve down Rue de la Calade, passing a view café, the town's fortified wall, and one of its two gates. At the end you'll run into the...

Museum of Santons

This free and fun "museum" displays a collection of *santons* ("little saints"), popular folk figurines that decorate local Christmas mangers. Notice how the Nativity scene "proves" once again that Jesus was born in Les Baux. These painted clay dolls show off local dress and traditions (with good English descriptions).

NEAR LES BAUX
▲▲Carrières de Lumières (Quarries of Light)

A 15-minute walk from Les Baux, this colossal quarry-cave with immense vertical walls offers a mesmerizing sound-and-slide experience. Enter a darkened world filled with floor-to-ceiling images and booming music. Wander through a complex of cathedral-like aisles, transepts, and choirs (no seating provided) as you experience the spectacle. There's no storyline to follow, but information panels by the café give some background. The show lasts 40 minutes and runs continuously. If you'd like an intermission, you can exit the "show" into a part of the quarry that opens to the sky and take a break at the café before re-entering. Dress warmly, as the cave is cool.

Cost and Hours: €13, covered by Pass Provence combo-ticket; daily 9:30-19:30, Nov-March 10:00-18:00; tel. 04 90 54 47 37, www.carrieres-lumieres.com.

Sleeping and Eating in Les Baux

Sleeping: Take your pick of a small inn just outside Les Baux or another one within the lower town.

$$ Le Mas d'Aigret*** is a 10-minute walk east of Les Baux on the road to St-Rémy (D-27). From this comfy refuge, you can gaze up at the castle walls rising beyond the heated swimming pool, or enjoy valley views from the groomed terraces. The rooms are tastefully appointed—10 have great views and decks or terraces (convenient half-pen-

sion dinner and breakfast option, air-con, *pétanque* courts, tel. 04 90 54 20 00, www.masdaigret.com, contact@masdaigret.com).

$ Hostellerie de la Reine Jeanne** is just inside the gate to Les Baux, across from the TI. The easygoing owners rent four good-value rooms above their popular restaurant (family rooms, air-con, for view deck ask for *chambre avec terrasse*, tel. 04 90 54 32 06, www.la-reinejeanne.com, marc.braglia@wanadoo.fr).

Eating: You'll find quiet cafés with views as you follow my walking directions through Les Baux's lower town. The recommended **$ Hostellerie de la Reine Jeanne** offers friendly service and good-value meals indoors or out (open daily).

There are also a few worthwhile places in the untouristed village of **Maussane,** a few minutes' drive south of Les Baux (and 15 minutes from Arles). **Place de la Fontaine,** the town's central square, makes a good stop for café fare. **$ Pizza Brun** has tasty wood-fired pizza to take out or eat in with fun seating indoors and out (closed Mon, 1 Rue Edouard Foscalina; with your back to Place de la Fontaine, walk to the right for about 10 minutes and look for colored tables in an alleyway; tel. 04 90 54 40 73).

St-Rémy-de-Provence

Sophisticated and sassy, St-Rémy (sahn ray-mee) gave birth to Nostradamus and cared for a distraught artist. Today, it caters to shoppers and Van Gogh fans. A few minutes from the town center, you can visit the once-thriving Roman city called Glanum and the psychiatric ward where Vincent van Gogh was sent after lopping off his earlobe. Best of all is the chance to elbow your way through St-Rémy's raucous Wednesday market. A ring road hems in a fun-filled pedestrian-friendly center that's fully loaded with fine foods, beauticians, art galleries, and the latest Provençal fashions.

GETTING THERE

By Car: From Les Baux, St-Rémy is a spectacular 15-minute drive over the hills and through the woods. Roads D-5 and D-27 each provide scenic routes between these towns, making a loop drive between them worthwhile (the most scenic approach is on D-27).

Parking in St-Rémy is tricky; it's easiest at the pay lot by the TI. You can park for free but less centrally by the cemetery (see the "St-Rémy Area" map).

By Bus: It's one hour from Arles via **bus #54** (5/day Mon-Fri, 3/day Sat, none on Sun) or **bus #57** (6/day, daily July-Aug, Sat-Sun only in early May-June and Sept, none in off-season) and 45 minutes from Avignon via bus #57 (12/day Mon-Fri, 6/day Sat-Sun). If arriving in St-Rémy by bus, get off on the ring road at the République stop and continue uphill. The TI is a block up Avenue Durand Maillane (to the right).

By Taxi: From Les Baux, allow €20 one-way; from Avignon, count on €40 (mobile 06 14 81 34 85 or 06 25 17 00 73).

By Bike: Rent all sorts of bikes (including electric bikes) at **Sun-e-Bike** (2 Rue Camille Pelletan, tel. 04 32 62 08 39, www.location-velo-provence.com).

Orientation to St-Rémy-de-Provence

From St-Rémy's circular center, it's a 20-minute walk along a busy road with no sidewalk to Glanum and the St. Paul Monastery (Van Gogh's psychiatric hospital).

Tourist Information: The TI is two blocks toward Les Baux from the ring road (Mon-Sat 9:00-12:30 & 14:00-18:30, Sun 10:00-12:30, tel. 04 90 92 05 22, www.saintremy-de-provence.com). Pick up bus schedules, hiking maps, and a town map that includes Van Gogh's favorite painting locations. The TI can also call a cab for you.

Helpful Hints: St-Rémy's Wednesday **market** swallows Place de République with clothing, fabric, and bric-a-brac, and spreads along the town's traffic-free lanes selling anything Provençal. You'll find produce on picturesque Place Pelisser (by City Hall). The market wraps up by about 12:30.-

Sights in St-Rémy-de-Provence

St-Rémy's key sights—the ruins at Glanum and the hospital where Vincent van Gogh was treated—are an unappealing 20-minute walk south of the TI. If you're driving, you can park for free at the St. Paul Monastery (coming from Les Baux, it's the first right after passing Glanum) and walk a few minutes on a footpath to Glanum from there (or pay to park at the Glanum site; leave nothing of value in your car).

▲St. Paul Monastery and Hospital
(Le Monastère St. Paul de Mausole)

The still-functioning psychiatric hospital (Clinique St. Paul) that treated Vincent van Gogh from 1889 to 1890 is a popular pilgrimage for Van Gogh fans. Here you'll enter Van Gogh's temporarily peaceful world: a small chapel, intimate cloisters, a re-creation of his room, and a small lavender field with several large displays featuring copies of his paintings. There's also a display about sculptor Camille Claudel, who also sought solace in St-Rémy following a tumultuous affair with Auguste Rodin.

PROVENCE

St-Rémy Area

To Maillane

To Isle-sur-la-Sorgue & Avignon

AVE. F. MISTRAL

AVE. ALBERT SCHWEITZER

N

To A-7 Freeway, Cavaillon & Luberon via D-99

D-99

D-5

AVE. MAL DE LATTRE

D-99

D-571

POOL

Most scenic route to Les Baux & Arles

MISTRAL

AVE. ALBERT GLEIZES   AVE. LOUIS

D-99A

OLD TOWN

RING ROAD

AVE. JEAN MOULIN

POST

4

BUS & TAXI STOP

AVE. DE LA LIBERATION

CHEMIN DE LA COMBETTE

AVE. DU SOUVENIR FRANÇAIS

AVE. DURAND MAILLANE

AVE. PASTEUR

i

2

(Free)

3

AVE. J. D'ARBAUD   F. BARONCELLI

CH. LA CROIX DES VERTUS

CHEMIN GAULOIS

1

AVE. VINCENT VAN GOGH

AVE. ANTOINE DE LA SALLE

300 Meters

300 Yards

"LES ANTIQUES" ROMAN ARCH & TOWER

■ **ST. PAUL MONASTERY**

Free

P Pay

D-5

■ **GLANUM RUINS**

To Les Baux & Arles

1 Le Mas des Carassins Hôtel & Restaurant

2 Mas des Tourterelles Chambres

3 Hôtel du Soleil

4 Bike Rental

Cost and Hours: €5; daily 9:30-18:30, Oct-March 10:15-16:30, closed Jan-mid-Feb; tel. 04 90 92 77 00, www.saintpauldemausole.fr.

Visiting the Hospital: Inside, read the thoughtful English explanations about Van Gogh's tortured life. Amazingly, in his 53 weeks here, the artist completed 143 paintings and more than

100 drawings. In and around the complex, you'll see copies of his works—some positioned right where he painted them. Several are located through the gift shop in a lavender garden. Stand among flame-like cypress trees, gazing over the Alpilles mountains, and realize you're in the midst of some of Van Gogh's most famous creations.

You'll also find memories here of another troubled artist, Camille Claudel (1864-1943), whose parents had her committed to a nearby mental ward after her anguished affair with sculptor Auguste Rodin. Watch for a re-creation of her kitchen and see a short video about her life.

▲Glanum Ruins

These crumbling stones are the foundations of a Roman market town, located at the crossroads of two ancient trade routes between

Italy and Spain. While the ruins are, well...ruined, their setting at the base of the rocky Alpilles is splendid. It's also unshaded and can be very hot (making it easier to enjoy early or late).

A stubby Roman arch and tall tower stand across the road from the site as proud reminders of the town's glory days. These lonely monuments marked the entry to Glanum 2,000 years ago. The plump triumphal arch was designed to impress visitors with scenes of Rome's power, and the tower was built as a mausoleum by one of Glanum's most distinguished families.

Cost and Hours: €8; daily 9:30-18:30; Oct-March Tue-Sun 10:00-17:00, closed Mon; parking-€3/day, tel. 04 90 92 23 79.

Visiting the Ruins: Start at the helpful little museum at the entrance, with good English explanations of key buildings and the excavation process, as well as a model of Glanum in its prime. The free English handout and information panels scattered about the site provide more context to the ruins you'll see. Serious students of ancient Rome will want to spring for the well-done *Itineraries* book (€7).

The Roman site was founded in 27 BC and occupied for about 30 years. About 2,500 people lived in Glanum at its zenith (the Roman city was about seven times bigger than the ruins you see today). And though this was an important town, with grand villas, temples, a basilica, a forum, a wooden dam, and aqueducts, it was not important enough to justify an arena or a theater (such as those in Arles, Nîmes, and Orange). Stroll up Glanum's main street and see remains of a market hall, a forum, thermal baths, reservoirs, and more. The view from the belvedere justifies the uphill effort. These ruins highlight the range and prosperity of the Roman Empire.

Sleeping in St-Rémy-de-Provence

Unless otherwise noted, the following hotels have easy parking and air-conditioning.

$$ Le Mas des Carassins,*** a 15-minute walk from the center, is well-run by Michel and Pierre. Luxury is affordable here, with two generously sized pools, ample outdoor lounging spaces, big gardens, and everything just so. The 22 rooms are split between the more traditional main building (which I prefer) and the newer annex, which comes with larger rooms and more modern decor (American-style breakfast, table tennis, great dinner option—see below, 1 Chemin Gaulois, tel. 04 90 92 15 48, www.masdescarassins.com, info@masdescarassins.com).

$$ Mas des Tourterelles Chambres, a Provençal farmhouse in a pleasant neighborhood, is a 10-minute walk from the town center. It has six sharp rooms and an apartment, pool, and small garden with outdoor picnic facilities including a fridge (2-night minimum, air-con in top-floor rooms—others don't need it, 21 Chemin de la Combette, tel. 09 54 64 83 30 or mobile 06 15 87 24 55, www.masdestourterelles.com, contact@masdestourterelles.com). Turn right at the top of Place de la République onto Chemin de la Combette; after 400 yards look for the brown sign down a lane on the left (just after the second speed bump).

$$ Hôtel du Soleil,** a 10-minute walk from St-Rémy's center, is a sharp hotel, with fresh white stone and beige decor throughout. Its spotless rooms cluster around a courtyard/parking area and pool (five rooms have small terraces, a block above the TI at 35 Avenue Pasteur, tel. 04 90 92 00 63, www.hotelsoleil.com, info@hotelsoleil.com).

$ Sommeil des Fées Chambres rents five simple, clean, and comfortable rooms in the center of St-Rémy. They also run a good restaurant, La Cuisine des Anges, described later (4 Rue du 8 Mai 1945, tel. 04 90 92 17 66, www.angesetfees-stremy.com).

Eating in St-Rémy-de-Provence

The town is packed with restaurants, each trying to outdo the other. Join the evening strollers and compare.

$$$ Le Mas des Carassins offers a four-course food experience worth booking ahead. One *menu* is prepared each night and served in a country-classy setting inside or out. Service is friendly, kids are welcome, and the cuisine is utterly delicious. Review their website to see what's cooking before booking a table (see listing under "Sleeping in St-Rémy," earlier).

$ Crêperie Lou Planet, on pleasant Place Favier, is cheap and peaceful, with outdoor seating in summer, tasty crêpes, good salads, and inexpensive, good house wine (daily April-Sept 12:00-22:00, behind Hôtel de Ville at Place Favier, next to Musée des Alpilles).

$$ Bar-Tabac des Alpilles, popular with locals, has an old-school-meets-new-world feel, with wine barrels, wood tables, and modern art. The menu offers just enough choice, including salads, *plats*, and a fairly priced *menu*. Dinner is served in two seatings, at 19:15 and 20:45; best to book ahead (daily, except closed Tue-Wed for dinner, 21 Boulevard Victor Hugo, tel. 04 90 92 02 17).

$$ Café de la Place, on Place de la République behind the parking lot, is a hit with St-Rémy's young people (as well as aging travel writers). Come for a coffee, a drink, or a good meal of basic café fare (big *terrasse*, open daily, tel. 04 90 92 02 13).

$$ La Cuisine des Anges is a welcoming place serving tasty cuisine with a Mediterranean accent in a pleasant courtyard or dining room (closed Thu, 4 Rue du 8 Mai 1945, tel. 04 90 92 17 66).

$$$ L'Aile ou la Cuisse is St-Rémy's vintage bistro, with a warm, classy interior and traditional cuisine (closed Tue-Wed, 5 Rue de la Commune, tel. 04 32 62 00 25).

Orange

Orange is notable for its grand Roman arch and exceptional Roman Theater. Called "Arausio" in Roman times, Orange was a thriving city in those days—strategically situated on the Via Agrippa, connecting the important Roman cities of Lyon and Arles. It was founded as a comfortable place for Roman army officers to enjoy their retirement. Did the emperor want thousands of well-trained, relatively young guys hanging around Rome? No way. What to do? "How about a nice place in the south of France...?"

Today's Orange (oh-rahnzh) is a busy, workaday city with a gritty charm that reminds me of Arles. Leafy café-lined squares, a handful of traffic-free streets, a fine Hôtel de Ville (City Hall), and that theater all give the town some serious street appeal. For some,

PROVENCE

Orange works well as a base, with its quick access to the Côtes du Rhône wine villages by car (slower but OK by bus) and quick rail access to Avignon (which even drivers should consider).

Orientation to Orange

TOURIST INFORMATION

The unnecessary TI is located next to the fountain and parking area at 5 Cours Aristide Briand (Mon-Sat 9:00-12:30 & 14:00-18:00—no lunch break July-Aug, Sun 9:00-12:30; shorter hours and closed Sun Oct-March; tel. 04 90 34 70 88, www.orange-tourisme.fr).

Market Day: Thursday is market day, and it's a big deal here, with all the town's streets and squares crammed with produce and local goods for sale until 12:30. I like this market because it focuses on locals' needs and not touristy kitsch.

ARRIVAL IN ORANGE

By Train: Orange's train station is a level 15-minute walk from the Roman Theater (or an €8 taxi ride, mobile 06 66 71 58 02). Sadly, there's no bag storage in Orange. To walk into town from the station, head straight out of the station (down Avenue Frédéric Mistral), merge left onto Orange's main shopping street (Rue de la République), then turn left on Rue Caristie; you'll run into the Roman Theater's massive stage wall.

By Bus: All buses stop at Cours Pourtoules, two blocks from the Roman Theater; the bus to Vaison-la-Romaine also stops at the train station.

By Car: Follow *Centre-Ville* signs, then *Office du Tourisme* or *Théâtre Antique* signs; park as close to the Roman Theater's huge wall as you can. If coming from Avignon on D-907, park where you see *Parking Théâtre* signs; if coming from the autoroute, park near the TI on Cours Aristide Briand. If arriving on a Thursday morning—market day—expect lots of traffic and scarce parking; the road leading to the train station (15-minute walk to the theater) is your best bet. There's lots of free parking by the Roman arch, a 10-minute walk from the town center (leave nothing visible in your car).

Sights in Orange

▲▲▲Roman Theater (Théâtre Antique)

Orange's ancient theater is the best preserved in existence, and the only such theater in Europe with its (awesome) acoustic wall still standing. Built in the first century AD, the huge theater celebrated the glory of the empire and cemented Rome's presence in Provence.

Cost and Hours: €9.50, drops to €8.50 one hour before clos-

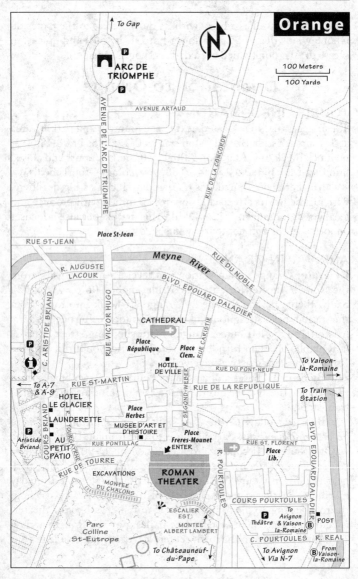

ing; ticket includes good audioguide (not available within an hour of closing) and entry to the small museum across the street; daily April-Sept 9:00-18:00, June-Aug until 19:00; Oct and March 9:30-17:30; Nov-Feb 9:30-16:30; closing times can change for evening performances or rehearsals, tel. 04 90 51 17 60, www.theatre-antique.com.

Video and Multimedia: In a passageway at the very top of the tiered seats, you'll find a worthwhile 15-minute **video history** of the theater plus the amusing *Ghosts of the Theater* **multimedia show,** which covers four periods of performance history (including rock concerts).

Cheap Trick: Vagabonds wanting a partial but free view of the theater (or others wanting a view from above) can find it in the Parc de la Colline St-Eutrope. Walk around to the left of the theater (see the "Orange" map), and find the steps to the right, just after the *tabac*. Climb the steps, keep left at the first fork, and continue for a little over 100 yards, then take the steps to the right to the top. From here, follow the *Point de Vue* sign to the right. Benches and grassy areas make this a good picnic spot (no WCs), and you can scamper about for views of the theater from different angles.

Visiting the Theater: If you pay to enter, to the right you'll see a huge dig devoted to the Temple to the Cult of the Emperor (English explanations posted). But we'll turn left, into the theater.

Climb the steep stairs to find a seat high up to appreciate the massive acoustical theater wall, one of the greatest surviving examples of Roman architecture. Contemplate the idea that 2,000 years ago, Orange residents enjoyed grand spectacles here, with high-tech sound and lighting effects—such as simulated thunder, lightning, and rain. If you've been to Arles' Ancient History Museum, conjure up the theater model there and imagine this place covered with brilliant white marble.

From the center of the acoustic wall, a grandiose **Caesar** overlooks everything, reminding attendees of who's in charge. If it seems like you've seen this statue before, you probably have. Countless identical sculptures were mass-produced in Rome and shipped throughout the empire to grace buildings like this for propaganda purposes. To save money on shipping and handling, only the heads of these statues were changed with each new ruler. The permanent body wears a breastplate emblazoned with the imperial griffon (body of a lion, head and wings of an eagle) that only

the emperor could wear. When a new emperor came to power, new heads were made in Rome and shipped off throughout the empire to replace the pop-off heads on these statues. (Imagine Barack Obama's head on George W. Bush's body—on second thought...)

The horn has blown. It's time to find your **seat:** row 2, number

30. Sitting down, you're comforted by the "EQ GIII" carved into the seat (*Equitas Gradus* #3...three rows for the Equestrian order). You're not comforted by the hard limestone bench (thinking it'll probably last 2,000 years). The theater is filled with people. Thankfully, you mix only with your class, the nouveau riche—merchants, tradesmen, and city big shots. The people seated above you are the working class, and way up in the "chicken roost" section is the scum of the earth—slaves, beggars, prostitutes, and youth hostellers. Scanning the orchestra section (where the super-rich sit on real chairs), you notice the town dignitaries hosting some visiting VIPs.

OK, time to worship. Around the stage, they're parading a bust of the emperor from its sacred home in the adjacent temple. Next is the ritual animal sacrifice called *la pompa* (so fancy, future generations will use that word for anything full of such...pomp). Finally, you settle in for an all-day series of spectacles and dramatic entertainment. All eyes are on the big stage door in the middle— where the Angelina Jolies and Brad Pitts of the day will appear. (Lesser actors use the side doors.)

With an audience of 10,000 and no amplification, **acoustics** were critical. A partial roof made of wood was originally suspended over the stage, somewhat like the glass-and-iron roof you see today (installed to protect the stage wall). The original was designed not to protect the stage from the weather, but to project the voices of the actors into the crowd (see if you can eavesdrop on people by the stage). For further help, actors wore masks with leather caricature mouths that functioned as megaphones. The theater's side walls originally rose as high as the stage wall and supported a retractable awning (called a velarium) that gave the audience some protection from the sun or rain. (When you leave the theater, look up to the stage wall from the outside and notice the supports for poles that held the velarium in place, like the masts and sails of a ship.)

The Roman Theater was all part of the "give them bread and circuses" approach to winning the support of the masses. Its spectacles grew from 65 days of games per year when the theater was first built (and when Rome was at its height) to about 180 days each year by the time Rome finally fell.

Nearby: Pop into the **Musée d'Art et d'Histoire** across the street (included with ticket, free audioguide) to see a few theater details and a rare Roman land register, ordered by Emperor Vespasian in AD 79. Carved on marble, this was an official record of property ownership—each square represented a 120-acre plot of land. The fine mosaics and carvings displayed here humanize what are otherwise stony ancient ruins.

PROVENCE

▲Roman "Arc de Triomphe"

This 60-foot-tall arch is in the center of a pleasant traffic circle, a level 15-minute walk north of the theater. Technically the only real Roman arches of triumph are in Rome's Forum, built to commemorate various emperors' victories. But this arch was the model for those in Rome, preceding the famous arches of Septimius Severus and Constantine. It was erected in about AD 19 to commemorate the Roman general Germanicus and one of the bloodiest battles in the conquest of Gaul. The facade is covered with reliefs of military exploits, including naval battles and Romans beating up on barbarians and those rude, nasty Gauls. (Around the arch, you'll find easy free parking and a picnic site.)

Hôtel de Ville

Orange owns a fine City Hall, worth the short detour to appreciate it (in the heart of the old town on Place Georges Clemenceau).

Sleeping and Eating in Orange

Sleeping: $ Hôtel le Glacier,*** across from the TI, is run by English-speaking and affable Philippe. It's a good value, with easy parking, a comfortable lobby with a bar, and well-designed rooms (book directly for a free upgrade when available, elevator, air-con, a few parking spaces, 46 Cours Aristide Briand, tel. 04 90 34 02 01, www.le-glacier.com, info@le-glacier.com).

Eating: Orange has several inviting squares with ample eating choices in all price ranges. A few cafés/restaurants are across from the theater. You'll find more choices by wandering the lanes toward the Hôtel de Ville. For a more refined meal, **$$$ Au Petit Patio** delivers elegant dining and fine cuisine (closed Wed-Thu for dinner and all-day Sun, 58 Cours Aristide Briand, tel. 04 90 29 69 27).

Orange Connections

From Orange by Train to: Avignon (hourly, 20 minutes), **Arles** (4/day direct, 35 minutes, more frequent with transfer in Avignon), **Lyon** (16/day, 2 hours).

By Bus to: Vaison-la-Romaine (bus #4, 10/day Mon-Sat, 2/day Sun, 1 hour), **Avignon** (bus #2, 14/day Mon-Sat, 3/day Sun, 45 minutes). For all bus service, check www.cars-lieutaud.fr or www.voyages-arnaud.com.

Buses to **Vaison-la-Romaine** and other wine villages depart from the train station and from Cours Pourtoules (see map on page 658). Because of occasional route changes, bus #4 to Vaison-la-Romaine may depart across from the bus shelter (look for blue bus icon or verify with any bus driver at the shelter).

PROVENCE

Côtes du Rhône Villages

The sunny Côtes du Rhône wine road—one of France's most engaging—starts at Avignon's doorstep and winds north along a mountainous landscape carpeted with vines, studded with warm stone villages, and carpeted with fields of fragrant lavender, all presided over by the wind-scarred Mont Ventoux. The wines of the Côtes du Rhône (grown on the *côtes*, or hillsides, of the Rhône River valley) are easy on the palate and on your budget, as are the area's good-value restaurants. But this hospitable area offers lots more than wine—its hill-capping villages inspire travel posters, its Roman ruins add historical perspective, and the locals seem as excited about their region as you are.

PLANNING YOUR TIME

If you're sleeping in this area, Vaison-la-Romaine is a handy home base. It offers reasonable bus connections with Avignon and Orange, bike rental, and a mini Pompeii in the town center. To delve further into the region's highlights, follow my driving tour of favorite wine villages, or pedal along peaceful roads to nearby towns. The vineyards' centerpiece, the Dentelles de Montmirail mountains, are laced with hiking trails.

To explore this area, allow two nights for a decent dabble. Drivers should head for the hills (read this section's self-guided driving tour before deciding where to stay). If you're without wheels, Vaison-la-Romaine or Orange make the only practical home bases (or, maybe better, consider a minivan tour for this area).

GETTING AROUND THE COTES DU RHONE

By Car: Pick up Michelin maps #332 or #527. Landmarks like the Dentelles de Montmirail and Mont Ventoux help you get your bearings. I've described my favorite driving route in this region ("Côtes du Rhône Wine Road Drive") near the end of this section.

By Bus: From Orange, buses run regularly to Vaison-la-Romaine and Avignon Monday to Saturday, though for most, taking the train from Avignon to Orange and then the bus to Vaison-la-Romaine is best. There's only scant service between Orange and several of the wine villages described in this section (see "Orange Connections," earlier, for details). All routes provide scenic rides through this area. A useful website for figuring out your bus options is www.pacamobilite.fr.

By Train: Trains from Avignon (hourly, 20 minutes) will get you as far as Orange (and bus connections).

By Minivan Tour: There's no shortage of people willing to take you for a ride through this marvelous region—so buyer beware. For my recommendations on wine-focused tours, more general tours, and private guides, see "Tours in Provence" on page 578.

Vaison-la-Romaine

With quick access to vineyards, villages, and Mont Ventoux, this lively little town of 6,000 makes a good base for exploring the Côtes du Rhône region. You get two villages for the price of one: Vaison-la-Romaine's "modern" lower city has Roman ruins, a lone pedestrian street, and the lively, café-lined main square—Place Montfort. The car-free medieval hill town looms above, with meandering cobbled lanes, a handful of cafés and art galleries, and a ruined castle.

Orientation to Vaison-la-Romaine

The city is split in two by the Ouvèze River. A Roman-era bridge connects the lower town (Ville-Basse) with the hill-capping medieval upper town (Ville-Haute).

TOURIST INFORMATION

The TI is in the lower city, between the two Roman ruin sites, at Place du Chanoine Sautel (July-Aug Mon-Fri 9:00-18:45, Sat-Sun 9:00-12:30 & 14:00-18:45; Sept-June Mon-Sat 9:30-12:00 & 14:00-17:45, Sun 9:30-12:00—except closed Sun mid-Oct-March; tel. 04 90 36 02 11, www.vaison-ventoux-tourisme.com). Say *bonjour* to the *charmante* and ever-so-patient staff, ask about festivals and other

events, and pick up information on walks and bike rides.

ARRIVAL IN VAISON-LA-ROMAINE

By Bus: Bus stops are near the Cave la Romaine winery on the edge of the lower town. Tell the driver you want the stop for the *Office de Tourisme*. When you get off the bus, walk five minutes down Avenue Général de Gaulle to reach the TI and recommended hotels.

By Car: Follow signs to *Centre-Ville*, then *Office de Tourisme*, and park in or near the big lot across from the TI. Parking is free in Vaison-la-Romaine.

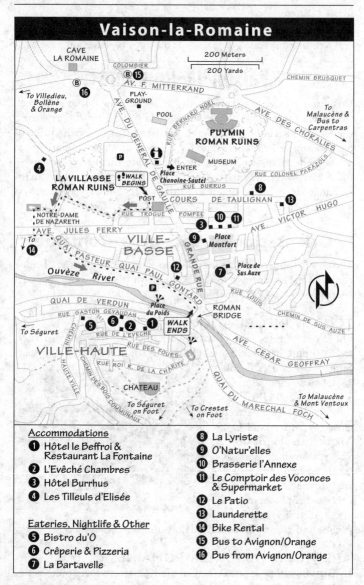

Vaison-la-Romaine

200 Meters

200 Yards

Accommodations
1. Hôtel le Beffroi & Restaurant La Fontaine
2. L'Evêché Chambres
3. Hôtel Burrhus
4. Les Tilleuls d'Elisée

Eateries, Nightlife & Other
5. Bistro du'O
6. Crêperie & Pizzeria
7. La Bartavelle
8. La Lyriste
9. O'Natur'elles
10. Brasserie l'Annexe
11. Le Comptoir des Voconces & Supermarket
12. Le Patio
13. Launderette
14. Bike Rental
15. Bus to Avignon/Orange
16. Bus from Avignon/Orange

HELPFUL HINTS

Market Day: Sleep in Vaison-la-Romaine on Monday night, and you'll wake to an amazing Tuesday market. If you spend a Monday night, ask your hotelier where you can park—avoid parking at market sites and where signs indicate *Stationnement Interdit le Mardi*, or you won't find your car where you left it.

Supermarket: A handy **Casino** is on Place Montfort in the thick of the cafés (Mon-Sat 7:30-13:00 & 15:30-19:30, Sun 9:00-13:00).

Laundry: The self-service **Laverie la Lavandière** is on Cours Taulignan, near Avenue Victor Hugo (daily 8:00-22:00, English instructions). The friendly owners, who work next door at the dry cleaners, will do your laundry while you sightsee (dry cleaners closed Sun).

Bike Rental: The TI has a list. **Sun-e-bike** is the most central, with electric and regular bikes (160 Avenue René Cassin, tel. 09 54 94 99 14, www.sun-e-bike.com). For help with bike rental and biking plans, contact John and Monique at the recommended **L'Ecole Buissonnière Chambres** (see listing under "Sleeping in Vaison-la-Romaine").

Taxi: Call 04 90 36 00 04 or 04 90 46 89 42.

Car Rental: You can rent cars by the day, though they must be returned to Vaison-la-Romaine and supply is limited; ask at the TI for locations.

Local Guide: Scottish by birth and an attorney by profession, **Janet Henderson** offers enthusiastic and educational walks of Vaison-la-Romaine that bring those Roman ruins and medieval buildings to life (€30/person, minimum 3 people or €90, allow 2.5 hours, www.provencehistorytours.com, janet.henderson@wanadoo.fr).

Tourist Train: The **Petit Train** stops in front of the TI and does a 35-minute loop around the town (€5, free for kids under 12, daily July-Aug 10:00-17:00, Sept-June 14:00-17:00).

Cooking Classes: Charming **Barbara Schuerenberg** offers reasonably priced cooking classes from her view home in Vaison-la-Romaine, where you'll pick herbs from the garden to use in the recipes (€90, cash only, includes lunch, 4-person maximum, tel. 04 90 35 68 43, www.cuisinedeprovence.com, cuisinedeprovence@gmail.com).

After-Dinner Fun: You won't party late in this quiet town but there are a few fun places to consider. Place Montfort has most of the action: **Brasserie L'Annexe** has the warmest interior, while **Le Comptoir des Voconces** is the happening hangout with a pub-like ambience. Below the Roman bridge, **Le Patio** has cool wine-bar action at the back of its restaurant (closed Wed and Sun, 4 Rue de Ventoux).

Sights in Vaison-la-Romaine

Vaison's top sight is its Gallo-Roman ruins—Puymin and Villasse. Start your sightseeing day at the Puymin site, then follow my short self-guided walk to tie together the rest of Vaison's sights. Pick up the detailed city map from the tourist office before you begin.

PROVENCE

Roman Ruins

A modern road splits the town's Gallo-Roman ruins into two well-presented sites, Puymin and La Villasse. The Puymin side has more

to see and gives a good introduction to these ruins, thanks to its small museum offering a look at life during the Roman Empire (see below). For helpful background about Roman civilization, read "The Romans in Provence" on page 581.

Cost and Hours: €9 ticket admits you to both sites; daily June-Sept 9:30-18:30, shorter hours off-season, closed Jan-Feb; good audioguide-€3, tel. 04 90 36 50 48, www.vaison-la-romaine.com.

Visiting the Puymin Ruins: Near the entry are the scant but worthwhile ruins of a sprawling mansion. Find the faint remains of a colorful frescoed wall and mosaic floors, as well as a few wells, used before Vaison's two aqueducts were built. Climb the short hill to the good little **museum** (pick up your audioguide here; exhibits also well explained in an English loaner booklet). Artifacts include

lead water pipes, well-preserved mosaic floors, and a few models of ancient buildings. Be sure to see the 12-minute **film** (plays in English every other showing) that takes you inside the homes and daily life of wealthy Vaison residents some 2,000 years ago. A five-minute walk behind the museum brings you to a largely rebuilt (but still used) 6,000-seat theater—just enough seats for the whole town (of yesterday and today).

• *Exiting the Puymin site will deposit you just above the TI—and the start of my self-guided walk, next.*

Self-Guided Walk to the Roman Bridge from the Roman Ruins

Give yourself 45 minutes for this level, crosstown ramble. We'll start just across from the TI, where there is a parking lot. Lean against the railing there overlooking the Villasse archaeological site.

La Villasse Ruins: When the Romans took over Provence (second century BC), the people of Vaison-la-Romaine sided with their vanquishers, earning themselves a preferred "federated" rela-

PROVENCE

tionship with Rome (rather than being a simple colony). This, along with a healthy farming economy (olives and vineyards) and good weather made it a most prosperous place...as a close look at these sprawling ruins demonstrates.

About 6,000 people called Vaison-la-Romaine home 2,000 years ago. The Roman town extended all the way from where you're standing to the Ouvèze River (to the left, or south). The ancient forum lies between you and the river (not excavated). Vaison was a river port, boasting aqueducts, a big theater, baths, a forum, busy shopping streets, and the trophy homes of wealthy businessmen.

When the barbarians arrived in the fifth century AD, the Romans were forced out, and the townspeople fled from their un-walled, unprotected low neighborhoods into the hills. The town's population has only recently recovered from those barbaric times, with the number of residents again reaching Roman-era levels.

If you have a ticket, you can walk through the Villasse ruins, though you can see everything from the sidewalks that run along the perimeter—which is our plan. What you can see between both Puymin and Villasse is only about 10 percent of the Roman town's extent—most is still buried under today's city.

Make your way to the corner of Rue Trogue Pompée, just be-hind the post office. The ruins sit behind a stone and iron fence that runs the length of the street. Stop in about 20 steps, just before reaching the tall arch. Spot the wire mesh that covers parts of a Roman sewer that was used until the 1900s. That tall arch was the centerpiece of a public Roman bath. Notice the public latrines a few steps farther along. That stone channel in front of the toilets had running water that men used to rinse the public sponge (usually attached to a stick—before the invention of toilet paper). Hmmm.

The stone-paved street running perpendicularly below you was lined with shops. The columns and remnants on the left side are what's left of two mega-homes. You won't see the homes of poorer folks as they were built from materials that did not last.

Continue along the pedestrian walkway that hugs the ruins. Just below, find an original (if faded) mosaic under a tiled roof. Nearby, there's a linear channel that was once lined in marble and used as a fish pond (some parts of it are now planted).

• *Turn left as you leave the ruins behind. You'll pass a lovely garden, then turn right at the first little path you come to. Stop when you reach the back of...*

Notre-Dame de Nazareth Cathedral: As you approach this medieval church, look at its base to find the stubs of Roman col-umns that form its foundation. This church wasn't built until 600 years after the Romans left, thanks to a lack of security in the lower town and a complete loss of Roman-era building techniques. The first church built over the Roman ruins was abandoned in the

PROVENCE

Middle Ages, when residents fled to the relative safety of the upper town; the present building dates from the 11th to 12th century.

Walk left, then right, to view the church from its side. Appreciate the simple exterior. This is a fine example of Romanesque architecture: heavy arches, few windows, and little exterior decoration. Notice the delicate frieze under the eaves.

• *With your back to the church, walk out to the street and turn left on Avenue Jules Ferry, then veer right on Quai Louis Pasteur. After several blocks, angle through the parking lot and find a spot above the river.*

Medieval Hill Town: Look up to the medieval village. From the fourth century onward, Vaison-la-Romaine was ruled by a prince-bishop. When the sitting prince-bishop came under attack by the count of Toulouse in the 12th century, he built the abandoned castle you see on the top of this rocky outcrop (about 1195). Over time, the townspeople followed, vacating the lower town and building their homes behind the upper town's fortified wall—where they would remain until after the French Revolution. The castle, which the count of Toulouse successfully claimed, protected the town for a while, but the count was eventually chased out by the armies of a Cathar-hating pope and a land-grabbing French king. The bell tower crowned by a lovely 18th-century wrought-iron bell cage (beautiful at night) tolled to announce curfew (the hill town was sealed tight after-hours), to warn of danger, or to signal important public events.

• *Continue along the river to the corner of the parking area closest to the Roman bridge.*

Roman Bridge: The Romans cut this sturdy, no-nonsense vault into the canyon rock 2,000 years ago, and it has survived ever since. Until the 20th century, this was the only way to cross the Ouvèze River. A vicious 1992 flood crested well above the bridge, and locals still talk of how water flowed through the windows and doors of the buildings on your left. The flood destroyed several other modern bridges downstream, but couldn't budge the 55-foot Roman arch supporting the bridge.

• *Exit the parking lot, turning right, and make your way to the bridge.*

Read the information panel on the left side of the bridge, then find the small dark plaque *(Septembre 22-92...)* on the wall to the right, showing the high-water mark of the record flood that killed 30 people. A 50-yard detour down the road (with the river to your right) leads to fun views of the hill town's rock-hugging Catholic church (it replaced Notre-Dame de Nazareth when folks fled the lower town).

• *Our walk is over. From here, you have two choices: Explore the medieval lanes of the upper town, or meander the shops and main square of the lower town.*

Upper Town (Ville-Haute): To reach the upper town, hike

across the Roman bridge and up to the right (passing a WWI memorial), looping around and through the medieval gate, under the lone tower. Although there's nothing of particular importance to see in the medieval town, the cobbled lanes and enchanting fountains make you want to break out a sketchpad. Look for occasional English information plaques as you meander. The château itself is closed, and the view from the steep, uneven trail to its base does not merit the effort.

Lower Town (Ville-Basse): To reach Place Montfort, the TI, and the main parking lots, from the Roman bridge do an about-face and walk up the pedestrian-only Grande Rue, Vaison's main shopping street. The modern town centers on café-friendly Place Montfort. Tables grab the north side of the square, conveniently sheltered from the prevailing mistral wind while enjoying the generous shade of the ubiquitous plane trees.

Wine Tasting

Cave la Romaine, a five-minute walk up Avenue Général de Gaulle from the TI, offers a big variety of good-value wines from nearby villages in a pleasant, well-organized tasting room (free tastes, Mon-Sat 9:00-12:30 & 14:00-18:30, Sun 9:00-12:00, Avenue St-Quenin, tel. 04 90 36 55 90, www.cave-la-romaine.com).

▲Hiking

Stop at the TI for detailed information on hikes into the hills above Vaison-la-Romaine.

It's about 1.5 hours to the quiet hill town of Crestet, though views begin immediately. To find the trail, drive or walk on Chemin des Bois Communaux, the road behind the castle in the upper town (with the rock base and castle on your left), continue onto Chemin des Fontaines (blue signs), and stay the course as far as you like (follow yellow *Crestet* signs). Cars are not allowed on the road after about a mile.

To find the five-mile trail to Séguret (allow 2 hours), take the same road above Vaison-la-Romaine and look for a yellow sign *(Sablet/Coste Belle)* to the right. For either route, consider hiking one way and taking a taxi back (best to arrange a pickup in advance in Vaison-la-Romaine—ask your hotelier).

Biking

The TI has details on several manageable bike routes, with good directions in English, as well as information on mountain-biking trails (also available at bike shops). The easiest is the yellow itinerary to Séguret and Sablet (shortcuts back to Vaison are described, allowing for loop rides of one to three hours). If the air's calm, the five-mile ride to cute little Villedieu (with the recommended La Maison Bleue restaurant) is a delight. The bike route is signed along

PROVENCE

small roads; from Vaison-la-Romaine, find the road to Villedieu at the roundabout by Cave La Romaine (see "Vaison-la-Romaine" map). Alternatively, get a good map and connect the following villages for an enjoyable 11-mile loop ride: Vaison-la-Romaine, St-Romain-en-Viennois, Puyméras, Faucon, and St-Marcellin-lès-Vaison.

Sleeping in Vaison-la-Romaine

Hotels in Vaison-la-Romaine are a good value and are split between the upper medieval village (with all the steps) and the lower main town (with all the services). Those in the upper village (Ville-Haute) are quieter, cozier, cooler, and give you the feeling of sleeping in a hill town (some come with views), with all the services of a real town just steps away. But they require a 10-minute walk down to the town center and Roman ruins. None of the hotels listed has an elevator, and few have air-conditioning.

If you have a car, consider staying in one of the Côtes du Rhône villages near Vaison-la-Romaine. I've listed a few nearby places here; for more suggestions see the "Côtes du Rhône Wine Road Drive," later.

IN THE UPPER TOWN

If staying in the upper village with a car, follow signs to *Cité Médiévale* and park just outside the upper village entry (driving into the Cité Médiévale itself is a challenge, with tiny lanes and nearly impossible parking).

$$ Hôtel le Beffroi* hides deep in the upper town, just above a demonstrative bell tower (which stops demonstrating at 22:00). The hotel offers 16th-century red-tile-and-wood-beamed-cozy lodgings with nary a level surface. The rooms—split between two buildings a few doors apart—are Old World comfy, and some have views. You'll enjoy antique-filled public spaces, a view-filled garden, a small pool with more views, and animated Nathalie at reception (several good family rooms, closed mid-Jan-March, Rue de l'Evêché, tel. 04 90 36 04 71, www.le-beffroi.com, hotel@le-beffroi.com). The hotel has a **$$$ restaurant** with pleasant outdoor seating in fine weather (see "Eating in Vaison-la-Romaine," later).

$ L'Evêché Chambres, a few doors away from Hôtel le Beffroi, is a five-room melt-in-your-chair B&B. The charming owners (the Verdiers) have an fine sense of interior design and are passionate about books, making this place feel like a cross between a library and an art gallery (the *solanum* suite is worth every euro, Rue de l'Evêché, tel. 04 90 36 13 46, eveche.free.fr, eveche@aol.com).

IN THE LOWER TOWN

$ Hôtel Burrhus** is equal parts contemporary art gallery and funky-creaky hotel—but a good value. It's a central, laid-back place, with a broad, terrific terrace over Place Montfort and surprisingly big rooms (for maximum quiet, request a back room). Its floor plan will confound even the ablest navigator (air-con, 1 Place Montfort, tel. 04 90 36 00 11, www.burrhus.com, info@burrhus.com).

$ Les Tilleuls d'Elisée is a terrific *chambres d'hôte* in a stone, blue-shuttered home near the Notre-Dame de Nazareth Cathedral, 10 minutes' walk below the TI. Anne and Laurent Viau run this comfortable five-room place with grace and great rates. Relax in the garden with views to the upper town and ask about wine tastings in their small cellar (includes breakfast, air-con, 1 Avenue Jules Mazen, tel. 04 90 35 63 04, www.vaisonchambres.info, anne.viau@vaisonchambres.info).

NEAR VAISON-LA-ROMAINE

$ L'Ecole Buissonnière Chambres is run by an engaging Anglo-French team, John and Monique, who share their peace and quiet 10 minutes north of Vaison-la-Romaine. This creatively restored farmhouse has three character-filled rooms and comfy public spaces. Getting to know John, who has lived all over the south of France, is worth the price of the room. The outdoor kitchen allows guests to picnic in high fashion in the tranquil garden (family rooms, includes breakfast, cash only; between Villedieu and Buisson on D-75—leave Vaison following signs to *Villedieu*, then follow D-51 toward Buisson and turn left onto D-75—Route de Villedieu; tel. 04 90 28 95 19, www.buissonniere-provence.com, ecole.buissonniere@wanadoo.fr).

Eating in Vaison-la-Romaine

Vaison-la-Romaine offers a handful of good dining experiences—arrive by 19:30 in summer or reserve ahead, particularly on weekends. And while you can eat very well on a moderate budget in Vaison, it's well worth venturing to nearby Côtes du Rhône villages to eat. I've listed three nearby places; for recommendations farther afield, see the "Côtes du Rhône Wine Road Drive," later. Wherever you dine, begin with a fresh glass of Muscat from the nearby village of Beaumes-de-Venise.

IN THE UPPER TOWN

$$$ Restaurant La Fontaine, located at the recommended **Hôtel le Beffroi,** serves traditional cuisine of average quality in the lovely hotel gardens when the weather agrees, and in the pleasant dining

PROVENCE

room when it doesn't. If they're serving in the garden, you won't find a better setting in Vaison (closed Wed, tel. 04 90 36 04 71).

$$$ Bistro du'O dishes up creative and well-presented Franco-Provençal cuisine in a smart, stone-arches-meet-wood-tables setting in the lower part of the Ville Haute (closed Sun-Mon, Rue Gaston Gevaudan, tel. 04 90 41 72 90).

$ You'll also find a simple *crêperie* with a view deck and a decent **pizzeria** on the main street leading up to the old town. Both have indoor and outdoor seating, some views over the river, and cheap, basic food (good for families).

IN THE LOWER TOWN

$$ La Bartavelle, run by friendly Berangère, is a good place to savor traditional French cuisine, with tourist-friendly mix-and-match choices of local options. The €30 *menu* gets you four courses, including a great cheese tray; the €23 *menu* offers top-end main-course selections and dessert (excellent foie gras and seafood plate—*assiette de pêcheur,* closed Mon, also closed Sun evening off-season; outside terrace, air-con, 5 Rue Camille Pelletan, tel. 04 90 36 02 16).

$$ La Lyriste is an unpretentious and intimate place to experience true Provençal cuisine, with Sandra taking your orders and her husband doing the cooking (closed Mon, 45 Cours Taulignan, tel. 04 90 36 04 67).

$$ O'Natur'elles is a sweet little place, especially for lunch. It's ideal for vegetarians, but good for all persuasions as the all-organic dishes can be served with or without meat. The cuisine is delicious, but the place is small (closed Wed, may open Sat for dinner—ask about other nights, reservations smart, 38 Place Montfort, tel. 04 90 65 81 67).

Cafés on Place Montfort: Come here for classic **$$** café fare and to observe the daily flow of life in Vaison-la-Romaine. Outdoor tables are ideal but can come with smokers. The popular **Brasserie l'Annexe** is best, with a good selection of fine quality dishes ranging from big salads to tempting *plats du jour* (open daily).

NEAR VAISON-LA-ROMAINE

$ La Maison Bleue, about four miles north of Vaison-la-Romaine on Villedieu's delightful little square, serves good pizzas and salads with great outdoor ambience. Skip it if the weather forces you inside (March-Oct Thu-Sun open for lunch and dinner, closed Mon-Wed except July-Aug closed Mon only, tel. 04 90 28 97 02).

$ Auberge d'Anaïs, at the end of a short dirt road 10 minutes from Vaison-la-Romaine, is a fun Provençal experience, ideal for a relaxing lunch or dinner *en plein air* (not worth it in bad weather). Outdoor tables gather under cheery lights with immediate vineyard views and classic Provençal cuisine. Ask for a table *sur la terrasse* (closed Sun-Mon, tel. 04 90 36 20 06). Heading east of Vaison-la-Romaine, follow signs to *Carpentras,* then *St. Marcellin-lès-Vaison.* Signs will guide you from there.

$$ La Fleur Bleue is a good find, serving fresh and local cuisine in a charming blue-shuttered farmhouse (open for lunch and dinner, closed Wed, reservations smart, Chemin du Sublon, a mile from Crestet on the road toward Malaucène, tel. 04 90 36 23 45, www.lafleurbleue.fr).

Vaison-la-Romaine Connections

The most central **bus stop** is a few blocks up Avenue Général de Gaulle from the TI near the main winery, Cave la Romaine. Buses to Orange and Avignon stop on the winery side (see "Vaison-la-Romaine" map for location). Buses to Nyons, Crestet, and Carpentras depart from the bus station farther east on that road.

From Vaison-la-Romaine by Bus to: Avignon (#4 to Orange, transfer to #2, 10/day Mon-Sat, 2/day Sun, 1.5 hours—train from Orange is faster), **Orange** (bus #4, 10/day Mon-Sat, 2/day Sun, 1 hour), **Nyons** (3-5/day, none on Sun, 45 minutes), **Crestet** (lower village below Crestet, bus #11, 5/day Mon-Sat, none on Sun, 5 minutes), **Carpentras** (bus #11, 5/day Mon-Sat, none on Sun, 1 hour).

Côtes du Rhône Wine Road Drive

SEGURET LOOP

This self-guided driving tour provides a crash course in Rhône Valley wine, an excuse to meet the locals who make the stuff, and breathtaking scenery—especially late in the day, when the famous Provençal sunlight causes colors to absolutely pop. Allow at least a half-day for this 35-mile loop drive, which starts in the village of Séguret, skirts Vaison-la-Romaine, and then winds clockwise around the Dentelles de Montmirail, visiting the mountaintop village of Crestet, adorable little Suzette, and the renowned wine villages of Beaumes-de-Venise and Gigondas. (You can, of course, start anywhere along this circular route.)

Even if wine isn't your thing, don't miss this scenic drive. This region is not only about wine; you'll pass orchards of apricots, figs, and cherries, as well fields of table grapes. As you drive, notice how some vineyards grow at angles—they're planted this way to compensate for the strong effect of the mistral wind.

Planning Your Drive: Our tour starts a bit south of Vaison-la-Romaine in little Séguret. By **bike,** or for a **more scenic drive** from

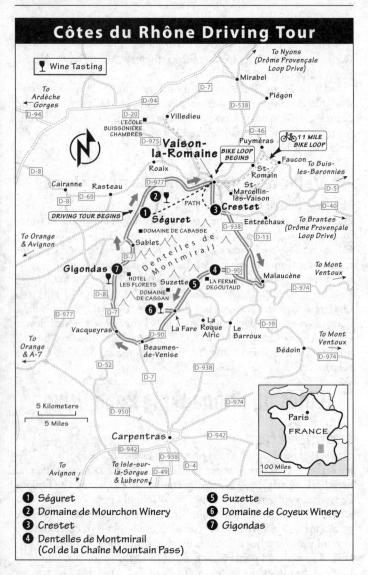

Côtes du Rhône Driving Tour

♥ Wine Tasting

🚲 11 MILE BIKE LOOP

DRIVING TOUR BEGINS

BIKE LOOP BEGINS

PATH

To Nyons (Drôme Provençale Loop Drive)

To Ardèche Gorges

To Orange & Avignon

To Orange & A-7

To Avignon

To Isle-sur-la-Sorgue & Luberon

To Buis-les-Baronnies

To Brantes (Drôme Provençale Loop Drive)

To Mont Ventoux

L'ECOLE BUISSONIERE CHAMBRES

DOMAINE DE CABASSE

HOTEL LES FLORETS

DOMAINE DE CASSAN

LA FERME DEGOUTAUD

Dentelles de Montmirail

5 Kilometers
5 Miles

Paris
FRANCE
100 Miles

1 Séguret
2 Domaine de Mourchon Winery
3 Crestet
4 Dentelles de Montmirail
(Col de la Chaîne Mountain Pass)
5 Suzette
6 Domaine de Coyeux Winery
7 Gigondas

Vaison-la-Romaine, cross to the Cité Médiévale side of the river, then follow D-977 signs downriver to Séguret (park in lots P-2 or P-3). Theft is a problem in this beautiful area—leave absolutely nothing in your car.

Wineries: I've listed several wineries *(domaines)* along the way. Remember that the wineries you'll visit are serious about their wines—and they hope that you'll take them seriously, too. At private wineries, tastings are not happy-go-lucky chances to knock back a few glasses and buy a T-shirt with the property's label on it. Show genuine interest in the wines, and buy some if you like it.

Eating: Drivers on this route can enjoy a wealth of country-Provençal dining opportunities in rustic settings (even within 15 minutes of Vaison-la-Romaine). It's a great opportunity to experience rural France. All restaurants listed have some outdoor seating and should be considered for lunch or dinner.

❶ Séguret

Blending into the hillside with a smattering of shops, two cafés, made-to-stroll lanes, and a natural spring, this hamlet is understandably popular. Séguret makes for a good coffee or ice cream stop and has a good café-restaurant.

Séguret's name comes from the Latin word *securitas* (meaning "security"). The town's long bulky entry arch came with a massive gate, which drilled in the message of the village's name. In the Middle Ages, Séguret was patrolled 24/7—they never took their *securitas* for granted. Find the drawing of the medieval town with its high-flying castle on the arch's wall. A castle once protected Séguret, but all that's left today is a tower that you can barely make out (though trails provide access).

Walk through the arch and up a block. To appreciate how the homes' outer walls provided security in those days, drop down the first passage on your right (near the fountain). These tunnel-like exit passages, or *poternes*, were needed in periods of peace to allow the town to expand below. You will come across **La Maison d'Eglantine** tucked in here, serving delicious cakes, coffee, and tea in a cozy room with views.

Moving along, you could follow Rue Calade up to the unusual 12th-century St. Denis church for views (the circular village you see below is Sablet). We'll veer right and down instead, aiming for the **santon shop** (worth a peek for its displays). At Christmas, this entire village transforms itself into one big crèche scene. From here, drop down and return to your car past the recommended **Restaurant/Café Côté Terrasse.**

Sleeping and Eating: Sure, it's a hotel and restaurant, but winemaking is also part of the business at **$$ Domaine de Cabasse,***** a lovely spread flanked by vineyards at the foot of Séguret (with views and a walking path to the village). Free tastings are offered every evening from April through September. Each of the 23 rooms has tasteful decor, air-conditioning, and views over vines; all the first-floor rooms have balconies or decks (elevator, big heated pool, discount for 2-3 night stay if reserved directly with hotel; on D-23 between Sablet and Séguret, entry gate opens automatically... and slowly, tel. 04 90 46 91 12, www.cabasse.fr, hotel@cabasse.fr). It's worth booking ahead for their **$$** classy country **restaurant.**

PROVENCE

$ Le Bouquet de Séguret Chambres d'Hôte is a lovely Provençal refuge perched just above Séguret with vineyard and village views, a pool, and owners Jos and Ingrid—who spoil their guests with optional home-cooked dinners, wine tastings, and afternoon tea (near Domaine de Cabasse at 252 Route de Sablet, tel. 04 90 28 13 83, www.lebouquetdeseguret.com, info@lebouquetdeseguret.com).

With a terrific setting in the center of the village, **$$ Restaurant/Café Côté Terrasse** offers all-day café service as well as lunch and dinners. They deliver big portions, reasonable prices, good quality, and cheerful service, either on the terrace or in the modern interior (daily from 10:00, Rue des Poternes, tel. 04 90 28 03 48).

• *Signs near Séguret's upper parking lots lead you up, up, and away to our next stop, the nearby Domaine de Mourchon (leave bread crumbs or track your route up to find your way back down).*

❷ Domaine de Mourchon Winery

This high-flying winery blends state-of-the-art technology with traditional winemaking methods (a shiny ring of stainless-steel vats holds grapes grown on land plowed by horses). The wines have won the respect of international critics. Take advantage of the amazing deal they've arranged to deliver wine stateside for nearly the same price you'd pay at the winery. Free and informative English tours of the vineyards are usually offered on Wednesdays at 17:00, followed by a tasting, though you're welcome to taste anytime they're open (winery open Mon-Sat 9:00-18:00, Sun by appointment only; from Easter-Oct, call to verify; tel. 04 90 46 70 30, www.domainedemourchon.com).

• *Next, drop back down to Séguret, head toward Vaison-la-Romaine, and once past the city follow signs for Carpentras/Malaucène. After passing through "lower" Crestet on the main highway, look for signs for a side road leading up to Le Village. Drivers can park at the second lot on the approach to the town, then hike up through the village on foot, or bypass the lower lots to keep climbing toward Place du Château at the top of town.*

❸ Crestet

This quiet village—founded after the fall of the Roman Empire, when people banded together in high places like this for protection from marauding barbarians—followed the usual hill-town evolution. The outer walls of the village did double duty as ramparts and house walls. The castle above (from about 850) provided a final safe haven when the village was attacked.

Wander the peaceful lanes and appreciate the amount of work it took to put these stones in place. Notice the elaborate water channels. Crestet was served by 18 cisterns in the Middle Ages. Imagine hundreds of people living here with animals roaming everywhere. The bulky Romanesque church is built into the hillside; if it's open, peek in to see the unusual stained-glass window behind the altar.

Eating: The village's only business, the café-restaurant **$$ Le Panoramic,** well signed at the top of town, serves basic omelets, salads, crêpes, and *plats* from what must be Provence's greatest view tables. Stop for a coffee or drink and enjoy the panorama (April-Nov daily 10:30-22:00, closed in bad weather and Dec-March, tel. 04 90 28 76 42).

Nearby: A fine lunch stop about a mile from Crestet is **$$ La Fleur Bleue** (see "Eating in Vaison-la-Romaine," earlier).

• *Drivers should carry on and reconnect with the road below, following signs to Malaucène. Entering Malaucène, turn right on D-90 (direction: Suzette) just before the gas station. After a few minutes you'll approach a pass. Look for signs on the left to Col de la Chaîne (Chain Pass).*

❹ Dentelles de Montmirail (Col de la Chaîne Mountain Pass)

Get out of your car at the pass (elevation: about 1,500 feet) and enjoy the breezy views. The peaks in the distance—thrusting up like the back of a stegosaurus or a bad haircut (you decide)—are the Dentelles de Montmirail, a small range running just nine miles basically north to south and reaching 2,400 feet in elevation. This region's land is constantly shifting. Those rocky tops were the result of a gradual uplifting of the land, which was then blown bald by the angry mistral wind. The village below the peaks is Suzette (you'll be there soon).

Now turn around and face Mont Ventoux. Are there clouds on the horizon? You're looking into the eyes of the Alps (behind Ventoux), and those "foothills" help keep Provence sunny.

• *Time to push on. With the medieval castle of Le Barroux topping the horizon in the distance (off to the left), drive on to little...*

❺ Suzette

Tiny Suzette floats on its hilltop, with a small 12th-century chapel, wine tastings, a handful of residents, and the gaggle of houses where they live. Park in Suzette's lot, then find the big orientation board above the lot. Look out to the broad shoulders of Mont Ventoux. At 6,000 feet, it always seems to have some clouds hanging around. If it's clear, the top looks like it's snow-covered; if you drive up there, you'll see it's actually white stone.

Back across the road from the orientation table is a simple tasting room for **Château Redortier** wines (unreliable hours, but well-explained wine list provided). Good picnic tables lie just past Suzette on our route.

• *Continue from Suzette in the direction of Beaumes-de-Venise. You'll drop down into the lush little village of La Fare. Just after leaving the village is the...*

❻ Domaine de Coyeux Winery

A private road winds up and up to this impossibly beautiful setting, with the best views of the Dentelles I've found. Olive trees frame the final approach, and *Le Caveau* signs lead to a modern tasting room (you may need to ring the buzzer) within a big winery. The owners and staff are sincere and take your interest in their wines seriously—skip it if you only want a quick taste or are not interested in buying. These wines have earned their good reputation, and some are now available in the US (winery  generally open daily 10:00-12:00 & 14:00-18:00, except closed Sun off-season and no midday closure July-Aug; tel. 04 90 12 42 42, www.domainedecoyeux.com, some English spoken).

• *Drive on toward Beaumes-de-Venise. Navigate through Beaumes-de-Venise, following signs for Vacqueyras (a famous wine village with a Thursday market), and then signs for Gigondas and Vaison par la route touristique. As you enter Gigondas, follow signs to the TI and park on or near the tree-shaded square.*

❼ Gigondas

This upscale village produces some of the region's best reds and is ideally situated for hiking, mountain biking, and driving into the mountains. The TI has lists of wineries and *chambres d'hôtes*, and tips for good hikes or drives (Mon-Sat 10:00-12:30 & 14:30-18:00, closed Sun, 5 Rue du Portail, tel. 04 90 65 85 46, www.gigondas-dm.fr). Take a short walk up through the village lanes to find a good viewing platform over the heart of the Côtes du Rhône vineyards (leaving from the recommended Du Verre à l'Assiette restaurant, veer right just after the Nez Bar à Vins, then make a quick left uphill); you'll find even better views a little higher at the church.

Several good tasting opportunities lie on the main square.

Le Caveau de Gigondas is the best, where Sandra and Barbara await your visit in a handsome tasting room with a large and free selection (daily 10:00-12:00 & 14:00-18:30, close to the TI on the main town square, tel. 04 90 65 82 29, www.caveaudugigondas. com). Here you can compare wines from 75 private producers in an intimate, low-key surrounding. The provided list of wines is helpful.

Sleeping and Eating: The shaded red tables of **$$ Du Verre à l'Assiette** ("From Glass to Plate") entice lunchtime eaters, as does the good interior ambience (open for lunch daily except Wed, dinner Fri-Sat nights, and every night but Wed mid-June-mid-Sept, located diagonally across from TI, Place du Village, tel. 04 90 12 36 64). **$ Nez Bar à Vins,** with pleasant atmosphere inside and out, is a cool-if-trendy place to enjoy a glass of wine and light appetizers; you'll find it along a pedestrian lane a block up from the main square (closed Sun-Mon, Place du Rouvis, tel. 04 90 28 99 59).

$$ Hôtel les Florets,*** with tastefully designed rooms, is a half-mile above Gigondas, buried in the foothills of the Dentelles de Montmirail. It comes with an excellent restaurant, a vast terrace with views, a pool, and hiking trails into the mountains (no air-con, annex rooms by pool have front patios, tel. 04 90 65 85 01, www.hotel-lesflorets.com, accueil@hotel-lesflorets.com). Their traditional, family-run **$$$ restaurant** is well worth the price—particularly if you dine on the magnificent terrace. Dinners blend classic French cuisine with Provençal accents, served with class by English-speaking Thierry. The weighty wine list is literally encyclopedic (closed Wed, also closed Thu for lunch, service can be slow).

• *From Gigondas, follow signs to the circular wine village of Sablet—with generally inexpensive yet tasty wines (the TI and wine coopérative share a space in the town center)—then back to Séguret, where our tour ends.*

Hill Towns of the Luberon

Just 30 miles east of Avignon, the Luberon region hides some of France's most captivating hill towns and sensuous landscapes. Those intrigued by Peter Mayle's best-selling *A Year in Provence* love joyriding through the region, connecting I-could-live-here villages, crumbled castles, and meditative abbeys. Mayle's book describes the ruddy local culture from an Englishman's perspective as he buys a stone farmhouse, fixes it up, and adopts the region as his new home. *A Year in Provence* is a great read while you're here—or, better, get it as an audiobook and listen while you drive.

The Luberon terrain in general (much of which is a French regional natural park) is as enticing as its villages. Gnarled vineyards and wind-sculpted trees separate tidy stone structures from abandoned buildings—little more than rock piles—that challenge city slickers to fix them up. Mountains of limestone bend along vast ridges, while colorful hot-air balloons survey the scene from above.

There are no obligatory museums, monuments, or vineyards in the Luberon. Treat this area like a vacation from your vacation. Downshift your engine. Brake for views, and lose your car to take a walk. Get on a first-name basis with a village.

What follows is a rundown of my favorite villages and stops in this beautiful area. The D-900 highway cuts the Luberon in half like an arrow. The villages I describe sit just north and south of it.

GETTING AROUND THE LUBERON

By Car: Luberon roads are scenic and narrow. With no major landmarks, it's easy to get lost—and you will—but getting lost is the point. Consider buying the Michelin map #332 or #527 to navigate, and look for free maps available at local TIs. Popular towns charge a small fee to park. Expect headaches parking in Isle-sur-la-Sorgue during its market days.

By Bus: Isle-sur-la-Sorgue is connected with Avignon's town center by the Trans Vaucluse bus line #6 (12/day Mon-Sat, 2/day Sun, 45 minutes, central stop—called Robert Vasse—is near the post office in Isle-sur-la-Sorgue, ask for schedule at TI or download French-only schedule from www.voyages-raoux.fr/lignes/index.php). Buses also connect Isle-sur-la-Sorgue with the Marseille airport (4/day direct, 2 hours, www.info-ler.fr, look for

Carpentras-Marseille line). Without a car or minivan tour, skip the more famous hill towns of the Luberon.

By Train: Trains get you to Isle-sur-la-Sorgue (station called "L'Isle-Fontaine de Vaucluse") from Avignon (8/day on weekdays, 5/day on weekends, 30 minutes) or from Marseille (6/day, 1.5 hours). If you're day-tripping by train, check return times before leaving the station.

By Minivan Tour: I list several minivan tour companies and private guides who can guide you through this marvelous region (see "Tours in Provence" on page 578).

By Taxi: Contact **Luberon Taxi** (based in Maubec off D-3, mobile 06 08 49 40 57, www.luberontaxi.com).

By Bike: Isle-sur-la-Sorgue makes a good base for biking, with level terrain and good rental options. Hardy bikers can ride from Isle-sur-la-Sorgue to Gordes, then to Roussillon, connecting other villages in a full-day loop ride (30 miles round-trip to Roussillon and back, with lots of hills). Several appealing villages are closer to Isle-sur-la-Sorgue and offer easier biking options. **Sun-e-Bike** rents electric bikes and has a network of partners with spare batteries scattered across the Luberon, extending the range of your e-bike trip. They can also arrange bike tours and shuttle your bags between hotels (1 Avenue Clovis Hugues in Bonnieux, tel. 04 90 74 09 96, www.sun-e-bike.com).

Isle-sur-la-Sorgue

This sturdy market town—literally, "Island on the Sorgue River"—sits within a split in its crisp, happy little river at the foot of the Luberon. It's a workaday town that feels refreshingly real after so many adorable villages.

Although Isle-sur-la-Sorgue is renowned for its market days (Sun and Thu), it's an otherwise pleasantly average town with no important sights and a steady trickle of tourism. It's lively on weekends but calm most weeknights. The town revolves around its river, the church square, and two pedestrian-only streets, Rue de la République and Rue Carnot.

The TI has an essential town map, hiking information (ask about trails accessible by short drives), biking itineraries, and a line on rooms in private homes, all of which are outside town (April-Sept Mon-Sat 9:00-12:30 & 14:30-18:00, until 17:30 Oct-March,

PROVENCE

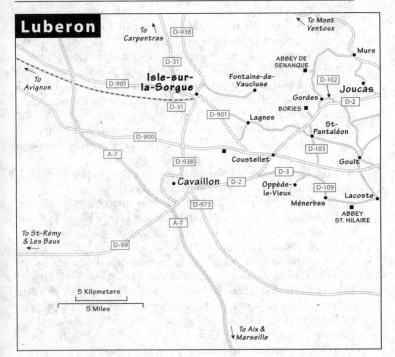

Luberon

To Carpentras

D-938

To Mont Ventoux

Murs

To Avignon

D-901

D-31

ABBEY DE SENANQUE

D-102

Isle-sur-la-Sorgue

Fontaine-de-Vaucluse

Joucas

Gordes

D-2

D-31

BORIES

St-Pantaléon

D-901

Lagnes

D-900

A-7

D-938

Coustellet

D-103

Goult

Cavaillon

D-2

Oppède-le-Vieux

D-3

D-109

Lacoste

D-973

Ménerbes

ABBEY ST. HILAIRE

A-7

To St-Rémy & Les Baux

D-99

5 Kilometers

5 Miles

To Aix & Marseille

Sun 9:00-12:30; in town center next to church, tel. 04 90 38 04 78, www.oti-delasorgue.fr).

Visiting Isle-sur-la-Sorge: In Isle-sur-la-Sorgue—called the "Venice of Provence"—the Sorgue River's extraordinarily clear and shallow flow divides like cells, producing water, water everywhere. The river has long nourished the region's economy, but today, antique shops keep the town afloat. Navigate by the town's splintered streams and nine mossy waterwheels, which, while still turning, power only memories of the town's wool and silk industries. At its peak, Isle-sur-la-Sorgue had 70 waterwheels; in the 1800s, the town competed with Avignon as Provence's cloth-dyeing and textile center.

Find **Le Bassin,** where the Sorgue River crashes into the town and separates into many branches (carefully placed lights make this a beautiful sight after dark).

With its source (a spring) a mere five miles away, the Sorgue River never floods and has a constant flow and temperature in all seasons. Despite its exposed (flat) location, Isle-sur-la-Sorgue prospered in the Middle Ages, thanks to the natural protection this river provided.

In the town's center, peek into Notre-Dame des Anges church with its festive Baroque interior and colorful walls (closed 12:00-15:15). The town erupts into a carnival-like market frenzy

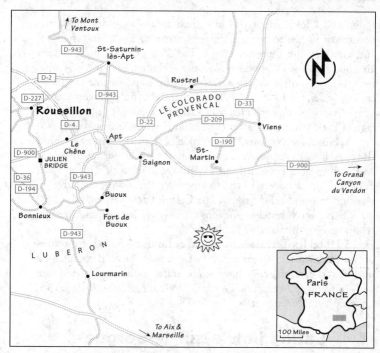

each Sunday and Thursday, with hardy crafts and local produce. The Sunday market is astounding and famous for its antiques; the Thursday market is still impressive but focused more on produce and bric-a-brac than antiques.

Sleeping in and near Isle-sur-la-Sorgue

Pickings are slim for good sleeps in Isle-sur-la-Sorgue, though the few I've listed provide reliable values. A *laverie automatique* (launderette) is in the town center, just off Rue de la République on Impasse de l'Hôtel de Palerme (open 24/7).

$$$ La Prévôté*** has the town's highest-priced digs. Its five meticulously decorated rooms—located above a classy restaurant—are adorned in earth tones, with high ceilings, a few exposed beams, and carefully selected furnishings. Séverine manages the hotel while chef-hubby Jean-Marie controls the kitchen (includes breakfast, limited check-in/check-out times, no elevator, rooftop deck with hot tub, no parking, one block from the church at 4 Rue J. J. Rousseau, tel. 04 90 38 57 29, www.la-prevote.fr, contact@la-prevote.fr).

$$ Sous l'Olivier is 10 minutes from Isle-sur-la-Sorgue, off D-900 near Petit Palais. Here big Julien, quiet Carole, and sons

Hugo and Clovis adopt you into their sprawling old stone farm-house, with grass to burn, a big pool, yards of chairs and lounges, and views to the Luberon range. The six rooms are big but lack air-conditioning. A good breakfast is included, and the €34 din-ner is a family affair, worth every euro (three apartments available, cash only, tel. 04 90 20 33 90, www.chambresdhotesprovence.com, souslolivier@orange.fr). Heading east on D-900, it's near the vil-lage of Petit Palais, just after the David Ferronerie shop).

$ Hôtel les Névons,*** two blocks from the center (behind the post office), is concrete motel-modern outside, with well-priced and comfortable-enough rooms within, a roof deck with a small pool, and quick access to the town center (family rooms, air-con, elevator, free and safe parking, 205 Chemin des Névons, tel. 04 90 20 72 00, www.hotel-les-nevons.com, hotel-les-nevons@orange.fr). Easygoing Benjamin's in charge.

$ Hôtel les Terrasses by David et Louisa** rents eight rooms over a pleasant restaurant right on Le Bassin. Several rooms look out over the river, most have some traffic noise and queen-size beds (air-con, 2 Avenue du Général de Gaulle, tel. 04 90 38 03 16, louisaetdavid@orange.fr).

Eating in Isle-sur-la-Sorgue

Cheap and mediocre restaurants are a dime a dozen in Isle-sur-la-Sorgue. You'll see several brasseries on the river, good for views and basic café fare.

For a cheap breakfast or a light riverside meal find **$ La Passe-relle,** where charming Jennifer and Vincent serve salads, quiche, a *plat du jour,* and more (daily until 20:00, summers until 22:00, 18 Quai Jean Jaurès, mobile 06 62 18 23 57).

Begin your dinner with a glass of wine at the cozy wine and cheese shop **$ Chez Stéphane.** Or for a light meal, order a selec-tion of cheeses from charming Stéphane (great to share) with your wine and call it good (wine barrel tables outside or find the bar hiding in the rear; daily 9:30-19:30, Fri-Sat until 21:00, 12 Rue de la République, tel. 04 90 20 70 25).

$$ Les Terrasses by David et Louisa is an appealing riverside wine-bar-bistro with a warm interior and ample choices. The cui-sine is a blend of French traditional and Provençal (closed Wed, 2 Avenue du Général de Gaulle, tel. 04 90 38 03 16).

$$ Le Nego is a relaxed place with generous outdoor seating and a large selection of reasonably priced, regional fare that works well for riverfront dining (daily, 12 Quai Jean Jaurès, tel. 04 90 20 88 83).

$$$$ La Balade des Saveurs is a refreshing change from the many run-of-the-mill riverfront places. Here, the owners deliver

PROVENCE

fresh, fairly priced Provençal cuisine at riverside tables or in their elegantly sky-lit interior (closed Mon-Tue, 3 Quai Jean Jaurès, tel. 04 90 95 27 85, www.balade-des-saveurs.com).

$$$$ La Prévôté is the place in town to do it up in the elegant French style. Its lovely dining room is country-classy but not stuffy, and the cuisine blends traditional French with regional specialties. A stream runs under the restaurant, visible through glass windows (closed Tue, on narrow street that runs along left side of church as you face it, 4 Rue J. J. Rousseau, tel. 04 90 38 57 29, www.la-prevote.fr).

Roussillon

With all the trendy charm of Santa Fe on a hilltop, photogenic Roussillon requires serious camera and café time. An enormous deposit of ochre, which gives the earth and its buildings that distinctive reddish color, provided this village with its economic base until shortly after World War II. This place is popular; visit early while the rising sun highlights the ochre cliffs, or come late and stay for dinner.

The little **TI** is in the center, across from the Chez David restaurant. Say bonjour to sweet Pascale. Hotel hunters can leaf through their binders describing area hotels and *chambres d'hôtes*. Walkers should get info on trails from Roussillon to nearby villages (TI hours unreliable, usually Mon-Sat April-Oct 9:30-12:30 & 14:00-18:00, Nov-March 14:00-17:30, closed Sun year-round, Place de la Poste, tel. 04 90 05 60 25, http://otroussillon.pagesperso-orange.fr).

Parking lots are available at every entry to the village (free if you're staying overnight and have arranged it with your hotel). **Parking des Ocres** (also called "P2") is the largest lot on the hill toward the ochre cliffs. Day-trippers should head straight here, as spots are more available and the view of Roussillon is striking. Leave nothing of value visible in your car.

Parking Sablons is next to the recommended Maison des Ocres. Parking St-Michel is below the town on the way to Joucas and Gordes.

Visiting Roussillon: Climb from any parking lot to the village center, cross the cute square, and then climb under the bell tower and the church. Continue past the church to the summit and find the orientation table and the **viewpoint.** During the Middle Ages, a castle occupied this space on the top of the appropriately named Red Mountain (Mont Rouge), and watched over the village below.

Stroll back to the pretty 11th-century **Church of St. Michel,** and appreciate the natural air-conditioning and the well-worn center aisle.

Linger over *un café,* or—if it's later in the day—*un pastis,* in the picturesque village square **(Place de la Mairie).** Watch the stream of shoppers. Is anyone playing *boules* at the opposite end? You could paint the entire town without ever leaving the red-and-orange corner of your palette. Many do. While Roussillon receives scads of day-trippers, mornings and evenings are romantically peaceful on this square.

Roussillon was Europe's capital for ochre production until World War II. A stroll to the south end of town, beyond the upper parking lot, shows you why: Roussillon sits on the world's largest known ochre deposit. Two radiant orange paths—the ▲▲ **Ochre Cliffs Trail** (Le Sentier des Ocres)—lead around the richly colored, Bryce Canyon-like cliffs; allow 35 minutes for the shorter path and 55 minutes for the longer one (€2.50, €7.50 combo-ticket with Ochre Conservatory—described next; May-June and Sept 9:30-18:30, July-Aug 9:00-19:30, shorter hours off-season, closed Jan).

For a good introduction to the history and uses of ochre, visit the ▲ **Ochre Conservatory (Conservatoire des Ocres et de la Couleur),** an intriguing reconstructed ochre factory. Grab a pamphlet to follow the well-done self-guided tour, which shows how ochre has been used since prehistoric times and how it is converted from an ore to a pigment—allow 45 minutes (€7, €7.50 combo-ticket with ochre cliffs, daily 10:00-18:00 but closed for lunch, July-Aug until 19:00, about a half-mile below Roussillon toward Apt on D-104, tel. 04 90 05 66 69, www.okhra.com).

Sleeping in and near Roussillon

The TI posts a list of hotels and *chambres d'hôtes.*

$$$ Le Clos de la Glycine*** delivers Roussillon's plushest accommodations with nine lovely rooms located dead-center in the village (some view rooms, air-con, parking options, located at the recommended restaurant Chez David—they prefer you pay for half-pension, across from the TI on Place de la Poste, tel. 04 90 05 60 13, www.luberon-hotel.fr, contact@luberon-hotel.fr).

$$ Maison des Ocres,*** well-located on the edge of the village center at the Sablons parking area, is a stylish place with a spacious lounge, handsome, well-configured rooms (many with decks or balconies), a few good family rooms, and a lovely pool (private parking, Route de Gordes, tel. 04 90 05 60 50, www.lamaisondesocres-hotel.com, contact@lamaisondesocres-hotel.com). Coming from Gordes and Joucas, it's the first building you pass in Roussillon.

$$$ Hôtel la Clé des Champs,*** more like an elegant bed-and-breakfast, is a lovely nine-room Provençal splurge warmly run by René and Armelle. Carefully appointed rooms are clustered about a heated pool, there's a hammam and hot tub, and dinners are available several days each week for €38 (between Roussillon and Joucas, off D-2 on Chemin du Garrigon, tel. 04 90 05 63 22, www.hotelcledeschamps.com, contact@hoteldeschamps.com)

$$ At Le Mas Destonge, Stéphane and Dominique welcome you into their impeccable Provençal retreat located in a small neighborhood 10 minutes from Roussillon. Their five beautifully decorated rooms come with cozy lounges, a sweet patio, a common kitchen, and a big pool (on D-227 in Hameau Des Riperts, tel. 04 90 05 63 13, www.destonge.com, destonge@gmail.com).

$$ Hôtel les Sables d'Ocre** offers 22 well-maintained, motel-esque rooms, a big pool, the greenest grass around, air-conditioning, and fair rates (a half-mile from Roussillon toward Apt at intersection of D-108 and D-104, tel. 04 90 05 55 55, www.sablesdocre.com, sablesdocre@orange.fr).

$ Le Clos des Cigales is a good forested refuge run by friendly Philippe. Of their five blue-shuttered, stylish bungalows, two are doubles and three are two-room family friendly suites with tiny kitchenettes; all have private patios facing a big pool (family rooms, includes breakfast, table tennis, hammock, 5 minutes from Roussillon toward Goult on D-104, tel. 04 90 05 73 72, www.leclosdescigales.com, philippe.lherbeil@wanadoo.fr).

Located in the center of lovely little Joucas, **$ Hostellerie des Commandeurs**** has quite comfortable, good-value rooms and is kid-friendly, with a big pool and a sports field/play area next door. Ask for a south-facing room *(côté sud)* for the best views. All rooms have showers, air-conditioning, and mini fridges (above park at village entrance, hotel open March-Oct, tel. 04 90 05 78 01, www.lescommandeurs.com, hostellerie@lescommandeurs.com). The traditional **$$ restaurant** offers Provençal cuisine at fair prices (restaurant closed Wed). Village kids like to hang out around the bar's pool table.

Eating in Roussillon

Restaurants change with the mistral here—what's good one year disappoints the next. But I have found a few reliable places that offer a good range of prices and cuisine. Consider my suggestions, then go with what looks best.

A good place to splurge is at **$$$$ Chez David,** at the recommended hotel Le Clos de la Glycine. You can enjoy a fine meal on the terrace or from an interior window table with point-blank views over the ochre cliffs (daily, Place de la Poste, tel. 04 90 05 60 13).

$$ La Treille hangs just above the village square and serves good-value meals on a small terrace or under soft arches in an upstairs room. *Souris d'agneau*—lamb shank—is the chef's specialty, though his daily specials are also worth considering (best to book ahead for an outside table, closed Wed and Sun, Rue du Four, tel. 04 90 05 64 47).

$ Le Bistrot de Roussillon is ideally situated on Roussillon's delightful square and serves simple café fare at good prices. Dine at outdoor tables on the square (my favorite), inside in a pleasant dining room, or on a small terrace out back with views to the ochre cliffs (daily, Place de la Mairie, tel. 04 90 05 74 45).

$ Chez Nino cascades down the hillside with three view terraces. The chef is Sicilian and his wife is Moroccan, and the simple fare combines elements of both with regional cuisine (lunch or early dinner only, daily until 19:00, a block behind the TI on Rue des Bourgades, tel. 04 90 74 29 17).

More Luberon Towns and Sights

I'd make a loop out of these villages and sights, doing them in the order described below. If you're sleeping in or near Roussillon, start there (mornings are peaceful) then follow signs to Gordes, then Oppède-Le-Vieux, and so on (making a counterclockwise loop through the Luberon). If you're staying elsewhere (like Isle-sur-la-Sorgue), start with Gordes, then Oppède-le-Vieux (ending with Roussillon). Bonnieux looks best from a distance, but it's a good place for lunch or to stay overnight. Each town is about a 10-minute drive from the last and the route is well signed.

Gordes

The Luberon's most impressively situated hill town is worth a quick stop to admire its setting. As you approach Gordes, veer right when you see the viewpoint icon. Get out, stroll along the road, and admire the sensational view. Now consider this: In the 1960s Gordes was a ghost town of derelict buildings with no economy. Today Gordes is renovated top to bottom (notice how every stone seems perfectly placed) and filled with people who live in a world without calluses. Many Parisian big-shots and moneyed foreigners invested heavily, restoring dream homes and putting property values and café prices out of sight for locals. Beyond its stunning views, the village has pretty lanes lined with trendy boutiques and restaurants but little else of interest.

Abbey Notre-Dame de Sénanque

This still-functioning and beautifully situated Cistercian abbey was built in 1148 as a back-to-basics reaction to the excesses of Benedictine abbeys. Come first thing and stop at a pullout for a bird's-eye view as you descend from Gordes, then wander the abbey's perimeter. The abbey church is always open and free (except during Mass, but you're welcome to attend) and highlights the utter simplicity sought by these monks. In late June through much of July, the five hectares of lavender fields that surround the abbey make for breathtaking pictures and draw loads of visitors.

Abbey interior areas that you can visit include Sénanque's church, the small cloisters, the refectory, and a *chauffoir*, a small heated room where monks could copy books year-round. The interior, which doesn't measure up to the abbey's spectacular setting, is a letdown—skip the tour and just wander the grounds.

Cost and Hours: €7.50 with or without a tour. French-only tours are mandatory daily 11:00-17:00, but individual visits are allowed Mon–Sat 9:00-11:00, or you can attend Mass at various times in the abbey's church. There are no individual visits on Sunday or holidays, and no visits at all 12:45-14:30. Reservations for tours are recommended (English booklet with translations available, see website for times, tel. 04 90 72 05 72, www.senanque.fr, visites@ndsenanque.net). Modest dress is required for entry—shoulders and knees must be covered.

▲Oppède-le-Vieux

This off-the-beaten-path fixer-upper of a village was completely abandoned in 1910, and today has a ghost town-like feel (it once housed 200 people). Climb the 20-minute path up to the small church and castle ruins for views. Back down in the village center, consider a meal with views of the castle ruins at **$ Le Petit Café,** where all-business Laurent is in charge (closed Wed and mid-Dec-Feb). Le Petit Café also offers simple but comfy **$** rooms, all with nice views (usually closed for check-in Tue-Wed, includes breakfast, air-con, rooftop terrace, tel. 04 90 76 74 01, www.lepetitcafe. fr, info@lepetitcafe.fr).

Ménerbes

Ménerbes, still (in)famous as the village that drew author Peter Mayle's attention to this region, has an upscale but welcoming feel in its small center (small parking fee). Wine bars, cafés, and a smattering of galleries gather where key lanes intersect. To explore the linear rock-top village, follow *Eglise* signs.

Find **$$$$ Maison de la Truffe et du Vin,** which offers "truffle discovery workshops," fine meals, and wine tastings (Place de l'Horloge, tel. 04 90 72 38 37, www.vin-truffe-luberon.com). Pass the Hôtel de Ville for more views (the church is closed but the views aren't) then double back and find Rue Corneille, which leads to the town's cute château (closed to public). Find the even cuter prison room outside the château and walk back along the path.

A fine lunch or snack awaits at the **$ Auzet Salon de Thé,** with a cozy interior or view tables from the small terrace. You'll find cheap quiche and savory pies with salad, delicious baked goods, and more (52 Rue du Portail Neuf, tel. 04 90 72 37 53).

Lacoste

Little Lacoste slumbers across the valley from Bonnieux in the shadow of its looming castle. This town is worth a stop to wander its pretty lanes to the base of the castle for views and to stop for a meal at **$ Café de France,** with its outdoor tables overlooking Bonnieux (reasonably priced omelets, quiche, and *plats;* daily, lunch only off-season, tel. 04 90 75 82 25).

Bonnieux

Spectacular from a distance, this town lacks a pedestrian center, though the Friday-morning market briefly creates one. The main reason to visit here is to enjoy the views from a well-positioned restaurant or hotel.

Sleeping: Located in Bonnieux's center, **$$ Hôtel le Clos du Buis***** is a 10-room delight, run by eager-to-please Lydia and Sophie. Rooms are lovingly decorated—some have private decks, their veranda allows fine views over the Luberon, and the garden pool is a peaceful retreat (includes breakfast, air-con, free parking, guest kitchen, in the middle of town on Rue Victor Hugo, tel. 04 90 75 88 48, www.leclosdubuis.fr, contact@leclosdubuis).

The country-elegant *chambres d'hôte* **$$$ Mas del Sol,** between Bonnieux and Lacoste, is perfect for connoisseurs of the Luberon, but it may be closing in 2020. Young Lucine and Richard Massol rent five bright, spacious rooms that come with views, vines, olives, and a big breakfast. The setting is unbeatable, and the stylish pool and gardens will knock your socks off (guest kitchen for family picnics, €40 three-course dinners with wine and coffee possible, tel. 04 90 75 94 80, www.mas-del-sol.com, contact@mas-del-sol.com). From D-900, take the D-36 turnoff to Bonnieux and look for *Mas del Sol* signs on the right after about three kilometers (two miles).

Eating: To eat with a view, find **$ Les Terrasses,** serving basic café cuisine on a sensational view terrace at the top of the village (open daily for lunch and dinner, Cours Elzéar Pin, tel. 04 90 75 99 77). To dine in Provence elegance sans view, find **$$$ Restaurant l'Arôme** with a formal-but-warm dining room and a streetside terrace, (closed Wed, across from Hôtel le Clos du Buis at 2 Rue Lucien Blanc, tel. 04 90 75 88 62).

Julien Bridge (Pont Julien)

Due south of Roussillon, just below D-900 (see "Luberon" map, earlier), this delicate, three-arched bridge, named for Julius Caesar, survives as a testimony to Roman engineers—and to the importance of this rural area 2,000 years ago. It's the only surviving bridge on what was the main road from northern Italy to Provence—the primary route used by Roman armies. The 215-foot-long Roman bridge was under construction from 27 BC to AD 14. Mortar  had not yet been invented, so (as with Pont du Gard) the stones were carefully set in place. Amazingly, the bridge survives today, having outlived Roman marches, hundreds of floods, and decades of automobile traffic. A new bridge finally rerouted traffic from this beautiful structure in 2005.

THE FRENCH RIVIERA

La Côte d'Azur: Nice • Villefranche-sur-Mer • Along the Three Corniches • Monaco • Antibes • Inland Riviera

A hundred years ago, celebrities from London to Moscow flocked to the French Riviera to socialize, gamble, and escape the dreary weather at home. Today, budget vacationers and heat-seeking Europeans fill belle époque resorts at France's most sought-after fun-in-the-sun destination.

Some of the Continent's most stunning scenery and intriguing museums lie along this strip of land—as do millions of sun-worshipping tourists. Nice has world-class museums, a splendid beachfront promenade, a seductive old town, and all the drawbacks of a major city (traffic, crime, pollution, and so on). The day-trip possibilities are easy and exciting: Fifteen minutes east of Nice, little Villefranche-sur-Mer stares across the bay to woodsy and exclusive Cap Ferrat; the eagle's-nest Eze-le-Village surveys the scene from high above; Monaco offers a royal welcome and a fairy-tale past; Antibes has a thriving port and silky sand beaches; and the inland hill towns present a rocky and photogenic alternative to the beach scene. Evenings on the Riviera, a.k.a. la Côte d'Azur, were made for a promenade and outdoor dining.

CHOOSING A HOME BASE

My favorite home bases are Nice, Antibes, and Villefranche-sur-Mer.

Nice is the region's capital and France's fifth-largest city. With convenient train and bus connections to most regional sights, this is the most practical base for train travelers. Urban Nice also has museums, a beach scene that rocks, the best selection of hotels in all price ranges, and good nightlife options. A car is a headache in Nice.

The French Riviera

RIVIERA

To Digne — Entrevaux

Alpes Maritimes

ITALY
To Genoa

To Grand Canyon du Verdon, Digne & Chamonix

D-6202

A-8

Venti-miglia

ROUTE NAPOLÉON

D-6085

Gorges du Loup

Gourdon   Tourrettes

La Turbie   Menton

MONACO

Vence   Eze-le-Village

Le Bar   **St-Paul**   **Villefranche-sur-Mer**

Grasse   **Nice**

Cap Ferrat

Biot

Vallauris   **Antibes**

A-8

Juan-les-Pins

To Arles & Avignon   Cannes

A-8   D-6098

Massif de l'Estérel   **SCENIC DRIVE**

Mediterranean Sea

D-559

Fréjus

St-Raphaël

D-559

St-Tropez

10 Kilometers
10 Miles

Paris

FRANCE

100 Miles

Nearby **Antibes** is smaller, with a bustling center, a lively night scene, great sandy beaches, grand vistas, good walking trails, and a stellar Picasso museum. Antibes has frequent train service to Nice and Monaco. It's the most convenient overnight stop for drivers, with light traffic and easy hotel parking.

Villefranche-sur-Mer is the romantic's choice, with a serene setting and small-town warmth. It has sand-pebble beaches; quick public transportation to Nice, Monaco, and Cap Ferrat; and a small selection of hotels and good restaurants in most price ranges.

PLANNING YOUR TIME

Ideally, allow a full day for Nice, a day for Monaco and the Corniche route that connects it with Nice, and a half-day for Antibes, Villefranche-sur-Mer, or Cap Ferrat (or better, a full day combining Villefranche and Cap Ferrat). Monaco and Villefranche-sur-Mer are radiant at night, and Antibes is enjoyable by day (good beaches and hiking) and night (fine choice of restaurants and a lively after-hours scene). Hill-town-loving travelers should add a day to explore the charming villages of St-Paul-de-Vence and Vence.

French Riviera at a Glance

▲▲▲**Nice** Classy resort town with beaches, seafront promenade, a fine palette of museums, and a ramble-worthy old town. See page 703.

▲▲▲**Villefranche-sur-Mer** Romantic pastel-orange beach village with a yacht-filled harbor and small-town ambience. See page 743.

▲▲**Along the Three Corniches** Scenic coastal roads highlighted by the exclusive woodsy Cap Ferrat peninsula, flowery hill-capping Eze-le-Village, and the Roman monument of Trophée des Alpes. See page 753.

▲▲**Monaco** Tiny independent municipality known for its classy casino and Grand Prix car race. See page 764.

▲▲**Inland Riviera** Up and away from the beaches, postcard-perfect St-Paul-de-Vence, crammed with boutiques and tourists, and appealing little Vence, host to a Matisse chapel. See page 790.

▲**Antibes** Laid-back beach town with a medieval center, worthwhile Picasso museum, sandy beaches, and view hikes. See page 776.

HELPFUL HINTS

Medical Help: Riviera Medical Services has a list of English-speaking physicians all along the Riviera. They can help you make an appointment or call an ambulance (tel. 04 93 26 12 70, www.rivieramedical.com).

Sightseeing Tips: Mondays and Tuesdays can frustrate market lovers and museumgoers. Closed on Monday: Nice's Modern and Contemporary Art Museum, Fine Arts Museum, and Cours Saleya produce and flower market; Antibes' Picasso Museum and market hall (Sept-May). Closed on Tuesday: Chagall, Matisse, Masséna, and Archaeological museums in Nice. Matisse's Chapel of the Rosary in Vence is closed Sunday and Monday and in the morning on Wednesday and Saturday.

The **French Riviera Pass** includes entry to many Riviera sights and activities, including Nice's Chagall Museum, Monaco's Oceanography Museum, and Villa Ephrussi de Rothschild on Cap Ferrat (€26/24 hours, €38/48 hours, €56/72 hours, tel. 04 92 14 46 14, http://en.frenchrivierapass.com). This pass is worthwhile if you have an aggressive sightseeing plan or want to do some bigger-ticket items like the included hop-on, hop-off Le Grand Tour Bus in Nice (see "Tours in Nice," later).

A €10 **combo-ticket for Nice** covers all of the city's museums, except the Chagall Museum.

Events: The Riviera is famous for staging major events. Unless you're actually taking part in the festivities, these occasions give you only room shortages and traffic jams. Here are the three biggies: **Nice Carnival** (two weeks in Feb, www.nicecarnaval.com), **Cannes Film Festival** (12 days in mid-May, www.festival-cannes.com), and the **Grand Prix of Monaco** (4 days in late May, www.acm.mc). To accommodate the busy schedules of the rich and famous (and really mess up a lot of normal people), the film festival and car race often overlap.

Connecting to the Alps: If driving from the Riviera north to the Alps region (see next chapter), consider taking La Route Napoléon. After getting bored in his toy Elba empire, Napoléon gathered his entourage, landed on the Riviera, bared his breast, and told his fellow Frenchmen, "Strike me down or follow me." France followed. But just in case, he took the high road, returning to Paris along the route known today as La Route Napoléon. (Waterloo followed shortly afterward.) The route is beautiful (from south to north, follow signs: *Digne*, *Sisteron*, and *Grenoble*). Little Entrevaux is worth a quick leg-stretch. Climb high to the citadel for great views and appreciate the unspoiled character of the town. An assortment of pleasant villages with inexpensive hotels lies along this route, making an overnight easy.

GETTING AROUND THE RIVIERA

Trains and buses do a good job of connecting places along the coast, with bonus views along many routes. Buses also provide reasonable service to some inland hill towns. Nice makes the most convenient base for day trips, though public transport also works well from Riviera towns such as Antibes and Villefranche-sur-Mer. Driving can be challenging in this congested region (traffic, parking, etc.).

By Public Transportation

In the Riviera, buses are often less expensive and more convenient while trains are faster and more expensive. For an overview of the most useful train and bus connections, see the "Public Transportation in the French Riviera" chart (confirm all connections and last train/bus times locally). You'll also find details under each destination's "Connections" section. For a scenic inland train ride, take the narrow-gauge train into the Alps (see page 725).

If taking the train or bus, have coins handy. Ticket machines don't take euro bills, some US credit cards may not work, smaller train stations may be unstaffed, and bus drivers can't make change for large bills.

Buses: Most of the area's top destinations are connected by bus, and tickets are cheap. This is an amazing deal in the Riviera. Any one-way bus or tram **ticket** costs €1.50 (€10 for 10 tickets) whether you're riding just within Nice or to Villefranche-sur-Mer, Monaco, or Antibes. This ticket is good for 74 minutes of travel in one direction anywhere within the bus system (but does not cover airport buses). Outside of the Inland Riviera, you can buy a single bus ticket from the

driver or from machines at stops, and validate it in the machine on board (10-ride or all-day tickets must be purchased at machines or at Lignes d'Azur offices). At Inland Riviera destinations such as Vence and St.-Paul-de-Vence, buy bus tickets at a *tabac*. Your ticket allows transfers between the buses of the Lignes d'Azur (the region's main bus company, www.lignesdazur.com) and the TAM (Transports Alpes-Maritimes); if you board a TAM bus and need a transfer, ask for *un ticket correspondance*. A €5 all-day ticket is good on Nice's city buses, tramway, and selected buses serving nearby destinations (such as Villefranche, Cap Ferrat, and Eze-le-Village). The general rule of thumb: If the bus number has one or two digits, it's covered with the all-day ticket; with three digits, it's not.

You'll be able to get around most of the Riviera on the following major bus routes:

- **Bus #100** runs eastbound from **Nice** along the Low Corniche (3-4/hour) stopping in **Villefranche-sur-Mer** (20 minutes), **Beaulieu-sur-Mer** (**Villa Kérylos**; 30 minutes), **Eze-Bord-de-Mer** (40 minutes, transfer to #83 to Eze-le-Village), **Monaco** (1 hour), and **Menton** (1.5 hours).
- **Bus #81** runs eastbound from **Nice** (2-3/hour) to **Villefranche-sur-Mer** (15 minutes), **Beaulieu-sur-Mer** (**Villa Kérylos**; 20 minutes), and all **Cap Ferrat** stops, ending at **St-Jean-Cap-Ferrat** (30 minutes).
- **Buses #82 and #112** run from **Nice** and upper **Villefranche-sur-Mer** to **Eze-le-Village** (together they depart about hourly; only #82 runs on Sunday; 30 minutes to reach Eze from Nice). **Bus #112,** which runs along the scenic Middle Corniche, continues from Eze-le-Village to **Monte Carlo** in Monaco (6/day, none on Sun, 20 minutes).
- **Bus #200** goes from **Nice** westbound (4/hour Mon-Sat, 2/

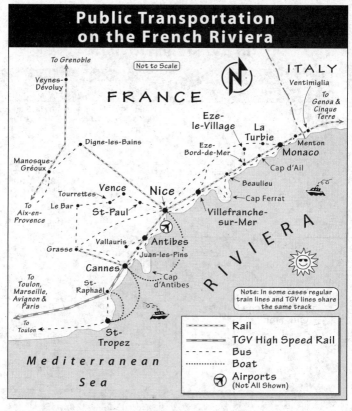

Public Transportation on the French Riviera

Not to Scale

FRANCE

ITALY

To Grenoble

Veynes-
Dévoluy

Ventimiglia

*To Genoa &
Cinque Terre*

Digne-les-Bains

Eze-
le-Village

La
Turbie

Menton

Manosque-
Gréoux

Eze-
Bord-de-Mer

Monaco

Cap d'Ail

Tourrettes

Vence

Nice

Beaulieu

*To
Aix-en-
Provence*

Le Bar

St-Paul

Cap Ferrat

Villefranche-
sur-Mer

Vallauris

Antibes

RIVIERA

Grasse

Juan-les-Pins

Cannes

St-
Raphaël

Cap
d'Antibes

*To
Toulon,
Marseille,
Avignon &
Paris*

Note: In some cases regular
train lines and TGV lines share
the same track

*To
Toulon*

St-
Tropez

*Mediterranean
Sea*

Rail

TGV High Speed Rail

Bus

Boat

Airports
(Not All Shown)

hour Sun) to **Cagnes-sur-Mer** (1 hour), **Antibes** (1.5 hours), and **Cannes** (2 hours).

- For the inland towns, **bus #400** runs from **Nice** (2/hour) to **St-Paul-de-Vence** (45 minutes) and **Vence** (50 minutes).

Trains: These are more expensive but much faster than the bus (Nice to Monaco by train is about €4), and there's no quicker way to move about the Riviera (http://en.voyages-sncf.com). Speedy trains link the Riviera's beachfront destinations. (Never board a train without a ticket or valid pass—fare inspectors accept no excuses. The minimum fine: €70.)

By Car

This is France's most challenging region to drive in. Beautifully distracting vistas (natural and human), loads of Sunday-driver tourists, and every hour being lush-hour in the summer make for a dangerous combination. Parking can be exasperating. Bring lots of coins and patience.

The Riviera is awash with scenic roads. To sample some of the

RIVIERA

Public Transportation in the French Riviera

From \ To		Cannes	Antibes	Nice
Cannes		N/A	**Train:** 2/hr, 15 min **Bus:** #200, 2-4/hr, 35 min	**Train:** 2/hr, 30 min **Bus:** #200, 2-4/hr, 2 hrs
Antibes		**Train:** 2/hr, 15 min **Bus:** #200, 2-4/hr, 35 min	N/A	**Train:** 2/hr, 20 min **Bus:** #200, 2-4/hr, 1.5 hrs
Nice		**Train:** 2/hr, 30 min **Bus:** #200, 2-4/hr, 2 hrs	**Train:** 2/hr, 20 min **Bus:** #200, 2-4/hr, 1.5 hrs	N/A
Villefranche-sur-Mer		**Train:** 2/hr, 50 min	**Train:** 2/hr, 40 min	**Train:** 2/hr, 10 min **Bus:** #100, 3-4/hr, 20 min; also #81, 2-3/hr, 15 min
Cap Ferrat		**Bus/Train:** #81 to Beaulieu-sur-Mer (2-3/hr, 10 min), then train to Cannes (2/hr, 1 hr)	**Bus/Train:** #81 to Beaulieu-sur-Mer (2-3/hr, 10 min), then train (2/hr, 40 min) **Bus:** #81 to Nice (2-3/hr, 30 min), then #200 (2-4/hr, 1.5 hrs)	**Bus:** #81, 2-3/hr, 30 min
Eze-le-Village		**Bus/Train:** #83 to Eze-Bord-de-Mer (8/day, 15 min), then train (2/hr, 1 hour)	**Bus/Train:** #83 to Eze-Bord-de-Mer (8/day, 15 min), then train (2/hr, 45 min)	**Bus/Train:** #83 to Eze-Bord-de-Mer (8/day, 15 min), then train (2/hr, 15 min) **Bus:** #82/#112, hourly, 30 min
Monaco		**Train:** 2/hr, 70 min	**Train:** 2/hr, 50 min	**Train:** 2/hr, 20 min **Bus:** #100, 3-4/hr, 1 hour

Note: Bus frequencies are given for Monday-Saturday (Sunday often has limited or no bus service).

Villefranche-sur-Mer	Cap Ferrat	Eze-le-Village	Monaco
Train: 2/hr, 50 min	**Train/Bus:** 2/hr, 1 hr to Beaulieu-sur-Mer, then bus #81 (2-3/hr, 10 min)	**Train/Bus:** 2/hr, 1 hr to Eze-Bord-de-Mer, then bus #83 (8/day, 15 min)	**Train:** 2/hr, 70 min
Train: 2/hr, 40 min	**Train/Bus:** 2/hr, 40 min to Beaulieu-sur-Mer, then bus #81 (2-3/hr, 10 min) **Bus:** #200 to Nice (2-4/hr, 1.5 hrs), then #81 (2-3/hr, 30 min)	**Train/Bus:** 2/hr, 45 min to Eze-Bord-de-Mer, then bus #83 (8/day, 15 min)	**Train:** 2/hr, 50 min
Train: 2/hr, 10 min **Bus:** #100, 3-4/hr, 20 min; also #81, 2-3/hr, 15 min	**Bus:** #81, 2-3/hr, 30 min	**Train/Bus:** 2/hr, 15 min to Eze-Bord-de-Mer, then bus #83 (8/day, 15 min) **Bus:** #82/#112, hourly, 30 min	**Train:** 2/hr, 20 min **Bus:** #100, 3-4/hr, 1 hour
N/A	**Bus:** #81, 2-3/hr, 15 min	**Train/Bus:** 2/hr, 5 min to Eze-Bord-de-Mer, then bus #83 (8/day, 15 min) **Bus:** #100 to Eze-Bord-de-Mer, then transfer to #83; also #82/#112 from upper Villefranche	**Train:** 2/hr, 10 min **Bus:** #100, 3-4/hr, 40 min
Bus: #81, 2-3/hr, 15 min	N/A	**Bus:** 30-min walk or bus #81 to Beaulieu-sur-Mer (3-4/hr, 10 min), then #83 to Eze-le-Village (8/day, 20 min)	**Bus:** 20-min walk or bus #81 to #100 (3-4/hr, 20 min)
Bus/Train: #83 to Eze-Bord-de-Mer (8/day, 15 min), then train (2/hr, 5 min) **Bus:** #83 to Eze-Bord-de-Mer, then transfer to #100; also #82/#112 to upper Villefranche	**Bus:** #83 to Beaulieu-sur-Mer (8/day, 20 min), then walk 30 min or transfer to #81)	N/A	**Bus:** #112, 6/day, 20 min
Train: 2/hr, 10 min **Bus:** #100, 3-4/hr, 40 min	**Bus:** #100, 3-4/hr, 20 min (plus 20-min walk or transfer to #81)	**Bus:** #112, 6/day, 20 min	N/A

Riviera's best scenery, connect Provence and the Riviera by driving the splendid coastal road between Cannes and Fréjus (D-6098 from Cannes/D-559 from Fréjus). Once in the Riviera, the most scenic and thrilling road trip is along the three coastal roads—called "corniches"—between Nice and Monaco (see "Along the Three Corniches," later).

By Boat

Trans Côte d'Azur offers seasonal boat service from Nice to Monaco (tel. 04 92 98 71 30, www.trans-cote-azur.com). For details, see the "By Boat" section under "Nice Connections," later.

TOURS IN THE RIVIERA

Most hotels and TIs have information on economical shared minivan excursions from Nice (per person: roughly €50-70/half-day, €80-120/day).

Local Guides with Cars

These two energetic and delightful women adore educating people about this area's culture and history, and have comfortable minibuses: **Sylvie Di Cristo** (€600/day, €350/half-day for up to 8 people, mobile 06 09 88 83 83, http://frenchrivieraguides.com, dicristosylvie@gmail.com) and **Ingrid Schmucker** (€490/day for 2 people, €530/day for 3-4 people, €580 for 5-6, €200/half-day to explore old Nice on foot, mobile 06 14 83 03 33, https://kultours.fr, kultours06@gmail.com). Their websites explain their programs well, and they are happy to adapt to your interests.

Charming Fouad Zarrou runs **France Azur Excursions** and offers a fun experience. His tours are more about exploring the region's natural beauty, food, and wine than its cultural history. He provides comfortable transportation in his minivan (figure €300/half-day, mobile 06 20 68 10 70, http://franceazurexcursions.com, contact@franceazurexcursions.com).

Local Guides Without Cars

For a guided tour of Nice or the region using public transit or with a guide joining you in your rental car, consider **Pascale Rucker,** an art-loving guide with 25 years of experience who teaches with the joy and wonder of a flower child (€160/half-day, €260/day, mobile 06 16 24 29 52, pascalerucker@gmail.com). **Boba Vukadinovic-Millet** is an effective teacher, ideal for those wanting to dive more deeply into the region's history and art. She can arrange chauffeur-driven rental options (car, minivan, minibus, bus) for you if needed (from €250/half-day, from €350/day, mobile 06 27 45 68 39, www.yourguideboba.com, boba@yourguideboba.com).

Food Tours

For food and wine walking tours and cooking classes offered in Nice, see "Tours in Nice," later.

THE RIVIERA'S ART SCENE

The list of artists who have painted the Riviera reads like a Who's Who of 20th-century art. Pierre-Auguste Renoir, Henri Matisse, Marc Chagall, Georges Braque, Raoul Dufy, Fernand Léger, and Pablo Picasso all lived and worked here—and raved about the region's wonderful light. Their simple, semi-abstract, and—most importantly—colorful works reflect the pleasurable atmosphere of the Riviera. You'll experience the same landscapes they painted in this bright, sun-drenched region, punctuated with views of the "azure sea." Try to imagine the Riviera with a fraction of the people and development you see today.

But the artists were mostly drawn to the uncomplicated lifestyle of fishermen and farmers that has reigned here since time began. As the artists grew older, they retired in the sun, turned their backs on modern art's "isms," and painted with the wide-eyed wonder of children, using bright primary colors, basic outlines, and simple subjects.

A collection of modern- and contemporary-art museums dot the Riviera, allowing art lovers to appreciate these masters' works while immersed in the same sun and culture that inspired them. Many of the museums were designed to blend pieces with the surrounding views, gardens, and fountains, thus highlighting that modern art is not only stimulating, but sometimes simply beautiful.

THE RIVIERA'S CUISINE SCENE

The Riviera adds an Italian-Mediterranean flair to the food of Provence. While many of the same dishes served in Provence are available in the Riviera (see "Provence's Cuisine Scene" on page 583), there are differences, especially if you look for anything Italian or from the sea. When dining on the Riviera, I expect views and ambience more than top-quality cuisine.

A fresh and colorful *salade niçoise* makes the perfect introduction to the Riviera's cuisine. Surprisingly, the authentic version contains no potatoes or green beans but consists of ripe tomatoes, plenty of raw vegetables (such as radishes, green peppers, celery, and perhaps artichoke or fava beans), as well as tuna (usually canned), anchovy, hard-boiled egg, and olives. This is my go-to salad for a tasty, healthy, cheap (€14), and fast lunch. I like to spend a couple of extra euros and eat it in a place with a nice ambience and view.

For lunch on the go, look for a *pan bagnat* (like a *salade niçoise* stuffed into a crusty roll drizzled with olive oil and wine vinegar). Other tasty bread treats include *pissaladière* (bread dough topped with caramelized onions, olives, and anchovies), *fougasse* (a spindly, lace-like bread sometimes flavored with nuts, herbs, olives, or ham), and *socca* (a thin chickpea-and-olive-oil crêpe, seasoned with pepper and often served in a paper cone by street vendors).

The Riviera specializes in all sorts of fish and shellfish. Bouillabaisse is the Riviera's most famous dish; you'll find it in seafront villages and cities. It's a spicy fish stew based on recipes handed down from sailors in Marseille. This dish often requires a minimum order of two and can cost up to €40-60 per person. Far less pricey than bouillabaisse and worth trying is the local *soupe de poissons* (fish soup). It's a creamy soup flavored like bouillabaisse, with anise and orange, and served with croutons and *rouille* sauce (but has no chunks of fish).

Other fishy options include *fruits de mer* (platters of seafood—including tiny shellfish, from which you get the edible part only by sucking really hard), herb-infused mussels, stuffed sardines, squid (slowly simmered with tomatoes and herbs), and tuna *(thon)*. The popular *loup flambé au fenouil* is grilled sea bass, flavored with fennel and torched with *pastis* prior to serving.

For details on dining in France's restaurants, cafés, and brasseries, getting takeout, and assembling a picnic—as well as a rundown of French cuisine—see the "Eating" section in the Practicalities chapter.

Wines of the Riviera: Do as everyone else does: Drink wines from Provence. Bandol (red) and cassis (white) are popular and from a region nearly on the Riviera. The only wines made in the Riviera are Bellet rosé and white, the latter often found in fish-shaped bottles.

Nice

Nice (sounds like "niece"), with its spectacular Alps-meets-Mediterranean surroundings,
is the big-city highlight
of the Riviera. Its traffic-
free Vieux Nice—the
old town—blends Ital-
ian and French flavors to
create a spicy Mediter-
ranean dressing, while its
big squares, broad seaside

walkways, and long beaches invite lounging and people-watching.
Nice may be nice, but it's jammed in May, July, and August—reserve ahead and get a room with air-conditioning. Nice gets quiet
and mild in April and October. Everything you'll want to see in
Nice is either within walking distance, or a short bike, bus, or tram
ride away.

Orientation to Nice

Focus your time on the area between the beach and the train tracks
(about 15 blocks apart). The city revolves around its grand Place

Masséna, where pedestrian-
friendly Avenue Jean Médecin
meets Vieux Nice and the Promenade du Paillon parkway (with
quick access to the beaches). It's
a 20-minute walk (or about €15
by taxi) from the train station
to the beach, and a 20-minute
stroll along the promenade from
the fancy Hôtel Negresco to the
heart of Vieux Nice.

A 10-minute ride on the smooth tram through the center of
the city connects the train station, Place Masséna, Vieux Nice, and
Place Garibaldi. A new, mostly underground tram line paralleling
the Promenade des Anglais runs from the port to the airport and is
convenient for tourists.

TOURIST INFORMATION

Nice has several helpful TIs (tel. 08 92 70 74 07, www.nicetourisme.
com), including the main branches at the **train station** and at #5
Promenade des Anglais (both daily 9:00-18:00, July-Aug until
19:00), and possibly by the fountains near **Place Masséna,** called

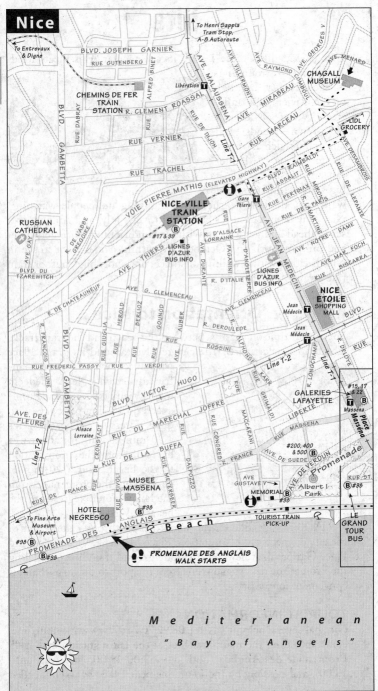

Nice

To Entrevaux & Digne

BLVD. JOSEPH GARNIER
RUE GUTENBERG

To Henri Sappia Tram Stop, A-8 Autoroute

CHEMINS DE FER TRAIN STATION

R. CLEMENT ROASSAL

Libération 🚋

AVE. MALAUSSENA

AVE. VILLEMONT

AVE. MIRABEAU

AVE. RAYMOND COMBOUL

AVE. GEORGES V

AVE. MENARD

CHAGALL MUSEUM

RUE DE DILON

RUE DABRAY

RUE VERNIER

RUE MARCEAU

LIDL GROCERY

AVE. DESAMBROIS

RUE TRACHEL

Line T-1

BLVD. GAMBETTA

VOIE PIERRE MATHIS (ELEVATED HIGHWAY)

BLVD. RAIMBALDI

RUE ASSALIT

RUE DE LEPANTE

Gare Thiers

NICE-VILLE TRAIN STATION

🛈

🚋

RUE PERTINAX

RUE MIRONS

RUE DE PARIS

RUSSIAN CATHEDRAL

R. DE L'ABBE GREGOIRE

AVE. GAY

#17 & 99 Ⓑ

R. D'ALSACE-LORRAINE

RUE LAMARTINE

RUE NOTRE DAME

LIGNES D'AZUR BUS INFO

BLVD. DU TZAREWITCH

AVE. THIERS

RUE DURANTE

RUE D'ANGLETERRE

PAGANINI

AVE. JEAN MEDECIN

AVE. MAR. FOCH

BISCARRA

R. DE CHATEAUNEUF

R. FRANÇOIS

AVE. DURANTE

R. D'ITALIE

LIGNES D'AZUR BUS INFO

NICE ETOILE SHOPPING MALL

BLVD.

AVE. G. CLEMENCEAU

AVE. CLEMENCEAU

Jean Médecin 🚋

R. DELOYE

RUE

RUE FREDERIC PASSY

R. DE JOSEPH GARNIER

HEROLD

GIUGLIA

BERLIOZ

GOUNOD

AUBER

R. DEROULEDE

ROSSINI

ALPHONSE KARR

Jean Médecin 🚋

RUE VERDI

Line T-2

AUNE

BLVD. VICTOR HUGO

RUE

RUE GRIMALDI

Line T-1

GALERIES LAFAYETTE

#15, 17 & 22 🚋

Place Massena

AVE. DES FLEURS

BLVD. GAMBETTA

RUE DU MARECHAL JOFFRE

RUE CONGRES

LIBERTE

RUE MASSENA

Massena

Alsace Lorraine

RUE DE CRONSTADT

RUE DE LA BUFFA

MACCARANI

FRANCE

AVE. DE SUEDE

#200, 400 & 500 Ⓑ

Promenade

RUE MEYERBEER

MUSEE MASSENA

RUE RIVOLI

DALPOZZO

AVE. GUSTAVE V

MEMORIAL 🛈

AVE. DE VERDUN

Albert I Park

RUE ST.

Ⓑ #98

RUE DE FRANCE

HOTEL NEGRESCO

Ⓑ #98

#98 ■

To Fine Arts Museum & Airport

#98 Ⓑ

PROMENADE DES ANGLAIS

Beach

TOURIST TRAIN PICK-UP

LE GRAND TOUR BUS

Ⓑ #98

👣 PROMENADE DES ANGLAIS WALK STARTS

⚓

Mediterranean

"Bay of Angels"

RIVIERA

RIVIERA

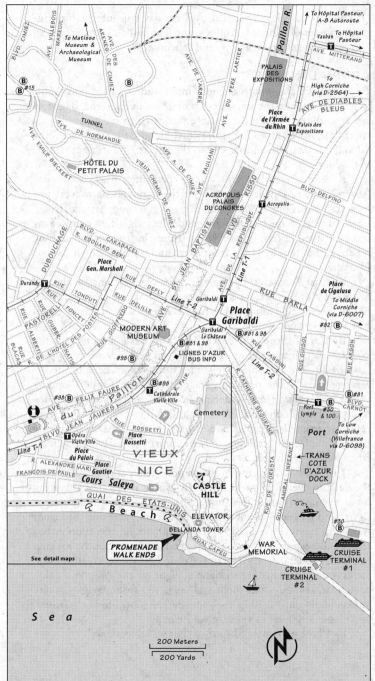

To Hôpital Pasteur, A-8 Autoroute
To Hôpital Pasteur
Vauban
AVE. MITTERAND

BLVD. CIMIEZ
AVE. VILLEBOIS MAREUIL
AVE. DES ARENES DE CIMIEZ
AVE. DU PERE CARTIER
AVE. DE L'ARBRE
Paillon R.
PALAIS DES EXPOSITIONS
To High Corniche (via D-2564)
To Matisse Museum & Archaeological Museum
B #15
B
Place de l'Armée du Rhin
AVE. DE DIABLES BLEUS
TUNNEL DE NORMANDIE
AVE. EMILE BIECKERT
AVE. A. DE CIMIEZ
VIEUX CHEMIN DE CIMIEZ
AVE. PAULIANI
Palais des Expositions
HÔTEL DU PETIT PALAIS
ST. JEAN BAPTISTE
ACROPOLIS-PALAIS DU CONGRES
BLVD. RISSO
Acropolis
BLVD DELFINO
DUBOUCHAGE
BLVD. GAKABACEL
R. EDOUARD BERI
AVE. DE LA REPUBLIQUE
Line T-1
RUE BARLA
Place de Cigalusa
To Middle Corniche (via D-6007)
Durandy
Place Gen. Marshall
RUE TONDUTI
RUE DEFLY
RUE DELILLE
AVE. GIOFFREDO
Line T-2
Garibaldi
Place Garibaldi
B #82
RUE PASTORELLI
RUE GUBERNATIS
RUE DE L'HOTEL DES POSTES
RUE FONCET
RUE ALBERTI
RUE BLACAS
MODERN ART MUSEUM
Garibaldi
Le Château
B #81 & 98
RUE CASSINI
RUE GUSOL
RUE ARSON
#98
B #81 & 98
LIGNES D'AZUR BUS INFO
Line T-2
B #81
BLVD CARNOT
#98 B
AVE. FELIX FAURE
Paillon
B #98
Cathédrale Vielle Ville
Cemetery
R. CATHERINE SEGURANE
Port Lympia
#30 & 100
To Low Corniche (Villefranche via D-6098)
Port
BLVD. JEAN JAURES
RUE DE L'AIR
RUE ROSSETTI
Opéra Vielle Ville
Place Rossetti
VIEUX NICE
TRANS COTE D'AZUR DOCK
Place du Palais
R. ALEXANDRE MARI
Place Gautier
RUE DE FORESTA
QUAI AMIRAL INFERNET
FRANÇOIS DE PAULE
Cours Saleya
CASTLE HILL
ELEVATOR
BELLANDA TOWER
#30 B
QUAI DES ETATS-UNIS
Beach
WAR MEMORIAL
CRUISE TERMINAL #1
See detail maps
PROMENADE WALK ENDS
QUAI CAPEU
CRUISE TERMINAL #2
Sea
200 Meters
200 Yards
N

"Pavillon" (may close in 2020). Ask for day-trip information (including maps of Monaco, Antibes, and Cannes) and details on boat excursions, bus stop locations, and schedules.

ARRIVAL IN NICE

By Train: All trains stop at Nice's main station, called Nice-Ville. With your back to the tracks, car rentals are to the right. Bag storage is to the left inside the station; you can also stash your bags a short block away at the recommended Hôtel Belle Meunière. The TI and bus stops (including #99 to the airport) are straight out the main doors.

A nearby tram line zips you to the center in a few minutes (several blocks to the left as you leave the station, departs every few minutes, direction: Hôpital Pasteur; see "Getting Around Nice," later. To walk to the beach, Promenade des Anglais, or many of my recommended hotels, cross Avenue Thiers in front of the station, go down the steps by Hôtel Interlaken, and continue down Avenue Durante.

By Bus: For arrival by bus, see "Nice Connections," at the end of this section. The region's primary bus company, Lignes d'Azur, has an information office across from the train station (see "Helpful Hints," next page).

By Car: To reach the city center from the autoroute, take the *Nice Centre* exit and follow signs. Ask you hoteliers where to park (allow €20-30/day; some hotels offer deals but space is limited—arrange ahead). The parking garage at the Nice Etoile shopping center on Avenue Jean Médecin is near many recommended hotels (ticket booth on third floor, about €28/day, 18:00-8:00). Other centrally located garages have similar rates. On-street parking is strictly metered (usually a 2-hour limit) every day but Sunday, when it is typically free.

You can avoid driving in the center—and park for free during the day (no overnight parking)—by stashing your car at a parking lot at a remote tram or bus stop. Look for blue-on-white *Parcazur* signs (find locations at www.lignesdazur.com), and ride the bus or tram into town (10/hour, 15 minutes, buy round-trip tram or bus ticket and keep it with you—you'll need it later to exit the parking lot; for tram details, see "Getting Around Nice," later). The easiest lot to use is Parcazur Henri Sappia, right off the *Nice Nord* autoroute exit. It always has room and saves you from navigating city streets (daily until 2:30 in the morning). As lots are not guarded, don't leave anything of value in your car.

By Plane or Cruise Ship: See "Nice Connections."

HELPFUL HINTS

Theft Alert: Nice has its share of pickpockets (especially at the train station, on the tram, and trolling the beach). Stick to main streets in Vieux Nice after dark.

Sightseeing Tips: The Cours Saleya produce and flower market is closed Monday, and the Chagall and Matisse museums are closed Tuesday. All Nice museums—except the Chagall Museum—share the same €10 combo-ticket (valid 24 hours, €20/7 days, buy at any participating museum).

Baggage Storage: You can store your bags inside the train station (€5-10/bag per day), at the recommended **Hôtel Belle Meunière** (€5/bag per day), or at the **Bagguys** in Vieux Nice (€8/bag per day, daily 10:00-19:00, 22 Rue Centrale, info@bagguys.fr).

Grocery Store: Small grocery shops are easy to find. The big **Monoprix** on Avenue Jean Médecin and Rue Biscarra has it all (open daily, see map on page 736).

Boutique Shopping: The chic streets where Rue Alphonse Karr meets Rue de la Liberté and then Rue de Paradis are known as the "Golden Square." If you need pricey stuff, shop here.

Renting a Bike (and Other Wheels): Bike-rental shops are a breeze to find in Nice, and several companies offer bike tours of the city. Bikes *(vélos)* can be taken on trains. **Holiday Bikes** has multiple locations, including one across from the train station, and they have electric bikes (www.loca-bike.fr). **Roller Station** is well-situated near the sea and rents bikes, rollerblades, skateboards, and Razor-style scooters (bikes-€5/hour, €10/half-day, €15/day, leave ID as deposit, open daily, 49 Quai des Etats-Unis—see map on page 732, tel. 04 93 62 99 05).

Car Rental: Renting a car is easiest at Nice's airport, which has offices for all the major companies. Most companies are also represented at Nice's train station and near the southwest side of Albert I Park.

Lignes d'Azur Bus Tickets: Useful information offices are at 17 Rue Thiers (kitty-corner from the train station, information only), at 1 Rue d'Italie (sells tickets and passes), and at 4 Boulevard Jean Jaurès (the main office where you can buy tickets and passes). Office hours vary (generally Mon-Fri 9:00-18:00 or 19:00, Sat until 15:00, closed Sun). Ask for their helpful "Passenger Guide" with information on buses to all Riviera destinations in English.

Views: For panoramic views, climb Castle Hill (see "Sights in Nice," later) or take a one-hour boat trip (see "Tours in Nice," later).

Beach Tips: To make life tolerable on the rocks, swimmers should buy a pair of the cheap plastic beach shoes sold at many shops.

Go Sport at #13 on Place Masséna is a good bet (open daily, see map on page 732). Locals don't swim in July and August, as the warming sea brings swarms of stinging jellyfish. Ask before you dip.

GETTING AROUND NICE
By Public Transportation

Although you can walk to most attractions, smart travelers make good use of the buses and trams within Nice. For information on getting around the Riviera from Nice, see "Nice Connections."

Tickets: Buses and trams are covered by the same €1.50 single-ride ticket, or you can pay €10 for a 10-ride ticket that can be shared (each use good for 74 minutes in one direction, including transfers between bus and tram). The €5 all-day pass is valid on city buses and trams, as well as buses to some nearby destinations (but not airport buses). You must validate your ticket in the machine on every trip—imitate how the locals do it. Buy single tickets from the bus driver or from the ticket machines on tram platforms (coins only—press the green button once to validate choice and twice at the end to get your ticket). Passes and 10-ride tickets are also available from machines at tram stops and from two Lignes d'Azur offices (see "Helpful Hints," earlier), but not from drivers. Info: www.lignesdazur.com.

Buses: The bus is handy for reaching the Chagall and Matisse museums and the Russian Cathedral (for specifics, see listings under "Sights in Nice"). Route diagrams in the buses identify each stop.

Trams: Nice has a modern and efficient L-shaped tram line (T-1) that runs to the train station and a new line (T-2) that connects the city center to the airport (http://tramway.nice.fr). T-1 trams to the train station run every few minutes along Avenue Jean Médecin and Boulevard Jean Jaurès, and connect the main train station with Place Masséna and Vieux Nice (Opéra stop), the port (Place Garibaldi stop), and buses east along the coast (Vauban stop). These trams also

stop near the Chemins de Fer de Provence train station (Libération stop)—the departure point for the scenic narrow-gauge rail journey.

Boarding the tram in the direction of Hôpital Pasteur takes you toward the beach and Vieux Nice (direction: Henri Sappia goes the other way). The new T-2 tramway goes from the airport through the city center to Nice's Port Lympia, paralleling the Promenade des Anglais a few blocks inland.

By Taxi or Uber

While pricey, **cabs** are useful for getting to Nice's less-central sights (figure €8 for shortest ride, €15 from Promenade des Anglais to the Chagall Museum). Cabbies normally pick up only at taxi stands *(tête de station)*, or you can call 04 93 13 78 78. **Uber** works here like it does at home (including your US app and account), though there are fewer cars here, and the price is not much cheaper than a taxi. Still, drivers are often nicer and more flexible, and you usually get a car without much delay.

Tours in Nice

ON WHEELS
Hop-On, Hop-Off Bus

Le Grand Tour Bus provides a useful 14-stop, hop-on, hop-off service on an open-deck bus with good headphone commentary. The route includes the Promenade des Anglais, the old port, Cap de Nice, and the Chagall and Matisse museums. From April to October, it also runs to Villefranche-sur-Mer (1-day pass-€23, 2-day pass-€26, buy tickets on bus, 2/hour, daily 10:00-19:00, 1.75-hour loop with Villefranche-sur-Mer, main stop near where Promenade des Anglais and Quai des Etats-Unis meet—across from the Albert I Park, tel. 04 92 29 17 00, www.nice.opentour.com). While it's not the best way to get to the Chagall and Matisse museums, this bus is a good value if you're looking for a city overview and want to also visit these museums or spend time in Villefranche-sur-Mer (best seats are up top on the left as you face forward).

Tourist Train

For €10, you can spend 45 minutes on the tourist train tooting along the promenade, through the old city, and up to Castle Hill (2/hour, daily 10:00-18:00 or 19:00, recorded English commentary, meet train at the Monument du Centenaire statue at Albert I Park, across from the Promenade des Anglais, tel. 02 99 88 47 07).

Bike Tour

Tina Balter at **Lifesparkz Bike Tours** offers well-designed, customized bike tours for individuals or small groups of all abilities (mobile 06 40 52 94 39, www.lifesparkz.net).

BY BOAT
▲Trans Côte d'Azur Cruise

To see Nice from the water, hop this one-hour tour run by Trans Côte d'Azur. You'll cruise in a comfortable yacht-size vessel to Cap

Nice at a Glance

▲▲▲**Promenade des Anglais** Nice's sun-struck seafront promenade. See page 711.

▲▲▲**Chagall Museum** The world's largest collection of Marc Chagall's work, popular even with people who don't like modern art. **Hours:** Wed-Mon 10:00-18:00, Nov-April until 17:00, closed Tue year-round. See page 720.

▲▲**Vieux Nice** Charming old city offering enjoyable atmosphere and a look at Nice's French-Italian cultural blend. See page 715.

▲**Matisse Museum** Modest collection of Henri Matisse's paintings, sketches, and paper cutouts. **Hours:** Wed-Mon 10:00-18:00, mid-Oct-mid-June from 11:00, closed Tue year-round. See page 722.

▲**Russian Cathedral** Finest Orthodox church outside Russia. **Hours:** Daily 9:30-17:30. See page 724.

▲**Castle Hill** Site of an ancient fort boasting great views. **Hours:** Park closes at 20:00 in summer, earlier off-season. See page 724.

Modern and Contemporary Art Museum Enjoyable collection from the 1960s and '70s, usually including Warhol and Lichtenstein. **Hours:** Tue-Sun 10:00-18:00, closed Mon. See page 723.

Ferrat and past Villefranche-sur-Mer, then return to Nice with a final lap along Promenade des Anglais.

Guides enjoy pointing out mansions owned by famous people, including Elton John and Sean Connery (€19; April-Oct Tue-Sun 2/day, usually at 11:00 and 15:00, no boats Mon or in off-season; verify schedule, arrive 30 minutes early to get best seats).

The boats leave from Nice's port, Bassin des Amiraux, just below Castle Hill—look for the ticket booth *(billeterie)* on Quai de Lunel. The same company also runs boats to Monaco (see "Nice Connections").

ON FOOT
Local Guides and Walking Tours

If interested in hiring a local guide for Nice and other regional destinations, see page 700 for suggestions.

The TI on Promenade des Anglais organizes weekly walking

tours of Vieux Nice in French and English (€12, Sat morning at 9:30, 2.5 hours, reservations necessary, departs from TI, tel. 08 92 70 74 07).

Food Tours and Cooking Classes

Charming Canadian Francophile **Rosa Jackson,** a food journalist, Cordon Bleu-trained cook, and longtime resident of France, runs a cooking school—Les Petits Farcis—and offers a good food-market tour in Vieux Nice for small groups (€80-120/person based on group size). She also teaches cooking classes that include a morning shopping trip to the market on Cours Saleya and an afternoon cooking session for €195/person, and a pastry course for €80/person (12 Rue Saint Joseph, mobile 06 81 67 41 22, www.petitsfarcis. com).

A Taste of Nice Food Tours runs daily scratch-and-taste tours in Vieux Nice that combine cultural history with today's food scene. You'll stop for 10 different tastings of classic Niçois products. Tours meet daily except Monday at 10:00 on Quai des Etats-Unis at the Opéra Plage (€70/4 hours, tel. 09 86 65 75 17, www.atasteofnice. com, booking@atasteofnice.com).

Walks in Nice

To get acquainted with Nice, combine the following two self-guided walks. "Promenade des Anglais" covers the sun-drenched seaside that made Nice famous, while "Vieux Nice" takes you through the historic old town of this engaging Franco-Italian city.

PROMENADE DES ANGLAIS WALK

This leisurely, level self-guided walk, worth ▲▲▲, is a straight line along this much-strolled beachfront. It begins near the landmark Hôtel Negresco and ends just before Castle Hill. While this one-mile section is enjoyable at any time, the first half makes a great stroll before or after breakfast or dinner (meals served at some beach cafés). If extending this stroll to Castle Hill, it's ideal to time things so you wind up on top of the hill at sunset. Allow one hour at a promenade pace to reach the elevator up to Castle Hill. To trace the route of this walk, see the "Nice" map, earlier.

• *Start your walk at the pink-domed...*

Hôtel Negresco

Built in 1913, Nice's finest hotel is also a historic monument, offering up the city's most expensive beds and a museum-like interior.

If you wonder why such a grand hotel has such an understated entry, it's because today's front door was originally the back door. In the 19th century, elegant people avoided the sun, and any posh hotel that cared about its clientele would design its entry on the shady north side. If you walk around to today's "back" you'll see a grand but unused front door.

The hotel is technically off-limits if you're not a guest, but if you're decently dressed and explain to the doorman that you'd like to get a drink at Negresco's classy-cozy Le Relais bar, you'll be allowed past the registration desk. You can also explain that you want to shop at their store, which also might get you in—*bonne chance.*

If you get in, you can't miss the huge **Salon Royal** ballroom. The chandelier hanging from its dome is made of 16,000 pieces of crystal. It was built in France for the Russian czar's Moscow palace...but thanks to the Bolshevik Revolution in 1917, he couldn't take delivery. Bronze portrait busts of Czar Alexander III and his wife, Maria Feodorovna—who returned to her native Denmark after the revolution—are to the right, facing the shops. Circle the interior of the ballroom and admire the soft light from the glass dome that Gustave Eiffel designed two decades after his more famous tower in Paris, then wander the perimeter to enjoy both historic and modern art. Fine portraits include Emperor Napoleon III and wife Empress Eugénie (who acquired Nice for France from Italy in 1860).

• *Across the street from the Hôtel Negresco (to the east) is...*

Villa Masséna

When Nice became part of France, France invested heavily in what it expected to be the country's new high society retreat—an elite resort akin to Russia's Sochi. This fine palace was built for Jean-Andre Masséna, a military hero of the Napoleonic age. Take a moment to stroll around the lovely garden. Immediately on your right, find a memorial to the 86 people who died in the 2016 terrorist attack on the Promenade des Anglais, with pictures, stuffed animals, and names engraved in granite (garden is free, open daily 10:00-18:00). The Masséna Museum inside the villa (described later in "Sights in Nice") offers an interesting look at belle-époque Nice.

• *From Villa Masséna, head for the beach and begin your Promenade des Anglais stroll. But first, grab a blue chair and gaze out to the...*

Bay of Angels (Baie des Anges)

Face the water. The body of Nice's patron saint, Réparate, was supposedly escorted into this bay by angels in the fourth century. To your right is where you might have been escorted into France—Nice's airport, built on a massive landfill. The tip of land beyond the runway is Cap d'Antibes. Until 1860, Antibes and Nice were in different countries—Antibes was French, but Nice was a protectorate of the Italian kingdom of Savoy-Piedmont, a.k.a. the Kingdom of Sardinia. In 1850, the people here spoke Italian or Nissart (a local dialect) and ate pasta. As the story goes, the region was given a choice: Join newly united Italy or join France, which was enjoying prosperous times under the rule of Napoleon III. The majority voted in 1860 to go French...and *voilà!*

The lower green hill to your left is Castle Hill (where this walk ends). Farther left lie Villefranche-sur-Mer and Cap Ferrat (marked by the tower at land's end, and home to lots of millionaires), then Monaco (which you can't see, with more millionaires), then Italy. Behind you are the foothills of the Alps, which trap threatening clouds, ensuring that the Côte d'Azur enjoys sunshine more than 300 days each year. While 350,000 people live in Nice, pollution is carefully treated—the water is routinely tested and is very clean. But with climate change, the warmer water is attracting jellyfish in the summer, making swimming a stinging memory.
• *With the sea on your right, begin strolling.*

The Promenade

This area was the favorite haunt of 19th-century British tourists, who wanted a place to stroll in their finery while admiring the sea views (locals called it "Little London"). When first built, the promenade was a dusty path about six feet wide and about 10 blocks long. It's been widened and lengthened over the years to keep up with tourist demand, including increased bicycle use. As you walk, be careful to avoid the bike lane.

Nearby sit two fine belle-époque establishments: the West End and Westminster hotels, both boasting English names to help those original guests feel at home. (The West End is now part of the Best Western group...to help American guests feel at home.) These hotels symbolize Nice's arrival as a tourist mecca in the 19th century, when the combination of leisure time and a stable economy allowed visitors to find the sun even in winter.

Find the easel showing a painting of La Jetée Promenade—Nice's elegant pier and first casino, built in 1883. Even a hundred years ago, there was sufficient tourism in Nice to justify constructing a palatial building to house this leisure activity imported from Venice. La Jetée Promenade stood east of those white-covered pilings just offshore, until the Germans dismantled it during World War II to salvage its copper and iron. When La Jetée was thriving, it took gamblers two full days to get to the Riviera by train from Paris. The painting shows what an event strolling the Promenade was—it was all about dressing up, being seen, and looking good.

Although La Jetée Promenade is gone, you can still see the striking 1927 Art Nouveau facade of the **Palais de la Méditerranée,** once a magnificent complex housing a casino, luxury hotel, and theater. It became one of the most famous destinations in all of Europe until it was destroyed in the 1980s to make room for a new hotel (the Hyatt Regency). The facade of the grand old building was spared the wrecking ball, but the classy interior was lost forever.

Despite the lack of sand, the pebble beaches here are still a popular draw. You can go local and rent beach gear—about €15 for a *chaise longue* (long chair) and a *transat* (mattress), €5 for an umbrella, and €5 for a towel. You'll also pass several beach restaurants. Some of these eateries serve breakfast, all serve lunch, some do dinner, and a few have beachy bars...tailor-made for a break from this walk.

Albert I Park is named after the Belgian king who defied a German ultimatum at the beginning of World War I. While the English came first, the Belgians and Russians were also big fans of 19th-century Nice. That tall statue at the edge of the park commemorates the 100-year anniversary of Nice's union with France. The happy statue features two beloved women embracing the idea of union (Marianne—Ms. Liberty, Equality, and Brotherhood, and the symbol of the Republic of France—and Catherine Ségurane, a 16th-century heroine who helped Nice against the Saracen pirates).

The park is part of a long, winding greenbelt called the Promenade du Paillon. The Paillon River flows under the park on its way to the sea. This is the historical divide between Vieux Nice and the new town.

Continuing along the promenade you'll soon enter the **Quai des Etats-Unis** ("Quay of the United States"). This name was given as a tip-of-the-cap to the Americans for finally entering World War I in 1917. The big, blue chair statue celebrates the inviting symbol of this venerable walk and kicks off the best stretch of beach—quieter and with less traffic. Check out the laid-back couches at the **Plage Beau Rivage** lounge and consider a beachfront drink.

Those tall, rusted **steel girders** reaching for the sky were erected in 2010 to celebrate the 150th anniversary of Nice's union with France. (The seven beams represent the seven valleys of the Nice region.) Done by the same artist who created the popular Arc of the Riviera sculpture in the parkway near Place Masséna, this "art" justifiably infuriates many locals as an ugly waste of money.

A block ahead on the left, the elegant back side of Nice's opera house faces the sea. The tiny bronze Statue of Liberty (right in front of you as you face the opera) reminds all that this stretch of seafront promenade is named for the USA.

The top level of the long, low galleries on the left was British tourists' preferred place for a stroll before the Promenade des Anglais was built. The ground floor served the city's fishermen. Behind the galleries bustles the **Cours Saleya Market**—long the heart and soul of Vieux Nice, with handy WCs under its arches.

Farther along, on the far-right side of the Quai des Etats-Unis (opposite Le Camboda restaurant), find the three-foot-tall white ❼ **metal winch** at the ramp to the beach. Long before tourism—and long before Nice dredged its harbor—hardworking fishing boats rather than vacationing tourists lined the beach. The boats were hauled in through the surf by winches like this and tied to the iron rings on either side.

• *You could end your walk here, but the view from the point just past the Hôtel la Pérouse is wonderful. Either way, you have several great options: Continue 10 minutes along the coast to the port, around the foot of Castle Hill (fine views of the entire promenade and a monumental war memorial carved into the hillside); hike or ride the elevator up to Castle Hill (catch the elevator next to Hôtel Suisse; see listing for Castle Hill in "Sights in Nice," later) head into Vieux Nice (you can follow my "Vieux Nice Walk"); or grab a blue chair or piece of beach and just be on vacation—Riviera style.*

VIEUX NICE WALK

This self-guided walk through Nice's old town, known as Vieux Nice and worth ▲▲, gives you a helpful introduction to the city's bicultural heritage and its most interesting neighborhoods. For the route, see the "Vieux Nice Hotels & Restaurants" map on page 732.

Allow about one hour at a leisurely pace for this level walk from Place Masséna to Place Rossetti. It's best done in the morning (while the outdoor market thrives—consider coffee or breakfast at a café along the Cours Saleya), and preferably not on a Sunday, when things are quiet. This ramble is also a joy at night, when fountains glow and pedestrians control the streets.

• *Start where Avenue Jean Médecin hits the people-friendly Place Masséna—the successful result of a long, expensive city upgrade and the new center of Nice.*

Place Masséna

The grand Place Masséna is Nice's drawing room, where old meets new, and where the tramway bends between Vieux Nice and the train station. The square's black-and-white pavement feels like an elegant outdoor ballroom, with the sleek tram waltzing across its dance floor. While once congested with cars, the square today is crossed only by these trams, which swoosh silently by every couple of minutes. The men on pedestals sitting high above are modern-art additions that arrived with the tram. For a mood-altering experience, return after dark and watch the illuminated figures float yoga-like above. Place Masséna is at its sophisticated best after the sun goes down.

This vast square dates from 1848 and pays tribute to Jean-André Masséna, a French military leader during the Revolutionary

RIVIERA

and Napoleonic wars. Not just another pretty face in a long lineup of French military heroes, he's considered among the greatest commanders in history—anywhere, anytime. Napoleon called him "the greatest name of my military Empire." No wonder this city is proud of him.

Standing on the square with your back to the fountains, start a clockwise spin tour: The **modern swoosh sculpture** at palm-tree height in the parkway is meant to represent the "curve of the French Riviera"—the arc of the bay. To the right stretches modern Nice, born with the arrival of tourism in the 1800s. **Avenue Jean Médecin,** Nice's Champs-Elysées, cuts from here through the new town to the train station. Looking up the avenue, you'll see the tracks, the freeway, and the Alps beyond. Once crammed with cars, buses, and delivery vehicles tangling with pedestrians, Avenue Jean Médecin was turned into a walking and cycling nirvana in 2007. Businesses along it flourish in the welcoming environment of generous sidewalks and no traffic.

Appreciate the city's Italian heritage—it feels more like Venice than Paris. The portico flanking Avenue Jean Médecin is Italian, not French. The rich colors of the buildings reflect the taste of previous Italian rulers.

Now turn to the fountains and look east to see Nice's ongoing effort to "put the human element into the heart of the town." An ugly concrete bus station and parking structures were demolished not long ago, and the **Promenade du Paillon** (named for the river which it covers) was created to fill the space. Today, this pedestrian-friendly parkway extends from the sea to the Museum of Modern Art—a modern-day Promenade des Anglais. Forming a key spine for biking, walking, and kids at play, the Promenade du Paillon is a delight any time of day. Past the fountain stands a bronze statue of the square's namesake, Masséna. The hills beyond separate Nice from Villefranche-sur-Mer.

To the right of the Promenade du Paillon lies **Vieux Nice,** with its jumbled and colorful facades below Castle Hill. Looking closer and further to the right, the **statue of Apollo** has horsey hair and holds a beach towel (in the fountain) as if to say, "It's beer o'clock, let's go."

• *Walk past Apollo into Vieux Nice (careful of those trams). A block down Rue de l'Opéra you'll see a grouping of rusted girders (described earlier). Turn left onto Rue St. François de Paule.*

Rue St. François de Paule

This colorful street leads into the heart of Vieux Nice. On the left is the Hôtel de Ville (City Hall). Peer into the **Alziari olive oil shop** (at #14 on the right). Dating from 1868, the shop produces top-quality stone-ground olive oil. The proud and charming owner, Gilles Piot, claims that stone wheels create less acidity, since grinding with metal creates heat (see photo in back over the door). Locals fill their own containers from the huge vats.

A few awnings down, **La Couqueto** is a colorful shop filled with Provençal fabrics and crafts, including lovely folk characters *(santons)*. Walk in for a lavender smell sensation—is madame working the sewing machine upstairs? The *boulangerie* next door is ideal for a cheap lunch and has good outdoor seating.

Next door is Nice's grand **opera house,** built by a student of Charles Garnier (architect of Monte Carlo's casino and opera house). Imagine this opulent jewel back in the 19th century, buried deep in Vieux Nice. With all the fancy big-city folks wintering here, this rough-edged town needed some high-class entertainment. And Victorians needed an alternative to those "devilish" gambling houses. (Queen Victoria, so disgusted by casinos, would actually close the drapes on her train window when passing Monte Carlo.) The four statues on top represent theater, dance, music, and party poopers.

Across the street, **Pâtisserie Auer**'s grand old storefront would love to tempt you with chocolates and candied fruits. It's changed little over the centuries. The writing on the window says, "Since 1820 from father to son." Wander in for a whiff of chocolate and a dazzling interior. The twin gold royal shields on the back mirrors remind shoppers that Queen Victoria indulged her sweet tooth here.

• *Continue on, sifting your way through a cluttered block of tacky souvenir shops to the big market square.*

Cours Saleya

Named for its broad exposure to the sun *(soleil)*, Cours Saleya (koor sah-lay-yuh)—a commotion of color, sights, smells, and peo-

ple—has been Nice's main market square since the Middle Ages (flower market all day Tue-Sun, produce market Tue-Sun until 13:00, antiques on Mon). While you're greeted by the ugly mouth of an underground parking lot, much of this square itself was a parking lot until 1980, when the mayor of Nice had this solution dug. If you're early enough for coffee, pause for a break at **Café le Flore**'s outdoor tables in the heart of the market (a block up on the left).

The first section is devoted to the Riviera's largest **flower market.** In operation since the 19th century, this market offers plants and flowers that grow effortlessly and ubiquitously in this climate, including the local favorites: carnations, roses, and jasmine. Locals know the season by what's on sale (mimosas in February, violets in March, and so on). Until the recent rise in imported flowers, this region supplied all of France with flowers. Still, fresh flowers are cheap here, the best value in this expensive city. The Riviera's three big industries are tourism, flowers, and perfume (made from these flowers...take a whiff).

The boisterous **produce section** trumpets the season with mushrooms, strawberries, white asparagus, zucchini flowers, and more—whatever's fresh gets top billing. What's in season today?

The market opens up at Place Pierre Gautier. It's also called Plassa dou Gouvernou—you'll see bilingual street signs here that include the old Niçois language, an Italian dialect. This is where farmers set up stalls to sell their produce and herbs directly.

From the steps, look up to the **hill** that dominates to the east. In the Middle Ages, a massive castle stood there with soldiers at the ready. Over time, the city sprawled down to where you are now. With the river guarding one side (running under today's Promenade du Paillon parkway) and the sea the other, this mountain fortress seemed strong—until Louis XIV leveled it in 1706. Nice's medieval seawall ran along the line of two-story buildings where you're standing.

Now, look across Place Pierre Gautier to the large "palace." The **Ducal Palace** was where the kings of Sardinia, the city's Italian rulers until 1860, resided when in Nice. (For centuries, Nice was under the rule of the Italian capital of Turin.) Today, the palace is the local police headquarters. The land upon which the Cours Saleya sits was once the duke's gardens and didn't become a market until Nice's union with France.

• *Continue down Cours Saleya. The faded golden building that seals the end of the square is where Henri Matisse spent 17 years. I imagine he was inspired by his view. The* **Café les Ponchettes** *is perfectly positioned for you to enjoy the view too if you want a coffee break. At the café, turn onto...*

Rue de la Poissonnerie

Look up at the first floor of the first building on your right. **Adam and Eve** are squaring off, each holding a zucchini-like gourd. This scene represents the annual rapprochement in Nice to make up for the sins of a too-much-fun Carnival (Mardi Gras, the pre-Lenten festival). Residents of Nice have partied hard during Carnival for more than 700 years.

Next, check out the small **Baroque church** (Notre-Dame de l'Annonciation, closed 12:00-14:30) dedicated to Ste. Rita, the patron saint of desperate causes and desperate people (see display in window). She holds a special place in locals' hearts, making this the most popular church in Nice. Drop in for a peek at the dazzling Baroque decor. The first chapel on the right is dedicated to St. Erasmus, protector of mariners.

• *Turn right on the next street, where you'll pass one of Vieux Nice's most happening bars (the recommended Distilleries Ideales), with a swash-buckling interior that buzzes until the wee hours. Pause at the next corner and study the classic Vieux Nice scene in all directions. Now turn left on Rue Droite and enter an area that feels like Little Naples.*

Rue Droite

In the Middle Ages, this straight, skinny street provided the most direct route from river to sea within the old walled town. Pass the recommended restaurant Acchiardo. Notice stepped lanes leading uphill to the castle. Pop into the Jesuit **Eglise St-Jacques** church (also called Eglise du Gésu) for an explosion of Baroque exuberance hidden behind that plain facade.

We're turning left onto Rue Rossetti...but if you continued another block along Rue Droite you'd find the **Palais Lascaris** (c. 1647), home of one of Nice's most prestigious families. Today it's a museum and worth a quick look (peek in the entry for free or take a tour, covered by Nice museum €10 combo-ticket, Wed-Mon 10:00-18:00, from 11:00 off-season, closed Tue year-round). Inside you'll find a collection of antique musical instruments—harps, guitars, violins, and violas (good English explanations)—along with elaborate tapestries and a few well-furnished rooms. The palace has four levels—but only two are open to the public: The ground floor was used for storage, the first floor was devoted to reception rooms (and musical events), the owners lived a floor above that, and the servants lived at the top. Look up and make faces back at the guys under the balconies.

• *Shortly after making a left on Rue Rossetti, you'll cross Rue Benoît Bunico.*

In the 18th century, this street served as a **ghetto** for Nice's Jews. At sunset, gates would seal the street at either end, locking people in until daylight. To identify Jews as non-Christians, the men were required to wear yellow stars and the women to wear yellow scarves. Wander a few steps up the street to find the white columns and archway across from #19 that mark what was the synagogue until 1848, when revolution ended the notion of ghettos in France.

• *Continue down Rue Rossetti to...*

Place Rossetti

The most Italian of Nice's piazzas, Place Rossetti comes alive after dark—in part because of the **Fenocchio gelato shop,** popular for its many innovative flavors.

Check out the **Cathedral of St. Réparate**—an unassuming building for a big-city cathedral. It was relocated here in the 1500s, when Castle Hill was temporarily converted to military use. The name comes from Nice's patron saint, a teenage virgin named Réparate, whose martyred body floated to Nice in the fourth century accompanied by angels. The beautiful interior is worth a wander.

• *This is the end of our walk. From here you can hike up Castle Hill (from Place Rossetti, take Rue Rossetti uphill; see Castle Hill listing near the end of "Sights in Nice." Or you can have an ice cream and browse the colorful lanes of Vieux Nice...or grab Apollo and hit the beach.*

Sights in Nice

Some of Nice's top attractions—the Promenade des Anglais, the beach, and the old town—are covered earlier in my self-guided walks. But Nice offers some additional worthwhile sights, covered here.

MUSEUMS

A combo-ticket covers all of Nice's museums except the Chagall Museum (see details under "Helpful Hints"). The Chagall Museum requires a separate admission (and is well worth it).

The first two museums (Chagall and Matisse) are a long walk northeast of Nice's city center. Because they're in the same direction and served by the same bus line (see "Getting There," next page), try to visit them on the same trip. From Place Masséna, the Chagall Museum is a 10-minute bus ride, and the Matisse Museum is a few stops beyond that.

▲▲▲Chagall Museum
(Musée National Marc Chagall)

Even if you don't get modern art, this museum—with the world's largest collection of Marc Chagall's work in captivity—is a delight.

After World War II, Chagall returned from the United States to settle first in Vence and later in St-Paul-de-Vence, both not far from Nice. Between 1954 and 1967, he painted a cycle of 17 large murals designed for, and donated to, this museum. These paintings, inspired by the biblical books of Genesis, Exodus, and the

Song of Songs, make up the "nave," or core, of what Chagall called the "House of Brotherhood."

Cost and Hours: €8, €2 more during frequent special exhibits; Wed-Mon 10:00-18:00, Nov-April until 17:00, closed Tue year-round; ticket includes helpful audioguide (though Chagall would suggest that you explore his art without guidance); must check day-packs, idyllic **$** garden café (salads and *plats*), tel. 04 93 53 87 20, http://en.musees-nationaux-alpesmaritimes.fr.

Getting There: The museum is located on Avenue Docteur Ménard. **Taxis** from the city center cost about €15. **Buses** connect the museum with downtown Nice. From downtown, catch bus #15 (Mon-Sat 6/hour, Sun 3/hour, 10 minutes). Catch the bus from the east end of the Galeries Lafayette department store, near the Masséna tram stop, on Rue Sacha Guitry (see map on page 732). Watch for a *Musée Chagall* sign on the bus shelter where you'll get off (on Boulevard de Cimiez).

Visiting the Museum: This small museum has six rooms: two rooms (the main hall and Song of Songs room) with the 17 murals, two rooms for special exhibits, an auditorium with stained-glass windows and a good film, and a mosaic-lined pond (viewed from inside). It takes about one hour to see the whole thing.

In the **main hall** you'll find the core of the collection (Genesis and Exodus scenes). Each painting is a lighter-than-air collage of images that draws from Chagall's Russian folk-village youth, his Jewish heritage, the Bible, and his feeling that he existed somewhere between heaven and earth. He believed that the Bible was a synonym for nature, and that both color and biblical themes were key for understanding God's love for his creation. Chagall's brilliant blues and reds celebrate nature, as do his spiritual and folk themes. Notice the focus on couples. To Chagall, humans loving each other mirrored God's love of creation.

The adjacent **octagonal room** houses five more paintings. The paintings in this room were inspired by the Old Testament Song of Songs. Chagall was one of the few "serious" 20th-century artists to portray unabashed love. Where the Bible uses the metaphor of earthly, physical, sexual love to describe God's love for humans, Chagall uses unearthly colors and a mystical ambience to celebrate human love. These red-toned canvases are hard to interpret literally, but they capture the rosy spirit of a man in love with life.

Back near the entry, the wall **mosaic** (which no longer reflects in the filthy reflecting pond) evokes the prophet Elijah in his chariot of fire (from the Second Book of Kings)—with Chagall's addition of the 12 signs of the zodiac, which he used to symbolize time.

The **auditorium** is worth a peaceful moment to enjoy three Chagall stained-glass windows depicting the seven days of creation. This is also where you'll find a wonderful film (52 minutes) on Chagall, which plays at the top of each hour (not available during special exhibits).

Leaving the Museum: From here, you can return to downtown Nice or head to the Matisse Museum. **Taxis** usually wait in front of the museum. For the **bus** back to downtown Nice, turn right out of the museum, then make another right down Boulevard de Cimiez, and ride bus #15 heading downhill. To continue to the Matisse Museum, catch #15 using the uphill stop located across the street.

To **walk** to the train station area from the museum (20 minutes), turn right out of the museum grounds and follow the first street to the right (hugging the museum). Drop down ramps and staircases, turn left at the bottom under the freeway and train tracks, then turn right on Boulevard Raimbaldi.

Nice's Other Museums
▲Matisse Museum (Musée Matisse)

This small, underachieving museum fills an old mansion in a park surrounded by scant Roman ruins, and houses a limited sampling of works from the various periods of Henri Matisse's artistic career. The museum offers an introduction to the artist's many styles and materials, both shaped by Mediterranean light and by fellow Côte d'Azur artists Picasso and Renoir.

Background: Matisse, the master of leaving things out, could suggest a woman's body with a single curvy line—letting the viewer's mind fill in the rest. Ignoring traditional 3-D perspective, he expressed his passion for life through simplified but recognizable scenes in which dark outlines and saturated, bright blocks of color create an overall decorative pattern.

As you tour the museum, look for Matisse's favorite motifs—including fruit, flowers, wallpaper, and sunny rooms—often with a window opening onto a sunny landscape. Another favorite subject is the *odalisque* (harem concubine), usually shown sprawled in a seductive pose and with a simplified, masklike face. You'll also see a few souvenirs from his travels, which influenced much of his work.

Cost and Hours: Covered by €10 Nice museum combo-ticket; Wed-Mon 10:00-18:00, mid-Oct-mid-June from 11:00, closed Tue year-round, 164 Avenue des Arènes de Cimiez, tel. 04 93 81 08 08, www.musee-matisse-nice.org.

Getting There: Take a cab (€20 from Promenade des Anglais). Alternatively, hop bus #15, direction: Rimiez, from the east end of Galeries Lafayette (from train station, catch #17, direction: Cimiez Hôpital). Get off at the Arènes-Matisse bus stop (look for the crumbling Roman arena that once held 10,000 spectators), then walk 50 yards into the park to find the pink villa.

Leaving the Museum: Turn left from the museum into the

park, exiting at the Archaeological Museum, and turn right at the street. The bus stop across the street is for bus #17, which goes to the train station, and #20, which heads to the port. For bus #15 (frequent service to downtown and the Chagall Museum), continue walking—with the Roman ruins on your right—to the small roundabout, and find the shelter (facing downhill).

Modern and Contemporary Art Museum (Musée d'Art Moderne et d'Art Contemporain)

This ultramodern museum features an explosively colorful, far-out, yet manageable collection focused on American and European-American artists from the 1960s and 1970s (Pop Art and New Realism are highlighted. The exhibits cover three floors, one of which is devoted to temporary shows. The permanent collection usually includes a few works by Andy Warhol, Roy Lichtenstein, and Jean Tinguely. You should also find rooms dedicated to Yves Klein and Niki de Saint Phalle. English explanations are posted in some rooms, and there's a good timeline of Riviera artists from 1947 to 1977. Don't leave without exploring the views from the rooftop terrace.

Cost and Hours: Covered by €10 Nice museum combo-ticket, Tue-Sun 10:00-18:00, mid-Oct-mid-June from 11:00, closed Mon year-round, near Vieux Nice on Promenade des Arts, tel. 04 93 62 61 62, www.mamac-nice.org.

Fine Arts Museum (Musée des Beaux-Arts)

Housed in a sumptuous Riviera villa with lovely gardens, this museum lacks a compelling collection but holds 6,000 artworks from the 17th to 20th centuries. Start on the first floor and work your way up to enjoy paintings by Monet, Sisley, Bonnard, and Raoul Dufy, as well as a few sculptures by Rodin and Carpeaux.

Cost and Hours: Covered by €10 Nice museum combo-ticket, Tue-Sun 10:00-18:00, mid-Oct-mid-June from 11:00, closed Mon year-round, inconveniently located at the western end of Nice, take bus #12 from train station to Rosa Bonheur stop and walk to 3 Avenue des Baumettes; tel. 04 92 15 28 28, www.musee-beaux-arts-nice.org.

Archaeological Museum (Musée Archéologique)

This museum displays various objects from the Romans' occupation of this region. It's convenient—just below the Matisse Museum—but is of little interest except to ancient Rome aficionados (scant information in English). Entry includes access to the poorly maintained Roman bath ruins (ask for the English handout).

Cost and Hours: Covered by €10 Nice museum combo-ticket, Wed-Mon 11:00-18:00, closed Tue, near Matisse Museum at 160 Avenue des Arènes de Cimiez, tel. 04 93 81 59 57.

RIVIERA

Masséna Museum (Musée Masséna)

Like Nice's main square, this museum was named in honor of Jean-André Masséna (born in Antibes), a highly regarded commander during France's Revolutionary and Napoleonic wars. The beachfront mansion is worth a look for its lavish decor and lovely gardens alone (few English labels in museum, but a €3 booklet in English may be available). The gardens on the seaward side of the museum have a memorial to the 86 people who died in the terrorist attack on the Promenade des Anglais in 2016.

Cost and Hours: Covered by €10 Nice museum combo-ticket, always free to enter gardens, Wed-Mon 10:00-18:00, mid-Oct-mid-June from 11:00, closed Tue year-round, 35 Promenade des Anglais, tel. 04 93 91 19 10.

OTHER SIGHTS IN NICE

▲Russian Cathedral (Cathédrale Russe)

Nice's Russian Orthodox church—claimed by some to be the finest outside Russia—is worth a visit. Five hundred rich Russian families wintered in Nice in the late 19th century, and they needed a worthy Orthodox house of worship. Dowager Czarina Maria Feodorovna and her son, Nicholas II, offered the land for the construction, which began in 1903. Nicholas underwrote much of the project and gave this church to the Russian community in 1912. (A few years later, Russian comrades who *didn't* winter on the Riviera assassinated him.) Here in the land of olives and anchovies, these proud onion  domes seem odd. But, I imagine, so did those old Russians. The park around the church stays open at lunch and makes a nice setting for picnics.

Cost and Hours: Free; daily 9:30-17:30 except during services, chanted services Sat at 18:00, Sun at 10:00; no tourist visits during services, no shorts, Avenue Nicolas II, tel. 04 93 96 88 02, www.sobor.fr.

▲Castle Hill (Colline du Château)

This hill—in an otherwise flat city center—offers sensational views over Nice, the port (to the east, created for trade and military use in the 15th century), the foothills of the Alps, and the Mediterranean. The views are best early, at sunset, or whenever the weather's clear.

Nice was founded on this hill. Its residents were crammed onto the hilltop until the 12th century, as it was too risky to live in the flatlands below. Today you'll find a playground, a café, and a cemetery—but no castle—on Castle Hill.

Cost and Hours: Park is free and closes at 20:00 in summer, earlier off-season.

Getting There: You can get to the top by foot, by elevator (free, daily April-Sept 9:00-19:00, until 20:00 in summer, Oct-March 10:00-18:00, next to beachfront Hôtel Suisse), or by pricey tourist train (see "Tours in Nice," earlier).

See the "Promenade des Anglais Walk" for a pleasant stroll that ends near Castle Hill.

Leaving Castle Hill: After enjoying the views and hilltop fun, you can walk via the cemetery directly down into Vieux Nice (just follow the signs), descend to the beach (via the elevator or a stepped lane next to it), or hike down the back side to Nice's port (departure point for boat trips and buses to Monaco and Ville-franche-sur-Mer).

EXCURSION FROM NICE
Narrow-Gauge Train into the Alps (Chemins de Fer de Provence)

Leave the tourists behind and take the scenic train-bus-train combination that runs between Nice and Digne through canyons, along whitewater rivers, and through tempting villages (4/day, departs Nice from Chemins de Fer de Provence Station, two blocks from the Libération tram stop, 4 Rue Alfred Binet, tel. 04 97 03 80 80, www.trainprovence.com).

An appealing stop on the scenic railway is little **Entrevaux,** a good destination that feels forgotten and still stuck in its medieval shell (about €25 round-trip, 1.5 scenic hours from Nice). Cross the bridge, meet someone friendly, and consider the steep hike up to the citadel (€3, TI tel. 04 93 05 45 73).

Nightlife in Nice

The city is a walker's delight after dark. Promenade des Anglais, Cours Saleya, Vieux Nice, Promenade du Paillon, and Place Mas-séna are all worth an evening wander. I can't get enough of the night scene on Place Masséna and around the adjacent fountains.

Nice's bars play host to a happening late-night scene, filled with jazz, rock, and trolling singles. Most activity focuses on Vieux Nice. Rue de la Préfecture and Place du Palais are ground zero for bar life, though Place Rossetti and Rue Droite are also good targets. **Distilleries Ideales** is a good place to start or end your evening, with a lively international crowd, a *Pirates of the Caribbean* interior, and a *Cheers* vibe (lots of beers on tap, where Rue de la Poissonnerie and Rue Barillerie meet, happy hour 18:00-

21:00). **Wayne's Bar** and others nearby are happening spots for the younger, Franco-Anglo backpacker crowd (15 Rue Préfecture; see "Vieux Nice Hotels & Restaurants" map). Along the Promenade des Anglais, the classy Le Relais bar at **Hôtel Negresco** is fancy-cigar old English with frequent live jazz. To savor fine views over Nice, find the **Hotel Aston La Scala**'s seventh-floor bar/terrace, which is a good spot for a drink any night but offers jazz and blues on Thursdays and Fridays and a DJ on Saturdays (daily 17:00 to late, on the Promenade du Paillon at 12 Avenue Félix Faure, tel. 04 92 17 53 00).

Sleeping in Nice

Don't look for charm in Nice. Seek out a good location and modern, reliable amenities (like air-conditioning). The price rankings given here are for April through October. Prices generally drop considerably November through March and sometimes in April, but go sky-high during the Nice Carnival (in February), the Cannes Film Festival (May), and Monaco's Grand Prix (late May). Between the film festival and the Grand Prix, the second half of May is slammed. Nice is also one of Europe's top convention cities, and June is convention month here.

For parking, ask your hotelier or see "Arrival in Nice—By Car," earlier, under "Orientation to Nice."

IN THE CITY CENTER

The train station area offers Nice's cheapest sleeps, but the neighborhood feels sketchy after dark. The cheapest places are older, well-worn, and come with some street noise. Places closer to Avenue Jean Médecin are more expensive and in a more comfortable area.

$$$$ Hôtel du Petit Palais** is a little belle-époque jewel with 25 handsome rooms tucked neatly into a residential area on the hill several blocks from the Chagall Museum. It's bird-chirping peaceful and plush, with tastefully designed rooms, a garden terrace, and small pool. You'll walk 15 minutes down to Vieux Nice (or use bus #15), free street parking is usually easy to find (17 Avenue Emile Bieckert, tel. 04 93 62 19 11, wwww.petitpalaisnice.com, reservation@petitpalaisnice.com).

$$ Hôtel Vendôme* gives you a whiff of the belle époque, with pink pastels, high ceilings, and grand staircases in a mansion set off the street. The modern rooms come in all sizes; many have balconies (limited pay parking—book ahead, 26 Rue Pastorelli at the corner of Rue Alberti, tel. 04 93 62 00 77, www.hotel-vendome-nice.com, contact@vendome-hotel-nice.com).

$$ Hôtel St. Georges, five blocks from the station toward the sea, offers a practical location, a pleasant backyard patio, and friendly Houssein at the reception. Rooms are dark and basic but adequate and fairly priced (family rooms, limited parking—book ahead, 7 Avenue Georges Clemenceau, tel. 04 93 88 79 21, www. hotelsaintgeorges.fr, contact@hotelsaintgeorges.fr).

$ **Hôtel Durante*** **** rents quiet rooms in a happy orange building with rooms wrapped around a flowery courtyard. All but two rooms overlook the well-maintained patio. The rooms have adequate comfort (mostly modern decor), the price is right, and the parking is free on a first-come, first-served basis (family rooms, 16 Avenue Durante, tel. 04 93 88 84 40, www.hotel-durante.com, info@hotel-durante.com).

$ **Hôtel Ibis Nice Centre Gare,*** **** 100 yards to the right as you leave the station, provides a secure refuge in this seedy area. It's big (200 rooms), modern, has well-configured rooms and a pool, and is next to a handy parking garage (bar, café, 14 Avenue Thiers, tel. 04 93 88 85 85, www.ibishotel.com, h1396@accor.com).

$ **Hôtel Belle Meunière,*** in an old mansion built for Napoleon III's mistress, attracts budget-minded travelers with cheap rates a block below the train station. Simple but well-kept, the place has adequate rooms and charismatic Mademoiselle Marie-Pierre presiding with her perfect English (family rooms, air-con, no elevator but just three floors, laundry service, limited pay parking, 21 Avenue Durante, tel. 04 93 88 66 15, www.bellemeuniere. com, hotel.belle.meuniere@cegetel.net).

¢ **B&B Nice Home Sweet Home** is a good budget value. Laid-back Genevieve (a.k.a. Jennifer) Levert rents out four large rooms and one small single in her home. Her cavernous rooms are artfully decorated, with high ceilings, big windows, and space to spread out (cheaper rooms with shared bath, no air-conditioning, elevator, one floor up, laundry services, kitchen access, 35 Rue Rossini at intersection with Rue Auber, mobile 06 50 83 25 85, glevert@free.fr).

Hostel: The fun, good-value ¢ **Auberge de Jeunesse les Camélias** has a handy location, modern facilities, and lively evening atmosphere. Rooms accommodate four to eight people and come with showers and sinks—WCs are down the hall (includes breakfast, rooms closed 11:00-15:00 but can leave bags, laundry, kitchen, safes, bar, 3 Rue Spitalieri, tel. 04 93 62 15 54, www.hihostels.com, accueil.nice@hifrance.org).

NEAR THE PROMENADE DES ANGLAIS

These hotels are close to the beach. The Negresco and West End are big, vintage Nice hotels that open onto the sea from the heart of the Promenade des Anglais.

$$$$ **Hôtel Negresco***** ** owns Nice's most prestigious ad-

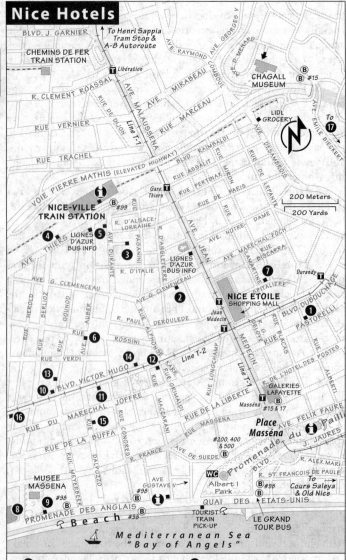

Nice Hotels

1. Hôtel Vendôme
2. Hôtel St. Georges
3. Hôtel Durante
4. Hôtel Ibis Nice Centre Gare
5. Hôtel Belle Meunière
6. B&B Nice Home Sweet Home
7. Auberge de Jeunesse les Camélias Hostel
8. Hôtel Negresco
9. Hôtel West End
10. Hôtel Splendid
11. Hôtel Villa Victoria
12. Hôtel Le Grimaldi
13. Hôtel Gounod
14. Hôtel Carlton
15. Hôtel les Cigales
16. Hôtel Victor Hugo
17. To Hôtel du Petit Palais

RIVIERA

dress on the Promenade des Anglais and knows it. Still, it's the kind of place that if you were to splurge just once in your life... Rooms are opulent, tips are expected, and it seems the women staying here have cosmetically augmented lips (some view rooms, *très* classy bar, 37 Promenade des Anglais, tel. 04 93 16 64 00, www. hotel-negresco-nice.com, reservations@hotel-negresco.com).

$$$$ Hôtel West End**** opens onto the Promenade des Anglais with formal service and decor, classy public spaces, and high prices (some view rooms, 31 Promenade des Anglais, tel. 04 92 14 44 00, www.hotel-westend.com, reservation@westendnice. com).

$$$ Hôtel Splendid**** is a worthwhile splurge if you miss your Marriott. The panoramic rooftop pool, bar/restaurant, and breakfast room almost justify the cost...but throw in plush rooms, a free gym, and spa services, and you're as good as at home (pay parking, 50 Boulevard Victor Hugo, tel. 04 93 16 41 00, www. splendid-nice.com, info@splendid-nice.com).

$$$ Hôtel Villa Victoria**** is a service-oriented place managed by cheery and efficient Marlena and her staff, who welcome travelers into a classy old building with a spacious lobby overlooking a sprawling and wonderful rear garden-courtyard. Rooms are comfortable and well-kept, but those facing the street come with some noise (pay parking, 33 Boulevard Victor Hugo, tel. 04 93 88 39 60, www.villa-victoria.com, contact@villa-victoria.com).

$$$ Le Grimaldi**** is a lovely place with a beautiful lobby and 48 spacious rooms with high ceilings and tasteful decor (big breakfast extra, a few suites and connecting rooms ideal for families, 15 Rue Grimaldi, tel. 04 93 16 00 24, www.le-grimaldi.com, info@le-grimaldi.com).

$$ Hôtel Gounod*** is a fine value behind Hôtel Splendid. Because the two share the same owners, Gounod's guests are allowed free access to Splendid's pool, hot tub, and other amenities. Most rooms are quiet, with high ceilings and traditional decor (family rooms, pay parking, 3 Rue Gounod, tel. 04 93 16 42 00, www.gounod-nice.com, info@gounod-nice.com).

$$ Hôtel Carlton*** is a good deal. It's a well-run, unpretentious, and comfortable place with spacious, simply decorated rooms, many with decks (26 Boulevard Victor Hugo, tel. 04 93 88 87 83, www.hotel-carlton-nice.com, info@hotel-carlton-nice.com, helpful Lionel at the reception).

$$ Hôtel les Cigales,*** a few blocks from the Promenade des Anglais, is a sweet little place with 19 sharp and richly colored rooms and a cool upstairs terrace, all well-managed by friendly Veronique and Elaine (RS%, 16 Rue Dalpozzo, tel. 04 97 03 10 70, www.hotel-lescigales.com, info@hotel-lescigales.com).

$ Hôtel Victor Hugo, a traditional and spotless seven-room hotel, is an adorable time-warp place where Gilles warmly welcomes guests. All rooms are on the ground floor and come with kitchenettes and air-conditioning. While it's a short walk from the Promenade des Anglais, it's a hefty walk from Vieux Nice (RS%, includes breakfast, 59 Boulevard Victor Hugo, tel. 04 93 88 12 39, www.hotel-victor-hugo-nice.com).

IN OR NEAR VIEUX NICE

Most of these hotels are either on the sea or within an easy walk of it. (Hôtel Lafayette and the Villa Saint Exupéry Beach hostel are more central).

$$$$ Hôtel la Perouse,** built into the rock of Castle Hill at the east end of the bay, is a fine splurge. This refuge-hotel is top-to-bottom flawless in every detail—from its elegant rooms (satin curtains, velour headboards) and attentive staff to its rooftop terrace with hot tub, sleek pool, and lovely **$$$$** garden restaurant. Sleep here to be spoiled and escape the big city (good family options, 11 Quai Rauba Capeu, tel. 04 93 62 34 63, www.hotel-la-perouse.com, lp@hotel-la-perouse.com).

$$$$ Hôtel Suisse,** below Castle Hill, has brilliant sea and city views for a price—sleep elsewhere if you don't land a view. It's surprisingly quiet given the busy street below (most view rooms have balconies, 15 Quai Rauba Capeu, tel. 04 92 17 39 00, www.hotels-ocre-azur.com, hotel.suisse@hotels-ocre-azur.com).

$$$ Hôtel Albert 1er* is a fair deal in a central, busy location on Albert I Park, two blocks from the beach and Place Masséna. The staff is formal and the rooms are well-appointed and spotless, with heavy brown tones. Some have views of the bay, while others overlook the park or a quiet interior courtyard (4 Avenue des Phocéens, tel. 04 93 85 74 01, www.hotel-albert-1er.com, info@hotel-albert1er.com).

$$$ Hôtel Mercure Marché aux Fleurs** is ideally situated near the sea and Cours Saleya. Rooms are sharp, standard doubles are tight, and prices can be either reasonable or exorbitant (superior rooms worth the extra euros—especially those with views, 91 Quai des Etats-Unis, tel. 04 93 85 74 19, www.hotelmercure.com, h0962@accor.com).

$$ Hôtel de la Mer is an intimate, 12-room place with an enviable position overlooking Place Masséna, just steps from Vieux Nice and the beach. Rooms are modern, comfortable, and well-priced (4 Place Masséna, tel. 04 93 92 09 10, www.hoteldelamernice.com, hotel.mer@wanadoo.fr). They also run the **$$$$ Suites Masséna** in the same building, with seven huge, modern, high-ceilinged rooms—designed for two but with room for three (tel. 04 93 13 48 11, www.lessuitesmassena.com).

$$ Room With a Vue rents four well-designed rooms (several with small balconies) right on Cours Saleya above the Pain et Cie bakery/café (3 Louis Gassin, tel. 04 93 62 94 32, roomwithavue@gmail.com, enthusiastic manager Fred).

$$ Hôtel Lafayette,* located a block behind the Galeries Lafayette department store, is a modest, homey place with 17 mostly spacious, well-designed and good-value rooms. All rooms are one floor up from the street—some traffic noise sneaks in (RS%, 32 Rue de l'Hôtel des Postes—see "Vieux Nice Hotels & Restaurants" map, tel. 04 93 85 17 84, www.hotellafayettenice.com, info@hotellafayettenice.com).

Hostel: ¢ **Villa Saint Exupéry Beach** is a sprawling place with more than 200 beds, split between a building with private rooms (figure **$**) and the hostel next door (dorms with 4-8 beds). The owners and many staff are English so communication is easy. The vibe is young and fun, with a bar, cheap restaurant, community kitchen, air-con, elevator, and *beaucoup* services including laundry, yoga classes, free walking tour of Vieux Nice, and scuba diving (no curfew, 6 Rue Sacha Guitry, tel. 04 93 16 13 45, www.villahostels.com, beach@villahostels.com).

NEAR THE AIRPORT

Several airport hotels offer a handy and cheap port-in-the-storm for those with early flights or who are just stopping in for a single night: **$$ Hôtels Campanile** (www.campanile.fr) and **$$$ Nouvel** (www.novotel.com) are closest; **$$ Hôtel Ibis Budget Nice Aéroport** (www.ibis.com) is cheap and a few minutes away, though two other Ibis hotels are closer and a bit pricier. Free shuttles connect these hotels with both airport terminals.

Eating in Nice

You'll find plenty of regional dishes and lots of Italian influence blended with classic French cuisine in this Franco-Italian city. My favorite dining spots are in Vieux Nice. It's well worth booking ahead for these places. If Vieux Nice is too far, I've listed some great places handier to your hotel. Promenade des Anglais is ideal for picnic dinners on warm, languid evenings or a meal at a beachside restaurant. For a more romantic and peaceful meal, head for nearby Villefranche-sur-Mer (described later). Avoid the fun-to-peruse but terribly touristy eateries lining Rue Masséna.

IN VIEUX NICE

Nice's dinner scene converges on Cours Saleya, which is entertaining enough in itself to make the generally mediocre food a fair deal. It's a fun, festive spot to compare tans and mussels. Most of my recommendations are on side lanes inland from here. Even if

Vieux Nice Hotels & Restaurants

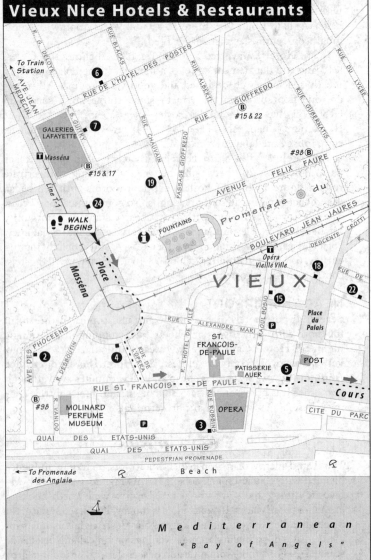

Accommodations
1 Hôtel la Perouse & Hôtel Suisse
2 Hôtel Albert 1er
3 Hôtel Mercure Marché aux Fleurs
4 Hôtel de la Mer & Suites Masséna
5 Room With a Vue & Pain et Cie Bakery
6 Hôtel Lafayette
7 Villa Saint Exupéry Beach Hostel

Eateries, Nightlife & Other
8 Le Safari
9 Acchiardo
10 Chez Palmyre
11 Olive et Artichaut
12 Koko Green
13 Cave du Fromager
14 Bistrot d'Antoine

RIVIERA

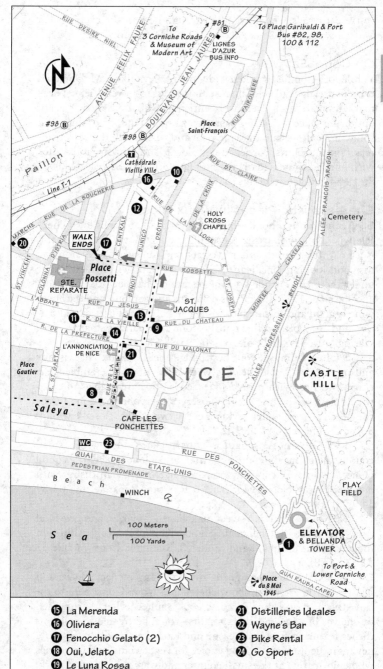

RUE DESIRE NIEL

AVENUE FELIX FAURE

BOULEVARD JEAN JAURES

To
3 Corniche Roads
& Museum of
Modern Art

To Place Garibaldi & Port
Bus #82, 98,
100 & 112

#81 B

LIGNES
D'AZUR
BUS INFO

#98 B

#98 B

Paillon

Place
Saint-François

RUE PAIROLIERE

Line T-1

MARCHE

RUE DE LA BOUCHERIE

Cathédrale
Vieille Ville

T

RUE ST. CLAIRE

RUE DE LA CROIX

16

10

HOLY
CROSS
CHAPEL

ALLEE FRANCOIS ARAGON

Cemetery

20

ST. VINCENT

COLONNA D'ISTRIA

12

R. CENTRALE

B.UNICO

R. DROITE

DE LA
LOGE

WALK
ENDS

17

Place
Rossetti

STE.
REPARATE

L'ABBAYE

BENOIT

RUE DU JESUS

RUE ROSSETTI

ST. JOSEPH

MONTEE DU CHATEAU

BENOIT

R. ST. GAETAN

R. DE LA VIEILLE

11

13

ST. JACQUES

9

R. DE LA PREFECTURE

14

RUE DU CHATEAU

ALLEE PROFESSEUR

L'ANNONCIATION
DE NICE

21

RUE DU MALONAT

Place
Gautier

RUE DE LA POISSONNERIE

17

N I C E

CASTLE
HILL

8

Saleya

CAFE LES
PONCHETTES

WC 23

QUAI DES ETATS-UNIS

RUE DES PONCHETTES

PEDESTRIAN PROMENADE

PLAY
FIELD

B e a c h

WINCH

S e a

100 Meters

100 Yards

ELEVATOR
& BELLANDA
TOWER

1

To Port &
Lower Corniche
Road

Place
du 8 Mai
1945

QUAI RAUBA CAPEU

15 La Merenda
16 Oliviera
17 Fenocchio Gelato (2)
18 Oui, Jelato
19 Le Luna Rossa
20 Comptoir du Marché

21 Distilleries Ideales
22 Wayne's Bar
23 Bike Rental
24 Go Sport

you're eating elsewhere, wander through here in the evening. For locations, see the "Vieux Nice Hotels & Restaurants" map.

RIVIERA

On Cours Saleya

While local foodies would avoid Cours Saleya like a McDonald's, the energy of wall-to-wall restaurants taking over Vieux Nice's market square each evening is enticing. **$$$ Le Safari** is a fair option for Niçois cuisine, pasta, pizza, and outdoor dining. This sprawling café-restaurant, convivial and rustic with the coolest interior on the Cours, is packed with locals and tourists, and staffed with hurried waiters (daily noon to late, 1 Cours Saleya, tel. 04 93 80 18 44, www.restaurantsafari.fr).

Characteristic Places in Vieux Nice

$$ Acchiardo is a homey-but-lively eatery that mixes loyal clientele with hungry tourists. As soon as you sit down you know this is a treat. It's a family affair overseen by Monsieur Acchiardo and his good-looking sons, Jean-François and Raphael. A small plaque under the menu outside says the restaurant has been run by father and son since 1927. The food is delicious and copious, and the house wine is good and reasonable (Mon-Fri 19:00 until late, closed Sat-Sun and Aug, often a line out the door, reservations smart, indoor seating only, 38 Rue Droite, tel. 04 93 85 51 16).

$ Chez Palmyre, your best budget bet in Vieux Nice, is tiny and popular, so book ahead (a week is advised). The ambience is rustic and fun, with people squeezed onto shared tables to enjoy the homestyle cooking. Philippe serves everyone the same three-course, €17 *menu,* which changes every two weeks (closed Sat-Sun, 5 Rue Droite, tel. 04 93 85 72 32).

$$$ Olive et Artichaut is a sharp bistro-diner with a small counter, black-meets-white floor tiles, and a foodie vibe. It's a good choice to dine on carefully prepared Mediterranean dishes with creative twists (closed Mon-Tue, 6 Rue Ste. Réparate, tel. 04 89 14 97 51).

$$ Koko Green is a sweet little haven for vegan and raw-food types and is run by a delightful Franco-Kiwi couple (open Thu-Sun for lunch, Sat for lunch and dinner, 1 Rue de la Loge, mobile 07 81 63 14 88).

$$$ Cave du Fromager is run by young owners Maeva and Mattieu, who are crazy about cheese and wine. Come here to escape the heat and dine in cozy, cool, vaulted cellars surrounded by shelves of wine and cheery lights. You'll be treated to delicious dishes featuring fresh fish, pasta, and ham—most with cheese as a key ingredient. This is a good choice for vegetarians, and for singles who enjoy eating at the small counter and watching the chef work.

Book ahead (closed Tue, just off Place du Jésus at 29 Rue Benoît Bunico, tel. 04 93 13 07 83, www.lacavedufromager.com).

$$ Bistrot d'Antoine has street appeal inside and out. It's a warm, vine-draped place whose menu emphasizes affordable Niçois cuisine and good grilled selections. It's popular, so call a day or two ahead to reserve a table. The upstairs room is quieter than the outdoor tables and ground-floor room (closed Sun-Mon, 27 Rue de la Préfecture, tel. 04 93 85 29 57).

$$ La Merenda is a shoebox where you'll sit on small stools and dine on simple homestyle dishes in a communal environment. The menu changes with the season, but the hardworking owner, Dominique, does not. This place fills fast, so arrive early, or better yet, drop by during lunch to reserve for dinner—seatings are at 19:00 and 21:00 (closed Sat-Sun, cash only, 4 Rue Raoul Bosio, no telephone).

$$ Oliviera venerates the French olive. This fun shop/restaurant offers olive oil tastings and a menu of Mediterranean dishes paired with specific oils (like a wine pairing). Adorable owner Nadim speaks excellent English, knows all of his producers, and provides animated "Olive Oil 101" explanations with your meal. It's a good place for vegetarians—try his guacamole-and-apple dish; the pesto is also excellent (lunch only, closed Sun-Mon, cash only, 8 bis Rue du Collet, tel. 04 93 13 06 45).

And for Dessert...

Gelato lovers should save room for the tempting ice-cream stands in Vieux Nice (open daily until late). **Fenocchio** is the city's favorite, with mouthwatering displays of dozens of flavors ranging from lavender to avocado (two locations: 2 Place Rossetti and 6 Rue de la Poissonnerie). Gelato connoisseurs should head for **Oui, Jelato,** where the quality is the priority rather than the selection (5 Rue de la Préfecture, on the Place du Palais).

IN THE CITY CENTER
Near Nice Etoile, on Rue Biscarra

An appealing lineup of bistros overflowing with outdoor tables stretches along the broad sidewalk on Rue Biscarra (just east of Avenue Jean Médecin behind Nice Etoile, all closed Sun). Come here to dine with area residents away from most tourists. Peruse the choices—all five places are different and reservations are normally not needed.

Near Place Masséna

$$ Le Luna Rossa is a small neighborhood place serving delicious French-Italian dishes. Owner Christine and her staff welcome diners with enthusiastic service and reasonable prices. Pasta dishes

RIVIERA

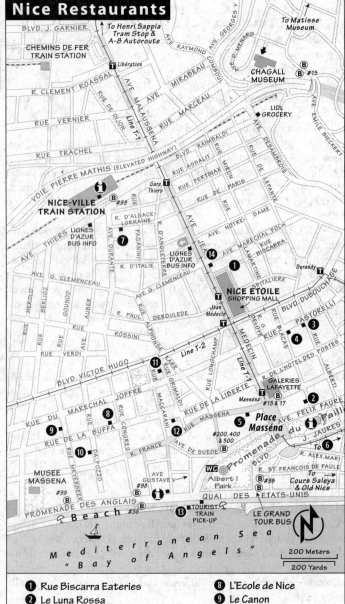

Nice Restaurants

1. Rue Biscarra Eateries
2. Le Luna Rossa
3. L'Ovale
4. Les 5 Sens
5. La Maison de Marie
6. To Comptoir du Marché
7. Voyageur Nissart
8. L'Ecole de Nice
9. Le Canon
10. Coco & Rico
11. Mon Petit Café
12. Crêperie Bretonne
13. Restaurant Le Galet
14. Monoprix (Grocery)

are copious and served in cast-iron pans, and the *assortiment* main course is a great sampler dish. Dine inside or outside on a sidewalk terrace (may be closing in 2020, just north of parkway at 3 Rue Chauvain, tel. 04 93 85 55 66).

$ L'Ovale takes its name from the shape of a rugby ball. Come here for an unpretentious and local café-bistro experience. Owner David serves traditional dishes from southwestern France (rich and meaty). Dining is inside only. Consider the cassoulet, the hearty *salade de manchons* with duck and walnuts, or the €18-23 three-course *menus* (daily, 29 Rue Pastorelli, tel. 04 93 80 31 65).

$$$ Les 5 Sens ("The Five Senses") is a lively and dressy restaurant serving classic French fare at higher-end prices that justify the cost for discerning diners (daily, 37 Rue Pastorelli, tel. 09 81 06 57 00).

$$ La Maison de Marie is a surprisingly high-quality refuge off Nice's touristy restaurant row. The interior tables are candlelit, white-tablecloth classy, while the tables in the courtyard enjoy a relaxed bistro feel. Expect some smokers outside. The *menu* is a good value (daily, 5 Rue Masséna, tel. 04 93 82 15 93).

$$ Comptoir du Marché, named for its red wood counter, feels like a wine shop-meets-bistro-meets-bakery with cozy ambience in and out. It's at a busy pedestrian corner and serves traditional French cuisine with a smile (closed Sun-Mon, 8 Rue du Marché, tel. 04 93 13 45 01).

Near the Train Station

$ Voyageur Nissart has blended good-value cuisine with friendly service since 1908. Kind owner Max and his able assistant Cédric are great hosts, and the quality of their food makes this place both very popular and a good choice for travelers on a budget (book ahead, leave a message in English). Try anything *à la niçoise*, including the fine *salade niçoise* (good €18 three-course *menus*, inexpensive wines, indoor and outdoor seating, closed Mon, a block below the train station at 19 Rue d'Alsace-Lorraine, tel. 04 93 82 19 60, www.voyageurnissart.com).

Near the Promenade des Anglais

$$ L'Ecole de Nice brings wine-shop decor to a cozy-but-modern restaurant, and serves a limited selection of delicious dishes complemented by a vast selection of wines. The set-price *menu*—less than €30 for three courses—is a swinging deal (closed Sun, 16 Rue de la Buffa, tel. 04 93 81 39 30).

$$$ Le Canon is a fine, if trendy, choice run by two friends intent on serving top-quality and inventive dishes that emphasize the region's local, fresh, and in-season ingredients (closed Sat-Sun, 23 Rue Meyerbeer, tel. 04 93 79 09 24).

$$$ Coco & Rico is a good place away from the tourist fray with creative homemade dishes. The cuisine and wine list represent many regions of France, with a focus on what's fresh (may close in 2020, indoor and outdoor seating, 3 Rue Dalpozzo, tel. 04 83 50 09 60).

$$$ Mon Petit Café delivers fine, traditional cuisine to appreciative diners in a warm, candlelit setting with rich colors and fine glassware, or on a pleasant front terrace. Book ahead for this dressy place and expect top service and mouth-watering cuisine (closed Sun-Mon, 11 bis Rue Grimaldi, tel. 04 97 20 55 36, www.monpetitcafe-nice.com).

$ Crêperie Bretonne is the only *crêperie* I list in Nice. Dine on the broad terrace or inside, with relaxed service and jukebox-meets-gramophone ambience. Their top-end, house-special crêpes are creative and enticing. Split a salad to start—try the goat cheese salad with honey (closed Sun, on Place Grimaldi, tel. 04 93 82 28 47).

Dining on the Beach

$$$ Restaurant Le Galet is your best eat-on-the-beach option. The city vanishes as you step down to the beach. The food is nicely presented, and the tables feel elegant, even at the edge of the sand. Arrive for the sunset and you'll have an unforgettable meal (open for dinner May-mid-Sept, 3 Promenade des Anglais—see "Nice Restaurants" map, tel. 04 93 88 17 23). Sunbathers can rent beach chairs and have drinks and meals served literally on the beach (lounge chairs-€16/half-day, €19/day).

Nice Connections

GETTING AROUND THE RIVIERA

Nice is perfectly situated for exploring the Riviera by public transport. Monaco, Eze-le-Village, Villefranche-sur-Mer, Antibes, Vence, and St-Paul-de-Vence are all within about a one-hour bus or train ride. With a little planning, you can link key destinations in an all-day circuit (for example: Nice, Monaco, and Eze-le-Village or La Turbie, then loop back to Nice). For a comparison of train and bus connections from Nice to nearby coastal towns, see the "Public Transportation in the French Riviera" sidebar on page 698. It's also possible to take a boat to several destinations in the Riviera.

By Train

From Nice-Ville Station to: Cannes (2/hour, 30 minutes), **Antibes** (2/hour, 20 minutes), **Villefranche-sur-Mer** (2/hour, 10 minutes), **Eze-le-Village** (2/hour, 15 minutes to Eze-Bord-de-

Mer, then infrequent bus #83 to Eze, 8/day, 15 minutes), **Monaco** (2/hour, 20 minutes), **Menton** (2/hour, 35 minutes).

By Bus

Regardless of length, most one-way rides on regional buses (except express airport buses) cost €1.50. Tickets are good for up to 74 minutes of travel in one direction, including transfers. For more info on buses in the Riviera, see page 696. To connect to regional destinations, use the following bus lines and stops (see "Nice Hotels" and "Vieux Nice Hotels & Restaurants" maps for stop locations; www.lignesdazur.com).

Eastbound Buses: Due to the new T-2 tram that ends at the port, expect some changes to stop locations for these buses. Trams T-1 and/or T-2 will get you close to these stops, and transfers are free from tram to bus for all lines but #100.

Bus #100 runs from Nice's port through **Villefranche-sur-Mer** (3-4/hour, 20 minutes), **Monaco** (1 hour), and **Menton** (1.5 hours). Bus #81 runs from the Promenade des Arts stop to **Villefranche-sur-Mer** (2-3/hour, 15 minutes) and around **Cap Ferrat** (30 minutes to **St-Jean-Cap-Ferrat**). Buses #82 and #112 to **Eze-le-Village** leave from the Vauban tram stop (about hourly; only #82 runs on Sundays; 30 minutes). For **La Turbie**, buses run 6/day and take 45 minutes (Mon-Sat take #116 from Vauban tram stop; on Sun catch #T-66 from Pont St. Michel tram stop).

Westbound Buses: Bus #200 goes to **Antibes** (4/hour Mon-Sat, 2/hour Sun, 1.5 hours) and **Cannes** (2 hours). Bus #400 heads to **St-Paul-de-Vence** (2/hour, 45 minutes) and **Vence** (1 hour). Bus #94 also serves Vence (1-2/hour, 1 hour). All use the Albert I/Verdun stop on Avenue de Verdun, a 10-minute walk along the parkway west of Place Masséna. You must buy tickets before boarding these buses.

By Boat

In summer, Trans Côte d'Azur offers scenic trips several days a week from Nice to Monaco.

Boats to **Monaco** depart at 9:30 and 16:00, and return at 11:00 and 17:00. The morning departure can be combined with the late-afternoon return from Monaco, allowing you a full day with Prince Albert II (€39 round-trip, €32 if you don't get off in Monaco, 45 minutes each way, June-Sept Tue, Thu, and Sat only). Drinks and WCs are available on board. Reservations are required (tel. 04 92 00 42 30, www.trans-cote-azur.com). The same company also runs one-hour round-trip cruises along the coast to Cap Ferrat (see listing under "Tours in Nice," earlier).

GETTING TO DESTINATIONS BEYOND THE RIVIERA
By Long-Distance Bus and Train

Ouibus and Flixbus run long-distance bus service from Nice; see "Transportation" in the Practicalities chapter. Compare schedules and fares with trains.

Most long-distance train connections from Nice to other French cities require a change in Marseille. The Intercité train to Bordeaux (serving Antibes, Cannes, Toulon, and Marseille—and connecting from there to Arles, Nîmes, and Carcassonne) requires a reservation.

From Nice by Train to: Marseille (18/day, 2.5 hours), **Cassis** (hourly, 3 hours, transfer in Toulon and/or Marseille), **Arles** (11/day, 4 hours, most require transfer in Marseille or Avignon), **Avignon** (10/day, most by TGV, 4 hours, many require transfer in Marseille), **Lyon** (hourly, 4.5 hours, may require change), **Paris'** Gare de Lyon (hourly, 6 hours, may require change), **Aix-en-Provence** TGV Station (10/day, 2-3 hours, usually changes in Marseille), **Chamonix** (4/day, 10 hours, requires multiple changes), **Beaune** (7/day, 7 hours, 1-2 transfers), **Florence** (6/day, 8 hours, 1-3 transfers), **Milan** (3 Thello trains/day, 4 hours, www.thello.com; or 4/day, 5 hours, most with transfers), **Venice** (5/day, 9 hours, 1-3 transfers), **Barcelona** (2/day via Montpellier or Valence, 9 hours, more with multiple changes).

By Plane

Nice's easy-to-navigate airport (Aéroport de Nice Côte d'Azur, airport code: NCE) is literally on the Mediterranean—with landfill runways, a 30-minute drive west of the city center. The two terminals are connected by shuttle buses *(navettes)*. Both terminals have TIs, banks, ATMs, trams, and buses to Nice (tel. 04 89 88 98 28, www.nice.aeroport.fr). Planes leave roughly hourly for Paris (one-hour flight, about the same price as a train ticket, check www.easyjet.com for the cheapest flights to Paris' Orly airport).

Linking the Airport and City Center

By Taxi: A taxi into the center is expensive considering the short distance (figure €35 to Nice hotels, €60 to Villefranche-sur-Mer, €70 to Antibes, about €5 more at night and on weekends, small fee for bags). Nice's airport taxis are notorious for overcharging. Before riding, confirm your fare. It's always a good idea to ask for a receipt *(reçu)*.

By Tram: The T-2 tramway, which opened in 2019, serves both airport terminals and runs frequently into Nice, paralleling the Promenade des Anglais and ending at Nice's Port Lympia.

The tram is handy for those sleeping at hotels near the Promenade des Anglais and Place Masséna.

By Bus: Two bus lines connect the airport with the city center, offering good alternatives to high-priced taxis. Note that these routes may be influenced by the new tram line; check routes before riding. **Bus #99** (airport express) runs to Nice's main train station (€6, 2/hour, 8:00-21:00, 30 minutes, drops you within a 10-minute walk of many recommended hotels). To take this bus to the airport, catch it right in front of the train station (departs on the half-hour). If your hotel is within walking distance of the station, #99 is your best budget bet.

Bus #98 runs along Promenade des Anglais and along the edge of Vieux Nice (€6, 3-4/hour, from the airport 6:00-23:00, to the airport until 21:00, 30 minutes, see the "Nice" map at the beginning of this section for stops).

For all buses, buy tickets from the driver. To reach the bus information office and stops at Terminal 1, turn left after passing customs and exit the doors at the far end. Buses serving Terminal 2 stop across the street from the airport exit (information kiosk and ticket sales to the right as you exit).

By Airport Shuttle: These services vary in reliability but can be cost-effective for families or small groups. Airport shuttles are better for trips from your hotel to the airport, since they require you to book a precise pickup time in advance. Shuttle vans offer a fixed price (about €30 for one person, a little more for additional people or to Villefranche-sur-Mer). Your hotel can arrange this, and I would trust their choice of company.

Linking the Airport and Nearby Destinations

To get to **Villefranche-sur-Mer** from the airport, take bus #98 (described above) to Place Garibaldi. From there, use the same ticket to transfer to bus #81. Or take the new T-2 tram to the last stop (Port Lympia). At the port, you can use the same ticket to transfer to bus #81 or buy a separate ticket for bus #100 (see the "Nice" map at the beginning of this section for bus-stop locations). Allow €60 for a taxi.

To reach **Antibes,** take bus #250 from either terminal (about 2/hour, 40 minutes, €11). For **Cannes,** take bus #210 from either terminal (1-2/hour, 50 minutes on freeway, €22). Express bus #110 runs from the airport directly to **Monaco** (2/hour, 50 minutes, €22).

By Cruise Ship

Nice's port is at the eastern edge of the town center, below Castle Hill; the main promenade and Vieux Nice are on the other side of the hill. Cruise ships dock at either side of the mouth of this port:

Terminal 1 to the east or Terminal 2 to the west.

**Getting into the City Cen-
ter:** The new T-2 tram connects
the port to the city center and
airport. Take the tram to Vieux
Nice or to the T-1 tram transfer
at Jean Médecin. You can then
ride the T-1 tram to Place Masséna for the start of my "Vieux
Nice Walk" or to catch a bus to the Chagall or Matisse museums
(#15).

If arriving at Terminal 2 and heading to Vieux Nice, you can
skip the walk to Place Garibaldi and stroll directly there by heading around the base of the castle-topped hill, with the sea on your
left (10-15 minutes).

Other options to get into town include a **taxi** from the terminals (about €20 to points within Nice) or the **hop-on, hop-off bus,**
which has a stop at the top of the port (see page 709).

Getting to Nearby Destinations: To visit Villefranche-sur-
Mer or Monaco, it's best to take **bus #100** (the train is faster, but
the bus stop is much closer to Nice's port). The bus stops along the
top of the port, near the right end of Place de l'Ile de Beauté (see
"Nice" map at the beginning of this section).

To take the **train** to Villefranche-sur-Mer, Monaco, Antibes,
Cannes, or elsewhere, take the T-2 tram to the Jean Médecin stop
and transfer to the T-1 tram, then ride it to the Gare Thiers stop
and walk one long block to the main train station.

Taxis at the terminals charge about €40 one-way to Villefranche-sur-Mer, or €95 one-way to Monaco.

Villefranche-sur-Mer

In the glitzy world of the Riviera, Villefranche-sur-Mer offers travelers an easygoing slice of small-town Mediterranean life. From here, convenient day trips let you gamble in Monaco, saunter the Promenade des Anglais in Nice, indulge in seaside walks and glorious gardens in Cap Ferrat, and enjoy views from Eze-le-Village and the Grande Corniche.

Villefranche-sur-Mer feels more Italian than French, with pastel-orange buildings; steep, narrow lanes spilling into the sea; and pasta on menus. Luxury yachts glisten in the bay. Cruise ships make regular calls to Villefranche-sur-Mer's deep harbor, creating periodic rush hours of frenetic shoppers and bucket-listers. Sand-pebble beaches, a handful of interesting sights, and quick access to Cap Ferrat keep other visitors just busy enough.

Orientation to Villefranche-sur-Mer

TOURIST INFORMATION

The TI is just off the road that runs between Nice and Monaco, located in a park (Jardin François Binon) below the Nice/Monaco bus stop, labeled *Octroi* (daily 9:00-18:30; mid-Sept-mid-June Mon-Sat 9:00-12:30 & 14:00-17:30, closed Sun; tel. 04 93 01 73 68, www.villefranche-sur-mer.com). Pick up regional bus schedules and information on seasonal sightseeing boat rides. The TI has an excellent brochure-map showing seaside walks around neighboring Cap Ferrat and information on the Villa Ephrussi de Rothschild's gardens.

ARRIVAL IN VILLEFRANCHE-SUR-MER

By Bus: Get off at the Octroi stop. To reach the old town, walk downhill past the TI along Avenue Général de Gaulle, take the first stairway on the left, then make a right at the street's end. The hop-on, hop-off bus from Nice stops at the citadel entrance in the old town.

By Train: Not all trains stop in Villefranche-sur-Mer (you may need to transfer to a local train in Nice or Monaco). Villefranche-sur-Mer's train station is just above the beach, a short stroll from the old town and most of my recommended hotels (taxis won't take such a short trip).

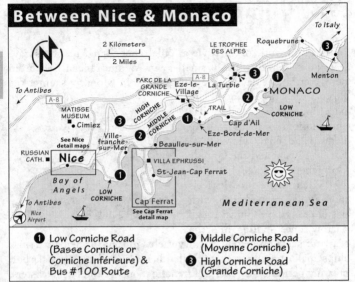

Between Nice & Monaco

To Italy

2 Kilometers
2 Miles

LE TROPHEE DES ALPES   Roquebrune

PARC DE LA GRANDE CORNICHE   Eze-le-Village   La Turbie   Menton

To Antibes   A-8   MONACO

MATISSE MUSEUM   HIGH CORNICHE   LOW CORNICHE

Cimiez   MIDDLE CORNICHE   TRAIL   Cap d'Ail

Ville-franche-sur-Mer   Eze-Bord-de-Mer

See Nice detail maps   Beaulieu-sur-Mer

RUSSIAN CATH.   Nice   VILLA EPHRUSSI   St-Jean-Cap Ferrat

Bay of Angels   LOW CORNICHE

To Antibes   Cap Ferrat   Mediterranean Sea

Nice Airport   See Cap Ferrat detail map

❶ Low Corniche Road (Basse Corniche or Corniche Inférieure) & Bus #100 Route

❷ Middle Corniche Road (Moyenne Corniche)

❸ High Corniche Road (Grande Corniche)

By Car: From Nice's port, follow signs for *Menton, Monaco,* and *Basse Corniche.* In Villefranche-sur-Mer, turn right at the TI (first signal after Hôtel la Flore) for parking and hotels. For a quick visit to the TI, park at the pay lot just below the TI. You'll pay to park in all public parking areas except from 19:00 to 9:00. Parking around the citadel is reasonable (about €2/hour) but the most central lot at the harbor is pricey (Parking Wilson, €26/day). Parking is free near Port de la Darse. Some hotels have their own parking.

By Plane: Allow an hour to connect from Nice's airport to Villefranche-sur-Mer (for details, see page 741).

By Cruise Ship: See "Villefranche-sur-Mer Connections."

HELPFUL HINTS

Market Day: A fun bric-a-brac market enlivens Villefranche-sur-Mer on Sundays (on Place Amélie Pollonnais by Hôtel Welcome, and in Jardin François Binon by the TI). On Saturday and Wednesday mornings, a market sets up in Jardin François Binon. A small trinket market springs to action on Place Amélie Pollonnais whenever cruise ships grace the harbor.

Wi-Fi: There's free Wi-Fi near the TI in the Jardin François Binon, at the port, and in cafés on Place Amélie Pollonnais.

Electric Bike Rental: The adventurous can try **Eco-Loc** electric bikes as an alternative to taking the bus to Cap Ferrat, Eze-le-Village, or even Nice. You get about 25 miles on a fully charged battery (after that you're pedaling; €20/half-day, €30/day, mid-April-Sept daily 9:00-17:00, deposit and ID required, best to reserve 24 hours in advance; helmets, locks, and baskets available; pick up bike by the cruise terminal entrance at the port, mobile 06 66 92 72 41, www.ecoloc06.fr).

Spectator Sports: Lively *boules* action takes place each evening just below the TI and the huge soccer field (for more on this sport, see the sidebar on page 580).

RIVIERA

GETTING AROUND VILLEFRANCHE-SUR-MER

By Bus: Little **minibus #80** saves you the sweat of walking uphill (and gets you within a 15-minute walk of Mont-Alban Fort, described later), but runs only about once per hour from the old port to the top of the hill, stopping at Place Amélie Pollonnais (by the cruise terminal), Hôtel la Fiancée du Pirate, and the Col de Villefranche stop (for buses to Eze-le-Village), before continuing to the outlying suburban Nice Riquier train station (€1.50, runs daily 7:00-19:00, see the "Villefranche-sur-Mer" map for stop locations, schedule posted at stops and available at TI). Also, consider the **hop-on, hop-off bus** that makes a loop trip from the citadel to Nice (see page 709).

    By Taxi: Taxis wait between the cruise terminal and Place Amélie Pollonnais. Beware of taxi drivers who overcharge. Normal weekday, daytime rates to outside destinations should be about €25 to Cap Ferrat, €40 to central Nice or Eze-le-Village, and €70 to the airport or Monaco. For a reliable taxi, call **Didier** (mobile 06 15 15 39 15). For a general taxi call tel. 04 93 55 55 55.

Villefranche-sur-Mer Town Walk

For tourists, Villefranche is a tiny, easy-to-cover town that snuggles around its harbor under its citadel. This quick self-guided walk laces together everything of importance, starting at the waterfront near where cruise-ship tenders land and finishing at the citadel.

• *If arriving by bus or train, you'll walk five minutes to the starting point. Go to the end of the short pier directly in front of Hôtel Welcome, where we'll start with a spin tour (spin to the right) to get oriented.*

    The Harbor: Look out to sea. Cap Ferrat, across the bay, is a landscaped paradise where the 1 percent of the 1 percent compete for the best view. The Rothschild's pink mansion, Villa Ephrussi (about dead center, hugging the top) is the most worthwhile sight to visit in the area. To its right, in the saddle of the hill, the next big home, with the red-tiled roof, belonged to the late Paul Allen. Geologically, Cap Ferrat is the

RIVIERA

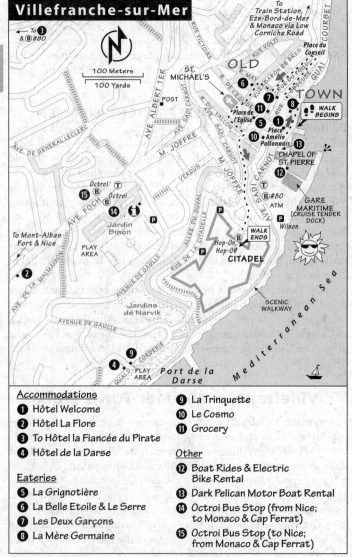

Villefranche-sur-Mer

To Train Station,
Eze-Bord-de-Mer
& Monaco via Low
Corniche Road

To ③
& Ⓑ#80

N

100 Meters
100 Yards

OLD TOWN

Place du
Conseil

ST. MICHAEL'S

POST

Place de
l'Eglise

Place
Amélie
Pollonnais

WALK
BEGINS

CHAPEL OF
ST. PIERRE

Ⓑ#80
ATM

GARE
MARITIME
(CRUISE TENDER
DOCK)

Octroi
Octroi

Jardin
Binon

PLAY
AREA

To Mont-Alban
Fort & Nice

Wilson

WALK
ENDS

Hop-On,
Hop-Off

CITADEL

SCENIC
WALKWAY

Jardins
de Narvik

AVENUE DE GAULLE

Port de la
Darse

PLAY
AREA

Mediterranean Sea

Accommodations
1 Hôtel Welcome
2 Hôtel La Flore
3 To Hôtel la Fiancée du Pirate
4 Hôtel de la Darse

Eateries
5 La Grignotière
6 La Belle Etoile & Le Serre
7 Les Deux Garçons
8 La Mère Germaine

9 La Trinquette
10 Le Cosmo
11 Grocery

Other
12 Boat Rides & Electric
Bike Rental
13 Dark Pelican Motor Boat Rental
14 Octroi Bus Stop (from Nice;
to Monaco & Cap Ferrat)
15 Octroi Bus Stop (to Nice;
from Monaco & Cap Ferrat)

southern tip of the Alps. The range emerges from the sea here and arcs all across Europe, over 700 miles, to Vienna.

At 2,000 feet, this is the deepest natural harbor on the Riviera and was the region's most important port until Nice built its own in the 18th century. Today, ships bring tourists rather than pirates. The bay is generally filled with beautiful yachts. (In the evenings, you might see well-coiffed captains being ferried in by dutiful mates to pick up statuesque call girls.)

Up on the hill, the 16th-century citadel (where this walk ends) is marked by flags. The yellow fisherman's chapel (with the little-toe bell tower) has an interior painted by Jean Cocteau. Hôtel Welcome offers the balconies of dreams. Up the skinny lane just right of the hotel stands the baroque facade of St. Michael's Church. The waterfront, lined by fancy fish restaurants, curves to the town beach. Fifty yards above the beach stands the train station and above that, supported by arches, is the Low Corniche road, which leads to Monaco. Until that road was built in the 1860s, those hills were free of any development all the way to Monaco. The big yellow building just above can be rented for €300,000 a month (as Madonna did once for a birthday).

• *Leave the pier and walk left 30 yards past the last couple of fishing boats surviving from the town's once-prominent fishing community to find a small bronze bust of Jean Cocteau, the artist who said, "When I look at Villefranche, I see my youth." A few more steps take you to the little chapel he painted.*

Chapel of St. Pierre (Chapelle Cocteau): This chapel is the town's cultural highlight. Cocteau, who decorated the place, was a Parisian transplant who adored little Villefranche-sur-Mer and whose career was distinguished by his work as an artist, poet, novelist, playwright, and filmmaker. Influenced by his pals Marcel Proust, André Gide, Edith Piaf, and Pablo Picasso, Cocteau was a leader among 20th-century avant-garde intellectuals. At the door, Marie-France—who is passionate about Cocteau's art—collects a €3 donation for a fishermen's charity. She then sets you free to enjoy the chapel's small but intriguing interior. She's delighted to give you a small tour if you ask (Wed-Sun 9:30-12:30 & 14:00-18:00, usually closed Mon-Tue, hours vary with cruise-ship traffic and season).

• *From the chapel, turn right and stroll the harbor promenade 100 yards past romantic harborside tables.* **Restaurant La Mère Germaine** *is named for Mother Germaine, who famously took care of US Navy troops in World War II (step inside to see sketches and old photos on the wall). Immediately after the restaurant, a lane leads up into the old town. Walk up a few steps until you reach a long tunnel-like street.*

Rue Obscure, the Old Town, and St. Michael's Church: Here, under these 13th-century vaults, you're in another age. Turn right and walk to the end of Rue Obscure (which means "dark street"). At the end, wind up to the sunlight past a tiny fountain at Place du Conseil, and a few steps beyond that to a viewpoint overlooking the harbor.

Turn around and stroll back past the fountain, straight down the lane, and gently downhill. Notice the homes built under the heavy arches. At Place des Deux Garçons (the square with a name-sake restaurant), turn right on Rue May and climb the stepped lane. Take your first left at the restaurant to find St. Michael's Church, facing a delightful square with a single magnolia tree (Place de l'Eglise). The deceptively large church features an 18th-century organ, a particularly engaging crucifix at the high altar, and (to the left) a fine statue of a recumbent Christ—carved, they say, from a fig tree by a galley slave in the 1600s.

• *Leaving St. Michael's, go downhill halfway to the water, where you hit the main commercial street. Go right on Rue du Poilu (browsing a real-estate window if you'd like to move here), then curve left, pass the square, and walk up to the...*

Citadel: The town's mammoth castle was built in the 1500s by the Duke of Savoy to defend against the French. When the region joined France in 1860, the castle became just a barracks. Since the 20th century, it's housed the police station, City Hall, a summer outdoor theater, and art galleries. The single fortified entry—origi-nally a drawbridge over a dry moat (a.k.a. kill zone)—still leads into this huge complex.

The exterior walls slope thickly at the base, indicating that they were built in the "Age of Black Powder"—the 16th century—when the advent of gunpowder made thicker, cannonball-deflect-ing walls a necessity for any effective fortification. The bastions are designed for smarter crossfire during an attack.

• *And that concludes our introductory walk. For a brilliant seaside stroll (described next), drop back down below the citadel to the harbor parking lot (Parking Wilson) and find the stone path that leads to the right.*

Activities in Villefranche-sur-Mer

▲Seafront Walks

A seaside walkway originally used by customs agents to patrol the harbor leads under the citadel and connects the old town with the workaday harbor (Port de la Darse). At the port you'll find a few cafés, France's Institute of Oceanography (an outpost for the Uni-versity of Paris oceanographic studies), and an 18th-century dry dock. This scenic walk turns downright romantic after dark. You can also wander the other direction along Villefranche-sur-Mer's waterfront and continue beyond the train station for postcard-per-fect views back to Villefranche-sur-Mer (ideal in the morning—go before breakfast).

Hike to Mont-Alban Fort

This fort, with a remarkable setting on the high ridge that separates Nice and Villefranche-sur-Mer, is a good destination for hikers (also accessible by car and bus; info at TI). From the TI, walk on the main road toward Nice about 500 yards past Hôtel La Flore. Look for wooden trail signs labeled *Escalier de Verre* and climb about 45 minutes as the trail makes long switchbacks through the woods up to the ridge. Find your way to Mont-Alban Fort (interior closed to tourists) and its sensational view terrace over Villefranche-sur-Mer and Cap Ferrat. To visit with a much shorter hike, minibus #80 drops you a 15-minute walk away (by the recommended Hôtel Fiancée du Pirate). Bus #14 from Nice drops you just five minutes away (catch it at Masséna/Guitry stop by Galeries Lafayette department store).

Boat Rides (Promenades en Mer)

To view this beautiful coastline from the sea, consider taking a quick **sightseeing cruise** with AMV (€12-22, some stay in the bay, others go as far as Monaco, select days June-Sept, departs across from Hôtel Welcome, tel. 04 93 76 65 65, www.amv-sirenes.com). You can also rent your own **motor boat** through Dark Pelican (€110/half-day, €175/day, deposit required, on the harbor at the Gare Maritime, tel. 04 93 01 76 54, www.darkpelican.com).

Sleeping in Villefranche-sur-Mer

You have a handful of great hotels in all price ranges to choose from in Villefranche-sur-Mer. The ones I list have sea views from at least half of their rooms—well worth paying extra for.

$$$$ Hôtel Welcome** has the best location in Villefranche-sur-Mer, and charges for it. Anchored seaside in the old town, with all of its 35 plush, balconied rooms overlooking the harbor and a lounge/wine bar that opens to the water, this place lowers my pulse and empties my wallet (pricey garage—must reserve, 3 Quai Amiral Courbet, tel. 04 93 76 27 62, www.welcomehotel. com, resa@welcomehotel.com).

$$ Hôtel La Flore** is a fine value—particularly if your idea of sightseeing is to enjoy a panoramic view from your spacious bedroom balcony (even street-facing rooms have nice decks). The hotel is warmly run and good for families. Several rooms in the annex sleep four and come with kitchenettes, views, and private hot tubs. It's a 15-minute uphill hike from the old town, but the parking is free and the bus stops for Nice and Monaco are close by (on main road at 5 Boulevard Princesse Grace de Monaco, tel. 04 93 76 30 30, www.hotel-la-flore.fr, infos@hotel-la-flore.fr).

$$ Hôtel la Fiancée du Pirate** is a family-friendly view refuge high above Villefranche-sur-Mer on the Middle Corniche (best for drivers, although it is on bus lines #80, #82, and #112 to Eze-le-Village and Nice). Don't be fooled by the modest facade—Eric and Laurence offer 15 lovely and comfortable rooms, a large pool, a hot tub, a nice garden, and a terrific view lounge area. The big breakfast features homemade crêpes (RS%, laundry service, free parking, 8 Boulevard de la Corne d'Or, Moyenne Corniche/N-7, tel. 04 93 76 67 40, www.fianceedupirate.com, info@fianceedupirate.com).

$ Hôtel de la Darse** is a shy little hotel burrowed in the shadow of its highbrow neighbors and the only budget option in Villefranche. It's a great value with handsome rooms, but isn't central—figure 10 scenic minutes of level walking to the harbor and a steep 15-minute walk up to the main road (hourly minibus #80 stops in front; handy for drivers, free parking usually available close by). Seaview rooms are easily worth the extra euros (no elevator, tel. 04 93 01 72 54, www.hoteldeladarse.com, info@hoteldeladarse.com). From the TI, walk or drive down Avenue Général de Gaulle (walkers should turn left on Allée du Colonel Duval into the Jardins de Narvik and follow steps to the bottom).

Eating in Villefranche-sur-Mer

Locals don't come here in search of refined cuisine and nor should you. For me, dining in Villefranche-sur-Mer is about comfort

food, attitude, and ambience. Comparison-shopping is half the fun—make an event out of a predinner stroll through the old city. Saunter past the string of pricey candlelit places lining the waterfront and consider the smaller, less expensive eateries embedded in the old town.

$$$ La Grignotière, hiding in the back lanes, features Mediterranean comfort food. Servings are generous and tasty. Consider the giant helping of spaghetti and *gambas* (prawns) or the chef's personal-recipe bouillabaisse, all served by gregarious Brigitte and gentle Chantal (cozy seating inside, a few tables outside, daily, 3 Rue du Poilu, tel. 04 93 76 79 83).

$$ La Belle Etoile is the romantic's choice, with a charming interior filled with white tablecloths and soft lighting. This intimate place, serving fine Mediterranean cuisine, is a few blocks above the harbor on a small lane (closed Tue-Wed, 1 Rue Baron de Bres, tel. 04 97 08 09 41).

$$$ Les Deux Garçons offers candlelit tables on a quiet square and a refined cuisine that attracts locals in search of a special dinner (closed Wed, 18 Rue du Poilu, tel. 04 93 76 62 40).

$ Le Serre, nestled in the old town near St. Michael's Church, is a simple, cozy place that opens at 18:00 for early diners. Hardworking owner Sylvie serves well-priced dinners to a loyal local clientele and greets all clients with equal enthusiasm. Choose from the many thin-crust pizzas (named after US states), salads, and meats. Try the *daube niçoise* meat stew or the great-value, three-course *menu* (open evenings only, cheap house wine, 16 Rue de May, tel. 04 93 76 79 91).

$$$$ La Mère Germaine, right on the harbor, is the only place in town classy enough to lure a yachter ashore. It's dressy, with formal service and high prices. The name commemorates the current owner's grandmother, who fed hungry GIs during World War II. Try the bouillabaisse, served with panache (daily, reserve for harborfront table, 9 Quai de l'Amiral Courbet, tel. 04 93 01 71 39, www.meregermaine.com).

$ La Trinquette is a relaxed, low-key place away from the fray on the "other port," next to the recommended Hôtel de la Darse (a lovely 10-minute walk from the other recommended restaurants). Gentle Jean-Charles runs the place with charm, delivering reliable cuisine, friendly vibes at good prices, and a cool live-music scene on weekends (daily in summer, closed Wed off-season, 30 Avenue Général de Gaulle, tel. 04 93 16 92 48).

$$ Le Cosmo serves brasserie fare on the town's appealing main square (daily, Place Amélie Pollonnais, tel. 04 93 01 84 05).

Grocery Store: A handy **Casino** is a few blocks above Hôtel Welcome at 12 Rue du Poilu (Thu-Tue 8:00-12:30 & 15:30-19:30 except closed Sun afternoon and all day Wed).

Dinner Options for Drivers: If you have a car and are staying a few nights, take a short drive to Eze-le-Village or La Turbie for a late stroll, an early dinner, or a sunset drink. If it's summer (June-Sept), the best option of all is to go across to a restaurant on one of Cap Ferrat's beaches, such as **$$$ Restaurant de la Plage de Passable,** for a before-dinner drink or a dinner you won't soon forget.

Villefranche-sur-Mer Connections

For a comparison of connections by train and bus, see the "Public Transportation in the French Riviera" sidebar on page 698.

BY TRAIN
Trains are faster and run later than buses (until 24:00). It's a level, 10-minute walk from the port to the train station.

From Villefranche-sur-Mer by Train to: Monaco (2/hour, 10 minutes), **Nice** (2/hour, 10 minutes), **Antibes** (2/hour, 40 minutes), **Eze-Bord-de-Mer** (2/hour, 5 minutes) then transfer to bus #83 for Eze-le-Village (see "Getting to Eze-le-Village," later).

BY BUS
In Villefranche-sur-Mer, the most convenient bus stop is Octroi, just above the TI.

Bus #81 runs from Villefranche-sur-Mer in one direction to **Nice** (15 minutes) and in the other direction through **Beaulieu-sur-Mer** (5 minutes) to **Cap Ferrat,** ending at the port in the village of **St-Jean** (15 minutes; for other transportation options, see "Getting to Cap Ferrat," later). The last bus departs from Nice around 20:15, and from St-Jean around 20:50.

Bus #100 runs along the coastal road from Villefranche-sur-Mer westbound to **Nice** (3-4/hour, 20 minutes) and eastbound to **Beaulieu-sur-Mer** (10 minutes), **Monaco** (40 minutes), and **Menton** (1.25 hours). The last bus from Nice to Villefranche leaves at about 21:00 and from Villefranche to Nice at about 22:00.

To reach **Eze-le-Village** by bus you have two choices; walk or take bus #80 to upper Villefranche-sur-Mer, then catch bus #82 or #112, which together provide about hourly service to Eze-le-Village (only #82 runs on Sun). You can also take bus #100 or #81 to the Plage Beaulieu stop in nearby Beaulieu-sur-Mer, then catch bus #83 to Eze-le-Village, 8/day).

For more on these buses, including ticket info, routes, and frequencies, see page 696.

BY CRUISE SHIP

Tenders deposit passengers at a slick terminal building (Gare Maritime) at the Port de la Santé, right in front of Villefranche-sur-Mer's old town.

Getting into Town: It's easy to **walk** to various points in Villefranche-sur-Mer. The town's charming, restaurant-lined square is a straight walk ahead from the terminal, the main road (with the TI and bus stop) is a steep hike above, and the train station is a short stroll along the beach. **Minibus #80,** which departs from in front of the cruise terminal, saves you some hiking up to the main road and bus stop (described earlier).

Getting to Nearby Towns: To connect to other towns, choose between the **bus** or **train.** Leaving the terminal, you'll see directional sights pointing left, to *Town center/bus* (a 10- to 15-minute, steeply uphill walk to the Octroi bus stop with connections west to Nice or east to Monaco); and right, to *Gare SNCF/train station* (a 10-minute, level stroll with some stairs at the end). See train and bus connections above.

Taxis wait in front of the cruise terminal and charge exorbitant rates (minimum €15 charge to train station, though most will refuse such a short ride). For farther-flung trips, see the price estimates under "Getting Around Villefranche-sur-Mer," earlier. For an all-day trip, you can try negotiating a flat fee (say, €300 for a 4-hour tour).

Along the Three Corniches

Nice, Villefranche-sur-Mer, and Monaco are linked by three coastal routes: the Low, Middle, and High Corniches. The roads are nicknamed after the decorative frieze that runs along the top of a building (cornice). Each Corniche (kor-neesh) offers sensational views and a different perspective. The villages and sights in this section are listed from west to east in the order you'll reach them when traveling from Villefranche-sur-Mer to Monaco.

The corniches are peppered with impressive villas such as La Leopolda, a sprawling estate with a particularly grand entry that's named for its 1930s owner, King Leopold II of Belgium (who owned the entire peninsula of Cap Ferrat in addition to this estate). Those driving up to the Middle Corniche from Villefranche-sur-Mer can look down on this yellow mansion and its lush garden, which fill an entire hilltop. The property was later owned by the Agnelli family (of Fiat fame and fortune), and then by the Safra family (Brazilian bankers). Its current value is more than a half-billion dollars.

THE CORNICHE ROADS

For an overview of these three roads, see the "Between Nice & Monaco" map.

Low Corniche: The Basse Corniche (also called "Corniche Inférieure") strings ports, beaches, and seaside villages together for a traffic-filled ground-floor view. It was built in the 1860s (along with the train line) to bring people to the casino in Monte Carlo. When this Low Corniche was finished, many hill-town villagers descended to the shore and started the communities that now line the sea. Before 1860, the population of the coast between Villefranche-sur-Mer and Monte Carlo was zero. Think about that as you make the congested trip today.

Middle Corniche: The Moyenne Corniche is higher, quieter, and far more impressive. It runs through Eze-le-Village and provides breathtaking views over the Mediterranean, with several scenic pullouts.

High Corniche: Napoleon's crowning road-construction achievement, the Grande Corniche caps the cliffs with staggering views from almost 1,600 feet above the sea. Two thousand years ago, this was called the Via Aurelia, used by the Romans to conquer the West.

By Car

Drivers can find the three routes from Nice by driving up Boulevard Jean Jaurès, past Vieux Nice and the port. For the Low Corniche (to Villefranche-sur-Mer and Cap Ferrat), follow signs to N-98 *(Monaco par la Basse Corniche)*, which leads past Nice's port. Signs for N-7 and the Middle Corniche *(Moyenne Corniche)* appear shortly after the turnoff to the Low Corniche. Signs for the High *(Grande)* Corniche appear a bit after that; follow D-2564 to *Col des 4 Chemins* and the *Grande Corniche*.

The Best Route from Nice to Monaco: This breathtaking drive, worth ▲▲▲, takes the Middle Corniche from Nice or Ville-franche-sur-Mer to Eze-le-Village, then uphill following signs to the *Grande Corniche* and *La Turbie*. For cloud-piercing, 360-de-gree views, take Boulevard Maréchal Leclerc uphill from Eze-le-Village's western edge and follow signs for *Parc de la Grande Corniche*. The road becomes the winding Route de la Revère, which has viewpoints galore with views north to the Alps, straight down to the village, and along the Riviera from Naples to Barcelona (well, almost). Bring a picnic, as benches and tables are plentiful. Continue east from here along the Grande Corniche to La Turbie, keeping an eye out for brilliant views back over Eze-le-Village, then finish by dropping down into Monaco.

By Bus

Buses travel along each Corniche; the higher the route, the less frequent the buses (see the "Between Nice & Monaco" map). **Bus #100** runs along the **Low Corniche** from Nice to Monaco (3-4/hour). **Bus #112** provides the single best route to enjoy this area as it connects Monaco and Nice via Eze-le-Village along the **Middle Corniche** (6/day, none on Sun). **Bus #T-66** connects Nice with La Turbie along the **High Corniche** (3-6/day), and **bus #11** does the same from Monaco (6/day).

Cap Ferrat

This exclusive peninsula, rated ▲▲, decorates Villefranche-sur-Mer's views. Cap Ferrat is a peaceful eddy off the busy Nice-Monaco route (Low Corniche). You could spend a leisurely day on this peninsula, wandering the sleepy port village of St-Jean-Cap-Ferrat (usually called "St-Jean"), touring the Villa Ephrussi de Rothschild mansion and gardens, and walking on sections of the beautiful trails that follow the coast. If you owned a house here, some of the richest people on the planet would be your neighbors.

Tourist Information: The main TI is near the harbor in St-Jean (Mon-Sat 9:30-18:30, Sun 10:00-17:30; Oct-April Mon-Sat 9:00-17:00, closed Sun; 5 Avenue Denis Séméria, bus #81 stops here at the *office du tourisme*). A smaller TI is near the Villa Ephrussi (closed Sat off-season, closed Sun year-round, 59 Avenue Denis Séméria, tel. 04 93 76 08 90, www.saintjeancapferrat-tourisme.fr).

PLANNING YOUR TIME

Here's how I'd spend a day on the Cap: From Nice or Villefranche-sur-Mer, take bus #81 to the Villa Ephrussi de Rothschild stop (called Passable), then visit the villa. Walk 30 minutes, mostly downhill, to St-Jean for lunch (many options, including grocery shops for picnic supplies) and poke around the village. Take the 45-minute walk on the Plage de la Paloma trail (ideal for picnics). After lunch, take bus #81 or walk the beautiful 30-minute trail to the Villa Kérylos in Beaulieu-sur-Mer and maybe tour that villa (see "Walks Around Cap Ferrat," later). Return to Villefranche-sur-Mer, Nice, or points beyond by train or bus.

Here's an **alternative plan** for the star-gazing, nature-loving beach bum: Visit Villa Ephrussi then walk to St-Jean for lunch, hike six miles around the entirety of Cap Ferrat (2-3 hours), and enjoy the late afternoon on the beach at Plage de Passable. At sunset, have a drink or dinner at the recommended Restaurant de la Plage de Passable, then walk or catch a taxi back.

GETTING TO CAP FERRAT

From Nice or Villefranche-sur-Mer: Bus #81 (direction: *Port de St-Jean*) runs to all Cap Ferrat stops (for info on tickets, route, and frequency, see page 696). For the Villa Ephrussi de Rothschild, get off at the Passable stop (allow 30 minutes from Nice and 10 minutes from Villefranche-sur-Mer's Octroi stop). The return bus (direction: *Nice*) begins in St-Jean.

Warning: In high season, late-afternoon buses back to Villefranche-sur-Mer or Nice along the Low Corniche can be jammed (worse on weekends), potentially leaving passengers stranded at stops for long periods. To avoid this, either take the train or board bus #81 on the Cap itself (before it gets crowded).

Cap Ferrat is quick by **car** (take the Low Corniche) or **taxi** (allow €30 one-way from Villefranche-sur-Mer, €65 from Nice).

Sights on Cap Ferrat

▲VILLA EPHRUSSI DE ROTHSCHILD

In what seems like the ultimate in Riviera extravagance, Venice, Versailles, and the Côte d'Azur come together in the pastel-pink Villa Ephrussi. Rising above Cap Ferrat, this 1905 mansion has views west to Villefranche-sur-Mer and east to Beaulieu-sur-Mer.

Cost and Hours: Palace and gardens-€14, includes audioguide; mid-Feb-Oct daily 10:00-18:00, July-Aug until 19:00; Nov-mid-Feb Mon-Fri 14:00-18:00, Sat-Sun 10:00-18:00; tel. 04 93 01 33 09, www.villa-ephrussi.com.

Getting There: With luck, drivers can find a free spot to park along the entry road just inside the gate. The nearest bus stop is

RIVIERA

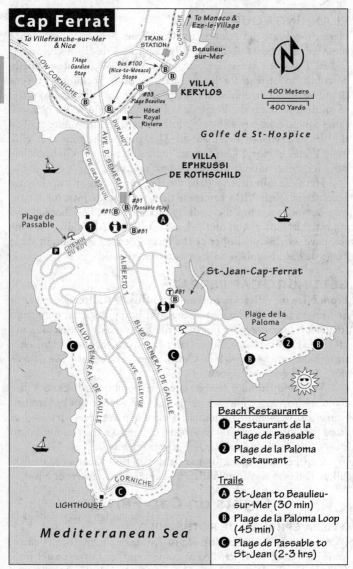

Cap Ferrat

To Villefranche-sur-Mer & Nice

To Monaco & Eze-le-Village

TRAIN STATION

Beaulieu-sur-Mer

l'Ange Gardien Stop

Bus #100 (Nice-to-Monaco) Stops

VILLA KERYLOS

#83 Plage Beaulieu

Hôtel Royal Riviera

LOW CORNICHE

AVE. DE GRASSEUIL

AVE. D. SEMERIA

Golfe de St-Hospice

VILLA EPHRUSSI DE ROTHSCHILD

Plage de Passable

#81

#81 (Passable stop)

CHEMIN DU ROY

P

ALBERTO 1

#81

St-Jean-Cap-Ferrat

#81

Plage de la Paloma

BLVD. GENERAL DE GAULLE

BLVD. GENERAL DE GAULLE

AVE. BELLEVUE

CORNICHE

LIGHTHOUSE

Mediterranean Sea

400 Meters

400 Yards

Beach Restaurants
1 Restaurant de la Plage de Passable
2 Plage de la Paloma Restaurant

Trails
A St-Jean to Beaulieu-sur-Mer (30 min)
B Plage de la Paloma Loop (45 min)
C Plage de Passable to St-Jean (2-3 hrs)

Passable, just a few minutes after the bus turns onto Cap Ferrat (bus #81, 5-minute walk uphill to the villa). If returning to Nice or Villefranche-sur-Mer by bus, check the posted schedule, and keep in mind that you're only a minute from the time-point listed for Port de St-Jean.

Visiting the Villa: Buy your ticket at the side of the building with the gift shop and get the small map of the gardens, then walk to the main entrance and pick up an audioguide. Start with the well-furnished belle-époque ground floor (well described by the audioguide). Upstairs, an 18-minute film (with English subtitles) explains the gardens and villa and gives you good background on the life of rich and eccentric Béatrice, Baroness de Rothschild, the French banking heiress who built and furnished the place.

As you stroll through the upstairs rooms, you'll pass royal furnishings and personal possessions, including the baroness's porcelain collection and her bathroom case for cruises. Her bedroom, sensibly, has views to the sea on both the port and starboard sides, and toward the bow, stretching like the prow of a vast cruise ship, is her garden. Don't miss the view from her private terrace.

The gorgeous **gardens** are why most come here. (The audioguide does not cover the gardens.) The ship-shaped gardens were inspired by Béatrice's many ocean-liner trips. She even dressed her small army of gardeners like sailors. Behind the mansion, stroll through the seven lush gardens re-created from locations all over the world—and with maximum sea views. Don't miss the Jardin Exotique's wild cactus, the rose garden at the far end, and the view back to the house from the "Temple of Love" gazebo. Cross the stepping-stone bridge by the playful fountains, if you dare.

An appropriately classy **$$ garden-tearoom** serves drinks and lunches with a view (12:00-17:30).

Walks from the Villa Ephrussi: It's a lovely 30-minute stroll, mostly downhill and east, from the Villa Ephrussi to the Villa Kérylos in Beaulieu-sur-Mer (described later) or to the port of St-Jean. To get to either, make a U-turn left at the stop sign below the Villa Ephrussi and follow signs along a small road toward the Hôtel Royal Riviera on Avenue Henri Honoré Sauvan (see "Cap Ferrat" map). Walk about five minutes down; when the road comes to a T, keep straight, passing a gate down a pedestrian path, which ends at the seafront trail (on Place David Niven)—go left to reach the Villa Kérylos, or head right to get to St-Jean. It's about 15 minutes to either destination once you join this path.

To get to Plage de Passable from the Villa Ephrussi, turn left on the main road just below the villa; after 50 yards you'll find signs leading down to the beach.

Plage de Passable

This pebbly little beach, located below the Villa Ephrussi, comes with great views of Villefranche-sur-Mer. It's a peaceful place, popular with families. One half is public (free, with snack bar, shower, and WC), and the other is run by a small restaurant (€30 includes changing locker, lounge chair, and shower; they have 260 "beds," but still reserve ahead in summer or on weekends as this is a prime spot, tel. 04 93 76 06 17). If you were ever to do the French Riviera rent-a-beach ritual, this would be the place.

To park near the beach (curbside or in a nearby lot), figure about €12/day in metered spots (free mid-Oct-April). Bus #81 stops a 10-minute walk uphill from the beach, near Villa Ephrussi.

For me, the best reason to come here is for dinner. Arrive before sunset, then watch as darkness descends and lights flicker over Villefranche-sur-Mer's heavenly setting. **$$$ Restaurant de la Plage de Passable** is your chance to dine on the beach with romance and class (with good-enough food) while enjoying terrific views and the sounds of children still at play (daily late May-early Sept, always make a reservation, tel. 04 93 76 06 17).

Plage de la Paloma

This half-private, half-public beach is a 10-minute walk from St-Jean-Cap-Ferrat. For €26 you get a lounge chair and the freedom to relax on the elegant side. Or enjoy the pebbly free beach (with shower and WC).

$$$ Plage de la Paloma Restaurant is inviting for dining on the beach, with salads for lunch and elegant dinners (daily from 12:00 and from 20:00, closed late Sept-Easter, tel. 04 93 01 64 71, www.paloma-beach.com).

ST-JEAN-CAP-FERRAT

This quiet harbor town lies in Cap Ferrat's center, yet is off most tourist itineraries and feels overlooked. St-Jean houses yachts, boardwalks, views, and boutiques packaged in a "take your time, darling" atmosphere. It's a few miles off the busy Nice-to-Monaco road—convenient for drivers. A string of restaurants line the port, with just enough visitors and locals to keep them in business. St-Jean is especially peaceful at night.

For picnics, the short pedestrian street in St-Jean has all you need (grocery store, bakery, charcuterie, and pizza to go), and you'll have no trouble finding portside or seaside seating. There's a big **Casino grocery** on the port below the main drag. Plage de la Paloma, described earlier, is a 10-minute walk away.

▲▲WALKS AROUND CAP FERRAT

The Cap is perfect for a walk; you'll find well-maintained and well-marked foot trails covering most of its length. You have several easy, mostly level options of varying lengths. The TIs in Villefranche-sur-Mer and St-Jean have maps of Cap Ferrat with walking paths marked.

Between St-Jean and Beaulieu-sur-Mer (30 minutes)

A level walk takes you past sumptuous villas, great views, and fun swimming opportunities. From St-Jean's port, walk along the har-

RIVIERA

bor and past the beach with the water on your right. Head up the steps to Promenade Maurice Rouvier and continue; before long you'll see smashing views of the whitewashed **Villa Kérylos**. In 1902, an eccentric millionaire modeled his mansion after an ancient Greek villa from the island of Delos (€12, includes audioguide; daily 10:00-19:00, Oct-May until 17:00; tel. 04 93 01 47 29, www.villakerylos.fr).

To get from Beaulieu-sur-Mer to St-Jean or the Villa Ephrussi, start at the Villa Kérylos (with the sea on your left), walk toward the Hôtel Royal Riviera, and find the trail. If going to St-Jean, stay left at the Villa Sonja Rello (about halfway down); if going to the Villa Ephrussi, after about 20 minutes look for signs leading uphill at Place David Niven (walk up the path to Avenue Henri Honoré Sauvan, then keep going). If you're walking from St-Jean to the Villa Ephrussi, turn left off the trail at Place David Niven.

Plage de la Paloma Loop Trail (45 minutes)
A few blocks east of St-Jean's port, a scenic trail offers an easy sampling of Cap Ferrat's beauty. From the port, walk or drive about a quarter-mile east (with the port on your left, passing Hôtel La Voile d'Or); parking is available at the port or on streets near Plage de la Paloma. You'll find the trailhead where the road comes to a T—look for a *Plage Paloma* sign pointing left, but don't walk left. Cross the small gravel park *(Jardin de la Paix)* to start the trail, and do the walk counterclockwise. The trail is level and paved, yet uneven enough that good shoes are helpful. Plunk your picnic on one of the benches along the trail, or eat at the restaurant on Plage de la Paloma at the end of the walk (described earlier).

Eze-le-Village

Capping a peak high above the sea, flowery and flawless Eze-le-Village (pronounced "ehz"; don't confuse it with the seafront town of Eze-Bord-de-Mer) is entirely consumed by tourism. This *village d'art et de gastronomie* (as it calls itself) is home to perfume outlets, stylish boutiques, steep cobbled lanes, and magnificent views. Touristy as it Eze, its stony state of preservation and magnificent hilltop setting over

the Mediterranean affords a fine memory. Day-tripping by bus to Eze-le-Village from Nice, Monaco, or Villefranche-sur-Mer works

RIVIERA

well. While Eze-le-Village can be tranquil early and late, during the day it is mobbed by cruise-ship and tour-bus groups. Come early or late in the day.

GETTING TO EZE-LE-VILLAGE

There are two Ezes: Eze-le-Village (the spectacular hill town on the Middle Corniche) and Eze-Bord-de-Mer (a modern beach resort far below the "village" of Eze). Parking in Eze-le-Village may be a headache as construction is under way for a new underground garage.

From Nice and upper Villefranche-sur-Mer, buses #82 and #112 together provide about hourly service to Eze-le-Village (only #82 runs on Sun, 30 minutes from Nice).

From Nice, Villefranche-sur-Mer, or Monaco, you can also take the train or the Nice-Monaco bus (#100) to Eze-Bord-de-Mer, getting off at the Gare d'Eze stop. From there, take the infrequent #83 shuttle bus straight up to Eze-le-Village (8/day, daily about 9:00-18:00, schedule posted at stop, 15 minutes). Those coming from Villefranche-sur-Mer can also take buses #81 or #100 and transfer to bus #83 at the Plage Beaulieu stop in Beaulieu-sur-Mer.

To connect Eze-le-Village directly with Monte Carlo in Monaco, take bus #112 (6/day Mon-Sat, none on Sun, 20 minutes).

A taxi between the two Ezes or from Eze-le-Village to La Turbie will run you about €30; allow €65 to Nice's port (mobile 06 09 84 17 84 or 06 18 44 47 93).

Orientation to Eze-le-Village

Tourist Information: The helpful TI is adjacent to Eze-le-Village's main parking lot, just below the town's entry. Ask here for bus schedules. Call at least a week in advance to arrange a €12, one-hour English-language tour of the village that includes its gardens (TI open daily 9:00-18:00, July-Aug until 19:00, Nov-March until 16:00 and closed Sun, Place de Gaulle, tel. 04 93 41 26 00, www.eze-tourisme.com).

Helpful Hints: The stop for **buses** to Nice is across the road by the Avia gas station, and the stops for buses to Eze-Bord-de-Mer and Monaco are on the village side of the main road, near the Casino grocery. Public **WCs** are just behind the TI and in the village behind the church. For food, there's a handy **Casino**

grocery at the foot of the village by the bus stop (daily 8:00-19:30) and a sensational picnic spot at the beginning of the trail to Eze-Bord-de-Mer. Or try **$ Le Cactus** near the entry to the old town (daily until about 19:30, tel. 04 93 41 19 02). For a splurge, dine at **$$$$ Château de la Chèvre d'Or** (see the walk, next).

Eze-le-Village Walk

This self-guided walk gives you a quick orientation to the village.

• *From the TI, hike uphill into the town. You'll come to an exclusive hotel gate and the start of a steep trail down to the beach, marked* Eze/Mer. *For a panoramic view and an ideal picnic perch, side-trip 90 steps down this path (for details, see "Hike to Eze-Bord-de-Mer," later). Continuing up into the village, find the steps immediately after the ritzy hotel gate and climb to...*

Place du Centenaire: In this square, a stone plaque in the flower bed (behind the candy stand) celebrates the 100th anniversary of the 1860 plebiscite, the time when all 133 Eze residents voted to leave the Italian Duchy of Savoy and join France. A town map here helps you get oriented.

• *Now pass through the once-formidable town gate and climb into the 14th-century village.*

As you walk, stop to read the information plaques (in English) and contemplate the change this village has witnessed in the last 90 years. Eze-le-Village was off any traveler's radar until well after World War II (running water was made available only in the 1930s), yet today hotel rooms outnumber local residents two to one (66 to 33).

• *Wandering the narrow lanes, consider a detour to **Château de la Chèvre d'Or** for its elegant bar-lounge and sprawling view terrace (high prices but high views). Continue on, following signs to the...*

Château Eza: This was the winter getaway of the Swedish royal family from 1923 until 1953; today it's a 15-room hotel. The château's tearoom (Salon de Thé), on a cliff overlooking the jagged Riviera and sea, offers another scenic coffee or beer break—for a price. The view terrace is also home to an expensive-but-excellent **$$$$** restaurant (open daily, tel. 04 93 41 12 24).

• *Backtrack a bit and continue uphill (follow signs to* Jardin Exotique*). The lane ends at the hilltop castle ruins—now blanketed by the...*

Jardin d'Eze: You'll find this prickly festival of cactus and exotic plants suspended between the sea and sky at the top of Eze-le-Village. Since 1949, the ruins of an old château have been home to 400 different plants 1,400 feet above the sea (€6, usually daily 9:00-19:00, Oct-May until about 16:00, well described in English, tel. 04 93 41 10 30). At the top, you'll be treated to a commanding 360-degree view, with a helpful *table d'orientation*. On a clear day (they say...) you can see Corsica. The castle was demolished by Louis XIV in 1706. Louis destroyed castles like this all over Europe (most notably along the Rhine), because he didn't want to risk having to do battle with their owners at some future date.

• As you descend, follow the pastel bell tower and drop by the...

Eze Church: Though built during Napoleonic times, this church has an uncharacteristic Baroque fanciness—a reminder that 300 years of Savoy rule left the townsfolk with an Italian savoir faire and a sensibility for decor. Notice the pulpit with the arm holding a crucifix, reminding the faithful that Christ died for their sins.

Sights in Eze-le-Village

Fragonard Perfume Factory
This factory, with its huge tour-bus parking lot, lies on the Middle Corniche, 100 yards below Eze-le-Village. Designed for tour groups, it cranks them through all day long. If you've never seen mass tourism in action, this place will open your eyes. (The gravel is littered with the color-coded stickers each tourist wears so that salespeople know which guide gets the kickback.) Drop in for an informative and free tour (2/hour, 15 minutes). You'll see how the perfume and scented soaps are made before being herded into the gift shop.

Cost and Hours: Daily 8:30-18:30; best Mon-Fri 9:00-11:00 & 14:00-15:30, when people are actually working in the "factory," tel. 04 93 41 05 05.

Hike to Eze-Bord-de-Mer
A steep trail leaves Eze-le-Village from the foot of the hill-town entry, near the fancy hotel gate (100 yards up from the main road), and descends 1,300 feet to the sea along a no-shade, all-view trail. The trail is easy to follow but uneven in a few sections—allow 45 minutes (good walking shoes are essential; expect to be on all fours in certain sections). Once in Eze-Bord-de-Mer, you can catch a bus or train to all destinations between Nice and Monaco. While walking this trail in the late 1800s, Friedrich Nietzsche was moved to write his unconventionally spiritual novel, *Thus Spoke Zarathustra*.

Le Trophée des Alpes

High above Monaco, on the Grande Corniche in the overlooked village of La Turbie, lies the ancient Roman "Trophy of the Alps," one of this region's most evocative historical sights (with dramatic views over the entire country of Monaco as a bonus). Rising well above all other buildings, this massive monument, worth ▲, commemorates Augustus Caesar's conquest of the Alps and its 44 hostile tribes. It's exciting to think that, in a way, Le Trophée des Alpes (also called "Le Trophée d'Auguste" for the emperor who built it) celebrates a victory that kicked off the Pax Romana—joining Gaul and Germania, freeing up the main artery of the Roman Empire, and linking Spain and Italy.

Circumnavigate the hulking structure. Notice how the Romans built a fine stone exterior using 24 massive columns that held together a towering cylinder filled with rubble and coarse concrete. Find the huge inscription on the back side of the monument. Flanked by the vanquished in chains, the towering inscription (one of the longest such inscriptions surviving from ancient times) tells the story: It was erected "by the senate and the people to honor the emperor."

A guardian will escort you halfway up the monument and give you a detailed explanation in English if you ask. The good little one-room **museum** shows a model of the monument, a video, and information about its history and reconstruction. There's also a translation of the dramatic inscription, which lists all the feisty alpine tribes that put up such a fight.

Cost and Hours: €6, Tue-Sun 9:30-13:00 & 14:30-18:30, off-season 10:00-13:30 & 14:30-16:30, closed Mon year-round, audioguide-€3 but English explanations are posted throughout; tel. 04 93 41 20 84, www.la-turbie.monuments-nationaux.fr.

Getting There: If visiting by **car,** take the High Corniche to La Turbie, ideally from Eze-le-Village (La Turbie is 10 minutes east of, and above, Eze-le-Village), then look for signs to *Le Trophée d'Auguste.* Once in La Turbie, drive to the site by turning right in front of the La Régence café. Those coming from farther afield can take the efficient A-8 to the La Turbie exit. To reach Eze-le-Village from La Turbie, follow signs to *Nice,* and then look for signs to *Eze-le-Village.*

From Nice, you can get here Monday through Saturday on **buses** #116 or #T-66 (6/day each from the Vauban tram stop); on Sunday take bus #T-66 (from the Pont St. Michel tram stop). From Monaco, bus #11 connects to La Turbie (8/day Mon-Sat, 5/day Sun, 30 minutes). La Turbie's bus stop is near the post office (La Poste) on Place Neuve.

Eating in La Turbie: The sweet old village of La Turbie sees almost no tourists, but it has plenty of cafés and restaurants. Your best bet is the welcoming **$$ Restaurant La Terrasse,** with tables under umbrellas and big views (daily for lunch and dinner, near the post office at the main parking lot, 17 Place Neuve, tel. 04 93 41 21 84). Charming owners Jacques and Helen speak flawless English.

Monaco

Despite high prices, wall-to-wall daytime tourists, and a Disney-esque atmosphere, Monaco is a Riviera must. Monaco is on the go. Since 1929, cars have raced around the port and in front of the casino in one of the world's most famous auto races, the Grand Prix de Monaco. The modern breakwater—constructed elsewhere and towed in by sea—enables big cruise ships to dock here, and the district of Fontvieille, reclaimed from the sea, bristles with luxury high-rise condos. But don't look for anything too

deep in this glittering tax haven. Many of its 36,000 residents live here because there's no income tax—there are only about 6,000 true Monegasques.

This minuscule principality (0.75 square mile) borders only France and the Mediterranean. The country has always been tiny, but it used to be...less tiny. In an 1860 plebiscite, Monaco lost two-thirds of its territory when the region of Menton voted to join France. To compensate, France suggested that Monaco build a fancy casino and promised to connect it to the world with a road (the Low Corniche) and a train line. This started a high-class tourist boom that has yet to let up.

Although "independent," Monaco is run as a part of France. A French civil servant appointed by the French president—with the blessing of Monaco's prince—serves as state minister and manages the place. Monaco's phone system, electricity, water, and so on, are all French.

The glamorous romance and marriage of the American actress Grace Kelly to Prince Rainier added to Monaco's fairy-tale mystique. Princess Grace first came to Monaco to star in the 1955 Alfred Hitchcock movie *To Catch a Thief,* in which she was filmed racing along the Corniches. She married the prince in 1956 and adopted the country, but tragically, the much-loved princess died in 1982 after suffering a stroke while driving on one of those same scenic roads. She was just 52 years old.

The death of Prince Rainier in 2005 ended his 56-year-long enlightened reign. Today, Monaco is ruled by Prince Albert Alexandre Louis Pierre, Marquis of Baux—son of Prince Rainier and Princess Grace. Monaco is a special place: There are more people in Monaco's philharmonic orchestra (about 100) than in its army (about 80). Yet the princedom is well-guarded, with police and cameras on every corner. (They say you could win a million dollars at the casino and walk to the train station in the wee hours without a worry.) Stamps are printed in small quantities and increase in value almost as soon as they're available. And collectors snapped up the rare Monaco versions of euro coins (with Prince Albert's portrait) so quickly that many Monegasques have never even seen one.

Orientation to Monaco

The principality of Monaco has three tourist areas: Monaco-Ville, Monte Carlo, and La Condamine. **Monaco-Ville** fills the rock

high above everything else and is referred to by locals as Le Rocher ("The Rock"). This is the oldest part of Monaco, home to the Prince's Palace and all the key sights except the casino. **Monte Carlo** is the area around the casino. **La Condamine** is the port, which lies between Monaco-Ville and Monte Carlo. From here it's a 20-minute walk up to the Prince's Palace or to the casino, or a few minutes by frequent bus to either (see "Getting Around Monaco," later).

TOURIST INFORMATION

The main TI is at the top of the park above the casino (Mon-Sat 9:00-19:00, Sun 11:00-13:00, 2 Boulevard des Moulins, tel. 00-377/92 16 61 16 or 00-377/92 16 61 66, www.visitmonaco.com). Another TI is at the train station (daily mid-June-mid-Sept 9:00-18:00, off-season Tue-Sat until 17:00, closed 12:30-14:00, closed Sun-Mon).

ARRIVAL IN MONACO

By Bus #100 from Nice and Villefranche-sur-Mer: Bus riders need to pay attention to the monitor showing the next stop. Cap d'Ail is the town before Monaco, so be on the lookout after that (the last stop before Monaco is called "Cimetière"). You'll enter Monaco through the modern cityscape of high-rises in the Font-vieille district. When you see the rocky outcrop of old Monaco, be ready to get off.

There are three stops in Monaco. In order from Nice, they are Place d'Armes (at the base of Monaco-Ville), Princesse Antoinette (on the port), and Monte Carlo-Casino (in front of the TI on Boulevard des Moulins).

Most riders will get off at **Place d'Armes** to visit Monaco-Ville first. Use the crosswalk in front of the tunnel, then keep right and

RIVIERA

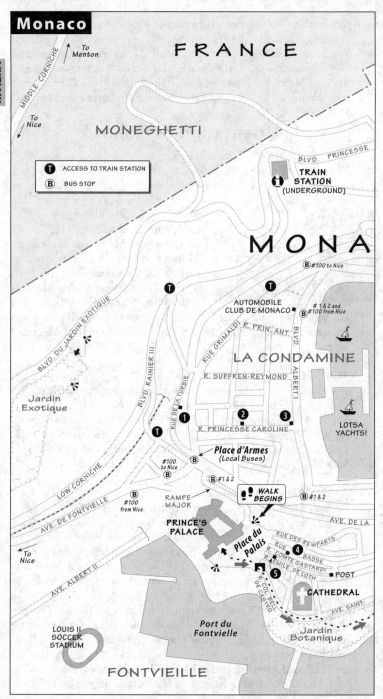

Monaco

T ACCESS TO TRAIN STATION

B BUS STOP

FRANCE

To Menton

To Nice

MIDDLE CORNICHE

MONEGHETTI

BLVD. PRINCESSE

TRAIN STATION
(UNDERGROUND)

MONA

B #100 to Nice

T

T

AUTOMOBILE CLUB DE MONACO

B # 1 & 2 and #100 from Nice

RUE GRIMALDI

R. PRIN. ANT.

BLVD. ALBERT 1

BLVD. DU JARDIN EXOTIQUE

BLVD. RAINIER III

LA CONDAMINE

R. SUFFREN-REYMOND

Jardin Exotique

RUE DE LA TURBIE

1

2

3

R. PRINCESSE CAROLINE

LOTSA YACHTS!

T

Place d'Armes
(Local Buses)

B

#100 to Nice

B

LOW CORNICHE

RAMPE MAJOR

B #1 & 2

B #100 from Nice

AVE. DE FONTVIELLE

WALK BEGINS

B #1 & 2

PRINCE'S PALACE

Place du Palais

AVE. DE LA

RUE DES REMPARTS

RUE BASSE

R. COMTE GASTARDI

4

R. EMILE DE LOTH

■ POST

To Nice

AVE. ALBERT II

R. COL. BEL DE CASTRO

5

CATHEDRAL ✝

AVE. SAINT

LOUIS II SOCCER STADIUM

Port du Fontvielle

Jardin Botanique

FONTVIEILLE

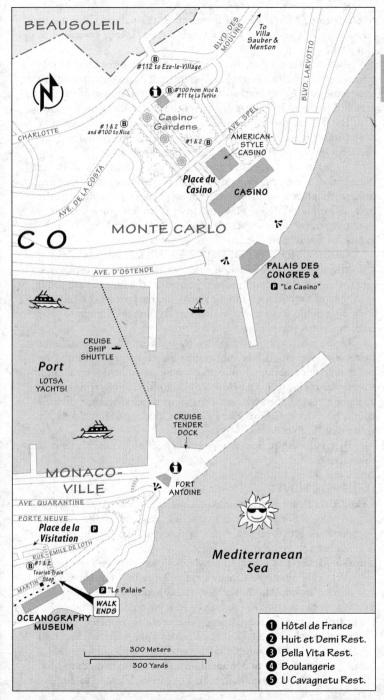

RIVIERA

BEAUSOLEIL

BLVD. DES MOULINS

To Villa Sauber & Menton

BLVD. LARVOTTO

N

(B) #112 to Eze-le-Village

(i) (B) #100 from Nice & #11 to La Turbie

CHARLOTTE

#1 & 2 and #100 to Nice (B)

Casino Gardens

#1 & 2 (B)

AVE. SPEL

AVE. DE LA COSTA

AMERICAN-STYLE CASINO

Place du Casino

CASINO

C O

MONTE CARLO

PALAIS DES CONGRES & 🅿 "Le Casino"

AVE. D'OSTENDE

Port

LOTSA YACHTS!

CRUISE SHIP SHUTTLE

CRUISE TENDER DOCK

MONACO-VILLE

FORT ANTOINE

AVE. QUARANTINE

PORTE NEUVE

Place de la Visitation 🅿

RUE EMILE DE LOTH

(B) #1 & 2 Tourist Train Stop

MARTIN

🅿 "Le Palais"

WALK ENDS

OCEANOGRAPHY MUSEUM

Mediterranean Sea

300 Meters
300 Yards

❶ Hôtel de France
❷ Huit et Demi Rest.
❸ Bella Vita Rest.
❹ Boulangerie
❺ U Cavagnetu Rest.

find bus stops #1 and #2 and the ramp to the palace. Casino-first types wait for the **Monte Carlo-Casino** stop. There's no reason to exit at the port stop.

By Train from Nice: The long, entirely underground train station is in the center of Monaco. From here, it's a 15-minute walk to the casino or the port, and about 15 minutes to the base of the palace (and frequent local buses). The station has no baggage storage.

The TI, train-ticket windows, and WCs are up the escalator at the Italy end of the station. There are three exits from the train platform level (one at each end and one in the middle).

To reach Monaco-Ville and the palace, take the exit at the Nice end of the tracks (signed *Sortie Fontvieille/Le Rocher*), which leads through a long tunnel and along a pedestrian plaza to the base of Monaco-Ville at Place d'Armes (turn left when you reach the busy street). From here, it's about a 15-minute hike up to the palace, or five minutes by bus (#1 or #2) plus a short walk.

To reach Monaco's port and the casino, take the middle exit, following *Sortie Port Hercule* signs down the steps and escalators, and then *Accès Port* signs until you pop out at the port, where you'll see the stop for buses #1 and #2 across the busy street. From here, it's a 20-minute walk to the casino (up Avenue d'Ostende to your left), or a short trip via bus #1 or #2.

If you plan to return to Nice by train in the evening (after ticket windows close), buy your return tickets on arrival or use the ticket machines (about €4 in coins or use a credit card with a chip).

By Car: Follow *Centre-Ville* signs into Monaco (warning: traffic can be heavy), then watch for the signs to parking garages at *Le Casino* (for Monte Carlo) or *Le Palais* (for Monaco-Ville). You'll pay about €12 for four hours.

By Cruise Ship: See "Monaco Connections," near the end of this section.

HELPFUL HINTS

Grand Prix Prep: If you come anytime from early April through May, you'll encounter construction detours as the country prepares for its largest event of the year, the Grand Prix de Monaco.

Combo-Tickets: If you plan to see both of Monaco's big sights (Prince's Palace and Oceanography Museum), buy the €20.50 combo-ticket. Another combo-ticket includes the Prince's private car collection in Fontvieille (not covered in this book).

Changing of the Guard: This popular event takes place daily (in good weather) at 11:55 at the Prince's Palace. Arrive by 11:30 to get a good viewing spot.

Loop Trip from Nice to Monaco: From Nice, you can get to Monaco by bus or train, then take a bus from Monaco to Eze-le-

Village or La Turbie, and return to Nice from there by bus. For bus numbers, frequencies, and stop locations, see "Monaco Connections," near the end of this section.

Evening Events: Monaco's cultural highlights include its **Philharmonic Orchestra** (tel. 00-377/98 06 28 28, www.opmc. mc) and **Monte Carlo Ballet** (tel. 00-377/99 99 30 00, www. balletsdemontecarlo.com).

Passport Stamp: For an official memento of your visit, get your passport stamped at the TI.

Post Office: The handiest post office for local stamps is in Monaco-Ville (described on my self-guided walk; Mon-Fri 8:00-19:00, Sat until 13:00, closed Sun).

GETTING AROUND MONACO

By Local Bus: Buses #1 and #2 link all areas with frequent service (10/hour, fewer on Sun, buses run until 21:00). If you pay the driver, a single ticket is €2, 6 tickets €11, and a day pass €5.50; save by using red curbside machines, where you get 12 tickets for €11. You can split a 6- or 12-ride ticket with your travel partners. Bus tickets are good for a free transfer if used within 30 minutes.

For a **cheap and scenic loop ride** through Monaco, ride bus #2 from one end to the other and back (25 minutes each way). You'll need two tickets and must get off the bus at the last stop and then get on again.

By Open Bus Tour: You could pay €23 for a hop-on, hop-off open-deck bus tour that makes 12 stops in Monaco, but I wouldn't. If you want a scenic tour of the principality that includes its best views, take local bus #2 for much less (see above).

By Tourist Train: An efficient way to enjoy a scenic blitz tour, **Monaco Tours** tourist trains begin at the Oceanography Museum and pass by the port, casino, and palace (€10, 2/hour, 30 minutes, recorded English commentary).

By Taxi: If you've lost all track of time at the casino, you can call the 24-hour taxi service (tel. 00-377/93 15 01 01)...assuming you still have enough money to pay for the cab home.

Monaco-Ville Walk

All of Monaco's major sights (except the casino) are in Monaco-Ville, packed within a few Disneyesque blocks. This self-guided walk connects these sights in a tight little loop, starting from the palace square.

• *To get from anywhere in Monaco to the palace square (Monaco-Ville's sightseeing center and home of the palace), take bus #1 or #2 to the end of the line at Place de la Visitation. Turn right as you step off the bus and*

walk five minutes down Rue Emile de Loth. You'll pass the post office, a
worthwhile stop for its collection of valuable Monegasque stamps.

Palace Square (Place du Palais)

This square is the best place to get oriented to Monaco. Facing the palace, walk to the right and look out over the city (er...principality). This rock gave birth to the little pastel Hong Kong look-alike in 1215, and it's managed to remain an independent country for most of its 800 years. Looking beyond the glitzy port, notice the faded green dome roof: It belongs to the casino that put Monaco on the map in the 1800s. The casino was located away from Monaco-Ville because Prince Charles III (r. 1856-1889) wanted to shield his people from low-life gamblers.

The modern buildings just past the casino mark the eastern limit of Monaco. The famous Grand Prix runs along the port and then up the ramp to the casino (at top speeds of 180 mph). Italy is so close, you can almost smell the pesto. Just beyond the casino is France again (it flanks Monaco on both sides)—you could walk one-way from France to France, passing through Monaco, in about 60 minutes.

The odd statue of a woman with a fishing net is dedicated to the glorious reign of **Prince Albert I** (1889-1922). The son of Charles III (who built the casino), Albert I was a true Renaissance Man. He had a Jacques Cousteau-like fascination with the sea (and built Monaco's famous aquarium, the Oceanography Museum) and was a determined pacifist who made many attempts to dissuade Germany's Kaiser Wilhelm II from becoming involved in World War I.

Escape the crowds for a moment with a short detour up the street, keeping the view on your left. Gawk at the houses lining the street and imagine waking up to that view every day.

• *Head toward the palace, passing electric car chargers (Prince Albert is an environmentalist), and find a statue of a monk grasping a sword.*

Meet **François Grimaldi,** *a renegade sword-carrying Italian dressed as a monk, who captured Monaco in 1297 and began the dynasty that still rules the principality. Prince Albert is his great-great-great... grandson, which gives Monaco's royal family the distinction of being the longest-lasting dynasty in Europe.*

Now walk to the...

Prince's Palace (Palais Princier)

A medieval castle once sat where the palace is today. Its strategic setting has had a lot to do with Monaco's ability to resist attackers. Today, Prince Albert and his wife live in the palace, while poor Princesses Stephanie and Caroline live down the street. The palace guards protect the prince 24/7 and still stage a **Changing of the Guard** ceremony with all the pageantry of an important nation (daily at 11:55 in good weather, fun to watch but jam-packed, arrive by 11:30). An audioguide takes you through part of the prince's lavish palace in 30 minutes. The rooms are well-furnished and impressive, but interesting only if you haven't seen a château lately. Even if you don't tour the palace, get close enough to check out the photos of the last three princes in the palace entry.

Cost and Hours: €8, includes audioguide, €20.50 combo-ticket includes Oceanography Museum; hours vary but generally daily 10:00-18:00, July-Aug until 19:00, closed Nov-March; buy ticket at the *Billeterie* at the souvenir stand 75 yards opposite the palace entrance; tel. 00-377/93 25 18 31, www.palais.mc.

• *Head to the west end of the palace square. Below the cannonballs is the district known as...*

Fontvieille

Monaco's newest, reclaimed-from-the-sea area has seen much of the principality's post-WWII growth (residential and commercial—notice the lushly planted building tops). Prince Rainier continued—some say, was obsessed with—Monaco's economic growth, creating landfills (topped with apartments, such as in Fontvieille), flashy ports, more beaches, a big sports stadium marked by tall arches, and a rail station. (An ambitious new landfill project is in the works and would add still more prime real estate to Monaco's portfolio.) Today, thanks to Prince Rainier's past efforts, tiny Monaco is a member of the United Nations. (If you have kids with you, check out the nifty play area just below.)

• *With your back to the palace, leave the square through the arch at the far right (onto Rue Colonel Bellando de Castro) and find the...*

Cathedral of Monaco (Cathédrale de Monaco)

The somber but beautifully lit cathedral, rebuilt in 1878, shows that Monaco cared for more than just its new casino. It's where centuries of Grimaldis are buried, and where Princess Grace and Prince Rainier were married. Inside, circle slowly behind the altar (counterclockwise). The second tomb is that of Albert I, who did much to put Monaco on the world stage. The second-to-last tomb—inscribed *"Gratia Patricia, MCMLXXXII"* and displaying the 1956 wedding photo of Princess Grace and Prince Rainier—is where the princess was buried in 1982. Prince Rainier's tomb lies next to hers (cathedral open daily 8:30-19:15).

• *Leave the cathedral and dip into the immaculately maintained **Jardin***

Botanique, with more fine views. In the gardens, turn left. Eventually you'll find the impressive building housing the...

Oceanography Museum (Musée Océanographique)

Prince Albert I had this cliff-hanging museum built in 1910 as a monument to his enthusiasm for things from the sea. The museum's aquarium, which Jacques Cousteau captained for 32 years, has 2,000 different specimens, representing 250 species. You'll find Mediterranean fish and colorful tropical species (all well described in English). Rotating exhibits occupy the entry floor. Upstairs, the fancy Albert I Hall is filled with ship models, whale skeletons, oceanographic instruments and tools, and scenes of Albert and his beachcombers hard at work—but sadly, only scant English information. Don't miss the elevator to the rooftop terrace view café.

Cost and Hours: €11-16, kids-€7-12 (price depends on season), €20.50 combo-ticket includes Prince's Palace; daily 10:00-19:00, longer hours July-Aug, Oct-March until 18:00; down the steps from Monaco-Ville bus stop, at the opposite end of Monaco-Ville from the palace; tel. 00-377/93 15 36 00, www.oceano.mc.

• *The red-brick steps across from the Oceanography Museum lead up to stops for buses #1 and #2, both of which run to the port, the casino, and the train station. To walk back to the palace and through the old city, turn left at the top of the brick steps. If you're into stamps, walk down Rue Emile de Loth to find the **post office**, where philatelists and postcard writers with panache can buy—or just gaze in awe at—the impressive collection of Monegasque stamps.*

Sights in Monaco

Jardin Exotique

This cliffside municipal garden, located above Monaco-Ville, has eye-popping views from France to Italy. It's home to more than a thousand species of cacti (some giant) and other succulent plants, but worth the entry only for view-loving botanists (some posted English explanations provided). Your ticket includes entry to a skippable natural cave, an anthropological museum, and a view snack bar/café. You can get similar views over Monaco for free from behind the souvenir stand at the Jardin's bus stop; or, for even grander vistas, cross the street and hike toward La Turbie.

Cost and Hours: €7.20, daily 9:00-19:00, Oct-April until about dusk, take bus #2 from any stop in Monaco or take the elevator up from the Nice end of the train station and follow signs, tel. 00-377/93 15 29 80, www.jardin-exotique.com.

▲Monte Carlo Casino (Casino de Monte-Carlo)

Monte Carlo, which means "Charles' Hill" in Spanish, is named for the prince who presided over Monaco's 19th-century makeover. In the mid-1800s, olive groves stood here. Then, with the construction of casino and spas, and easy road and train access (thanks to France), one of Europe's poorest countries was on the Grand Tour map—*the* place for the vacationing aristocracy to play. Today, Monaco has the world's highest per-capita income.

The Monte Carlo casino is intended to make you feel comfortable while losing your retirement nest egg. Charles Garnier designed the place (with an opera house inside) in 1878, in part to thank the prince for his financial help in completing Paris' Opéra Garnier (which the architect also designed). The central doors provide access to slot machines, gaming rooms, and the opera house. The gaming rooms occupy the left wing of the building. Cruise ship visitors can jam the entry during afternoons.

The odd bubble-like structures that line the parkway above the casino are temporary, and house high-end boutiques relocated from nearby for a long-term construction project. Ignore the tacky American-style casino that hides behind the outdoor café across from the hotel.

Cost and Hours: Tightwads can view the atrium entry, classy bar/café, and slot-machine room for free; daily 9:00-late. Touring the casino costs €17 (€12 off-season); daily 9:00-12:15; you'll see the atrium area and inner-sanctum gaming rooms with an audioguide, take photos, and have your run of the joint. Gamblers pay €10; daily 14:00 until the wee hours, must be 18 and show ID; no shorts, T-shirts, hoodies, tennis shoes, or torn jeans. Whether you gamble or not, expect lines at the entrance from May through September; tel. 00-377/92 16 20 00, www.montecarlocasinos.com.

Visiting the Casino: Enter through sumptuous **atrium.** This is the lobby for the 520-seat opera house (open Nov-April only for performances). A model of the opera house is at the far-right side of the room, near the bar-café. The **first gambling rooms** (Salle Renaissance, Salon de l'Europe, and Salle des Amériques) offer European and English roulette, plus Trente et Quarante, Punto Banco—a version of baccarat—and slot machines. The more glamorous **game rooms** (Salons Touzet, Salle Medecin, and Terrasse Salle Blanche) have those same games and Ultimate Texas Hold 'em poker, but you play against the cashier with higher stakes.

RIVIERA

The **park** behind the casino is a peaceful place with a good view of the building's rear facade and of Monaco-Ville.

Eating: The casino has two dining options. The **$$$$ Train Bleu** restaurant is for deep pockets for whom price is no object and elegance is everything. **$$$ Le Salon Rose** offers brasserie food—big salads and pasta dishes in a classy setting. If you paid to tour the casino or to gamble, show your ticket for a discount.

Take the Money and Run: The stop for buses returning to Nice and Villefranche-sur-Mer, and for local buses #1 and #2, is on Avenue de la Costa, at the top of the park above the casino (at the small shopping mall; for location, see the "Monaco" map). To reach the train station from the casino, take bus #1 or #2 from this stop, or find Boulevard Princesse Charlotte (parallels Avenue de la Costa one block above) and walk 15 minutes.

Sleeping and Eating in Monaco

Sleeping: Centrally located in Monaco-Ville, **$$ Hôtel de France**** is comfortable, well run by friendly Sylvie and Christoph, and reasonably priced—for Monaco (includes breakfast, air-con, no elevator; exit west from train station, 10-minute walk to 6 Rue de la Turbie, tel. 00-377/93 30 24 64, www.hoteldefrance.mc, hoteldefrance@monaco.mc).

Eating on the Port: Several cafés serve basic, inexpensive fare (day and night) on the port. Troll the places that line the flowery and traffic-free Rue Princesse Caroline between Rue Grimaldi and the port. **$$$ Huit et Demi** is a reliable choice, with a white-tablecloth-meets-director's-chair ambience and good outdoor seating (closed Sun, 7 Rue Princesse Caroline, tel. 00-377/93 50 97 02). A few blocks below, **$$ Bella Vita**—an easygoing place for salads, Italian fare, and classic French dishes—has a large terrace and modern interior (daily, serves nonstop from morning to late, 21 Rue Princesse Caroline, tel. 00-377/93 50 42 02).

Eating in Monaco-Ville: You'll find sandwiches—including the massive *pan bagnat,* basically *salade niçoise* on country bread—and quiche at the yellow-bannered **$ Boulangerie** (daily until 19:00, near Place du Palais at 8 Rue Basse). At **$$ U Cavagnetu,** just a block from Albert's palace, you'll dine cheaply on specialties from Monaco—pizza and such (daily, serves nonstop 11:00-23:00, 14 Rue Comte Félix Gastaldi, tel. 00-377/97 98 20 40). Monaco-Ville has other pizzerias, *crêperies,* and sandwich stands, but the neighborhood is dead at night.

Monaco Connections

BY TRAIN

For a comparison of train and bus connections, see the "Public Transportation in the French Riviera" sidebar on page 698. Most trains heading west will stop in Villefranche-sur-Mer, Nice, and Antibes (ask). The last train leaves Monaco for Villefranche-sur-Mer and Nice at about 23:30.

From Monaco by Train to: Villefranche-sur-Mer, Nice, Antibes, or **Cannes** (2/hour).

BY BUS

Frequent **bus #100,** which runs along the Low Corniche back to **Nice** (1 hour), and **Villefranche-sur-Mer** (40 minutes) is often slammed. For a better chance of securing a seat, board at the stop near the TI on Avenue de la Costa (see the "Monaco" map, earlier) rather than the stop near Place d'Armes. The last bus leaves Monaco for Nice at about 21:30. In the other direction bus #100 goes to **Menton** (30 minutes). For bus details, including tickets, routes, frequencies, and travel times, see page 696.

Bus #112, which goes along the scenic Middle Corniche to **Eze-le-Village** then on to Nice (6/day Mon-Sat, none on Sun, 20 minutes to Eze), departs Monaco from Place de la Crémaillère, one block above the main TI and casino park. Walk up Rue Iris with Barclays Bank to your left, curve right, and find the bus shelter across the street at the green La Crémaillère café.

Bus #11 to **La Turbie** (9/day Mon-Sat, 5/day Sun, 30 minutes) stops in front of the TI (same side of street).

Bus #110 express takes the freeway from the Place d'Armes stop to **Nice Airport** (2/hour, 50 minutes, €22).

BY CRUISE SHIP

Cruise ships tender passengers to the end of Monaco's yacht harbor, a short walk from downtown. It's a long walk or a short bus ride to most sights in town. To reach other towns, such as Villefranche-sur-Mer or Nice, you can take public transportation. To summon a taxi (assuming none are waiting when you disembark), look for the gray taxi call box near the tender dock—just press the button and wait for your cab to arrive.

Getting into Town: To reach **Monaco-Ville,** which towers high over the cruise terminal, you can either hike steeply and scenically up to the top of the hill, or walk to Place d'Armes and hop on bus #1 or #2, which will take you up sweat-free. It's a 15-minute, level walk to the bus stop from the port: Cross Boulevard Albert I, follow green *Gare S.N.C.F./Ferroviare* signs, and take the public elevator to Place d'Armes.

RIVIERA

The ritzy skyscraper zone of **Monte Carlo** is across the harbor from the tender dock, about a 25-minute walk. You can also ride the little electric "bateau bus" shuttle boat across the mouth of the harbor (works with a bus ticket). To reach the upper part of Monte Carlo—with the TI and handy bus stops (including for Eze-le-Village and La Turbie)—catch bus #1 or #2 at the top of the yacht harbor, along Boulevard Albert I.

Getting to Sights Beyond Monaco: Monaco is connected to most nearby sights by both train and bus. See the "Arrival in Monaco" section, earlier, as well as the bus and train connection information in this section for details.

The train station is about a 20-minute walk from the tender harbor—first walk to Place d'Armes (directions earlier under "Getting into Town"), then follow Rue Grimaldi to find stairs and an elevator to the station. For buses, see earlier for bus stop locations and frequencies. If taking bus #112 to Eze-le-Village or bus #11 to La Turbie, first ride bus #1 or #2 to the TI and casino, then follow the directions above.

Antibes

Antibes has a down-to-earth, easygoing ambience. Its old town is a warren of narrow streets and red-tile roofs rising above the blue Med, protected by twin medieval towers and wrapped in extensive ramparts. Visitors making the short trip from Nice can browse Europe's biggest yacht harbor, snooze on a sandy beach, loiter through an enjoyable old town, and hike along a sea-swept trail. The town's cultural claim to fame, the Picasso Museum (closed on Mondays), shows off its appealing collection in a fine old building.

Though much smaller than Nice, Antibes has a history that dates back just as far. Both towns were founded by Greek traders in the fifth century BC. To the Greeks, Antibes was "Antipolis"—the town *(polis)* opposite *(anti)* Nice. For the next several centuries, Antibes remained in the shadow of its neighbor. By the turn of the 20th century, the town was a military base—so the rich and famous partied elsewhere. But when the army checked out after World War I, Antibes was "discovered" and enjoyed a particularly roaring '20s—with the help of party animals like Rudolph Valentino and the rowdy (yet silent) Charlie Chaplin. Fun seekers even invented water-skiing right here in the 1920s.

Orientation to Antibes

Antibes' old town lies between the port and Boulevard Albert I and Avenue Robert Soleau. Place Nationale is the old town's hub of activity. Stroll above the sea between the old port and Place Albert I (where Boulevard Albert I meets the water). Good beaches lie just beyond Place Albert I, and the walk there leads to fine views. Fun play areas for children are along this path and on Place des Martyrs de la Résistance (close to recommended Hôtel Relais du Postillon).

TOURIST INFORMATION

The TI is a few blocks from the train station at 42 Avenue Robert Soleau (July-Aug daily 9:00-19:00; Sept-June Mon-Sat 9:00-12:30 & 14:00-18:00, Sun 9:00-13:00; shorter hours and closed Sun in winter; tel. 04 22 10 60 10, www.antibes-juanlespins.com). Hikers should get the free tourist map of the Sentier Touristique de Tire-poil hike (see "Sights in Antibes," later).

ARRIVAL IN ANTIBES

By Train: Bus #14 runs frequently (except Sun) from below the train station along Avenue de la Libération to the city bus station (*gare routière;* near several recommended hotels and the old town), and continues to the fine Plage de la Salis, with quick access to the Phare de la Garoupe trail (2/hour, none on Sun, bus stop 100 yards to right as you exit train station). **Taxis** usually wait in front of the station.

To **walk** from the station to the port, the old town, and the Picasso Museum (15 minutes), cross the street in front of the station, skirting left of the café, and follow Avenue de la Libération downhill as it bends left. At the end of the street, head to the right along the port. If you walk on the water's edge, you'll see the yachts get bigger as you go.

To walk directly to the TI and recommended hotels in the old town, turn right out of the station and walk down Avenue Robert Soleau.

There's no baggage check in Antibes. The last train back to Nice leaves at about midnight.

By Bus: Antibes has two bus stations—one mostly for regional buses and one only for city buses. **Regional buses** (#200 &

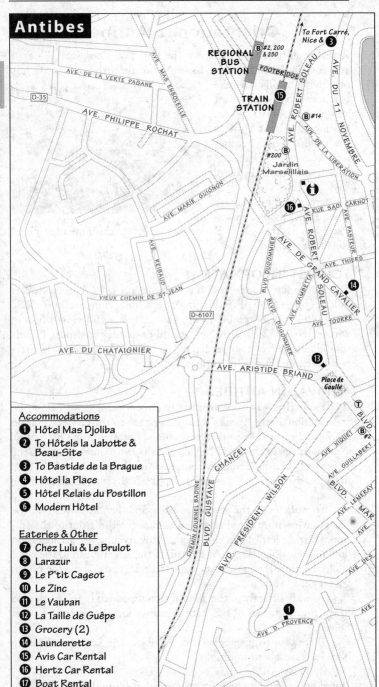

Antibes

Accommodations
1. Hôtel Mas Djoliba
2. To Hôtels la Jabotte & Beau-Site
3. To Bastide de la Brague
4. Hôtel la Place
5. Hôtel Relais du Postillon
6. Modern Hôtel

Eateries & Other
7. Chez Lulu & Le Brulot
8. Larazur
9. Le P'tit Cageot
10. Le Zinc
11. Le Vauban
12. La Taille de Guêpe
13. Grocery (2)
14. Launderette
15. Avis Car Rental
16. Hertz Car Rental
17. Boat Rental

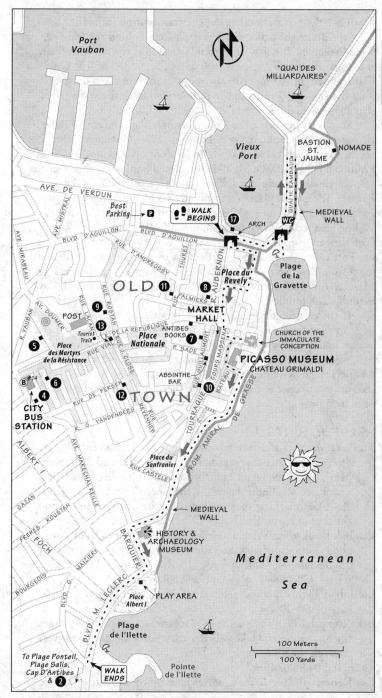

Port Vauban

"QUAI DES MILLIARDAIRES"

Vieux Port

BASTION ST. JAUME

NOMADE

AVE. DE VERDUN

Best Parking

P

WALK BEGINS

17

ARCH

WC

MEDIEVAL WALL

BLVD. D'AGUILLON

QUAI H. RAMBAUD

Plage de la Gravette

AVE. MISTRAL

AVE. MIRABEAU

RUE D'ANDREOSSY

RUE THURET

RUE D'AUBERNON

Place du Revely

OLD

RUE ROSTAN

RUE LACAN

RUE PALMIERS

11

8

MARKET HALL

AV. DOLMER

POST

9

13

Tourist Train

RUE DE LA REPUBLIQUE

Place Nationale

Antibes Books

7

R. SADE

Place des Martyrs de la Résistance

R. VAUBAN

5

RUE VIAL

RUE J. CLOSE

RUE GUILLAUMONT

Church of the Immaculate Conception

PICASSO MUSEUM
CHATEAU GRIMALDI

B #14

6

ABSINTHE BAR

COURS MASSENA

4

CITY BUS STATION

RUE DE FERSEL

12

RUE REVENNES

TOWN

10

RUE TOURAQUE

PROM. DE GRASSE

R. G. VANDENBERG

PROM. AMIRAL DE GRASSE

ALBERT I

AVE. MARÉCHAL FEILLE

Place du Sanfranier

RUE CASTELET

GAZAN

FRÈRES ROUSTAN

FOCH

MEDIEVAL WALL

BOURGEOIS

BLVD. G. MAIZIÈRE

BARQUIER

HISTORY & ARCHAEOLOGY MUSEUM

Mediterranean

Sea

BLVD. M. LECLERC

Place Albert I

PLAY AREA

Plage de l'Ilette

To Plage Ponteil, Plage Salis, Cap D'Antibes & 2

WALK ENDS

Pointe de l'Ilette

100 Meters

100 Yards

#250) use the bus station behind the train station (called the *Pôle d'Echange;* take the pedestrian overpass from behind the train station to reach it). Buses to and from Nice stop at the far right (east) end (info office open Mon-Fri 7:00-19:00, Sat 9:00-12:30 & 14:00-17:00, closed Sun). Bus #200 also stops in front of the train station (find the shelter 50 yards to the right as you leave the station) and near Place de Gaulle.

Some **city buses** use the *Pôle d'Echange* (like handy bus #2), but all serve the bus station in the old town on Place Guynemer, a block below Place Général de Gaulle (info desk open Mon-Fri 7:30-19:00, Sat 8:30-12:00 & 14:30-17:30, closed Sun, www.envibus.fr).

By Car: Day-trippers follow signs to *Centre-Ville,* then *Port Vauban.* The easiest place to park is a convenient but pricey underground parking lot located outside the ramparts near the archway leading into the old town (€10/4 hours, €24/12 hours, just south of Port Vauban—see the "Antibes" map). A free lot is available opposite Fort Carré (north of the port). It's a 15-minute walk to the old town from here; you can also catch bus #14. Street parking is free Monday through Friday (12:00-14:00 & 19:00-8:00), and all day Saturday and Sunday.

If you're sleeping in Antibes, follow *Centre-Ville* signs, then signs to your hotel. The most appealing hotels in Antibes are best by car, and Antibes works well for drivers—compared with Nice, parking is easy, traffic is minimal, and it's a convenient springboard for the Inland Riviera. Pay parking is available at Antibes' train station, so drivers can ditch their cars here and day-trip from Antibes by train.

HELPFUL HINTS

Markets: Antibes' old-time market hall (Marché Provençal) hosts a vibrant produce market (daily until 13:00, closed Mon Sept-May), and a lively antiques/flea market fills Place Nationale and Place Audiberti, next to the port (Thu and Sat 7:00-18:00). A clothing market winds through the streets around the post office on Rue Lacan (Thu 9:00-18:00).

English Bookstore: With a welcoming vibe, **Antibes Books** has a good selection of new and used books; check out their many guidebooks—including mine (13 Rue Georges Clemenceau, tel. 04 93 61 96 47, www.antibesbooks.com).

Laundry: There's a launderette at 19 Avenue du Grand Cavalier (daily 8:00-20:45).

Bike Rental: The TI has a list of places where you can rent bikes (including electric bikes). Bikes are a good way for nondrivers to reach the hikes described later.

Taxi: Tel. 04 93 67 67 67.

Car Rental: The big-name agencies have offices in Antibes (closed

RIVIERA

Mon-Sat 12:00-14:00 and all day Sun). The most central are **Avis** (at the train station, tel. 04 93 34 65 15) and **Hertz** (a few blocks from the train station at 52 Avenue Robert Soleau, tel. 04 92 91 28 00).

Boat Rental: You can motor your own seven-person yacht thanks to **Antibes Bateaux Services** (€100/half-day, at the small fish market on the port, mobile 06 15 75 44 36, www.antibes-bateaux.com).

GETTING AROUND ANTIBES

Antibes' buses (Envibus) cost €1 and are handiest for carless travelers wanting access to Cap d'Antibes. **Bus #14** links the train station, city bus station, old town, and Plage de la Salis. It also takes you to Fort Carré, where free parking is available. **Bus #2** provides access to the best beaches, the path to La Phare de la Garoupe, and the Cap d'Antibes trail. It runs from the Pôle d'Echange bus station (behind the train station) through the city center and down Boulevard Albert I (daily 7:00-19:00, every 40 minutes). Pick up a schedule at the bus station.

Antibes Walk

This 40-minute self-guided walk will help you get your bearings, and works well day or night.

• *Begin at the old port (Vieux Port) at the southern end of Avenue de Verdun. Stand at the port, across from the archway with the clock.*

Old Port: Locals claim that this is Europe's first and biggest pleasure-boat harbor, with 1,600 stalls. That star-shaped stone structure crowning the opposite end of the port is **Fort Carré,** which protected Antibes from foreigners for more than 500 years.

The pathetic remains of a once-hearty **fishing fleet** are moored in front of you. The Mediterranean is pretty much fished out. Most of the seafood you'll eat here comes from fish farms or the Atlantic.

• *With the port on your left, walk a block past the sorry fleet and duck under the first open arch to the shell-shaped...*

Plage de la Gravette: This normally quiet public beach is tucked right in the middle of old Antibes. Walk out onto the paved area. Consider the scale of the ramparts that protected this town. Because Antibes was the last fort before the Italian border, the French king made sure the ramparts were top-notch. The twin towers crowning the old town are the church's bell tower and the tower topping Château Grimaldi (today's Picasso Museum). As you face the old town, forested Cap d'Antibes is the point of land in the distance to the left. Is anyone swimming? Locals don't swim much in July and August because of jellyfish—common now in warmer water. Throughout the Mediterranean, you'll see red flags warning of dangerous storms or tides. Many beaches now also have white flags with jellyfish symbols warning that swimming might be a stinging experience.

• *For a close-up look at the megayachts and a walk along the ramparts, follow this fun detour. Otherwise, skip ahead to the "Old Antibes" directions.*

Antibes' Megayacht Harbor: Take a three-block detour to the north as you leave Plage de la Gravette for a glimpse at the epitome of conspicuous consumption. You'll walk along the harbor under the ramparts known as Bastion St. Jaume.

You'll eventually reach a restricted area harboring massive yachts. Climb the ramparts on your right and make your way to the **modern white sculpture.** *Nomade*—a man of letters looking pensively out to sea—was created in 2010 by the Spanish artist Jaume Plensa (find the posted English explanations nearby). You can sit in the sculpture and ponder how human communication forms who we are and links all people. Looking north, the Alps make a beautiful backdrop when it's clear.

Browse the line of huge pleasure craft stern-tied to the pier (which was built in the 1970s with financial aid from mostly Saudi Arabian yacht owners, who wanted a decent place to tie up). Locals call this the *Quai des Milliardaires* ("billionaire's dock").

Old Antibes: Return along the upper walkway then enter Antibes' old town through the arch under the clock.

• *You can walk directly up the main street to get to our next stop, but here's a more scenic option: Passing through the gate, turn immediately left, and then walk up the steps in the small square. Walk straight through the arch at #14 and into picturesque Place du Revely. Cross Place du Revely to the right, and go down the ramp under several arches, then turn left when you reach the main drag into the old town and Antibes' market hall, Le Marché Provençal.*

Market Hall: Antibes' market hall bustles under a 19th-century canopy, with flowers, produce, Provençal products, and beach accessories. The market wears many hats: produce until 13:30 (daily except closed Mon Sept-May), handicrafts most afternoons (Thu-Sun), and fun outdoor dining in the evenings, on Cours Masséna.

On the right (at the corner of Rue Sade), a pretty shop hides an atmospheric **absinthe bar** in its ninth-century vaulted cellar. You're welcome to go through the shop (or enter via Rue Sade) and descend to find an amazing collection of absinthe fountains, the oldest dating from the 1860s. The owner will gladly show you his memorabilia. You can even taste the now-legal drink to better understand Picasso's paintings. On Friday and Saturday nights, the basement is transformed into an absinthe-infused jazz bar lounge with 1920s ambience.

• *Double back to the entry of the market and find Rue Christian Chessel leading uphill to the pretty pastel...*

Church of the Immaculate Conception: Built on the site of a Greek temple, this is worth a peek inside. A church has stood on this site since the 12th century. This one served as the area's cathedral until the mid-1200s. The stone bell tower standing in front of the church predates it by 600 years, when it was part of the city's defenses. Many of those heavy stones were pillaged from Antibes' Roman monuments.

• *Looming above the church on prime real estate is the white-stone...*

Château Grimaldi: This site was home to the acropolis of the Greek city of Antipolis and later a Roman fort. Later still, the château was the residence of the Grimaldi family (a branch of which still rules Monaco). Today it houses Antibes' Picasso Museum. Its proximity to the cathedral symbolized the sometimes too-cozy relationship between society's two dominant landowning classes: the Church and the nobility. (In 1789, the French Revolution changed all that.)

• *After visiting the **Picasso Museum** (see "Sights in Antibes," next), work your way through the warren of pretty lanes, then head out to the water, turn right along the ramparts, and find a sweeping sea view. As you walk, you'll pass a charming neighborhood (La Commune Libre du Safranier) on your right, making a lovely return route. As you wander, look for forested **Cap d'Antibes** (to the south), crowned by its lighthouse and studded with mansions (a proposed hike here is described later). The Cap was long the refuge of Antibes' rich and famous, and a favorite haunt of F. Scott Fitzgerald and Ernest Hemingway.*

*The rampart walk leads to the **History and Archaeology Museum**. After taking a quick spin through its galleries (see "Sights in Antibes," next), continue hugging the shore past Place Albert I until you see the smashing views back to old Antibes. Benches and soft sand await. You're on your own from here—energetic walkers can continue on the trail, which leads to the lighthouse (see "Hikes," later in this section); others can return to old Antibes and wander around in its peaceful back lanes.*

Sights in Antibes

▲▲Picasso Museum (Musée Picasso)

Sitting serenely where the old town meets the sea, this compact three-floor museum offers a manageable collection of Picasso's paintings, sketches, and ce-ramics. Picasso lived in this castle for part of 1946, when he cranked out an amazing amount of art (most of the paintings you'll see are from this short but prolific stretch of his long and varied career). He was elated by the end of World War II, and his works show a celebration of color and a rediscovery of light after France's long nightmare of

war. Picasso was also reenergized by his young and lovely compan-ion, Françoise Gilot (with whom he would father two children). The resulting collection (donated by Picasso) put Antibes on the tourist map.

Cost and Hours: €8; Tue-Sun 10:00-18:00, mid-Sept-mid-June closed Tue-Sun 13:00-14:00, closed Mon year-round; tel. 04 92 90 54 20).

Visiting the Museum: The museum's highlight is on the top floor, where you'll find the permanent collection of Picasso's works. Visitors are greeted by a large image of Picasso and a display of photographs of the artist at work and play during his time in An-tibes.

The first gallery room (up the small staircase to your left) houses several famous works, including the lively, frolicking, and big-breasted *La Joie de Vivre* painting (from 1946). This Greek bac-chanal sums up the newfound freedom in a just-liberated France and sets the tone for the rest of the collection. You'll also see the colorless, three-paneled *Satyr, Faun and Centaur with Trident* and several ceramic creations. As you leave this room don't miss the adorable (pregnant?) goat.

Throughout, you'll see both black-and-white and colorful ink sketches that challenge the imagination—these show off Picasso's skill as a cartoonist and caricaturist. Look also for the cute Basque fishermen *(Pecheur attablé)* and several Cubist-style nudes *(nus cou-chés)*, one painted on plywood.

Near the end, don't miss the wall devoted to Picasso's ceramic plates. In 1947, inspired by a visit to a ceramics factory in nearby Vallauris, Picasso discovered the joy of this medium. He was smit-ten by the texture of soft clay and devoted a great deal of time to exploring how to work with it—producing over 2,000 pieces in one year. In the same room, the wall-sized painting *Ulysses and the Sirens* screams action and anxiety. Lashed to the ship mast, Ulysses survives the temptation of the sirens.

History and Archaeology Museum (Musée d'Histoire et d'Archéologie)

More than 2,000 years ago, Antibes was the center of a thriving maritime culture. It was an important Roman commercial port with aqueducts, theaters, baths, and so on. This museum—the only place to get a sense of the city's ancient roots—displays Greek, Roman, and Etruscan odds and ends in two simple halls but sadly, no English descriptions. Your visit starts at an 1894 model of Antibes and continues past displays of Roman coins, cups, plates, and scads of amphorae.

Cost and Hours: €3; Tue-Sun 10:00-12:00 & 14:00-18:00, shorter hours off-season, closed Mon year-round, on the water between Picasso Museum and Place Albert I, tel. 04 92 95 85 98.

Fort Carré

This impressively situated, mid-16th-century citadel, on the headland overlooking the harbor, protected Antibes from Nice (which until 1860 wasn't part of France). You can tour this unusual star-shaped fort for the fantastic views over Antibes, but there's little to see inside (€3, Tue-Sun 10:00-12:30 & 13:30-18:00, until 16:30 off-season, closed Mon year-round).

▲Beaches *(Plages)*

Good beaches stretch from the south end of Antibes toward Cap d'Antibes. They're busy but manageable in summer and on weekends, with cheap snack stands and good views of the old town. The closest beach to the old town is at the port

(Plage de la Gravette), which seems calm in any season.

HIKES

I list two good hikes below. Orient yourself from the seaside rampart walk below the Picasso Museum or from the bottom of Boulevard Albert I (where it meets the beach). That tower on the hill is your destination for the first hike. The longer Cap d'Antibes hike begins over that hill, a few miles farther away. The two hikes are easy to combine by bus, bike, or car.

RIVIERA

▲▲Chapelle et Phare de la Garoupe Hike

The territorial views—best in the morning, skippable if it's hazy—from this viewpoint more than merit the 20-minute uphill climb from Plage de la Salis (a few blocks after Maupassant Apartments, where the road curves left, follow signs and the rough, cobbled Chemin du Calvaire up to lighthouse tower). An orientation table explains that you can see from Nice to Cannes and up to the Alps.

Getting There: Take bus #2 or #14 to the Plage de la Salis stop and find the trail a block ahead. By car or bike, follow signs for *Cap d'Antibes*, then look for *Chapelle et Phare de la Garoupe* signs.

▲▲Cap d'Antibes Hike
(Sentier Touristique de Tirepoil)

Cap d'Antibes is filled with exclusive villas and mansions protected by high walls. Roads are just lanes, bounded on both sides by the

high and greedy walls in this home of some of the most expensive real estate in France (and where "public" seems like a necessary evil). But all the money in the world can't buy you the beach in France, so a thin strip of rocky coastline forms a two-mile long, parklike zone with an extremely scenic, mostly paved but often rocky trail (Sentier Touristique de Tirepoil).

As you walk, you'll have fancy fences with security cameras on one side and dramatic sea views on the other. The public space is rarely more than 50 yards wide and often extremely rocky—impassible if not for the paved trail carved out of it for the delight of hikers.

At a fast clip you can walk the entire circle in just over an hour. Don't do the hike without the tourist map (available at hotels or the TI). You can do it in either direction (or in partial segments; see "Getting There," next page). I've described the walk starting at its western end going counterclockwise.

From the La Fontaine bus stop walk five minutes down Avenue Mrs. L. D. Beaumont to the gate of the Villa Eilenroc. Enter through the gate to the trail skirting the villa on your left, and walk five more minutes to the rocky coastal trail. Now turn left and follow the trail for nearly an hour around Cap Gros. There's no way to get lost without jumping into the sea or scaling villa security walls. You return to civilization at a tiny resort (Plage de la Garoupe), with an expensive restaurant, a fine beach (both public and private), and a fun and inexpensive beachside bar/café. From here it's a 10-minute walk up Avenue André Sella to your starting point and the bus stop. With a car (or bike), you could start and end at Plage de la Garoupe. For a shorter version, walk from Plage de la Garoupe to Cap Gros and back.

Getting There: Drivers will find parking easier at the trail's eastern end (Plage de la Garoupe), though some street parking is available a few blocks from the trail's western end (look near Hôtel Beau-Site). Pedestrians should start at the trail's western end. Take bus #2 from Antibes for about 15 minutes to the La Fontaine stop at Rond-Point A. Meiland (next to the recommended Hôtel Beau-Site), then follow the route described earlier.

Sleeping in Antibes

Several sleepable options are available in the town center, but my favorite Antibes hotels are farther out and most convenient for drivers.

OUTSIDE THE TOWN CENTER

$$ Hôtel Mas Djoliba*** is a traditional manor house with chirping birds and a flower-filled moat. While convenient for drivers, it's workable for walkers (10-minute walk to Plage de la Salis, 15 minutes to old Antibes). Bigger rooms are worth the additional cost, and several rooms come with small decks (several good family rooms, no elevator but just three floors, *boules* court and loaner balls; 29 Avenue de Provence—from Boulevard Albert I, look for gray signs two blocks before the sea, turn right onto Boulevard Général Maizière, and follow signs; tel. 04 93 34 02 48, www.hotel-djoliba.com, contact@hotel-djoliba.com, Delphine).

$$ Hôtel la Jabotte** is a cozy little hotel hidden along an ignored alley a block from the best beaches and a 20-minute walk from the old town. Run with panache by Nathalie, the hotel's rich colors and decor show a personal touch. The immaculate rooms have smallish bathrooms and individual terraces facing a cute, central garden where you'll get to know your neighbor (no TVs, free breakfast for Rick Steves readers, sauna, bikes, and a kayak available; 13 Avenue Max Maurey, take the third right after passing Hôtel Josse, tel. 04 93 61 45 89, www.jabotte.com, info@jabotte.com). The hotel will shuttle clients to the train station, hiking trails, restaurants, etc. in their small tuk-tuk vehicle for a small fee.

$$ Hôtel Beau-Site,*** my only listing on Cap d'Antibes, is a 10-minute drive from town. It's a terrific value if you want to get away...but not *too* far away. (Without a car, you'll feel isolated.) Helpful Nathalie and Francine welcome you with a pool, a comfy patio garden, and secure pay parking. Rooms are spacious and comfortable, and several have balconies (electric bikes available, 141 Boulevard Kennedy, tel. 04 93 61 53 43, www.hotelbeausite.

net, contact@hotelbeausite.net). The hotel is a 10-minute walk from Plage de la Garoupe on the Cap d'Antibes loop hike (described earlier).

$ Bastide de la Brague is an easygoing bed-and-breakfast hacienda up a dirt road a 10-minute drive east of Antibes. The fun-loving family (wife Isabelle, who speaks English, and hubby Franck) rent seven rooms—the best rooms are upstairs; several are ideal for families, and breakfast is included (55 Avenue No. 6, tel. 04 93 65 73 78, www.labastidedelabrague.com, bastidebb06@gmail.com). Antibes bus #10 drops you five minutes away, and if arranged in advance, they can pick you up at the Biot or Antibes train station.

IN THE TOWN CENTER

$$$ Hôtel la Place* is central, pricey, and cozy. It overlooks the ugly bus station with tastefully designed rooms and a comfy lounge (no elevator, 1 Avenue 24 Août, tel. 04 97 21 03 11, www.la-place-hotel.com, contact@la-place-hotel.com).

$ Hôtel Relais du Postillon is a mellow, central place above a peaceful café with 16 impeccable rooms at very fair rates. The furnishings are tasteful, and several rooms have small balconies or terraces (tiny elevator, pay parking, 8 Rue Championnet, tel. 04 93 34 20 77, www.relaisdupostillon.com, relais@relaisdupostillon.com).

$ Modern Hôtel, in the pedestrian zone behind the city bus station, is suitable for budget-conscious travelers. The 17 standard-size rooms are simple and spick-and-span (no elevator, 1 Rue Four-millière, tel. 04 92 90 59 05, www.modernhotel06.com, modern-hotel@wanadoo.fr).

Eating in Antibes

Antibes is a fun and relaxed place to dine out. But there are precious few really good options in Antibes, and those get booked up on weekends in particular (when you're smart to book a day ahead). All but one of my recommendations are within a few blocks of each other, so it's easy to comparison shop.

Antibes' **Market Hall** (Marché Provençal) has great ambience and is popular with budget-minded diners each evening after the market stalls close. It's not *haute cuisine,* but prices are usually reasonable, and slurping mussels under a classic 19th-century canopy can make for a great memory. To start your soirée, consider a glass of wine from one of several wine bars that call the market hall home.

$$ Try Chez Lulu for an ultimate family-style dining adventure that seems utterly out of place on the Riviera. Diners fork over €27 and settle in, while charismatic owner Frank (who speaks

RIVIERA

flawless English), his wife Alice, and—when they're busy—their granddaughter dish out charcuterie, salads, soups, a main course, and desserts to be shared. Tables seat 6-10, and the setting is warm and convivial. Don't come for a romantic meal. You'll be on a first-name basis with your neighbors, cut your own bread, and serve your own soup (fun!). Book a day ahead or arrive early (from 19:00, closed Sun-Mon, tel. 04 89 89 08 92, 5 Rue Frédéric Isnard).

$$$$ Larazur is the love child of a young couple who both worked as chefs at Michelin-starred restaurants and wanted a quieter life in the south. Lucas does the cooking while Jeanne runs the restaurant. The setting is relaxed yet elegant, and the attention to quality is obvious (book ahead, closed Mon-Tue, 8 Rue des Palmiers, tel. 04 93 34 75 60, www.larazur.fr).

$$ Le P'tit Cageot is a find. The chef makes delicious Mediterranean cuisine affordable. The place is tiny, just 25 seats inside and out, so book ahead (closed Wed and Sun, 5 Rue du Docteur Rostan, tel. 04 89 68 48 66).

$$ Le Zinc is a cool little wine-bar bistro at the upper end of the market hall serving a limited selection of tasty cuisine. Book ahead or arrive early for an outside table (closed Mon, 15 Cours Masséna, tel. 04 83 14 69 20).

$$$ Le Vauban is a traditional and dressy place with red-velvet chairs and serious service. It's popular with locals for special events and its seafood (closed for lunch Mon and Wed, closed all day Tue, opposite 4 Rue Thuret, tel. 04 93 34 33 05, www.levauban.fr).

$$ Le Brulot, an institution in Antibes, is known for its Provençal cuisine and meat dishes (most cooked over an open fire). It's a small, rustic place with tables crammed every which way (big, splittable portions, come early or book ahead, closed Sun, 2 Rue Frédéric Isnard, tel. 04 93 34 17 76, www.brulot.fr).

$$$ La Taille de Guêpe is family-run by Olivier in the kitchen and Katy in the relaxing garden-like dining room. The chef has worked for several years with flowers; the colorful varieties you find on your plate are all edible and add a twist to the fresh, fine, and light food. The *moëlleux au chocolat* is a perfect way to end your meal. *Menus,* enjoyed with cheap and good local wine, are a good deal (reservations recommended, closed Sun-Mon, 24 Rue de Fersen, tel. 04 93 74 03 58).

Picnic on the Beach or Ramparts: Romantics on a shoestring can find grocery stores open until late in Antibes and assemble their own picnic dinner to enjoy on the beach or ramparts. There's a good **Carrefour City** market at 44 Rue de la République and a **Monoprix** on Place Général de Gaulle—both open late.

RIVIERA

Antibes Connections

For a comparison of train and bus connections, see the "Public Transportation in the French Riviera" sidebar on page 698.

From Antibes by Train: TGV and local trains deliver great service to Antibes' little station. Trains go to **Cannes** (2/hour, 15 minutes), **Nice** (2/hour, 20 minutes), **Villefranche-sur-Mer** (2/hour, 40 minutes), **Monaco** (2/hour, 50 minutes), and **Marseille** (hourly, 2.5 hours).

By Bus: All the buses listed below serve the Pôle d'Echange regional bus station (behind the train station). Handy **bus #200** ties everything together from Cannes to Nice, but runs at a snail's pace when traffic is bad. It goes west to **Cannes** (35 minutes) and east to **Nice** (1.5 hours). For bus details, including info on tickets, routes, frequencies, and travel times, see the "Getting Around the Riviera" section near the start of this chapter. **Bus #250** runs to **Nice Airport** (2/hour, 40 minutes).

Inland Riviera

For a verdant, rocky, fresh escape from the beaches, head inland and upward. Some perfectly perched hill towns and splendid scenery hang overlooked in this region more famous for beaches and bikinis. Driving is the easiest way to get around, though Vence and St-Paul-de-Vence are well served by bus from Nice (see "Nice Connections," on page 739). For a scenic inland train ride, take the narrow-gauge train from Nice into the Alps (see page 725).

St-Paul-de-Vence

This most famous of Riviera hill towns is also the most-visited village in France. I believe it. This incredibly situated village—with views to the sea and the Alps—is understandably popular. Every cobble and flower seems just so, and the setting is postcard-perfect. But it can also feel like an overrun and over-restored artist's shopping mall. Avoid visiting between 11:00 and 18:00, particularly on weekends. Beat  the crowds by skipping breakfast at your hotel to get here early, or come for dinner and experience the village at its tranquil best.

Orientation to St-Paul-de-Vence

Tourist Information: The helpful TI, just through the gate into the old town on Rue Grande, has maps with minimal explanations of key buildings, and rental *boules* for *pétanque* on the square (daily 10:00-18:00, June-Sept until 19:00, closes for lunch on weekends, tel. 04 93 32 86 95, www.saint-pauldevence.com).

Arrival in St-Paul-de-Vence: Pay to park close to the village, or park for free along the road to Fondation Maeght (look for *Parking Conseillé* signs) and walk down to the village. Free parking is also available at the entry to Fondation Maeght (a 20-minute walk from town). Bus #400 (connecting Nice and Vence) stops on the main road, just above the village.

However you arrive, if the traffic-free lane leading into the old town is jammed, walk along the road that veers up and left just after Café de la Place, and enter the town through its side door.

Sights in St-Paul-de-Vence

The Old Town
St-Paul's old town has no essential sights, though its perfectly cobbled lanes and peekaboo views delight most who come. You'll pass two vintage eateries before piercing the walls of the old town. The recommended **La Colombe d'Or** is a good spot for a meal. Back when the town was teeming with artists, this historic hotel/restaurant served as their clubhouse. Its walls are covered with paintings by Picasso, Miró, Braque, Chagall, and others who traded their art for free meals. **Café de la Place** is a classic spot to have a coffee and croissant while watching waves of tourists crash into town (daily from 7:00). On the square, serious *boules* competitions take place. Find the cool *boules* sculpture there.

After entering the walls of St-Paul, meander deep to find its quieter streets and panoramic views. How many art galleries can this village support? Imagine the time it took to create the intricate stone patterns in the street you're walking along. Visit **Marc Chagall's grave** in the cemetery at the opposite end of town, a 10-minute walk keeping straight along the main drag (from the cemetery entrance, turn right, then left to find Chagall's grave). Walk up the stairs to the **view platform** above the cemetery and try to locate the hill town of Vence at the foot of an impressive mountain. Is the sea out there somewhere?

▲Fondation Maeght
This inviting, pricey, and far-out private museum is situated a steep walk or short drive above St-Paul-de-Vence. Fondation Maeght (fohn-dahs-yohn mahg) offers an excellent introduction to modern Mediterranean art by gathering many of the Riviera's most famous

artists under one roof. There are no English explanations for the interior displays.

Cost and Hours: €16, daily 10:00-18:00, July-Sept until 19:00, audioguide-€3 (covers primarily art in the gardens), great gift shop and cafeteria, tel. 04 93 32 81 63, www.fondation-maeght.com.

Getting There: The museum is a steep 20-minute uphill walk from St-Paul-de-Vence and the bus stop. Parking is usually available (and free) at the sight and in lower lots, signed *Parking Conseillé*.

Visiting the Museum: The founder, Aimé Maeght, long envisioned the perfect exhibition space for the artists he supported and befriended as an art dealer. He purchased this arid hilltop, planted 35,000 plants, and hired the Catalan architect José Luis Sert to enact his vision.

A sweeping lawn laced with amusing sculptures and bending pine trees greets visitors. On the right, a chapel designed by Georges Braque—in memory of the Maeghts' young son, who died of leukemia—features a moving purple stained-glass work over the altar. The unusual museum building is purposely low profile to let its world-class modern art collection take center stage. Works by Fernand Léger, Joan Miró, Alexander Calder, Georges Braque, Marc Chagall, and many others are thoughtfully arranged in well-lit rooms (the permanent collection is sometimes replaced by special thematic shows). Outside, in the back, you'll find a Gaudí-esque sculpture labyrinth by Miró and a courtyard filled with the wispy works of Alberto Giacometti—both designed by the artists for these spaces.

Eating in St-Paul-de-Vence

$$ Le Tilleul is a good place to dine well in St-Paul, either at inviting tables on the broad terrace or in its pleasant interior (daily, near the TI on Place du Tilleul, tel. 04 93 32 80 36, www.restaurant-letilleul.com).

Book well ahead for **$$$$ La Colombe d'Or,** a veritable institution in St-Paul where the menu hasn't changed in 50 years (see description earlier). Dine on good-enough cuisine inside by the fire to best feel its pulse (closed Nov-Dec, tel. 04 93 32 80 02, www.la-colombe-dor.com; for reservations, email contact@la-colombe-dor.com).

Vence

Vence, an appealing town set high above the Riviera, sees a fraction of the crowds that you'll find in St-Paul. While growth has sprawled beyond Vence's old walls and cars jam its roundabouts, the traffic-free lanes of the old city are a delight, the mountains are front and center, and the breeze is fresh. Vence bubbles with workaday life—and ample tourist activity in the day—but it's quiet at night, with far fewer visitors and cooler temperatures than along the coast. You'll also find terrific choices for affordable hotels and restaurants. Vence makes a handy base for travelers wanting the best of both worlds: a hill-town refuge near the sea.

Orientation to Vence

Tourist Information: Vence's fully loaded and helpful TI is at the southwest corner of the main square, Place du Grand Jardin (in the Villa Alexandrine, Mon-Sat 9:00-19:00, Sun 10:00-18:00; Nov-March 10:00-17:00 and closed Sun, tel. 04 93 58 06 38, www. vence-tourisme.fr). Pick up the city map with a well-devised self-guided walking tour, a list of art galleries, bus schedules, or *pétanque* instructions, and ask about guided walking tours in English.

Arrival in Vence: Bus #94 (fastest bus from Nice, about an hour) or #400 (from Nice, Cagnes-sur-Mer, and St-Paul-de-Vence, just over an hour) drops you at the Ara bus stop just off the round-about at Place Maréchal Juin, a 10-minute walk to the town center (along Avenue Henri Isnard or Avenue de la Résistance). If arriving by **car,** follow signs to *cité historique* and park in the underground Parking Grand Jardin, near the TI.

Helpful Hints: Market days are Tuesdays and Fridays until 13:00 on the Place du Grand Jardin and in the *cité historique* around Place Clemenceau. A big all-day antiques market is on Place du Grand Jardin every Wednesday. If you miss market day, a Mono-prix **supermarket** is on Avenue de la Résistance, across from the entrance to the Marie Antoinette parking lot (grocery store up-stairs, Mon-Sat 8:30-20:00, Sun 9:00-13:00). For a **taxi,** call 04 93 58 11 14.

Sights in Vence

Château de Villeneuve

This 17th-century mansion, adjoining an imposing 12th-century watchtower, bills itself as one of the Riviera's high temples of mod-ern art, with a rotating collection. Check with the TI to see what's showing in the temple. The museum offers a loaner guide with English explanations of the collection.

RIVIERA

Cost and Hours: €7, Tue-Sun 11:00-18:00, closed Mon, 2 Place du Frêne, tel. 04 93 58 15 78.

▲Chapel of the Rosary (Chapelle du Rosaire)

The chapel—a short drive or 20-minute walk from town—was designed by an elderly and ailing Henri Matisse as thanks to a Dominican nun who had taken care of him (he was 81 when the chapel was completed). While the chapel is the ultimate pilgrimage for his fans, the experience may underwhelm others. (Picasso thought it looked like a bathroom.) The chapel's design may seem basic—white porcelain tiles, simple black designs, and floor-to-ceiling windows—but it's a space of light and calm that only a master could have created.

Cost and Hours: €7; Tue, Thu, and Fri 10:00-12:00 & 14:00-18:00, Wed and Sat 14:00-18:00 (Nov-March until 17:00), closed Sun-Mon and mid-Nov-mid-Dec, 466 Avenue Henri Matisse, tel. 04 93 58 03 26, www.chapellematisse.fr.

Getting There: On foot, it's a 20-minute walk from Place du Grand Jardin. Walk down Avenue Henri Isnard all the way to the traffic circle. Turn right across the one-lane bridge on Avenue Henri Matisse, following signs to *St-Jeannet.* **By car,** follow signs toward *St-Jeannet,* cross the bridge, and start looking for parking—the chapel is about 400 yards after the bridge toward St-Jeannet.

Visiting the Chapel: The modest chapel holds a simple series of charcoal black-on-white tile sketches and uses three symbolic colors as accents: yellow (sunlight and the light of God), green (nature), and blue (the Mediterranean sky). Bright sunlight filters through the stained-glass windows and does a cheery dance across the sketches. Your entry ticket includes a 20-minute tour from one of the kind nuns who speak English. In the little museum, you'll find pictures of the artist, displays of the vestments Matisse designed for the priests, his models of the chapel, and sketches. Outside, there's a terrace with terrific views toward Vence.

Sleeping in and near Vence

These places tend to close their reception desks between 12:00 and 16:00. Make arrangements in advance if you plan to arrive during this time.

$$$ La Maison du Frêne, centrally located behind the TI, is a modern, art-packed B&B with four sumptuous suites. Energetic and art-crazy Thierry and Guy make fine hosts (RS%, includes good breakfast, kids under 12 free; next to the Château de Villeneuve at 1 Place du Frêne; tel. 04 93 24 37 83, www.lamaisondufrene.com, contact@lamaisondufrene.com).

$ Hôtel La Victoire is a solid value right on the main square next to the TI. Rooms are small but have all the comforts; it's warmly run and well maintained by Pierre (elevator one floor up, 1 Place du Grand Jardin, tel. 04 93 24 15 54, www.hotel-victoire.com, contact@hotel-victoire.com).

$ Auberge des Seigneurs feels medieval. Located in a 17th-century building, it has six simple but spacious rooms over a well-respected restaurant (Wi-Fi in lobby, no air-con, no elevator, 1 Rue du Docteur Binet, tel. 04 93 58 04 24, http://auberge-seigneurs.fr, sandrine.rodi@wanadoo.fr).

NEAR VENCE

$ The Frogs' House is situated in the untouristed hill town of St-Jeannet, a 15-minute drive from Vence. (It's so quiet, it's hard to believe a Riviera beach is only 10 miles away.) Benôit and Corinne welcome travelers with a full menu of good rooms, cooking lessons, restaurant recommendations, hikes in the area, and day trips. If you don't have wheels, they'll pick you up at the train station or airport. Rooms are small but sharp (includes hearty breakfast, some rooms with balconies, family rooms, full-house rentals available in winter, mobile 06 28 06 80 28, www.thefrogshouse.fr, info@thefrogshouse.com). Park in the lot at the bottom of St-Jeannet, a few blocks from this small hotel.

Eating in Vence

Tempting outdoor eateries litter the old town. Lights embedded in the cobbles illuminate the way after dark. The restaurants I list have similar prices and quality, and all have outside dining options.

At **$$ Les Agapes,** Chef Jean-Philippe goes beyond the standard fare with lavish presentations, creative food combinations, and moderate (for the Riviera) prices. Try the *sphere chocolat* dessert to round out your meal (closed Mon year-round, closed Sun off-season, reservations smart, 4 Place Clemenceau, tel. 04 93 58 50 64, www.les-agapes.net).

$$ La Litote is a favorite, with outdoor tables on a quiet, hidden square, a cozy interior, and traditional cuisine (closed Sun year-round, closed Mon off-season, 7 Rue de l'Evêché, tel. 04 93 24 27 82).

$ Le Michel Ange is a sweet, kid-friendly place on an adorable square serving excellent-value cuisine from pizza to pasta, as well as tasty, well-presented *plats du jour* (closed Sun-Mon, 1 Place Godeau, tel. 04 93 58 32 56).

For inexpensive, casual dining, head to Place du Peyra, where you'll find ample outdoor seating and early dinner service. At the basic **$$ Bistro du Peyra,** enjoy a relaxed dinner salad or pasta dish outdoors to the sound of the town's main fountain (closed Mon-Tue off-season, 13 Place du Peyra, tel. 04 93 58 67 63).

THE FRENCH ALPS

Annecy • Chamonix

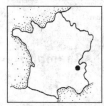

The Savoie region grows Europe's highest mountains and is the penthouse of the French Alps (the lower Alpes-Dauphiné lie to the south). More than just a pretty-peaked face, stubborn Savoie maintained its independence from France until 1860, when mountains became targets, rather than obstacles, for travelers. Savoie's borders once stretched south to the Riviera and far west across the Rhône River Valley. Home to the very first winter Olympics (1924, in Chamonix), today's Savoie is France's mountain-sports capital, showcasing 15,780-foot Mont Blanc as its centerpiece. Boasting wooden chalets overflowing with geraniums and cheese fondue in every restaurant, Savoie feels more Swiss than French.

The scenery is drop-dead spectacular. Serenely self-confident Annecy is a postcard-perfect blend of natural and man-made beauty. In Chamonix, it's just you and Madame Nature—there's not a museum or important building in sight. Take Europe's ultimate cable-car ride to the 12,602-foot Aiguille du Midi in Chamonix.

PLANNING YOUR TIME

Lakefront Annecy has boats, bikes, and hikes with mountain views for all tastes and abilities. Its arcaded walking streets and good transportation connections (most trains to Chamonix pass through Annecy) make it a convenient stopover,

FRENCH ALPS

French Alps

Lausanne

50 Kilometers
50 Miles

SWITZ.

Lake Geneva

A-9

Montreux

CHATEAU DE
CHILLON

A-1

Nyon

Evian-
les-Bains

Thonon-
les-Bains

N-5

D-902 D-22

Geneva

To
Lyon &
Paris

Annemasse

GENEVA
EAUX-VIVES
STN.

A-40

N-205

A-40

A-41

La
Roche-
sur-Foron

Morzine

Avoriaz

Champéry

SWITZ.

A-9

Vernayaz

Martigny

To
Zermatt
& Milan

D-902

Samoëns

Cluses

Flaine

A-40

Vallorcine

Argentière

N-506

Exit
#16

Annecy

See detail
map

D-909

Sévrier

D-41

Menthon

Talloires

St-Jorioz

Duingt

Le
Semnoz

D-42

Doussard

Lac
d'Annecy

D-909

La Clusaz

Col de
la Forclaz

D-1212

Flumet

D-1508

D-1212

FRANCE

Les
Bossons

See
detail
map

Les Praz

Chamonix

MTN.
LIFTS

St-
Gervais

Megève

MT. BLANC
TUNNEL

Mont
Blanc

La Palud

Courmayeur

Pré-St-Didier

S-26

To Aosta
& Torino

ITALY

To
Grenoble

Albertville

N-90

Paris
FRANCE

100 Miles

Bourg-St-Maurice

N-90

Aime

D-902

Tignes

Moûtiers

Courchevel

Val-d'Isère

but if you're pressed for time and antsy for Alps, slide your sled
to Chamonix. There you can skip along alpine ridges, glide over
mountain meadows, zip down the mountain on a luge (wheeled
bobsled), or meander riverside paths on a mountain bike. Plan a
minimum of two nights and one day in Chamonix, and try to work
in an additional night and a day in Annecy. Weather is everything
in this area: Check the forecast. If it looks good, make haste to
Chamonix; if it's gloomy, Annecy offers more distraction.

The Alps have twin peaks: the summer and winter seasons, when hotels and trails or slopes are slammed. June and November are dead quiet in Chamonix (many hotels and restaurants close) as locals recover from one high season and prepare for the next.

GETTING AROUND THE ALPS

Annecy and Chamonix are well-connected by train and bus. Buses run from Chamonix to nearby villages, and the Aiguille du Midi lift takes travelers from Chamonix to Italy over Europe's most scenic border crossing. If you have a car, pricey autoroutes make the going easy, and scenic drives near Annecy allow you to savor remarkable views.

Entering Switzerland by Car: Drivers passing through Switzerland need a "vignette" decal to use Swiss autoroutes (about €36, valid one calendar year, can be used on one car only)—even if only to reach Geneva's airport from bordering France (though locals suggest this section is not heavily patrolled, and skipping the autoroute via local roads through Geneva is possible but a headache). It's a €300 fine if you're caught sans decal. You can buy Swiss vignettes at Annecy's Mont Blanc Automobile Club (15 Rue de la Préfecture, Mon-Sat 9:00-12:00 & 14:00-18:00, closed Sun) or for a bit more on the autoroute at the border crossing.

SAVOIE'S CUISINE SCENE

Savoie cuisine is mountain-hearty. Its Swiss-similar specialties include *fondue savoyarde* (melted Beaufort and Comté cheeses and local white wine, sometimes with a dash of Cognac), raclette (chunks of melted cheese served with potatoes, pickles, sausage, and bread), *tartiflette* (hearty scalloped potatoes with melted cheese), *poulet de Bresse* (the best chicken in France), Morteau (smoked pork sausage), *gratin savoyard* (a potato dish with cream, cheese, and garlic), and fresh fish. Look also for *pierrades,* heated stone blocks delivered to your table along with thinly sliced meats, vegetables, potatoes, and more that you cook on the stone. Local cheeses are Morbier (look for a charcoal streak down the middle), Comté (like Gruyère), Beaufort (aged for two years, hard and strong), Reblochon (mild and creamy), and Tomme de Savoie (mild and semihard). Evian water comes from Savoie, as does Chartreuse liqueur. Apremont and Crépy are two of the area's surprisingly good white wines. The local beer, Baton de Feu, is more robust than other French beers.

Annecy

There's something for everyone in this lakefront city that knows how to entertain: mountain views, romantic canals, a hovering château, and swimming in—or boating on, or biking around—the

translucent lake. Sophisticated yet outdoors-oriented and bike-crazy, Annecy (ahn-see) is France's answer to Switzerland's Luzern, and, though you may not have glaciers knocking at your door as in nearby Chamonix, the distant peaks frame a darn pretty picture with Annecy's

lakefront setting. Don't bother with museums in Annecy: You're here for the vistas, arcaded streets, and outdoor activities. During the winter holidays, Christmas markets and festive decorations animate the city. Annecy is a joy before noon in any season, but high-season weekend afternoons will try your patience. Spend your mornings in the old town and afternoons around the lake.

Orientation to Annecy

Modern Annecy (pop. 50,000) sprawls for miles, but we're interested only in its compact old town, on the northwest corner of the lake (known as Lac d'Annecy, or Lake Annecy). The old town is split by the Thiou River (which looks more like a canal) and bounded by the château to the south, and the TI and Rue Royale to the north.

TOURIST INFORMATION

The TI is a few blocks from the old town, across from the big grass field, inside the Bonlieu shopping center (daily 9:00-18:30, some midday closures, Sun hours vary depending on season; 1 Rue Jean Jaurès, tel. 04 50 45 00 33, www.lac-annecy.com). Get a city map, the *Town Walks* walking-tour brochure (describes several themed walks and has basic historical information), the map of the lake showing the bike trail (and a good brochure about the bike trail), and, if you're staying awhile, the *Lac Annecy Magazine*. Ask about walking tours in English (€6.50, July-Aug only, normally Tue and Fri at 16:00). There's a handy WC across the hall from the TI. You'll also find TIs in most villages on the lake (many open weekends and summers only).

ARRIVAL IN ANNECY

By Train and Bus: The stations sit side by side. To reach the old town and TI, cross the street in front of the stations, turn left, and walk to the Hôtel des Alpes. Turn right on Rue de la Poste, then left on Rue Royale to reach the TI and some hotels, or continue straight to more recommended hotels. Baggage storage is available nearby (see "Helpful Hints," later).

By Car: Annecy can be a traffic mess in high season and on weekends. Smart drivers plan to arrive early, during lunch, or late. Avoid most of the snarls by taking exit #16 from the autoroute (headed north, it's signed *Annecy-Centre;* headed south, the sign reads *Albertville*). Avoid exit #17, the other Annecy option. From exit #16, follow *Annecy/Albertville* signs. Upon entering Annecy, follow signs to *Le Lac* or *Le Château* depending on the location of your hotel. (Don't follow signs for *Annecy-le-Vieux*.)

Refer to the map of Annecy for parking lots. The first 30 minutes are free; after that figure €1.30 per hour (about €16/24 hours). Ask your hotel for a free overnight parking pass for the Hôtel de Ville or Bonlieu parking lots. Upon arrival, ditch your car at the first lot you come to, then get advice from your hotel for more convenient parking. Parking Ste. Claire and Parking du Château work for the hotels I list away from the lake. On the lake, you can park near the big boat docks at the underground Hôtel de Ville lot or at Parking La Tournette, or a block farther along at Parking Stade Nautique. If all else fails, the big Parking Trésum, just off the lake, usually has spaces. The Colmyr and Marquisats parking lots are free but a 20-minute walk to town.

By Plane: From Geneva's airport (GVA, www.gva.ch), Annecy is a 45-minute autoroute drive (Swiss vignette required; see "Getting Around the Alps," earlier). Several bus companies connect the airport to Annecy (see www.gva.ch) or book a shuttle van in advance (www.genevashuttle.com). Or you can take Ouibus (www.ouibus.com) or make the cheap but scenic 2.5-hour slog by bus and train (10/day). Taxis charge an outrageous 200 Swiss francs. Geneva's airport has a helpful transportation desk at baggage claim.

From Lyon's St-Exupéry airport (LYS, www.lyonaeroports.com), allow 1.5 hours by car (all autoroute), 2 hours by Ouibus (4/day), or 2.5 hours by train (8/day).

HELPFUL HINTS

Market Days: A thriving outdoor food market occupies much of the old town center on Tuesday, Friday, and Sunday mornings until about 12:30. The biggest market in Annecy is on Saturday, but it's less central and geared toward locals (more

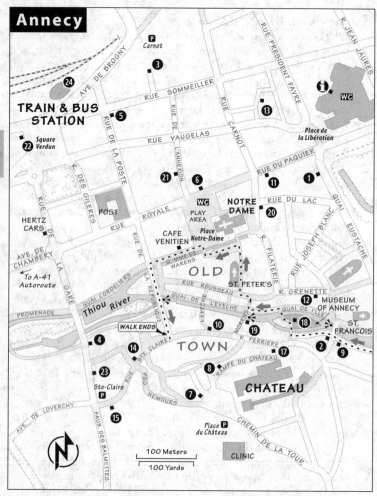

Annecy

FRENCH ALPS

clothes, fewer crafts; until 12:30, around Boulevard Taine—
several blocks behind the TI).

Supermarkets: The **Monoprix** is at the corner of Rue du Lac and
Rue Notre-Dame (Mon-Sat 8:30-19:50, closed Sun, supermarket upstairs). A smaller **Franprix** is on Rue de l'Annexion
just off Rue Royale (Mon-Sat 8:00-21:00, Sun 9:00-19:00).

Bike Alert: Pedestrians should be aware of bike riders and avoid
walking in bike lanes. If you ride a bike here, obey the same
rules you would when driving a car (look before merging, don't
stop in a travel lane, etc.).

Baggage Storage: Store your bags at the **Vival** grocery across from
the train station (€3/hour, or €12/day, 1 Rue de l'Industrie,
Mon 13:00-21:00, Tue-Sun 9:00-21:00, see the "Annecy"

FRENCH ALPS

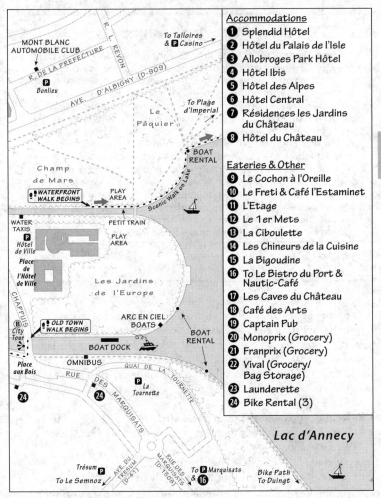

Accommodations
1. Splendid Hôtel
2. Hôtel du Palais de l'Isle
3. Allobroges Park Hôtel
4. Hôtel Ibis
5. Hôtel des Alpes
6. Hôtel Central
7. Résidences les Jardins du Château
8. Hôtel du Château

Eateries & Other
9. Le Cochon à l'Oreille
10. Le Freti & Café l'Estaminet
11. L'Etage
12. Le 1er Mets
13. La Ciboulette
14. Les Chineurs de la Cuisine
15. La Bigoudine
16. To Le Bistro du Port & Nautic-Café
17. Les Caves du Château
18. Café des Arts
19. Captain Pub
20. Monoprix (Grocery)
21. Franprix (Grocery)
22. Vival (Grocery/Bag Storage)
23. Launderette
24. Bike Rental (3)

map). Bike renters can leave their bags at all bike-rental shops (except Véloncey).

Laundry: Lav' Confort Express launderette is at the western edge of the old town near where Rue de la Gare meets Rue Ste. Claire (6:00-20:00, 6 Rue de la Gare).

Bike and Paddleboard Rental: Many places rent bikes for about €20/day (leave ID as deposit, includes helmet and basket, half-day rentals; electric, tandem, and kids' bikes/carriers available; hours generally daily 9:00-12:30 & 14:00-18:30). All but Véloncey can keep your bags while you ride. Ask the TI about a rental shop near your hotel.

Roul' ma Poule, near the lakefront bike path across from the lake steamers, rents rollerblades, bikes, and more (open

Brief History of Annecy

Humans have called Annecy home for more than 5,000 years. The city has had its ups and downs over the millennia (more ups than downs) and has thrived thanks to its proximity to Geneva's powerful counts and its easy access to routes over the Alps into Italy. In Roman times, Annecy was an important city of about 2,000 people, complete with a forum, temples, and thermal baths. After the Roman Empire fell, locals headed for the hills and occupied the area around the château. A few centuries later, they moved down to the banks of the Thiou River at the lake's mouth. The medieval town then spread to both sides of the river and was protected by the castle you see today. In 1401, Annecy became part of the Savoie region, eventually serving as capital of a large slice of the House of Savoie. The 1800s saw the rise of hydroelectric power in Annecy and the establishment of a reliable industrial base. The 1900s brought tourism to the lake, and Annecy hasn't looked back. Tourism drives their economy.

March-Oct, 4 Rue Marquisats, tel. 04 50 27 86 83, www. roulmapoule.com). They also rent paddleboards (about €15/half-day) from their shop in Annecy-le-Vieux (47 Avenue du Petit Port, tel. 04 50 23 31 15). **Cyclable** is also near the lake on Place aux Bois (more choices, open daily 9:00-19:00, tel. 04 50 51 51 50, www.cyclable.com). **Véloncey Bikes** is at the train station and requires a €250 deposit (closed Sun, tel. 04 50 51 38 90).

Car Rental: Avis is at the train station (tel. 04 50 52 87 10). **Hertz** is a block from the station (15 bis Avenue de la Gare, tel. 04 50 51 19 89).

Taxi: Call 04 50 45 05 67.

Bus Tour: Red open-top minibuses run hour-long loops around the old town and along sections of the lake—an easy introduction to Annecy. Board the **Annecy City Tour** bus by the view bridge where the river enters the old town (€13, May-Sept 3-4 trips/day, some English commentary, see the "Annecy" map for bus stop, details at TI or www.annecycitytour.com).

Bad Weather: If it's raining, consider a day trip to Lyon (10 trains/day, 2 hours, 6/day by bus, see "Annecy Connections" later). The last train back to Annecy usually leaves Lyon at about 21:00, allowing a full day in the big city.

Sights in Annecy

▲▲Old Town Walk

Most of the old town is wonderfully traffic-free. The river, canals, and arcaded streets are made for ambling, as described in the TI's *Town Walks* brochure (see "Tourist Information," earlier). This 45-minute walking tour includes aspects of the TI's walks and will get you familiar with Annecy *toute de suite*. Do it early to allow time for *une pause café* at a canalfront café, or do it in the evening so you can enjoy the old town's soft lighting. No sight in Annecy merits an entry fee. Cool your jets and learn to saunter—as you wander Annecy's lovely lanes you'll be following in the footsteps of Jean-Jacques Rousseau, who adored strolling here (see sidebar).

Start in the center of the **bridge** on Quai Eustache Chappuis (it's the bridge closest to the lake). With your back to the lake, take in the iconic view of the old town. You're looking down the Thiou River, which starts its puny 2.2-mile trek here (running from the lake into tributaries of the Rhône River). It splits the old town in two and has provided power and resources for Annecy's economy since the Middle Ages. The Museum of Annecy (Palais de l'Isle) covers the tiny island in the river straight ahead, the St. François de Sales Church (1610) sits to your right, and the château (built in 1219, described later) looms above to the left.

Stroll down the left side of the river toward the island. You'll soon spot twin metal gates allowing overflow from the Thiou to pass under the **St. François de Sales Church** and into the St. Dominique Canal. The pretty church was converted into a textile factory after the Revolution (and became a church again in 1923).

Keep straight along the river at the first bridge, skirting past the **Museum of Annecy,** and then cross onto the minuscule island at the next bridge. You'll pass the I-could-stay-a-while Café des Arts (opens at 10:00) and the entrance to the museum (described later).

Resume your walk by crossing to the other side of the Thiou and turn left on Quai de l'Ile. Notice the homes with doors right at river level. The river is carefully controlled with overflow gates and locks to maintain its level, allowing it to run safely through the heart of the city. At the next **bridge** (Pont Morens), look for the protruding outhouse on the upper floor of the building across the canal. This bridge was smothered with houses in the Middle Ages, when a central address was all-important and any available space was used for housing.

Turn your back to the canal and walk under those heavy arches, then make a left onto Rue J. Jacques Rousseau. You'll come to Annecy's plain **St. Peter's Cathedral** (built in 1535, and used by the Counts of Geneva during the Reformation). Turn right just before the cathedral on Passage de la Cathédrale, then make a left at the canal and walk to the next bridge. Notice the merging of two canals and wooden walkways. The canal running under the building is the Notre Dame Canal; the other is the Vassé Canal (both were instrumental in Annecy's economic development). Cross the bridge, take a short detour into the big square, **Place Notre-Dame,** to admire the flowers, then double back and continue along the canal. Consider a canalfront pause at the peaceful Café Vénitien (open daily at 8:00).

Continue on and turn left when you reach **Rue de la République.** When you get back to the Thiou River, stop on the bridge to take in the view over Quai de l'Evêché. Those metal gates (on either side of the bridge) once fed water to a turbine that powered a cotton factory in the late 1800s. Continue along Rue de la République, returning to the lake by taking a left along the arcaded and pedestrian-popular Rue Ste. Claire. Any lanes to the right lead up to the **Château Museum** (described later).

Museum of Annecy (Palais de l'Isle)

This serenely situated 13th-century building cuts like the prow of a ship through the heart of the Thiou River. Once a prison, it held captured French Resistance fighters during World War II. Today, you can still see several of the prison cells, but most of the museum is taken up with exhibits on local architecture since the war and is skippable.

Cost and Hours: €4, €7.20 combo-ticket includes Château Museum, Wed-Mon June-Sept 10:30-18:00, Oct-May 10:00-12:00 & 14:00-17:00, closed Tue year-round, free English leaflet.

Château Museum (Musée-Château d'Annecy)

The castle, built in 1219 by aristocrats from nearby Geneva, reminds us of the historic and important ties Annecy had with its big sister city. The castle itself cuts an impressive figure as it hangs above the lake in the old town. But there's little to see inside: a few rooms devoted to local folklore, anthropology, and natural history, and a modern-art collection that rotates regularly. Skip it.

Cost and Hours: €5.50, €7.20 combo-ticket with Museum of Annecy, same hours as Museum of Annecy.

▲Annecy's Waterfront

Stroll the bike/walking path in either direction for lake and mountain views. The best views are found walking east with the lake on your right. The peaks of Mont Veyrier and La Tournette dominate the left (east) side of the lake while Le Semnoz and the tallest viewable peak—La Sambuy at 7,200 feet—control the west and south views. A *petit* tourist train runs along the lake from near the small Pont des Amours to the Imperial Palace Hotel and beach (in good

Jean-Jacques Rousseau (1712-1778)

"Man is born free, and everywhere he is in chains. Those who think themselves the masters of others are indeed greater slaves than they." (The Social Contract, 1762)

Though born in Geneva, Jean-Jacques Rousseau was shaped in Annecy. He arrived here a 16-year-old runaway. He was taken in by a wealthy 29-year-old baroness, who lived on the street known today as Rue Jean-Jacques Rousseau. For the next 14 years, he lived in Annecy as a student, music teacher, flute player, and boyfriend of the baroness. Under the spell of the awesome beauty of the Alps and the free spirit of his mistress, Rousseau's basic philosophy was formed—that man in his pure natural state is good, but becomes corrupted by the artificial institutions of modern society.

At age 30, Rousseau moved to Paris, where he wrote a mildly successful opera and a wildly successful novel. Next came works on political philosophy that would literally "Revolution"-ize France.

Rousseau questioned the legitimacy of the authority of the state over the individual, who, he said, was "born free." He saw the state as little more than powerful people manipulating the weak to take more than their fair share. He examined the "social contract"—the unspoken agreement between rulers and ruled—in which citizens give up their rights in exchange for protection. Rousseau argued that a better social contract would be between the individual and the collective body of citizens. This contract would benefit everyone equally, respect the individual's inalienable rights, and give everyone a voice—i.e., democracy. His controversial writings threw gas on the already-simmering concept of revolution. When Rousseau went so far as to say that men (like animals) were born pure in nature, not tainted by the Christian idea of original sin, his books were banned, and he was exiled.

In 1767, on the lam and in disguise, Rousseau returned to Annecy. He lived there several years until the storm passed and he could return to Paris.

Rousseau's words encouraged people to rethink their roles as citizens and as human beings. His personal passions and love of nature inspired the 19th-century movement known as Romanticism. And much of that legacy can be traced to his formative years in a small town in the foothills of the awe-inspiring Alps.

weather only, 2/hour, €4 one-way, €6 round-trip, see "Annecy" map for departure point).

Beaches in and Around Annecy

Annecy's lake is ringed with good beaches offering great swimming and views. Some are private and charge a small fee, others are free. Most have grassy shores. **Plage d'Imperial** offers the most kid fun, with water slides and more (small fee, served by the tourist train, www.plage-imperial.com). A bit past Plage d'Imperial, **Plage d'Albigny** is a good, sandy public beach but also draws lots of people in summer (free). **Plage Municipale de Sevrier,** 10 minutes from Annecy, is a sandy beach with great views on the lake's bike path (free).

SCENIC RIDES, STROLLS, AND HIKES

Lakeside paths and short, steep hikes up hillsides offer rewarding views, even with clouds. Boats, bikes, and cars make this lake's villages, hikes, and views accessible. Here are a few suggestions for where to go around the lake.

▲▲Boating

This is one of Europe's cleanest, clearest lakes, and the water is warmer than you'd think (average summer water temperature is 72 degrees Fahrenheit).

On Your Own: To tool around the lake, rent a **paddle-boat** (*pédalos,* some equipped with a slide, about €20/hour for 2 people; some boats can handle 6 passengers) or a **motorboat** (*hors-bord,* no license needed; about €60/hour for 2 people, up to 7 people, several companies all have the same rates). **Water taxis** will take you for a personal cruise or to destinations along the lake such as Talloires or Duingt (figure €140/hour for up to 5 passengers for a cruise, mobile 06 28 06 74 87, info@water-taxi.fr).

Organized Cruises: Compagnie des Bateaux du Lac d'Annecy runs several worthwhile lake cruises. The **one-hour cruise** makes no stops but has frequent departures (€14.50, 8-10/day May-Aug, 6-8/day April and Sept-mid-Oct, generally 1/day off-season, no cruises in Jan). The **two-hour cruises,** called Circuit Omnibus, stop at several villages on a clockwise loop around the lake and allow one stopover—Duingt or Talloires, described later, are good choices (€19 for entire loop, less for shorter trips, 3-5/day late April-Sept); these are ideal for hikers and cyclists (see later). Another boat offers 2.5-hour **lunch cruises** for about €60 and elaborate **dinner and dancing** cruises (€60-90). Get schedules and prices for all boat trips at the TI or on the lake behind Hôtel de Ville (tel. 04 50 51 08 40, www.annecy-croisieres.com). Yet another company, **L'Arc en Ciel,** runs lake cruises in smaller boats (with some commentary) at similar prices (www.arcenciel-annecy.com).

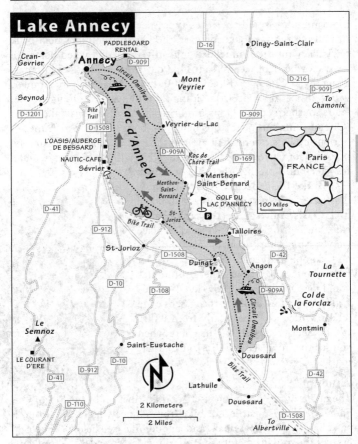

FRENCH ALPS

▲▲Biking Annecy's Lake Path

Annecy was made for biking. It's an ain't-it-great-to-be-alive way to poke around the lake (sun or clouds) and test waterfront cafés and grassy parks and beaches. A scenic lakefront bike trail runs along the entire west side of the lake. Even a short ride on the path is worth the effort, as there are no hills, you're separated from car traffic, and the lake and mountain views make you forget the hard seat. Expect big crowds on weekends. Wear sunglasses and bring water and a bathing suit.

Leave Annecy passing right by the big boats with the lake on your left, pedal as far as your legs take you, break for a lakefront café, and consider a swim at one of the many grassy beaches. You'll pass wheat fields, farms, towns, and lots of other riders (treat the trail like a highway—merge carefully, don't stop in your lane, etc.). My favorite easy ride is the seven-mile stretch from Annecy to the village of **Duingt** (described later)—steady pedalers make it in 45 minutes; smell-the-roses types need an hour. You can ride to Duingt and take your bike on the Circuit Omnibus boat back to Annecy (not recommended mid-July–mid-Aug, when boats are most crowded), or vice versa (€11, 3/day from Duingt, 45 minutes; generally at 11:45, 15:30, and 18:00; more departures in summer, verify at boat dock or TI). Riding 20 minutes past Duingt to the lake's southern end at Doussard brings some of the best lake views (Circuit Omnibus boat stops here, one-hour trip back to Annecy). Serious cyclists can make it around the lake in about 3-4 hours (be prepared for narrow roads on the stretches with no bike path, and a few steep hills on the other side of the lake).

Brake for a Break: About 15 min-utes after leaving Annecy you'll come to **L'Oasis/Auberge de Bessard** chalet/café, an inviting Shangri-la kind of place (serves smoothies, coffee, beer, salads, and complete meals; daily March-Oct from about 9:00). In another 10 minutes you'll pass the peaceful, low-key **Nautic-Café,** with a few tables at the water's edge (cheap coffee and beer, daily from 9:00). It's in Sevrier's marina: Turn left when you see the wood slat building on your left marked *Cercle de Voile/Club Kayak.*

▲Duingt

The quiet village of Duingt is a good destination by boat (see "Or-ganized Cruises," earlier) or bike from Annecy. Here you'll find a café, bakery, tiny boat dock, and a good hike (see below). Bike rid-ers exit the trail just before the rail tunnel, cross under the trail, and turn right (for the village center and the hike). If you arrive by boat, walk through the park with the lake on your right, and cross into the village. By car it's a 20-minute drive from Annecy. Park behind Duingt's church and walk along the asphalt lane past the little TI (open summers only) and the old rail tunnel (now the bike path).

Duingt's *boulangerie* sells good sandwiches, quiches, and drinks and is on the lakefront road, 50 yards toward Annecy from the Hôtel du Roselet. The small park between the castle and the boat dock has picnic tables and views.

Hike: A short, steep, and beautiful trail leading up to glorious lake views starts from the rear of the village (100 yards from the old rail tunnel toward the town center). Find signs to *Grotte N-D du Lac Belvedere,* and walk up the trail passing the Stations of the Cross. In another 20 minutes, great views and benches await at the end of the paved walkway. From here, a steep dirt trail continues up for even better vistas (some rocky, uneven sections).

▲▲Talloires

From this upscale and charming village, you can hike (and I mean hike) along the Roc de Chère trail up to jaw-dropping views over the village and Lake Annecy. To reach Talloires from Annecy, allow 30 minutes by car, 45 minutes by Circuit Omnibus boat (and 90 scenic minutes back as the boat does a one-way loop around the lake). The lack of bike paths makes Talloires a less appealing bike trip.

Those arriving by car can avoid the steep hike up the Roc de Chère trail by turning at signs for the Golf du Lac d'Annecy golf course between Menthon-St-Bernard and Talloires—you'll soon find hiking signs by the wood shelter (parking available). It's a 20-minute walk from there to the lake views.

If coming by boat, plan on about two hours for the hike. Walk from the Talloires dock, veering left up and up through the quaint village to the main road (D-909). Turn left on the road and follow the narrow sidewalk. A few minutes after passing Chalet Christine, find the short staircase leading left into the trees (after the hairpin curve). The trail climbs for 20 extremely steep minutes up a rocky path with some very uneven footing. You'll pass a map of the area's trails and come to benches with glorious views. Follow *Liaison Menthon-St-Bernard* signs to continue to that village (and catch the Circuit Omnibus boat there), or double back to Talloires.

You could hike the Roc de Chère trail from Menthon-St-Bernard's boat dock, but finding the trail takes patience: Turn right off the boat, walk to the big hotel/palace, turn left and walk 200 yards up the road, then take a right on a path marked *Roc de Chère*. This leads to a small road (turn right again), taking you up to the trail. If you need lunch in Talloires, find **$$ Café de la Place** (daily, tel. 04 50 64 40 74).

Driving Around the Lake

The busy roads that link villages along the lake (D-1508 on the west side and D-909 on the east) deliver mostly modest, though occasionally spectacular, lake views (better from D-909). They eventually lead to a scenic route to Chamonix and access to fantastic view drives (described next). Read the bike route description earlier for suggested stops along the lake's west side. Be prepared for afternoon traffic on weekends and on any day in summer.

Several roads off D-1508 and D-909 lead to remarkable views of this gorgeous area. Go early for clearest skies, go late for sunsets, and skip it if it's hazy. Both views below are worth ▲▲ in clear weather.

Le Semnoz: For majestic mountain panoramas near Annecy that include Mont Blanc, drive or take the summer-only bus up... and up...and up to Le Semnoz (about 5,000 feet). To **drive**, fol-

FRENCH ALPS

low D-41 from near the lake (see the "Lake Annecy" map). Allow about 30 minutes one-way and expect lots of bicycles on weekends. After leaving the city, you'll pass through Annecy's forest and climb past tree level to grandiose views over the high Alps, featuring Monsieur Blanc. Just before the top, you'll pass a fun summer luge (Luge d'Eté, about €4/ride in summer, July-Aug daily; May-June and Sept-Oct Wed, Sat-Sun, and holidays). Carry on, climbing above the luge area, pass the hotel, and park when you see the chalet-café **Le Courant d'Ere** (good for a drink and snacks, but meals are mediocre; open daily for lunch, tel. 04 50 01 23 17). Climb to the chairlift station above the café for a magnificent panorama in all directions. Ligne d'Eté **buses** to Le Semnoz (and this viewpoint) leave from the Annecy train station (€6 round-trip, 6/day, daily July-Aug, Sat-Sun only in June, none Sept-May, 40 minutes, stops at the luge, details at TI and www.sibra.fr).

Col de la Forclaz: For drop-dead gorgeous views that take in the entire lake, drive 18 miles from Annecy (allow 45 minutes one-way) to Col de la Forclaz. Start by taking D-1508 south toward Albertville. Three kilometers (about one mile) after leaving the lake at Doussard, turn left on D-42 (signed *Col de la Forclaz*), then wind your way up a narrow lane for five miles past lovely scenery to the Col de la Forclaz (3,600 feet). Look out for cyclists on this climb. At the top, you'll find a sensational viewpoint, cafés and restaurants, and paragliders galore. Several outfits offer a chance to jump off a cliff and sail over the lake, including the appropriately named Adrenaline Parapente (www.annecy-parapente.fr). This trip ties in well with the scenic route to Chamonix via D-1508; it also works as a loop back to Annecy (follow D-42 down to Menthon-St-Bernard from the Col de la Forclaz).

Sleeping in Annecy

Annecy is popular, particularly on weekends and during the summer. Hotel rates drop from about mid-October through late April and increase in summer. Most hotels can help you find free overnight parking (in lots, usually after 19:00 until 9:00 in the morning). Unless otherwise noted, these hotels do not have elevators.

IN THE TOWN CENTER

This part of town is pedestrian-friendly and comes with some noise.

$$$ Splendid Hôtel*** decorates Annecy's busy, parkfront street and makes an impression with its grand, American-style facade and comfy public spaces inside. Standard rooms are tight but quiet and well-appointed; ask about larger accommodations and the pricier fifth-floor rooms with nice decks and lake views (air-con, elevator, big beds, bar, terrace, fitness room, 4 Quai Eustache Chappuis, tel. 04 50 45 20 00, www.splendidhotel.fr, info@splendidhotel.fr).

$$$ Hôtel du Palais de l'Isle*** offers a romantic canalside location in the thick of the old town and 34 contemporary rooms—several with canal or rooftop views—and a comfy lounge (air-con, elevator, 13 Rue Perrière, tel. 04 50 45 86 87, www.palaisannecy.com, contact@palaisannecy.com).

$$ Allobroges Park Hôtel,*** near the train station, rents lovely rooms in a handsome mansion set off the street (small terrace, great breakfast, air-con, elevator, easy pay parking, 11 Rue Sommeiller, tel. 04 50 45 03 11, www.allobroges.com, info@allobroges.com).

$ Hôtel Ibis*** is a good choice, with updated, well-configured rooms (all with queen-size beds), a canalside lounge, and access to underground public parking. It's well-situated on the edge of the old town, a few blocks from the train station (air-con, elevator, 12 Rue de la Gare, tel. 04 50 45 43 21, https://ibis.accorhotels.com, h0538@accor.com).

$ Hôtel des Alpes,** a top value, has a homey feel with 32 pleasant rooms at a busy intersection a block from the train station. Rooms on the courtyard are quieter, but those facing the street have effective double-pane windows (family rooms, air-con, 12 Rue de la Poste, tel. 04 50 45 04 56, www.hotelannecy.com, info@hotelannecy.com).

$ Hôtel Central is just that and more. Run by your Annecy mother, Corinne, this modest, homey, and hyperdecorated place makes a fun stay. Each well-maintained room has a different theme, from Sevilla to India. It's at the back of a modest, ivy-covered courtyard (family rooms, 6 bis Rue Royale, tel. 04 50 45 05 37, hotelcentralannecy@orange.fr).

AT THE FOOT OF THE CHATEAU
These places are in a quiet area a steep five-minute walk up from the old town on Rampe du Château.

$$ Résidences les Jardins du Château, run by charming Austrian Martina and French Hervé, is an urban refuge above the fray near the château entry. It has a small garden and a picnic-perfect upstairs terrace, along with eight simple but good-enough rooms. No phones or TVs, but most rooms come with kitchenettes (good family rooms, cash only, 1 Place du Château, mobile 06 67 91 94 23, www.jardinduchateau.sitew.com, rent74@free.fr).

$ Hôtel du Château,** an unpretentious place run by unpretentious Romain and Amélie, sits barely below the château. It comes with a view terrace (nice for breakfast) and 16 simple, deep yellow, spotless rooms—about half have views. It's first-come, first-get for the few free parking spots (rental bikes available, 16

Rampe du Château, tel. 04 50 45 27 66, www.annecy-hotel.com, hotelduchateauannecy@gmail.com).

Eating in Annecy

Although the touristy old town is well-stocked with forgettable restaurants, I've found a few worthy places. And though you'll pay more to eat with views of the river or canal, the experience is uniquely Annecy. The ubiquitous and sumptuous *gelati* shops remind me how close Italy is. If it's sunny, assemble a gourmet picnic at the arcaded stores and dine lakeside.

$$ Le Cochon à l'Oreille ("The Pig's Ear") is a meat lover's nirvana. Just off the Thiou River, it welcomes diners with a leafy courtyard and a raucous, higgledy-piggledy interior. Amicable owners "Fred" and Jean speak enough English (and fluent pig) and are serious about their cooking (ask to see their pig collection). The accent is on fresh products and meat dishes (particularly ham and pork), though fish options are available. Melted cheese is not their thing (huge salads, good-value two-course meal, closed Mon, Quai du Perrière, tel. 04 50 45 92 51).

$$ Le Freti is a reliable restaurant for local cuisine at fair prices. It's *the* place to go for good fondue, raclette, or anything with cheese. There's fine outside seating under the arcade, and inside upstairs, where each booth comes with its own outlet for melting raclette (reservations smart, but not taken in summer—arrive early or expect a long wait, cheap wine, air-con, open daily for dinner, open for lunch weekends only in off-season, walk through door at 12 Rue Ste. Claire and go upstairs, tel. 04 50 51 29 52, www. lefreti.fr).

$$ Café l'Estaminet, a pub-like place with a cozy interior and a few waterside tables on the back terrace, dishes out salads, omelets, pasta, mussels, fries, and more for fair prices (daily in summer, off-season closed Sun evening and Mon, 8 Rue Ste. Claire, tel. 04 50 45 88 83).

$$ L'Etage is a good choice if you can't decide what you want. Well-prepared regional specialties and a good range of standard brasserie fare are served at respectable prices. Dine along the pedestrian street terrace or upstairs under wood beams around a big fireplace (fondue and raclette, daily, 13 Rue du Paquier, tel. 04 50 51 03 28).

$$ Le 1er Mets is made for foodies. It's an intimate, contemporary place with a focus on preparation, presentation, and service. The cuisine offers a little of everything, from rabbit to octopus (book well ahead, 2 Place Saint-Maurice, tel. 04 57 09 10 54, www. restaurant-1ermets.fr).

$$$ La Ciboulette is a lovely splurge. Dine with class without breaking the bank at a Michelin-starred restaurant on the terrace or in the lovely dining room (*menus* from €40, closed Sun-Mon, 10 Rue Vaugelas, tel. 04 50 45 74 57).

$$ Les Chineurs de la Cuisine is a nice place for a refined meal in the thick of the atmospheric Faubourg Ste. Claire area. Locals come here for French and regional classics. The interior mixes nostalgic knickknacks and fine dining ambience; outdoor tables are few and need to be booked ahead (daily, 26 Rue Ste. Claire, tel. 04 50 10 02 18, www.chineursdelacuisine.com).

$ La Bigoudine has been serving simple and cheap *savoyard* specialties for more than 20 years. It's a great budget value, with a modest-yet-cheery, two-level interior and good outside tables (closed Wed except in summer, 15 Faubourg Ste. Claire, tel. 04 50 51 31 22).

Lakefront Dining: Many cafés and restaurants ring Annecy's postcard-perfect lake. If you have a car and want views, prowl the many waterfront villages. **$$$ Le Bistro du Port,** a nautical place five minutes from Annecy by car, is beautifully situated on the boat dock at the southern end of Sévrier-Centre (daily, Port de Sévrier, turn off D-1508 at the McDonald's, tel. 04 50 52 45 00).

Dessert: Wherever you eat, don't miss an ice cream-licking stroll along the lake after dark.

Nightlife: Start or end your evening at one of these local and different-as-night-and-day places. At the cozy wine bar **Les Caves du Château,** you'll escape the crowds by heading just 20 steps up the Rampe du Château from busy Rue Ste. Claire. They offer a good choice of wines by the glass from throughout France and appetizers (daily except closed Mon Sept-June, 6 Rampe du Château, tel. 09 51 17 29 98).

Café des Arts is Annecy's most atmospheric café, marooned on the island at the Palais de l'Ile. With good prices, it attracts a mix of local hipsters and the odd tourist (daily 10:00-late, 4 Passage de l'Isle, tel. 04 50 51 56 40).

At the **Captain Pub** (arrr, matey!) you'll step down into a venerable pirate's pub deep in Annecy's old town. Half the place works as a **$$ restaurant** with nice seating inside and out, the other half is the pirate's den pub (open 11:00-late, 10 beers on tap, 50 more in bottles, 11 Rue du Pont Morens, tel. 04 50 45 79 80).

Annecy Connections

Check Ouibus (www.ouibus.com) and Flixbus (www.flixbus.com) for cheaper fares and sometimes better schedules.

From Annecy by Train or Bus to: Chamonix (train: 10/day, 2.5 hours, change in St-Gervais; bus: 5/day by Ouibus, 2 hours), **Lyon** (train: 10/day, 2 hours; bus: 6/day by Ouibus and Flixbus, 2.5

hours, some stopping at Lyon airport and Lyon-Perrache), **Beaune** (8/day, 4 hours, change in Lyon), **Nice** (4/day, 7 hours, start with bus or train to Lyon, more with 2-3 changes), **Paris'** Gare de Lyon (hourly, 4 hours, many with change in Lyon), **Geneva** (about hourly, 2 hours by bus/train; bus-and-train options also available from Geneva's airport in 2.5 hours).

Chamonix

Surrounded by snow-capped peaks, powerful—if receding—glaciers, and richly rewarding hiking trails,
Chamonix (shah-moh-nee) is France's
favorite alpine resort. Officially called
Chamonix-Mont Blanc, it's the largest of
five villages lining the valley at the base of
Mont Blanc. Ever since tourists eclipsed
cows as the town's economic base a couple
hundred years ago, Chamonix's purpose
has been to dazzle visitors with some of
Europe's top alpine thrills. But you'll also
learn a thing or two about glaciers and get
a look into the wild world of mountain
climbing. Chamonix is a busy place from
early July through late August and during

winter holidays, but it's plenty peaceful at other times. Chamonix's
sister city is, logically, Aspen, Colorado.

PLANNING YOUR TIME
Summers—or any time a sunny day follows a rainy stretch—bring crowds and long lift lines. Ride the lifts by 8:00 (crowds and clouds roll in later in the morning).

If you're a good hiker and have one sunny day, spend it this way: Start with the Aiguille du Midi lift (go very early, reservations possible and recommended July-Aug), take it all the way to Pointe Helbronner, double back to Plan de l'Aiguille, hike to Montenvers and its Mer de Glace (with good shoes and snow level permitting), explore there, then take the train down to Chamonix. End your day with a well-deserved drink at a view café in town.

If you can't get to Helbronner and have a Multipass lift ticket (described later), do the Aiguille du Midi and the walk to Montenvers, return to Chamonix and take the Le Brévent gondola to Planpraz. Find a seat at one of several magnificent view cafés and watch the parasailers launch into the abyss.

Orientation to Chamonix

The frothy Arve River splits Chamonix in two—with mountains (Mont Blanc and the Aiguilles Rouges peaks) towering on either side. The thriving pedestrian zone forms Chamonix's lively core. The TI is just above the pedestrian zone, and the train station is two long blocks across the river. To get your mountain bearings, head to the TI and find the big photo in front. And to see the town, follow my self-guided Chamonix Walk (described later) from that point.

Located where Switzerland, Italy, and France intersect, this town has always drawn an international crowd. Today about half of its foreign visitors are British—many have stayed and found jobs in hotels and restaurants.

TOURIST INFORMATION

Visit the TI to make plans. Get the mountain weather forecast, pick up the free town and valley map and the "panorama" map of all the valley lifts, and maybe the €5 *Carte des Sentiers* hiking map (see "Chamonix-Area Hikes" on page 834). Ask about snow levels and hours of lifts and trains, and consider buying the Multipass lift ticket (described later). The TI's helpful website and free app have updated sightseeing info, weather forecasts, and more (daily mid-June–mid-Sept and mid-Dec–mid-April 9:00-19:00; off-season generally Mon-Sat 9:00-12:30 & 14:00-18:00, closed Sun; tel. 04 50 53 00 24, www.chamonix.com, info@chamonix.com). Pull up a beachy sling chair outside the TI and plan your hike.

ARRIVAL IN CHAMONIX

By Train: Walk straight out of the station and up Avenue Michel Croz. In three blocks, you'll reach the town center; turn left at the big clock, then right for the TI. While the train station has no baggage storage, you can leave bags at the Absolute Café/Tabac shop (a block in front of the station on the right at 223 Avenue Michel Croz, €5/5 hours, €1/hour after that).

By Bus: The long-distance bus station is south of the town center (234 Avenue de Courmayeur, behind the bowling alley). It's a 15-minute walk to the town center (see the "Chamonix Town" map). Or take the free shuttle bus called Le Mulet (see page 823).

By Car: For many of my recommended hotels and the TI, take the Chamonix Nord turnoff—coming from Annecy and Geneva, it's the second exit after you pass under the Aiguille du Midi cable car—and follow signs to *Centre-Ville*. Take the exit before the Aiguille du Midi lift station for hotels south of the TI. Most parking is metered and well-signed; your hotel can direct you to free park-

Chamonix: A Quick History

1091 Chamonix is first mentioned in local documents.

1786 Jacques Balmat and Michel-Gabriel Paccard are the first to climb Mont Blanc.

1818 First ascent of Aiguille du Midi.

1860 The Savoie region (including Chamonix) becomes part of France. After a visit by Napoleon III, alpine tourism begins to boom.

1901 Train service reaches Chamonix, making it accessible to the masses.

1908 The cogwheel train to Montenvers is completed.

1924 The first Winter Olympics are held in Chamonix.

1930 Le Brévent *téléphérique* (gondola) opens to tourists.

1955 Aiguille du Midi *téléphérique* opens to tourists.

1965 The Mont Blanc tunnel is built.

2020 You visit Chamonix.

ing. From mid-July to late August, traffic and parking are a mess in Chamonix—plan ahead or arrive before 10:00 to get a spot.

The Mont Blanc tunnel (7.2 miles long, about a 15-minute drive) allows quick access between Chamonix and Italy (one-way-€46, round-trip-€58 with return valid for 1 week, www.tunnelmb.com).

By Plane: The nearest international airport is in Geneva, Switzerland (Genève airport, airport code: GVA, www.gva.ch; hourly trains, 4 hours with two changes; 2 hours by car, airport shuttle van, or bus—see "Chamonix Connections" at the end of this chapter. Also nearby is Lyon (St-Exupéry airport, airport code: LYS, www.lyonaeroports.com; linked by 4 buses/day, 3.5 hours on Ouibus; 3 hours by car).

HELPFUL HINTS

Crowd-Beating Tips: Trails are quieter the earlier you go. The only lift with serious crowd challenges is the big one: Aiguille du Midi. In high season (especially on a good day after a stretch of bad weather), take an early lift to beat the crowds and afternoon clouds (lift opens at 6:30 or 7:00 in summer, go no later than 8:00). Have breakfast on top.

Regardless of the weather, good restaurants in Chamonix can be booked solid for summer evenings. It's smart to make reservations.

Plan Ahead: Bright snow abounds up high, so bring sunglasses and dress for the cold. For Chamonix's weather, check at your hotel, the TI, or online at www.chamonix.com or www.chamonix-meteo.com. For current lift information and to book the Aiguille du Midi lift, use www.montblancnaturalresort.com (select "Area & Sites," then "Aiguille du Midi").

Open-Air Market: Chamonix's Saturday-morning market fills big Place Mont Blanc.

Supermarkets: Little **Casino** markets are plentiful. The **Super-U** is central and big (next to Le Génépy on Rue Joseph Vallot). Supplement your run-of-the-mill groceries with gourmet local specialties from **Le Refuge Payot** (two locations: 166 Rue Joseph Vallot and 255 Rue du Docteur Paccard).

Inexpensive Mountain Gear: The best deals on sunglasses, lightweight gloves, daypacks, and the like are at **Technique Extrême** (daily 9:00-19:00, 200 Avenue de l'Aiguille du Midi).

English Books: Small collections are kept at **Librarie Landru** (open daily, 74 Rue Joseph Vallot) and at **Maison de la Presse** (daily, 93 Rue du Docteur Paccard).

Laundry: There are two good self-service launderettes, both with long hours daily: One is a block up from the Aiguille du Midi lift at 174 Avenue de l'Aiguille du Midi; the other is in the Blanche Neige Gallerie on 266 Rue du Docteur Paccard, across from Le Refuge Payot.

Taxis: There's usually one at the train station. If not, try **Alp Taxi** (mobile 06 81 78 79 51, www.alp-taxi.com) or **Taxi Michel Buton** (mobile 06 07 19 70 36, www.taxi-buton-chamonix.com).

Car Rental: Europcar is across from the train station (Mon-Sat 9:00-12:00 & 14:00-18:00, closed Sun, 36 Place de la Gare, tel. 04 50 53 63 40, mobile 06 85 40 04 72).

Local Guides: Local guides can be hired through the TI or the local guides bureau (half-day in English-€200, full day-€300, visitechamonix@hotmail.fr).

Local Firewater: Pick up a little (5 cl) bottle of **génépi** liqueur, the local herb schnapps, and nip on it throughout your high-altitude adventures. It'll warm you and make you feel like a local.

GETTING AROUND (AND UP AND DOWN) THE VALLEY

Lifts and cogwheel trains are named for their highest destination (e.g. Aiguille du Midi, Montenvers, and Le Brévent). More details on individual lifts are given under "Sights in Chamonix," later. You can find current lift information and book the big Aiguille du Midi lift at www.montblancnaturalresort.com. You can also buy tickets (and reserve the Aiguille du Midi lift) at any of the valley lift stations.

FRENCH ALPS

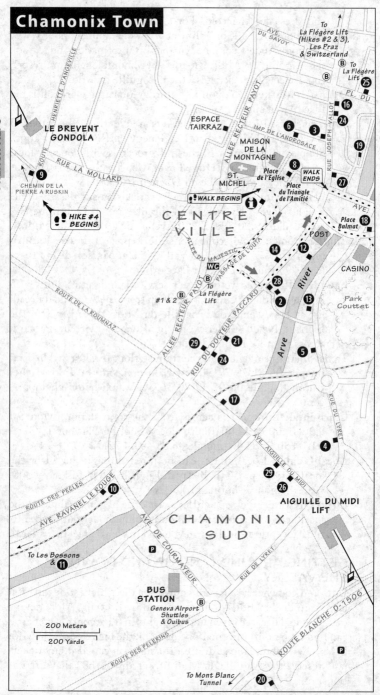

Chamonix Town

LE BREVENT GONDOLA

ROUTE HENRIETTE D'ANGEVILLE

CHEMIN DE LA PIERRE A RUSKIN

RUE LA MOLLARD

9

HIKE #4 BEGINS

AVE. DU SAVOY

To La Flégère Lift (Hikes #2 & 3), Les Praz & Switzerland

(B) To La Flégère Lift

25

PL. DU

ESPACE TAIRRAZ

MAISON DE LA MONTAGNE

ST. MICHEL

ALLÉE RECTEUR PAYOT

IMP. DE L'ANDROSACE

6

3

RUE JOSEPH VALLOT

16

24

19

8

Place de l'Eglise

WALK ENDS

27

WALK BEGINS

i

Place du Triangle de l'Amitié

AVE.

ALLÉE DU MAJESTIC

CENTRE VILLE

POST

Place Balmat

18

WC

PASSAGE DE L'OUTA

14

12

River

CASINO

B

28

Park Couttet

#1 & 2 (B) To La Flégère Lift

2

13

ROUTE DE LA ROUMNAZ

ALLÉE RECTEUR PAYOT

RUE DU DOCTEUR PACCARD

29

21

24

Arve

5

17

RUE DU LYRET

4

AVE. AIGUILLE DU MIDI

ROUTE DES PÈCLES

AVE. RAVANEL LE ROUGE

10

29

26

AIGUILLE DU MIDI LIFT

AVE. DE COURMAYEUR

CHAMONIX SUD

To Les Bossons &

11

P

RUE DE LYRET

BUS STATION

(B)

Geneva Airport Shuttles & Ouibus

200 Meters

200 Yards

ROUTE DES PÈLERINS

ROUTE BLANCHE D-1506

P

To Mont Blanc Tunnel

20

FRENCH ALPS

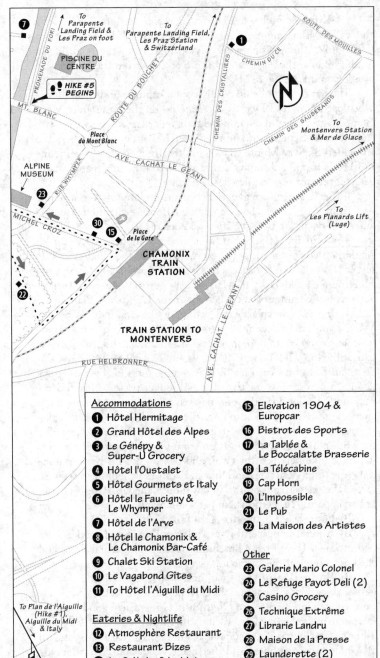

Accommodations
1. Hôtel Hermitage
2. Grand Hôtel des Alpes
3. Le Génépy & Super-U Grocery
4. Hôtel l'Oustalet
5. Hôtel Gourmets et Italy
6. Hôtel le Faucigny & Le Whymper
7. Hôtel de l'Arve
8. Hôtel le Chamonix & Le Chamonix Bar-Café
9. Chalet Ski Station
10. Le Vagabond Gîtes
11. To Hôtel l'Aiguille du Midi

Eateries & Nightlife
12. Atmosphère Restaurant
13. Restaurant Bizes
14. La Calèche & La Maison du Burger
15. Elevation 1904 & Europcar
16. Bistrot des Sports
17. La Tablée & Le Boccalatte Brasserie
18. La Télécabine
19. Cap Horn
20. L'Impossible
21. Le Pub
22. La Maison des Artistes

Other
23. Galerie Mario Colonel
24. Le Refuge Payot Deli (2)
25. Casino Grocery
26. Technique Extrême
27. Librarie Landru
28. Maison de la Presse
29. Launderette (2)
30. Absolute Café/Tabac (Bag Storage)

By Lift: Gondolas *(téléphériques)* climb mountains all along the valley. The mightiest one—Aiguille du Midi—leaves from Chamonix. Though sightseeing is optimal from the Aiguille du Midi gondola, there are more hiking options from the Le Brévent gondola and La Flégère lift.

The lift to Aiguille du Midi is open summer and winter (usually closed Nov-mid-Dec). The *télécabines* on the Panoramic Mont Blanc lift to Helbronner (atop the Italian border) run only from late June to early September, and even then only in good weather. The lift called Skyway Monte Bianco (on the Italian side of the mountain) runs from Helbronner down to Pontal d'Entrèves and rotates 360 degrees for panoramic views en route.

Other area lifts are generally open from January to mid-April and from mid-June to late September. Because maintenance closures can occur anytime, verify schedules for all lifts at the TI.

The **Multipass lift ticket** saves time and money for most, particularly if you're spending two or more days in the Chamonix valley. It allows unlimited access to all the lifts and trains (except the Helbronner gondola to Italy). You also get discounts for various activities in Chamonix, such as the Parc de Loisirs des Planards.

Your pass is a smart card, valid for the day (not 24 hours). With it you can scan your way to the top and ride lifts you'd otherwise skip. You could hop on a lift just to have a drink from a view café at the top (€64/1 day, €78/2 days, €88/3 days, €128/6 days, add €3 to all passes for card itself; kids 4-14—and kids over 64—pay about 15 percent less for two-day and longer passes, kids under 4 may not be allowed). The one-day pass is only a few euros more than the round-trip ticket to Aiguille du Midi, and a terrific value if you plan to do the round-trip lift from Chamonix to Aiguille du Midi plus the round-trip train from Chamonix to Montenvers (and not hike between the two), and/or ride the Le Brévent gondola (great for view cafés and hikes). Families benefit from reduced fares. The pass is sold online (www.montblancnaturalresort.com), at participating lift stations, and at some hotels.

By Foot: See "Chamonix-Area Hikes" on page 834.

By Bike: The peaceful river valley trail is ideal for bikes (and pedestrians). The TI has a brochure showing bike-rental shops and the best mountain-biking routes.

By Bus or Train: One road and one scenic rail line lace together the valley's towns and lifts. To help reduce traffic and pollution, your hotel offers a free **Chamonix Guest Card** good for local travel during your stay (also included with lift passes; €10/week at TI or €3/day on bus if not staying at a hotel). The cards are valid on all Chamonix-area buses and the scenic valley train (from Servoz to Vallorcine). This is a great value for those with time to explore the valley.

FRENCH ALPS

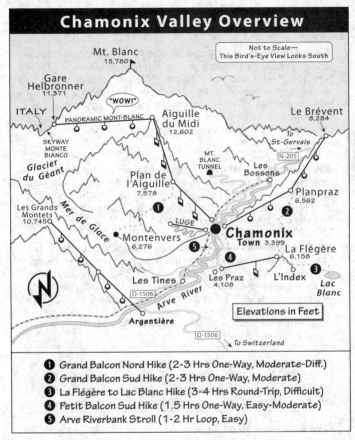

Chamonix Valley Overview

Not to Scale—
This Bird's-Eye View Looks South

Mt. Blanc
15,780

Gare
Helbronner
11,371

ITALY

"WOW!"

PANORAMIC MONT-BLANC

Aiguille
du Midi
12,602

Le Brévent
8,284

To
St-Gervais

SKYWAY
MONTE
BIANCO

N-205

*Glacier
du Géant*

MT.
BLANC
TUNNEL

Les
Bossons

Plan de
l'Aiguille
7,578

❶

Planpraz
6,562

Les Grands
Montets
10,745

Mer de Glace

LUGE

❷

Montenvers
6,276

❺

Chamonix
Town 3,399

La Flégère
6,158

❹

Les Tines

Les Praz
4,108

L'Index

❸

Lac
Blanc

D-1506

Arve River

Elevations in Feet

Argentière

D-1506

To Switzerland

❶ Grand Balcon Nord Hike (2-3 Hrs One-Way, Moderate-Diff.)
❷ Grand Balcon Sud Hike (2-3 Hrs One-Way, Moderate)
❸ La Flégère to Lac Blanc Hike (3-4 Hrs Round-Trip, Difficult)
❹ Petit Balcon Sud Hike (1.5 Hrs One-Way, Easy-Moderate)
❺ Arve Riverbank Stroll (1-2 Hr Loop, Easy)

Local buses #1 and #2 run to valley villages (2/hour, details in English at https://chamonix.montblancbus.com). The easiest stop to find in Chamonix is 200 yards to the right when you leave the TI (past Hôtel Mont Blanc—look for the bus shelters); the website shows other stops in Chamonix by route. Direction "Le Tour" on bus #2 and "Les Praz/Flégère" on bus #1 will take you toward Les Praz (for Hikes #2 and #3) and Switzerland (see "Chamonix-Area Hikes" map, later).

Le Mulet/Navette: These free minibuses circulate around Chamonix village (4/hour, mid-June-early Sept and mid-Dec-mid-April daily 8:00-19:00). They're especially handy to or from the Aiguille du Midi lift, which is a 15-minute walk from many hotels.

The train ride toward **Martigny** in Switzerland is gorgeous, and villages such as Les Praz and Tines (10 minutes by bus) offer quiet escapes from busy Chamonix.

Chamonix Activities at a Glance

▲▲▲**Aiguille du Midi Gondola** The valley's most spectacular and popular lift, taking you to magnificent views at 12,602 feet. From here you can ride cute *télécabines* over the Alps to the Italian border and back, take Chamonix's greatest hike to the Mer de Glace (from the halfway-up stop at Plan de l'Aiguille), or just enjoy the views. Whether hiking or just changing gondolas, be sure to enjoy some nature-loving time at Plan de l'Aiguille.

▲▲▲**Train to Montenvers** Cogwheel train to the eight-mile-long Mer de Glace, where you can walk inside the glacier, admire jagged mountain peaks, and have lunch with a view at the Montenvers hotel. Many people hike to Montenvers from halfway down the Aiguille du Midi lift.

▲▲▲**Le Brévent Gondola** Second-most-spectacular lift from Chamonix, allowing access to the mountain range on the opposite side of the valley from Mont Blanc—and the best view cafés in the valley (closed late April-mid-June and mid-Sept). Get off halfway at the Planpraz station for the Grand Balcon Sud hike to the La Flégère lift (although the hike is best in the other direction), or go all the way to Le Brévent for sky-high views and a restaurant.

▲▲▲**La Flégère Lift** Starting point for hikes to Lac Blanc and to the Grand Balcon Sud trail back to Planpraz (on the Le Brévent gondola). Refuge-Hôtel La Flégère, at the station, offers drinks, snacks, and accommodations, all with a view.

Arve Riverbank Stroll Several trails allow a level walk or bike ride in the woods between Chamonix and Les Praz. See paragliders make dramatic landings and enjoy mountain views outside Chamonix to the sound of the Arve River.

Chamonix Walk

Cut in half by a raging little river and with lifts reaching to staggering mountain peaks on either side of its valley, Chamonix really feels like a mountain resort. Yet hiding in its pedestrian-mall town center, among all the outdoor shops and restaurants, is a little history. This quick self-guided walk will help you understand the town that for a thousand years had more cows than people. Then, with the 19th century, came the realization that mountains make wonderful vacation destinations. Chamonix became the springboard to Europe's tallest peak and was transformed into an alpine resort.

• *Start at the map in front of the tourist office.*

Triangle of Friendship and TI: The big image of the surrounding peaks offers a fun review of the reasons you're here. From this point, you can see the Aiguille du Midi lift on one side of the valley and, opposite, the similarly staggering Le Brévent gondola. The town square is actually a triangle. Known as the Triangle of Friendship, it celebrates the peaceful and productive collaboration of France, Switzerland, and Italy (whose borders come together near here). Facing the TI is the Hôtel de Ville (look for the flags), which has been the City Hall since 1910. There is almost always some kind of cultural exhibition on the square.

• *Look for the church spire.*

St. Michael's Church and Maison de la Montagne: Facing the square is Chamonix's historic St. Michael's Catholic Church. The church is made from granite just like the surrounding mountains. Immediately inside the entry are stained-glass windows (circa 1925) celebrating winter sports, with saints looking down over the participants enjoying the local nature.

While most of the building is relatively new, its stone-spire base dates from Romanesque times (800 years ago), and there was a church on this spot centuries before that. In 1091 the owner of the valley had no use for this remote land and gave it to an Italian monastery. The monks built the first church and a priory next door, today's **Maison de la Montagne,** which houses the guide and mountaineering headquarters (for details, see "Chamonix-Area Hikes," later). Behind the church, a stony overpass leads to the Crystal Museum (see "Rainy Day Options," later).

• *From this triangular square, stroll past the TI and right, down Allée du Majestic. Keep straight along a parking lot. On the right is a public WC and behind that is the handy local bus stop. (This is the best town center stop for bus #1 or #2 to Flégère). At the WC, turn left across the parking lot and walk down a lane to the busy pedestrian street, Rue du Docteur Paccard. Then head left a few steps to the next square.*

Mountain Guides Fresco: Ahead is the eye-catching *Mountain Guides* fresco, created in 2010, with impressive 3-D effects and featuring a cast of 20 leading characters from Chamonix history. An info board in the square explains the story in English.

• *Continuing on beyond the fresco, you'll pass the cinema on the left (movies listed as "v.o."—version originale—are shown in their original languages) and the post office on the right (a rare place that actually changes cash). Hook right to the statue (immediately over the river) of two men looking up at the mountains, which marks...*

Place Balmat and the Arve River: The centerpiece of Place Balmat is the statue erected here in 1886—100 years after Jacques Balmat, a mountaineer, and Michel-Gabriel Paccard, a doctor, made the first ascent of 15,780-foot Mont Blanc. Shown in this statue is Balmat, pointing excitedly up to the summit, along with

FRENCH ALPS

scientist Horace de Saussure (the smart-looking guy), whom Balmat led to the top a year later. The statue was erected with funds donated by alpine clubs from as far afield as Boston (see the granite engraving). If you look up the river about a block there's another statue, this one of Paccard, erected in 1986 to honor the 200th anniversary of the first

ascent. Both Paccard and Balmat forever enjoy a fine view of the mountain they were the first to conquer.

Raging underneath is the **Arve River.** Born near the Swiss border, it flows to Geneva where it joins the Rhône River's run south to the Mediterranean. Sediment from glacial melt makes the water milky. (In winter, when little is melting, the river is smaller and much clearer.) In medieval times, the first bridge here was made of wood and used mostly by cows. Today's stone bridge dates from 1880. Historically, whenever there's a big melt and a heavy rain, the Arve would flood the town. But in the 1960s the river was channeled into a canal, and since then it's been regularly dredged to help prevent flooding.

• *Look across the street to the...*

Casino: This was once one of Chamonix's oldest hotels—built for Romantic Age travelers back when local guides carried aristocrats in sedan chairs up to see a glacier. The building has a northern Italian design—a reminder that this town (like Nice) was once part of the northern Italian kingdom of Savoy. Napoleon III came here in 1860, and from this building's balcony he welcomed the citizens of Chamonix after they had voted to join France. The hotel later became a casino, part of Chamonix's drive to be considered a real tourist resort.

• *Walk to the left of the casino and into a grassy park, created in 2014, when its original huge trees were cut down (you'll see the stumps and the massive timbers used for benches).*

Park Couttet: The grassy expanse covers a hill, or moraine (rocky debris left by a receding glacier)—a reminder that a glacier once filled this valley. Informative panels tell about the geology. Walk to the back of the park to find **La Maison des Artistes,** an eclectic granite mansion that dates from the 1920s. Today it's a popular jazz bar mixing great mountain views with booze and live music almost nightly in high season (closed Sun-Mon and in May & Oct).

• *Turn left on the street behind the park and walk 200 yards to the train station.*

Protestant Church: Across the street from the train station, hiding in a woodsy lot, is a small Protestant church—built in the 1860s for the many English visitors who traveled here on their Grand Tours. From here, with your back to the station, a walk straight down the main drag (Avenue Michel Croz) takes you back to the river, the statue of Paccard, and the center of Chamonix.

Sights in Chamonix

MOUNTAIN LIFTS, GONDOLAS, AND TRAINS
▲▲▲Aiguille du Midi

The Aiguille du Midi (ay-gwee doo mee-dee) is the most spectacular mountain lift in Europe—and the most popular ride in the valley. If the weather's clear, the price doesn't matter. Take an early lift and have breakfast above 12,000 feet. Remember, it's freezing cold up there and you'll need sunglasses.

Cost: From Chamonix to Plan de l'Aiguille—round-trip-€33 (one-way-€18); Aiguille du Midi—round-trip-€62 (one-way-€50, not including parachute). Tickets for the Panoramic Mont Blanc *télécabines* from Aiguille du Midi to Pointe Helbronner (Italy) are sold at both base and summit lift stations with no difference in price (round-trip-€30). As conditions can change, I wouldn't buy the Helbronner ticket until I'm at the top of Aiguille du Midi, where it's easy to purchase. If dropping into Italy on the Skyway Monte Bianco, buy that ticket at Helbronner (€50, baggage allowed).

Discounts: The prices listed above are for ages 15-64; kids 4-14 and over 64 cost about 15 percent less (family rates for 2 adults and 2 children ages 14 and under are also available). While going all the way up and only halfway down (and hiking from Plan de l'Aiguille) costs the same as a round-trip ticket, those with a round-trip ticket who hike over to Montenvers can use it to ride the train back into Chamonix, which saves €28.

Hours: Lifts generally run daily July-Aug 6:30 or 7:00-18:00, late May-June and Sept 8:10-16:30, and Oct-mid-May 8:10-15:30, closed mid-May-late May and Nov-mid-Dec. Be warned: Hours can change with the weather, among other reasons. Always confirm plans locally. Gondolas run every 10 minutes during busy times; the last return from Aiguille du Midi is generally one hour after the last ascent. The last *télécabine* departure to Pointe Helbronner is

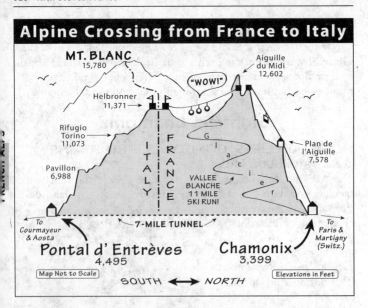

Alpine Crossing from France to Italy

MT. BLANC
15,780

Aiguille
du Midi
12,602

"WOW!"

Helbronner
11,371

Rifugio
Torino
11,073

ITALY

FRANCE

G

Plan de
l'Aiguille
7,578

a

c

Pavillon
6,988

VALLEE
BLANCHE
11 MILE
SKI RUN!

i

e

r

To
Courmayeur
& Aosta

7-MILE TUNNEL

Pontal d' Entrèves
4,495

Chamonix
3,399

To
Paris &
Martigny
(Switz.)

Map Not to Scale

Elevations in Feet

SOUTH ⟷ NORTH

about 14:30, and the last train down from Montenvers (for hikers) is between 17:00-18:00, depending on the season.

Crowd-Beating Strategies: To beat the hordes and clouds, ride the Aiguille du Midi lift (up and down) as early as you can (first lift departs at 6:30 or 7:00 in summer). To beat major delays in summer, leave no later than 8:00, no reservation needed. While you can reserve ahead for a later time, sights and trails will be busy the later you go. Crowds are worst on a sunny day after a string of bad days. If you arrive later in the day, you'll likely be assigned a lift time and will have to come back.

You can reserve at the information booth next to the lift, online at www.montblancnaturalresort.com, or in person at this or other lifts (reservations are nonrefundable). Reservations are taken from one to seven days in advance (no same-day reservations, usually booked up one day out—try to reserve at least two days ahead). Pick tickets up at the lift station 20 minutes before departure (the information booth at the Aiguille du Midi lift tells you which window to use for priority access). Reservations are not possible for the *télécabines* to Helbronner.

Time to Allow: Chamonix to Aiguille du Midi—20 minutes one-way, 2 hours round-trip, 3 hours in peak season; Chamonix to Helbronner—about 45 minutes one-way, 3 hours round-trip. (In peak season, you can get hung up by crowds at Helbronner.) On busy days, minimize delays returning to Chamonix by making a reservation for your return lift time upon arrival at the top of Aiguille du Midi. (When crowded, attendants hand out return-time cards as you arrive—ask for advice when you get to the top.)

Visiting the Aiguille du Midi

Pile into the *téléphérique* (gondola), try to grab a window spot, and soar to the tip of a rock needle 12,602 feet above sea level (you'll be packed into the gondola like sardines; take off your daypack to allow more room). Chamonix shrinks as trees fly by, soon replaced by whizzing rocks, ice, and snow. Change gondolas at Plan de l'Aiguille to reach the top. Notice the receding glaciers on the right as you ascend. No matter how sunny it is, it's cold and the air is thin. People are giddy with delight (those prone to altitude sickness or agoraphobia are less so). Fun things can happen at Aiguille du Midi if you're not too winded to join the locals in the halfway-to-heaven tango.

Aiguille du Midi Station and the Summit: In the station, you'll find several gift shops, cafeterias, view terraces, and many nooks and crannies to explore. The actual gondola station has shops and a view terrace, and an interesting exhibit about the history of the 1950s construction. The summit tower atop the peak looks like a spacecraft perched on an alp (look up as you walk out of the lift station).

A **skybridge** leads from the station past an information kiosk (which sells tickets for the Helbronner lift to Italy). Stop there to assess the crowds, the trip to Italy, and return-to-Chamonix options (remember, it may be quiet now, but later it can be horribly crowded with hours-long delays if you're sloppy). Ask about reserving a time for your descent back into Chamonix.

The skybridge deposits you in the **main building** with an elevator to the summit. Before riding the elevator up, you can explore. An exhibit called "Vertical Space Extreme" thrills with amazing photos and videos of daredevil mountaineers. A tubular walkway called "The Tube" gets you away from the crowds to quieter views. Spot the climbers and ponder the value of an ice ax. Stairs near The Tube's entry lead up to a heated room with an exhibit on Mont Blanc's fragile environment.

Follow *Vallée Blanche* signs to a drippy **"ice tunnel"** where skiers and mountain climbers make their exit. The views are sensational if you can get close (only skiers/climbers allowed past a certain point); merely observing is exhilarating. Skiers make the 13-mile run to the Mer de Glace

from here. Next to that is the gondola station for the Panoramic Mont Blanc lift to Helbronner (Italy).

The highlight of your ascent is riding the **elevator to the summit** (signed *Terrasse 3842*)—12,602 feet above sea level (pose with the much-photographed altitude sign). From this platform, the Alps spread out before you. Use the orientation posters to identify key peaks: You can see the main Swiss and Italian summits rising above 13,000 feet. If it's clear, you can see the bent little Matterhorn—the tall, shady pyramid listed in French on the observation table as "Cervin—4,505 meters" (14,775 feet). And looming on the other side is Mont Blanc, the Alps' highest point, at 4,810 meters (15,780 feet).

Use the telescopes to spot mountaineers (roped up and following guides); more than 2,000 people scale Mont Blanc each year. A long but not technically challenging climb, the summit was first conquered in 1786, more than 170 years before this lift was built. Find the giant's tooth, spot the *télécabines* to Italy, and identify lift stations of the Aiguilles Rouges mountain range across the valley, on the other side of Chamonix. That rusty tin-can needle above you serves as a communications tower. Check the temperature near the elevator.

At the summit, the "Step Into the Void" glass box offers a chance to stand in what feels like midair. (They'll take your photo for a fee.) But it can be a long wait for a small payoff.

Taking the Gondola to Italy: For your private glacial dream world, embark on the little red Panoramic Mont Blanc *télécabine* and sail south to Pointe Helbronner, the mountaintop Italian border station (typically open late June-early Sept). This line stretches three miles over ice, snow, and rocks. In a gondola for four (if it's not too crowded, you can usually get a private one for two if you ask), you'll dangle silently for 40 minutes as you glide over glaciers and past a forest of peaks to Italy. Hang your head out the window. Enjoy the silence. Explore every corner of your view. From Helbronner, you can turn around and return to Aiguille du Midi, or descend into Italy on the Skyway Monte Bianco lift (described later, under "Day Trips near Chamonix")—but for most there's really no point unless you're traveling on into Italy.

Helbronner station, at over 11,000 feet, has a whole different crowd (people coming up from Italy with no intention of going to Aiguille du Midi). There's a cafeteria, a crystal hall, an elevator down to a passage that leads to the Torino Refugio climber's refuge (with view terrace and restaurant), and, most importantly, spiraling stairs leading to a 360-degree viewing platform for killer views from the Matterhorn to Mont Blanc (called Monte Bianco here in Italy). Unfortunately, you need to keep an eye on the crowds and the slow line to assure your timely return to Aiguille du Midi.

Returning to Chamonix via Plan de l'Aiguille: To get from Aiguille du Midi to Chamonix, you'll need to change gondolas at **Plan de l'Aiguille.** Take some time here on your way down. Gondolas depart every few minutes, and those boarding here never have to wait. At Plan de l'Aiguille you'll find a scenic café with sandwiches, drinks, outdoor tables, paragliders jumping off cliffs (except in July-Aug), and rocky perches for private sunbathing. It's a great place to just relax. But the best reason to get off here is to follow the wonderful **trail to the Mer de Glace,** then catch the train back into Chamonix (for details, see "Chamonix-Area Hikes—Hike #1," later).

For a quick trip, find the Montenvers-Mer de Glace trail below the lift station and walk 15 minutes to the peaceful and cozy **$ Refuge-Plan de l'Aiguille,** where you can get reasonable meals (good omelets, pastas, salads, and mouthwatering tarts, made by welcoming manager Claude—no English, no problem) and drinks inside or out (open daily May-late Oct, mobile 06 65 64 27 53). It's a manageable hike for most travelers (or a great overnight for a steal—see "Sleeping in Chamonix," later).

Never hike all the way down to Chamonix from Plan de l'Aiguille or Montenvers-Mer de Glace; it's a long, steep walk through thick forests with few views. Ride the gondola down, and notice as you're finally dropping back into Chamonix the highway disappearing into the mountain—that's the Mont Blanc Tunnel.

▲▲▲Mer de Glace (Montenvers)

From Gare de Montenvers (the little station over the tracks from Chamonix's main train station), the cute cogwheel Train du Mon-

tenvers toots you up to tiny Montenvers (mohn-tuh-vehr). Sit on the left-hand side as you go up for good views among pine trees over the valley. There you'll see a dirty, rapidly receding glacier called the Mer de Glace (mayr duh glahs, "Sea of Ice") and fantastic views up the white valley (Vallée Blanche) of splintered, snow-capped peaks. (As the glacier recedes, it is literally pulling away from the train station; in coming years you'll see construction as the train tracks are extended to catch up with the ice.)

Cost and Hours: Round-trip-€33, one-way-€28, family rates available, prices include gondola and ice caves entry, daily 8:30-

FRENCH ALPS

17:00, July-Aug 8:00-18:00, 2/hour, 20 minutes, confirm first/last trip times with TI or call 04 50 53 12 54.

Visiting the Glacier: Find the **view deck** across from the train station. France's largest glacier, at eight miles long, is impressive from above and below. The swirling glacier extends under the dirt about a half-mile downhill to the left. Imagine that it recently reached as high as the vegetation below (see the dirt cliffs—called moraines—left behind in its retreat). In 1860, this glacier stretched all the way down to the valley floor (see the "Understanding the Alps" sidebar).

Use an **orientation table** as you look up to the peaks. **Aiguille du Dru**'s powerful spire, at about 11,700 feet, makes an irresistible target for climbers. It was first scaled in 1860 (long before the train you took here was built) and was recently free-climbed (no ropes, belays, etc.); the colored lines indicate different routes taken. The smooth snow field to the left of Dru's spire (Les Grands Montets) is the top of Chamonix's most challenging ski run, with a vertical drop of about 6,500 feet (down the opposite side). The path to the right (as you face the glacier) leads to a fine view café and a reconstruction of a crystal cave.

The glacier's **ice caves** are beneath you (and are skippable for most). Take the free, small gondola down and prepare to walk about 500 steps each way. (Several years ago, it was 280 steps.) This glacier is beating a hasty retreat—as you walk down you'll pass signs that bring this point home by showing the extent of the glacier over the years. The ice cave, a hypnotizing shade of blue-green, is actually a long tunnel dug about 75 yards into the glacier. Informative panels describe the digging of the cave.

The **Terminal Neige/Refuge du Montenvers,** a few minutes' walk toward Chamonix from the viewing platform outside the station, offers a full-service restaurant, view tables (fair prices, limited selection), and a warm interior (you can even bunk here in style—see "Sleeping in Chamonix," later). The hotel was built in 1880, when tourists arrived on foot or by mule.

The three-hour trail to Plan de l'Aiguille (see page 837 for a description) begins across from the hotel. Follow signs for *Le Signal/Plan de l'Aiguille* past two stone buildings and track the trail as it rises (sometimes steeply, with no shade) just above the Mer de Glace valley. For terrific views, hike this trail just a short distance. The views get better fast, and the higher you climb, the better they get as the peaks of the Aiguilles Rouges come into sight behind you. Bring a picnic. Le Signal is a brilliant destination—but a long climb (figure one hour).

A **Glaciorium** lies 50 yards behind the hotel along the main walkway. It houses a small but worthwhile exhibit on glaciers of the world with dioramas, a film, interactive displays, and terrific images that explain the life of a glacier (all well described in English). As you leave you're reminded that more than two-thirds of the world's drinking water comes from glaciers (free, daily 9:30-18:00 in summer, 10:00-16:00 in winter).

▲▲▲Lifts to Le Brévent and La Flégère

Though Aiguille du Midi gives a more spectacular ride, the Le Brévent and La Flégère lifts offer worthwhile hiking and viewing options, with unobstructed panoramas across to the Mont Blanc range and fewer crowds. The Le Brévent (luh bray-vahn) gondola is in Chamonix; the La Flégère (lah flay-zhair) lift is in nearby Les Praz (lay prah). The lifts are connected by a scenic hike or by bus along the valley floor (bus is free with Chamonix Guest Card, see Hike #2 in the next section); both have sensational view cafés. Both lifts are closed from late April to mid-June and again by mid-September (reopening when ski season starts, usually in Dec).

Le Brévent and Planpraz

This gondola, a steep 10-minute walk up the road above Chamonix's TI, is a worthwhile trip just for the ride and view cafés alone (ideal with a Multipass). It takes two gondolas to reach Le Brévent's top. The first gondola to Planpraz, with automated eight-person *télécabines*, runs every minute. Sit backward and watch Chamonix shrink away below (round-trip to Planpraz-€18, one-way-€14). Planpraz merits a little exploring—there are view restaurants and cafés and good hiking options. The free little funicular *(Funi)* takes you up to a view platform where you'll find parasailers and an easier start if you want to hike between Planpraz and La Flégère (my Hike #2 in reverse).

The second gondola to Le Brévent station leaves from Planpraz and runs every 5-15 minutes. At the top, you get 360-degree views, more hikes, an exhibit on how the region has evolved over 60,000 years, and a smashing view café. It's a fine stop, but for most, Planpraz is plenty high (round-trip from Chamonix to Le Brévent-€33, one-way-€24; daily 8:45-17:00, July-Aug 8:15-18:00, last return from Planpraz one hour after last ascent, closed late April-mid-June and mid-Sept, tel. 04 50 53 13 18).

La Flégère and L'Index

This lift runs from the neighboring village of Les Praz to La Flégère station every 15 minutes; to go higher, take the chairlift to L'Index (La Flégère round-trip-€18, one-way-€15 L'Index round-trip-€30, one-way-€25; daily 8:15-16:45, summer 8:00-17:30, last return from La Flégère 15 minutes after last ascent, closed late April-mid-June and mid-Sept, tel. 04 50 53 18 58). Hikes to Planpraz and Lac Blanc leave from the top of this station (see Hikes #2 and #3 in the

Understanding the Alps

The Alps were formed about 100 million years ago by the collision of two continents: the African plate pushing north against the stable plates of Europe and Asia. In the process, the sediments of the ancient Tethys Ocean (which occupied the general real estate of the modern Mediterranean) became smooshed between the landmasses. Shoving all this material together made the rocks and sediments fold, shatter, and pile on top of each other; over millennia, this growing jumble built itself up into today's Alps. Up in the mountains, look for folds and faults in the rocks that hint at this immense compression, which is still happening today: The Alps continue to rise by at least a millimeter each year (while erosion wears them down at about the same rate).

The current shape of the mountains and valleys is the handiwork of at least five ice ages over the last two million years. Glaciers flowed down the mountain valleys, scooped out beautiful alpine lakes, and carried rocks far away from where they formed. The Alps were the first mountains extensively studied by geologists, and many of the geological terms that describe mountains originated here. Once you learn how to recognize a few of the

 landforms shaped by glaciers, you can easily spot these features when you visit other alpine areas. Study glacier exhibits to train your eye to recognize what you're seeing.

Glaciers are big and blunt, so they make simple, large-scale marks on the landscape. If a valley is U-shaped, like Chamonix's (with steep sides and a rounded base), it's probably been scoured out by a glacier. (California's Yosemite Valley is another classic example.)

A **cirque** (French for "circus") is the amphitheater-like depression carved out at the upper part of a valley by a glacier. If two adjacent cirques erode back close to each other, a sharp, steep-sided ridge forms, called an **arête** (French for "fishbone").

next section). Les Praz is easy to reach from Chamonix by local bus (10 minutes—it's the first stop after Chamonix).

CHAMONIX-AREA HIKES

The **Maison de la Montagne** service center is a good first stop for serious hikers (located across from the TI, first-floor WC). On the second floor, the **Office de Haute-Montagne** (High Mountain Office) can help you plan your hikes and tell you about trail and snow conditions (daily 9:00-12:00 & 15:00-18:00, tel. 04 50 53 22 08, www.chamoniarde.com). The staff speaks enough English and

Cirques and arêtes are common in mountains that have had glaciers. More rarely, when three or more cirques erode toward one another, a pyramidal peak is created—called a **horn.** Switzerland's Matterhorn (visible—barely—from the Aiguille du Midi) is the world's most famous example. Glaciers flowed down all sides of this mountain, scooping material away as they went to leave its distinctive sharp peak.

A common feature left behind by retreating glaciers is a **moraine,** a pile of dirt and rocks that was carried along on the glacier as it advanced, then was dumped as the glacier melted (plainly visible around the Mer de Glace).

Alpine glaciers can only originate above the snowline, so if you see any of these landforms (U-shaped valleys, cirques, horns, or moraines) in lower elevations, you know that the climate there used to be colder. The effects of a warming climate have profoundly hit the glaciers of the Alps, which have lost at least a third of their volume since the 1950s. At that rate, some studies project that most here could virtually disappear by the end of the 21st century, affecting water storage and hydroelectric power generation, and making mountainsides less stable.

Another consequence of the warming climate is that winter weather no longer reliably produces snow at altitudes that it did in the past—which is bad news for Europe's huge ski industry. Seeing a future of ever-warmer winters, alpine resorts are putting their ingenuity to the test. This goes beyond snow machines: Many resorts are investing hugely in new spas, convention centers, and other attractions that don't require snow. Meanwhile, European governments strive to invest in environmentally friendly technologies in hopes of keeping their mountains white and their valleys green.

has vital weather reports and maps, as well as some English hiking guidebooks to consult. Ask to look at the trail guidebook (sold in many stores and at the TI, includes the helpful *Carte des Sentiers,* the region's hiking map).

At **Compagnie des Guides de Chamonix** on the ground floor, you can hire a mountaineering or climbing guide (about €220/half-day, €350/day, less per person for groups) to help you scale Mont Blanc, or hike to the Matterhorn and Zermatt (open daily 9:00-12:00 & 14:30-19:00, closed Sun-Mon off-season, tel.

FRENCH ALPS

Kids' Activities

Chamonix provides a wealth of fun opportunities for kids; ask the TI to suggest family-friendly activities. Here are a few options:

Parc de Loisirs des Planards: Chamonix's fun park for kids of all ages. It includes a luge (summer only) and a Parc d'Aventure with tree courses, Tarzan swings, trampolines, electric motorbikes, Jet Skis, and more (for details, see "Luge" listing under "Other Activities," later).

Piscine du Centre Sportif Richard Bozon: A large pool complex with a big waterslide, water garden, hot tub, and more (€6 for those 17 and under, €8 for adults, discount with Chamonix Guest Card, open June-early Sept Mon-Sat in the afternoon and all day Sun, closed early Sept-May).

Parc de Merlet: Animal sanctuary with trails that let you discover mountain animals (marmots, mountain goats, llamas, deer, and more). It's located in Coupeau above Les Houches, and comes with exceptional views (so parents get some scenery while kids get to see animals). You can get there by car (20-minute drive) or hike for two beautiful hours from Chamonix. If you drive, head to the very top parking lot, as you'll be hiking uphill for 20-30 minutes just to reach the entry. There's a lot more walking inside the park to find the animals—bring good shoes and water (€5 for kids 4-14, free for kids 3 and under, €8 for adults, view café with salads and regional dishes, no picnics allowed; July-Aug daily 9:30-19:30; May-June and Sept Tue-Sun 10:00-18:00, closed Mon and off-season; tel. 04 50 53 47 89, www.parcdemerlet.com).

04 50 53 00 88, www.chamonix-guides.com). Up a few steps is an adventure-sports office.

In this section, I describe three fairly strenuous hikes and three easier walks (see the "Chamonix-Area Hikes" map). Start early, when the weather's generally best. This is most important in summer as trails become more crowded as the day goes on. If hiking late in the day, confirm lift closing hours to avoid a long, steep hike down.

For your hike, bring sunglasses, sunscreen, rain gear, water, snacks, and maybe light gloves. Pack warm layers (mountain weather can change in a moment) and wear good shoes (trails are rocky and uneven). Take your time, watch your footing, don't take shortcuts, and say *"Bonjour!"* to your fellow hikers. Note that there's no shade on Hikes #1, #2, and #3.

▲▲Hike #1
Plan de l'Aiguille to Montenvers-Mer de Glace
(Le Grand Balcon Nord)

This three-hour hike (including breaks) is the most efficient way to incorporate a high-country adventure into your ride down from the valley's greatest lift, and check out a world-class glacier to boot. The spectacular, well-used trail rises but mostly falls (dropping 1,500 feet from Plan de l'Aiguille to Montenvers and the Mer de Glace) and is moderately difficult, provided the snow has melted (generally snow-covered until June; get trail details and conditions at

FRENCH ALPS

the Office de Haute-Montagne, listed earlier). A few stretches are steep and strenuous, with uneven footing and slippery rocks. Wear good shoes (hard soles are better) and watch your footing. Note the last train time from Montenvers-Mer de Glace back to Chamonix, or you'll be hiking another hour and a half straight down.

To experience this marvelous hike at its peaceful best, go early. In mid-July, I started the trail at 9:15 (after visiting the Aiguille du Midi) and didn't meet another hiker for over an hour. If you start very early, shade covers the trail for long stretches.

From the Aiguille du Midi lift, get off halfway down at Plan de l'Aiguille, *sortie* to the café/bar, then find signs leading down to *Montenvers-Mer de Glace*. Follow the main trail that is parallel to the gondola cables (avoid spur trails to the right). You'll drop steadily for 15 minutes down to a wonderful refuge (the recommended **Refuge-Plan de l'Aiguille,** good prices for meals and drinks), then go right, hiking the spectacularly scenic, undulating, and (for short periods) strenuous trail to Montenvers (overlooking the Mer de Glace glacier). Plan on lots of boulder-stepping and occasional stream crossings. Stop frequently to turn around and savor the views.

After hiking little more than an hour at a moderate yet steady

pace, the trail splits. Follow signs uphill to *Le Signal* (more scenic and easier), rather than to the left toward *Montenvers* (it looks easier, but becomes very difficult—and you miss the best views). At this point, you'll grind it out uphill for about 20 minutes, level off, and then climb more gradually to the

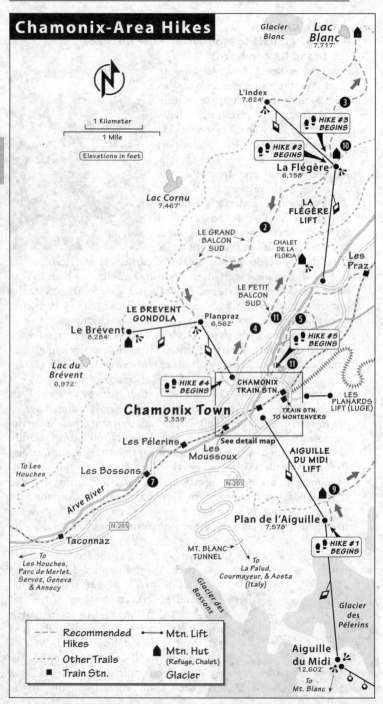

Chamonix-Area Hikes

Glacier Blanc

Lac Blanc 7,717'

L'Index 7,824'

HIKE #3 BEGINS ③

⑩

HIKE #2 BEGINS

La Flégère 6,158'

1 Kilometer
1 Mile

Elevations in feet

Lac Cornu 7,467'

LA FLÉGÈRE LIFT

② LE GRAND BALCON SUD

CHALET DE LA FLORIA

Les Praz

LE PETIT BALCON SUD

⑪ ⑤

LE BRÉVENT GONDOLA

Planpraz 6,562'

Le Brévent 8,284'

④

HIKE #5 BEGINS

⑪

Lac du Brévent 6,972'

HIKE #4 BEGINS

CHAMONIX TRAIN STN.

Chamonix Town 3,339'

TRAIN STN. TO MONTENVERS

LES PLANARDS LIFT (LUGE)

Les Pélerins

Les Moussoux

See detail map

AIGUILLE DU MIDI LIFT

To Les Houches

Les Bossons ⑦

⑨

Arve River

N-205

Plan de l'Aiguille 7,578'

HIKE #1 BEGINS

Taconnaz

MT. BLANC TUNNEL

To La Palud, Courmayeur, & Aosta (Italy)

To Les Houches, Parc de Merlet, Servoz, Geneva & Annecy

Glacier des Bossons

Glacier des Pélerins

Recommended Hikes
Other Trails
Train Stn.

Mtn. Lift
Mtn. Hut (Refuge, Chalet)
Glacier

Aiguille du Midi 12,602'

To Mt. Blanc

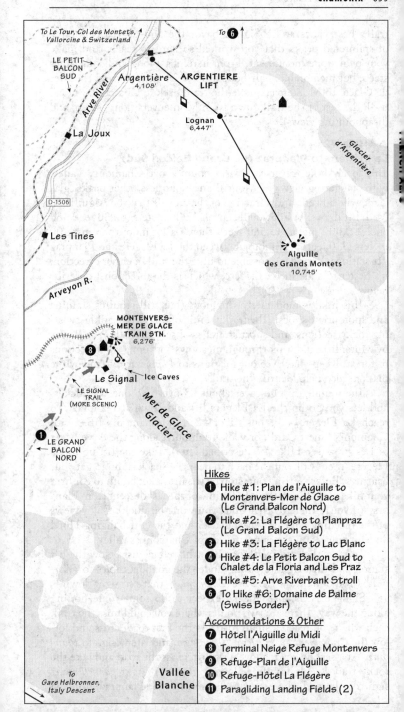

To Le Tour, Col des Montets, Vallorcine & Switzerland

To **6**

LE PETIT BALCON SUD

Arve River

Argentière 4,108'

ARGENTIERE LIFT

Lognan 6,447'

Glacier d'Argentière

La Joux

D-1506

Les Tines

Aiguille des Grands Montets 10,745'

Arveyon R.

MONTENVERS-MER DE GLACE TRAIN STN. 6,276'

8

Le Signal

Ice Caves

LE SIGNAL TRAIL (MORE SCENIC)

Mer de Glace Glacier

1

LE GRAND BALCON NORD

To Gare Helbronner, Italy Descent

Vallée Blanche

Hikes

1 Hike #1: Plan de l'Aiguille to Montenvers-Mer de Glace (Le Grand Balcon Nord)

2 Hike #2: La Flégère to Planpraz (Le Grand Balcon Sud)

3 Hike #3: La Flégère to Lac Blanc

4 Hike #4: Le Petit Balcon Sud to Chalet de la Floria and Les Praz

5 Hike #5: Arve Riverbank Stroll

6 To Hike #6: Domaine de Balme (Swiss Border)

Accommodations & Other

7 Hôtel l'Aiguille du Midi

8 Terminal Neige Refuge Montenvers

9 Refuge-Plan de l'Aiguille

10 Refuge-Hôtel La Flégère

11 Paragliding Landing Fields (2)

trail's best views at Le Signal. Savor the 360-degree panorama of splintered peaks that you worked so hard to reach, and make your own stone monument. From here, it's a long and sometimes steep, but memorable, half-hour drop to Montenvers and the Mer de Glace. In Montenvers, take the train back to Chamonix. Don't walk the rest of the trail down from Montenvers (long, steep, and disappointing views).

▲▲Hike #2
La Flégère to Planpraz (Le Grand Balcon Sud)

This lovely hike traverses for 2.5 hours above Chamonix Valley, with staggering views of Mont Blanc, countless other peaks, glaciers, wildflowers, and a fraction of the crowds that the Aiguille du Midi lift draws. While you'll start at 1,900 meters (6,230 feet) and end at 2,000 meters (6,560 feet), there's a lot more than just 100 meters (330 feet) of climbing between the La Flégère and Planpraz lift stations. While it's possible to hike the trail in either direction, it's better to start in La Flégère, which is the direction I describe below.

This hike is moderately strenuous (but still requires stamina and appropriate shoes). The trail is a mix of dirt paths, ankle-twisting rocky sections, and short stretches of service roads. You'll pass by winter lifts and walk through meadows and along small sections of forest. Keep your eyes out for signs to *Planpraz;* red-and-white markers also help identify the trail.

The round-trip rate saves about €3 over two one-way tickets and lets you go up the La Flégère lift and down at Planpraz. To reach La Flégère, take bus #1 or #2 from Chamonix (free with Chamonix Guest Card), or walk 40 minutes along the Arve River to Les Praz (see Hike #5, described later). Take the lift up to La Flégère, then walk out the back to near the snack stand to get your bearings. Before setting out, stop by the lift ticket booth to confirm your hike plan, the trail, and the time of the last descent from Planpraz (if you're there by that time, you won't be stuck). Enjoy views of the receding Mer de Glace glacier and the cliff-hanging Hôtel du Montenvers on the opposite side of Chamonix's valley.

To start the trail, walk down to the refuge just below the lift station and turn right, crossing under the gondola cables to *Planpraz.* (You don't want *Les Praz-Chamonix*—that's straight down.)

Signage is inconsistent, so expect to do some route-finding along the way. There are two points where you could miss the trail, each when you reach a small road. At the first road, cross and follow the *Croisement du Sentier à 100 m* sign, and later a sign to *Planpraz.* At a second road, above a ski lift, cross the road and take the rocky trail steeply uphill, following the *Le Brévent par Planpraz* sign. At the end, there's a steep climb to the (Planpraz) gondola station (great view cafés, parasailers, and a good history exhibit). Descend to Chamonix from here or take the gondola up to Le Brévent for more views.

▲▲Hike #3
La Flégère to Lac Blanc

This is the most demanding trail of those I list; it climbs steeply and steadily over a rough, boulder-strewn path for 2 hours to snowy Lac Blanc (pronounced "lock blah"). Some footing is tricky, and good shoes or boots are a must. I like this trail, as it gets you away from the valley edge and opens views to peaks you don't see from other hikes.

The destination is a snow-white lake framed by peaks and the nifty Refuge-Hôtel du Lac Blanc, which offers good lunches (and dinners, if you stay the night, summers only). The views on the return trip are breathtaking. Check for snow conditions on the trail (often a problem until July) and go early (particularly in summer), as there is no shade and this trail is popular.

Follow the directions for Hike #2 to La Flégère station, then walk out the station's rear door past the snack stand to get oriented. Track the trail as it drops way down to that winter chairlift station, then hooks hard left back up a steep hill. You can avoid this considerable down-and-up (and save 30 minutes) by taking the L'Index chairlift behind you (about €10 one-way, €11 round-trip, €30 from the base). Confirm that the trail from L'Index is free of snow, as this shortcut can be dicey, especially for kids. However you start, the trail is well-signed to Lac Blanc, and its surface improves as you climb.

▲Hike #4
Petit Balcon Sud to Chalet de la Floria and Les Praz

This trail runs above the valley on the Brévent side from the village of Les Houches to Argentière, passing Chamonix about halfway, and is handy when snow or poor weather make other hikes problematic. No lifts are required—just firm thighs for the climb up and down. Access paths link the trail to villages below. Once you're up, the trail rises and falls with some steep segments and uneven footing. The highlight of the trail is flower-covered **Chalet de la Floria** snack bar (allow one hour each way from Chamonix).

Reach the trail from Chamonix by starting at the Le Brévent gondola station (find signs to *Le Petit Balcon Sud*). Begin by walking along an asphalt road to the left of the lift leading uphill (on Chemin de la Pierre à Ruskin), which turns into a dirt road marked as the *Petit Balcon Sud* trail. After about 20 minutes on the dirt road, you'll see a *Petit Balcon Sud* sign pointing left and up a smaller trail. Bypass this turnoff (which doubles back above Chamonix with great views) and continue along the dirt road.

FRENCH ALPS

FRENCH ALPS

Winter Sports in Chamonix

Chamonix offers some of the best expert-level skiing in the world, a huge choice of terrain at reasonable prices (cheaper than Switzerland), access to lots of high-elevation runs (which means good snow and views), and great nightlife. Ski here for jaw-dropping views and a good balance between true mountaineer culture and touristy glitz.

The slopes are strung out along the valley for about 10 miles, so you must drive or catch the often-crowded shuttle buses to ski more than one area. There's also limitless *off-piste* (ungroomed) skiing, best explored with an experienced guide.

Nonskiers won't be bored. The lifts described in this chapter lead to top-notch views. Swimming, saunas, tennis, skating, and climbing are available at Chamonix's Centre Sportif. You can also relax in a spa, go bowling or dog-sledding, and hike along groomed winter footpaths.

When to Go
High season is usually from December to April. Chamonix is packed from Christmas through New Year's Day and busy February through April (during European winter and spring breaks). It's quieter in early December, in January after New Year's, and in May (Easter can be very busy). Thanks to easy access to high-elevation runs, you'll usually find good powder in late April and May, when it's less crowded. Chamonix is one of the great resorts for spring skiing, and you can usually find special spring package deals.

Tickets
Adult lift tickets covering Chamonix's three main areas, including the lower-elevation beginner areas, are about €53/day, €100/2 days, €145/3 days (longer options available, about 15 percent less for skiers older than 64 or younger than 16). Or consider the Mont Blanc Unlimited pass—covering all the areas in the Chamonix Valley (details on the websites listed later, under "Information").

Ski Rentals
Prices don't vary much, so go with something convenient to where you're staying and ask your hotel for deals with nearby shops. You'll pay about €15-26/day for skis and about €12/day for boots. **Technique Extrême** has the best deals on rentals and gear (tel. 04 50 53 38 25, 200 Avenue de l'Aiguille du Midi, www.technique-extreme.com). **Snell Sports** is a respected shop that's been around for many years (tel. 04 50 53 02 17, 104 Rue du Docteur Paccard, www.cham3s.com).

Where to Go
It's tough to find one area in Chamonix that offers a perfect mix of

FRENCH ALPS

terrain for every level of skier, but here's a rundown of Chamonix's key ski areas:

Le Brévent/La Flégère: A 10-minute walk from Chamonix's center, this area has one of the valley's better mixes of terrain. If you're staying in Chamonix and have just a day, ski Le Brévent/La Flégère. Runs are good for intermediates, with some expert options, but not great for beginners. You'll enjoy fantastic views of Mont Blanc.

Les Grands Montets: Above the village of Argentière (about 10 minutes from Chamonix by bus), this area is internationally renowned for its expert terrain (and killer views from the observation deck). Part of Les Grands Montets lies on the Argentière glacier, and there's plenty of vertical. Hire a local guide to explore the *off-piste* options.

Les Houches: A five-minute bus or train ride from Chamonix, Les Houches covers a large area with a variety of runs for most skill levels (good for families), but it has fewer expert options. This area is less crowded than other Chamonix Valley areas, and the tree skiing is good.

Domaine de Balme: The area above the nearby town of Le Tour offers good options for beginners, intermediates, and those looking for mellow cruising runs.

Lower Areas Good for Beginners: Le Savoy is at the bottom of Le Brévent, near Chamonix's center, with scads of kids and a few rope-tows. Les Planards is a short walk from the town center and the largest area for kids and beginners. These areas depend on good snow conditions.

The Vallée Blanche: This unique-to-Chamonix run starts on the sky-high Aiguille du Midi lift and takes you 13 miles down a glacier past astounding views and terrain to Montenvers (easy train back to Chamonix). It requires a lift ticket and hiring a guide or joining a group tour (figure about €320 for a private tour of up to 4 people, €25/additional person, maximum 6 people).

Ski Guides

You can hire a private guide for about €375 for your group or join another group. The Compagnie des Guides de Chamonix (CGC) puts together small groups for about €95/person (www.chamonix-guides.com, info@chamonix-guides.com). Groups can accommodate strong intermediate through advanced skiers. Guides also give experts the option to ski even more difficult terrain.

Information

For information about Chamonix and lift rates, check www.chamonix.com, www.leshouches.com, and www.montblancnaturalresort.com, or contact the Chamonix TI.

After about 30 more minutes, follow *la Floria* signs on a 20-minute round-trip detour to Chalet de la Floria, which has drinks, snacks, flowers, and magnificent views (daily mid-June-mid-Oct). From here, the trail continues above Les Praz to the north; junction trails lead back down to Chamonix or to Les Praz village. Following the junction trail to *Les Praz* eventually lands you on the main road; turn left to explore the village and to connect with the river trail back to Chamonix (the trail is immediately to the right after the bridge), or turn right on the road to reach the bus stop back to Chamonix (it takes bus #2 about 15 minutes to reach Les Praz from the time point posted in Le Tour; bus #1 starts a minute away at the Les Praz/La Flégère lift; and bus #21—summer only—starts about 17 minutes away at Col des Montets).

Hike #5
Arve Riverbank Stroll and Paragliding Landing Field

For a level, forested-valley stroll, bike ride, or jog, follow the Arve River toward Les Praz. At Chamonix's Hôtel Alpina, follow the path upstream past Chamonix's middle school, red-clay tennis courts, and find the green arrow to *Les Praz*. You'll cross a few bridges to the left, turn right along the rushing Arve River, and then follow Promenade des Econtres. Several trails loop through these woods; if you continue walking straight, you'll reach Les Praz in about an hour—an appealing destination with a number of cafés and a pleasing village green.

If you keep right after the tennis courts (passing piles of river sediment dredged to deter flooding), you'll come to a grassy landing field, signed *Parapente*, where paragliders hope to touch down. Walk to the top of the little grassy hill for fine Mont Blanc views and a great picnic spot.

Hike #6
Domaine de Balme—Hike to the Swiss Border

For a memorable and easy hike, consider this: Ride the local bus to Le Tour (free with Chamonix Guest Card, 2/hour, 25 minutes). From there, catch the gondola to Charamillon and from Charamillon a chairlift (€30 round-trip, lifts run about 9:00-17:00) takes you to Les Autannes at over 7,200 feet. At the top, it's an easy 20-minute walk in an alpine wonderland through meadows and past cows to the Swiss border at Col de Balme. There you'll find a stone marked with France on one side and Switzerland on the other and, nearby, a mountain hut. When you're ready to head back, backtrack the way you came and find the trail near the top of the chairlift. It's a one-hour hike down to the top of the gondola for the ride back down to Le Tour.

OTHER ACTIVITIES
▲Luge (Luge d'Eté)
Here's something for fun-seekers: Ride a plastic sled on rails up the hill, and then scream down a twisty, banked slalom course. Young or old, hare or tortoise, any fit person can manage a luge. *Freinez* signs tell you when to brake. The luge course is set in a grassy park with kids' play areas.

Cost and Hours: One ride-€7, six rides-€40, ask about double sleds, kids under 8 must ride with adult, entry includes all activities in Parc de Loisirs des Planards—see the "Kids' Activities" sidebar, earlier; generally July-Aug daily 10:00-18:30, mid-April-June and Sept-Oct Sat-Sun and select weekdays 13:30-18:00, check website for hours; 15-minute walk from town center, over the tracks from train station and past Montenvers train station; tel. 04 50 53 08 97, www.chamonixparc.com.

▲▲▲Paragliding (Parapente)
When it's sunny and clear, the skies above Chamonix sparkle with colorful parachute-like sails that circle the valley like birds of prey. For €110-120 plus the cost of the lift up to Planpraz (Le Brévent ski area) or Plan de l'Aiguille, you can launch yourself off a mountain in a tandem paraglider with a trained, experienced pilot and fly like a bird for about 20 minutes (true thrill-seekers can launch from Aiguille du Midi, €280, 40-minute ride). Most pilots will meet you at the lift station in Chamonix (usually from Le Brévent side, as it has the most reliable conditions, though you can ask them to fly you from Plan de l'Aiguille if you'll be there anyway and are pressed for time—not possible July-Aug). **Sean Potts** is English (no language barrier), has been paragliding in Chamonix for 25 years, and is easy to work with (www.fly-chamonix.com, info@fly-chamonix.com). You can also try **Summits Parapente** (smart to reserve a day ahead, open year-round, tel. 04 50 53 50 14, mobile 06 84 01 26 00, www.summits.fr).

For a sneak preview, walk to one of the two main landing areas and watch paragliders perfect their landings (see "Chamonix-Area Hikes—Hike #5," earlier).

RAINY-DAY OPTIONS
If the weather disagrees with your plans, stay cool and check out the following options.

Alpine Museum (Musée Alpin)
Situated in one of Chamonix's oldest "palaces," this place has good exhibits about Chamonix's evolution from a farming area to one focused on skiing. The museum shows off Chamonix's mountaineer-

ing, skiing, and mineralogical history (explanations in French only) and has exhibits on the first Winter Olympics, held right here.

Cost and Hours: €6, July-Aug daily 10:00-13:00 & 14:00-18:00, otherwise 14:00-18:00 and closed on Tue, 89 Avenue Michel Croz, tel. 04 50 53 25 93.

Espace Tairraz: Crystal Museum and Mountaineering Center (Musée des Cristaux and Espace Alpinisme)

The Espace Tairraz has two parts: a fascinating collection of crystals (with samples from all over the world in every color, shape, and size; get the English leaflet for some explanation), and a fascinating mountaineering museum covering the sport from 1786 to the present day. You'll learn of the great climbers through the ages, trace the evolution of mountain huts, and experience some of the best local ascents on video footage. The interactive climbing simulator is a hit with children and adults alike. Be aware that the center may be closed for renovations.

Cost and Hours: €6, daily 14:00-18:00, from 10:00 July-Aug, 615 Allée Recteur Payot, tel. 04 50 55 53 93.

Galerie Mario Colonel

One of Chamonix's most celebrated nature photographers displays his mesmerizing photographs of the scenery high above you. Don't miss the photos upstairs. These are so good you may not miss seeing the real thing.

Cost and Hours: Free, daily 10:00-12:30 & 15:00-19:30, no midday closure July-Aug, a block from the train station at 19 Rue Whymper, tel. 04 50 91 40 20, www.mario-colonel.com.

Day Trips near Chamonix

A Day in French-Speaking Switzerland

Plenty of tempting alpine and cultural thrills await just an hour or two away in Switzerland. A scenic road and rail route sneaks you from Chamonix to the Swiss town of Martigny. Train travelers cross without formalities, but drivers are charged a one-time fee of 40 Swiss francs (roughly €36) for a permit, known as a vignette, to use Swiss autobahns.

A Little Italy

The remote Valle d'Aosta and its historic capital city of Aosta offer a serious change of culture. The side trip is worthwhile if you'd like to taste Italy (spaghetti, gelato, and cappuccino), enjoy the town's great evening ambience, or view the ancient ruins in Aosta (often called the "Rome of the North").

Getting There: Take the spectacular lift (Aiguille du Midi–Helbronner—described earlier) to Italy. From Helbronner, ride the Skyway Monte Bianco lift, which stops at Pavillon du Mont Fréty on its way down to Pontal d'Entrèves (www.montebianco.com). It's an amazing ride—the gondola rotates 360 degrees as you sail along. From Pontal d'Entrèves, you can take the bus to Aosta (hourly, change in Courmayeur). Aosta's train station has connections to anywhere in Italy (about every 2 hours, usually on slow trains via Turin).

For a more down-to-earth experience, you can take the bus from Chamonix to Aosta via the Mont Blanc Tunnel. Flixbus offers good deals and comfort (www.flixbus.com); or try local SAT buses (about €20 one-way, €38 round-trip, reservation required in summer; 5/day July-mid-Sept; 2-3/day mid-Sept-June Mon-Sat, none Sun; 2 hours). Get schedules at 13 Avenue Michel Croz, near the Alpine Museum (tel. 04 50 53 00 95, www.sat-montblanc. com), or at Chamonix's bus station, 234 Avenue de Courmayeur. Drivers can travel straight through the Mont Blanc toll tunnel (one-way-€46, round-trip-€58 with return valid for 1 week, www. tunnelmb.com).

Sleeping in Chamonix

Reasonable hotels and dorm-like chalets abound in Chamonix, with easy parking and quick access from the train station. The TI can help you find budget accommodations anytime—either in person or by email (reservation@chamonix.com). Outside of winter, mid-July to August is most difficult, when some hotels have five-day minimum-stay requirements. Very few hotels offer air-conditioning, but most have elevators. Prices tumble off-season (outside July-Aug and Dec-Jan). Many hotels and restaurants are closed in May, June, and November, but you'll still find a room and a meal. If you want a view of Mont Blanc, ask for *côté Mont Blanc* (coat-ay mohn blah). Travelers who visit June through September should contemplate a night high above in a refuge-hotel.

Ask at your hotel about the free Chamonix Guest Card, which provides complimentary use of most buses and trains during your stay (described on page 822).

IN THE CITY CENTER
$$$ Hôtel Hermitage,**** a 10-minute walk from the town center, is a gorgeous chalet hotel with the coziest lounges in Chamonix and a lovely garden with views. It has a small bar, a small sauna, and 28 alpine-elegant rooms, all with balconies and reasonable prices considering the quality (big family rooms and suites, easy parking, closed mid-Sept-mid-Dec and mid-April-mid-June, near train station at 63 Chemin du Cé, tel. 04 50 53 13 87, www.hermitage-paccard.com, info@hermitage-paccard.com).

$$$ Grand Hôtel des Alpes**** rents top-comfort rooms in a grand old building with wads of character in Chamonix's traffic-free area. Rooms are big, cushy, and traditional, public spaces are wood-paneled cozy, and there's a garden terrace (private garage, 75 Rue du Docteur Paccard, tel. 04 50 55 37 80, www.grandhoteldesalpes. com, info@grandhoteldesalpes.com).

$$$ Le Génépy offers 10 apartments facing a central and peaceful courtyard just off Rue Joseph Vallot. Rooms are bright, modern, and well-designed with fully equipped kitchens. Apartments on the second and third floors come with views of Mont Blanc (arrange ahead for arrival after 19:00, 16 Impasse du Génépy, tel. 04 50 53 05 62, www.legenepy-chamonix.com, contact@legenepy-chamonix.com).

$$ Hôtel l'Oustalet*** is a chalet hotel warmly run by two sisters (Véronique and Agnès) who understand the importance of good service. The place is family-friendly, with lots of grass, a big pool, and six family suites. All rooms are wood-paneled, with views and balconies (terrific breakfast-€15, try the *teurgoule* rice pudding; sauna and Turkish bath, free and secure parking, near Aiguille du Midi lift at 330 Rue du Lyret, tel. 04 50 55 54 99, www.hotel-oustalet.com, infos@hotel-oustalet.com).

$$ Hôtel Gourmets et Italy*** is a 36-room place with comfy public spaces, a cool riverfront terrace, balcony views from many of its appealing rooms, and a small pool (some rooms with Mont Blanc view, family rooms, closed late April-early June and mid-Oct-mid-Dec, 2 blocks from casino on Mont Blanc side of river, 96 Rue du Lyret, tel. 04 50 53 01 38, www.hotelgourmets-chamonix. com, info@hotelgourmets-chamonix.com).

$$ Hôtel le Faucigny*** is peaceful with a Scandinavian feel and a welcoming vibe. This full-service hotel includes free loaner bikes, sauna and hot tub, and afternoon tea and treats in the linger-longer lounge. The front terrace provides a tranquil retreat with mountain views, and its 27 rooms are tight but comfortable and quite modern (great breakfast, no elevator, 118 Place de l'Eglise, tel. 04 50 53 01 17, www.hotelfaucigny-chamonix.com, reservation@hotelfaucigny-chamonix.com). The hotel also manages a beautiful chalet next door, $$$ Le Whymper, with 10 top-comfort rooms designed for small groups plus a pleasant central living room (rooms rented to individuals when not taken by groups, inquire at hotel, no elevator).

$$ Hôtel de l'Arve*** offers midrange comfort with a contemporary alpine feel in its 37 rooms, some right on the Arve River looking up at Mont Blanc, most with balconies. This hotel comes with a fireplace lounge, a pool table, a pleasant garden, a sauna, a climbing wall, and easy, free parking. Check their website for deals (family rooms, several "apartments" ideal for families, 60 Impasse

des Anémones, tel. 04 50 53 02 31, www.hotelarve-chamonix.com, reservation@hotelarve-chamonix.com).

$ Hôtel le Chamonix,** across from the TI and above a café, has simple alpine charm, with 16 paneled rooms at fair rates and no elevator. The rooms facing Mont Blanc have great views, are larger and brighter, and have little balconies...but also attract noise from *le café* below, which closes late on weekends (breakfast extra, 11 Rue de l'Hôtel de Ville, tel. 04 50 53 11 07, www.hotel-le-chamonix. com, hotel-le-chamonix@wanadoo.fr).

¢ Chalet Ski Station, filling a 300-year-old building, is a spartan but clean hostel that bustles with youthful energy. Gentle Veronique rents 44 beds to a young and sporty crowd who don't mind the steep 10-minute climb above town to the base of the Le Brévent gondola (self-serve kitchen, 6 Route des Moussoux, tel. 04 50 53 20 25, www.hostel-skistation-chamonix.com, chaletskistation@wanadoo.fr).

¢ Le Vagabond Gîtes offers the best cheap digs in Chamonix in a fun chalet just south of the town center. Dorm rooms have bunks, with basic showers and toilets down the hall; all rooms have sinks. The top floor has one family room. The staff is a mix of British expats, and the feel is relaxed, with a bar and outside terrace (private rooms available, includes breakfast, reception closed 10:00-16:30, 305 Avenue Ravanel le Rouge, tel. 04 50 53 15 43, www.gitevagabond.com, info@vaga.eu).

NEAR CHAMONIX

If Chamonix overwhelms you, spend the night in one of the valley's often-overlooked, lower-profile villages.

$$$ Hôtel l'Aiguille du Midi,*** a mountain retreat, lies near the train station in the village of Les Bossons, about two miles from Chamonix toward Annecy. It's run by the English-speaking Farini family in a parklike setting with point-blank views of Mont Blanc and the Bossons Glacier. This family-friendly place has a swimming pool, a clay tennis court, table tennis, a massage room, and a laundry room to boot. Most of the alpine-comfortable rooms come with modern bathrooms, many have decks with views, and several are good for families. A few budget rooms *(chambres économique)* lack views but have access to all the amenities. The classy restaurant offers à la carte and *menu* options, with *menus* from €35 (RS%, family rooms, elevator, easy by train, get off at Les Bossons, tel. 04 50 53 00 65, www.hotel-aiguilledumidi.com, info@hotel-aiguilledumidi.com).

REFUGES AND REFUGE-HOTELS NEAR CHAMONIX

Chamonix has the answer for hikers who want to sleep high above, but aren't into packing it in: refuge-hotels (generally open mid-June to mid- or late Sept, depending on snow levels). Refuge-hotels usually have some private rooms (but mostly dorm rooms), hot showers down the hall, and restaurants. Most require you to take dinner and breakfast there (a great value, and you don't have many alternatives anyway). Reserve in advance (a few days is generally enough), then pack a small bag for a memorable night among new international friends. The **Office de Haute-Montagne** in Chamonix can explain your options (see page 834).

$$ Terminal Neige Refuge Montenvers, Chamonix's oldest and classiest refuge, was built in 1880 as a simple climbing base for mountain guides before the train went there. Today's 16 wood-cozy rooms have been restored to their original look, and there's a 10-bed dorm room with comfy sleeping nooks. The dining room has alpine character, and the terrace tables have the views (at the Montenvers train stop, May-Sept & Nov-Dec, half-board required but reasonable, tel. 04 57 74 74 74, http://refuge.terminal-neige.com, contact@tn-refuge.com). For directions, see "Hike #1" on page 837.

¢ **Refuge-Plan de l'Aiguille** is a wonderful experience near Chamonix. It's a small, welcoming, fairly easy-to-reach refuge a 15-minute walk below the Plan de l'Aiguille lift, right on the trail between the Aiguille du Midi and Montenvers-Mer de Glace. It has a warm interior and a **$** café/restaurant with a killer view. The friendly cook and guardian Claude is a retired pastry chef, so the meals are good and the desserts heavenly (some private rooms, half-board required but reasonable, open May-late Oct, mobile 06 65 64 27 53, http://refuge-plan-aiguille.com, claudius74@hotmail.com).

¢ **Refuge-Hôtel La Flégère** hangs on the edge right at the La Flégère lift station. It's simple and big, but ideally located for hiking to Lac Blanc or Planpraz (open mid-June-mid-Sept only, fireplace, cool bar-café, mobile 06 03 58 28 14, www.autourdumontblanc.com, bellay.catherine@wanadoo.fr). For directions, see "Hike #2" on page 840.

Eating in Chamonix

You have plenty of dining options in Chamonix: cozy, traditional *savoyard* restaurants serving classic local dishes; rustic sports bars with typical brasserie fare; big, kitschy family-friendly eateries that smell like cheese from all the fondue and raclette they serve; and trendy, modern foodie haunts. You can sit on a terrace overlooking the rushing river or on the main square watching the steady stream of outdoor enthusiasts. Restaurants seek to satisfy ravenous hikers with the hearty and filling regional cuisine. The most popular beer is the local Mont Blanc amber (Rousse de Mt. Blanc), and water is free for the asking. Menus are often similar—it's the atmosphere that varies. Most restaurants open by 18:00 or serve nonstop, making early dinners easy.

IN THE TOWN CENTER

$$$ Atmosphère Restaurant is serious and pricey, but a fair value. Dressy and jazzy with a white-tablecloth ambience, they serve a mix of *savoyard* and French cuisine from an elegant menu. In high season two dinner seatings are offered on their long, skinny riverfront terrace: 19:15 and 21:15. To get a table literally over the torrent, make a reservation; skip this place if you can't dine riverside (daily, 123 Place Balmat, tel. 04 50 55 97 97, www.restaurant-atmosphere.com).

$$ Restaurant Bizes (Little Kisses) is a cool little place popular with foodies, offering fine dining (inside and out) in a small modern spot right on the rushing river. While they are enthusiastic about vegetarian and gluten-free dishes, they also do lots of grilling in their charcoal oven. With modern international dishes (ranging from smoked prawns to chicken curry), this place offers a fun break from heavy traditional fare (daily, 64 Rue du Lyret, tel. 09 51 92 25 03).

$$$ La Calèche is a kitschy, touristy, and traditional place with a fun, family-friendly energy, reasonable prices, and wild boars and stuffed birds on the walls. If you want to eat fondue or raclette (served in the traditional way) and feel like you're in an alpine museum (find the luge from the Chamonix 1924 Olympic Games), this is it. It's often still hopping when other places have closed for the night (daily, centrally located just off Place Balmat at 18 Rue du Docteur Paccard, tel. 04 50 55 94 68).

$ Elevation 1904 is a down-and-dirty climbers' haunt across from the train station, serving cheap and tasty sandwiches, burgers, pasta, and salads (daily until about 22:00, 263 Avenue Michel Croz, tel. 04 50 53 00 52).

$$ Bistrot des Sports is where you'll feel like you're hanging out with the locals. The lively bar has a fun energy, and the big back room is a casual, family-friendly restaurant with a French brasserie menu featuring big salads, regional specialties and fondue, pastas, and vegetarian dishes. Local craft beers, an enticing wine list, and plenty of wines by the glass add to the conviviality of the place. While you can sit outside, I'd come here to eat in (daily, kitchen closes at 21:30, 176 Rue Joseph Vallot, tel. 04 50 53 00 46).

$ Le Chamonix Bar-Café is a classic café with a cheap and accessible menu. Sitting below Chamonix's pretty little church (facing the TI) with terrific mountain views, they serve simple, tasty light meals. Their *tartine* (hot open-faced sandwiches) and *café gourmand* (coffee with a selection of desserts) are a hit (daily until 21:00, cash only, Place de l'Eglise, tel. 04 50 53 32 14).

$ La Maison du Burger is a simple takeout joint with a few plastic tables on the pedestrian street right downtown. They serve a fun array of burgers, toasted sandwiches, and crêpes—both sweet and savory (daily until 23:00, across from the recommended La Calèche restaurant).

Dining Well with a View: While many eateries offer great views, most serve mediocre food at inflated prices. Dining at a café on Place Balmat (by the statues), you'll hear the rush of the Arve River and have great views of mountains and people. But you can do better, so consider these places:

$$ La Tablée is my go-to place for a fine meal at good prices—even without its view of Mont Blanc (from its busy terrace tables). You'll find a mix of carefully prepared regional and traditional cuisine, and great salads. The interior is warm and the service is excellent (good *menu* deals, come early to land an outside table, opens at 18:00, daily, 75 Avenue de l'Aiguille du Midi, tel. 04 50 53 31 23).

$$ Le Boccalatte Brasserie sits just above La Tablée and is more about dishing fill-the-tank food than fine cuisine. Hardworking Thierry (from Alsace) serves meals in a casual interior and on a big, easygoing view terrace. The *tartiflette* with salad will fill you up, or choose from a large selection of salads, pizzas, and such. They have a good beer selection on tap, including Rousse de Mt. Blanc (daily 12:00-22:00, 59 Avenue de l'Aiguille du Midi, tel. 04 50 53 52 14).

$$ La Télécabine sits in a quiet corner and delivers a classy, peaceful experience. Just off the tourist center, it boasts a large selection of well-presented cuisine served on a spacious terrace with old gondolas and terrific Mont Blanc views (daily, next to the Casino at 27 Rue de la Tour, tel. 04 50 47 04 66).

$$$ Cap Horn offers a special experience only if you land a table on its riverfront terrace (behind the restaurant's main entry). The setting is elegant, the views beautiful, and the river serenades your dinner (large selection of *savoyard* and French dishes, daily, 74 Rue des Moulins, tel. 04 50 21 80 80).

Away from the Pedestrian Center: $$$ L'Impossible, housed in a beautiful farmhouse a 10-20-minute walk from most recommended hotels, is *the* place to go for refined organic cuisine with an Italian bias. This place offers gluten-free, lactose-free, and fat-free (well, maybe not) dishes without sacrificing flavor. Even if eating healthfully doesn't boost your boots, you'll appreciate the exquisite meals and attention to detail. Papa (who hails from Tuscany) cooks, while Mama serves (closed Tue except July-Aug,

5-minute walk from Aiguille du Midi lift on Route des Pélerins, tel. 04 50 53 20 36).

Après **Hike: Bistrot des Sports** is where locals hang their ice axes after a hard day in the mountains. Drinks are cheap, local beers are on tap, the crowd is loud, and the ambience works (see listing earlier for food).

Le Pub is aptly named and a good spot to raise a glass with the British crowd (225 Rue du Docteur Paccard, tel. 04 50 55 92 88).

La Maison des Artistes, in the park behind the casino, is the latest addition to the music scene in Chamonix. Started by popular French musician André Manoukian, it has a recording room and offers free concerts, mainly jazz (closed Sun-Mon all year and in May & Oct, 84 Chemin de la Tournette, www.maisondesartistes-chamonix.com).

Chamonix Connections

Bus and train service to Chamonix is surprisingly good. Some train routes pass through Switzerland to reach Chamonix (such as from Paris and Colmar) and require supplements if you have a France-only rail pass. You can avoid passing through Switzerland if you plan ahead, but it usually takes longer, and you miss some great scenery. The **route to Colmar** (via Bern and Basel) is beautiful and costs roughly €60 for the Swiss supplement. You'll get a fun taste of Switzerland's charms, and, though you'll make many transfers en route, they all work like a Swiss clock.

Chamonix's **bus station** is a few blocks from the Aiguille du Midi lift station at 234 Avenue de Courmayeur (Mon-Fri 8:15-12:00 & 14:00-17:15, daily with longer hours in high season, tel. 04 50 53 05 55). Flixbus, Ouibus, and Eurolines serve this station, as do some airport buses and shuttles. You'll also find an information office for regional SAT buses (Mon-Fri 9:00-12:00 & 14:30-18:30, tel. 04 50 53 00 95, www.sat-montblanc.com).

From Chamonix by Train to: Annecy (10/day, 2.5 hours, change in St-Gervais), **Lyon** (6/day, 4 hours), **Beaune** and **Dijon** (7/day, 7 hours, several changes), **Nice** (4/day, 10 hours, change in St-Gervais and Lyon), **Arles** (5/day, 7-8 hours, change in St-Gervais and Lyon), **Paris'** Gare de Lyon (7/day, more in summer and winter, 5.5-7 hours, some change in Switzerland), **Colmar** (hourly, 6 hours via Switzerland with 3-6 changes), **Martigny,** Switzerland (nearly hourly, 2 hours, scenic trip), **Geneva,** Switzerland and its airport (roughly hourly, 4 hours, 2 changes).

From Chamonix by Bus to: Geneva Airport (5/day, about 1.5 hours on Ouibus, www.ouibus.com; 4/day on Swisstours, www.stts.ch), **Paris** (check Eurolines for great deals on a night bus, www.eurolines.fr), **Courmayeur,** Italy (check Flixbus, www.flixbus.

com, or SAT buses 2-5/day, 45 minutes, reservation required in summer), **Aosta,** Italy (5/day in summer, fewer off-season and none on Sun, 2 hours, reservation required in summer, SAT buses). For more on buses to Italy, see "Day Trips near Chamonix," earlier.

From Chamonix to Geneva Airport by Shuttle: Mountain Dropoffs is a reliable outfit (www.mountaindropoffs.com); **Alpybus** is another good shuttle service with similar rates (www.alpybus.com). You can also try **Taxi Alpin** (mobile 06 64 93 44 22, www.taxialpin.fr).

BURGUNDY

Beaune • Burgundy Wine Villages • Abbey of Fontenay •
Vézelay • Château de Guédelon • Bourges • Cluny • Taizé

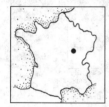

The rolling hills of Burgundy gave birth to superior wine, fine cuisine, spicy mustard, and sleepy villages smothered in luscious landscapes. This deceptively peaceful region witnessed Julius Caesar's defeat of the Gauls, then saw the Abbey of Cluny rise from the ashes of the Roman Empire to vie with Rome for religious influence in the 12th century. Burgundy's last hurrah came in the 15th century, when its powerful dukes controlled an immense area stretching north to Holland.

Today, bucolic Burgundy (roughly the size of Belgium) runs from about Auxerre in the north to near Lyon in the south. Crisscrossed with canals and dotted with quiet farming villages, it's also the transportation funnel for eastern France and makes a convenient stopover for travelers (car or train), with easy access north to Paris or Alsace, east to the Alps, and south to Provence.

Traditions are strong. In Burgundy, both the soil and the farmers who work it are venerated. Although many of the farms you see are growing grapes, only a small part of Burgundy is actually covered by vineyards.

This is a calm, cultivated, and serene region, where nature is as sophisticated as the people. If you're looking for quintessential French culture, you'll find it in Burgundy.

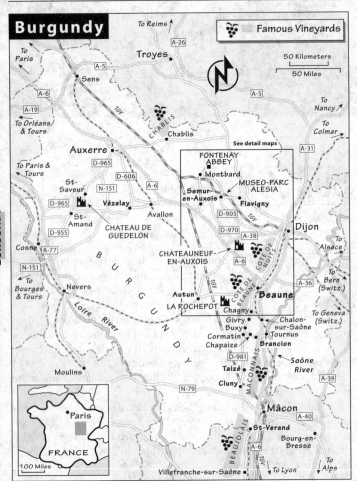

PLANNING YOUR TIME

With limited time, stay in or near Beaune. If you only have one day, spend the morning in Beaune and the afternoon exploring the surrounding vineyards and wine villages (good by bike, car, or minibus tour). If you have a car (cheap rentals are available), or good legs and a bike, the best way to spend your afternoon is by following my scenic vineyard drive to Château de la Rochepot.

With more time, visit unspoiled Flavigny-sur-Ozerain, the museum dedicated to the historic victory that won Gaul for Julius Caesar (in Alise-Ste-Reine), and France's best-preserved medieval abbey complex at Fontenay. These are close to each other and on the way to Paris, or doable as a long day trip from Beaune. The soul-stirring church at Vézelay is more famous but harder to reach, and

Burgundy at a Glance

▲▲**Beaune** Prosperous little wine capital and home to a land-mark medieval hospital that's now a fine museum. See page 860.

▲▲**Wine Villages and Vineyard Loops** Beautiful routes connecting wine villages, with plenty of tasting opportunities, pleasantly reachable by car or bike. See page 882.

▲▲**Between Burgundy and the Loire** Route linking the Romanesque hilltop church at Vézelay, the stained-glass wonders of Bourges Cathedral, and a medieval castle being built today—with 13th-century technology. See page 907.

▲**Between Beaune and Paris** Route linking Châteauneuf-en-Auxois (castle town), Alise-Ste-Reine (Roman battle site), and Fontenay (medieval abbey). See page 898.

▲**Between Beaune and Lyon** Romanesque churches and villages such as Brancion; the Middle Ages' most powerful abbey at Cluny; and a modern religious center at Taizé. See page 919.

is best done as an overnight trip, or en route to Paris or the Loire Valley. If you're connecting Burgundy with the Loire, don't miss the medieval castle construction at Guédelon and the fine "High" Gothic cathedral in Bourges (either of these pairs well with Vézelay). And if you're driving between Beaune and Lyon, take the detour to adorable Brancion and once-powerful Cluny, then head south along the Beaujolais wine route.

For up-to-date information on accommodations, restaurants, events, and shopping, see www.burgundyeye.com.

GETTING AROUND BURGUNDY

Trains link Beaune with Dijon to the north and Lyon to the south; some stop in the wine villages of Meursault, Nuits-St-Georges, Gevrey-Chambertin, and Santenay. Several buses per day cruise between vineyards north of Beaune on D-974, though precious few buses connect Beaune with villages to its south (see "Beaune Connections" on page 881). Bikes, hikes, minibus tours, and short taxi rides get you from Beaune into the countryside without a car. Drivers enjoy motoring on Burgundy's lovely roads; you'll cruise along canals, past manicured vineyards, and on tree-lined lanes. Navigate using the excellent (and free) map of the region available at all TIs.

BURGUNDY'S CUISINE SCENE

Arrive hungry. Considered by many to be France's best, Burgundian cuisine is peasant cooking elevated to an art. Entire lives are spent debating the best restaurants and bistros.

Several classic dishes were born in Burgundy: *escargots de Bourgogne* (snails served sizzling hot in garlic butter), *bœuf bourguignon*

(beef simmered for hours in red wine with onions and mushrooms), coq au vin (rooster stewed in red wine), and *œufs en meurette* (poached eggs in a red wine sauce, often served on a large crouton), as well as the famous Dijon mustards. Look also for delicious *jambon persillé* (cold ham layered in a garlic-parsley gelatin), *pain d'épices* (spice bread), and *gougères* (light, puffy cheese pastries). Those white cows (called Charolais) dotting the green pastures are Burgundian and make France's best steak and *bœuf bourguignon*.

Native cheeses are Époisses and Langres (both mushy and great), and my favorite, Montrachet (a tasty goat cheese). Crème de cassis (black currant liqueur) is another Burgundian specialty; look for it in desserts and snazzy drinks (try a *kir*).

BURGUNDY'S WINES

Along with Bordeaux, Burgundy is why France is famous for wine. From Chablis to Beaujolais, you'll find great fruity reds, dry whites, and crisp rosés. The

three key grapes are chardonnay (dry white wines), pinot noir (medium-bodied red wines), and gamay (light, fruity red wines, such as Beaujolais). Sixty percent of the wines are white, thanks to the white-only impact of the Chablis and Mâcon regions.

The Romans brought wine-making knowledge with them to Burgundy more than 2,000 years ago; medieval monks perfected the art a thousand years later, establishing the foundations for Burgundy's famous wines. Those monks determined that pinot noir and chardonnay grapes grew best with the soil and climate in this region, a lesson that is followed to the letter by winemakers today. The French Revolution put capitalists in charge of the vineyards (no longer a monkish labor of love), which led to quantity over quality and a loss of Burgundy's esteemed status. Phylloxera insects destroyed most of Burgundy's vines in the late 1800s, and forced growers to rethink how and where to best cultivate grapes in Burgundy. This led to a return of the monks' approach, with the veneration of pinot noir and chardonnay grapes, a focus on quality over quantity, and a big reduction in the land area devoted to vines.

Today the government controls how much farmers can produce (to sustain high quality). This has a huge effect—in Burgundy, the average yield is only about 40 hectoliters per hectare (about 1,000 gallons), whereas in California it's more than double that. There are about 4,200 wineries in 44 villages in Burgundy. (I review about a third of them in this chapter—it's a dirty job...) The wineries are tiny here (12-15 acres on average) thanks to Napoleon, who decided that land should be equally divided among a family's children when parents died. It's not unusual for a farmer to own just a few rows in a vineyard and piece together enough parcels to make a go of it.

In Burgundy, location is everything, and winery names take a back seat to the place where the grape is grown. Every village produces its own distinctive wine, from Chablis to Meursault to Chassagne-Montrachet. Road maps read like fine-wine lists. If the wine village has a hyphenated name, the second half usually comes from the town's most important vineyard (such as Gevrey-Chambertin, Aloxe-Corton, and Vosne-Romanée).

Burgundy wines are divided into four classifications: From top to bottom you'll find *grand cru, premier cru* (or *1er cru*), *village*, and *Bourgogne*. Each level allows buyers to better pinpoint the quality and origin of the grapes in their wine. With *Bourgogne* wines, the grapes can come from anywhere in Burgundy; *village* identifies the exact village where they were grown; and *grand cru* and *premier cru* locate the precise plots of land. As you drop from top to bottom, production increases—there is far more *Bourgogne* made than *grand cru*. In general, the less wine a vine produces, the higher the quality.

Look for *Dégustation Gratuite* (free tasting) signs, and prepare for serious wine tasting—and steep bottle prices, if you're not careful. For a more easygoing tasting experience, head for the hills: The less prestigious Hautes-Côtes (upper slopes) produce some terrific, inexpensive, and overlooked wines. The least expensive wines are Bourgogne and Passetoutgrain (both red) and whites from the Mâcon and Chalon areas (St-Véran whites are also a good value). If you like rosé, try Marsannay, considered one of France's best. And *les famous* Pouilly-Fuissé grapes are grown near the city of Mâcon. For tips on tasting, see the sidebar on page 872.

Beaune

You'll feel comfortable right away in this prosperous, popular, and perfectly French little wine capital, where life centers on the production and consumption of the prestigious Côte d'Or wines. *Côte d'Or* means "Gold Coast" (from when the sea covered the valley in the Jurassic era). Today, Burgundy's "gold coast" is a spectacle to enjoy in late October as the leaves turn around Beaune.

Medieval monks and powerful dukes of Burgundy laid the groundwork that established this town's prosperity. The monks cultivated wine and cheese, and the dukes cultivated power. A ring road (with a bike path) follows the foundations of the medieval walls, and parking lots just outside keep most traffic from seeping into the historic center. One of the world's most important wine auctions takes place here every year during the third weekend of November.

Orientation to Beaune

Beaune is compact (pop. 22,000), with a handful of interesting monuments and vineyards knocking at its door. Focus your Beaune ramblings on the town center, lassoed within its medieval walls and circled by a one-way ring road, and leave time to stroll into the vineyards. All roads and activities converge on the town's two squares, Place Carnot and Place de la Halle. Beaune is quiet on Sundays and Monday mornings. The city's monuments are beautifully lit at night, making Beaune ideal for a post-dinner stroll. The lighting gets downright dazzling from June to September, when a glimmering light show called "Les Chemins de Lumières" plays on seven important buildings (ask at TI or hotel for map).

TOURIST INFORMATION

The **main TI** is located across from the post office on the ring road's southeastern corner (look for the *Porte Marie de Bourgogne* sign above the doorway; daily June-Sept 9:00-19:00, April-May and Oct until 18:30, Nov-March 9:00-12:30 & 13:30-18:00, closes earlier Sun year-round; tel. 03 80 26 21 30, www.beaune-tourisme. fr). A small **TI annex** (called "Point-I") is in the market hall, across from Hôtel Dieu (daily 9:30-13:00 & 14:00-18:00).

Both TIs have extensive information on wine tasting in the area, a list of *chambres d'hôtes*, bus schedules, and an excellent, free regional road map. (Free bike maps are available, but the bike-rental shop probably has better ones.) The main TI rents audioguides (€5, 1.5 hours) and can also arrange a local guide (figure €200/4 hours, €350/all day, reserve ahead, guides@beaune-toursime.fr, or see my recommendations later). Don't miss the **Maison des Climats** display at the main TI (described under "Sights in Beaune," later).

The TI offers small discounts on some key sights in Burgundy (including the Abbey of Fontenay and Château of Clos Vougeot) and some wine cellars (including the recommended Patriarche Père et Fils). Buy tickets at the TI or online.

For a shortcut into Beaune's center from the main TI, walk out the back door, cross a small street, angle right, turn left through a long courtyard, and land on Place Carnot.

ARRIVAL IN BEAUNE

By Train: To reach the city center from the train station (no baggage storage), walk straight out of the station up Avenue du 8 Septembre, cross the busy ring road, and continue up Rue du Château. Follow it as it angles left and pass to the left of the mural, veering right onto Rue des Tonneliers. A left on Rue de l'Enfant leads to Beaune's pedestrian zone, Place Carnot, and the TI annex.

By Bus: Beaune has no bus station—only several stops along the ring road (see map on page 864 for stop locations). Ask the driver for *le Centre-Ville*. The Jules Ferry (zhul fair-ee) stop is the most central. (For details on bus service, see "Getting Around the Beaune Region" on page 882.)

By Car: Follow *Centre-Ville/Place de la Madeleine* signs and park for free in Place Madeleine (turnover is quick). The free Parking du Jardin Anglais at the north end of the ring road (see map on page 864) usually has spaces, and there are free parking spots all along the ring road. Parking inside Beaune's ring road is metered from 9:00 to 12:30 and 14:00 to 19:00; there's a convenient pay parking garage next to the main TI on the ring road.

HELPFUL HINTS

Market Days: Beaune hosts a smashing Saturday market and a meager Wednesday market. Both are on Place de la Halle and run until 12:30. The Saturday market fires up much of the old town and is worth planning ahead for. For either market, watch the action from the **Baltard Café** on Place de la Halle, then do as the locals do and have lunch at an outdoor café (see "Eating in Beaune," later, for ideas; sit down by 12:30 or forget it).

Supermarkets: Supermarché Casino has several small shops in Beaune, a store in the town center (next to 10 Rue Carnot), and a mothership store through the arch off Place Madeleine (daily 8:30-19:30 except closed Sun afternoon).

Laundry: Beaune's lone launderette is open daily 7:00-21:00 (65 Rue Lorraine).

BURGUNDY

Beaune's Best Wine and Food Stores

Beaune overflows with wine boutiques eager to convince you that their food products or wines are best. Here are a few to look for (to locate these, see the map on page 864).

The wine shop **Denis Perret** offers a good selection in all price ranges, though most are from large merchants (*négociants*). They can chill a white for your picnic and offer informal tastings by the glass, with some *grands crus* (Mon-Sat 9:00-12:00 & 14:00-19:00, Sun 14:00-19:00 except Oct-mid-April closed Sun, on Place Carnot, tel. 03 80 22 35 47, www.denisperret.fr).

For an exquisite selection of fruit liqueurs (such as crème de cassis—a Burgundian treat), fruit syrups, and Burgundian brandy, find **Védrenne** at 28 Rue Carnot (closed Sun afternoon).

For food, **Alain Hess** offers an elegant display of local cheeses, mustards, and other gourmet products (7 Place Carnot). At the corner, **Mulot-Petitjean Pain d'Epices** shows off exquisite packages of this tasty local spice bread, also handy as gifts (1 Place Carnot).

Bike Rental: See "Getting Around the Beaune Region—By Bike" on page 882.

Taxi: Call 06 11 83 06 10 or 06 09 35 63 12.

Car Rental: ADA is close to the train station (Mon-Sat 8:00-12:00 & 14:00-18:00, closed Sun, 26 Avenue du 8 Septembre, tel. 03 80 22 72 90). **Hertz** is outside the center at 52 Route de Serre (tel. 03 55 87 05 50). **Europcar** is also on the outskirts (53 Route de Pommard, tel. 03 80 22 32 24).

Beaune Greeters: The TI can arrange to have an English-speaking local show you their city for free. These kind folks donate their time in the hopes of helping travelers better appreciate their Burgundian home.

Best Souvenir Shopping: The **Athenaeum** has a great variety of souvenirs, wine and cookbooks in English, and a good children's section. They also offer informal wine tastings (three tastes-€5-15, daily 10:00-19:00, across from Hôtel Dieu at 7 Rue de l'Hôtel Dieu). **Le Vigneron** is another good place crammed with local products and clever Burgundian souvenirs (daily 9:00-19:00, just off Place Carnot at 6 Rue d'Alsace).

Tours in and Around Beaune

Tourist Train

A TGV-esque little "Visiotrain" putts around Beaune and nearby vineyards (€7.50, runs April-Oct 11:00-17:30, almost hourly departures from Hôtel Dieu, no morning trips on Wed and Sat market days, 45 minutes, waits for 10 people before it starts).

Local Guides

You have several great choices for walking or driving tours.

Kelly Kamborian is an effective teacher who trained as an archaeologist in the US. She has 20 years of experience guiding walking tours of Beaune, Dijon, and beyond, as well as driving tours of the region (€250/half-day, €380/day, mobile 06 63 41 21 10, kellykamborian@gmail.com).

For tours that focus on vineyards and Burgundian history, **Colette Barbier** is an engaging guide who is fluent in English and passionate about her region. Recently retired from the University of Burgundy, where she taught the history of gastronomy and wines for more than 25 years, she knows Burgundy as only a local can (her family has lived in the region for 250 years). Book well in advance (€300/half-day, €550/day, tel. 03 80 23 94 34, mobile 06 80 57 47 40, www.burgundy-guide.com, colettewinetour@gmail.com).

Delightful and wine-smart **Stephanie Jones** came from her native Britain to Burgundy to get a degree in oenology while working in Burgundian wine cellars. Today she leads informative, enjoyable, private tours of the vineyards (RS%: see website for rates, code: RS2020; prices are per person and decrease with more people, 2-person minimum, 6-person maximum; tel. 03 80 61 29 61, mobile 06 10 18 04 12, www.burgundywinetours.fr, stephnwine@aol.com).

Robert Pygott, British by birth but Burgundian by choice, offers relaxed and informative tours exploring Burgundy wines (€240-320/day, mobile 06 38 53 15 27, www.burgundydiscovery.com, robert@burgundydiscovery.com).

Minibus, Biking, and Walking Tours of Vineyards

Several outfits offer half- and all-day tours of the villages and vineyards around Beaune. Half-day tours generally provide just one tasting while all-day tours include three or more.

Likable Florian Garcenot at **Bourgogne Evasion/Active Tours** offers walking or biking tours into the vineyards and rents all sorts of bikes that can be delivered to your hotel. Some of his bike tours follow routes similar to those I describe later (see "Vineyard Loops near Beaune" on page 889), and include wine tastings and sightseeing. On the full-day bike tour, you'll be shuttled up to Château de la Rochepot and then sail downhill back to Beaune, stopping for lunch and at a few wineries (half-day walks from €20, 6-person minimum; half-day bike tour-€39, full-day bike tour-€137 including lunch; mobile 09 67 03 40 59, www.burgundybiketour.com, info@active-tours.fr).

Chemins de Bourgogne runs fun and informative tours, with

BURGUNDY

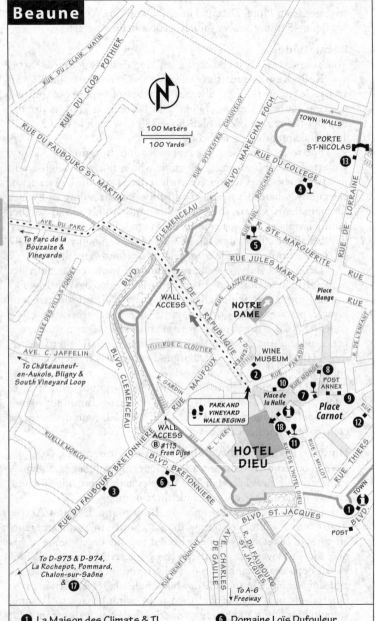

Beaune

N

100 Meters
100 Yards

1 La Maison des Climats & TI
2 Museum of the Wine of Burgundy
3 The Mustard Mill
4 Patriarche Père et Fils
5 Sensation Vin

6 Domaine Loïs Dufouleur
7 Denis Perret
8 Védrenne
9 Alain Hess & Mulot-Petitjean
  Pain d'Epices

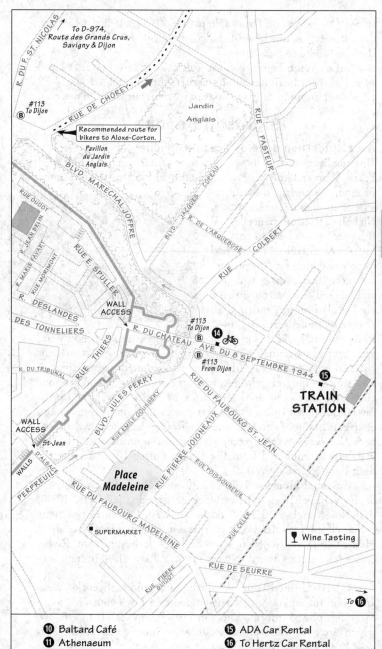

R. DU F. ST. NICOLAS

To D-974,
Route des Grands Crus,
Savigny & Dijon

RUE DE CHOREY

#113
To Dijon
B

Jardin
Anglais

RUE PASTEUR

Recommended route for
bikers to Aloxe-Corton.

Pavillon
du Jardin
Anglais

BLVD. MARECHAL JOFFRE

RUE OUDOT

R. JEAN BELIN

RUE MARIE FAVART

RUE MORIMONT

RUE E. SPULLER

BLVD. JACQUES COPEAU

R. DE L'ARQUEBUSE

RUE COLBERT

R. DESLANDES

DES TONNELIERS

WALL
ACCESS

R. DU CHATEAU

RUE THIERS

#113
To Dijon
B

14

#113
From Dijon
B

AVE. DU 8 SEPTEMBRE 1944

15

R. DU TRIBUNAL

BLVD. JULES FERRY

RUE EMILE GOUSSERY

RUE DU FAUBOURG ST. JEAN

TRAIN
STATION

WALL
ACCESS

St-Jean

WALLS D'ALSACE

PERPREUIL

**Place
Madeleine**

RUE PIERRE JOIGNEAUX

RUE POISSONNERIE

RUE DU FAUBOURG MADELEINE

SUPERMARKET

RUE GELER

🍷 Wine Tasting

RUE DE SEURRE

RUE PIERRE GUIDOT

To 16

BURGUNDY

⑩ Baltard Café	⑮ ADA Car Rental	
⑪ Athenaeum	⑯ To Hertz Car Rental	
⑫ Le Vigneron	⑰ To Europcar Rental	
⑬ Launderette	⑱ Tourist Train	
⑭ Bike Rental		

an SUV to get you off the beaten path (€60-70/half-day, €135/day, three itineraries, lunch not included, mobile 06 60 43 68 86, www. chemins-de-bourgogne.com).

Safari Wine Tours has four itineraries (€45-60, tours #2 and #4 are best for beginners; tours depart from TI, tel. 03 80 24 79 12, www.burgundy-tourism-safaritours.com, or call TI to reserve).

Sights in Beaune

▲▲▲Hôtel Dieu des Hospices de Beaune

This medieval charity hospital is now a museum. The Hundred Years' War and the plague (a.k.a. the Black Death) devastated Beaune, leaving three-quarters of its population destitute. Nicholas Rolin, chancellor of Burgundy (enriched, in part, by his power to collect taxes), had to do something for "his people" (or, more likely, was getting old and wanted to close out his life on a philanthropic, rather than a greedy, note). So, in 1443

Rolin paid to build this place. It was completed in just eight years and served as Beaune's hospital until 1971, when the last patient checked out. You'll notice Hospices de Beaune on wine labels in fine shops—they are Burgundy's largest landowner of precious vineyards, thanks to donations made by patients over the centuries (and still happening today). Besides its magnificently decorated courtyard, Hôtel Dieu is famous for Rogier van der Weyden's superb *Last Judgment* altarpiece, which Rolin commissioned. It's also wonderfully animated from the outside during Beaune's summer light show (see page 860).

Cost and Hours: €8.50, €12.30 combo-ticket with Museum of the Wine of Burgundy, includes audioguide, daily 9:00-18:30, mid-Nov-March 9:00-11:30 & 14:00-17:30, last entry one hour before closing; it's dead center in Beaune, dominating Place de la Halle; tel. 03 80 24 45 00, www.hospices-de-beaune.com. River-cruise tour groups crowd the place from 9:30 to 11:00 in high season.

❍ **Self-Guided Tour:** While the audioguide delivers key facts and good information, this self-guided tour gives your visit more meaning (posted information is in French only). Tour the rooms, which circle the courtyard, in a clockwise direction (following *Sens de la Visite* signs). Allow an hour for your visit.

• *To start, enter the courtyard and find the stone bench.*

Courtyard of Honor: Honor meant power, and this was all

about showing off. The exterior of the hospital and the town side of the courtyard are intentionally solemn, so as not to attract pesky 15th-century brigands and looters. The dazzling inner courtyard features a colorful glazed tile roof, establishing what became a style recognized in France as typically "Burgundian." The sturdy tiles, which last 300 years, are fired three times: once to harden, again to burn in the color, and finally for the glaze. They were last redone in 1902. The building is lacy Flamboyant Gothic with lots of decor—and boasts more weathervanes than any other building in France.

• *Now enter the hospice from the courtyard on the left side (follow Salle des Pôvres signs).*

Paupers' Ward (*Salle des Pôvres*): This grandest room of the hospital was the ward for the poorest patients. The vault, typical of big medieval rooms, was constructed like the hull of a ship. The screen separates the ward from the chapel at the front. Every three hours, the door was opened, and patients could experience Mass from their beds. Study the ceiling. Crossbeams are held by the mouths of creatively carved monsters—each mouth is stretched realistically, and each face has individual characteristics. Between the crossbars are busts of real 15th-century townsfolk—leading citizens, with animals humorously indicating their foibles (for example, a round-faced glutton next to a pig).

The carved wooden statue over the door you just entered shows a bound Christ—demonstrating graphically to patients that their Savior suffered and was able to empathize with their ordeal. Its realism shows that Gothic art had moved beyond the stiff formality of Romanesque carving. Behind the little window next to the statue was the nuns' dorm. The sisters (who were the first nurses) would check on patients from here. Notice the scrawny candleholder; if a patient died in the night, the candle was extinguished.

Find the small tables near the beds on the right. Rolin, who believed every patient deserved dignity, provided each patient with a pewter jug, mug, bowl, and plate. A painting on an easel at the left shows patients being treated in this room in 1949, 500 years after the hospital's founding. During epidemics, there were two to a bed. The ward didn't get heat until the 19th century (notice the heating grates on the floor), and the staff didn't get the concept of infection (and the basic practices of hand-washing) until the late 19th century (thanks to Louis Pasteur). Before then, most patients would have been better off left in a ditch outside.

• *Enter the chapel.*

Chapel: The hospice was not a place of hope. People came here to die. Care was more for the soul than the body. (Local guides are routinely instructed in writing by American tour companies not to use the word "hospice," because it turns off their clients. But this was a hospice, plain and simple, and back then, death was apparently less disturbing.) The stained glass shows Nicolas Rolin (lower left) and his wife, Guigone (lower right), dressed as a nun to show her devotion. Nicolas' feudal superior, the Duke of Burgundy, is portrayed above him; St. Nicholas is shown in green and St. Anthony in yellow (the saints you want on your side if death looks imminent).

Notice the action on Golgotha. As Jesus is crucified, the souls of the two criminals crucified with him (portrayed as miniature naked humans) are being snatched up—one by an angel and the other by a red devil. At the bottom, Mary cradles the dead body of Christ. You're standing on tiles with the love symbol (or "gallant device") designed by Nicolas and Guigone to celebrate their love (as noble couples often did). The letters N and G are entwined in an oak branch, meaning that their love was strong. The word *seule* ("only one") and the lone star declare that Guigone is the only star in Nicolas' cosmos.

• *Exit right to the next room...*

St. Hugue Ward: In the 17th century, this smaller ward was established for wealthy patients (who could afford Cadillac insurance plans). They were more likely to survive, and the decor displays themes of hope, rather than resignation: The series of Baroque paintings lining the walls shows the biblical miracles that Jesus performed. As the wealthy would lie in their beds, they'd stare at the ceiling—a painting with the bottom of an angel's foot, surrounded by the sick waiting to be healed by Jesus in his scarlet robe.

St. Nicolas Room: Originally divided into smaller rooms—one used for "surgery" (a.k.a. bloodletting and amputation), the other as an extension of the kitchen that you'll see next—this room now holds a model of the steep roof support and tools of the doctoring trade (amputation saws, caulking gun-size syringes, pans for bloodletting, and so on). The glass panel in the floor's center shows the stream running below; the hole provided a primitive but convenient disposal system after dinner or surgery. Living downstream from the hospital was a bad idea.

Operation of the hospice was primarily funded through auctions of its great wines (made from land donated by grateful patients over the years). Today, the auction of Hospices de Beaune wines is an internationally followed event, and gives the first indication of prices for the previous year's wines. Proceeds from the auction still support the "modern" hospital in Beaune.

• *Continue to the kitchen.*

Kitchen: Five nuns manned the kitchen at all times, preparing mostly soups and some meat dishes for their patients. Notice the 16th-century rotisserie. When fully wound, the cute robot would crank away, and the spit would spin slowly for 45 minutes.

The 19th-century stove provided running hot water, which spewed from the beaks of swans. This kitchen dished food until 1985 (serving its retirement home residents).

• *Before entering the pharmacy, peek out back to the garden and out-buildings. Before those buildings were added, this was a huge garden growing herbs and other plants used for medications. The buildings were added in the early 1900s to serve as a retirement home.*

Pharmacy: Inside the pharmacy, strange and wondrous con-coctions were mixed, cooked, distilled, and then stored in pottery jars. In the first room, the big bow over the mortar (large container) allowed the weighty pestle to be worked more easily for hours on end, grinding ingredients into fine pastes and powders. The alem-bic shows an ancient method for distilling medicines used in this pharmacy. A painting on the back wall shows the gardens before the retirement home addition. The second room displays jars whose shapes corresponded to the types of medications they contained—the biggest jar (by the window) was for *theriaca* ("panacea," or cure-all). The most commonly used medicine back then, it was a syrup of herbs, wine, and opium.

• *Continue to the St. Louis Ward, which provides access to the room with the Last Judgement.*

St. Louis Ward: A maternity ward until 1969, this room is lined with fine 16th- and 17th-century tapestries illustrating most-ly Old Testament stories. Dukes traveled with tapestries to cozy up the humble places they stayed in while on the road. The 16th-century pieces have better colors but inferior perspective. (The most precious 15th-century tapestries are displayed in the next room, where everyone is enthralled by the great Van der Weyden paint-ing.)

Rogier van der Weyden's *Last Judgment:* This exquisite painting, the treasure of Hôtel Dieu, was commissioned by Rolin in 1450 for the altar of the Paupers' Ward. He spared no cost, hir-ing the leading Flemish artist of his time. The entire altarpiece survives. The back side (on right wall) was sliced off so everything could be viewed at the same time. The painting is full of symbolism. Christ presides over Judgment Day. The lily is mercy, the sword is judgment, the rainbow promises salvation, and the jeweled globe at Jesus' feet symbolizes the universality of Christianity's message. As four angels blow their trumpets, St. Michael the archangel—very much in control—determines which souls are heavy with sin. Mary and the apostles pray for the souls of the dead as they emerge from their graves. But notice how both Michael and Jesus are expres-sionless—at this point, the cries of the damned and their loved ones are useless. In the back row are real people of the day.

The intricate detail, painted with a three-haired brush, is typi-cal of Flemish art from this period. While Renaissance artists employed mathematical tricks of perspective, these artists captured a sense of reality by painting minute detail upon detail.

The attendant will move the magnifying glass *(le loup)* for groups—and maybe for you if it's quiet—to help you appreciate the exquisite detail in the painting. You can also use the touch screen (outside the room) to zoom in. Stare at Michael's robe and wings. Check out John's delicate feet and hands. Study the faces of the damned; you can almost hear the gnashing of teeth. The feet of the damned show the pull of a terrible force. On the far left, notice those happily entering the pearly gates. On the far right, it's the flames of hell (no, this has nothing to do with politics).

Except for Sundays and holidays, the painting was kept closed and people saw only the panels that now hang on the right wall: on top, the Annunciation—the beginning of man's salvation; and at the bottom, Nicolas and Guigone piously at the feet of St. Sebastian, invoked to fight the plague, and St. Anthony, whom patients called upon for help in combating burning skin diseases.

The unusual 15th-century tapestry *A Thousand Flowers,* hanging on the left wall, tells the medieval story of St. Eligius.

Collégiale Notre-Dame
Built in the 12th and 13th centuries, during the transition from Romanesque to Gothic architecture, Beaune's cathedral was a "daughter of Cluny" (built in the style of the Cluny Abbey, described on page 923). The church features a mix of both styles: Its foundation is decidedly Romanesque while much of the rest is Gothic. View it from the square before entering. That porch was added in the 16th century and (sadly) masks the original facade. Enter the second chapel on the left to see the faint remains of frescoes depicting the life of Lazarus, and then, behind the altar, find five vibrant, 15th-century tapestries illustrating the life of the Virgin Mary (English explanations available for frame-by-frame descriptions).

Cost and Hours: Free to enter cathedral; tapestries on view generally 14:00-18:00, but hours change frequently.

La Maison des Climats (Burgundy's Land and Climates)
Located at the main TI, this helpful display covers the famous Côte d'Or vineyards. There are English explanations about the unique combination of land *(terroir)* and climate that have made this region ideal for wine production for the last 2,000 years.

In 2017, the Côte d'Or vineyards were added to the UNESCO World Heritage List as an outstanding example of grape cultivation and wine production, thus making them available for financial assistance for preservation. La Maison des Climats is a result of that designation (free, open same hours as the main TI).

Museum of the Wine of Burgundy (Musée du Vin de Bourgogne)

From this well-organized folk-wine museum, which fills the old residence of the Dukes of Burgundy, it's clear that the history and culture of Burgundy and its wine were fermented in the same bottle. Wander into the free courtyard (beautifully illuminated during summer light shows—see next listing) for a look at the striking palace, antique wine presses, and a concrete model of Beaune's 15th-century street plan (a good chance to appreciate the town's once-impressive fortified wall). Inside the museum, you'll find rooms devoted to the region's topography, tools of the trade, barrel making, traditional wine festivals, and more. English explanations are posted in every room.

Cost and Hours: €5, €11.30 combo-ticket with Hôtel Dieu; Wed-Mon 10:00-13:00 & 14:00-18:00 except closed Mon off-season, closed Dec and Tue year-round; in the Hôtel des Ducs on Rue d'Enfer, tel. 03 80 22 08 19, www.musees-bourgogne.org.

Getting There: With your back to the cathedral, turn left down the cobbled alley called Rue d'Enfer ("Hell Street," named for the fires of the Duke's kitchens once located on this street), keep left, and enter the courtyard of Hôtel des Ducs. There's also an entrance off Rue Paradis, opposite Le Petit Paradis restaurant.

Les Chemins de Lumières Light Show (Pathway of Lights)

Nightly from June through early September, and off-season on holiday weekends, Beaune puts on an entertaining light show accenting the exteriors of many buildings in the town center and along its ramparts walk. The main attractions are seven razzle-dazzle light shows (lasting about five minutes each) highlighting Beaune's most historic buildings. The most centrally located are Hôtel Dieu, Collégiale Notre-Dame church, the Museum of the Wine of Burgundy courtyard, and the bell tower at Place Monge (behind the Notre-Dame church). The lights start when daylight ends, making this ideal for an after-dinner event (TIs have maps with all the details).

The Mustard Mill (La Moutarderie Fallot)

The last of the independent mustard mills in Burgundy, owned by the Edmond Fallot company, opens its doors for guided tours in French (with a little English). They offer two tours: one with a hands-on focus on production (Découvertes tour) and another that highlights the history of mustard (Sensational Experience tour). The tours are long yet informative—you'll learn why Burgundy was the birthplace of mustard (it's about wine juice), and where they get their grains today (Canada). It takes over an hour to explain what could be explained in half that time—you'll see a short film, learn about the key machines used in processing mustard, and fin-

Wine Tasting in Burgundy

Many shops and wineries in the region offer informal and informative tastings (with the expectation that you'll buy something or pay a tasting fee). You can taste directly at the *domaine* (winery) or at a *caveau* representing a variety of wineries (I list several options for both). To sample older vintages you'll have to visit a winery because *caveaux* usually stock only younger wines. When visiting a cellar, don't mind the mossy ceilings. Many cellars have spent centuries growing this "angel's hair"—the result of humidity created by the evaporation of the wines stored there. For tips on wine tasting, see the sidebar on page 1124.

The limits on our ability to bring wines back to North America can lead to tricky dynamics, particularly at smaller places. Busy winemakers naturally prefer to spend their time with folks who can buy enough wine to make it worth their while—and in most cases, that's not you (as nice as you are). They hope you'll like their wines, buy several bottles or a dozen, and ask for them at your shop back home. Most places now charge an entry fee, allowing you to taste a variety of wines (with less expectation that you'll buy). If you're not serious about buying at least a few bottles, look for places that charge for tastings.

Taking Wine Home: Some shops and wineries can arrange ship-

ish with a tasting. But at the end there's a good boutique with a cool mustard-sampling counter.

Cost and Hours: €10, daily at 10:00 and 11:30, also on summer afternoons, call to reserve or book online—space is limited; free mustard tasting—daily 9:30-18:00, except closed at lunch in winter and Sun afternoon year-round; across ring road in the appropriately yellow building at 31 Rue du Faubourg Bretonnière, tel. 03 80 22 10 10, www.fallot.com.

Park and Vineyard Walk

Stroll across the ring road, through a pleasant Impressionist-like park, and into Beaune's beautiful vineyards. This walk is ideal for those lacking a car, families (good toys in park), and vine enthusiasts. The vine-covered landscape is crisscrossed with narrow lanes and stubby stone walls and provides memorable early morning and sunset views.

Follow Avenue de la République west from the center, cross the ring road, stay parallel to the stream along a few grassy blocks for about five minutes, and then veer right into the serene Parc de la Bouzaize (opens at 8:00 and closes a bit before sunset). Walk through the park alongside the pond and pop out at the right rear corner (find the path to a small opening in the iron fence behind the kid's play area). Turn left on the small road and keep left, hug-

ping (about €15 per bottle to ship a case, though you save about 20 percent on the VAT tax when shipping—so expensive wines are worth the shipping cost). To learn more about shipping wine, **Côte d'Or Imports** works with many sellers in Burgundy and has earned a reputation for safe and reliable shipping (www.cotedorpdx.com). The simplest solution for bringing six or so bottles back is to pack them well and check the box on the plane with you. Good packing boxes are usually available where you taste, or you can wrap them well and put them in a hard-sided suitcase. US customs allows one bottle duty-free; the duty on additional bottles is 10 percent.

Tasting in Beaune: Visit the cellars listed under "Wine Tasting in Beaune," later.

Visiting Vineyards by Car: Follow one of my two self-guided routes (starting on page 889), which can work well for bikers, too.

Visiting Vineyards Without Your Own Wheels: Rent a bike, take a taxi, or ride a train (long walks to villages from most stations) to nearby villages (see "Wine Villages and Sights near Beaune," next page), or take Transco bus #113 to wine villages on La Route des Grand Crus (see page 882). You can also book a minibus tour or hire a recommended local guide (see page 863).

ging the stone wall, then enter the Côte de Beaune vineyards. Find the big poster showing how the land is sliced and diced among different plots (called *clos*, for "enclosure"). Each *clos* is named; look for the stone marker identifying the area behind the poster as Clos Les Teurons *(1er cru)*. See "Burgundy's Wines," earlier, for more about the wines produced here.

Poke about Clos Les Teurons, noticing the rocky soil (wine grapes need to struggle). As you wander, keep in mind that subtle differences of soil and drainage between adjacent plots of land can be enough to create very different-tasting wines—from grapes grown only feet apart. *Vive la différence.* (Read "Wine Tasting in Burgundy" above to learn more.) A perfectly situated picnic table awaits under that lone tree up Chemin des Tilleuls.

Ramparts Walk

You can wander along sections of the medieval walls that protected Beaune from *les* bad guys. Much of the way is a paved lane used for parking, storage, and access to homes built into the wall, but you'll still get a feel for the ramparts' size and see vestiges of defensive towers. Find the path just inside the ring road that stretches counterclockwise from Avenue de la République to Rue de Lorraine (see map on page 876). The section near Avenue de la République is good for picnics, with shade, benches, and views to vineyards. You can enter or exit the ramparts at any cross street (free, always open).

WINE TASTING IN BEAUNE

Here are two good places to learn about Burgundy wines without leaving Beaune. For tastings in nearby wine villages, see page 883.

Patriarche Père et Fils

Home to Burgundy's largest and most impressive wine cellar, this is the best of the big wineries to visit in the city. With helpful video presentations at key points, you'll walk for about 500 yards exploring some of their three miles of underground passages. Your self-guided walk culminates in the atmospheric tasting rooms, where you'll try several Burgundian classics (3 whites and 7 reds); each bottle sits on top of its own wine barrel. The walk back to the elegant boutique and *sortie* helps sober you up.

Cost and Hours: €17 for 10 wines (mattress provided), reservation essential for private tours and tasting with guide—€250/small group, daily entry times 9:30-11:15 & 14:00-17:15, 5 Rue du Collège, tel. 03 80 24 53 78, www.patriarche.com.

Sensation Vin

For a good introduction to Burgundy wines, try the informative wine classes given by Céline or Damien. You'll gather around a small counter in the comfortable wine bar/classroom and learn while you taste. Since the young owners do not make wine, you'll get an objective education (with blind tastings) and sample from a variety of producers. Call, email, or book online to arrange a class/tasting.

Cost and Hours: Class length and wines tasted vary by season (€35 for 1.5-hour class with 7 wines, €165 for all-day tastings covering 12 wines, 2-person minimum—aspirin and pillow provided). Ask about their intimate tastings-in-the-vineyards class for two people (3-4 hours, €275/person; daily except closed Sun in winter, 2 Rue Paul Bouchard, tel. 03 80 22 17 57, www.sensation-vin.com, contact@sensation-vin.com).

Sleeping in Beaune

Beaune has accommodations with all levels of comfort in all price ranges. To sleep peacefully (and usually for less), choose one of the nearby wine villages (see page 883). Unless otherwise noted, the rooms listed next have air-conditioning but don't have elevators.

IN THE CENTER

$$$$ Hôtel le Cep**** is *the* venerable place to stay in Beaune, if you have the means. Buried in the town center, this historic build-

ing comes with fine public spaces inside and out, and 65 gorgeous wood-beamed, traditionally decorated rooms in all sizes (family rooms, fitness center, spa, pricey pay parking, 27 Rue Maufoux, tel. 03 80 22 35 48, www.hotel-cep-beaune.com, resa@hotel-cep-beaune.com).

$$$ Les Jardins de Loïs** is a four-star B&B run by welcoming winemakers Philippe and Anne-Marie. The five big rooms all overlook large gardens and show a no-expense-spared attention to comfort (also huge all-equipped apartment, includes custom-order breakfast; elevator, parking, on the ring road a block after Hôtel de la Poste at 8 Boulevard Bretonnière, tel. 03 80 22 41 97, mobile 06 73 85 11 06, www.jardinsdelois.com, contact@jardinsdelois.com). Their atmospheric wine cellar, **Domaine Loïs Dufouleur**, offers tastings for guests (arrange ahead).

$$ Hôtel Athanor* has a privileged location and charges for it. A block from Collégiale Notre-Dame church, you'll get modern, if tired, comfort with a touch of old Beaune. The lounge sports a pool table and a full-service bar. The hallways are faded and rooms are a tad pricey; some have a little street noise and less than half have air-conditioning (family rooms, elevator, 9 Avenue de la République, tel. 03 80 24 09 20, www.hotel-athanor.com, reservation@hotel-athanor.com).

$$ Hôtel des Remparts* is a peaceful oasis in a rustic manor house built around a soothing courtyard. It features attentive service, Old World comfort, many rooms with beamed ceilings, big beds, and a few good family suites (RS%, laundry service, bike rental, pay garage parking, just inside ring road between train station and main square at 48 Rue Thiers, tel. 03 80 24 94 94, www.hotel-remparts-beaune.com, hotel.des.remparts@wanadoo.fr, run by the formal Epaillys).

OUTSIDE THE WALLS

The first three hotels are a few blocks from the city center and train station, with easy parking. If you need to sleep cheap and have a car, there's a gaggle of motels between Beaune and the highway.

$$ Hôtel de la Paix,* a few steps off Place Madeleine, is a top Beaune choice, with rooms in two buildings. In the main building (with reception, breakfast room, bar, and comfy lounges), there are 30 three-star, handsome, well-appointed rooms, including several good family rooms and "apartments" sleeping up to six. In a nearby annex are seven good-value, comfortable two-star rooms and two family rooms (good breakfast, pay parking, 45 Faubourg Madeleine, tel. 03 80 24 78 08, www.hotelpaix.com, contact@hotelpaix.com).

$ Hôtel de France* is a simple but good place with fair prices and updated rooms that's easy for train travelers and drivers. It's

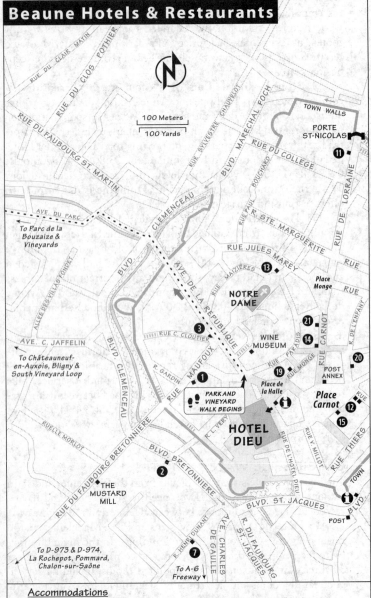

Beaune Hotels & Restaurants

N

100 Meters
100 Yards

RUE DU CLAIR MATIN
RUE DU CLOS POTHIER
RUE DU FAUBOURG ST. MARTIN
ALLEE DES VILLAS TONDET
AVE. DU PARC
To Parc de la Bouzaize & Vineyards
BLVD. CLEMENCEAU
AVE. C. JAFFELIN
To Châteauneuf-en-Auxois, Bligny & South Vineyard Loop
RUELLE MORLOT
RUE MAUFOUX
RUE GARDIN
R. L. VERY
BLVD. CLEMENCEAU
AVE. DE LA REPUBLIQUE
RUE C. CLOUTIER
RUE MAIZIERES
CLEMENCEAU
BLVD. MARECHAL FOCH
RUE SYLVESTRE CHAUVELOT
RUE DU COLLEGE
RUE PAUL BOUCHARD
R. STE. MARGUERITE
RUE JULES MAREY
RUE DE LORRAINE
TOWN WALLS
PORTE ST-NICOLAS
❶❶
NOTRE DAME
Place Monge
RUE
WINE MUSEUM
RUE PARADIS
RUE MONGE
RUE CARNOT
R. DE L'ENFANT
❷❶
❶❹
❶❾
POST ANNEX
❷⓿
Place Carnot
❶❷
❶❺
PARK AND VINEYARD WALK BEGINS
Place de la Halle
HOTEL DIEU
RUE DE L'HOTEL DIEU
RUE V. MILLOT
RUE THIERS
❶❸
❸
❶
❷
BLVD. BRETONNIERE
THE MUSTARD MILL
RUE DU FAUBOURG BRETONNIERE
BLVD. ST. JACQUES
AVE. CHARLES DE GAULLE
R. HENRI DUNANT
R. DU FAUBOURG ST. JACQUES
POST
TOWN
BLVD.
❶
To D-973 & D-974, La Rochepot, Pommard, Chalon-sur-Saône
❼
To A-6 Freeway

Accommodations

❶ Hôtel le Cep
❷ Les Jardins de Loïs
❸ Hôtel Athanor & Maison du Colombier
❹ Hôtel des Remparts
❺ Hôtel de la Paix

❻ Hôtel de France & Le Tast'Vin Restaurant
❼ Hôtel Ibis Beaune Centre
❽ Hôtel La Villa Fleurie
❾ Hôtel Rousseau

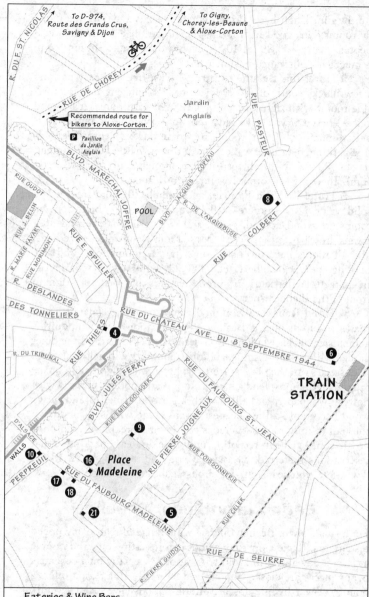

To D-974,
Route des Grands Crus,
Savigny & Dijon

To Gigny,
Chorey-les-Beaune
& Aloxe-Corton

R. DU F. ST. NICOLAS

RUE DE CHOREY

Jardin
Anglais

RUE PASTEUR

Recommended route for
bikers to Aloxe-Corton.

🅿 Pavillion
du Jardin
Anglais

BLVD. MARECHAL JOFFRE

RUE OUDOT

RUE J. BELIN

R. MARIE FAVART

RUE MORIMONT

RUE E. SPULLER

R. DESLANDES

DES TONNELIERS

R. DU TRIBUNAL

RUE THIERS

POOL

BLVD. JACQUES COPEAU

RUE DE L'ARQUEBUSE

RUE COLBERT

8

RUE DU CHATEAU

4

AVE. DU 8 SEPTEMBRE 1944

6

TRAIN
STATION

BLVD. JULES FERRY

RUE EMILE GOUSSERY

D'ALSACE

WALLS

PERPREUIL

10

RUE DU FAUBOURG ST. JEAN

RUE DU FAUBOURG MADELEINE

RUE PIERRE JOIGNEAUX

RUE POISSONNERIE

RUE CELER

9

16

*Place
Madeleine*

17

18

21

5

RUE DE SEURRE

R. PIERRE GUIDOT

BURGUNDY

Eateries & Wine Bars

10 Caveau des Arches
11 La Ciboulette
12 Les Pôpiettes
13 Le Goret
14 Brasserie le Carnot; Bien et Bon
15 Aux Hospices

16 Le Bistro des Cocottes
17 Les Caves Madeleine
18 L'Ardoise
19 Le Bistrot Bourguignon
20 Bistrot du Coin
21 Grocery (2)

run by fun, English-speaking owners Nicolas and Virginie (family rooms, bar, good bistro, pay garage parking, 35 Avenue du 8 Septembre, tel. 03 80 24 10 34, www.hoteldefrance-beaune.com, contact@hoteldefrance-beaune.com).

$ Hôtel Ibis Beaune Centre,*** with free and easy parking a few blocks south of Hôtel Dieu, has 73 efficient and comfortable rooms with tight but well-configured bathrooms. It's a good value—better if you have kids and want a pool. The bigger-and-better-appointed "Club" rooms are worth the extra euros (elevator, free parking, 5-minute walk to town center, 7 Rue Henri Dunant, tel. 03 80 22 75 67, https://ibis.accorhotels.com, h1363@accor.com). There are two other Ibis hotels in Beaune.

$ Hôtel La Villa Fleurie, an adorable 10-room refuge, is a solid value (a 15-minute walk from the center). First-floor-up rooms are wood-floored, plush, and *très* traditional; second-floor rooms are carpeted and cozy. Most rooms have queen-size beds, and all rooms have big bathrooms (family rooms, easy and free parking, 19 Place Colbert, tel. 03 80 22 66 00, www.lavillafleurie.fr, contact@lavillafleurie.fr). From Beaune's ring road, turn right in front of the Bichot winery.

¢ Hôtel Rousseau is a good-value frumpy old manor house that turns up its nose at Beaune's sophistication. Cheerful, quirky, and elusive owner Madame Rousseau, her pet birds, and the quiet garden will make you smile, and the tranquility will help you sleep. (Rousseau's run the place since 1959; her granddaughter and great-granddaughter now lend a hand). Rooms are spotless, covered with flowery wallpaper, and filled with big wood armoires and heavy wood bed frames. The cheapest rooms come with showers down the hall (family rooms, includes continental breakfast, cash only, no air-con, Wi-Fi in reception only, free and easy parking, email reservations preferred, 11 Place Madeleine, tel. 03 80 22 13 59, www.hotel-rousseau.com, hotelrousseaubeaune@orange.fr).

Eating in and near Beaune

For a small town, Beaune offers a wide range of reasonably priced restaurants. Review my suggestions before setting out, and reserve at least a day ahead to avoid frustration (especially on weekends). Many places are closed Sunday and Monday. This region offers a bounty of worthwhile upscale dining options (I've listed several), but before you book, check their wine lists (easiest to do online)—the prices may double your total dinner cost. For eating recommendations in the wine villages near Beaune, see page 883.

Wine Bars of Beaune

Beaune has several quality wine bars perfect for savoring the region's best offerings.

$$ Maison du Colombier operates as a wine bar and bistro. The picturesque outside terrace has views of the church; inside, stone walls meet wood beams, creating a cozy ambience with counter-height tables and stools (delicious tapas, *tartines,* and *plats,* closed Sun, 1 Rue Charles Cloutier, tel. 03 80 26 16 26).

$$ Le Bistrot Bourguignon is a laid-back wine bar/bistro with 15 types of *vin* available by the glass (order by number from display behind the bar). Come for a glass of wine and to use their Wi-Fi, or for a light dinner. Dine at the counter, the sidewalk tables, or in the casually comfortable interior (closed Sun-Mon, on pedestrian street at 8 Rue Monge, tel. 03 80 22 23 24).

$$ Bistrot du Coin is a warm and welcoming shoebox-size wine bar whose fun owner Alex clearly loves his work as much as he does making clients feel at ease. Prices are reasonable, though seating is limited to a few bar stools—clients spill outside onto the small square—and no food is served (Tue-Sat 17:00-24:00, closed Sun-Mon, 2 Place Ziem, mobile 06 99 42 65 43).

DINING IN THE TOWN CENTER

$$ Caveau des Arches is a reliable choice for Burgundian specialties; you'll experience romantic stone cellars with top service and fine table settings. It has a €26 *menu* with the classics, a €36 *menu* with greater choices, and a €58 *gourmand menu,* but portions can be small (closed Sun-Mon and Aug, impressive wine list, where the ring road crosses Rue d'Alsace—which leads to Place Madeleine—at 10 Boulevard Perpreuil, tel. 03 80 22 10 37, www.caveau-des-arches.com).

$$ La Ciboulette, intimate and family-run with petite Hélèna as your hostess, offers fine cuisine that mixes traditional Burgundian flavors with creative dishes and lovely presentation. It's worth the longer walk—and you can do your laundry next door while you dine (indoor seating only, closed Mon-Tue; from Place Carnot, walk out Rue Carnot to 69 Rue Lorraine; tel. 03 80 24 70 72).

$$ Les Pôpiettes is a lively place that's popular with locals and foodies. There's a communal table on one side, booths on the other, and a cheery ambience. The chef-owner produces cuisine that's an eclectic blend of delicious and inventive—though limited in choice—such as risotto and snails (inside dining only, closed

BURGUNDY

Tue-Wed, 10 Rue d'Alsace, tel. 03 80 21 91 81, www.les-popiettes.com).

$$$ Le Goret (slang for pig) turns its back on Beaune's sophistication, serving farmer-sized portions of regional dishes prepared by a jolly chef. Pork is their thing, and dietary concerns are not. This is the place to experience down-and-dirty Burgundy. There are no fixed *menus* (order from the pig chalkboards), and the selection is limited. You won't find first courses here, only big servings of well-garnished main courses and killer desserts (closed Sun-Mon and Thu evening, inside tables only, reserve ahead, behind Collégiale Notre-Dame at 10 Place Notre-Dame, tel. 03 80 22 05 94).

$$ Brasserie le Carnot is a perennially popular café with good inside seating and better exterior tables in the thick of the pedestrian zone. It serves pizza, salads, and pasta dishes as well as the usual café offerings (open daily, 18 Rue Carnot where it meets Rue Monge, tel. 03 80 22 32 93).

$ Bien et Bon serves cheap *le fast food* meals like crêpes, salads, and sandwiches with good outdoor seating (daily until 19:00, next to Brasserie le Carnot at 22 Rue Carnot, tel. 03 80 21 78 99).

$ Aux Hospices, in the middle of a cluster of places on the main square, serves simple, light meals at bargain prices. You'll get a fun outdoor experience, but there's good inside seating, too (daily, 32 Place Carnot, tel. 03 80 24 99 01).

DINING ON PLACE MADELEINE

Some of my favorite restaurants face this big square.

$ Le Bistro des Cocottes is a warm place where locals go for top regional cuisine at good prices. Interior tables buzz with regulars while terrace tables seem popular with tourists (closed Sun-Mon, 3 Place de la Madeleine, tel. 03 80 24 02 60).

$$$ Les Caves Madeleine serves owner/chef Martial's recipes, inspired by his grandmother's favorites. Step down into the warm little dining room and choose a private table—or better, join the communal table, where good food and wine kindle conversation and new friendships (making the place noisy for some). Service can be slow and wine by the glass or half-bottle is scarce (closed Wed and Sun, near Place Madeleine at 8 Rue du Faubourg Madeleine, tel. 03 80 22 93 30).

$$ L'Ardoise is a warm bistro serving creative versions of regional and classic French dishes with easygoing service (closed Sun-Mon, 14 Rue du Faubourg Madeleine, tel. 03 80 21 41 34).

NEAR THE TRAIN STATION

$$ Le Tast'Vin, across from the train station at the recommended Hôtel de France, has a tasty €26 *menu* and fun cheeseburgers with

Burgundian cheese in an air-conditioned room (closed Sat and Mon for lunch and all day Sun, 35 Avenue du 8 Septembre, tel. 03 80 24 10 34, www.hoteldefrance-beaune.com).

NEAR BEAUNE

A short drive from Beaune brings great rewards for fine dining at affordable prices. Along with L'Agastache, listed below, consider **Le Chevreuil** in Meursault, 10 minutes from Beaune (page 884); **Auprès du Clocher** in Pommard, just a few minutes away; or **Maison Lameloise**—one of France's top restaurants—a 20-minute drive south in Chagny (see page 886).

$$$ **L'Agastache**, an intimate place buried in the wine village of Volnay 10 minutes from Beaune, offers a break from Burgundian tradition. The charming front terrace gathers several tables, and the small interior mixes contemporary with tradition. It's run by a young Franco-Italian couple who prepare original and wonderfully presented dishes with a very limited selection—two- and three-course *menus* only—check their website to be sure you like the choices (closed Sun-Mon, 1 Rue de la Cave in Volnay, tel. 03 80 21 12 30, www.lagastache-restaurant.com).

Beaune Connections

For traveling to nearby wine villages, see "Burgundy's Wine Villages," next page.

From Beaune by Train to: Dijon (15/day, 20 minutes), **Paris** Gare de Lyon (nearly hourly, 2.5 hours, most require reservation and easy change in Dijon; more via Dijon to Paris' Gare de Bercy, no reservation required, 3.5 hours), **Bourges** (1/day direct, 2.5 hours, more with transfer in Nevers), **Colmar** (10/day, 3 hours via TGV between Dijon and Mulhouse, reserve well ahead, changes in Dijon and Mulhouse or Belfort), **Arles** (hourly, 5 hours, transfer in Lyon), **Chamonix** (7/day, 7 hours, several changes), **Annecy** (8/day, 4 hours, change in Lyon), **Amboise** (6/day, 6 hours, transfer at Nevers and/or St-Pierre-des-Corps; more with multiple connections).

Burgundy's Wine Villages

Exploring the villages and vineyards in the region near Beaune, by car or by bike, is a delight.

GETTING AROUND THE BEAUNE REGION

By Car: Driving provides the ultimate flexibility for touring the vineyards, though drivers should prepare for narrow lanes and use the handy buckets to spit back after tasting.

By Bike: Pedaling on a bike from Beaune takes you into the world-famous vineyards of the Côte d'Or within minutes. The many quiet service roads and bike-only lanes make this area wonderful for biking. (Beware of loose gravel on shoulders and along small roads.) A signed bike route, *La Voie Verte*, runs south from Beaune all the way to Cluny, and a new route from Beaune north toward Dijon should be in place by your visit. My favorite rides are described in detail in "Vineyard Loops near Beaune" (see later).

Well-organized, helpful, and English-speaking Florian and Cédric at **Bourgogne Randonnées** rent excellent bikes of all types, bike racks, kid bikes, and trailers, and offer maps and detailed itineraries. Ask about their favorite routes that follow only small roads and dedicated bike paths, and soak up their trustworthy wine-tasting tips. They can deliver a bike to your hotel anywhere in France if booked well ahead (standard bikes-€19/day, electric bikes-€35/day, includes helmet, daily 9:00-12:00 & 13:30-18:00, near Beaune train station at 7 Avenue du 8 Septembre, tel. 03 80 22 06 03, www.bourgogne-randonnees.fr, helloinfobr@aol.com).

ADA Car Rental (listed under "Helpful Hints," on page 862) and **Galmard Vehicle Rental** (18 Boulevard Jules Ferry, tel. 03 80 24 10 23) also rent bikes.

By Bus: Transco bus #113 links Beaune with all the important wine villages to the north along the famous Route des Grands Crus, and runs to Dijon's train station (7/day; http://viamobigo.fr). Buses to Dijon stop at the train station, and at two stops along Beaune's ring road (see map on page 864 and look for Transco decals in shelters). Bus service south of Beaune to villages like Meursault and Puligny-Montrachet is hopeless—take a taxi, hop a train (limited options), or rent a bike.

By Train: Trains stop intermittently in the wine villages of Meursault and Santenay to the south of Beaune. Trains also serve Nuits-St-Georges (best service), Vougeot (near Château de Clos Vougeot), and Gevrey-Chambertin to the north. Most of these stations require a 15-minute walk to the town center or main sight.

Bikes are generally allowed on local trains, though it's smart to check before you set out.

By Minibus Tour: Try **Chemins de Bourgogne** or **Safari Wine Tours** (see page 863).

By Taxi: Call Julien Dupont at **Allo Beaune Taxi** (mobile 06 11 83 06 10); for another taxi option, see page 862.

Wine Villages and Sights near Beaune

You'll find exceptional tasting, eating, and sleeping values in the workaday villages and towns within a 15-minute drive of Beaune. The Côte d'Or has scads of *chambres d'hôtes;* get a list at the TI and reserve ahead in summer. See also the suggestions along the Route des Grands Crus (page 895).

For driving/biking loops that tie these villages together, see page 889; for the Route des Grands Crus, see page 895.

SOUTH OF BEAUNE
Pommard

The small village of Pommard lies on the bike path just two miles south of Beaune. Walkers can follow the bike path and make it here in 45 minutes. Pommard has cafés, restaurants, and many tasting opportunities.

Appellation Chocolat makes its own *chocolat,* a fun and tasty diversion (Tue-Sat 9:30-19:00, closed Sun-Mon, a short block to the right off the main road at 5 Place de l'Europe, tel. 03 45 63 85 89).

Domaine Lejeune is a small family winery with an unusual twist—it has been handed from mother to daughter for seven generations, a rare occurrence in this traditionally male-dominated business. During the hour-long tour you'll see old-style wooden vats and the cellar before sampling three wines for free (Mon-Sat 9:00-12:00 & 14:00-18:00, best to call ahead, behind the church, tel. 03 80 22 90 88, www.domaine-lejeune.fr).

Eating in Pommard: Eat inside or outside at **$$ La Compagnie de Fanny,** a nifty little wine-bar-meets-diner that serves cheese-and-meat platters, bruschetta, and salads to happy clients (Thu-Sun 10:00-22:00, Mon until 18:00, Wed from 16:00, closed Tue, a short block off the main road at 12 Place de l'Europe, tel. 03 45 63 16 53). **$$ Hôtel du Pont,** on the main road, serves a good lunch at fair prices on a nice terrace (daily, Rue Marey Monge, tel. 03 80 22 03 41). To really do it up right, dine at **$$$$ Auprès du Clocher,** overlooking the bell tower, with stylish, contemporary decor, a formal yet intimate atmosphere, and a focus on *la cuisine gastronomique* (closed Tue-Wed, 1 Rue Nackenheim, tel. 03 80 22 21 79, www.aupresduclocher.com).

BURGUNDY

Meursault

This appealing town 10 minutes south of Beaune is like a mini-Beaune, with a vast main square ringed with a TI, cafés, wine shops, and a small grocery market. A good selection of hotels and restaurants is available in its compact center. Eat or sleep here for that small-town feel and quick access to Beaune, vineyards, and villages. The train station is a 20-minute walk from the town center (limited service).

Sleeping and Eating in Meursault: $$ Hôtel les Charmes,*** in the heart of town, is a good place with fine, traditional rooms and a homey Old World feel, thanks to the easygoing owners (*les* Grimprets). There's a veritable park in the back, a big pool, and easy parking (10 Place du Murger, tel. 03 80 21 63 53, www.hotellescharmes.com, contact@hotellescharmes.com).

These two good places feature Burgundian cuisine at fair prices and offer rooms at reasonable rates: **$$$ Hotel/Restaurant le Chevreuil**** attracts foodies and locals wanting a special Burgundian meal. With its country-elegant setting and lovely terrace in back, this place merits a detour from Beaune. They offer a good range of choices blending old and new. Come early for a glass of wine on the square (lunch deals, book ahead, closed Wed and Sun for dinner, 9 Place de la République, tel. 03 80 21 23 25, http://lechevreuil.fr, reception@lechevreuil.fr).

$ Hôtel du Centre** offers an unpretentious menu for lunch or dinner, a sweet courtyard, and simple, cheap rooms (restaurant closed Wed-Thu, 4 Rue de Lattre de Tassigny, tel. 03 80 21 20 75, www.hotel-du-centre-meursault.com, contact@hotel-du-centre-meursault.com).

Puligny-Montrachet

This village of around 400 people is situated about a 15-minute drive (or 60 minutes by bike) south of Beaune, on the scenic route to Château de la Rochepot (see page 890). It has just enough commercial activity to keep travelers well-fed, hydrated, and housed.

Located on the village's central roundabout, the user-friendly **Caveau de Puligny-Montrachet** has a convivial wine-bar-like tasting room, a smart outdoor terrace, and no pressure to buy. Knowledgeable owner Julien is happy to answer your every question. He has wines from 200 Burgundian vintners, from Chablis to Pouilly-Fuissé, but his forte is Puligny-Montrachet and Meursault whites, which is why I taste here. His reds are young and less ready to drink (€20/6 wines, can ship to the US; daily 9:30-13:00 & 15:00-19:00, closes at 18:00 in winter; tel. 03 80 21 96 78, www.caveau-puligny.com).

Sleeping in Puligny-Montrachet: $$$ Hôtel Le Montrachet delivers country-classy Burgundian comfort with formal service on Puligny-Montrachet's main square. Stay here and enjoy a meal at its recommended, well-respected restaurant (elevator, 10 Place du Pasquier de la Fontaine, tel. 03 80 21 30 06, www.le-montrachet.com, info@le-montrachet.com).

$$ Domaine des Anges, run by a British couple (John and Celine) who pamper their guests with the Queen's English, has lovely rooms, linger-longer lounges inside and out, laundry service, and afternoon tea every day. It's also ideally located in the center of Puligny-Montrachet (may be closing in 2020, no children under 16, Place du Pasquier de la Fontaine, tel. 03 80 21 38 28, mobile 06 23 86 63 91, domainedesanges@yahoo.fr).

$ Chambres les Gagères is a swinging deal with four cozy and spotless rooms—some with vineyard views, and all with a common kitchen and view terraces overlooking vineyards. Adorable Maria speaks little English but manages to get her point across (includes breakfast, 17 Rue Drouhin, tel. 03 80 21 97 46, mobile 06 15 97 64 71, www.les-gageres.fr, contact@les-gageres.fr).

Eating in Puligny-Montrachet: At **$$$$ Le Montrachet,** settle in for a truly traditional Burgundian experience—a justifiable splurge for refined and classy dining without stuffiness. It's a great choice for a gourmet lunch on a lovely terrace (€32 lunch *menu,* €65-97 dinner *menus,* pricey wine list; open daily; see Hôtel Le Montrachet listing, earlier, for contact info). Come early for a glass of wine before dinner with Julien at the Caveau de Puligny-Montrachet (described earlier).

$$ L'Estaminet des Meix, a contemporary café in the heart of the village, serves good brasserie fare at reasonable prices and has fun outdoor seating (€20 dinner *menu* includes snails, *bœuf bourguignon,* and dessert; closed Mon evening and all day Tue, Place du Pasquier de la Fontaine, tel. 03 80 21 33 01).

▲Château de la Rochepot

Splendid both inside and out, this pint-size, very Burgundian castle rises above its village, eight miles from Beaune.

Cost and Hours: €8.50 (skip the scarce €11 guided tours in French only); July-Aug daily 10:00-18:00; March-June & Sept-Nov Wed-Sun until 17:00 and closed Tue; closed Dec-Feb; tel. 03 80 20 04 00, www.larochepot.com.

Getting There: The highly recommended scenic route from Beaune to the château is described in the "South Vineyard Loop" (see later). Or, to reach the château more directly from Beaune, follow signs for *Chalon-sur-Saône* from Beaune's ring road, then follow signs to *Autun* for 15 lovely minutes. A café with drinks and light snacks stares point-blank at the castle entry.

Visiting the Castle: Cross the drawbridge under the Pot family coat of arms and knock three times with the ancient knocker to enter. If no one comes, knock harder, or find a log and ram the gate.

Construction began during the end of the Middle Ages (when castles were built to defend) and was completed during the Renaissance (when castles became luxury homes). So it's neither a purely defensive structure nor a palace—it's a bit of both. The castle was never attacked by foreigners, though the French Revolution laid waste to a good part of it. After being used as a quarry, it was purchased by a local family and rebuilt.

The furnishings are surprisingly cushy given the military look of the exterior. Enter through the guard's room, and appreciate the weight of a good suit of armor. The Captain's Room, surrounded by colorful nine-foot-thick walls and holding a fine 15th-century alarmed safe, makes becoming a captain seem worth the trouble.

The kitchen will bowl you over; the dining room sports a 15th-century walnut high chair. Look for paintings of the pre-Revolution castle to get a feel for its original appearance.

Climb the tower (fine views) and see the out-of-place Chinese room, sing chants in the resonant chapel, and make ripples in the 240-foot-deep well. (Can you spit a bull's-eye?) Paths outside lead you on a worthwhile walk around the castle. Don't leave without driving, walking, or pedaling up D-33 a few hundred yards toward St-Aubin for a romantic view.

Chagny

The only reason to come to this unexceptional town 20 minutes south of Beaune is to eat very well (trains allow access for non-drivers).

Eating in Chagny: Well-known as one of France's finest restaurants, **$$$$ Maison Lameloise** has Michelin's top rating (three stars). The setting is elegant (as you'd expect), the service is relaxed and patient (which you might not expect), the cuisine is Burgundy's best, and the overall experience is memorable. If you're tempted to dive into the top of the top of French cuisine, book this place well ahead (*menus* from about €150 at dinner and €82 at lunch, very pricey wines, open daily, 36 Place d'Armes, tel. 03 85 87 65 65, www.lameloise.fr). Or consider their nearby contemporary bistro **$$$ Pierre et Jean,** where you get the same quality with a simpler menu for less money (*menus* from €34, around the corner at 2 Rue de la Poste, tel. 03 85 87 08 67, www.pierrejean-restaurant.fr).

NORTH OF BEAUNE
Aloxe-Corton

This small, prestigious village has good tasting rooms (and not much more) for its remarkable red wines; it's just a 10-minute drive north of Beaune.

At the **Domaines d'Aloxe-Corton** *caveau*, you can sample four famous Aloxe-Corton wines in a comfortable and relaxed setting. Prices are affordable, and friendly Denis speaks enough English (small fee for tasting, free if you buy one bottle, Thu-Mon 10:00-13:00 & 15:00-19:00, no midday break on high-season weekends, closed Tue-Wed, tel. 03 80 26 49 85, http://aloxe.corton.free.fr). You'll find the *caveau* a few steps from the little square in Aloxe-Corton.

At **Mischief and Mayhem,** British-born-and-raised Fiona and Michael make fine wines and sell them at fair prices (€15-60, but little middle ground). They are thoroughly immersed in Burgundian life and can help you make sense of this region's wine culture. Tasting is by appointment only (tell them you're a Rick Steves reader). It's a few blocks below the church on D-115d to Ladoix-Serrigny at 10 Impasse du Puits, mobile 06 30 01 23 76, www.mischiefandmayhem.com.

Domaine Comte Senard is famous for its prestigious wines and *table d'hôte*, where you get a no-choice lunch *menu* (with lots of courses), with matching wines and thorough explanations from the wine steward—including a visit to their cellars (lunch served Tue-Sat 11:30-13:30, €69 with 4 wines, €95 with 6 wines, several of them *grands crus*). Book ahead for this convivial way to spend two hours learning about the local product. You can also just do a free tasting of two basic wines—or guided tastings with a sommelier (€28 for 4 fine wines for the first person, €15/person after that, Tue-Sat 10:00-11:30 & 14:00-17:30, closed Sun-Mon, reserve ahead by phone, 1 Rue des Chaumes, tel. 03 80 26 41 65, www.domainesenard.com, table@domainesenard.com).

Sleeping in Aloxe-Corton: $$$ Hôtel Villa Louise*** is a romantic place burrowed deep in this wine hamlet. Many of its 14 spacious and tastefully decorated rooms overlook the backyard vineyards and a large, grassy garden made for sipping the owner's wine—but, sadly, no picnics are allowed. There's a small covered pool, a cozy lounge, and tastings of the owner's wines (suites available, sauna, near the château at 9 Rue Franche, tel. 03 80 26 46 70, www.hotel-villa-louise.fr, contact@hotel-villa-louise.fr).

Magny-les-Villers

This Hautes-Côtes village is located 15 minutes north of Beaune via a beautiful wine road (drive up into Pernand Vergeles to find this road signed on the right).

Domaine Naudin-Ferrand is overlooked by most, but makes fine reds and whites at excellent prices, and offers an authentic, small-producer experience (simple tasting room with helpful Julie or Claire who speak English well). Its best values are wines from the Hautes-Côtes vineyards. Tasting is by appointment only—call or email (free for a short tasting of 2-3 basic wines, fee for more elaborate tastings; Mon-Fri 9:00-12:00 & 13:30-17:30 except closed Wed afternoon, Sat 14:00-18:00, closed Sun, Rue du Meix-Grenot—carefully track the faded signs, tel. 03 80 62 91 50, mobile 06 87 76 85 42, www.naudin-ferrand.com, julie@naudin-ferrand.com).

Savigny-lès-Beaune

About five minutes from Beaune, Savigny-lès-Beaune is a thriving village with all the services travelers need, but no central square or focal point to make me want to sleep here.

Savigny-lès-Beaune is home to **Henri de Villamont,** a big-time enterprise with a huge range of wines and a modern, welcoming tasting room. They grow their own grapes and also buy grapes from other vineyards, but make all the wines themselves. This allows them to create a vast selection of wines featuring grapes from virtually all the famous wine villages, from Pouilly-Fuissé to Chablis (free tasting, hours vary but generally Wed-Fri 10:00-12:30 & 13:30-18:00, by appointment only on other days, Rue du Dr. Guyot, tel. 03 80 21 52 13, www.hdv.fr).

Sights in Savigny-lès-Beaune: The medieval castle **Château de Savigny** comes with a moat and an eclectic collection that includes 100 fighter jets, Abarth antique racing cars, tractors and fire engines, 300 motorcycles, 6,000 airplane models, vineyards—and no furnishings (castle-€11, daily mid-April-mid-Oct 9:00-18:30, shorter hours off-season, last entry 1.5 hours before closing, English handout; wine tasting-€4 for 7 of the owner's wines, €3 for 5 wines; tel. 03 80 21 55 03, www.chateau-savigny.com).

Eating in Savigny-lès-Beaune: Beyond the château in the village, the **$$ R. De Famille** café-pizzeria faces a little square and has good outdoor seating (closed Mon). A grocery shop and a bakery are a few blocks past the café (grocery usually closed 12:30-15:00).

Vineyard Loops near Beaune

I've outlined two vineyard loops near Beaune, with recommendations for touring the Route des Grands Crus between Beaune and Dijon. These drives combine great scenery with some of my favorite wine destinations (for more on these towns, see "Wine Villages and Sights near Beaune," earlier). Certain segments are doable by bike depending on your fitness and determination. Before planning to take your bike on the train, check with the bike shop to be sure it's allowed on board.

Choosing a Route: If time is tight and you have a car, drive the beautiful **"South Vineyard Loop"** to Château de la Rochepot. The last part is a tough ride on a bike (unless it's electric), so bikers should only do the first section of this route (ideally to Puligny-Montrachet and back—an easy, level ride).

My **"North Vineyard Loop"** takes you through Aloxe-Corton to Savigny-lès-Beaune and is good by car or by bike (manageable hills and distances). I also list worthwhile stops on the famous **"Route des Grands Crus,"** connecting Burgundy's most prestigious wine villages farther north of Beaune, which should have a new bike path in place by the time of your visit.

Vineyard Tips: Along these routes, I avoid tasting at famous wine châteaux (such as those in Pommard and Meursault) and look for smaller, more personal places. Although you can drop in unannounced at a wine château or a *caveau* that represents multiple wineries (*comme un cheveu sur la soupe*—"like a hair on the soup"), at private wineries it's best to call ahead and arrange an appointment (ask your hotelier for help). At free tastings, you're expected to buy at least a bottle or two unless you're on a group tour.

Before heading out, read the section on Burgundian wines (page 858). You'll almost certainly see workers tending the vines. In winter, plants are pruned way back (determining the yield during grape harvest in the fall). Starting in spring, plants are trimmed to get rid of extraneous growth, allowing just the right amount of sun to reach the grapes. The arrival date of good weather in spring determines the date of harvest (100 days later).

South Vineyard Loop

Take this pretty, peaceful route, worth ▲▲, for the best approach to La Rochepot's romantic castle, and to glide through several of Burgundy's most reputed vineyards. Read ahead and note the open hours of wineries and sights along the route (you can also do this loop in reverse). There are good picnic spots along the way; one is just before entering Puligny-Montrachet from the north (turn right, pass the first picnic spot, and continue 100 yards farther to one closer to the hills). The entire loop is 28 miles.

Bikers can follow the first part of this route to Puligny-Mon-

BURGUNDY

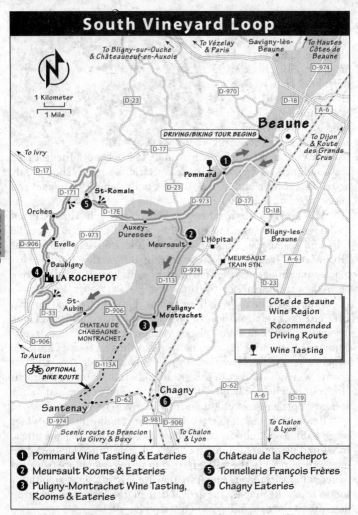

South Vineyard Loop

1 Kilometer
1 Mile

To Bligny-sur-Ouche & Châteauneuf-en-Auxois · To Vézelay & Paris · Savigny-lès-Beaune · To Hautes Côtes de Beaune

Beaune

DRIVING/BIKING TOUR BEGINS

To Dijon & Route des Grands Crus

To Ivry

Pommard ❶

St-Romain ❺

Orches

Auxey-Duresses

Meursault ❷ L'Hôpital

MEURSAULT TRAIN STN.

Bligny-les-Beaune

Evelle

Baubigny

❹ LA ROCHEPOT

St-Aubin

Puligny-Montrachet ❸

CHATEAU DE CHASSAGNE-MONTRACHET

To Autun

OPTIONAL BIKE ROUTE

Chagny ❻

Santenay

Scenic route to Brancion via Givry & Buxy

To Chalon & Lyon

Côte de Beaune Wine Region

Recommended Driving Route

Wine Tasting

❶ Pommard Wine Tasting & Eateries
❷ Meursault Rooms & Eateries
❸ Puligny-Montrachet Wine Tasting, Rooms & Eateries
❹ Château de la Rochepot
❺ Tonnellerie François Frères
❻ Chagny Eateries

trachet, along Burgundy's best bike path (connects the wine villages of Pommard, Volnay, Meursault, and Puligny-Montrachet for a level, 18-mile loop; allow two hours round trip). Only power riders or those with e-bikes should tackle the hills to La Rochepot.

From Beaune to Château de la Rochepot

By Car: Drivers leave Beaune's ring road, following signs for *Chalon-sur-Saône* (often abbreviated "Chalon-s/ S.," first turnoff after Auxerre exit), then follow signs to *Pommard/Autun*. When you come to Pommard, you'll pass several lunch and wine-tasting opportunities, including **Domaine Lejeune** (see page 883).

South of Pommard, the road gradually climbs past Volnay and terrific views. From here, follow signs into **Meursault** (*Centre-Ville* signs lead to its fine square, bakeries, grocery shops, and good restaurants; see page 884).

Drivers just passing through Meursault follow *Toutes Directions* to the lower end of the village, then turn right on D-113b, and follow signs for *Puligny-Montrachet*. Pass through low-slung vineyards south of Meursault, then enter **Puligny-Montrachet** (town and wineries described on page 884)—with good picnic spots on the right as you enter. At the big roundabout with a bronze sculpture of vineyard workers, find the **Caveau de Puligny-Montrachet** and a chance to sample from vines that produce "the world's best whites." A block straight out the door of the *caveau* leads to a small grocery and the town's big square (Place du Pasquier de la Fontaine), with **Hôtel-Restaurant Le Montrachet** and **Café de l'Estaminet des Meix.**

Go back to the roundabout and follow signs to *Chassagne-Montrachet* and *St. Aubin* (D-113a), leading through more manicured vineyards.

Continue on to **Château de la Rochepot** by making a hard right on D-906 to St-Aubin and following *La Rochepot* signs onto D-33. After heading over the hills and through the vineyards of the Hautes-Côtes (upper slopes), you'll come to a drop-dead view of the castle (stop mandatory). Turn right when you reach La Rochepot, and follow blue *Le Château* signs to the castle (described earlier under "Wine Villages and Sights near Beaune").

Returning to Beaune: After visiting the castle, turn right out of its parking lot. You'll crest the hill, then turn left following signs into Baubigny and track the D-17 through Evelle and rock-solid Orches. After Orches, climb to the top of Burgundy's world— keeping straight on D-17, you'll pass several **lookouts** on your right (simple dirt pullouts with exceptional views, the best is about 50 yards before the steel guardrail). Get out of your car and wander cliffside for a postcard-perfect Burgundian image. The village of St-Romain swirls below, and if it's really clear, look for Mont Blanc on the eastern horizon.

Next, drive down to **St-Romain,** passing Burgundy's most important wine-barrel maker, **Tonnellerie François Frères** (it's above the village in the modern building, www.francoisfreres. com). Inside, well-stoked fires heat the oak staves to make them flexible, and sweaty workers use heavy hammers to pound iron rings around the barrels as they've done since medieval times. The workshop is closed to the public, but discreet travelers can take quick peeks through the glass doors to the far left.

Next, follow signs for *Auxey-Duresses,* and then *Beaune* for a scenic finale to your journey.

By Bike: Take the vineyard bike path by leaving the ring road toward Auxerre, and turning left at the signal after Lycée Viticole de Beaune (look for bike-route icons and *Voie Verte Beaune-Santenay* signs). **Pommard** has lunch and wine-tasting stops (listed earlier). South of Pommard, follow bike icons along the bike-only path, then ride into **Meursault** (restaurants and more). Follow more bike icons out of town through low-slung vineyards to reach **Puligny-Montrachet** (described earlier).

From Puligny-Montrachet, double back to **Beaune** or continue on the bike path to **Santenay,** ride along the canal to **Chagny,** and take the train back to Beaune (2/hour weekdays, 1/hour weekends, ask for *la gare* in Chagny—it is poorly signed). Continuing to **Château de la Rochepot** is not recommended without an e-bike.

North Vineyard Loop

For an easy and rewarding spin by car—or ideally by bike—through waves of vineyards that smother traditional villages, follow this relatively level 10-mile loop from Beaune, worth ▲. It laces together three renowned wine villages—Aloxe-Corton, Pernand-Vergelesses, and Savigny-lès-Beaune—connecting you with Burgundian nature and village wine culture.

Planning Your Drive

With stops, allow a half-day by bike or 1.5 hours by car. Those wanting a little more should take the extension from Pernand-Vergelesses to Magny-les-Villers. Drivers can combine this loop with the "Route des Grands Crus" (all these options are described later).

Bring water and snacks, as there is precious little available until the end of this route. There's a fine picnic spot with shade on the small road halfway between Aloxe-Corton and Pernand-Vergelesses. Your tour concludes in Savigny-lès-Beaune, where you'll find a café-pizzeria, wine tastings, a small grocery, and a unique château.

From Beaune to Savigny-lès-Beaune

By Car: From Beaune's ring road, drivers take D-974 a few blocks north toward Dijon. Follow Savigny-lès-Beaune signs left at the signal, then quickly turn right. On the outskirts of town you'll cross over the autoroute, then veer right, following the second signs you see to Pernand-Vergelesses (D-18). Turn right at the first Aloxe-Corton sign, and glide into the town. Make a hard left at the stop sign and climb uphill to find a small parking area with several recommended wine-tastings close by.

By Bike: From Beaune's ring road, turn right on Rue de Cho-

BURGUNDY

North Vineyard Loop & Route des Grands Crus

North Vineyard Loop

1. Aloxe-Corton Wine Tastings & Hotels
2. La Grappe de Pernand Café
3. Domaine Naudin-Ferrand
4. Henri de Villamont Wine Tasting, Château de Savigny & R. De Famille Café-Pizzeria

Dijon

D-10 — D-905

Velars-sur-Ouche

D-108

Marsannay-la-Côte

D-122 — A-311

Urcy

Fixin

CÔTE DE NUITS

D-974

A-31 → To Nancy & Metz and Colmar via A-36

2 Kilometers
2 Miles

Quemigny-Poisot

D-35

D-31

Gevrey-Chambertin

10 TRAIN STN.

D-122

Ternant

9 Morey-St-Denis

Broindon

Chambolle-Musigny

8 TRAIN STN. A-31

7 Vougeot

D-25

Paris

FRANCE

100 Miles

D-35

Concoeur

5 Vosne-Romanée

6

ROUTE DES GRANDS CRUS

D-25

D-25

Nuits-St-Georges

D-8

Arcenant

D-115

D-8

TRAIN STN.

D-8

N

HAUTE CÔTE DE NUITS

Echevronne

Villers-la-Faye

CÔTE DE NUITS

D-974

HAUTE CÔTE DE BEAUNE

D-2

D-18

3

Magny-les-Villers

D-974

Pernand-Vergelesses

2

D-20F A-31

4 Savigny-lès-Beaune

1 Aloxe-Corton

D-20

D-2

→ To Paris

A-6

Ladoix-Serrigny

NORTH VINEYARD LOOP

CÔTE DE BEAUNE

Chorey

D-20

DRIVING/BIKING TOUR BEGINS

Beaune

TRAIN STN.

D-974

D-973

A-6

→ To La Rochepot

CÔTE DE BEAUNE

D-17

→ To Chalon & Lyon

Legend:
- Famous Wine Regions
- Recommended Driving Route
- 🍷 Wine Tasting

Route des Grands Crus

5. Ferme Fruirouge
6. Romanée-Conti Vineyards
7. Château du Clos de Vougeot
8. Le Caveau des Musignys & Le Millésime Restaurant
9. Caveau des Vignerons
10. Philippe LeClerc Winery, Hôtel les Grands Crus, Le Bar à Vins & La Jeanette

rey after passing the public pool, following signs for Gigny (just before D-974 to Dijon). Continue following signs toward Gigny into Chorey-les-Beaune. In Chorey-les Beaune, veer left onto Rue Pavelot, pass through two stop signs, then follow the lane as it enters the vineyards and eventually curves left. Cross busy D-974, go straight up the tree-lined road, veer right at the fork, then make a left at the stop sign and climb uphill into Aloxe-Corton.

Aloxe-Corton: This tiny town, with a world-class reputation among wine enthusiasts, is packed with top tasting opportunities (but no cafés). The easygoing **Domaines d'Aloxe-Corton,** English-owned **Mischief and Mayhem,** and more upscale **Domaine Comte Senard** all offer different kinds of tastings (see page 887).

• *Drivers and bikers leave Aloxe-Corton and head up the hill on Rue des Chaumes, following signs for Pernand-Vergelesses (you'll pass an idyllic picnic spot on the left in about 300 yards, just after passing a house). At the T-intersection with D-18, most bikers will want to turn left and pick up the directions for leaving Pernand-Vergelesses (below). Otherwise, turn right and head into...*

Pernand-Vergelesses: As you enter the village, look for a cute little café called **$ La Grappe de Pernand** (follow the umbrellas down to the right and find reasonably priced food and drink, closed Mon in off-season and Tue year-round, tel. 03 80 21 59 46).

Drivers and strong bikers should consider two worthwhile detours from Pernand-Vergelesses: Climbing well above the village leads to one of the best vineyard panoramas in Burgundy. To get there, enter Pernand-Vergelesses, turn right at the roundabout and head up into the village, turning right on Rue du Creux St. Germain, and then continuing straight and up along Rue Copeau. Curve up past the church until you see small *Panorama* signs. Drivers and bikers wanting to extend their ride can follow signs (just after passing the church, en route to the panorama) to **Magny-les-Villers** and track a scenic and hilly wine lane for about two miles to one of my favorite wineries, **Domaine Naudin-Ferrand** (see page 888). Just a short distance down this lane brings rewards; the views are best on your return to Pernand-Vergelesses.

• *Leaving Pernand-Vergelesses, bikers and drivers both follow the main road (D-18) back toward Beaune, and turn right into the vineyards on the first lane (at the Pernand-Vergelesses Premier Cru sign, about 400 yards from Pernand-Vergelesses). Keep left at the first fork and rise gently to lovely views. Drop down and turn right when you come to a T, then joyride along the vine service lanes (bikers should watch for loose gravel). The lane dumps you in the center of...*

Savigny-lès-Beaune: A left leads to **Henri de Villamont** winery, and a right leads to the village center, **Château de Savigny,** and the **R. De Famille** café-pizzeria (all described on page 888).

• *From Savigny-lès-Beaune, drive or pedal following signs back into*

*Beaune. To avoid busy D-18 into Beaune, bikers can take a slightly lon-
ger route following D-2a from Savigny, tracking signs to D-974, then
crossing it and taking the first right in Chorey-les-Beaune (along the
stone wall), and then following Route de Beaune signs. Turn right at the
"do not enter" sign then take your first left to reach Beaune's ring road.
Those with a car can continue along the "Route des Grands Crus," next.*

Route des Grands Crus

While I prefer the areas south and west of Beaune, a more northern
stretch of the Route des Grands Crus is a ▲ must for wine connoisseurs with a car, as it passes through Burgundy's most fabled
vineyards.

The first part, between Aloxe-Corton and Nuits-St-Georges,
forces you onto the unappealing highway (D-974). But from Vougeot north, the route improves noticeably if you stick to D-122.
Locals call this section the "Champs-Elysées of Burgundy." Between Vosne-Romanée and Gevrey-Chambertin, the road runs
past 24 *grand cru* wineries of the Côte de Nuits—pinot noir paradise, where 95 percent of the wines are red. The path of today's
busy D-974 road was established by monks in the 12th century to
delineate the easternmost limit of land on which good wine grapes
could be grown. (Land to the east of this road is fine for other crops
but not for wine.) For lunch fixings, you'll find grocery stores in
Nuits-St-Georges and in Gevrey-Chambertin.

Here's a rundown of my favorite places on the northern Route
des Grands Crus, listed from Beaune toward Dijon (for locations,
see the map on page 893). By car each stop is a few minutes from
the next once you get to Nuits-St-Georges.

Concoeur

Come to this little village high above the wine route (northwest of
Nuits-St-George) for a Back Door stop at the shop called **Ferme
Fruirouge**. Adorable owners Sylvain and Isabelle grow cherries,
raspberries, and black currants, and make crème de cassis, vin-
egars, mustards, and jams with passion. They (or their equally
adorable staff) will explain their time-honored process for craft-
ing these products. You can sample everything—including their
one-of-a-kind cassis-ketchup—and get free recipe cards in French
(Thu-Mon 9:00-12:00 & 14:00-19:00, closed Tue-Wed, 2 Place de
l'Eglise, tel. 03 80 62 36 25, www.fruirouge.fr, call ahead to arrange for a good explanation of their operation).

Vosne-Romanée

The fabled **Romanée-Conti** vineyards of this tiny hamlet produce the priciest wines in Burgundy (figure $6,000 per bottle minimum; sorry, all bottles are presold).

Vougeot

In many ways, this is the birthplace of great Burgundian wines. In the 12th century, monks from the abbey of Cîteaux (8 miles southeast from here) built the impressive stone **Château du Clos de Vougeot** to store equipment and make their wines. Their careful study of winemaking was the foundation for the world-famous reputation of Burgundian wines. It was here that monks discovered that pinot noir and chardonnay grapes were best suited to the local soil and climate. There's little to see inside except for the fine stone construction, four ancient and massive wine presses, and the room where the Confrérie des Chevaliers Tastevin (a Burgundian brotherhood of wine tasters) meets to celebrate their legacy—and to apply their label of quality to area wines, called *le Tastevinage*. As you enter, ask if they can play the well-done, 20-minute film about the château and the Confrérie des Chevaliers Tastevin in English (but since it's mostly images, it's still worth seeing in French, shown in the upstairs monks' dormitory). Skipping the entrance fee is a good option for some as you can still view the historic courtyard, see the cellar where Tastevin vintages are stored, and peruse the gift shop. The château has a good English handout and posted information on touchscreens, but no tastings (€7.50, daily April-Oct 9:00-18:30 except Sat until 17:00, Nov-March 10:00-17:00, tel. 03 80 62 86 09, well-signed just outside town, www.closdevougeot.fr).

Some of the region's most scenic vineyards lie north of Vougeot, along D-122, where the next three villages lie.

Chambolle-Musigny

Hiding in the northwest corner of the village of Chambolle-Musigny, **Le Caveau des Musignys** is a fine place to sample Burgundy's rich variety of wines. Say bonjour to *charmant* Annie, who will introduce you to the region's wines in a cool, vaulted tasting room. Representing 45 producers, she has wines from throughout Burgundy in all price ranges (recent vintages only for tasting). The whites and reds from the Hautes-Côtes are a good value, as are the midrange reds from Chambolle-Musigny and Vosne-Romanée (free tasting, shipping available, daily 9:30-18:00, a block north of the church at 1 Rue Traversière, parking available within a few blocks, tel. 03 80 62 84 01). You can eat upstairs in an elegant setting, where sharp, modern decor blends with traditional preparation, at the lovely **$$$ Le Millésime** (lunch *menus* except Sat, pricier dinner *menus,* indoor seating only, dazzling wine shelves, closed Sun-Mon, tel. 03 80 62 80 37).

Morey-St-Denis

This village houses more vineyards, a café, a bakery, and another worthwhile tasting stop at the **Caveau des Vignerons,** with reasonably priced wines from 13 small producers (each too small to have its own tasting room). Gentle Catherine speaks enough English to welcome you to her free tasting room, where you can sample wines from the Côtes de Nuits. They have a good selection of wines from Gevrey-Chambertin, though I prefer those from Morey-St-Denis (daily 10:00-13:00 & 13:30-18:30, next to the church, tel. 03 80 51 86 79).

Gevrey-Chambertin

For many pinot noir lovers, a visit to this flowery village is the pinnacle of their Burgundian pilgrimage. The appealing village has a TI (daily, 1 Rue Gaston Roupnel, tel. 03 80 34 38 40), a small grocery, a café, a pizzeria, a few restaurants, and a good-value hotel.

Gevrey-Chambertin produces nine of the 32 *grand cru* wines from Burgundy. All are pinot noirs (no whites in sight), and all use the suffix "Chambertin" ("Gevrey" is the historic name of the village; "Chambertin" is its most important vineyard. **Philippe LeClerc**'s domaine, nestled in the town center, owns an atmospheric wine cellar with good tastings and a nifty wine museum (€10 for museum and 6 tastes, free if you buy, daily 9:30-19:00, Rue des Halles, tel. 03 80 34 30 72, www.philippe-leclerc.com).

Sleeping in Gevrey-Chambertin: You can sleep well at **$ Hôtel les Grands Crus,***** with simple, spotless, and traditional rooms overlooking vineyards, plus a pleasant patio and free, secure parking. And it's an easy walk to the village center (air-con, at the northwest edge of town on Rue de Lavaux, tel. 03 80 34 34 15, www.hoteldesgrandscrus.com, hotel.lesgrandscrus@nerim.net).

Eating in Gevrey-Chambertin: Enjoy simple, inexpensive fare at the local watering hole, **$ Le Bar à Vins** café (three-course Burgundian *menu* for €18, closed Tue). For lunch, try the funky, fun, and casual **$ La Jeanette,** a little boutique that doubles as a diner with a sliver of outdoor tables and a 1950s interior (small selection but good value, Fri-Tue 10:00-19:00, closed Wed-Thu, 12 Rue du Gaizot, tel. 03 80 33 41 95).

Between Beaune and Paris

North of Beaune, you'll find a handful of worthwhile places that string together well for a full-day excursion: towering Châteauneuf-en-Auxois, remote Fontenay's abbey, pretty little Flavigny-sur-Ozerain, and Julius Caesar's victorious battlefield at Alise-Ste-Reine (with its good museum, MuséoParc Alésia).

As a bonus, following my driving tour of this area takes you along several stretches of the **Burgundy Canal** (Canal de Bourgogne). As in much of France, Burgundy's canals were dug 200 years ago, in the early Industrial Age, as an affordable way to transport heavy materials. The Burgundy canal was among the most important, linking Paris with the Mediterranean Sea. The canal is 145 miles long, with 209 locks, and rises over France's continental divide in Pouilly-en-Auxois, just below Châteauneuf-en-Auxois (where the canal runs underground for about two miles). Digging began in 1727 and the canal was completed in 1832—just in time for the invention of steam engines on rails, which soon eliminated the need for waterway transport (timing is, as they say, everything).

Back-Door Burgundy Towns and Sights

The towns and sights described below can be connected with my "Back-Door Burgundy Drive" outlined on page 904.

Châteauneuf-en-Auxois

This living hill town, hunkered in the shadow of its 14th-century castle, merits exploring. The perfectly medieval castle once monitored passage between Burgundy and Paris, with hawk-eye views from its 2,000-foot-high setting. *Châteauneuf* means "new castle," so you'll see many in France. This one is in the Auxois area, so it's Châteauneuf-en-Auxois. Park at the lot in the very upper end of the village (where the road ends), and don't miss the **panoramic viewpoint** nearby. The military value of this site is powerfully clear from here. Find the Burgundy Canal and the three reservoirs that have maintained the canal's flow for more than 200 years. The small village below is Châteauneuf's port, Vandenesse-en-Auxois—you'll be there shortly. If not for phylloxera—the vine-loving insect that ravaged France in the late 1800s, killing all its vineyards—you'd see more vineyards than wheat fields.

Saunter into the village, where every building feels historic and stocky farmers live side by side with tattooed artists. Walk into the courtyard, but skip the **château**'s interior (€5, Tue-Sun 10:00-

12:00 & 14:00-18:00, closed Mon, English handout). You'll get better moat views and see the more important castle entry by walking beneath the Hôstellerie du Château, and then turning right, following *Eglise* signs.

Sleeping and Eating in Châteauneuf-en-Auxois: A simple place, **$ Hôstellerie du Château**** houses an enticing budget-vacation ensemble: nine homey, inexpensive rooms with a rear garden overlooking the brooding floodlit castle at night (tel. 03 80 49 22 00, www.hostellerie-de-chateauneuf.com, contact@hostellerie-de-chateauneuf.com). Their **$$** good-value **restaurant** offers regional cuisine, salads, and grilled meats (closed Wed off-season). There are also several affordable cafés and restaurants along the town's main drag, including cozy **$ Orée du Bois,** which makes good crêpes, including one stuffed with snails (tel. 03 80 49 25 32).

Alise-Ste-Reine

A united Gaul forming a single nation animated by the same spirit could defy the universe.

—Julius Caesar, *The Gallic Wars*

Historians are convinced that Julius Caesar defeated the Gallic leader Vercingétorix on these lands surrounding the vertical village of Alise-Ste-Reine in 52 BC, thus winning Gaul for the Roman Empire and forever changing France's destiny. Visit the museum-park and stand where Caesar did, then drive above the village to see things from the Gauls' perspective.

▲MuséoParc Alésia

This circular museum, looking like a modern sports arena, does this important site justice with easy-to-follow exhibits and well-

delivered information (but no original artifacts from the battle). The circular structure symbolizes how, more than 2,000 years ago, Caesar ordered his outnumbered forces to surround the Gauls' *oppidum* (hilltop village), starving them out and winning a decisive victory (see sidebar).

Cost: €10, includes essential audioguide (kid version, too), skip the €2 extra for the archaeological site on the hills above.

Hours: Daily April-Sept 10:00-18:00, until 19:00 July-Aug, shorter hours off-season, closed Feb, tel. 03 80 96 96 23, www. alesia.com.

Visiting the Museum: With the help of the audioguide, touchscreens, and posted information, you'll gain a keen understanding of the events that led up to this battle, why it happened here, and how it unfolded. You'll learn much about the two protagonists, Caesar and Vercingétorix, their armies, and their motivations, and be drawn into the conflict with an 18-minute film.

Allow an hour for the museum's single floor of exhibits, then climb to the top floor for views from a Roman perspective. Finally, walk out back to inspect the full-scale reconstruction of a section of the Roman wall and lookouts that pinned the Gauls to that hilltop.

Staff dressed as Romans or Gauls are present in high season to answer your questions and give demonstrations (some English spoken). Pick up the chain-mail suit (30 pounds), and learn that it took more than half a mile of metal line to make one. To add more meaning to this sight, read "The Romans in Provence" (see page 581).

Nearby: Drive up through the village of Alise-Ste-Reine and follow the *Statue de Vercingétorix* signs leading to the park with the huge **statue** of the Gallic warrior overlooking his Waterloo (skip the archaeological site). Stand as he did—imagining yourself trapped on this hilltop—then find the orientation table under the gazebo and appreciate the peekaboo views through the trees.

Flavigny-sur-Ozerain

A few minutes from Alise-Ste-Reine, little Flavigny-sur-Ozerain's (flah-veen-yee sur oh-zuh-rain) red-tile roofs cover its hilltop with a movie-set panorama. The town had its 15 minutes of fame in 2000, when the movie *Chocolat* was filmed here, but otherwise this unassuming and serenely situated village feels permanently stuck in the past. Flavigny makes a good coffee or lunch stop, as there's little to do here but appreciate the setting, admire its beautiful church, and sample the local *anis* (anise) candies.

Flavigny has been home to an abbey since 719, when the first (Benedictine) abbey of St. Pierre was built. The town thrived during the Middle Ages thanks to its relative proximity to Vézelay (with its relics of Mary Magdalene) and the flood of pilgrims coming through en route to Santiago de Compostela in northwest Spain. The little town was occupied by the Brits during the Hundred Years' War (15th century), then ever-so-gradually slid into irrelevance. By the time the French Revolution rolled around, it had no religious or defensive importance and was left alone. The movie *Chocolat* (with Johnny Depp, Juliette Binoche, and Alfred Molina) put the town back on the map—at least for a while. The TI and *anis* shop have booklets of photos taken during the filming and can help you locate key buildings featured in the movie. Today, Flavigny has been reinvigorated by the return of 50 Benedictine monks to the Abbey of St. Joseph.

Park in the designated lot and enter the village, passing the

The Dying Gauls

In 52 BC, General Julius Caesar and his 60,000 soldiers surrounded Alésia (today's Alise-Ste-Reine), hoping to finally end the uprising of free Gaul and establish Roman civilization in central and northern France (they had long controlled the south). Holed up inside the hilltop fortress were 80,000 die-hard (long-haired, tattooed) Gauls under their rebel chief, Vercingétorix (pronounced something like "verse-an-zhet-or-eex"). Having harassed Caesar for months with guerrilla-war attacks, they now called on their fellow Gauls to converge on Alésia.

Rather than attack the fierce-fighting Gauls, Caesar's soldiers patiently camped at the base of the hill and began building a wall. In six weeks, they had completed a 12-foot-tall, stone-and-earth wall all the way around Alésia (11 miles around—blue line on the orientation table at the hilltop site), and then a second, larger one (13 miles around—red line on the orientation table), trapping the rebel leaders with the intention of starving them out. If the Gauls tried to escape, not only would they have to breach the two walls, they'd first have to cross a steep no-man's-land dotted with a ditch, a moat, and booby traps (including stakes in pits and buried iron spikes).

The starving Gauls inside Alésia sent their women and children out to beg for mercy from the Romans. The Romans (with little food themselves) refused. For days, the women and children wandered the unoccupied land, in full view of both armies, until they starved to death.

After months of siege, Vercingétorix's reinforcements finally arrived. With 90,000 screaming Gallic warriors (Caesar says 250,000) converging on Alésia, and 80,000 more atop the hill, Caesar ordered his men to move between the two walls to fight a two-front battle. The Battle of Alésia raged for five days—a classic struggle between the methodical Romans and the impetuous "barbarians." When it became clear the Romans would not budge, the Gauls retreated.

Vercingétorix surrendered, and Gallic culture was finished. During the rebellion, one in five Gauls had been killed, enslaved, or driven out. Roman rule was established for the next 500 years, and Vercingétorix spent his last years as a prisoner. In 46 BC, he was brought to Rome, where he was strangled to death in a public ritual.

café-restaurant along the Rue de l'Abbaye. You'll soon come to the charming **Anis de Flavigny shop** and factory at the former Abbaye de St-Pierre. The shop has a sweet little café, information about the village, and tours of its candy production (open daily). The candies are sold in pretty tins for €2.50 and make great souvenirs—the coffee-flavored ones are *très bon*. Pick up a village map here or from the **TI** (limited hours, a block down from the church on Rue de l'Eglise). And peek into the evocative ninth-century Carolingian crypt next door.

The town revolves around its medieval **Church of St. Genest,** with its mesmerizing interior (closed 12:30-14:30). Climb to the balcony for fine views up the nave (*Chocolat* movie fans can relive the young priest's anxious sermons). Outside the church, just below the recommended Grange restaurant, spot the location for the movie's chocolate shop (behind the rounded brown window sills).

Eating in Flavigny-sur-Ozerain: You'll eat for a steal at **$$ La Grange** ("The Barn") on cheap, farm-fresh fare, including luscious quiche, salads, *plats du jour*, fresh cheeses, pâtés, and delicious fruit pies (April-mid-Oct daily 12:30-18:00; open Sun only in off-season and closed Dec-Jan; across from church, look for brown doors and listen for lunchtime dining, tel. 03 80 35 81 78).

▲▲Abbey of Fontenay

The entire ensemble of buildings composing this isolated Cistercian abbey has survived, giving visitors perhaps the best picture of medieval abbey life in France.

In the Middle Ages, it was written, "To fully grasp the meaning of Fontenay and the power of its beauty, you must approach it trudging through the forest footpaths...through the brambles and bogs...in an October rain." Those arriving by car will still find Fontenay's secluded setting—blanketed in birdsong and with a garden lovingly used "as a stage set"—truly magical.

Cost and Hours: €10, daily 10:00-19:00, mid-Nov-March 10:00-12:00 & 14:00-17:00, tel. 03 80 92 15 00, www. abbayedefontenay.com. Private English tours can be booked by calling ahead (€100/group).

Getting There: The abbey is a 10-minute drive (4 miles) north of Montbard. There's no bus service—allow about €30 round-trip for a taxi from Montbard's train station (taxi mobile 06 08 26 61 55 or 06 08 82 20 61), or rent a bike at Montbard's TI (electric and standard) and ride 30 minutes each way (TI tel. 03 80 92 53 81).

Background: This abbey—one of the oldest Cistercian abbeys in France—was founded in 1118 by St. Bernard as a back-to-basics reaction to the excesses of Benedictine abbeys like Cluny. The Cistercians worked to recapture the simplicity, solitude, and poverty of the early Church. Bernard created "a horrible vast solitude" in the forest, where his monks could live like the desert fathers of the Old Testament. They chose marshland ("Cistercian" is derived from "marshy bogs") and strove to be separate from the world (which required the industrious self-sufficiency these abbeys were so adept at). The movement spread, essentially colonizing Europe religiously. In 1200, there were more than 500 such monasteries and abbeys in Europe.

Like the Cistercian movement in general, Fontenay flourished from the 13th to 15th century. A 14th-century proverb said, "Wherever the wind blows, to Fontenay money flows." Fontenay thrived as a prosperous "mini city" for nearly 700 years, until the French Revolution, when it became the property of the nation and was eventually sold.

Visiting the Abbey: Like visitors centuries ago, you'll enter through the abbey's **gatehouse.** The main difference: Anyone with a ticket gets in, and there's no watchdog barking angrily at you (through the small hole on the right). Pick up the excellent English self-guided tour flier with your ticket. Your visit follows the route described here (generally clockwise). Arrows keep you on course, and signs tell you which sections of the abbey are private (as its owners still live here).

Start at the stone bench 75 yards from the **abbey church.** Read the abbey flier for background. Enter the **church.** Inside it's pure Romanesque and built to St. Bernard's specs: Latin cross plan, no fancy stained glass, unadorned columns, earthen floors—nothing to distract from prayer. The lone statue is the 13th-century *Virgin of Fontenay,* a reminder that the church was dedicated to Mary. Breathe in the ethereal light. Quiet your mind and listen carefully to hear the brothers chanting.

Stairs lead from the end of the church to a vast 16th-century, oak-beamed **dormitory** where the monks slept—together, fully dressed, on thin mats. Monastic life was pretty simple: prayer, reading, work, seven services a day, one meal in the winter, two in the summer. Daily rations: a loaf of bread and a quarter-liter of wine.

Back down the stairs, enter the **cloister.** Stand in the center surrounded by a gaggle of unadorned, rounded arches—so beautiful in their simplicity. This was the heart of the community, where monks read, exercised, washed, did small projects—and, I imagine, gave each other those silly haircuts.

The shallow alcove (next to the church door) once stored prayer books; notice the slots for shelves. Next to that, the vaulted **chapter room** was where the abbot led discussions and community business was discussed. The adjacent **monks' hall** was a general-purpose room, likely busy with monks hunched over tables copying sacred texts (a major work of abbeys). The dining hall, or refectory, also faced the cloister (closed to the public).

Across the garden stands the huge abbey **forge.** In the 13th

BURGUNDY

century, the monks at Fontenay ran what many consider Europe's first metalworking plant. Iron ore was melted down in ovens with big bellows. Tools were made and sold for a profit. The hydraulic hammer, which became the basis of industrial manufacturing of iron throughout Europe, was first used here. Leaving the building, walk left around the back to see the stream, which was diverted to power the wheels that operated the forge. Water was vital to abbey life. The **pond**—originally practical, rather than decorative—was a fish farm (some whopper descendants still swim here).

Leave through the small museum and gift shop, which was the public **chapel** in the days when visitors were not allowed inside the abbey grounds. Upstairs you'll see a **model** of the abbey complex and appreciate the isolation these monks found here. Next to it a sign displays a quote from St. Bernard: *"We learn more from the woods than from books; the trees and rocks teach us things we could not learn elsewhere."*

Back-Door Burgundy Drive

This all-day, 125-mile loop links Châteauneuf-en-Auxois, Alise-Ste-Reine, and Fontenay, with short stops suggested in Flavigny-sur-Ozerain and Semur-en-Auxois. The trip trades vineyards for wheat fields, canals, and pastoral landscapes. You'll drive along the Burgundy canal and visit a Cistercian abbey, medieval villages, and the site of Gaul's last stand against the Romans. If you're heading to/from Paris, this tour works well en route or as an overnight stop; I've listed accommodations and described sights along the way in greater detail under "Back-Door Burgundy Towns and Sights," earlier.

Planning Your Drive: For this drive you'll need a good map (Michelin maps #320 or #519 work well). Here's how I'd spend this day: Get out early and joyride to MuséoParc Alésia in Alise-Ste-Reine (with at least a short stop in Châteauneuf-en-Auxois), tour the museum and battle site, have lunch a few minutes away in Flavigny, drive to Fontenay and tour the abbey, then consider a photo stop in Semur-en-Auxois on your way back (this plan also works for those continuing to Paris). Energetic sightseers could add Vézelay to this plan by getting on the road no later than 8:00 and focusing on Alise-Ste-Reine and Fontenay, then darting over to Vézelay on the way back.

The museum and battlefield at Alise-Ste-Reine and the Abbey of Fontenay are your primary goals; allow an hour to tour each. With no stops, this one-way drive from Beaune to Fontenay should take about an hour and a half. But you should be stopping—a lot. (Those in a hurry can get from Beaune to Fontenay in about an

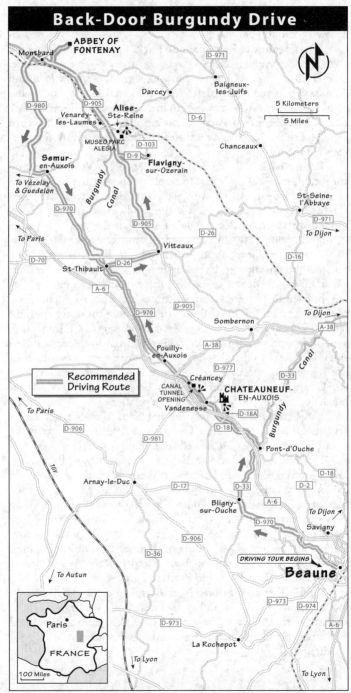

Back-Door Burgundy Drive

N

5 Kilometers

5 Miles

ABBEY OF FONTENAY

Montbard

D-971

Darcey

Baigneux-les-Juifs

D-980

D-905

Venarey-les-Laumes

Alise-Ste-Reine

D-6

MUSEO PARC ALESIA

D-103

Chanceaux

Semur-en-Auxois

D-9

Flavigny-sur-Ozerain

To Vézelay & Guedelon

Burgundy Canal

St-Seine-l'Abbaye

D-970

D-905

D-971

To Paris

D-26

To Dijon

D-70

Vitteaux

D-16

St-Thibault

D-26

A-6

D-970

D-905

Sombernon

To Dijon

A-38

Pouilly-en-Auxois

A-38

Canal

Recommended Driving Route

Créancey

D-977

D-33

CANAL TUNNEL OPENING

CHATEAUNEUF-EN-AUXOIS

To Paris

Vandenesse

D-18A

Burgundy

D-906

D-981

D-18

Pont-d'Ouche

TGV

Arnay-le-Duc

D-17

D-33

D-18

D-2

Bligny-sur-Ouche

A-6

To Dijon

D-970

Savigny

To Autun

D-906

D-36

DRIVING TOUR BEGINS

Beaune

Paris

FRANCE

100 Miles

D-973

D-974

To Lyon

La Rochepot

A-6

To Lyon

hour via the autoroute: Take exit #21 to Semur-en-Auxois, then follow D-980 to Fontenay.)

From Beaune to Fontenay and Back: Leave Beaune following signs for *Auxerre* and *Bligny-sur-Ouche;* from Bligny-sur-Ouche, take D-33 to Pont d'Ouche (following signs to *Pont du Pany* and *Dijon*), where you'll turn left along the canal (D-18), following signs to *Château de Châteauneuf.* In five minutes, you'll see the castle at **Châteauneuf-en-Auxois** looming above (see page 898). Turn right on D-18a and cross over the canal, then the freeway, for great views of the hill town, even if you're not visiting it.

Return back down to the canal, press on to Vandenesse, and turn right, crossing the canal (nice picnic spot on the "port," with views of Châteauneuf-en-Auxois). Next, turn left to **Créancey** (D-18) and pause once there. The Burgundy Canal tunnels underground for several miles through Pouilly-en-Auxois, as it passes its highest point between Paris and Dijon (rivers east of here flow to the Mediterranean, those to the west to the Atlantic). Look for small brown signs in Créancey reading *Entrée de Souterrain du Canal* for a short detour to see the canal tunnel's opening.

Stay on D-18 from Créancey through Pouilly-en-Auxois, and then follow signs (on D-970) to Vitteaux. In St-Thibault turn right on D-26 toward Vitteaux. Consider a quick stop in St-Thibault to view its evocative 13th-century church (English descriptions inside). Turn left in Vitteaux on D-905 and drive north toward Alise-Ste-Reine. Just before Alise-Ste-Reine, look for signs to **Flavigny-sur-Ozerain** (5 scenic minutes away on D-9). Save Flavigny for lunch and tour Alise-Ste-Reine before or after.

Signs lead from Flavigny's parking lot to Alise-Ste-Reine (described earlier), where Julius Caesar is said to have defeated the Gauls. Follow signs to *Alésia* and *MuséoParc.*

From here drop down to D-905, turn right (north), and follow signs to the secluded Cistercian Abbey of Fontenay (described earlier). After the abbey, continue up D-905 to Montbard, then turn onto D-980 and drive south, stopping to admire the rooftop view over Semur-en-Auxois (across from the Citroën shop, where D-980 and D-954 intersect). From there, take D-970 via Pouilly-en-Auxois and retrace your route to Beaune. For a quicker option, you can dart from Semur-en-Auxois across to the A-6 autoroute and take it to Beaune (or head north to Paris).

Public Transit Options: Nondrivers can get to Alésia by taking the train from Dijon to Les Laumes-Alésia (one-mile walk to site) and to the Abbey of Fontenay by taking the train to Montbard and a taxi or bike from there (see Abbey of Fontenay listing for details).

Between Burgundy and the Loire

These three sights—Vézelay and its Romanesque Basilica of Ste. Madeleine; the under-construction Château de Guédelon; and the underrated, overlooked city of Bourges, with its grand "High" Gothic cathedral—make good stops for drivers connecting Burgundy and the Loire Valley. Visiting all three in one day is impossible, so pick two and get an early start (allow 6 hours of driving from Beaune to the Loire, plus time to stop and visit the sights). The first two sights also work if you're linking Burgundy and Paris (skip Bourges, which requires a long detour).

Vézelay

For more than eight centuries, travelers have hoofed it up through this pretty little town to get to the famous hilltop church, the Basilica of Ste. Madeleine. In its 12th-century prime, Vézelay welcomed the medieval masses. Cultists of Mary Magdalene came to file past her (supposed) body. Pilgrims rendezvoused here to march to Spain to venerate St. James' (supposed) relics in Santiago de Compostela. Three Crusades were launched from this hill: the Second Crusade (1146), announced by Bernard of Clairveaux; the Third Crusade (1190), under Richard the Lionheart and King Philippe Auguste; and the Seventh Crusade (1248), by King (and Saint) Louis IX. Today, tourists flock to Vézelay's basilica, famous for its place in history, its soul-stirring Romanesque architecture—reproduced in countless art books—and for the relics of Mary Magdalene.

Tourist Information: Vézelay's TI is a block uphill as you climb through the village. Learn your options for visiting the basilica, including the TI's €3 audioguide that covers the church and town (12 Rue St. Etienne, daily in summer 10:00-13:00 & 14:00-18:00, until 19:00 July-Aug, closed Thu Oct-April, Sun Sept-June, and Mon Sept-March; tel. 03 86 33 23 69, http://en.vezelaytourisme.com, vezelay.otsi@wanadoo.fr).

Getting There: Vézelay is about 90 minutes northwest of Beaune. Drivers take the Nitry exit from A-6 and follow *Vézelay* signs for about 20 minutes. Pay parking is available at the lower end of the village (about €4/day). Train travelers go to **Sermizelles** and take the SNCF shuttle bus (check TI website for details, 2/day, free with rail pass; allows you about 6 hours in Vézelay or an easy overnight) or a taxi (6 miles, allow €20 one-way, mobile 06 74 53 45 76, www.cathytaxi-vezelay.fr). From Paris, Gare de Bercy trains run directly to Sermizelles (3/day direct, more with transfer in Auxerre, 3 hours); from other places, you'll transfer in Auxerre or Avallon.

Sights in Vézelay

▲▲Basilica of Ste. Madeleine

To accommodate the growing crowds of medieval pilgrims, the abbots of Vézelay enlarged their original church (1104), then rebuilt it after a disastrous 1120 fire. The building we see today—one of the largest and best-preserved Romanesque churches anywhere—was built in stages: nave (1120-1140), narthex (1132-1145), and choir (1215). The construction spanned the century-long transition from the Romanesque style (round barrel arches like the ancient Romans', thick walls, small windows) to Gothic (pointed arches, flying buttresses, high nave, lots of stained glass). Vézelay blends elements of both styles.

Cost and Hours: Free, daily 7:00-20:00; Mass Mon-Fri at 18:30, Sat at 12:30 and 18:30, Sun at 11:00.

Getting There: Allow 20 minutes to walk uphill from the parking lots and bus stop at the bottom of the village to the basilica. A free shuttle van runs along this climb daily in summer, weekends in spring and fall, none in winter (call the TI for updates). You'll be tempted by shops, galleries, and cafés as you ascend—just as pilgrims have for 800 years.

Tours: The TI's **audioguide** covers the basilica (described in "Tourist Information," earlier). The **Maison du Visiteur** center presentation focuses on the basilica's light and architecture (€8, 4/day; tours of basilica interior possible for individuals—usually in French with English handout for €10, or in English for private groups for about €130; located on main drag a few blocks below basilica, tel. 03 86 32 35 65, www.vezelay-visiteur.com, maisonduvisiteur@orange.fr). **Monk- or nun-guided basilica tours** are possible (tel. 03 86 33 39 50, www.basiliquedevezelay.org). Or be your own guide, either by following the route I describe next or buying the €8 **guidebook** as you enter.

Visiting the Basilica: The **facade**—with one tower missing its original steeple, another that's unfinished, and an inauthentic tympanum—isn't why you came. Step inside.

The **narthex,** or entrance hall, served several functions. Religiously, it was a place to cross from the profane to the sacred. Practically, it gave shelter to overflow pilgrim crowds (even overnight, if necessary) as they shuffled through one of the three doorways. And aesthetically, the dark narthex prepares the visitor for the radiant nave.

The **tympanum** (carved relief) over the central, interior doorway is one of Romanesque's signature pieces. It shows the risen

Mary Magdalene

France has a special affection for Mary Magdalene *(La Madeleine)*, and Vézelay is one of several churches dedicated to her—a rarity in Europe, where most churches honor Jesus' mother, the Virgin Mary.

The Bible says that Mary Magdalene, one of Jesus' followers, was exorcised of seven demons (Luke 8:2), witnessed the Crucifixion (Matthew 27:56), and was the first mortal to see the resurrected Jesus (Mark 16:9-11)—the other disciples didn't believe her.

Some theologians have fleshed out Mary's reputation by associating her with biblical passages that don't specifically name her—e.g., the sinner who washed Jesus' feet with her hair (Luke 7:36-50), the forgiven adulteress (John 8), or the woman with the alabaster jar who anointed Jesus (Matthew 26:7-13).

In medieval times, legends appeared (especially in France) that, after the Crucifixion, Mary Magdalene fled to southern France, lived in a cave, converted locals, performed miracles, and died in Provence. Renaissance artists portrayed her as a fanciful blend of Bible and legend: a redheaded, long-haired prostitute who was rescued by Jesus, symbolizing the sin of those who love too much.

In recent times, feminists have claimed Mary Magdalene was a victim of male-dominated Catholic suppression. Bible scholars cite passages in two ancient (but noncanonical) gospels that cryptically allude to Mary as Jesus' special "companion." *The Da Vinci Code*—a popular if unhistorical novel—seized on this, slathering it with medieval legend and asserting that Mary Magdalene was actually Jesus' wife who bore him descendants, and that her relics lie not in Vézelay but in a shopping mall in Paris.

Christ standing on a tomb with welcoming arms wide open, ascending to heaven in an almond-shaped cloud, shooting Holy Ghost rays at his apostles and telling them to preach the Good News to the ends of the earth. The whole diversity of humanity (appropriate, considering Vézelay's function as a gathering place) appears beneath: hunters, fishermen, farmers, pygmies, and men with long ears, feathers, and dog heads—the grotesque figures depicting those not touched by God's word. The signs of the zodiac arch over the scene.

Gaze through the central doorway into the **nave** at the rows and rows of arches that seem to recede into a luminous infinity. The nave is long, high, and narrow (200 feet by 60 feet by 35 feet), creating a tunnel effect formed by 10 columns and arches on each side. Overhead is the church's most famous feature—barrel vaults (wide arches) built of stones alternating between creamy white and light brown. The nave rises up between the low-ceilinged side aisles, lined with slender floor-to-ceiling columns that unite both stories. The interior glows with an even light from the unstained glass of the clerestory windows. The absence of distractions or bright colors makes this simple church perfect for meditation.

The capitals of the nave's **columns** are masterpieces of saints and Bible scenes carved by several sculptors. All are worth studying (the guidebook sold at the entry identifies each scene). Here are some you might recognize. Start on the right aisle and locate the Conversion of St. Eustace (third column up), depicting the Christian conversion of Roman general Placidus and the ensuing challenges to his faith. On the next (fourth) column find the well-known "Mystical Mill," showing Old Testament Moses and New Testament Paul working together to fill sacks with grain (and, metaphorically, the Bible with words). Cross to the left aisle and find David and Goliath (fourth column), Adam and Eve (ninth column), and Peter Freed from Prison (10th and final column).

The light at the end of the tunnel-like nave is the **choir,** radiating a brighter, blue-gray light. Constructed when Gothic was the rage, the choir has pointed arches and improved engineering, but for me it feels cold and sterile.

In the right transept stands a **statue** of the woman this church was dedicated to—not the Virgin Mary (Jesus' mother) but one of Jesus' disciples, Mary Magdalene. She cradles an alabaster jar of ointment she used (according to some Bible interpretations) to anoint Jesus.

Go down into the **crypt** for the ultimate medieval experience in one of Europe's greatest medieval churches. You're entering the foundations of the earlier ninth-century church that monks built here on the hilltop after Vikings had twice pillaged their church at the base of the hill. Step carefully across the crude floor, and pause on a pew to reflect on the pure, timeless scene. Notice the utter simplicity of these capitals compared to those you saw earlier. File past the small container with the **relics of Mary Magdalene.** In medieval times, Vézelay claimed to possess Mary's entire body, but the relics were later damaged and scattered by anti-Catholic Huguenots (16th century) and Revolutionaries (18th century), leaving only a few pieces.

Are they really her mortal remains? We only have legends—many different versions—that first appeared in the historical record around AD 1000. The most popular says that Mary Magdalene traveled to Provence, where she died, and that her bones were brought here by a monk to save them from Muslim pirates. In the 11th century, the abbots of Vézelay heavily marketed the notion that these were Mary's relics, and when the pope authenticated them in 1058, tourism boomed.

Vézelay prospered until the mid-13th century, when King Charles of Anjou announced that Mary's body was not in Vézelay, but had been found in another town. Vézelay's relics suddenly looked bogus, and pilgrims stopped coming. For the next five centuries, the church fell into disrepair and then was vandalized by secularists in the Revolution. The church was restored (1840-1860) by a young architect named Eugène Viollet-le-Duc, who would later revamp Notre-Dame in Paris and help plan the Statue of Liberty.

A **glorious view** over the Burgundian countryside hides in a park behind the basilica's cloisters (out the right transept).

Sleeping and Eating in Vézelay

Sleeping in Vézelay: Hotels are gathered at the base of the village on Place du Champ-de-Foire, near parking and the bus stop.

$$ Hôtel de la Poste et du Lion d'Or*** has 39 comfortable, country-classy rooms and a **$$$ restaurant** to match (air-con, pay parking, at the foot of the village, Place du Champ-de-Foire, tel. 03 73 53 03 20, www.hplv-vezelay.com, reservation@hplv-vezelay.com).

¢ Hôtel le Compostelle** offers a solid value with 18 spotless rooms and a view breakfast room (Place du Champ-de-Foire, www.lecompostellevezelay.com, le.compostelle@wanadoo.fr, tel. 03 86 33 28 63).

Eating in Vézelay: You'll find pleasant cafés with reasonable food all along the street leading to the church.

$$ Le Cheval Blanc serves tasty Burgundian cuisine at pleasant outside tables or in their cozy dining room (closed Wed-Thu, Place du Champ-de-Foire, tel. 03 86 33 22 12).

$ La Dent Creuse has the best terrace tables at the lower end of the village (left side), with decent salads, pizza, and such (daily until 21:00, Place du Champ-de-Foire, tel. 03 86 33 36 33).

$ Le Vézelien bar/café, halfway up to the basilica, features cheap omelets and a small selection of salads and *plats*, with appealing seating outside and in (closed Tue-Wed, 1 Place du Grand Puits, tel. 03 86 33 25 09).

Café Calabus offers tea, coffee, and other drinks in an atmospheric setting just below the basilica (Rue St. Pierre).

Château de Guédelon

A historian's dream (worth ▲▲, or ▲▲▲ for kids), this castle is being built by 35 enthusiasts using only the tools, techniques, and materials available in the 13th century.

GETTING THERE

Guédelon lies an hour west of Vézelay on D-955, between St-Amand-en-Puisaye and St-Sauveur-en-Puisaye. Finding it requires patient route-finding skills and time. Allow 2.5 hours from Paris or Beaune at a steady pace. Coming from Paris, take exit #18 off the A-6 autoroute (well before Auxerre) and follow D-3 to Toucy; then join D-955 south. Coming from Beaune, exit A-6 at Nitry, then carefully track signs to Vézelay (take a break to visit its basilica), Clamecy, Entrains-sur-Nohain, St-Amand-en-Puisaye, and finally Guédelon (direction: St-Fargeau). The castle is inaccessible by public transport.

ORIENTATION

Cost: €14 for adults, €12 for kids 5-17, cheaper online, free for kids 4 and under.

Hours: Castle open July-Aug daily 9:30-18:30; April-June and Sept-early Nov Thu-Mon 10:00-18:00, closed Tue-Wed; closed late Nov-March (tel. 03 86 45 66 66, www.guedelon.fr).

Tours: There's a good English handout, some posted information, and English-speaking workers on site. Expertly guided tours in English are available most days in July and August for an additional €3/person; check online for times. Guided private tours can be arranged at other times of year and are well worth the investment (1.5-hour tour-€160, contact sarah.preston@guedelon.fr).

Services: There's a picnic area and good-value lunch café with many options inside.

VISITING THE CASTLE

The project is the dream of two individuals who wanted to build a medieval castle (this one is based on plans drafted in 1228). Started in 1997, it will ultimately include four towers surrounding a central courtyard with a bridge and a moat (images of the finished castle are on postcards and in books in the gift shop). The goal of this exciting project is to give visitors a better appreciation of medieval construction, and for the builders to learn about  medieval techniques while they work. The castle won't be complete for another 12 years or so, so you still have time to watch the process.

Enter the project to the sound of chisels chipping rock and the sight of people dressed as if it were 800 years ago. Human-powered hamster wheels carefully hoist up to 1,000 pounds of stone up tower walls (the largest tower will reach six stories when completed). Carpenters whack away at massive beams, creating supports for stone arches, while weavers demonstrate how clothing was made (a sheep's pen provides raw materials). Thirteen workstations help visitors learn about castle construction, from medieval rope-making to blacksmithing. Ask the workers questions—some speak English. If it's been raining, be prepared for mud—you are, after all, on a construction site.

You can also visit the working reconstruction of a medieval flour mill, a quarter-mile walk from the construction site along a woodland path—wear good walking shoes.

Kids can't get enough of Guédelon. It's a favorite for local school field trips, so expect lots of children. And if you can't get enough, there's a program for those wanting to help with the work (must speak French, check their website for details).

SLEEPING NEAR GUEDELON

Guédelon is remote. To sleep nearby, try **$ Hôtel Les Grands Chênes,***** where British Rachael and French Alain have restored a pretty manor home with a nice pool among trees, lakes, and waves of grass (family rooms, on D-18 between St-Fargeau and St-Amand-en-Puisaye, tel. 03 86 74 04 05, www.hotellesgrandschenes.com, contact@hotellesgrandschenes.com).

Bourges

Nestled between rolling vineyards and thick forests in the geographical center of France, unpretentious Bourges (pronounced "boorzh") is among France's most overlooked and authentic cities. Here you'll uncover a wonderful collection of medieval houses, a Gothic cathedral to rival any you've seen, and a down-to-earth, Midwest-like friendliness. Situated three hours due south of Paris, two hours west of Beaune, and 1.5 hours east of Amboise, Bourges is a handy stopover on the drive through the French heartland between Burgundy and the Loire.

Little-known Bourges has a big story to tell, thanks largely to its strategic location between two once-powerful regions, Burgundy and the Loire. It began as a Celtic city, became one of the first Christian towns in Gaul, and later served as the northern boundary of the sophisticated Kingdom of Aquitaine. Bourges reached its peak in the Middle Ages, when its great cathedral was built. It was home to future King Charles VII (r. 1422-1461), the man who, at Joan of Arc's insistence, rallied the French and drove out the English. During that Hundred Years' War, Bourges was a provisional

BURGUNDY

capital of France, which explains its impressive legacy of medieval architecture.

TOURIST INFORMATION

If the cathedral had a transept, the TI would lie outside the south portal (generally Mon-Sat 9:00-19:00; Sun 10:00-18:00 except Oct-March 14:00-17:00; 21 Rue Victor Hugo, tel. 02 48 23 02 60, www.bourges-tourisme.com). Pick up a town map. Wine lovers should ask for the *Route des Vignobles* map, and historians the *Route Jacques Cœur* map.

ARRIVAL IN BOURGES

By Train: From the station, it's about a half-mile walk south to the town center and cathedral. Head straight out onto Avenue Henri Laudier and turn left onto Rue du Commerce to find the TI.

By Car: Parking Mairie-Cathédrale is on the south side of the cathedral (small fee, free on Sun). The stairs up to the street land you in front of the TI. Parking Séraucourt/Centre Historique on Rue de Séraucourt, several blocks south of the cathedral, is free.

HELPFUL HINTS

Street Markets: Bourges is known for its good morning markets (all close by 13:00). The biggest is held on Saturdays on Place de la Nation. A smaller Thursday market takes place near the cathedral on Place des Maronniers, and Place St-Bonnet has a good market on Sundays.

Sound-and-Light Show: Bourges' **Nuits Lumière** starts at sundown every night in July and August, and every Thursday, Friday, and Saturday in June and September. The town's facades, courtyards, and monuments are colorfully illuminated, accompanied by medieval and Renaissance music.

Music Festival: Every April, Bourges hosts **Printemps de Bourges,** a huge music festival.

Laundry: Try **Laverie Excelclean** (1 Rue Wittelsheim, daily 7:00-21:00, mobile 06 80 24 64 41), or ask at the TI.

Sights in Bourges

The city's medieval lanes, lined with half-timbered buildings, are best appreciated on foot. The only sights in Bourges that charge admission are the Palais Jacques Cœur and the cathedral tower/crypt (both worth paying for). The handful of municipal museums are all free.

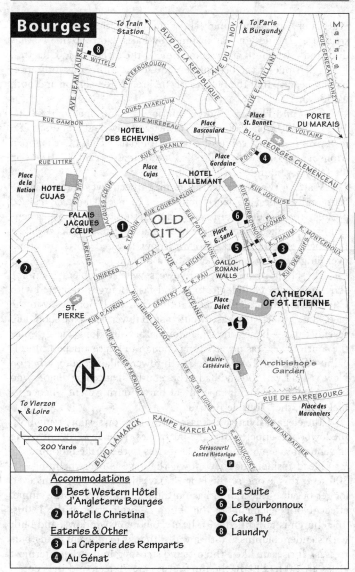

Bourges

To Train Station
To Paris & Burgundy

BLVD DE LA REPUBLIQUE
AVE DU 11 NOV.

Marais

RUE GENERAL CHANZY

AVE JEAN JAURES

R. WITTELS

PETERBOROUGH

RUE E. VAILLANT

PORTE DU MARAIS

RUE GAMBON

COURS AVARICUM

RUE MIREBEAU

Place St. Bonnet

R. VOLTAIRE

BLVD GEORGES CLEMENCEAU

HOTEL DES ECHEVINS

Place Bascoulard

RUE E. BRANLY

Place Gordaine

POISO

RUE LITTRE

Place Cujas

HOTEL LALLEMANT

RUE JOYEUSE

Place de la Nation

HOTEL CUJAS

RUE DES ARENES

R. JACQUES CŒUR

RUE COUERSARLON

RUE BOURBONNOUX

PL. LACOMBE

RUE MONTGENOUX

PALAIS JACQUES CŒUR

R. TEMOIN

OLD CITY

RUE PORTE JAUNE

Place G. Sand

R. THAUM.

R. DES JUIFS

LINIERES

R. ZOLA

RUE MICHEL

GALLO-ROMAN WALLS

RUE PAU

ST. PIERRE

RUE D'AURON

RUE HENRI DUCROT

RUE MOYENNE

GENETRY

Place Dolet

CATHEDRAL OF ST. ETIENNE

RUE JACQUES FERNAULT

Mairie-Cathédrale

P

Archbishop's Garden

To Vierzon & Loire

AVE DU 95 LIGNE

RUE DE SARREBOURG

Place des Maronniers

200 Meters
200 Yards

N

BLVD. LAMARCK

RAMPE MARCEAU

R. SERAUCOURT

RUE JEAN BAFFIER

Séraucourt/ Centre Historique

P

BURGUNDY

Accommodations
1 Best Western Hôtel d'Angleterre Bourges
2 Hôtel le Christina

Eateries & Other
3 La Crêperie des Remparts
4 Au Sénat

5 La Suite
6 Le Bourbonnoux
7 Cake Thé
8 Laundry

▲▲Cathedral of St. Etienne

One of Europe's great Gothic churches, Bourges' Cathedral of St. Etienne is known for its simple but harmonious design, flying buttresses, stained glass, and mammoth size. A Christian church has stood on this spot since the third century, including a Roman-esque cathedral where Eleanor of Aquitaine received her crown in 1137. The present church was started in 1195, and finished just 55 years later—an astonishingly short amount of time for such a large structure. The design was inspired by Paris' Notre-Dame Cathedral, and it was built at the same time as the cathedral in Chartres. Bourges is one of the best-preserved Gothic cathedrals in France, having been spared the ravages of the French Revolution and both world wars.

Cost and Hours: Church interior-free and open daily 8:30-19:15, Oct-March 9:00-17:45; tower and crypt-€8 for both, €6 for tower only, €12 combo-ticket with Palais Jacques Cœur; open Mon-Sat 9:45-11:30 & 14:00-17:30, Sun 14:00-17:30, tel. 02 48 65 49 44, www.bourges-cathedrale.fr.

Visiting the Cathedral: The magnificent **west facade** is exceptionally wide (135 feet), dominated by five elaborately carved portals. The five doors reflect the church's unique interior—a central nave, flanked on each side by two aisles. The frightening Last Judgment over the central doorway shows a seated Christ presiding over Judgment Day and deserves your attention.

The church's mismatched **towers** were a problem from the start. In an age of build-'em-high-and-fast, Bourges competed with Chartres to erect the ultimate Gothic cathedral. Bourges won the race, but at a cost. The hastily built south tower had to be shored up several times—hence the squat tower that sits alongside it. Since the south tower was never strong enough to house any bells, locals call it "The Deaf Tower." The north tower collapsed altogether on New Year's Eve 1506 and had to be rebuilt, financed by donors who were granted an indulgence to eat butter during Lent—hence its nickname, the "Tour de Beurre."

The elegant **flying buttresses** form two rows, supporting both the lower and upper walls. The buttresses slope upward, enfolding the church in a pyramid shape as it rises to the peaked roofline.

Head inside. The view down the **nave** is overwhelming—at 300 feet, this is one of the longest naves in France. It seems even longer because the church has no transept to interrupt the tunnel effect. Notice elements of the "High" Gothic style of the 1200s: The church is tall, filled with light from many windows, and built with slender columns and thin walls (thanks to efficient flying buttresses). It rises up like a three-tiered step-pyramid—the outermost aisles are 30 feet high, the inner aisles are 70 feet, and the central nave is a soaring 120 feet from floor to rib-arched ceiling.

The best **stained glass** (c. 1215) is at the far end of the church, in the apse. Also, the Jacques Cœur Chapel (on the north side near the ambulatory) has a colorful Annunciation in stained glass.

The towering **astronomical clock,** on the south side of the nave, celebrates the most famous wedding the cathedral witnessed: that of hometown boy (and future king) Charles VII and Marie d'Anjou. The old clock, from 1424, still works.

Climbing the Tower: The 396 steps up the north tower yield terrific views and justify the exhaustion.

Crypt: To see the crypt, you need to join a tour in French... but you don't have to pay attention. Once inside, find the tomb statue of Duke Jean de Berry (1340-1416), the great collector of illuminated manuscripts and patron of this church. He lies on his back atop a black marble slab, dressed in ermine. At his feet sleeps a muzzled bear, representing the duke's quiet ferocity. Nearby, the colorfully painted Holy Sepulchre statues (c. 1530) tell the story of Christ's body being prepared for burial. See how realistic the marble looks as the mourners tug the ends of Christ's shroud—remarkably supple.

Nearby: The Archbishop's Garden (Jardin de l'Archevêché), just behind the cathedral, has a fine classical design and point-blank views of the flying buttresses. On Sundays when the weather agrees, old-school *guinguette* balls (picture a Renoir scene) are held here.

▲Medieval Quarter Stroll

Bourges' old city (Vieille Ville) is lassoed within Rues Bourbon-noux, Mirebeau, Coursarlon, Edouard Branly, and des Arènes. You'll see richly decorated Renaissance mansions, many of which house small museums (worth entering). These mix with France's greatest concentration of half-timbered homes (more than 500), most of them connected below street level by a labyrinth of underground passages. Look for Hôtel Lallemant (home to the Musée des Arts Decoratifs), Hôtel des Echevins (Musée Estève, with contemporary paintings by Maurice Estève), and Hôtel Cujas (Musée du Berry, with Roman tombstones and the famously expressive mourner statues from the Duke of Berry's elaborate tomb). For a historic stroll by the Gallo-Roman walls, take the steps up on the narrow lane between #44 and #50 on Rue Bourbonnoux and immediately turn left. Joan of Arc stayed in one of these fourth-century towers.

▲Palais Jacques Cœur

Bourges matters to travelers because of Jacques Cœur (c. 1395-1456), financier and minister to King Charles VII, who was born in Bourges. Monsieur Cœur helped establish Bourges as a capital for luxury goods and arms manufacturing. He also bankrolled Joan of Arc's call to save France from the English. His extravagant home is an impressive example of a Gothic civil palace, combining all the best elements of a château in an urban mansion. To visit the palace, join a French-only tour or pick up the English handout and go on your own.

Cost and Hours: €8, €12 combo-ticket with cathedral crypt and tower, new audioguide available for €3, daily 10:00-12:15 &

14:00-17:15, April-Sept until 18:00, 10 bis Rue Jacques-Cœur, tel. 02 48 24 79 42, www.palais-jacques-coeur.fr.

Sleeping and Eating in Bourges

Hotels and restaurants are a good value here. Ground zero for dining in Bourges is Place Gordaine and the nearby streets, where you'll find easygoing cafés and bistros.

Sleeping: $$$ Best Western Hôtel d'Angleterre Bourges**** is a fine place and as central as it gets (includes buffet breakfast, air-con, lounge bar, 1 Place des Quatre-Piliers, tel. 02 48 24 68 51, www.bestwestern-angleterre-bourges.com, hotel@bestwestern-angleterre-bourges.com).

$ Hôtel le Christina*** is a good hotel 10 blocks from the cathedral (air-con, 5 Rue de la Halle, tel. 02 48 70 56 50, www.le-christina.com, info@le-christina.com).

Eating: $ La Crêperie des Remparts offers a great range of inexpensive crêpes and salads (closed Sun-Mon, 59 Rue Bourbonnoux, tel. 02 48 24 55 44).

$$ Au Sénat is a local favorite for good-value traditional cuisine (closed Wed year-round and Thu in winter, on Place Gordaine at 8 Rue de la Poissonnerie, tel. 02 48 24 02 56).

$$$ La Suite in the old city is a fine, handsome place to do it up right (closed Sun-Mon, 50 Rue Bourbonnoux, tel. 02 48 65 96 26).

$$ Le Bourbonnoux offers good *menus,* fair prices, and copious servings (closed Fri, Sat for lunch, and Sun evening; 44 Rue Bourbonnoux, tel. 02 48 24 14 76).

$ Cake Thé is run by friendly Aude, who makes everything in this grand 14th-century vaulted cellar—her lemon meringue tart is a delight. Peaceful seating inside and out (lunch only, closed Mon, 74 bis Rue Bourbonnoux, parallel to the street by the ramparts, 02 48 24 94 60).

Bourges Connections

From Bourges by Train to: Paris (15/day, 2-3 hours, most with 1 change), **Amboise** (roughly hourly—though fewer midday, 2-3 hours, 1 change), **Beaune** (2/day, 3 hours, transfer in Nevers or Moulins-sur-Allier), **Sarlat-la-Canéda** (6/day, 7 hours, 2 changes).

Between Burgundy and Lyon

Drivers traveling south from Beaune should think about detouring into the lovely, unspoiled Mâconnais countryside. Brancion, Chapaize, Cluny, and Taizé are short drives from one another, about 30 minutes west of the autoroute between Mâcon and Tournus (see map on page 856). Drivers day-tripping to this area from Beaune should take the autoroute south to Tournus (then D-14 to Brancion), and take D-981 back to Beaune (described next). Route D-14 from Brancion meets D-981 at Cormatin.

For a romp through vineyards and unspoiled villages, connect Cluny and Beaune along D-981 (via Cormatin, Buxy, and Givry). Notice how many villages have signs to their *Eglise Romaine* (Romanesque churches are a dime a dozen here). Be on the lookout for bikers and a surprising château on the west side of the road in cute little Sercy (just south of Buxy).

Nondrivers can reach Cluny and Taizé by bus (see info under each listing for details).

Brancion and Chapaize

An hour south of Beaune by car (12 miles west of Tournus on D-14) are two tiny villages, each with "daughters of Cluny"—churches that owe their existence and architectural design to the nearby and once-powerful Cluny Abbey. Between the villages you'll pass a Stonehenge-era menhir (standing stone) with a cross added on top at a later point—evidence that this was sacred ground long before Christianity (from Brancion, it's on the right just after passing the bulky Château de Nobles).

Brancion

This is a classic feudal village. Back when there were no nations in Europe, control of land was delegated from lord to vassal. The

Duke of Burgundy ruled here through his vassal, the Lord of Brancion. His vast domain—much of south Burgundy—was administered from this tiny fortified town. Within the town's walls, the feudal lord had a castle, a church, and all the necessary administrative buildings to deliver justice, collect taxes, and so on. Strategically perched on a hill between two river valleys, he enjoyed a complete view of his domain. Brancion's population peaked centuries ago at 60. Today, it's home to a handful of full-time residents.

The **castle,** part of a network of 17 castles in the region, was destroyed in 1576 by Protestant Huguenots. After the French Revolution, it was sold as a quarry and spent most of the 19th century being picked apart. Though the flier gives a brief tour and the audioguide a longer one, the small castle is most enjoyable for its evocative angles and the lush views from the top of its keep (€6, daily 10:00-12:30 & 13:00-18:30, until 17:00 Oct-mid-Nov, closed mid-Nov-March, audioguide-€2).

Wandering from the castle to the church, you'll pass L'Auberge du Vieux Brancion, a 15th-century market hall that was used by farmers from the surrounding countryside until 1900, a handful of other buildings from that period and a few cafés.

The 12th-century warm-stone **church** is the town's highlight. Circumnavigate the small building—this is Romanesque at its pure, unadulterated, fortress-of-God best (thick walls, small windows, once colorfully painted interior, no-frills exterior). Notice the stone roof (made using a flat flagstone called *lauze*) and the orange-tinted stone of the church walls. Inside, you'll see faint paintings surviving from 1330, some moved to canvas in the early 1900s and displayed today (find English explanations). From its front door, enjoy a lord's view over one glorious Burgundian estate.

Sleeping and Eating in Brancion: ¢ L'Auberge du Vieux Brancion serves traditional Burgundian fare and offers a perfectly tranquil place to overnight, despite the simple and frumpy rooms (family rooms, cheaper rooms with shared bath, tel. 03 85 51 03 83, mobile 06 83 50 92 91, www.brancion.fr, contact@brancion.fr).

Chapaize

This hamlet, a few miles west of Brancion on D-14, grew up around its Benedictine monastery—only its 11th-century church survives. It's a pristine place (cars park in a lot at the edge of town) peppered with flowers, appealing cafés, and rustic decay. The classic Romanesque church gets all the attention. Enter through its cemetery and notice the stone roof. The WWI monument near the entry, with so many names from such a tiny hamlet, is a reminder of the 5.6 million young French men who were wounded or died in the war that *didn't* end all wars. Inside the church, study the fine stonework by Lombard masons and appreciate how it contrasts with the church in Brancion (different rock, higher nave, funky pillars). The leaning structure seems determined to challenge the faith of parishioners (the nave collapsed once already—900 years ago). Wander around the back for a view of the belfry, and then ponder Chapaize across the street while sipping a café au lait.

Cluny

People come from great distances to admire Cluny's great abbey that is no more. This mother of all abbeys once vied with the Vati-

can as the most important power center in Christendom (Cluny's abbot often served as mediator between Europe's kings and the pope). The building was destroyed during the French Revolution, and, frankly, there's not a lot to see today. Still, the abbey makes a worthwhile visit for history buffs and pilgrims looking to get some idea of the scale of this vast complex.

The pleasant little town that grew up around the abbey maintains its medieval street plan, with plenty of original buildings and even the same population it had in its 12th-century heyday (4,500). That's stability. As you wander the town, which claims to be the finest surviving Romanesque town in France, enjoy the architectural details on everyday buildings. Many of the town's fortified walls, gates, and towers survive.

Getting There: Drivers park at designated lots (best free lot is Parking le Rochefort). Bus #701 makes several trips to Cluny from Mâcon and Chalon-sur-Saône on the same line (6/day, 30 minutes from Mâcon, 1.5 hours from Chalon-sur-Saône; tel. 03 80 11 29 29, http://viamobigo.fr). There is no train station in Cluny.

Orientation to Cluny

Everything of interest is within a few minutes' walk of the **TI,** 100 yards to the right as you face the abbey entrance (daily April-Sept 9:30-18:30, except closed for lunch in April; Oct-March Mon-Sat 9:30-12:30 & 14:30-17:00, closed Sun except in Oct; 6 Rue Mercière, tel. 03 85 59 05 34, www.cluny-tourisme.com).

The TI is at the base of the **Tour des Fromages**—"Cheese Tower"—so named because it was used to age cheese (or perhaps for the way tourists smell after climbing to the top). The tower offers a city view but through wire screens (€2, €4 with 3-D tablet that shows how the town looked in the Middle Ages, same hours as TI).

A **farmers market** animates the old town each Saturday morning.

Sights in Cluny

Site of Cluny Abbey

It's free to view the site of the former abbey. The best point from which to appreciate the abbey's awesome dimensions is from just below the Museum of Art and Archaeology (called Palais Jean de Bourbon, 100 yards up from the Hôtel de Bourgogne).

Find the marble table that shows the original floor plan (*vous êtes ici* means "you are here"). Look out to the remaining tower (there used to be three). You're standing above the front of the central nave, the largest of five naves that stretched all the way to those towers.

Some of today's old town stands on the site of what was the largest church in Christendom. It was almost two football fields long (555 feet) and crowned with five soaring towers. The whole complex (church plus monastery) covered 25 acres. Revolutionaries destroyed it in 1790, and today the National Stud Farm and a big school obliterate much of the floor plan of the abbey. Only one tower and part of the transept still stand (5 percent of its original size). The visitor's challenge: Visualize it. Get a sense of its grandeur, more easily done by entering the museum's lobby to see a model of how Cluny looked 800 years ago (free to see model, museum included with abbey ticket, see description below).

Walk downhill past the replica nubs that recall the once-massive columns, work your way down the nave and around the right at the bottom, and climb a stairway to find today's abbey entry.

Abbey Interior

Once inside the one-time abbey complex (now a mishmash of bits of the original church and other, more recent buildings), follow *Suite de la Visite* signs. Information displays (in English) designed to introduce the abbey and provide historical context help put the pieces of the ruined building back together. You'll see a 12-minute 3-D film giving a virtual tour of the 1,100-year-old church that helps you grasp the tragedy of its destruction (use headset for translation and pick up your 3-D glasses). Consult the English flier to tour what little of the abbey still stands. You'll gaze up to the tallest Romanesque vault in the world (100 feet tall) in the lone remaining bell tower (awesome) and see parts of an adjacent transept. Your visit ends at the flour mill *(Le Farinier)*; make sure to go upstairs to see the intricate wood roof supports. (A left turn out of the abbey exit leads quickly to the old town and TI.)

Cost and Hours: €9.50 ticket, covers abbey interior and Museum of Art and Archaeology; both sights open daily 9:30-18:00, July-Aug until 19:00, Oct-March until 17:00; audioguide-€4.50 for abbey only, tel. 03 85 59 15 93, www.cluny-abbaye.fr. Historians should invest in *The Abbey of Cluny* guidebook (€7), sold at

History of Cluny and Its (Scant) Abbey

In 1964, St. Benedict (480-547), founder of the first monastery (at Montecassino, south of Rome) from which a great monastic movement sprang, was named the patron saint of Europe. Christians and non-Christians alike recognize the impact that monasteries had in establishing a European civilization out of the dark chaos that followed the fall of Rome.

The Abbey of Cluny was the ruling center of the first great international chain of monasteries in Europe. It was the heart of an upsurge in monasticism, of church reform, and an evangelical revival that spread throughout Europe—a phenomenon that historians call the Age of Faith (11th and 12th centuries). From this springboard came a vast network of abbeys, priories, and other monastic orders that kindled the establishment of modern Europe.

In 910, 12 monks founded a house of prayer at Cluny, vowing to follow the rules of St. Benedict. The cult of saints and relics was enthusiastically promoted, and the order was independent and powerful. From the start, the abbot of Cluny answered only to the pope (not to their local bishop or secular leader). The abbots of the other Cluniac monasteries were answerable only to the abbot of Cluny (not to their local bishop or prince). This made the abbot of Cluny arguably the most powerful person in Europe.

The abbey's success has been attributed to a series of wise leaders. In fact, four of the first six abbots actually became saints. They preached principles of piety (they got people to stop looting the monasteries) and practiced shrewd fundraising (convincing wealthy landowners to will their estates to the monasteries in return for perpetual prayers for the benefit of their needy and frightened souls).

From all this grew the greatest monastic movement of the High Middle Ages. A huge church was built at Cluny, and by 1100 it was the headquarters of 10,000 monks who ran nearly a thousand monasteries and priories across Europe. Cluny peaked in the 12th century, then faded in influence (though monasteries continued to increase in numbers and remain a force until 1789).

BURGUNDY

the abbey only, or take a free 90-minute tour (in English) when available.

Museum of Art and Archaeology (Palais Jean de Bourbon)
The small abbey museum fills the Palace of the Abbot, 100 yards straight out from the entrance to the abbey interior. The modest collection features some fine artifacts from the medieval town of Cluny and provides context for your visit to the abbey site. There's a terrific model of the village and abbey complex during the Middle Ages. You'll also see a beautifully carved stone frieze from a man-

sion in Cluny (first floor up, some English explanations) and fragments of the main entry (Grand Portail) to the abbey church set within a model of the doorway. There's also a short film in French that helps even non-French speakers imagine the original abbey (near the ticket counter).

Cost and Hours: Same ticket and hours as the abbey interior—see previous listing.

National Stud Farm (Les Haras Nationaux)

Napoleon (who needed *beaucoup de* horses for his army of 600,000) established this farm in 1806. Today, 50 thoroughbred stallions kill time in their stables. If the stalls are empty, they're out doing their current studly duty...creating strapping racehorses. Since 2010, the complex has been home to the National School of Equestrian Activities. French-only tours are offered from the entry gate next to Hôtel de Bourgogne (€7, 75 minutes, usually at 11:00 and 15:30, more in summer, no tours in winter, verify times before coming, tel. 03 85 59 85 19).

Sleeping and Eating in Cluny

If you're spending the night, bed down at the homey, traditional, and spotless **$ Hôtel de Bourgogne,***** built into the wall of the abbey's right transept and central for enjoying the town. All rooms are comfortable, some have views of the abbey tower, and there's a peaceful interior courtyard (pay parking garage, Place de l'Abbaye, tel. 03 85 59 00 58, www.hotel-cluny.com, contact@hotel-cluny.com).

$ Brasserie du Nord owns the best abbey view from its outdoor tables (skip the mod interior) and serves standard café fare at fair prices (daily, tel. 03 85 59 09 96, 1 Place du Marché).

Nearby: $ More Travel Guesthouse offers good rooms and a personal touch 20 minutes south of Cluny (see page 963).

Taizé

To experience the latest in European monasticism, drop by the booming Christian community of Taizé (teh-zay), a few miles north of Cluny on the road to Brancion. The normal, uncultlike ambience of this place—with thousands of mostly young, European pilgrims asking each other, "How's your soul today?"—is remarkable. Even if this sounds a little airy, you might find the 30 minutes it takes to stroll from one end of the compound to the other a worthwhile detour. Notice how everyone of any age seems to be in a good mood. A visit to Taizé can be a thought-provoking experience, particularly after a visit to Cluny. A thousand years ago, Cluny had a similar power to draw the faithful in search of direction and meaning in life.

Getting There: Drivers follow *La Communauté* signs in Taizé and park in a dirt lot. Bus #701 (free with rail pass) serves Taizé from Chalon-sur-Saône to the north (4/day, 1 hour) and from Mâcon to the south (6/day, 1 hour; tel. 03 80 11 29 29, http://viamobigo.fr) or Taxi Veronique (mobile 06 71 11 60 81).

Tourist Information: At the southern (Cluny) end, the Welcome Office provides an orientation and daily schedule, and makes a good first stop (daily 9:30-12:20 & 14:30-20:20). Ask to see the short film about Taizé.

Visiting Taizé: Taizé is an ecumenical movement—prayer, silence, simplicity—welcoming Protestant as well as Catholic Christians. Though it feels Catholic, it isn't. (But, as some of the brothers are actually Catholic priests, Catholics may take the Eucharist here.) The Taizé style of worship is well known among American Christians for its hauntingly beautiful chants—songbooks and CDs are the most popular souvenirs here. The Exposition (next to the church) is the thriving community shop, with books, CDs, handicrafts, and other souvenirs.

The community welcomes visitors who'd like to spend a few days getting close to God through meditation, singing, and simple living. Although designed primarily for youthful pilgrims in meditative retreat (there are about 5,000 here in a typical week), people of any age are welcome to pop in for a meal or church service. Time your visit for one of the services (Mon-Sat at 8:15, 12:20, and 20:30; Sun at 10:00 and 20:30; Catholic and Protestant communion available daily).

During services, the bells ring and worshippers file into the long, low, simple, and modern Church of Reconciliation. It's dim—

candlelit with glowing icons—as the white-robed brothers enter. The service features responsive singing of chants (from well-worn songbooks that list lyrics in 19 languages), reading of biblical passages, and silence, as worshippers on crude kneelers stare into icons. The aim: "Entering together into the mystery of God's presence." (Secondary aim: Helping Lutherans get over their fear of icons.)

Sleeping and Eating in Taizé: Those on retreat fill their days with worship services; workshops; simple, relaxed meals; and hanging out in an international festival of people searching for meaning in their lives. Visitors are welcome for free. The cost for a real stay is about €25-40 per day (based on a sliding scale; those under 18 stay for less) for monastic-style room and board. Adults (over age 30) are accommodated in a more comfortable zone, but count on **¢ simple dorms.** Call or email first if you plan to stay overnight (reception open Mon-Fri 10:00-12:00 & 18:00-19:00, tel. 03 85 50 30 02). The Taizé community website explains everything—in 29 languages (www.taize.fr).

The **$$ Oyak** (near the parking lot) is where those in a less monastic mood can get a beer or burger.

LYON

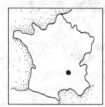

Straddling the mighty Rhône and Saône rivers between Burgundy and Provence, Lyon has been among France's leading cities since Roman times. In spite of its workaday, business-first facade, Lyon is France's most historic and culturally important city after Paris. You'll experience two different-as-night-and-day cities: the Old World cobbled alleys, pastel Renaissance mansions, and colorful shops of Vieux Lyon; and the more staid but classy, Paris-like buildings and shopping streets of the Presqu'île. Once you're settled, this big city feels relaxed, welcoming, and surprisingly untouristy. It seems everyone's enjoying the place—and they're all French.

PLANNING YOUR TIME

Just 70 minutes south of Beaune and two hours north of Avignon, Lyon is France's best-kept urban secret. Lyon deserves two nights and a full day. With frequent and fast service to Paris, Provence, Burgundy, and the Alps, the city makes a handy overnight stop for train travelers. Those who spend the night can experience its renowned cuisine (at appetizing prices) and enjoy one of Europe's most beautifully floodlit cities.

For a full day of sightseeing, take a funicular up to Fourvière Hill, visit the Notre-Dame Basilica, and tour the Roman Theaters and Lugdunum Gallo-Roman Museum. Ride the other funicular back down to Vieux Lyon and have a French (read: slow) lunch, then explore the old town and its hidden passageways. Finish your day touring the Museum of Fine Arts, Resistance Center, or Lumière Museum (covering the history of early filmmaking). Most of Lyon's important sights are closed on Monday and/or Tuesday.

Dine well in the evening (book ahead if possible; your hotelier can help) and cap your day enjoying a stroll through the best-lit city in France.

LYON'S CUISINE SCENE

In Lyon, how well you eat determines how well you live. The best restaurants are all the buzz—a favorite conversation topic likely to generate heated debate. Here, great chefs are more famous than professional soccer players. (Paul Bocuse, who died in 2018, was the chef MVP.) With an abundance of cozy, excellent restaurants in every price range, it's hard to go wrong—unless you're an intermediate eater and order tripe (cow intestines, also  known as *tablier de sapeur*), *foie de veau* (calf's liver), or *tête de veau* (calf's head). Beware: These questionable dishes are common in small bistros *(bouchons)*. Look instead for these classics: St. Marcellin cheese, *salade lyonnaise* (croutons, fried bits of ham, and a poached egg on a bed of lettuce), green lentils *(lentilles)* served on a salad or with sausages, *quenelles de brochet* (fish dumplings in a creamy sauce), and *filet de sandre* (local whitefish).

LYON-AREA WINES

Fruity and fresh Gamay Beaujolais grapes, which grow in vineyards just north of Lyon, produce a light, easy-to-drink red wine. Beaujolais vines are grown on granite rock slopes, yielding wines with a distinct flavor. While there are several premier *crus* producing lovely wines, the area is most famous for its simple Beaujolais Nouveau wines, opened just six weeks after bottling. The arrival of the new Beaujolais is cause for lighthearted celebration and mischief in this otherwise hard-to-impress country. At midnight on the third Thursday of November, the first bottles are opened to great fanfare, road rallies carry the new wine to destinations throughout France, and cafés everywhere post signs announcing its arrival.

Big, luscious reds made from mostly syrah grapes grow on steep slopes to the city's south. Look for Saint-Joseph and (my favorite) Crozes-Hermitage wines. In the village of Condrieu, only viognier grapes are allowed to grow; they produce a rich and perfumy white wine.

Orientation to Lyon

Despite being France's third-largest city (after Paris and Marseille), with about 1.5 million inhabitants in its metropolitan area,

the traveler's Lyon (home to 485,000 people) is peaceful and manageable. Traffic noise is replaced by pedestrian friendliness in the old center—listen to how quiet this big city is. Notice the emphasis on environmentally friendly transport: Electric buses have replaced diesel buses in the historic core, bike lanes run everywhere, and pedal taxis (called *cyclopolitains*, seek-loh-poh-lee-tan) are used instead of traditional taxis for short trips (about €1/kilometer). Lyon's network of more than 5,000 city-owned rental bikes was in place years before Paris started its program.

The people of Lyon are happy to remind visitors that their city may not be the capital of France, but it *is* the ancient Gallo-Roman capital, the city that introduced Christianity to France, the Renaissance capital (with the finest surviving Renaissance district), the capital of Nazi resistance during World War II, and a cuisine capital. And, while Paris may call itself "the City of Light," Lyon is a leader in artistic urban lighting—as you'll see each evening.

You'll hear the term "Gallo-Roman" a lot here. The Romans conquered the Gauls (the dominant proto-French tribe) and incorporated them into their culture as they established their vast empire. For several centuries, this substantial part of the Roman empire was a Gaulish, or Gallo-Roman, civilization.

The city evolved as it grew, starting on the hill in Gallo-Roman times, moving to a fortified town on the banks of the Saône River with the fall of Rome and through the Renaissance, then filling the Presqu'île (peninsula, pron. press-keel) between the two rivers in the 19th century, before sprawling west of the Rhône in modern times.

Today Lyon provides the organized traveler with a full day of activities. Sightseeing can be enjoyed on foot from any of my recommended hotels, though it's smart to make use of trams, funiculars, and the Métro. Lyon's sights are concentrated in

LYON

three areas: **Fourvière Hill,** with its white Notre-Dame Basilica glimmering over the city; historic **Vieux Lyon,** which hunkers below on the bank of the Saône River; and the **Presqu'île** (home to my recommended hotels), lassoed by the Saône and Rhône rivers. Huge Place Bellecour, which lies in the middle of the Presqu'île, seems oversized...unless it's hosting an event.

TOURIST INFORMATION

Stop at the well-equipped TI for a city map (with good enlargements of central Lyon and Vieux Lyon; hotels have similar maps), a map of Lyon's murals, and an event schedule (daily 9:00-18:00, corner of Place Bellecour, free public WCs behind the TI building, tel. 04 72 77 69 69, www.lyon-france.com). The TI sells the worthwhile Lyon City Card (described next) and rents an audioguide for touring Lyon (see "Tours in Lyon," later). The TI also has a brochure on the Beaujolais wine road north of Lyon. Ask about a pocket Wi-Fi device that gives you service all over town; you can leave it in any mailbox before departing Lyon (€8/day, €4 with Lyon City Card).

Sightseeing Pass: Those planning a busy, full day of sightseeing via the public transit system should invest in the **Lyon City Card** (€25/1 day, €35/2 consecutive days, €45/3 consecutive days, half-price for kids under age 16, sold at TI and most participating museums, may be cheaper online, https://lyoncitycard.com). This pass covers 22 Lyon museums plus buses, trams, funiculars, the Métro, and the river shuttle boat *Le Vaporetto.* It also covers a river cruise (April-Oct), a tram tour of the hilly Croix-Rousse neighborhood, and a walking tour of Vieux Lyon with a live guide (or use of the TI's audioguide), and provides discounts on other activities. The one-day pass pays for itself if you visit the Gallo-Roman Museum and the Resistance and Deportation History Center, plus take a guided walking tour and use public transit.

ARRIVAL IN LYON

By Train: Lyon has two train stations—Part-Dieu and Lyon-Perrache. Many trains stop at both, and some through trains connect the two stations. Both stations are well-served by Métro, bus, tram, and taxi (figure €15 to taxi from either station to my recommended hotels near Place Bellecour), and both have the standard car-rental companies. Only Part-Dieu has baggage storage (daily 6:15-23:00) and free Wi-Fi in the waiting area. The all-day transit ticket is a great value—buy it upon arrival at either station if you plan to do much sightseeing that day (unless you plan to get a Lyon City Card). For more on public transportation, see "Getting Around Lyon," later.

Arriving at Part-Dieu Station: This is where most visitors arrive. There are two exits from the station: Porte du Rhône and Porte des Alpes. Bag check is near the *Porte des Alpes* exit. To reach Place Bellecour in the **city center** (close to most hotels and the TI), exit by following *Sortie Porte du Rhône* signs, keep right, then enter the Métro station and buy your ticket from the machine. Take blue Métro line B toward Gare d'Oullins, transfer at Saxe-Gambetta to line D/Gare de Vaise, and get off at Bellecour. At Bellecour, follow *Sortie Rue République* signs.

The other main exit, signed as *Sortie Porte des Alpes*, offers access to the handy **airport** train (the Rhône Express, described below under "By Plane"). Taxis wait outside either exit.

Arriving at Perrache Station: This station is within a 20-minute walk of Place Bellecour. Follow green *Place Carnot* signs out of the station, then cross Place Carnot and walk up pedestrian Rue Victor Hugo to reach the TI and most of my recommended hotels. Or take the Métro (direction: Vaulx-en-Velin) two stops to Bellecour and follow *Sortie Rue République* signs.

By Car: The city center has good signage and is manageable to navigate, though you'll hit traffic on surrounding freeways. If autoroutes A-6/7 are jammed (not unusual), you'll be directed to bypass freeways if just passing through Lyon. Follow *Centre-Ville* and *Presqu'île* signs, and then follow *Office de Tourisme* and *Place Bellecour* signs. Park near Place Bellecour at Parking des Célestins or Parking Antonin Poncet (yellow *P* means "parking lot"), or get advice from your hotel. The TI's map identifies all public parking lots. Overnight parking (generally 19:00-8:00) is only €5, but day rates are €2 per hour (figure about €32/24 hours). Garages near Perrache station are cheaper than those near Bellecour.

By Plane: Lyon's sleek little airport, St-Exupéry, is 15 miles from the city center, and is a breeze to navigate (ATMs, English information booths, code: LYS, tel. 08 26 80 08 26, www.lyonaeroports.com). It has air and rail connections to major European cities, including two flights per hour to Paris' Charles de Gaulle Airport and direct TGV ("InOui") service to many French cities. Car rental is a snap. Four **Rhône Express** shuttles per hour make the 30-minute trip from the airport (follow red tram car icons) to Part-Dieu Station, described earlier (€16 one-way, €28 round-trip; buy ticket from machine with bills, coins, or chip-and-PIN credit card—conductors can help, or at www.rhonexpress.fr/en). Allow €60 for a taxi or Uber if you have baggage.

HELPFUL HINTS

City Murals: Lyon is famous for its colorful and monumental wall murals. You'll find them in many neighborhoods (the TI has a map; keep your eyes up). Locations include Fourvière Hill near the Notre-Dame Basilica *(Les Fresques de la Sarra);* the

LYON

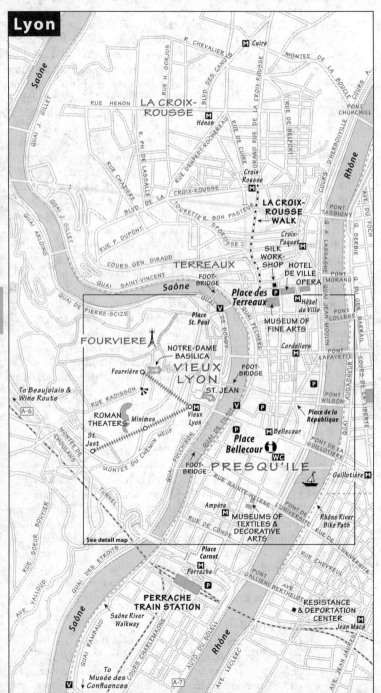

Lyon

Saône

R. CHEVALIER

M Cuire

MONTÉE DE LA BOUCLE

COURS A.

RUE H. GORJUS

QUAI J. GILLET

RUE HENON

LA CROIX-ROUSSE

BLVD. DES CANUTS

RUE DE BELFORT

PONT CHURCHILL

Hénon M

RUE PH. DE LASSALLE

R. PH. DE LASSALLE

RUE DENFERT-ROCHEREAU

RUE DE CUIRE

GRAND RUE DE LA CROIX-ROUSSE

COURS D'HERBOUVILLE

Rhône

QUAI J. GILLET

RUE CHAZIÈRE

CROIX-ROUSSE

BLVD. DE LA

Croix-Rousse M

LA CROIX-ROUSSE WALK

PONT TASSIGNY

AVE. DU FOCH

QUAI ARLOING

RUE P. DUPONT

TOURETTE R. BON PASTEUR

R. SPORTISSE

Croix-Paquet M

SILK WORK-SHOP

HOTEL DE VILLE OPERA

Q. A. LASSAGNE

Q. SERBIE

COURS GEN. GIRAUD

TERREAUX

Place des Terreaux P

QUAI SAINT-VINCENT

Saône

FOOT-BRIDGE

M Hôtel de Ville

PONT MORAND

QUAI DE PIERRE-SCIZE

QUAI DE BONDY

QUAI PÉCHERIE

MUSEUM OF FINE ARTS

QUAI JEAN JEAN MOULIN

PONT COLLÈGE

Place St. Paul

FOURVIÈRE

NOTRE-DAME BASILICA

Cordeliers M

PONT LAFAYETTE

PONT AUGAGNEUR

VIEUX LYON

FOOT-BRIDGE

Fourvière

ST. JEAN

PONT WILSON

COURS DE LA LIBERTÉ

To Beaujolais & Wine Route

A-6

RUE RADISSON

M Vieux Lyon

V P

Place de la République

ROMAN THEATERS

Minimes

St. Just

QUAI FULCHIRON

QUAI DE TILSIT

P

Place Bellecour

M Bellecour

i

WC

PONT DE LA GUILLOTIÈRE

MONTÉE DU CHEMIN NEUF

FOOT-BRIDGE

PRESQU'ILE

Guillotière M

MONTÉE DE CHOULANS

RUE SAINTE-HÉLÈNE

PONT DE L'UNIVERSITÉ

Rhône River Bike Path

RUE SŒUR BOUVIER

TUNNEL

Ampère M

MUSEUMS OF TEXTILES & DECORATIVE ARTS

RUE DE L'UNIVERSITÉ

RUE DE CONDÉ

See detail map

RUE CHEVREUL

AVE. VALLOUD

Place Carnot

RESISTANCE & DEPORTATION CENTER

QUAI DES ÉTROITS

Perrache M

PONT GALLIENI BERTHELOT

AVE. JEAN JAURÈS

PERRACHE TRAIN STATION

P

AVE. BERTHELOT

Jean Macé M

Saône

Saône River Walkway

QUAI RAMBAUD

COURS CHARLEMAGNE

Rhône

AUTO DU SOLEIL

AVE. LECLERC

To Musée des Confluences

V

A-7

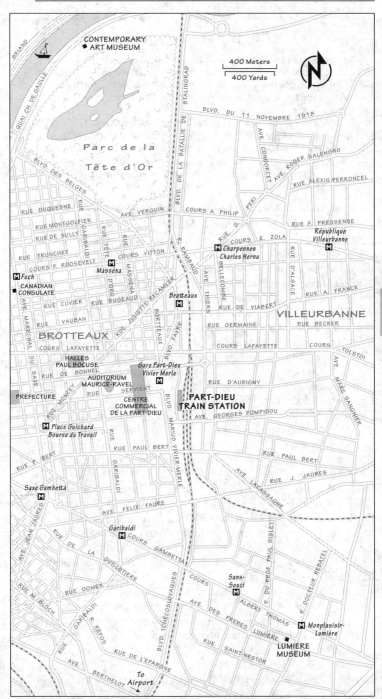

BRIAND

QUAI CH. DE GAULLE

CONTEMPORARY ART MUSEUM

400 Meters
400 Yards

N

Parc de la Tête d'Or

BLVD. DU 11 NOVEMBRE 1918

BLVD DES BELGES

BLVD DE LA BATAILLE DE STALINGRAD

AVE. CONDORCET

AVE. ROGER SALENGRO

RUE ALEXIS PERRONCEL

RUE DUQUESNE

AVE. VERGUIN

COURS A. PHILIP

PERI

RUE G.

RUE F. PRESSENSE

RUE MONTGOLFIER

RUE DE SULLY

GARIBALDI

RUE TÊTE D'OR

COURS VITTON

COURS E. ZOLA

République
Villeurbanne

RUE TRONCHET

RUE MASSÉNA

Masséna

Charpennes
Charles Hernu

BELLECOMBE

RUE D'ALSACE

COURS F. ROOSEVELT

RUE JULIETTE RÉCAMIER

R. RAMBAUD

AVE. THIERS

RUE A. FRANCE

Foch

CANADIAN
CONSULATE

RUE CUVIER

RUE BUGEAUD

Brotteaux

RUE DE VIABERT

VILLEURBANNE

RUE VAUBAN

BORTTEAUX

RUE GERMAINE

RUE BECKER

BROTTEAUX

COURS LAFAYETTE

BLVD FAYRE

COURS LAFAYETTE

COURS

TOLSTOI

DU SAXE

HALLES
PAUL BOCUSE

RUE DE BONNEL

Gare Part-Dieu
Vivier Merle

RUE D'AUBIGNY

AVE. MARC SANGNIER

AUDITORIUM
MAURICE-RAVEL

SERVIENT

PART-DIEU
TRAIN STATION

PREFECTURE

RUE MONCEY

RUE

CENTRE
COMMERCIAL
DE LA PART-DIEU

BLVD MARIUS VIVIER-MERLE

AVE. GEORGES POMPIDOU

Place Guichard
Bourse du Travail

RUE

RUE PAUL BERT

RUE PAUL BERT

GARIBALDI

AVE. LACASSAGNE

RUE J. JAURES

RUE P. BERT

Saxe Gambetta

AVE. JEAN JAURES

AVE. FELIX FAURE

Garibaldi

COURS GAMBETTA

R. DU PROF. PAUL SIGLEY

RUE DE LA GUILLOTIERE

COURS

BLVD. TCHECOSLOVAQUES

Sans-
Souci

R. DOCTEUR REBATEL

RUE M. BLOCH

RUE DOMER

AVE. DES FRERES LUMIERE

ALBERT THOMAS

Monplaisir-
Lumière

RUE

GARIBALDI

R. REPOS

RUE DE L'EPARGNE

RUE SAINT-NESTOR

LUMIERE
MUSEUM

AVE. BERTHELOT

To
Airport

LYON

Illuminated Lyon

The golden statue of Mary above Notre-Dame Basilica was placed atop a 16th-century chapel on December 8, 1852. Spontaneously, the entire city welcomed her with candles in their windows. Each December 8 ever since, the city glows softly with countless candles.

This tradition has spawned an actual industry. Lyon is famous as a model of state-of-the-art floodlighting, and the city hosts conventions on the topic. Each night, more than 200 buildings, sites, and public spaces are gloriously flood-lit. Go for an after-dinner stroll and enjoy the view from Pont Bonaparte after dark.

Croix-Rousse neighborhood (*Mur Peint des Canuts*, Europe's largest mural); and several in the Presqu'île area. If visiting **Les Halles de Lyon** market hall, look for *Thank you Monsieur Paul*, honoring Lyon's beloved chef Bocuse.

Market Days: A small market stretches along the Saône River near the Passerelle du Palais de Justice bridge (daily until 12:30). Tuesday through Sunday, it's produce; Monday, it's textiles. On Sunday morning, a crafts and contemporary art market is on the other side of the bridge near the Court of Justice. Another bustling morning produce market takes place on Boulevard de la Croix-Rousse (Tue-Sun until 12:30, biggest on Sun, see page 950).

Festivals and Events: Lyon celebrates the Virgin Mary with candlelit windows during the Festival of Lights each year in early December (www.lumieres.lyon.fr). Les Nuits de Fourvière—with dance, music, and theater—takes place from early June to early August in the Roman Theaters (www.nuitsdefourviere.com).

Useful Website: For helpful information in English about visiting Lyon, check out www.angloinfo.com/lyon.

Bookstore and Wi-Fi: Raconte Moi La Terre is a traveler's bookstore (no books in English) and resource center with a café; it's also a good place to get online (Mon 12:00-19:30, Tue-Sat 10:00-19:30, closed Sun, free Wi-Fi in café, air-con, 14 Rue du Plat—see map on page 958, Métro: Bellecour, tel. 04 78 92 60 22, www.racontemoilaterre.com).

Laundry: A launderette is at 7 Rue Mercière on the Presqu'île, near the Alphonse Juin bridge; another is between Place Bellecour and Perrache station, a few steps off Rue Victor Hugo at 19 Rue Ste. Hélène. Both have long hours daily (see map on page 958 for locations).

Driver: Design your own half-day or full-day tour with a car and driver (mobile 06 65 38 75 08, www.lugdunum-ips.com, contact@lugdunum-ips.com).

Children's Activities: The Parc de la Tête d'Or is vast, with row-boat rentals, a miniature golf course, pony rides, a free zoo and botanical gardens, and easy access to the riverside bike path (across Rhône River from the Croix-Rousse neighborhood, Métro: Masséna, www.loisirs-parcdelatetedor.com).

GETTING AROUND LYON
By Public Transit

Lyon has a user-friendly public transit system, with five modern tram lines (T1-T4 and the Rhône Express line to the airport), four underground Métro lines (A-D), an extensive bus system, and two funiculars to get you up that hill. The subway is similar to Paris' Métro (e.g., routes are signed by *direction* for the last stop on the line) but is more automated (buy tickets at coin-op machines), cleaner, less crowded, and less rushed (drivers linger longer at stops). Study the wall maps to find your direction; ask a local if you're not certain. Yellow signs lead to transfers, and green signs lead to exits *(Sortie).*

Tickets: You can transfer between Métro, tram, and bus lines with the same ticket (valid one hour) and can do round-trips, but you must revalidate your ticket whenever boarding (1 hour-€1.90, 1 day-€5.80, 10 rides-€16.90, evening ticket-€3, all tickets cover funicular). The **one-day ticket** is a great deal (even if you only use the funicular and visit one of the outlying museums—Resistance Center or Lumière Museum) and a great time-saver, as you only have to buy a ticket once. Also remember that the Lyon City Card (described earlier, under "Tourist Information") covers transit.

To use the ticket machines, change the display language to English. Then use the black roller to *selectionner* your ticket and firmly push the top button twice to *confirmer* your request. Pay with coins or a chip-and-PIN credit card. In the Métro, insert your ticket in the turnstile, then reclaim it.

By Taxi or Uber

Lyon is not a good taxi town; locals are accustomed to walking and using the excellent tram and subway system. You generally don't hail cabs in the street, there are few taxi stands, and the minimum fare is a steep €7. If you do need a taxi, try Taxi Lyon at tel. 06 82 55 69 34. Uber works here, but not as efficiently as in Paris.

By Bike

While you wouldn't really sightsee by bike, fine riverside bike paths and big parks make Lyon a fun place for a joyride. You can rent electric or standard bikes at **La Bicycletterie** (Mon-Sat 8:30-

Lyon at a Glance

▲▲**Lugdunum Gallo-Roman Museum and Roman Theaters**
Fine museum covering Roman Lyon. **Hours:** Museum—Tue-Fri
11:00-18:00, Sat-Sun from 10:00, closed Mon; theaters—daily
7:00-19:00, May-Sept until 21:00 except during Les Nuits de
Fourvière festival in early June-early Aug, when they can close
as early as 17:00. See page 941.

▲▲**Vieux Lyon** The city's fascinating traffic-free historic core,
with intriguing covered *traboules* (passageways). **Hours:** Passageways usually open daily 8:00-19:30. See page 943.

▲**Notre-Dame Basilica** Lyon's ornate version of Paris' Sacré-
Cœur. **Hours:** Daily 7:00-19:00; Mass usually at 7:15, 11:00, and
17:30. See page 939.

▲**Museum of Fine Arts** One of France's most important fine-
arts museums. **Hours:** Wed-Mon 10:00-18:00, Fri from 10:30,
closed Tue. See page 949.

▲**Resistance and Deportation History Center** Displays and
videos telling the inspirational story of the French Resistance.
Hours: Wed-Sun 10:00-18:00, closed Mon-Tue. See page 952.

▲**Lumière Museum** A museum of film, dedicated to the Lumière brothers' pivotal contribution. **Hours:** Tue-Sun 10:00-
18:30, closed Mon. See page 953.

LYON

19:00, closed Sun, 16 Rue Romarin, tel. 04 37 92 04 96). You can
also use handy, city-owned **Vélo'v Bikes:** Purchase a day ticket
(€4/24 hours, discount with Lyon City Card; buy at machines with
a chip-and-PIN credit card, online with any credit card, or (easiest)
with the app (www.velov.grandlyon.com). You can pick the bike up
at one location, and leave it at another. The first 30 minutes are free,
then the cost rises quickly to encourage short-term use.

Tours in Lyon

On Foot
TI Offerings: The TI's **audioguide** (€10/day) offers good self-
guided walking tours of Vieux Lyon. Live **guided walks** of Vieux
Lyon are usually offered at 14:30 daily from July through early September and on weekends year-round (€12, 2 hours, several in English, some start near Vieux Lyon Métro station—verify days and
times with TI or sign up online, www.visiterlyon.com).

"**Free**" (**Tip-Based**) **Walks:** Hardworking Nicolas (a.k.a.

Nico) leads fun and informative 2.5-hour town walks from the Presqu'île to Vieux Lyon, and up to the Croix-Rousse district. While the walks are advertised as free, a generous tip is expected if you enjoyed the experience (Mon-Sat at 10:00; Mon, Wed, and Fri night walks at 21:00 following a different route; no need to book ahead—meet at Louis XIV statue in Place Bellecour; tel. 07 69 61 34 29, www.lyonexplorer.com).

By Bus

Lyon City Tours: This company offers two options for exploring (tel. 04 78 56 32 39, www.lyoncitytour.fr). **The Lyon City Bus** is a hop-on, hop-off tour with 14 stops covering Presqu'île, Fourvière Hill, stretches of the Saône river, and the Confluence area (€21, daily 10:00-18:00, 2/hour). The red **Lyon City Tram** runs a one-hour loop from Place des Terreaux to the Croix-Rousse district and back (€9, daily 10:15-17:30, 6/day).

Wine Tours and Sightseeing Excursions: Kanpai Tours runs minivan trips to the Beaujolais and northern Rhône Valley wine regions near Lyon (€90/half-day, €110/day for individuals, €400-800/day for private groups up to 8, tel. 06 84 52 14 99, www.kanpai-tourisme.com, kanpai.tours@gmail.com).

By Boat

For a short cruise on the Saône River with nice views of Vieux Lyon, hop aboard *Le Vaporetto*. This shuttle boat makes a 30-minute trip between Vieux Lyon and the Confluence shopping mall, with a stop at Pont Bonaparte along the way (€4 one-way, daily 9:30-21:00; departures posted at stops: every 80 minutes from Pont de la Feuillée in Vieux Lyon starting at 10:20, from Confluence mall starting at 9:30; busy on weekends, no service mid-Dec-Feb). For stops, see map on page 932.

Pont Bonaparte Spin Tour

This central bridge, just a block from Place Bellecour, is made to order for a day-or-night self-guided spin tour.

• *Stand on the bridge and face the golden statue of the Virgin Mary marking the Notre-Dame Basilica on Fourvière Hill. (It's actually capping the smaller chapel, which predates the church by 500 years.) The basilica is named for the Roman Forum* (fourvière) *upon which it sits. Now begin to look clockwise.*

The **Metallic Tower** (a pint-sized version of Paris' Eiffel Tower) is called La Tour Métallique. It was finished five years after the Eiffel Tower, in 1894, as part of a local world's fair (leftover parts?). Originally an observation tower, today it functions only as a TV tower. The husky, twin-towered church on the riverbank below (St. Jean Cathedral) marks the center of the old town. A block upstream, the Neoclassical columns are part of the Court of Justice (where Klaus Barbie, head of the local Gestapo—a.k.a. "the Butcher of Lyon"—was sentenced to life in prison). Way upstream, the hill covered with tall, pastel-colored houses is the **Croix-Rousse district,** former home of the city's huge silk industry. With the invention of the Jacquard looms (1805), which required 12-foot-tall ceilings, new factory buildings were needed and the new weaving center grew up on this hill. In 1850, in good Industrial Revolution style, it was churning with 30,000 looms.

You are standing over the **Saône River,** which, along with the Rhône, makes up Lyon's duo of power rivers. The Saône drains the southern area of the Vosges Mountains in Alsace and runs for about 300 miles before joining the Rhône (barely south of here), which flows to the Mediterranean. The Place Bellecour side of the river (behind you) is the district of Presqu'île. This strip of land is sandwiched by the two rivers and is home to Lyon's Opera House, City Hall, theater, top-end shopping, banks, and all my recommended hotels. A morning market sets up daily under the trees (upriver, just beyond the red bridge). The simple riverfront cafés *(buvettes)* are ideal for a drink with a view (best at night).

Speaking of bridges, most of Lyon's bridges—including the one you're standing on—were destroyed by the Nazis as they checked out in 1944. Looking downstream, the stately mansions of Lyon's well-established families line the left side of the river. Across the river, still downstream, the 19th-century Neo-Gothic **St. Georges Church** marks the neighborhood of the first silk weavers. The ridge behind St. Georges is dominated by a big building—once a seminary for priests, now a state high school—and leads us back to Mary.

• *Walk across the bridge and continue two blocks to find the funicular station and ride up Fourvière Hill to the basilica (catch the one marked* Fourvière, *not* St. Just*). Sit up front and admire the funicular's funky old technology (€3 round-trip, Métro/tram tickets valid). Or you can skip Fourvière Hill and go directly into the old town* **(Vieux Lyon)** *by turning right at* **St. Jean Cathedral.**

Sights in Lyon

FOURVIERE HILL
On Fourvière Hill, you can tour the basilica, enjoy a panoramic city view, visit the Roman Theaters and Lugdunum Gallo-Roman Museum, then catch another funicular back down and explore the old town. I've listed key sights next according to this route.

▲Notre-Dame Basilica
(Basilique Notre-Dame de Fourvière)

This ornate, gleaming church fills your view as you exit the funicular. In about the year 1870, the bishop of Lyon vowed to build a worthy tribute to the Virgin Mary if the Prussians spared his city. They did, so construction started in earnest, with more than 2,000 workers on site (similar divine deal-making led to the construction of the basilica of Sacré-Cœur in Paris). Building began in 1872, and the church was ready for worship just in time for the outbreak of the next war, World War I.

Cost and Hours: Free, daily 7:00-19:00.

Church Services: Mass usually at 7:15, 11:00, and 17:30 plus Sun at 9:30 (in the chapel to the right on weekdays; in the basilica on Sat eve and Sun at 9:30 and 17:30).

Rooftop Tours: The lengthy "Original Tour" takes you to the attic and rooftop for splendid views over the city (€10, 1.5 hours, French only, 3-4 tours run daily June-Sept between 11:00-16:00; April-May and Oct-Nov tours run Wed and Sat-Sun only; no tours Dec-March). Check the schedule and reserve "Visite Insolite" online at www.fourviere.org. You can also book at the basilica just before the scheduled tour, but since they're limited to 18 people, it's wise to book in advance online.

Visiting the Basilica: Before entering, view the fancy facade, the older chapel on the right (supporting the statue of Mary), and the top of the Eiffel-like TV tower on the left.

Climb the steps and enter. Notice that everything—floor, walls, ceiling—is covered with elaborate mosaics. Scenes glittering on the walls tell stories of the Virgin (in Church history on the left, and in French history on the right). You won't find a more Mary-centered church. It's all about our lady—Notre Dame. Amble slowly down the center aisle, enjoy the dazzling neo-Byzantine (late 1800s) decor, and examine these main scenes lining the nave on the left and right:

First Scene (left): In 431, the Council of Ephesus declared Mary to be the "Mother of God."

First Scene (right): The artist imagines Lugdunum (Lyon)—the biggest city in Roman Gaul, with 50,000 inhabitants—as the first Christian missionaries arrive. The first Christian martyrs in France (killed in AD 177) dance across heaven with palm branches.

Second Scene (left): In 1571, at the pivotal sea battle of Lepanto, Mary provides the necessary miracle as the outnumbered Christian forces beat the Ottomans.

Second Scene (right): Joan of Arc appears in three dramatic scenes. From right to left, she hears messages from Mary; she rallies the French against the English at the Siege of Orléans in 1429 (Joan, with the bright halo, pops on her horse; the timid French King Charles VII—whom Joan inspired to take a stand and fight the English—is buried in the crowd); and Joan is ultimately burned at the stake in Rouen at age 19 (1431).

Third Scene (left): In 1854, Pope Pius I proclaims the dogma of the Immaculate Conception in St. Peter's Square (establishing the belief among Catholics that Mary was conceived without the "Original Sin" of apple-eating Adam and Eve). To the left of the Pope, angels carry the tower of Fourvière Church; to the right is the image of the Virgin of Lourdes (who miraculously appeared in 1858).

Third Scene (right): Dashing King Louis XIII offers the crown of France heavenward to the Virgin Mary. (The empty cradle between the king and queen hints that while he had Mary on the line, he asked, "Could I please have a son?" Louis XIV was born shortly thereafter.) Above marches a parade of pious French kings and emperors, from Clovis and Charlemagne to Napoleon (on the far right—with the white cross and red coat). Below are the great Marian churches of France (left to right): Chartres; Paris' Sacré-Cœur, Notre-Dame, and Val-de-Grâce; Reims (where most royalty was crowned); and this church.

These six scenes in mosaic all lead to the altar where Mary reigns as Queen of Heaven.

Lower Church and Adjacent Chapel: Exit under Joan of Arc and descend (passing Hail Marys in a couple dozen languages as you climb down the stairs) to the crypt directly below. There you'll find a lower church, dedicated to Mary's earthly husband, Joseph. Priorities here are painfully clear: Money ran out for Joseph's church. Strolling around Joseph's church you'll see models of beloved Marys from around the world (to welcome the many pilgrims), walls lined with plaques thanking Mary for prayers answered, and a rare altar featuring Joseph.

Return up the same stairs, leave the basilica, and step into the adjacent 16th-century chapel to the Virgin (pull the door). Back outside, glance up to see the glorious statue of Mary that overlooks Lyon.

City View: Just around this chapel (past the church museum) is a commanding **view** of Lyon. Below you lies the old town with its Renaissance roofs sporting uniform chimneys. The peninsula between the two rivers is the Presqu'île, with its elegant and uniform 19th-century architecture.

You can see parts of both rivers and north from the Croix-Rousse district south to Pont Bonaparte, with greater Lyon spread out before you in the distance. The black barrel-vaulted structure to the left is the Opera House, and the rose-colored skyscraper in the distance is called, appropriately, "Le Crayon" (The Pencil). The skyline's latest addition and tallest building is the tower nicknamed "La Gomme" (The Eraser). The big green space filling the bend in the river beyond the Opera House is Lyon's massive park (La Tête d'Or). On a clear afternoon, you'll get a glimpse of Mont Blanc (the highest point in Europe, just left of the pencil-shaped skyscraper).

• *To get to the Roman Theaters and Gallo-Roman Museum, walk back to the funicular station and turn left down Rue Roger Radisson. The museum hides in the concrete bunker down the steps, where Rue Roger Radisson meets Rue Cléberg.*

▲▲Lugdunum Gallo-Roman Museum and Roman Theaters (Lugdunum-Musée and Théâtres)

The fine Gallo-Roman museum was built on the hillside with views of the two Roman Theaters, and it makes clear Lyon's importance in Roman times.

Cost and Hours: Museum—€4, includes essential and well-produced audioguide, €7 if special exhibits are on, free first Sun of the month, open Tue-Fri 11:00-18:00, Sat-Sun from 10:00, closed Mon; theaters—free, daily 7:00-19:00, May-Sept until 21:00 except during Les Nuits de Fourvière festival early June-early Aug, when they can close as early as 17:00; 17 Rue Cléberg.

Information: Tel. 04 72 38 49 30, www.lugdunum.grandlyon.com.

Les Nuits de Fourvière: From early June through early August, the theaters host an open-air festival of concerts, theater, dance, and film. Check programs at the TI and purchase tickets here at the theaters (box office at gate exit toward the Minimes funicular station, Mon-Sat 11:00-18:00, closed Sun), or online at www.nuitsdefourviere.com.

Visiting the Museum and Theaters: Visit the museum first, then tour the theaters.

• *Before entering the museum, get an overview of the site by taking a few steps left down Rue Cléberg to find a ramp leading to the museum's rooftop (open the gate).*

From the **museum rooftop** you can see the two ancient theaters, with the Gallo-Roman forum spread below the basilica. Founded as Lugdunum in AD 43, this city held an estimated 50,000 people—four or five times the population of Roman Paris by the first century. Lyon was a critical transportation hub for the administration of Roman Gaul (and much of what became modern-day France—a lot like today).

LYON

The city became the central metropolis of the Three Gauls—the integrated Roman provinces of Aquitania (Aquitaine), Belgica (Belgium), and Lugdunensis (Lyon region)—and Emperors Claudius and Caracalla were both born here in Lyon (for more on the Romans, see "The Romans in Provence" on page 581). In the third century, Lugdunum's need for water grew, and the aqueduct system became inadequate. Inhabitants abandoned the high town and, using the original town as a kind of quarry, rebuilt down below along the riverbank.

• *Now enter the* **museum.** *The route described here gives an overview of the museum's highlights, which take on more meaning with the excellent audioguide. The collection takes you on a chronological stroll—illustrated with artifacts found in Lyon—down several floors through ancient Lyon.*

First is a brief glimpse at **prehistoric objects.** The unusual remains of a bronze chariot are Celtic (the tribes Rome conquered), dating from the seventh century BC.

Next, dive into the Gallo-Roman rooms. Sit close to the **model** of Lyon with its hills and rivers and listen on your audioguide to the history of Lugdunum while following its evolution on the model. It was a city of 50,000 in its second-century AD glory days. Gauls and Romans lived and worked side by side in Roman Lyon. Notice that the forum stood where the basilica does today, hanging on the cliff edge. (You'll see those ruins—across the river—if you follow my walking route of today's Croix-Rousse neighborhood.)

The curved stones you pass next were arena seats—inscribed with the names of big shots who sat there. Soon after, look for a big, black-bronze **tablet** and marvel at the amazing penmanship. Carved into it is the transcription of a speech given by Emperor Claudius in AD 48—his (long-winded) account of how he integrated the Gauls into the empire by declaring them eligible to sit in the Roman Senate (also recorded: the interjections of senators begging him to get to the point already—see the English translation behind, on the wall). A few steps farther is a stone Roman **pump** that looks like an engine block (the TV screen illustrates out how it worked).

Next are displays of Roman **coins and tools,** a model of a few key Roman buildings in Lyon, and fragments of a second-century AD **calendar.** Notice how each month is made of two fortnights, how the gods each have their day (like Christian saints would on later calendars), and the tiny holes used so a movable peg could mark the day. A bit farther along, behind the model of the big and small theaters (with originals out the window), check out the mechanics of a Roman theater **stage curtain,** which was raised instead of lowered. Go ahead...push the button.

The last section of the museum shows how Roman Lyon's

wealthy merchants built large homes with interior courtyards often tiled with mosaics. Ancient **amphora** (jugs) recall the thriving river trade. Your visit ends with displays on Roman religious life and the arrival of Christianity. Fifth-century **tombstones** come with early Christian symbolism.

• *Take the elevator up to exit the museum, return your audioguide, and enter the **Roman Theaters**.*

The closer **big theater** was built under the reign of Emperor Augustus and expanded by Hadrian—at its zenith, it could hold

10,000 spectators. Today it seats 3,000 for concerts. The **small theater,** an "odeon" (from the Greek "ode" for song), was acoustically designed for speeches and songs. The grounds are peppered with gravestones and sarcophagi. Find a seat in the big theater and read the description of Orange's Roman theater on page 657 for context.

• *The ancient road between the Roman Theaters leads down and out, where you'll find the Minimes funicular station (to the right as you leave). Take the funicular to Vieux Lyon (not St. Just), where it deposits you only a few steps from St. Jean Cathedral. Take some time to explore Vieux Lyon. Or, from the Vieux Lyon funicular stop, you can take Métro line D directly to the Lumière Museum or (with an easy transfer) to the Resistance and Deportation History Center (both described later).*

VIEUX LYON (OLD LYON)
St. Jean Cathedral

Stand back in the square for the best view of the cathedral (brilliant at night and worth returning for). This mostly Gothic cathedral took 200 years to build. It doesn't soar as high as its northern French counterparts; influenced by their Italian neighbors, churches in southern France aren't nearly as vertical as their sisters to the north. This cathedral, the seat of the "primate of the Gauls" (as Lyon's bishop is offi-

cially titled), serves what's considered the oldest Christian city in France.

Cost and Hours: Free, Mon-Fri 8:15-19:45, Sat-Sun until 19:00.

Facade: Before entering the cathedral, enjoy the carvings decorating the west facade. Nearby Geneva was the epicenter of Calvinism—a radically puritan Reformation sect that forbade images—and (in the 16th century) loved destroying them. As the Calvinist iconoclasts swept into Lyon, the statues on the cathedral were the first to go (notice the empty niches and the headless bodies). They missed some lovely smaller scenes though: Enjoy the intimate details (e.g., Genesis scenes from 15th century) carved into the small panels at eye level just to the right of the central door.

Interior: Notice the beautiful 13th- and 14th-century stained glass in "The Window of Redemption" above the altar. While the medieval faithful would know each scene, 21st-century workers, not so much. The panel to the right of the altar shows how the scenes were replaced in the wrong order after the 2015 restoration.

Under the north (left) transept is a medieval astronomical clock (1383); it has survived wars of all kinds, including the French Revolution. Impressively, its 650-year-old mechanism can compute Catholic holidays, including those that change each year, such as Easter.

Nearby: Outside (make two right turns as you leave) are the ruins of a mostly 11th-century church, destroyed during the French Revolution when the cathedral was turned into a "temple of reason." What's left of a baptistery from an early Christian church (c. AD 400—back when you couldn't enter a church until you were baptized) is under glass.

▲▲Heart of Vieux Lyon

Vieux ("Old") Lyon offers the best concentration of well-preserved Renaissance buildings in France. The city grew rich from its trade fairs and banking, and was the center of Europe's silk industry from the 16th to 19th century. The most prominent vestiges of Lyon's Golden Age are the elegant pastel buildings of the old center, which were inspired by Italy and financed by the silk industry. Busy Rue St. Jean, leading north from the cathedral to Place du Change, is the main drag. With the rise of Lyon's popularity with river cruise groups, this area is becoming *très* touristy. It's flanked by parallel pedestrian streets (Rue Juiverie and Rue du Bœuf are quieter and more appealing) and punctuated with picturesque squares and courtyards (entrances shown on "Vieux Lyon" map). A fine example of an Italian courtyard can be found at 8 Rue Juiverie. The pedestrian-friendly lanes of Vieux Lyon were made for ambling, window-shopping, and café lingering.

• *Stroll along Rue St. Jean and take a short detour by making a left up Rue de la Bombarde to the colorful courtyard of...*

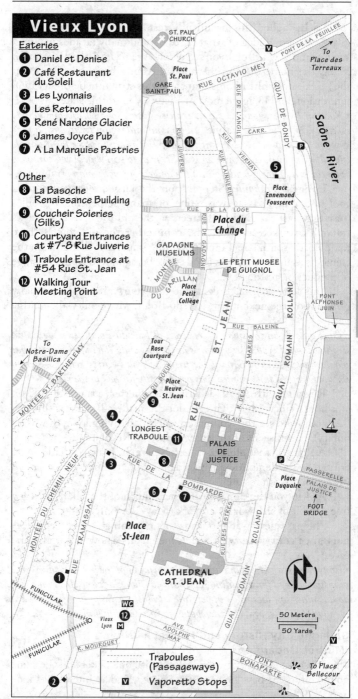

Vieux Lyon

Eateries

1. Daniel et Denise
2. Café Restaurant du Soleil
3. Les Lyonnais
4. Les Retrouvailles
5. René Nardone Glacier
6. James Joyce Pub
7. A La Marquise Pastries

Other

8. La Basoche Renaissance Building
9. Coucheir Soieries (Silks)
10. Courtyard Entrances at #7-8 Rue Juiverie
11. Traboule Entrance at #54 Rue St. Jean
12. Walking Tour Meeting Point

ST. PAUL CHURCH

PONT DE LA FEUILLEE

To Place des Terreaux

Place St. Paul

RUE OCTAVIO MEY

GARE SAINT-PAUL

QUAI DE BONDY

Saône River

RUE DE L'ANGILE

RUE JUIVERIE

RUE LAINERIE

RUE VERNAY

CARR.

Place Ennemond Fousseret

RUE DE LA LOGE

Place du Change

RUE DE GADAGNE

GADAGNE MUSEUMS

LE PETIT MUSEE DE GUIGNOL

MONTÉE DU GARILLAN

Place Petit Collège

RUE ST. JEAN

RUE BALEINE

3 MARIES

ROLLAND

PONT ALPHONSE JUIN

To Notre-Dame Basilica

MONTÉE ST. BARTHELEMY

Tour Rose Courtyard

RUE DU BOEUF

Place Neuve St. Jean

RUE DES

RUE PALAIS

QUAI ROMAIN

LONGEST TRABOULE

PALAIS DE JUSTICE

PASSERELLE

RUE DE LA

Place Duquaire

PALAIS DE JUSTICE

BOMBARDE

FOOT BRIDGE

MONTÉE DU CHEMIN NEUF

RUE TRAMASSAC

Place St-Jean

RUE DES ESTRÉES

ROLLAND

QUAI ROMAIN

CATHEDRAL ST. JEAN

FUNICULAR

WC

Vieux Lyon M

AVE. ADOLPHE MAX

50 Meters

50 Yards

R. MOURGUET

PONT BONAPARTE

To Place Bellecour

------ Traboules (Passageways)

V Vaporetto Stops

LYON

La Basoche: This beautifully restored Renaissance building gives you a good idea of what hides behind many facades in Vieux Lyon—and a whiff of Lyon's Golden Age. (Until the Revolution it was the home of a brotherhood of young lawyers.) Check out the black-and-white photos that show this structure before its 1968 renovation, and imagine most of Vieux Lyon in this state.

• *Back on Rue St. Jean, **A La Marquise** pastry shop sells Lyon's dessert specialty:* la tarte à la praline, *an almond and cream treat with a sugary coating that's as sweet as it is pink. This is a fine place for a sample (closed Mon-Tue). Continue up Rue St. Jean to #54 where you can push open the heavy doors leading into the longest of Lyon's many* traboules.

Longest *Traboule:* Stepping off the busy street, you enter a cool and quiet passageway—one of many serpentine traboules (passageways) that link the streets of the old town. The old city's traboules worked as shortcuts, connecting the old town's three main north-south streets and providing important shelter from the elements as unfinished silk goods were being moved from one stage of production to the next.

This long *traboule* links three tiny courtyards and eventually pops out on the next street, Rue du Bœuf, where our walk continues.

• *Once outside on the small quiet street of Rue du Bœuf, turn right and stroll downhill. You'll stay on this lane to its end. You're following what would have been the flow of the neighborhood's "dirty water"—down the gutter of the lane, which was periodically flushed to the river.*

Rue du Bœuf: At #21 is **Brochier Soieries,** a traditional Lyon silk house since 1890 that sells locally-made silks. Peek through the window to see the "computerized" silk weaving loom (it was all binary), reminiscent of the early Industrial Revolution.

A little further along is **Place Neuve St. Jean,** a small square created by the demolition of an old building. It's lined with *bouchons* (traditional Lyon restaurants).

At #16 you can pop into another branch of the silk house for a free exhibit of **silk worms** at work (May-Nov only).

The passageway at #16 leads to a charming and peaceful **Renaissance courtyard** with a rich merchants' showoff spiral staircase.

• *Continue straight down Rue du Bœuf to find (on the left) a Renaissance mansion named for a leading merchant family, Gadagne. It's home to a double museum, showing puppets and city history. Step into its courtyard to enjoy the scene, and consider popping into the museum.*

Gadagne City History and Puppet Museum (Musées Gadagne)

This museum (actually two museums with one ticket and the same hours) offers the best look at Lyon's history and an interactive, kid-

Exploring *Traboules*

There are many *traboules* (covered passageways) in Lyon's old town—giving visitors a hide-and-seek opportunity to discover pastel courtyards, lovely loggias, and delicate arches. *Traboules* are generally accessible from 8:00 until 19:30. To access them, press the button next to the street-front door to release the door, push the buttons to illuminate dark walkways, and slide the door-handle levers shut when leaving. You're welcome to explore—but please be respectful of the residents, and don't go up any stairs. Spiral staircases are often shared by several houses.

In the courtyards, gaze up and imagine the elegance of the original Renaissance inhabitants in the 16th century, when Lyon was the last great French city—before the Italian world and the gateway to Renaissance culture. Then imagine the later squalor when these became tenements inhabited by the poor, sharing a single fountain in each courtyard before the age of modern plumbing.

While you wander Vieux Lyon, look for door plaques giving a history of each building and *traboule.* After walking through these hidden passageways, you'll understand why Lyon's old town was an ideal center for the Resistance fighters to slip in and out of as they confounded the Nazis.

LYON

friendly look at puppets from around the world. The **Lyon History Museum** offers a serious swing through the story of Lyon, taking you from the city's Roman period to the present day—and every era in between. Interesting rooms devoted to its silk industry show looms and sample fabrics. The **Puppets of the World Museum** celebrates Guignol puppetry, the still-vibrant tradition first created in Lyon by an unemployed silk worker. Here you can see (and play with) examples of beautifully crafted Guignol puppets from around the world.

Cost and Hours: €9, includes audioguide and English brochure, Wed-Sun 11:00-18:30, closed Mon-Tue, 1 Place du Petit Collège, tel. 04 78 42 03 61, www.gadagne.musees.lyon.fr. The museum's pleasant rooftop terrace comes with an inviting café.

• *Walk to the end of Rue du Bœuf. At the T-intersection, go right, downhill into...*

Place du Change: This was the banking center of medieval Lyon. The city's finance industry developed after it began hosting trade fairs in 1420. Its centerpiece is France's first stock exchange, La Loge, which was completely renovated in the 18th century (creating a stark contrast to the Renaissance architecture around it). It's now a Reformed church.

• *A short block down Rue de la Fronde leads to more puppets, on display and for sale, at* **Le Petit Musée de Guignol.** *Two minutes along, on the*

river below Place du Change, ice-cream connoisseurs must stop at the
recommended **René Nardone Glacier.** *From here it's a short walk north*
into Presqu'île to Place des Terreaux and the Museum of Fine Arts (cross
Pont de la Feuillée and continue straight four blocks).

PRESQU'ILE

Presqu'île literally means "almost an island." This peninsula between the two rivers is Lyon's shopping spine, with thriving pedestrian streets (see map on page 958). The neighborhood's northern
focal point is the...

Place des Terreaux

This stately square hosts the City Hall (Hôtel de Ville), the Museum of Fine Arts, and an action-packed fountain by Frédéric-

Auguste Bartholdi (the French
sculptor who designed the Statue of Liberty). The fountain features Marianne (the Lady of the
Republic) riding a four-horse-
powered chariot, symbolically
leading Lyon's two great rivers
to the sea. It was originally destined for the city of Bordeaux,
which (ultimately) realized that
it could not afford the price tag, so the sculptor shopped it at the
1889 World Expo in Paris. There, Lyon's mayor fell in love and had
to have it. After Bartholdi modified it to fit Lyon's needs, the massive fountain was installed here in 1891. Originally in the square's
center, it was relocated in 1992 when they built a parking garage
below the square (imagine moving this thing).

Atelier de Soierie

This silk workshop, just off Place des Terreaux on Rue Romarin
(behind Café le Moulin Joli, a Resistance hangout during World
War II), welcomes the public to drop in to see silk printing and
screen painting by hand. At one end of the workshop is a wall full
of 100-year-old print blocks. At the other is a kitchen cooking up
buckets of artfully mixed paint in 20 colors (a nearly lost art that
today is performed primarily by machines). Within the shop, you'll
see stretched silk canvases, buckets of dye, and artists in action.
Friendly staff members speak some English and are happy to field
questions while they work. Climb the staircase to visit a boutique
selling handmade silk creations—mostly scarves and ties. Prices
range from €25 to €250. A handy brochure explains in English
how to tie a scarf French-style.

   Cost and Hours: Free entry, Mon-Fri 9:30-13:00 & 14:00-

18:30, Sat opens and closes 30 minutes earlier, closed Sun, tel. 04 72 07 97 83.

▲Museum of Fine Arts (Musée des Beaux-Arts)

Located in a former abbey that was secularized by Napoleon in 1803 and made into a public museum, this fine-arts museum has an impressive collection, ranging from Egyptian antiquities to Impressionist paintings. The inner courtyard is a pleasant place to take a peaceful break from city streets. The helpful museum map (pick up when you enter) and audioguide make touring it a pleasure. Plan your arrival carefully, as several key sections close for lunch. A bar/café with calming terrace seating is on the first floor, next to the bookstore.

Cost and Hours: €8, Wed-Mon 10:00-18:00 except Fri—when it opens at 10:30, closed Tue, audioguide-€1, picnic-perfect courtyard, 20 Place des Terreaux, Métro: Hôtel de Ville, tel. 04 72 10 17 40, www.mba-lyon.fr.

Visiting the Museum: After passing the ticket taker, walk up a short flight of stairs to the Chapel, a dreamy Orsay-like display of 19th- and 20th-century statues, including works by Rodin, Carpeaux, and Bartholdi. The next flight of steps leads to *Les Antiquités* (first floor on map), a fine collection of ancient artifacts (especially Egyptian—the Temple Gate from Medamud is mesmerizing) medieval art, Islamic art, and Art Nouveau (furniture). This first floor is closed 12:30-14:00.

The second floor displays a pretty selection of paintings from the last six centuries (no famous works, but a good Impressionist collection). You'll see Renaissance and Baroque paintings by Veronese, Cranach, Rubens, and Rembrandt, and Impressionist works by Monet, Manet, Matisse, Pissarro, Gaugin, Cézanne, and more. The small modern art section shows some works by Picasso, Dufy, Léger, and Braque.

The highlight is a series of Pre-Raphaelite-type works called *Le Poème de l'Ame* ("The Poem of the Soul"), by Louis Janmot (in the Salle Janmot, down a flight of stairs between the Impressionist and France/Europe in 19th-century sections). This cycle of 18 paintings and 16 charcoal drawings traces the story of the souls of a boy and a girl as they journey through childhood, adolescence, and into adulthood. They struggle with fears and secular temptations before gaining spiritual enlightenment on the way to heaven. The boy loses his faith and enjoys a short but delicious hedonistic fling that leads to misery in hell. But a mother's prayers intercede, and he reunites with the girl to enjoy heavenly redemption.

Museums of Textiles and Decorative Arts
(Musées des Tissus et des Arts Décoratifs)

These museums, between Place Bellecour and Perrache station, fill two buildings (sharing a courtyard and connected with an interior hallway). Expect some room closures, as both are undergoing renovation. There is no English information in these museums.

Cost and Hours: €10, covers both museums, Tue-Sun 10:00-18:00, closed Mon, 34 Rue de la Charité, Métro: Bellecour, tel. 04 78 38 42 00, www.mtmad.fr.

Visiting the Museums: The **Museum of Textiles** was founded in the mid-1800s to "maintain the commercial advantage of Lyon's silk manufacturers by showing their discerning taste for the arrangements and color settings of original motifs." It holds arguably the world's most valuable collection of textiles, going back over 4,000 years and touching all corners of the world. The museum shows off some breathtaking silk work—you'll see tunics, shawls, dresses, coats, capes, and more from around the world and made from a variety of fabrics.

The **Museum of Decorative Arts** fills a luxurious mansion and is decorated to the hilt with 18th-century furniture, textiles, and tapestries in a plush domestic setting. Entire rooms from aristocratic Lyonnaise homes have been re-created, including an 18th-century kitchen. There's plenty of china and a dazzling display of designer teakettles and coffee servers.

Shopping and Eating on the Presqu'île

There's more to this "almost-an-island" than the sights listed here. Join the river of shoppers on sprawling Rue de la République (north of Place Bellecour) and the teeming and less fancy Rue Victor Hugo pedestrian mall (south of Place Bellecour). Smart clothing boutiques line Rue Président Edouard Herriot. Peruse the *bouchons* (characteristic bistros—especially characteristic in the evening) of Rue Mercière.

Passage de l'Argue is an Old World, covered shopping passage from the 1800s that predates shopping malls (between 78 Rue Président Edouard Herriot and 43 Rue de Brest). And **Grand Café des Négociants** is ideal for an indoor break. This *grand café*, which has been in business since 1864, feels like it hasn't changed since then, with its soft velvet chairs, painted ceilings, and glass chandeliers (daily, 1 Place Francisque Régaud, near Cordeliers Métro stop, tel. 04 78 42 50 05).

For more eating recommendations, see the "Eating in Lyon" section, later.

La Croix-Rousse Walk

This is a mostly straight, downhill stroll along a long, stepped pedestrian lane in the La Croix-Rousse neighborhood. On the

20-minute stroll from top to bottom, you'll pass hip cafés, art galleries, creative graffiti, and used-clothing shops on your way to the Presqu'île.

Hilly, untouristy, and SoHo-esque, this neighborhood to the north of Presqu'île hummed with some 30,000 silk looms in the 1800s. Today this part of town is popular with Lyon's bohemian-chic crowd, drawn here by abandoned, airy apartment spaces (built in the age of the Jacquard loom, which required exceptionally high ceilings). The French nickname for this crowd is "Bobo"—bourgeois bohemian—people with money and education but who don't show it. It's a progressive and green community, where people eat vegetarian and drive electric cars.

The smartest way to visit the district is to take the Métro to the top (line C to **La Croix-Rousse**), then follow a series of scenic slopes and stairs back down (see map on page 932).

Outside the Croix-Rousse stop, a produce market stretches across the square and down **Boulevard de la Croix-Rousse** (daily except Mon, until about 12:30, best on Sun). The statue at the center of the square is Monsieur Jacquard, inventor of the loom that powered Lyon's economy in the mid-1800s.

Start your downhill stroll from behind the Métro stop along **Rue des Pierres Plantées** to a little square with a big view. Pause to appreciate the views from the top of the parklike Montée de la Grande Côte, and notice how the small concrete square may be used as a soccer field, a tricycle track, an outdoor café, and any other purpose the neighbors can find for it. Continue down the stairs, straight through the gardens along the **Montée de la Grande Côte** and two more stepped blocks. From here, you'll go down the steps and begin your descent along the straight vertical spine of the neighborhoods. At **Rue des Tables Claudiennes,** detour a block to the right for a view over the Roman Amphitheater of the Three Gauls. This ruined arena was once the same size as the one in Arles, holding 20,000 spectators. Parts of the arena were destroyed in the 1800s for city development; serious excavation did not begin until the 1960s. Return to the hill and continue your descent. At the end of the street, jog left, and pass through **Place des Capucins.** Turn left at the Eglise de Scientologie, continue down the stairs, and you end up back in the more high-powered commercial world of the Presqu'île at the stately **Place des Terreaux.**

Confluence Neighborhood

At the southern tip of the Presqu'île, where the Rhône and Saône rivers converge, you can experience France's cutting-edge, urban-design energy. Called **La Confluence,** this expansive urban renewal project (one of Europe's most ambitious), features futuristic offices, sustainable residential buildings, shopping, and vast public spaces in an area that recently was a vast wasteland. When completed, the Confluence project will double the size of Lyon's commercial center—that's right, double. While worthwhile for urban design types, this area is of average interest for most travelers.

To reach La Confluence, you can **cruise** down the Saône River on the shuttle boat *Le Vaporetto,* from either the northern end of Vieux Lyon or near Pont Bonaparte, to the Confluence shopping mall dock. Here you'll see the Confluence project's latest showpiece, the Place Nautique—a pleasure-boat marina.

From the **dock,** it's a 15-minute walk along the river (not along the tram route) to the Presqu'île's southern end and the Musée des Confluences. As you follow the **pedestrian walkway** you'll pass revamped dock warehouses, wild-and-crazy office buildings, and restaurant barges. The skippable **Musée des Confluences** is worth a look from the outside for its daring design. Inside, the permanent collection recounts the sweeping story of human existence (€9, Tue-Fri 11:00-19:00, Thu until 22:00, Sat-Sun 10:00-19:00, closed Mon, 86 Quai Perrache, tel. 04 28 38 11 90, www.museedesconfluences.fr).

To return, catch the **T1 tram** (in front of museum, direction: Feyssine) back to the Confluence mall and board *Le Vaporetto* to Vieux Lyon, or continue on the T1 to the Perrache stop where you can connect to the Métro and other tram lines (see map on page 932).

EAST BANK OF THE RHONE

Along with two worthwhile museums, Lyon's east bank of the Rhône River is a destination itself. The inviting and people-friendly riverside people zone between Pont Lafayette and Pont de la Guillotière is lined with restaurant and bar boats, bike lanes, and a mostly younger crowd enjoying the moment. It's great for a drink or light meal: Prices are reasonable and the scene is local, laid back, and fun. Foodies will also want to visit the Les Halles de Lyon Paul Bocuse for a lively food market experience (described under "Eating in Lyon," later).

▲Resistance and Deportation History Center
(Centre d'Histoire de la Résistance et de la Déportation)
This museum gives visitors a thorough understanding of how Lyon became an important city in the Resistance, what life was like for its members, and the clever strategies they employed to fight the Germans. You'll also learn about the fate of the Jews in Lyon during the war.

Located near Vichy (capital of the French puppet state) and neutral Switzerland, Lyon was the center of the French Resistance from 1942 to 1945. These "underground" Resistance heroes fought the Nazis tooth and nail. Bakers hid radios inside loaves of bread to secretly contact London. Barmaids passed along tips from tipsy Nazis. Communists in black berets cut telephone lines while printers countered Nazi propaganda with anonymous pamphlets. Farmers hid downed airmen in haystacks and housewives spread news from the front with their gossip. Without their bravery, the liberation of France would have been much more difficult.

Cost and Hours: €8, Wed-Sun 10:00-18:00, closed Mon-Tue, audioguide-€1 (also downloadable as an app), 14 Avenue Berthelot, tel. 04 78 72 23 11.

Getting There: The easiest way to reach the museum is to ride the Métro to Perrache station, exit the station and cross the tram tracks, and transfer to the T2 tram. You can also take Métro line B to Jean Macé, exit toward the elevated train line, and transfer to the T2 tram (going right). Get off the tram at Centre Berthelot. Otherwise it's a 20- to 30-minute hike from Place Bellecour.

Visiting the Museum: The museum's "Lyon, A City at War 1939-1945" exhibit is rich with artifacts. While you can request the binder with English translations, I'd use the excellent audioguide. Visit the 43 displays in numeric order. Everything's on one floor until the end, where you climb down into a clandestine basement printing office. There are two videos, each with English subtitles (45-minute documentary about Klaus Barbie trial at exhibit start, plays 5 times/day; 10-minute clip on liberation of Lyon at exhibit end, loops continually).

Though these days it's dedicated to the history of the Resistance, this building actually served as a Nazi torture chamber and Gestapo headquarters under Klaus Barbie (who was finally tried and convicted in 1987 here in Lyon after extradition from Bolivia). More than 11,000 people were killed or deported to concentration camps during his reign.

▲Lumière Museum (Musée Lumière)

Antoine Lumière and his two sons, Louis and Auguste—the George Eastmans of France—ran a huge factory with 260 workers in the 1880s, producing four million glass photographic plates a day. Then, in 1895, they made the first *cinématographe*, or movie. In 1903, they pioneered the "autochrome" process of painting frames to make "color photos." This museum tells their story.

Cost and Hours: €7, Tue-Sun 10:00-18:30, closed Mon, essential audioguide-€3, tel. 04 78 78 18 95, www.institut-lumiere. org.

Getting There: Take Métro line D to the Monplaisir-Lumière stop. The museum is in the large mansion with the tiled roof on the square, kitty-corner from the Métro stop at 25 Rue du Premier-Film.

Visiting the Museum: The museum fills Villa Lumière, the family's belle époque mansion, built in 1902. Many interesting displays and the audioguide do a great job of explaining filmmaking history and the laborious yet fascinating process of creating moving images. You'll never again take the quality of today's movies for granted.

Before your visit, pick up the informative museum plan. The museum's highlights are the many antique cameras (ground floor) and the screens playing the earliest "movies." The first film reels held about 950 frames, which played at 19 per second, so these first movies were only 50 seconds long. About 1,500 Lumière films are catalogued between 1895 and 1907. The very first movie ever made features workers piling out of the Lumière factory at the end of a workday—mesmerizing in its day not for the plot or action, but simply because of the technology that produced moving images. After their initial success, the Lumières sent cameramen to capture scenes from around the world, connecting diverse cultures and people in a way that had never been done before.

Upstairs are exhibits on still photography and the Lumière living quarters (furnished c. 1900). One room has tablets where you can select movies to watch (notice that each movie is tagged with its "Catalog Lumière" number). The cinema features an hour-long selection of short movies with commentaries, along with recent feature-length films in many languages, including English. Across the park from the mansion is a shrine of what's left of the warehouse where the first movie was actually shot. In a wonderful coincidence, *lumière* is the French word for light.

Nightlife in Lyon

Lyon has France's second-largest cultural budget after Paris, so there are always plenty of theatrical productions and concerts to attend (in French, of course). The TI has the latest information and schedules. From mid-June through mid-September, the terrace-café at the Opera House hosts an outdoor jazz café with free concerts (usually Mon-Sat, www.opera-lyon.com).

After dinner, stroll through Lyon to savor the city's famous illuminations (see sidebar on page 934).

For lively bar and people-watching scenes in Presqu'île, prowl Rue de la Monnaie (angles off "restaurant row" Rue Mercière to the south) and the streets between Place des Terreaux and the Opera House. The **James Joyce** Irish pub, in the heart of Vieux Lyon, is a cozy English-speaking place (daily, 68 Rue St. Jean, tel. 04 78 37 84 28).

Sleeping in Lyon

Hotels in Lyon are a steal compared with those in Paris. Weekends are generally discounted (Sundays in particular) in this city that lives off business travelers. Prices rise and rooms disappear when trade fairs are in town, so it's smart to reserve your room in advance. All my listings are on the Presqu'île except for the youth hostel. Hotels have elevators and air-conditioning—a godsend when it's hot (hottest June-mid-Sept)—unless otherwise noted. Expect to push buttons to gain access to many hotels.

ON OR NEAR PLACE DES CELESTINS

Book ahead to sleep in this classy yet unpretentious neighborhood (Métro: Bellecour). Just a block off the central Place Bellecour and a block to the Saône River, this area gives travelers easy access to Lyon's sights. Join shoppers perusing the upscale boutiques, or watch children playing in the small square fronting the Théâtre des Célestins. Warning: Weekend nights can be noisy if you score a room facing Place des Célestins.

$$$ Hôtel Globe et Cecil** is the most professional and elegant of my listings, with refined comfort on a refined street and a service-oriented staff. Its rooms are tastefully decorated and mostly spacious (good breakfast, 21 Rue Gasparin, tel. 04 78 42 58 95, www.globeetcecilhotel.com, accueil@globeetcecilhotel.com).

$$ Hôtel des Artistes,** ideally located on Place des Célestins, is a comfortable, business-class hotel that offers a fair value on weekdays and a good value on weekends (standard rooms are comfortable but tight, 8 Rue Gaspard-André, tel. 04 78 42 04 88, www.hotel-des-artistes.fr, reservation@hotel-des-artistes.fr).

$$ Hôtel des Célestins,** just off Place des Célestins, is warmly run by Cornell-grad Laurent. Its cheery rooms aren't cheap but are filled with thoughtful touches. Streetside rooms have more light and are bigger (beautiful suites ideal for families or those in need of room to roam, completely nonsmoking, laundry service, 4 Rue des Archers, tel. 04 72 56 08 98, www.hotelcelestins.com, info@hotelcelestins.com).

$ Elysée Hôtel,* a few blocks off Place des Célestins, is a simple little hotel with excellent rates and two-star comfort. Gentle Monsieur Larrive is your host (elevator from first floor up, 92 Rue Président Edouard Herriot, tel. 04 78 42 03 15, www.hotel-elysee.fr, accueil@hotel-elysee.fr).

$ Hôtel du Théâtre* has no air-conditioning and requires stamina to reach the lobby, as it's 40 steps from street level. But the hotel is well-located on Place des Célestins and offers a solid deal. Owners Monsieur and Madame Kuhn run a tight ship, and most of the rooms and bathrooms are spacious and bright (no elevator,

10 Rue de Savoie, enter from hotel's rear, tel. 04 78 42 33 32, www. hotel-du-theatre.fr, contact@hotel-du-theatre.fr).

OTHER PLACES ON THE PRESQU'ILE

$$ Hôtel la Résidence,*** south of Place Bellecour and my closest listing to Perrache station, has 65 plain but good-value rooms. Most are spacious and have high ceilings and bathtub-showers (family rooms, 18 Victor Hugo, tel. 04 78 42 63 28, www.hotel-la-residence.com, hotel-la-residence@wanadoo.fr).

$ Le Boulevardier,** a quirky budget option located a few blocks south of Place des Terreaux, has 14 rooms above a nostalgic café. The rooms have character—some with antique furniture and toys, and others with church views (larger rooms worth the extra euros, no air-con but fans, 5 Rue de la Fromagerie, tel. 04 78 28 48 22, www.leboulevardier.fr, hotelboulevardier@gmail.com).

HOSTEL

¢ Auberge de Jeunesse HI Lyon is impressively situated—it's only a 10-minute steep walk above Vieux Lyon. Open daily (except 13:00-14:00 & 20:00-21:00), it has a lively common area with kitchen access and a snack bar (includes breakfast, book only through website, small safes available, 45 Montée du Chemin Neuf, Métro: Vieux Lyon, or take funicular to Minimes, exit station and make a left U-turn, then follow station wall downhill to Montée du Chemin Neuf; tel. 04 78 15 05 50, www.hihostels.com, lyon@hifrance.org).

Eating in Lyon

Dining is a ▲▲▲ attraction in Lyon and, compared to Paris, the value is good. Half the fun is joining the procession of window shoppers mulling over where they'll *diner ce soir.* In the evening, the city's population seems to double as locals emerge to stretch their stomachs. The tried-and-true *salade lyonnaise*  (usually filling) followed by *quenelles* (dumplings) is a classic Lyon meal. (While the *quenelle* is a local favorite, for some it's just a big doughy dumpling.) You won't want dessert.

Lyon's characteristic *bouchons* are small bistros that evolved from the days when Mama would feed the silk workers after a long day. True *bouchons* are simple places with limited selection and seating ("just like Mama's"), serving only traditional fare and special 46-centiliter *pot* (pron. "poh") wine pitchers. The lively pedestrian streets of Vieux Lyon and Rue Mercière on the Presqu'île are *bouchon* bazaars, worth strolling even if you dine elsewhere. Though food quality may be better away from these popular restaurant rows, you can't beat the atmosphere. Many of Lyon's restaurants close on Sunday and Monday and during August, except along Rue Mercière. If you plan to dine somewhere special, reserve ahead (ask your hotelier for help).

IN OR NEAR VIEUX LYON

Come to Vieux Lyon for a charming atmosphere. For the epicenter of restaurant activity, go to Place Neuve St. Jean, and survey the scene and *menus* before sitting down. Most of these places are located on the map on page 945.

$$$ Daniel et Denise is formal, dressy, and worth booking ahead. Reputed chef Joseph Viola has created a buzz by providing wonderful cuisine at affordable prices in a classic *bouchon* setting (indoor seating only, closed Sun-Mon, 36 Rue Tramassac, tel. 04 78 42 24 62, www.danieletdenise.fr).

$$ Café Restaurant du Soleil serves Lyon's tastiest *quenelles*, offering five types, including the traditional *brochet* (pike), scallops (my favorite), and original varieties made with wild garlic. The atmosphere and setting, both inside and out, is unforgettable (no lunch Sun-Mon, 2 Rue Saint Georges, tel. 04 78 37 60 02).

$ Les Lyonnais is a block off the Rue du Bœuf action, making it a bit quieter. Its lighthearted interior has rich colors, wood tables, and a photo gallery of loyal customers. Stéphane runs the place with grace, offering a good €25 *menu* with *salade lyonnaise* and *quenelles*, or fine and filling €14 salads (closed Mon, small terrace, 1 Rue Tramassac, tel. 04 78 37 64 82).

$$ Les Retrouvailles serves tasty, more modern Lyonnaise cuisine in a charming setting under wood-beam ceilings with an open kitchen. Tables are grouped around a central buffet displaying delectable desserts. Your dining experience is thoughtfully overseen by owners Pierre *(le chef)* and Odile (*menus* from €27, indoor dining only, dinner only, closed Sun, 38 Rue du Bœuf, tel. 04 78 42 68 84).

$$ Restaurant de Fourvière, atop Fourvière Hill with a spectacular view overlooking Lyon, serves fine traditional cuisine in a superb setting. Choose from the modern interior or the better, leafy terrace, both with views. Reserve well ahead for a view table (*menus* from €30, may be closed in 2020, 9 Place de Fourvière, near Notre-Dame Basilica—see map on next page, tel. 04 78 25 21 15, www.restaurant-fourviere.fr).

Ice Cream: René Nardone Glacier, with pleasant outdoor seating on the river near Place du Change, serves up some of Lyon's

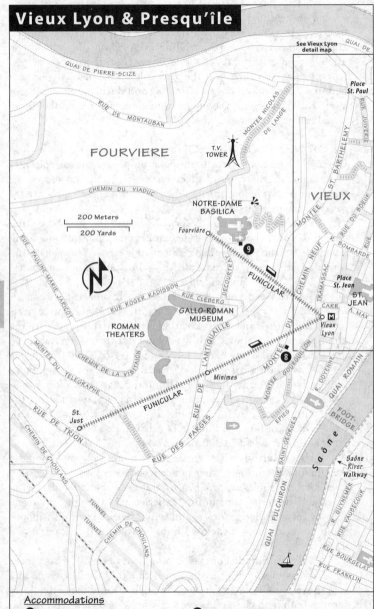

Vieux Lyon & Presqu'île

QUAI DE PIERRE-SCIZE

RUE DE MONTAUBAN

FOURVIERE

T.V. TOWER

CHEMIN DU VIADUC

NOTRE-DAME BASILICA

Fourvière

200 Meters
200 Yards

FUNICULAR

RUE ROGER RADISSON

RUE CLEBERG

GALLO-ROMAN MUSEUM

ROMAN THEATERS

RUE PAULINE-MARIE JARICOT

CHEMIN DE LA VISITATION

Minimes

MONTEE DU TELEGRAPHE

FUNICULAR

RUE DE L'ANTIQUAILLE

St. Just

RUE DE TRION

RUE DES FARGES

CHEMIN DE CHOULANS

TUNNEL

TUNNEL CHEMIN DE CHOULANS

See Vieux Lyon detail map

QUAI DE

Place St. Paul

RUE JUIVERIE

ST. BARTHELEMY

VIEUX

MONTEE

RUE DU BOEUF

R. BOMBARDE

CHEMIN NEUF

TRAMASSAC

Place St. Jean

ST. JEAN

A. MAX

CARR.

M Vieux Lyon

MONTEE DU

MONTEE GOURGUILLON

EPIES

RUE SAINT-GEORGES

R. DOYENNE

QUAI ROMAIN

FOOT-BRIDGE

Saône

Saône River Walkway

QUAI FULCHIRON

R. GUYNEMER

RUE VAUBECOUR

RUE BOURGELAT

RUE FRANKLIN

LYON

Accommodations

1 Hôtel Globe et Cecil
2 Hôtel des Artistes
3 Hôtel des Célestins
4 Elysée Hôtel
5 Hôtel du Théâtre
6 Hôtel la Résidence
7 Le Boulevardier
8 Auberge de Jeunesse HI Lyon

Eateries & Other

9 Restaurant de Fourvière
10 To Le Bouchon des Filles & Archange

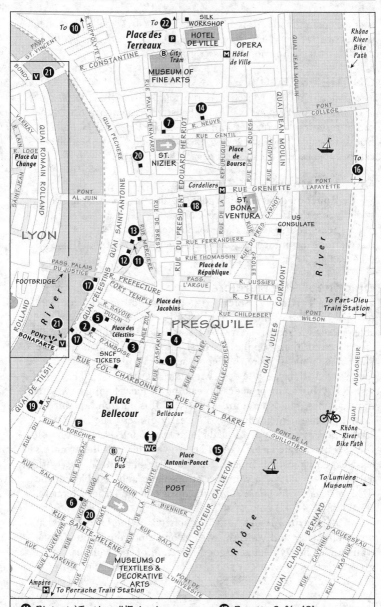

⑪ Bistrot à Tartines/L'Epicerie	⑰ Buvette Cafés (2)
⑫ L'Arbre à Thé	⑱ Grand Café des Négociants
⑬ Bistrot de Lyon	⑲ Bookstore & Wi-Fi
⑭ L'Harmonie des Vins	⑳ Launderette (2)
⑮ Brasserie le Sud	㉑ Le Vaporetto Boat Stop (2)
⑯ To Les Halles de Lyon Paul Bocuse	㉒ To Bike Rental

best ice cream, made fresh daily next door. Ask Armelle about her peanut ice cream (May-Sept daily 8:30-24:00, off-season 9:00-20:00, 3 Place Ennemond Fousseret).

ON THE PRESQU'ILE
The pedestrian Rue Mercière is the tourist-friendly epicenter of *bouchons* on the Presqu'île. Along this street, an entertaining can-can of restaurants stretches four blocks from Place des Jacobins to Rue Grenette. Enjoy surveying the scene and choose whichever eatery appeals. See the map on page 958 for locations.

Near the Museum of Fine Arts
$$ Le Bouchon des Filles is a cozy, traditional *bouchon* on a quiet street where the two *"filles"* ("girls") offer a good-value *menu* including a cheese course (open daily for dinner plus Fri-Sun for lunch, reservations recommended, 20 Rue Sergent Blandan, tel. 04 78 30 40 44).

On or near Rue Mercière
$ Bistrot à Tartines/L'Epicerie is a young and fun place for tasty *tartines* (big slice of bread topped with goodies) offered at unbeatable prices by a friendly staff. You can split a *tartine* and save money (and room for their popular desserts). The interior, which feels like an antique general store, has good seating inside and out (daily, food served all day, 2 Rue de la Monnaie, tel. 04 78 37 70 85).

$ L'Arbre à Thé provides a break in this meat-loving city, with light quiches, salads, and great desserts. This cute and quaint tea salon is convenient for lunch or an early dinner (Tue-Sat 11:30-19:00, closed Sun-Mon, 4 Rue du Petit David, tel. 04 72 40 06 68).

$$ Bistrot de Lyon, famed chef-owner Jean-Paul Lacombe's least-expensive establishment, feels touristy but still bustles with authentic, circa-1900 Lyonnaise atmosphere and reliable cuisine (€22 *quenelles*, €13 *salade lyonnaise*, open daily, 64 Rue Mercière, tel. 04 78 38 47 47).

$$ L'Harmonie des Vins is a convivial wine bar/bistro that oozes character and warmth, with a long zinc counter and stone walls under heavy beams, a good selection of local dishes, and a great selection of wines by the glass or bottle (closed Sun-Mon, 9 Rue Neuve, tel. 04 72 98 85 59).

Refined Dining
$$$ Archange is a softly lit, white-tablecloth place accommodating 26 happy diners, all eager to sample the popular chef's creations that infuse a hint of Asian influence with refined French cuisine (*menus* only—no à la carte). Ask your hotelier to book your table ahead (dinner and indoor seating only, closed Mon, near Place des

Terreaux at 6 Rue Hippolyte Flandrin, tel. 04 78 28 32 26, www.
archangecafe.com).

$$$ Brasserie le Sud is one of four places in Lyon where you
can sample the cuisine of the late legendary chef Paul Bocuse at
affordable prices. His brasseries feature international cuisine from
different parts of the world (each named for the corner it repre-
sents—north, south, east, and west). Le Sud is the most accessible,
with a sunny Mediterranean menu and feel. It's dressy, with three
dining zones: bright and spacious inside, under a big awning, and
outside facing a big modern square. With professional service,
nicely presented and reliably tasty dishes, and great prices, it's un-
derstandably popular. While the *prix fixe* menus are the most eco-
nomical, order à la carte to enjoy the full range of the kitchen (daily,
reservations recommended, 11 Place Antonin-Poncet, a few blocks
off Place Bellecour, tel. 04 72 77 80 00, www.nordsudbrasseries.
com).

ON THE EAST BANK OF THE RHONE
Les Halles de Lyon Paul Bocuse

As a cuisine capital, Lyon has a thriving market to serve its many
creative chefs. The modern Les Halles is away from the normal
tourist action, but foodies and market enthusiasts enjoy a visit or
a meal here. It's a complete food festival—crammed with butch-
ers, fishmongers, pastry specialists, cheese shops, and colorful pro-
duce stands, with food stands and mini restaurants mixed in. For
a memorable lunch or early-by-French-standards dinner, drop by
and survey your many dining options (indoor and outdoor, daily
11:00-14:30, also Wed-Sat 18:00-21:00; take T1 tram to Part
Dieu-Servient stop, walk to Rue Garibaldi, and turn right—it's
under a round concrete structure at 102 Cours Lafayette).

Lyon Connections

After Paris, Lyon is France's most important rail hub. Train travel-
ers find this gateway to the Alps, Provence, the Riviera, and Bur-
gundy an easy stopover. And now the Eurostar connects Lyon with
London in a little over five hours.

Two main train stations serve Lyon: **Part-Dieu** and **Perrache.**
Most trains officially depart from Part-Dieu, though many also
stop at Perrache, and trains run between the stations (service can
be infrequent). Double-check your train's departure station.

From Lyon by Train to: Paris (hourly, 2 hours), **Annecy** (10/
day, 2 hours; also 6/day by bus, 2.5 hours), **Chamonix** (6/day, 4
hours, most change at St-Gervais), **Strasbourg** (7/day, 4 hours),
Dijon (hourly, 2 hours), **Beaune** (hourly, 2 hours), **Avignon** (hour-
ly, 70 minutes, slower to Centre-Ville station), **Arles** (hourly, 3

hours, most change in Avignon, Marseille, or Nîmes), **Nice** (6/day, 4.5 hours), **Carcassonne** (4/day, 4 hours), **Venice** (2/day, 9 hours, change in Turin), **Rome** (3/day, 9 hours, change in Milan or Turin), **Florence** (4/day, 8-12 hours), **Geneva** (8/day, 2 hours), **Barcelona** (1/day direct, 5 hours, more with change in Perpignan, Narbonne, or Valence), **London** (1/day "direct" but border check at Lille, 5.5 hours on Eurostar, more with easy change in Lille).

From Lyon by Bus: Ouibus and Flixbus leave from Perrache station (and the airport).

Near Lyon: The Rhône Valley

The Rhône Valley is the narrow part of the hourglass that links the areas of Provence and Burgundy. The region is bordered to the west by the soft hills of the Massif Central, and with the rolling foothills of the Alps just to the east, it's the gateway to the high Alps (the region is called Rhône-Alpes). The mighty Rhône River rumbles through the valley from its origin in the Swiss Alps to its outlet 500 miles away in the Mediterranean near Arles.

Vineyards blanket the western side of the Rhône Valley, from those of the Beaujolais just north of Lyon to the steep slopes of Tain-Hermitage below Lyon. On the eastern side of the river and closer to Avignon are the vineyards of the famous Côtes du Rhône.

The Rhône Valley has always provided the path of least resistance for access from the Mediterranean to northern Europe, and today, Roman ruins litter the valley between Lyon and Orange.

BEAUJOLAIS WINE ROUTE

Between Lyon and Mâcon (near Cluny, in Burgundy), the Beaujolais region makes for an appealing detour, thanks to its beautiful vineyards and villages and easygoing wine tasting (for more on Beaujolais wines, see page 928).

The Beaujolais wine road starts 45 minutes north of Lyon and runs from Villefranche-sur-Saône to Mâcon. The *Route du Beaujolais* winds up, down, and around the hills just west of the A-6 autoroute and passes through Beaujolais' most important villages: Chiroubles, Fleurie, Chénas, and Juliénas. Look for *Route du Beaujolais* signs, and expect to get lost more than a few times (Lyon's TI has a route map, and you can check there for more information).

Note that while Villefranche-sur-Saône may be the Beaujolais capital, it's an unappealing city that's best avoided. Focus your time on the small villages, and look for *dégustation* (tasting) signs.

From Lyon to Mâcon: To enjoy the best of this wine route, start by making your way to the hill of **Fleurie** with its chapel and viewpoint, then pass Moulin à Vent's famous vineyards and see its trademark windmill. In Juliénas, the old church has been transformed into a cellar and tasting room and is used as a bar by the locals. You'll find more serious wines at **Le Château de Juliénas,** an authentic castle with impressive vaulted cellars (www.chateaudejulienas.com). If it's lunchtime, enjoy the convivial atmosphere of **$$ Joséphine à Table** in the village of Saint-Amour, which is also home to two Michelin-star restaurants. It's the local winemakers' hangout; arrive early or reserve a day before (closed Sun-Mon, tel. 03 85 37 10 26, www.josephineatable.fr).

Continuing north, you'll enter the Mâconnais white wine region, passing signs to the famous villages of Pouilly and Fuissé as you near Mâcon. The 45-minute hike to the 1,600-foot-high **Solutré Rock** (a prehistoric site) offers grandiose views over the Saône valley, vineyards, and the twin shorter sister Vergisson Rock.

For a high-priced but thorough introduction to this region's wines, visit **Le Hameau Dubœuf** in Romanèche-Thorins. The king of Beaujolais, Georges Dubœuf, has constructed a Disney-esque introduction to wine at his museum, which immerses you in the life of a winemaker and features impressive models, exhibits, films, and videos. You'll be escorted from the beginning of the vine to present-day winemaking, with a focus on Beaujolais wines. It also has a lovely garden with fragrant flowers, fruits, herbs, and spices that represent the rich aromas present in wine (€19, keep receipt for discount if you intend to visit the Abbey of Cluny—see page 922, includes a small tasting, free English headphones and a *petit train* ride, plan to spend half a day, daily 10:00-18:00; in Romanèche-Thorins, follow signs labeled *Le Hameau Dubœuf* from D-306, then *La Gare* signs, and look for the old train-station-turned-winery; tel. 03 85 35 22 22, www.hameauduboeuf.com).

Train Alternative: Without a car, consider seeing the wine route by train. Trains between Lyon and Mâcon stop at several wine villages, including Romanèche-Thorins (6 trains/day from Lyon).

Sleeping on the Beaujolais Wine Route: A young French couple who lived in the US for over a decade, Virginie (who also leads tours for my company) and Olivier rent three rooms at **$ More Travel Guesthouse** in scenic St-Vérand, 20 minutes south of Cluny and two miles from Juliénas (includes breakfast, cash or PayPal only, ask about homemade dinners and nearby train station pickup, Virginie also offers day trips and wine tastings, tel. 06 52 90 88 61, https://virginiemoretravel.wordpress.com, virginiemoretravel@gmail.com).

LYON

ALSACE

Colmar • Route du Vin • Strasbourg

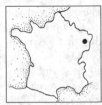

The province of Alsace stands like a flower-child referee between Germany and France. Bounded by the Rhine River on the east and the Vosges Mountains on the west, this is a green region of Hansel-and-Gretel villages, ambitious vineyards, and vibrant cities. Food and wine are the primary industry, topic of conversation, and perfect excuse for countless festivals.

Alsace has changed hands between Germany and France several times because of its location, natural wealth, naked vulnerability—and the fact that Germany considered the mountains the natural border, while the French saw the Rhine as the dividing line.

On a grander scale, Alsace is Europe's cultural divide, with Germanic nations to the north and Romantic ones to the south. The region is a fault line marking the place where cultural tectonic plates collide—it's no wonder the region has been scarred by a history of war.

Through the Middle Ages, Alsace was part of the Holy Roman Empire when German culture and language ruled. After the devastation of the Thirty Years' War (1618-1648), Alsace started to become integrated into France—revolutionaries took full control in 1792. But in 1871, after France's defeat in the Franco-Prussian War, Alsace "returned" to Germany. Almost five decades later, Germany lost World War I—and Alsace "returned" to France. Except for a miserable stint as part of the Nazi realm from 1940 to 1945, Alsace has been French ever since.

Having been a political pawn for 1,000 years, Alsace has a hybrid culture: Natives who curse do so bilingually, and the local cuisine features sauerkraut with fine wine sauces. In recent years,

Alsace

To Frankfurt

A-62

A-8

A-6

10 Kilometers

10 Miles

A-8

Saarbrücken

A-80

A-27

Paris

FRANCE

100 Miles

GERMANY

To Metz, Verdun, Reims & Paris

F R A N C E

Wissembourg

To Frankfurt

A-35

To Verdun, Reims & Paris

A-4

Haguenau

Baden-Baden

TGV

D-1061

Sarrebourg

A-4

Saverne

Rhine River

To Lunéville

N-4

L O R R A I N E

D-1004

Strasbourg

Kehl

A-5

28

Baccarat

LE STRUTHOF

D-1420

A-35

TGV

D-1083

Rhine

GERMANY

B L A C K   F O R E S T

N-59

D-1420

D-424

See detail map

St-Dié

N-59

Sélestat

294

Kaysersberg

D-415

Colmar

A-5

Col de Bonhomme

D-415

Breisach

Freiburg

Eguisheim

31

To Epinal

A-35

Rhine River

A-35

TGV

N-66

D-83

Mulhouse

317

A-36

TGV

A-35

Ronchamp

N-19

Belfort

A-3

A-36

Basel

To Zürich

To Besançon, Dijon & Beaune

To Bern

SWITZERLAND

V O S G E S   M T N S.

A L S A C E

ALSACE

Alsace and its sister German region just across the border have been growing farther apart linguistically—but closer commercially. People routinely cross the border to shop and work. And, while Alsace's Germanic-based dialect is fading, schools on the German side are encouraged to teach French as the second language and vice versa. Street names are commonly shown in both French and Alsatian.

Of the 1.8 million people living in Alsace, about 270,000 live in Strasbourg (its biggest city) and 70,000 live in Colmar. Colmar is one of Europe's most enchanting cities—with a small-town warmth and world-class art. Strasbourg is a big-city version of Colmar, worth a stop for its venerable cathedral and to feel its high-powered and trendy bustle. The small villages that dot the wine road between them are like petite Colmars and provide a delightful and charming escape from the two cities.

PLANNING YOUR TIME

The ideal plan: Make Colmar your home base and spend two or three days in the region. I suggest a day each in Colmar, the villages of the Route du Vin, and Strasbourg. If you have a car and like small towns, think about basing yourself in Eguisheim. Urban Strasbourg, with its soaring cathedral and vigorous center, is a headache for drivers but a quick 30-minute train ride from Colmar—do it by train as a day trip from Colmar or as a stopover on your way in or out of the region. If you have only one day, get an early start for a morning along the Route du Vin, when it's quieter, and enjoy an afternoon and evening in Colmar.

The somber WWI battlefields of Verdun and the bubbly vigor of Reims in northern France (see next chapter) are closer to Paris than to Alsace and follow logically if your next destination is Paris. The high-speed TGV-Est train links Paris with Reims, Verdun, Strasbourg, Colmar, and destinations farther east, bringing the Alsace within two hours of Paris and giving train travelers easy access to Reims or Verdun *en route* between Paris and Alsace.

GETTING AROUND ALSACE

Frequent trains make the trip between Colmar and Strasbourg a snap (2/hour, 30 minutes). Distances are short and driving is easy—though a good map helps. Connecting Colmar with neighboring villages is doable via the region's sparse bus service or on a bike if you're in shape. Minivan excursions are handy for those without cars and depart from Colmar or Strasbourg. Taking a taxi between towns is another worthwhile option (distances are short so prices are fair). Once in the Route du Vin villages, you can hike or rent bikes to explore further.

Early Crockpots

For old-school Alsatian comfort food, order the ubiquitous *Baeckeoffe*, which is still served at your table in traditional pottery. The dish gets its name from where it was cooked—in the "baker's oven." For centuries Alsatian women combined the week's leftover pork, beef, and veal with potatoes, *onions*, and leeks in a covered clay pot, then added white wine. Carrying the pot on their way to church on Sunday, the women would pass by the bakery and put their pot in one of the large stone ovens, still warm from baking the morning bread. During the three-hour Mass, the meat would simmer and be perfectly stewed in time for lunch. The pottery, which is still produced and sold locally, remains an integral part of every Alsatian household.

ALSACE'S CUISINE SCENE

Alsatian cuisine is a major tourist attraction in itself. You vill not escape the German influence: sausages, potatoes, onions, and

sauerkraut. Look for *choucroute garnie* (sauerkraut and sausage), the more traditionally Alsatian *Baeckeoffe* (see sidebar), *Rösti* (an oven-baked potato-and-cheese dish), *Spätzle* (soft egg noodles), *quenelles* (dumplings made of pork, beef, or fish), fresh trout, and foie gras. For lighter fare, try the *poulet au Riesling,* chicken cooked slowly in Riesling wine (*coq au Riesling* is the same dish done with rooster). At lunch, or for a lighter dinner, try a *tarte à l'oignon* (like an onion quiche) or *tarte flambée* (like a thin-crust pizza with onion and bacon bits). If you're picnicking, buy some stinky Munster cheese. Dessert specialties are *tarte alsacienne* (fruit tart) and *Kugelhopf glacé* (a light cake mixed with raisins, almonds, dried fruit, and cherry liqueur).

ALSATIAN WINES

Thanks to Alsace's Franco-Germanic culture, its wines are a kind of hybrid. The bottle shape, grapes, and much of the wine terminology are inherited from its German past, though wines made today are distinctly French in style (and generally drier than their German sisters). Alsatian wines are named for their grapes—unlike in Burgundy or Provence, where wines are commonly named after villages, or in Bordeaux, where wines are often named after châteaux. White wines rule in Alsace. Sample at least a few of the four "noble grapes" of the Alsace: riesling, gewürztraminer, pinot gris, or muscat. You'll also see a local version of Champagne, called Crémant d'Alsace, and a variety of *eaux-de-vie* (strong fruit-flavored brandies). For more information, see the "Wines of the Alsace" sidebar on page 996.

Colmar

Colmar feels made for wonderstruck tourists—its essentially traffic-free city center is a fantasy of steeply pitched roofs, pastel stucco, and antique timbers. Plus, it offers a few heavyweight sights in a comfortable, midsize-town package. Historic beauty was usually a poor excuse for being spared the ravages of World War II, but it worked for Colmar. The American and British military were careful not to bomb the half-timbered old burghers' houses, characteristic tiled roofs, and cobbled lanes of Alsace's most beautiful city. The town's distinctly French shutters combined with the ye-olde German half-timbering gives Colmar an intriguing ambience.

Today, Colmar is alive with colorful buildings, impressive art treasures, and German tourists. Antique shops welcome browsers, homeowners fuss over their geraniums, and locals seem genuinely proud of their clean and beautiful city.

Orientation to Colmar

There isn't a straight street in Colmar's historic center—count on getting lost. Thankfully, most streets are pedestrian-only, and it's a lovely town to be lost in. Navigate by church steeples and the helpful signs that seem to pop up whenever you need them. For tourists, the town center is Place Unterlinden (a 20-minute walk from the train station), where you'll find Colmar's most important museum, the TI, and a big Monoprix supermarket/department store. City buses and tourist trains depart nearby.

Colmar is busiest from May through September and during its festive Christmas season (www.noel-colmar.com). Weekends draw crowds all year (book lodging well ahead). A popular music festival fills hotels the first two weeks of July (www.festival-colmar.com),

ALSACE

and the local wine festival keeps things flowing nicely in July and August.

TOURIST INFORMATION

The efficient TI is next to the Unterlinden Museum on Rue Unterlinden (Mon-Sat 9:00-18:00, Sun 10:00-13:00, closed for lunch in winter, tel. 03 89 20 68 92, www.tourisme-colmar.com). Get information about concerts and festivals in Colmar and in nearby villages, and ask about Folklore Evenings held on summer Tuesdays (described later, under "Nightlife in Colmar"). The TI has a good city map, a bike map, and a list of launderettes. Route du Vin travelers should pick up the free map and get information on bike rental, bus schedules, and where to catch the bus to Route du Vin villages.

ARRIVAL IN COLMAR

By Train and Bus: The old and new (TGV) parts of Colmar's train station are connected by an underground passageway. Follow *Sortie/Avenue de la République* signs to exit the station. Day-trippers can check their bags at **Colmar Vélo** to the left as you leave the old station (see "Helpful Hints").

The old part of the train station was built during Prussian rule using the same plans as the station in Danzig (now Gdańsk, Poland). Check out the charming 1991 window that shows two local maidens about to be run over by a train and rescued by an artist. Opposite, he's shown painting their portraits.

Connecting to the Town Center: It's a 15-minute walk: Exit straight out of the old station past Hôtel Bristol, turn left on Avenue de la République, and keep walking. Or hop any Trace bus from the station (immediately to the left at the station) and ride to the Champ de Mars stop (Place Rapp) or the Théâtre stop, next to the Unterlinden Museum (€1.30, see the "Colmar" map, later). Taxis wait curbside to the left of the exit and charge €7 for any downtown ride.

Connecting to Route du Vin villages: Buses to the villages arrive and depart from the front of the old station and from stops closer to the city center. As you walk out of the station, bus #145 to Kaysersberg leaves from the far left, and stops for buses #106 and #109 to Riquewihr and Ribeauvillé are to the far right (see "Alsace's Route du Vin," later).

By Car: Follow signs for *Centre-Ville,* then *Place Rapp* (where there's a huge underground garage, first hour free, €21/24 hours). Hotels can advise you where to park—they may have private spots or get deals at pay lots. Parking is metered along streets and in most lots in the city center, but free from 19:00-9:00 and on residential streets just outside the city center (around Boulevard St-Pierre and

Rue Bartholdi near the recommended Le Maréchal and Turenne hotels). The parking lot at Place Scheuer-Kestner north of the town center is €6/day and free overnight. Half the spots are free at Parking de la Vieille Ville/Parking de la Montagne Verte near Hôtel St. Martin.

When entering or leaving on the Strasbourg side of town (north), look for the big Statue of Liberty replica—designed to commemorate the 100th anniversary of the death of sculptor Frédéric-Auguste Bartholdi. At two traffic circles closer to Colmar (look for a red devil sculpture in the middle) are the imposing army barracks built by the Germans after annexing the region in 1871.

HELPFUL HINTS

Closed Day: Colmar's top sight, the Unterlinden Museum, is closed on Tuesday.

Market Days: Markets take place in and around the vintage market hall (*marché couvert;* Tue-Sat generally 8:00-18:00, Sun 10:00-14:00, no market Mon). Textiles are on sale Thursdays on Place de la Cathédrale (all day) and Saturdays on Place des Dominicains (afternoons only). A flea market happens Fridays in summer on Place des Dominicains. The Saturday morning market on Place St. Joseph is where locals go for fresh produce and cheese (over the train tracks, 15 minutes on foot from the center, no tourists).

Department/Grocery Store: The big **Monoprix,** with a supermarket, is across from the Unterlinden Museum (Mon-Sat 8:00-20:00, closed Sun). A small **Petit Casino** supermarket stands across from the recommended Hôtel St. Martin (Mon-Sat 8:30-19:00, closed Sun).

Wine Tasting in Colmar: For a fun in-town tasting experience, visit **Maison Jund.** Winemakers André and Myriam Jund and family own 44 acres of vineyards and grow all 7 of the Alsatian grapes. Son Sébastien hosts the tastings in excellent English. Allow one hour (€6, call for appointment, 12 Rue de l'Ange, tel. 03 89 41 58 72, www.martinjund.com, martinjund@hotmail.com). They also run a recommended guesthouse (listed later, under "Sleeping in Colmar").

Laundry: 5àsec, across the street from the Champ de Mars park, offers wash, dry, and fold service (32 Avenue de la République, Mon-Sat 8:45-19:00, closed Sun, tel. 03 89 41 75 73). The TI has a list of other launderettes.

Bike Rental: Colmar Vélo rents bikes at the train station (€8-12/day, electric bike-€20/day, €150 deposit and ID required, behind bike racks on the left as you leave the old station, Mon-Fri 8:00-12:00 & 14:00-19:00, Sat-Sun 9:00-19:00, closed Sun off-season, tel. 03 89 41 37 90). Closer to the center, rent at **Lulu Cycles** (closed Sun, 4 Rue d'Ingersheim, tel. 03 89 41 42 66, www.lulucycles.com). I prefer renting a bike along the Route du Vin in Eguisheim, Kaysersberg, or Ribeauvillé.

Taxis: The minimum Colmar fare of €7 gets you anywhere in town. Fares to nearby villages are reasonable—it's just €15 for a cab to Eguisheim. You can find a taxi at the train station (to your left as you walk out, past the Trace buses), or call 06 79 50 99 96. You can also try William (tel. 03 89 23 10 33, mobile 06 14 47 21 80) or Michele (mobile 06 72 94 65 55).

Car Rental: Avis is the only rental office at the train station (tel. 03 89 23 16 89). The TI has a list of other options. Warning: Some car rental offices are located well outside the city center; verify the location before booking.

Tours in Colmar

Local Guides

Colmar offers no scheduled city walks in English, but private English-speaking **guides** are available through the TI if you book in advance (€170/3 hours, tel. 03 89 20 68 95, guide@tourisme-colmar.com). **Muriel Brun** works independently and is a fine teacher of all things Alsatian (tel. 03 89 79 70 92, muriel.h.brun@calixo.net). **Stéphan Reitter** is another top choice (st.reitter@laposte.net, tel. 03 89 29 00 24 or mobile 06 18 16 22 72).

Tourist Train

Colmar has two competing choo-choo trains (green and white) that jostle along the cobbles of the old part of town offering visitors a relaxing, barely narrated half-hour tour under a glass roof (€7, departures daily 9:00-18:30). Both trains leave across from the Unterlinden Museum, follow similar routes, and offer kid discounts.

In the summer, **horse-drawn carriages** are also an option.

Canal Cruise

Little flat-bottomed boats glide silently on a straight stretch of the city's canal, making a simple 30-minute lap back and forth with little or no narration (€6, departures every 10 minutes, daily 10:00-12:00 & 13:30-18:30). With eight others, you'll pack onto the boat, gliding peacefully—powered by a silent electric motor—through a lush garden world under willows. While the route is kind of pathetic, the tranquility is enjoyable. Try to sit in front for an unobstructed view. Boats depart from Petite Venise (those leaving from the bridge at St. Pierre offer a better tour, tel. 03 89 41 01 94, info@barques-colmar.fr).

ALSACE

Colmar Old Town Walk

This self-guided walk—good by day, romantic by night—is a handy way to link the city's three worthwhile sights (Little Venice, the Unterlinden Museum, and the Dominican Church—see this chapter's "Colmar" map to help navigate). Supplement my commentary by reading the sidewalk information plaques that describe points of interest along the way. Allow an hour for this walk at a leisurely pace (longer if you enter sights). Colmar is particularly pretty after dark on Fridays and Saturdays and during festivals, when the lighting is changed to give different intensities and colors—and to impress visiting VIPs.

• Start in front of the Customs House (where Rue des Marchands hits Grand Rue). Face the old...

Customs House (Koïfhus): Colmar is so attractive today because of its trading wealth. And that's what its Customs House was all about. The city was an economic powerhouse in the 15th, 16th, and 17th centuries because of its privileged trading status.

In the Middle Ages, most of Europe was fragmented into chaotic little princedoms and dukedoms. Merchant-dominated cities were natural proponents of the formation of large nation-states (proto-globalization), and they banded together for free trade and mutual defense. Rather than being ruled by some duke or prince, these "trading leagues" worked directly with the emperor.

The Hanseatic League was the super-league of northern Europe. Prosperous Colmar was a leading member of a similar but much smaller league of 10 Alsatian cities, called the Decapolis (founded 1354).

Looking up at the Customs House, imagine how this "Alsatian Big Ten" enjoyed special tax and trade privileges, including the right to build fortified walls and run their internal affairs. As "Imperial" cities, they were ruled directly by the Holy Roman Emperor rather than by one of his lesser princes. This was preferable and, by banding together, they negotiated to protect this special status and won the Holy Roman Emperor's promise not to sell them to some other, likely more aggressive, prince. The 10 mostly Alsatian towns of the Decapolis enjoyed this status until the 17th century.

This street—Rue des Marchands—is literally "Merchants Street," and throughout the town you'll notice how street names bear witness to the historic importance and power of merchants in Colmar. Thirty yards in front of the Customs House, find the carved plaque in the wall at #23. This is a "stone of banishment," declaring that the town's merchants kicked a noble family out of Colmar, and that the family could never live here again.

Step up closer to the Customs House. Delegates of the Decapolis would meet here to sort out trade issues, much like the European Union does in nearby Strasbourg today. In Colmar's heyday, this was where the action was. Notice the fancy green and yellow roof tiles. Note also the plaque above the door to the right with the double eagle of the Holy Roman Emperor—a sign that this was an Imperial city.

Walk under the archway to Place de l'Ancienne Douane and face the Frédéric-Auguste Bartholdi statue of General Lazarus von Schwendi—arm raised (Statue of Liberty-style) and clutching a bundle of local pinot gris grapes. He's the man who brought that grape from Hungary to Alsace.

From here, do a 360-degree spin to appreciate a gaggle of gables. This was the center of business activity in Colmar, with trade routes radiating to several major European cities. All goods that entered the city were taxed here. Today, it's the festive site of outdoor cafés and, on many summer evenings, fun wine tastings (open to all). Through much of the summer, local vintners each get 10 days to share their wine here at the site of the town's medieval wine fair.

• *Follow the statue's left elbow and walk down Petite Rue des Tanneurs (not the larger "Rue des Tanneurs"). The half-timbered commotion of higgledy-piggledy rooftops on the downhill side of the fountain marks the...*

Tanners' Quarter: These 17th- and 18th-century rooftops competed for space in the sun to dry their freshly tanned hides, while the nearby river channel flushed the waste products. When the industry moved out of town, the neighborhood became a slum. It was restored in the 1970s—Colmar was a trendsetter in the government-funded renovation of depressed old quarters. Residents had to play along or move out. At the street's end, carry on a few steps, and then turn back. Notice the openings just below the roofs where hides would be hung out to dry. Stinky tanners' quarters were always at the edge of town. You've stepped outside the old center and are looking back at the city's first defensive wall. The oldest and lowest stones you see in the buildings are from 1230, now built into the row of houses; later walls encircled the city farther out.

• *Walk with the old walls on your right to the first street, Rue des Tanneurs. Turn left (at the Old Market Hall), then cross the bridge for an iconic Colmar view. Turn right onto Quai Poissonnere and walk to the next bridge, where you'll re-cross the river to enter the market hall on its far side.*

Old Market Hall: Colmar's historic market hall is where locals have come since 1865 to buy fish, produce, and other products (originally delivered by flat-bottomed boat). You'll find picnic fixings and produce, sandwiches and bakery items, wine tastings, and clean WCs. Several stands are run like cafés, and there's even a

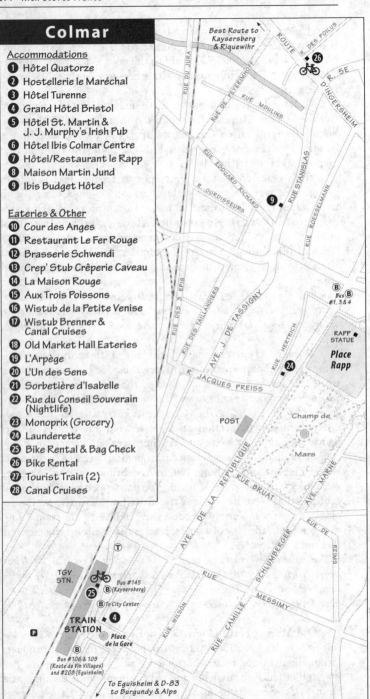

Colmar

Accommodations

1 Hôtel Quatorze
2 Hostellerie le Maréchal
3 Hôtel Turenne
4 Grand Hôtel Bristol
5 Hôtel St. Martin &
  J. J. Murphy's Irish Pub
6 Hôtel Ibis Colmar Centre
7 Hôtel/Restaurant le Rapp
8 Maison Martin Jund
9 Ibis Budget Hôtel

Eateries & Other

10 Cour des Anges
11 Restaurant Le Fer Rouge
12 Brasserie Schwendi
13 Crep' Stub Crêperie Caveau
14 La Maison Rouge
15 Aux Trois Poissons
16 Wistub de la Petite Venise
17 Wistub Brenner &
   Canal Cruises
18 Old Market Hall Eateries
19 L'Arpège
20 L'Un des Sens
21 Sorbetière d'Isabelle
22 Rue du Conseil Souverain
   (Nightlife)
23 Monoprix (Grocery)
24 Launderette
25 Bike Rental & Bag Check
26 Bike Rental
27 Tourist Train (2)
28 Canal Cruises

Best Route to
Kaysersberg
& Riquewihr

ROUTE
R. DES POILUS
R. 5E
D'INGERSHEIM

RUE DU JURA
RUE DE PFEFFINHOFF
RUE MOULINS
RUE STANISLAS

RUE EDOUARD RICHARD
R. OURDISSEURS
RUE ROESSELMANN

9

RUE DES 3 EPIS
RUE DES TAILLANDIERS
AVE. J. DE TASSIGNY
RUE HERTRICH

Bus
#1, 3 & 4
B B

RAPP
STATUE

Place
Rapp

24

R. JACQUES PREISS

POST

Champ de

Mars

AVE. DE LA REPUBLIQUE
RUE BRUAT
AVE. MARNE
RUE DE
REIMS
SCHLUMBERGER

T

TGV
STN.

Bus #145
B (Kaysersberg)

25

B To City Center

TRAIN
STATION

4

Place
de la Gare

P

B
Bus #106 & 109
(Route du Vin Villages)
and #208 (Eguisheim)

RUE WILSON
RUE CAMILLE
RUE
MESSIMY

To Eguisheim & D-83
to Burgundy & Alps

To Strasbourg via
D-83/D-1083
Bus #106 & 109
(Route du Vin
Villages)

DIVISION

RUE LA CAVALERIE

CINEMA

Pl. Scheurer-
Kestner

RUE DES ANCETRES

RUE GOLBERY

RUE DU REMPART

RUE DU CHANTIER

RUE DE THANN

RUE CLOCHES

RUE DU NORD

RUE RAPP

Bus #208
to Eguisheim

Bus
#1, 3 & 4

UNTERLINDEN
MUSEUM

Place de
la Mairie

POST

R. RUEST

RUE ETROITE

RUE ST-ELOI

6

KLEBER

WALK ENDS

Place
d'Unter-
linden

23

27 27

RUE DES CLEFS

8

RUE VAUBAN

RUE THEINHEIM

RUE DES LABOUREURS

MAISON
DES
TETES

Canal

DOMINICAN
CHURCH

RUE JETES

R. D'ALSPACH

BISCUITS

BOULANGERS

R. SERRURIERS

ST. NICHOLAS

R. PRETRES

R. MOUTON

RUE DE LA GRENOUILLERE

Square
Hansi

RUE DES MARCHANDS

19

Place de la
Cathédrale

ST. MARTIN

R. L'EGLISE

GRAND RUE

PROTESTANT
CHURCH

R. CIGOGNE

OLD

BLVD. DU CHAMP DE MARS

R. WEIN.

7 1

BARTHOLDI
MUSEUM

RUE BETHE

RUE AUGUSTINS

20

MAISON
PFISTER

21 5

11

12

WALK BEGINS

Place du
2 Février

TOWN

Place
Douane

10

Montagne
Verte

Pl. de
Marché aux Fruits

CUSTOMS
HOUSE

22 13

TANNEURS

PETITE RUE
DES TANNEURS

Lauch River

R. CHAUFOUR

R. PFEFFEL

GRAND RUE

MOLLY

R. ST-JEAN

RUE DES ECOLES

14

OLD
MARKET
HALL

18

QUAI POISS.

RUE SCHWENDI

RUE ST-JOSSE

RUE BLES

PETITE

LE PETIT
VIGNERON

17

16

R. POISSONNERIE

15

RUE DES FLEURS

Pl. des Six
Montagnes
Noires

R. MANEGE

"PONT DE
FANNY"

VENISE

2

RUE TURENNE

RUE SCHWENDI

28

BLVD. ST-PIERRE

3

ROUTE DE BALE

200 Meters

200 Yards

LE
KRUTENAU

RUE BARTHOLDI

N

ALSACE

bar (Tue-Sat 8:00-18:00, Sun 10:00-14:00, closed Mon). Outside, on the market hall's northwest corner at Rue des Ecoles, find the fountain with a copy of Bartholdi's joyful sculpture, *Le Petit Vigneron (Young Alsatian Wine Grower).*

• *Return to the flower-bedecked Rue des Ecoles bridge leading to...*

Petite Venise: This neighborhood, a collection of Colmar's most colorful houses lining the small canal, is popular with tour-

ists during the day. But at night it's romantic, with fewer crowds. It lies between the town's first wall (built to defend against arrows) and its later wall (built in the age of gunpowder). Medieval towns needed water. If they weren't on a river, they'd often redirect parts of nearby rivers to power their mills and quench their thirst. Colmar's river was canalized this way for medieval industry—to provide water for the tanners, to allow farmers to barge their goods into town (see the steps leading from docks into the market hall), and so on.

• *Turn right and walk along the flower-box-lined canal to the end of Rue de la Poissonnerie.*

Half-Timbered Houses: As you stroll, notice the picturesque houses. The pastel colors are just from this generation—designed to pump up the cuteness of Colmar for tourists. But the houses themselves are historic and real as can be. See the sidebar to learn more about this unique architectural style.

Enjoy the creaky houses toward the end of Rue de la Poissonnerie, as the lane narrows into a sort of alleyway. When you emerge, on your right is "Pont de Fanny," a bridge so popular with tourists for its fine views that you see lots of fannies lined up along the railing. Walk to the center of the bridge, and add yours to the scene. Look for examples of the flat-bottomed gondolas used to transport goods on the small river. Today, they give tourists sleepy, scenic, 30-minute canal tours (described on page 971).

• *Cross the bridge, walk a short block, and find a fountain in the square to your left.*

La Fontaine Roesselmann: Another Bartholdi work, this one was commissioned to honor Jean Roesselmann, a 13th-century town provost who died defending his beloved city when the bishop of Strasbourg tried unsuccessfully to seize it.

• *Take the second right leading from the square onto...*

Grand Rue: Walk for several blocks to the Customs House where this walk began. As you stroll, enjoy the amazing Alsatian architecture and be thankful that WWII bombs spared this town. (Freiburg, about this size, just over the border in Germany, was

Half-Timbered Houses of Alsace

In medieval times when these towns were established, houses of the rich were made of stone while budget builders made half-timbered structures. The process: Build your frame with pine beams; create a weave of little branches between the beams, which you'd fill with mud, straw, and gunk; let it dry; and plaster over it. (This is called "wattle and daub" in England.) Timbers were soaked in vinegar and then treated with ox blood to be waterproof. If you find unrestored timbers, you can see the faint red tint of the blood.

When the French elite, accustomed to the fine stone buildings of Paris, moved here in the 18th century, they disguised the cheap wattle and daub with a thick layer of plaster. There's disagreement about the reason. One theory says that to them, the half-timbers looked cheap...and German. To be French was à la mode and that meant no half-timbers. Or, perhaps plastering these homes occurred by decree as a fire safety move. These houses often have a stone wall protruding above the roof tiles—built to stop fires. Back when roofs were made with wood shingles (rather than today's safer terra-cotta), fire was a serious problem. Another theory says that the plaster was applied to protect the wood beams.

Today the half-timbered style has become charming to locals and tourists alike, so the current owners have peeled away the plaster to reveal the old beams.

Rich or poor, all homes sat on a stone base. This prevented them from sinking into the marshy ground, kept the moist ground from rotting the timbers, and preserved the ground floor in case of a fire—commonplace back then. You can identify true stone homes by their windowsills: Wooden sills mean they're half-timbered; stone sills indicate the entire building is built of stone.

Notice how upper floors are cantilevered out. This was a structural support trick and a tax dodge, as real-estate taxes were based on the square footage of the ground floor. The bright colors that cover many of these homes are a post-WWII addition.

ALSACE

80 percent destroyed and consequently has very little of this Old World charm.)

With your back to the Customs House, look uphill along **Rue des Marchands**—one of the most scenic intersections in town. (The ruler of Malaysia was so charmed by this street that he had it re-created in Kuala Lumpur.)

• *Walk uphill on Rue des Marchands for a couple of blocks, and you'll come face-to-face with the...*

Maison Pfister (Pfister House): This richly decorated merchant's house dates from 1537. Here the owner displayed his wealth for all to enjoy (and to envy). The external spiral-staircase turret (with slanted windows), a fine loggia on the top floor, and the bay windows (called oriels) were pricey add-ons. The painted walls indicate this guy was one of those big-city liberal elites with a taste for Renaissance humanism.

The cozy wine shop, Vinum, on the ground floor sells fine wines, but they're actually most proud of their locally made whisky. David enjoys offering tastings, so go ahead, take a hit and see what you think—ask, *"Déguster un whisky Alsatian?"*

Now that you're in a happy mood, stand outside facing the Pfister House for a little review. Find the four main styles of Colmar architecture: Gothic (move to the right to see a part of the church), medieval half-timbered structures, Renaissance (that's Mr. Pfister's place), and (across the lane on your right) the urbane and elegant shutters and ironwork of Paris from the 19th century.

• *As you move past the spiral staircase, check out the attached building (at #9).*

Meter Man: The man carved into the side of this building was a drapemaker; he's shown holding a bar, Colmar's local measure of about one meter (almost equal to a yard). In the Middle Ages, it was common for cities to have their own units of length; it's one reason that merchants supported the "globalization" efforts of their time to standardize measuring systems.

The building shows off the classic half-timbered design—the beams (upright, cross, angular supports) are grouped in what's called (and looks like) "a man." Typical houses are built with a man in the middle flanked by two "half men."

Two doors farther up the street on the left is the **Bartholdi Museum,** located in the home of the famous sculptor Frédéric-Auguste Bartholdi, creator of the Statue of Liberty. If it's open, step into the courtyard if it's open and admire the bronze statue called *The Grand Pillars of the World* (for more on the museum, see page 985).

Next door (at #28) is an inviting café, Au Croissant Doré, with a charming Art Nouveau facade, delicate interior, and friendly staff.

• *A passage opposite the Bartholdi Museum leads you through the old guards' house to the...*

Church of St. Martin: The city's cathedral-like church replaced a smaller Romanesque church that stood here earlier. It was erected in 1235 after Colmar became an Imperial city and needed a bigger place of worship. Colmar's ruler at the time was Burgundian, so the church has a Burgundian-style tiled roof. Walk to your right to see the stork nest atop the church's apse. Two storks have made this nest their home, and locals have named the pair Martin and Martine.

The side door still has the round Romanesque tympanum, starring St. Martin, from the earlier church. Notice how it fits into the pointed Gothic arch. This was the lepers' door—marked by the four totem-like rows of grotesque faces and bodies. They could "go to church" but had to stay outside, away from other parishioners.

Walk left, under three expressive gargoyles, to the west portal. Facing the front of the church, notice that the relief over the main door depicts not your typical Last Judgment scene but the Three Kings who visited Baby Jesus. The Magi, whose remains are nearby in the Rhine city of Cologne, Germany, are popular in this region. The church's beautiful Vosges-stone exterior radiates color in the early evening. The dark interior holds a few finely carved and beautifully painted altarpieces.

• *Continue past the church, go left around Jupiler Café, and wander up the pedestrian-only Rue des Serruriers ("Locksmiths Street") to the...*

Dominican Church: Compare the Church of St. Martin's ornate exterior with this simple Dominican structure. While both churches were built at the same time, each makes different statements. The "High Church" of the 13th century was fancy and corrupt. The Dominican order was all about austerity. It was a time of crisis in the Roman Catholic Church. Monastic orders (as well as heretical movements like the Cathars in southern France) preached a simpler faith and way of life. In the style of St. Dominic and St. Francis, they tried to get Rome back on a Christ-like track. This church houses the exquisite *Virgin in the Rosebush* by Martin Schongauer (described on page 984). If the church is open, pop in to see this exquisite painting; it takes just a few minutes and is a highlight of the town.

• *Continue straight past the Dominican Church, where Rue des Serruriers becomes Rue des Boulangers—"Bakers Street." Stop at #16.*

Skyscrapers and Biscuits: The towering green-and-brown house, dating from the 16th century, was one of Colmar's tallest buildings from that age. Notice how it contrasts with the string of buildings to the right, which are lower, French-style structures—likely built after a fire cleared out older, higher buildings.

As this is Bakers Street, check out the one right here at #16. Maison Alsacienne de Biscuiterie sells traditional biscuits (cookies), including boxed Christmas delights year-round. Macarons and biscuits are sold by weight.

• *Turn right on Rue des Têtes (notice the beautiful swan sign over the pharmacie at the corner). Walk a block to the fancy old house festooned with heads (on the right) and cross the street to view its facade.*

Maison des Têtes ("House of Heads"): Colmar's other famous merchant's house, built in 1609 by a big-shot winemaker (see the grapes hanging from the wrought-iron sign and the happy man at the tip-top), is playfully decorated with about 100 faces and masks. On the ground floor, the guy showing his bellybutton in the window's center has pig's feet.

Look four doors to the right to see a bakery sign (above the big pretzel), which shows the *boulangerie* basics in Alsace: croissant, *Kugelhopf,* and baguette. Notice the colors of the French flag indicating that this house supported French rule.

Behind you, study the early-20th-century store sign trumpeting the tasty wonders of a butcher who once occupied this spot (with the traditional maiden with her goose about to be force-fed).
• *Continue another block to a peaceful square where a canal runs under linden trees. Our walk is over. The venerable church and convent on your left house Colmar's top attraction, the* **Unterlinden Museum** *(enter from the big empty square around the building to the right).*

Sights in Colmar

▲▲▲Unterlinden Museum
This museum is Colmar's touristic claim to fame. Its extensive yet manageable collection ranges from Roman Colmar to medieval winemaking exhibits to Monet and Renoir, and from traditional wedding dresses to paintings that give vivid insight into the High Middle Ages. But its highlight is one of the most unforgettable masterpieces of medieval Europe: Matthias Grünewald's gloriously displayed Isenheim Altarpiece.

Cost and Hours: €13, Wed-Mon 10:00-18:00, until 20:00 first Thu of month, closed Tue, good audioguide-€2, 1 Rue d'Unterlinden, tel. 03 89 20 15 50, www.musee-unterlinden.com.

⊙ Self-Guided Tour
The air-conditioned museum has three parts: the 13th-century convent cloisters and chapel (where you'll spend most of your time), the underground galleries, and the new Ackerhof wing (modern art and temporary exhibits).
• *After showing your ticket, step into the...*

Cloister *(Cloître):* This soothing space was the largest 13th-century cloister in Alsace. Because the nuns didn't leave the convent, this cloister was the one place they could feel the air and see the sky. This Dominican convent, founded by (and for) noblewomen in 1230, functioned until the French Revolution, when the building became a garrison.

• *Rooms with museum exhibits branch off from the cloister.*

Medieval and Renaissance Art: Keep straight to find the first room, dedicated to Marin Schongauer, a local artist who painted multipaneled altarpieces and gained wide fame as an engraver. His most famous work—the Virgin in the Rosebush—is displayed in Colmar's Dominican Church, but the Unterlinden Museum claims the largest collection of his paintings.

As you enjoy the medieval and Renaissance art displayed in this part of the museum, remember that Alsace was historically German and part of the upper Rhine River Valley. The Three Kings (of Bethlehem fame) are prominently featured throughout this region because their remains are believed to have ended up in Cologne's cathedral (nearby, on the Rhine). Throughout the museum you'll see small photos of engravings, illustrating how painters were influenced by other artists' engravings (such as Schongauer's). Most German painters of the time were also engravers (that's how they made money—engraving versions of their art that could be duplicated to maximize sales).

• *In the next room find the small...*

15th-Century Stained-Glass Windows: Note the fine details painted into the glass, originally intended for "God's eyes only"—they were too tiny for worshippers to see from the floor below. The glass is a jigsaw puzzle connected by lead. Around here, glass this old is rare—most of it was destroyed by rampaging Protestants in the religious wars following the Reformation.

• *Next comes Grünewald's gripping...*

Isenheim Altarpiece (c. 1515): This complex work is actually a polyptych—a series of two-sided paintings on hinges that pivot like shutters. As the church calendar progressed, priests would change which parts of the altarpiece were visible to the congregation by opening or closing these panels. (The museum has disassembled the altarpiece so that visitors can view all the individual panels. To understand how the altarpiece was originally put together, see the models on the side walls.)

Designed to help people in a medieval hospital endure horrible skin diseases (specifically St. Anthony's Fire, later called rye ergotism)—long before the age of painkillers—this altarpiece is one of the most powerful paintings ever produced. Germans know it like Americans know the *Mona Lisa.*

• *Invest the time here to study each panel (and if you have the museum's audioguide, listen to each one described).*

Panel 1, Crucifixion: Stand in front of this panel as if you were a medieval peasant, and feel the agony and suffering of the Crucifixion. It's an intimate drama. Jesus' suffering and death are drilled

home: The horizontal crossbar bends not so much from Jesus' weight as from his agony. His stretched, extended arms are pulled from their sockets, his fingers grotesquely contorted in pain—reminding the faithful that Jesus suffered for them. His mangled feet are swollen with blood. In turn, the intended viewers—the hospital's patients—would have felt that Jesus understood their distress, because he looks like he has a skin disease (though the marks on his body represent lash marks from whipping).

Study the faces and the Christian symbolism. The composition of the trio on the left is as sorrowful as it is powerful. John the Evangelist supports a swooning, white-faced Mary; she's wrapped in the white shroud that will cover Jesus' body in the tomb. Mary Magdalene, overcome by anguish, is on her knees. On the right, John the Baptist is shown with a little lamb—the symbol of Jesus' sacrifice.

The outer panels feature two saints who helped the sick: St. Sebastian (on the left, called upon by those with the plague) and St. Anthony (on the right, called upon by those with ergot poisoning from rotten rye).

The predella (the horizontal painting below) shows the Lamentation over Jesus. His mourners wring their hands in sorrow. Jesus' fingernails are black—as is the case with any corpse—and the cruel crown of thorns now rests at his feet.

• *Walk around to the other side of this panel.*

Panels 2-3, Resurrection and Annunciation: The Resurrection scene on the left is unique in art history. (Grünewald was a mysterious genius—an artistic loner who had no master and no students.) Jesus rockets out of the tomb as man is transformed into God. As if proclaiming once again, "I am the Light," he is radiant. His shroud is the color of light: Roy G. Biv. Within the rainbow is the "resurrection of the flesh." Jesus' perfect white flesh would have offered hope to the patients who meditated on the scene. The happy finale is a psychedelic explosion of Resurrection joy.

The right panel depicts the Annunciation. The angel (accompanied by a translucent dove—barely visible—representing the Holy Spirit) is telling Mary she'll give birth to the son of God. The normally sanguine Mary looks unsettled. She's shown reading the Bible passage that tells of this event.

• *Now turn around to see...*

Panels 3-4, Nativity and Concert of Angels: Grünewald set his nativity scene (on the right) in the Rhineland, in a landscape that would have been familiar to him and the viewers of his artwork. The tender, loving, and much-adored Mary cradles (an unusually oversized) Baby Jesus—true to the Dominican belief that she was the intercessor for all in heaven. The infant plays with a rosary—a newly popular device in the late 15th century for organizing one's prayers. Two angels tell shepherds of the birth while God, high above, oversees the victory of good over evil. The heavenly jam session (on the left) is the Concert of Angels.

• *Walk around to view the reverse side.*

Panels 4-5, Temptation of St. Anthony and St. Anthony Visits St. Paul: Looking at these last panels, zoom in on the agonizing Temptation of St. Anthony (on the left). Anthony is being ravaged by demons who look like the cast of an animated horror film. The figure in the lower left corner embodies the condition of those seeking treatment for St. Anthony's Fire. His left arm has rotted to a stump, and his skin is a torturous mess. God the Father appears high above, as if coming to the rescue, consistent with a Christian message of hope. In the scene on the right, set in the desert of Thebes, Anthony visits St. Paul, the hermit (wearing a spiffy palm-frond cloak) amid trees covered in lichen.

• *Finally, turn around to see the sculpted part of the altarpiece.*

Panel 6, St. Anthony on His Throne: Carved in wood by Nikolaus Hagenauer, St. Anthony sits on his throne like a king, flanked by church fathers St. Augustine (left) and St. Jerome (right). Small mortals bring gifts—a chicken and a pig. Below, Jesus shares a last supper with his 12 apostles.

• *Nearby steps lead up to an exhibit of...*

Decorative and Folk Art: This exhibit circles the cloister from one floor above and deserves a look. You'll see wrought-iron signs, cast-iron ovens, massive church bells, and chests with intricate locking systems. There are also ornate armoires, medieval armor, muskets, pottery, kitchen tools, and antique jewelry boxes.

• *Double back to the museum entry, and go down one floor to find...*

Gallo-Roman Archaeology and Gothic Art: Follow *Archéologie* signs and find a room dedicated to the Mosaic of Bergheim, a portion of a luxurious mosaic from a third-century Roman villa in the town of Bergheim, which was discovered and moved here in 1848. It's surrounded by Gallo-Roman carvings from the same age.

The next two rooms display 14th-century Gothic statues and capitals from Colmar's Church of St. Martin and other area churches. Study the exquisite Romanesque detail of the capitals

ALSACE

and the faces of the statues. Notice how some faces look eerily realistic, while others seem very stylized. Even though they endured the elements outdoors for more than 500 years, it's still clear that they were sculpted with loving attention to detail. The masons knew their fine stonework would not be seen from below—it was, again, "for God's eyes only." The reddish stone is quarried from the Vosges Mountains, giving these works their unusual coloring. Notice the faint remnants of paint still visible on some statues—then imagine all of these works brightly painted.

• *In the next rooms you'll see a painting by Lucas Cranach and more fine stained glass windows. Farther on, don't miss the...*

Alsatian Cellar (Cave Alsacienne): Open the door into this dark, shrine-like wine room containing 17th-century oak presses (once turned by animals) and finely decorated casks. Wine revenue was used to care for Colmar's poor. Nuns owned many of the best vineyards around, and production was excellent. So was consumption. Find the cask with Bacchus and his big tummy straddling a keg. The quote from 1781 reads: "My belly's full of juice. It makes me strong. But drink too much and you lose dignity and health."

• *Drop down another level to find...*

The Rest of the Museum: Follow signs reading *Arts 19e-20e siècles* to find a gallery showcasing 19th- and 20th-century paintings, including works by Monet, Renoir, Leger, Bonnard, and Dubuffet. One floor up from this gallery is the museum's small modern art collection, including a work by Picasso and a copy of his *Guernica* painting by another artist. The Ackerhof and Piscine sections house more modern art and temporary exhibits.

Other Sights in Colmar
▲▲Dominican Church (Eglise des Dominicains)

This beautiful Gothic church is simple—in keeping with the austerity integral to the Dominican style of Christianity. It's plain on the outside and stripped-down on the inside.

Instead of gazing at art, worshippers would focus on the word of God preached from the pulpit.

Cost and Hours: €2, April-Dec daily 10:00-13:00 & 15:00-18:00, June-Oct Fri-Sat no midday closure, closed Jan-March, tel. 03 89 41 27 20.

Visiting the Church: This church houses a mesmerizing medieval masterpiece—Martin Schongauer's angelically beautiful *Virgin in the Rosebush* (1473), which looks as if it were painted yesterday. Here, graceful Mary is shown as a loving and welcoming mother. Jesus clings to her, reminding the viewer of the warmth of his relationship with Mary. The Latin on her halo reads, "Pick me also for your child, O very Holy Virgin." Rather than telling a particular Bible story, this is a general scene, designed to meet the personal devotional needs of any worshipper.

Nature is not a backdrop; Mary and Jesus are encircled by it. Schongauer's robins, sparrows, and goldfinches bring extra life to an already impressively natural rosebush. The white rose (over Mary's right shoulder) anticipates Jesus' crucifixion. Angels hold Mary's heavenly crown high above. The frame, with its angelic orchestra, dates only from 1900 and feels to me a bit over-the-top...as Neo-Gothic tends to be.

The painting was located in the Church of St. Martin until 1972, when it was stolen. It was recovered, then moved to the better-protected Dominican Church. Detailed English explanations are in the nave to the right of the painting as you face it. The contrast provided by the simple Dominican setting heightens the elegance of this Gothic masterpiece.

As for the rest of the church, the columns are thin to allow worshippers to see the speaker, even if the place is packed. The windows are precious 14th-century originals depicting black-clad Dominican monks busy preaching. Notice how windows face the sun on the south side while the north side is walled against the cloister. If you look at the columns in the rear of the nave, you can see how 14th-century Colmar's street level was about two feet below today's.

▲Bartholdi Museum

This little museum recalls the life and work of the local boy who gained fame by sculpting America's much-loved Statue of Liberty. Frédéric-Auguste Bartholdi (1834-1904) was a dynamic painter/ photographer/sculptor with a passion for the defense of liberty and freedom. Although Colmar was his home, he spent most of his

career in Paris, refusing to move back here while Alsace was German. While Lady Liberty is his most famous work, you'll see several enjoyable Bartholdi statues gracing Colmar's squares.

The entry courtyard is free and dominated by a bronze statue, *Les Grands Soutiens du Monde (The Great Pillars of the World)*. It was cast in 1902—two years before Bartholdi died—and shares his personal philosophy. The world is supported by three figures representing patriotism, hard work, and justice. Mr. Hard Work holds a stack of books, symbolizing intellectual endeavors, and a hammer, a sign for physical labor. Ms. Justice has her scales. And Mr. Patriotism holds a flag and a sword—sheathed but ready to be used if necessary. All have one foot stepping forward: ahead for progress, the spirit of the Industrial Age.

Cost and Hours: €6, March-Dec Wed-Mon 10:00-12:00 & 14:00-18:00, closed Tue and Jan-Feb, audioguide-€2, in heart of the old town at 30 Rue des Marchands, tel. 03 89 41 90 60, www.musee-bartholdi.fr. Curiously, even though entry is free on the Fourth of July, there are no English descriptions posted. The English handout near the ticket desk gives ample background about the artist but little room-by-room information.

Visiting the Museum: As you tour the museum, notice how Bartholdi's patriotic pieces tend to have one arm raised—*Vive la France*...God bless America...Freedom!

Ground Floor: You'll see exhibits covering Bartholdi's works commissioned in Alsatian cities (including nine for Colmar), commonly dedicated to city bigwigs and military heroes. The highlight is the *Young Alsatian Wine Grower* who, guzzling from his small cask, offers a fun contrast to Bartholdi's more staid subjects.

First Floor: Climbing the stairs, you'll pass a portrait of the artist at the first landing. Rooms to the left re-create Bartholdi's high-society flat in Paris. The red-carpeted dining room is lined with portraits of his aristocratic family. In the far corner room, find two beautiful portraits by Jean Benner—paintings of the sculptor and another of his mother, who sits on a red chair. Bartholdi is depicted facing his mother, with whom he was very close: He wrote her daily letters while working in New York. Many see his mother's face in the Statue of Liberty.

In the long hallway leading past the staircase, a room dedicated to Bartholdi's most famous French work, the *Lion of Belfort*, celebrates the Alsatian town that fought so fiercely in 1871 that it was never annexed into Germany. Photos show the red sandstone lion sitting regally below the mighty Vauban fortress of Belfort—a symbol of French spirit standing strong against Germany. Small models give a sense of its gargantuan scale. (If you're linking Burgundy with Alsace by car, you'll pass the city of Belfort and see signs directing you to the *Lion*.)

The rest of the floor shows off Bartholdi's other French works. Small wax models let you trace his creative process. Glass cases are filled with the tools of his trade. The last room shows sculptures of important figures in French history—the statue of Vercingétorix is wild and mesmerizing.

Second Floor: The next (and top) floor is dedicated to Bartholdi's American works—the paintings, photos, and statues that Bartholdi made during his many travels to the States. You'll see statues of Columbus pointing as if he knew where he was going, and Lafayette (who was only 19 years old when he came to America's aid) with George Washington.

One room is dedicated to the evolution and completion of Bartholdi's dream of a Statue of Liberty. The sculptor devoted years of his life to realizing the vision of a statue of liberty for America that would stand in New York City's harbor. Fascinating photos show the Eiffel-designed core in Bartholdi's French workshop, the frame being covered with plaster, and then the hand-hammered copper plating, which was ultimately riveted to the frame. The statue was created in Paris, then dismantled and shipped to New York in 1886...10 years late. The big ear in the exhibit is half-size.

Though the statue was a gift from France, the US had to come up with the cash to build a pedestal. This was a tough sell, but Bartholdi was determined to see his statue erected. On 10 trips to the US, he worked to raise funds and lobbied for construction, bringing with him a painting (shown here) and a full-size model of the torch—which the statue would ultimately hold. (Lucky for Bartholdi and his cause, his cousin was the French ambassador to the US.)

Eventually, the project came together—the pedestal was built, and the Statue of Liberty (kind of the "anti-wall") has welcomed waves of immigrants into New York ever since. Thank you, Frédéric-Auguste Bartholdi.

Nightlife in Colmar

No one would come to Colmar solely for its nightlife. But if you're out after dinner, there are a few good old town options.

Floodlit Town Stroll: Colmar puts lots of creative energy into its floodlit cityscapes, making evening strolls memorable. You could retrace the route of this chapter's guided walk simply to enjoy the lights and architecture.

Wine Festival Stalls: Every July and August, five local vintners take 10 days each to show off local wines at a small wine festival. It's held under the historic arches of the Customs House (daily 12:00-23:00, self-service, no food, great prices for nice wine).

Folk Dance Tuesdays: On Tuesdays in May to September, there's likely Alsatian folk dancing at the town's Folklore Evening (Soirée Folklorique, starts at 20:30) to give your wine tasting a little color.

Bar Scene: Rue du Conseil Souverain (stretching from the Customs House to the "Pont de Fanny") has a fun run of watering holes where you can enjoy mellow outdoor seating with the locals on balmy evenings or interiors of your choice when it's cold. **Les Incorruptibles** attracts younger locals, with a DJ on weekends, some

Alsatian edginess, and gourmet Belgian beers (1 Rue des Ecoles).
Pub James'On has a big, pubby-warm interior and draws a marginally more mature crowd (2 Rue du Conseil Souverain). **Sport's
Café** is a big-screen, Red Bull-and-foosball place. This is the place
to be if there's a big sporting event on TV and you want to share
it with a gang of French enthusiasts (3 Rue du Conseil Souverain).
J. J. Murphy's Irish Pub, a short block away, invites you to take a
trip to Ireland at the bar, where you can enjoy a classic pub vibe and
Murphy's Irish Stout on tap (48 Grand Rue).

Sleeping in Colmar

Hotels are a reasonable value in Colmar. They're busy on weekends in May, June, September, and October, and every day in July
and August. Hotels have air-conditioning, buffet breakfasts, and
elevators unless otherwise noted. If you have trouble finding a bed,
ask the TI for help or look in a nearby village, where small hotels
and bed-and-breakfasts are plentiful (see my recommendations in
nearby Eguisheim, later).

$$$ Hôtel Quatorze** is a high-end boutique hotel blend-
ing sleek, daringly modern design and a central location. It offers
14 rooms tucked behind a quiet patio (14 Rue des Augustins, tel. 03
89 20 45 20, www.hotelquatorze.com, info@hotelquatorze.com).

$$$ Hostellerie le Maréchal,** in the heart of La Petite
Venise, holds Colmar's most characteristic rooms. Though the
rooms are on the small side (three-star quality and prices), the setting is romantic, the decor is warm, and the service is professional
(pay garage parking, 4 Place des Six Montagnes Noires, tel. 03
89 41 60 32, www.le-marechal.com, info@le-marechal.com). The
hotel is famous for the quality of its well-respected **$$$$ restaurant;** many French clients travel to dine here (€35-85 menus, reserve ahead).

$$ Hôtel Turenne** is less central (a 10-minute walk from
the city center) and greets you with a big, open lobby, interior patio,
and top service. Its 90 very comfortable rooms are split between an
older, more traditional wing (cheaper) and a new wing with more
modern rooms. All rooms are well-appointed and come with ac-
cess to a spa and secure private parking (family rooms, 10 Route de
Bâle, tel. 03 89 21 58 58, www.turenne.com, infos@turenne.com).

$$ Grand Hôtel Bristol** has little personality but works if
you want American-like comfort at the train station with a spa and
fitness room (7 Place de la Gare, tel. 03 89 23 59 59, www.grand-
hotel-bristol.com, reservation@grand-hotel-bristol.com).

$$ Hôtel St. Martin,** ideally situated near the old Customs
House, is a family-run place that began in 1361 as a coaching inn.
It has 40 mostly traditional, well-equipped rooms with big beds.

The rooms are woven into its antique frame and joined together by a small courtyard (some rooms with no elevator access, family rooms, limited free public parking nearby at Parking de la Vieille Ville/Montagne Verte, pay parking in private garage at Parking Josse, 38 Grand Rue, tel. 03 89 24 11 51, www.hotel-saint-martin.com, colmar@hotel-saint-martin.com).

$$ Hôtel Ibis Colmar Centre,*** on the ring road, is economical—renting tight rooms with small bathrooms at acceptable rates (10 Rue St. Eloi, tel. 03 89 41 30 14, https://ibis.accorhotels.com, h1377@accor.com).

$$ Hôtel le Rapp,*** conveniently located off Place Rapp and near a big park, offers rooms for many budgets, a full-service bar and a good restaurant. The cheapest rooms are tight but smartly configured; the bigger rooms are tasteful, usually with king-size beds. There's also a small basement pool, a sauna, and a Turkish bath (family rooms, 1 Rue Weinemer, tel. 03 89 41 62 10, www.rapp-hotel.com, rapp-hotel@calixo.net). The **$$ Restaurant le Rapp** is a traditional place to savor a slow, elegant meal served with grace and fine Alsatian wine (closed Sun-Mon).

¢ Maison Martin Jund holds my favorite budget beds in Colmar. This ramshackle yet historic half-timbered house—the home of likeable winemakers André and Myriam and their grown kids—feels like a medieval treehouse soaked in wine and filled with flowers. The rooms are modest but spacious and comfortable enough. Some have air-conditioning and many have kitchenettes (big family apartments, fun tasting room—see "Helpful Hints" earlier, no elevator, 12 Rue de l'Ange, tel. 03 89 41 58 72, www.martinjund.com, location.alsace68@gmail.com). Leave your car at Parking de la Mairie. There is no real reception—though good-natured Myriam or her daughter Cécile will likely be around (call if arriving after 20:00).

¢ Ibis Budget Hôtel offers bright, efficient, cookie-cutter rooms with three beds—one bed is a bunk—and ship-cabin bathrooms (secure pay parking, 10-minute walk from city center at 15 Rue Stanislas, tel. 08 92 68 09 31, https://ibis.accorhotels.com, h5079@accor.com).

Eating in Colmar

Colmar is full of good restaurants offering traditional Alsatian or creative French menus for €20-35. Worth careful consideration (and reservations) are: L'Arpège (fun and foodie), Wistub de la Petite Venise (romantic Alsatian), Cour des Anges (foodie, Bohemian-mellow), and L'un des Sens (peaceful wine bar with Alsatian tapas).

IN THE OLD CITY CENTER

The venerable Customs House, with a canal cutting right behind it on Place de l'Ancienne Douane, marks the touristic and historic center of Colmar. Dine here under the stars on a balmy evening to enjoy the floodlit scene of half-timbered buildings and strolling musicians. While you'll be sitting side-by-side in a mosh pit of tourists, it's hard to beat the location and fun vibe.

$ Cour des Anges is an easygoing delight serving organic, locally grown products to discerning regulars in a quiet Alsatian courtyard or cozy interior just steps away from the tourist mobs. The chef "revisits" traditional dishes in tasty ways. Order family-style here to maximize the experience—sharing delicious salads, homemade *tarte flambée*, "revisited" *choucroute* or crêpes, and more (closed Sun-Mon, 4 Place de l'Ancienne Douane, tel. 03 89 24 98 02).

$$ Restaurant Le Fer Rouge, facing the Customs House, is popular and serves Alsatian classics (daily, 52 Grand Rue, tel. 03 89 20 80 69). Nearby are plenty of places specializing in *tarte flambée* (the "Alsatian pizza").

$ Brasserie Schwendi has fun, German pub energy inside with six beers on tap and hustling waiters. The big terrace with tight, regimented seating fills up on warm evenings. Choose from a dozen filling, robust Swiss *Rösti* plates or *tarte flambée*—I like the *strasbourgeoise flambée* (daily 12:00-22:30, facing the Customs House at 3 Grand Rue, tel. 03 89 23 66 26).

$ Crep' Stub Crêperie Caveau is my favorite for crêpes in the old center, with great outside seating—at the gray tables around the big tree on Place de l'Ancienne Douane—or inside in a cute little back room (closed Mon, 10 Rue des Tanneurs, tel. 03 89 24 51 88).

$$ La Maison Rouge, with a folk-museum interior and sidewalk seating, has reasonably priced, beautifully presented Alsatian cuisine and an understandably loyal following. You'll be greeted by a *jambon à l'os*—ham cooking on the bone (try the veal cordon bleu with Munster, closed Sun-Mon, 9 Rue des Ecoles, tel. 03 89 23 53 22).

IN PETITE VENISE

$$$ Aux Trois Poissons is an intimate and refined place across from the old market hall without a hint of Alsatian decor or cuisine (pleasant indoor and outdoor seating). The traditionally French menu emphasizes fish, though meat dishes are also available (tasty steak tartare, closed Sun-Mon, 15 Quai de la Poissonnerie, tel. 03 89 41 25 21).

$$ Wistub de la Petite Venise's caring owners Virginie and Julien buck the touristy trend, combining a wood-warm, chalet ambience with the energy of an open kitchen. The limited menu, heavy on the meaty classics, is reliably tasty. Chef Julien is particularly proud of his *jambonneau, choucroute,* and foie gras (no outside seating, closed Wed, 4 Rue de la Poissonnerie, tel. 03 89 41 72 59).

$$ Wistub Brenner offers quality, seasonal specialties and attentive service in a good atmosphere. Book ahead or arrive early for a table on the fun terrace. Their formula is freedom: You can choose any first course to go along with any main course on their €30 menu deal (daily, 1 Rue Turenne, tel. 03 89 41 42 33).

Lunch in Petite Venise: For the best selection of quick, inexpensive, and memorable lunch options, grab a bite in the **$ Old Market Hall** in Petite Venise. There are a handful of enticing little eateries to choose from and the fun atmosphere can't be beat (Tue-Sat 8:00-18:00, Sun 10:00-14:00, closed Mon). You can also get a dish to go or a picnic and find a nice canalside perch just outside.

OTHER MEMORABLE DINING OPTIONS

$$$ L'Arpège offers a special experience, like eating in a Monet painting where each waiter's mission is to be sure you leave evangelical about Chef Jean-Martin's cooking. He gives classic French dishes a creative modern twist with seasonal and organic ingredients, always respects the vegetarians with a serious dish, and finishes with a delightful dessert. Inside you'll enjoy candlelight and sleek rocking chairs. Outside, you dine in a homey and beautifully lit garden. It's romantic either way (reservations essentially required, closed Sun-Tue, 24 Rue des Marchands, tel. 03 89 24 29 64, www.larpegebio.com).

$ L'un des Sens is your Midnight in Paris rendezvous—a cool little wine bar three blocks from the nearest tourist offering. You'll discover a laid-back interior and an idyllic leafy courtyard with rickety little tables. They have a long wine list and a short food list: ideal for enjoying nice French wines with a shared tapas-style meal featuring local meats, cheeses, fancy foie gras, and a couple of hot dishes. Three small portions will likely be enough for a couple (reservations helpful, Tue-Sat 17:00-22:00, closed Sun-Mon, 18 Rue Berthe Molly, tel. 03 89 24 04 37, www.lun-des-sens.alsace, helpful Chantal speaks English and serves while Annabelle does the food prep).

Sweet Tooth: Sorbetière d'Isabelle sells fine sorbet and sweets; you can eat at an outdoor table or get it to go (daily until at least 19:00, later in July-Aug and on busy weekends, near Maison Pfister at 13 Rue des Marchands).

Colmar Connections

From Colmar by Train to: Strasbourg (about 2/hour, 35 minutes), **Reims** (TGV: 10/day, 2 hours, most change in Strasbourg), **Verdun** (5/day, 2.5-5 hours, 2-3 changes, many with 30-minute bus ride from Gare de Meuse), **Beaune** (10/day, 3.5 hours, fastest by TGV via Mulhouse, reserve ahead, possible changes in Mulhouse or Belfort and Dijon), **Paris'** Gare de l'Est (12/day with TGV, 2.5 hours, 3 direct, others change in Strasbourg), **Amboise** (13/day, 6 hours, most with transfer in Strasbourg and Paris), **Basel,** Switzerland (hourly, 45 minutes), **Freiburg,** Germany (hourly bus to Breisach then direct train, 1.5 hours), **Karlsruhe,** Germany (TGV: 7/day, 2 hours, best with change in Strasbourg; non-TGV: hourly, 2-3 hours, change in Strasbourg and Appenweier or Offenburg; from Karlsruhe, it's 1.5 hours to Frankfurt, 3 hours to Munich).

Alsace's Route du Vin

Alsace's Route du Vin (Wine Road) is an asphalt ribbon that ties 90 miles of vineyards, villages, and medieval fortress ruins into an understandably popular tourist package. With France's driest cli-

mate, this sunny stretch of vine-covered land has made for good wine since Roman days. Colmar and Eguisheim are well located for exploring the 30,000 acres of vineyards blanketing the hills from Marlenheim to Thann.

This is France's smallest wine region. It's long (75 miles) and skinny (a mile wide on average), with vineyards strategically planted between the flood line of the marshy plains and the frost line of the higher ground. Everyone scrambles for the finest land. Medieval towns grew low into regular farmland rather than high into the vineyards. Local folk wisdom reminded young brides to marry into a family that grew grapes. The region's 50 *grand cru* vineyards (the highest quality) get the privilege of putting up their names on big signs along the hillsides.

The towns with evocative castle ruins are often strategically located at the ends of valleys. Their names can reveal their histories—towns ending with "heim" and "wihr" were born as farmsteads (Eguisheim was Egui's farm, and I guess Riquewihr was the farm of a guy named Rick).

Peppering the landscape are Route du Vin villages, full of quaint half-timbered architecture corralled within medieval walls (for a practical review of what to look for as you wander through these towns, see the "Half-Timbered Houses of Alsace" sidebar, earlier). You can't miss how seriously these villages take their flowers. The *Ville Fleurie* flower competition revs up village pride through an annual contest designed to improve the beauty of the villages. Winners are awarded from one to four flower petals; these ratings are posted on signs as you enter the village. While this contest takes place throughout France, it seems particularly important in Alsace.

As you tour the Route du Vin, you'll see stork nests on church spires and City Halls, thanks to a campaign to reintroduce the birds to this area. (Those nests can weigh over 1,000 pounds, posing a danger if they fall and forcing villagers to shore them up.) Storks make a noise something like a woodpecker. If you hear such a sound, look up: Nests can be on top of any building. Look also for crucifixion monuments scattered about the vineyards—intended to get a little divine intervention for a good harvest.

PLANNING YOUR TIME

If you have only a day, focus on towns within easy striking range of Colmar. World War II hit many Route du Vin villages hard. While some of the towns are amazingly preserved from centuries past, others were entirely rebuilt after the war. It all depended on where the war went in 1944. Among the villages that emerged from World War II unscathed are the four I cover most extensively in this chapter: Eguisheim, Kaysersberg, Riquewihr, and Bergheim.

A sampling of two of the touristy villages is enough for most (visit them early to minimize crowds), then add a less-touristed place (like Bergheim or Turckheim, each of which can be seen in under an hour). Driving distances between villages are generally short. If taking a minibus tour, you can see a representative sampling in a half-day or cover the highlights of the entire region in a full day (including a few wine tastings). For those without wheels it's more work (by bike), time-consuming (by bus), or pricier but manageable (by taxi).

Towns are most alive during their weekly morning (until noon) farmers markets (Mon—Kaysersberg and Bergheim; Fri—Turckheim; Sat—Ribeauvillé and Colmar). Riquewihr and Eguisheim have no market days.

GETTING AROUND THE ROUTE DU VIN
By Car

Drivers can pick up a detailed map of the Route du Vin at any area TI. To reach the Route du Vin north of Colmar, leave Colmar fol-

ALSACE

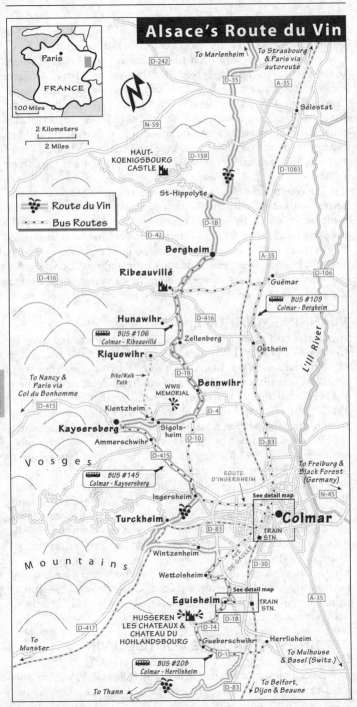

Alsace's Route du Vin

Paris
FRANCE
100 Miles

2 Kilometers
2 Miles

ALSACE

🍇 Route du Vin
⋯⋯ Bus Routes

To Marlenheim
To Strasbourg & Paris via autoroute

D-242
D-35
A-35
Sélestat

N-59

D-159
HAUT-KOENIGSBOURG CASTLE
D-1083

St-Hippolyte

D-1B
D-42

Bergheim
A-35

D-416
Ribeauvillé
D-106
Guémar

BUS #109
Colmar - Bergheim

Hunawihr
D-416
Zellenberg

BUS #106
Colmar - Ribeauvillé
Ostheim
Riquewihr

To Nancy & Paris via Col du Bonhomme
D-415
Bike/Walk Path
D-1B
WWII MEMORIAL
Bennwihr
D-4

L'ILL River

Kientzheim
Sigols-heim
D-10

Kaysersberg
Ammerschwihr
D-83

V o s g e s
D-415

To Freiburg & Black Forest (Germany)
N-45

BUS #145
Colmar - Kaysersberg

ROUTE D'INGERSHEIM
See detail map

Ingersheim

Turckheim
Colmar

D-83
TRAIN STN.

M o u n t a i n s
Wintzenheim

AV. DE GAULLE
D-30

To Munster
Wettolsheim

See detail map
A-35
TRAIN STN.

Eguisheim

HUSSEREN LES CHATEAUX & CHATEAU DU HOHLANDSBOURG
D-1B
D-14
Gueberschwihr
Herrlisheim

D-417
D-1
To Mulhouse & Basel (Switz.)

BUS #208
Colmar - Herrlisheim

D-83
To Thann
To Belfort, Dijon & Beaune

lowing signs to Ingersheim. Look for *Route du Vin* signs. For the quickest way to Eguisheim from Colmar, head for the train station and take D-30 and then D-83 south toward Belfort. In general, it's better to navigate by town names rather than road numbers.

Many drivers discreetly use some of the scenic wine-service lanes known as *sentiers viticoles*. If you do, drive at a snail's pace. I've recommended my favorite segments.

By Train or Bus

The only Route du Vin village accessible by train from Colmar is pleasant little Turckheim (12/day, 10 minutes, described later).

Several bus companies connect Colmar with villages along the Route du Vin daily except Sunday, but deciphering schedules and locating bus stops in Colmar is tricky. I have done this for you (later), but things can change; confirm bus schedules and stop locations by asking at any TI or by using the helpful website (in English) www.vialsace.eu/en. Schedules are posted at most stops.

Buses to Route du Vin villages stop at Colmar's train station (see under "Arrival in Colmar") and in Colmar's city center near the Unterlinden Museum (at the Théâtre stop—with shelters labeled *quai,* each identified with a letter—or a few blocks away by the cinema). The TI can show you the exact locations of these bus stops.

Here's a rundown of service to key Route du Vin villages from Colmar (see Alsace's Route du Vin map to locate these bus routes). Remember, there's no Sunday service on any of these routes.

Kaysersberg has reasonable service (Kunegel bus #145, direction: Le Bonhomme, 7/day, 30 minutes, Théâtre stop Quai G. At the Colmar train station, find the last stop to the left as you leave the station (signed as *145*).

Riquewihr, Hunawihr, and **Ribeauvillé** have decent service (bus #106, roughly 8/day, 45 minutes, big midday service gaps in summer). Buses leave from the bus stop near Place Scheurer-Kestner, behind the cinema on Rue de la 5ème Division (direction: Illhaeusern). See the "Colmar" map, earlier, for stop locations. They also stop at the train station (to the right as you exit).

Bergheim and **Ribeauvillé** are served by bus #109 (roughly 3/day, 30 minutes, direction: St-Hippolyte, same bus stops as #106).

Eguisheim has one bus per day, which departs Colmar about noon and returns from Eguisheim at about 17:00 (Mon-Sat only, 15 minutes). Look for bus #208 (direction: Herrlisheim, leaves from Théâtre stop Quai F, or from the train station, to the right as you exit). Eguisheim is so close that many get there by bike or taxi.

Château du Haut-Kœnigsbourg has a shuttle bus from the Sélestat train station (explained on page 1001).

ALSACE

Wines of the Alsace

Romans planted the first grapevines in Alsace more than 2,000 years ago. Wine and Rhine worked together to form the backbone of the region's medieval economy. Barrels of wine were shipped on the nearby Rhine River to international destinations (Scandinavia, the Low Countries, and Britain were big buyers). This created enormous wealth for Alsatians; their investments financed many of the beautiful buildings and villages we see today. Until the 17th century, Alsace produced more (and better) wine than any other region in the Holy Roman Empire. The Thirty Years' War, French Revolution, and Franco-Prussian War buried Alsace's wine dominance. Two world wars didn't help. Today Alsace is struggling to get its foot back in the door of international wine markets—where the big money is.

To help earn this recognition, they eagerly welcome visitors.

Most Route du Vin towns have wineries that give tours (some charge a fee), and scores of small producers open their courtyards with free and fun tastings. The cooperatives at Eguisheim, Bennwihr, Hunawihr, and Ribeauvillé, created after the destruction of World War II, provide a good look at modern and efficient methods of production. Before you set off, review "French Wine-Tasting 101" on page 1124.

The simplest wines are blended from several grapes and usually called **Edelzwicker.** Despite being cheapest, these wines can be delicious and offer very good value.

Here are the key grapes to look for; the first four are the "noble grapes" of the Alsace:

Riesling is the king of Alsatian grapes. It's more robust than sylvaner, but far drier than the German style. The name comes from the German word that describes its slightly smoky smell, with a note

By Taxi

Allow €15 from Colmar to Eguisheim (€25 round-trip) and €35 from Colmar or Eguisheim to Kaysersberg or Riquewihr. For a group of four with limited time, this is a smart option. For recommendations, see page 971.

By Minivan Tour

All three companies listed next offer private group tours as well as these shared tours. These prices are per person.

of *goût petrol* ("gasoline taste").

Pinot gris is more full-bodied, spicier, and distinctly different from other pinot gris wines you may have tried.

Muscat is best as a before-dinner wine. Compared with other French muscat wines, the Alsatian version is dry, usually with a strong floral taste.

Gewürztraminer is "the lady's wine"—its bouquet is like a rose-bush, its taste is fruity, and its aftertaste is spicy—as its name implies (*gewürtz* means "spice" in German). Drink this with pâtés and local cheeses.

Pinot noir, the local red wine, is light and fruity. While a few good exceptions exist, if you want a red wine with body, look beyond Alsace. Pinot noir is generally served chilled.

Sylvaner—fresh and light, fruity and cheap—is a good wine for a hot day.

Pinot blanc is easy to drink as it's a middle-of-the-road but refreshing wine. It's neither too fruity or sweet nor too strong or dry—it's also not too memorable.

Crémant d'Alsace, the Alsatian sparkling wine, is good—and much cheaper than Champagne. You'll also see *eaux-de-vie,* powerful fruit-flavored brandies—try the *framboise* (raspberry) flavor.

Wine Tasting Tips

I like to taste at wineries in villages along the Route du Vin. As you explore, look for the word *degustation.* It's usually free and informal. Just step up to the bar, enjoy a little small talk, and ask to taste. Vintners generally want you to follow a logical progression, and while they prefer that you buy a bottle or two—usually for between €6 and €15—it's OK to just taste (hopefully while showing genuine interest in their wines). Make a goal of getting to know the various grapes and which you like best. Don't hesitate to use the spittoons. A smart taster can sample plenty of wine without getting tipsy. (If you're bent on getting tipsy, finish things off with a taste of the local brandies, the *eaux-de-vie.)* In case you really get "Alsauced," the French term for headache is *mal à la tête.*

Ophorus Tours offers well-run trips from Colmar and Strasbourg to villages along the Route du Vin that include good wine tastings, informative walking tours, and time to wander (€125/full day, €75/half-day, tel. 05 56 15 26 09, www.ophorus.com, info@ophorus.com).

Alsascope also offers tours departing from Colmar and Strasbourg (€120/full day, €65/half-day, mobile 06 82 87 50 73, www.alsascope.fr, info@alsascope.fr).

Vinotours offers tours with a wine focus (€130/full day, €80/

half-day, mobile 06 51 94 05 17, www.vinotours-alsace.fr, contact@ vinoroute.fr).

Private Guides: Muriel Brun and **Stéphan Reitter** are excellent guides for the Route du Vin (see page 971).

By Bike

Alsace is among France's best biking regions. The Route du Vin has an abundance of well-marked trails and *sentiers viticole* (wine-service roads) that run up and down the slopes, offering memorable views and the fewest cars but lots of sweat (rent an electric bike). Colmar's TI has a good bike map, and bike rental shops know all the routes. Bikers can rent in Colmar, Turckheim, Eguisheim, Kaysersberg, or Ribeauvillé. (I've listed rental options for each.) All but Turckheim have electric bikes for rent and all make great starting points.

Riding round-trip between Ribeauvillé and Kaysersberg via Hunawihr and Riquewihr along the upper *sentier viticole* yields sensational views but very hilly terrain (you can reduce some of the climbing by following lower wine-service lanes).

A bike path runs south from Colmar to Eguisheim following the river for a stretch (described on bike map available at Colmar's TI). One of the most beautiful wine-service lanes in Alsace runs south from Eguisheim through Husseren to Gueberschwihr.

Bike tours work well, too. Service-oriented **Alsa Cyclo** in Eguisheim runs tours using electric bikes (€45-85 for 2-4 hours with a guide, see "Orientation to Eguisheim," later).

On Foot

Hikers can stroll along *sentier viticole* service roads and paths into vineyards from each town on short loop trails (each TI has brochures), or connect the villages on longer walks. Consider taking a bus or taxi from Colmar to one village and hiking to another, then taking a bus or taxi back to Colmar (Riquewihr and Kaysersberg make good combinations—see details on page 1012). Hikers can also climb high to the ruined castles of the Vosges Mountains (Ribeauvillé is the best starting point).

Towns and Sights
Along the Route du Vin

These sights are listed in the order you'll encounter them starting from Colmar.

SOUTH OF COLMAR
Vieil-Armand WWI Memorial (Hartmannswillerkopf)
This powerful memorial evokes the slaughter of the Western Front in World War I, when Germany and France bashed heads for years in a war of attrition. It's up a windy road above Cernay (20 miles south of Colmar). From the parking lot, walk 10 minutes to the vast cemetery, and walk 30 more minutes through trenches to a hilltop with a grand Alsatian view. Here you'll find a stirring memorial statue of French soldiers storming the trenches in 1915-1916—facing near-certain death—and rows of simple crosses marking the graves of those who lost their lives here.

Gueberschwihr
This sweet little village 15 minutes south of Colmar sees almost no tourists and offers an excellent wine-tasting experience at **Domaine Ernest Burn,** where sincere Simone takes you on a tasting tour of their well-respected wines in an atmospheric tasting room (daily, best to call ahead, 8 Rue Basse, www.domaine-burn.fr, tel. 03 89 49 20 68). Follow the gorgeous wine lane due north from Gueberschwihr's center to Eguisheim through Husseren.

Eguisheim
This is the most charming village of the region (described later).

NORTHWEST OF COLMAR
Turckheim
With a picturesque square and a garden-filled moat, this quiet town is refreshingly untouristy. It's an ideal destination for non-drivers, with quick trains from Colmar and easy bike rental. Drivers will find easy parking by the station.

Its 13th-century walls are some of the oldest in the region. Drivers and train riders enter Turckheim through its walls at the France Gate, where—once upon a time—all foreign commerce entered. Just inside the wall you'll see the **TI,** offering a helpful town map with a suggested stroll (Rue Wickram, tel. 03 89 27 38 44, www.turckheim.com). Turckheim's main drag (Grand Rue) runs east from here and makes for a nice wander among bakeries and shops. Rent bikes a block past the TI at the classy **Hôtel des Deux Clefs** reception desk (long hours, 3 Rue du Conseil, tel. 03 89 27 06 01, www.hotellerie-deuxclefs.fr).

Turckheim has a rich history and has long been famous for its wines. It gained town status in 1312, became a member of the Decapolis league of cities in 1354, and was devastated in the Thirty Years' War. In the 18th century it was rebuilt, thanks to the energy of Swiss immigrants. Reviving an old tradition, from May to October there's a town crier's tour each evening at 22:00 (in Alsatian and French).

Turckheim's **"Colmar Pocket" Museum** (Musée Mémorial des Combats de la Poche de Colmar), chronicling the American push to take Alsace from the Nazis, is a hit with WWII buffs (€4, minimal English information; daily 14:00-18:00, Sat-Sun also 10:00-12:00; closed Nov-March; tel. 03 89 80 86 66, www.musee. turckheim-alsace.com).

Kaysersberg
This is the most historic town after Colmar. It has an intriguing medieval center, Dr. Albert Schweitzer's house, and plenty of hiking opportunities (described on page 1008).

Bennwihr
After this town was completely destroyed during World War II, the only object left standing was the compelling statue of two girls depicting Alsace and Lorraine (outside its modern church). The war memorials next to the statue list the names of those who died in both world wars. During World War II, 130,000 Alsatian men aged 17-37 were forced into military service under the German army (after fighting against them). Most were sent to the deadly Russian front.

Riquewihr
This adorable town is the most touristed on the Route du Vin—and understandably so. If you find crowds tiresome, this town is exhausting (described on page 1014).

Hunawihr
This bit of wine-soaked Alsatian cuteness is far less visited than its more famous neighbors, and features a 16th-century fortified church that today is shared by both Catholics and Protestants (the Catholics are buried next to the church; the Protestants are buried outside the church wall). Park at the village washbasin *(lavoir)* and follow the path between vines up to the church, then loop back through the village. Kids enjoy Hunawihr's small nature-conservation park, **Centre de Réintroduction,** where they'll spot otters *(loutre),* over 150 storks *(cigogne),* and more (€10.50, daily 10:00-17:30, shorter hours April and Oct, closed Nov-March, other animals take part in the afternoon shows—times listed on website, tel. 03 89 73 72 62, www.centredereintroduction.fr). A nearby **butterfly exhibit** (Le Jardin des Papillons) houses thousands of the delicate insects from around the world (€8, includes audioguide, daily 10:00-18:00, until 17:00 March-April and Oct, closed Nov-Easter, tel. 03 89 73 33 33, www.jardinsdespapillons.fr).

Bergheim

With a well-preserved gate and charming architecture, sleepy Bergheim is happily untouristed. It's my vote for the best nontouristy stop on the Route du Vin (described on page 1017).

Ribeauvillé

This town, less visited by Americans, is well situated for hiking and biking. It's a linear place with a long pedestrian street (Grand Rue). A steep but manageable trail leads from the top of the town into the Vosges Mountains to three castle ruins, and is ideal for hikers looking for a walk in the woods and sweeping views. Follow Grand Rue uphill to the Hôtel aux Trois Châteaux and find the cobbled lane leading up from there. St. Ulrich is the most interesting of the three ruins (allow 2 hours round-trip, or just climb 10 minutes for a view over the town—get info at TI at 1 Grand Rue, tel. 03 89 73 23 23, www.ribeauville-riquewihr.com). It's a short, sweet, and really hilly bike loop from Ribeauvillé to Hunawihr and Riquewihr (can be extended to Kaysersberg). You can **rent a bike** at Ribo' Cycles (Tue-Sat 9:00-12:00 & 14:00-18:00, Sat until 17:00, closed Sun-Mon, 17 Rue de Landau, tel. 03 89 73 72 94, www.ribocycles.fr).

▲Château du Haut-Kœnigsbourg

This granddaddy of Alsatian castles stands atop a rocky spur of the Vosges Mountains, 2,500 feet above the flat Rhine plain. From here you'll get an eagle's-nest perspective over the Vosges and villages below. Be aware that the castle gets hammered with visitors in high season, particularly on weekends.

Cost and Hours: €9, daily April-Sept 9:15-18:00, June-Aug until 18:45; Oct-March 9:30-17:45; Nov-Feb closes for lunch and a half-hour early; audioguide-€5, about 15 minutes north of Ribeauvillé, above St-Hippolyte, tel. 03 69 33 25 00, www.haut-koenigsbourg.fr.

Tours: An English leaflet and posted descriptions give a reasonable overview of key rooms and history, but the one-hour audioguide is a good investment.

Getting There: A €2.50 shuttle bus runs to the castle from the Sélestat train station (8/day mid-April-mid-May and mid-June-mid-Sept, weekends only off-season, none Jan-mid-March, 30 minutes, timed with trains, call château for schedule or check website). Your shuttle ticket saves you €2 on the château entry fee. If driving in high season, expect to park along the road well below the castle (unless you come early). Parking can be a zoo in the summer—it's limited to roadside spaces.

Visiting the Castle: While the elaborate castle was rebuilt barely 100 years ago, it's a romantic's dream, dramatically situated along its sky-high ridge. Its exhibits give helpful insight into this 15th-century mountain fortress.

Started in 1147 as an Imperial castle in the extensive network that served the Holy Roman Empire, Haut-Kœnigsbourg was designed to protect valuable trade routes. It was under constant siege and eventually destroyed by rampaging Swedes in the 17th century. The castle sat in ruins until the early 1900s, when an ambitious restoration campaign began (a model in the castle storeroom shows the castle before its renovation).

Today's castle—well-furnished by medieval standards—highlights Germanic influence in Alsatian history with decorations and weapons from the 15th through 17th centuries. Don't miss the top-floor Grand Bastion with its elaborate wooden roof structure and models showing its construction. There are cannons and magnificent views in all directions.

Eguisheim

Just a few miles south of Colmar's suburbs, this circular, flower-festooned little wine town (pop. 1,500, 33 wineries), often busy with tourists, is a delight. Come here first thing to experience the village at its peaceful best (or spend the night). In 2013 it was named France's favorite town, adding to its touristic fame. Eguisheim ("ay-gush-I'm") is ideal for a relaxing lunch and vineyard walks. If you have a car, it makes a good small-town base for exploring Alsace. It's also a cinch to day-trip here by car (easy parking) or taxi (€15 from Colmar), and manageable by bike (see "Getting Around the Route du Vin—By Bike," earlier), but barely accessible by bus.

Orientation to Eguisheim

The **TI** has information on bus schedules, festivals, vineyard walks, and Vosges Mountain hikes (generally Mon-Sat 9:30-12:30 & 13:30-18:00, Sun 10:30-13:30, shorter hours off-season, 22 Grand Rue, tel. 03 89 23 40 33, www.tourisme-eguisheimrouffach.com). They're happy to call a taxi for you. A handy WC sits behind the TI.

Eguisheim's **bus stop** is at the upper end of the village, close to Place Charles de Gaulle (see map, same stop for both directions).

The *Petit Train* leaves from the town center, a block east of the TI, and runs a scenic route through Eguisheim and into the vineyards (€7, 40 minutes, hourly).

Alsa Cyclo Tours is a good outfit that rents top-quality bikes with GPS and recorded directions in English (electric bike-€25/half-day, €35/day; regular bike-€15/half-day, €25/day; GPS-€3; May-Oct daily 9:00-18:00, just off the main square at 3 Rue de Pairis, tel. 03 69 45 96 48 or 06 34 41 19 04, www.alsacyclotours. alsace). They also offer bike tours from Colmar (€45-85 for 2-4 hours with a guide, includes electric bike).

Eguisheim Walk

Draw a circle and then cut a line straight through it. That's your plan with this inviting little town. The main drag (Grand Rue) cuts through the middle, with gates at either end and a stately town square in the center. And, while Eguisheim's town wall is long gone, it left a circular lane (Rue du Rempart—Nord and Sud) lined with gingerbread-cute houses. (For more on this type of architecture, see the "Half-Timbered Houses of Alsace" sidebar in the "Colmar" section, earlier.) Rue du Rempart Sud is more picturesque than Rue du Rempart Nord, but the Nord ramparts feel more real and lived in. I'd walk the entire circle.

• *Start your self-guided walk near the TI and circle the former ramparts clockwise, walking up Rue du Rempart Sud (just after the Auberge du Rempart hotel).*

Rue du Rempart Sud: Be on the lookout for small information plaques as you stroll. The most enchanting and higgledy-piggledy view in town is right at the start of the loop (at the tight Y in the road; go left and uphill). You'll see that what was once the wall is now lined with 16th- and 17th-century houses—a cancan of half-timbered charm. You're actually walking a lane between the back of fine homes (on the left) and their barns (on the right).

Look for emblems of daily life: The holes peppering exposed beams were from nails used to hold a plaster covering (at #27). You'll see religious and magical symbols (at #35), dates of construction with initials of owners on lintel stones, little hatch doors leading to wine or coal cellars, and so on. Hearts cut into shutters once meant there was a fair maiden in that household looking for a man. (Everything looks sharp because the government subsidizes the work locals do on their exteriors.)

Along the way, you may bump into Chez Thierry's *saucisson*

ALSACE

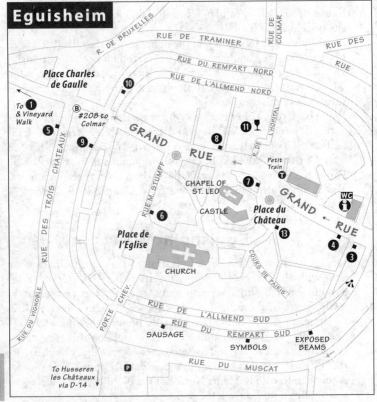

stand (at #49) with plenty of tasty samples and Frederic Hertzog's farmhouse cheese shop (try the Munster cheese—made in the town of Munster just up the valley).

Rue du Rempart Nord: The loop takes a decidedly hip turn along its northern half, as you pass an art gallery, a cool coffee shop, and a trendy bar. The second half also comes with lots of fixer-uppers and fewer tourists.

As you explore the town, you may come upon some of its 20 "tithe courtyards." Farmers who worked on land owned by the Church came to these courtyards to pay their tithes (10 percent of their production). With so many of these courtyards, it's safe to conclude that this was great farm country.

• *When you've finished the loop, walk up Grand Rue to Eguisheim's main square...*

Place du Château Saint-Léon: The square is lined with fine houses; many were mansions for the managers of wealthy estates and vineyards owned by absentee landowners.

Fountains like the one here were important meeting points back when women would gather here to collect water, wash, and

Accommodations
1. To Hôtel St. Hubert & Thérèse Bombenger Chambres
2. Auberge Alsacienne
3. Auberge du Rempart
4. Le Hameau d'Eguisheim & Ginglinger Winery
5. Jean-Luc Meyer Chambres

Eateries & Other
6. Caveau Heuhaus
7. Restaurant/Charcuterie-Café A Edel
8. Auberge de Trois Châteaux
9. Le Pavillion Gourmand
10. Le Café
11. Paul Schneider Winery
12. Wolfberger Winery
13. Alsa Cyclo Tours

share gossip. The fountain sports a statue of St. Leo IX—the only Alsatian pope. Leo was likely born here in 1002. A bishop at just 24, he was famed for his pastoral qualities, tending the sick and poor, and working to reform the Church (which had grown corrupt). Elected in 1048, Leo's pontificate lasted just five years.

Above the fountain stands the town "castle" (now just a private mansion built on the historic site of the castle) and the Chapel of St. Leo IX. The octagonal footprint of the castle survives from the 13th century. There's been some kind of castle here for a thousand years—the first was the fortress of a local duke. After the French Revolution, the castle was state-owned and, as the state so often did during that no-nonsense age, sold and dismantled it. But a local bishop later built a chapel on this spot.

• *As you approach the church, you can see a stork nest on the bell tower and a statue of St. Leo IX above the doorway.*

Chapel of St. Leo IX: This chapel honors Eguisheim's home-town saint. Built in the Neo-Romanesque style popular in 19th century and consecrated in 1894, it's of little historic importance. But it's beautiful inside and worth a peek to see how a Romanesque church may have been painted. Inside, the paintings, stained glass, and carvings are all in the Romanesque Revival style. After the paganism of the French Revolution, romantics in the late 1800s used this style to signal a spiritual revival—a new Golden Age of Christianity.

Linger awhile to soak it all in (drop a 50-cent coin into the box by the church entry for light). Flanking the altar, two fine stained-glass angels majestically spread their wings. To the right of the altar is a reliquary with a piece of Leo's jaw. To the left is a statue of Leo.

• *Your Eguisheim walk is done—time to taste some of the wine that made all this small-town beauty possible.*

Sights in Eguisheim

Wine Tasting

Don't leave without visiting one of Eguisheim's many cozy wineries.

Pierre Henri Ginglinger is an organic winery offering fine wines and a café-like tasting room across from the TI (daily, 33 Grand Rue, tel. 03 89 41 32 55, www.vins-ginglinger.com).

Paul Schneider's independent winery, located in a one-time hospice, is still family-run after three generations. You can buy a glass of their wine (€3), or pay €5-8 to sample a good mix of wines in the traditionally furnished tasting room. Ask English-fluent Claire Schneider to explain the abstract paintings on the walls (also found on the labels of their Grands Crus)—they give a modern twist to some old Alsatian traditions. Drop in to taste but call ahead for a short tour of the two cellars where they produce 100,000 bottles a year (daily 9:00-12:00 & 13:30-18:30, 1 Rue de l'Hôpital, tel. 03 89 41 50 07, www.vins-paul-schneider.fr, vins.paul.schneider@wanadoo.fr).

Wolfberger Winery is a big and slick corporate alternative to the others listed here. Located at the lower end of town, it offers a history exhibition, a big shopping section, and a welcoming bar with a helpful staff eager to introduce you to their wine one tiny tasting glass at a time (tastings daily 8:00-12:00 & 14:00-18:00, 6 Grand Rue, tel. 03 89 22 20 20, www.wolfberger.com).

Views over Eguisheim

If you have a car, you can follow signs up the *Route Les Cinq Châteaux* to *Les Husseren*, then walk 30 minutes to the ruined castle towers for a good view of the Vosges Mountains above and vineyards below. For even better views, you can drive to Château du Hohlandsbourg and ramble its ramparts (www.chateau-hohlandsbourg.com).

By mountain bike or on foot, find any path through the vineyards above Eguisheim for great views (the TI has a free map).

Sleeping in Eguisheim

$$ Hôtel St. Hubert** offers 15 spotless rooms with modern, German comfort and an indoor pool and sauna. The 10-minute walk from the town center is rewarded with vineyards out your window (family rooms, 4 rooms have patios, view breakfast room and outside tables where you can touch the vines, reception open 8:00-12:00 & 15:00-21:00, 6 Rue des Trois Pierres, tel. 03 89 41 46 88, www.hotel-st-hubert.com, reservation@hotel-st-hubert.com, welcoming owner Maxime).

$ Auberge Alsacienne*** is conveniently located near the lower parking area with reasonably priced, sharp, and modern rooms in a picturesque building with a well-respected restaurant (easy parking, 12 Grand Rue, tel. 03 89 41 50 20, www.auberge-alsacienne.net, contact@auberge-alsacienne.net.

$ Auberge du Rempart is laid back and a solid value: bright, airy rooms, big beds, and surprisingly elaborate decor above a lively café/restaurant deep inside the town. Rooms get some noise from the restaurant on warm nights (rooms with air-con cost more, great family suite, near TI at 3 Rue du Rempart Sud, tel. 03 89 41 16 87, www.auberge-du-rempart.com, contact@auberge-du-rempart.com). The reception desk in the restaurant is usually open only during lunch and after 18:00.

CHAMBRES D'HOTES

$$ Le Hameau d'Eguisheim, on the grounds of the Pierre Henri Ginglinger winery (convenient tastings), offers five big, bright, tastefully decorated rooms that includes breakfast. Stéphanie has transformed the 17th-century place into a cozy abode with a nice upstairs terrace (33 Grand Rue, tel. 03 89 24 18 66, www.hameau-eguisheim.com, contact@hameau-eguisheim.com). She also rents several studios for up to six people (3-night minimum, fully equipped kitchen but no breakfast).

¢ Winemaker **Jean-Luc Meyer** rents modern rooms, some with balcony, and apartments for 2 to 12 people (2-night minimum, includes breakfast in their tasting room, kitchenettes, good family options, 4 Rue des Trois Châteaux, tel. 03 89 24 53 66, www.vins-meyer-eguisheim.com, info@vins-meyer-eguisheim.com).

¢ Thérèse Bombenger is sweet, speaks some English, and has a contemporary French home just above Eguisheim with three rooms and nice views into the vineyards and over town (includes breakfast, communal fridge and microwave, across from Hôtel St. Hubert at 3 Rue des Trois Pierres, tel. 03 89 23 71 19, mobile 06 61

94 31 09, bombenger.marie-therese@wanadoo.fr). She'll pick you up at the station in Colmar if scheduled in advance, and she'll do your laundry if you ask nicely.

Eating in Eguisheim

$ Caveau Heuhaus is a fun, old-time place just a few steps off the main drag that serves a delicious *tarte flambée* and *plats* nonstop from 10:30 to 22:00 (closed Thu, 7 Rue Monseigneur Stumpf, tel. 03 89 41 85 72).

$ Restaurant/Charcuterie-Café A Edel, on Place du Château St. Léon IX, has inviting sit-down lunches, *tarte flambée* and quiche served with small salads, and good to-go selections. Eat in or get all you need for a fun picnic (closed at 18:00, 2 Place du Château St. Léon IX, tel. 03 89 41 22 40).

$$ Auberge des Trois Châteaux, straight out of Hansel and Gretel, has cozy ambience and is the place in town for traditional dinner (affordable plats du jour, closed Tue-Wed, 26 Grand Rue, tel. 03 89 23 70 61).

$ Auberge du Rempart offers casual outdoor dining in a pleasant courtyard around a big fountain. Come here for wood-fired *tarte flambée,* as well as lighter meals (daily for lunch, closed Sun-Mon for dinner, near TI at 3 Rue du Rempart Sud, tel. 03 89 41 16 87).

$$ Le Pavillion Gourmand is dressy, serving gourmet French and Alsatian cuisine from lamb to duck to pork, all with modern touches. Eat in a smart dining room or outside on the streetfront terrace (closed Tue-Wed, 101 Rue du Rempart Sud, tel. 03 89 24 35 88).

$$ Le Café, a cool hangout morning and night, is run by English-speaking Reiner (drinks and light snacks only, inviting outdoor seating, on Rue Allmend Nord at top of village, daily 10:00-22:00, tel. 09 70 44 76 06).

Kaysersberg

The domain of Germanic princes for much of its history, Kaysersberg ("Emperor's Mountain") was of strategic importance, thanks to its location guarding the important route over the Vosges Mountains that links Colmar with the rest of France. Today, philosopher-physician Albert Schweitzer's hometown offers a cute jumble of 15th-century homes under a romantically ruined castle with easy vineyard trails at its doorstep, and plenty of tourists. Reasonable bus service from Colmar makes Kaysersberg a convenient day trip (bus #145, direction: Le Bonhomme, 7/day, 30 minutes, schedule at www.vialsace.eu).

Orientation to Kaysersberg

The **TI** is two blocks from the town's main entry, inside Hôtel de Ville at 39 Rue du Général de Gaulle (Mon-Sat 9:00-12:30 &  14:00-18:00, closed Sun except June-Sept Sun 9:30-12:30, tel. 03 89 78 22 78, www. kaysersberg.com). Pick up town and valley maps, bus schedules, and detailed descriptions of hiking trails between wine villages (see "Walking/Biking Trails from Kaysersberg," later).

All buses from Colmar serve the Rocade Verte stop at a parking lot on the village's south side, just outside the town walls (best stop for return trip). Drivers find pay lots along the town's ring road. Porte Basse Parking works best, but all lots are a quick and easy walk to the center.

Find **WCs** next to the TI and across from the Schweitzer Museum. **Alsa Cyclo Tours** rents top-quality bikes (Place de l'Hôtel de Ville , tel. 03 69 45 98 40, www.alsacyclotours.alsace).

Kaysersberg Walk

• *Start your self-guided town stroll in the center of Kaysersberg at the main square, Place de la Mairie.*

From the Main Square to the Church: Face the Hôtel de Ville (City Hall) and start up the main drag, Rue de Général de Gaulle, to its left. After a few steps, you'll find a round arch from 1604 on the right. Walking through it, you'll go past a former gunpowder storehouse—now a hall used for free art exhibits (TI access from here, too). Enjoy the art, then walk into a typical **Alsatian courtyard** with a wooden gallery, cascades of geraniums, and a public WC. The painting from 1993 celebrates the 700th anniversary of Kaysersberg's status as an Imperial city. In 1293, the Holy Roman Emperor gave Kaysersberg trade and tax status and the right to build strong city walls (making the townsfolk very happy, as you can see in the painting). Later, in 1354, the town was a founding member of the Decapolis.

Return to the street, turn right, and continue up Rue de Général de Gaulle. The neighboring region of Lorraine is known for its handmade glass, and at **Verrerie d'Art de Kaysersberg** (across from the church), you can see glassblowers at work and browse their showroom (Tue-Sat 10:00-12:30 & 14:00-17:30).

Opposite the glassworks (on the side of the church), read some of the names on the **war memorial**—that's a lot of war dead for a small town. We're in France now, but all of this fighting was done

Albert Schweitzer
(1875-1965)

I don't know what your destiny will be, but one thing I do know: The only ones among you who will be really happy are those who have sought and found how to serve.

—Albert Schweitzer

Albert Schweitzer—theologian, musician, philosopher, and physician—was an unusually gifted individual who never hesitated to question accepted beliefs and practices. He is probably most famous for his work with sufferers of leprosy and tuberculosis in Africa.

Born to German parents in 1875 in Kaysersberg, he studied philosophy and theology at the University of Strasbourg, eventually becoming a pastor at his church. Not satisfied with that, Schweitzer studied music and soon gained fame as a musical scholar and organist. After trying his hand at writing with *The Quest of the Historical Jesus,* which challenged contemporary secular views of Jesus, he shifted his attention to medicine. He married Helene Bresslau, and the couple left for Africa and founded a missionary hospital in Gabon (then called Lambaréné). During World War I, Schweitzer and his wife were forced out of Africa by the French.

After the war, Schweitzer returned to Gabon on his own, where he remained for most of the rest of his life. He received the 1952 Nobel Peace Prize for his service to humanity, particularly for founding the Albert Schweitzer Hospital in Gabon, where he died in 1965. He was 90 years old.

for Germany. In World War I they fought on the Western Front. After Hitler annexed Alsace in World War II, local boys were sent to Russia and Poland (far from home, so they could kill the enemy with less guilt and couldn't desert). Notice also the noncombatant victims *(victimes civiles):* Some were sent to death camps and others died in bombing raids. In 1944 Allied bombers destroyed 45 percent of Kaysersberg—and that included many of its citizens.

• *Now turn your attention to the church.*

Church of the Holy Cross: In front of the church stands a **fountain** featuring the Roman Emperor Constantine—holding a cross and honored here because he was the first Christian emperor. Up on the simple Romanesque facade of the church is his mom, Helen (also holding a cross). She converted her son to Christianity and, according to Church lore, brought pieces of the True Cross to Rome from Jerusalem.

The church dates from the 13th and 14th centuries. Gothic was in high gear elsewhere, but back then Alsace was about a hundred years behind the artistic curve. Look at the tympanum (carved relief over the door, surviving from the 13th century) and notice how crude and naive it is. The carved red sandstone figures remind me of Archaic Greek statues.

Step inside (free, daily 9:00-18:00). The nave is Romanesque, but the side aisles, dating from the 15th century when the church was expanded, are more Gothic. The medieval stained glass was destroyed in 1944; what you see is modern. The moving statue of a crucified Christ is carved out of linden wood and painted. Notice the attempt to manage the perspective by making Jesus' legs shorter than they actually would have been.

Walk up close to the altarpiece (from 1518) and study the finely carved Passion of Christ. These scenes show the events of Jesus' last week—from entering Jerusalem (on the left) to the Resurrection (on the right). The carvings are high relief in the center but low relief in the wings so it will all fit when closed.

On the right side of the nave (as you leave, under the window in the transept), check out the wooden statue of the Deposition, showing Christ after his death by crucifixion. That small metal chest below kept the communion bread back in the 16th century.

• *Continue walking up this busy street.*

From the History Museum to the Bridge: At #62, the **Kaysersberg History Museum** has a lovely courtyard restaurant but a forgettable three-room exhibit of religious and domestic artifacts—without a word of English (free, closed Tue and off-season, enter from the courtyard between the twin gables). The nearby **Biscuiterie La Table Alsacienne,** tempting visitors with all the traditional baked goods, is more interesting.

Continue along the main drag. The huge house standing near the bridge was an old inn and bathhouse. **Maison Herzer,** on the right at #101, dates from 1592. Its finely restored ornamentation includes fun faces (could be the owners) and a gargoyle-supported pulley high above to lift hay to the attic. Look down the picturesque lane to its left and notice how some buildings have settled in the soft ground.

Just before the bridge, walk a few steps upstream to see where the town's canal starts—an example of the importance of waterpower in the Middle Ages.

Kaysersberg's Bridge: The bridge was fortified on the upstream side to stop enemy boats from entering town. Look downstream; the helter-skelter roofs were for drying the hides of a tannery. On this 16th-century bridge, find the emblems of the Holy Roman Empire (double eagle) and of Kaysersberg (two bags with a belt to tie goods to the trader's horse). These signs—plus the saint-in-a-cage at the end of the bridge (Constantine with the Holy

Cross and Christ)—meant this bridge offered both political and religious protection for people coming and going.

At the end of World War II, as the Nazis were preparing to retreat, they planned to destroy the bridge. Locals reasoned with the commander, agreeing to dig an antitank ditch just beyond the bridge—and the symbol of the town was saved.

Cross the bridge and look back above the **bathhouse** with its stork nest. (Storks are choosy and often don't like man-made nest cages like this one.) High on the ridge is the town's 12th-century castle and city wall. Consider again the strategic importance of this place, in its day the last fortified point between a German realm and a French invasion.

• *Your walk is finished. The castle is an easy climb and the Albert Schweitzer Museum is 200 yards beyond the bridge at the top of the town.*

SIGHTS IN KAYSERSBERG
Wine Tasting
The **Cave des Vignerons de Kaysersberg** owns a modern tasting room representing 150 winemakers from around Kaysersberg, including several Grands Crus, and offers free and easy wine tastings with an English-speaking staff (Wed-Sun 10:30-13:00 & 14:00-18:30, closed Mon-Tue, near TI at 20 Rue du Général de Gaulle, tel. 03 89 47 18 43).

Albert Schweitzer Museum
The home of Dr. Albert Schweitzer is a small museum offering two rooms of scattered photos and artifacts from his time in Africa. Schweitzer was a Renaissance man who opened people's eyes to conditions in the Third World (€2.50, daily 9:00-12:00 & 14:00-19:00, shorter hours off-season, 126 Rue du Général de Gaulle, tel. 03 89 47 36 55).

Walking/Biking Trails from Kaysersberg
Trails start near the TI. To find them, turn left out of the TI and walk out of the walls under the arch. Look for signs leading to a worthwhile 10-minute climb to the ruined **castle** (free, always open, great views, 113 steps up a dark stairway to the top of the tower). Loop back down behind the castle and enter the town near its 16th-century bridge. Wandering into the vineyards brings more views. Avoid trails leading from here to Riquewihr (a better trail is described next).

For a scenic 1.5-hour hike—or 40-minute bike ride—over vine-covered hills to **Riquewihr,** turn right on the main trail near the TI. Everyone starts on a bike path *(piste cyclable)* toward **Kientzheim** (well-marked with green crosses and bike icons). Hikers follow the green crosses left after about five minutes and join a hiking trail. Bikers follow the bike icons through Kientzheim, then join the *sentier viticole* bike path as it turns left and climbs through vineyards to wonderful views and on to Riquewihr.

NEAR KAYSERSBERG
World War II Sights

The Second World War careened wildly back and forth through this region. Some towns were entirely destroyed. Others made it through unscathed. Towns with gray rather than red-tiled roofs were rebuilt after 1945. Kientzheim has an American-made tank parked in its front yard, a wine museum in its castle grounds, and a network of tiny streams trickling down its streets (as was commonplace around here before World War II). The towns of Sigolsheim (which was the scene of fierce fighting—note its sterile, rebuilt Romanesque church) and nearby Bennwihr are modern, as they were taken and lost numerous times by the Allies and Nazis and completely ruined.

The hill just north of Kaysersberg houses a **World War II Memorial** and is still called "Bloody Hill" by locals (as it was nicknamed by German troops). From Kaysersberg, follow signs to *Kientzheim* and on to *Sigolsheim,* then follow *Nécropole* signs to find a spectacular setting (best at sunset), with a monument to the American divisions that helped liberate Alsace in World War II (find the American flag). Up the lane, a beautiful cemetery is the final resting place of 1,600 men who fought in the French army (many gravestones are Muslim, for soldiers from France's North African colonies—Morocco, Algeria, and Tunisia). From this commanding viewpoint you can survey the entire southern section of the Route du Vin and into Germany. The castle hanging high to the north is the Château du Haut-Kœnigsbourg (described earlier).

Eating in Kaysersberg

If you're hungry, **$ L'Enfariné Boulangerie Café** is good for a quiet, light lunch or a coffee break with no tourists around. Try their simple, delicious quiches and toasted sandwiches (Tue-Sun 6:30-19:00, closed Mon, a block from the TI at 29 Rue du Général de Gaulle, tel. 03 89 47 63 58). At the other end of town (near the Schweitzer Museum), you can enjoy Alsatian fare, coffee, or dessert at **$ Bratschall Manala** (good prices, service inside or out, 104 Rue du Général de Gaulle, tel. 03 89 47 38 49). A fun **Monday-morning market** happens across from the Schweitzer Museum, and a smaller food-and-drink market is at the Porte Basse parking lot on Friday evenings (16:30-19:00).

Riquewihr

This little village, wrapped in vineyards, is so picturesque today because it was so rich centuries ago, thanks to wine exports. Its old-time wealth is evident by its many stone houses—more here than in any other village in Alsace. The village is a touristic fruitcake of shops, cafés, galleries, cobblestones, and flowers. Arrive early or visit very late as midday crowds (many from river cruise ships) can trample its ample charms.

Orientation to Riquewihr

Buses drop you off at the lower end of the village; drivers can park in spaces along the ring road or at the lots on either end of town (€3/2 hours). Park below if you can (or find more parking encircling the village). Wherever you park, find the Hôtel de Ville's archway at the town's lower end (where my short walk starts); the main drag runs uphill from here. The **TI** is halfway up at 2 Rue de la 1ère Armée (closed daily 12:30-14:00, tel. 03 89 73 23 23, www.ribeauville-riquewihr.com). A WC is behind the TI. For a taxi, call 03 89 73 73 71 or mobile 06 46 84 40 05. Market day is Friday morning (on Place des Trois Eglises).

Riquewihr Walk and Wine Crawl

Start your self-guided walk at the bottom of town, in front of the **Hôtel de Ville.** We'll walk straight up the Rue de Général de Gaulle and emerge on the other end of town.

Notice the three flags: Europe, France, and Alsace. In this bubbling town of 1,300 people, you realize that without wine and tourism, this place would have no economy. After passing under the arch, find the historic map and engraving (left) that help you imagine Riquewihr in 1644 and appreciate its double wall and moat.

Strolling up Riquewihr's main street, **Rue de Général de Gaulle,** savor the architecture. (For help appreciating the half-timbered houses, see the "Half-Timbered Houses of Alsace" sidebar in the "Colmar" section, earlier.) Iron signs, designed to help illiterate shoppers know what's for sale, date from the 15th century. Gird yourself, as on this walk you'll also drop into three very different Alsatian wineries. All offer free tastings (hoping that you'll buy something) and English-speaking staff.

On the first corner above the Hôtel de Ville, a *degustation* sign marks a stone stairway leading down into the tasting cellar of **Caves Dopff et Irion.** They provide a spacious, user-friendly wine-tasting experience and a special counter for *eau-de-vie* tastings (daily in season, 10:00-18:00 or 19:00).

Back in daylight, continue your walk into town. The beautiful vineyards around the village belonged to absentee princes. The impressive **mansions** you'll see were the domains of men who managed the estate of a feudal lord and, in return, got a cut of the production. At #14 you can see what would have been considered a skyscraper in the 16th century—the highest half-timbered building in Alsace when it was built. Gaze left to see the massive stork nest atop #16. At #18, notice the broad arches for wagonloads of grapes. Venture into the courtyard (filled with restaurant tables; lookie-loos are welcome) with its traditional Alsatian galleries. At the entry is a collection of 200-year-old iron stove plates. Decorated with old German texts, these were placed behind the fire to protect the back wall and reflect heat out. In the far back corner, just past the old well, you'll find the mammoth 1817 wine press that drained juice directly into the cellar.

At the town's **main intersection** (TI to the left), a street leads to two churches (Protestant to the right, Catholic to the left, neither of sightseeing interest). Survey the scene with surviving 16th-century architecture all around. Before the age of private plumbing, public fountains were scattered through town. Notice the fine wood carvings decorating the corners, and the iron sign advertising the vintner, Hugel, with the harvest team ready to bring in the grapes.

It's time for a tasting at **Caves Hugel.** This fine winemaker has an intimate tasting room overlooking the main drag (daily 9:00-12:00 & 13:00-18:00, check out their classy English flier). You'll feel (and taste) the pride of 13 generations of family tradition.

To continue your wine education, head up to #29, on the left, for another tasting. Through a round arch, stone steps lead into the 16th-century cellar of **Cave Zimmer** (pleasant courtyard café outside). While the business is too small to export to the US, the Zimmer family, with a tradition dating back to 1848, is happy to let you taste their work (10:00-19:00 daily, 33 Rue du Général de Gaulle).

Staggering farther up the main street, you'll see an iron sign for the **town gourmet** at #42. The word "gourmet" originated here in France, where each town in winemaking regions had an official wine judge, appraiser, and middleman. The gourmet was instrumental in effectively connecting the vintner with the thirsty market. He facilitated sales and set prices. To judge the wine, he needed to have fine food to complement the tasting. The town appointed the gourmet, and the position—quite lucrative as you

ALSACE

can see by this fine house—was then handed down from father to son. While the traditional function of the gourmet died out in the 1930s, the concept of the person with the best food in town—the gourmet—survives to this day. Wander through the gourmet's courtyards. Notice the nails on timbers designed to hold stucco.

After two more blocks of Riquewihr townscapes, you'll come to one of the most impressive guard towers in Alsace—Le Dolder, from 1291. The Dolder Museum inside the tower has small rooms covering its history—but doesn't merit the climb or €3 entry fee.

Walk under two guard towers and turn left outside the walls to stroll along the beautifully preserved ramparts. In Alsace, older towns were fortified with **walls** built to withstand arrows. When they grew bigger—and war technology advanced to gunpowder and cannons—the townspeople built a stouter wall outside the original wall. In this case, it left an area in the middle for "newer" 18th-century houses. Notice how homes were built on top of the defensive walls. Double back into town after passing the old wine press and find adorable Rue des Remparts—and explore.

Sights in Riquewihr

Tourist Train

At the town entry, you'll see the *petit train* that choo-choos through the town and then along a very scenic path above Riquewihr into the vineyards (€7, departs every 45-60 minutes, 30 minutes).

Wine Tasting

The vines surrounding Riquewihr produce some of Alsace's most prestigious wines. The village is lined with good places to sample them. Among the many options in town, I like Caves Dopff et Irion, Caves Hugel, and Cave Zimmer (all described earlier in my town walk).

Scenic Routes from Riquewihr

A path with grand views leads from the town's lower end. Follow the road a few blocks to the right as you face Hôtel de Ville. Hike up a stepped path for about 75 yards, then turn right on the trail to find views over Riquewihr and a bench to enjoy them from. Another 100 level yards lead to a paved lane (go left and up) and terrific views of hilltop Zellenberg and vineyards to the north. For the same views with a car, take D-311 from the roundabout at the town's lower end toward Ribeauvillé. Drive just a short block and find the metal signs on the left *(sentier viticole)* and follow the small lanes up to wonderful views.

On the town's south side, another *sentier viticole* leads to Kientzheim (then Kaysersberg). Start from the TI and head out Rue de la 1ère Armée, then follow bike icons to Kientzheim on this beautiful walk or bike ride. The lane rises, then drops into the village—revealing views all the way (allow 90 minutes to hike at a steady pace to Kaysersberg, 40 minutes by bike). Drivers are not allowed on this path.

Bergheim

While cutesy towns draw the crowds, Bergheim is a quiet Route du Vin village. And it's quick and easy: There's free parking all around the town, but the lot at the southern end is most convenient (with a WC and the stop for bus #109). This is also where my self-guided walk starts. Strolling through Bergheim, you'll pass a handful of quiet cafés and a smattering of other businesses and shops (including a small grocery). There's no TI but there's little need for one.

Bergheim Walk

On this 30-minute loop stroll you'll walk through the wall, down Grand Rue, past the City Hall, and along some smaller lanes back to where you started.

Start your walk at the southern parking lot with three big plane trees (easy to find when coming from Riquewihr or Ribeau-

villé). Stroll across to the small flowery park (picnic tables at the ready) and marvel at the massive trunk of an ancient linden tree, then turn around and head into the village.

Bergheim never sprawled beyond its 14th-century walls thanks to the higher land value of the surrounding vineyards. Study the design of the **towering gate:** Night watchman surveyed the town for fires from the bell tower high above. The carved relief on the left recalls how this town—empowered, unusually, by Holy Roman Emperor Leopold II to grant asylum—provided sanctuary for people running from the law from 1530 to 1667. A total of 744 characters—like this guy happily mooning those pursuing him—took refuge in Bergheim.

Bergheim's main drag, the **Grand Rue,** is lined by a narrow little canal for the first block. Notice the small iron gate 50 yards down. When lowered, the canal filled with water so that the laundry women could do their chores. The canal flows under the old laundry building (today a sweet café), on the side of which you can see a faded painting of women doing the wash.

As you stroll look for buildings with gates and courtyards ideal for horse carriages. Notice the fine **half-timbered houses** and the old iron hanging signs (look for *sommelier*, the local wine steward.) This town, unlike its more touristy neighbors, still has a healthy economy that's not tourist dependent—with enough locals to keep a newsstand in business, a shop that sells nothing but foie gras, a small grocery store, and cars rather than tour groups on its streets.

It's hard to grasp how old these places are. A highlight of the Unterlinden Museum in Colmar is the "Mosaic of Bergheim," which once decorated the floor of a third-century Roman mansion in this town. If you were to dig beneath your feet, you'd find the remains of an ancient Roman town.

Bergheim's nondescript **church** at its northern end comes with a stork nest on top, a lush garden, and an insect hotel (for pollination).

Stepping outside the **town walls,** look to the left to see the fortifications: inner walls (14th century) and outer walls (16th century). The inner wall was tall and skinny (handy for warding off arrows) and the outer wall was more squat and stout (better for protecting against cannon fire). The area in between was a moat; now it's a handy place for gardens and car parking.

Continue a few steps outside the walls to visit the **war memorial,** dedicated not to heroes who died for their country but to the "victims of war." Alsace was part of Germany during World War I. And in World War II many Alsatians were also forced to fight for the Nazis, who sent them to the Eastern Front. Look for the "Tambow" plaque, memorializing a Russian POW camp where 5,000-10,000 Alsatian men died, and the rest were kept captive until 1947.

Double back into town, and after a block turn right at the stop sign. Follow the street's curve left and pop out onto **Place du Dr. Pierre Walter** in front of the City Hall, a delightful spot where the town's Monday market is held (until 13:00). You'll see the strikingly untouristy Eglantine Shop (artisanal jams and herbs), a nice wine-café for lunch, and a photogenic line of pastel half-timbered homes. The skinny pink one is just a single window wide. To finish your town loop, continue back toward the gate you entered through, noticing a fun balcony to the right that's bedecked with flowers (and witches blowing in the breeze). A few blocks beyond that is the tower's happy sanctuary seeker, still mooning all who pass.

From the roundabout by the southern lot, white signs lead to the solitary and peaceful **German Military Cemetery** *(Deutscher Soldatenfriedhof)*. It's a scenic five-minute drive to the parking lot and a five-minute steep hike from there. You reach a sad bluff blanketed with the tombs of 5,307 German soldiers who died in 1944 and 1945, three names per tombstone, nearly all very young. Almost no one goes here, but I find walking among these tombstones with a view of the Alsatian landscape they fought over thought-provoking.

Strasbourg

Strasbourg is France's seventh-largest city (with 275,000 people) and offers your best chance to experience urban Alsace. It feels like a giant Colmar with rivers and streetcars. Long a humanist and intellectual center, today it has a delightful big-city energy. Walking its people-friendly streets, you'll find generous space devoted to pedestrians and bikes, sleek trams, meandering waterways, and a mix of university students, Eurocrats, and street people. Located on the Franco-German border and with a name that means the "city of streets," it's the ultimate European crossroads.

PLANNING YOUR TIME

Strasbourg makes a good day trip from Colmar. And, thanks to high-speed TGV-train service, it's also a handy stop for train travelers en route to or from Paris (baggage storage available). The city has four main sights: its amazing cathedral, the Strasbourg Historical Museum, the Alsatian Museum, and the characteristic Petite France (Little France) quarter. While you could easily enjoy an entire day here, for a day trip from Colmar (for example) you'll need at least four hours to hit the highlights.

Orientation to Strasbourg

TOURIST INFORMATION

Strasbourg's TI faces the cathedral (daily 9:00-19:00, 17 Place de la Cathédrale, tel. 03 88 52 28 28, www.otstrasbourg.fr, info@otstrasbourg.fr). You can learn about special events (like the summer sound-and-light show at the cathedral), buy the €1.50 city map (which describes a decent walking tour that supplements the one in this chapter), or rent an audioguide for a 1.5-hour tour that covers the cathedral and old city in more detail. The TI also has bike maps for the city and surrounding areas.

Sightseeing Pass: The **Strasbourg Pass** (€21.50), valid three consecutive days, is a great value for busy sightseers. It includes one

ALSACE

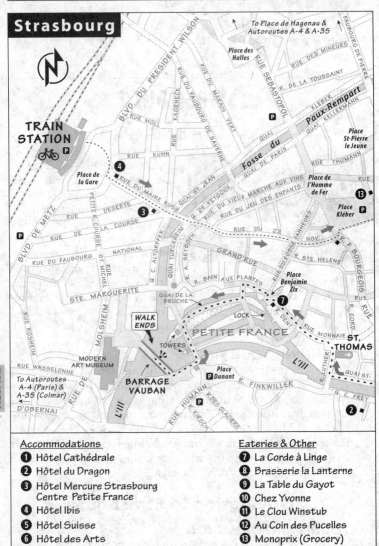

Accommodations
1 Hôtel Cathédrale
2 Hôtel du Dragon
3 Hôtel Mercure Strasbourg Centre Petite France
4 Hôtel Ibis
5 Hôtel Suisse
6 Hôtel des Arts

Eateries & Other
7 La Corde à Linge
8 Brasserie la Lanterne
9 La Table du Gayot
10 Chez Yvonne
11 Le Clou Winstub
12 Au Coin des Pucelles
13 Monoprix (Grocery)

free museum entry and a half-off coupon for another, a discount on the town audioguide, a free boat cruise, a *petit train* tour, and free entry to the cathedral narthex view and the astrological clock tour. The simpler one-day Museum Pass gets you into the town's museums for €12 (sold at participating museums).

ARRIVAL IN STRASBOURG

By Train: TGV trains serve Strasbourg's gleaming train station (free Wi-Fi). Baggage storage is available (platform 1, daily 8:30-

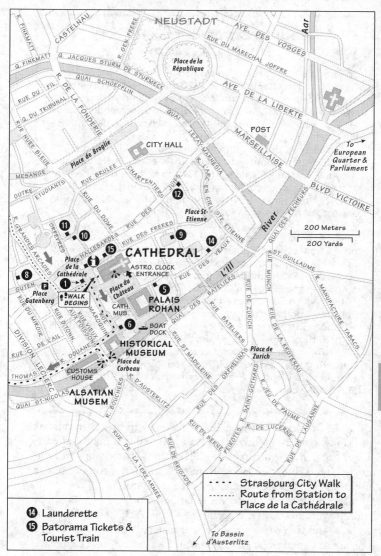

14 Launderette

15 Batorama Tickets & Tourist Train

---- Strasbourg City Walk

.... Route from Station to Place de la Cathédrale

18:30). WCs are across from the stairs to platform 2. Ticket counters are on the north *(nord)* side. Rail-pass holders have access to the Salon Grand Voyageur lounge (see "Strasbourg Connections" at the end of this chapter for more).

To **walk** to the cathedral in 15 urban minutes, exit straight out of the station, cross the big square (Place de la Gare) then walk up Rue du Maire Kuss, and follow the map above.

To get from the train station to the city center by **public transportation,** catch the tram under the station (€1.80, €3.50 round-

Reading Strasbourg's History in its Cityscape

The people of Strasbourg have had a dizzying history: harsh Germanization after the Franco-Prussian War in 1870, extreme Frenchification after World War I, a brutal period under Nazi rule during World War II, and then the intense need to purge all that was German after 1945. The cityscape reflects these changes.

Neustadt, the city's grid-planned district of grand buildings and grand boulevards around Place de la République, was built by the Prussians after 1870 to be a modern, healthy, and easy-to-police center of town filled with Historicism (Neo-Gothic, Neo-Baroque, Neoclassical, and so on...like Vienna) and lots of Art Nouveau (a.k.a. Jugendstihl).

When the Council of Europe was born in 1949 with the goal of winning an enduring European peace, Churchill proposed that it be headquartered in Strasbourg, a living symbol of the hope for perpetual amity between France and Germany. Today, a huge and modern complex northeast of the city center houses the European Court of Human Rights, the European Parliament (which shares administrative responsibilities for the European Union with Brussels and Luxembourg), and other European institutions. An EU visitors center, Lieu d'Europe, is in the 18th-century Villa Kayserguet on Rue Boecklin.

Nowadays, Strasbourg exudes a bicultural gentleness. Bordering the west bank of the Rhine River, the city provides the ultimate blend of Franco-Germanic culture, architecture, and ambience.

ALSACE

trip, €4.50 day pass; buy from machines on platforms, then validate in skinny machines). Take tram #A (direction: Illkirch Graffenstaden) or tram #D (direction: Kehl Bahnhof) three stops to Langross-Grand Rue, two blocks from the cathedral. (You can return to the station, Gare Centrale, from the same stop.)

By Car: From Colmar, you're far better off day-tripping in by train. If you must drive, take *sortie* #4 from A-35 and follow *Centre-Ville* and *Cathédrale* signs. Park at metered street spaces or in a central lot signed as *La Petite France, Gare Centrale*, or *la Cathédrale* (€4/hour, €20/24 hours).

For less money and stress, park outside of town and take the tram in. Follow signs from the same autoroute exit to the *Elsau P+R* (Parking & Relais) lot at the Elsau tram station outside the city center (€4.50/day includes round-trip tram tickets for up to 7 people; take green-line "F" tram in direction: Centre-Ville, exit at Homme de Fer stop). Validate your parking ticket at the tram platform scanner both going and returning.

By Plane: The user-friendly Strasbourg-Entzheim airport

(airport code: SXB, tel. 03 88 64 67 67, www.strasbourg.aeroport.fr), with frequent, often inexpensive flights to Paris, is connected by train to the main rail station (€2.60, 10-minute trip).

HELPFUL HINTS

Quiet Transportation: Beware of quiet trams and bicycles—look both ways before crossing streets.

Free Museums: All museums described in this chapter are free the first Sunday of the month.

Laundry: You'll find a handy launderette at 15 Rue des Veaux, near my recommended hotels (daily 7:00-21:00).

Bike Rental: Vélhop is one level below street level at the train station, with a helpful office that makes renting easy (daily 9:00-19:00, €6/day, €150 deposit, tel. 09 60 17 74 63, www.velhop.strasbourg.eu).

Taxi: Call 03 88 27 13 13 or mobile 06 80 43 22 25.

Car Rental: All major companies are at or near the train station.

Route du Vin Tour: See page 996 for recommended minivan tours of the Route du Vin.

Local Guide: Charming and smart **Audrey Riehm** works with a team of top-quality private guides (€100/hour, €200/half-day, www.guides-alsace.fr).

Free City Tours: An earnest guide team offers free city walks that, while informative, are works in progress. The 1.75-hour tour can be in German, French, and/or English depending on who shows up (skip it if all three languages will be used). Look for the *Free Tour* sign in front of the cathedral after 10:30 and expect to reward your guide with a tip (at 11:00 Sat-Sun, more days may be added, www.strasburg-tours.com).

Tourist Train: Strasbourg's *Petit Train* does a scenic loop around the city's historic core, running from the cathedral (across from TI) to the Barrage Vauban dam and back (€7, May-Sept 10:30-17:30).

Sights in Strasbourg

I've linked Strasbourg's main sights with walking directions: You can connect the sights to form your own fine city walk.

• *Start on the square in front of the cathedral, far enough back to take in the whole scene.*

Place de la Cathédrale

Since Roman times, this square around the cathedral has been the heart of the city—the stage upon which Strasbourg's life plays out. The dark half-timbered building to your left, next to the TI, was the home of a wealthy merchant in the 16th century and symbolizes the virtues of capitalism that Strasbourg has long revered. Goods were sold under the ground-floor arches; owners lived above.

Strasbourg made its medieval mark as a trading center, milking its position at the crossroads of Europe and its access to the important Rhine River to charge tolls for the movement of goods. With all that trade wealth, it could build its glorious cathedral.

Strasbourg's location drew all kinds of people to the city (just like today), making it susceptible to new ideas. Just as the city flipped from German to French and back, it also flipped from Catholic to Protestant and back. As at Wittenberg, Martin Luther's theses were posted on the cathedral's main doors during the Reformation, and after the wars of religion, this cathedral was Protestant for more than 100 years. Then, Louis XIV returned it to Catholicism in 1681.

Grand Rue

As you wander the town, sooner or later you're likely to walk on Grand Rue, the longest street in Strasbourg. Laid out by the Romans, it now links the cathedral with the Petite France quarter. If you find yourself on it, enjoy the mix of historic architecture: protruding oriel windows mark buildings from the German Renaissance, while buildings with wrought iron are likely French from the 1700s.

▲▲▲Strasbourg Cathedral (Cathédrale de Notre-Dame)

If this church, with its cloud-piercing spire and red sandstone, drops your jaw today, imagine its impact on medieval tourists. The

cathedral somehow survived the French Revolution, the Franco-Prussian War, World War I, and World War II. Today, it's the big draw of the city; a steady stream of visitors go through a security check and flow like a river through the building. Don't be swept by the crowds—the interior is worth savoring slowly.

Cost and Hours: Free, Mon-Sat 8:30-11:15 & 12:45-17:45, Sun 13:00-17:30. The midday closing is for a special €3 viewing of the astronomical clock.

Narthex Climb: For €6, you can climb 330 steps to the top of the narthex for an amazing view over Strasbourg, Alsace, the Rhine, and the Black Forest (access on right side of cathedral, daily April-Sept 9:30-20:00, Oct-March 10:00-17:15).

Visiting the Cathedral: Start with the exterior. The delicate Gothic style of the cathedral (begun in 1176, finished in 1439) is the work of a succession of about 50 master builders. An earlier church burned down in the 12th century, and Strasbourg was so wealthy that it rebuilt *très* fancy—with a lacy, innovative, see-through design—and tall (at 466 feet, it was the world's tallest spire until the mid-1800s). A matching second tower was planned but was never built due to concern over stress on the foundations.

Notice the dark-red **stone** that differentiates this cathedral from other great Gothic churches in France. The stones, which date mostly from the 13th and 14th centuries, were quarried from the northern part of the Vosges Mountains. You'll see this stone on fine buildings throughout Strasbourg (which contrasts with the softer, yellower stone of Colmar's churches). Study the intricate carvings on the facade. Look for the sculpture over the lower section of the left portal (calm yet vicious, spear-toting Virtues getting revenge on those nasty Vices).

Enter the cathedral and walk down the center (displays explain highlights in English). The **nave** is notable for its width. An exquisite, gold-leafed organ hangs high above. Admire the elaborately carved stone pulpit, a Flamboyant Gothic masterpiece from the 1400s.

Enjoy the cathedral's marvelous **stained glass**—80 percent is original, surviving from the 12th to 15th centuries. Scenes on the nave's lower left show various rulers of Strasbourg while those on the right depict Bible stories. The rose window is 36 feet wide. Its golden wheat symbolizes the fertile land of Alsace. The cathedral's windows traveled a lot during World War II: hidden by the French in southwestern France first; then carted to northern Germany by the Nazis; and finally saved and returned by the Monuments Men (British and American troops dedicated to returning art to its rightful place after 1945).

Walk to the **choir,** take a seat, and gaze into the Byzantine-like scene with 14th-century paintings still lining the apse. The central high window was replaced after World War II, funded by the European Union. Notice the "brought to you by" EU flag above Mary and Jesus.

Walk to the right side of the apse (near the clock) to see another innovative-at-the-time feature, the eight-sided **"pillar of the angels."** This column is pretty wild for the 14th century—structural yet so decorative, with exquisite carving and expressive faces.

The intricate **astronomical clock** from the 1500s—with more features than my smart phone—was a wonder of its age. It worked like clockwork for generations...until it broke in the 1700s. The workings were replaced in 1842 and—with the help of its "Ecclesiastical Computer" (lower left) that recalibrates the entire thing each year—it's been back at it ever since. Every quarter-hour people

ALSACE

gather for a tiny show (the bell rings and a stage of life—young or old—parades past the grim reaper).

The church is cleared out every day but Sunday between 11:15 and 12:45 for a boring presentation of the clock. Visitors can pay to enter the church from its far right side and see a 20-minute movie (with English) that explains the clock's workings. Then, at 12:30, they witness the clock do its full routine—the biggest of the day. (All in all, this is too crowded and not worth the time.)

• *Next door to the cathedral on Place du Château, you'll find four museums housed in two buildings. These will appeal mostly to aficionados with particular interests or those who have a full day in Strasbourg.*

Art and Artifact Museums
Palais Rohan, a stately former palace, contains three museums: The **Archaeological Museum** presents Alsatian civilization through the millennia (includes audioguide). The **Museum of Decorative Arts** feels like a mini-Versailles in the heart of Strasbourg (pick up the English explanations). And the **Museum of Fine Arts** holds a well-displayed collection of paintings from the Middle Ages to the Baroque period. The **Museum of the Cathedral** (Musée de l'Œuvre Notre-Dame), next door, has plenty of church artifacts, mostly from the cathedral (includes good audioguide).

Cost and Hours: €6.50 each, €12 day pass covers all four; open Wed-Mon 10:00-18:00, closed Tue; both buildings on Place du Château.

• *Facing the cathedral, go right down Rue du Maroquin, enjoying the fine old buildings and restaurants. Turn right on Place de la Grande Boucherie and go one block to find the Strasbourg Historical Museum.*

▲▲Strasbourg Historical Museum
This wonderful museum takes you on a sweep through the city's complex and fascinating history, with artifacts, good English descriptions, and a fine (included) audioguide. You'll learn the impact of becoming a free Imperial city—how Strasbourg was fortified with concentric walls and eighty towers, which were then destroyed by Louis XIV as he centralized France in the 1680s. There's an exhibit about Johannes Gutenberg, who worked here from 1434 to 1444, a section about the French Revolution, and a description of how the Prussians rebuilt the city after destroying much of it in 1870, ushering in its glory days (1880 to 1914). There's a sad section about the Nazi years and a happy finale with Strasbourg's leadership role in the EU.

Cost and Hours: €6.50, Tue-Sun 10:00-18:00, closed Mon, 2 Rue du Vieux-Marché-aux-Poissons, tel. 03 68 98 51 60, www.musees.strasbourg.eu/musee-historique.

• *From the history museum, cross the river on the Pont du Corbeau and look back. Survey the city from this historic Ill River crossing. The history museum fills a former slaughterhouse. Across the street, along the river is the very long 14th-century Customs House where taxes were paid on all river trade. Look back at the lacy spire of the cathedral in the distance. River cruises depart a block to your right (see "Activities in Strasbourg," later); across the street (behind you) is the Alsatian Museum.*

▲Alsatian Museum

One of Strasbourg's oldest and most traditional houses hosts this extensive and well-presented collection of Alsatian folk art. Thanks to its many artifacts, audioguide, and printed English explanations, you'll learn much about Alsatian life and traditions from birth to death. Rooms you'd find in traditional homes are beautifully re-created here (wrapped around a fine old courtyard), and models explain the ins and outs of half-timbered construction. You'll see tools, pottery, elaborate furnishings, toys, and folk costumes from Alsatian culture through the centuries. There's also a room devoted to Jewish culture in Alsace.

Cost and Hours: €6.50, includes audioguide, Wed-Mon 10:00-18:00, closed Tue, 23 Quai St. Nicholas, tel. 03 88 52 50 01, www.musees.strasbourg.eu.

• *Backtrack across the bridge and continue along the river past the Customs House. At the second bridge turn right and follow Rue Martin Luther to the big, blocky church.*

St. Thomas Church

The big, bold red sandstone blocks seem to boast: This is the biggest Protestant church in France. While the architecture is medieval, in 1529 the Reformation hit, the Catholic ornamentation was swept away, and it's been Protestant ever since. Today the church is known for its fine acoustics, prestigious 1741 Silbermann organ (which was played by Mozart), and its frequent concerts (open 10:00-18:00, 11 Rue Martin Luther).

• *Turn left through Place Saint-Thomas and follow the pedestrian Rue de la Monnaie ("Street of Money") into the old commercial zone. Wander down the lane until you reach the convivial, riverside Place Benjamin Zix.*

▲Petite France

Strasbourg's popular Petite France ("Little France") quarter is where the river is split into several canals with weirs, a lock, and a swing bridge—all reminders of a time when trade came by river and watermills powered local industry. This was the craft guild's district of town, busy with tanners, millers, and fishermen. Many of the charming 16th- and 17th-century half-timbered buildings have open lofts used for drying hides.

The district's nickname predates all this industry. In the 1400s there was a hospice here for people suffering from what Germans

ALSACE

called "the French Disease" (syphilis). The district was slated for redevelopment but was saved by a progressive French minister of culture in the 1970s. Today, these fine buildings are protected and give us a sense of this pre-electricity world. Place Benjamin Zix is a Hansel-and-Gretel fantasy—a delight even with hordes of visitors. And the canalside parks farther out provide a peaceful place for locals to relax.

• *Follow the water from Place Benjamin Zix and cross the canal on the small bridge, then turn right and walk through the park to its far end. From there, across the road and the water, you'll see the...*

Barrage Vauban

This big dam was built in 1690 over the River Ill as part of Strasbourg's defenses. Known as "the Great Lock," during times of attack, it could flood the land south of the city, mucking up the enemy's plans. It was used to create just such a flood in 1870 when the Prussians attacked. Today it's just a scenic viewpoint and a reminder to be thankful for peace in Europe.

• *Turn left on the road (Ponts Couverts) and cross two bridges to the river's far bank. Turn right and walk to the Barrage where you can take steps or a lift to the top of the dam.*

From atop the Barrage Vauban you get a fine perspective of four guard towers that protected the six waterways leading into Strasbourg's old city. Both ends of the dam also have steps leading down to street level. From here it's just a 15-minute walk back to the train station (see the "Strasbourg" map).

Activities in Strasbourg

Boat Ride (Batorama) on the Ill River

To see the cityscape from the water, take a loop cruise around Strasbourg on the Ill River. The glass-topped boats are air-conditioned and sufficiently comfortable— both sides have fine views. You'll pass through two locks as you circle the old city clockwise. A highlight is cruising by the European Parliament buildings and the European Court of Human Rights. Buy tickets at their shop next to the TI at 18 Place de la Cathédrale, or from machines at the boat docks (buy early in the  day for the best choice of departure times).

Cost and Hours: €13, 70 minutes, good audioguide; April-Oct daily 9:45-19:30, until later in high season, shorter hours off-season, dock is outside cathedral's right transept—where Rue Rohan meets the river, tel. 03 88 84 13 13, www.batorama.fr.

Traditional Music and Dancing

On Sunday mornings from late July to late August, look for Alsatian folk dancing on Place Gutenberg (starting at about 10:45). During the same season on Mondays, Tuesdays, and Wednesdays from 20:30 to 22:00, listen to traditional music on various squares around town (Mon—Place des Tripiers, Tue—in La Petite France on Place Benjamin Zix, and Wed—Place du Marché aux Cochons de Lait).

Cathedral Sound-and-Light Shows

Every night from mid-July to early September, a sound-and-light show bathes the soaring cathedral in colorful lights (free, runs every 30 minutes until 24:30, from 22:30 in July, 22:15 in Aug, and 21:15 in Sept).

Christmas Market

From the last Saturday of November until December 31, the city bustles and sparkles with its delightful Christkindelsmärik, held on several squares in the old town (hotel rates climb, and rooms book up well in advance).

Sleeping in Strasbourg

Strasbourg is quieter in the summer (July-Aug), when 4,000 Eurocrats leave town and hotel prices fall—and slammed when the parliament is in session, throughout December (thanks to the Christmas market), and during major conferences. All hotels listed next have elevators and air-conditioning unless otherwise noted.

$$$ Hôtel Cathédrale*** is pricey and a little tired with a Jack-and-the-beanstalk spiral stairway. But this modern-yet-atmospheric place lets you stare at the cathedral point-blank from your room—for a price (rooms without views reasonably priced, laundry service, bicycles available for guests, 12 Place de la Cathédrale, tel. 03 88 22 12 12, www.hotel-cathedrale.fr, booking@hotel-cathedrale.fr).

$$ Hôtel du Dragon*** is a tasteful, modern, well-run, and spotless business-class place with an outdoor patio (12 Rue du Dragon, tel. 03 88 35 79 80, www.dragon.fr, sleep@dragon.fr).

$$ Hôtel Mercure Strasbourg Centre Petite France*** has all the comforts a few blocks from the station-area seediness toward the cathedral (3 Rue du Maire Kuss, tel. 03 88 32 80 80, www.mercure.com, h1813@accor.com).

$ Hôtel Ibis*** faces the train station and delivers its usual comfort and amenities at fair rates (10 Place de la Gare, tel. 03 88 23 98 98, https://ibis.accorhotels.com, h3018@accor.com).

$ Hôtel Suisse,** across from the cathedral, is a welcoming, central, and solid two-star value with sharp rooms and a delightful front terrace (cozy lounge-café, no air-con or elevator, 2 Rue de la Râpe, tel. 03 88 35 22 11, www.hotel-suisse.com, info@hotel-suisse.com, engaging owner Edith).

$ Hôtel des Arts,** located in the thick of things above a busy café, is a simple, sparse budget option. It has tight bathrooms but is comfortable enough and offers good value. Rooms in front can be noisy (no elevator, 10 Place du Marché aux Cochons de Lait, tel. 03 88 37 98 37, www.hotel-arts.com, info@hotel-arts.com).

Eating in Strasbourg

Atmospheric *winstubs* (wine bars) serving affordable salads and *tarte flambée* are a snap to find. If the weather's nice, I'd head for Petite France and choose ambience over cuisine—dine outside at the café/*winstub* that appeals. Stock up on picnic supplies at the Monoprix (Mon-Sat 8:30-20:30) on Place Kléber or at gourmet Alsatian specialty shops on Rue des Orfèvres and take them to the park near Barrage Vauban.

IN AND NEAR LA PETITE FRANCE

$$ La Corde à Linge (The Clothesline), right on Place Benjamin Zix, is a good choice for location, vibe, and price (big salads, burgers, and several intriguing *Spätzle plats*, tel. 03 88 22 15 17).

$ Brasserie la Lanterne, between Petite France and the cathedral, is a down-and-dirty Alsatian microbrewery filled with students and young, hip locals. This place is known for its home brews and cheap cuisine (including *tarte flambée*), and makes me want to plot a revolution (daily 16:00-late, near Place Kléber at 5 Rue de la Lanterne, tel. 03 88 32 10 10).

NEAR THE CATHEDRAL

For a full-blown dining experience, skip the touristy restaurants on the cathedral square and along Rue du Maroquin. Consider these nearby places instead.

For outdoor dining with ambience (ideal for lunch or dinner) head behind the cathedral a few blocks to Place du Marché Gayot, where relaxed places line the atmospheric square. **$ La Table du Gayot** at #8 is a top choice with well-priced salads and *plats* (daily for lunch, closed Sun for dinner, tel. 03 88 36 30 27).

The next two places are one block behind the TI:

$$ Chez Yvonne (marked *S'Burjerstuewel* above windows), right out of a Bruegel painting, has a tradition of quality cuisine at fair prices. Try the *coq au Riesling* or *choucroute garnie* or the *salade alsacienne* (reservations smart, daily from 18:00, 10 Rue du Sanglier, tel. 03 88 32 84 15, www.restaurant-chez-yvonne.net).

$$ Le Clou Winstub, half a block left down Rue du Chaudron at #3, is *très* cozy and Alsatian-traditional as it gets (closed Sun, dinner served from 18:00, tel. 03 88 32 11 67).

$$ Au Coin des Pucelles is an institution for discerning locals. The kind owners welcome diners at shared tables in a warm atmosphere and serve generous portions of Alsatian dishes—the *choucroute* is tops (open 19:00 until late, closed Sun, reservations recommended, 12 Rue des Pucelles, tel. 03 88 35 35 14, www. aucoindespucelles.fr).

Strasbourg Connections

Strasbourg makes a good side-trip from Colmar or a stop on the way to or from Paris. If you have time to kill at the station and have a rail pass, find the **Salon Grand Voyageur** by track 1 (near the *Consigne Baggage*) and enjoy a peaceful lounge with free filtered water, coffee, and good WCs.

From Strasbourg by Train to: Colmar (2/hour, 35 minutes), **Reims** (hourly, 2 hours, change at Gare Champagne-Ardenne), **Verdun** (5/day, 2 hours, 1-2 transfers), **Paris'** Gare de l'Est (hourly with TGV, under 2 hours, just as fast but cheaper by Ouigo trains, www.oui.sncf), **Lyon** (5/day direct, 4 hours), **Baden-Baden,** Germany (TGV: 1/day direct, 30 minutes; otherwise hourly, 70 minutes, change in Appenweier or Offenburg), **Karlsruhe,** Germany (TGV: 4/day direct, 40 minutes; otherwise hourly, 1-1.5 hours, with change in Appenweier or Offenburg), **Munich,** Germany (TGV; 5/day, 4 hours, most with 1 change; non-TGV train: 5/day, 5 hours, 2 changes), **Basel,** Switzerland (regional train: 2/hour, 1.5 hours).

ALSACE

REIMS & VERDUN

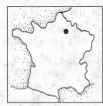

Different as night and day, bubbly Reims and brooding Verdun offer worthwhile stops between Paris and Alsace. The administrative capital of the Champagne region, bustling, modern Reims greets travelers with cellar doors wide open. It features a lively center, a historic cathedral, and, of course, Champagne tasting. Too-often overlooked, quiet Verdun is famous for the brutal WWI battles that surrounded the small city and pummeled the countryside, and offers an exceptional opportunity to learn about the Great War. High-speed TGV trains make these destinations accessible to all travelers.

PLANNING YOUR TIME

Organized travelers can see Reims and Verdun in a day and a half as they travel between Paris and the Alsace (with an overnight in Reims). Plan on most of a day for Reims and at least a half-day for Verdun. It's about 70 miles between the two towns, making a day trip from Reims to Verdun doable if you have a car, but it's challenging by train. Day-tripping by train from Paris to Reims is a breeze, but getting to Verdun from Paris requires planning (think about spending a night).

GETTING AROUND REIMS AND VERDUN

A car is sans doubt the most efficient way to tour this region. You'll do fine without one in Reims: The town is easily walkable, and excellent public transportation links its major sights. But for touring Verdun battlefield sights, it's close to essential to rent a car—whether you choose to drive yourself or arrange for a private guide to accompany you. Other options for touring the Verdun sights include a hop-on, hop-off bus or a taxi (see "Getting Around the Battlefields," later.)

Many find Reims a good place to pick up a rental car for a longer trip after leaving Paris. Train travelers from Paris will reach Reims before drivers get out of the city. Verdun is just off the A-4 autoroute (an hour from Reims, 2.5 hours from Paris, and 3 hours from Colmar).

Frequent high-speed TGV trains link central Paris and Reims in 45 minutes, and a few TGV trains link Paris and Verdun in 1.5 hours. Several trains per day connect Charles de Gaulle Airport to Reims (via its Champagne-Ardenne train station) in about one hour. Most train connections between Reims and Verdun take about three hours each way.

CHAMPAGNE'S CUISINE SCENE

Contrary to popular belief, Champagne is wine that can easily accompany an entire meal. Locals drink Champagne with everything here. And just as the Burgundians cook many of their meat and poultry dishes with their local red wine, the Champenois cook with bubbly (on menus you'll see *à la champenoise*).

This is a "meaty" region: Most menus will offer foie gras, raw *tartares*, loads of beef, and some dishes you may choose to avoid, such as *rognons, ris de veau, tête de veau, pieds de porc, andouillette*, and *boudin noir* (kidneys, sweetbreads, calf's head, pig's feet, tripe sausage, and blood sausage, respectively). Despite its reputation, I find *boudin noir* delicious. *La potée champenoise* (also called *La Joute*) is like a *pot-au-feu* stew, made of smoked ham, chicken, sausage, and vegetables with lots of cabbage. *Boudin blanc* is a moist, white sausage made from pork or chicken, eggs, cream, and spices. Many salads and starters include *jambon de Reims,* the local smoked ham. *Andouillette de Troyes* is a tripe sausage that you can smell from across the room. Ample rivers make for flavorful trout *(truite)* dishes. You may also find rooster cooked in the rare local red wine known as Bouzy Rouge *(coq au vin de Bouzy)*.

Brie de Meaux cheese, made on Champagne's border, is the most flavorful Brie, as it's unpasteurized. Other local cheeses include Cendré de Champagne (similar to Brie but the size of a large Camembert, with a thin ash covering), Chaource (a young, creamy, and mild cheese in a cylindrical shape), and Langres (orange-colored rind, creamy and pungent, usually aged). All of these listed cheeses have edible rinds.

Biscuits roses de Reims (pink cookies) are on every bakery shelf in town. Traditionally dunked in Champagne, this ladyfinger-style treat also goes well with afternoon coffee or tea and is often used in local desserts, such as *charlotte aux biscuits roses* (trifle). Fruit-flavored brandies are a common way to end an evening.

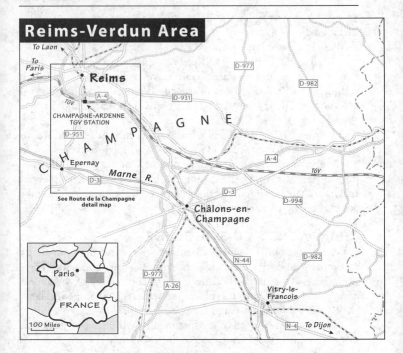

Reims-Verdun Area

To Laon
To Paris
Reims
D-977
D-982
A-4
TGV
D-931
CHAMPAGNE-ARDENNE
TGV STATION
C   H   A   M   P   A   G   N   E
D-951
A-4
TGV
C   H   A   M   P   A   G   N   E
Epernay
Marne R.
D-994
D-3
D-3
See Route de la Champagne
detail map
Châlons-en-
Champagne
D-982
N-44
Paris
D-977
D-982
A-26
Vitry-le-
Francois
FRANCE
100 Miles
N-4   To Dijon

Reims

With its Roman gate, Gothic cathedral, Champagne *caves*, and vibrant pedestrian zone, Reims feels both historic and youthful. And thanks to the TGV bullet train, it's less than an hour's ride from Paris.

Reims (pronounced like "rance") has a turbulent history: This is where 25 French kings were crowned, where Champagne first bubbled, where WWI devastation met miraculous reconstruction during the Art Deco age, and where the Germans officially surrendered in 1945, bringing World War II to a close in Europe. The town's sights give you an entertaining peek at the entire story.

PLANNING YOUR TIME

You can see Reims' essential sights in an easy day, either as a day trip from Paris or as a stop en route to or from Paris. Because some trains connect Charles de Gaulle Airport directly with Reims, this can be a handy first- or last-night stop. Take a morning train from Paris and explore the cathedral and city center before lunch, then spend your afternoon below ground, in a cool, chalky Champagne cellar or *cave* (pronounced "kahv"). You can be back at your Parisian hotel by dinner.

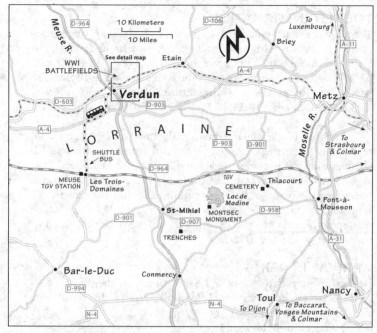

With a car, it's worth taking a few hours to joyride the Champagne road that leaves from Reims' back step (described later). Day-tripping drivers can arrange to pick up their car near either of the Reims train stations and visit the city before continuing on (storing bags at the rental office or in the car at the train station's secure parking).

To best experience contemporary Reims, explore the busy shopping streets between the cathedral and the Reims-Centre train station. Rue de Vesle, Rue Condorcet, and Place Drouet d'Erlon are most interesting. Try to visit Reims on a Saturday, when the market erupts inside the dazzling Halles Boulingrin, and surrounding streets are lively. Sundays are *très* quiet and worth avoiding—handy buses don't run, and so much is closed that it's hard to get a feel for the town.

Orientation to Reims

Reims' hard-to-miss cathedral marks the city center and makes an easy orientation landmark. Most sights of interest are within a 15-minute walk from the Reims-Centre train station. City buses and taxis connect the harder-to-reach Champagne *caves* with the central train station and cathedral. The city is ambitiously renovating its downtown, converting large areas into pedestrian-friendly zones.

REIMS & VERDUN

TOURIST INFORMATION

The main TI is one block away from the cathedral at 6 Rue Rock-efeller (Easter-Sept Mon-Sat 9:00-19:00, Sun 10:00-18:00, Oct-Easter Mon-Sat 9:00-18:00, Sun 10:00-12:30 & 13:30-17:00; tel. 03 26 77 45 00, www.reims-tourisme.com). A smaller TI lies just outside the Reims-Centre **train station** (Mon-Sat 8:30-12:30 & 13:30-18:00, Sun 10:00-11:30 & 12:30-16:00, Oct-Easter closed Sun).

At either TI, pick up free maps of the town center, the bus and tram routes, and the Champagne *caves*. Ask at the cathedral TI about renting a tablet videoguide for visiting the cathedral and city.

TIs will call a taxi (about €10) to get you to any Champagne house that you book. TIs also have information on minivan excursions into the vineyards and Champagne villages. For more information on reservations and reaching the *caves*, see "Reims' Champagne *Caves*" on page 1049.

ARRIVAL IN REIMS

By Train: From Paris' Gare de l'Est station, take the direct TGV to the **Reims-Centre** station (12/day, 50 minutes). In Reims, the small TI is to your right as you exit; a taxi office is to your left (taxis wait in front of the station at busy times).

Trains also run directly from Charles de Gaulle Airport to the **Champagne-Ardenne TGV** station five miles away from Reims-Centre station (4/day, 45 minutes). Other TGV trains from Paris destined for Germany or Alsace also stop at the Champagne-Ardenne station. From there, take a local "milk-run" (TER) train to Reims-Centre (TER usually leaves 15 minutes after TGV arrival, 15 minutes to Reims-Centre station), or ride tram #B into the city center (3/hour, 20 minutes, direction: Neufchâtel; walk downhill from the station to find the tram stop; see "Getting Around Reims" for ticket information).

By Car: Day-trippers should follow *Cathédrale* signs, and park in metered spots on or near the cathedral or in the well-signed Parking Cathédrale structure. If you'll be staying the night, take the *Reims-Centre* exit from the autoroute for most of my recommended hotels, and park in the Erlon parking garage—enter from Boulevard du Général Leclerc.

REIMS & VERDUN

HELPFUL HINTS

Department Store: Monoprix is inside the Espace Drouet d'Erlon shopping center (Mon-Sat 9:00-20:00, Sun until 13:00, basement level, 53 Place Drouet d'Erlon, follow *FNAC* signs).

Baggage Storage: Stash your bags a minute from the train station at the **Ibis Reims Centre Hotel** (turn left directly as you exit the station, small fee, 28 Boulevard Joffre, tel. 03 26 40 03 24).

Laundry: You'll find a launderette a 10-minute walk south of the cathedral (long hours daily, 49 Avenue Gambetta).

Bike Rental: Manu Loca Vélo delivers bikes within about 10 miles of Reims (reservations required, mobile 06 51 27 24 10, manulocavelo@hotmail.fr).

Taxi: Taxi offices are at the train station and at 40 Rue Carnot, next to the Opéra. Or you can call 03 26 03 03 00.

Car Rental: Single-day or longer car rental in Reims is usually reasonable even when booked late. **Avis** is just outside the central train station at 20 Rue Pingat (tel. 03 26 47 10 08, use the *Clairmarais* exit from the station, turn right, and walk 200 yards); another office is in front of the Champagne-Ardenne TGV station (tel. 03 61 58 82 71). **Europcar** is at 76 Boulevard Lundy (tel. 09 77 40 32 61); **Hertz** is at 26 Boulevard Joffre (tel. 03 26 47 98 78). Rental agencies are usually open Mon-Sat 8:00-12:00 & 14:00-18:00; most are closed Sun and some close early Sat afternoon.

Bus Tours: Reims City Tour offers a one-hour circuit of the city (€10-15, 3-5 trips/day in summer, fewer in winter, recorded commentary). Purchase tickets from the main TI or online, departure behind the cathedral (www.reims-citytour.com).

Champagne Tours: See page 1049.

GETTING AROUND REIMS

By Bus or Tram: Reims has an integrated network of colorful buses, trams, and an electric shuttle bus (www.citura.fr, French only, but excellent maps). You can purchase tickets from the driver on the bus and shuttle but not on trams; it's better to use the ticket machines at any tram stop (€1.60/1 hour, €4/24 hours, €12.50/10 1-hour tickets that can be shared; coins only, no credit cards). Your ticket is valid for unlimited transfers between all buses and trams, even a round-trip on the same line. Each time you board a bus or tram, hold your ticket to the validation machine until you hear a beep.

The **tram** system's two lines—#A and #B—connect Reims' two train stations and travel on to a few stops in town (about every 10 minutes, fewer on Sun). To get from either station to the cathedral, main TI, and town center, take a tram to the Opéra stop.

The bright-green **CityBus** electric shuttle (#C) makes a loop

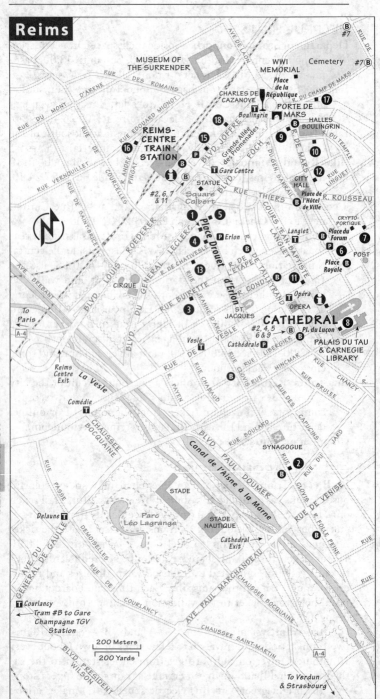

Reims

MUSEUM OF
THE SURRENDER

WWI
MEMORIAL
Place de
la République

Cemetery #7 Ⓑ

CHARLES DE
CAZANOVE

Ⓑ #7

PORTE DE
MARS

17

Boulingrin

HALLES
BOULINGRIN

18

REIMS-
CENTRE
TRAIN
STATION

16

15

9

10

12

#2, 6, 7
& 11

STATUE
Square
Colbert

1

5

Erlon

4

13

3

CITY
HALL

Place de
l'Hôtel
de Ville

CRYPTO-
PORTIQUE

Place du
Forum

7

Langlet

6

POST

Place
Royale

11

Opéra

OPÉRA

CATHEDRAL

#2, 4, 5
6 & 9

8

Pl. du Luçon

PALAIS DU TAU
& CARNEGIE
LIBRARY

CIRQUE

ST.
JACQUES

Vesle

Cathédrale

Canal de l'Aisne à la Marne

SYNAGOGUE

2

STADE

Parc
Léo Lagrange

STADE
NAUTIQUE

Cathedral
Exit

Comédie

CHAUSSEE
BOCQUAINE

Reims
Centre
Exit

La Vesle

To
Paris
A-4

Delaune

Courlancy
← Tram #B to Gare
Champagne TGV
Station

To Verdun
& Strasbourg →
A-4

200 Meters
200 Yards

REIMS & VERDUN

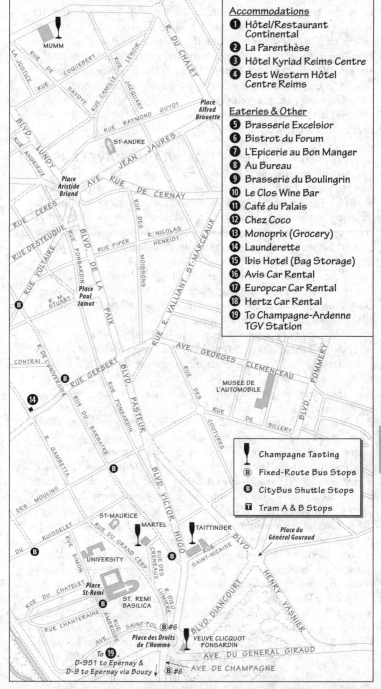

Accommodations

1 Hôtel/Restaurant Continental
2 La Parenthèse
3 Hôtel Kyriad Reims Centre
4 Best Western Hôtel Centre Reims

Eateries & Other

5 Brasserie Excelsior
6 Bistrot du Forum
7 L'Epicerie au Bon Manger
8 Au Bureau
9 Brasserie du Boulingrin
10 Le Clos Wine Bar
11 Café du Palais
12 Chez Coco
13 Monoprix (Grocery)
14 Launderette
15 Ibis Hotel (Bag Storage)
16 Avis Car Rental
17 Europcar Car Rental
18 Hertz Car Rental
19 To Champagne-Ardenne TGV Station

Champagne Tasting
B Fixed-Route Bus Stops
B CityBus Shuttle Stops
T Tram A & B Stops

REIMS & VERDUN

from the Reims-Centre station to the cathedral; then to the St. Remi and St. Timothée stops (close to Martel and Taittinger *caves*); then to the Carnegie Library, Place du Forum, and Halles Boulingrin (near recommended restaurants); and then back to the station (30 minutes for full loop). Wave at the driver to stop (Mon-Sat 9:00-19:00, no service Sunday, free for up to 5 people with Erlon parking garage receipt).

Regular **fixed-route buses** also cover the city center; the most useful ones are listed under each sight.

BLITZ WALKING TOUR FOR TRAIN TRAVELERS

If you're racing through Reims, here's a quick walking plan that follows the order of its main sights. These highlights can be seen on foot in a three-hour sightseeing stroll from the train station (add another two hours to visit a cellar, and another hour each per museum visit). Pick up a town map from the TI just outside the train station before you begin, and see the complete sight descriptions under "Sights in Reims," later.

If you plan to visit the Museum of the Surrender, check their hours locally first (you can start there and do this walk in reverse—especially fun on a Wed, Fri, or Sat morning, when the market at Halles Boulingrin is in full swing).

From the station (which retains its original 1860 facade), walk directly into the park out front. Find the statue of hometown boy Jean-Baptiste Colbert, the finance minister of Louis XIV back in the 17th century.

The **park,** or Grande Allée des Promenades, was originally a garden outside the city walls. In 1848, when it was clear that Reims didn't need a protective wall, the fortifications were demolished to create a three-mile-long circular boulevard. Look at your town map to see the "left foot"-shaped outline left by the wall.

From Colbert, angle to the right, cross what was the wall, and walk along **Place Drouet d'Erlon.** This long, pedestrianized street-like square marks the commercial center of town. It's Reims' "little Champs-Elysées." Stroll two long blocks up to the square's centerpiece: a **fountain** and column crowned by a glistening gold-winged figure of Victory. (The original Victory, from 1906, was melted down by the Nazis—the current one is a recent replacement.) The fountain—with four voluptuous women—celebrates the four major rivers of this district.

While World War II left the city unscathed, World War I devastated Reims. It was the biggest city on France's Western Front, and it was hammered. Sixty-five percent of Reims was destroyed by shelling, and in 1918 only 70 buildings remained undamaged. The area around you was entirely rebuilt in the 1920s. If it looks eclectic, that's because the mayor at the time said to build any way you like—just build. Make a little spin tour to survey the facades.

All around you'll see the stylized features—geometric reliefs, motifs in ironwork, rounded corners, and simple concrete elegance—of **Art Deco.** The only hints that this was once a medieval town are the narrow lots that struggle to accommodate today's buildings. Continue along the square to check out the building at #15, which is fake half-timbered (in concrete), and the three Art Deco facades at #19-21. Where Place Drouet d'Erlon ends (at a small fountain), pop into the **Waida Pâtisserie** at #5 for a pure, typical Art Deco interior.

While at Waida, consider picking up a quiche and some pastries to enjoy on the cathedral square. They also sell *biscuits roses de Reims*—light, rose-colored egg-and-sugar cookies that have been made since 1756. They're the locals' favorite munchie to accompany a glass of Champagne—you're supposed to dunk them, but I like them dry (many places that sell these treats offer free samples).

From here, cut over to the left (Rue Condorcet works), then take a right on Rue de Talleyrand; you can't miss **Reims Cathedral.**

The **cathedral museum** (Palais du Tau) and **Carnegie Library** are next to the church. From the Cathédrale stop near the TI, you can catch the electric CityBus #C to the Taittinger and Martel Champagne *caves* (see "Reims' Champagne Caves," later), or continue your walk via **Place du Forum** (the former Roman forum) to **Porte de Mars** (the old Roman gate). Near Porte de Mars you can't miss the restored 1927 **Art Deco covered market hall** (Halles Boulingrin). From here, the **Museum of the Surrender** is a short walk across the intersection, behind the train station. Just like that, you've seen the highlights of the city. Now it's time for a nice glass of Champagne.

Sights in Reims

▲▲▲REIMS CATHEDRAL

The cathedral of Reims is a glorious example of Gothic architecture, and one of Europe's greatest churches. (Expect to see scaffolding during ongoing restoration work.) It celebrated its 800th birthday in 2011. Clovis, the first Christian king of the Franks, was baptized at a church on this site in AD 496, establishing France's Christian roots, which still hold firm today. Since Clovis' baptism, Reims Cathedral has served as *the* place for the coronation of 26 French kings, giving it a more important role in France's political history than Notre-Dame Cathedral in Paris. This cathedral is to France what Westminster Abbey is to England.

And there's a lot more history here. A self-assured Joan of

Arc led a less-assured Charles VII to be crowned here in 1429. Thanks to Joan, the French rallied around their new king to push the English out of France and finally end the Hundred Years' War. During the French Revolution, the cathedral was converted to a temple of reason (as was Paris' Notre-Dame). After the restoration of the monarchy, the cathedral hosted the crowning of Charles X in 1825—the last coronation here. During World War I about 300 shells hit the cathedral, damaging statues and windows and destroying the roof, but the structure survived. Then, during the 1920s, it was completely rebuilt, thanks in large part to financial support from John D. Rockefeller Jr.

Luckily, World War II spared the church, and since then it has come to symbolize reconciliation. A French plaque set in the pavement just in front recalls the 1962 Mass of Reconciliation between France and Germany. A German version of the marker was added in 2012, commemorating 50 years of friendship and celebrating the belief that another war today between these two nations would be unthinkable.

Cost and Hours: Free, daily 7:30-19:15, helpful information boards in English throughout the church (www.reims-cathedral.culture.fr). You can rent tablet-based videoguides at the cathedral TI, but my self-guided tour below works well for most.

Getting There: The cathedral is a 15-minute walk from the Reims-Centre station. Follow *sortie* signs for Place de la Gare, then walk to the TI on the right and follow the map on page 1038. You can also catch the green electric CityBus #C from in front of the station (5-minute ride to the cathedral).

Cathedral Tower: An escorted one-hour tour climbs the 250 steps of the tower to explore the rooftop and get a close-up look at the Gallery of Kings statuary (€8, €11 combo-ticket with Palais du Tau; reserve tickets on cathedral website on day of your visit, get hours at TI or Palais du Tau, where you'll pick up tickets and meet escort).

Cathedral Sound-and-Light Show (Rêve de Couleurs): For a memorable experience, join the crowd in front of the cathedral for a free, 25-minute sound-and-light show on most summer evenings. The colorful lights and booming sound take you through the ages, evoking the building's design and construction, the original appearance of the statuary, the coronations that occurred here, the faith of the community, and—during the centennial of the Great War—the shelling it absorbed during World War I. Sit directly in front of the cathedral or settle more comfortably into a seat at a café with a clear view through the trees. The show generally starts when it's dark—between 21:30 and 23:00 (TI has the schedule, nightly except Mon July-Aug, Wed-Sun only in June). Sometimes a second show commences 10 minutes after the first show ends.

⊘ Self-Guided Tour: Begin your visit by admiring the cathedral's **West Portal.** It's perhaps the best west portal anywhere. Built under the direction of four different architects, it is remarkable for its unity and harmony. The church was started in about 1211 and mostly finished just 60 years later. The 260-foot-tall towers were added in the 1400s; the spires intended to top them were never installed for lack of money.

Like the cathedrals in Paris and Chartres, this church is dedicated to **"Our Lady"** (Notre Dame). Statues depicting the crowning of the Virgin take center stage on the facade. For eight centuries Catholics have prayed to the Mother of God, kneeling here to ask her to intervene with God on their behalf. In 1429, Joan of Arc received messages here from Mary encouraging her to rally French troops against the English at the Siege of Orléans (a statue of Joan from 1896 is over your left shoulder as you face the church).

An ornate facade like this comes with a cohesive and carefully designed message. Study the carving. A good percentage of the statues are original and date from around 1250. There are **three main doors,** each with a theme carved into the limestone.

On the left is the **Passion** (the events leading up to and including the Crucifixion). Among the local saints shown below is the famous Smiling Angel, whose jovial expression has served the city well as its marketing icon. The central portal is dedicated to the **Virgin Mary,** featuring the Coronation of Mary with scenes from her life below. And on the right is the **Last Judgment,** with scenes from the apocalypse. Above the great rose window are reliefs of David (with his dog) and Goliath. Notice the fire damage, from 1914, around the rose window (fire melts limestone). Across the top is the **Gallery of Kings,** depicting 56 of France's kings. They flank the country's first Christian king, Clovis, who appears to be wearing a barrel—he's actually kneeling prayerfully at a baptismal font. These anonymous statues, without egos, are unnamed kings whose spiritual mission is to lead their people to God.

Before going inside, step around to the right side and study the exoskeletal nature of the church's structure. Braces on the outside—**flying buttresses**—soar up the sides of the church. These massive "beams" are critical to supporting the building, redirecting the weight of the roof outward (and into the ground), rather than downward on the supporting walls. With the support provided by the columns, arches, and buttresses, the walls—which no longer needed to be so solid and thick—became window holders.

The architects of Reims Cathedral were confident in their building practices. Gothic architects had learned by trial and error—many church roofs caved in as they tested their theories and strove to build ever higher. Work on Reims Cathedral began decades after the Notre-Dame cathedrals in Paris and Chartres, allowing architects to take advantage of what they'd learned from those magnificent earlier structures.

Contemplate the lives of the people in Reims who built this huge building in the 13th century. Construction on a scale like this required a wholesale community effort—all hands on deck. The builders of the Reims Cathedral gave it their all, in part because this was the church of France—where its kings were crowned. Most townsfolk who participated donated their money or their labor knowing that neither they, nor their children, would likely ever see it completed—such was their pride, dedication, and faith. Imagine the effort it took to raise the funds and manage the workforce. Master masons supervised, while the average Jean did much of the sweat work.

Now, step inside and stand at the back of the nearly 500-foot-long **nave.** The weight of the roof is supported by a few towering columns that seem to sprout crisscrossing pointed arches. This load-bearing skeleton of columns, arches, and buttresses allowed the church to grow higher. Sun pours through the **stained glass,** bathing visitors and worshippers in divine light.

Take a look at the wall of **52 statues** stacked in rectangular blocks inside the door. (Cover the light from the door with this book to see better.) Imagine the 13th-century technology employed to carve each of these blocks in the nearby workshop and then install them so seamlessly here. These blocks continue the stories told by the statues on the outside.

Walk up the central aisle until you find a **plaque in the floor** marking the site of Clovis' baptism in 496. Back then, a much smaller, early-Christian Roman church stood here. And back then you couldn't enter a church until you were baptized. Baptisteries stood outside churches, like the one that welcomed Clovis into the Christian faith.

Walk ahead to the **choir.** The set of candlesticks and crucifix at the high altar were given to the church by Charles X on the occasion of his coronation in 1825. Look back at the west wall. The original windows were lost in World War I; these, rebuilt from photographs, date from the 1930s.

Walk into the **south transept.** The WWI-destroyed windows here were replaced in 1954 by the local Champagne makers. The windows' scenes portray the tending of vines (left), the harvest (center), and the time-honored double-fermentation process (right).

Notice, around the edges, the churches representing all the grape-producing villages in the area.

Looking high above at the ceiling, you'll see evidence of **bomb damage** from 1917, when the roof took direct hits and collapsed. (The lighter bricks show the repair job from the 1920s.) The gray/white "grisaille" windows in this transept were installed in the 1970s. Many of the darker, more richly colored medieval glass windows were replaced by clear glass in the 18th and 19th centuries (when tastes called for more light).

The **apse** (east end, behind the altar) holds a luminous set of **Marc Chagall stained-glass windows** from 1974. Chagall's ex-

pressive style lends itself to stained glass, and he enjoyed opportunities to adorn great churches with his windows. The left window illustrates scenes from the Old Testament, with the Tree of Jesse (with Jesse himself sleeping at the bottom) reaching up to Mary with the Christ Child. In the central panels, the cohesion of the Old and New Testament scenes is emphasized by the ladder that connects one to the other. On the right, the Tree of Jesse—which is essentially a genealogical diagram of Christ's lineage—is extended to symbolically include the royalty of France, thus affirming the divine power of the monarchs and stressing their responsibility to rule with wisdom and justice. Featured are Clovis (at the bottom, with his bishop); St. Louis IX (seen at the cathedral and then dispensing justice); Charles VII (on the right in green); and Joan of Arc, in blue, holding her sword (on the far right).

For the cathedral's 800th anniversary, in 2011, six modern, **abstract windows** were installed on either side of the Chagall windows. Just to the left is a 1901 statue of Joan of Arc, her face carved from ivory.

From here, behind the high altar, enjoy the best view of the entire nave. Seen from this distance, the west wall is an ensemble seemingly made entirely of glass. Look at the confidence of the design. Even the corners outside the rose window were glass, made without stone. The architects pulled out all the stops in this triumph of Gothic.

OTHER REIMS SIGHTS
Palais du Tau

This former Archbishop's Palace, named after the Greek letter *T (tau)* for its shape, houses artifacts from the cathedral next door and

REIMS & VERDUN

a pile of royal goodies. You'll look into the weathered eyes of original statues from the cathedral's facade, and see precious tapestries, coronation jewels, and more.

Cost and Hours: €8, €11 combo-ticket includes cathedral tower tour, Tue-Sun 9:30-18:30, Sept-April Tue-Sun 9:30-12:30 & 14:00-17:30, closed Mon year-round. The €3 audioguide is overkill for most—follow my tour below and supplement it with the free English brochure, good bookshop, tel. 03 26 47 81 79, www.palais-du-tau.fr.

Visiting the Palace: The collections are in two distinct parts—the royal chapel and treasury with jewels and artifacts, and the cathedral museum with statues and tapestries. Most of the exhibits are on the upper level.

On the **ground floor** (Room 1), you'll start in the hall dedicated to the rebuilding of the cathedral after WWI bombings and the enlightened philanthropy of John D. Rockefeller Jr. When the roofs of Gothic churches burned, the lead that covered them melted and cascaded down like flowing rivers. Here, the gargoyles with once-molten lead spewing out of their storm-drain mouths make that much easier to envision.

Upstairs, the **royal chapel** (Room 5) was where the king would spend the night before his coronation, secluded in prayer. Inlaid in the floor are fleurs-de-lis, symbol of the French monarchy. At the altar are six candlesticks used at Napoleon's wedding in 1810.

Flanking the entry to the chapel are **treasury rooms** (Rooms 6 and 7) filled with royal valuables. On the left are examples that survived the melt-it-down mania of the French Revolution. Imagine the fury of the revolutionaries, who would melt down precious crowns and chalices to satisfy their practical need for gold and silver. Very little survived that wasn't buried away—these varied treasures were excavated from royal tombs in the 1920s (and survive in perfect condition). Don't miss the ninth-century talisman worn by Charlemagne and the exquisite chalice used by French royalty in the 12th century.

Room 8 is filled with gold-plated silver regalia made for the coronation of Charles X in 1825. The new pieces were necessary because the historic regalia had been melted down.

In the next room (9) ponder the royal portraits and the 60-pound mantle of the divine king. Think of the dramatic swings in France's history: A generation after you cut off a king's head, you welcome a new king as if he were divine.

Turning right into Room 10, where the **cathedral museum** section begins, let your gaze soar high. An original 13th-century statue of Goliath measures a whopping 17.7 feet. In the next rooms, find cases with tiny statues with traces of original paint. Admire the amazing detail of the carving.

The highlight and grand finale (Room 15) is the original centerpiece of the cathedral's west facade: the fire-damaged Coronation of Mary group, carved in the 12th century. In the same room, six figures from the Gallery of Kings stand as if guarding 16th-century tapestries. Originally hung around the choir in the center of the cathedral, the themes of these tapestries illustrating the Virgin's life supported the prayers and preaching of the faithful.

▲Carnegie Library (Bibliothèque Carnegie)

The legacy of the Carnegie Library network, funded generously by the 19th-century American millionaire Andrew Carnegie and his

steel fortune (notice the American flag above the main entrance on the left), extends even to Reims. Carnegie believed knowledge could put an end to war, and he built several thousand such libraries around the world (he dedicated $200,000 for the one in Reims). Built in 1921 in the flurry of interwar reconstruction, this beautiful Art Deco building still houses the city's public library. Considering that admission is free and it's just behind the cathedral, it's worth a quick look.

Visitors are welcome to poke around but are asked not to enter the reading room. In the onyx-laden entry hall, small marble mosaics celebrate different fields of knowledge, and a chandelier hangs down like the sleek dress of a circa-1920s flapper. Peek through the reading room door to admire the stained-glass windows of this temple of thought. The gorgeous wood-paneled card-catalogue room takes older visitors back to their childhoods. Go ahead, finger the laboriously created typewritten files, and imagine the technology available back in 1928, the year the library was inaugurated.

Cost and Hours: Free; Tue-Wed and Fri-Sat 10:00-13:00 & 14:00-19:00 except Sat until 18:00, Thu 14:00-19:00 only, closed Sun-Mon; Place Carnegie, tel. 03 26 77 81 41. The CityBus #C shuttle runs to the Carnegie stop.

Place du Forum

Reims' main square recalls the forum, or market, that marked the center of the ancient city. Legend has it that Reims was founded by Remus (brother of Romulus), and so the tribe that lived here came to be called "Remes." This old town of 50,000 people was the capital of the Roman province of Gaullia-Belgica. From Place du Forum, you can climb down steps into the **Cryptoportique,** a first-century AD Roman gallery. About 10 feet below today's street level, this cool retreat was once the cloister that defined a sacred temple zone in the middle of the Roman Forum (free, daily 14:00-18:00, closed Oct-May). This is also a pleasant place to dine al fresco on warm summer evenings (see "Eating in Reims," later).

Porte de Mars

The only aboveground monument surviving from ancient Reims is this entry gate to the city (free, always open, at Place du Boulingrin). The Porte de Mars, built in the second century AD, was one of four principal entrances into the ancient Gallo-Roman town. Inspired by triumphal arches that Rome built to herald war victories, this one was constructed to celebrate the Pax Romana (the period of peace and stability after Rome had vanquished all its foes). Unlike most other structures here, the gate was undamaged in World War I, but it bears the marks of other eras, such as its integration into the medieval ramparts.

Near the Porte de Mars (on Place de la République) stands a huge **WWI memorial.** Reims, the biggest city on the Western Front during the Great War, endured 1,051 days of shelling during those four years.

Covered Market Hall (Halles Boulingrin)

Built in 1927, this jewel of Art Deco architecture reopened in 2012 for the first time in 20 years after an estimated €31 million renovation. The vaulted roof consists of a mere 2.75 inches of reinforced concrete and rises 65 feet. Its splendid, bustling morning market spills over to include surrounding streets (open Sat 6:00-14:00, also Wed and Fri 7:00-13:00; tiny organic market Fri 16:00-20:00, closed other days, 50 Rue de Mars).

▲Museum of the Surrender (Musée de la Reddition)

Anyone interested in World War II will enjoy visiting the place where US General Dwight Eisenhower and the Allies received

the unconditional surrender of all German forces on May 7, 1945. The news was announced the next day, turning May 8 into Victory in Europe (V-E) Day. There's an extensive collection of artifacts, but the most thrilling sight is the war room (or Signing Room), where Allied operations were managed.

Start with the good 10-minute video in the theater on the main floor. Then climb upstairs to the museum and Signing Room. Imagine running the European Theater of Operation from here, as General Eisenhower did from February to May 1945 (after the

Allies gained control of the airspace). The walls are covered with floor-to-ceiling maps showing troop positions, fuel supplies, where train lines were functioning, and so on. Progress was painstakingly marked and updated daily. The chairs around the table, with name tags in their original spots, show where the signatories sat.

Cost and Hours: €5, Wed-Mon 10:00-18:00 (may close at lunchtime—check hours locally), closed Tue, 12 Rue Franklin Roosevelt, tel. 03 26 47 84 19, www.musees-reims.fr.

Getting There: It's a 10-minute walk from the Reims-Centre train station.

REIMS' CHAMPAGNE *CAVES*

Reims, the capital of the Champagne region, offers many opportunities to visit its ▲▲ world-famous chalk Champagne cellars *(caves)*. The oldest were dug by the Romans as they mined chalk and salt in the 1st century BC. Hundreds of years later, Champagne producers converted the caves—with their perfect and constant temperatures—into wine storage.

Which *cave* should you visit? Martel offers the most personal and best-value tour. Taittinger and Mumm have the most impressive cellars (Mumm is also close to the city center and offers one of the best tours in Reims). Veuve Clicquot is popular with Americans and fills up weeks in advance. Cazanove is closest to the train station and the cheapest, but you get what you pay for. Wherever you go, bring a sweater, even in summer, as the *caves* are cool and clammy.

How to Visit: All charge entry fees, most have several daily English tours, and most require a reservation (only Taittinger allows drop-in visits). Call, email, or visit the website for the schedule and to secure a spot on a tour. The TI can make reservations for the Mumm and Martel cellars, and they offer minivan excursions into the nearby vineyards. **Cris-Event Champagne Tours** gets rave reviews and can be booked directly (€85/person for half-day, €190/person all day, includes lunch, tel. 03 26 53 03 06, www.cris-event.fr). **France Bubble Tours** is another good option (€115-190/person for all-day tour, tel. 02 47 79 40 20, www.france-bubbles-tours.com).

Getting to the *Caves*: Mumm and Cazanove are both in the city and easy to reach on foot. Without a car, the others involve a long **walk** (40 minutes) or a 15-minute **shuttle bus** (except on Sun) or **taxi** ride (for more, see under "*Caves* Southeast of the Cathedral"). A **taxi** from either train station to the farthest Champagne *cave* will cost about €10 each way. To return, ask the staff at the *caves* to call a taxi for you. The meter starts running once they are called, so count on €5 extra for the return trip.

Champagne in the City Center
Mumm

Mumm ("moome") is one of the easiest *caves* to visit, as it's a short walk from the central train station. Reservations are essential, especially on weekends (book in advance online). Choose which tasting you want when getting your ticket (the cheapest Cordon Rouge tasting is fine for most, though you can pay more for the same tour with extra "guided" tastings). You'll see a quick promotional video explaining the Champagne-making process, then follow a guided walk taking you through the industrial-size chalk cellars, where 25 million bottles are stored (Mumm is Champagne's largest producer), and a museum of old Champagne-making tools and traditions. The tour ends with your tasting choice.

Cost and Hours: €20-50 depending on tasting level, includes one-hour tour; tours March-Oct daily 9:30-11:30 & 14:00-16:30, Nov-Feb Mon-Sat 9:30-10:50 & 14:00-16:00, closed Sun; 34 Rue du Champ de Mars—go to the end of the courtyard and follow *Visites des Caves* signs; tel. 03 26 49 59 70, www.mumm.com, guides@mumm.com.

Getting There: It's a 15-minute walk from the Reims-Centre train station or from the cathedral. From the station, turn left on Boulevard Joffre and walk to Place de la République; pass through the square, and continue along on Rue du Champ de Mars (to the left of the Europcar office). You can also take bus #7 from the station (direction: Béthany) to the Justice stop, turn right (south) onto Rue de la Justice, and then left onto Rue du Champ de Mars. To return to the station on bus #7, turn left from Mumm and walk a block down Rue du Champ de Mars to the bus shelter (direction: Apollinaire).

Charles de Cazanove

If you're in a rush and not too concerned about quality, Cazanove is closest to the train station and has a cheap and basic tasting. (Martel's tasting for same price is far superior; see "Martel," later.) There are no chalk *caves* and no Champagne is made on-site (€15, includes "tour" with 3 tastings; daily 10:00-13:00 & 14:00-19:00, 5-minute walk from the station up Boulevard Joffre to 8 Place de la République, tel. 03 26 88 53 86, www.champagnedecazanove.com).

Caves Southeast of the Cathedral

Taittinger and Martel, offering contrasting looks at two very different *caves*, are a few blocks apart, and can easily be combined in one visit. Veuve Clicquot Ponsardin is a bit farther out and pricey—but it has impressive cellars and that memorable name. It's also a big draw for American travelers and must be booked well in advance.

Getting There from the Town Center: It's a 30-minute **walk** to Taittinger and Martel. Starting from behind the cathedral's south transept, walk straight down Rue de l'Université, then Rue du Barbâtre. Veuve Clicquot is another 15 minutes farther on foot (see map on page 1038). If that's too far, there's a handy **taxi stand** at 40 Rue Carnot, next to the Opéra (about €10).

To reach Taittinger and Martel by **bus,** take the small green **CityBus** #C from the train station or from the Cathédrale stop (near TI one block in front of the cathedral)—and ride 10 minutes to the St. Timothée stop (ask the driver to point you in the right direction). Use the same stop to return to the cathedral or station.

To get near Veuve Clicquot, take bus #6 from the train station (to the Droits de l'Homme stop, 4/hour, direction: ZI Farman, return stop is on opposite side of big roundabout on Boulevard Dieu Lumière, bus stop Cimitière du Sud, direction: Gare Centre).

Taittinger

One of the biggest, slickest, and most renowned of Reims' *caves*, Taittinger (tay-tan-zhay) runs morning and afternoon tours in English through their vast and historic cellars (call for times, best to show up early, no reservation necessary, about 30 people per tour). After seeing their 10-minute promo-movie (hooray for Taittinger!), descend with your guide for 40 chilly minutes in a chalky underworld of *caves*, the deepest of which were dug by ancient Romans. You'll tour part of the three miles of *caves*, see ruins of an abbey and a Roman chalk quarry, pass some of the three million bottles stored here, and learn all you need to know about the Champagne-making process from your well-informed guide. Popping corks signal that the tour's done and the tasting's begun.

Cost and Hours: €19-45 depending on tasting level, includes cellar tour, can reserve ahead online, April-mid-Nov daily 9:30-17:30; mid-Nov-March Mon-Fri 9:30-13:00 & 13:45-17:30, closed Sat-Sun; 9 Place St. Niçaise, tel. 03 26 85 84 33, www.taittinger.fr, visites@taittinger.fr.

Martel

This small operation with less extensive *caves* offers a homey contrast to Taittinger's big-business style, and it's a great deal. Call to set up a visit and expect a small group that might be yours alone. Friendly Emmanuel runs the place with a relaxed manner. Only 20 percent of their product is exported, so you won't find much of their Champagne in the US. A visit includes an informative 10-minute film, a tour of their small cellars (which are peppered with rusted old winemaking tools), and a tasting of three Champagnes in a casual living-room atmosphere.

Cost and Hours: €16, one-hour tour and tasting, daily 10:00-11:30 & 14:00-17:30, reservations not required but advised, TI can call ahead for you, 17 Rue des Créneaux, tel. 03 26 82 70 67, www. champagnemartel.com, boutique@champagnemartel.com.

Veuve Clicquot Ponsardin

Because it's widely exported in the US, Veuve Clicquot is inundated with American travelers willing the pay the high price to visit their cellars. Reservations are required and fill up three weeks in advance, so book before your trip—it's easy on their website (figure €28-60 for tour and tasting, Place des Droits de l'Homme, tel. 03 26 89 53 90, www.veuve-clicquot.com, visitscenter@veuve-clicquot.fr).

ROUTE DE LA CHAMPAGNE DRIVE

Drivers can joyride over the hills just south of Reims (the pretty Montagne de Reims area) and through the vineyards, experiencing the chalky soil and rolling landscape of vines that produce Champagne's prestigious sparkling wines. This leisurely 50-mile loop drive takes about three hours, including stops.

There are thousands of small-scale producers of Champagne in these villages—unknown outside France and producing fine-quality Champagne without the high costs and flash associated with big brand-name houses in Reims and Epernay (figure about €15-25/bottle). These less famous producers harvest the grapes themselves and make wine only from their own grapes (identified as *"récoltant manipulant"* or just *"RM"* on bottles and elsewhere).

Planning Your Drive

The Reims TI has maps of the Route de la Champagne and a *Discovery Guide* for the Marne region. Roads are well marked: Brown *Route Touristique de la Champagne* signs lead along much of our route and take you to some great viewpoints. The only rail-accessible destination along this route is Epernay.

It takes a little work to line up visits to wine producers in this area, and you must call ahead to tour a cellar rather than just taste, but this usually pays off with a more intimate, rewarding cultural experience. Ask your hotelier or a TI for help, or check in with Les Vignerons Indépéndents de Champagne (Independent Winemakers of Champagne, offers a selection of Champagne *caves* open for tastings Sat-Sun only April-Oct, tel. 03 26 59 55 22, www. vignerons-independants-champagne.com).

If you're doing this drive without reservations, it's easier on a weekend, when more places are open and more likely to welcome drop-in tasters. If you plan to picnic, you'll find all you need in the sweet little town of Aÿ. There's also a bakery and a small grocery in Bouzy (unpredictable hours).

If you're pressed for time, you can still sample the vineyard

Pop Pop, Fizz Fizz

Like perfume and Cognac, Champagne is synonymous with good living and good form in France. When invited to a French home for dinner, your aperitif choice always includes Champagne, as it is the proper way to start an evening with friends. Though many wine-growing regions in France produce sparkling wines (called Crémant, Mousseux, or Blanquette), only grapes from this region can be called Champagne. The beverage produced here is commonly regarded as the finest sparkling wine in the world.

Given the notoriety of the Champagne region, surprisingly little of its land is planted in vines (about 60,000 acres), and sparkling wines have little history compared to France's other famous wines. While the Romans planted the first grapes here, Champagne was not "invented" until the late 17th century, and then it was by virtue of necessity—the local climate and chalky soil did not produce competitive still wines.

Champagne is made from three grapes: the red pinot noir and pinot meunier, and the white chardonnay. Most Champagne is roughly an equal blend of these grapes, though some smaller producers will make Champagne from 100 percent of any one of the three grapes. Then it's called *blanc de blancs* ("white from white," from chardonnay) or *blanc de noirs* ("white from black"—in France red grapes are considered black grapes—from pinot noir and pinot meunier).

To guarantee quality, the rules governing Champagne production are the strictest in France. The *méthode champenoise* involves two fermentations, the first in casks to make a still wine and the second in bottles (after more sugar and yeast are added) to trap the bubbles. As wine turns bubbly, sediment forms in the bottle and must be removed. In the traditional manner, it's done by hand in a painstaking process of turning and tilting each bottle slightly each day. Nowadays this is mostly done by machines. Once inverted, and the sediment collected in the neck of the bottle, the bottle is opened and the solids are ejected or "disgorged." The Champagne is then topped up, corked, and cellared for additional aging. Most bottles are aged for two to five years, then sold, as Champagne does not improve with age. Champagne is usually blended from several vintages to maintain consistency in taste.

Champagnes are classified by their level of sweetness: *brut* and *extra-brut* are dry (and very dry); *demi-sec* is sweeter; and *doux,* the sweetest, is intended for dessert courses. Bottles labeled *tête de cuvée* are as good as it gets; from there, the ranking proceeds to *grand cru* (from top vines), *premier cru* (next best), and *cru* (table Champagne). The smaller the bubbles, the better the Champagne. The signature aromas of Champagne include brioche, toast, and baked bread, due to the yeast cells present during the second fermentation.

scenery by driving just 15 minutes south from Reims, or by working parts of this route into your drive to or from Reims (the best
stop is Hautvillers).

From Reims to Louvois

• *From Reims, take A-4 (direction: Châlons-en-Champagne), then soon
exit south to Cormontreuil on D-9, following signs to Louvois (first
tasting opportunity).*

You'll pass through the usual commercial fringe before popping out into lovely scenery just 15 minutes after leaving Reims.
If you toured Mumm's cellars, you'll notice their hilltop property
with a windmill well off in the distance (on the left) as you climb
the Montagne de Reims. Remember that the best grapes are grown
along the slopes of the Montagne de Reims.

Louvois

Consider a stop at **Guy de Chassey,** where drop-ins are welcome
to enjoy a tasting (assuming the place isn't busy). Call ahead if
you want to tour their property (daily 10:00-18:00, may be closed
12:00-14:00, closed Aug and mid-Dec-mid-March, on the roundabout as you enter town at 1 Place de la Demi-Lune, tel. 03 26 57
04 45, www.champagne-guy-de-chassey.com).
• *Take D-34 out of town. A little after leaving Louvois, look for Route
de la Champagne signs leading left along a vineyard lane into the appropriately named village of Bouzy. Take the short detour off to the point
de vue for a fine view over the village and vines.*

Bouzy

There are 30 producers of Champagne in little Bouzy alone, some
of whom are famous for their Bouzy Rouge (a still red wine made
only from pinot noir grapes, and not made every year). Most places
require reservations to visit, but drop-ins are welcome for the fun
tasting at **Champagne Herbert Beaufort.** You'll likely be served
by a family member. Arrive at 10:30 or 15:30 for visits to their
cellars (free tastings, Mon-Fri 9:30-11:30 & 14:00-17:30, Sat 9:30-
11:30 & 14:30-17:00, Sun 10:00-12:00 in summer, closed Sun Oct-
Easter, first *domaine* on your left coming from Louvois on D-34 at
32 Rue de Tours, tel. 03 26 57 01 34, www.champagnebeaufort.fr).
• *From Bouzy, leave the vineyards following D-19 to Tours-sur-Marne,
then turn right onto D-1 and carefully track signs to Aÿ.*

Aÿ

This lively little town (pronounced "eye") boasts of producing 100
percent *grand cru* Champagne from all its vineyards. Detour into
the pleasant town center, and park near Hôtel de Ville and Café du

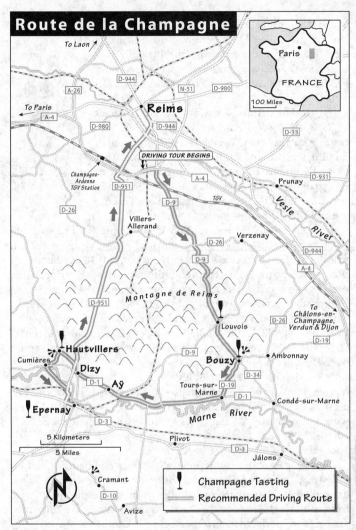

Route de la Champagne

To Laon

Paris

FRANCE

100 Miles

To Paris

Reims

DRIVING TOUR BEGINS

Champagne-
Ardenne
TGV Station

Prunay

Vesle River

TGV

Villers-
Allerand

Verzenay

Montagne de Reims

Louvois

To
Châlons-en-
Champagne,
Verdun & Dijon

Hautvillers

Cumières

Dizy

Aÿ

Bouzy

Ambonnay

Tours-sur-
Marne

Condé-sur-Marne

Epernay

Marne River

5 Kilometers

5 Miles

Plivot

Jálons

N

Cramant

Champagne Tasting

Recommended Driving Route

Avize

REIMS & VERDUN

Midi. Within a few blocks you'll find bakeries, charcuteries, cafés, and a good grocery store (which sells cold drinks).

• *Back on D-1, drive into the next town—Dizy (what you get after too much Bouzy, Aÿ!)—and follow signs up the hill to Hautvillers. You'll pass Moët et Chandon vineyards on your way.*

Hautvillers

If you have time for only one stop, make it Hautvillers (meaning "High Village"). This is the most attractive hamlet in the area, with strollable lanes, houses adorned with wrought-iron shop signs, and a seventh-century abbey church with the tomb-stone of the monk Dom Pérignon. Park near the Café Hautvillers, across from the little TI (tel. 03 26 57 06 35, www.tourisme-hautvillers.com). From here it's a nice walk to the town's sights (all well-signed).

The **abbey church** is worth a wander (great WCs) for its wood-accented interior alone. According to the story, in about 1700, after much fiddling with double fermentation, it was here that Dom Pérignon stumbled onto the bubbly treat. On that happy day, he ran through the abbey, shouting, "Brothers, come quickly...I'm drinking stars!" Find his tombstone in front of the altar.

To taste your own stars, find **Champagne G. Tribaut** (300 yards from the café), and meet animated Valerie or her assistant, who love their work and the family's product (€10 for tasting of three Champagnes). Ask them about Ratafia, a local fortified wine served as an aperitif. You can linger over your glass of bubbly in the comfortable view reception room as you survey the sea of vineyards, but it's best to call or email a day ahead to let them know you'll be stopping by (9:00-12:00 & 13:30-18:00, closed Sun Jan-Feb, tel. 03 26 59 40 57, www.champagne.g.tribaut.com, contact@champagne-hautvillers.com).

Another option is **Au 36,** a slick wine shop/tasting room that represents many producers. The passionate staff will help you understand the differences among grape varieties (€10-15 tastings with 3 contrasting Champagnes, good prices for purchase, daily 10:30-18:00, a block from Café Hautvillers at 36 Rue Dom Pérignon, tel. 02 26 51 58 37).

For a spectacular picnic spot (with tables and benches, but no WCs) and **sweeping views** over vineyards and the Marne River, drive to the abbey church and follow Rue de l'Eglise past it for three minutes. Get out of the car and wander among the vineyards. That picture-perfect village down below is Cumières.

• *Exit the town downhill, toward the river to Cumières, then turn left on D-1 and follow signs home to Reims (about 20 minutes back on the speedy D-951). You could also pass through Cumières and drive two miles into Epernay, home to Moët et Chandon. True connoisseurs can continue along the Route Touristique de Champagne south of Epernay toward Vertus, along the chardonnay grape-filled Côte des Blancs.*

CHAMPAGNE IN EPERNAY

Champagne purists may want to visit Epernay, about 16 miles from Reims (and also well-connected to Paris—two daily local TER trains run through Epernay on the way to Reims). Epernay is most famously home to Moët et Chandon, which sits along Avenue de Champagne, the Rodeo Drive of grand Champagne houses.

Arrival in Epernay: Trains run frequently between Reims-Centre station and Epernay (12/day, 35 minutes). From the Epernay station, walk five minutes straight up Rue Gambetta to Place de la République, and take a left to find Avenue de Champagne. Moët et Chandon is at #20, and the TI is at #7 (mid-April-mid-Oct Mon-Sat 9:30-12:30 & 13:30-19:00, Sun 10:30-13:00 & 14:00-16:30; in off-season closes at 17:30 and on Sun; tel. 03 26 53 33 00, www.ot-epernay.fr).

Tasting in Epernay: The granddaddy of Champagne companies, **Moët et Chandon** offers 60- to 90-minute tours with pricey tasting possibilities (€25-40 for one or two tastes, no reservation needed, kids 10-18 can join the tour for €10—but no tasting, under 10 free, daily 9:30-11:30 & 14:00-16:30, closed weekends off-season, closed Jan, 20 Avenue de Champagne, tel. 03 26 51 20 20, www.moet.com).

To sip a variety of different Champagnes from smaller producers, stop by the wine bar **C Comme Champagne** (meaning "C like Champagne"). Start with a peek in the wine cellar, then snuggle into an armchair and order by the taste, glass, or bottle (daily 10:00-20:00, except Wed opens at 15:00, 8 Rue Gambetta, tel. 03 26 32 09 55).

Sleeping in Reims

$$$ Hôtel Continental**** is a boutique hotel on lively Place d'Erlon with plush, quite modern rooms in every size, shape, and price (RS%, good family options; air-con, elevator, pay parking, 5-minute walk from central train station at 93 Place Drouet d'Erlon, tel. 03 26 40 39 35, www.continental-hotel.fr, reservation@continental-hotel.fr).

$$ La Parenthèse has five well-equipped rooms (some have cathedral views) with kitchenettes and is situated closer to the river with easy car access and pay parking. A pleasant garden and public spaces are available. The owners live off-site, so check-in must be arranged in advance (2-night minimum, make deposit through PayPal and pay balance in cash only, no air-con, 83 Rue Clovis, tel. 03 26 40 39 57, www.laparenthese.fr, contact@laparenthese.fr).

$ Hôtel Kyriad Reims Centre* is a good three-star hotel with modern comforts (air-con, 29 Rue Buirette, tel. 03 26 47 39 39, www.kyriad.com/en/hotels/kyriad-reims-centre, reims.centre@kyriad.fr).

$ Best Western Hôtel Centre Reims* delivers crisp and modern comfort at fair rates in surprisingly quiet rooms, despite being right on the lively square (family rooms, elevator, air-con, 75

Place Drouet d'Erlon, tel. 03 26 47 39 03, www.hotel-centre-reims.fr, contact@hotel-centre-reims.fr).

Eating in Reims

Dining in Reims is as much about the area you eat in as the restaurant you choose. I've described areas to troll for dinner as well as a few specific restaurants. If you're just looking for cheap picnic fixings, head to the grocery store at Monoprix (see "Helpful Hints," earlier).

PLACE DROUET D'ERLON

This bustling line of cafés and restaurants serves mostly cheap and so-so meals but has the city's best people-watching and café action. Linger over a drink at one of the cafés on the square, then eat elsewhere. You'll find exceptions to the forgettable offerings at the recommended **$$$ Hôtel Continental's** restaurant, with quiet, inside-only dining, contemporary decor, and top service thanks to the helpful staff (good three-course *menu* includes a drink or half-bottle of wine, closed Sun evenings, 93 Place Drouet d'Erlon, tel. 03 26 40 63 83). Also consider across the square at **$$$ Brasserie Excelsior,** with an established clientele, a woody brasserie interior, and fine terrace tables outside (open daily, 96 Place Drouet d'Erlon, tel. 03 26 91 40 50).

PLACE DU FORUM AND CATHEDRAL SQUARE

The quiet but popular Place du Forum attracts a young professional crowd at several bistros with good outdoor seating; it's best for a more wine-focused, intimate meal with locals. Cathedral Square is ideal for picnicking while you admire the impressive church, eating outdoors under the towering cathedral facade. This spot is sensational after dark, when the floodlighting and sound-and-light show make the view a performance.

$$ Bistrot du Forum is an informal place with small wooden tables, a cool zinc bar, and good terrace seating. They serve hearty salads (try the one with *boudin blanc*), bruschetta-like *tartines*, and burgers, as well as traditional meat and fish dishes. You'll also find a good selection of wines (and Champagne, *bien sûr*) by the glass (long hours daily, 6 Place Forum, tel. 03 26 47 56 58).

Just off the Place du Forum, on Rue Courmeaux, you'll find **$$ L'Epicerie au Bon Manger,** a foodie refuge whose mantra is "In Good We Trust." They have a handful of tables, stacks of organic local wines (by smaller, hard-to-find producers), smelly cheese, and charcuterie to go or to enjoy sitting down. It's a handy place if you're eating outside the rigid French lunch hours, because they serve nibbles all day (Tue-Sat 10:00-20:00, Thu-Fri until 22:00, closed Sun-Mon, 7 Rue Courmeaux, tel. 03 26 03 45 29).

$$ Au Bureau, one of a handful of eateries on Cathedral Square, is worth it only if you grab a table outside and are OK with average café fare and indifferent service—but it's a good place to linger over coffee (daily until late, at the cathedral at 9 Place du Cardinal Luçon, tel. 03 26 35 84 83).

ELSEWHERE IN REIMS

Near the Covered Market Hall (Halles Boulingrin): The pedestrian street Rue du Temple, along the south side of the market hall, is filled with cafés and brasseries—all with inviting outdoor terraces and a pleasant atmosphere. It's especially lively on Saturday mornings during the weekly market. **$$ Brasserie du Boulingrin** is a grand old Reims institution serving traditional French cuisine (including fresh oysters and a seafood platter) at reasonable prices (closed Sun; 10-minute walk from the Reims-Centre train station at 31 Rue de Mars, next to the Covered Market Hall, tel. 03 26 40 96 22). Consider a glass of Champagne or wine in the cozy courtyard of the **Le Clos** wine bar at #25 (18:00 until late, closed Sun-Mon, live music some evenings, tel. 03 26 07 74 69).

Near Opéra: $$$ Café du Palais is appreciated by older locals who don't mind paying a premium to eat a meal or sip coffee wrapped in 1930s ambience. Reims' most venerable café-bistro stands across from the Opéra and is good even just for a glass of wine (serves hot food during lunch hours and snacks the rest of the day, Tue-Sat 9:00-20:30, closed Sun-Mon, 14 Place Myron Herrick, tel. 03 26 47 52 54).

Near City Hall: $$ Chez Coco is a cool little bistro with a few front terrace tables, a cozy interior, and well-prepared and presented cuisine (Tue-Sat 11:00-22:00, Sun 8:00-16:00, closed Mon, 12 Rue de Mars, tel. 03 26 25 15 60).

Reims Connections

Reims has two train stations—Reims-Centre and Champagne-Ardenne. Most trains to or from Paris use Reims-Centre, while TGV trains traveling to or from points east (such as Strasbourg or Colmar) use Champagne-Ardenne (5 miles from the center of Reims; frequent connection by local TER train or by tram to Reims-Centre station). Trains that stop at Reims-Centre don't stop at Champagne-Ardenne. For more on Reims' train stations, see "Arrival in Reims" on page 1036.

From Reims-Centre Station by Train to: Paris Gare de l'Est (8/day by TGV, 45 minutes; 2/day by local train, 2 hours), **Epernay** (12/day, 35 minutes), **Verdun** (4/day, 3 hours, 1-2 changes).

From Reims Champagne-Ardenne Station by Train to: Paris Gare de l'Est (via TGV: 4/day, 40 minutes), **Strasbourg** (via TGV: hourly, 2 hours), **Colmar** (via TGV: 10/day, 2 hours, most change in Strasbourg), **Verdun** (4/day, 1-3 hours, TGV to Meuse or Metz, then bus to Verdun).

Verdun

While World War I was fought a hundred years ago, and there are no more survivors to tell its story, the WWI sights and memorials scattered around Europe do their best to keep the devastation from fading from memory.

Perhaps the most powerful WWI sightseeing experience a traveler can have is at the battlefields of Verdun, where, in 1916, roughly 300,000 lives were lost in what is called the Battle of 300 Days and Nights.

Today, the lunar landscape left by WWI battles is buried under thick forests—all new growth. But there are plenty of rusty remnants of the battle and memorials to the carnage left to be experienced.

A string of battlefields lines an eight-mile stretch of road outside the town of Verdun. From here (with a tour, rental car, shuttle bus, or taxi) you can ride through the eerie moguls left by the incessant shelling, pause at melted-sugar-cube forts, ponder plaques marking spots where towns once existed, and visit a vast cemetery. In as little as three hours you can see the most important sights and appreciate the horrific scale of the battles.

TOURIST INFORMATION

Verdun's TI is east of Verdun's city center (just across the river—cross at Pont Chaussée, on Avenue du Général Mangin; generally Mon-Sat 9:00-18:00, June-Sept until 19:00, Sun 10:00-17:00—shorter hours Sun off-season; tel. 03 29 86 14 18, www.tourisme-verdun.fr, contact@tourisme-verdun.fr). Ask for the free Pass Lorraine, which is good for discounts at some sights in the region. The pleasant park nearby provides a good picnic setting.

ARRIVAL IN VERDUN

By Train: Verdun is served by two train stations: the Meuse TGV station (18 miles from Verdun) and the Verdun station (within walking distance of town).

Several daily TGV trains from Paris' Gare de l'Est serve the **Meuse TGV station;** a 30-minute shuttle bus connects the TGV station with Verdun's station (free with ticket to Verdun or a rail pass, leaves shortly after train arrives). This high-speed service puts Verdun within 1.5 hours of Paris (compared with 3.5 hours by local train—see "Verdun Connections," later).

Verdun's main train station is 15 minutes by foot from the TI. Shuttle buses to the Meuse TGV station leave from the front of a glassy building 75 yards to the left as you walk out of the station. To reach the town center and TI, exit the station (no baggage check), cross the parking lot and the roundabout, and keep straight down Avenue Garibaldi, then follow *Centre-Ville* signs on Rue St. Paul. Turn left on the first traffic-free street in the old center (Rue Chaussée) and cross the river to the TI.

By Car: Drivers can bypass the town center and head straight for the TI or the battlefields. To find the TI, follow signs to *Centre-Ville,* then *Office de Tourisme.* To reach the battlefields, follow signs reading *Verdun Centre-Ville,* then signs toward *Longwy,* then find signs to *Douaumont* and *Champs de Bataille* (battlefields) on D-112, then D-913. The sights covered here fall in a line along this drive (just follow signs to *Fort de Douaumont* and *Ossuaire*). The map in this book is adequate for this drive.

Orientation to Verdun Town

While the Battle of Verdun took place in the hills outside town, the town of Verdun itself is worth a stroll—except on Sundays and Mondays, when most shops and businesses are closed. It's a handy base for exploring the battlefield sights.

Verdun's strategic location has left it with a hard-fought history. Locals call it "the most decorated town in France;" the number of war memorials would suggest they're right. It's a monochrome place, with bullet holes still pocking its stony buildings. And it's small, with only 16,000 people—4,000 fewer than at the start of World War I. Most of the action lies along the Meuse River on the broad esplanade of Quai de Londres, where you'll find a commotion of recreation boats mostly from the Low Countries and Germany (enjoying a system of former industrial canals) and scads of cafés, restaurants, and locals.

The town's mighty 14th-century gate squats on the river (near the TI), looking warily east. The city's state-of-the-art (in the 17th century) fortifications still seem poised to repel German armies. Just across the river, a thicker wall—built in 1871 in anticipation of an attack—supports a mammoth monument to the French victims of German invaders in both world wars.

Verdun's old town is crowned by its **Victory Monument,** high above the river, with a cascading fountain connecting it to the pedestrian heart of town. The fountain's centerpiece, a towering warrior, plants his sword in the ground in a declaration of peace. He's flanked by twin cannons—made by the French for the Russians but ultimately used by the Germans against the French at Verdun. While the monument originally honored French and Allied troops, today it honors Germans as well. Now that a century has passed, the German flag flies next to French and European Union flags. The varied sights of the Verdun battlefields have risen above national bias, memorializing all victims of that senseless war, and celebrating peace.

Verdun has a special place in the hearts of the French, as nearly every soldier in World War I was cycled in and out of this killing field. In 1916 Verdun was the departure point for soldiers heading to the battlefields (as it is today for visitors). The **Citadelle Souterraine** was the site where French soldiers assembled and had their last good bed, meal, and shower before heading into the shelling zone. The citadel, with 2.5 miles of tunnels cut into a rock, was a teeming military city. How big? Its bakery cranked out 23,000 rations of bread every day. Today, it tries to give the public a glimpse at life on the front with a 30-minute ride on a Disneyesque wagon that comes with a recorded narration (€9, open daily 9:00-18:30). While interesting, if your time if limited, it's better spent at other battlefield sights.

Eating and Sleeping in Verdun: A good selection of eateries lines the river on Quai de Londres. **$ Bolzon Charcuterie** on the pedestrian-only Rue Chaussée (#21) has good salads, quiche, and dishes to go. There's only one café at the battlefields (at the Verdun Memorial Museum). If you're short on time, consider assembling a picnic in Verdun or at an autoroute minimart.

Verdun makes an inexpensive and handy overnight stop. The comfortable **$ Hotel de Montaulbain***** is in the heart of the old town (4 Rue de la Vieille Prison, mobile 06 13 56 47 08, www.hoteldemontaulbain.fr, contact@hoteldemontaulbain.fr).

Verdun Connections

High-speed TGV trains serve the Verdun area from the Meuse TGV station, 30 minutes south of Verdun. Regular but slower trains also run to Verdun's station. For TGV connections listed next, allow an additional 30 minutes to ride a shuttle bus to Verdun's train station (included with ticket to Verdun or rail pass).

From Verdun by Train to: Strasbourg (5/day, 2 hours, 1-2 transfers), **Colmar** (5/day, 2.5-5 hours, 2-3 changes), **Reims-Centre** (4/day, 3 hours, 1-2 changes), **Reims Champagne-Ardenne** (4/day, 1-3 hours, bus to Meuse or Metz, then TGV to Reims), **Paris** Gare de l'Est (5/day direct via shuttle bus and TGV, 1.5 hours; 4/day by regional train, 3.5 hours with transfer).

Battlefields of Verdun

Verdun's battlefields are littered with monuments and ruined forts. For most travelers, a half-day is enough. We'll concentrate on the three most important sights, the Verdun Memorial Museum, Douaumont Ossuary, and Fort Douaumont.

Information: Sights are adequately described in English (some provide audioguides). The TI and all sights sell books in English. At the TI, the simple but adequate booklet *Verdun du Ciel* provides helpful details (€5). Serious students will read ahead, and there's no shortage of literature about the Battle of Verdun. Alistair Horne's *The Price of Glory* sorts through the complex issues and offers perspectives from both sides of the conflict.

Eating: There are only two places to eat along this route. One is the rooftop café at Verdun Memorial Museum; the other is a café near the Ossuary. Consider picking up supplies in Verdun and using the picnic area near the trenches at Fort Souville (see later).

GETTING AROUND THE BATTLEFIELDS

The most interesting battlefield sights lie along an easy eight-mile stretch of road from the town of Verdun. To lace these sights together, you have four choices:

By Car: Cheap car rental is available a block from the Verdun train station at **AS Location** (€48/day with 110 km/60 miles included—that's plenty, Mon-Fri 8:30-12:00 & 14:00-18:00, sometimes open Sat, closed Sun, 22 Rue Louis Maury, tel. 03 29 86 58 58, www.location-vehicule-verdun55.fr, fg.location@sfr.fr). I've included basic route tips in my "Verdun Battlefield Drive," later.

By Bus: The Verdun tourist information office offers a very limited number of bus tours to the battlefields. Most visitors will find a car rental or taxis a far better option, but you can also give them a try (tel. 03 29 86 14 18, www.tourismeverdun.fr, contact@tourisme-verdun.fr).

By Taxi: Taxi rates are about €30/hour. For roughly €40 round-trip, taxis can drop a carload at one sight and pick up at another (walk between sights). Ask to be dropped at "Fort de Douaumont" and picked up three hours later at the "Ossuaire de Douaumont" or five hours later at the "Mémorial de Verdun"; figure about 30 minutes of level walking between each of these sights). Taxis normally meet trains at the station; otherwise they park at the TI (see http://taxi-verdun.com, mobile 06 81 95 26 98).

By Private Guide: To get the most out of your visit, you can hire a private guide to join your car for a tour. **Ingrid Ferrand** (mobile 06 79 45 30 98, ingrid.ferrand@nordnet.fr), **Florence Lamousse** (tel. 03 29 85 21 83, www.lorrainetouristique.com, florence.lamousse@aliceadsl.fr), and **Guillaume Moizan** (mobile 07 70 06 66 61, guillaume.moizan.guide@gmail.com) are good English-speaking guides (€200/half-day, €350/day).

BACKGROUND

After the annexation of Alsace and Lorraine following the German victory in the Franco-Prussian War in 1871, Verdun found itself just 25 miles from the German border. This was too close for comfort for the French, who invested mightily in new fortifications ringing Verdun, hoping to discourage German thoughts of invasion. It was as if the French knew they'd be seeing German soldiers again before too long.

The plan failed. World War I erupted in August 1914, and after a lengthy stalemate, in 1916 the Germans elected to strike a powerful knockout punch at the heart of the French defense, to demoralize them and force a quick surrender. They chose Verdun as their target. By defeating the best of the French defenses, the Germans would cripple the French military and morale. The French chose to fight to the bitter end. Three hundred days of nonstop trench warfare ensued. France eventually prevailed, but at a terrible cost. This is as far as Germany ever got.

World War I introduced modern technology to the age-old business of war. Tanks, chemical weapons, monstrous cannons, rapid communication, and airplanes made their debut, conspiring to kill nearly 10 million people in just four years. This senseless war started with little provocation, raged on with few decisive battles, and ended with nothing resolved, a situation that sowed the seeds of World War II.

The Battle of Verdun was fought from February through December of 1916. This was one chapter in a horrific battle of attrition in which Germany and France decided to wage a fierce fight, knowing they would suffer unprecedented losses. Each side calculated that the other would drop first.

During the "Hell of Verdun" (hell for troops and hell for locals), Germany and France dropped 60 million artillery shells on each other. Most of the casualties were caused by shells bursting

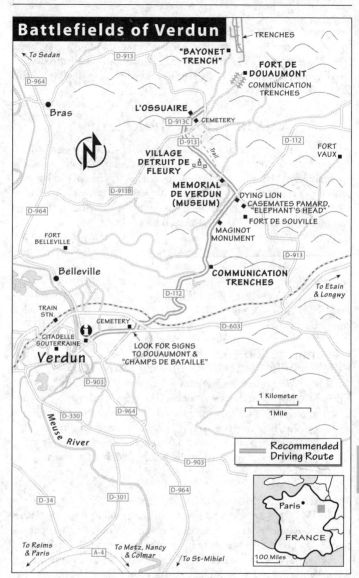

Battlefields of Verdun

To Sedan
D-913
"BAYONET TRENCH"
TRENCHES
FORT DE DOUAUMONT
COMMUNICATION TRENCHES
D-964
Bras
L'OSSUAIRE
D-913C
CEMETERY
D-913
D-112
FORT VAUX
Trail
VILLAGE DETRUIT DE FLEURY
D-913B
MEMORIAL DE VERDUN (MUSEUM)
DYING LION
CASEMATES PAMARD, "ELEPHANT'S HEAD"
FORT DE SOUVILLE
D-964
FORT BELLEVILLE
MAGINOT MONUMENT
Belleville
D-913
COMMUNICATION TRENCHES
To Etain & Longwy
D-112
TRAIN STN.
CEMETERY
D-603
CITADELLE SOUTERRAINE
Verdun
LOOK FOR SIGNS TO DOUAUMONT & "CHAMPS DE BATAILLE"
D-903
Meuse River
D-330
D-964
1 Kilometer
1 Mile
D-903
Recommended Driving Route
D-34
D-301
D-964
Paris
FRANCE
To Reims & Paris
A-4
To Metz, Nancy & Colmar
To St-Mihiel
100 Miles

REIMS & VERDUN

into lethal fragments. An estimated 95 percent of the deaths at Verdun were from artillery shrapnel. Shells were fired from as far away as nine miles, with poor accuracy. Death by friendly fire was commonplace.

Today, soft, forested lands hide the memories of World War I's longest battle. Millions of live munitions are still scattered in vast cordoned-off areas. It's not unusual for French farmers or hikers to be injured by until-now unexploded mines. It's difficult to imagine today's lush terrain as it was just a few generations ago...a gray, treeless, crater-filled landscape, smothered in mud and littered with shattered weaponry and body parts as far as the eye could see. But as you visit, it's good to try.

Verdun Battlefield Drive

All the sights described here are along (or just off) the same road. As Fort Douaumont is the most distant stop, follow signs for *Douaumont*. With the simple map in this book, you should have no problem. Along the way (within easy view of the road), you'll see the sights described next. Your major stops: the museum, the huge cemetery/ossuary, and the pulverized fort.

• *Leave Verdun on D-603 (direction: Longwy), and then take a left on D-112. Departing Verdun, on the first corner you see six field cannons—German guns made by Skoda that were state of the art in 1914. (Renault, Peugeot, Skoda—seemingly all industry was geared toward machines of destruction.) Behind those guns are 5,000 gravestones—most dated 1916. Following signs to Champs de Bataille, from here you enter a lumpy forest that has grown over what was smooth farmland.*

Communication Trenches near Fort Souville (Massif Fortifié de Souville)

At this parking and picnic area, find a curving trench and craters, similar to those that mark so much of the land here. A few communication trenches like this remain—they protected reinforcements and supplies being shuttled to the front, and sheltered the wounded being brought back. But the actual trenches defining the front in this area were destroyed during the battles or have since been filled in. The nearby Fort Souville is not safe to visit.

Monument to Maginot

André Maginot served as France's minister of war in the 1920s and '30s, when the line of fortifications that later came to bear his name was built. The Maginot Line, which stretches from Belgium to Switzerland, was a series of underground forts and tunnels built after World War I in anticipation of World War II and another German attack. The Germans solved the problem presented by this formidable line of French defense by going around it through Belgium. The monument (showing a wounded Maginot being carried to safety) is here because André Maginot's family was from this region, and he was wounded near Verdun.

Monument to the Dying Lion

At the intersection with D-913, a statue of a dying lion marks the place where, after giving it their all, the German forces were stopped. The German military commanders had hoped for a quick victory at Verdun so troops could be sent to fight the British in the Somme offensive. The war was dragging on, hunger was setting in among the German citizenry, and the German leadership feared a revolt. They needed a boost—but the offensive failed. This was the site of massive artillery barrages: Imagine no trees here, only a brown lunar-like terrain with countless shell holes 20 feet deep. A short detour (turn right on D-913 at the intersection) takes you to a small sight signed *Casemates Pamard*, which is an armored machine gun nest nicknamed "Elephant's Head" for the way the 1917 structure looks. (Access was only by tunnel from the nearby Fort Souville.)

• *Return to the intersection, and continue straight ahead on D-913 (following signs to Ossuaire and Douaumont). Along the way you'll pass the...*

▲▲Verdun Memorial Museum (Mémorial de Verdun)

This museum delivers gripping exhibits on the 300 days of the Battle of Verdun, with lots of information in English. Allow a minimum of one hour to visit.

Cost and Hours: €11, discount with free Pass Lorraine—get at Verdun TI, daily 9:30-19:00, until 17:00 in winter, closed Jan; last entry one hour before closing; rooftop snack bar, tel. 03 29 88 19 16, http://memorial-verdun.fr.

Visiting the Museum: The ground floor sets the scene with videos and exhibits that take you into the battle. Start 10 steps past the turnstile at a small screen for a breathtaking five-minute review of "why WWI." The museum is rich in artifacts and pairs both German and French exhibits. Displays help you imagine the experiences of men on the front line. You'll see soldiers' personal effects, uniforms, guns, trucks, and more. A battlefield replica lies below you, visible through the glass floor, complete with mud, shells, trenches, and WWI military equipment. You'll learn about shrapnel, medical help in the trenches, and leaps in technology (from X-ray machines to machine guns shooting through airplane propeller blades). It was the end of horses and the start of ergonomic helmets. Sitting under a wall of faces, page through letters to loved ones sent from the trenches.

The upper floor continues with exhibits providing a broader context for the Battle of Verdun and World War I, from trench art to the role of women in World War I to propaganda. You can't help but see how, before 1914, propaganda, nationalism, and isolation from other cultures (lack of travel) was a tragically explosive mix. Your visit finishes on the top floor with a terrace overlooking the actual battlefields.

From this museum, it's a chilling 10-minute walk through the wooded yet bomb-pitted terrain to the destroyed village of Fleury, and a 20-minute walk on a trail to the cemetery at the base of the ossuary (trail starts across the road from the museum).

Destroyed Village of Fleury (Village Détruit de Fleury)

Thirty villages caught in the hell of Verdun were destroyed. Nine—like Fleury—were never rebuilt. Though gone, these villages (sign-posted as *Villages Détruites*) have not been forgotten: Each has a ceremonial mayor who represents the villages and works on preserving their memory.

Photos at the roadside pullout show Fleury before and after its destruction. Stroll through the cratered former townscape. The rebuilt church stands where the village church once did. Plaques locate the butcher, the baker, and so on. There's also a memorial to two French officers who were executed by the French military because, by leaving the battlefield briefly to take a wounded soldier to safety, they disobeyed the order to "stand your ground until the last drop of blood." Ponder the land around you. Not one square meter was left flat or unbombed.

• Drive on, *following signs to the tall, missile-like building surrounded by a sea of small white crosses.*

▲Douaumont Ossuary (L'Ossuaire de Douaumont)

This is the tomb of countless unknown French and German soldiers who perished in the muddy trenches of Verdun. In the years after the war, a local bishop wandered through the fields of bones—the bones of an estimated 100,000 French soldiers and even more German soldiers. Concluding there needed to be a respectful final resting place, he began the project in 1920. It was finished in 1932. The unusual artillery shell-shaped **tower** and cross design of this building symbolizes war...and peace (imagine a sword plunged into the ground up to its hilt). Over time, fewer visitors come as pilgrims and more as tourists. Yet even someone who's given little thought to the human cost of this battle of attrition will be deeply moved by this somber place.

Cost and Hours: Free entry, €6 for film and tower; Mon-Fri 9:00-18:00, Sat-Sun 10:00-18:00, July-Aug until 18:30; shorter hours off-season, closed Jan; tel. 03 29 84 54 81, www.verdun-douaumont.com.

Eating: The nearby **$$ Café Abri des Pèlerins** is the only place to eat among all these Verdun monuments (closed Wed, just beyond the Ossuary on the road to Douaumont, 1 Place Monseigneur Ginisty, tel. 03 29 85 50 58).

Visiting the Ossuary: Park behind the **theater/shop/tower.** Look through the low windows in the back of the building at the bones of countless unidentified soldiers. From there, steps lead down to the shop and theater where you can see the excellent 20-minute film (shows on the half-hour; English speakers get headphones) and hike 200 steps up the tower (skippable). Appropriate attire is required, and men are asked to remove their hats.

The **Mémorial Ossuaire** is a humbling, moving tribute to the soldiers who believed the propaganda that this "Great War" would be the war to end all wars. The building has 22 sections with 46 granite graves, each holding remains from different sectors of the battlefields. Those who donated to the construction (in the 1920s) got a plaque for their loved one: the soldier's name, rank, regiment, and dates of birth and death. In the chapel, stained-glass windows (circa 1920) honor priests, nurses, stretcher bearers, and mothers—all of whom contributed and suffered.

Outside, in front, walk through the **cemetery** and reflect on a war that ruined an entire generation, leaving more than 70 percent of all French soldiers dead, wounded, or missing. Rows of 16,000 Christian crosses and Muslim headstones (the latter gathered together and oriented toward Mecca), all with red roses, decorate the cemetery.

Just beyond the main cemetery you'll find memorials to the Muslim and Jewish victims of Verdun. The Muslim memorial (built in 2006, across the street from the cemetery) recalls the 600,000 "colonial soldiers" (most of whom came from North Africa) who fought for France. These men, often thrown into the most suicidal missions, were considered instrumental in France's ultimate victory at Verdun (a fact overlooked by anti-immigration, right-wing politicians in France today).

French Jews also fought and died in great numbers. The Jewish memorial (which you'll pass as you drive out of the ossuary) survived World War II. That's because the Nazi governor of this part of France, who had fought at Verdun and respected soldiers of any faith, covered it up.

• *Leaving the ossuary parking lot, follow signs to the...*

Bayonet Trench (Tranchée des Baïonnettes)

There is a legend that an entire company of French troops was buried in their trench by an artillery bombardment—leaving only their bayonets sticking above the ground to mark their standing graves. The memorial to this "bayonet trench" is a few hundred yards beyond the ossuary. The bulky concrete monument, donated by the US and free to enter (notice the inscription reading *"Leurs frères d'Amérique,"* meaning "Brothers from America") opened in 1920, and was the first such monument at Verdun.

In fact, most of the Third Company of the 137th Infantry Regiment was likely wiped out here because they had no artillery support and died in battle—still tragic, just not quite as vivid as the myth. The notion of the bayonet trench could have come from the German habit of making "gun graves"—burying dead French soldiers with their guns sticking up so that their bodies could be found later and given a proper burial. Walking around this monument provides a thought-provoking opportunity to wander into the silent and crater-filled second-growth forest that now blankets the battlefields of Verdun.

• *Backtrack toward the ossuary, and follow signs to Fort de Douaumont. Between the ossuary and the fort, on either side of the road, you'll pass what remains of the London Communication Trench. This served as a means of communication and resupply for Fort Douaumont. As you explore, be careful of rusty rebar spiking up randomly.*

▲Fort Douaumont (Fort de Douaumont)

This was the most important stronghold among 38 hilltop fortifications built to protect Verdun after Germany's 1871 annexation of Alsace and the Moselle region of Lorraine. First constructed in 1882, it was built atop and into the hillside and ultimately served as a strategic command center for both sides at various times. Soldiers were protected by a thick layer of sand (to muffle explosions) and a wall of concrete five to seven feet thick. Inside, there are two miles of cold, damp hallways.

Cost and Hours: €4, includes excellent 45-minute audio-guide, daily May-June 10:00-18:30, July-Aug until 19:00, shorter hours off-season, closed Jan; tel. 03 29 84 41 91.

Visiting the Fort: Experiencing these corridors will add to your sympathy for the soldiers who were forced to live here like moles. Climb to the bombed-out top of the fort and check out the round, iron-gun emplacements that could rise and revolve. The massive central gun turret was state of the art in 1905, antiquated in 1915, and essentially useless when the war arrived in 1916. From the top, look out at fields leading to Germany.

Notice again the beautiful sight of a German flag waving with the French and European flags as if to exclaim, "We won't do this again." Say what you like about the European Union, its great accomplishment has been to weave together the economies of France and Germany, uniting them and effecting a shared empathy. In 1914, Germans and French could kill each other carelessly because most Frenchmen had never met a German and vice versa. Today, thanks largely to the EU, it's a different world, with a solid foundation for European peace.

OTHER WWI BATTLEFIELDS AND MEMORIALS

To see the place where US Army General John Pershing's troops fought, take a side trip 45 minutes south to **St-Mihiel.** Here you'll find full-scale battle trenches (the French used sandbags, the Germans used concrete) and appreciate how close the opposing sides were. Nearby you can visit the **American Cemetery and Memorial,** and a bit farther on, the **Montsec Monument,** with a fine tribute to American soldiers and good views over the battlefields. The Verdun TI can provide maps, directions, and other information for this trip.

Countless WWI sites and memorials stretch all along the Western Front from Flanders (near the English Channel) to Hartmannswillerkopf (near the Swiss border) and welcome the public. In this book I've laid out what I consider the most interesting and powerful single day of WWI sightseeing at Verdun, but travelers with more interest and time can make an entire tour out of visiting these WWI sights.

Following the centennial celebrations (2014-2018), the many WWI sights and memorials are better equipped than ever to make your visit meaningful and rewarding. Tourist information is plentiful (online, in books, and as you travel), and many top-quality guides and tour companies can ensure that you know where to go and what you're looking at.

REIMS & VERDUN

FRANCE: PAST & PRESENT

FRENCH HISTORY IN AN ESCARGOT SHELL

About the time of Christ, Romans "Latinized" the land of the Gauls. With the fifth-century AD fall of Rome, the barbarian Franks and Burgundians invaded. Today's France evolved from this unique mix of Latin and Celtic cultures.

While France wallowed with the rest of Europe in medieval darkness, it got a head start in its development as a nation-state. In 507, Clovis, the king of the Franks, established Paris as the capital of his Christian Merovingian dynasty. Clovis and the Franks would eventually become Louis and the French. The Frankish military leader Charles Martel stopped the spread of Islam by beating the Spanish Moors at the Battle of Poitiers in 732. And Charlemagne, the most important of the "Dark Age" Frankish kings, was crowned Holy Roman Emperor by the pope in 800. Charles the Great presided over the "Carolingian Renaissance" and effectively ruled an empire that was vast for its time.

The Treaty of Verdun (843), which divided Charlemagne's empire among his grandsons, marks what could be considered the birth of Europe. For the first time, a treaty was signed in vernacular languages (French and German), rather than in Latin. This split established a Franco-Germanic divide, and heralded an age of fragmentation. While petty princes took the reigns, the Frankish king ruled only Ile de France, a small region around Paris.

Vikings, or Norsemen, settled in what became Normandy. Later, in 1066, these "Normans" invaded England. The Norman king, William the Conqueror, consolidated his English domain, accelerating the formation of modern England. But his rule also muddied the political waters between England and France, kicking off a centuries-long struggle between the two nations.

In the 12th century, Eleanor of Aquitaine (a separate country

France Almanac

Official Name: Officially République Française, but everyone calls it France.

Size: At 215,000 square miles, it's Western Europe's largest nation (but Texas is still 20 percent bigger); population is nearly 67 million people (similar to the combined populations of California and Texas).

Geography: The terrain consists of rolling plains in the north and mountains in the southwest (Pyrenees), southeast (Alps), and south-central (Massif Central). Capping the country on both ends are 1,400 miles of coastline (Mediterranean and Atlantic). The Seine River flows east-west through Paris, the Rhône rumbles north-south 500 miles from the Alps to the Mediterranean, and the Loire travels east-west, roughly dividing the country into north and south. Mont Blanc (15,780 feet) is Western Europe's highest point.

Latitude and Longitude: 46°N and 2°E (similar latitude to the states of Washington and Maine).

Major Cities: Nearly one in five lives in greater Paris (12 million in the metropolitan area, 2.3 million in the city). Marseille, on the Mediterranean coast, and Lyon, in the southeast, both have about 1.5 million people.

Economy: The Gross Domestic Product is $2.5 trillion (slightly bigger than California's $2.4 trillion); GDP per capita is about $43,600 (US is about $57,500). Though the French are among the world's biggest wine producers, they drink much of it themselves. France's free-market economy is tempered by the government, which collects some of Europe's highest taxes (21 percent of GDP—compared to 11 percent in the US) and invests both in industry and social spending. Despite the stereotypes, the French work as much as their EU neighbors—that is, 20 percent less than Americans (but with greater per-hour productivity).

Government: President Emmanuel Macron heads a centrist government along with president-appointed Prime Minister Édouard Philippe. The upper-house Senate (348 seats) is chosen by an electoral college; the National Assembly (577 seats) by popular vote.

Flag: The Revolution produced the well-known *tricolore,* whose three colors are vertical bands of blue, white, and red.

The Average Jean: The average French person is 41 years old, will live 82 years, and consumes a glass and a half of wine a day. The average worker enjoys five weeks of holiday and vacation a year.

Soccer Champions: In 2018 France won the World Cup for the second time in two decades—which makes almost every citizen proud *(Allez les Bleus!)*. This would be like the entire US winning the Super Bowl—not just a city, but the whole country watched with excitement, then celebrated with 20 years of pent-up gusto.

in southwest France) married Louis VII, king of France, bringing Aquitaine under French rule. They divorced, and she married Henry of Normandy, soon to be Henry II of England. This marital union gave England control of a huge swath of land from the English Channel to the Pyrenees. For 300 years, France and England would struggle over control of Aquitaine. Any enemy of the French king would find a natural ally in the English king.

In 1328, the French king Charles IV died without a son. The English king (Edward III), Charles IV's nephew, was interested in the throne, but the French resisted. This quandary pitted France, the biggest and richest country in Europe, against England, which had the biggest army. They fought from 1337 to 1453 in what was modestly called the Hundred Years' War.

Regional powers from within France actually sided with England. Burgundy took Paris, captured the royal family, and recognized the English king as heir to the French throne. England controlled France from the Loire north, and things looked bleak for the French king.

Enter Joan of Arc, a 16-year-old peasant girl driven by religious voices. France's national heroine left home to support Charles VII, the dauphin (boy prince, heir to the throne but too young to rule). Joan rallied the French, ultimately inspiring them to throw out the English. In 1430, Joan was captured by the Burgundians, who sold her to the English, who then convicted her of heresy and burned her at the stake in Rouen. But the inspiration of Joan of Arc lived on, and by 1453 English holdings on the Continent had dwindled to the port of Calais. (For more on Joan of Arc, see page 229.)

By 1500, a strong, centralized France had emerged, with borders similar to those of today. Its kings (from the Renaissance François I through the Henrys and all those Louises) were model divine monarchs, setting the standards for absolute rule in Europe.

Outrage over the power plays and spending sprees of the kings—coupled with the modern thinking of the Enlightenment (whose leaders were the French *philosophes*)—led to the French Revolution of 1789. In France, it was the end of the *ancien régime*, as well as its notion that some are born to rule, while others are born to be ruled.

The excesses of the Revolution in turn led to the rise of Napoleon, who ruled the French empire as a dictator. Eventually, *his* excesses ushered him into a South Atlantic exile, and after another half-century of monarchy and empire, the French settled on a compromise role for their leader. The modern French "king" is ruled by a constitution. Rather than dress in leotards and powdered wigs, the president goes to work in a suit and carries a briefcase.

The 20th century spelled the end of France's reign as a military and political superpower. Devastating wars with Germany in 1870, 1914, and 1940—and the loss of her colonial holdings—left France with not quite enough land, people, or production to be a top player on a global scale. But the 21st century may see France rise again: Paris is a cultural capital of Europe, and France—under the EU banner—is a key player in unifying Europe as a single economic power. And when Europe becomes a superpower, Paris may yet be its capital.

CONTEMPORARY POLITICS IN FRANCE

Today, the political issues in France are the economy, terrorism, its relationship with the European Union, and immigration.

French unemployment remains high (over 10 percent, even higher for youth) and growth has flatlined. France has not balanced its books since 1974, and public spending—at 56 percent of GDP—chews up a bigger chunk of output than any other eurozone country. The overwhelming challenge for French leadership is to address its economic problems while maintaining the high level of social services that the French people expect from their government.

France also has its economic strengths: a well-educated workforce, an especially robust service sector and high-end manufacturing industry, and more firms big enough to rank in the global Fortune 500 than any other European country. Ironically, while France's economy may be one of the world's largest, the French remain skeptical about the virtues of capitalism and its requisite work ethic. Globalization conflicts in a fundamental way with French values—many fear losing what makes their society unique in the quest for a bland, globalized world. Business conversation outside the office is generally avoided, as it implies a fascination with money that the French find vulgar; it's considered gauche even to ask what someone does for a living (in part because they think there's much more to a person than their occupation). In France, CEOs are not glorified as celebrities—chefs are.

The French believe the economy should support social good, not vice versa. This has produced a cradle-to-grave social security system of which the French are proud. France's poverty rate is half of that in the US, proof to the French they are on the right track. On the other hand, if you're considering starting a business in France, think again—taxes are daunting (figure a total small-business tax rate of around 66 percent—and likely to increase). And a job-security entitlement makes it difficult for employers to find motivated staff. You'll feel this impact in small hotels and restaurants where owners run themselves ragged trying to do everything themselves.

French voters are notorious for their belief in the free market's

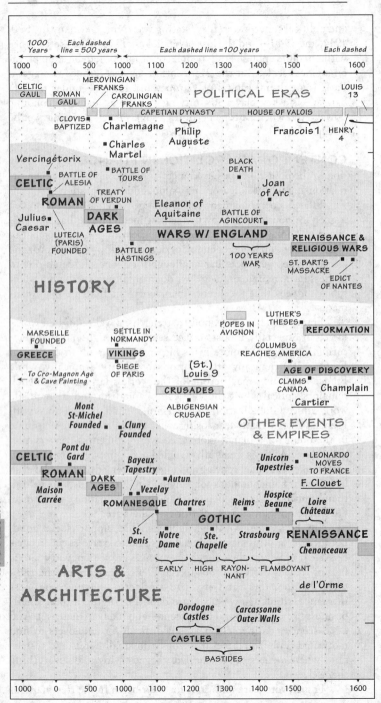

PAST & PRESENT

French History & Art Timeline

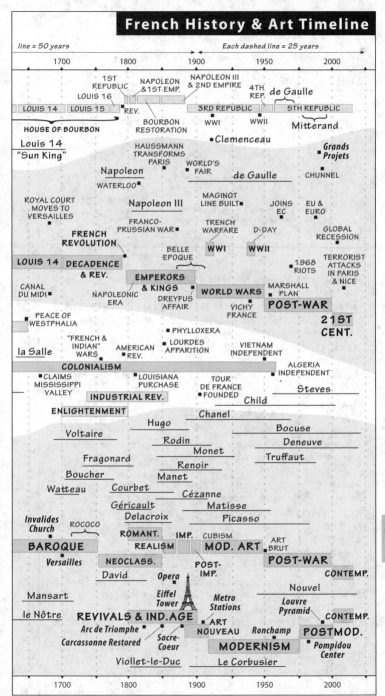

line = 50 years   *Each dashed line = 25 years*

1700   1800   1900   1950   2000

1ST REPUBLIC
LOUIS 16
NAPOLEON & 1ST. EMP.
NAPOLEON III & 2ND EMPIRE
4TH REP.
de Gaulle
LOUIS 14   LOUIS 15   REV.
3RD REPUBLIC
5TH REPUBLIC
HOUSE OF BOURBON
BOURBON RESTORATION
WWI   WWII
Mitterand
Louis 14 "Sun King"

HAUSSMANN TRANSFORMS PARIS
Clemenceau
Grands Projets
Napoleon
WORLD'S FAIR
de Gaulle
CHUNNEL
WATERLOO
ROYAL COURT MOVES TO VERSAILLES
Napoleon III
MAGINOT LINE BUILT
JOINS EC
EU & EURO
FRANCO-PRUSSIAN WAR
TRENCH WARFARE
D-DAY
GLOBAL RECESSION
FRENCH REVOLUTION
WWI   WWII
BELLE EPOQUE
LOUIS 14   DECADENCE & REV.
1968 RIOTS
TERRORIST ATTACKS IN PARIS & NICE
EMPERORS & KINGS
WORLD WARS
MARSHALL PLAN
CANAL DU MIDI
NAPOLEONIC ERA
DREYFUS AFFAIR
VICHY FRANCE
POST-WAR
PEACE OF WESTPHALIA
21ST CENT.
PHYLLOXERA
"FRENCH & INDIAN" WARS
LOURDES APPARITION
la Salle
AMERICAN REV.
VIETNAM INDEPENDENT
COLONIALISM
ALGERIA INDEPENDENT
CLAIMS MISSISSIPPI VALLEY
LOUISIANA PURCHASE
TOUR DE FRANCE FOUNDED
Steves
INDUSTRIAL REV.
Child
ENLIGHTENMENT
Chanel
Hugo
Bocuse
Voltaire
Rodin
Deneuve
Monet
Truffaut
Fragonard
Renoir
Boucher
Manet
Watteau
Courbet
Cézanne
Géricault
Matisse
Delacroix
Picasso
Invalides Church
ROCOCO
BAROQUE
ROMANT.
REALISM
IMP.
CUBISM
MOD. ART
ART BRUT
POST-WAR
Versailles
NEOCLASS.
POST-IMP.
CONTEMP.
David
Opera
Nouvel
Mansart
Eiffel Tower
Metro Stations
Louvre Pyramid
CONTEMP.
le Nôtre
REVIVALS & IND. AGE
ART NOUVEAU
Ronchamp
POSTMOD.
Arc de Triomphe
Carcassonne Restored
Sacre-Coeur
MODERNISM
Pompidou Center
Viollet-le-Duc
Le Corbusier

1700   1800   1900   1950   2000

Typical Church Architecture

History comes to life when you visit a centuries-old church. Even if you wouldn't know your apse from a hole in the ground, learning a few simple terms will enrich your experience. Note that not every church has every feature, and a "cathedral" isn't a type of church architecture, but rather a designation for a church that's a governing center for a local bishop.

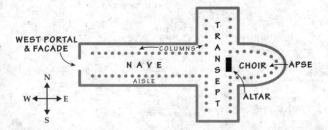

Aisles: The long, generally low-ceilinged arcades that flank the nave.

Altar: The raised area with a ceremonial table (often adorned with candles or a crucifix), where the priest prepares and serves the bread and wine for Communion.

Apse: The space beyond the altar, often bordered with small chapels.

Barrel Vault: A continuous round-arched ceiling that resembles an extended upside-down U.

Choir: A cozy area, often screened off, located within the church nave and near the high altar where services are sung in a more intimate setting.

Cloister: Covered hallways bordering a square or rectangular open-air courtyard, traditionally where monks and nuns got fresh air.

Facade: The front exterior of the church's main (west) entrance, usually highly decorated.

Groin Vault: An arched ceiling formed where two equal barrel vaults meet at right angles. Less common usage: medieval jock strap.

Narthex: The area (portico or foyer) between the main entry and the nave.

Nave: The long, central section of the church (running west to east, from the entrance to the altar) where the congregation sits or stands through the service.

Transept: In a traditional cross-shaped floor plan, the transept is one of the two parts forming the "arms" of the cross. The transepts run north-south, perpendicularly crossing the east-west nave.

West Portal: The main entry to the church (on the west end, opposite the main altar).

Typical Castle Architecture

Castles were fortified residences for medieval nobles. Castles come in all shapes and sizes, but knowing a few general terms will help you understand them.

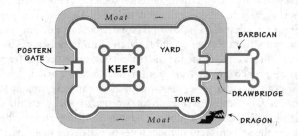

Barbican: A fortified gatehouse, sometimes a stand-alone building located outside the main walls.

Crenellation: A gap-toothed pattern of stones atop the parapet.

Drawbridge: A bridge that could be raised or lowered, using counterweights or a chain-and-winch.

Great Hall: The largest room in the castle, serving as throne room, conference center, and dining hall.

Hoardings (or Gallery or Brattice): Wooden huts built onto the upper parts of the stone walls. They served as watch towers, living quarters, and fighting platforms.

Keep (or Donjon): A high, strong stone tower in the center of the complex; the lord's home and refuge of last resort.

Loopholes (or Embrasures): Narrow wall slits through which soldiers could shoot arrows.

Machicolation: A stone ledge jutting out from the wall, with holes through which soldiers could drop rocks or boiling liquid onto wall-scaling enemies below.

Moat: A ditch encircling the wall, sometimes filled with water.

Parapet: Outer railing of the wall walk.

Portcullis: An iron grille that could be lowered across the entrance.

Postern Gate: A small, unfortified side or rear entrance. In wartime, it became a "sally-port" used to launch surprise attacks, or as an escape route.

Towers: Square or round structures with crenellated tops or conical roofs serving as lookouts, chapels, living quarters, or the dungeon.

Turret: A small lookout tower rising from the top of the wall.

Wall Walk (or Allure): A pathway atop the wall where guards could patrol and where soldiers stood to fire at the enemy.

Yard (or Bailey): An open courtyard inside the castle walls.

heartless cruelty. France is routinely plagued with strikes, demonstrations, and slowdowns as workers try to preserve their hard-earned rights in the face of a competitive global economy.

Another ongoing issue French leaders are working to address is immigration, which is shifting the country's ethnic and cultural makeup in ways that challenge French society. Traditionally, every French citizen has been expected to speak French. Ten percent of France's population is now of North African descent, mainly immigrants from former colonies. Many immigrants are Muslim, raising cultural questions in this heavily Catholic society (two out of three French are at least nominally Roman Catholic) with a history of official state secularism. In 2011 the government (quite controversially) made it illegal for women to wear a full, face-covering veil *(niqāb)* in public. Debates continue about whether banning the veil enforces democracy—or squelches diversity.

A series of terrorist attacks in France in recent years has battered the nation's self-confidence. Locals have had to adjust to life with armed soldiers patrolling rail stations and streets. Many of the attackers were immigrants—and French citizens. Each attack raises serious questions about immigration, policing, class divisions, and what it means to be French. Together they have undermined the nation's self-confidence.

France is part of the European Union, the "United States of Europe" that has successfully dissolved borders and implemented a common currency, the euro. France's governments have been decidedly pro-EU and critical to the EU's success. But many French are Euroskeptics, afraid that EU meddling threatens their job security and social benefits. Britain's 2016 vote to leave the EU ("Brexit") raised the question: Is a Frexit possible? The EU can survive sans Britain but probably not sans France. For now, that possibility seems to have been shelved with President Emmanuel Macron, who is pro-EU.

France is governed by a president elected by popular vote every five years. The president then selects the prime minister, who in turn chooses the cabinet ministers. Collectively, this executive branch is known as the *gouvernement*. The parliament consists of a Senate (348 seats) and Assemblée Nationale (577 seats).

In France, voters have an array of political parties to choose from, making compromise and coalition-building essential to keeping power. Even the biggest parties rarely get more than one-third of the seats in parliament. And, because the parliament can force the *gouvernement* to resign at any time, it's essential that the *gouvernement* work with them.

For a snapshot of the current political landscape, look no further than the 2012 and 2017 elections. (French elections last only several months, with just one TV debate—yes, the French election season is that short).

In 2012, socialist François Hollande defeated center-right incumbent Nicolas Sarkozy. But when Hollande's term became fraught by scandal, rocked by terrorist events, and weighed down by a flat economy, Hollande opted against running for re-election in 2017. That left the field wide open.

The 2017 election was a wild ride, with events never seen before in France. Eleven candidates competed in the French version of a primary, reducing the field to two for the final vote. For the first time since de Gaulle, neither of the two finalists were from the traditional right and left parties. (Imagine a US presidential election sans Republican or Democrat!) Emmanuel Macron, a centrist businessman, had no party affiliation and had never held elected office. Marine Le Pen, though a politician, represented the far-right National Front party (now called the National Rally—*Rassemblement National* in French), once a pariah party tarnished by accusations of anti-Semitism.

Le Pen rallied support by proposing to limit immigration and step back from the EU. Macron proposed a moderate stay-the-course plan that attracted both liberals and moderate conservatives. The tone of the debates was uncharacteristically nasty—something totally unheard of in genteel France. The French were presented with a stark choice: moderate vs. extreme. In the end, they overwhelmingly chose the moderate path. Macron won with a whopping 66 percent of the vote. Still, Le Pen's result was the best yet for a far-right candidate.

Elected at 39, Macron is France's youngest leader since Napoleon Bonaparte (and looks even younger). His success was completely unpredicted. He won as an outsider, representing a change from traditional party politics. (Sound familiar?)

After an almost flawless first year in office, Macron's second year was a different story—his popularity dropped from 64 percent to below 30 percent. The working class felt abandoned by Macron, calling him "the president of the rich" (thanks to more business-friendly policies, like canceling the 70 percent wealth tax and easing labor laws, making it easier for companies to fire employees). His proposal to raise the tax on gasoline led to the first true crisis of his presidency. The "yellow vest" anti-government protestors have created havoc and dominated the French news. With an election coming in 2022, Macron has work to do to restore the country's faith in his ability to connect with the working class.

What is clear is that, regardless of the shifting winds of politics, France has a social structure that stretches back 1,000 years.

For more about French history, consider Europe 101: History and Art for the Traveler *by Rick Steves and Gene Openshaw, available at* www.ricksteves.com.

PAST & PRESENT

Top French Notables in History

Madame and Monsieur Cro-Magnon: Prehistoric hunter-gatherers who moved to France (c. 30,000 BC), painted cave walls at Lascaux and Font-de-Gaume, and eventually settled down as farmers (c. 10,000 BC).

Vercingétorix (72 BC-46 BC): This long-haired warrior rallied the Gauls against Julius Caesar's invading Roman legions (52 BC). Defeated by Caesar, France fell under Roman domination, resulting in 500 years of peace and prosperity. During that time, the Romans established cities, built roads, taught in Latin, and converted people to Christianity.

Charlemagne (742-814): For Christmas in 800, the pope gave King Charlemagne the title of Emperor, thus uniting much of Europe under the leadership of the Franks ("France"). Charlemagne stabilized France amid centuries of barbarian invasions. After his death, the empire was split, carving the outlines of modern France and Germany.

Eleanor of Aquitaine (c. 1122-1204): The beautiful, sophisticated ex-wife of the King of France married the King of England, creating an uneasy union between the two countries. During her lifetime, French culture was spread across Europe by roving troubadours, theological scholars, and skilled architects pioneering "the French style"—a.k.a. Gothic.

Joan of Arc (1412-1431): When France and England fought the Hundred Years' War (1337-1453), this teen—guided by voices in her head—rallied the French troops. Though Joan was captured and burned as a heretic, the French eventually drove England out for good, establishing the current borders. Over the centuries, the church upgraded Joan's status from heretic to saint (canonized in 1920).

François I (1494-1547): This Renaissance king ruled a united, modern nation, making it a cultural center that hosted the Italian Leonardo da Vinci. François set the tone for future absolute monarchs, punctuating his commands with the phrase, "For such is our pleasure."

Louis XIV (1638-1715): Charismatic and cunning, the "Sun King" ruled Europe's richest, most populous, most powerful nation-state. Every educated European spoke French, dressed in Louis-style leotards and powdered wigs, and built Versailles-like palaces. Though Louis ruled as an absolute monarch (distracting the nobility with courtly games), his reign also fostered the arts and philosophy, sowing the seeds of democracy and revolution.

Marie-Antoinette (1755-1793): The wife

of Louis XVI came to symbolize (probably unfairly) the decadence of France's ruling class. When Revolution broke out (1789), she was arrested, imprisoned, and executed—one of thousands guillotined on Paris' Place de la Concorde as an enemy of the people.

Napoleon Bonaparte (1769-1821): This daring young military man

became a hero during the Revolution, fighting Europe's royalty. He went on to conquer much of the Continent, become leader of France, and eventually, rule as a dictator with the title of emperor. In 1815, an allied Europe defeated and exiled Napoleon, reinstating the French monarchy—though future kings and emperors (including Napoleon's nephew, who ruled as Napoleon III) were somewhat subject to democratic constraints.

Claude Monet (1840-1926): His Impressionist paintings captured the soft-focus beauty of the belle époque—middle-class folk enjoying drinks in cafés, walks in gardens, and picnics along the Seine. At the turn of the 20th century, French culture reigned supreme while its economic and political clout was fading, and was soon shattered by World War I.

Charles de Gaulle (1890-1970): This career military man helped France survive occupation by Nazi Germany with his rousing radio broadcasts and unbending faith in his countrymen. He left politics after World War II, but after France's divisive wars in Vietnam and Algeria, he became president of the Fifth Republic in 1959. De Gaulle shocked allies by granting Algeria independence, blocking Britain's entry into the Common Market, and withdrawing from the military wing of NATO. Student riots in the late 1960s eventually led to his resignation in 1969.

Recent French Notables: Which French personalities of the last century will history remember? Marcel Marceau (1923-2007), world-famous mime? Brigitte Bardot (b. 1934), film actress, crusader for animal rights, and popularizer of the bikini? President François Mitterrand (1916-1996), the driving force behind Paris' La Grande Arche and Opéra Bastille? Chef Paul Bocuse (1926-2018), inventor of nouvelle cuisine? Yves Saint Laurent (1936-2008), the great fashion designer? Jean-Marie Le Pen (b. 1928), father of the far-right National Rally party...and 2017 presidential runner-up Marine Le Pen? Bernard Kouchner (b. 1939), cofounder of Doctors Without Borders? Zinédine Zidane (b. 1972), star soccer player, whose Algerian roots helped raise the status of Arabs in France? Or will it be actress Catherine Deneuve (b. 1943), NBA star Tony Parker (b. 1982), or wrestler-turned-actor Andre the Giant (1946-1993)? (Giants all.)

PRACTICALITIES

This chapter covers the practical skills of European travel: how to get tourist information, pay for things, sightsee efficiently, find good-value accommodations, eat affordably but well, use technology wisely, and get between destinations smoothly. For more information on these topics, see www.ricksteves.com/travel-tips.

Tourist Information

The French national tourist office is a wealth of information. **Before your trip,** scan their website—http://us.france.fr. It has particularly good resources for special-interest travel and plenty of free-to-download brochures. Paris' official TI website, www.parisinfo.com, offers practical information on hotels, special events, museums, children's activities, fashion, nightlife, and more.

In France, a good first stop is generally the tourist information office (abbreviated **TI** in this book). TIs are in business to help you enjoy spending money in their town, but even so, I still make a point to swing by to confirm sightseeing plans, pick up a city map, and get information on public transit, walking tours, special events, and nightlife. Anticipating a harried front-line staffer, prepare a list of questions and a proposed plan to double-check. Some TIs have information on the entire country or at least the region, so try to pick up maps and get information for destinations you'll be visiting later in your trip. Towns with a lot of tourism generally have English-speaking guides available for private hire through the TI (about €100 for a two-hour guided town walk).

The French call TIs by different names: *Office de Tourisme* and *Bureau de Tourisme* are used in cities; *Syndicat d'Initiative* and *Information Touristique* are used in small towns. Also look for *Accueil* signs in airports and at popular sights. These information booths are staffed with seasonal helpers who provide tourists with limited, though generally sufficient, information. Smaller TIs are often closed from 12:00 to 14:00 and on Sundays.

Other Helpful Services: Several private companies offer trip-planning services for a fee. **Detours in France** offers self-drive itinerary packages, hotel bookings, and guided tours of any region in France (tel. 09 83 20 71 56, www.detours-in-france.com). **Paris Webservices** focuses on Paris-specific assistance (tel. 01 45 56 91 67 or 09 52 06 02 59, www.pariswebservices.com, contactpws@ pariswebservices.com).

Travel Tips

Emergency and Medical Help: For any emergency service—ambulance, police, or fire—call **112** from a mobile phone or landline. Operators, who in most countries speak English, will deal with your request or route you to the right emergency service. For hearing-assisted help for all services, dial 114. If you get sick, do as the French do and go to a pharmacist for advice. Or ask at your hotel for help—they'll know the nearest medical and emergency services.

ETIAS Registration: Beginning in 2021, US and Canadian citizens may be required to register online with the European Travel Information and Authorization System (ETIAS) before entering certain European countries (quick and easy process, $8 fee, valid 3 years). A useful private website with more details is www. schengenvisainfo.com/etias.

Theft or Loss: To replace a passport, you'll need to go in person to an embassy or consulate (see next). If your credit and debit cards disappear, cancel and replace them (see "Damage Control for Lost Cards," later). File a police report, either on the spot or within a day or two; you'll need it to submit an insurance claim for lost or stolen rail passes or travel gear, and it can help with replacing your passport or credit and debit cards. For more information, see www. ricksteves.com/help.

US Consulate and Embassy: Embassy visits usually require

PRACTICALITIES

an appointment online or by phone. Paris—tel. 01 43 12 22 22 (2 Avenue Gabriel, to the left as you face Hôtel Crillon, Mo: Concorde, https://fr.usembassy.gov). Marseille—tel. 01 43 12 48 85 (Place Varian Fry, 13286 Marseille, https://fr.usembassy.gov/embassy-consulates/marseille).

Canadian Consulate and Embassy: Paris—tel. 01 44 43 29 00 (130 Rue du Faubourg Saint-Honoré, Mo: Saint-Philippe-du-Roule or Miromesnil, www.canadainternational.gc.ca/france). Nice—tel. 04 93 92 93 22 (10 Rue Lamartine, nice@international.gc.ca). For 24/7 emergency assistance call collect to Canada 613/996-8885 or email sos@international.gc.ca.

Time Zones: France, like most of continental Europe, is generally six/nine hours ahead of the East/West Coasts of the US. The exceptions are the beginning and end of Daylight Saving Time: Europe "springs forward" the last Sunday in March (two weeks after most of North America), and "falls back" the last Sunday in October (one week before North America). For a handy time converter, use the world clock app on your mobile phone or download one (see www.timeanddate.com).

Business Hours: You'll find much of rural France closed weekdays from 12:00 to 14:00 (lunch is sacred). On Sunday, most businesses are closed (family is sacred), though some small shops such as *boulangeries* (bakeries) are open until noon, special events and weekly markets pop up, and museums are open all day (but public transportation options are limited). On Mondays, some businesses are closed until 14:00 and possibly all day. Smaller towns are often quiet and downright boring on Sundays and Mondays, unless it's market day.

Watt's Up? Europe's electrical system is 220 volts, instead of North America's 110 volts. Most newer electronics (such as laptops, battery chargers, and hair dryers) convert automatically, so you won't need a converter, but you will need an adapter plug with two round prongs, sold inexpensively at travel stores in the US. Avoid bringing older appliances that don't automatically convert voltage; instead, buy a cheap replacement in Europe.

Discounts: Discounts for sights are generally not listed in this book. However, seniors (age 60 and over), youths under 18, and students and teachers with proper identification cards (www.isic.org) can get discounts at many sights—always ask. To inquire about a senior discount, ask, *"Réduction troisième âge?"* (ray-dewk-see-ohn trwah-zee-ehm ahzh). Some discounts are available only to European citizens.

Online Translation Tips: Google's Chrome browser instantly translates websites; Translate.google.com is also handy. The Google Translate app converts spoken English into most European languages (and vice versa) and can also translate text it "reads" with your phone's camera.

Exchange Rate

1 euro (€) = about $1.20

To convert prices in euros to dollars, add about 20 percent: €20 = about $24, €50 = about $60. (Check www.oanda.com for the latest exchange rates.) Just like the dollar, one euro (€) is broken down into 100 cents. Coins range from €0.01 to €2, and bills from €5 to €200 (bills over €50 are rarely used).

Money

Here's my basic strategy for using money in Europe:

- Upon arrival, head for a cash machine (ATM) at the airport and withdraw some local currency, using a debit card with low international transaction fees.
- Pay for most purchases with your choice of cash or a credit card. You'll save money by minimizing your credit and debit card exchange fees. The trend is for bigger expenses to be paid by credit card, but cash is still the standby for small purchases and tips.
- Keep your cards and cash safe in a money belt.

PLASTIC VERSUS CASH

Although credit cards are widely accepted in Europe (particularly in Paris), cash is sometimes the only way to pay for cheap food, taxis, tips, and local guides. Some businesses (especially smaller ones, such as B&Bs and mom-and-pop cafés and shops) may charge you extra for using a credit card—or might not accept credit cards at all. Having cash on hand helps you out of a jam if your card randomly doesn't work.

I use my credit card to book and pay for hotel reservations, to buy advance tickets for events or sights, and to cover most expenses. It can also be smart to use plastic near the end of your trip, to avoid another visit to the ATM.

WHAT TO BRING

I pack the following and keep it all safe in my money belt.

Debit Card: Use this at ATMs to withdraw local cash.

Credit Card: Handy for bigger purchases (at hotels, shops, restaurants, travel agencies, car-rental agencies, and so on), payment machines, and ordering online.

Backup Card: Some travelers carry a third card (debit or credit; ideally from a different bank), in case one gets lost, demagnetized, eaten by a temperamental machine, or simply doesn't work.

A Stash of Cash: For an emergency reserve, in most of Europe

PRACTICALITIES

bring dollars. But in France consider bringing €200 in €20-50 bills (bring euros, as dollars can be hard to change in France).

BEFORE YOU GO

Use this pretrip checklist.

Know your cards. Debit cards from any major US bank will work in any standard European bank's ATM (ideally, use a debit card with a Visa or MasterCard logo). As for credit cards, Visa and MasterCard are universal, American Express is less common, and Discover is unknown in Europe.

Know your PIN. Make sure you know the numeric, four-digit PIN for all your cards, both debit and credit. Request it if you don't have one and allow time to receive the information by mail.

All credit and debit cards now have chips that authenticate and secure transactions. Europeans insert their chip cards into the payment machine slot, then enter a PIN. American cards should work in most transactions—but you'll need a PIN at self-service machines at train stations, tollbooths, gas pumps, or parking lots.

Report your travel dates. Let your bank know that you'll be using your debit and credit cards in Europe, and when and where you're headed.

Adjust your ATM withdrawal limit. Find out how much you can take out daily and ask for a higher daily withdrawal limit if you want to get more cash at once. Note that European ATMs will withdraw funds only from checking accounts; you're unlikely to have access to your savings account.

Ask about fees. For any purchase or withdrawal made with a card, you may be charged a currency conversion fee (1-3 percent) and/or a Visa or MasterCard international transaction fee (1 percent). Consider getting a new debit or credit card. Reputable no-fee cards include those from Capital One, as well as Charles Schwab debit cards. Most credit unions and some airline loyalty cards have low-to-no international transaction fees.

IN EUROPE
Using Cash Machines

European cash machines have English-language instructions and work just like they do at home—except they spit out local currency instead of dollars, calculated at the day's standard bank-to-bank rate.

In most places, ATMs are easy to locate—in France ask for a *distributeur* (dee-stree-bew-tur). When possible, withdraw cash from a bank-run ATM located just outside that bank. Ideally use it during the bank's opening hours so if your card is munched by the machine, you can go inside for help.

PRACTICALITIES

If your debit card doesn't work, try a lower amount—your request may have exceeded your withdrawal limit or the ATM's limit. If you still have a problem, try a different ATM or come back later—your bank's network may be temporarily down.

Avoid "independent" ATMs, such as Travelex, Euronet, Moneybox, Cardpoint, and Cashzone. These have high fees, can be less secure than a bank ATM, and may try to trick users with "dynamic currency conversion" (see below).

Exchanging Cash

Avoid exchanging money in Europe; it's a big rip-off. In a pinch you can always find exchange desks at major train stations or airports—convenient but with crummy rates. Anything over 5 percent for a transaction is piracy. Banks generally do not exchange money unless you have an account with them.

Using Credit Cards

US credit cards no longer require a signature for verification, but don't be surprised if a European card reader generates a receipt for you to sign or prompts you to enter a PIN (it's important to know the code for each of your cards). After entering your PIN, you may need to press "validate," usually shown as a "V" on the keypad or touch screen. If a cashier is present, you should have no problems.

In France, self-service payment machines (transit-ticket kiosks, parking, freeway tollbooths, etc.) can be a headache, as US cards may not work in unattended transactions even if you know the PIN (though this is rare with updated cards). If that happens, look for a cashier who can process your card manually—or pay in cash. (If all else fails, you could give cash to a French person in return for using their card).

Drivers Beware: Be aware of potential problems using a US credit card to fill up at an unattended gas station, enter a parking garage, or exit a toll road. Carry cash in bills under €50 and be prepared to move on to the next gas station if necessary. When approaching a toll payment plaza, look for coin icons (meaning cash) or a green arrow. For more tips, see the "Driving" section, later.

Dynamic Currency Conversion

If merchants offer to convert your purchase price into dollars (called dynamic currency conversion, or DCC), refuse this "service." You'll pay extra for the expensive convenience of seeing your charge in dollars. If an ATM offers to "lock in" or "guarantee" your conversion rate, choose "proceed without conversion." Other prompts might state, "You can be charged in dollars: Press YES for dollars, NO for euros." Always choose the local currency.

Security Tips

Pickpockets target tourists. To safeguard your cash, wear a money belt—a pouch with a strap that you buckle around your waist like a belt and tuck under your clothes. Keep your cash, credit cards, and passport secure in your money belt, and carry only a day's spending money in your front pocket or wallet.

Before inserting your card into an ATM, inspect the front. If anything looks crooked, loose, or damaged, it could be a sign of a card-skimming device. When entering your PIN, carefully block other people's view of the keypad.

Don't use a debit card for purchases. Because a debit card pulls funds directly from your bank account, potential charges incurred by a thief will stay on your account while the fraudulent use is investigated by your bank.

To access your accounts online while traveling, be sure to use a secure connection (see the "Tips on Internet Security" sidebar, later in this chapter).

Damage Control for Lost Cards

If you lose your credit or debit card, report the loss immediately to the respective global customer-assistance centers. With a mobile phone, call these 24-hour US numbers: Visa (tel. +1 303/967-1096), MasterCard (tel. +1 636/722-7111), and American Express (tel. +1 336/393-1111). From a landline, you can call these US numbers collect by going through a local operator. European toll-free numbers can be found at the websites for Visa and MasterCard.

For another option (with the same results), you can call these toll-free numbers in France: Visa (tel. 08 00 90 11 79), MasterCard (tel. 08 00 90 13 87), and American Express (tel. 08 05 54 05 24).

You'll need to provide the primary cardholder's identification-verification details (such as birth date, mother's maiden name, or Social Security number). You can generally receive a temporary card within two or three business days in Europe (see www.ricksteves.com/help for more).

If you report your loss within two days, you typically won't be responsible for unauthorized transactions on your account, although many banks charge a liability fee of $50.

TIPPING

Tipping *(donner un pourboire)* in France isn't as automatic and generous as it is in the US. For special service, tips are appreciated, but not expected. As in the US, the proper amount depends on your resources, tipping philosophy, and the circumstances, but some general guidelines apply.

Restaurants: At cafés and restaurants, a service charge is included in the price of what you order, and it's unnecessary to tip extra, though you can for helpful service. For details on tipping in restaurants, see "Eating," later.

Taxis: For a typical ride, round up your fare a bit (for instance, if the fare is €13, pay €14). If the cabbie hauls your bags and zips you to the airport to help you catch your flight, you might want to toss in a little more. But if you feel like you're being driven in circles, skip the tip.

Services: In general, if someone in the tourism or service industry does a super job for you, a small tip of a euro or two is appropriate...but not required. If you're not sure whether (or how much) to tip, ask a local for advice.

GETTING A VAT REFUND

Wrapped into the purchase price of your French souvenirs is a Value-Added Tax (VAT) of about 20 percent. You're entitled to get most of that tax back if you purchase more than €175 (about $210) worth of goods at a store that participates in the VAT-refund scheme. Typically, you must ring up the minimum at a single retailer—you can't add up your purchases from various shops to reach the required amount. (If the store ships the goods to your US home, VAT is not assessed on your purchase.)

Getting your refund is straightforward...and worthwhile if you spend a significant amount on souvenirs.

Get the paperwork. Have the merchant completely fill out the necessary refund document, called a *bordereau de détaxe*. You'll have to present your passport. Get the paperwork done before you leave the store to ensure you'll have everything you need (including your original sales receipt).

Get your stamp at the border or airport. Process your VAT document at your last stop in the European Union (such as at the airport) with the customs agent who deals with VAT refunds. Arrive an additional hour before you need to check in to allow time to find the customs office—and wait. Some customs desks are positioned before airport security; confirm the location before going through security.

It's best to keep your purchases in your carry-on. If they're not allowed as carry-on (such as knives), pack them in your checked bags and alert the check-in agent. You'll be sent (with your tagged bag) to a customs desk outside security; someone will examine your bag, stamp your paperwork, and put your bag on the belt. You're not supposed to use your purchased goods before you leave. If you show up at customs wearing your chic new shoes, officials might look the other way—or deny you a refund.

Collect your refund. You can claim your VAT refund from refund companies, such as Global Blue or Planet, with offices at major airports, ports, or border crossings (either before or after security, probably strategically located near a duty-free shop). At Paris' Charles de Gaulle, you'll find them at the check-in area (or ask for help at a Paris Tourisme desk). These services (which extract a 4 percent fee) can refund your money in cash immediately or credit your card (within two billing cycles). Otherwise, you'll need to mail the stamped refund documents to the address given by the shop where you made your purchase.

CUSTOMS FOR AMERICAN SHOPPERS

You can take home $800 worth of items per person duty-free, once every 31 days. Many processed and packaged foods are allowed, including vacuum-packed cheeses, dried herbs, jams, baked goods, candy, chocolate, oil, vinegar, mustard, and honey. Fresh fruits and vegetables and most meats are not allowed, with exceptions for some canned items. As for alcohol, you can bring in one liter duty-free (it can be packed securely in your checked luggage, along with any other liquid-containing items).

To bring alcohol (or liquid-packed foods) in your carry-on bag on your flight home, buy it at a duty-free shop at the airport. You'll increase your odds of getting it onto a connecting flight if it's packaged in a "STEB"—a secure, tamper-evident bag. But stay away from liquids in opaque, ceramic, or metallic containers, which usually cannot be successfully screened (STEB or no STEB).

For details on allowable goods, customs rules, and duty rates, visit http://help.cbp.gov.

Sightseeing

Sightseeing can be hard work. Use these tips to make your visits to France's finest sights meaningful, fun, efficient, and painless.

MAPS AND NAVIGATION TOOLS

A good map is essential for efficient navigation while sightseeing. The maps in this book are concise and simple, designed to help you locate recommended destinations, sights, and local TIs, where you can pick up more in-depth maps. More detailed maps are sold at newsstands and bookstores.

You can also use a mapping app on your mobile device. Be aware that pulling up maps or turn-by-turn walking directions on the fly requires an internet connection: To use this feature, it's smart to get an international data plan. With Google Maps or City Maps 2Go, it's possible to download a map while online, then go offline and navigate without incurring data-roaming charges—though you can't search for an address or get real-time walking directions. A handful of other apps, including Apple Maps, Off-Maps, and Navfree, also allow you to use maps offline.

PRACTICALITIES

PLAN AHEAD

Set up an itinerary that allows you to fit in all your must-see sights. For a one-stop look at opening hours in the bigger cities, see the "At a Glance" sidebars for Paris, Normandy, Nice, Lyon, the Loire Valley châteaux, Provence, the French Riviera, and the Dordogne's prehistoric sights. Most sights keep stable hours, but you can easily confirm the latest by checking with the TI or visiting museum websites.

Don't put off visiting a must-see sight—you never know when a place will close unexpectedly for a holiday, strike, or restoration. Given how precious your vacation time is, I recommend getting reservations for any must-see sight that offers them (see page 27). Many museums are closed or have reduced hours at least a few days a year, especially on holidays such as Christmas, New Year's, and Labor Day (May 1). A list of holidays is in the appendix; check online for possible museum closures during your trip. In summer, some sights may stay open late; in the off-season, hours may be shorter.

Going at the right time helps avoid crowds. This book offers tips on the best times to see specific sights. Try visiting popular sights very early (arrive at least 15 minutes before opening time) or very late. Evening visits are usually peaceful, with fewer crowds. For example, Paris' Louvre and Orsay museums are open selected evenings, and the abbey at Mont St-Michel is open on summer evenings.

Many French monuments and cities (and some villages) are beautifully lit at night, making evening walks a joy. Sound-and-light shows *(son et lumière)* are outdoor events held at major buildings after dark; you'll take a seat and watch an array of colored lights illuminate the facade (e.g., of the town's cathedral) while a narrator or audioguide melodramatically tells the story of the place. These spectacles, which usually require a fee, can be a fun experience (though once is usually enough for most).

At Mont St-Michel and Carcassonne, it's best to arrive at about 17:00, spend the night, and explore in the evening and the next morning before the crowds descend. Visit these sights first thing or late in the day: Versailles, Château de Chenonceau, Les Baux, Roussillon, St-Paul-de-Vence, the Dordogne's riverfront villages, St-Cirq-Lapopie, and Pont du Gard.

If you plan to hire a local guide, reserve ahead by email. Popular guides can get booked up.

Study up. To get the most out of the self-guided tours and sight descriptions in this book, read them before you visit. The Louvre is more interesting if you understand why the *Venus de Milo* is so disarming.

AT SIGHTS

Here's what you can typically expect:

Entering: Several cities offer sightseeing passes (listed in this book) that can be worthwhile values. For example, most adult travelers visiting Paris should buy a Paris Museum Pass, which can speed you through lines and save you money. Without the pass, advance tickets can save time in line at popular sights (see page 59). It's always smart to reserve a ticket for the Eiffel Tower (not covered by Paris Museum Pass; for details, see page 91).

You may not be allowed to enter some sights if you arrive less than 30 to 60 minutes before closing time. And guards start ushering people out well before the actual closing time, so don't save the best for last.

Many sights have a security check, and some are fairly rigorous. Allow extra time for these lines. Some sights require you to check daypacks and coats. (If you'd rather not check your daypack, try carrying it tucked under your arm like a purse as you enter.)

At churches—which often offer interesting art (usually free) and a cool, welcome seat—a modest dress code (no bare shoulders or shorts) is encouraged though rarely enforced.

Photography: If the museum's photo policy isn't clearly posted, ask a guard. Generally, taking photos without a flash or tripod is allowed. Some sights ban selfie sticks; others ban photos altogether.

Temporary Exhibits: Museums may show special exhibits in addition to their permanent collection. Some exhibits are included in the entry price, while others come at an extra cost (which you may have to pay even if you don't want to see the exhibit).

Expect Changes: Artwork can be on tour, on loan, out sick, or shifted at the whim of the curator. Pick up a floor plan as you enter, and ask museum staff if you can't find a particular item. Say the title or artist's name, or point to the photograph in this book and ask for its location by saying, *"Où est?"* (oo ay).

Audioguides and Apps: Many sights rent hand-held audioguides, which generally offer worthwhile recorded descriptions in English. Many audioguides have a standard output jack so if you bring your own earbuds, you can often enjoy better sound. To save money, bring a Y-jack and share one audioguide with your travel partner. Increasingly, museums and sights offer apps—often free—that you can download to your mobile device (check their websites). And, I've produced free, downloadable audio tours for my Historic Paris and Rue Cler walks, plus tours of the Louvre, Orsay Museum, Versailles, and Père Lachaise Cemetery. Look for the ∩ in this book. For more on my audio tours, see page 28.

Services: Important sights usually have a reasonably priced on-site café or cafeteria (handy places to rejuvenate during a long visit). The WCs at sights are free and generally clean.

Before Leaving: At the gift shop, scan the postcard rack or thumb through a guidebook to be sure that you haven't overlooked something that you'd like to see. Every sight or museum offers more than what is covered in this book. Use the information in this book as an introduction—not the final word.

Sleeping

Good-value accommodations in France are generally easy to find. Choose from one- to five-star hotels (two and three stars are my

mainstays), bed-and-breakfasts (*chambres d'hôtes,* usually cheaper than hotels), hostels, campgrounds, and homes (*gîtes,* rented by the week).

Extensive and opinionated listings of good-value rooms are a major feature of this book's Sleeping section. Rather than list accommodations scattered throughout a town, I choose

hotels in my favorite neighborhoods that are convenient to your sightseeing.

My recommendations run the gamut, from dorm beds to fancy rooms with all the comforts. I like places that are clean, central, relatively quiet at night, reasonably priced, friendly, small enough to have a hands-on owner or manager, and run with a respect for French traditions. I'm more impressed by a handy location and a fun-loving philosophy than flat-screen TVs and a spa. Most of my recommendations fall short of perfection. But if I can find a place with most of these features, it's a keeper.

Book your accommodations as soon as your itinerary is set, especially if you want to stay at one of my top listings or if you'll be traveling during busy times. Reserving ahead is particularly important for Paris—the sooner, the better. Wherever you're staying, be ready for larger crowds in May and September and during these holiday periods: Easter weekend, Labor Day, Ascension weekend, Pentecost weekend, Bastille Day and the week during which it falls, and the winter holidays (mid-Dec-early Jan). Note that many holiday weekends fall in May, jamming French hotels. In August and at other times when business is slower, some Paris hotels offer lower rates to fill their rooms. Check hotel websites for the best deals.

Sleep Code

Hotels in this book are ranked according to the average price of a standard double room without breakfast in high season.

$$$$	**Splurge:**	Most rooms over €250
$$$	**Pricier:**	€190-250
$$	**Moderate:**	€130-190
$	**Budget:**	€70-130
¢	**Backpacker:**	Under €70
RS%	**Rick Steves discount**	
*	**French hotel rating system**	(0-5 stars)

Unless otherwise noted, credit cards are accepted, hotel staff speak basic English, and free Wi-Fi is available. Comparison-shop by checking prices at several hotels (on each hotel's own website, on a booking site, or by email). For the best deal, book directly with the hotel. Ask for a discount if paying in cash; if the listing includes **RS%**, request a Rick Steves discount.

See the appendix for a list of major holidays and festivals in France.

Some people make reservations as they travel, calling ahead a few days to a week before their arrival. It's best to call hotels at about 9:00 or 10:00, when the receptionist knows which rooms will be available. Some apps—such as HotelTonight—specialize in last-minute rooms, often at business-class hotels in big cities. If you encounter a language barrier, ask the fluent receptionist at your current hotel to call for you.

RATES AND DEALS

I've categorized my recommended accommodations based on price, indicated with a dollar-sign rating (see sidebar). The price ranges suggest an estimated cost for a one-night stay in a standard double room with a private toilet and shower in high season, don't include breakfast, and assume you're booking directly with the hotel (not through a booking site, which extracts a commission). Room prices can fluctuate significantly with demand and amenities (size, views, room class, and so on), but relative price categories remain constant.

Room rates are especially volatile at larger hotels that use "dynamic pricing" to set rates. Prices can skyrocket during festivals and conventions, while business hotels can have deep discounts on weekends when demand plummets. Of the many hotels I recommend, it's difficult to say which will be the best value on a given day—until you do your homework.

Booking Direct: Once your dates are set, compare prices at several hotels. You can do this by checking Hotels.com, Booking.

com, and hotel websites. But to get the best deal, contact hotels directly. When you go direct, the owner avoids the commission paid to booking sites, thereby leaving enough wiggle room to offer you a discount, a nicer room, or a free breakfast. If you prefer to book online or are considering a hotel chain, it's to your advantage to use the hotel's website. French hotels recently won the right to undercut Booking.com and Hotels.com prices on their websites; virtually all offer lower rates if you book direct. If the price they quote is higher than the offer on a booking site, let the hotel know, and they'll usually adjust the rate.

Getting a Discount: Some hotels extend a discount to those who pay cash or stay longer than three nights. And some accommodations offer a special discount for Rick Steves readers, indicated in this guidebook by the abbreviation "RS%." Discounts vary: Ask for details when you reserve. Generally, to qualify for this discount, you must book direct (not through a booking site), mention this book when you reserve, show it upon arrival, and sometimes stay a certain number of nights. In some cases, you may need to enter a discount code (which I've provided in the listing) in the booking form on the hotel's website. Rick Steves discounts apply to readers with either print or digital books. Understandably, discounts do not apply to promotional rates.

Room Taxes: Hotels in France must charge a daily tax *(taxe du séjour)* of about €1-4 per person per day (based on the number of stars the hotel has). Some hotels include it in their prices, but most add it to your bill.

TYPES OF ACCOMMODATIONS
Hotels

In this book, the price for a double room will normally range from €70 (very simple; toilet and shower down the hall) to €400 (grand lobbies, maximum plumbing, and the works), with most clustering around €100-140 (with private bathrooms).

Most hotels also offer single rooms and some offer larger rooms for four or more people (I call these "family rooms" in the listings). Some hotels can add an extra bed (for a small charge) to turn a double into a triple. In general, a triple room is cheaper than the cost of a double and a single. Three or four people can economize by requesting one big room.

The French have a simple hotel rating system based on amenities and rated by stars (indicated in this book by aster-

French Hotel-Room Lingo

Know your options. Hoteliers often don't mention the cheaper rooms—they assume you want a private bathroom or a bigger room. Here are the types of rooms and beds:

French	English
une chambre avec douche et WC	room with private shower and toilet
une chambre avec bain et WC	room with private bathtub and toilet
une chambre avec cabinet de toilette	room with a toilet (shower down the hall)
une chambre sans douche ni WC	room without a private shower or toilet
chambres communiquantes	connecting rooms (ideal for families)
une chambre simple, une single	a true single room
un grand lit	double bed (55 in. wide)
deux petits lits	twin beds (30-36 in. wide)
un lit queen-size	queen-size bed (63 in. wide)
un king size	king-size bed (usually two twins pushed together)
un lit pliant	folding bed
un berceau	baby crib
un lit d'enfant	child's bed

isks, from * through *****). One star is modest, two has most of the comforts, and three is generally a two-star with a fancier lobby and more elaborately designed rooms. Four-star places give a bit more comfort than those with three. Five stars probably offer more luxury than you'll have time to appreciate. Two-star-and-above hotels are required to have an English-speaking staff, though nearly all hotels I recommend have someone who speaks English.

The number of stars does not always reflect room size or guarantee quality. One- and two-star hotels are less expensive, but some three-star (and even a few four-star) hotels offer good value, justifying the extra cost. Unclassified hotels (no stars) can be bargains...or depressing dumps.

Within each hotel, prices vary depending on the size of the room, whether it has a tub or shower, and the bed type (tubs and twins cost more than showers and double beds). If you have a preference, ask for it. Hotels often have more rooms with tubs (which the French prefer) and are inclined to give you one by default. You can save lots by finding the rare room without a private shower or toilet.

Most French hotels now have queen-size beds—to confirm, ask, *"Avez-vous des lits queen-size?"* (ah-vay-voo day lee queen-size). Some hotels push two twins together under king-size sheets and blankets to make *le king-size*. If you'll take either twins or a double, ask for a generic *une chambre pour deux* (room for two) to avoid being needlessly turned away. Many hotels have a few family-friendly rooms that open up to each other *(chambres communiquantes)*.

Arrival and Check-In: Hotel elevators are becoming more common, though many older buildings still lack them. You may have to climb a flight of stairs to reach the elevator (if so, you can ask the front desk for help carrying your bags up). Elevators are typically small—packing light helps, or if you're driving, consider keeping bulky things in your car.

The EU requires that hotels collect your name, nationality, and ID number. When you check in, the receptionist may ask for your passport and may keep it for anywhere from a couple of minutes to a couple of hours. (If not comfortable leaving your passport at the desk for a long time, ask when you can pick it up.)

If you're arriving in the morning, your room probably won't be ready. Check your bag safely at the hotel and dive right into sightseeing.

Hotel lobbies, halls, and breakfast rooms are off-limits to smokers, though they can light up in their rooms. Still, I seldom smell any smoke in my rooms. Some hotels have nonsmoking rooms or floors—ask.

In Your Room: Most hotel rooms have a TV and free Wi-Fi (although in old buildings with thick walls, the Wi-Fi signal might be available only in the lobby). Many have a telephone, though some hotels have removed them.

The latest trend is to provide quilts as the only bed covering. While comfortable, they're warm in summers (forcing me to use air-conditioning)—ask the hotel for a sheet *(uhn drah)* for cooler sleeping.

Extra pillows and blankets are often in the closet or available on request. To get a pillow, ask for *"Un oreiller, s'il vous plaît"* (uhn oh-ray-yay, see voo play). Towels and linens aren't always replaced every day so hang your towel up to dry.

Breakfast and Meals: Most hotels offer breakfast, but it's rarely included in the room rates—pay attention when comparing rates between hotels (though some offer free breakfast to Rick Steves readers or with direct booking—ask). The price of breakfast correlates with the price of the room: The more expensive the room, the more expensive the breakfast. This per-person charge rises with the number of stars the hotel has and can add up, particularly for families. While hotels hope you'll buy their breakfast, it's optional unless otherwise noted; to save money, head to a bakery or café instead.

Some hoteliers, especially in resort towns, strongly encourage their peak-season guests to take *demi-pension* (half-pension)—that is, breakfast and either lunch or dinner. By law, they can't require you to take half-pension unless you are staying three or more nights, but, in practice, some do during high season. And though the food is usually good, it limits your ability to shop around. I've indicated where I think *demi-pension* is a good value.

Hoteliers uniformly detest it when people bring food into bedrooms. Dinner picnics are particularly frowned upon: Hoteliers worry about cleanliness, smells, and attracting insects. Be tidy and considerate.

Checking Out: While it's customary to pay for your room upon departure, it can be a good idea to settle your bill the day before, when you're not in a hurry and while the manager's in. Some hoteliers will ask you to sign their *Livre d'Or* (literally "Golden Book," for client comments). They take this seriously and enjoy reading your remarks.

Hotelier Help: Hoteliers can be a good source of advice. Most know their city well, and can assist you with everything from public transit and airport connections to calling an English-speaking doctor, or finding a good restaurant, a late-night pharmacy, or a self-service launderette (*laverie automatique,* lah-vay-ree oh-to-mah-teek).

Hotel Hassles: Even at the best places, mechanical breakdowns occur: sinks leak, hot water turns cold, toilets may gurgle or smell, the Wi-Fi goes out, or the air-conditioning dies when you need it most. Report your concerns clearly and calmly at the front desk.

To guard against theft in your room, keep valuables out of sight. Some rooms come with a safe, and other hotels have safes at the front desk. I've never bothered using one and in a lifetime of travel, I've never had anything stolen from my room.

For more complicated problems, don't expect instant results. Above all, keep a positive attitude. Remember, you're on vacation. If your hotel is a disappointment, spend more time out enjoying the place you came to see.

Modern Hotel Chains: France is littered with ultramodern hotels, providing drivers with low-stress accommodations and often located on cheap land just outside town. The clean and inexpensive Ibis Budget chain (about €55/room for up to three people), the more attractive and spacious standard Ibis hotels (€100-170 for a double), and the cushier Mercure and Novotel hotels (€170-300 for a double) are all run by the same company, Accor (www.accorhotels.com). Though hardly quaint, these can be a good value (look for deals on their websites), particularly when they're centrally located; I list several in this book. Other chains to consider are Kyriad, with moderate prices and good quality (www.kyriad.com) and the familiar-to-Americans Best Western (www.bestwestern.com). Château and Hotels Collection has more cushy digs (www.chateauxhotels.com).

Bed & Breakfasts

B&Bs (*chambres d'hôte*, abbreviated "CH") generally are found in smaller towns and rural areas. They're usually family-run and a good deal, offering double the cultural intimacy for less than most hotel rooms. While you may lose some hotel conveniences—such as lounges, TVs, daily bed-sheet changes, and credit-card payments—I happily make the trade-off for the personal touch and lower rates. It's always OK to ask to see the room before you commit. And though some CHs post small *Chambres* or *Chambres d'hôte* signs in their front windows, many are found only through the local tourist office.

I recommend reliable CHs that offer a good value and/or unique experience (such as CHs in renovated mills, châteaux, and wine *domaines*). For a list of over 17,000 *chambres d'hôte* throughout France, check www.chambres-hotes.fr. You can see images of places to stay, make a reservation, and get directions for any listing on the website. While *chambres d'hôte* have their own star-rating system, it doesn't correspond to the hotels' rating system. To avoid confusion, I haven't listed these stars for CHs. But virtually all of my recommended CHs have private in-room bathrooms and Wi-Fi, and some have common rooms with refrigerators and kitchenettes. Doubles generally cost €60-80; fancier places are about €100-120. Breakfast is usually included, but not always—ask. *Tables d'hôte* are CHs that offer an optional home-cooked dinner (usually a great value, must be requested in advance). And though your hosts may not speak English, they will almost always be enthusiastic and pleasant.

Gîtes

Countryside *gîtes* (pronounced "zheet") are usually urbanites' second, countryside homes, rentable by the week, from Saturday to Saturday.

Gîtes are best for drivers (they're usually rural, with little public-transport access) and ideal for families and small groups (since they can sleep many for the same price). Homes range in comfort from simple cottages and farmhouses to restored châteaux (BYO soap, shampoo, etc.). Sheets or linens may be included or provided for a bit extra. Like hotels, all *gîtes* are rated for comfort from one to four *épis* (ears of corn). Two or three *épis* generally indicate suffi-

Making Hotel Reservations

Reserve your rooms as soon as you've pinned down your travel dates. For busy national holidays, it's wise to reserve far in advance (see the appendix).

Requesting a Reservation: For family-run hotels, it's generally cheaper to book your room directly via their website, email, or a phone call. For business-class hotels, reserve directly through the hotel's official website (not a booking website). For complicated requests, send an email. Almost all my recommended hotels take reservations in English.

Here's what the hotelier wants to know:

- Type(s) of rooms you want and size of your party
- Number of nights you'll stay
- Your arrival and departure dates, written European-style as day/month/year (for example, 18/06/20 or 18 June 2020)
- Special requests (en suite bathroom, cheapest room, twin beds vs. double bed, quiet room)
- Applicable discounts (such as a Rick Steves reader discount, cash discount, or promotional rate)

Confirming a Reservation: Most places will request a credit-card number to hold your room. If you're using an online reservation form, look for *https* or a lock icon at the top of your browser. If you book directly, you can email, call, or fax this information.

Canceling a Reservation: If you must cancel, it's courteous—and smart—to do so with as much notice as possible, especially for smaller family-run places (which describes many of the hotels I list). Cancellation policies can be strict; read the fine print before

cient quality, but I'd look for three for more comfort. Prices generally range from €500 to €1,500 per week, depending on house size and amenities such as pools. Some owners may not speak English, so be prepared to do business in French.

For more information on *gîtes*, visit www.gites-de-france.com (with the most rentals) or www.gite.com. Also check sites like Airbnb and HomeAway/VRBO (see next page).

Short-Term Rentals

A short-term rental—whether an apartment, house, or room in a local's home—is an increasingly popular alternative, especially if you plan to settle in one location for several nights. For stays longer than a few days, you can usually find a rental that's comparable to—and cheaper than—a hotel room with similar amenities. Plus, you'll get a behind-the-scenes peek into how locals live.

Many places require a minimum stay and have strict cancellation policies. And you're generally on your own: There's no hotel reception desk, breakfast, or daily cleaning service.

From: rick@ricksteves.com
Sent: Today
To: info@hotelcentral.com
Subject: Reservation request for 19-22 July

Dear Hotel Central,

I would like to stay at your hotel. Please let me know if you have a room available and the price for:

• 2 people
• Double bed and en suite bathroom in a quiet room
• Arriving 19 July, departing 22 July (3 nights)

Thank you!
Rick Steves

you book. Many discount deals require prepayment, with no refunds for cancellations.

Reconfirming a Reservation: Always call or email to reconfirm your room reservation a few days in advance. For *chambres d'hôtes* or very small hotels, I call again on my day of arrival to tell my host what time to expect me (especially important if arriving late—after 17:00).

Phoning: For tips on calling hotels overseas, see the "How to Dial" sidebar, later.

Finding Accommodations: Aggregator websites such as Airbnb, FlipKey, Booking.com, and the HomeAway family of sites (HomeAway, VRBO, and VacationRentals) let you browse properties and correspond directly with European property owners or managers. If you prefer to work from a curated list of accommodations, consider using a rental agency such as InterhomeUSA.com or RentaVilla.com. Agency-represented apartments typically cost more, but this method often offers more help and safeguards than booking direct.

To find a place, try the resources listed above, or one of these: **France Homestyle,** run by Claudette, a service-oriented French woman from Seattle who handpicks every home and apartment she lists (US tel. 206/325-0132, www.francehomestyle.com, info@francehomestyle.com), or **Ville et Village,** which has a bigger selection of higher-end places (US tel. 510/559-8080, www.villeetvillage.com). For a list of rental agencies in Paris, see page 142.

Before you commit, be clear on the location. I like to virtu-

PRACTICALITIES

Using Online Services to Your Advantage

From booking services to user reviews, online businesses are playing a greater role in travelers' planning than ever before. Take advantage of their pluses—and be wise to their downsides.

Booking Sites

Hotel booking websites, including Priceline's Booking.com and Expedia's Hotels.com, offer one-stop shopping for hotels. While convenient for travelers, they present a real problem for small, independent, family-run hotels. Without a presence on these sites, these hotels become almost invisible. But to be listed, a hotel must pay a sizeable commission...and promise that its own website won't undercut the price on the booking-service site.

Here's the work-around: Use the big sites to research what's out there, then book directly with the hotel by email or phone, in which case hotel owners are free to give you whatever price they like. Ask for a room without the commission mark-up (or ask for a free breakfast if not included, or a free upgrade). If you do book online, be sure to use the hotel's website. French hotels now have the right to offer rooms on their site below rates on third-party websites; most will give you lower rates by booking direct.

As a savvy consumer, remember: When you book with an online booking service, you're adding a middleman who takes roughly 20 percent. To support small, family-run hotels whose world is more difficult than ever, book direct.

Short-Term Rental Sites

Rental juggernaut Airbnb (along with other short-term rental sites) allows travelers to rent rooms and apartments directly from locals, often providing more value than a cookie-cutter hotel. Airbnb fans appreciate feeling part of a real neighborhood and getting into a daily routine as "temporary Europeans." Depending on the host, Airbnb can provide an opportunity to get to know a local person, while keeping the money spent on your accommo-

ally "explore" the neighborhood using the Street View feature on Google Maps. Also consider the proximity to public transportation, and how well-connected the property is with the rest of the city. Ask about amenities (elevator, air-conditioning, laundry, Wi-Fi, parking, etc.). Reviews from previous guests can help identify trouble spots.

Think about the kind of experience you want: Just a key and an affordable bed...or a chance to get to know a local? There are typically two kinds of hosts: those who want minimal interaction with their guests, and hosts who are friendly and may want to interact with you. Read the promotional text and online reviews to help shape your decision.

dations in the community.

Critics view Airbnb as a threat to "traditional Europe," saying it creates unfair, unqualified competition for established guesthouse owners. In some places, the lucrative Airbnb market has forced traditional guesthouses out of business and is driving property values out of range for locals. Some cities have cracked down, requiring owners to occupy rental properties part of the year (and staging disruptive "inspections" that inconvenience guests).

As a lover of Europe, I share the worry of those who see residents nudged aside by tourists. But as an advocate for travelers, I appreciate the value and cultural intimacy Airbnb provides.

User Reviews

User-generated review sites and apps such as Yelp and TripAdvisor can give you a consensus of opinions about everything from hotels and restaurants to sights and nightlife. If you scan reviews of a restaurant or hotel and see several complaints about noise or a rotten location, you've gained insight that can help in your decision-making.

But as a guidebook writer, my sense is that there is a big difference between the uncurated information on a review site and the vetted listings in a guidebook. A user-generated review is based on the limited experience of one person, who stayed at just one hotel in a given city and ate at a few restaurants there. A guidebook is the work of a trained researcher who forms a well-developed basis for comparison by visiting many restaurants and hotels year after year.

Both types of information have their place, and in many ways, they're complementary. If something is well reviewed in a guidebook and it also gets good online reviews, it's likely a winner.

Confirming and Paying: Many places require you to pay the entire balance before your trip. It's easiest and safest to pay through the site where you found the listing. Be wary of owners who want to conduct your transaction offline to avoid fees; this gives you no recourse if things go awry. Never agree to wire money (a key indicator of a fraudulent transaction).

Apartments or Houses: If you're staying somewhere for four or more nights, it's worth considering an apartment or house (shorter stays aren't worth the hassle of arranging key pickup, buying groceries, etc.). Apartment and house rentals can be especially cost-effective for groups and families. European apartments, like hotel rooms, tend to be small by US standards. But they often come

PRACTICALITIES

Traveling with Kids

With a good mix of big-city excitement and rural fun, France appeals to kids of all ages. Both of this book's authors have kids, and we've used our substantial experience traveling with them to improve our advice. Our kids' favorite places have been Mont St-Michel, the Alps, Loire châteaux, Carcassonne, and Paris (especially the Eiffel Tower and Seine River boat ride)—and any hotel with a pool. Here are some tips for traveling with kids in France:

Plan Ahead

• Minimize hotel changes by planning three-day stops. Aim for hotels with restaurants, so older kids can go back to the room while you finish a pleasant dinner. Most hotels have some sort of crib you can use. If you're staying for a week or more in one place, one great option is to rent an apartment or *gîte* (see page 1101).

• Car-rental agencies usually rent car seats, though you must reserve one in advance. According to French law, kids under 10 must be in a car seat in the back seat.

• Choose items that are small and convenient for use on planes, trains, and in your hotel room, such as compact travel games, a deck of cards, or a tablet. Bring your own drawing paper, pens, and crayons (expensive in France).

• For longer drives, audio books can be fun for the whole family. I recommend Peter Mayle's *A Year in Provence,* but searching "France for kids" will yield many results.

• Older kids can stay in touch with friends at home with Wi-Fi texting apps. Wi-Fi hotspots are a godsend (at hotels, many cafés and TIs, and all Starbucks and McDonald's). Most parents find it worth the peace of mind to buy a supplemental international plan for the whole family: Adults can stay connected to teenagers while allowing them maximum independence (see page 1128).

Eating Tips

• Eat dinner early (19:00-19:30 at restaurants, earlier at cafés). Skip romantic eateries. Try relaxed cafés (or fast-food restaurants) where kids can move around without bothering others.

• Kid-friendly foods that are commonly available and easy to order include crêpes (available at takeout stands), *croque monsieurs* (grilled ham-and-cheese sandwiches), and *tartines* (open-faced sandwiches). Plain pasta is available at many cafés and some bistros (ask for *pâtes nature*). For breakfast, try a *pain au chocolat* (chocolate-filled pastry) or dip your baguette in a *chocolat chaud* (hot chocolate). Fruit, cereals, and yogurt are usually available. Carry a baguette to snack on. In the south of France, pizza is omnipresent.

• If your kids love peanut butter, bring it from home (it's hard to find in France)...or help them acquire a taste for Nutella, the tasty hazelnut-chocolate spread available everywhere. Look for organic *(bio)* stores, where you can find numerous nut butters and Chocolade, a less-sugary version of Nutella.

• Picnics work well. *Boulangeries* are good places to grab off-hour snacks when restaurants aren't serving. (See page 1111 for picnic tips.)

• For older kids, be aware that the drinking age is 16 for beer and wine and 18 for the hard stuff: Your waiter will assume that your teen will have wine with you at dinner. Teens are also welcome in most bars and lounges (there's no 21-and-older section).

Sightseeing Tips

• To make your trip fun for everyone in the family, mix heavy-duty sights with kids' activities, such as playing minigolf or *boules,* renting bikes or canoes, and riding the little tourist trains popular in many towns.

• I've listed public pools in many places (especially the south), but be warned: Public pools in France commonly require a small, Speedo-like bathing suit for boys and men (American-style swim trunks won't do)—though they usually have these little suits to loan. At hotel pools, either kind of suit will do.

• For memories that will last long after the trip, keep a family journal. Pack a diary and a glue stick. While relaxing at a café over a *citron-pressé* (lemonade), take turns writing down the day's events, and include mementos such as ticket stubs from museums, postcards, or stalks of lavender.

Parenting, French-Style

• Famous for topless tanning, French women are equally comfortable with public breastfeeding—no need for cover-ups here. Changing tables are nonexistent, so bring a roll-up changing mat and get comfortable changing your baby on your knees, on a bench, or wherever you find enough space.

• French grandmothers take their role seriously and won't hesitate to recommend that you put more sunscreen on your child in the summer, or add a layer of clothing if it's breezy.

• Rather than saying bonjour to French children, say *coucou* (coo-coo) if they are young and *salut* (sal-oo) if they are preteens or older.

with laundry machines and small, equipped kitchens, making it easier and cheaper to dine in.

Rooms in Private Homes: Renting a room in someone's home is a good option for those traveling alone, as you're more likely to find true single rooms—with just one single bed, and a price to match. These can range from air-mattress-in-living-room basic to plush-B&B-suite posh. Some places allow you to book for a single night; if staying for several nights, you can buy groceries just as you would in a rental house. While you can't expect your host to also be your tour guide—or even to provide you with much info—some may be interested in getting to know the travelers who come through their home.

Other Options: Swapping homes with a local works for people with an appealing place to offer (don't assume where you live is not interesting to Europeans). A good place to start is HomeExchange. To sleep for free, Couchsurfing.com is a vagabond's alternative to Airbnb. It lists millions of outgoing members who host fellow "surfers" in their homes.

Hotel Barges

These are a fun option in canalside towns; I've listed a few in this book. If you're interested in renting one for more than a night or two, try **Papillon Barge** (www.burgundycanalvacations.com), **French Country Waterways** (www.fcwl.com), or the cheaper bed-and-breakfast **Barge Nilaya** (May-Sept mobile 06 89 18 80 67, Oct-April UK mobile—from the US dial 011-44-7909-151-611, www.bargenilaya.com). For a comprehensive source on enjoying the rivers and canals of France, check www.french-waterways.com.

Hostels

A hostel *(auberge de jeunesse)* provides cheap beds in dorms where you sleep alongside strangers for about €35 per night. Travelers of any age are welcome if they don't mind dorm-style accommodations and meeting other travelers. Most hostels offer kitchen facilities, guest computers, Wi-Fi, and a self-service laundry. Hostels almost always provide bedding, but the towel's up to you (though you can usually rent one for a small fee). Family and private rooms are often available.

Independent hostels tend to be easygoing, colorful, and informal (no membership required; www.hostelworld.com). You may pay slightly less by booking directly with the hostel. **Official hostels** are part of Hostelling International (HI) and share an online booking site (www.hihostels.com). HI hostels typically require that you either have a membership card or pay a bit more per night.

Hip Hop Hostels is a clearinghouse for budget hotels and hostels in Paris. It's worth a look for its good selection of cheap accommodations (tel. 01 48 78 10 00, www.hiphophostels.com).

Camping

In Europe, camping is more of a social than an environmental experience. It's a great way for American travelers to make European friends. Campsites average about €25 per night, and almost every destination recommended in this book has a campground within a reasonable walk or bus ride from the town center and train station. A tent, pillow, and sleeping bag are all you need. Some campgrounds have small grocery stores and washing machines, and some even come with cafés and miniature golf. Local TIs have camping information. You'll find more detailed information in the annually updated *Michelin Camping France,* available in the United States and at most French bookstores.

Eating

The French eat long and well. Relaxed and tree-shaded lunches with a chilled rosé, three-hour dinners, and endless hours of sitting

in outdoor cafés are the norm. Here, celebrated restaurateurs are as famous as great athletes, and mamas hope their babies will grow up to be great chefs. Cafés, cuisine, and wines should become a highlight of any French adventure: It's sightseeing for your palate. Even if the rest of you is sleeping in a cheap hotel, let your taste buds travel first-class in France.

You can eat well without going broke—but choose carefully: You're just as likely to blow a small fortune on a mediocre meal as you are to dine wonderfully for €20. Read the information that follows and consider my restaurant suggestions in this book.

For listings in this guidebook, I look for restaurants that are convenient to your hotel and sightseeing. When restaurant-hunting, choose a spot filled with locals, not the place with the big neon signs boasting, "We Speak English and Accept Credit Cards." Venturing even a block or two off the main drag leads to higher-quality food for a better price.

In Paris, restaurant lunches are a great value, as most places offer the same quality and similar selections for far less than at dinner. If you're on a budget or just like going local, try making lunch your main meal, then have a lighter evening meal at a café.

PRACTICALITIES

RESTAURANT PRICING

I've categorized my recommended eateries based on the average price of a typical main course, indicated with a dollar-sign rating (see sidebar). Expensive specialties, fine wine, appetizers, and dessert can significantly increase your final bill.

The categories also indicate the personality of a place: **Budget** eateries include street food, takeaway, order-at-the-counter shops, basic cafeterias, bakeries selling sandwiches, and so on. **Moderate** eateries are nice (but not fancy) sit-down restaurants, ideal for a straightforward, fill-the-tank meal. Most of my listings fall in this category—great for a good taste of local cuisine.

Pricier eateries are a notch up, with more attention paid to the setting, presentation, and (often inventive) cuisine. **Splurge** eateries are dress-up-for-a-special-occasion-swanky—typically with an elegant setting, polished service, elaborate cuisine, and an expansive (and expensive) wine list.

BREAKFAST

Most hotels serve an optional breakfast, which is usually pleasant and convenient (generally €10-20, price rises proportionately with room cost). They almost all offer a buffet breakfast (cereal, yogurt, fruit, cheese, ham, croissants, juice, and hard-boiled eggs). Some add scrambled eggs and sausage. Before committing to breakfast, check to see if it's included in your room rate; if not, scan the offerings to be sure it's to your liking. Once committed, it's self-service and as much as you want. Coffee is often self-serve from a machine or a thermos. If there's no coffee machine and you want to make your own *café au lait,* find the hot milk and mix it with your coffee. If your hotelier serves your coffee, ask for *café avec du lait.* For your basic American-style coffee (black and not too strong), ask for *café Americain.*

Breakfast is a great time to try the country's delightful array of breads, pastries, and pies. Many hotels and B&Bs take pride in serving these extremely fresh—often with a different selection each day.

If all you want is coffee or tea and a croissant, the corner café or bakery offers more atmosphere and is less expensive (though you get more coffee at your hotel). Go local at a café and ask for *une tartine* (ewn tart-een), a baguette slathered with butter or jam. If you crave eggs for breakfast, order *une omelette* or *œufs sur le plat* (fried eggs). Some cafés and bakeries offer worthwhile breakfast deals with juice, croissant, and coffee or tea for about €8-12 (for more on coffee and tea drinks, see the "Beverages" section, later).

To keep it cheap, pick up some fruit at a grocery store and pastries at your favorite *boulangerie* and have a picnic breakfast, then

Restaurant Code

Eateries in this book are categorized according to the average cost of a typical main course. Drinks, desserts, and splurge items can raise the price considerably.

$$$$	**Splurge:** Most main courses over €30
$$$	**Pricier:** €25-30
$$	**Moderate:** €15-25
$	**Budget:** Under €15

In France, a crêpe stand or other takeout spot is **$**; a sit-down brasserie, café, or bistro with affordable plats du jour is **$$**; a casual but more upscale restaurant is **$$$**; and a swanky splurge is **$$$$**.

savor your coffee at a café bar *(comptoir)* while standing, like the French do.

PICNIC DINING AND FOOD TO GO

Whether going all out on a perfect French picnic or simply grabbing a sandwich to eat on an atmospheric square, dining with the town as your backdrop can be one of your most memorable meals.

Picnics

Great for lunch or dinner, French picnics can be first-class affairs and adventures in high cuisine. Be daring. Try the smelly cheeses, ugly pâtés, prissy quiches, and minuscule yogurts. Shopkeepers are accustomed to selling small quantities of produce. Get a succulent salad to go, and ask for a plastic fork. If you need a knife or corkscrew, borrow one from your hotelier (but don't picnic in your room, as French hoteliers uniformly detest this). Though drinking wine in public places is taboo in the US, it's *pas de problème* in France. Plastic bags are not available at markets in France; you'll need your own bag (cheap at stores) or daypack for carrying items.

Assembling a Picnic: Visit several small stores to put together a complete meal. Shop early, as many shops close from 12:00 or 13:00 to 15:00 for their lunch break. Say *"Bonjour madame/monsieur"* as you enter, then point to what you want and say, *"S'il vous plaît."* For other terminology you might need while shopping, see the sidebar.

At the *boulangerie* (bakery), buy some bread. A baguette usually does the trick, or choose from the many loaves of bread on display: *pain aux céréales* (whole grain with seeds), *pain de campagne* (country bread, made with unbleached bread flour), *pain complet* (wheat bread), or *pain de seigle* (rye bread). To ask for it sliced, say *"Tranché, s'il vous plaît."*

At the *pâtisserie* (pastry shop, which is often the same place

Picnic Vocabulary

English	French
please	*s'il vous plaît* (see voo play)
a plastic fork	*une fourchette en plastique* (ewn foor-sheht ahn plah-steek)
a plastic cup	*un goblet en plastique* (uhn goh-blay ahn plah-steek)
a paper plate	*une assiette en papier* (ewn ah-see-eht ahn pahp-yay)
napkins	*les serviettes* (lay sehr-vee-eht)
a small box	*une barquette* (ewn bar-keht)
a knife	*un couteau* (uhn koo-toh)
a corkscrew	*un tire-bouchon* (uhn teer-boo-shohn)
sliced	*tranché* (trahn-shay)
a slice	*une tranche* (ewn trahnsh)
a small slice	*une petite tranche* (ewn puh-teet trahnsh)
more	*plus* (plew)
less	*moins* (mwan)
It's just right.	*C'est bon.* (say bohn)
That'll be all.	*C'est tout.* (say too)
Thank you.	*Merci.* (mehr-see)

you bought the bread), choose a dessert that's easy to eat with your hands. My favorites are *éclairs* (*chocolat* or *café* flavored), individual fruit *tartes* (*framboise* is raspberry, *fraise* is strawberry, *citron* is lemon), and *macarons* (made of flavored cream sandwiched between two meringues, not coconut cookies like in the US).

At the **crémerie** or **fromagerie** (cheese shop), choose a sampling of cheeses *(un assortiment)*. I usually get one hard cheese (like Comté, Cantal, or Beaufort), one soft cow's milk cheese (like Brie or Camembert), one goat's milk cheese (anything that says chèvre), and one blue cheese (Roquefort or Bleu d'Auvergne). Goat cheese usually comes in individual portions. For all other large cheeses, point to the cheese you want and ask for *une petite tranche* (a small slice). The shopkeeper will show you the size of the slice about to be cut, then look at you for approval. If you'd like more, say, *"Plus."* If you'd like less, say *"Moins."* If it's just right, say *"C'est bon!"*

At the **charcuterie** or **traiteur** (for deli items, prepared salads, meats, and pâtés), I like a slice of *pâté de campagne* (country pâté made of pork) and *saucissons secs* (dried sausages, some with pepper crust or garlic—you can ask to have it sliced thin like salami). I get a fresh salad, too. Typical options are *carottes râpées* (shredded carrots in a tangy vinaigrette), *salade de betteraves* (beets in vinaigrette), and *céleri rémoulade* (celery root with a mayonnaise sauce). The food comes in takeout boxes, and they may supply a plastic fork.

At a *cave à vin* you can buy chilled wines that the merchant is usually happy to open and recork for you.

At a *supermarché, épicerie,* or *magasin d'alimentation* (small grocery store or minimart), you'll find plastic cutlery and glasses, paper plates, napkins, drinks, chips, and a display of produce. *Supermarchés* are less colorful than smaller stores, but cheaper, more efficient, and offer adequate quality. Department stores often have supermarkets in the basement. On the outskirts of cities, you'll find the monster *hypermarchés.* Drop in for a glimpse of hyper-France in action.

The best shopping option is to visit open-air markets *(marchés),* which are fun and photogenic, but shut down around 13:00 (many are listed in this book; local TIs have complete lists). There's more information about these wonderful experiences in the "Market Day" sidebar, later.

To-Go Food

You'll find plenty of to-go options at *crêperies,* bakeries, and small stands. Baguette sandwiches, quiches, and pizza-like items are tasty, filling, and budget-friendly (about €5).

Sandwiches: Anything served *à la provençale* has marinated peppers, tomatoes, and eggplant. A sandwich *à l'italienne* is a grilled *panini* (usually referred to as *pannini*). Here are some common sandwiches:

Fromage (froh-mahzh): Cheese (white on beige)

Jambon beurre (zhahn-bohn bur): Ham and butter (boring for most but a French classic)

Jambon crudités (zhahn-bohn krew-dee-tay): Ham with tomatoes, lettuce, cucumbers, and mayonnaise

Fougasse (foo-gahs): Bread rolled up with salty bits of bacon, cheese, or olives

Poulet crudités (poo-lay krew-dee-tay): Chicken with tomatoes, lettuce, maybe cucumbers, and always mayonnaise

Saucisson beurre (saw-see-sohn bur): Thinly sliced sausage and butter

Thon crudités (tohn krew-dee-tay): Tuna with tomatoes, lettuce, and maybe cucumbers, but definitely mayonnaise

Quiche: Typical quiches you'll see at shops and bakeries are *lorraine* (ham and cheese), *fromage* (cheese only), *aux oignons* (with onions), *aux poireaux* (with leeks—my favorite), *aux champignons* (with mushrooms), *au saumon* (salmon), or *au thon* (tuna).

Crêpes: The quintessentially French thin pancake called a crêpe (rhymes with "step," not "grape") is filling, usually inexpensive, and generally quick. Place your order at the *crêperie* window or kiosk, and watch the chef in action. But don't be surprised if

Market Day

Market day *(jour de marché)* is a big deal throughout France. They have been a central feature of life in rural areas since the Middle Ages. No single event better symbolizes the French preoccupation with fresh products—and their strong ties to the soil—than the weekly market. Many locals mark their calendars with the arrival of fresh produce.

Markets *(marchés)* combine products from area farmers and artisans, and offer a mind-boggling array of choices, from the perishable (produce, meats, cheeses, breads, and pastries) to the nonperishable (kitchen wares, inexpensive clothing, brightly colored linens, and pottery). *Les marchés brocantes* specialize in quasi-antiques and flea-market bric-a-brac (think rummage sale). Many marchés have good selections of produce and some brocantes.

Notice the signs as you enter towns indicating the *jours du marché* (essential information to any civilized soul, and a reminder not to park on the streets the night before—be on the lookout for *stationnement interdit* signs that mark "no parking" areas). Most *marchés* take place once a week in the town's main square; larger *marchés* spill into nearby streets.

they don't make the crêpe for you from scratch; at some *crêperies,* they might premake a stack of crêpes and reheat them when they fill your order.

Crêpes generally are *sucrée* (sweet) or *salée* (savory). Technically, a savory crêpe should be made with a heartier buckwheat batter, and is called a *galette.* However, many cheap and lazy *crêperies* use the same sweet batter *(de froment)* for both their sweet-topped and savory-topped crêpes. A *socca* is a chickpea crêpe.

Standard crêpe toppings include cheese *(fromage;* usually Swiss-style Gruyère or Emmental), ham *(jambon),* egg *(œuf),* mushrooms *(champignons),* chocolate, Nutella, jam *(confiture),* whipped cream *(chantilly),* apple jam *(compote de pommes),* chestnut cream *(crème de marrons),* and Grand Marnier.

Usually, the bigger the market, the greater the overall selection—particularly of nonperishable goods. Bigger towns (such as Beaune and Arles) may have two weekly markets. The biggest market days are usually on weekends, so that everyone can go.

Market day is as important socially as it is commercially—it's a weekly chance for locals to resume friendships and get the current gossip. Here neighbors can catch up on Henri's barn renovation, see photos of Jacqueline's new grandchild, and relax over un café. Dogs are tethered to café tables while friends exchange kisses. Tether yourself to a table and observe: three cheek-kisses for good friends (left-right-left), a fourth for friends you haven't seen in a while. (The appropriate number of kisses varies by region—Paris, Lyon, and Provence have different standards.) It's bad form to be in a hurry on market day. Allow the crowd to set your pace.

It's a joy to assemble picnics at an open-air market. Most perishable items are sold directly from the producers—no middlemen, no credit cards, just really fresh produce (*du pays* means "grown locally"). Sometimes you'll meet a widow selling a dozen eggs, two rabbits, and a wad of herbs tied with string. But most vendors follow a weekly circuit of markets they feel works best for them, showing up in the same spot every week, year in and year out. Notice how much fun they have chatting up their customers and one another. Many vendors speak enough English to assist you in your selection. Markets usually end by 13:00—in time for lunch, allowing the town to reclaim its streets and squares.

RESTAURANT AND CAFE DINING

To get the most out of dining out in France, slow down. Give yourself time to dine at a French pace, engage the waiter, show you care about food, and enjoy the experience as much as the food itself.

French waiters probably won't overwhelm you with friendliness. As their tip is already included in the bill (see "Tipping," later), there's less schmoozing than we're used to at home. Notice how hard they work. They almost never stop. Cozying up to clients (French or foreign) is probably the last thing on their minds. They're often stuck with client overload, too, because the French rarely hire part-time employees, even to help with peak times. To get a waiter's attention, try to make meaningful eye contact, which is a signal that you need something. If this doesn't work, raise your hand and simply say, *"S'il vous plaît"* (see voo play)—"please."

This phrase also works when you want to ask for the check. In French eateries, a waiter will rarely bring you the check unless you request it. To the French, having the bill dropped off before asking for it is akin to being kicked out—*très gauche*. But busy travelers are often ready for the check sooner rather than later. If you're in a hurry, ask for the bill when your server comes to clear your plates or checks in to see if you want dessert or coffee. To request your bill, say, *"L'addition, s'il vous plait."* If you don't ask now, the wait staff may become scarce as they leave you to digest in peace. (For a list of other restaurant survival phrases, see the appendix.)

Note that all café and restaurant interiors are smoke-free. Today the only smokers you'll find are at outside tables, which—unfortunately—may be exactly where you want to sit.

Tipping: At cafés and restaurants, a 12-15 percent service charge is always included in the price of what you order (*service compris* or *prix net*), but you won't see it listed on your bill. Unlike in the US, France pays servers a decent wage (a favorite café owner told me that his waiters earn more than some high school teachers). Because of this, most locals only tip a little, or not at all. When dining, expect reasonable, efficient service. If you don't get it, skip the tip. If you feel the service was good, tip a little—about 5 percent; maybe 10 percent for terrific service. To tell the waiter to keep the change when you pay, say *"C'est bon"* (say bohn), meaning "It's good." If you are using a credit card, leave your tip in cash—credit-card receipts don't even have space to add a tip. Never feel guilty if you don't leave a tip.

Cafés and Brasseries

French cafés and brasseries provide user-friendly meals and a relief from sightseeing overload. They're not necessarily cheaper than many restaurants and bistros, and famous cafés on popular squares can be pricey affairs. Their key advantage is flexibility: They offer long serving hours, and you're welcome to order just a salad, a sandwich, or a bowl of soup, even for dinner. It's also OK to share starters and desserts, though not main courses.

Cafés and brasseries usually open by 7:00, but closing hours vary. Unlike some restaurants, which open only for dinner and sometimes for lunch, many cafés and all brasseries serve food throughout the day (usually with a limited menu during off hours), making them the best option for a late lunch or an early dinner. *Service Continu* or *Service Non-Stop* signs indicate continued service throughout the day. Small-town cafés often close their kitchens from about 14:00 until 18:00.

Check the price list first, which by law should be posted prominently (though I see fewer posted every year). There are two sets of prices: You'll pay more for the same drink if you're seated at a table *(salle)* than if you're seated or standing at the bar or counter *(comptoir)*. (For tips on ordering coffee and tea, see the "Beverages" section, later.)

Vegetarians, Allergies, and Other Dietary Restrictions

Many French people think "vegetarian" means "no red meat" or "not much meat." If you're a strict vegetarian, be specific: Tell your server what you don't eat—and it can be helpful to clarify what you do eat. Write it out on a card and keep it handy.

But be reasonable. Think of your meal (as the French do) as if it's a finely crafted creation by a trained artist. The chef knows what goes well together, and substitutions are considered an insult to his training. Picky eaters should try their best to just take it or leave it.

However, French restaurants are willing to accommodate genuine dietary restrictions and other special concerns, or at least point you to an appropriate choice on the menu. These phrases might help:

French	English
Je suis végétarien/végétarienne. (zhuh swee vay-zhay-tah-ree-an/vay-zhay-tah-ree-ehn)	I am vegetarian.
Je ne peux pas manger de _____ . (zhuh nuh puh pah mahn-zhay duh _____)	I cannot eat _____ .
Je suis allergique à _____ . (zhuh sweez ah-lehr-zheek ah _____)	I am allergic to _____ .
Pas de _____ . (pah duh _____).	No _____ .

At a café or a brasserie, if the table is not set, it's fine to seat yourself and just have a drink. However, if it's set with a placemat and cutlery, you should ask to be seated and plan to order a meal. If you're unsure, ask the server before sitting down.

Ordering: A salad, crêpe, quiche, or omelet is a fairly cheap way to fill up. Each can be made with various extras such as ham, cheese, mushrooms, and so on. Omelets come lonely on a plate with a basket of bread.

Sandwiches, generally served day and night, are inexpensive, but most are very plain (*boulangeries* serve better ones). To get more than a piece of ham *(jambon)* on a baguette, order a *sandwich jambon crudités* (garnished with veggies). Popular sandwiches are the *croque monsieur* (grilled ham-and-cheese) and *croque madame* (*monsieur* with a fried egg on top).

Salads are typically meal size and often can be ordered with warm ingredients mixed in, such as melted goat cheese, fried gizzards, or roasted potatoes. One salad is perfect for lunch or a light dinner. See the "French Cuisine" section later for a list of classic salads.

PRACTICALITIES

The daily special—*plat du jour* (plah dew zhoor), or just *plat*—is your fast, hearty, and garnished hot plate for about €14-22. At most cafés, feel free to order only *entrées* (which in French means the starter course); many people find these lighter and more interesting than a main course. A vegetarian can enjoy a tasty, filling meal by ordering two *entrées*.

Regardless of what you order, bread is free but almost never comes with butter; to get more bread, just hold up your basket and ask, *"Encore, s'il vous plaît?"*

Restaurants

Choose restaurants filled with locals. Consider my suggestions and your hotelier's opinion, but trust your instincts. If a restaurant doesn't post its prices outside, move along.

Restaurants open for dinner around 19:00 and are most crowded about 20:00 (21:00 in cities). The early bird gets the table. Last seating is usually about 21:00 (22:00 in cities and on the French Riviera; possibly later in Paris).

Tune into the quiet, relaxed pace of French dining. The French don't do dinner and a movie on date nights; they just do dinner. The table is yours for the night. Notice how quietly French diners speak in restaurants and how few mobile phones you see during a meal, and how this improves your overall experience. Go local.

Ordering: In French restaurants, you can choose something off the menu (called the *carte*), or you can order a multicourse, fixed-price meal (confusingly, called a *menu*). Or, if offered, you can get one of the special dishes of the day *(plat du jour)*. If you ask for *un menu* (instead of *la carte*), you'll get a fixed-price meal.

Ordering **à la carte** gives you the best selection. I enjoy going à la carte especially when traveling with others and eating family style (waiters are usually happy to accommodate this approach and will bring small extra plates). It's traditional to order an *entrée* (a starter—not a main dish) and a *plat principal* (main course), though it's becoming common to order only a *plat principal*. *Plats* are generally more meat-based, while *entrées* usually include veggies. Multiple-course meals, while time-consuming (a positive thing in France), create the appropriate balance of veggies to meat. Elaborate meals may also have *entremets*—tiny dishes served between courses. Wherever you dine, consider the waiter's recommendations and anything *de la maison* (of the house), as long as it's not an organ meat (tripe, *rognons*, or andouillette).

Two people can split an *entrée* or a big salad (small-size dinner salads are usually not offered á la carte) and then each get a *plat principal*. At restaurants, it's inappropriate for two diners to share one main course. If all you want is a salad or soup, go to a café or brasserie.

Fixed-price *menus*—which usually include two, three, or four courses—are always a better deal than eating à la carte, providing you want several courses. At most restaurants offering fixed-price *menus*, the price for a two- or three-course *menu* is only slightly higher than a single main course from the à la carte list (though the main course is usually larger than the one you get with the fixed-price *menu*). With a three-course *menu* you'll choose a starter of soup, appetizer, or salad; select from three or four main courses with vegetables; and finish up with a cheese course and/or a choice of desserts. It sounds like a lot of food, but portions are a bit smaller with fixed-price *menus*, and what we cram onto one large plate they spread out over several courses. If you're dining with a friend, one person can get the full *menu* while the other can order just a *plat* (and share the *menu* courses). Also, many restaurants offer less expensive and less filling two-course *menus*, sometimes called *formules*, featuring an *entrée et plat*, or *plat et dessert*. Many restaurants have a reasonable *menu-enfant* (kid's meal).

Wine and other drinks are extra, and certain premium items add a few euros, clearly noted on the menu (*supplément* or *sup.*).

Lunch: If a restaurant serves lunch, it generally begins at 12:00 and goes until 14:00, with last orders taken at about 13:30. If you're hungry when restaurants are closed (late afternoon), go to a *boulangerie*, brasserie, or café (see previous section), or find a grocery store. Even fancy places usually have affordable lunch *menus* (often called *formules* or *plat de midi*), allowing you to sample the same gourmet cooking for a lot less than the price of dinner.

In the south, I usually order *une entrée* and *un plat* from *la carte* (often as a two-course *menu* or *formule*), then find an ice-cream or crêpe stand and take a dessert stroll. If that sounds like too much, just order *un plat* (but don't skip the dessert stroll!).

Restaurants are almost always a better value in the countryside than in Paris. If you're driving, look for red-and-blue *Relais Routier* decals on main roads outside cities, indicating that the place is recommended by the truckers' union. These truck-stop cafés offer inexpensive and hearty fare.

FRENCH CUISINE

Most restaurants serve dishes from several regions, though some focus on a particular region's cuisine. Among the listings in this book are restaurants specializing in food from Provence, Burgundy, Alsace, Normandy, Brittany, Dordogne, Languedoc, and the Basque region.

General styles of French cooking include *cuisine gastronomique* (classic, elaborately prepared, multicourse meals); *cuisine semi-gastronomique* or *bistronomie* (the finest-quality home cooking); *cuisine des provinces* (traditional dishes of specific regions); and *nouvelle cuisine* (a focus on smaller portions and closer attention to the texture and color of the ingredients). Sauces are a huge part of French cooking. In the early 20th century, the legendary French chef Auguste Escoffier identified five French "mother sauces" from which all others are derived: *béchamel* (milk-based white sauce), *espagnole* (veal-based brown sauce), *velouté* (stock-based white sauce), *hollandaise* (egg yolk-based white sauce), and *tomate* (tomato-based red sauce).

The following list of items should help you navigate a typical French menu. Galloping gourmets should bring a menu translator. The most complete (and priciest) menu reader around is *A to Z of French Food* by G. de Temmerman (look for the cheaper app). The *Marling Menu-Master* is also good. The *Rick Steves French Phrase Book & Dictionary*, with a menu decoder, works well for most travelers. For dishes specific to each region, see the "Cuisine Scene" sections throughout this book.

If you're interested in learning to cook French cuisine (not just eat it), look for my listings of food tours and cooking classes or check out L'Atelier des Chefs, a network of cooking schools located in many cities throughout France, with top classes at good rates (from €17, www.atelierdeschefs.fr).

First Course *(Entrée)*

Crudités: A mix of raw and lightly cooked fresh vegetables, usually including grated carrots, celery root, tomatoes, and beets, often with a hefty dose of vinaigrette dressing. If you want the dressing on the side, say, *"La sauce à côté, s'il vous plaît"* (lah sohs ah koh-tay, see voo play).

Escargots: Snails cooked in parsley-garlic butter. You don't even have to like the snail itself. Just dipping your bread in garlic butter is more than satisfying. Prepared a variety of ways, the classic is *à la bourguignonne* (served in their shells).

Foie gras: Rich and buttery in consistency—and hefty in price—this pâté is made from the swollen livers of force-fed geese (or ducks, in *foie gras de canard*). Put small chunks on bread—don't spread it, and never add mustard. For a real French experience, try this dish with a sweet white wine (such as a Muscat).

Huîtres: Oysters, served raw any month, are particularly popular at Christmas and on New Year's Eve, when every café seems to have overflowing baskets in their window.

Œuf mayo: A simple hard-boiled egg topped with a dollop of flavorful mayonnaise.

Pâtés and **terrines:** Slowly cooked ground meat (usually pork, though game, poultry liver, and rabbit are also common) that is highly seasoned and served in slices with mustard and *cor-*

nichons (little pickles). Pâtés are smoother than the similarly prepared but chunkier *terrines*.

Soupe à l'oignon: Hot, salty, filling—and hard to find in Paris—French onion soup is a beef broth served with a baked cheese-and-bread crust over the top.

Salads *(Salades)*

With the exception of a *salade mixte* (simple green salad, often difficult to find), the French get creative with their *salades*. Here are some classics:

Salade de chèvre chaud: This mixed-green salad is topped with warm goat cheese on small pieces of toast.

Salade de gésiers: Though it may not sound appetizing, this salad with chicken gizzards (and often slices of duck) is worth a try.

Salade composée: "Composed" of any number of ingredients, this salad might have *lardons* (bacon), Comté (a Swiss-style cheese), Roquefort (blue cheese), *œuf* (egg), *noix* (walnuts), and *jambon* (ham, generally thinly sliced).

Salade gourmande: The "gourmet" salad varies by region and restaurant but usually features cured and poached meats served on salad greens with a mustard vinaigrette.

Salade niçoise: A specialty from Nice, this tasty salad usually includes greens topped with ripe tomatoes, raw vegetables (such as radishes, green peppers, celery, and perhaps artichoke or fava beans), tuna (usually canned), anchovy, hard-boiled egg, and olives.

Salade paysanne: You'll usually find potatoes *(pommes de terre)*, walnuts *(noix)*, tomatoes, ham, and egg in this salad.

Main Course *(Plat Principal)*

Duck, lamb, and rabbit are popular in France, and each is prepared in a variety of ways. You'll also encounter various stew-like dishes that vary by region. The most common regional specialties are described here.

Bœuf bourguignon: A Burgundian specialty, this classy beef stew is cooked slowly in red wine, then served with onions, potatoes, and mushrooms.

Cabillaud: Cod is France's favorite fish, and you'll find it on French menus. It's cooked in many ways that vary by region, but most commonly with butter, white wine, and herbs.

Confit de canard: A favorite from the southwest Dordogne region is duck that has been preserved in its own fat, then cooked in its fat, and often served with potatoes (cooked in the same fat). Not for dieters. (Note that *magret de canard* is sliced duck breast and very different in taste.)

Coq au vin: This Burgundian dish is rooster marinated ever so slowly in red wine, then cooked until it melts in your mouth. It's served (often family-style) with vegetables.

Daube: Generally made with beef, but sometimes lamb, this is a long and slowly simmered dish, typically paired with noodles or other pasta.

Escalope normande: This specialty of Normandy features turkey or veal in a cream sauce.

Gigot d'agneau: A specialty of Provence, this is a leg of lamb often grilled and served with white beans. The best lamb is *pré salé*, which means the lamb has been raised in salt-marsh lands (like at Mont St-Michel).

Le hamburger: This American import is all the rage in France. Cafés and restaurants serve it using local sauces, breads, and cheeses. It's fun to see their interpretation of our classic dish.

Poulet rôti: Roasted chicken on the bone—French comfort food.

Saumon and **truite:** You'll see salmon and trout *(truite)* dishes served in various styles. The salmon usually comes from the North Sea and is always served with sauce, most commonly a sorrel *(oseille)* sauce.

Steak: Referred to as *pavé* (thick hunk of prime steak), *bavette* (skirt steak), *faux filet* (sirloin), or *entrecôte* (rib steak), French steak is usually thinner and tougher than American steak and is always served with sauces (*au poivre* is a pepper sauce, *une sauce roquefort* is a blue-cheese sauce). Because steak is usually better in North America, I generally avoid it in France (unless the sauce sounds good). You will also see *steak haché,* which is a lean, gourmet hamburger patty served *sans* bun. When it's served as *steak haché à cheval*, it comes with a fried egg on top.

By American standards, the French undercook meats: Their version of rare, *saignant* (seh-nyahn), means "bloody" and is close to raw. What they consider medium, *à point* (ah pwan), is what an American would call rare. Their term for well-done, or *bien cuit* (bee-yehn kwee), would translate as medium for Americans (and overdone for the French).

Steak tartare: This wonderfully French dish is for adventurous types only. It's very lean, raw hamburger served with savory seasonings (usually Tabasco, capers, raw onions, salt, and pepper on the side) and topped with a raw egg yolk. This is not hamburger as we know it, but freshly ground beef.

Cheese Course *(Le Fromage)*

The cheese course is served just before (or instead of) dessert. It not only helps with digestion, it gives you a great opportunity to sample the tasty regional cheeses—and time to finish up your wine. Between cow, goat, and sheep cheeses, there are more than 350 different ones to try in France. Some restaurants will offer a cheese platter *(plateau de fromages),* from which you select a few different kinds. A good platter has at least four cheeses: a hard cheese (such as Cantal), a flowery cheese (such as Brie or Camembert), a blue or Roquefort cheese, and a goat cheese.

To sample several types of cheese from the cheese plate, say, *"Un assortiment, s'il vous plaît"* (uhn ah-sor-tee-mahn, see voo play). You'll either be served a selection of several cheeses or choose from a large selection offered on a cheese tray. If you serve yourself from the cheese tray, observe French etiquette and keep the shape of the cheese: Shave off a slice from the side or cut small wedges.

A glass of good red wine is a heavenly complement to your cheese course. With three-course *menus,* the last course is usually a choice between *"fromage"* or *"dessert."*

Dessert *(Le Dessert)*

If you order espresso, it will always come after dessert. To have coffee with dessert, ask for *"café avec le dessert"* (kah-fay ah-vehk luh day-sayr). See the list of coffee terms next. Here are the types of treats you'll see:

Baba au rhum: Pound cake drenched in rum, served with whipped cream.

Café gourmand: An assortment of small desserts selected by the restaurant, served with an espresso—a great way to sample several desserts.

Crème brûlée: A rich, creamy, dense, caramelized custard.

Crème caramel: Flan in a caramel sauce.

Fondant au chocolat: A molten chocolate cake with a runny (not totally cooked) center. Also known as *moelleux* (meh-leh) *au chocolat.*

Fromage blanc: A light dessert similar to plain yogurt (yet different), served with sugar or herbs.

Glace: Ice cream—typically vanilla, chocolate, or strawberry.

Ile flottante: A light dessert consisting of islands of meringue floating on a pond of custard sauce.

Mousse au chocolat: Chocolate mousse.

Profiteroles: Cream puffs filled with vanilla ice cream, smothered in warm chocolate sauce.

Riz au lait: Rice pudding.

Sorbets: Light, flavorful, and fruity ices, sometimes laced with brandy.

Tartes: Open-face pie, often filled with fruit.

Tarte tatin: Apple pie like grandma never made, with caramelized apples, cooked upside down, but served upright.

PRACTICALITIES

French Wine-Tasting 101

France is peppered with wineries and wine-tasting opportunities. For some, trying to make sense of the vast range of French wines can be overwhelming, particularly when faced with a no-nonsense winemaker or sommelier. Do your best to follow my tips, and don't linger if you don't feel welcome.

Visit several private wineries or stop by a *cave coopérative* or a *caveau* to taste wines from a number of local vintners in a single, less intimidating setting. (Throughout this book, I've tried to identify which vineyards are most accepting of wine novices.) At wineries, you'll have a better experience if you call ahead to let them know you're coming (even if it's open all day; ask your hotelier for help). Avoid visiting places between noon and 14:00: Many wineries close midday, and those that don't are staffed by people who would rather be at lunch.

Winemakers and sommeliers are usually happy to work with you...especially if they can figure out what you want. It helps to know what you like (drier or sweeter, lighter or full-bodied, fruity or more tannic, and so on). The people serving you may know those words in English, but you're wise to learn the key words in French (see the "French Wine Lingo" section).

French wines usually have a lower alcohol level than American or Australian wines. While Americans commonly like a big, full-bodied wine, most French prefer subtler flavors. They judge a wine by how well it pairs with a meal—and a big, oaky wine would overwhelm most French cuisine. The French enjoy sampling younger wines and divining how they will taste in a few years, allowing them to buy bottles at cheaper prices and stash them in their cellars. Americans want it now—for today's picnic.

At tastings, vintners and wine shops are hoping you'll buy a bottle or two (otherwise you may be asked to pay a small tasting fee). They understand that North Americans can't take much wine with them, but they do hope you'll look for their wines when you're back home. Some places will ship wine—ask.

BEVERAGES

In stores, unrefrigerated soft drinks, bottled water, and beer are one-third the price of cold drinks. Bottled water and boxed fruit juice are the cheapest drinks. Avoid buying drinks to-go at street-side stands; you'll pay far less in a shop.

In bars and at eateries, be clear when ordering drinks—you can easily pay €10 for an oversized Coke and €15 for a supersized beer at some cafés. When you order a drink, state the size in cen-

Here are some phrases to get you started when wine-tasting:

Hello, madam/sir.
Bonjour, madame/monsieur.
(bohn-zhoor, mah-dahm/muhs-yuh)

We would like to taste a few wines.
Nous voudrions déguster quelques vins.
(noo voo-dree-ohn day-gew-stay kehl-kuh van)

We would like a wine that is _____ and _____ .
Nous voudrions un vin _____ et _____ .
(noo voo-dree-ohn uhn van _____ ay _____)

Fill in the blanks with your favorites from this list:

English	French
red	*rouge* (roozh)
white	*blanc* (blahn)
rosé	*rosé* (roh-zay)
light	*léger* (lay-zhay)
full-bodied	*robuste* (roh-bewst)
fruity	*fruité* (frwee-tay)
sweet	*doux* (doo)
tannic	*tannique* (tah-neek)
fine	*fin, avec finesse* (fan, ah-vehk fee-nehs)
ready to drink (mature)	*prêt à boire* (preh tah bwar)
not ready to drink	*fermé* (fair-may)
oaky or woody	*boisé* (bwah-zay)
from old vines	*de vieilles vignes* (duh vee-yay-ee veen-yuh)
sparkling	*pétillant* (pay-tee-yahn)

tiliters (don't say "small," "medium," or "large," because the waiter might bring a bigger drink than you want). For something small, ask for 25 *centilitres* (vant-sank sahn-tee-lee-truh; about 8 ounces); for a medium drink, order 33 cl (trahnte-twah; about 12 ounces—a normal can of soda); a large is 50 cl (san-kahnt; about 16 ounces); and a super-size is one liter (lee-truh; about a quart—which is more than I would ever order in France). The ice cubes melted after the last Yankee tour group left.

Water, Juice, and Soft Drinks

The French are willing to pay for bottled water with their meal (*eau minérale;* oh mee-nay-rahl) because they prefer the taste over tap water. Badoit is my favorite carbonated water (*l'eau gazeuse;* loh gah-zuhz) and is commonly available. To get a free pitcher of tap water, ask for *une carafe d'eau* (ewn kah-rahf doh). Otherwise, you may unwittingly buy bottled water.

In France *limonade* (lee-moh-nahd) is Sprite or 7-Up. For a fun, bright, nonalcoholic drink of 7-Up with mint syrup, order *un diabolo menthe* (uhn dee-ah-boh-loh mahnt). For 7-Up with fruit syrup, order *un diabolo grenadine* (think Shirley Temple). Kids love the local orange drink, Orangina, a carbonated orange juice with pulp (though it can be pricey). They also like *sirop à l'eau* (see-roh ah loh), flavored syrup mixed with carbonated water.

For keeping hydrated on the go, hang on to the half-liter mineral-water bottles (sold in grocery stores for about €1-2) and refill. Buy juice in cheap liter boxes, then drink some and store the extra in your water bottle. Of course, water quenches your thirst better and cheaper than anything you'll find in a store or café. I drink tap water throughout France, filling up my bottle in hotel rooms.

Coffee and Tea

The French define various types of espresso drinks by how much milk is added. To the French, milk is a delicate form of nutrition: You need it in the morning, but as the day goes on, too much can upset your digestion. Therefore, the amount of milk that's added to coffee decreases as the day goes on. The average French person thinks a *café au lait* is exclusively for breakfast, and a *café crème* is only appropriate through midday. You're welcome to order a milkier coffee drink later in the day, but don't be surprised if you get a funny look.

By law, a waiter must give you a glass of tap water with your coffee or tea if you request it; ask for *"un verre d'eau, s'il vous plaît"* (uhn vayr doh, see voo play).

Here are some common coffee and tea drinks:

Café (kah-fay): Shot of espresso

Café allongé, a.k.a. *café long* (kah-fay ah-lohn-zhay; kah-fay lohn): Espresso topped up with hot water—like an Americano

Noisette (nwah-zeht): Espresso with a dollop of milk (best value for adding milk to your coffee)

Café au lait (kah-fay oh lay): Espresso mixed with lots of warm milk (used mostly for coffee made at home; in a café, order *café crème*)

Café crème (kah-fay krehm): Espresso with a sizable pour of steamed milk (closest thing you'll get to an American-style latte)

Grand crème (grahn krehm): Double shot of espresso with a bit more steamed milk (and often twice the price)

Décaféiné (day-kah-fee-nay): Decaf—available for any of the above

Thé nature (tay nah-tour): Plain tea

Thé au lait (tay oh lay): Tea with milk

Thé citron (tay see-trohn): Tea with lemon

Infusion (an-few-see-yohn): Herbal tea

Alcoholic Beverages

The legal drinking age is 16 for beer and wine and 18 for the hard stuff—at restaurants it's normal for wine to be served with dinner to teens.

Wine: Wines are often listed in a separate *carte des vins*. House wine is generally cheap and good (about €3-8/glass). At a restaurant, a bottle or carafe of house wine costs around €10-15. To order inexpensive wine at a restaurant, ask for table or house wine in a pitcher, rather than a bottle. Finer restaurants usually offer only bottles of wine.

Here are some important wine terms:

Vin de table (van duh tah-bluh): House wine

Verre de vin rouge (vehr duh van roozh): Glass of red wine

Verre de vin blanc (vehr duh van blahn): Glass of white wine

Pichet (pee-shay): Pitcher

Demi-pichet (duh-mee pee-shay): Half-carafe

Quart (kar): Quarter-carafe (ideal for one)

Bouteille (boo-teh-ee): Bottle

Demi-bouteille (duh-mee boo-teh-ee): Half-bottle

Beer: Local *bière* (bee-ehr) costs about €5 at a restaurant and is cheaper on tap (*une pression;* ewn pres-yohn) than in the bottle. France's best-known beers are Alsatian; try Kronenbourg or the heavier Pelfort (one of your author's favorites). Craft beers *(bière artisanale),* usually from outside Paris, are gaining in popularity; Brittany produces some of the best, though all regions seem to be making craft beers these days. *Un Monaco* is a red drink made with beer, grenadine, and lemonade.

Aperitifs: Champagne is a popular way to start your evening in France. For a refreshing before-dinner drink, order a *kir* (pronounced "keer")—a thumb's level of *crème de cassis* (black currant liqueur) topped with white wine (upgrade to a *kir royal* if you'd like it made with champagne). Also consider a glass of Lillet, a sweet, flowery fortified wine from Bordeaux.

After Dinner: If you like brandy, try a *marc* (regional brandy—e.g., *marc de Bourgogne*) or an Armagnac, cognac's cheaper twin brother. *Pastis,* the standard southern France aperitif, is a sweet anise (licorice) drink that comes on the rocks with a glass of water. Cut it to taste with lots of water.

Staying Connected

One of the most common questions I hear from travelers is, "How can I stay connected in Europe?" The short answer is: more easily and cheaply than you might think.

The simplest solution is to bring your own device—mobile phone, tablet, or laptop—and use it just as you would at home (following the tips next, such as getting an international plan or connecting to free Wi-Fi whenever possible). Another option is to buy a European SIM card for your US mobile phone. Or you can use European landlines and computers to connect. Each of these options is described next, and more details are at www.ricksteves.com/phoning. For a very practical one-hour talk covering tech issues for travelers, see www.ricksteves.com/mobile-travel-skills.

USING A MOBILE PHONE IN EUROPE

Here are some budget tips and options.

Sign up for an international plan. To stay connected at a lower cost, sign up for an international service plan through your carrier. Most providers offer a simple bundle that includes calling, messaging, and data. Your normal plan may already include international coverage (T-Mobile's does).

Before your trip, call your provider or check online to confirm that your phone will work in Europe, and research your provider's international rates. Activate the plan a day or two before you leave, then remember to cancel it when your trip's over.

Use free Wi-Fi whenever possible. Unless you have an unlimited-data plan, you're best off saving most of your online tasks for Wi-Fi (pronounced *wee-fee* in French). You can access the internet, send texts, and even make voice calls over Wi-Fi.

Most accommodations in Europe offer free Wi-Fi, but some—especially expensive hotels—charge a fee. Many cafés (including Starbucks and McDonald's) have free hotspots for customers; look for signs offering it and ask for the Wi-Fi password when you buy something. You'll also often find Wi-Fi at TIs, city squares, major museums, public-transit hubs, important train stations, airports, aboard trains and buses, and at some autoroute (highway) rest stops.

Minimize the use of your cellular network. Even with an international data plan, wait until you're on Wi-Fi to Skype, download apps, stream videos, or do other megabyte-greedy tasks. Using a navigation app such as Google Maps over a cellular network can take lots of data, so do this sparingly or use it offline.

Limit automatic updates. By default, your device constantly

checks for a data connection and updates apps. It's smart to disable these features so your apps will only update when you're on Wi-Fi. Also change your device's email settings from "auto-retrieve" to "manual" (or from "push" to "fetch").

When you need to get online but can't find Wi-Fi, simply turn on your cellular network just long enough for the task at hand. When you're done, avoid further charges by manually turning off data roaming or cellular data (either works) in your device's Settings menu. Another way to make sure you're not accidentally using data roaming is to put your device in "airplane" mode (which also disables phone calls and texts), and then turn your Wi-Fi back on as needed.

Use Wi-Fi calling and messaging apps. Skype, WhatsApp, FaceTime, and Google Hangouts are great for making free or low-cost voice calls or sending texts over Wi-Fi. With an app installed on your phone, tablet, or laptop, you can log on to a Wi-Fi network and contact friends or family members who use the same service. If you buy credit in advance, with some of these services you can call or send a text anywhere for just pennies per minute.

Some apps, such as Apple's iMessage, will use the cellular network if Wi-Fi isn't available: To avoid this possibility, turn off the "Send as SMS" feature.

USING A EUROPEAN SIM CARD

With a European SIM card, you get a European mobile number and access to cheaper rates than you'll get through your US carrier. This option works best for those who want to make a lot of local calls, need a local phone number, or want faster connection speeds than their US carrier provides. It's simple: You buy a SIM card in Europe to replace the SIM card in your "unlocked" US phone or tablet (check with your carrier about unlocking it) or buy a basic cell phone in Europe.

SIM cards are sold at department-store electronics counters, some newsstands, and vending machines, but if you need help setting it up, buy one at a mobile-phone shop (you may need to show your passport). Costing about $5-10, SIM cards usually include prepaid calling credit, with no contract and no commitment. Expect to pay $20-40 more for a SIM card with a gigabyte of data.

There are no roaming charges for EU citizens using a domestic SIM card in other EU countries. Theoretically, providers don't have to offer Americans this "roam-like-at-home" pricing, but most do. To be sure, buy your SIM card at a mobile-phone shop and ask if non-EU citizens also have roam-like-at-home pricing.

When you run out of credit, you can top your SIM card up at newsstands, tobacco shops, mobile-phone stores, or many other

How to Dial

International Calls

Whether phoning from a US landline or mobile phone, or from a number in another European country, here's how to make an international call. I've used one of my recommended Paris hotels as an example (tel. 01 47 05 25 45).

Initial Zero: Drop the initial zero from international phone numbers—except when calling Italy.

Mobile Tip: If using a mobile phone, the "+" sign can replace the international access code (for a "+" sign, press and hold "0").

US/Canada to Europe

Dial 011 (US/Canada international access code), country code (33 for France), and phone number.

▶ To call the Paris hotel from home, dial 011 33 1 47 05 25 45.

Country to Country Within Europe

Dial 00 (Europe international access code), country code, and phone number.

▶ To call the Paris hotel from Spain, dial 00 33 1 47 05 25 45.

Europe to the US/Canada

Dial 00, country code (1 for US/Canada), and phone number.

▶ To call from Europe to my office in Edmonds, Washington, dial 00-1-425-771-8303.

Domestic Calls

To call within France (from one French landline or mobile phone to another), simply dial the phone number, including the initial 0 if there is one.

▶ To call the Paris hotel from Nice, dial 01 47 05 25 45.

More Dialing Tips

French Phone Prefixes: France doesn't use area codes. French phone prefixes vary by region or type of call. For instance, all Paris landline numbers start with 01, and all landlines in Provence and the Riviera begin with 04.

businesses (look for your SIM card's logo in the window), or possibly online.

WITHOUT A MOBILE PHONE

It's possible to travel in Europe without a mobile device. You can make calls from your hotel, and check email or browse websites using public computers.

Most **hotels** charge a fee for placing calls—ask for rates before you dial. Prepaid international phone cards *(cartes international)* are

Any number beginning with 06 or 07 is a mobile phone, and costs more to dial.

Toll and Toll-Free Calls: France's toll-free numbers start with 0800-0805 and are called *numéro vert* (green number). Any 08 number followed by 10-99 is a toll call (generally €0.10-0.50/minute; cost announced in French; you can hang up before being billed). International rates apply to US toll-free numbers dialed from France—they're not free.

More Phoning Help: See www.howtocallabroad.com.

European Country Codes		Ireland & N. Ireland	353 / 44
Austria	43	Italy	39
Belgium	32	Latvia	371
Bosnia-Herzegovina	387	Montenegro	382
Croatia	385	Morocco	212
Czech Republic	420	Netherlands	31
Denmark	45	Norway	47
Estonia	372	Poland	48
Finland	358	Portugal	351
France	33	Russia	7
Germany	49	Slovakia	421
Gibraltar	350	Slovenia	386
Great Britain	44	Spain	34
Greece	30	Sweden	46
Hungary	36	Switzerland	41
Iceland	354	Turkey	90

not widely used in France, but can be found at some newsstands, tobacco shops, and train stations. Dial the toll-free access number, enter the card's PIN code, then dial the number.

Public computers are not always easy to find. Some hotels have one in their lobby for guests to use; otherwise you may find one at a public library (ask your hotelier or the TI for the nearest location). On a European keyboard, use the "Alt Gr" key to the right of the space bar to insert the extra symbol that appears on

Tips on Internet Security

Make sure that your device is running the latest versions of its operating system, security software, and apps. Next, ensure that your device and key programs (like email) are password- or passcode-protected. On the road, use only secure, password-protected Wi-Fi hotspots. Ask the hotel or café staff for the specific name of their Wi-Fi network, and make sure you log on to that exact one.

If you must access your financial info online, use a banking app rather than accessing your account via a browser. A cellular connection is more secure than Wi-Fi. Avoid logging onto personal finance sites on a public computer.

Never share your credit-card number (or any other sensitive information) online unless you know that the site is secure. A secure site displays a little padlock icon, and the URL begins with *https* (instead of the usual *http*).

some keys. If you can't locate a special character (such as @), simply copy and paste it from a Web page.

MAIL

You can mail one package per day to yourself worth up to $200 duty-free from Europe to the US (mark it "personal purchases"). If you're sending a gift to someone, mark it "unsolicited gift." For details, visit www.cbp.gov, select "Travel," and search for "Know Before You Go."

The French postal service works fine, but for quick transatlantic delivery (in either direction), consider services such as DHL (www.dhl.com). French post offices are referred to as *La Poste* or sometimes the old-fashioned PTT, for "Post, Telegraph, and Telephone." Hours vary, though most are open weekdays 8:00-19:00 and Saturday morning 8:00-12:00. Stamps are also sold at *tabacs*. It costs about €1 to mail a postcard to the US. One convenient, if expensive, way to send packages home is to use the post office's Colissimo XL postage-paid mailing box. It costs €50-90 to ship boxes weighing 5-7 kilos (about 11-15 pounds).

Transportation

Figuring out how to get around in Europe is one of your biggest trip decisions. **Cars** work well for two or more traveling together (especially families with small kids), those packing heavy, and those delving into the countryside. **Trains** and **buses** are best for solo travelers, blitz tourists, city-to-city travelers and those who want to leave the driving to others. Smart travelers can use short-hop **flights** within Europe to creatively connect the dots on their itineraries. Just be aware of the potential downside of each option: A car is an expensive headache in any major city; with trains and buses you're at the mercy of a timetable; and flying entails a trek to and from a usually distant airport.

If your itinerary mixes cities and countryside, my advice is to connect cities by train (or bus) and to explore rural areas by rental car. Arrange to pick up your car in the last big city you'll visit, then use it to lace together small towns and explore the countryside. For more detailed information on transportation throughout Europe, see www.ricksteves.com/transportation.

In cities, arriving by train in the middle of town makes hotel-hunting and sightseeing easy. But in France, many destinations are small, remote places far from a station, such as Honfleur, Mont St-Michel, D-Day beaches, Loire Valley châteaux, Dordogne caves, and villages in Provence and Burgundy. In such places, taking trains and buses can require great patience, planning, and time. If you'll be relying on public transportation, focus on fewer destinations, or hire one of the excellent minivan tour guides I recommend.

I've included two sample itineraries—by car and by public transportation—to help you explore France smoothly; you'll find these on pages 20 and 22.

TRAINS

France's SNCF rail system (short for Société Nationale Chemins de Fer) sets the pace in Europe. Its high-speed trains (TGV, tay zhay vay; *Train à Grande Vitesse*—also called "InOui") have inspired bullet trains throughout the world. The TGV, which requires a reservation, runs at 170-220 mph. Its rails are fused into one long, continuous track for a faster and smoother ride. The TGV has changed commuting patterns throughout France by putting most of the country within day-trip distance of Paris.

Any staffed train station has schedule information, can make reservations, and can sell tickets for any destination. For more on train travel, see www.ricksteves.com/rail.

Schedules

Schedules change by season, weekday, and weekend. Verify train times and frequencies shown in this book—online, go to www.bahn.com (Germany's excellent all-Europe schedule site), or check locally at train stations. The French rail website is www.sncf.com; for online sales, go to https://en.oui.sncf/en. If you'll be traveling on one or two long-distance trains without a rail pass, it's worth looking online, as advance-purchase discounts can be a great deal.

Bigger stations may have helpful information agents roaming the station (usually in bright red or blue vests) and at *Accueil* or

French Train Terms and Abbreviations

SNCF (Société Nationale des Chemins de Fer): This is the Amtrak of France, operating all national train lines that link cities and towns.

TGV (*Train à Grande Vitesse;* also called "InOui"): SNCF's network of high-speed trains (twice as fast as regular trains) that connect major cities in France. These trains always require a reservation.

Intercité: These trains are the next best to the TGV in terms of speed and comfort and, like TGV trains, they require a reservation.

TER (Transport Express Régional): These trains serve smaller stops within a region. For example, you'll find trains called TER Provence (Provence-only trains) and TER de Bourgogne (trains operating only in Burgundy). No reservations are needed.

Paris Region

For more on Paris transit, see page 39.

RATP (Réseau Autonome de Transports Parisiens): This company operates subways and buses within Paris.

Le Métro: This network of subway lines serves central Paris.

RER (Le Train): This commuter rail and subway system links central Paris with suburban destinations.

Transilien: It's similar to Le Train system, but travels farther afield, serving the Ile-de-France region around Paris. Rail passes cover these lines.

International Trains Operating in France

Eurostar: Connects French cities of Paris, Lille, and Calais with London via the Chunnel.

ICE (Intercity Express): High-speed German-run trains connecting major cities in Europe.

Thalys: High-speed trains linking Paris with cities in Belgium, the Netherlands, and Germany.

TGV Lyria: High-speed trains connecting France and Switzerland.

Information offices or booths. Make use of their help; don't stand in a ticket line if all you need is a train schedule or to confirm a departure time.

Rail Passes

The single-country Eurail France Pass can be a good value for long-distance train travelers. Each day of use of your France Pass allows you to take as many trips as you want on one calendar day (you could go from Paris to Beaune in Burgundy, enjoy wine tasting, then continue to Avignon, stay a few hours, and end in Nice—though I wouldn't recommend it).

Be aware that France's fast TGV and international trains require paid seat reservations (up to €20 within France and more for international, especially if your pass doesn't cover both ends of travel). Particularly on international trains, places for rail-pass holders can be limited—which means trains may "sell out" for pass holders well before they've sold out for ticket buyers. Reserving these fast trains at least several weeks in advance is recommended (for strategies, see "Reservations," later).

You'll save money with the second-class version of the France Pass, but first class gives you more options when reserving popular TGV routes. A first-class pass also grants you access to "Salon des Grand Voyageurs" lounges in railway stations at Paris (Est, Nord, Montparnasse, and Gare de Lyon), Strasbourg, Bordeaux, Marseille, Nantes, Rennes, Lille Flandres, Lille Europe, and Lyon Part-Dieu. These first-class lounges are more basic than airport lounges—but they do offer free coffee and water, good chairs, Wi-Fi, WCs, and a place to charge your phone.

For very short trips in France, buy second-class point-to-point tickets. Longer rides are where you can really save money with either a rail pass or advance-purchase ticket discounts. Note that if you're connecting the French Alps with Alsace, you might travel through Switzerland, a route that requires France Pass holders to buy a ticket for that segment (about €50).

If your trip extends beyond France, consider the **Eurail Global Pass,** covering most of Europe. If you buy two separate passes for neighborhing countries, note that you'll use a travel day on each when crossing the border. For more detailed advice on figuring out the smartest rail-pass options for your train trip, visit www.ricksteves.com/rail.

Buying Tickets

Online: While there's no deadline to buy any train ticket, the fast, reserved TGV trains get booked up. Buy well ahead for any TGV you cannot afford to miss. Tickets go on sale as far as four months in advance, with a wide range of prices on any one route. The cheapest tickets sell out early and reservations for rail-pass holders also go particularly fast.

To buy the cheapest advance-discount tickets (up to 60 percent less than full fare), visit https://en.oui.sncf/en three to four months ahead of your travel date. (A pop-up window may ask you to choose between being sent to the Rail Europe website or staying on the SNCF page—click "Stay.") Next, choose "Train," then "TGV." Under "Book your train tickets," pick your travel dates, and choose "France" as your ticket collection country. The cheap-

Public Transportation in France

Legend:
- Rail
- Eurostar Rail
- TGV High-Speed Rail
- Bus
- Boat
- ✈ Airports (Not All Shown)

Note: In some cases regular train lines and TGV lines share the same track

50 Kilometers
50 Miles

ENGLAND

To Ireland
London
Eurostar
Dover
Folkstone
Poole
Portsmouth
Newhaven
Boulogne

English Channel

Cherbourg
Le Tréport
Dieppe
Le Havre
Roscoff
Arromanches
Honfleur
Rouen
Brest
Morlaix
Mont St-Michel
St-Malo
Bayeux
Caen
Lisieux
Avranches
Versailles
Lamballe
Pontorson
Dinan
Dol
Chartres
Quimper
TGV
Vannes
Rennes
Le Mans
Orléans
Quiberon
Redon
Blois
Angers
Tours
Amboise
Nantes
Saumur
Chenonceaux
Langeais
Chinon
Tours St-Pierre des Corps TGV Stn.
Azay
Vierzon

Atlantic Ocean

Poitiers
FRA
La Rochelle
Oradour-sur-Glane
Cognac
Saintes
Limoges
Angoulême
Perigueux
Brive
Libourne
Sarlat-la-Canéda
Bordeaux ✈
Les Eyzies
Souillac
St-Emilion
Le Buisson
Beynac
Cahors
Biarritz
Agen
Guernica
TGV
Montauban
Bilbao ✈
St-Jean-de-Luz
Dax
Bayonne
Hendaye
PRIVATE RAIL
Toulouse ✈
San Sebastián
Irun
St-Jean Pied-de-Port
Pau
Miranda de Ebro
Lourdes
Pamplona
Burgos
Foix
La Tour
SPAIN
ANDORRA
To Madrid
To Barcelona

PRACTICALITIES

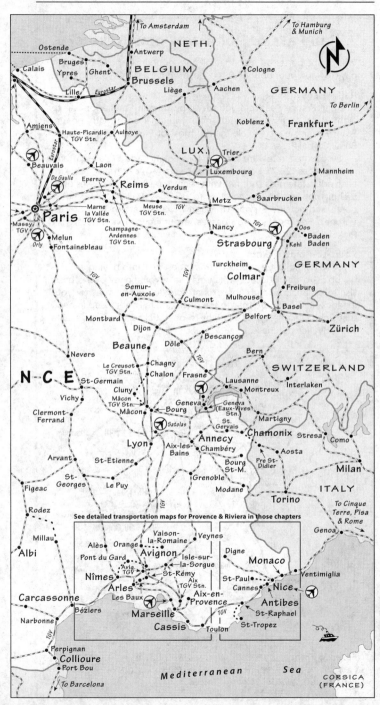

See detailed transportation maps for Provence & Riviera in those chapters

PRACTICALITIES

Rail Pass or Point-to-Point Tickets?

Will you be better off buying a rail pass or point-to-point tickets? It pays to know your options and choose what's best for your itinerary.

Rail Passes

A Eurail France Pass lets you travel by train in France for one to eight days (consecutively or not) within a one-month period. France is also covered (along with most of Europe) by the classic Eurail Global Pass.

Discounted rates are offered for seniors (age 60 an up) and youths (ages 12-27). Up to two kids (ages 4-11) can travel free with each adult-rate pass (but not with senior rates). All rail passes offer a choice of first or second class for all ages. Rail passes are best purchased outside Europe (through travel agents or Rick Steves' Europe). For more on rail passes, including current prices, visit RickSteves.com/rail.

Point-to-Point Tickets

If you're taking just a couple of train rides, look into buying individual point-to-point tickets, which may save you money over a pass. Use this map to add up approximate pay-as-you-go fares for your itinerary, and compare that to the price of a rail pass. Keep in mind that significant discounts on point-to-point tickets may be available with advance purchase.

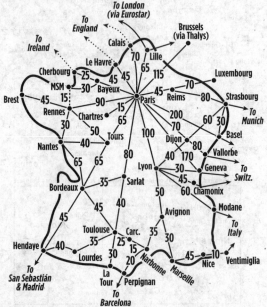

Fares in France:

Map shows approximate costs, in US dollars, for one-way, second-class tickets on faster trains.

est (nonrefundable) tickets are called "Prems"; be sure it also says "TGV" (avoid iDTGV trains—they're very cheap, but this SNCF subsidiary doesn't accept PayPal). Choose the eticket delivery option (which allows you to print at home) and pay with your PayPal account to avoid credit-card approval issues. These low-rate tickets may not be available from Rail Europe or other US agents.

After the "Prems" rates are sold out, you can buy other fare types on the French site with a US credit card if it has been set up for the "Verified by Visa," "MasterCard SecureCode," or "American Express SafeKey" program. For a credit-card purchase, choose "USA" as your ticket collection country.

Otherwise, US customers can order through a US agency, such as at www.ricksteves.com/rail, which offers both etickets and home delivery, but may not have access to all the cheapest rates; or Trainline (www.trainline.eu), which sells the "Prems" fare and iDTGV tickets.

Travelers with smartphones have the option of saving tickets and reservations directly to their phones (choose "m-ticket"). For more details, see https://en.oui.sncf/en/mobile.

In France: You can buy train tickets in person at SNCF Boutiques or at any train station, either from a staffed ticket window or from a machine. You can buy tickets on regional trains for a €7-15 surcharge depending on the length of your trip, but you must find the conductor immediately upon boarding; otherwise it's a €50 minimum charge.

The ticket machines available at most stations are great time savers when other lines are long. While most machines accept American chip cards if you know the PIN code, be prepared with euro coins and bills just in case. Some machines have English instructions, but for those that don't, here are the prompts. (Turn the dial or move the cursor to your choice, and press *"Validez"* to agree to each step.)

1. *Quelle est votre destination?* (What's your destination?)
2. *Billet Plein Tarif* (Full-fare ticket—yes for most.)
3. *1ère ou 2ème* (First or second class; normally second is fine.)
4. *Aller simple ou aller-retour?* (One-way or round-trip?)
5. *Prix en Euro* (The price should be shown if you get this far.)

Reservations

Reservations are required for any TGV or Intercité train, *couchettes* (sleeping berths) on night trains, and some other trains where indicated in timetables. You can reserve any train at any station any time before your departure or through SNCF Boutiques. If you're buying a point-to-point ticket for a TGV or Intercité train, you'll reserve your seat when you purchase your ticket.

Popular TGV routes can fill up quickly. It's wise to book well

Coping with Strikes

Going on strike *(en grève)* is a popular pastime in this revolution-happy country. Because bargaining between management and employees is not standard procedure, workers strike to get attention. Trucks and tractors block main roads and autoroutes (they call it Opération Escargot—"Operation Snail's Pace"), baggage handlers bring airports to their knees, and museum workers make artwork off-limits to tourists. Métro and train personnel seem to strike every year—probably during your trip. What does the traveler do? You could *jeter l'éponge* (throw in the sponge) and go somewhere less strike-prone (Switzerland's nice), or learn to accept certain events as out of your control. Strikes in France have become unpredictable in length, but if you're aware of them, you can usually plan around them. Your hotelier will know the latest (or can find out). Make a habit of asking your hotel receptionist about strikes and checking with the TI. This website gives up-to-date information on train disruptions: https://en.oui.sncf/en/help.

ahead for any TGV, especially on the busy Paris-Avignon-Nice line. If the TGV trains you want are fully booked, ask about TER trains serving the same destination, as these don't require reservations.

If you're using a rail pass, reservations cost €10-20 for domestic travel, depending on the kind of train they're for and where you buy them. Seat reservations on Thalys and international TGV trains usually range from €10 to €38, with the price depending on route and class of service (and can cost up to €60 in first class on TGV Lyria trains to Swiss destinations). These international routes also allocate a very limited number of seats for rail-pass holders. Eurostar trains (to and from London only) accept the larger multi-country passes (plus seat reservation).

Rail-pass holders can book TGV reservations directly at French stations up to departure, if still available, or book etickets at www.raileurope.com. Given the possible difficulty of getting TGV reservations with a rail pass, I recommend making those reservations online before you leave home.

For trains other than the TGV and Intercité, reservations are generally unnecessary, but are advisable during busy times (for example, Friday and Sunday afternoons, Saturday mornings, weekday rush hours, and holiday weekends; see "Holidays and Festivals" in the appendix).

Baggage Check

I've noted when baggage check (*Consigne* or *Espaces Bagages*) is

Train-Ticket French

Hello, madam/sir, do you speak English?
Bonjour, madame/monsieur, parlez-vous anglais?
(bohn-zhoor, mah-dahm/muhs-yur, par-lay-voo ahn-glay)

I would like a departure for Avignon, on 10 May, about 9:00, the most direct way possible.
Je voudrais un train pour Avignon, pour le 10 Mai, vers 9:00, le plus direct possible.
(zhuh voo-dray uhn tran poor ah-veen-yohn, poor luh dees may, vehr nuhf, luh plew dee-rehk poh-see-bluh)

available (only at a handful of the biggest stations, can depend on current security concerns—be prepared to keep your bag; about €5-10/bag per day depending on size). For security reasons, all luggage should carry a tag with the traveler's first and last name and current address (though it's not enforced). This applies to hand luggage as well as bigger bags that are stowed. Free tags are available at many train stations.

Other baggage-check options include hotels and shops near train stations (ask at the station or the TI). Major museums and monuments often have free baggage check for visitors. Even if the sight is not particularly interesting to you, the entry fee may be worth it if you need to stow your bags for a few hours.

Train Tips
At the Station
- Arrive at the station at least 30 minutes before your departure, when platform numbers are typically posted. (In Paris, your ticket must be scanned to access the platform—see below.) Large stations have separate information *(accueil)* windows; at small stations the ticket office gives information.
- Small stations are minimally staffed; if there is no agent at the station, go directly to the tracks and look for the overhead sign that confirms your train stops at that track.
- Larger stations have platforms with monitors showing TGV layouts (numbered forward or backward) so you can figure out where your car *(voiture)* will stop on the long platform and where to board each car.
- Travelers with first-class tickets or rail passes can gain access to lounges at some stations (see "Rail Passes" earlier).

Validating Tickets, Reservations, and Rail Passes
- At major stations (including all Paris stations) you'll need to scan your ticket at turnstiles to access the tracks. Smaller sta-

PRACTICALITIES

tions continue to use the old system of validating your ticket in yellow machines near the platform or waiting area. Print-at-home tickets and etickets downloaded to your phone don't require validation.

- If you have a rail pass, get it activated at a ticket window before using it the first time (don't stamp it in the machine). If you're traveling with a pass and have a reservation for a certain trip, you must activate the reservation by stamping it.
- If you have a rail flexipass, write the date on your pass each day you travel (before or immediately after boarding your first train).
- Note that a Eurail pass must be kept in its cover, and you must fill in trip details on the cover as you go.

On the Train

- Before getting on a train, confirm that it's going where you think it is. For example, if you want to go to Bayeux, ask the conductor or any local passenger, *"À Bayeux?"* (ah bah-yuh).
- Some longer trains split off cars en route. Make sure your train car is continuing to your destination by asking, for example, *"Cette voiture va à Avignon?"* (seht vwah-toor vah ah ah-veen-yohn; meaning, "This car goes to Avignon?").
- If a non-TGV train seat is reserved, it'll likely be labeled *réservé*, with the cities to and from which it is reserved.
- If you don't understand an announcement, ask your neighbor to explain: *"Pardon madame/monsieur, qu'est-ce qui se passe?"* (kehs kee suh pahs; "Excuse me, what's going on?").
- Verify with the conductor all the transfers you must make: *"Correspondance à Lyon?"* ("Must I transfer to get to Lyon?")
- To guard against theft, keep your bags in sight (directly over-head is ideal but rarely available—the early boarder gets the best storage space). If you must store them in the lower racks by the doors (available in most cars), pay attention at stops. Your bags are most vulnerable to theft before the train takes off and whenever it stops.
- Note your arrival time, so you'll be ready to get off.
- Use the train's free WCs before you get off (but not while the train is stopped in a station).

BUSES

Buses usually provide the cheapest transportation between European cities. (They're also the cheapest way to cross the English Channel; book at least two days in advance for the best fares.)

Eurolines is the old standby, but two relative newcomers—Ouibus and FlixBus—are cutting prices drastically while offering speedy service, snacks for purchase, Wi-Fi, easy booking, and lots of destinations in France. All of these companies usually provide service between train stations or between train stations and airports within France, as well as to international destinations. The bus is also a handy way to connect Parisian airports with other destinations in France, such as Blois, Rouen, and Caen, for example.

Ouibus has routes mostly within France, but serves some other European cities as well (toll tel. 08 92 68 00 68, www.ouibus.com). German-run **FlixBus** connects key cities within France and throughout Europe, often from secondary airports and train stations (handy eticket system and easy-to-use app, tel. 01 76 36 04 12, www.flixbus.com). **Eurolines'** buses depart from Paris' Gare Routière du Paris-Gallieni station in the suburb of Bagnolet (28 Avenue du Général de Gaulle, Mo: Gallieni, toll tel. 08 92 89 90 91; from the US, dial 011 33 1 41 86 24 21, www.eurolines.com).

A few bus lines are run by the SNCF rail system and are covered by your rail pass (show rail pass at station to get free bus ticket), but most bus lines are not covered. Bus stations *(gare routière)* are usually located next to train stations. Train stations usually have bus information where train-to-bus connections are important—and vice versa for bus companies.

Regional Bus Tips

These tips apply to buses you'll use to explore an area from your home base (for instance, getting to Vaison-la-Romaine from Avignon).

- Read the train tips described earlier—many also apply to buses (check schedules in advance, arrive at the station early, confirm the destination before you board, find out if you need to transfer, etc.).
- The bus company websites I've listed in this book are usually in French only. Here are some key phrases you'll see: *horaires* (schedules), *en semaine* (usually Monday through Saturday, sometimes through Friday), *samedi* (Saturday), *dimanche* (Sunday), *jours fériés* (holidays), *LMMJV (Monday, Tuesday, Wednesday, Thursday, Friday), année* (bus runs all year on the days listed), *vac* (runs only during summer vacations), *scol/scolaire* (runs only when school is in session), *ligne* (route or bus line), and *réseau* (network—usually all routes).
- Use TIs to help plan your trip and verify times (TIs have regional bus schedules).
- Be aware that service is sparse or nonexistent on Sunday. Wednesday bus schedules often are different during the school year, because school is out this day (and regional buses generally operate school service).
- Confirm a bus stop's location in advance (rural stops are often not signed) and be at bus stops at least five minutes early.

Regional Minivan Excursions

Worthwhile day tours are generally available in regions where bus and train service is sparse. For the D-Day beaches, Loire Valley châteaux, Dordogne Valley villages and caves, Cathar castles near Carcassonne, Provence's villages and vineyards, the Route du Vin (Wine Road) in Alsace, other Normandy and Brittany sights (including Mont St-Michel), and wine tasting in Burgundy, I list reliable companies that provide this helpful service at fair rates. Some of these minivan excursions just offer transportation between the sights; others add a running commentary and information on regional history.

TAXIS AND RIDE-BOOKING SERVICES

Most European taxis are reliable and reasonable. In many cities, two people can travel short distances by cab for little more than the cost of bus or subway tickets. If you like ride-booking services such as Uber, their apps usually work in Europe just like they do in the US: Request a car on your mobile phone (connected to Wi-Fi or data), and the fare is automatically charged to your credit card. In France, Uber services generally work in only the largest cities and are not much cheaper than taxis.

RENTING A CAR

It's cheaper to arrange most car rentals from the US, so research and compare rates before you go. Most of the major US rental agencies (including Avis, Budget, Enterprise, Hertz, and Thrifty) have offices throughout Europe. Also consider the two major Europe-based agencies, Europcar and Sixt, and the French agency, ADA (www.ada.fr). Consolidators such as Auto Europe/Kemwel (www.autoeurope.com—or the sometimes cheaper www.autoeurope.eu), compare rates at several companies to get you the best deal.

Wherever you book, always read the fine print. Ask about add-on charges—such as one-way drop-off fees, airport surcharges, or mandatory insurance policies—that aren't included in the "total price."

Rental Costs and Considerations

Figure on paying roughly $250 for a one-week rental for a basic compact car. Allow extra for supplemental insurance, fuel, tolls, and parking.

Manual vs. Automatic: Almost all rental cars in Europe are manual by default—and cars with a stick shift are generally cheaper. If you need an automatic, request one in advance. When selecting a car, don't be tempted by a larger model, as it won't be as maneuverable on narrow, winding roads or when squeezing into tight parking lots.

PRACTICALITIES

Age Restrictions: Some rental companies impose minimum and maximum age limits. Young drivers (25 and under) and seniors (69 and up) should check the rental policies and rules section of car rental websites. If you're considered too young or too old, look into leasing (covered later), which has less stringent age restrictions.

Choosing Pickup/Drop-off Locations: Always check the hours of the locations you choose. Except at airports and major train stations, most rental offices close from midday Saturday until Monday morning and, in smaller towns, at lunchtime.

When selecting an office, plug the address into a mapping website to confirm the location. A downtown site is generally cheaper—and might seem more convenient than the airport. But pedestrianized and one-way streets can make navigation tricky when returning a car at a big-city office or urban train station. Wherever you select, get precise details on the location and allow ample time to find it.

If you want a car for only a day or two (e.g., for the Côtes du Rhône wine route, Luberon villages, D-Day beaches, or Loire Valley châteaux), you'll likely find it easy to rent on the spot just about anywhere in France. In many cases, this is a worthwhile splurge. All you need is your American driver's license and a major credit card (figure €60-90/day; some include unlimited mileage, others give you 100 kilometers—about 60 miles—for free).

Picking Up Your Car: Before driving off in your rental car, check it thoroughly and make sure any damage is noted on your rental agreement. Rental agencies in Europe tend to charge for even minor damage, so be sure to mark everything. Find out how your car's gearshift, lights, turn signals, wipers, radio, and fuel cap function, and know what kind of fuel the car takes (diesel vs. unleaded). When you return the car, make sure the agent verifies its condition with you. Some drivers take pictures of the returned vehicle as proof of its condition.

Car Insurance Options

When you rent a car in Europe, the price typically includes liability insurance, which covers harm to other cars or motorists—but not the rental car itself. To limit your financial risk in case of damage to the rental, choose one of these options: Buy a Collision Damage Waiver (CDW) with a low or zero deductible from the car-rental company (roughly 30-40 percent extra), get coverage through your credit card (free, but more complicated), or get collision insurance as part of a larger travel-insurance policy.

Basic **CDW** costs $15-30 a day and typically comes with a $1,000-2,000 deductible, reducing but not eliminating your financial responsibility. When you reserve or pick up the car, you'll be offered the chance to "buy down" the basic deductible to zero (for an additional $10-30/day; this is sometimes called "super CDW" or "zero-deductible coverage").

If you opt for **credit-card coverage,** you must decline all coverage offered by the car-rental company, which means they can place a hold on your card for up to the full value of the car. In case of damage, it can be time-consuming to resolve the charges. Before relying on this option, quiz your credit-card company about how it works.

If you're already purchasing a **travel-insurance policy** for your trip, adding collision coverage can be an economical option. For example, Travel Guard (www.travelguard.com) sells affordable renter's collision insurance as an add-on to its other policies; it's valid everywhere in Europe except the Republic of Ireland, and some Italian car-rental companies refuse to honor it, as it doesn't cover you in case of theft.

For more on car-rental insurance, see www.ricksteves.com/cdw.

Leasing

For trips of three weeks or more, consider leasing (which automatically includes zero-deductible collision and theft insurance). By technically buying and then selling back the car, you save money on taxes and insurance. Leasing provides you a brand-new car with unlimited mileage and a 24-hour emergency assistance program. You can lease for as little as 21 days to as long as five and a half months; Idea Merge offers two-week leases. Car leases must be arranged from the US; some companies allow drop off in different countries.

These reliable companies offer 21-day lease packages: **Auto France** (Peugeot cars only, US tel. 800-572-9655, www.autofrance.net); **Idea Merge** (ask about two-week leases; Citroën only, US tel. 503/715-5810, www.ideamerge.com); and **Kemwel** (Peugeot only, US tel. 877-820-0668, www.kemwel.com).

RV and Campervan Rental

Even given the extra fuel costs, renting your own rolling hotel can be a great way to save money, especially if you're sticking mainly to rural areas. Keep in mind that RVs in France are much smaller than those you see at home. Consider: Van It (rents pop-top VW Eurovan campers that are easy to maneuver on small roads, mobile 06 95 99 61 46, www.van-it.com); **Idea Merge** (best resource for small RV rental, see listing earlier); and **Origin** (current-model Volkswagen vans fully equipped for 2-3 people, rates less than RVs, mobile 06 80 01 72 77, www.origin-campervans.com).

Navigation Options

If you'll be navigating using your phone or a GPS unit from home, remember to bring a car charger and device mount.

Your Mobile Phone: The mapping app on your phone works fine for navigation in Europe, but for real-time turn-by-turn directions and traffic updates, you'll need mobile data access. And driving all day can burn through a lot of very expensive data. The economical workaround is to use map apps that work offline. By downloading in advance from Google Maps, Apple Maps, Here WeGo, or Navmii, you can still have turn-by-turn voice directions and maps that recalibrate even though they're offline.

You must download your maps before you go offline—and it's smart to select large regions. Then turn off your data connection so you're not charged for roaming. Call up the map, enter your destination, and you're on your way. Even if you don't have to pay extra for data roaming, this option is great for navigating in areas with poor connectivity.

GPS Devices: If you want the convenience of a dedicated GPS unit, consider renting one with your car ($10-30/day). These units offer real-time turn-by-turn directions and traffic without the data requirements of an app. The unit may come loaded only with maps for its home country; if you need additional maps, ask. Also make sure your device's language is set to English before you drive off.

A less expensive option is to bring a GPS device from home. Be sure to buy and install the European maps you'll need before your trip.

Maps and Atlases: Even when navigating primarily with a mobile app or GPS, I always make it a point to have a paper map. It's invaluable for getting the big picture, understanding alternate routes, and filling in when my phone runs out of juice. The free maps you get from your car-rental company usually don't have enough detail. It's smart to buy a better map before you go, or pick one up at European gas stations, bookshops, newsstands, and tourist shops.

Michelin maps are available throughout France at bookstores, newsstands, and gas stations (about €6 each, cheaper than in the US). The Michelin #721 France map (1:1,000,000 scale) covers this book's destinations with good detail for drivers. Drivers should also consider the soft-cover Michelin France atlas (the entire country at 1:200,000, well-organized in a €20 book with an index and maps of major cities). Spend a few minutes learning the Michelin key to get the most sightseeing value out of these maps.

DRIVING

It's a pleasure to explore France by car, but you need to know the rules.

Road Rules: Seat belts are mandatory for all, and children under age 10 must be in the back seat with a special seat. In city and town centers, traffic merging from the right (even from tiny side streets) may have the right-of-way *(priorité à droite)*. So even when you're driving on a major road, pay attention to cars merging from the right. In contrast, cars entering the countless suburban round-abouts must yield *(cédez le passage)*. You can't turn right on a red light, U-turns are illegal, and on expressways it's illegal to pass drivers on the right.

STOP AND LEARN THESE ROAD SIGNS

Speed Limit (km/hr)	Yield	No Passing	End of No Passing Zone
One Way	Intersection	Main Road	Expressway
Roundabout Ahead	Danger	No Entry	All Vehicles Prohibited
No Through Road	Restrictions No Longer Apply	Traffic on right has priority	No Stopping
Parking	No Parking	Customs or Toll Road	Peace

When navigating France's narrow village lanes, you'll likely encounter short sections where cars must pass single file, one direction at a time (to control speeds). At those spots, you'll see a sign with thick and thin arrows pointing up and down. A thick (white) arrow pointing up in the direction you're traveling means you have priority to pass through the section; a red arrow indicates you must yield to cars coming the other way.

Be aware of typical European road rules; for example, many countries require headlights to be turned on at all times (in France, they must be used in any case of poor visibility), and nearly all forbid handheld mobile-phone use. Ask your car-rental company about these rules, or check the "International Travel" section of the US State Department website (www.travel.state.gov, search for your country in the "Country Information" box, then click "Travel and Transportation").

Speed Limits: Because speed limits are by road type, they typically aren't posted, so it's best to memorize them:

- Two-lane D and N routes outside cities and towns: 80 km/hour, 90 km/hour if the road has a divider separating the lanes.

- Two-lane roads in villages: 50 km/hour (unless posted at 30 km/hour)
- Divided highways outside cities and towns: 90-110 km/hour
- Autoroutes (toll roads): 130 km/hour (unless otherwise posted)

If it's raining, subtract 10 km/hour on D and N routes and 20 km/hour on divided highways and autoroutes. Speed-limit signs are a red circle around a number; when you see that same number again in gray with a broken line diagonally across it, this means that limit no longer applies. Speed limits drop to 30-50 km/hour in villages (always posted) and must be respected.

Road speeds are monitored regularly with cameras—a mere two kilometers over the limit yields a pricey ticket (a minimum of about €70). The good news is that signs warn drivers a few hundred yards before the camera and show the proper speed (see image on the next page). Look for a sign with a radar graphic that says

PRACTICALITIES

French Road Signs

Signs You Must Obey

Allumez vos feux	Turn on your lights
Cédez le Passage	Yield
Déviation	Detour
Dépassement Interdit	No passing
Parking Interdit/Stationnement Interdit	No parking
Priorité à Droite	Right-of-way is for cars coming from the right
Ralentissez	Slow down
Rappel	Remember to obey the sign
Vous n'avez pas la priorité	You don't have the right of way (when merging)

Signs for Your Information

Autres Directions	Other directions (follow when leaving a city)
Centre Commercial	Shopping center (not city center)
Centre-Ville	City center
Feux	Traffic signal

Pour votre sécurité, contrôles automatiques. The French use these cameras not to make money but to slow down traffic—and it works.

Tire Pressure: In Europe, tire pressure is measured in *bars* of pressure. To convert to PSI (pounds per square inch) the formula is: *bar* × 14.5 = PSI (so 2 *bars* would be 2 × 14.5, or 29 PSI). To convert to *bar* pressures from PSI, the formula is: PSI × 0.07 = *bar* (so 30 PSI × 0.07 would be 2.1 *bar*). Your car's recommended tire pressure is usually found on a sticker mounted on the driver-side doorframe.

Pulling to the Side of the Road: All rental cars are equipped with a yellow safety vest and triangle. You must wear the vest and display the triangle whenever you pull over on the side of the road (say, to fix a flat tire). If you don't, you could be fined.

Fuel: Gas *(essence)* is expensive—about $7 per gallon. Diesel

Horodateur	Ticket-vending machine for parking
Parc de Stationnement/Parking	Parking lot
Route Barrée	Road blocked
Rue Piétonne	Pedestrian-only street
Sauf Riverains	Local access only
Sens Unique	One-way street
Sortie des Camions	Work truck exit
Suivre... (e.g., Pont du Gard, suivre Nîmes)	Follow... (e.g., for Pont du Gard, follow signs for Nîmes)
Toutes Directions	All directions (follow when leaving a city)

Signs Unique to Autoroutes

Aire	Rest stop with WCs, telephones, and sometimes gas stations
Bouchon	Traffic jam ahead
Fluide	No traffic ahead
Péage	Toll
Par Temps de Pluie	When raining (modifies speed limit signs)
Télépéage	Automated tollbooths

(gazole) costs less—about $6.50 per gallon. Know what type of fuel your car takes before you fill up. Many Americans get marooned by filling with unleaded in a diesel car. Many rentals are diesel; if yours is one of them, use the yellow pump. Fuel is most expensive on autoroutes and cheapest at big supermarkets. Your US credit and debit cards may not work at self-serve pumps—so you may need to find gas stations with attendants (all autoroute stations have them, as do most countryside stations during business hours)—and be sure to know your card's PIN (explained earlier, under "Money").

Plan ahead for Sundays, as most gas stations in town are closed. I fill my tank every Saturday. If stuck on a Sunday, use an autoroute, where the gas stations are always staffed.

Autoroutes and Tolls: Autoroute tolls are pricey, but the alternative to these super-"feeways" usually means being marooned in countryside traffic—especially near the Riviera. Autoroutes save enough time, gas, and nausea to justify the cost. Mix high-speed "autorouting" with scenic country-road rambling.

You'll usually take a ticket when entering an autoroute and pay when you leave. Figure roughly €1 in tolls for every 15 kilometers driven on the autoroute (or about €15 for two hours). Cash (coins or bills under €50) is your best payment option as some US credit cards won't work (for more on paying at tollbooths, see the sidebar). Estimate your distance and toll costs, then make sure that you have enough cash before entering the autoroute.

Autoroute gas stations are open on Sundays and usually come with well-stocked minimarts, clean restrooms, sandwiches, maps, local products, cheap vending-machine coffee, and Wi-Fi. Many have small cafés or more elaborate cafeterias with reasonable prices. For more information, see www.autoroutes.fr.

Highways: Roads are classified into departmental (D), national (N), and autoroutes (A). D routes (usually yellow lines on maps) are often slower but the most scenic. N routes and important D routes (red lines) are the fastest after autoroutes (orange lines on maps). Green road signs are for national routes; blue are for autoroutes. Some roads in France have had route-number changes (mostly N roads converting to D roads). If you're using an older map, the actual route name may differ from what's on your map. Navigate by destination rather than road name...or buy a new map. There are plenty of good facilities, gas stations (most closed Sun), and rest stops along most French roads.

Parking: Finding a parking place can be a headache in larger cities. Ask your hotelier for ideas, and pay to park at well-patrolled lots (blue P signs direct you to parking lots in French cities). Parking garages require that you take a ticket with you and pay at a machine (called a *caisse*) on your way back to the car or at a machine at the exit. American chip cards should work in these machines; otherwise, use euro coins (some accept bills, too). If your credit card does not work and you don't have enough coins, find the garage's *accueil* office, where the attendant can help or direct you to a nearby shop where you can change bills into coins. Overnight parking in garages (usually 19:00-8:00) is generally reasonable (priciest in cities).

Metered parking is strictly monitored in France. At parking machines, prepare to enter your car's license plate number and the amount of time you need, then take the receipt and place it on your dash. While the first 30 minutes is often free, you still need to input your license number and get a ticket. Metered parking is sometimes free 12:00-14:00 and usually free 19:00-9:00 and on Sunday (varies by city and parking area). Look for a small machine selling time (called an *horodateur*, usually one per block), and plug in a few coins or your credit card. Avoid spaces outlined in blue, as they require a special permit.

Theft: Theft is a problem, particularly in southern France. Thieves easily recognize rental cars and assume they are filled with a tourist's gear. Try to make your car look locally owned by hiding

French Tollbooths

For American drivers, getting through the toll payment stations on France's autoroutes is mostly about knowing which lanes to avoid—and having cash and a chip-and-PIN credit card on hand. Don't assume that your US credit card will work even if it has a chip—have cash as a backup.

When approaching the tollbooths, slow down to study your options (and pull off to the side if you need time to consider your choices). Skip lanes marked only with a lowercase "t"—they're reserved for cars using the automatic Télépéage payment system. Follow green arrows to get a ticket (green-arrow lanes are sometimes combined with Télépéage lanes).

When exiting the autoroute, follow the coins icon (usually in white), meaning cash or chip-and-PIN cards are accepted. If you don't see these icons, take the green-arrow lane. Avoid the "t"-only (Télépéage) lane or the credit-card-only lane. Tollbooths are entirely automated (if you have a problem at the tollbooth, press the red button for help). Even machines that take cash usually have a credit card slot—give it a try (know your PIN). Have smaller bills ready (payment machines won't accept €50 bills). Shorter autoroute sections have periodic tollbooths, where you can pay by dropping coins into a basket (change is given for bills, but keep a good supply of coins handy to avoid waiting for an attendant).

To estimate how much cash to have on hand for tolls, use the planning tool at ViaMichelin.com.

the "tourist-owned" rental-company decals and putting a French newspaper in your back window. Be sure all of your valuables are out of sight and locked in the trunk—or, even better, with you or in your room. And don't assume that just because you're parked on a main street that you'll be fine. Thieves work fast.

Driving Tips

- France is riddled with roundabouts—navigating them is an art. The key is to know your direction and be ready for your turnoff. If you miss it, take another lap (or two). See the diagram on next page.
- At intersections and roundabouts, French road signs use the name of an upcoming destination for directions—the highway number is usually missing. That upcoming destination could be a major city, or it could be the next minor town up the road. Check your map ahead of time and get familiar with the names of towns and cities along your route—and even major cities on the same road beyond your destination.
- When navigating into cities, approach intersections cautiously,

How to Navigate a Roundabout

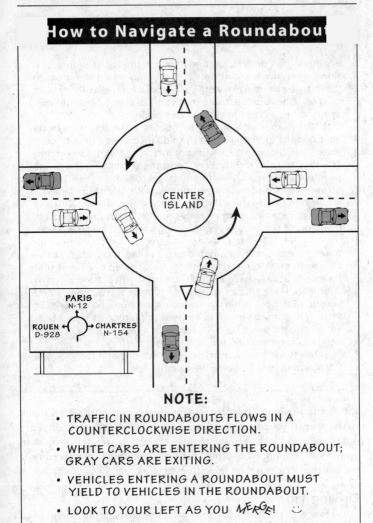

NOTE:

- TRAFFIC IN ROUNDABOUTS FLOWS IN A COUNTERCLOCKWISE DIRECTION.
- WHITE CARS ARE ENTERING THE ROUNDABOUT; GRAY CARS ARE EXITING.
- VEHICLES ENTERING A ROUNDABOUT MUST YIELD TO VEHICLES IN THE ROUNDABOUT.
- LOOK TO YOUR LEFT AS YOU MERGE! ☺

stow the map, and follow the signs to *Centre-Ville* (city center). From there, head to the TI *(Office de Tourisme)* or your hotel.

- When leaving or just passing through cities, follow the signs for *Toutes Directions* or *Autres Directions* (meaning "anywhere else") until you see a sign for your specific destination. Look also for *Suivre* signs telling you to follow *(suivre)* signs for the (usually more important) destination listed.
- Driving on any roads but autoroutes will take longer than you think, so allow plenty of time for slower traffic (tractors, trucks, and hard-to-decipher signs all deserve blame). First-

PRACTICALITIES

timers should estimate how long they think a drive will take... then double it. I pretend that kilometers are miles (for distances) and base my time estimates accordingly.

- While locals are eating lunch (12:00-14:00), many sights (and gas stations) are closed, so you can make great time driving—but keep it slow when passing through villages.
- Be very careful when driving on smaller roads—many are narrow and flanked by little ditches that lure inattentive drivers. I've met several readers who "ditched" their cars (and had to be pulled out by local farmers).
- On autoroutes, keep to the right lanes to let fast drivers by, and be careful when merging into a left lane, as cars can be coming at high speeds.
- Motorcycles will scream between cars in traffic. Be ready—they expect you to make space so that they can pass.
- Keep a stash of coins handy for parking and small autoroute tolls.

BIKING

You'll find areas in France where public transportation is limited and bicycle touring might be a good idea. For many, biking is a romantic notion, and the novelty wears off after the first hill or headwind. Realistically evaluate your physical condition, be clear on the limitations present, and consider an electric bike. Electrically assisted bikes are now available everywhere in France—making biking a reasonable option for many. For a good touring bike, figure about €15 for a half-day and €20 for a full day (double that for electric bikes). You'll pay more for better equipment; generally the best bikes are available through bike shops, not at train stations or other outlets.

Whether on an electric or standard bike, start with an easy pedal, then decide how ambitious you feel. Most find that one hour on a narrow, hard seat is enough. I've listed bike-rental shops where appropriate (TIs can also guide you), and suggested a few of my favorite rides. French cyclists often do not wear helmets, though most rental outfits have them (for a small fee).

FLIGHTS

To compare flight costs and times, begin with a travel search engine: Kayak.com is the top site for flights to and within Europe, easy-to-use Google Flights has price alerts, and Skyscanner.com includes many inexpensive flights within Europe.

Flights to Europe: Start looking for international flights about four to six months before your trip, especially for peak-season travel. Depending on your itinerary, it can be efficient and no more expensive to fly into one city and out of another. If your flight requires a connection in Europe, see our hints on navigating Europe's top hub airports at www.ricksteves.com/hub-airports.

Flights Within Europe: Flying between European cities has become surprisingly affordable. If you're visiting one or more French cities on a longer European trip—or linking up far-flung French cities (such as Paris and Nice)—a flight can save both time and money. Before buying a long-distance train or bus ticket, first check the cost of a flight on one of Europe's airlines, whether a major carrier or a no-frills outfit like EasyJet, Vueling, or Ryanair. Also check Air France for specials. Be aware of the potential drawbacks of flying with a discount airline: nonrefundable and non-changeable tickets, minimal customer service, time-consuming treks to secondary airports, and stingy baggage allowances (also an issue on major airlines). To avoid unpleasant surprises, read the small print about the costs for "extras" such as reserving a seat, checking a bag, or checking in and printing a boarding pass.

Flying to the US and Canada: Because security is extra tight for flights to the US, be sure to give yourself plenty of time at the airport. It's also important to charge your electronic devices before you board because security checks may require you to turn them on (see www.tsa.gov for the latest rules).

Resources from Rick Steves

Begin Your Trip at Ricksteves.com

My mobile-friendly **website** is *the* place to explore Europe in preparation for your trip. You'll find thousands of fun articles, videos, and radio interviews; a wealth of money-saving tips for planning your dream trip; travel news dispatches; a video library of my travel talks; my travel blog; my latest guidebook updates (www.ricksteves.com/update); and my free Rick Steves Audio Europe app. You can also follow me on Facebook, Instagram, and Twitter.

Our **Travel Forum** is a well-groomed collection of message boards where our travel-savvy community answers questions and shares their personal travel experiences—and our well-traveled staff chimes in when they can be helpful (www.ricksteves.com/forums).

Our **online Travel Store** offers bags and accessories that I've designed to help you travel smarter and lighter. These include my popular bags (rolling carry-on and backpack versions, which I helped design...and live out of four months a year), money belts, totes, toiletries kits, adapters, guidebooks, and planning maps (www.ricksteves.com/shop).

Our website can also help you find the perfect **rail pass** for your itinerary and your budget, with easy, one-stop shopping for rail passes, seat reservations, and point-to-point tickets (www.ricksteves.com/rail).

Rick Steves' Tours, Guidebooks, TV Shows, and More

Small Group Tours: Want to travel with greater efficiency and less stress? We offer more than 40 itineraries reaching the best destinations in this book...and beyond. Each year about 30,000 travelers join us on about 1,000 Rick Steves bus tours. You'll enjoy great guides and a fun bunch of travel partners (with small groups of around 24 to 28 travelers). You'll find European adventures to fit every vacation length. For all the details, and to get our tour catalog, visit www.ricksteves.com or call us at 425/608-4217.

Books: *Rick Steves France 2020* is just one of many books in my series on European travel, which includes country and city guidebooks, Snapshots (excerpted chapters from bigger guides), Pocket Guides (full-color little books on big cities), "Best Of" guidebooks (condensed, full-color country), and my budget-travel skills handbook, *Rick Steves Europe Through the Back Door.* A more complete list of my titles—including phrase books; cruising guides; and travelogues on European art, history, and culture—appears near the end of this book.

TV Shows and Travel Talks: My public television series, *Rick Steves' Europe,* covers Europe from top to bottom with over 100 half-hour episodes—and we're working on new shows every year (watch full episodes on my website for free). My free online video library, Rick Steves Classroom Europe, offers a searchable database of short video clips on European history, culture, and geography (Classroom.RickSteves.com). And to raise your travel I.Q., check out the video versions of our popular classes (covering most European countries as well as travel skills, packing smart, cruising, tech for travelers, European art, and travel as a political act; see www.ricksteves.com/travel-talks).

Radio: My weekly public radio show, *Travel with Rick Steves,* features interviews with travel experts from around the world. It airs on 400 public radio stations across the US, or you can hear it as a podcast. A complete archive of programs is available at www.ricksteves.com/radio.

Audio Tours on My Free App: I've also produced dozens of free, self-guided audio tours of the top sights in Europe. For those tours and other audio content, get my free **Rick Steves Audio Europe app,** an extensive online library organized into handy geographic playlists. For more on my app, see page 28.

PRACTICALITIES

APPENDIX

Holidays and Festivals

This list includes selected festivals in major cities, plus national holidays observed throughout France. Many sights and banks close on national holidays—keep this in mind when planning your itinerary. Before planning a trip around a festival, verify the dates with the festival website, France's national tourism website (http://us.france.fr), or my "Upcoming Holidays and Festivals in France" web page (http://www.ricksteves.com/europe/france/festivals). Hotels get booked up on Easter weekend, Labor Day, Ascension Day, Pentecost, Bastille Day, and the winter holidays.

Here is a sampling of events and holidays in 2020:

Jan 1	New Year's Day
Feb-March	Carnival (Mardi Gras) parades and fireworks, Nice (www.nicecarnaval.com)
April 10-13	Easter weekend (Good Friday-Easter Monday)
April-Oct	International Garden Festival, Chaumont-sur-Loire (www.domaine-chaumont.fr)
May 1	Labor Day
May 8	VE (Victory in Europe) Day

APPENDIX

Mid-May	Cannes Film Festival, Cannes (www.festival-cannes.fr)
Late May	Monaco Grand Prix auto race (www.grand-prix-monaco.com)
May 21	Ascension
May 31-June 1	Pentecost Sunday/Monday
June 6	Anniversary of D-Day Landing, Normandy
Mid-June	Le Mans Auto Race, Le Mans—near Loire Valley (www.lemans.org)
June 21	Fête de la Musique (music festival), free concerts and dancing in the streets throughout France
June-July	Nights of Fourvière, Lyon (theater and music in a Roman theater, www.nuitsdefourviere.com)
July	Nice Jazz Festival (www.nicejazzfestival.fr); Avignon Festival, theater, dance, music (www.festival-avignon.com); Beaune International Music Festival; Chorégies d'Orange, Orange (performed in Roman theater, www.choregies.fr); "Jazz à Juan" International Jazz Festival, Antibes/Juan-les-Pins (www.jazzajuan.com); Jousting matches and medieval festivities, Carcassonne; Colmar International Music Festival (www.festival-colmar.com); International Music and Opera Festival, Aix-en-Provence (www.festival-aix.com)
July	Tour de France, national bicycle race culminating on the Champs-Elysées in Paris (www.letour.fr)
July 14	Bastille Day (fireworks, dancing, and revelry all over France)
July-Aug	International Fireworks Festival, Cannes (www.festival-pyrotechnique-cannes.com)
Aug 15	Assumption
Sept	Jazz at La Villette Festival, Paris (www.jazzalavillette.com)
Sept	Fall Arts Festival (Fête d'Automne), Paris; Wine harvest festivals in many towns
Early Oct	Grape Harvest Festival in Montmartre, Paris (www.fetedesvendangesdemontmartre.com)
Nov 1	All Saints' Day
Early Nov	Dijon International and Gastronomic Fair, Dijon, Burgundy (www.foirededijon.com)
Nov 11	Armistice Day
Late Nov	Wine Auction and Festival (Les Trois Glorieuses), Beaune

Late Nov- Dec 24	Christmas Markets, Strasbourg, Colmar, and Sarlat-la-Canéda
Early Dec	Festival of Lights (celebration of Virgin Mary, candlelit windows), Lyon
Dec 25	Christmas Day
Dec 31	New Year's Eve

Books and Films

To learn more about France past and present, check out a few of these books and films. To learn what's making news in France, you'll find *France 24 News* online at www.France24.com/en.

Nonfiction

A to Z of French Food, a French to English Dictionary of Culinary Terms (G. de Temmerman, 1995). This is the most complete (and priciest) menu reader around—and it's beloved by foodies. You can find it cheaper in France (try FNAC department stores) or by downloading the app.

Almost French: Love and a New Life in Paris (Sarah Turnbull, 2003). Turnbull takes an amusing look at adopting a famously frosty city.

The Course of French History (Pierre Goubert, 1988). Goubert provides a readable summary of French history.

Culture Shock! France (Sally Adamson Taylor, 2012). Demystify French culture and the French people with this good introduction.

D–Day, June 6, 1944: The Battle for the Normandy Beaches (Stephen E. Ambrose, 1994). Relying on 1,400 interviews with war veterans, Ambrose spins a detailed history of this fateful day.

A Distant Mirror (Barbara Tuchman, 1987). Respected historian Barbara Tuchman paints a portrait of 14th-century France.

French or Foe? (Polly Platt, 1994). This best seller, along with its follow-up, *Savoir-Flair!*, is helpful (if somewhat dated) for interacting with the French and navigating the intricacies of their culture.

I'll Always Have Paris (Art Buchwald, 1996). The American humorist recounts life as a Paris correspondent during the 1940s and 1950s.

Is Paris Burning? (Larry Collins and Dominique Lapierre, 1964). Set in the last days of the Nazi occupation, this book tells the story of the French resistance and how a German general disobeyed Hitler's order to destroy Paris.

La Seduction: How the French Play the Game of Life (Elaine Sciolino, 2011). Sciolino, former Paris bureau chief of the *New York*

Times, gives travelers a fun, insightful, and tantalizing peek into how seduction is used in all aspects of French life—from small villages to the halls of national government.

The Longest Day: The Classic Epic of D-Day (Cornelius Ryan, 1959). Ryan's classic recounts the hours before and after the D-Day Normandy invasion.

Marling Menu-Master for France (William E. Marling, 1971). A compact guide for navigating French cuisine and restaurant terminology.

A Moveable Feast (Ernest Hemingway, 1964). Hemingway recalls Paris in the 1920s.

My Life in France (Julia Child, 1996). The inimitably zesty chef recounts her early days in Paris.

Paris to the Moon (Adam Gopnik, 2000). This collection of essays and journal entries explores the idiosyncrasies of life in France from a New Yorker's point of view. His literary anthology, *Americans in Paris,* is also recommended.

Portraits of France (Robert Daley, 1991). Part memoir, part travelogue, this is a charming reminiscence of the writer's lifelong relationship with France, including marrying a French girl on his first trip there.

The Road from the Past: Traveling Through History in France (Ina Caro, 1994). Caro's enjoyable travel essays take you on a chronological journey through France's historical sights.

Sixty Million Frenchmen Can't Be Wrong (Jean-Benoît Nadeau and Julie Barlow, 2003). This is a must-read for anyone serious about understanding French culture, contemporary politics, and what makes the French tick.

The Sweet Life in Paris (David Lebovitz, 2009). Funny and articulate, pastry chef and cookbook author Lebovitz delivers oodles of food suggestions for travelers in Paris.

Travelers' Tales: Paris and *Travelers' Tales: France* (edited by James O'Reilly, Larry Habegger, and Sean O'Reilly, 2002). Notable writers explore Parisian and French culture.

Two Towns in Provence (M. F. K. Fisher, 1964). Aix-en-Provence and Marseille are the subjects of these two stories by the celebrated American food writer. She also writes about her life in France in *Long Ago in France: The Years in Dijon* (1929).

Wine & War: The French, the Nazis, and the Battle for France's Greatest Treasure (Don and Petie Kladstrup, 2001). This compelling story details how French vintners preserved their valuable wine amidst the chaos of World War II.

A Year in Provence and *Toujours Provence* (Peter Mayle, 1989/1991). Mayle's memoirs include humorous anecdotes about restoring and living in a 200-year-old farmhouse in a remote area of the Luberon.

Fiction

All the Light We Cannot See (Anthony Doerr, 2014). A moving tale of occupied France seen through the experiences of a blind French girl and a lonely German boy whose paths cross in war-torn St-Malo.

Birdsong: A Novel of Love and War (Sebastian Faulks, 1993). This novel follows a 20-year-old Englishman into WWI France, and into the romance that follows.

Chocolat (Joanne Harris, 1999). A woman and her daughter stir up tradition in a small French town by opening a chocolate shop two days before Lent (also a movie starring Juliette Binoche and filmed in the Dordogne region).

City of Darkness, City of Light (Marge Piercy, 1996). Three French women play pivotal roles behind the scenes during the French Revolution.

The Hotel Majestic (Georges Simenon, 1942). Ernest Hemingway was a fan of Simenon, a Belgian writer who often set his Inspector Maigret detective books, including this one, in Paris.

Labyrinth (Kate Mosse, 2005). This thriller set in Carcassonne jumps back and forth between present-day archaeological intrigue and the medieval Cathar crusade.

Madame Bovary (Gustave Flaubert, 1886). Emma Bovary's yearning for luxury and passion ultimately lead to her demise in this literary classic.

Murder in the Marais (Cara Black, 1999). Set in Vichy-era Paris, private investigator Aimée Leduc finds herself at the center of a murder mystery.

A Place of Greater Safety (Hilary Mantel, 1992). Three young men come to Paris in 1789—Maximilien Robespierre, Camille Desmoulins, and George-Jacques Danton—and the rest is history.

Suite Française (Irène Némirovsky, 2004). Némirovsky, a Russian Jew who was living in France and died at Auschwitz in 1942, plunges readers into the chaotic WWII evacuation of Paris, as well as daily life in a small rural town during the ensuing German occupation.

A Tale of Two Cities (Charles Dickens, 1859). Dickens' gripping tale shows the pathos and horror of the French Revolution.

A Very Long Engagement (Sebastien Japrisot, 1991). A woman searches for her fiancé, supposedly killed in the line of duty during World War I (also a movie starring Audrey Tautou).

Film and TV

Amélie (2001). A charming young waitress searches for love in Paris.

Before Sunset (2004). Nine years after meeting on a train to Vienna,

Jesse and Celine (played by Ethan Hawke and Julie Delpy) are reunited in Paris.

Breathless (1960). A Parisian petty thief (Jean-Paul Belmondo) persuades an American student (Jean Seberg) to run away with him in this groundbreaking classic of French New Wave cinema.

Cyrano de Bergerac (1990). A homely, romantic poet woos his love with the help of another, better-looking man (look for scenes filmed at the Abbey of Fontenay).

Dangerous Liaisons (1988). This inside look at sex, intrigue, and revenge takes place in the last days of the French aristocracy in pre-Revolutionary Paris.

Dirty Rotten Scoundrels (1988). Steve Martin and Michael Caine star in this comedy, filmed in and around Villefranche-sur-Mer.

The Gleaners & I (2000). Working-class men and women gather sustenance from what's been thrown away in this quiet, meditative film by Agnès Varda.

Grand Illusion (1937). French WWI prisoners hatch a plan to escape a German POW camp. Considered a masterpiece of French film, the movie was later banned by the Nazis for its anti-fascism message.

The Intouchables (2011). A quadriplegic Parisian aristocrat hires a personal caregiver from the projects, and an unusual and touching friendship ensues.

Jean de Florette (1986). This marvelous tale of greed and intolerance follows a hunchback as he fights for the property he inherited in rural France. Its sequel, *Manon of the Spring* (1986), continues with his daughter's story.

Jules and Jim (1962). François Truffaut, the master of the French New Wave, explores a decades-long love triangle in this classic.

La Grande Bouffe (1973). In this hilarious comedy about French food, French sex, and French masculinity, Marcello Mastroianni leads a rat pack of middle-aged men in a quest to eat themselves to death.

La Haine (1995). An Arab boy is critically wounded and a police gun finds its way into the hands of a young Jewish skinhead in this intense examination of ethnic divisions in France.

La Vie en Rose (2007). Marion Cotillard won the Best Actress Oscar for this film about the glamorous and turbulent life of singer Edith Piaf, who famously regretted nothing (many scenes were shot in Paris).

Les Misérables (2012). A Frenchman trying to escape his criminal past becomes wrapped up in Revolutionary intrigues (based on Victor Hugo's 1862 novel).

The Longest Day (1962). This meticulous re-creation of the D-Day invasion won two Oscars and features an all-star cast including John Wayne, Richard Burton, Robert Mitchum, and Henry Fonda.

Loving Vincent (2017). The first fully painted animated feature film, this movie follows an investigation into Vincent van Gogh's final days before his death in Auvers-sur-Oise.

Marie Antoinette (2006). Kirsten Dunst stars as the infamous French queen (with a Californian accent) at Versailles in this delicate little bonbon of a film about the misunderstood queen.

Midnight in Paris (2011). Woody Allen's sharp comedy shifts between today's Paris and the 1920s mecca of Picasso, Hemingway, and Fitzgerald.

Paths of Glory (1957). Stanley Kubrick directed this WWI story about the futility and irony of war.

The Red Balloon (1956). A small boy chases his balloon through the streets of Paris, showing how beauty can be found even in the simplest toy.

The Return of Martin Guerre (1982). A man returns to his village in southwestern France from the Hundred Years' War—but is he really who he claims to be?

Ridicule (1996). A nobleman navigates the opulent court of Louis XVI on his wits alone.

Ronin (1998). Robert De Niro stars in this crime caper, which includes a car chase through Paris and scenes filmed in Nice, Villefranche-sur-Mer, and Arles.

Saving Private Ryan (1998). This intense and brilliant story of the D-Day landings and their aftermath won Steven Spielberg an Oscar for Best Director.

The Silence of the Sea (1949). A Frenchman and his niece, forced to house a German officer in Nazi-occupied France, resist through silent protest.

The Sorrow and the Pity (1969). This award-winning documentary about the Nazi occupation doesn't pull any punches about French collaboration, which is why it was banned by French TV.

Three Colors trilogy (1990s). Krzysztof Kieślowski's stylish trilogy (*Blue, White,* and *Red*) is based on France's national motto— "Liberty, Equality, and Fraternity." Each features a famous French actress as the lead (*Blue,* with Juliette Binoche, is the best).

Welcome (2009). A young Kurdish refugee in Calais, France faces the harsh realities of illegal immigration as he tries to join his girlfriend in England.

Conversions and Climate

NUMBERS AND STUMBLERS
- Europeans write a few of their numbers differently than we do: 1 = 1, 4 = 4, 7 = 7.
- In Europe, dates appear as day/month/year, so Christmas 2020 is 25/12/20.
- Commas are decimal points and decimals are commas. A dollar and a half is $1,50, one thousand is 1.000, and there are 5.280 feet in a mile.
- When counting with fingers, start with your thumb. If you hold up your first finger to request one item, you'll probably get two.
- What Americans call the second floor of a building is the first floor in Europe.
- On escalators and moving sidewalks, Europeans keep the left "lane" open for passing. Keep to the right.

METRIC CONVERSIONS
A **kilogram** equals 1,000 grams (about 2.2 pounds). One hundred **grams** (a common unit at markets) is about a quarter-pound. One **liter** is about a quart, or almost four to a gallon.

A **kilometer** is six-tenths of a mile. To convert kilometers to miles, cut the kilometers in half and add back 10 percent of the original (120 km: 60 + 12 = 72 miles). One **meter** is 39 inches—just over a yard.

1 foot = 0.3 meter	1 square yard = 0.8 square meter
1 yard = 0.9 meter	1 square mile = 2.6 square kilometers
1 mile = 1.6 kilometers	1 hectare = 2.47 acres
1 ounce = 28 grams	1 centimeter = 0.4 inch
1 quart = 0.95 liter	1 meter = 39.4 inches
1 kilogram = 2.2 pounds	1 kilometer = 0.62 mile
32°F = 0°C	

CLOTHING SIZES
When shopping for clothing, use these US-to-European comparisons as general guidelines (but note that no conversion is perfect).

Women: For pants and dresses, add 32 in France (US 10 = French 42). For blouses and sweaters, add 8 for most of Europe (US 32 = European 40). For shoes, add 30-31 (US 7 = European 37/38).

Men: For shirts, multiply by 2 and add about 8 (US size 15 = European 38). For jackets and suits, add 10. For shoes, add 32-34.

Children: Clothing is sized by height—in centimeters (2.5 cm = 1 inch), so a US size 8 roughly equates to 132-140. For shoes up to size 13, add 16-18, and for sizes 1 and up, add 30-32.

FRANCE'S CLIMATE

First line, average daily high; second line, average daily low; third line, average days without rain. For more detailed weather statistics for destinations in this book (as well as the rest of the world), check www.wunderground.com.

	J	F	M	A	M	J	J	A	S	O	N	D
Paris												
	43°	45°	54°	60°	68°	73°	76°	75°	70°	60°	50°	44°
	34°	34°	39°	43°	49°	55°	58°	58°	53°	46°	40°	36°
	14	14	19	17	19	18	19	18	17	18	15	15
Nice												
	50°	53°	59°	64°	71°	79°	84°	83°	77°	68°	58°	52°
	35°	36°	41°	46°	52°	58°	63°	63°	58°	51°	43°	37°
	23	22	24	23	23	26	29	26	24	23	21	21

Fahrenheit and Celsius Conversion

Europe takes its temperature using the Celsius scale, while we opt for Fahrenheit. For a rough conversion from Celsius to Fahrenheit, double the number and add 30. For weather, remember that 28°C is 82°F—perfect. For health, 37°C is just right. At a launderette, 30°C is cold, 40°C is warm (usually the default setting), 60°C is hot, and 95°C is boiling. Your air-conditioner should be set at about 20°C.

Packing Checklist

Whether you're traveling for five days or five weeks, you won't need more than this. Pack light to enjoy the sweet freedom of true mobility.

Clothing

- ☐ 5 shirts: long- & short-sleeve
- ☐ 2 pairs pants (or skirts/capris)
- ☐ 1 pair shorts
- ☐ 5 pairs underwear & socks
- ☐ 1 pair walking shoes
- ☐ Sweater or warm layer
- ☐ Rainproof jacket with hood
- ☐ Tie, scarf, belt, and/or hat
- ☐ Swimsuit
- ☐ Sleepwear/loungewear

Money

- ☐ Debit card(s)
- ☐ Credit card(s)
- ☐ Hard cash (US $100-200)
- ☐ Money belt

Documents

- ☐ Passport
- ☐ Tickets & confirmations: flights, hotels, trains, rail pass, car rental, sight entries
- ☐ Driver's license
- ☐ Student ID, hostel card, etc.
- ☐ Photocopies of important documents
- ☐ Insurance details
- ☐ Guidebooks & maps

Toiletries Kit

- ☐ Basics: soap, shampoo, toothbrush, toothpaste, floss, deodorant, sunscreen, brush/comb, etc.
- ☐ Medicines & vitamins
- ☐ First-aid kit
- ☐ Glasses/contacts/sunglasses
- ☐ Sewing kit
- ☐ Packet of tissues (for WC)
- ☐ Earplugs

Electronics

- ☐ Mobile phone
- ☐ Camera & related gear
- ☐ Tablet/ebook reader/laptop
- ☐ Headphones/earbuds
- ☐ Chargers & batteries
- ☐ Phone car charger & mount (or GPS device)
- ☐ Plug adapters

Miscellaneous

- ☐ Daypack
- ☐ Sealable plastic baggies
- ☐ Laundry supplies: soap, laundry bag, clothesline, spot remover
- ☐ Small umbrella
- ☐ Travel alarm/watch
- ☐ Notepad & pen
- ☐ Journal

Optional Extras

- ☐ Second pair of shoes (flip-flops, sandals, tennis shoes, boots)
- ☐ Travel hairdryer
- ☐ Picnic supplies
- ☐ Water bottle
- ☐ Fold-up tote bag
- ☐ Small flashlight
- ☐ Mini binoculars
- ☐ Small towel or washcloth
- ☐ Inflatable pillow/neck rest
- ☐ Tiny lock
- ☐ Address list (to mail postcards)
- ☐ Extra passport photos

PRONUNCIATION GUIDE FOR PLACE NAMES

When using the phonetics: Try to nasalize the n sound (let the sound come through your nose). Note that the "ahn" combination uses the "ah" sound in "father," but the "añ" combination uses the "a" sound in "sack." Pronounce the "ī" as the long "i" in "light." If your best attempt at pronunciation meets with a puzzled look, just point to the place name on the list.

In Paris

Arc de Triomphe ark duh tree-ohnf

arrondissement ah-rohn-dees-mohn

Bateaux-Mouches bah-toh moosh

Bon Marché bohn mar-shay

Carnavalet kar-nah-vah-lay

Champ de Mars shahn duh mar

Champs-Elysées shahn-zay-lee-zay

Conciergerie kon-see-ehr-zhuh-ree

Ecole Militaire eh-kohl mee-lee-tehr

Egouts ay-goo

Fauchon foh-shohn

Galeries Lafayette gah-luh-ree lah-fay-yet

gare gar

Gare d'Austerlitz gar doh-stehr-leets

Gare de l'Est gar duh less

Gare de Lyon gar duh lee-ohn

Gare du Nord gar dew nor

Gare St. Lazare gar san lah-zar

Garnier gar-nee-ay

Grand Palais grahn pah-lay

Grande Arche de la Défense grahnd arsh duh lah day-fahns

Ile de la Cité eel duh lah see-tay

Ile St. Louis eel san loo-ee

Jacquemart-André zhahk-mar-ahn-dray

Jardin des Plantes zhar-dan day plahnt

Jeu de Paume juh duh pohm

La Madeleine lah mah-duh-lehn

Le Hameau luh ah-moh

Les Halles lay ahl

Les Invalides lay-zan-vah-leed

Orangerie oh-rahn-zhuh-ree

Louvre loov-ruh

Marais mah-ray

marché aux puces mar-shay oh poos

Marmottan mar-moh-tahn

Métro may-troh

Monge mohnzh

Montmartre mohn-mart

Montparnasse mohn-par-nahs

Moulin Rouge moo-lan roozh

Musée d'Orsay mew-zay dor-say

Musée de l'Armée mew-zay duh lar-may

Notre-Dame noh-truh-dahm

Opéra Garnier oh-pay-rah gar-nee-ay

Orsay or-say

palais pah-lay

Palais de Justice pah-lay duh zhew-stees

Palais Royal pah-lay roh-yahl

Parc de la Villette park duh la vee-leht

Parc Monceau park mohn-soh

Père Lachaise pehr lah-shehz

Petit Palais puh-tee pah-lay

Pigalle pee-gahl

Place Dauphine plahs doh-feen

Place de la Bastille plahs duh lah bah-steel

Place de la Concorde plahs duh lah kohn-kord

Place de la République plahs duh lah ray-poo-bleek

Place des Vosges plahs day vohzh

Place du Tertre plahs dew tehr-truh

Place St. André-des-Arts plahs san tahn-dray day-zart

Place Vendôme plahs vahn-dohm

Pompidou pohn-pee-doo

pont pohn

Pont Alexandre III pohn ah-

leks-ahn-druh twah
Pont Neuf pohn nuhf
Promenade Plantée proh-mehn-ahd plahn-tay
quai kay
Rive Droite reeve dwaht
Rive Gauche reeve gohsh
Rodin roh-dan
rue rew
Rue Cler rew klehr
Rue Daguerre rew dah-gehr
Rue de Rivoli rew duh ree-voh-lee
Rue des Rosiers rew day roz-ee-ay
Rue Montorgueil rew mohn-tor-goy
Rue Mouffetard rew moof-tar
Sacré-Cœur sah-kray-koor
Sainte-Chapelle sant-shah-pehl
Seine sehn
Sèvres-Babylone seh-vruh-bah-bee-lohn
Sorbonne sor-buhn
St. Germain-des-Prés san zhehr-man-day-pray
St. Julien-le-Pauvre san zhew-lee-ehn-luh-poh-vruh
St. Séverin sahn say-vuh-ran
St. Sulpice sahn sool-pees
Tour Eiffel toor ee-fehl
Trianon tree-ahn-ohn
Trocadéro troh-kah-day-roh
Tuileries twee-lay-ree
Venus de Milo vuh-news duh mee-loh

Outside Paris

Abri du Cap Blanc ah-bree dew cah blahn
Aiguille du Midi ah-gwee dew mee-dee
Aïnhoa an-oh-ah
Albi ahl-bee
Alet ah-lay
Alise Ste-Reine ah-leez sant-rehn
Aloxe-Corton ah-lohx kor-tohn
Alsace ahl-sahs
Amboise ahm-bwahz
Annecy ahn-see
Antibes ahn-teeb
Aosta (Italy) ay-oh-stah

Apt ahp
Aquitaine ah-kee-tehn
Arles arl
Arromanches ah-roh-mahnsh
Autoire oh-twahr
Auvergne oh-vehrn
Avignon ah-veen-yohn
Azay-le-Rideau ah-zay luh ree-doh
Bayeux bī-yuh
Bayonne bī-yuhn
Beaucaire boh-kehr
Beaujolais boh-zhoh-lay
Beaune bohn
Bedoin buh-dwan
Bennwihr behn-veer
Beynac bay-nak
Biarritz bee-ah-reetz
Blois blwah
Bonnieux bohn-yuh
Bordeaux bor-doh
Brancion brahn-see-ohn
Brittany bree-tah-nee
Bruniquel brew-nee-kehl
Caen kahn
Cahors kah-or
Cajarc kah-zhark
Calais kah-lay
Camargue kah-marg
Cambord kahn-bor
Cancale kahn-kahl
Carcassonne kar-kah-suhn
Carennac kah-rehn-ahk
Carsac kar-sahk
Castelnaud kah-stehl-noh
Castelnau-de-Montmiral kah-stehl-noh-duh-mohn-mee-rahl
Caussade koh-sahd
Cavaillon kah-vī-ohn
Cénac say-nahk
Céret say-ray
Chambord shahn-bor
Chamonix shah-moh-nee
Champagne shahn-pahn-yuh
Chapaize shah-pehz
Chartres shart
Château de Rivau shah-toh duh ree-voh
Château du Haut-Kœnigsbourg shah-toh dew oh-koh-neegs-boorg
Châteauneuf-du-Pape shah-toh-nuhf-dew-pahp
Châteauneuf-en-Auxois shah-

toh-nuhf-ehn-ohx-wah
Chaumont-sur-Loire shoh-mohn-sewr-lwahr
Chenonceau shuh-nohn-soh
Chenonceaux shuh-nohn-soh
Cherbourg shehr-boor
Cheverny shuh-vehr-nee
Chinon shee-nohn
Cluny klew-nee
Colleville kohl-veel
Collioure kohl-yoor
Collonges-la-Rouge koh-lohnzh-lah-roozh
Colmar kohl-mar
Cordes-sur-Ciel kord-sewr-see-yehl
Côte d'Azur koht dah-zewr
Cougnac koon-yahk
Courseulles-sur-Mer koor-suhl-sewr-mehr
Coustellet koo-stuh-lay
Digne deen-yuh
Dijon dee-zhohn
Dinan dee-nahn
Dinard dee-nar
Domme dohm
Dordogne dor-dohn-yuh
Eguisheim eh-geh-shīm
Entrevaux ahn-truh-voh
Epernay ay-pehr-nay
Espelette eh-speh-leht
Eze-Bord-de-Mer ehz-bor-duh-mehr
Eze-le-Village ehz-luh-vee-lahzh
Faucon foh-kohn
Flavigny-sur-Ozerain flah-veen-yee-sewr-oh-zuh-ran
Font-de-Gaume fohn-duh-gohm
Fontenay fohn-tuh-nay
Fontevraud fohn-tuh-vroh
Fontvieille fohn-vee-yeh-ee
Fougères foo-zher
Fougères-sur-Bièvre foo-zher-sewr-bee-ehv
Gaillac gī-yahk
Gigondas zhee-gohn-dahs
Giverny zhee-vehr-nee
Gordes gord
Gorges de l'Ardèche gorzh duh lar-dehsh
Grenoble gruh-noh-bluh
Grouin groo-an

Guédelon gway-duh-lohn
Hautes Corbières oht kor-bee-yehr
Hendaye ehn-dī
Honfleur ohn-flur
Huisnes-sur-Mer ween-sewr-mehr
Hunawihr uhn-ah-veer
Ile Besnard eel bay-nar
Isle-sur-la-Sorgue eel-sewr-lah-sorg
Juan-les-Pins zhwan-lay-pan
Kaysersberg kī-zehrs-behrg
Kientzheim keentz-īm
La Charente lah shah-rahnt
Lacoste lah-kohst
Langeais lahn-zhay
Languedoc-Roussillon long-dohk roo-see-yohn
La Rhune lah rewn
La Rochepot lah rohsh-poh
La Roque St-Christophe lah rohk san-kree-stohf
La Roque-Gageac lah rohk-gah-zhahk
Lascaux lah-skoh
Lastours lahs-toor
La Trophée des Alpes lah troh-fay dayz ahlp
La Turbie lah tewr-bee
Le Bugue luh bewg
Le Crestet luh kruh-stay
Le Havre luh hah-vruh
Lémeré lay-muh-ray
Le Ruquet luh rew-kay
Les Baux lay boh
Les Eyzies-de-Tayac lay zay-zee-duh-tī-yahk
Les Praz lay prah
Les Vosges lay vohzh
Limoges lee-mohzh
Loches lohsh
Loire lwahr
Longues-sur-Mer long-sewr-mehr
Loubressac loo-bruh-sahk
Lourmarin loo-mah-ran
Luberon lew-beh-rohn
Lyon lee-ohn
Malaucène mah-loh-sehn
Marne-la-Vallée-Chessy marn-lah-vah-lay-shuh-see
Marseille mar-say
Martel mar-tehl

Mausanne moh-sahn
Ménerbes may-nehrb
Millau mee-yoh
Minerve mee-nerv
Mirabel mee-rah-behl
Modreuc mohd-rewk
Mont Blanc mohn blahn
Mont St-Michel mohn san-mee-shehl
Mont Ventoux mohn vehn-too
Montenvers mohn-tuh-vehr
Montfort mohn-for
Montignac mohn-teen-yahk
Mortemart mort-mar
Munster mewn-stehr
Nantes nahnt
Nice nees
Normandy nor-mahn-dee
Nyons nee-yohns
Oradour-sur-Glane oh-rah-door-sewr-glahn
Orange oh-rahnzh
Padirac pah-dee-rahk
Paris pah-ree
Pech Merle pehsh mehrl
Peyrepertuse pay-ruh-per-tewz
Pointe du Hoc pwant dew ohk
Pont du Gard pohn dew gahr
Pontorson pohn-tor-sohn
Provence proh-vahns
Puycelsi pwee-suhl-cee
Puyméras pwee-may-rahs
Queribus kehr-ee-bews
Reims rans (rhymes with France)
Remoulins ruh-moo-lan
Rennes rehn
Ribeauvillé ree-boh-vee-yay
Riquewihr reek-veer
Rocamadour roh-kah-mah-door
Rouen roo-ahn
Rouffignac roo-feen-yahk
Roussillon roo-see-yohn
Route du Vin root dew van
Sablet sah-blay
Sare sahr
Sarlat-la-Canéda sar-lah lah cah-nay-duh
Savigny-les-Beaune sah-veen-yee-lay-bohn
Savoie sah-vwah
Séguret say-goo-ray
Semur-en-Auxois suh-moor-ehn-ohx-wah
Sigolsheim see-gohl-shīm
Souillac soo-ee-yahk
St-Cirq-Lapopie san-seerk lah-poh-pee
St-Cyprien san-seep-ree-ehn
St-Emilion san-tay-meel-yohn
St-Geniès san-zhuh-nyehs
St-Jean-de-Luz san-zhahn-duh-looz
St-Jean-Pied-de-Port san-zhahn-pee-yay-duh-por
St-Malo san-mah-loh
St-Marcellin-lès-Vaison san-mar-suh-lan-lay-vay-zohn
St-Rémy san-ray-mee
St-Romain-en-Viennois san-roh-man-ehn-vee-ehn-nwah
St-Suliac san-soo-lee-ahk
St-Paul-de-Vence san-pohl-duh-vahns
Ste-Mère Eglise sant-mehr ay-gleez
Stes-Maries-de-la-Mer sant-mah-ree-duh-lah-mehr
Strasbourg strahs-boorg
Suzette soo-zeht
Taizé teh-zay
Tarascon tah-rah-skohn
Tours toor
Turckheim tewrk-hīm
Ussé oo-say
Uzès oo-zehs
Vacqueyras vah-kee-rahs
Vaison-la-Romaine vay-zohn lah roh-mehn
Valançay vah-lahn-say
Valréas vahl-ray-ahs
Vence vahns
Verdun vehr-duhn
Versailles vehr-sī
Veynes vay-nuh
Vézelay vay-zuh-lay
Vierville-sur-Mer vee-yehr-veel-sewr-mehr
Villandry vee-lahn-dry
Villefranche-de-Rouergue veel-frahnsh-duh-roo-ehrg
Villefranche-sur-Mer veel-frahnsh-sewr-mehr
Villeneuve-lès-Avignon veel-nuhv-lay-zah-veeh-yohn
Vitrac vee-trahk
Vouvray voo-vray
Villedieu vee-luh-dyuh

French Survival Phrases

When using the phonetics, try to nasalize the <u>n</u> sound.

English	French	Pronunciation
Good day.	*Bonjour.*	boh<u>n</u>-zhoor
Mrs. / Mr.	*Madame / Monsieur*	mah-dahm / muhs-yuh
Do you speak English?	*Parlez-vous anglais?*	par-lay-voo ah<u>n</u>-glay
Yes. / No.	*Oui. / Non.*	wee / noh<u>n</u>
I understand.	*Je comprends.*	zhuh koh<u>n</u>-prah<u>n</u>
I don't understand.	*Je ne comprends pas.*	zhuh nuh koh<u>n</u>-prah<u>n</u> pah
Please.	*S'il vous plaît.*	see voo play
Thank you.	*Merci.*	mehr-see
I'm sorry.	*Désolé.*	day-zoh-lay
Excuse me.	*Pardon.*	par-doh<u>n</u>
(No) problem.	*(Pas de) problème.*	(pah duh) proh-blehm
It's good.	*C'est bon.*	say boh<u>n</u>
Goodbye.	*Au revoir.*	oh ruh-vwahr
one / two / three	*un / deux / trois*	uh<u>n</u> / duh / trwah
four / five / six	*quatre / cinq / six*	kah-truh / sa<u>n</u>k / sees
seven / eight	*sept / huit*	seht / weet
nine / ten	*neuf / dix*	nuhf / dees
How much is it?	*Combien?*	koh<u>n</u>-bee-a<u>n</u>
Write it?	*Ecrivez?*	ay-kree-vay
Is it free?	*C'est gratuit?*	say grah-twee
Included?	*Inclus?*	a<u>n</u>-klew
Where can I buy / find...?	*Où puis-je acheter / trouver...?*	oo pwee-zhuh ah-shuh-tay / troo-vay
I'd like / We'd like...	*Je voudrais / Nous voudrions...*	zhuh voo-dray / noo voo-dree-oh<u>n</u>
...a room.	*...une chambre.*	ewn shah<u>n</u>-bruh
...a ticket to ___.	*...un billet pour ___.*	uh<u>n</u> bee-yay poor ___
Is it possible?	*C'est possible?*	say poh-see-bluh
Where is...?	*Où est...?*	oo ay
...the train station	*...la gare*	lah gar
...the bus station	*...la gare routière*	lah gar root-yehr
...tourist information	*...l'office du tourisme*	loh-fees dew too-reez-muh
Where are the toilets?	*Où sont les toilettes?*	oo soh<u>n</u> lay twah-leht
men	*hommes*	ohm
women	*dames*	dahm
left / right	*à gauche / à droite*	ah gohsh / ah drwaht
straight	*tout droit*	too drwah
pull / push	*tirez / poussez*	tee-ray / poo-say
When does this open / close?	*Ça ouvre / ferme à quelle heure?*	sah oo-vruh / fehrm ah kehl ur
At what time?	*À quelle heure?*	ah kehl ur
Just a moment.	*Un moment.*	uh<u>n</u> moh-mah<u>n</u>
now / soon / later	*maintenant / bientôt / plus tard*	ma<u>n</u>-tuh-nah<u>n</u> / bee-a<u>n</u>-toh / plew tar
today / tomorrow	*aujourd'hui / demain*	oh-zhoor-dwee / duh-ma<u>n</u>

APPENDIX

In a French Restaurant

English	French	Pronunciation
I'd like / We'd like...	Je voudrais / Nous voudrions...	zhuh voo-dray / noo voo-dree-oh<u>n</u>
...to reserve...	...réserver...	ray-zehr-vay
...a table for one / two.	...une table pour un / deux.	ewn tah-bluh poor uh<u>n</u> / duh
Is this seat free?	C'est libre?	say lee-bruh
The menu (in English), please.	La carte (en anglais), s'il vous plaît.	lah kart (ah<u>n</u> ah<u>n</u>-glay) see voo play
service (not) included	service (non) compris	sehr-vees (noh<u>n</u>) koh<u>n</u>-pree
to go	à emporter	ah ah<u>n</u>-por-tay
with / without	avec / sans	ah-vehk / sah<u>n</u>
and / or	et / ou	ay / oo
special of the day	plat du jour	plah dew zhoor
specialty of the house	spécialité de la maison	spay-see-ah-lee-tay duh lah may-zoh<u>n</u>
appetizers	hors d'oeuvre	or duh-vruh
first course (soup, salad)	entrée	ah<u>n</u>-tray
main course (meat, fish)	plat principal	plah pra<u>n</u>-see-pahl
bread	pain	pa<u>n</u>
cheese	fromage	froh-mahzh
sandwich	sandwich	sahnd-weech
soup	soupe	soop
salad	salade	sah-lahd
meat	viande	vee-ahnd
chicken	poulet	poo-lay
fish	poisson	pwah-soh<u>n</u>
seafood	fruits de mer	frwee duh mehr
fruit	fruit	frwee
vegetables	légumes	lay-gewm
dessert	dessert	day-sehr
mineral water	eau minérale	oh mee-nay-rahl
tap water	l'eau du robinet	loh dew roh-bee-nay
milk	lait	lay
(orange) juice	jus (d'orange)	zhew (doh-rah<u>n</u>zh)
coffee / tea	café / thé	kah-fay / tay
wine	vin	va<u>n</u>
red / white	rouge / blanc	roozh / blah<u>n</u>
glass / bottle	verre / bouteille	vehr / boo-tay
beer	bière	bee-ehr
Cheers!	Santé!	sah<u>n</u>-tay
More. / Another.	Plus. / Un autre.	plew / uh<u>n</u> oh-truh
The same.	La même chose.	lah mehm shohz
The bill, please.	L'addition, s'il vous plaît.	lah-dee-see-oh<u>n</u> see voo play
Do you accept credit cards?	Vous prenez les cartes?	voo pruh-nay lay kart
tip	pourboire	poor-bwahr
Delicious!	Délicieux!	day-lees-yuh

For more user-friendly French phrases, check out *Rick Steves French Phrase Book and Dictionary* or *Rick Steves French, Italian & German Phrase Book*

INDEX

INDEX

INDEX

MAP INDEX

Start your trip at

Our website enhances this book and turns

Explore Europe

At ricksteves.com you can browse through thousands of articles, videos, photos and radio interviews, plus find a wealth of money-saving travel tips for planning your dream trip. And with our mobile-friendly website, you can easily access all this great travel information anywhere you go.

TV Shows

Preview the places you'll visit by watching entire half-hour episodes of Rick Steves' Europe (choose from all 100 shows) on-demand, for free.

rickersteves.com

your travel dreams into affordable reality

Radio Interviews

Enjoy ready access to Rick's vast library of radio interviews covering travel tips and cultural insights that relate specifically to your Europe travel plans.

Travel Forums

Learn, ask, share! Our online community of savvy travelers is a great resource for first-time travelers to Europe, as well as seasoned pros.

Travel News

Subscribe to our free Travel News e-newsletter, and get monthly updates from Rick on what's happening in Europe.

Classroom Europe

Check out our free resource for educators with 300+ short video clips from the Rick Steves' Europe TV show.

Audio Europe™

Pack Light and Right

Gear up for your next adventure at ricksteves.com

Light Luggage

Pack light and right with Rick Steves' affordable, custom-designed rolling carry-on bags, backpacks, day packs and shoulder bags.

Accessories

From packing cubes to moneybelts and beyond, Rick has personally selected the travel goodies that will help your trip go smoother.

Shop at **ricksteves.com**

Experience maximum Europe

Save time and energy

This guidebook is your independent-travel toolkit. But for all it delivers, it's still up to you to devote the time and energy it takes to manage the preparation and logistics that are essential for a happy trip. If that's a hassle, there's a solution.

Rick Steves Tours

A Rick Steves tour takes you to Europe's most interesting places with great

great tours, too!

with minimum stress

guides and small groups of 28 or less. We follow Rick's favorite itineraries, ride in comfy buses, stay in family-run hotels, and bring you intimately close to the Europe you've traveled so far to see. Most importantly, we take away the logistical headaches so you can focus on the fun.

travelers—nearly half of them repeat customers—along with us on four dozen different itineraries, from Ireland to Italy to Athens. Is a Rick Steves tour the right fit for your travel dreams? Find out at ricksteves.com, where you can also request Rick's latest tour catalog. Europe is best experienced with happy travel partners. We hope you can join us.

Join the fun

This year we'll take thousands of free-spirited

See our itineraries at ricksteves.com

A Guide for Every Trip

BEST OF GUIDES

Full-color guides in an easy-to-scan format. Focused on top sights and experiences in the most popular European destinations

Best of England
Best of Europe
Best of France
Best of Germany
Best of Ireland
Best of Italy
Best of Scotland
Best of Spain

COMPREHENSIVE GUIDES

City, country, and regional guides printed on Bible-thin paper. Packed with detailed coverage for a multi-week trip exploring iconic sights and venturing off the beaten path

Amsterdam & the Netherlands
Barcelona
Belgium: Bruges, Brussels, Antwerp & Ghent
Berlin
Budapest
Croatia & Slovenia
Eastern Europe
England
Florence & Tuscany
France
Germany
Great Britain
Greece: Athens & the Peloponnese
Iceland
Ireland
Istanbul
Italy
London
Paris
Portugal
Prague & the Czech Republic
Provence & the French Riviera
Rome
Scandinavia
Scotland
Sicily
Spain
Switzerland
Venice
Vienna, Salzburg & Tirol

E BEST OF ROME

Italy's capital, is studded with remnants and floodlit fountain From the Vatican to the Colos-th crazy traffic in between, Rome rful, huge, and exhausting. The he heat, and the weighty history

of the Eternal City where Caesars walked can make tourists wilt. Recharge by taking siestas, gelato breaks, and after-dark walks, strolling from one atmospheric square to another in the refreshing evening air.

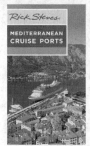

POCKET GUIDES

Compact color guides for shorter trips

Amsterdam
Athens
Barcelona
Florence
Italy's Cinque Terre
London
Munich & Salzburg

Paris
Prague
Rome
Venice
Vienna

SNAPSHOT GUIDES

Focused single-destination coverage

Basque Country: Spain & France
Copenhagen & the Best of Denmark
Dublin
Dubrovnik
Edinburgh
Hill Towns of Central Italy
Krakow, Warsaw & Gdansk
Lisbon
Loire Valley
Madrid & Toledo
Milan & the Italian Lakes District
Naples & the Amalfi Coast
Nice & the French Riviera
Normandy
Northern Ireland
Norway
Reykjavík
Rothenburg & the Rhine
Sevilla, Granada & Southern Spain
St. Petersburg, Helsinki & Tallinn
Stockholm

CRUISE PORTS GUIDES

Reference for cruise ports of call

Mediterranean Cruise Ports
Scandinavian & Northern European
  Cruise Ports

Complete your library with...

TRAVEL SKILLS & CULTURE

*Study up on travel skills and gain
insight on history and culture*

Europe 101
Europe Through the Back Door
Europe's Top 100 Masterpieces
European Christmas
European Easter
European Festivals
For the Love of Europe
Travel as a Political Act

PHRASE BOOKS & DICTIONARIES

French
French, Italian & German
German
Italian
Portuguese
Spanish

PLANNING MAPS

Britain, Ireland & London
Europe
France & Paris
Germany, Austria & Switzerland
Iceland
Ireland
Italy
Spain & Portugal

Credits

RESEARCHER
To help update this book, Rick and Steve relied on...

Virginie Moré

After living for 10 years in Los Angeles, Montana, and Florida, Virginie has been back in France for a few years. Originally from Brittany, she now lives in southern Burgundy with her husband Olivier, where they are running a small, old-farm guesthouse. Along with doing book research, she teaches Americans about French culture and history while leading Rick Steves' Europe tours and guiding small private groups in this beautiful, off-the-beaten-path wine region.

CONTRIBUTOR
Gene Openshaw

Gene has co-authored a dozen *Rick Steves* books, specializing in writing walks and tours of Europe's cities, museums, and cultural sights. He also contributes to Rick's public television series, produces tours for Rick Steves Audio Europe, and is a regular guest on Rick's public radio show. Outside of the travel world, Gene has co-authored *The Seattle Joke Book*. As a composer, Gene has written a full-length opera called *Matter*, a violin sonata, and dozens of songs. He lives near Seattle with his daughter, enjoys giving presentations on art and history, and roots for the Mariners in good times and bad.

ACKNOWLEDGMENTS
Thanks to Steve's wife, Karen Lewis Smith, for her assistance covering French cuisine, and to Steve's children, Travis and Maria, for help with children's activities. The co-authors would also like to thank David Price, who lives in Avignon and is a fine source of information about key sights in Provence.

PHOTO CREDITS
Front Cover: Saint-Jacques-le-Majeur church and vineyards in Hunawihr, Alsace © Olimpio Fantuz / SIME / eStock Photo

Title Page: Along the Seine, Paris © Dominic Arizona Bonuccelli

Back Cover: Dreamstime.com: © Vitalyedush, © Pitrs10, © Xantana

Alamy: p.61 © Hemis / Alamy Stock Photo

Additional Photography: Dominic Arizona Bonuccelli, Abe Bringolf, Mary Ann Cameron, Rich Earl, Barb Geisler, Cameron Hewitt, David C. Hoerlein, Sandra Hundacker, Michaelanne Jerome, Suzanne Kotz, Lauren Mills, Virginie Moré, Gene Openshaw, Paul Orcutt, Michael Potter, Steve Smith, Robyn Stencil, Rick Steves, Gretchen Strauch, Rob Unck, Laura VanDeventer, Wikimedia Commons (PD-Art/PD-US). Photos are used by permission and are the property of the original copyright owners.

Avalon Travel
Hachette Book Group
1700 Fourth Street
Berkeley, CA 94710

Text © 2019 by Rick Steves' Europe, Inc. All rights reserved.
Maps © 2019 by Rick Steves' Europe, Inc. All rights reserved.

Printed in Canada by Friesens.
First printing November 2019.

ISBN 978-1-64171-144-9

For the latest on Rick's lectures, guidebooks, tours, public television series, and public radio show, contact Rick Steves' Europe, 130 Fourth Avenue North, Edmonds, WA 98020, 425/771-8303, rick@ricksteves.com, www.ricksteves.com.

The publisher is not responsible for websites (or their content) that are not owned by the publisher.

Rick Steves' Europe
Managing Editor: Jennifer Madison Davis
Assistant Managing Editor: Cathy Lu
Special Publications Manager: Risa Laib
Editors: Glenn Eriksen, Tom Griffin, Suzanne Kotz, Rosie Leutzinger, Jessica Shaw, Carrie Shepherd
Editorial & Production Assistant: Megan Simms
Editorial Interns: Amelia Benich, Maxwell Eberle
Researcher: Virginie Moré
Contributor: Gene Openshaw
Graphic Content Director: Sandra Hundacker
Maps & Graphics: David C. Hoerlein, Lauren Mills, Mary Rostad
Digital Asset Coordinator: Orin Dubrow

Avalon Travel
Senior Editor and Series Manager: Madhu Prasher
Editors: Jamie Andrade, Sierra Machado
Copy Editor: Maggie Ryan
Proofreader: Kelly Lydick
Indexer: Stephen Callahan
Production & Typesetting: Lisi Baldwin, Rue Flaherty
Cover Design: Kimberly Glyder Design
Maps & Graphics: Kat Bennett

Although every effort was made to ensure that the information was correct at the time of going to press, the author and publisher do not assume and hereby disclaim any liability to any party for any loss or damage caused by errors, omissions, sudden cheese urges, or any potential travel disruption due to labor or financial difficulty, whether such errors or omissions result from negligence, accident, or any other cause.

COLOR MAPS

France • West Paris • East Paris

ENGLAND

English Channel

GERMANY

D-DAY BEACHES

Honfleur

Mont St-Michel

Bayeux

Giverny

Reims

Verdun

Dinan

PARIS

ALSACE

Colmar

LOIRE VALLEY

Amboise

BURGUNDY

Beaune

Atlantic Ocean

DORDOGNE

Annecy

Chamonix

100 Kilometers

100 Miles

Sarlat-la-Canéda

ALPS

PONT DU GARD

Les Baux

Villefranche-sur-Mer & Monaco

Carcassonne

ARLES

NICE

LANGUEDOC-ROUSSILLON

Antibes

RIVIERA

FRANCE

Mediterranean Sea

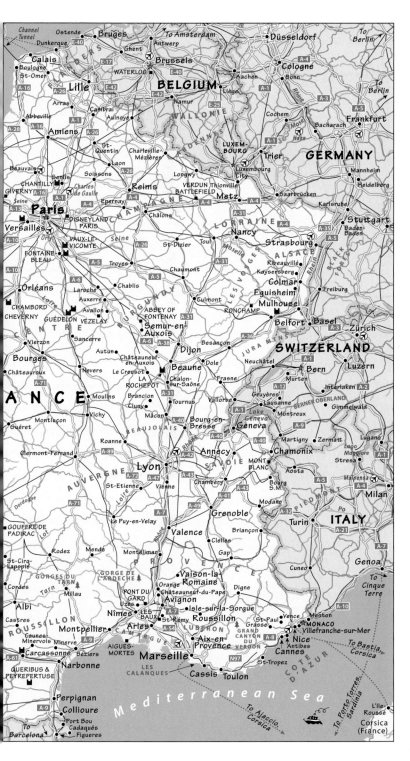

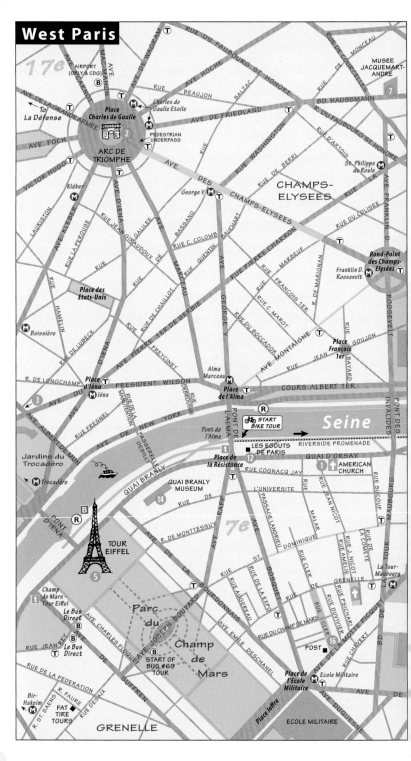

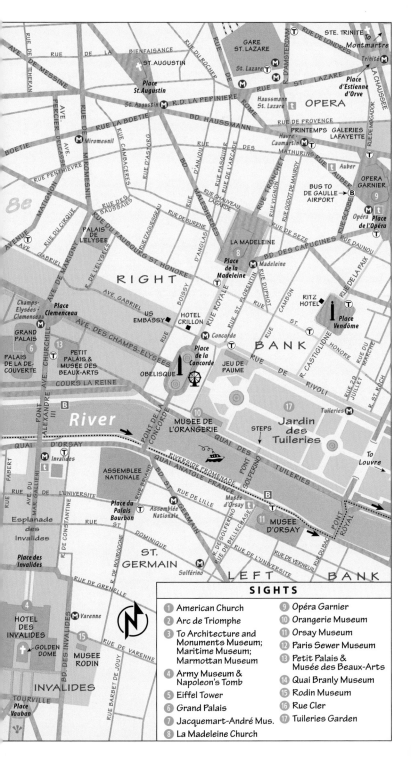

SIGHTS

1. American Church
2. Arc de Triomphe
3. To Architecture and Monuments Museum; Maritime Museum; Marmottan Museum
4. Army Museum & Napoleon's Tomb
5. Eiffel Tower
6. Grand Palais
7. Jacquemart-André Mus.
8. La Madeleine Church
9. Opéra Garnier
10. Orangerie Museum
11. Orsay Museum
12. Paris Sewer Museum
13. Petit Palais & Musée des Beaux-Arts
14. Quai Branly Museum
15. Rodin Museum
16. Rue Cler
17. Tuileries Garden

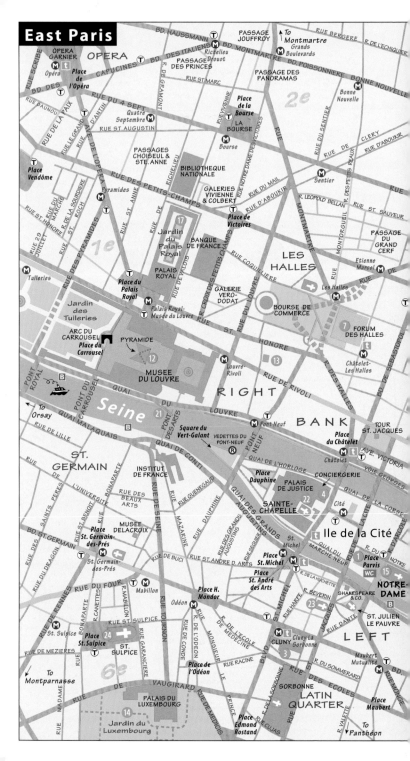